THE ENCYCLOPEDIA
OF
ORGANIC GARDENING

New Revised Edition

by the Staff of
Organic Gardening® magazine

 Rodale Press Emmaus, Pennsylvania

Library of Congress Cataloging in Publication Data

Organic gardening and farming.
      The encyclopedia of organic gardening.

      1.   Organic gardening—Dictionaries.   I.   Smyser, Steve.   II.   Title.
SB453.5.O72   1978   631.5′8   77-25915
ISBN 0-87857-225-2 hardcover
ISBN 0-87857-351-8 hardcover deluxe

12	14	16	18	20	19	17	15	13	hardcover
				8	10	9			hardcover deluxe

Printed in 1985.

The Encyclopedia of Organic Gardening

Editors

Anna Carr

Mary Ellen Chauner

William H. Hylton

Steven W. Smyser

Carol Stoner

Michael Stoner

Roger B. Yepsen, Jr.

Copy Editors

Susan Greene

Marjorie Hunt

Pat Olver

Ann Snyder

Illustrator Erick Ingraham

Design Terri Lepley

Layout Carol Stickles

Photographers Margaret Smyser and
the Rodale Press photography staff

Special Assistance

Shirley DeEsch

Lori Eisenberg

Julie Ruhe

Contributors

Jeff Cox

Catharine O. Foster

Maurice Franz

M. C. Goldman

Jerry Goldstein

Rudy Keller

Gene Logsdon

Carol Smyser McHarg

Ray Poincelot

Carole Turko

Ray Wolf

A Note on the Revised Edition

When it first appeared in 1959, THE ENCYCLOPEDIA OF ORGANIC GARDENING appealed primarily to what was at that time a rather specialized segment of the gardening community—those people who believed that there exists a strong direct relationship between the health of our bodies and the health of the soil in which we grow our food.

Over the past 18 years the ENCYCLOPEDIA has helped millions of gardeners throughout the world to restore the fertility of their soil, grow more bountiful crops, eat better food, and increase their personal productivity and self-reliance. Dog-eared, dilapidated copies adorning the shelves of garden sheds, greenhouses and potting benches everywhere bear witness to the book's enduring value as a practical gardening guide, a comprehensive source of all those bits and pieces of gardening wisdom of which even the veteran grower has occasional need.

As the ecological hazards of applying toxic, highly soluble herbicides and pesticides to our prime food-producing soils become increasingly well documented, and the permanence of an agricultural system epitomized by its gluttonous consumption of fossil fuels and soil-depleting chemical fertilizers becomes increasingly suspect, the organic alternative grows steadily in importance.

While most of the basic elements of organic husbandry—composting, mulching, natural soil fertility management, insect and disease control, etc.—were treated in depth in the original edition, important new information relating to these subjects has surfaced so rapidly in recent years that a thorough revision was needed to bring the ENCYCLOPEDIA up to date.

Receiving special attention in the revision are the many new developments in the fields of entomology, agronomy, nutrition, and microbiology. The great strides that have been made in the areas of biological pest control, for instance, are summarized in the new INSECT CONTROL entry. New information on plants that naturally like or dislike growing in association with one another is contained in the expanded COMPANION PLANTING entry. There is a new entry on INTENSIVE GARDENING that describes the raised-bed, concentration planting method that can so greatly expand the productive capabilities of city gardeners and others with limited space.

The extensively rewritten GREENHOUSES entry brings the reader up to date on improved methods of natural insect control, recommended soil mixtures, new construction and glazing materials, and recently developed techniques for cutting heating costs in the greenhouse.

The practice of municipalities composting their sewage sludge and applying it to agricultural lands was something of a novelty in this country in 1959. Today, confronted with sewage disposal problems of monumental proportions, a steadily expanding number of local governments are turning to composting and farmland application of nutrient-rich sludge. Farmers and gardeners, for their part, are finding improved ways of putting this valuable source of organic fertilizer to use, as is described in the new MUNICIPAL COMPOSTING and SEWAGE SLUDGE entries.

Along with these many new entries, each of the more than 2,300 entries from the 1959 edition was reviewed, researched and revised to include the most recent, most reliable information available. In the case of the individual plant entries, this has meant the inclusion of new information on ranges of plant hardiness, improved cultural practices and important new varieties. Only those varieties and cultivars listed in the catalogs of established seed and nursery suppliers are included.

After considerable debate, it was decided to retain the system of listing most plants by their common names rather than their Latin botanical equivalents. The botanical name then follows immediately after the common name entry. The reader seeking information on *Helianthus,* for example, is directed by cross-reference to SUNFLOWER. *Agaricus campestris* is covered under MUSHROOM, and *Phaseolus vulgaris* under KIDNEY BEAN. When a plant has no common name it is listed under its botanical name. Botanical names are given in the standard binomial (two-word) manner, with the genus followed by the species and, where necessary, the variety. Cultivars are distinguished by single quotation marks. For the most part, the International Rules of Botanical Nomenclature have been followed so that the plant names used conform with those in Bailey's *Hortus Third* (New York: Macmillan Publishing Co., 1976). In a few, special cases, the 9th edition of Alfred Byrd Graf's *Exotica* (East Rutherford, NJ: Roehrs Co., 1976) has been the reference.

A national survey conducted in 1976 revealed that nearly 30 million American households (close to 50 percent) were growing at least a portion of their own food. Our fondest hope for this revision is that it will furnish an increasingly large proportion of those gardeners with the information, confidence and incentive needed to care for their gardens the natural way.

Steven W. Smyser
April 1978

Introduction

Thirty years ago, Sir Albert Howard, the British agricultural scientist, began to express in his writings a natural and whole concept of plant and animal husbandry. Town wastes, he said, should be returned to the soil as compost. Artificial fertilizers and poisonous insecticides became suspect to him as improper tools of sound agriculture. The slow but devastating erosion of good lands everywhere could be stopped, said Sir Albert, if we would let Nature be our teacher. The seed of the organic idea had been planted, and it took root on every continent.

In the early years of what came to be known as the organic movement, growth was slow. Here and there a few conservation-minded people were impressed with Sir Albert's reasoning and began trying to teach his ideas to others. Soon, though, garden and farm magazines headed by "organic" editors were being published in the United States, England, Australia, New Zealand, and Germany. These magazines became the principal method of communication in the organic field. Because the usual government channels of education and science were largely closed to those with organic leanings, the magazines became clearing houses of organic activity.

Magazines, though, are not the most efficient tool for permanent reference. They are cumbersome to store and to refer to. Today, there is a tremendous demand for the basic facts about organic methods in a permanent reference book. THE ENCYCLOPEDIA OF ORGANIC GARDENING has been created to meet that demand.

This book, though, is broader in scope than you may think when first reading the title. It is actually an encyclopedia covering the whole field of horticulture, from the organic point of view. Even people who are unacquainted with the organic idea will find it a useful reference work. THE ENCYCLOPEDIA OF ORGANIC GARDENING will tell you how to plant, how to cultivate, how to fertilize, and how to harvest. It will help you identify plants, cure plant disease and prevent insect attack. In short, it will help you solve your garden problems.

It has been many months since the first editorial meeting on THE ENCYCLOPEDIA OF ORGANIC GARDENING took place. And, in fact, the idea for a complete reference book about the organic method goes back many more years.

Our editorial objectives were to publish a comprehensive, readable book that would give *practical* information on the entire realm of organic gardening, and to describe the relationship between soils and actual gardening and farming practices.

We realized that this was an ambitious undertaking; we hoped that a book of this nature would give new impetus to the already well-established organic gardening idea. To reach our goal, many gardening authorities were contacted; and much research was done. We received encouragement from everyone. Authors of articles in *Organic Gardening and Farming®* gave us permission to use their material, and notified us they'd be willing to help in any way possible.

Special attention has been given to the subjects of major importance to organic gardeners. Composting, mulching, fertilizing, soils, vegetable gardening, flower gardening, orcharding and fruit trees, house plants, landscaping, nut trees, plant diseases and insect control, shrubs, borders—these topics are covered in detail.

Basic as well as more advanced information is given on growing plants in cold frames and greenhouses, for propagating plants by division, cuttings or layering. Growing details are given as well for thousands of plants in individual entries. In keeping with our desire to make the ENCYCLOPEDIA a practical book, most plants are listed under their well-known popular names instead of the Latin name. Cross-references will lead you from one related subject to another. For example, if you want information on liming your soil, the entry under LIME tells you which form is best, how much to apply, and why lime is useful to plants. A reference to ACIDITY–ALKALINITY will take you to a further discussion telling you, among other things, which plants need lime, which ones do not.

Every gardening topic that we've considered of interest has been described thoroughly. For example, the subject of layering—an important one to many—was discussed in such a way that accurate coverage is given to *all* of the different methods. The same was true of lawns, pruning, house plants, berries, humus, protecting plants, herbs, and roses.

And now the book is done. It is with a feeling of accomplishment that we realize that the last entry has been made. And we're sure this feeling is shared by the many others whose efforts went into the ENCYCLOPEDIA. People like Thomas Powell and Dorothy Franz, and the many other authors whose names are listed following their articles.

J. I. Rodale
Robert Rodale
Jerome Olds

November 1958

THE ENCYCLOPEDIA
OF
ORGANIC GARDENING

A

ABELIA

These small to medium-sized shrubs of the Honeysuckle family have numerous attractive small flowers varying in color from white to pink or purple. They attain a height of three to ten feet and bloom June through October. Some varieties are hardy as far north as Pennsylvania.

Abelias do best in a sunny, fairly protected place. They prefer a well-drained soil, enriched with compost, leaf mold or peat moss. Propagation can be done in any of three ways: with cuttings of green wood in summer, which should be rooted under glass; with cuttings of ripened wood in autumn; or with layers in springtime.

A. floribunda, with showy rose red flowers, can be grown in a greenhouse in cool climates and outdoors in areas where there is little or no frost.

ABIES   *See* FIR

ABSINTHE   *See* WORMWOOD

ACACIA

Acacias are quick-growing trees and shrubs that produce dense clusters of very small,

usually yellow flowers. They are generally short-lived, reaching their full maturity in about 30 years and then starting to die. This short life span and their brittleness make them unsuitable street trees.

The best known is the silver wattle (*A. decurrens* var. *dealbata*), suited to such states as Arizona, California, Florida, Oklahoma, and Texas. Although hardier varieties are being developed, most current acacias cannot endure too much frost. Winter temperatures below 20°F. (−6.67°C.) will be damaging.

In suitable climates, these trees are easily grown outdoors. Once established, acacias generally are drought resistant, but for quick growth they need good soil and sufficient water.

Propagating can be done with seeds, soaking them first in hot water and then cold, and then planting while the seeds are still wet. Acacias can also be propagated from cuttings of half-ripened wood, from which a delicate taproot develops.

ACCENT PLANT

This term refers to a shrub or tree (sometimes a group) that is used to accentuate some feature in the garden design. A sense of form and arrangement requires careful use of an accent plant in just the right place, curtailing overuse and overaccenting.

See also LANDSCAPING.

1

ACEROLA   (*Malpighia glabra*)

Also called Barbados cherry, acerola is a bushy tree native to the tropical and semi-tropical regions of the Western Hemisphere. When the Spaniards came to Puerto Rico in the late fifteenth century, they found these "acerola" trees growing wild in various sections of the island. There are no records to show that any serious attempts to domesticate these trees were undertaken at this time.

Often attaining a height of ten feet, the tree has fairly deep, penetrating roots, and adapts itself easily to poor soil conditions without much care. Its trunk is short and slender —about two feet in length and four inches in diameter.

The buds are small, arranged singly and in clusters on slender, short stems. Flowers are also very small, about ¾ inch in diameter when fully open. Depending on the variety, their color can range from rose to deep pink.

The fruits, which look like cherries, produce a red orange juice with a pleasant tart flavor. Their vitamin C content is highest just before the cherries ripen. Tests have shown that juice from the acerola contains more than 85 times as much vitamin C as fresh orange juice.

The acerola needs full sun and moist soil. It can be grown in the house or greenhouse.

ACHILLEA   *See* YARROW

ACHIMENES

Growing erect or prostrate, with multi-colored tubular flowers, and leaves ranging in color from light green to bronze, achimenes are popular plants for hanging baskets and window boxes.

Achimenes grow from small rhizomes that are planted as soon as they are received in late winter or early spring, about ½ inch deep in a light porous compost made of leaf mold, or of any combination of leaf mold, peat moss, vermiculite, and loam.

Water the containers lightly and set them in the basement or under a greenhouse bench away from frost and where they will not get too wet, dry or hot. A temperature of 50°F. (10°C.) during storage is satisfactory. Don't let them dry out.

As soon as the sprouts show above the soil in the spring (in about three weeks), move them to a lighted window and top-dress with well-rotted manure. They need considerable light, but resent full sunlight except in the early morning and evening. Repot in March or April and put in a greenhouse with a 60°F. (15.56°C.) temperature.

In fall, as the number of flowers decreases, cut down on the water and allow the plants to dry off. When entirely dry, cut the stems above the soil and set the pot, with soil and tubers undisturbed, in the basement or under the greenhouse bench. Do not disturb them until the tubers sprout again in the spring, except to sprinkle the soil with water from time to time if needed.

The plants will make a fine show if left in the same soil and container for two seasons. If three to five tubers were planted in a five- or six-inch pot the first spring, the second season should find the pot full of blooming plants. Repot before the third season, however, using fresh compost.

Achimenes can also be propagated by cuttings.

ACIDANTHERA

These African herbs of the Iris family have long sword-shaped leaves and spikes of three to six white and purple flowers that open from leaf clusters along the 2½-foot stalk.

The corms should be planted at the end of May or in early June when the ground is warming up. The plants do best in full sunshine. Soak the corms in warm water for 24 hours before planting for a quick start because acidanthera needs about four months to bloom outdoors. Start them indoors in March like tuberous begonias for blooms in early August.

After the first frost the corms should be harvested with the stems intact, tied in a bundle and slipped into a paper bag which is hung from the ceiling of a warm cellar or room. The stalks should be removed in March.

ACIDITY—ALKALINITY

Acidity and alkalinity of soils are the result of 1) the chemical composition of the rock from which the soil is derived, and 2) the partial or complete decomposition of vegetation. The degree of acidity or alkalinity of the soil, measured in terms of pH, is known as the soil's reaction. A basic indicator of soil health and fertility, soil reaction is easy to determine and, in most cases, easy to control.

In years past, a gardener or farmer tasted his soil. If it tasted sour, he knew that it wasn't good for raising crops. The same thing went for a bitter taste. But if it tasted sweet, he knew that he could expect high yields. He may not have known it, but the soil that tasted sour was too acid to raise good general crops, and the soil that tasted bitter was too alkaline to produce the yields he wanted.

A few plants, like blueberries, flourish in fairly acid soil, but most garden crops, lawn grasses, trees, and shrubs prefer soils that are just slightly acid (pH 6.5 to 6.0). Moreover, microorganisms and chemical elements in the soil work more vigorously to make nutrients available to plants when the soil is nearly neutral rather than too acid or alkaline. Excessive acidity in the soil may cause calcium, phosphorus and magnesium to be changed into forms that plants cannot use, causing them to suffer a deficiency of these elements.

Alkaline soils are most characteristic of salt marshes, the alkali deserts of the West, and some limestone areas. In humid regions soil under cultivation tends to become increasingly acid. This is because soil water dissolves the more alkaline substances like calcium, sodium, magnesium, and potassium faster than acidic materials like carbon. Thus the alkalis leach out sooner than the acids.

It isn't completely understood why plants won't tolerate highly acid conditions. Slowdown of beneficial bacterial action is part of the reason; increased toxicity from certain trace elements like aluminum is another. Deficiency of calcium and magnesium is a third possibility. The best explanation may be that in acid soils, chemical reaction can lock up major nutrients, especially phosphorus, making them unavailable to plants.

Heavy use of inorganic, high-analysis fertilizers causes soil to become more acid, as does heavy use of sulfur-containing fungicides. Organic gardeners don't have to worry about that, but the same result can stem from using organic fertilizers that have an acidifying effect.

Acidity and alkalinity are measured in pH units, the "pH" being a symbol for the relative

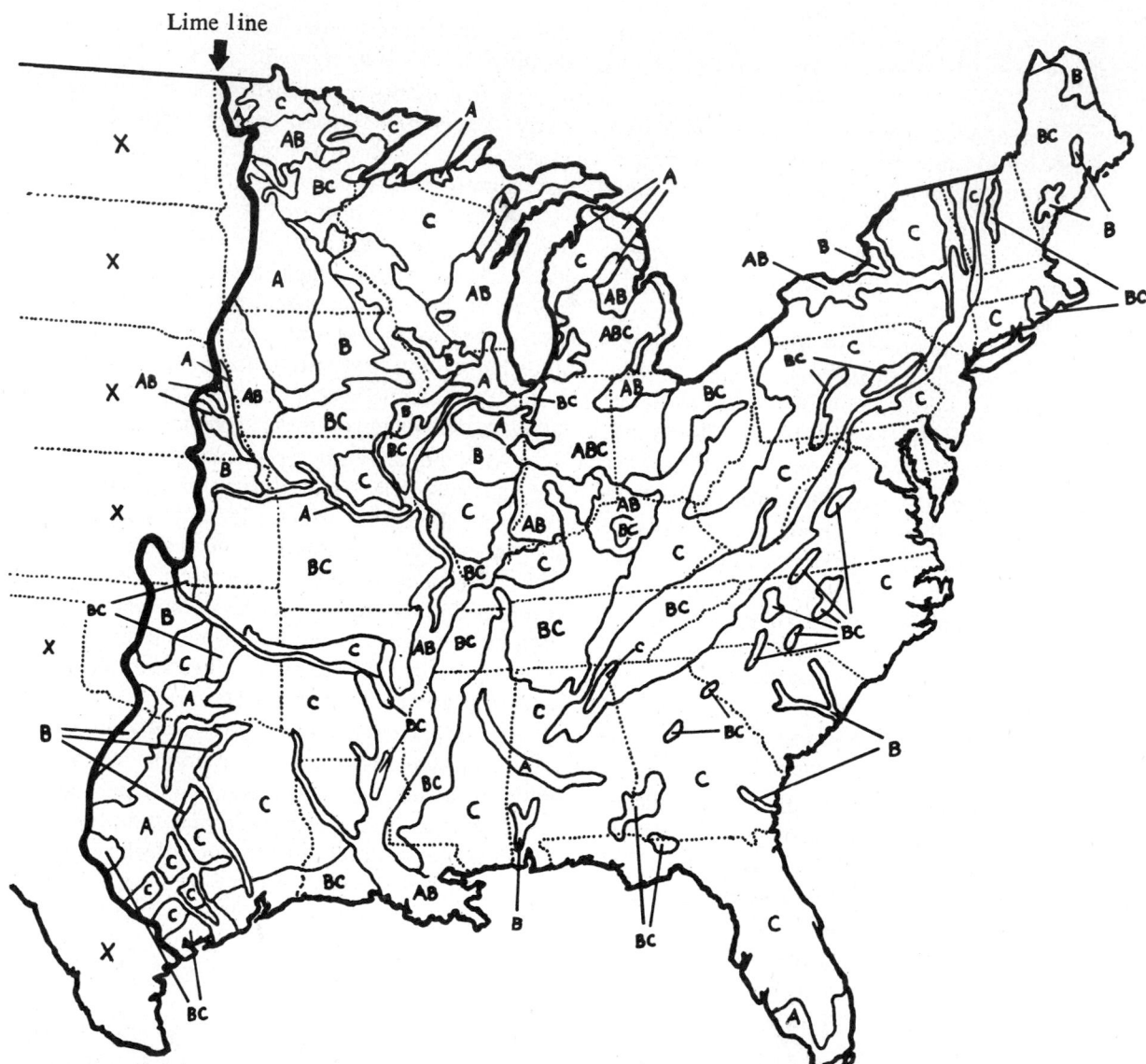

East of the "lime line," soils are generally acid and often require liming.

X. *Soils rich in lime*
A. *Soils fairly rich in lime, but some surfaces may be acid*
B. *Acid soils with some lime available to deep-rooted plants*
C. *Very acid soils*

AB. *Soils with high to medium amounts of lime*
BC. *Soils with medium to low amounts of lime*
ABC. *Mixed soils with high, medium and low amounts of lime*

(Courtesy of U.S. Department of Agriculture)

amount of hydrogen in a substance. Essentially, the pH value (power of hydrogen) assigned a substance is indicative of its rate of breakdown or ionization of water into the hydrogen ion (a positively charged atom) and an oxygen-hydrogen ion (a negatively charged molecule). Soil alkalinity or acidity, then, is determined by the reaction of various mineral and organic compounds with moisture in the soil.

On a pH scale from 1 to 14, 1 is extremely acid and 10 or more extremely alkaline. A peat bog can have a pH as low as 3; an arid desert alkaline soil as high as 10 or 11. A pH of 7 is neutral.

Plants are very often listed according to their pH preference, but this is an imperfect indicator since soils vary so greatly. Some plants respond differently to pH in different soils. Other plants tolerate a comparatively wide pH range.

Obviously, for high yields, the gardener or farmer should know the pH of his soil. Then he can either grow the kinds of plants that do best on soil of this particular pH, or he can take steps to change the soil pH to within the desirable range for the plants he wishes to grow.

For the majority of common plants, a pH of 6.5 to 7 is optimum. Soils in this pH range offer the most favorable environment for the microorganisms that convert atmospheric nitrogen into a form available to plants. It also offers the best environment for the bacteria that decompose plant tissue and form humus. In this pH range, all of the essential mineral nutrients are available to plants in sufficient quantities, and generally in a much greater amount than at any other pH. Also, soil having a pH within this range has better tilth, because a good crumb structure is more easily maintained.

Too acid a soil means that the bacteria which decompose organic matter cannot live. Manganese and aluminum are so soluble in very acid soil that they may be present in amounts toxic to plants. Yet strong acidity decreases total nutrient availability, and plants may literally starve to death for one essential mineral nutrient while having so much of another that it poisons them.

On the other hand, too alkaline a soil is not desirable. Strong alkalinity decreases total nutrient availability. It causes loss of soil structure and development of "puddling." Strong alkalinity dissolves and disperses humus. "Black alkali" is caused by the accumulation of alkali and humus at the surface of the soil. Strong alkalinity causes a concentration of some salts in such quantities that they are toxic to plants and may completely inhibit their growth. In some of the desert regions the soils are so strongly alkaline that no plants of any kind will grow.

Soils developed from acid minerals are generally acid. Those developed from high-lime deposits are generally alkaline. Soils high in calcium generally have pH values up to 7.5. Large amounts of calcium carbonate in the soil, however, may run the pH up to 8.5. Soils high in sodium usually have very high pH values.

The effect of neutralizing a strongly acid soil is to increase and maintain a good supply of available nitrates and other essential plant nutrients. This is accomplished by furnishing microorganisms with a more favorable environment so that they are more active in converting ammonia or nitrogen into nitrates and in decomposing organic matter. Thus, the benefit of adding organic matter to the soil is utilized.

A steady release of nutrients to the growing plants is maintained. However, in very acid soils, this is slowed down greatly. The best pH range for utilizing organic matter is between 6 and 8.

Testing Your Soil: A good soil test is the surest way to determine the pH of your soil. A simple test for pH you can do yourself is with blue litmus paper, available from drugstores. Blue litmus turns pink when brought into contact with an acid (even a weak acid like vinegar) and turns back to blue if dipped in limewater.

Get three or four samples of your garden's soil, trying to collect samples from several different spots and from different depths. Mix up all the soil you've collected in a clean bucket, then pour clean rainwater over it. Place several pieces of litmus paper into the mud you've made in the bucket, being careful that your hands are clean of any acid substance before you handle the paper. Wait ten seconds and withdraw one piece of the paper. Rinse it off with clean water. If pinkness shows immediately, the soil is quite acid. The intensity of the pink is a further indication of degree of acidity.

Pull another piece of the paper out in about five minutes. If pink, the soil needs lime, but not as much as when the color changes right away. If after 15 minutes the blue paper shows little or no change to pink, your soil probably doesn't need lime.

This method is far from precise, but it can give you a rough idea of where your soil stands.

Correcting Acid Soil: If your soil is too acid, it may be brought back to a favorable pH by applying limestone. Agricultural-ground limestone is the commonest and safest liming material. Of the two types of ground limestone, calcitic and dolomitic, the latter is preferred because it contains magnesium in addition to calcium, thus fertilizing the soil as well as neutralizing it.

General guidelines for applying limestone are as follows: to increase pH by one unit, spread on every 1,000 square feet of sandy soil 30 pounds of limestone; on a sandy loam, spread 50 pounds; on a loam, 70 pounds; and on a heavy clay, 80 pounds.

Another good material with which to lime soil is unleached hardwood ashes. If you have a fireplace or wood stove, save the ashes. If you can't put them directly on the soil, store in a dry place, since rain quickly leaches out the lime and potash in them. Coal ashes are of little or no value.

Spread your liming material on top of the soil in the fall *after* you have plowed, rototilled or spaded deeply. Lime should not be plowed under, as it leaches down into the soil too rapidly. On lawns and pastures, the preferred time for spreading is late summer. It is best not to apply lime with other fertilizers. Do not apply lime around acid-loving plants or on any area where runoff water might carry the lime downhill to such plants. Lime is poison to blueberries, azaleas and the like.

When using ground limestone, don't expect a tremendous response the first year you apply it. The year after will be better. Liming should be repeated every fourth or fifth year, depending on the indications of soil tests.

Where it is really needed, liming produces dramatic results. Because of this, there is a temptation to overlime, especially on a small garden plot. Overliming is as bad as not liming at all. A pH of 7.0 is a signal you've overdone it.

Correcting Alkaline Soil: A slight alkalinity can sometimes be cured with a little borax

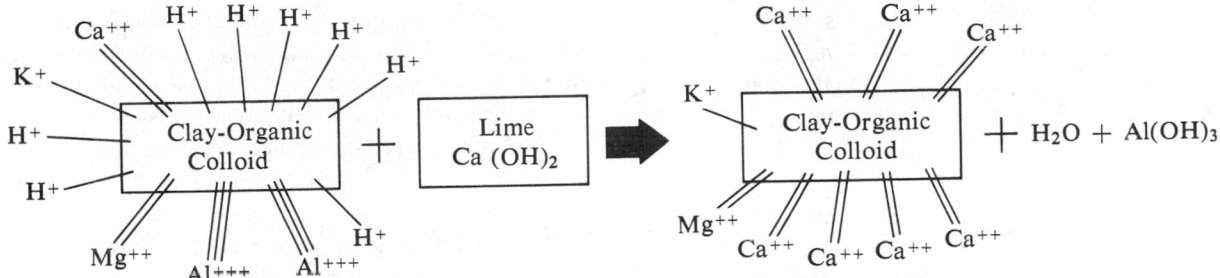

Acid Soil + Lime = Neutral Soil + Water + Aluminum Hydroxide

When lime is added to an acid soil, calcium and magnesium ions replace hydrogen ions, resulting in a more alkaline soil.

and manganese, but be guided at all times by soil tests when using these trace mineral elements. It doesn't take much boron to kill a plant.

Farmers in semiarid regions often use gypsum (calcium sulfate) to reclaim alkali beds and add calcium to soil that is excessively alkaline. By replacing the sodium of alkali soils with calcium, gypsum can often improve drainage and aeration. As a hydrate, however, in which the sulfate is chemically combined with water, gypsum is not strictly a natural product, and is thus avoided by many organic growers.

A better way to acidify soil is with naturally acid organic materials—acid muck from swamps, oak leaves, oak sawdust, or ground-up oak bark, cottonseed meal or acid peat moss.

Increasing the organic matter content can be of benefit too. Organic matter contains natural acid-forming material and produces acids directly on decomposition. These acids combine with excess alkali and neutralize it. Organic matter can be applied in great quantity without damaging the soil. It acts as a buffer against both excess alkalinity and excess acidity.

Incorporating good compost helps correct an adverse soil pH to the range wherein most common plants thrive. Even where the pH of a soil is less than optimum for the plants being raised, plants will commonly thrive if there is sufficient organic matter present.

Acid Soil Plants: The following plants prefer a pH of 4 to 5.5:

Azalea	Marigold
Bayberry	Mountain laurel
Blackberry	Oak
Blueberry	Peanut
Butterfly weed	Pecan
Cardinal flower	Potato
Chrysanthemum	Radish
Cranberry	Raspherry
Flax	Rhododendron
Heath	Spruce
Heather	Sweet potato
Huckleberry	Trailing arbutus
Lily	Watermelon
Lily-of-the-valley	Yew
Lupine	

The following plants require a somewhat acid soil but can tolerate a pH of 5.5 to 6.5:

Apple	Blazing-star
Balloon flower	Butterfly weed

Cornflower
Gardenia
Gloxinia
Gold-banded lily
Gypsophila
Lupine

Nicotiana
Pansy
Pumpkin
Redtop grass
Rice
Turnip

Alkaline Soil Plants: Moderately alkaline soil favors the growth and productiveness of' many garden plants. Certain alkaline soil plants such as peas, clover and alfalfa become stunted or even sickly in acid soil. The more common alkaline-soil plants in the garden will tolerate a pH of 6.5 and up. They are:

Alyssum
Asparagus
Bean
Beet
Cabbage
Cantaloupe
Carnation
Cauliflower
Celery
Cucumber
Geum
Iris

Lettuce
Mignonette
Nasturtium
Onion
Parsnip
Pea
Phlox
Rhubarb
Salsify
Squash
Sweet pea

See also LIME, pH.

ACID SOILS   *See* ACIDITY–ALKALINITY

ACONITE   *See* ACONITUM

ACONITUM

These late-blooming, hardy perennials of the Buttercup family have mostly blue flowers shaped like hoods or old-fashioned helmets in spikes at the tops of the stems. Common names include aconite, monkshood and wolfsbane. The leaves are glossy and finely divided like those of buttercups. Many species are poisonous, containing in varying amounts the alkaloid aconitine, which acts on the central nervous system and has medicinal value. The alkaloid is present in the leaves but is most highly concentrated in the dark, fleshy, carrot-shaped roots. While it is unlikely that these would be eaten by mistake, the plants should not be located near food crops, and children should be warned to leave them alone.

Several species have great ornamental value. They bloom in late summer and fall when blue colors are scarce in the garden, and they add a spirelike effect to the border. All require a deep, rich, moist but well-drained soil high in organic matter. Water should never stand around the roots. They prefer partial shade and will need frequent watering if grown in full sun. Aconitums resent being moved once established, and this should not be necessary for five years or more because they are long-lived and never invasive. Propagate by division in early spring or early fall after flowering. Dig a generous root ball and be careful not to break the young roots when separating the clump. Plant them two feet from other plants and leave them alone.

A. napellus, native to central Europe, is the most poisonous species. It has blue flowers on four-foot stems in August and early September. Bicolor has blue flowers with white centers, and Spark's Variety has violet blue flowers late in September. Stake them in open locations.

Often called *A. Fischeri, A. Carmichaelii* is valuable where a shorter type is wanted, as it grows only to 3½ feet. The pale blue flowers appear from mid-August to mid-September. The taller Barker's Variety needs to have its four- to five-foot stems staked. The amethyst blue flowers come in August and September.

A. *uncinatum,* clambering monkshood, is a native of the eastern mountains. It grows to two or three feet and has violet blue flowers from August to October, depending on location. It is a good specimen for the wild flower garden.

The true wolfsbane, A. *lycoctonum,* grows to four feet and produces yellow flowers from early to midsummer.

ACORN

The acorn is the fruit, or nut, of the oak tree. Although today the acorn is regarded as a nut fit only for squirrels, it has been used as a standard food for ages and rates high in food value for human consumption. Some acorns are good to eat in the natural state, and most can be made palatable by removing the bitter tannin.

Typically, acorns of the white oak group (including the chestnut oak, swamp oak and bur oak) are sweeter than those of the black (or red) oak group, and can be made into a meal for muffins. Husk the acorns and grind them in a mill. Mix the meal with hot water, and pour into a jelly bag to leach away the tannin; a second or third washing may be necessary. Spread the meal out to dry and then parch it in an oven. Use acorn meal as you would cornmeal.

ACTINIDIA

Deciduous climbing shrubs or vines popular for their handsome foliage, actinidias are an excellent choice for covering trellises and arbors. Two species, A. *arguta* (tara vine) and A. *chinensis* (kiwi berry), produce many-seeded fruits that have a gooseberry flavor.

Actinidias do best in a somewhat moist location with rich soil, and they will climb well in either full sun or partial shade. Propagate them by seeds sown in spring, by cuttings of half-ripened wood in summer or by layering.

ACTINOMYCETES

This group of soil microorganisms, on the basis of their organization, occupies a position somewhere between true molds and bacteria. Sometimes classified with fungi, they are also called thread bacteria. Although actinomycetes resemble molds in structure, they are unicellular and about the same diameter as bacteria.

Actinomycetes develop best in well-aerated, moist soils with optimum development occurring at a pH of from 6 to 7.5. Their growth at a pH below 5 is negligible.

They are found in some 90 species, and form about 20 percent of all the microorganisms in the average soil. Soils very high in organic matter may contain 40 percent actinomycetes. Although the largest proportion of them will be found in the top foot or so of soil, actinomycetes often extend to greater depths than the other soil organisms; they frequently work many feet below the surface at their job of breaking down dead plant matter, making food for the deeper-reaching roots of new plants.

Wherever found, they are important soil-makers. One researcher discovered that actinomycetes reduce the gray, fibrous mud in lake bottoms to rich black mud, a process accompanied by the movement of iron and calcium to the upper mud layer.

Their activities are much the same in soil. They attack the roots, stems, straws, and leaves of dead plants sheet-composted or plowed into the soil, converting them rapidly and efficiently into a dark brown mass very much like peat (their work is the first step in the formation of peat or brown coal). They secrete digestive enzymes that decompose the three most complex and abundant organic compounds in vegetable matter: protein, starch and cellulose. The cellulose, and the "woody" lignin material, too, are said to be "lignified." This is a humidification process resulting in the formation of black coloring substances and the synthesis, or building up, of cell matter into soil organic matter.

When large numbers of actinomycetes are at work, a musty, earthy odor rises like a rotting log in the woods or a damp haycock out in the field.

The actinomycetes do not fix nitrogen from the air, but instead liberate ammonia from complex proteins and reduce nitrates to nitrites. They steal very little nitrogen from soil reserves, needing only one part of nitrogen for every fifty parts of cellulose they break down. And the humic material they produce, being very fine, has the ability to absorb nitrogenous materials and chemical compounds, residues of soil fertility which plants can then draw upon from the humus as needed.

The more fertile the soil, the higher its organic matter content and the more actinomycetes it will contain.

One species of actinomycetes causes potato scab, and other species produce antibiotics which are valuable as sources of medicines.

ACTIVATORS

Also called an inoculant, a compost acti- vator is any substance which will stimulate biological decomposition in a compost pile. Several commercial activators are available.

Artificial activators are chemically synthesized compounds such as ammonium sulfate or phosphate, urea, ammonia, or any of the common commercial nitrogen fertilizers. These materials are not recommended for the organic garden or farm.

There are two areas in which an activator can possibly influence a compost heap. It can introduce strains of microorganisms that are effective in breaking down organic matter, and it can increase the nitrogen content of the heap, thereby providing extra food for microorganisms.

Claims have sometimes been made that special cultures of bacteria will hasten the breakdown of material in a compost heap and will also produce a better quality of finished compost. Products are manufactured which are reported to be effective in improving the action of a compost heap. These include pure strains of bacteria naturally present in decomposition, as well as products containing such things as "hormones," "biocatalysts," etc.

Experiments conducted at the University of California have indicated that there is no benefit to be gained from the use of an activator which relies only on the introduction of new microorganisms to a heap. The composting process was neither accelerated nor the finished compost improved.

Nitrogen Activators: It is generally agreed that the most common cause of compost heap "failures" is a lack of nitrogen. A heap that doesn't heat up or decay quickly is usually made from material low in nitrogen, since nitrogen is essential as a source of energy for the bacteria and fungi that do the composting work. Thus it is advisable to add nitrogen supplements or activators, such as bone meal, cottonseed meal, tankage, manure, or blood meal. How much to add depends on the nature of the material to be composted. Low-nitrogen materials like straw, sawdust, corncobs, and old weeds should have at least two or three pounds of nitrogen supplements added per 100 pounds of raw material. If plenty of manure, grass clippings, fresh weeds, and other relatively high-nitrogen materials is available to be mixed with the compost, little if any nitrogen supplement will be necessary.

Some of the commercial compost activators that are sold are high in nitrogen, and it is probably this nitrogen value which accounts for their effectiveness, if any.

The general conclusion is that commercial activators are not essential to efficient composting, since microorganisms are already present in the organic materials to be decomposed, and these are quite capable of doing the job if the proper environmental conditions are met. While certain commercial activators and supplements may improve the overall nutrient value of the compost (and even this is doubtful), it appears false to credit them with accelerating the decomposition process.

See also COMPOSTING.

ADOBE SOILS

Adobe is the Spanish word for sun-dried mud brick; earth from which such bricks can be made is called adobe soil. Usually red or yellow in color, adobe occurs in many parts of the American Southwest where, in conjunction with a dry climate and "hard" water, it confronts the gardener with numerous special problems.

Adobe soil is heavy clay, sometimes with an admixture of silt. It is likely to be rich in minerals, but almost entirely deficient in humus. Of all soil types it is one of two (sand is the other) that will benefit most conspicuously from organic gardening methods.

Being heavy, it requires aeration. In its natural state it will contain no earthworms (ants and tunneling gophers aerate it for the native vegetation). It will be alkaline, with a pH of at least 7.5 and probably higher. Because of this, some essential nutrients, phosphorus and iron among them, will be unavailable.

The first step will be to add humus. This may not be easy, but the results make any effort worthwhile. By doing this every one of the problems named above will be minimized, some entirely eliminated. The soil will become easier to till. Moisture will seep down and be held instead of running off. In this converted adobe, earthworms may be planted and will flourish. Since humus is a neutralizer, the alkalinity will be brought down to a point suitable for many garden plants. Even the vital iron, which has been there all the time (the red in adobe is iron oxide), and the locked-up phosphates may be freed to some extent. They should be supplemented, however, by using ground phosphate rock, and, if iron-deficiency symptoms appear, by the application of acid organic materials such as peat moss, sawdust and oak leaves.

See also ACIDITY–ALKALINITY.

ADONIS

This genus of the Buttercup family is comprised of ornamentals such as the pheasant's-eye and 40 other Eurasian species. These herbs have finely divided leaves, showy red or yellow flowers, and grow from nine to 18 inches high. The fruits are achenes.

Of easy culture, adonis grows in any light, moist, fairly rich soil and will do well in either full sun or partial shade. The perennial species are recommended for borders.

The annuals of the adonis group are propagated by seeds sown ¼ inch deep in sandy loam in autumn or very early spring. With perennials, dividing in the first part of spring is best.

A. aestivalis and *A. annua* are yellow and purplish annuals that are naturalized in eastern North America.

AERATION

Soil contains two types of pores, macropores and micropores. Macropores generally allow the ready exchange of air and movement of water. In micropores, both air and water movement is restricted. Fine-textured soils have a large proportion of pore space, but since the space is filled with micropores that can hold water, the soil can easily become waterlogged. In silt loam soils in good condition, the total pore space is often nearly 50 percent of the total and is likely to be shared evenly by water and air.

Soil aeration is directly related to the porosity of the soil. Proper aeration of the soil is important to proper plant growth. Well-aerated soil consists of a large proportion of macropores, allowing sufficient quantities of the right gases to be available to aerobic organisms to encourage best functioning and growth. Poor aeration results in a decrease in the activity of soil microorganisms. When oxidation of organic matter slows, aerobic organisms are unable to function properly. Higher plants are adversely affected in several ways. Root and top growth is slowed, absorption of nutrients and water is decreased and certain inorganic compounds toxic to plant growth may form.

Role of Soil Air: Air is needed in the soil for the decomposition of organic matter, and is necessary for the proper functioning of soil microorganisms and oxidation of mineral matter. In poorly aerated soil, few minerals are available for plant sustenance. The presence of sufficient oxygen helps to balance the supply of carbon dioxide, and in the process of plant respiration, oxygen is absorbed by plant roots. Better soil aeration enables plants to develop a bigger root system and results in higher yields. In the process of plant growth, the leaves absorb carbon dioxide from the atmosphere and give off oxygen. The reverse takes place in the roots, which take in oxygen and give off carbon dioxide. In the decay of organic matter, carbon dioxide is given off.

The composition of soil air differs somewhat from that of the atmosphere above ground. In the soil much of the air is dissolved in the soil water, but as such it is available to the needs of plants. Humidity is greater in the soil, a condition necessary for the optimum functioning of soil organisms. The carbon dioxide content is much higher in soil air and the percentage of oxygen and nitrogen less. While too much of this gas is detrimental, enough is needed to provide the needs for the biochemical activities that begin to take place before the nutrients enter the roots.

Causes of Poor Aeration: Properly aerated soil has both sufficient space for air to be present in the soil and allows unimpeded air flow in and out of this space. The amount of space available for air to be present in the soil is largely dependent on the water content of the soil. A high water content means that little or no room is left for gases in the soil. A waterlogged condition is so detrimental to plant growth that even a short period may seriously endanger some plants. This may occur either in poorly drained soils composed of fine particles or in well-drained soil if enough water is rapidly applied. Prevention of this type of poor aeration necessitates removing water from the land, either by controlled runoff or drainage; the latter can be particularly effective.

Poor aeration can also be due to restricted flow of air from the atmosphere into soil pores. Most of the gaseous interchange with the atmosphere occurs through diffusion, which is hampered by a lack of macropores in the soil. On heavily textured topsoils and in compact subsoils, the rate of gaseous movement is particularly slow.

Some chemical fertilizers harden the soil and reduce aeration. Nitrate of soda is a typical offender. In yearly applications of this fertilizer, plants use up much of the nitrate but little of the soda. This keeps piling up in the soil, and combines with carbon to form carbonate of soda (washing soda). Where large amounts of nitrate of soda are used, the soil can become so hard that it can be cultivated only after a rain.

Improving Aeration: Drainage and air exchange are both improved in soils of good structure. The best way to maintain good soil porosity is to incorporate organic matter into the soil by turning under green manure and farm manures, or adding compost to your soil.

The earthworm is a great aid to soil aeration. The earthworm will burrow down six feet and more, leaving its passageways as means for the entry of air. Applications of organic matter automatically multiply the earthworm population. In well-run organic farms and gardens there should be millions of earthworms per acre.

The subsoiler made by many tractor manufacturers is pulled through the soil at depths of ten to 20 inches, shattering hardpans and improving aeration. The soil must not be wet when subsoiling is going on or the hardpan will not be broken.

A legume crop is a good natural subsoiler on soil with a high enough oxygen content to support it. Alfalfa roots have been known to go down 15 feet or more. The decaying roots of this crop after harvest provide air passageways to very low depths.

Tilling is an excellent means of improving soil aeration and reducing the carbon dioxide content of the soil. When one plows or tills corn and then cultivates three times while the crop grows, much air is mixed with the soil, weeds are killed and crop yields increase.

See also CARBON DIOXIDE, COMPOSTING, CULTIVATION, GREEN MANURE, MANURE, ORGANIC MATTER, OXYGEN, SUBSOILING.

AEROBIC COMPOSTING

Aerobic composting is composting done in the presence of oxygen. It is characterized by high temperatures and an absence of foul odors. It is more rapid than anaerobic composting, which is composting done in the absence of oxygen. Most modern composting processes are aerobic.

See also ANAEROBIC COMPOSTING, COMPOSTING.

AESCHYNANTHUS

Formerly called *Trichosporum,* this genus of the Gesneria family contains several trailing or climbing plants that produce showy clusters of crimson flowers throughout the summer. *A. radicans,* the lipstick vine, has tubular, bright red flowers. *A. pulcher,* the royal-red bugler, has yellow-throated crimson flowers.

In its native tropical habitat, the aeschynanthus grows rampantly on trees and dead logs. They are occasionally grown in greenhouses having a winter temperature of 60 to 70°F. (15.56 to 21.11°C.), with shade from strong sun. The best way to propagate them is to insert three-inch-long cuttings in an osmunda/sphagnum moss/charcoal mixture and keep them at a moist temperature of 75 to 85°F. (23.89 to 29.44°C.) until rooted.

AFRICAN DAISY

Many different members of the Daisy family are commonly called African daisy.

Arctotis acaulis is an annual having silvery, hairy leaves and daisylike flowers with white petals and blue black centers. It prefers a hot, dry location. The plants tend to bloom heavily for a short time, but bloom can be extended by keeping the flower heads picked.

Lonas annua is the original African daisy, once used frequently by florists. It is a profusely blooming annual growing about one foot tall. No longer widely grown, it is generally cultivated only in botanical gardens.

Gazania ringens is a perennial used in borders and summer gardens; it has yellow rays with dark centers.

Grown as an annual in all but the warmest regions of the world, African daisies are compact, bushy plants with large, soft leaves and flowers that come in a range of brilliant colors.

Dimorphotheca sinuata is a half-hardy annual with apricot petals and deep violet centers; it is also called Cape marigold.

See also Cape Marigold, Gazania.

AFRICAN LILY
(*Agapanthus africanus*)

Also called lily-of-the-Nile, this tuberous-rooted herb of the Lily family has many long, narrow, dark leaves, from among which arises a stem two or three feet high. This bears a large umbel of very handsome, blue funnel-shaped flowers. Dwarf types include Peter Pan, with deep blue flowers on 18-inch stems, and Rancho Dwarf, a white form with stems 24 inches high. Unlike the amaryllis, the African lily blooms with its leaves, which adds to its beauty. All are ideal for patio planting.

The easiest way to grow it is in pots or tubs which are stored in a light cellar or other dry place during the winter. During the resting period give the plant just enough water to prevent the leaves from falling. In the spring, when danger of frost is past, the plants are put outdoors to flower and make their growth. Pot them in large containers in equal parts of loam, leaf mold, well-rotted manure, and sharp sand. Feed weekly with fish emulsion or dilute compost tea. They can hardly be overwatered. With heavy feeding they multiply rapidly; divide them in spring when necessary.

AFRICAN VIOLETS   (*Saintpaulia*)

No house plant has grown in popularity as rapidly as the African violet. Varieties have multiplied and their collection has become an obsession with some people, but it is only in recent years that they have really started to come into their own.

The African violet has a quiet charm and is one of the most generous of plants with its blossoms. Many plants flower without ceasing for well over a year. Frequently a well-grown plant will carry 30 or more open flowers at the same time, almost hiding the foliage under its crown of beauty.

In their natural home, African violets grow in the woods in limestone regions near streams and waterfalls. The plants grow close to rocks and boulders where they get constant shade and where the rocks act to keep the temperature of the soil at a uniform level.

Anyone can grow good, robust African violets by observing a few basic rules regarding proper lighting, temperature, watering, humidity, and fertilizing.

Proper lighting is very important—too much light may cause burning, too little will check growth and flowering. Light from an east window from September to March, and from a north window from March to September, should give excellent results.

During the months when artificial heat is necessary, house temperatures should be about 70 to 72°F. (21.11 to 22.22°C.) during the day, falling to 65°F. (18.33°C.) at night.

Watering: Proper humidity and watering cannot be overstressed. Many troubles will be avoided if greater care is given these two essentials. To avoid water spotting the leaves, water plants with tepid water when the sun is not shining on them.

Pots three inches or smaller should be watered from the bottom. Pour enough water into the saucer and permit the plant to "drink" for a half hour; then pour off the excess. Larger potted plants should be watered from the top. Do not overwater as this cuts off the air from the plants, and air is of the utmost importance.

Insufficient humidity causes leaf curl and bud drop. To increase the humidity, fill plant saucers with moist gravel, place pans of water near radiators or use plant sprayer.

Plants should not be watered on cloudy or rainy days, unless, of course, they are very dry. It is well to check them daily, since allowing the soil to get too dry affects the tiny root hairs that absorb the food for the plant. These tiny hairs become incapable of absorbing water when dried out, causing a setback to the plant until new root hairs are grown.

If the water in your area is chlorinated, draw some off for watering and allow it to stand for 24 hours before using it on your plants. Try to use rain or spring water when available.

To feed the plant, choose a clear bright day, water the plant, wait several hours to prevent burning of root hairs, and apply a liquified organic plant food according to the directions of the container. It is well to make a V-shaped hole against the side of the pot and apply fertilizer slowly at this point. Fertilizer should always be applied to the surface of the soil, and the watering following fertilizing should be surface watering; then return to usual method.

A three-inch pot will accommodate a plant for a long period of time. It is time to repot when there is a network of root hairs and a nine- to 12-inch spread to the plant.

Repotting: For repotting, the soil should be a loose, friable one consisting of one-third good garden soil, one-third sand and one-third peat or leaf mold. To this mixture add one teaspoonful of bone meal for each quart of mix. The soil should be slightly acid, about pH 6.5. For the beginner and the inexperienced gardener, it is advisable to use one of the well-prepared organic soil mixes on the market. These mixes are complete and especially prepared for African violets.

When potting, remember that the roots are delicate and the fine root hairs absorb the nourishment, so care must be taken to pot loosely, gently firming the soil about the roots. The potting mixture should be moist, not wet.

Place a piece of broken flowerpot over the drainage hole of a large pot, then a ¼-inch layer of chicken grit (or crushed oyster shells or flowerpot chips), followed by a wad of sphagnum moss and the potting soil. Place just enough potting soil in the pot so that when the root ball is set on it, the crown of the plant is ¼ to ½ inch below the rim of the pot. Now fill in the sides of the pot, tapping gently to settle the soil and prevent air pockets.

If pots are to be watered from below, omit the drainage material and just cover the drainage hole with broken pot chips.

The newly potted plants are ready for a bath to cleanse the leaves of dust and soil. Place them in the bathtub and sprinkle lightly with tepid water from a watering can equipped with a fine nozzle, until leaves are clean and soil settled in the pot. Leave the pots in the tub and keep them shaded and out of drafts until the leaves are dry. If leaves become wet and the room temperature is too cool, the leaves will spot.

Stem or petiole rot can occur where violet leaves touch the rims of clay pots. To prevent this condition, plant only in plastic pots or lip clay pot rims in paraffin.

Propagation: The early spring months through summer are the time for propagating leaves. Cut a few leaves from the center of a plant for best results. Trim the leaf stalk to about 1½ inches in length and insert in a glass of water or vermiculite. By using a large pot, a number of leaves can be rooted at the same time. When leaves have been set in position in vermiculite, add water gently until the granular mixture is damp.

When the plantlets are ready to be potted, have ready a mixture of half soil and half vermiculite. Place a piece of flowerpot over the drainage hole, add some of the soil mixture, set one crown to a pot (1½-inch size), and finish potting. Add water meagerly. Remove suckers as they appear. Feed once a week with liquid organic fertilizer.

When plantlets have outgrown the small pot, repot to a slightly larger one using a rich potting mixture made for African violets, as the ones described earlier. Try to keep plants root-bound to force blooms. If plants must develop roots, they will not develop buds at the same time.

Varieties: Here are a few African violets that are worthy of space in your collection.

Strike Me Pink is everything the name implics with its diminutive roselike blossoms and cupped, fluted-edged leaves, which are dark, glossy green with white throats.

Double Pink Cheer is a slightly darker pink rosette; the flower rises above oval pinked-margined leaves supported by longer petioles than Strike Me Pink.

The lighter green foliage of the Fringed Snow Prince is topped with tall stems of fringed, dainty white blossoms. This one, coupled with contrasting varieties of deeper colors, adds much pleasure and interest to any collection.

Bluc Pom, with its lovely double bloom of deep blue and fragile pale green foliage, is also appealing.

See also HOUSE PLANTS.

AFTERMATH

Aftermath is the late summer and fall growth of grasses which have been cut earlier in the same season. It is sometimes called rowen.

AGARICUS   *See* MUSHROOM

AGAVE

Native to the southwestern United States and Mexico, these succulents are plants that grow until they flower, then they die. Some species are used to produce pulque and mescal, popular Mexican drinks, and sisal hemp.

They are fine garden plants in low frost regions, but most are poor house plants because of their large size. The best for house plants are varieties of the century plant, *A. americana* cv. 'Marginata' and *A. a.* cv. 'Medio-picta', and the species *A. Victoriae-Reginae*. Agaves prefer a sunny southern exposure and a well-drained cactus soil that should dry thoroughly between waterings. Propagation is by suckers. Potted plants will probably never bloom.

See also SUCCULENTS.

AGERATUM

Sometimes called flossflower, ageratum is a profusely blooming, tender annual with fluffy flowers borne in dense heads. The dwarf varieties are high on the list of garden flowers used for borders, edgings, rock gardens, window boxes, and small beds. The tall varieties are good for cut flowers and may also be dried for winter arrangements. Ageratum is a constant bloomer, and the popular blue violet color combines with practically any other garden color.

Culture: Seeds can be started indoors and seedlings transplanted outside as soon as they are big enough to handle and all danger of frost has passed. Seeds can also be planted directly in the open ground where the plants are to flower, when the soil has warmed up in the spring. Care must be taken to water them when the weather remains dry. Ageratums will do well in sun or in semishade.

A finely pulverized seedbed is essential. The soil should be spaded to a depth of six to eight inches. Incorporating compost, woods soil or other humus is ideal. This will provide a rich soil that will hold moisture well. Ageratum develops a heavy fibrous root system and is quite drought resistant once it becomes established. Keep it moist in the early stages of growth.

The seed of ageratum is very fine, so barely cover it with a light layer of fine soil. This may be easily accomplished by sifting the soil through a box or pan with a fine wire mesh on the bottom. After covering the seed, use a flat board or block to tamp the soil into close seed-soil contact. Do this lightly so as not to pack the soil.

After the plants are a few inches high, thin to 6 to 8 inches for the dwarf varieties and 10 to 12 inches apart for the tall-growing varieties. When the plants begin to bloom, keep the shabby seed heads picked. This is easily done with a lawn-edging shears and not only improves the appearance of the plants but will also encourage profuse blooming throughout the entire season. In the fall, just before frost, you can pot plants of the dwarf varieties and take them indoors for several more weeks of blooming.

Varieties: The dwarf and compact forms are generally preferred to the tall varieties. Of the dwarf varieties the blue violet color is the most popular. Among this group Blue Cap, Midget Blue, Blue Ball, Blue Perfection, Blue Blazer, and Tetra Blue are good varieties. Imperial Dwarf White and Summer Snow are good white varieties. If you wish to use alternate plants of blue and white in a bedding or

The soft, compact flowers of the ageratum can be dried for winter arrangements.

edging scheme, be careful to get varieties that mature at the same height or some will grow up to cover the others. Possible combinations are Blue Blazer and Summer Snow or Snow Carpet and Midget Blue. Tall Blue and Tall White are good varieties in the taller-growing group. These make wonderful cut flowers for bouquets all summer and may also be dried and kept for winter arrangements. Cut the flowers just as they open, bunch about a dozen stalks together and hang from the ceiling of your basement. They require a dark, moisture-free place to dry satisfactorily. If dried in the light, the blue violet color will fade considerably more than in the dark.

AGGREGATE SOIL

Referring to soil structure, an aggregate consists of many fine soil particles held in a single cluster, such as a clod or crumb. The ideal soil structure is granular, where the rounded aggregates of soil lie loosely and readily shake apart. When the granules are especially porous, the term crumb is applied.

AGRICULTURAL EXPERIMENT STATIONS
See EXTENSION SERVICES, COOPERATIVE; GOVERNMENT SERVICES

AGROSTEMMA   *See* LYCHNIS

A HORIZON   *See* SOIL HORIZON

AILANTHUS

The best-known ailanthus is the tree-of-heaven, also called stinkweed for its malodorous male flowers. The tree of *A Tree Grows in Brooklyn,* it seems to thrive on the worst that the city environment has to offer. Soot, smoke and other air pollutants apparently do not faze the tree-of-heaven. While it does best in a light, moist soil, it will grow just about anywhere.

This tree is suited to the city environment, but is seldom chosen as an ornamental in areas where other attractive trees will grow; the tree-of-heaven spreads its seeds so successfully that it is often regarded as a weed, and the fast-growing, brittle branches litter the ground after a windstorm. It can be propagated either by seeds or root cuttings.

AIR LAYERING
See LAYERING, PROPAGATION

AIR PLANT
See EPIPHYTE, KALANCHOE

AJUGA   (*Ajuga reptans*)

Often called bugleweed, this herb of the Mint family is commonly found in moist lowlands, though it will grow well in most varieties of garden soils. It is distinguished by the glands dotting the lower parts of its leaves and the irregular, two-lipped flowers which resemble small bugles. The flowers are white, blue and occasionally red, making ajuga a frequent choice for borders and rock gardens. Propagation is by division or seeds.

Ajuga has been valued as an astringent for many decades. Once a popular remedy for throat and bronchial inflammations, bugleweed is today regarded by some as an effective remedy for diarrhea and dysentery.

See also HERB.

ALBINO FLOWERS

True albinos are white sports or breaks from a normally colored species. These can be differentiated from nonalbinos, the stems and foliage of which are pure green. Albino plants are generally short-lived because they lack the chlorophyll necessary for photosynthesis.

ALBRECHT, DR. WILLIAM A.

(1888–1975) Dr. Albrecht was an eminent agricultural scientist whose studies in the fields of soil microbiology, nitrogen fixation, inoculation of legumes, amino acids in soil fertility, animal husbandry, and nutrition achieved worldwide recognition. As a student of nature as well as a scientist, Albrecht recognized the fundamental relation between sound, natural soil care and the health and welfare of humans. Vitally concerned with trace metal deficiencies, he was also among the first to realize the importance of nutritional quality versus yield per se. He challenged the tendency of agricultural research to measure yields merely in terms of bushels or cash returns per acre or man-hours. "Qualities that deal with life, not quantities of materials alone," was his maxim.

For over 20 years he was the chairman of the Department of Soils at the University of Missouri, where he taught since 1916. During World War II he served as an instructor of soils at the U.S. Army University in Biarritz, France. He was a consulting editor for several magazines, including *Soil Science,* and his writings appeared frequently in the pages of *Organic Gardening and Farming®*. Upon retirement from formal teaching, Dr. Albrecht remained as Professor Emeritus of Soils at the University of Missouri until his death in 1975. The majority of Albrecht's thoughts are summarized in his book *Soil Fertility and Animal Health,* published in 1958, and *The Albrecht Papers* (Acres, U.S.A., 1976).

ALCHEMILLA

These somewhat weedy perennial herbs of the Rose family make hardy rock garden and low border plants. They produce small green or yellow flowers, small dry fruit and attractive silver gray leaves.

Easily grown in full sun and any well-drained garden soil, alchemillas are propagated by seeds or root division.

ALDRIN
See CHLORINATED HYDROCARBONS

ALFALFA   (*Medicago sativa*)

A perennial, herbaceous legume, alfalfa is the standard by which other legumes are compared. Plants bear purple or yellow flowers in loose racemes and the leaves are pinnately trifoliate and arranged alternately on the stem. Pods are twisted and spiraled, and contain small, kidney bean-shaped seeds. The root system can be extensive, developing a thick taproot that penetrates the soil 23 feet or more. Alfalfa develops a crown at or near the surface of the soil from which grow five to 25 or more stems; as stems mature or are cut, more grow from the crown. Plants grow from two to three feet high.

Alfalfa is suitable for general feeding purposes, pasture, as an excellent cover crop, and is valuable as a green manure, furnishing nitrogen for future crops. Alfalfa grows virtually everywhere in the United States, with highest yields reported from the North Central states; cultivars have even survived −57°F. (−49.44°C.) temperatures in Alaska.

Alfalfa does best on well-drained, deep

Although well adapted to a wide range of climatic and soil conditions, alfalfa performs best in regions where rainfall is moderate, winters are cool and soils are deep and well drained.

loams with porous subsoils. It does not thrive on either acid or highly alkaline soils, preferring a pH of 6.5 to 7. Areas east of the Mississippi generally need lime for best results. Potassium and phosphorus may also be necessary, since alfalfa needs these for a good yield. Alfalfa does well on dry soils if irrigated. For best results, alfalfa seeds should be inoculated with rhizobia bacteria before planting.

In many parts of the United States, farmers seed alfalfa in spring. In certain areas, however, other times of the year are recommended for best results. In the Southwest, plantings should not be made in the heat of summer and are usually made in December. If you are unsure about the best planting time for alfalfa in your area, check with neighboring farmers or with the state agricultural extension service.

Alfalfa is a very heavy feeder, and each stand needs a good supply of plant food. Manure has been found to be very satisfactory, supplying the crop with needed trace elements as well as humus. Regular applications of rock phosphate and potash are essential.

Alfalfa is usually planted with a nurse crop. It can be broadcast seeded in winter wheat or similar crops early in spring, but best results are obtained by drilling seed with oats or other spring-planted grains. Use 10 to 12 pounds of seed per acre when seeded with a single grass, 5 to 6 pounds per acre in other mixtures. The nurse crop will control most weeds and although the alfalfa stand will not be quite as heavy as it would be if planted alone, the grain crop will make up for the loss.

Like other legumes, alfalfa is valuable for its ability to fix nitrogen in the soil. The plants draw nitrogen from the air and rhizobia bacteria in nodules on the plant roots change the nitrogen into a form the plant can use.

ALFALFA

Stage	Analysis in %			
	Minerals	Protein	Fiber	Fat
Bud	10.3	19.6	28.0	2.4
1/10 bloom	10.2	18.1	30.1	2.4
1/2 bloom	9.7	16.9	32.6	2.6
Full bloom	9.6	15.9	33.3	2.1
Seeds ripe	8.5	14.5	35.3	2.1

Nitrogen-fixing abilities are greatly enhanced by inoculation before planting; the USDA estimates that alfalfa fixes between 100 and 200 pounds of nitrogen per acre, depending on conditions. *See also* LEGUME.

Alfalfa makes an excellent green manure crop as well, returning additional nitrogen to the soil as it decomposes—often as much as 100 pounds per acre. In addition, it averages 2 to 3 percent potash, often returning 75 pounds or more potash to the soil as it decomposes, depending on crop yield.

Alfalfa is also excellent pasture. When grazed, it is usually mixed with timothy, orchardgrass or smooth bromegrass. Excellent for swine, alfalfa is also used for sheep and cattle; mixed stands reduce the hazard of bloat, but even such pasturage is best supplemented with grain rations for improved stock energy. Rotational grazing of alfalfa pastures is best.

Alfalfa makes excellent hay. It is high in protein, often offering 11 pounds of digestible protein per 100 pounds, as opposed to 7.2 pounds for clover, depending on growing and curing conditions and time of harvest. Although it has a lower net energy value than grass hay, it is a good source of calcium, vitamins A and D, niacin, and riboflavin.

The quality of the hay ultimately depends on the stage at which it is cut, and the type of curing it receives. Hay of a good green color and a large leaf content, cured without wetting, has the highest feeding value. Generally, the earlier hay is cut, the higher its protein and vitamin content, the lower its fiber content, and the greater its digestibility. However, continuous cutting at bud or prebud stage will severely reduce the tonnage per acre and prematurely kill the stand by reducing the food reserves in the roots. One cutting per year may be made at prebloom stage without damaging the stand if done early in the year.

Obviously, a balance must be made between nutritional value and cutting time. The best time to cut alfalfa is at the early flower stage—from first flower to 1/10 bloom. When bloom is delayed or spotty, cutting may be gauged by the amount of new growth at the crown. However, a cutting should not be made in the fall later than four weeks before the average date of the first killing frost. This will permit considerable top growth so that the roots can store enough food for winter.

Time of cutting is more important in determining hay quality than any other single factor. It influences protein content as well as minerals, fiber and fat as shown in the table above.

ALGAE

Most algae are microscopic green plants that live as single cells or in large colonies of unicellular entities. Three of the seven phyla or classifications of algae are seaweeds: green algae (sea lettuce), brown algae from the kelp beds off the California coast, and red algae, found mostly in subtidal areas. Algae are valuable contributors to water, soil and industry, provided they are controlled against usurping plant and mineral resources.

Although most algae are green, some types are blue, blue green, yellow, orange, red, brown, black, or colorless. A few change colors. Most algae conduct photosynthesis daily, and some eat bacteria, plant tissue and other organic matter just as animals do.

Common pond scum, the growth covering sides of trees, and the seaweeds washed up on our beaches are all algae. Algae also exist in fishbowls and large aquariums. They make the water cloudy and cover the glass with green slime unless eaten by snails or other animals which keep their numbers down.

Marine algae, as opposed to freshwater algae, are often recognized as a potential food source, especially in the Orient. Kombu, made from boiled and dried kelp, is a staple in Japan.

Freshwater algae are also being studied as a food resource, specifically *Chlorella*. *Chlorella* have potentially high fat or protein content, depending on the manner of cultivation.

Algae have contributed to various industrial practices. Kelps and rockweeds have served as potassium and iodine sources. Agar-agar, obtained from red alga *Gelidium*, is used as a solidifying agent in culture media at science laboratories. Algae are also a stiffening agent in food processing and clarifier of liquid products. Alginates, the salts extracted from kelps, are employed in the manufacture of ice cream.

Algae sometimes present a threat to neighboring plant life and mineral resources. One effective method of checking growth of pond scum is to create surface turbulence by blowing air over the pond or bubbling it up through the water. Other useful types of algae control include stocking the pond with snails, geese, ducks, and other species which feed on algae and keep it in check.

Obviously not all algae grow in ponds or saltwater. Some algae live on tree bark, others live in protozoa (one-celled animals), or together with fungi in the form of lichens. Even hot sulfur springs, coral reefs, the Dead Sea, and glaciers in the polar regions have algae.

Algae are very active in association with limestone. In the tropics and subtropics, certain marine algae coat themselves thickly with lime and contribute to the formation of coral reefs which eventually become calcareous soils. Layers of the mineral travertine are formed by algae in hot springs containing large amounts of calcium and magnesium in solution. Marl deposits on shallow lake bottoms and calcareous pebbles result from algal action. It is thought that the siliceous sinter deposits around hot springs may also be produced by algae.

In the economy of the soil, algae may play a surprising role. Under favorable weather conditions providing warmth and moisture, the growth of algae in the upper three inches of a soil may add as much as six tons of organic matter per acre.

To do this, algae must take about a quarter-of-a-million (250,000) cubic feet of carbon dioxide out of the air. They use the energy in sunlight to produce the organic matter in their cells from this enormous amount of carbon dioxide gas.

The role of algae in connection with soil organic matter is even more interesting. Their growth results in a net production of organic matter, since they convert carbon dioxide gas into cell material.

Although other microbes, such as the bacteria and fungi, are important in transforming organic matter generally and in changing it into humus, their activities always result in a net decrease of organic matter. They oxidize some of the original material to carbon dioxide which passes into the atmosphere. It is the algae which help turn this carbon dioxide back to organic matter and plow it into the soil, so to speak.

Other aspects of soil algae are equally interesting and important. Certain of the so-called blue green algae are nitrogen-fixers. At the same time that they produce soil organic matter from carbon dioxide, these legumelike microbes enrich the soil with nitrogen since they make their cell protein from nitrogen in the air.

The important soil-forming activities of lichens probably depend on the nitrogen-fixing ability of the algal partners in these fungus-alga associations. Lichens on bare rock surface far above timberline can get their required nitrogen only from the atmosphere. By fixing nitrogen both for themselves and for the fungi with which they are intimately combined, algae make life possible for the resulting lichen.

It is also significant that blue green algae are among the first living creatures to become established on volcanic ash and lava, after it has cooled, and there initiate the slow process of soil formation. Primitive algae thus create conditions which permit more advanced plants to develop. In rice fields algae are believed to benefit the rice plants by taking up some of the carbon dioxide and providing oxygen which the submerged roots require for "breathing."

Algae are among the most important microbes in the soil. They are not responsible for serious crop losses as are certain disease-producing fungi and bacteria. In soil or water they work unobtrusively, but constructively.

See also LICHEN, MICROORGANISM.

ALKALIGRASS   *See* ZIGADENUS

ALKALI SOILS

Alkali soils fall into two groups. The first is soil in which an accumulation of soluble salts—usually the chlorides and sulfates of sodium, calcium and magnesium, and sometimes potassium—is present. This is called white alkali or saline soil. The second is soil in which there are large amounts of absorbed sodium that either are directly toxic to plants or harm them by making the soil impermeable by water. This is called black or true alkali soil. White alkali is the most common type, found in almost all arid and semiarid regions.

White alkali soil is easily recognized—it frequently has a white crust on its surface and shows streaks of salt within the soil. White alkali soils generally have good structure, and a pH seldom rising above 8.5. *See also* SALINE SOIL.

Both types may be caused either by a high water table which brings the soluble salts to the surface by capillary movement, or by the depositing of these salts in the soil by irrigation water. Digging into the rock substrata under the subsoil in many of these areas will reveal large amounts of sodium there. If excessive irrigation or other factors raise the ground-water level, sodium will rise with it and be left in the surface soil when the water evaporates. This causes black alkali soil, most damaging to crops because it has poor structure and puddles and packs easily. White alkali soils are similarly formed, but they contain less sodium and do not pack.

What happens to plants in an alkali environment? The strong soil solution has a corrosive effect on the roots and stems, causing an actual shrinkage of the tissues that makes them less able to take up water. The large amounts of salts in the soil displace needed nutrients, causing nutritional deficiencies, especially of phosphorus, iron and manganese.

Sodium causes a breakdown of the soil humus and clay. This results in the loss of good soil structure and the beginning of puddling and erosion. Water infiltration and root penetration are hindered, and aeration is reduced. The anaerobic conditions thus produced make toxic compounds of many of the elements present. Microbial life ceases, and the soil is dead.

Alkali soils, from the very nature of their development, are usually deficient in organic matter and nitrogen.

Rebuilding Alkali Soils: Drainage is very important for reclaiming alkali soils, especially where the water table is high. The soil should be permeable to a depth well below the root zone. The groundwater level should never come nearer the surface than at least ten feet. In the case of hardpans, subsoiling is a must to insure good drainage. Tile drains are sometimes necessary.

Once adequate drainage is established, leaching will help remove the salts. Irrigation water should be applied well in excess of the amount needed by the crop. If the irrigation water itself contains harmful salts to any degree, apply extra-large quantities to make sure these salts, too, wash down. Don't conserve water at the expense of soil conservation! Each field should be carefully leveled, of course, so the water will enter the soil uniformly.

There are a number of other ways to restore the soil's organic content. Acid peats can be purchased in carload lots. Or, collect waste organic materials; apply as a mulch or partially disk into the soil. Apply 40 to 50 tons per acre in conjunction with frequent irrigations to promote leaching of the salts.

In India, cheap organic materials like manure, oilcake and such by-products of the sugar industry as molasses and press-mud, effected excellent reclamation. Gypsum was almost totally ineffective.

Besides building up the soil's structure, organic matter exerts a "buffer" action, lessening the toxicity of the strong salts to plants. It also lowers the pH and improves the soil's capacity to supply available nitrogen.

Manure or sludge (20 tons or more to the acre) is also excellent, as is growing crops like sweet clover. Plowing in a green manure crop increases the carbon dioxide content of the soil air, causing displacement of the harmful sodium by calcium. Other good alkali-resistant crops are sugar beets, cotton, rye, sorghum, and barley. Alfalfa is very good because it requires a flooding type of irrigation that aids leaching, and its tough roots help break up the packed soil. Always prepare a good seedbed, have the soil moist to insure germination, and use more seed than usual.

In California, the Bermudagrass that often infests alfalfa fields has been found to be a fine alkali soil reclaimer. It provides valuable pasturage while at the same time preparing the soil for less alkali-resistant crops.

Keep a mulch on soil wherever possible to retard evaporation. The soil should always be moist enough to keep any salts in it dilute. Irrigate often and lightly. Soils that show a marked tendency toward becoming alkali should have organic matter added to them as often as practical.

See also ACIDITY—ALKALINITY, LIME, pH.

ALLAMANDA

These tropical vines and shrubs make excellent plants for the greenhouse and are often grown outdoors in the South. Yellow or rose violet bell-shaped flowers bloom abundantly, and the vines climb trellises and fences rapidly.

Allamandas are simple to grow; a favorite potting mixture is about one part sand, two parts loam and one part leaf mold. To aid drainage, add charcoal.

Plants should be watered frequently and fertilized every few weeks with liquid manure. From late autumn to early spring, however, watering should be almost eliminated.

Yellow bell (*A. nerifolia*) is one of the lower-growing varieties, reaching about five feet.

ALLIGATOR PEAR   *See* AVOCADO

ALLIUM

This hardy genus of vegetables and herbs gives us the chive, garlic, leek, onion, and shallot. (*See* CHIVES, GARLIC, LEEK, ONION, SHALLOT.) The genus also includes several

Ornamental alliums need no special treatment and will bloom in spring and summer.

hardy ornamental species that bloom early to sprinkle a variety of colors around new garden borders. Bulbs of the Allium family generally can be planted in the fall or, for late-blooming crops, very early in the spring.

ALLUVIAL SOIL
See ALLUVIUM, AZONAL SOIL

ALLUVIUM

Fine material such as mud or clay carried and deposited by streams is called alluvium. There are three types of alluvial deposits: floodplains, alluvial fans and deltas. Great alluvial valleys and deltas include the Nile, the Mississippi, the Amazon, and other large river valleys, many of them the homes of early civilizations. Some of these soils are supplemented annually by a thin covering of fresh alluvium from eroding rocks which is added to the surface during periods of high water in the river.

Alluvial material ranges in texture from fine clay to large rocks and even boulders. Fine sediments are washed into the drainage valley from the watershed surface. When the current is swift, the carrying capacity of the stream is high, but as the rate of flow decreases first the coarse and then the fine materials settle out. A common characteristic of all alluvial material is stratification, layers of different-sized particles overlying each other.

Most alluvium is carried and deposited during floods because it is at this period that erosion is most active and the carrying capacity of streams is at a maximum. When a flooding stream overflows its banks, its carrying power is suddenly reduced as the flow area increases and velocity decreases. This causes the coarse sands and gravels to settle along the bank where they sometimes form conspicuous ridges called natural levees. As the water reaches the floodplains of the valley, the rate of flow is slow enough to permit the silt to settle. Finally the water is left in quiet pools, from which it seeps away or evaporates, leaving the fine clay. Levees are characterized by good internal drainage during periods of low water, whereas floodplains exhibit poor internal drainage.

Large mature valleys like the Mississippi are characterized by rivers with many meanders which develop in a well-recognized cycle. As a stream swings back and forth across its floodplain, cutting new channels in flood periods, sections of the old bed, known as oxbows, are left as lakes and swamps which fill with sediments during subsequent overflows.

Terracing: Terraces are developed from floodplains as streams cut deeper channels because of lowered outlets. Several terraces may be found along a stream or a lake which has undergone repeated changes in level. Extensive terraces were formed as the glaciers receded and their outwash plains were no longer covered with water. Terraces usually are quite well drained and may be droughty, exhibiting clear stratification. They are likely to be rather infertile.

Streams flowing from hills or mountains into dry valleys or basins drop their sediments in a fanlike deposit as the water spreads out. These alluvial fans are usually coarse textured, being composed of sands and gravels, are well or excessively drained, and low in organic matter.

Floodplains as well as deltas are, in general, rich in plant nutrients and comparatively high in organic matter content. Special crops such as vegetables and fruits frequently are grown on the latter formations because the soil warms up quickly and their good drainage and coarse texture permit free root development.

Delta Soils: Delta soils are formed when the fine sediment carried by a current is not deposited in the floodplain but flows into the body of water to which the smaller stream is tributary. Insufficient current and wave action allows the material to accumulate, beginning formation of a delta, which is enlarged as more material accumulates. Deltas are extremely fertile when subject to flood control and drainage.

Some sediments carried by water are deposited in the ocean or in large bodies of saltwater, such as along much of the Atlantic Coast and extending around the Gulf. These coastal plains can be quite important agriculturally if raised and well drained.

See also AZONAL SOIL.

ALMOND   (*Prunus dulcis*)

Almonds are members of the Rose family and relatives of the peach as well. Native to the Orient and North Africa, almonds were known to all early Mediterranean cultures and are referred to in Greek mythology.

There are two types, bitter and sweet. Sweet almonds are cultivated as food; bitter almonds, which contain prussic acid, are grown mostly for their rootstocks on which sweet almonds are grafted. They are not sold in this country.

Almonds are raised for ornamental and nutritional reasons. Like other nuts, almonds are high in vitamin B and protein. One cup of shelled almonds contains 26 grams of protein, 77 grams of fat, 28 grams of carbohydrates, 332 milligrams of calcium, and small amounts of vitamins B_1 and B_2, iron, and niacin.

The almond tree is as hardy as the peach but its production is more limited because it blossoms a month earlier, making the flowers more susceptible to spring frosts. The nuts ripen from peachlike, fuzzy fruits into the ripe almond and are ready for gathering in late August or September.

The warmer part of the United States is more reliable for almond tree growth. In California almonds are an important crop. California varieties are Nonpareil, IXL, Peerless, Drake, Texas, and Mission. Two or more varieties must be planted together since all are self-sterile.

Propagation is by budding named varieties onto peach or almond seedlings. Bitter almond rootstocks are usually used since they are less expensive than the sweet almond stocks.

Budding takes place in the early autumn. In the following spring, stock is cut back to the bud, which is permitted to grow for a season. At the end of this period, the one-year tree is ready for planting in the orchard.

The almond requires a sandy, well-drained soil, neutral or tending slightly to the alkaline. Since good drainage is essential, plenty of humus should be present to hold moisture while permitting excess water to drain away.

The roots of the tree run deep. It is advisable to break up the topsoil thoroughly and to as great a depth as possible before planting, and then fertilize with plenty of organic matter.

Many commercial growers plant cover crops which are then turned under for green manure, protecting the ground and enriching the soil. This practice should not be necessary on the small homestead where only a few trees are planted.

Compost should be worked in late in the autumn. Place a straw mulch under the tree but not close to the trunk.

Almond trees begin to bear in three or four years and should be in full production in 12 years. Nuts should be harvested when those in the center of the tree are ripe. Nuts which fall to the ground before the regular harvesttime should be cleaned up daily to prevent disease.

After harvesting, shell and dry the nuts. The kernels should be spread for drying in a shady location until the meat is crisp. Kernels can be stored in airtight jars and kept in cool places.

See also NUT TREES.

ALOCASIA

These handsome tropical foliage plants are planted outdoors in southern Florida and California and used in greenhouses in the North. Leaves are arrow shaped and frequently veined and variegated, and flowers are borne in a spathe, like Jack-in-the-pulpit.

A humusy soil is ideal, and it should be kept evenly moist. An east or west exposure, or shaded southern one, is needed. Temperatures at night should be no lower than 70°F. (21.11°C.). Propagation is by suckers or root cuttings. Good species include *Alocasia indica, A. macrorhiza, A. odora,* and *A. sanderiana.* Their heights vary from three to 15 feet.

ALOE

These perennial succulents, with large leaves and tubular red or yellow flowers, make very decorative plants. Their stiff appearance gives a "desert" effect.

Aloe plants often stay healthy for years in the same pot and flower abundantly. Potting mixture recommended is three parts sandy loam, one part broken brick (for drainage), and an addition of some lime, compost or manure. Pot firmly and be sure surplus water can easily leave the soil. Water very little, except when the plant is growing rapidly.

Aloe thrives in low humidity and full sun or partial shade. Propagation is by seed, division or cuttings.

Aloe vera is sometimes called the "burn plant" as its juices are very soothing to minor burns.

Aloe vera *thrives with very little care or watering and can remain in the same pot for several years.*

ALPINE

This term is applied to very high altitude plants—strictly speaking, those above the timberline of a mountain. Many alpine plants are delightful and have been adapted to northern rock gardens.

In their native homes most choice rock garden plants are snow covered from early fall to late spring. In our climate they must be well mulched to prevent their roots being heaved out of the ground by alternate freezing and thawing. Salt hay, peat moss, oak leaves, and evergreen boughs are all light mulching material and will protect the plants while not smothering them with weight. Peat moss and oak leaves should be used in large quantities only on plants that like an acid soil.

See also ROCK GARDEN.

ALPINE FIR   *See* FIR

ALSIKE CLOVER   *See* CLOVER

ALSTROEMERIA

These South American plants produce large red, purple or yellow flowers and are usually grown in a greenhouse or outdoors in southern gardens. They should have some shade (a low ground temperature) and a soil well supplied with sand, leaf mold or other humus, plus a good amount of bone meal.

The Peruvian lily (*A. Pelegrina*), with spotted lilac flowers, can be planted outdoors in the spring, blooms throughout the summer, and should be dug and stored in a cool, dry place for the winter. *A. P.* cv. 'Alba', which produces umbels of white flowers, is considered one of the best for potted culture.

Alstroemerias grow from tuberous roots which should be divided frequently to maintain the vigor of the plant. Do this during the dormant winter period before the plants are set out in the garden for the summer blooming season.

ALTHAEA   (*Althaea officinalis*)

A perennial herb introduced from Europe, althaea now grows wild in sunny marshes near the sea in Massachusetts and Connecticut and along tidal rivers in New York and Pennsylvania. It grows up to four feet tall and has pink flowers in July and August. The roots, leaves and flowers are sometimes used medicinally.

The plant grows well in almost any loose garden soil of moderate fertility but tends to winter-kill under cultivation in situations where the ground freezes to a considerable depth and no mulch or other protection is provided. The plant can be propagated from seed or from divisions of the old roots made early in spring. The seed is sown in shallow drills at least three feet apart, and the seedlings thinned to stand 12 inches apart in the row.

Hollyhock, a member of the genus *Alcea,* is closely related to this plant.

ALUMINUM SULFATE
See FERTILIZER, CHEMICAL

ALYCE CLOVER   *See* CLOVER

ALYSSUM

This spring-blooming perennial is also known as madwort because it was supposed to help in treating sickness brought about by the bite of a mad dog. Fine for rock gardens and in front of borders, low-growing alyssums have a decorative foliage and numerous clusters of small white or yellow blossoms. They grow in any well-drained soil and should have prolonged sun. Propagation is by division, cuttings or seed.

See also BORDER, SWEET ALYSSUM.

AMARANTH   (*Amaranthus*)

Amaranth is the generic term for a group of annual herbs. They are widely distributed, vigorous growers, thriving in heat and full sunshine. Often grown in the United States as an ornamental, the plant is an important food source in many other parts of the world. The stalks can be served like asparagus; the leaves can be eaten raw in salads or cooked like spinach; and the mature pods can be ground for flour or popped like corn. The nutritional equal of spinach, amaranth leaves have the further advantages of a milder flavor and a lower oxalic acid content. Oxalic acid is known to tie up calcium in the body, making it unavailable to the system.

The high-protein amaranth grains are produced in large sorghumlike seed heads. Some analyses show amaranth seed to have a protein content over 18 percent, more than wheat or corn. Because of its amino acid

Amaranth grain contains a higher percentage of protein than either wheat or corn.

makeup, amaranth flour when combined with whole wheat or corn makes a protein as nutritious as meat.

Widely available in the wild, where it is often known as pigweed, amaranth can also be cultivated. Sow the seeds ¼ inch deep in the garden after all danger of frost is past, or start seeds indoors, being sure to give the seedlings plenty of light. The plants require well-drained soil which has been spaded deeply and enriched with plant food. They should have good air circulation. Under proper conditions the plants branch freely while still quite small. When in full bloom some varieties stand up to ten feet tall with every branch ending in a globular flower. Where they are grown in a soil richly supplied with humus, they may be expected to add another foot to their normal height. When grown for seed production, plants often produce 1½ ounces of edible seed.

All amaranths have an extensive flowering season, starting in June and lasting well into August. They are among the easiest of all annuals to grow, showing a high endurance to summer heat and drought. For best results, however, they should never suffer from a lack of water. When growing *Amaranthus* as an ornamental, do not enrich the soil as poor soil brings out the bright colors of the leaves.

AMARYLLIS

The lovely garden amaryllis (*Hippeastrum vittatum, A. Belladonna,* and *A. reginae* and their hybrids), are members of Amaryllidaceae. Native to South America and South Africa, many amaryllis grown today are hybrids of native varieties and are highly prized for their large flowers. The lilylike or bell-shaped flowers are red, pink, white, and combinations of these colors.

In frost-free climates, amaryllis are grown in the open field or in beds and borders around the home. They are excellent landscape subjects for use as individual specimens, in mass plantings, in beds, or as part of the border planting around home grounds and in park plantings. They are easily grown indoors.

It is common occurrence with many to fail with amaryllis after the first or second year. The reason for failure lies in the care given the bulbs, especially in the initial watering and subsequent care after blooming. (Blooming is proof that the bulb is of mature blooming size and had previously formed bloom buds.)

To water a bulb too much after the growth starts may cause it to rot. A newly potted, dormant amaryllis should be kept fairly dry until signs of life begin to show, except for an initial watering to settle the soil around the bottom of the bulb. It should be watered sparingly by syringing the bulb itself until you are sure there are roots growing. Once the leaf tip emerges from the center of the bulb, and after the bloom stem has cleared the scales, it is definite that roots are feeding the bulb and it is time to apply more water to the soil regularly, keeping it moist but not soggy.

However, to start the foliage into full growth before the bloom and bud appear may cause the bud to rot or abort and there can be a healthy set of leaves growing and no evidence of a bloom coming. It is wise not to water the bulb until the bloom bud shows, regardless of how promising the foliage looks.

Culture: Grow bulbs in a mixture of three parts rich loam, one part well-rotted leaf mold and another of well-rotted cow manure, with some sand and bone meal. Set the bottom third of the bulb in the soil mixture. Water

To produce healthy, flowering amaryllis, water the plant sparingly until the leaves and flower stalk begin to emerge from the bulb. After the flower bud has appeared, fertilize and increase watering.

carefully, and, once the bloom bud clears the neck of the bulb, use liquid manure or fish emulsion once a week or every ten days depending upon the growing conditions, until the color begins to show in the blossom buds through the sheath. Full sunlight is best for sturdiness, and a temperature between 55 and 60°F. (12.78 and 15.56°C.) is best. Tie the bloom stem loosely to a stake to prevent its being broken. The blooms can be cut and used as cut flowers.

When blooming ends in February, March or April, the plant is given less water and kept somewhat cooler for a while. As weather becomes warmer the feeding of liquid manure or fish emulsion is started again. As space and light permit, the pots can be placed in April or May in a cold frame or somewhat sheltered place, to gradually harden them off for outside planting. Sink the pot to the rim in a flower bed or among shrubs, and continue weekly feeding; water as needed.

In the fall, as the foliage matures, water should be gradually withheld and the pots lifted in cool weather before frost and placed in a cool cellar to "ripen" (allow the foliage to die off) until around the first of the year. Around Christmas or later, the bulbs should be checked for bloom buds showing, or possible injury, and all old foliage and loose dried scales cleaned off.

In late January or early February, scratch about an inch of the dry soil out of the pot with your fingers and replace it with rich, old compost mixed with a little bone meal. Amaryllis bulbs flower best when they are pot-bound, so do not repot them for two to three seasons. By replacing the top layer of soil each year, fertility is maintained.

When repotting becomes necessary, do it only when the bulb is thoroughly dormant and the soil is dry. Upend the pot and tap the bulb out. Carefully crumble the dry soil out from among the roots with your fingers. Be careful not to break any live, white roots. Repot, as suggested above.

Dutch hybrid amaryllis are widely available to gardeners. The Ludwig, Warmenhaven and van Meuveven strains are all excellent and come in many shades of red, pink and white. Buy the largest bulbs you can. They are worth the expense.

Propagation: Amaryllis can be easily grown from seed and will bloom at 18 months old, if grown correctly. Fertilization is easily done by hand, the pollen from one bloom being placed upon the pistil of another when the pistil is somewhat separated into three segments and becomes quite moist and sticky.

Cut the bloom petals back nearly to the neck of the flower after pollinating it, to show definitely that it has been fertilized. There is no further use for the bloom as it draws energy from the bulb that should now help form healthy seed.

The seed is gathered when the pod has turned brown and the three sections are about to open. Sow in a mixture of leaf mold and sand and cover very lightly. The seeds should be kept moist and warm. After two small leaves have formed, the tiny plants and bulblets are potted into small containers and kept growing in a healthy state, gradually increasing the richness of the soil to that used for mature bulbs. Usually no larger size pot than a four-inch is needed before blooming. There are differences, however, individualistic traits sometimes showing up in a bulb larger than usual, as well as others being long delayed both in size and bloom.

AMAZON LILY
(*Eucharis grandiflora*)

This native of the Andes is a fine plant for the window garden. It has long-stemmed basal leaves and clusters of dazzling white, trumpetlike blossoms with a perfume subtle yet potent enough to permeate the house. It should be potted to half the depth of the bulb in a coarse, fibrous, humus-rich soil with charcoal and sand, placed in an east window with other amaryllids and watered whenever dry.

During spring and fall, feed it once a month with liquid manure or fish emulsion.

Bulbs require a semidormant period to induce flowering. This can be managed by gradually letting the soil dry off for four to five weeks after blooming. Never let the soil become so dry that the foliage dies. When leaves wilt, water sparingly; then begin watering more heavily when the plant begins to throw new shoots. *Eucharis* requires warm conditions, so do not allow temperatures to drop below 55°F. (12.78°C.). In the greenhouse, do not expose the plant to direct summer sun.

AMELANCHIER

Also known as shadbush, serviceberry and Juneberry, this genus of deciduous shrubs or small trees produces purple red clusters of edible fruit that resemble small apples.

There are about 25 species, three of them arborescent. Besides their value for food, they are extraordinarily handsome, especially when seen in the earliest days of spring just before the landscape breaks into green. They then raise a mass of snow white blossoms that stand out like tiny clouds against the gray brown of the wood's edges and old fields that are their favorite haunts. Their lovely appearance is aided by the woolly white or red uncurling leaves, which later become a delicate green and then a clear yellow before dropping in the fall. The bark is a soft ashy gray or red brown. The trunk is often branched at the ground, but in the dense forest will sometimes rise in a clear bole with little taper to heights of 40 feet. *A. spicata*, *A. stolonifera* and *A. sanguinea* are best for fruit. *A. laevis*, or Juneberry, is the most handsome species when in bloom.

Most species are hardy in the North and thrive well in a dry climate in a variety of soils. Propagation is by seeds sown in spring.

AMERICAN ELM   *See* ELM

AMERICAN LOTUS
(*Nelumbo lutea*)

The yellow ten-inch flowers, exotic blue green leaves and angular seedpods of this lotus distinguish it as one of the most attractive plants of our native flora. The round leaves, which are attached in the center to a long petiole or leaf stem, are usually one to two feet wide and stand two or more feet out of the water. Younger leaves may float on the surface before emerging to their mature height.

The leaves rise from a strong and thick tuberous rhizome which creeps in the mud on the bottom of ponds or slow-moving streams. In the middle of each tuber there is a large cavity extending throughout its length, with five or six smaller cavities within, all serving as air passages.

The American lotus, which may be easily grown in a sunken garden or naturalized in a large pond, is hardy north to New Jersey. It should be planted in a container of rich loam and dropped into the pond.

AMINO ACIDS

These consist of nitrogen-containing organic compounds, large numbers of which join together in the formation of a protein molecule.

AMMONIA

This is a colorless gas composed of one atom of nitrogen and three atoms of hydrogen.

Liquefied under pressure, ammonia is used as a fertilizer.

See also FERTILIZER, CHEMICAL.

AMMONIUM CHLORIDE
See FERTILIZER, CHEMICAL

AMMONIUM NITRATE
See FERTILIZER, CHEMICAL

AMMONIUM SULFATE
See FERTILIZER, CHEMICAL

AMORPHA

Good bee plants, these low- to medium-sized shrubs of the Pea family are cultivated for their pinnate foliage and dense spikes of deep blue flowers. Most are hardy as far north as Massachusetts.

Amorphas generally do well in average garden soil, in sunny and somewhat dry conditions. Also known as false indigo, these shrubs are well suited for borders of shrubs.

AMYLASE   *See* ENZYME

ANACHARIS   *See* AQUARIUM

ANAEROBIC COMPOSTING

Anaerobic composting is a composting system that excludes oxygen. The process is characterized by low temperatures and a malodorous intermediate product. It is slower than aerobic composting, which is composting done in the presence of oxygen. The main advantage

to anaerobic composting is that the composting can be carried on with a minimum of attention. A big problem, of course, is that it is difficult to exclude air from the composting material.

See also AEROBIC COMPOSTING, COMPOSTING.

ANCHUSA

Once used as a salad herb but now grown for its showy flower clusters, this coarse-growing perennial is of easy culture in any good garden soil. *A. azurea* cv. 'Dropmore', which grows three to five feet high, is covered with bright blue flowers from early June to September. An earlier bloomer, *A. barrelieri*, has blue flowers with a white tube and yellow throat. It grows to two feet and should be set in the second border row, back of the edgings.

Anchusa prefers sun, but tolerates some shade. If stalks are cut back after the first flowering, and the plants fertilized with bone meal, you will get blossoms until frost. Propagation is by seed, division, or root cuttings.

Brunnera macrophylla (formerly *A. myosotidiflora*) is the species often called Russian or Siberian forget-me-not. It grows to one foot, producing many flowers the size and color of its namesake in May and June. It does very well in masses in moist semishade, and is one of the most easily grown spring flowers. It looks very nice planted near yellow or orange trollius, which flowers at the same time and prefers similar conditions.

ANDROMEDA

Andromedas are low evergreen shrubs, with small, bell-shaped pink flowers. They are hardy in the North and grow best in an acid, humus-rich, moist sandy soil without full sun.

Andromedas germinate well from seeds, especially if sown in sphagnum, and attain a height of about one foot. They are also easily propagated by division or by layering. The most familiar species is bog-rosemary, *A. polifolia.* It is hardy to −50°F. (−45.5°C.), but dislikes hot summer weather. This is a good plant for the bog or water garden.

See also EVERGREEN, LYONIA.

ANEMONE

Also called windflowers, these popular perennial herbs of the Buttercup family vary widely in form, color and size. All require partial shade and rich, sandy loam. Propagation is by root division in early spring or by seed sown very shallow in a finely raked bed during fall or early spring.

The showy horticultural forms are divided into three types: the early spring group, the bulbous group of spring and early summer, and the tall Oriental forms of late summer and fall.

The Early Spring Group: *Anemone blanda,* the bulbous Greek windflower, grows about four inches high with finely cut leaves and blue, pink or white daisylike flowers. They bloom in early spring and are excellent subjects for the rock garden or locations in light deciduous shade. Foliage disappears in early summer. Plant them in large colonies near other small spring bulbs like scilla and chionodoxa. *Anemone Pulsatilla,* the true pasque flower of Eurasia, has very silky hairs ¾ to one inch long. Its flowers are blue to red purple, 1½ to 2½ inches across and bloom in early April. Many cultivars and varieties are known, including the white *A. P.* cv. 'Alba'. This pulsatilla group thrives best in well-drained soil, or stony places in some shade.

The Bulbous Group: The bulbous group of anemones blooms almost whenever desired, depending on the culture and the time the corms are planted. In sections where it is too cold in winter, corms should be cured or ripened after the flowering period by being lifted from the ground to dry and store. If left in the ground to cure they must be protected against excess moisture; the corms cannot stand frost. The corms are of unusual structure, some resembling a three-cornered horn. Florists use this group extensively indoors for late winter and early spring blooms. Home gardeners can easily force these anemones into winter bloom. When the corms are received, soak them overnight in room-temperature water, then plant them one inch deep and two inches apart in a good sandy loam in a bulb pan. Planting is done in September or October. Place the pan in a dark place that never gets warmer than 55°F. (12.78°C.) until growth starts. Then move the plants to a cool, bright window and begin to water freely, feeding every two weeks with diluted fish emulsion or weak compost tea.

A. coronaria, the poppy-flowered anemone, has large flowers in red, white and indigo. Popular controlled varieties with single blooms include DeCaen, St. Brigid and Victoria Giant. Many double forms are also to be had in a variety of colors, although the scarlet ones are predominant. One cultivar known as *Anemone coronaria* cv. 'Chrysanthemiflora' is a seedling produced in 1848, looking much like a full chrysanthemum; *Anemone* x *fulgens,* the scarlet windflower, resembles a scarlet daisy having a black center. It can be forced like *A. coronaria.*

The Tall Oriental Forms: The tall anemones of late summer and fall are the Oriental forms *Anemone hupehensis* (Japanese anemone) and *Anemone vitifolia,* the grape-leaved windflower from China and India, which is somewhat hardier than *A. hupehensis.* These are two to four feet tall with long, slender, flexible stems bearing white and rose purple to carmine flowers two to three inches across. These are excellent to use in a hardy border or colony in a partially shaded place. They bloom from late summer to frost. There are beautiful cultivars of the group, particularly in the white color from the cultivar Alba; Whirlwind is a beautiful, semidouble white. September Charm is a good semidouble pink, and Alice is rose carmine.

ANGELICA
(*Angelica Archangelica*)

In the first two years of growth, angelica puts forth leaves on "blooming" stems.

A plant with myriad culinary and medicinal uses, angelica is difficult to classify because it has both annual and perennial tendencies. With careful manipulation, you can grow it as a near-perennial—a plant that will last several years—albeit at the loss of angelica's most pleasant annual show: its spectacular yellow green bloom of flowers that appear early in May. By pruning the flowers, and so preventing seed formation, you can encourage angelica to return for another year.

Medicinally, angelica is said to have properties as a tonic, stimulant, diaphoretic, carminative, and expectorant. One of the simplest and most popular ways to enjoy angelica is in a tea made by infusing fresh leaves or bruised roots.

In the kitchen, there'll be scant leavings for the compost pile because nearly every inch of angelica, from its roots to the seeds in its umbel-tipped pods, is usable. The roots can be eaten raw, with butter. Stalks are considered a delicacy in parts of the North Atlantic community where angelica flourishes. They can be eaten raw, like carrots, or prepared with butter or hollandaise like asparagus. Leaves are a pleasant garnish on meat dishes and may be added, fresh or dried, to soups, stews and vegetable courses. Angelica seeds can be used as a flavoring in clear dishes where leaf fragments would be undesirable. Seeds should be crushed before adding.

In addition, the seeds and roots have great commercial value as an ingredient of elegant liqueurs and even in wines.

A lover of cool climates and rich soils, angelica is fairly easy to grow in most of North America. Choose a semishady spot and keep it mulched well to hold moisture and discourage weeds. Its seed germinates easily if sown for the next season in late July or early August, but take care not to cover it. It needs light to germinate, and so should be sprinkled, then hand-pressed into light soil that has been raked and graded beforehand. Old root clusters can be divided in fall or spring to produce angelica growths. Maturing plants should be thinned to stand in rows 18 inches apart. Use plenty of well-rotted compost or manure to prepare the bed.

Harvesting leaves can be done whenever leaves are mature. Stems should be cut in June or July. The seeds should be gathered just as the pod turns from green to yellow. Be careful not to shatter seedpods; they are delicate and will burst if dropped. Roots can be taken in the fall of the first growing season. If dried roots are wanted, slice the thicker parts to hasten drying.

Two other types of angelica are known in North America: American angelica or masterwort (*A. atropurpurea*), similar to *A. archangelica* but of lesser potency and greater acidity; and wild angelica (*A. sylvestris*), valuable for the yellow dye it yields.

See also HERB.

ANHYDROUS

This is an adjective, meaning without water or being dry. For example, anhydrous ammonia is water-free as opposed to the water solution of ammonia known as household ammonia. Anhydrous ammonia is a nitrogen-rich chemical fertilizer used by many farmers. The fertilizer is often referred to simply as "anhydrous."

See also FERTILIZER, CHEMICAL.

ANIMAL PESTS
See entries for individual animals

ANISE   (*Pimpinella anisum*)

Anise is an annual herb which has been widely cultivated throughout the world. The dried fruits, which are usually called seeds, have been for centuries used to flavor pastries, candies and beverages.

The plant requires a light, fertile, sandy loam that is well drained and can be so pulverized that the small seed can be planted at a uniform depth and the very small young seedlings cultivated. A frost-free season of at least 120 days is required, and uniform rainfall throughout the growing season is essential because the plant is unfavorably affected by sudden changes from wet to dry periods. The temperature throughout the growing season should be fairly uniform without excessively hot periods, especially following rainfall. When the seed is near maturity alternate rainy and dry periods cause it to become brown, which greatly reduces its quality, and under such

A tender annual herb, anise produces seeds which are used to flavor pastries, candies and beverages, and leaves which are excellent in salads.

sents some difficulties in that the umbels ripen progressively and the seed ripens unevenly within each umbel.

In countries where the plants are grown commercially, they are either pulled out of the ground or the tops are cut off by hand. The material thus obtained is tied in bundles and then stacked in a conical pile with the fruiting heads toward the center. This is usually done when all the seed of the umbel is still green. The seed then continues to ripen and when mature does not discolor and shatter from the plant. In foreign countries the seed is usually flailed out, but it can doubtless be threshed by machinery. After the threshed seed is cleaned it is bagged for the market. The oil is extracted from the seed by steam distillation. Under favorable conditions a seed yield of 400 to 600 pounds per acre can be expected.

Attractive in the herb garden, anise grows to two feet high. Its leaves are often used in salads.

conditions the harvesting of the seed is difficult.

The seed is planted about ½ inch deep in the field in rows 18 to 30 inches apart at the rate of one to two seeds per inch. At this rate about five to ten pounds of seed are required to plant one acre. Growers in some European countries broadcast the seed, but as a rule weeds are a major difficulty and if these are present at harvest they are likely to affect the market value of both the seed and the oil. If it is necessary to broadcast the seed, and cultivation is therefore impossible, it is important that the land be fallow and in clean culture the previous season. The harvesting of anise pre-

ANISE HYSSOP
(*Agastache Foeniculum*)

Sometimes called fragrant giant hyssop, this is a valuable honey plant that blooms from early summer until frost.

The seed of anise hyssop is quite small and grows slowly in the early stages. The small plants will not compete successfully with fast-growing annual weeds which infest most cultivated land. Thus, under most conditions, there must be weeding or cultivation at least until the bed is established.

The abundant seed supply of anise hyssop furnishes summer and fall feed for some small songbirds. It grows well in ordinary garden soil

and attracts bees to its flowers as well as sweet clover does.

See also HONEY PLANTS.

ANNONA

This genus of tropical evergreen trees and shrubs is cultivated for its edible fruits. *A. Cherimola* grows to 18 feet and has summer-blooming brown flowers and yellow green fruit called cherimoya. *A. muricata* grows to 30 feet and has yellow flowers and a pulpy fruit called soursop.

Annonas do best in a heavy loam soil, and can tolerate temperatures as low as 25°F. (−3.89°C.). Most begin bearing fruit when three or four years old. Generally, they suffer less from insect pests than most other fruit trees and require little pruning.

Fruits should be picked when mature, and not permitted to fall to the ground and get bruised.

ANNUALS

To the botanist, an annual is any plant which grows from seed, produces its flowers, matures its seeds, and dies in one season. To the gardener, an annual is any plant which, sown in the spring, will produce summer or fall blossoms and not live over the winter.

Many species of plants called annuals are, in their native home, perennial herbs (flowering plants that perpetuate their growth from year to year) or biennials (plants that live two years from seed, but bloom mostly the second year). Since these plants are generally too tender to survive northern winters, it is better to treat them as annuals.

Most annuals are grown directly from seed, but some are grown from tubers or bulbs. For example, crocus and lilies are actually perennials that die back each year while the roots remain alive. This growth habit earns them the name of "false annuals."

Annuals are classified by degree of hardiness. *Hardy* annuals may be sown outdoors before frosts have entirely ceased. Some, such as sweet peas, can be sown in autumn. *Half-hardy* annuals need warmth to get a good start and can be sown indoors in very early spring. Once established, they are quite hardy in the garden. *Tender* plants require more warmth for germination than the half-hardy group; a temperature range of 60 to 70°F. (15.56 to 21.11°C.) is considered correct.

Most annuals are easy to handle, inexpensive, ideal for temporary plantings, fine as fill-ins after perennials have stopped blooming. They offer a color range from pure white to a deep black. They range in size from prostrate to tall-growing; there are fragrant and scentless, day- and night-blooming annuals.

As cut flowers, annuals are almost indispensable. Sweet peas, asters, calendulas, larkspurs, marigolds, snapdragons, and zinnias are all easily grown decorative flowers. They are used for bedding plants, edgings, in rock gardens, and as climbers for covering trellises and arbors.

Culture: The preparation of the permanent bed should be given careful attention. Most annuals do best in an open sunny location and in soil to which has been added large amounts of manure, leaf mold, etc. The usual time to start a flower bed is early spring, as most seeds germinate best during the moist spring weather. Before digging the flower bed, mark out the dimensions, using a spade to get a clean-cut edge. Any good garden soil will usually produce a fine array of flowers if spaded to the proper depth and broken up to make a fine seedbed. Heavy and moist soils can be made lighter by adding a good quantity of sharp sand.

A layer of well-rotted stable manure is then spread evenly over the surface, two to three inches thick, and spaded into the soil so that it is completely covered. After spading, use a steel rake to give a fine, smooth surface to the seedbed.

Starting Plants in a Seedbed: In many cases the seedbed is used for raising seedlings which later are transplanted to their permanent place in the garden. The seedbed provides an ideal location for the germination and early growth of the seedling.

The bed must be well drained and should be located where it receives the full warmth of sunny spring days. The soil should be perfectly smooth and fine. Sow the seed thinly in shallow drills and cover lightly with fine soil. Each row should be labeled to show the variety of seed sown, as the seedlings must be identified before being set out. Frequent stirring of the soil between the rows encourages quick growth of the seedlings and helps keep down weeds. The seedbed is valuable for raising plants of almost all annuals, except those which transplant poorly, such as poppies, and the more tender ones, which should be started in the house or hotbed.

Starting Plants in the House or Hotbed: Tender plants require considerable warmth and sunshine to start growth. In nearly every home there is a bright sunny window that can serve as a nursery for such plants. For such a window-sill nursery, fill two- or three-inch-deep boxes nearly full with fine rich soil or compost. Settle the soil firmly in the boxes, and for very fine seeds, water it well two hours before seed is sown. Scatter the seeds thinly and evenly over the surface. Sprinkle lightly with fine soil, barely covering the seed, and press the surface firmly with a small block so that the seeds will not wash out when watered. While the seeds are sprouting, keep the soil slightly moist, being careful not to overwater nor to allow it to become dry.

When the young seedlings are well started, they should be carefully lifted and replanted to give them more room. As they increase in size and strength they should be transplanted to larger pots so they will be strong and bushy when the time comes for setting them in the flower bed. *See also* COLD FRAME, HOTBED.

Sowing Outdoors: Seed of the hardier annuals can be sown outdoors in the early spring, directly into the bed where the plants are to bloom. If the bed is to be planted solidly to one type flower, the seed may be sown thinly over the surface of the freshly prepared bed and lightly raked in. Where a border is desired, a shallow drill may be made around the edge of the bed with a small stick. The seed should be sown thinly in the drill and lightly covered with fine surface soil.

Transplanting: Choose a late afternoon after a good soaking rain, if possible, for transplanting the seedlings. If the soil has become dry, it would be well to water the seedbed thoroughly a few hours before transplanting. Use a trowel or a stick to loosen the soil around the roots, carefully dig up each plant with all the roots possible, and set in a hole sufficiently large to allow the roots to be spread out in planting. Draw the soil over the roots and slightly up around the stem, and press it firmly into place. A good watering after transplanting will help the plants to become established in their new location. If the following day is warm and clear, shade with a newspaper during the hottest part of the day.

The Care and Cultivation of the Flower Bed: When the young seedlings or transplanted plants are well established, the surface of the bed should be frequently loosened with a small hoe or cultivator. Mulching is even more effective for keeping weeds down and encouraging quick growth of the plants. In dry periods, plants may be kept growing by watering them thoroughly.

The neat and attractive appearance of the flower bed will be much enhanced if all the blossoms are cut off and removed as soon as they fade. This will also prolong the flowering period. In the fall the blossoming period may be further prolonged by covering the flower bed with sheets or newspapers on cold nights, as often there are several weeks of mild weather after the first light frost which injures the more tender plants.

What to Plant in March or April: Sown indoors, or in the hotbed or cold frame, these plantings will furnish specimens to set out in May.

Ageratum	Ipomoea
Aster	Lantana
Begonia	Large-flowered and
Browallia	double petunias
Canna	Lemon verbena
Celosia	Lobelia
Cobaea	Marigold
Cockscomb	Ricinus
Coleus	Salvia
Cypress vine	(Flowering sage)
Dahlia	Torenia
Geranium	Verbena
Heliotrope	

What to Plant in April: The following may be started in the seedbed or in the garden where they are to grow and bloom when the trees begin to leaf out.

Abronia	Gaillardia
Ageratum	Godetia
Anchusa	Gypsophila
Annual chrysan-	Larkspur
themums	Lobelia
Aster	Marigold
Balloon vine	Mignonette
Brachycome	Nasturtium
Browallia	Ornamental grasses
Calendula	Pansy
Calliopsis	Petunia
Canary-bird flower	Phlox
Candytuft	Poppy
Carnation	Salpiglossis
Centaurea	Scabiosa
Cosmos	Snapdragon
Cypress vine	Stocks
Datura	Sunflower
Dianthus	Sweet alyssum
Eschscholtzia	Sweet pea
Everlasting	Verbena
Forget-me-not	Zinnia

What to Plant in May: Seeds of the following require considerable warmth to start them into growth, and the young plants are liable to injury from cool nights. Therefore it is best to defer planting the seeds in the open ground until the trees are in bloom, as the nights are then quite warm. If plantings of the varieties in the preceding list have been omitted, they can still be made at this time along with the following:

Abutilon	Ipomoea
Balsam	Lemon verbena
Begonia	Momordica
Celosia	Moonflower
Cleome	Morning-glory
Cobaea	Nicotiana
Cockscomb	Portulaca
Coleus	Ricinus
Dahlia	Salvia
Euphorbia	Sensitive plant
Four-o'clock	Torenia

ANTHURIUM

These tropical American plants with attractive foliage are widely grown by florists. They are noted for their nodding spikes of yellow flowers set off by a large, waxy, heart-shaped scarlet bract, which becomes green upon maturation. Anthuriums are grown in tropical gardens or greenhouses, since they require a nighttime minimum temperature of 62 to 65°F. (16.67 to 18.33°C.) and high humidity levels. A soil rich in humus, which is never allowed to dry, and a location without direct sun will produce good plants. In containers, an annual topdressing and repotting every three years will be necessary. More than 600 good species exist.

ANTIBIOTIC

An antibiotic is a chemical substance either synthesized or derived from a mold or bacteria that inhibits the activity or life processes of other microorganisms. Antibiotics are used to control infectious diseases of man, to treat and control diseases in animals and food crops, and to stimulate the growth of animals.

The antibiotic age opened with the discovery of penicillin in 1941. Since then, over 3,000 antibiotics have been found in soils from all over the United States, and from such widespread places as Africa, India, Italy, and the Philippines.

Antibiotics have practically eliminated human deaths from blood poisoning, mastoiditis, certain types of pneumonia, and typhoid, scarlet and childbirth fevers. They are effective aids against many other diseases, and help reduce the recovery period for still more illnesses. Used properly, they have saved the lives of numerous farm animals, too.

"Used properly" are the key words to the whole question of antibiotics. If such drugs are used indiscriminately—too often, at too low or high a dose, or for too brief a period of time—bacterial resistance to these drugs may develop, possibly reducing their effectiveness when used at a later date.

Effects on Human Health: A 1973 survey of brand-name antibiotics indicated the production of 40 doses for every man, woman and child in the United States. Although some of these were intended for export or animals, the number earmarked for human consumption remains discomfortingly high. Although antibiotics kill or neutralize only bacteria, some physicians prescribe them for viral diseases such as the common cold, sore throat and bronchitis, often at the insistence of patients who have come to expect a "miracle cure" for every illness.

Even when a patient has a bacterial infection, an antibiotic may not offer a sure cure. Physicians must diagnose precisely if they intend to use a "narrow-spectrum" antibiotic which will kill only certain types of bacteria, and this precise diagnosis often requires a bacterial culture, a costly and time-consuming process. To save time and money doctors often prescribe instead a broad-spectrum antibiotic, one which is powerful enough to knock out a broad range of bacteria. Such hit-or-miss prescriptions present a number of dangers.

Medical societies report increasing incidence of allergic reactions to antibiotics. Vomiting, nausea and kidney problems have been among the adverse reactions to prescribed drugs. Estimates of the annual number of hospital deaths associated with drug misuse run from 2,000 to 14,000.

In addition, indiscriminate and widespread use of antibiotics has brought about the development of many types of bacteria resistant to such drugs. Certain bacteria can be induced by an antibiotic to synthesize an enzyme which destroys the drug molecule. When antibiotics are administered, those bacteria which do not possess the proper defensive characteristics are destroyed, but mutants with resistant characteristics can multiply and prosper. Also, it has recently been found that resistance to one or more antibiotics can be transferred from a resistant bacteria cell to a nonresistant bacterium by mere cell contact, even if the cells are of different species. Therefore, a resistant, harmless cell can transfer its drug-resistant characteristics to a previously nonresistant disease-causing species, making it immune to treatment by antibiotics. Thus, people treated with antibiotics for a particular illness may find themselves immune to the same treatment should their illness recur or a different illness strike.

Even if you have never been given antibiotics when ill, you get small amounts of these potent drugs every day in your food. Livestock feeds contain antibiotics, used as disease preventatives and growth stimulators. When adverse conditions (low birth weight, poor diet quality, dirty environment, and stresses such as uneven temperature) are present, feed antibiotics can result in a much greater than 10 percent average increase in meat production. However, under ideal conditions, antibiotics may provide little or no advantage. Drug residues higher than the tolerances set by the FDA have been found in meats.

Use on Plants: A mere glance at the results of antibiotics on crops can make them seem highly attractive. Not only do they kill off disease bacteria, but they stimulate growth and yields (probably by destroying growth-retarding bacteria). Corn germination has been doubled and its growth rate accelerated by Terramycin applied to the seed. Penicillin-treated soil, in one test, produced radishes three times as heavy as normal. An antibiotic dip for seed potatoes gave an increased yield of 72 bushels per acre, and tomatoes sprayed with an antibiotic solution gave a 42 percent increase. Bigger yields and better market quality were reported for many crops.

But, it has already been proven that plant disease bacteria, just like those that cause human disease, can develop resistance to antibiotics—one company reports the appearance of a bean blight bacteria resistant to a streptomycin concentration as high as 500 ppm. Often the wonder drug is as toxic to the plant as to the disease organism: Actidione, an antibiotic that attacks fungi, damaged peach trees when applied as a preharvest spray for brown rot. When applied to the soil to prevent damping-off of alfalfa seedlings, Actidione destroyed the damping-off organisms, but greatly slowed the seedlings' growth.

Most antibiotics act as systemics. This means they enter the plant's tissues, moving through and thoroughly saturating them. Some antibiotics, scientists believe, are changed into more active toxicants in the plant—giving the consumer an even stronger poison to worry about.

Other wonder drugs, like Thiolutin, now being tested for plant use, are highly toxic to man. Another, actinomycetin—highly beneficial when produced naturally in the soil by the actinomycetes—is the deadliest poison known to man.

There is a strong residue problem with a number of the antibiotics: streptomycin-terramycin residues have been found on apple surfaces a month after spraying with a 100 ppm solution. (When bacteria develop resistance to an antibiotic, synergism—combining with another antibiotic or chemical—may be resorted to, increasing the already dangerous amounts in the plant.) Some antibiotic residues last a whole season.

Organic soil, it has been proven time and again, has a very strong antibiotic reaction. A soil rich in humus has a huge microbial population, one of whose duties is the production of substances that protect plants from disease.

An unbalanced microbial population, many experts are beginning to realize, is one of the chief causes of many of today's crop troubles. Only one bacteria in 30,000 is harmful, but let chemicals or poor management destroy that one bacteria's enemies, and you have plant disease.

Selman Waksman, a world-renowned microbiologist, believes it is far more important to human life to feed the good microbes than to destroy the bad. By incorporating large amounts of organic wastes into our soils, we keep the good bacteria busy producing materials to nourish and protect our plants—without loading up our foods with foreign substances that may do us great harm.

ANTS

Ants build nests or mounds in the garden, and often spread aphids to plants, but few species actually eat vegetable plants. They can be kept off plants by banding the trunk or stem with cotton batting painted with a sticky preparation, available commercially. Ants will back away from lines of bone meal or powdered charcoal poured on the ground. To keep ants from carrying aphids into the house, squeeze

the juice of a lemon at the point of entry and leave the sliced peel there.

See also APHIDS, INSECT CONTROL.

APHIDS

These small, variously hued, soft-bodied insects are known to most gardeners. Aphids cluster on leaves and stems, where they suck sap, causing curling and cupping of leaves. Severe infestations cause a general loss of plant vigor and stunting, with reduced yields. Aphids excrete excess sugars and sap in a liquid called honeydew, which makes leaf surfaces sticky and supports the growth of a black mold that can block light from leaves. Ants feed on honeydew, and so valuable is this food source that some species of ants tend the aphids as man does cows, taking them to underground shelters in cold weather. Such ants tend to aggravate aphid problems, distributing the pests to new and greener plants.

Aphid populations can explode into infestations because of the insect's ability to reproduce live young parthenogenetically (without fertilization). After one or two such genera-

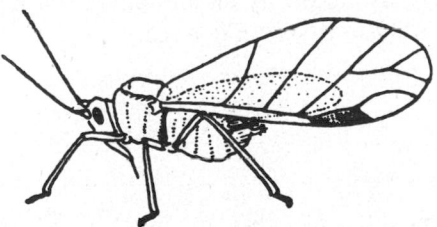

Aphids, or plant lice, destroy foliage by sucking plant sap and introducing certain viral diseases. A forceful spray of clear or soapy water helps to eliminate them.
(Courtesy of U.S. Department of Agriculture)

tions, winged aphids are born, and these fly off to other plants. When males and females mate towards the end of the season, eggs are produced, enabling the insect to overwinter. The number of aphids can be kept down with naturally occurring controls such as ladybugs, lacewings (both commercially available) and wasp parasites. Damp weather favors diseases connected with aphids.

Properly fed plants tend to be less troubled by aphids; too much nutrient can be as bad as too little, however, and high nitrogen levels have been found to encourage several aphid species.

As prevalent and numerous as this pest may be, there are many effective organic controls. If few plants are involved, the infested leaves can simply be rubbed gently between thumb and forefinger. Nasturtiums, garlic, chives, coriander, anise, and petunias will all help keep aphids from damaging neighboring plants. Sprays as simple as water, or as exotic as a tea of quassia and larkspur, work well. Effective sprays can also be made from rhubarb leaf tea, tobacco tea and elder leaf tea. Aphids are drawn to a trap made by pouring slightly soapy water into a yellow plastic dishpan; set the pan near the vulnerable plants. Winged aphids have been found to shy away from plants surrounded by an aluminum foil mulch.

See also INSECT CONTROL.

APIOS

This genus of hardy vining herbs of the Pea family thrives in moist, rich soil and is propagated by seed or tubers.

A. americana is a species native to eastern North America. The pealike, brownish, violet-scented flowers appear in clusters in the summer and are followed by long, flat, thickish, many-seeded pods. The tuberous roots were once an important source of food to the North American Indians.

APPLE   (*Malus pumila*)

Cultivated in Europe for more than 2,000 years, the apple was introduced to this country soon after the Europeans first arrived. Today, Washington, New York, Michigan, California, Pennsylvania, and Virginia are the leading producers of apples. The number of trees has dropped since early in this century, but yields have remained about the same thanks to superior sites, soils and better orchard management. Per capita consumption of apples has suffered as better transportation has made citrus fruit more available. The most popular varieties are Red Delicious, Golden Delicious, McIntosh, Rome Beauty, Jonathan, and York. Such old standbys as Baldwin, Grimes, Northern Spy, and Wealthy are losing popularity.

Apples will grow in almost any soil, but do best in a clay loam. A general rule is that they thrive in soils suited to common cereals and potatoes. A sloped site promotes air drainage, thus minimizing frost damage, but also encourages soil erosion. Such steep sites can be grown to alfalfa sod, and the growth cut two or three times a season.

Trees must be provided with plenty of organic matter, such as a heavy mulch of alfalfa or grass clippings. Sweet clover, seeded late in July, makes an excellent winter ground cover. Leave it standing through the following summer or turn it under in spring. If the surface soil is low in fertility, rye will do better than clover but must be turned under before it develops fully, as it tends to grow woody when mature and could threaten young trees.

Mulches should be deep enough to smother the weeds beneath the branches. Increase the depth of the mulches as the years pass: a five-year-old tree can use 100 pounds of straw; trees two to four years old will need proportionately less.

Natural forms of nitrogen can be applied in the fall after the foliage has dropped. Use 2¼ pounds of dried blood or 4½ pounds of cottonseed meal per tree. If too much nitrogen reaches a tree late in the season, the resultant growth may be susceptible to winter injury.

Young trees have shallow root systems, and are therefore more vulnerable to shortages of water and nutrients than well-established trees. Larger trees also can rely on food reserves in the bark and wood in hard times.

To protect trees from field mice and other small animals, place fine-mesh wire screens or wrap two thicknesses of aluminum foil around the base in the fall. Also, staking a new tree may be necessary where wind or heavy snow might cause it to grow crooked. Placing a four-inch barrier of one- to two-inch crushed rock on the bottom, sides and top of the planting hole is also effective.

In late winter or early spring, while trees are dormant and before their buds begin to swell, a dormant oil spray should be applied. This mixture of 3 percent miscible oil and water smothers many insect eggs before hatching.

Planting: Buy healthy one- or two-year-old trees about three to five feet tall and plant them after the leaves have fallen, from late October into early November. Freshly dug trees can also be planted early in spring, but in spring land dries slowly and the growing season may be well advanced by the time the orchard is planted. Young apple trees withstand the shock of transplanting best when they are dormant, another good reason for fall planting. By planting your trees before the ground freezes, some new growth of the roots will take place at once and the trees will have a good start on the season when spring comes.

Set the trees 40 feet apart in and between the rows. Make the holes for them just large enough to accommodate the root development of each tree. Set the trees an inch lower in the ground than they stood in the nursery; a young apple tree will not root any deeper by deep planting, and may suffer for it.

Trees of at least two varieties should be planted within 50 feet of one another, because pollination of one variety by the pollen from another is usually required for the trees to bear.

Nutrition: If your soil is very acid, broadcast one pound of lime and ½ pound of phosphate rock per tree over the entire orchard before planting. One-half this amount may well be sufficient for young trees grown in a cover crop that is mowed for mulch. If apple trees are grown in sod and mulched with nonlegume hay, add dried blood or other nitrogenous fertilizer. Increase the amount with each recurring season, reaching a maximum application of two pounds of nitrogen for seven- or eight-year-old trees. Apply nitrogenous material in a circle about three feet wide under the outer extremities of the branch spread.

A deficiency of nitrogen will show up as small, yellowish leaves. If the foliage rolls and scorches that indicates a lack of potassium in the soil. A liberal mulch of manure (or a clover mulch to which lime has been added) mixed with the right amount of potash rock to the acre, will adjust the potassium deficiency.

Falling Apples: The fall of apples, if not in excess, is a natural phenomenon, nature's way of removing improperly pollinated fruit. This also removes fruit that the tree could not normally bring to maturity without exhausting its nutrient supply. Two abscission periods generally occur. The "first drop" begins shortly after petal fall and lasts for two or three weeks. The so-called "June drop," which begins a few days after the completion of the first drop, is somewhat of a misnomer since it normally spans two to four weeks anywhere from late May to early June. Excessive drop may be caused by a deficiency of boron or magnesium, or by too little moisture, and heavy applications of nitrogen may encourage drop.

Apple Scab: Apple scab spends the winter on dead fruit and dead leaves on or under the tree. It can be prevented largely by carefully removing all dead leaves and fruit to the compost heap and mulching under the tree. A dormant oil spray will also help.

Old Trees: Apple trees may bear crops for 30 to 50 years. If the trunk or branches are badly rotted or about a quarter of the top is dead through disease or winter injury, it is not ordinarily worthwhile to attempt salvage. However, here's some general advice when trying to bring new life into old neglected trees:

Cut out old wood and prune heavily to strong, new growth; remove all suckers not necessary to replace the top; prune out interlacing branches to open the trees to light and the circulation of air; break up the soil around the tree, working in a great deal of compost, manure and organic materials; apply organic nitrogen such as dried blood, cottonseed meal or nitrogen-rich sludge, about 25 to 35 pounds per tree; mulch heavily. Do this regularly for several seasons.

Vitamin C Content: Apples are an important source of vitamin C, although the varieties differ greatly in their level of this vitamin. While five Delicious apples provide a minimum amount of vitamin C, one could get the same amount from two Winesaps or one Baldwin. Yellow Newton and Northern Spy are other good sources. McIntosh, Jonathan and York Imperial rate low in vitamin C.

Baldwin is widely grown in the eastern United States. It is sensitive to the climatic extremes existing west of Lake Michigan, however. Northern Spy, another high-C apple, is also adaptable to the midcontinent and eastern

When properly pruned and fed, apple trees may blossom and bear fruit for 30 to 50 years.

To rejuvenate an old, neglected apple tree, begin by removing all dead wood, broken limbs and suckers. The second year, thin the regular wood and cut all limbs that grow toward the center of the tree. Continue to prune and shape the tree during the winter of each succeeding year.

region. Northern Spy is an excellent dessert or eating apple, but is not too useful for cooking. Baldwin is just the reverse. It is good for making pies and applesauce, but not too good for eating fresh. So by planting both of those trees you will get a good supply of both cooking and eating apples that are rich in vitamin C.

Tests have shown that most of the vitamin C in apples is right in or under the skin, and the skin can contain five times as much of the vitamin as the flesh. It is interesting that small apples are richer in vitamin C than large apples; small apples have more area of skin per pound of fruit, and this greater percentage of skin is probably the cause of the higher vitamin C content. It is fortunate that apples lose very little of their vitamin C in storage. If stored at 36°F. (2.22°C.), Baldwin apples will lose no vitamin C over a period of five or six months. However, if the storage temperature gets up to 45°F. (7.22°C.), some of the vitamin content will be lost.

Selecting a Location: Each variety does best in certain regions of the country. In the Northeast, the Great Lakes keep the growing season cool and summer rainfall is usually dependable. Growers in the central Atlantic region worry more about rainfall. Warmer temperatures dictate that most orchards be placed at fairly high elevations in the Appalachians. Warm temperatures in the Ohio Basin region cause more importance to be placed on a sufficient rainfall; droughts tend to be quite serious. Soils that can hold water well to a depth of three to four feet will minimize the threat of damage. In the north central states, cold winters are the grower's main concern. Cold-resistant varieties have been developed, and include Haralson, Honeygold, Red Baron, Joan, Secor, Anoka, and Regent. Sunny summers and relative freedom from spring frost damage make the West Coast an excellent apple-growing area, although large orchards often must be irrigated.

In general, the primary consideration determining what variety can be grown is temperature. Talk with growers in the immediate area and extension service agents about the dangers of spring frost, in particular, and the suitability of temperature the rest of the year.

A persistent heavy wind may render a site unsuitable, making spraying difficult and affecting fruit set. The best sites are elevated rolling or sloping fields; low-lying areas tend to collect cold air.

Although they cost a bit more initially, dwarf apple trees offer several advantages to the home orchardist. Most standard apple varieties take five to ten years to bear fruit; dwarf trees bear from one to three years after planting. A dwarf produces an average of one to three bushels (50 to 150 pounds) of fruit per season —plenty for the average family—and the fruit is as large or larger than that of the standard tree. Because they grow only six to eight feet high—15 feet in the case of semidwarfs— dwarfs are easy to spray and pick from. They also require much less space; you can plant six dwarfs in the amount of space required for one standard tree.

Gardeners interested in growing some of the colorful old apple varieties of yesteryear, either for their superior regional adaptability or exceptional taste, should consider grafting scions of old varieties like American Beauty, Rhode Island Greening and Cox Orange. Individuals and groups who raise these old favorites can often be traced through local nurseries, horticultural societies or county agricultural extension offices. Other old-time varieties that once flourished in backyards and small orchards include Ben Davis, Black Gilliflower, Blue Pearmain, Esopus Spitzenburg, Maiden's Flush, Pound Sweet, Twenty Ounce, and Fameuse. Some nurseries that specialize in old varieties are Baum's Nursery, New Fairfield, Connecti-

cut; Leuthardt, East Moriches, New York; Mellinger's, North Lima, Ohio; and Waynesboro Nursery, Waynesboro, Virginia. Further information on obtaining grafting wood for antique varieties may be obtained from the Worcester Historical Society, 30 Elm Street, Worcester, MA 01608.

See also CIDER, FRUIT TREES, INSECT CONTROL, ORCHARD, WINE.

APPLE POMACE

The waste from apple processing plants, when available, is good material for composting.

Apple pomace decays readily if mixed with material that provides for proper aeration. Its value in the wet state is not high, since the nitrogen content is only .2 percent. But when the ash content of apple skins was analyzed, it appeared that they had over 3 percent phosphoric acid. Since apple pomace can be had in quantities where it is available at all, a goodly amount of phosphoric acid may be obtained from it at a low cost, often gratis. The potash content is, of course, much higher, amounting to about 12 percent of the ash, which corresponds to .75 percent of the pomace. It would seem best to use apple pomace for mulching in the orchard whenever feasible, possibly mixed with straw to permit penetration of air. If pomace is used as a mulch in areas near human habitation, the sour, vinegary odor in late stages of decay can be objectionable. Also, it attracts and supports large populations of fruit flies, sugar ants and other harmless but annoying insects.

In the compost heap, apple pomace should be mixed with straw, leaves or other coarse material, or used in thin layers because heavy layers tend to become compact and, as a result of this, fail to break down.

Apple pomace contains large amounts of seeds which are storage organs containing valuable nutritive substances, especially phosphorus and nitrogen. Hence the fertilizer value of the seed part must also be considered of value to organic gardening.

Composition	Protein %	Carbohydrate %	Mineral %
Wet	1.3	13.9	0.9
Dried	4.5	62.2	2.2
Silage	1.6	12.6	1.0

APPLE TREE BORER
See INSECT CONTROL

APRICOT   (*Prunus Armeniaca*)

With an individual and superior flavor, ripening a week or two earlier than peaches, apricots deserve space in every orchard. They are as easy to grow as peaches and, requiring the same temperature, frequently outlive them. Deep, fertile, well-drained soil of fine texture is best for apricots. Loam to clay loam soils are preferable to sandy soils which tend to warm early. Shallow hardpan should be avoided, and wet subsoil can kill the apricot tree.

As the apricot belongs to the Plum family, it is a simple matter to graft plum, peach or apricot scions on the same stock. If early-, middle- and late-ripening varieties are used, one can have fruit from the same tree all season long—an ideal arrangement for gardeners with limited land.

The stocks on which apricots are budded affect their adaptability. Those whose host tree is a myrobalan plum stand heavy soils better; those on seedling peach and apricot stocks are best for hungry overporous land.

One drawback to apricot culture is that the flower buds, which open very early, risk being injured by late spring frosts. To overcome this, select a cool and not overly sunny spot, planting in a northern or western exposure to delay the opening of the buds. Avoid full shade. Where possible, an eastern aspect should be avoided because the morning sun does not allow frostbitten buds to recover gradually, as they can when the sunlight does not strike them immediately.

Try to plant apricots at some distance from the vegetable garden and strawberry patch. Tomatoes, potatoes, Persian melons, and strawberries all harbor verticillium wilt, which causes blackheart in apricot trees.

Apricot trees should be planted in early spring before the buds begin to swell. In California they are planted between the middle of January and the first of March. Throughout the rest of the country they should be planted as soon as the soil can be prepared.

Two-year-old, six-foot whips are good for planting. The average apricot tree covers a circle 25 to 30 feet in diameter when fully grown; this means that apricots should be set at least this distance apart, and eventually they will need this space available to them on all sides. But shorter-lived brambles and bush fruits may be planted closer to them until they need their full room.

One self-pollinating apricot tree will yield 200 to 250 pounds of fruit in a good year. If fruit is to be dried, five pounds of fresh fruit will yield one pound dried. The best types are:

Perfection and Goldrich, excellent large-fruited cultivars. Alfred and Curtis, which are resistant to most diseases and can be grown in northern regions where spring frosts are not too severe.

Blenheim, the leading California cultivar; Moorpark, an old English, home-garden variety; and Scout. Scout is non-self-pollinating.

Early Golden, which has large fruits, almost as big as peaches, and is an old-time reliable sort.

Kok-pshar, Manchu and Zard, three recent introductions from central and northern China. These extra-hardy cultivars are suited to climates where winter temperatures dip as low as $-40°F.$ ($-40°C.$).

Several varieties suited to the Great Plains region have been developed by the South Dakota Experimental Station.

Young fruits should be thinned rigorously; otherwise, lean years may alternate with fruiting years. Important: When they are half-grown, snip out one of every two fruits that touch.

Multi-variety trees—apricot, peach and plum on one tree—are recommended for the garden that is limited in area.

Apricots, both dried and fresh, contain large quantities of vitamin A (7,500 units in three fresh fruits; 13,700 units in 100 grams dried fruit) and moderate quantities of the B vitamins, as well as some iron and calcium.

Insect Control: Branch and twig borers may be frustrating to many apricot growers.

These brown or black beetles are about ½ inch long and are cylindrical. They can be found burrowing into fruit buds or limb jointures, causing the branches to die and the trees to become weakened.

Prune off infected twigs from smaller fruit trees and remove all prunings from the vicinity of the tree as soon as possible. If infested wood is held for fuel, dipping it for a moment in stove oil will kill the larvae under the bark. Maintain as much vigor as possible in the orchard to eliminate these pests. This is accomplished by a sound system of mulching and tree feeding to encourage the vitality of the tree.

Cankerworms or measuring worms are wingless crawling insects which lay their eggs in the spring and fall in the limbs of trees. These slender, dark green worms chew on the edges of the leaves while they attack the apricot trees. Since these worms do not have wings in their egg-laying adult stage, they must crawl up the trunks of the trees to deposit the eggs of the next brood. By placing a band of sticky material like Tanglefoot® or an inverted funnel of window screen around the trunk, the moths will be prevented from climbing the tree.

The small greenish insect covered with a powderlike substance that can be seen crawling up the twigs of apricot, plum and prune trees is the mealy plum aphid. Should it strike, the foliage will become curled from loss of vital plant juices, the tree will become weak and stunted, and the fruit will split. Fruit is often spoiled by being covered by the sooty mold that is excreted.

Aphids can destroy trees that are unhealthy and weak. Best control for the organic gardener is to revitalize his tree by the use of organic fertilizers.

The brownish snout beetle that feeds in curved excavations and lays its eggs in the fruit is the plum curculio. It also devours leaves and petals until the fruit appears.

See also FRUIT TREES, INSECT CONTROL, ORCHARD.

AQUACULTURE

Fish farming holds great promise for the problem of diminishing world protein resources. Raising fish in ecologically balanced ponds or pools on a commercial or homestead scale is becoming a more common practice in America for many reasons. Fish convert approximately 85 percent of what they eat into protein food as contrasted with approximately 10 percent converted by beef cattle. Properly managed, a small pond can produce as many pounds of protein as a large pasture. In addition, fish are guarded by more natural pest control organisms than land animals, whose protectors have been destroyed by pesticides. The prospect of raising largemouth bass, bluegills, redear sunfish, catfish, crayfish, and other species has appealed to the organic gardener or farmer seeking inexpensive and balanced protein for his family.

Pond Construction: Farm ponds can be inexpensively constructed and ecologically maintained through natural feeding, fertilization and a good water supply. Water should be clear, with a pH between 6 and 9. In general, the water source should be higher than the fish pond itself for gravity flow.

The prime location for a fish pond is a low, wet area immune to natural flooding and with soil high in clay content. A Soil Conservation Service agent can evaluate a potential pond site upon request. In general, the land area should be flat with gradual slopes for drainage or spillover.

Size and shape of the fish pool are normally determined by the surrounding environment and desired fish production. For most small fish farming projects, ponds average one or two acres. Shapes vary from naturally irregular forms which result from dammed streams or brooks to square and rectangular figures specifically designed for fish harvesting nets. Large ponds should be shaped with the long axis at a right angle to prevailing winds in order to reduce wind and water erosion.

Water depth and temperature depend on the type of fish raised and the climate. Trout ponds work best at a depth of about four feet, with water under 70°F. (21.11°C.). Trout farmers recommend oxygenated water, free of weeds. (Weeds are welcomed by warm-water pond farmers raising bass, bluegills or sunfish, since they provide food and shelter from predator fish.) Warm-water ponds should be between three and six feet deep, and up to ten feet deep in freezing climates.

Pond construction involves clearing away all bushes and trees blocking the area and smoothing the pond bottom, followed by concrete work and pipe laying for foundation and drainage. A "catching pond" or harvest basin should be constructed at the lower end of the pond for harvesting. When the pond is drained, fish can be collectively removed by nets or seines in this basin.

There are two types of pond construction —the dug pond formed by digging a sunken shape out of the earth, and the levee pond made by natural levees or by mechanically digging out a level pond bottom. Levee ponds allow for drainage naturally since they are higher than ground level.

Raising the Fish: When the pond is fully constructed and the clear water allowed to stand for a week or two, it is time for fish stocking. Stocking rates depend on fish size, pond surface area and desired yield. For the first year, stocking 500 to 600 two- to four-inch fingerlings per acre will yield eight-inch rainbow or brook trout. It is estimated that through supplemental feeding, 2,000 fingerlings can be stocked per acre to produce 1,000 pounds of ten-inch trout.

Raising carp may prove even more productive to commercial and homestead farmers than the trout. Carp can be stocked 4,000 to 12,000 two-inch fingerlings per acre for top yields, providing there is supplemental feeding. Carp are perfect for organic food growers, since they derive most food from the pond and reduce the raiser's need for commercial food pellets and other supplies.

Catfish are also commonly stocked in American fish ponds. Low in fats and carbohydrates but high in vitamins, minerals and protein, catfish are likely to be seen with increasing frequency on the American dinner table. Channel, blue and white catfish, stocked 750 to 1,000 four-inch fingerlings to the acre in the spring, will yield nine-ounce fish each fall.

Beside their food value, bluegill sunfish and largemouth bass are stocked for forage and predation. The U.S. Fish and Wildlife Service suggests stocking 100 bass to 1,000 bluegill per pond acre. Bluegills feed off insects and small crustacea. The bass, in turn, keep bluegills from overpopulating the pond by feeding on them.

Crustacea such as crayfish and mussels can also be raised in small ponds. Crayfish are good water purifiers and can produce as much as 1,000 pounds of protein per acre.

Feeding, like pond site selection and construction, depends on the types of fish raised and their stages of development. Commercial food pellets are available for supplemental feeding, but a more natural diet consisting of table scraps, small crustacea, minnows, sunfish, earthworms, soybeans, and algae is recommended.

Pond harvesting is usually best the second year after stocking. There are three harvesting techniques—fishing, seining and draining. Fishing requires continual work and attention to the balance of species remaining in the pond, especially when predators and their prey are involved. Seining involves the mechanical removal of 70 to 90 percent of the fish in an efficient manner using nets with one edge weighted with sinkers. Draining the fish pool concentrates the catch into a harvest basin for slow and safe removal. These techniques can be used alone or in combination to harvest fish pond crops.

Hybridizing of fish is now becoming common practice to prevent overpopulation of stocked lakes. This is effected by getting the fish to produce more males than females and thereby causing the first generation to produce 90 percent males, the second 99 percent and the third 100 percent. With this method, the pond can produce for ten to 15 years before being restocked.

Indoor Culture: Small-scale fish farming need not be confined to the outdoors. Carp, catfish, sunfish, and other species can be raised in a six by six-foot tank (three feet deep) in the basement if a few essential conditions are met. Since there is no soil present to act as a buffer against the ill-smelling fish wastes, filtration and aeration systems must be provided.

Fish in indoor tanks may be fed a combined diet of commercial pellets and kitchen wastes. Feeding should be calculated on the basis of body weight: with pellets, fish should receive an amount equal to 4 percent of their body weight per day; with kitchen wastes, 10 percent of body weight. This formula is designed to produce a 3 percent weight gain per day.

As exothermic creatures, fish are extremely sensitive to temperature, oxygen supply and other environmental conditions. Water quality is critical, and anyone attempting to raise fish indoors should be prepared to do regular monitoring of dissolved oxygen, pH and nitrogen ammonia levels.

Aquaculture is a science open to the future. Experimenters like Dr. William McLarney and the New Alchemy Institute in Woods Hole, Massachusetts, continue to compile data on backyard fish farming, working with heated geodesic-dome-covered ponds housing tilapia and other exotic species of fish. Others, such as Rodale Resources in Emmaus, Pennsylvania, and the Institute of Local Self-Reliance in Washington, D.C., are innovating in the areas of water filtration, fish feeding and harvesting techniques.

See also PONDS.

AQUARIUM

Living systems of aquatic plants and animals for exhibition, scientific analysis or decoration, aquariums are balanced when aquatic plants and animals exist in respiratory cooperation. Fish exhale carbon dioxide and eliminate wastes which the plants absorb as fertilizer. Plants use the carbon dioxide and emit oxygen during photosynthesis which the fish inhale. Cooperation exists in this sense.

Sufficient daylight, uniform water temperature and prepared fish foods are all that are needed to support most freshwater fish. A large variety of aquatic plants is good for aquariums.

There are no rules to follow in artistic aquarium planting except the general ones of proportion which apply to all garden compositions, indoors or outdoors. Mass the tall plants at the back and corners for background effects. Bushy plants should be placed at the side or in the corners and specimen plantings can be made of different varieties. In a large aquarium of more than five gallons capacity, nothing is better than *Vallisneria*. Commonly called eelgrass, it is a tall, thin plant with ribbonlike strands which swing to right and left below the water surface. It is used in clumps or as a solid mass across the back of the tank.

For the sides and corners *Caboma, Anacharis* and *Ludwigia* are extremely good. The latter provides a spot of color for the planting, as the leaves are green in front and purple red in back. *Anacharis* is pinched back as it grows rapidly and will soon crowd the tank.

Sagittaria is a good specimen plant; so is spatterdock. Moneywort, a low green plant dainty in appearance, and hairgrass will carpet the aquarium with small grasslike needles which provide the fish with a good hiding place. There are many other aquatic plants which may be used, such as water hyacinths or water lilies.

Many fine vines, bulbs and plants will thrive in water. English ivy, once established, requires little care and will climb stucco walls or trail from a mantel with attractive effects. Nasturtiums, cut before heavy frosts, will bloom indoors all winter. Fertilizer is added to the water each week for good growth. The Chinese evergreen (*Aglaonema modestum*) and Roman hyacinths are all easily grown in water.

In starting his aquarium the beginner should keep in mind the following four basic functions that plant life performs:

1. Its ability, under the influence of light, to develop free oxygen and to absorb carbon dioxide. This function is absolutely vital to the animal life in the aquarium.

2. Absorption through its underwater roots and leaves of the fecal matter excreted by the animal life.

3. Helping keep the water clear by competing successfully for food with microscopic vegetal organisms. *Salvinia,* duckweed and *Azolla* are excellent for this purpose.

4. Providing a breeding ground for the fish. Many fish deposit their eggs on the leaves of the plants and the younger fish subsequently seek refuge there from their cannibalistic elders. *Riccia* is especially recommended for this purpose.

AQUATIC GARDENING
See AQUARIUM, LILY POND, WATER GARDEN

AQUATIC WEED CONTROL

Aquatic weeds are often a threat to water plant and animal life. In the South, water hyacinth, American lotus and alligator weed have interfered with fishing and aquatic plants. In the West, weed growth clogs irrigation ditches, slowing water flow and increasing evaporation rates.

There are several mechanical and natural methods of controlling aquatic weeds today. One special harvesting machine uses a cutting bar to remove as much as one ton of weeds from lakes, streams or ponds in about 30 minutes. Harvested weeds are used for mulching or composting.

A more biological approach has also been employed in aquatic weed control. Freshwater snails and weed-eating fishes feed on many varieties of aquatic weeds. The Congo tilapia, grass and other carp strains have proven effective in controlling majas and aquatic weeds such as potamogeton, elodes, chara, giant duckweed, bladderwort, needle rush, pithophora, giant spirogyra, and southern watergrass weeds.

AQUILEGIA   *See* COLUMBINE

ARABIAN JASMINE   *See* SAMBAC

ARACEAE

This is a large family of perennial herbs known for its stunning spathes, as in the Jack-in-the-pulpit and the calla lily. Most Araceae are tropical plants containing a milky, bitter juice that is often poisonous.

ARALIA

Hardy throughout most of the United States, this genus of ornamental herbs, shrubs and small trees is cultivated for its distinctive foliage, small white flowers and black berrylike fruits.

Shrubby kinds: Of the tall (30 to 40 feet), spiny-stemmed aralias, *A. spinosa* (Hercules'-club or devil's-walking-stick), *A. elata* (Japanese angelica) and *A. chinensis* are most common.

Herbaceous kinds: *A. californica* (elk clover) is a stout perennial native to the Pacific Northwest. *A. racemosa* (American spikenard), *A. hispida* (bristly sarsaparilla) and *A. nudicaulis* (wild sarsaparilla) are herbaceous species found in eastern North America.

Indoor kinds: *A. japonica* (ivy-leaf aralia) makes a fine house plant. Its glossy, dark green leaves, which may be four inches or more across, hold on the plant extremely well, showing no tendency to yellow or drop. For a bushy shape, ivy-leaf aralia should be cut back several times during its first two years; for a taller, more slender plant, allow it to branch normally as it matures.

Aralias need good drainage, fairly heavy watering and a warm situation. They may be grown in a partially sunny exposure but do best when given full bright light without direct sunlight. Pot them in good, humusy soil. Propagation is by seeds sown in frames in spring or by root cuttings over bottom heat. One fine point about this plant is the ease and speed with which cuttings may be rooted in a glass of plain water. When roots on the cuttings are ½ to one inch long, pot these new little plants in small, clean clay pots.

ARBOR

An arbor is usually a support for grapes or other viny plants. But arbors can be far more than simply that. They can also serve as a place to get away from it all, a secluded spot for a bit of solitude and privacy even in the bustling suburbs, and a place to cool off on a hot summer night.

Arbors are easy to construct from wood and wire. They are basically a sturdy framework. The sides and top are covered with latticework or wire to offer more support for plants (wire lasts longer than wood, although wood can be treated with a preservative such as Cuprinol for longevity). Used wood may be used to save money on construction.

If you want to use an arbor as a place of relaxation, make sure it's big enough to move around in. An ideal size is 7 feet wide by 6½ feet high by 24 feet long. If you want an arbor that is cool, locate its length along the path of evening breezes and keep both ends open. If privacy is desired, the ends may be closed and a central entrance provided; you may wish to design a T-, U- or L-shaped arbor.

As vines grow around the framework, plants or grass planted inside the arbor will eventually die off from hard usage and lack of sunlight. Once this bare earth floor is packed by the passage of traffic, there will be little tendency to muddiness and it will remain cool and moist. Furniture used in the arbor should be flat-footed so it will not gouge the earthen floor.

The most reliable grapes to plant are Concord and Fredonia, but most varieties will flourish on an arbor. A structure 24 feet long will support eight vines nicely, four spaced evenly on each side.

Every five years or so, the accumulation of old wood makes an all-out pruning necessary. This should be done late in the fall. It can be accomplished by sawing all branches along the sides at a height of about three feet from the ground. The whole loose growth can then be raised on one side and rolled back over the top so that it comes clear in a complete mass to be carried away for compost or mulch use.

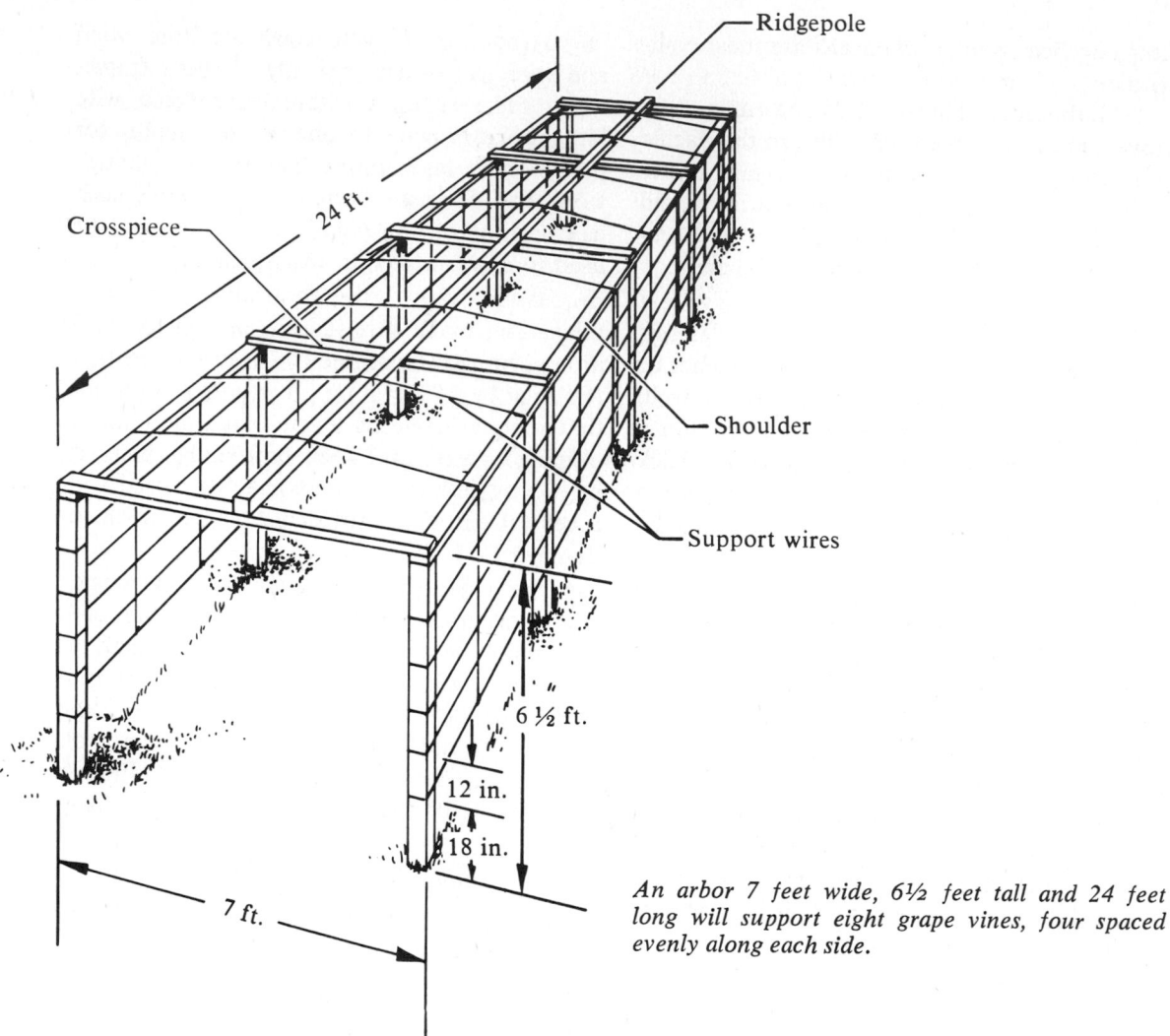

Ridgepole

Crosspiece

24 ft.

Shoulder

Support wires

6 ½ ft.

12 in.

18 in.

7 ft.

An arbor 7 feet wide, 6½ feet tall and 24 feet long will support eight grape vines, four spaced evenly along each side.

It will probably take two years for the arbor to become fully shaded by grape leaves, which give maximum shade while permitting free movement of air. No other leaves can equal the grape in this respect, but until the vines are sufficiently developed, ample shade can be had by planting climbing beans or morning glories. Tomatoes thrive against the support of an arbor, the ripe fruit adding a delightful touch of brightness in the late summer.

ARBORETUM

Defined as a place where trees and shrubs are cultivated for scientific and educational purposes, many of today's arboretums are located on private estates, public parks and several experiment stations. Of the more than 100 botanical gardens in the United States, some of the best known are the Arnold Arboretum of Harvard University, Brooklyn Arboretum, Longwood Gardens, Missouri Arboretum, Strybing Arboretum of San Francisco, Huntington Gardens of Los Angeles, and Fairchild Arboretum of Florida.

Arnold Arboretum has an outstanding collection of woody plants on its 265 acres in Jamaica Plains, outside Boston. This landscape garden features silver birch and weeping willow trees, in addition to weeping hemlock, a native American tree.

Brooklyn Arboretum is a 50-acre ornamental and educational garden in New York. It features three Japanese gardens, a rose garden where the All-American rose collection is displayed and a huge greenhouse containing a special bonsai collection. The arboretum offers educational programs in horticulture, botany and conservation.

Longwood Gardens, near West Chester, Pennsylvania, encompasses 1,000 acres of hemlocks, oaks and maples in addition to Italianate ornamental gardens and floodlit fountains. Longwood is also known for its fine displays of water lilies, roses, orchids, and heaths.

Missouri Arboretum offers something special in its 75 suburban acres—the Climatron. The Climatron is the first conservatory ever built on Buckminster Fuller's geodesic principle. It houses more than 100 taxa of tropical species. The garden also offers educational programs on gardening, greenhouse management and elementary horticulture.

Located in a corner of Golden Gate Park in San Francisco, Strybing Arboretum is basically an English landscape garden, recognized for its collection of magnolias.

Huntington Gardens comprises 207 acres of trees and plants surrounding the famous Hunt Library and Art Gallery in Los Angeles. Huntington is known for its fine Japanese garden, Italian statues and sculpture. Included is a ten-acre desert garden which features 25,000 desert plants including Cactaceae and Euphorbiaceae.

Fairchild Arboretum began as 83 acres of trees and tropical plants in Florida. Its palmetum contains the world's largest collection of palms, with over 500 species displayed. Also featured are mosses, orchids and philodendron.

ARBORVITAE (*Thuja*)

Evergreen trees and shrubs of the Cypress family, arborvitae have attractive scalelike leaves and small cones and come in a wide variety of shapes and sizes. Some are low shrubs popular for foundation plantings, while others grow to 200 feet. Still others are suitable for dense hedges, shrubby borders and windbreaks. Arborvitae prefer a moist, rich soil, a cool climate free of dust and smoke, and a modicum of summer sun. Propagation is by seed or cuttings of mature wood.

Thuja is derived from the Greek *thyos,* meaning sacrifice, a reference to the resin of some species which was used as incense. *Gerard's Herbal* notes the introduction of *T. occidentalis* in Britain before the sixteenth century, when members of the Cartier expedition to Canada used the leaves to cure scurvy. That expedition resulted in the eventual cultivation of the trees in France and later throughout Europe and Asia.

The leaves and twigs were officially recognized as stimulants, emmenagogues and irritants for many decades in the United States. Today the oil is distilled for use as an insect repellent and as an ingredient of soap liniment.

T. occidentalis, ranging from Canada to the mountains of North Carolina and Tennessee, grows to 50 feet high and has aromatic, scaled leaves that yield a yellowish dye.

T. plicata, native to western North America, is the giant arborvitae or western cedar, that grows along the Pacific slope. Its sturdy wood is used for shingles, siding and even mine props. *T. p.* var. *Pendula* is grown as an ornamental with long branches. *T. p.* var. *Pygmaea,* with its low bushy growth, is cultivated for foundation planting.

See also EVERGREEN.

ARCTOSTAPHYLOS

These evergreen shrubs of the Heath family produce red fruit and clusters of small, white or pink bell-shaped flowers. Fine honey plants native to the Pacific Coast, arctostaphylos grow best in a sandy loam enriched with peat. One species, the bearberry (*A. Uva-ursi*), makes an attractive evergreen ground cover in the northern temperate regions. The edible berry has a very bland taste, and the plant is the source of a yellow gray dye.

ARECA   *See* PALM

ARGEMONE

These annual or perennial herbs of the Poppy family bear large yellow, white or purple flowers throughout the summer. They are easily grown from seed in a light sandy soil and full sun.

ARID CLIMATE

Arid refers to a very dry climate, such as in parts of the Southwest, where desert or semi-desert conditions exist. Generally there is only enough water for widely spaced desert plants. Annual rainfall varies from ten to 20 inches. The soil is generally low or deficient in nitrogen and organic matter. Shrubs and bunchgrasses are the principal vegetation in areas where the rainfall is less than ten inches annually. The soils are light in color, alkaline in reaction and often high in lime content and mineral nutrients.

See also DESERT GARDEN.

ARMERIA

Often selected as border and rock garden plants, armerias prefer light, sandy soils and full sun. Sea pink or thrift (*A. maritima*) grows about one foot high and has pink, purple or white flowers and evergreen foliage.

See also ROSE PINK.

ARNICA

Arnica is a perennial herb often grown as an alpine or rock garden specimen and occasionally as a common border plant. Tincture of *Arnica montana,* a European native, has popular medicinal value in the treatment of sprains and bruises.

Arnica needs a good-quality, high-acid soil and a cool climate. It can be sown in early spring in a cold frame, or cultivated from root divisions, which is the preferred method.

The flowers, which make attractive dried arrangements, are yellow orange and cluster atop one- to two-foot stalks ringed with hairy, basal leaves.

ARROWWOOD
(*Viburnum dentatum*)

A ten- to 15-foot shrub that does well in open areas, the arrowwood offers creamy flowers in late May and early June and blue black berries and wine-colored foliage in the fall. It is hardy in practically every section of the United States. Moist soil and a somewhat sunny position are best.

See also VIBURNUM.

ARTEMISIA
See SOUTHERNWOOD, TARRAGON, WORMWOOD

ARTICHOKE, GLOBE
(*Cynara Scolymus*)

Native to the Mediterranean region, the globe artichoke is finding increasing popularity among gardeners in the damp mild coastal regions of this country. Generally three to five feet tall, this coarse, herbaceous perennial has large, lobed leaves to three feet long and good-sized heads that take on a violet shade as they ripen. The base of the scales of the unripe flower head, along with the bottom part of the artichoke, are eaten either cooked or raw.

A warm-weather perennial, the globe artichoke reaches heights of three to five feet and puts forth tremendous, coarse leaves. The large green flower heads are eaten raw or cooked.

Artichokes are best planted as started seedlings in trenches eight inches deep, lined with one inch of compost or rotted manure. While it does best in rich sandy loam, the artichoke will grow on any kind of soil, so long as it is trenched, pulverized and well manured. Plant roots five to six inches below the surface, cover with soil and tamp firmly. When plants are six inches tall, mulch heavily to preserve moisture. Cut away all but six of the suckers that develop at the base when plant reaches eight inches and transplant the suckers to make a new row. Plant these singly two feet apart, in rows at least four feet apart, or in groups of three in triangles, at least four feet apart in the row. Protect the young suckers with hot caps, evergreen boughs or some other protecting material. Cut plants back to the ground in fall. In cool areas, protect through the winter with an inverted bushel basket with leaves.

During dry weather furnish artichokes with copious amounts of manure water or compost tea. Deep, thorough watering is best, followed by a liberal mulching of half-rotted manure between the rows.

Crops are produced in spring in warmer areas; in summer farther north. Halfway through the growing season, apply a small handful of fertilizer around the base of each plant, and repeat after harvest. When harvesting, cut with one inch of stem. The preferred method of preparing artichokes is to harvest a head while still green and unopened, when it is about the size of an orange. Heads are placed in a pot of cold water, salted and cooked for 45 minutes after the water has begun to boil. Individual leaves are then picked off and eaten one by one, starting at the outside. The thickened bottom portion of the leaf is dipped in melted butter or a basil vinaigrette and its fleshy part stripped between the teeth. When all the leaves have been eaten and the hairy "choke" at the heart removed, the meaty and delicious artichoke heart—the best part of the plant—reveals itself.

The variety most commonly grown in this country is large Green Globe, which normally buds in its second year.

Although it bears a slight resemblance in taste, the globe artichoke is completely unrelated to the Jerusalem artichoke (*Helianthus tuberosus*), a North American sunflower.

ARTICHOKE, JERUSALEM
(*Helianthus tuberosus*)

The Jerusalem artichoke, a large, potato-shaped tuber, is characterized by its sweet nut-like flavor. Contrary to popular notion, it neither tastes nor looks like the green or globe artichoke, and is not even related to it botanically.

Jerusalem is actually a corruption of the Italian *girasole*, meaning "turning to the sun," and this artichoke is really a prolific member of the Sunflower family.

Culture: Jerusalem artichokes grow in almost any type of soil that gets a little sunshine, including sandy soil. They are free from disease, highly productive and completely frost-hardy, but spread very rapidly, and unless cultivated with some care, will become troublesome as weeds. For this reason, it is best to give them an out-of-the-way planting a reasonable distance from other vegetables or flowers. To check spreading, dig roots in late fall or early spring and thoroughly remove them.

Planting artichoke tubers is very much like planting potatoes, and is done from cut pieces each having a seed or "eye." Unlike potatoes, this frostproof vegetable can be set out in the fall as well as early spring. A good location may be along the garden edge where the six- to eight-foot-tall artichokes won't overshadow other plants. They are also useful where their screening effect and large, colorful blooms will improve the landscape. (Some grow to heights of a modest 12 feet or so!)

In two rows, plant one medium piece per hill, a foot apart, in two- or three-foot rows. In beds, set tubers four by four feet apart. As indicated, plants multiply quickly and soon choke out any venturesome weeds. Mulching is a good idea in row plantings, and compost applications maintain desirable fertility—although soil and climate extremes won't stop this persistent plant.

The sturdy artichoke's bright blossoms,

upper stalk and leaf growth don't go to waste, either. Where they're not used for livestock or poultry feeding, the tops can be cut and fed to the compost or mulch-material piles.

Since freezing doesn't injure the tubers, they may be left in the ground indefinitely after fall frosts, a fresh supply being dug as needed throughout the off-season. In fact, leaving them in the ground is a practical storage method for this vegetable whose tender skin doesn't make it a particularly good indoor keeper. Those that are brought in should be kept quite moist —if necessary given a daily soaking in water prior to use. It is best to dig up only the amount you plan to use immediately.

With the arrival of spring, tubers left in the ground should be dug either for eating or replanting. If an increased supply *is* wanted, some may simply be left to multiply.

Native to the Americas, Jerusalem artichoke is cultivated for its fleshy tubers which are fine, nutritious and low-starch substitutes for potatoes.

A 25-foot row will supply the average family for one year.

Nutritional Value: The artichoke is 100 percent *starchless*. It stores its carbohydrates in the form of inulin rather than starch, and its sugar as levulose the way most healthful fruits and honey do. It has practically no caloric value. Because of these facts, medical authorities strongly recommend it as a substitute for other carbohydrates on the diabetic's menu, and in the diet of all who should or must restrict their starch and caloric intake.

The Jerusalem artichoke offers a good source of some minerals and vitamins (particularly potassium and thiamine)—a result of its being a plant-world union of tuber roots and luxuriant sunflower growth.

ASEXUAL

Asexual propagation refers to any method of reproducing plants without the union of germ cells. The most common methods are cuttings of roots, stems and leaves, layering and root division.

ASH   (*Fraxinus*)

The ash tree is primarily important as timber, although the flowering ash makes a showy tree for home landscaping with its large clusters of white flowers. The main growing requirement for ash trees is sufficient moisture.

The wood is strong and elastic, and is used to make oars, long tool handles and baseball bats. Ash makes a fine firewood, and can even be burned green. The seeds grow so readily that young trees may be looked upon as weeds.

ASPARAGUS

In the early spring the home garden offers few pleasures greater than the cutting of the luscious early spears of an established asparagus planting. It was because of its habit of producing early shoots that the ancient Greeks named the plant *asparagos,* meaning to swell.

Until modern times asparagus was a medicinal plant. The early and abundant supply of green spears restored men who must have struggled through the long winter upon a poorly balanced diet. But like many other medicinal plants asparagus later became a garden favorite, and its popularity is still increasing.

Planting: It is possible to grow fine asparagus plants from seed if care is taken to see that the seedbed is properly drained and well pulverized and that the seedlings are transplanted without too much injury to the root system. But an established planting reaches the cutting stage much sooner if one-year-old roots of the best disease-resistant varieties are used.

To establish a planting of asparagus it is best to select a site to one side of the garden. This site should be free from shade; the soil should be rich, deep and well drained. The location should be so arranged that the permanence of the planting will not interfere with the cultivation of the rest of the garden.

In the spring as early as the ground can be worked, a trench 12 inches deep and about ten inches wide should be dug along the line where the first row is to stand. In the bottom of this trench place a three-inch layer of mature compost humus. If well-rotted manure is plentiful, this may be added. This layer should then be well dug into the bottom of the trench. The second row should be made not closer than four feet from the first.

One-year-old crowns should then be placed in position about 18 inches apart and ten inches below the level of the garden. The crowns should be covered with a two-inch layer of sifted compost humus and well watered. During the summer the trench should be slowly filled with a mixture of fine topsoil and composted material. Cultivation will tend to fill the trench, but it is advisable not to do the filling too rapidly or the growing plants are likely to be stifled.

Whatever care you take in the setting out will be well repaid to you later. Careful siting is important. The careful, deep preparation of the area is of great value because the powerful fleshy roots of the asparagus plant often thrust their way five to six feet downward and spread out almost an equal distance in their search for the heavy supply of plant nutrients needed for the production of the large spears. Because of this, the plants require more garden space than their feathery brush would seem to indicate, and because of the great depth to which the roots develop, you will find it wise to see that an ample supply of rich organic matter is deeply placed before setting out the crowns.

After the planting is established it will thrive with little care for many years. But as with all vegetables, asparagus should be kept free from weeds and the damaging influence of trees, and should receive each season a liberal supply of added organic material. This supply can be arranged in two ways.

In the spring the rows should be ridged. Ordinarily this is done by drawing up to the row a good quantity of the topsoil between the rows by using a hoe. If you use compost instead of topsoil to form these ridges, this will serve two purposes—bleaching the shoots by excluding sunlight, and adding valuable plant nutrients to the soil.

After the cutting season, it is good practice to sow a cover crop of cowpeas, soybeans, etc. These should be planted between the rows of asparagus. A cover crop of this type discourages the growth of weeds and when dug under adds greatly to the organic content of the soil.

But the organic material added during ridging is the most important. This ridge should be several inches high; if shallow, the shoots will tend to open before assuming sufficient length. Even if you decide to grow "green asparagus," that is, unbleached asparagus, you will find it necessary to form shallow ridges to overcome the tendency of the crown to get too close to the surface. This slow upward movement is caused by the formation each year of new storage roots on the uppermost side of the crown.

Harvest: If a good growth is made the first year, it is possible to cut the shoots lightly the following spring, but it is generally better to encourage plant growth and to delay cutting for another season. Spears should be cut when about six inches high. Some gardeners cut them two inches below the ground level, others at the surface.

In cutting, place the knife blade close to the spear, run it downward the desired depth, then turn it enough to cut cleanly through the spear but no more. Careless jabbing during cutting time can cause very serious injury to a planting of asparagus.

As winter approaches, the rows of asparagus should be lightly mulched with straw or similar material to prevent frost from penetrating too severely into the crowns. The brush

When harvesting, cut asparagus spears cleanly, avoiding injury to other parts of the plant.

should not be removed or burned but should remain as a part of the mulch. This mulch should be removed in the spring and the ground lightly cultivated.

Pests and Diseases: The asparagus beetle is considered a serious menace; it is very difficult to get rid of and does much damage. But most of the serious damage done by this beetle occurs when it is allowed to overwinter in the adult stage by finding concealment in fallen sticks, trash, leaves, and the like. In this case it emerges in the early spring to feed upon the young asparagus shoots. Garden cleanliness and fall cultivation will prevent the insects from overwintering. An old method for controlling asparagus beetles was to turn chickens, ducks or guinea hens loose in the asparagus planting. These birds invariably do an efficient job of wiping out the beetles and their larvae.

Asparagus rust is a plant disease affecting asparagus. Small reddish pustules appear first on the main stalks. These pustules, when they burst, release a fine rust-colored cloud of spores. Sometimes an entire planting is rapidly infected and dies. But the degree to which asparagus rust does damage is very largely dependent upon local conditions. The spores require dampness for germination. Areas subject to heavy dews and damp mists are poor locations for asparagus.

Varieties: Mary Washington is a reliable, rust-resistant variety and a favorite of many gardeners. Roberts Strain is also rust-resistant and is a heavy producer. Paradise is an early variety and very productive.

ASPARAGUS BEETLE
See INSECT CONTROL

ASPEN   See POPLAR

ASPIDISTRA

Commonly called the cast-iron plant, this Chinese member of the Lily family lives up to its name. Quite tolerant, it even manages to survive in dry, overheated apartments. The dark green arching leaves, four inches wide and 2½ feet long, spring directly from the rootstock. Small, purple brown, bell-shaped flowers are borne near the soil line and are pollinated by snails in their native environment. Once quite popular in Victorian times, it is now regaining prominence.

In its unfussy manner it will thrive in an all-purpose soil kept evenly moist. Since it can grow even in a northern exposure, it can bring green color to an otherwise drab area of your home. Propagation is by rootstock division.

The old Victorian standby was *Aspidistra elatior*. Newer cultivars include *A. elatior* cv. 'Variegata' and cv. 'Minor'. As their names indicate, they are a variegated and dwarf form, respectively.

ASTER

The name aster refers to two distinct genera of plants, both members of the Composite or Daisy family. It is the botanic name of the hardy asters which are perennials, and it is also the popular name of the tender China asters which are annuals. The China aster (*Callistephus*) has been developed until it is now one of our most popular garden annuals.

Culture: For early bloom, the seeds should be sown in early April in flats or pots. Use a soil mixture of one-third sand, one-third garden soil and one-third compost. Sow the seed in shallow drills about three inches apart and cover with a light layer of soil. Keep evenly moist, but not soaked, until the seedlings are up and growing well. When they have their first true leaves or are crowding, transplant them into paper cups or flats with at least four inches between plants. Do not delay the transplanting so long that the plants become spindly.

As the weather becomes warmer, gradually harden off the plants by setting them outside during the pleasant part of the day. When all danger of frost is over, the seedlings are ready to be transplanted to their permanent location. Set the plants in full sun about ten to 12 inches apart in rows about 1½ to two feet apart or in groups, as you prefer. Add some wood ashes to the soil in early spring or at least two weeks before planting the seedlings; otherwise add well-rotted manure or compost. A light sprinkling of lime on an acid or neutral soil surface a few weeks before planting is beneficial, as they like a slightly alkaline soil. Aster seeds can also be planted directly in the garden after the soil has warmed up if you are unable to start seedlings indoors.

Cultivate regularly throughout the growing season to keep down weeds. A good mulch can, of course, help control these and lighten the chore considerably. The roots of the aster are fine and close to the surface of the soil, so shallow cultivation is essential. During dry weather, water thoroughly about once a week.

Uses: There are several features which make the China aster one of the most desirable of the annual flowers. They are excellent cut flowers. They have good lasting quality, have long stems, are not easily damaged, and they have a wide color range. Bloom may be had from July until frost in October. They also

The China aster produces hardy, long-lasting flowers from midsummer through October.

make a wonderful display in the garden, as you may use them as a border plant, mass in groups in an informal fashion or intermix them with chrysanthemums.

Varieties: There have been so many types and varieties developed that it is difficult to discuss them all. Each variety has its own list of colors, some having many shades and tones. Consult seed catalogs for varieties, which can range from compact six-inch dwarfs useful for bedding and edging to three-foot giants for the back of the border. Annual asters are highly susceptible to a wilt disease which can kill plants or cause deformed leaves and flowers. The best new strains have been bred to be wilt resistant; choose these over older, wilt-susceptible varieties.

The late-blooming, hardy perennial asters are known as Michaelmas daisies in England, where the first hybrids were developed from wild American species. They are not very popular here, perhaps because two of the principal parents, the New England and New York asters, are common weeds in American meadows and hedgerows.

They come in a vast number of varieties, with color ranging from white and red through the deepest blues and purples, and they vary from one to six feet in height. All of them grow and spread rapidly. Their beauty makes them an excellent subject for massing in beds or for the perennial border, and many of them make fine cut flowers. They bloom from late summer through fall when chrysanthemums do, and are hardier and easier to grow. Gardeners who haven't time to maintain chrysanthemums properly should use the hardy asters to provide the last show of the season in the garden.

There are so many varieties that space permits listing of only a few. Consult nursery catalogs for more complete lists. All have daisylike single flowers with yellow centers. Autumn Glory is a fine red variety growing to four feet. Blue Radiance is a long-blooming, three-foot, light blue one. Coombe Violet is intense violet purple and four feet tall. Harrington's Pink has pure pink flowers on four-foot stems and does not need to be divided as often as the others. Finalist, a three-foot violet blue, is the latest-blooming variety, flowering till mid-November. Some good semidwarfs, growing 12 to 15 inches, are Snowball, white; Countess of Dudley, pink; and Professor Kippenberg, blue. *Aster* x *frikartii* Wonder of Staffa is a European hybrid valuable for its long July to October bloom period. It is good in dry soil, but needs winter protection in the coldest regions. Flowers are lavender blue on two-foot stems. *A. yunnanensis* Napsbury has blue flowers on 18-inch stems and blooms from May to July.

Grow them in average to rich, well-drained soil in full sun. Each year or every other year divide the clumps in spring, planting only the strongest divisions from the outside of each clump. Each division should have two or three shoots. With small varieties, set the divisions 12 to 24 inches apart; with vigorous ones, set them 24 to 36 inches apart. The tall varieties will need staking, which is most easily and inconspicuously done as the English do it. Push twiggy branches into the ground around the plants as growth starts in spring, using branches which are nearly as tall as the plant will be at maturity. The stems will grow up through the twigs and lean on them, and the developing foliage will hide the branches from view. The semidwarf asters which grow only 12 to 15 inches high do not need staking. Height of tall varieties can be regulated somewhat by pinching out the growing tips in June. This should induce shorter, bushier growth. Old clumps left undivided too long can be thinned by cutting out at the ground all but four or five of the stems in spring. This should improve flowering and help prevent mildew by improving air circulation.

ASTILBE

These plants of the Saxifrage family are native to Korea, Japan and China. In appearance they are similar to spireas and sometimes are incorrectly sold as such. Fluffy spikes of white, pink, red, or purple flowers appear from June to August on cultivars which vary in height from six inches to six feet. Smaller ones are used in perennial flower beds and larger ones in foundation or landscape plantings.

They prefer cooler temperatures and bright sun, and the soil should not be allowed to dry out. Propagation is by seed or division in the spring or fall. *Astilbe japonica* cv. 'Gladstone' is often used as a potted plant which is forced for Easter.

AUBRIETA

A purple rockcress growing to six inches, aubrieta is an excellent mat-forming plant for the rock garden, wall garden or sloping bank. Seeds may be sown in the open ground or in flats and transplanted. The most popular species, *A. deltoidea,* has many forms; some are dwarf and have lavender flowers, while others have larger leaves and pink, purple, crimson, and lilac flowers. Aubrietas prefer a well-drained soil and full sun. The plants may be carried over the winter in cold frames or with other protection.

AUSTRALIAN PINE
See CASUARINA

AUTUMN CROCUS
See COLCHICUM

AVAILABILITY

This is the state or quality of being present in a form that is usable. In reference to soil nutrients, this means being in a form that plants can readily absorb and assimilate. It is possible for a soil to have major and minor nutrients, but to have them unavailable to plants. In general, humus is a major factor in availability: if the soil is rich in humus, the nutrients are available; if the soil is humus-poor, the nutrients may be locked in nonavailable forms. Soil reaction (the pH of the soil) is another factor contributing to availability.

See also ACIDITY–ALKALINITY, FERTILIZER.

AVENS   *See* GEUM

AVOCADO   (*Persea americana*)

In Florida, Southern California and other frost-free regions, the avocado is a practical fruit and shade tree for the home grounds, thriving either in or out of the lawn area. A heavy mulch or cover crop should be maintained beneath the tree to conserve soil moisture and keep weeds in check. Avocado flowers are borne in winter, when subfreezing temperatures will destroy the crop. Its bearing habit is cyclical; heavy crops are invariably followed by lighter yields. Protection must be provided from strong winds and intense dry heat.

Planting: Avocados are planted from November through May. The planting hole should be at least twice as large as the root ball, to give the tender roots room to establish themselves.

In the bottom of the hole place two shovelsful of well-rotted compost mixed with the same quantity of good topsoil, preferably a rich sandy loam. If the hole is three feet deep, these amounts could be increased. Add enough topsoil to bring the top of the ball of roots level with the ground. Place the tree on this in the center of the hole and fill in with good soil in which some compost is mixed. This will put humus in the soil. Firm the mixture around the ball of roots as the filling in proceeds. When the hole is almost filled in, have a gentle stream of water from the hose run in to settle the soil, so there will be no air pockets. Let the water run long enough so it will reach down below the ball of roots, then fill in with more soil to bring it up to ground level. Make a basin around the tree to hold water. Give a thorough watering once or twice a week until the newly planted tree is established. When it has put out eight or nine inches of new growth, once in two weeks should be enough to water unless the soil has very free drainage and the weather is very hot. Keep the water running from 45 to 60 minutes. Temperatures and soil conditions vary in different districts. No set of rules can be given that will cover all sections, and a little experience will show what is the right amount. If there is good drainage any excess water will drain away.

As the trees grow, additional feeding may be given by applying a trowelful of blood meal and two of bone meal once in six weeks during spring and summer. Do not apply after August, for the new growth may be nipped in sections where there is danger of frost. Always give deep watering after applying fertilizer.

Do not cut off lower branches. They protect the trunk from sunburn. There are preparations on the market with which to paint the trunk for sun protection.

No pruning is required except to keep the tree in shape, well balanced and symmetrical in growth. In old trees keep all dead wood cut out. Never expose large bare branches to the sun as they are easily sunburned.

Cultivation should not be done near the roots, as they resent being disturbed. Keep a mulch of compost, leaves or old steer manure on the ground around the trees throughout the year. There will have to be several fresh applications of compost, as it will wash into the soil. The mulch should be three to four inches deep. Keep it several inches away from the trunk of the tree. Water the trees well before putting on the mulch.

The Florida-grown, so-called "West Indian," types of avocado are characterized by smooth skin and large size; the "Mexican" varieties grown in California are smaller with rough, darker skins.

Varieties: The following are some good varieties for the home garden.

Duke is a hardy variety for interior valleys and colder districts. It has a green, oval fruit of pleasant flavor. The tree is large, well branched and is one of the fastest growing avocados, with the fruit ripening in September and October.

Fuerte has a fruit of fine quality and is the leading commercial variety. The tree is large and spreading, and it grows well in the California coastal belt. It ripens in various localities anywhere from November to May.

The fruit of the Edranal variety has a rich, nutty flavor, and does not discolor when fully ripe. The tree is of upright growth, excellent for the home garden, as it requires less room than other varieties. It has large fruit with small seed and ripens from May to August.

Anaheim has a large, green, oval fruit that ripens from May to August. The tree is of upright growth and bears heavily.

Hass has one of the longest ripening seasons and produces a heavy crop each year. This purple black avocado is of fine flavor, and is perhaps the leading summer-ripening avocado grown commercially. It is excellent in the California coastal and foothill areas, ripening from May through October.

Ryan has fruit of finest quality and ripens after Fuerte, bearing a heavy crop each year. The fruit, pear shaped and green, ripens from May to October.

Nabal is particularly good in coastal areas. The fruit is round with seed and smooth skin. The flesh is rich and of exceptionally fine flavor, ripening from June to September.

Pueblo is a very fine home variety which is hardy to frost. From November to January the small trees bear heavy crops of large dark pear-shaped fruit with superior flavor.

Nutritional Value: Avocados are rich in vitamins A, C and E. Other nutrients include thiamine, riboflavin, niacin, pantothenic acid, biotin, potassium, calcium, and iron. Avocados are high in unsaturated fatty acids. Because of their high unsaturated fatty acid content, they are credited with the ability to lower the cholesterol level in the bloodstream.

Avocados also make fine potted plants indoors. To start the seed, place it large end down in the mouth of a jar full of water. Insert toothpicks in the seed. When a root forms and shoots appear, it is ready to pot. Grow near a sunny window, and pinch off terminal growth to prevent spindliness.

AXIL

This is the point at which a branch, stalk or leaf diverges from the stem to which it is attached.

AZALEA

This shrub is either evergreen or deciduous, and with the advent of spring it comes into its glory. Suddenly the tip of each branch bursts into bloom; for sheer beauty few other plants are its equal.

Actually the azalea is the lazy gardener's dream plant. Rarely, if ever, will an insect or disease do serious damage to a vigorous azalea. Most of the plant's ailments are caused by poor nutrition or an unsuitable location.

Its requirements are simple but rigid: acidic soil, a heavy mulch, constant moisture with good drainage, filtered sunlight and no cultivation.

The required acidic soil should be achieved by organic means. Decayed pine needles have high acidity. Oak leaf mold and the decayed sawdust from oak, cypress or hemlock are also acidic. If the soil is alkaline, it would be best to dig out the area and replace with acidic soil. This may seem like a lot of trouble, but it will make care of the plant simpler.

Acidic soil may be obtained from pine or other coniferous forests or from the woods where acid-loving plants such as mountain laurel and blueberry are growing. Coarse sand and leaf mold will make a loose, crumbly soil that retains moisture yet gives good drainage. The azalea will thrive in such soil, and after planting, the acidity can be maintained by proper mulching.

The importance of mulching azaleas cannot be overemphasized. The roots are extremely shallow—most of them lie within three or four inches of the surface—and they must be kept moist at all times. They must also be protected from the heat of summer and the cold of winter, and they must never be disturbed by cultivation. A mulch of at least four inches is necessary. The mulch will keep down weeds and is the natural home of frogs and lizards which eat many insect enemies of the plant.

Pine needles, oak leaves and sawdust from oak, cypress and hemlock make excellent mulches. Many growers find that a combination of pine needles and oak leaves is especially good. The needles keep the leaves from blowing and are high in acidity but slow in decaying. The oak leaves decay more rapidly and, while lower in acidity, are higher in food value. Seaweed added to the mulch from time to time will add trace minerals. Manure is not recommended for azaleas because of its alkaline reaction.

The most common symptom of an ailing azalea is chlorosis or a yellowing of the leaves. This usually means that the soil is not sufficiently acidic. It may be prevented by proper planting and mulching. If the condition appears in spite of these precautions, check the water supply. Sometimes the water contains lime which counteracts the acidity of the mulches.

Other than the food from the decaying mulch, azaleas require only a feeding of cottonseed meal once a year to keep them in good condition. This feeding should be given immediately after the blooming season and applied at the rate of 2½ pounds per 100 square feet. It should be sprinkled over the mulch and watered in. Because of the shallow roots, do not dig any fertilizers into the soil.

If the plant seems to lack vigor, a second feeding may be applied three weeks later, but never after the last of June. Later feeding will encourage new growth that will not be hardened before the heat of summer begins.

Azaleas need some sun to bloom satisfactorily, but the direct rays of the summer sun are usually harmful. The buds for the coming spring form during the summer and fall, and the plants need plenty of moisture during that time. Any baking by the sun will result in a shortage of blossoms. The plants wilt quickly if not kept moist and are slow in recovering after even a single drying out. They will thrive best in the edge of woods where they get filtered sunlight, or in sheltered locations. They also need some protection from the wind, which will damage the blossoms during the blooming season.

Winter hardiness varies with the different varieties and with the condition of the individual plant. In general, the Indica varieties are perfectly hardy only in the South, while the Kurumes are grown successfully as far north as Long Island.

Plants grown in dense shade or those which are overfed or fed late do not withstand cold well. All growth should be matured before winter. The plant will survive severe cold if the roots are protected, but the flower crop may be injured by unseasonable cold, especially after the buds are showing color.

Azaleas are pruned to keep them at the desired size and to make them produce more flowers. Ideally, the plant should be thick headed and well branched since a flower forms at the tip of each branch. Pruning should be done immediately after blooming so that the blossoms can form during the summer.

The colors range from white through pink, lavender, salmon, orange, and red. In small gardens a single color is most effective, especially when combined with plants of the same color which are in bloom at the same time.

The azalea is exacting in its requirements, but once those are met no other plant is more rewarding. Other than its uses as an outdoor plant, it is a long-lasting cut flower. Furthermore, because of the compact, shallow roots it is easily transplanted. During blooming season the entire plant may be lifted, potted and moved into the house. Then it can be replanted without damage.

AZOFICATION

This term refers to the process by which the azotobacter organisms add nitrogen to the soil.

See also AZOTOBACTER.

AZONAL SOIL

These are soils without well-developed soil profiles because of extreme youth, steep relief or very sandy parent material. They are found within any of the zonal soil regions. Azonal soils are of three types.

Alluvial Soils: These comprise recently deposited materials such as in valley bottoms, on deltas and along rivers on which the soil-forming forces have acted for only a comparatively short time. Alluvial soils are widely distributed throughout the world, and when properly drained can be productive. *See also* ALLUVIUM.

Lithosol: *Lith,* from Greek, means stone; hence lithosols are skeletal soils, which are more or less weathered materials and rock fragments. There are stony parent materials and, commonly, stony ground surface, as on steep slopes and in rough, rocky, mountain areas. They show little soil development and are not very significant agriculturally.

Regosols: These are very young soils located on deep, nonconsolidated mineral deposits, but are not stony. They are largely confined to sand dunes and steeply sloping glacial drift.

AZOTOBACTER

A group of soil bacteria that fixes nitrogen from atmospheric sources. Unlike legume bacteria, azotobacter exist in the soil independent of association with higher plants; they use soil organic matter as a source of energy, rather than carbohydrates from a host plant. When the bacteria die, the nitrogen incorporated in their bodies is left in the soil in the form of proteins and related compounds.

Nitrogen fixation is greatly encouraged by organic matter with a high carbon content. The bacteria are sensitive to calcium, and activity decreases in acidic soil. A pH higher than 6.5 gives the best results in a mineral soil.

Indications are that azotobacter are responsible for a large amount of nitrogen fixed annually. It is clear, however, that the presence of nitrates from high-nitrogen, artificial fertilizers decreases their efficiency. Russia has for many years experimented with azotobacter as a soil inoculant for increasing crop production. Recent tests in the United States indicate that azotobacter inoculants will significantly increase yields over untreated crops, although not all tests have been conclusive.

See also NITROGEN.

B

BABY BLUE-EYES
See Nemophila

BABY'S-BREATH
(*Gypsophila elegans*)

The white, rose or carmine flowers of the many varieties of annual baby's-breath are fine for filling in bare spots. This quick-growing annual with tiny flowers on wiry stems adds daintiness to any arrangement. Baby's-breath blooms quickly from the time of sowing, but passes quickly into seed production; therefore several plantings at monthly intervals are recommended if the blossoms are wanted over a long period. Baby's-breath needs full sunlight and open, not-too-rich soils. Period of bloom extends from June 15 to October; height attained is ten to 18 inches.

See also Gypsophila.

BACHELOR'S-BUTTON
(*Centaurea Cyanus*)

Often called cornflower or blue bonnet, this garden annual normally produces blue flowers, but occasionally it will have white, pink or purple blooms. It grows to about two to three feet high. Sow seed in fall or early spring and thin plants to one foot apart. It will seed itself readily and often comes up as a volunteer for several years without reseeding. Many gardeners cut the plants six inches from the top after the first blooming period to encourage a second flowering. Fertilizing with liquid manure is effective. Plants are hardy and will bloom until frost.

BACILLUS THURINGIENSIS

Of the microorganisms that make insects ill, *Bacillus thuringiensis* is by far the best known. Though safe to humans, it has a devastating effect on moth and butterfly larvae, both of which are prime economic pests.

BT, as it is often called, appears on the market under several trade names—Dipel, Thuricide and Biotrol—in the form of a soluble powder. The powder is suspended in water and sprayed on plant surfaces, where it is ingested by the pest. The BT spores then germinate into plants that occupy more and more of the victim's body. A toxic crystal is also produced and is thought to be partially responsible for the insecticidal effect.

BT is useful on both vegetable and fruit crops, aiding in the control of a number of well-known pests: tent caterpillar, fall webworm, codling moth worm, peach tree borer, corn earworm, European corn borer, cabbageworm, cabbage looper, and gypsy moth caterpillar.

See also Insect Control.

BACTERIA

See ACTINOMYCETES, DISEASE, FUNGUS, MICROORGANISM, SOIL

BALFOUR, LADY EVE

(1898–   ) Author of *The Living Soil,* and a dynamic leader in the field of organiculture in Great Britain, in 1946 she became the first president of England's Soil Association. The Soil Association has added much prestige and important research to the organic method. It is devoted to the furtherance of research into the biological aspects of soil fertility, and to the dissemination of knowledge on the subject.

BALLOON FLOWER
(*Platycodon grandiflorum*)

The balloon flower is a most attractive perennial plant, with large, showy, bell-shaped flowers. Blossoms are pure white, blue or white with blue veinings, and appear in July and August. Occasionally there are double-petaled blooms.

Balloon flowers may be propagated either by rootstock or from seed. The seeds germinate readily and may provide at least some blossoms the first year. Seeds should be started indoors in March, and will germinate in eight to ten days. When about two inches high, transplant them to their permanent location, in a well-drained soil in full sun about a foot apart. Stems reach a height of about 18 inches.

Do not disturb them once established, as they develop a taproot which should not be broken. Growth does not begin until late in the spring, so be careful not to injure the dormant crowns when working the bed. Balloon flower is a choice, low-maintenance perennial, providing bloom at a time when many other perennials have finished flowering.

Fast-growing, compact and very frost-resistant, balloon flowers make fine border plants for the garden bed.

BALM   (*Melissa officinalis*)

A somewhat weedy perennial growing to about two feet in height, balm has a strong lemon scent.

The leaves are sometimes used for tea, and sprigs are put into cool drinks to impart a lemony taste. Oil from the leaves is used in perfumes.

Balm is best planted where it is not too conspicuous because of its weedy habit. It has a tendency to spread and must be kept within bounds.

It thrives in poor soil in a warm, sunny spot, and can be propagated from seed sown in spring, or by dividing.

BALM-OF-HEAVEN
See UMBELLULARIA

BALSAM FIR
See CHRISTMAS TREE FARMING, FIR

BAMBOO
(Bambusa, Dendrocalamus, Phyllostachys, Sasa)

The bamboo is an easy-to-grow and highly useful plant, which organic techniques have enabled to grow even in the North. Bamboo is usually thought of as a tropical crop, and it is indeed one of the staples of Oriental agriculture, serving dozens of human needs. The Chinese and other Asian peoples use it for food, clothing, weapons, and all sorts of containers. They even construct their houses of it, build bridges and lay bamboo water pipes to carry drinking and irrigation water.

One bamboo prized for its delicately flavored shoots is Moso (*P. pubescens*). It is a giant bamboo, growing as tall as 80 feet, with canes up to eight inches in diameter. Its wide-spreading branches and feathery foliage make Moso one of the most handsome and impressive-looking bamboos.

A new Moso plantation should be established with the plants set 15 feet apart each way. They take about five to eight years to reach full size. Thereafter, in early spring the tasty shoots appear (actually they are the sprouting buds which, if not cut, will develop into full-sized canes or culms). They often grow at a fantastic rate and attain full maturity in about three years.

Another fine edible bamboo is sweetshoot (*P. dulcis*), known in China by the exotic name of "pak-koh-poo-chi." It grows to a maximum of about 30 feet, with stems up to three inches in diameter, and offers very sweet, tender shoots.

Bamboo is grown most extensively in the tropics, but several varieties will thrive in southern and western coastal regions of the United States.
(Courtesy of U.S. Forest Service)

The list of varieties that produce edible shoots is bigger than anyone first thought. *P. bambusoides,* the giant timber or Madake bamboo that grows well in the South and East, produces tasty shoots as does the interesting green sulfur bamboo, *P. viridis.* Its shoots give off a lovely delicate aroma when cooked. Beechey bamboo, *Bambusa Beecheyana,* also produces edible shoots.

The shoots of at least two other species, *B. Oldhamii* and *B. glaucescens,* are reported to be dug up before they emerge from the ground and used for food in the Dutch East Indies.

Cooking Bamboo Shoots: Gourmets recommend cutting the shoots into ⅛-inch-thick slices after peeling off the outer covering. Virtually all varieties, with the exception of sweetshoot, have a more or less bitter taste, so it is best to parboil them for six to eight minutes and then change the water. Further cooking for about 20 minutes will bring out their delicate flavor while retaining the firm, crisp texture.

Cooked this way, bamboo shoots taste very much like young field corn. You can serve them as a vegetable hot with butter, cold as a salad or in mixed salads, or use them in meat stews. They go well in numerous other American dishes, and of course in dozens of Oriental ones, too.

Bamboo House Plants: A particularly impressive one for a window with full sun is the Chinese-goddess bamboo.

The same is true of the fascinating Buddha's belly bamboo, *Bambusa ventricosa,* so called because the portions between the nodes swell out oddly. This variety grows 55 feet tall outdoors, but will stay in miniature for years when potted.

Many of these bamboos may be grown from Virginia south along the Gulf Coast, and in the milder areas of the West Coast. In colder parts of the country, edible bamboo benefits from a two- to three-inch mulch, perhaps of hay. Contrary to what many people believe, bamboo does not prefer constantly flooded land. It needs a fertile soil with abundant moisture, but will not stand poorly drained soils that stay saturated for long periods. Ridges close to wet soil are suitable, provided the roots are not in the wet portion.

BANANA   *(Musa)*

This is one of the most popular and important tropical fruits. Long-keeping and easily shipped, it is tasty, very digestible and rich in several major minerals and some vitamins.

Banana plants are rapid-growing herbs 5 to 25 feet tall. Their stalks or trunks are succulent, being actually composed of compressed layers of leaf sheaths. After bearing once, the stalks die back to the plant's true stem, which is an underground rhizome. New suckers on which further fruit is borne are constantly rising from a healthy, productive rhizome. On a plant that is growing well, a sucker bears within 12 to 18 months after its emergence from the soil, but the length of time required to develop fruit may vary with soil and climate.

A hole 30 by 36 inches and 18 inches deep should be prepared for planting either rhizomes or suckers. Dwarf Cavendish may be planted eight to ten feet apart; others should stand no closer than 12 to 15 feet. Plant the sucker or rhizome a foot deep, and fill the hole with a mixture of topsoil and compost or rotted manure.

While the plant is young, remove all but one sucker, which should be allowed to bear its fruit and be cut back before another sucker is permitted to grow. Older plants may be allowed to develop one new sucker every three months. A plant will grow and bear well for four to six years, after which it should be dug out, the soil enriched and new suckers or rhizome pieces planted. After its first fruit has ripened, the plant may be allowed to grow three to five suckers at a time, depending upon its vigor. All others should be cut out.

Bananas are gross feeders. Because of their heavy growth they need plenty of fertilizer and a large amount of moisture. They do best where the rainfall averages 60 to 100 inches per year. In areas where it is less than that, they will need frequent watering.

A heavy rich mulch should be maintained under the plants at all times. This may be rotted manure, compost or a mixture of manure and leaves or grass.

Because they contain no viable seeds, bananas must be propagated by separating the suckers from the parent plants or by making cuttings of the rhizomes. Suckers two to eight months old are used and are moved in March or April.

Seven- to ten-pound cuttings of the rhizomes are removed, each with two buds, by cutting with a spade or mattock. Rhizome cuttings can be replanted immediately or held for a few days, exposed to the air, then planted.

Bananas require about 100 days to mature after the young flower buds appear. Bananas which are cut seven to 14 days before ripening may be hung in a cool shady place to develop their flavor and sugar. Their nutritional value will be the same as that of tree-ripened fruit.

After the bunches are cut down from the plant, the ends of the stalk are trimmed and the bananas are held at room temperature until thoroughly ripe. Stalks of the plant are cut back and are chopped into small pieces which are added to the mulch around the roots.

Varieties: The two main varieties are the common banana, which is the imported type widely eaten as raw fruit, huge quantities being picked and shipped green and ripening to yellow only as they reach the consumer; and the Chinese dwarf banana (*M. acuminata* cv. 'Dwarf Cavendish') which grows only four to six feet high and bears many small, very tasty fruits. Since it is hardier than most varieties, this dwarf banana is better suited to culture in this country, and many are grown as fruiting ornamentals in gardens as well as potted indoor plants. The Gros Michel is the largest eating variety, with a mild, tender flavor. These should be cooked if green.

Nutrient Value: Varieties which are used only for cooking are, in general, richer in vitamins than those which are eaten raw. In one medium-sized banana of the cooking variety, there are 420 units vitamin A; .04 milligrams vitamin B_1; .06 milligrams vitamin B_2; .6 milligrams niacin; 12 milligrams vitamin C; and about 100 calories. In a dessert variety the amounts are approximately as follows: 120 units vitamin A; .03 milligrams vitamin B_1; .05 milligrams vitamin B_2; .6 milligrams niacin; 9 milligrams vitamin C; and 85 calories.

BANANA RESIDUES

Analyses have shown that banana skins and stalks are extremely rich in both phosphoric acid and potash, rating from 2.3 to 3.3 percent in phosphoric acid and from 41 to 50 percent in potash, on an ash basis. The nitrogen content is considered relatively high. When available in quantity, it would be thoroughly practical to utilize banana residues for gardening purposes. Table cuttings and kitchen refuse containing banana skins are valuable also for the reason that these materials contain large amounts of bacteria which effect quick breakdown and act as activators for the rest of the compost material.

BANEBERRY   (*Actaea*)

Perennial shrubs of the Buttercup family, baneberries have serrated leaves, spikes of fluffy white flowers and glossy, red or white poisonous berries. They are often seen in rich soils of northeastern woods, and grow best in the garden in a shady spot, in rich, fairly moist soil. The white form (*A. pachypoda*) does better in a neutral to slightly acid soil; the red baneberry (*A. rubra*) prefers a more acid soil. Both can be transplanted in spring or fall.

BANTAMS

Bantams, or banties, are small domestic fowl that have been bred from larger breeds of chickens. They do not represent a separate species, but are simply miniature members of the standard breeds, weighing about one-fourth as much as their larger counterparts and producing very small eggs. Although they are reliable layers and provide excellent meat, they are normally raised for show or simply kept as backyard pets. Their ability to patrol the vegetable patch for insects without scratching too deeply makes them favorites among gardeners.

Bantams require the same general care and feeding as larger chickens, but are content with less space. A flock of 12 birds should be provided with a coop and a small pen at least 20 square feet with a run of equal size. Since they are good fliers, surround their pen with a six-foot fence and, if necessary, a wire top. Like other chickens, banties need a perch that is well off the ground. They prefer to roost very high, sometimes even sleeping in the rafters of their coop or, if raised outside, in the trees.

There are over 300 varieties of banties, the most familiar being Rhode Island Red, Cornish, Plymouth Rock, and various Wyandottes. Both Rhode Island Red and Cornish Rock, a cross between Cornish and Plymouth Rock, lay very well. Either breed can be expected to produce about 160 eggs per year, but since banty hens like to hide their eggs, you may not collect that many. Gather them several times a day, checking in underbrush in and around the pen. A wooden egg left where you find the eggs will encourage the hen to continue laying them in that spot.

For more information on raising, breeding and enjoying bantams, contact the American Bantam Association, P.O. Box 464, Chicago, IL 60690. This organization sponsors shows and conventions and publishes several newsletters and magazines, among them the *Bantam Standard*.

See also CHICKEN.

BAPTISIA

Called blue, wild or false indigo, this native plant somewhat resembles the lupine. The pea-shaped blue blossoms are borne in long racemes in late May and early June.

B. australis grows three to four feet tall and should be used at the back of the border. It performs well under a variety of soil conditions in full sun or partial shade. It has no serious pests.

While individual plants will grow into sizable clumps in time, they do not crowd out their neighbors. Division should not be necessary for at least five years; indeed, the plants develop deep, massive root systems which are difficult to dig up. The tall stems usually do not need staking. This plant is recommended to any gardener who wishes a good return for little effort. Plants may be bought or propagated from seed. The seedpods left to mature on the stalks look good in dried arrangements, and the seed itself is attractive to wintering birds.

See also PERENNIALS.

BARBADOS CHERRY   See ACEROLA

BARBERRY   (*Berberis*)

The barberries are handsome deciduous or evergreen shrubs often grown as hedges. Most species have brilliant fall foliage, orange yellow flowers and reddish or purplish fruit. Alternate, usually smooth leaves clustered on spiny branches generally distinguish the barberry from its close relative, the *Mahonia,* which has pinnate leaves borne on spineless racemes.

Barberries germinate easily from seeds, which should be sown in flats or broadcast in beds in fall; in most cases, they will germinate by the following spring. Barberries can also be propagated from green cuttings of young wood taken in June and placed in sand in a shady bed.

Best results with barberries will be obtained if they are planted in moist, well-drained, light loamy soil, although the deciduous ones can stand drier conditions.

Varieties: Species of deciduous barberries generally bloom in the spring and early summer with the attractive purplish fruit developing in late summer, fall or early winter. *B. Thunbergii,* commonly called Japanese barberry, is a popular choice for low ornamental hedges and walk borders with its scarlet fall foliage, pale yellow flowers and bright red fruit. It is a dense, spreading shrub, growing two to five feet tall, and is hardy throughout most of the United States. *B. vulgaris,* the common barberry, grows from four to eight feet tall and is attractive year-round. In the spring its foliage is light green and its flowers golden yellow, while in the fall it develops brilliant scarlet to purple fruits which last throughout the winter.

Evergreen varieties of the barberry are marginally hardy in the northeastern states unless somewhat protected in winter. *B. buxifolia,* often called Magellan barberry, is a graceful shrub, with orange yellow flowers and deep purple fruits. It grows to a height of one to three feet. *B. verruculosa* is another hardy and handsome shrub, growing to three feet. Dwarf and spreading, its dense, lustrous, dark green foliage and violet black fruit make it a valued ornamental.

Pests: Barberry should not be planted near an area of concentrated wheat growing as it hosts a fungus that causes wheat rust.

BARK

Bark is the normal waste material of the lumber, pulp and paper industries; it can be utilized as an inexpensive and unusually effec-

Obtainable from lumber mills, chopped bark makes a clean, inexpensive and effective garden mulch.

tive soil builder. Bark can loosen the soil and improve its moisture-holding capacity, serve as a base for fertilizer, control the rate at which the plants obtain their food from the soil, and be used as a mulch.

Chopped bark is perhaps the most attractive mulching material available, and is used in large quantities in parks and professionally landscaped homes. Redwood, red cedar and cypress barks are relatively impervious to decay and will last for years. Oak and pine barks are high in acid and should have an extra sprinkling of lime put on the soil under them, or be used with acid-loving plants.

BARK BEETLES
See INSECT CONTROL

BARK GRAFTING   *See* GRAFTING

BARLEY   (*Hordeum vulgare*)

Barley was one of the first cereals to be cultivated by man, and is grown over a large

extent of the world at present. There are varieties of barley that will grow in the Arctic Circle. As a feed for livestock, barley compares favorably with corn, and in regions where corn is unadapted, barley is successfully used for fattening cattle and swine. On the average, barley contains 3 percent more protein than corn and can be substituted for corn in feed mixes. Some people prefer the taste of barley-fed beef.

Varieties: There are two botanically distinct types of barley: six-row and two-row. The six-row varieties are more common and are

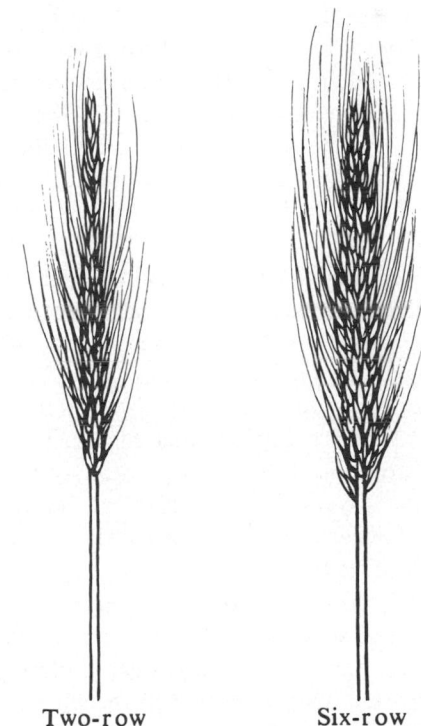

Two-row   Six-row

Two-row types of barley are grown in the Pacific Northwest and northern Great Plains regions, while the more common six-row varieties are cultivated throughout the upper Middle West and eastern United States.

divided into three families: Malting Barley, grown in the upper Midwest, tall, bearded and spring planted; the Coast group, grown in California and Arizona as a fall crop; and the Tennessee Winter group, grown east of the Mississippi as livestock feed. The two-row barleys are grown in the Pacific Northwest and on the northern Great Plains, spring planted, and used for feed and for malting.

Because of the different purposes of the grain, there are many varieties of barley available and new ones are being constantly developed. Most new varieties are bred to be stiffer strawed to prevent lodging. There are varieties adapted to every area.

Barley may have bearded heads or be beardless. Bearded barley has a slender bristle about three inches long, called an "awn," attached to each seed. Beardless varieties are generally preferred for forage, but the bearded varieties have proven resistant to deer in Pennsylvania.

Grow barley as you would wheat. Some varieties are spring planted and some are fall planted. Barley ripens sooner than wheat; spring-planted barley ripens in 60 to 70 days, fall-planted barley about 60 days after spring growth begins. Barley thus fits well into a double-cropping scheme and a variety of crop rotations. Be careful when planting barley with a drill because bearded varieties may cause planting tubes to clog.

Barley is harvested the same as wheat: cut, bundled and shocked to dry. Wear a shirt when harvesting barley as the awns can irritate your skin. Barley may be stored in the bundle and fed to stock without threshing.

Diseases and Pests: Yellow dwarf virus, an aphid-transmitted virus, attacks barley at the seedling stage, and damages older grain, but is not very common.

Fungus diseases do bother barley, especially in humid parts of the South. Resistant varieties have been developed, so the best thing to do is to check out which varieties are more resistant to the diseases encountered in your area.

Greenbugs and corn leaf aphids both attack barley, but infestations are usually not severe. Even commercial growers do not use chemicals, but rely instead on natural predators.

Uses: Barley can be stored and used in a bundle for stock feed. Animals like it less than wheat because of the hulls, and will consume more if the barley is ground.

You can feed sprouted barley to chickens with good results. The grain can be easily sprouted if the head-end of the whole bundle is soaked in water until the grains sprout. Allow about five days at 60°F. (15.56°C.). You will soon learn how fast the barley sprouts and how many bundles you'll have to keep soaking in order to have a constant supply of the sprouted grain. The chickens will eat the sprouts right out of the heads, and the straw will provide good bedding.

Sprouted barley can also be used to make malt for making beer.

Barley should be hulled for table use. The blender will do a fair job of hulling if you winnow or sift the hulls out, although you won't get all of them. Another method is to take the screen out of a hammer mill and slow the RPM's to half grinding speed. In any case, roasting the grain makes hulling easier.

Hulled barley can be stored as wheat.
See also WHEAT.

BARREL ROOT CELLAR

A very satisfactory root cellar for the small home garden is easily made from a large

Place the barrel in a trench and cover with alternate layers of dirt and straw. Pack clean, dry vegetables with sand or peat moss to prevent the spread of decay and help maintain a proper moisture level.

barrel. A strong, well-made one will last many years. Dig a trench a little larger than the barrel so that it can be set into the ground at an angle of about 45 degrees. Before placing the barrel in the trench, drop in a few large stones or bricks to facilitate drainage. Cover the barrel all around with about six inches of dirt, then six inches of straw or leaves and finally with about two inches of dirt to hold the organic matter in place. After the vegetables are packed in the barrel, place the cover over the top and then pile about a foot of straw, leaves or hay on the cover with a board and a rock to keep the covering in place. This covering is easily removed when you want to get into the root cellar.

See also STORAGE.

BASALT

Basalt rock is widely distributed in the United States, the New England coast being especially seamed with deposits. It contains significant amounts of phosphorus, potassium, calcium, magnesium, and iron.

Basalt can be applied directly to the soil, as one would do with phosphate or potash rock. At Griesheim, Germany, researchers believe that basalt, if left on the soil surface, increases the temperature of the soil, but if worked in, it temporarily reduces it. Their practice is to leave the basalt powder on the surface of the soil one year and plow it in the next season. Basalt added to compost heaps lowers the temperature of the heap but enables the compost to decompose. Although these heaps have more nutrients, they have not produced a temperature high enough to kill bacteria. In fact, earthworms can work in compost heaps with basalt added.

In large applications, apply two tons to the acre every three or four years.

BASIC SLAG

This is a by-product that results when iron ore is smelted to form pig iron. Large amounts of limestone and dolomite used in smelting unite with impurities in the ore to form a sludge which rises to the surface of the molten mass and is poured off. When hard, this sludge is called slag and contains lime, magnesium, silicon, aluminum, manganese, and various trace minerals, the mineral content varying according to variations in the mixture.

For agricultural purposes, slag must be finely ground. It is best used as a liming agent, and is better than lime because of its trace element and magnesium content.

Slag is alkaline and does best on moist clays and loam, and on peaty soils deficient in lime; it can be used on light soils if a potash mineral is used with it. It should be applied in autumn and winter. An average application is from one to several tons per acre. Slag is especially adapted to the needs of leguminous crops, such as beans, peas, clovers, vetches, and alfalfas.

Avoid slags with a high sulfur content.
See also ACIDITY–ALKALINITY, LIME.

BASIL, SWEET
(*Ocimum Basilicum*)

A pretty annual about 18 inches tall, sweet basil has light green, rather broad leaves and spikes of small white florets. There are several species of basil in cultivation, at least one having attractive purple leaves.

The spicily scented leaves are one of the most popular of all herbs used in cooking. They are considered especially good with tomato dishes, and are used fresh or dried.

The light green leaves are attractive, especially while the plants are young, and the purple-leaved kind gives an interesting color in the herb or window garden.

Basil grows easily from seed planted when danger of frost is over. Green leaves can be picked about six weeks after planting. For drying, it is best to cut them just before the flowers open.
See also HERB.

BASKET FLOWER
See CENTAUREA

BASSWOOD   *See* LINDEN

BAT GUANO   *See* GUANO

BAYBERRY   *See* MYRICA

BAY TREE
See LAUREL, UMBELLULARIA

BEAN RUST   *See* DISEASE

BEANS   (*Phaseolus*)

Beans are one of the most valuable plants grown because they not only produce food for human consumption, but improve the fertility and physical condition of the soil. Nitrogen, a most valuable plant food, is added to the soil by the beneficial bacteria in the nodules which grow on the roots. These bacteria are capable of absorbing the free nitrogen from the air, which, after the plants are harvested, is left in the soil. When enough organic matter is present, or if beans follow a legume sod crop, it is possible to have excellent yields with no added fertilizer. A small amount of phosphorus near the seeds, however, will usually enhance early growth.

Bush beans (also known as snap beans) are an excellent source of vitamins A and B_2 and a good source of B_1 and C. They also provide calcium and iron.

Culture: Bush beans should be included in every garden because of the ease in growing and the wealth in harvesting them. Although beans are essentially warm-season plants, they can be grown successfully in all sections of the country. Most varieties grow slowly at temperatures below 60°F. (15.56°C.) and perform best in the range of 75 to 85°F. (23.89 to 29.44°C.).

The bush beans, while responding to rich soil and thorough cultivation, will succeed in almost any garden soil, from heavy clay to light sandy soils. The soil should not be too acid and should receive a generous amount of rotted manure or compost.

Beans are sensitive to soil levels of zinc. Deficiencies are not uncommon on alkaline soils—especially where pH is well above 7—due to their free lime content. Nitrogen is best supplied from organic matter and from the nodule bacteria. Beans require only a little nitrogen at a time.

The seed is sown directly in the garden after the last spring frost. Sow the seed thinly in rows 18 to 30 inches apart for hand-cultivation. Plant one to two inches apart. When the plants are two or three inches high they may be thinned to four to six inches apart.

A continuous supply of beans throughout the growing season may be assured by successive plantings. Make additional sowings when the other crop is up and growing. Plant until midsummer, or until about 60 days before danger of the first killing frosts in the fall.

Weeds can be a nuisance in beans, especially at harvesttime. Those most frequently seen are lamb's-quarters, redroot pigweed, ragweed, foxtails, and quackgrass. The best control comes from good seedbed preparation —starting early in spring and continuing until planting time.

The cultivation of the crop consists of stirring the soil frequently during the entire season of growth. Scrape the weeds away and don't hoe deeply. The roots are close enough to the surface so that any deep or extensive cultivation will result in undesirable root pruning. It is essential that all weeds be kept down and that during times of drought a mulch is used to preserve moisture. Beans should be cultivated only when the leaves are turned up in the driest and lightest part of the day. Air can then flow under the leaves and around the stem.

As evening approaches, the leaves become damp and droop down to where they can become damaged. Never cultivate while dew or rain are on the leaves since this spreads disease from one leaf to another.

Make the first cultivation about the time the first two full leaves are out, and the second and third as weeds become obvious, and the last before runners appear and growth becomes too dense. Never cultivate after pods are formed.

Diseases and Pests: Beans are subject to a number of bacterial and viral diseases, especially in years of high temperature, high humidity and high rainfall. Dry beans are more vulnerable than snap beans because they are permitted to grow to maturity. Early stages of these diseases characteristically look like watery spots, then leaves yellow, die and drop prematurely. Beans dry up and appear to mature but remain small in size and show shrunken yellow seedcoat abnormalities.

Treatment of bean diseases is not very practical. The best solution is prevention in the form of purchasing good seed, avoiding cultivation when the plants are wet and subscribing to a definite program of rotations in the field or garden. Beans should not be grown more than once, or twice at most, on the same land without other crops being grown in rotation. Besides discouraging disease, rotations help reduce insect populations and rejuvenate soil organic matter. Beans may be rotated with almost any type of crop, since, as nitrogen-fixing legumes, they tend to improve soil fertility. To take full advantage of this property, plant heavy feeders such as sweet corn or cole crops in fields where beans grew the previous season. Avoid growing beans or any other legume in the same position for more than two consecutive seasons.

The Mexican bean beetle, a brown, spotted bug which characteristically appears on young plants, prefers late-season crops to early ones. If you plan to put up your bean harvest, plant as early in the spring as weather permits. To avoid the ravages of the beetle larvae, pick off the beetle when it is first detected. Any yellowish or brownish eggs on the undersides of leaves should be destroyed.

Other occasional bean pests include the tarnished plant bug, black bean aphid, alfalfa caterpillar, alfalfa looper, corn borer, and potato leafhopper. And once the beans are placed in storage, the bean weevil must be avoided at all cost.

Mosaic and anthracnose can be prevented by purchasing disease-resistant seeds. Anthracnose is spread by dissemination of spores. To avoid spreading the spores, do not touch or walk among the plants after a rain.

Varieties: There are two types of bush beans, the green podded and the yellow podded or wax beans. The variety or the color makes little difference except in individual preference. The quality is practically the same in all, provided they are pulled from the vine and eaten at the proper stage of maturity.

Bean cultivars are almost endless, some having no name and being perpetuated only within a family or circle of friends. Beans are self-pollinating and thus two cultivars can be grown side by side with no danger of cross-pollination.

Of the green bush varieties, Bountiful and Blue Lake are both flat podded and develop beans from six to seven inches long. Stringless Green Pod, Wade, Black Valentine, and Improved Tendergreen grow round pods from five to six inches long. Bountiful and Leka Lake are especially good for canning. Tendercrop and Topcrop are mosaic resistant. Of the yellow bush varieties, Pencil Pod Wax, Golden Wax, Eastern Butterwax, and Surecrop Stringless Wax are good varieties. Pencil Pod Wax and Butter Wax are yellow varieties well suited to canning. Kentucky Wonder is an early climber, as is the heavy-yielding Romano Italian.

The pole beans, including lima, snap and kidney varieties, require staking. A popular

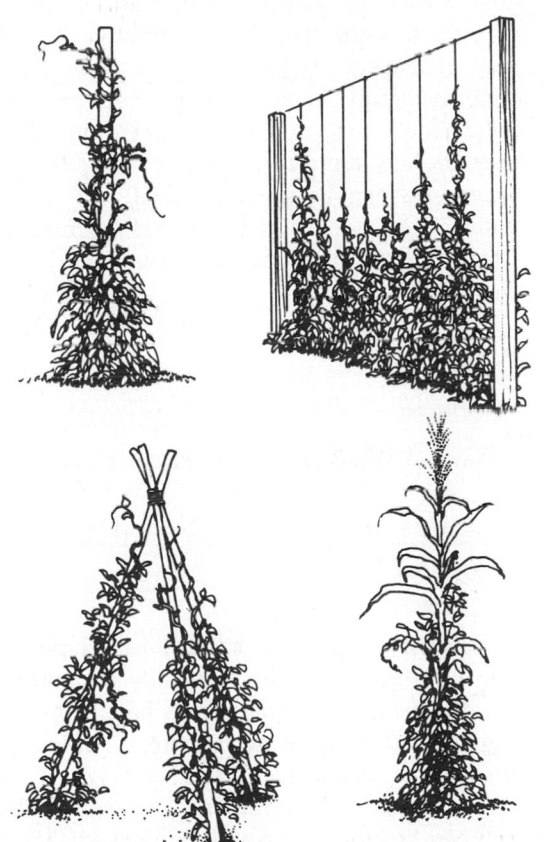

Whether trained to single poles, trellises, "tepees," or stalks of growing corn plants, pole beans produce heavier yields than bush beans, and in very little space.

method of staking is to stick three or four eight-foot-tall saplings or bamboo poles into the ground six inches deep, tepee fashion, and to tie them securely at the top. When the first tendrils appear on the young plants, train them around the pole and the plant will then climb by itself. Pole beans also may be trained along wire or strong cord, on trellises or any other support that permits the tendrils to twine. Sow two or three seeds at the base of each pole of tepee-type stakes, one inch deep.

Harvesting: Snap beans should be picked while the pods are immature. The seeds should still be small, the tips soft and the bean should snap readily. The plants should be watched carefully as the proper time of harvesting lasts only a few days. If the pods are allowed to ripen fully, the plants stop producing and will die. Bush beans usually have several pickings, a few days apart or every day if the weather is warm.

Beans are among those vegetables that are best when harvested young and eaten just after they are picked—an important reason for growing your own.

Drying Snap Beans: If, at harvesttime, you find you have too many beans to use in the near future, think about drying them for future use. Drying beans is not difficult, and will reward the family during the winter.

There are several ways of going about drying the beans. One woman, who has "dried 'em all my life," does it the easiest way there is. She simply leaves the bean plants alone until they're partially dried. She then pulls them up, shakes the earth off the roots, ties them up in bunches of three or four, and hangs them up in a dry place. She forgets all about them until wintertime when she wants beans.

Another woman picks the beans when they are so ripe that the pods show signs of drying up. The pods are then spread on papers or cookie tins and placed in the sun to dry. This is a slow process but not a time-consuming one. The important thing to remember is that the drying beans must be placed indoors before sundown and not put out until the sun is up and shining brightly. Besides turning them each day so they dry evenly, there is nothing else to do until they have thoroughly dried. By this time, the pods are so brittle that they crumble when you handle them.

If the weather is against your drying program (not enough sunny days), then the beans may be hulled and canned before they are thoroughly dry. If, however, they have thoroughly dried, then storing them in a dry place is imperative, for if the beans become damp, they may be wormy. Many people have had success by storing them in jars in a dry place.

Dry Beans: In addition to the snap beans, string beans and limas, all of which may be dried if desired, there are the many varieties like pinto, pea, horticultural, and navy beans that are grown specifically for stewing and baking. These varieties should not be harvested until they are thoroughly matured (normally 90 to 100 days) and the beans become hard. Once the beans have matured and the leaves are well yellowed, a light frost won't hurt but a hard freeze will damage beans that still have too high a water content. Bite one to determine hardness. You will barely be able to dent a bean of proper dryness. Harvesting when soft invites molding. To help avoid this, pull dry beans by hand and place the bunches upside down with the roots in the air for two to three days. Old-timers stacked them around a pole—roots to the pole—until the stack was five to seven feet high. Threshing may be done with a flail or bean thresher any

time after the pods are crisp and the beans are firm.

See also KIDNEY BEAN, LIMA BEAN.

BEARBERRY
(*Arctostaphylos Uva-ursi*)

An attractive evergreen ground cover that turns bronze in the winter, uva-ursi can be a valuable asset to beekeepers because its white and pink flowers are highly attractive to the honey producers. It thrives best in temperate North American climates, being a native of the Pacific Coast. It should be planted in early spring or late summer. In wintertime, frozen clumps also can be gathered wild and transplanted. Uva-ursi grows in sections reaching to six feet long. It puts down roots at each joint, so light soil is preferred.

See also ARCTOSTAPHYLOS, GROUND COVERS, UVA-URSI.

BEAUTYBUSH   *See* KOLKWITZIA

BEDDING

Literally, this term applies to all plants suitable for garden beds, especially decorative ones. In practice, bedding plants have come to designate certain types which are set into the garden in a somewhat formal design. Frequently, these are perennials or subshrubs which can be closely sheared or pinched. Usually, they are propagated by cutting, rather than seeds, and bought each spring from nurseries or florists who have established them in greenhouses over the winter.

Many hardy annuals, some true perennials and a number of tender subshrubs are used as bedding to lend both cover and distinct, lasting color to the garden. They extend the bloom period and help fill in those sections where early-flowering plants have lost their blooms and foliage. In addition, bedding plants are used to create complementary borders and edgings, to improve banked areas and to add often-lacking fragrance.

The list of suitable bedding plants is a long one. Among those best known and popularly adapted are the following: calendula, baby's-breath, sweet alyssum, poppy, portulaca, marigold, nasturtium, zinnia, verbena, garden pinks, carnation, ageratum, snapdragon, African daisy, China aster, moonflower, Canterbury-bells, cockscomb, coleus, cosmos, dahlia, chrysanthemum, larkspur, candytuft, chamomile, forget-me-not, petunia, phlox, salvia, and periwinkle.

BEE BALM   (*Monarda didyma*)

This native perennial plant is also called horsemint and Oswego tea because of the tea which is made from its leaves.

In the wild state the flowers are brilliant red, but cultivated varieties offer blooms in white, rose, maroon, and lavender. They are attractive to bees, hummingbirds and butterflies. Bee balm is a bushy plant growing 1½ to three feet tall.

Plants spread quickly and should be divided about every three years, at which time the woody center should be discarded. Propagation is also by seed. Bee balm, which is remarkably resistant to disease and insect attack, prefers a moist soil and full sun or part shade.

BEECH   (*Fagus*)

The beeches are hardy deciduous trees, attractive in shape, foliage and color, and very useful as shade and ornamental trees. Characterized by rounded tops and smooth gray bark, the beeches are a spreading type, reaching heights of 80 to 90 feet. While they prefer an alkaline soil, they will also grow in moderately acid locales, and do especially well when protected with a mulch of their own leaves. This is a long-lived tree (its beauty develops with age), and is appreciably free from insects and

The European beech is a somewhat hardier and taller variety than the American.
(*Courtesy of U.S. Forest Service*)

disease. Upright types are adaptable for hedges if given frequent pruning. Propagation is by seeds stratified in winter and sown in the spring. Transplant in the spring, and allow a nurseryman to prune the roots.

The American beech (*F. grandifolia*) holds its blue green leaves in the winter, has a light gray smooth bark that invites penknife inscriptions and usually grows to about 60 feet. The nut has been used as hog feed, a potherb and, when roasted, as a substitute for coffee. This tree is a surface feeder, and it is difficult to grow other plants within its dripline.

European beech (*F. sylvatica*) has darker foliage and bark than the American species, and is hardier in cultivation. Growing as high as 90 feet, it displays bright leaves which turn a deep red brown in autumn and remain through most of the winter.

BEEFWOOD   *See* CASUARINA

BEEKEEPING

Most people who know little about bees assume that hives have to be kept in the country where there is plenty of open space and much vegetation. While such settings are ideal, bees can be kept in much less likely places as well. Suburban backyards are usually fine (provided local laws permit and neighbors don't mind), and even some protected small-city rooftops can be suitable for a few beehives.

If you're interested in learning more about the how-to's of beekeeping, here's a short course, but it is suggested that you follow up the subject by pursuing some outside sources. *American Bee Journal* and *Gleanings in Bee Culture* as well as many books on the subject offer beginners sound information and advice. There are on-campus and correspondence courses at most state universities, and meetings of local and state beekeepers are good places for beginners to learn some tips. Beekeeping supply mail-order houses are also good sources of information on equipment and techniques. And don't neglect to visit—and learn from—experienced beekeepers in your own community.

To get started you'll need some basic equipment, namely, a hive consisting of one or

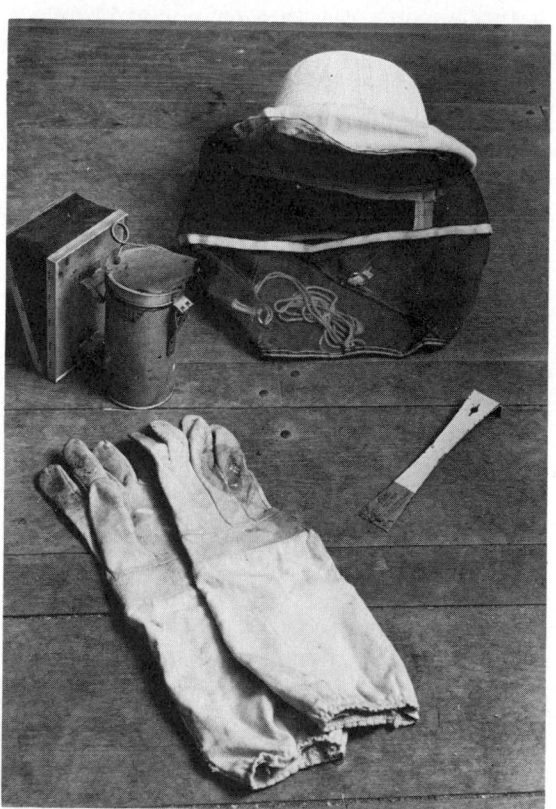

Only a few tools are necessary for a small beekeeping operation: a hat and veil, a hive tool, long, heavy gloves, and a smoker.

more standard (deep) boxes or supers and possibly one or more shallow supers. Each super holds ten frames, and inside each frame is a thin sheet of beeswax, called foundation, on which bees build their comb. You'll also want to buy a bottom board on which the hive stands and an inner and outer cover. A smoker to calm the bees, a hive tool to pry open the hives and separate the frames, gloves, and a hat and veil complete the basic equipment.

Other equipment includes bee escapes, which permit bees to exit, but not reenter supers of honey where they are not wanted; a queen excluder, which prevents queens but not worker bees from going from one super to another; a wiring board, used to embed wire in sheets of foundation to give them support; feeders that are used to feed bees honey or syrup when their own supplies run out; an extractor to remove honey from the combs; and a capping knife to slice the top layer of beeswax from the comb and release the honey.

Of course, you'll also need bees. You can get yours by catching a swarm of wild bees or by buying packaged bees through bee supply houses. For the beginner, packaged bees are easier and safer to handle. They usually come in a three-, four-, five-, or six-pound package that will, in a short time, grow into a bursting, energetic 85,000 bee colony. Packages arrive with a queen inside in her own apartment, and since you must transfer them at once, you need to have ready a large, empty hive in advance. Bees should be ordered in late winter so that they will arrive in early spring and have time to get established before the major honey flow begins in late June or early July.

Although there are many races of bees, the three most popular among American beekeepers are Italian, Caucasian and Carniolan bees. Italian bees are generally recommended for the beginner because they are relatively easy to work and produce good amounts of honey. They don't produce a great amount of propolis, which can glue up the inside of hives, and seem to withstand cold well. Italians are also relatively resistant to European foulbrood, an infectious disease of bees.

You must decide on whether you want to make section (comb) honey, or extracted honey. If you choose the latter, you will need an extractor and a few additional items of equipment. Extracted honey has many advantages over comb honey. It is easier to store; easier to use in cooking; there is no wax when you eat it; and you reuse the combs in which the bees store honey as only the caps are cut off and the honey is expelled by the centrifugal force of the extractor.

Beekeeping, a Simplified Method: Here is a method of beekeeping that is especially suitable for the small diversified enterprise that may well include gardening, fruit growing, poultry, or any other line of endeavor now practiced by millions of homeowners on relatively small holdings.

The secret is to make two standard, full-depth hive bodies the home of the bees the year around. Package bees are first hived in a single full-depth body; as soon as they fill it, the second is added. Two full-depth bodies give the bees abundant room, allow them to store honey enough for their own use so that feeding should never be necessary and help prevent swarming (when a queen leaves the hive with a band of workers to start a new colony). All the complicated manipulation described in some methods is done away with. The beginner may open his hives and study his bees if he wishes, or they will do very well with no more attention than is advised in the description of seasonal operation.

Bees should be checked at midday when it is warm and the sun is bright. At this time there is good flight to and from the colony, most bees are foraging and the beekeeper will find it easier to inspect the colonies.

Light-colored, smooth-finished materials should be worn when inspecting the colonies. Rough materials irritate bees, causing them to sting more readily. The face and ankles most attract bees. A good veil and boots will protect the beekeeper against stings in these areas.

The procedure of seasonal operation, beginning in the spring of the year, for established colonies in two full-depth bodies, is as follows:

When settled warm weather arrives, the hives are opened to be sure that each colony has a laying queen, plenty of honey to use and is otherwise in normal condition. If an occasional colony seems short of food, honey is borrowed; that is, combs exchanged with one that has an abundance. Bees should never, never be fed honey from a hive in which disease is even suspected, and many beekeepers prefer to feed sugar syrup to obviate against inter-colony spread of diseases.

If a colony has died, as one will once in a while, the dead bees are brushed from the combs and the whole hive scraped and cleaned. These combs are then given to an extra strong colony, not only to protect the combs from wax moths, but to give the strong colony more room. The exception here is a colony that has been infected by American foulbrood (AFB), a dreaded killer, or another infectious disease. Such combs and frames are best burned and the inside of the hive bodies well scorched with a blowtorch before reusing.

Normal colonies in two full-depth hive bodies will need more room at about the second month of settled warm weather or at the start of some major bloom. Over much of the United

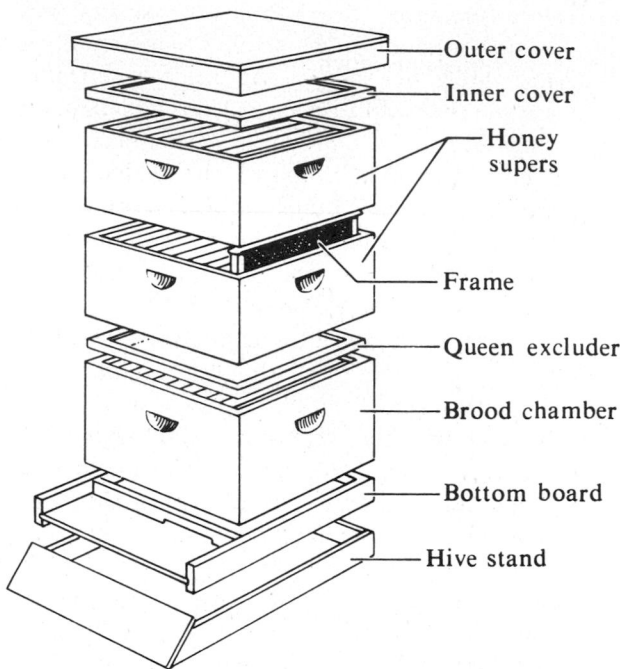

The standard beehive consists of several boxes or supers, each with ten frames on which the workers build their combs. The brood is hatched in the large bottom super while the smaller upper ones are used for storing honey. As the season progresses, more storage supers are added.

States this will be at the outset of clover bloom. For the purpose of easier handling it is best to use shallow supers for this extra room, although more full-depth bodies may be used if you are capable of heavy lifting. When filled with honey the shallow super weighs about 45 to 50 pounds, the full-depth body about 80 pounds.

The rule followed in giving extra room is to add one or more supers at any time that the colony shows signs of being crowded. The term "boiling over with bees" aptly describes a crowded colony, and extra room should be given before this stage becomes acute. If there is any question of when extra room is needed, it is better to give it a week early than a week late. At least one of the major causes of swarming is a crowded condition within the hive, and by giving abundant room, swarming is reduced to a minimum. The occasional swarm that does develop may be hived if convenient, but if it does get away, don't be too concerned.

As fall approaches, the honey gathered (that in the honey supers only—don't take any from the bottom one or two brood chambers) should be removed and the hives gradually reduced to two full-depth bodies. It is important to remember that in this method honey is never removed from the two lower bodies. The success of the whole thing revolves around having a strong colony of bees in a large self-sustaining hive.

Location of Hives: Hives should be located on hive stands four to eight inches high in a protected area. Thus, bottom boards will not be in contact with the ground when it is damp, and grass growing in the area will not shade the hives. Weeds must be kept low in the vicinity of the hives.

Bees must always have fresh water; they use it to dilute food, feed larvae and cool the hives when too warm. If there is no fresh water source, like a pond, stream or spring, within a two-mile radius of the hives, you will have to supply water for your bees.

In all sections of the country, hives should be located out of prevailing winds. In the North they will usually need some extra protection for winter. If you are located in a section having severe winters, first, determine that the hive has abundant stores. Second, reduce the entrance to prevent mice from entering and to help keep out the cold. Finally,

give added protection by first wrapping the hive in a mineral wool blanket and then capping that with tarred building paper.

In the desert areas of the western states it is too warm to place colonies directly in the sunlight. The beekeeper in these areas must construct a shaded area for the hives. It must be remembered that often colonies cannot obtain enough nectar and pollen in deserts and heavily wooded areas of the country to sustain themselves through the year. Mountainous areas do not have large foraging areas, but in certain cases one colony might survive.

Requeening: Some commercial and hobby beekeepers practice annual requeening and others only requeen hives which have failing queens.

Swarming is less of a problem when there is a young queen present in the colony. She produces more of the secretions that maintain social order and has a strong colony that can withstand disease. A young queen also lays more eggs and lays them earlier in the spring and later in the fall. The best time to requeen is in August. September is a satisfactory month, but at this time not all colonies will readily accept a new queen. The common method of requeening is to first find and kill the old queen. Second, place a queen cage with a young queen in the brood nest. In a day or two the young queen will be released by the bees. This method is not recommended for beginners and those not familiar with bee behavior.

The preferred method of requeening is to introduce a young queen into a nucleus colony in mid-July. The nucleus colony should contain one frame of brood and two or three frames of bees. Under these conditions the new queen is almost always accepted. The queen in the old colony can be found and killed around August 1.

Next, the old queen's brood nest is covered with a single sheet of newspaper. The nucleus colony is placed on top of the sheet. Over this honey supers are placed. If there are too many bees in the supers, shake them out or place a second sheet of newspaper between the nucleus and honey supers. Colony odors will be the same and the young queen will be accepted by the time the sheet is chewed away.

The beekeeper must wait a week or two before placing a queen excluder in the colony. At this time the young queen may be successfully driven into the lower brood chamber.

See also BEES, HONEY, HONEY PLANTS.

BEES

Bees play an important role in nature's scheme of things. There are some 5,000 species of bees in North America. Most of them are important only to wild plants, but several hundred pollinate cultivated crops (over 100 species, for instance, visit alfalfa).

Value of Bees: The value of those which pollinate only wild plants should not be minimized: they help to keep vital cover on millions of acres not used for farming.

Once we took pollination of our crops for granted. But it's a different story today. In the past 50 years, under the pressures of a growing population, more and more land was put under cultivation. But the more crops we planted, the faster we destroyed the basic means for a full crop return. Forests were cut down, woods and wasteland destroyed and burrows ripped up, destroying the homes of the wild bees.

Concentrated plantings of one crop over large acreages left the bees no wild plants to live on when the crop was not blooming; with nothing to fill in the gap in their food supply, they starved and disappeared practically overnight. And when indiscriminate spraying with powerful insecticides came along, the wild bees per acre could almost be counted on the fingers of one hand.

We simply do not have enough honeybees. Farmers in every state, according to the Department of Agriculture, could benefit by having more hives on or near their farms. Some areas need two or three times the number of hives they now have, to insure adequate pollination of the crops grown there.

This is where an increase in wild bees would be of immense help. Such an increase would bolster the efforts of hard-working domestic honeybees and show up in a direct rise in crop yields.

Wild Bees: Wild bees have certain characteristics that make them more valuable than their domesticated cousins. They are hardier, working in cold, rainy or windy weather, when honeybees will not venture from their cozy hives. Thus, they provide good sets of seed and fruit even in bad weather. In parts of New England and eastern Canada, this is especially important to apple growers, for the weather is usually bad there during apple-blooming time.

Practically all wild bees form no colonies, in the sense that the honeybee does. The exception to this is the bumblebee, who lives in a colony of some 50 to 500 individuals, with a queen and worker castes. Many new drones and queens are produced each year, but only the fertilized queens live through the winter, each one forming a new colony in the spring.

The other wild bees are solitary dwellers. Each female functions both as queen and worker. She builds her own nest, sealing her eggs in cells with honey-moistened pollen balls for the young to feed on. Once this is done, she has no further contact with her offspring.

Wild bees will nest almost anywhere. Sweat bees and mining bees construct underground burrows. Carpenter bees and leaf cutters chisel their nests in timber, or use old beetle holes. Some wild bees nest in the natural channels of hollow- or pithy-stemmed plants; others make their homes in abandoned snail shells or cavities in porous rocks.

The majority, however, are soil nesting. Almost any type of soil, moist or dry, loose or packed, flat or vertical, can be their home. Alkali bees, in some areas the major pollinators of alfalfa, nest in fairly sandy soil, often in "communities" of several thousand nests less than an inch apart. Seed growers, knowing that communities like these will insure pollination of their alfalfa for two miles around, protect them from disturbance. If small pieces of land are left unfarmed near the alfalfa fields, the alkali bees will also spread to them and establish new communities there in one season.

Tests by various experiment stations showed that on a cultivated plot situated next to overgrown land, wild bees were four times as numerous as on tilled plots surrounded by other tilled land. To increase your wild bees you can preserve some uncultivated or eroded land specifically for bees. Sometimes bee broods found on land that is to be tilled can be moved into these areas. On cropland, avoid working, flooding or trampling the burrows of ground-nesting bees whenever possible.

Field borders, fencerows, ditch banks, and the sides of roadways should be planted to nectar-producing plants. Kudzu and bicolor or *Lespedeza cuneata* make excellent bee pasturage, or use whatever is suitable for your region. Pithy-stemmed plants like elderberry, sumac and tree-of-heaven make fine nesting sites. They provide erosion protection and food and cover for other wildlife, too. Multiflora rose fences are very good, and bunch-type perennial grasses along the tops of banks are soil stabilizers as well as nesting sites.

Trees for windbreaks and streambank protection that also provide bee food and homes include the Russian olive, American elm, catalpa, honey locust, basswood, sycamore, wild plum, and many others. In woodlot management, make sure bee trees are not cut down.

Bee plants are often synonymous with soil-saving plants. The legumes used for green manures, orchard cover crops and in rotations provide bee food in plenty. Often a small planting of clover may be all that is necessary, with regular crop plants, to sustain a goodly population of wild bees all year. Improved pastures and grassed waterways should have some clover in their planting mixtures.

Bumblebees will nest in cans containing a handful of mattress stuffing or similar material, hung up in sheltered places in your outbuildings. Certain other species can be induced to set up housekeeping in cans with lids and entrance spouts, partially buried in well-drained soil. Some farmers break open bee trees in the woods, carrying the bees home in any handy container to be set up in suitable places around their farms. When walking through your fields, you can break over the stalks of hollow-stemmed plants like canebrake, teasel, milk-thistle, and wild parsnip, to provide nesting and hibernating places.

Some species of native bees are more efficient pollinators than honeybees. Red clover blooms, having little nectar and the pollen at the bottom of a deep corolla tube, are often passed up by the honeybee; but the long-tongued bumblebee does an excellent job on them. Honeybees can steal the nectar from alfalfa blooms without "tripping" them to release the pollen. But alkali, leaf cutter and bumblebees are pollen collectors who trip every blossom they visit.

On rangelands, where it is impractical to supply honeybees for pollination, wild bees have a big responsibility to keep the range plants reproducing year after year. Every range reseeding program should include adapted legumes and other honey-producing plants to increase the wild bees, and thus improve the fodder and fertility of the range.

Honeybees (Domestic): The honeybee is a social insect. The queen, drone and worker bees cannot live alone. All members of the honeybee colony divide labor to facilitate work, and there is never a time when the whole colony sleeps. Honeybees take rest periods throughout the day.

The single function of the drones (males) is to mate with the queen. They become sexually mature at ten to 12 days. During the afternoon virgin queens fly to "drone congregation areas" where mating takes place. Drones die in the mating process and are not present in the colony during the winter.

The queen is the most important part of the colony for two reasons—she lays eggs to insure the survival of the colony and controls the social order of the colony with the chemical substances she secretes. The queen is different from worker bees in that she has no wax glands, no pollen baskets on her hind legs and no modifications on her forelegs. She is also larger and her abdomen is longer and more slender.

Worker bees are female and perform all other tasks for the colony. The worker bee cleans cells, at first, and later feeds larvae. Her next duty is to guard the hive. After these tasks are completed, the worker bee begins to work in the fields. The ability of the worker bee to change from one task to another insures the survival of the colony. She lives for six weeks during the peak honey season, and six months in the winter.

There are three races of domestic (honey) bees: Carniolans, Caucasians and Italians.

Carniolan bees of the Alpine strain can be distinguished by their dark gray abdominal segments with bands of white hairs. These bees are the finest gray bees in existence and the largest of hive bees. The Alpine strain is less inclined to swarm than other bees and are extremely prolific.

Carniolans are very gentle, quiet on the combs, good breeders, and have a long life. These bees are economic consumers of stores, honest workers and winter-hardy. They build regular combs with white cappings well suited for comb honey production. They are brave in defending their hives, but gentle to humans.

Carniolan queens are darker than the workers, and drones are large and gray colored with or without visible bands.

Caucasian bees are somewhat parallel or merit a good second to the Carniolans in comb honey production. The Mountain Gray Caucasian can be compared to the Alpine Carniolan except it is smaller and intensely propolizing. The Caucasians are more immune to American foulbrood than other standard bees.

Italian bees are most commonly used in America and enjoy a high productivity. "Pure" Italians are three banded. Extra-yellow strains of four bands are found in the United States. The queens are yellower than the workers, and the drones are darker.

Italian bees are more reliable in their swarming habits, but are really no better or worse than other honeybees. However, these bees may rob and may be a menace. Their defense of their home is normal and they are fair in accepting new queens. In general, Italians are known for their good dispositions.

See also BEEKEEPING, HONEY, HONEY PLANTS.

BEET (*Beta vulgaris*)

Beets are one of the most important home-grown vegetables. They are a relatively easy crop to grow, quite resistant to insects and diseases, use little garden space, are reasonably easy to store, and are a good source of vitamins. Beets and beet greens can provide a valuable part of your diet.

Culture: Beets can be grown all over the country, but seem to be particularly adapted to northern sections. They may be grown in the South during the cooler months of late winter and early spring.

Beets prefer a well-drained soil that has been enriched with an application of rotted manure or compost. Hot, dry weather and soil cause beet roots to become stringy and tough. All stones or other obstacles should be removed from the top four inches of soil to allow for good root development.

Plant the seeds in rows approximately three feet apart. With two feet left between plants, ½ ounce of seed will sow a 100-foot row. When planting in warm weather, it may be a good idea to soak the seeds for as long as 12 hours. When plants reach two inches in growth, it is time to thin them. Thinned out plants need not be wasted—replant them in the rows and apply water. In a few days they will look as healthy as the others. To insure the best continuous yield, sow seed every three to four weeks until 90 days before the first frost. Shallow cultivation of weed growth and an occasional dousing of water are the only requirements for healthy beet growth.

Pests: Major beet offenders are the spinach flea beetle, leaf spot and leaf miner. None of these enemies will cause serious damage to plants grown on fertile soil. Crop rotation will discourage disease and infestation. *See also* DISEASE, INSECT CONTROL.

Harvest: "Baby" beets are harvested when one to 1½ inches in diameter. Simply pull the beets out of the ground, but, when removing the tops, leave an inch or two attached to the roots so they will not bleed.

Beets for storage are often left in the ground until just before the first frost. Those being used for long storage should have their tops cut off close to the roots. Remember to separate the diseased and decayed beets from the bunch before storing.

One method of underground storage is to place beets in a plastic basket in a hole three feet deep and four feet square. Place a sheet of plastic on top of the beets, followed by a layer of cornstalks and straw. Beets can also be stored indoors in a cool, dark cellar if placed in moist sand.

Varieties: There are two types of beets—the early growing and the late or maincrop type. Of the early type which prefer spring planting, Ruby Queen, Early Wonder and Crosby's Egyptian Redhart are popular. Detroit Dark Red matures in about 60 days and produces a fine-grained vegetable. Cylindra is a Danish variety that is long in shape and has a tender quality.

Winter Keeper and Detroit Dark Red are longer maturers and store well through the winter.

Nutritional Value: The stems of beets and their greens are high in vitamin A, providing over twice the RDA. The ascorbic acid content is also high and amounts to half of the RDA (22 mg.).

BEET WASTES

In the sugar beet growing regions, beet wastes are easily available. Much of that material can be used for ensiling or feeding, but plenty could be composted. Numerous analyses of beet roots showed that their potash content varied from .7 to 4.1 percent; the variation in nitrogen is less pronounced, and an average might be .4 percent, while phosphorus ranges from .1 to .6 percent. The leaves are not very different in their makeup, although their content in calcium and magnesium far exceeds that of the roots. Beet pulp is difficult to compost. Treat as apple pomace.

See also APPLE POMACE.

BEGGAR'S TICKS
(*Bidens frondosa*)

This member of the Daisy family belongs to a wide group of wild "pest plants" (those that cause skin irritation or infection, have poisonous berries or leaves, or injurious thorns). A vigorous-growing weed, from a few inches to five feet or more in height, the beggar's tick has a pair of down-pointed barbed spines at one end of the seed, which makes them cling stubbornly to clothing. The plant grows in damp, open areas, especially along lakeshores, and sometimes even in relatively dry waste places. Control of beggar's ticks, also called Spanish-needles, devil's pitchfork and bur marigold, can be aided by improving drainage on moist land and mowing before weed formation to prevent reinfestation.

BEGONIAS

This great group of tropical foliage and flowering ornamental plants, for gardening purposes, can be divided into two groups: tuberous rooted and fibrous rooted (common bedding varieties).

Begonias thrive in a warm, humid atmosphere. East, south or west windows give correct exposures for most varieties in the winter, and the Rex types seem to like north windows, or shaded east windows.

If your begonias do not have enough humidity, the edges of the leaves are likely to

To achieve full flowering, wax begonias require several hours of sunshine daily.

turn brown, and they will yellow and fall from the plant prematurely. Set the pots in larger containers, pack peat or sphagnum moss between the two and keep this moist at all times. The air rising around your plants will then have a mist of humidity in it that will make them grow like mad.

You can also set the plants in trays at least two inches deep filled with moist sand or peat moss. A tinsmith will construct one of these at small cost.

Begonias are not especially fussy about potting soils, but they like a light, porous soil which should be pressed gently but firmly about the roots, not packed hard as for geraniums and ivies. Here is an ideal soil mixture for them: two parts sandy loam; one part clean, sharp sand; one-half part well-rotted cow manure; and one-half part well-rotted leaf mold, with crushed charcoal added to keep the soil "sweet," and to insure the good drainage essential for begonias.

Begonias detest being overpotted and do not grow in pots without drainage holes in the bottom. Water from the top of the pot with lukewarm water until it runs from the bottom and do not water again until the top of the soil feels dry. If you are new at window gardening, pinch some of the soil between your fingers; if it sticks, it is wet enough; if it powders and falls from your fingers, water.

Begonias are very free of pests and diseases. Overwatering or poor drainage may cause black rot in the roots which spreads up through the plant. If you want to save it, take cuttings from still healthy growth and root in water, or in a mixture of equal parts peat moss and sand.

Begonias love terrarium conditions. If you do not have a regular container for this, a discarded aquarium is ideal. Place ½ inch of pebbles and crushed charcoal in the bottom. Then place at least three inches of regular potting soil in the terrarium, but add another part of the sand to insure good drainage.

These terrariums, which grow best in an eastern or northern exposure, may become "catch-alls" for your house plant cuttings, but they'll produce some nice surprises. Cover the top with a piece of window glass, keeping it slightly raised by placing a match under the edge for ventilation.

Do not overwater a terrarium. Keep the soil just moist at all times. Rex begonias especially will grow lush, beautiful foliage in a terrarium.

Other kinds of begonias include the popular, easy to grow, Semperflorens or wax begonias. They come in single- or double-flowered varieties. The cane types are among the most popular; our grandmothers grew and loved angel-wing begonias. The hirsute and rhizomatous groups offer more variety. The beefsteak begonia is one of dozens of rhizomatous varieties sporting beautiful foliage, not to mention beautiful clusters of flowers in pink and white. Tuberous-rooted begonias for growing in the summer seem to fall into a category entirely different from the winter-window-garden begonias.

Tuberous Begonias: These are excellent choices for shady spots. The tuberous begonias are native to Central and South America, where they can be found in cool, moist, shady places where the soil is rich and well supplied with humus.

Plant tubers in spring when the soil is moist, but not wet; remove a few inches of topsoil and cultivate the remaining soil, removing stones and working in compost. If the soil is heavy, work in additional organic materials, sand or peat moss. The goal is to have a spongy, loose, humus-rich soil.

Plant tubers directly in the bed—level with the soil surface and with the hollow side up. Water them lightly at first until the plants grow strongly; then keep the beds moist. Mulch them with about two inches of hulls, moss, etc.

Tuberous begonias generally begin to flower in July and continue until frost. Some gardeners produce earlier blooms—often in June—by starting tubers inside the house or greenhouse in March. Start them in shallow trays filled with peat moss, placing tubers close together. The trays should be kept in a shady place at a temperature around 60°F. (15.56°C.). Transplant the plantlets in May.

Begonias from Seed: Seed-sowing is a popular form of propagation. It provides many plants at a minimum of expense and the plants are more vigorous than those raised from cuttings. On the other hand, seedlings are not always true to species if they have been grown where insects can cross-pollinate them. Seeds from hybrids usually revert to some of their ancestral characteristics and the resulting plant may be handsome. Unfortunately, many unnamed or falsely named seedlings have been distributed, adding to the existing confusion in the begonia world.

Seed-sowing calls for scrupulous attention to details and for unremitting care for many weeks, but the reward is heartwarming. The plant lover will have all the plants he wants for himself, and plenty to give to friends and neighbors, or to sell.

There are many ingenious ways to start begonia seeds. One of the oldest ways is to use a "brick grandmother"—an old-fashioned red clay brick is good, because it is porous. Sterilize the soil and pack a thick layer on the brick, then set it in a pan and add water until the brick is half submerged. When the brick and soil are moist, scatter the seeds on the moist soil, pressing down firmly. Keep enough water in the pan to keep the soil moist at all times.

Some growers like to use a flat-sided, wide-mouthed bottle, partially filled with the soil mixture. Lay the bottle on the side and scatter the seeds with a long-handled implement. Cover the bottle neck loosely, to admit some air. When the seedlings are ready to transplant, slip a wide-bladed knife under them and draw carefully out of the wide bottle neck.

Seedlings sometimes show spotted leaves, even if they were not from spotted leaf varieties. As they get larger, the spots disappear, and the leaf takes on the appearance of the parent.

The fresher the seed, the better the germination, although there are always some sterile seeds. Begonia seeds bruise easily and this destroys fertility. They should always be packed in cotton wool to prevent bruising. Usually seeds germinate in nine to 15 days, but sometimes weeks or even months will elapse before the seedlings appear. The Semperflorens begonias will bloom in six months from seed, the tuberous kinds in about the same time, but most of the fibrous kinds will not bloom until they are a year or more old.

BELLADONNA
(*Atropa belladonna*)

The poisonous alkaloids present in all parts of this perennial herb are used in the preparation of a number of important medicines.

Native to the Mediterranean region and central Asia, belladonna thrives in cool, moist climates. Although it is not grown commercially in North America, plants can be found in special drug-plant or botanical gardens in the northeastern and central states and in the damp regions of the Northwest.

Commercially, belladonna is usually propagated from seed, although new fields can be planted with divisions of the fleshy rootstocks of old plants. Since individual seeds vary greatly in the time required for germination, it sometimes takes four or five weeks to obtain a good stand of seedlings from a given lot of seed. About one ounce of seed will provide enough plants for one acre.

The seed is sown thickly in pots or well-drained boxes in late winter in a cool greenhouse, a cold frame or outdoor seedbed early in spring, much like tobacco. When the seedlings grown indoors are large enough to handle they should be transplanted to light rich soil in small individual pots or seed flats. As soon as danger of frost is over they should be transplanted to a deeply plowed and well-prepared field by hand or with transplanting machines and set about 20 inches apart in rows 30 inches or more apart.

Belladonna grows to three feet and has inconspicuous flowers and poisonous large black berries.

BELLFLOWER   *See* CAMPANULA

BELLWORT   *See* UVULARIA

BEN FRANKLIN TREE
See FRANKLINIA

BENJAMIN BUSH   *See* SPICEBUSH

BENTGRASS   *See* LAWN

BERGAMOT

Two different related plants are known as bergamot. The first and most common is *Mentha citrata,* sometimes called lemon mint. It is a perennial, growing one to two feet tall with pink flowers in spikes. Like other mints, it can be propagated by seed, division or cuttings.

Wild bergamot (*Monarda fistulosa*) is a close relative of bee balm and is propagated by spring division of plants.

See also BEE BALM, MINT.

BERMUDAGRASS
(*Cynodon dactylon*)

Also commonly known as wiregrass, Bermudagrass is an extremely tenacious, long-lasting perennial grass, first found in the tough growing conditions of the Bengal region of India and introduced into the United States about 1751. It produces aboveground runners (stolons) that root by themselves and form the crowns of new plants at the nodes, and fleshy underground runners (rhizomes) that also develop into new plants.

In the United States, Bermudagrass is best adapted to the southern states—wherever mean daily temperatures are above 50°F. (10°C.). Although it can be a problem—and extremely difficult to eradicate—on lawns, Bermudagrass makes a good pasture when planted with legumes. It is more drought resistant than dallisgrass, carpetgrass or bahiagrass, and will make

One of the most stubborn lawn weeds, Bermuda-grass is also an excellent pasture grass grown throughout the southern United States.

good growth on any moderately well-drained soil with adequate moisture and nutrients.

Bermudagrass may be propagated by seeding or by planting vegetative sprigs, although the latter is more common. For pastures, most legumes will make good growth in association with Bermudagrass but clovers are most commonly planted. A number of cultivars have been developed.

To eradicate Bermudagrass from the lawn, try mulching with at least eight inches of hay, leaves or corn fodder. Where ground freezes, till in fall so that roots are exposed to the air through the winter months.

BERRIES

So many are the advantages of berries and other small fruits that it is difficult to see how any gardener can resist growing them. Besides their delicious flavor, berries are generally less susceptible to insect damage and disease. Strawberries, for example, often aren't sprayed even in commercial plantings.

NUTRITIVE VALUE OF BERRIES AND GRAPES PER CUP

FRUIT (1 cup, fresh) (125 to 150 grams)	Calories (Food Energy)	Fat Gm.	Protein Gm.	Calcium Mg.	Phosphorus Mg.	Iron Mg.	Vit. A I.U.	Vit. B₁ Mg.	Vit. B₂ Mg.	Vit. C Mg.
Blackberries	82	1.4	1.7	46	46	1.3	280	.05	.06	30
Blueberries	85	.8	.8	22	18	1.1	400	.04	.03	23
Currants	60	.2	1.3	40	36	1.0	130	.04	. . . .	40
Gooseberries	59	.3	1.2	33	42	.8	440	. . .	. . . .	49
Grapes (American type)	84	1.7	1.7	20	25	.7	90	.07	.05	5
Grapes (European type)	102	.6	1.2	26	33	.9	120	.09	.06	6
Loganberries	90	.9	1.4	50	27	1.7	280	.04	.10	34
Raspberries (Black)	100	2.1	2.0	54	50	1.2	. . .	.03	.09	32
Raspberries (Red)	70	.5	1.5	49	46	1.1	160	.03	.08	29
Strawberries	54	.7	1.2	42	40	1.2	90	.04	.10	89

Berry bushes usually bear fruit much sooner than do full-sized fruit trees. Most bushes will start bearing the second year after planting. The bushes also take up much less room than even dwarf trees.

The food values of fresh berries are high, as shown by the chart.

See also entries for individual berries, BRAMBLE FRUITS.

BETONY	*See* STACHYS
B HORIZON	*See* SOIL HORIZON
BIBLE LEAF	*See* COSTMARY

BIENNIALS

Biennials are plants which normally require two years to complete their life cycle (blooming the second season after seed is sown) before they produce seed and die. One group, known as the true biennials, includes Canterbury-bells, sweet William, foxglove, hollyhocks, and rose campion. These are best sown in mid-June to mid-July to obtain healthy vigorous plants the following year.

The second group of biennials includes those plants that are not very hardy, such as pansies, forget-me-nots, English daisies, and English wallflowers. Generally it is best to sow this group in August to avoid danger of winter-killing. It is also good practice to winter them in cold frames in regions where temperatures drop below 20°F. (−6.67°C.). In any case, all biennials should be protected from weather extremes and heaving during warm spells with a heavy mulch applied after the ground has frozen.

As a biennial, the leek does not flower until its second year at which time an elongated stem appears, terminated by several thousand flowers.

When starting biennials, prepare the soil as for any good seedbed, making the soil fine, moistening it and adding leaf mold, peat moss or other humus material. A good practice is to mix the tiny seeds with dry sand in order to get even distribution in the rows.

Be careful when watering the seeds; if they get too little water, they'll dry out; if too much, damping-off may result.

Once the seedlings have about four to six leaves and can be easily handled, it's time to transplant. Water sufficiently until they are well established and mulch to conserve moisture.

BINDWEED   (*Convolvulus*)

These annual and perennial twining vines are among the most stubborn of all weeds to eradicate. Best control is continuous cultivation—which kills by starvation of the roots through the continual removal of the top growth. Cultivation every two weeks is necessary and the best time to start is immediately after harvest in the summer or about two weeks after the plant starts growth in the spring.

A relative of the morning-glory, bindweed is best eradicated by frequent hoeing and chopping.

Continue at intervals of 14 days as long as growth continues, making about ten to 12 cultivations a season. If no plants are to be seen at the time a cultivation is due, that cultivation may be skipped. The depth of cultivation is not very important but make it deep enough to do a good job. Plows, duck-foot field cultivators and rotary rod-weeders all do a satisfactory job. *All* plants must be cut off at the time of cultivation. Extend the treatment to about ten feet beyond the patch. Unfortunately, it takes from two to three seasons for complete eradication. Soil erosion may result from this cultivation so be sure to use all plant residues. Winter rye planted in late September and plowed or disked the following spring and the cultivation started again helps. Do not allow the rye to pass the boot stage.

Close relatives to the bindweed include the California rose (*Calystegia hederacea*), a perennial climber of about 20 feet; and dwarf morning-glory (*Convolvulus tricolor*), an annual often recommended where blue flowers are desired in the garden color scheme.

BIO-DYNAMIC METHOD

The bio-dynamic method was first described over 50 years ago in Germany by Rudolf Steiner, the founder of anthroposophy. Steiner assumed that material science describes only one realm, the physical, and neglects those effects in nature which have their causes in spheres other than the earth's.

The "true farm," in bio-dynamic terms, lives and works as a single organism, supporting itself in all its functions and requiring outside help only as a temporary remedy. The density of livestock is based on the availability of land for crops, pasture and hayfield. Their composted manures, in turn, should be of sufficient quantity to fertilize the soil. Outside fertilizers—and this excludes chemical fertilizers—are again viewed as a temporary corrective measure which should be unnecessary with proper management.

The handling of manures has become a prime skill within bio-dynamic circles. All manures in their raw state are rejected as direct fertilizer and are subjected to a rigorous composting process to yield life-enriched material with stable humus compounds. The preservation of nitrogen alone is worth the effort, because it is well known that this element has an immense influence upon the yield of crops. Spreading fresh manure in gardens or fields may waste up to 50 percent of the nitrogen before the manure can be incorporated into the soil.

In bio-dynamic terms, a soil can be considered to have been fertilized if the grower has succeeded in increasing the soil life. From this viewpoint, compost becomes the one most powerful tool for achieving an increased soil-life population and generating or stimulating its seasonal productivity. The compost heap may be looked upon as a breeding place of soil microbes and other soil life which will be later "injected" into a field in order to spread and continue its digestive and excretive functions.

The bio-dynamic concept also incorporates the theory of planetary influences upon plant life. These forces are believed to manifest themselves in rhythmic patterns and even physical manifestations such as plant color and fragrance. In bio-dynamic practice, for example, the optimum dates for seeding and planting are determined by the phase and constellation of the moon. The results become especially apparent in the growth of viable seeds for reproduction.

The relation of insects to plants is viewed within the context of the living eco-system within which both function. The negative factors which cause a plant to become susceptible to insect attack are: 1) monoculture; 2) placement of a plant into climates or environments which are not native to it; and 3) wrong composition, structure, acidity, drainage, or fertility of soils. In establishing any crop, the grower should always be aware of how and to what extent these potentially damaging effects can be weakened or neutralized.

The next requirement—a more positive one—is to envision the plant as a whole. That includes not just the visible part above the ground, but the part which makes up the root system. Both parts of the plant are intimately immersed in the insect sphere and connected to insect life. The plant needs insect life above and below to exist, and in the natural habitat a certain ratio always exists between the upper and lower sphere of insect activity. If this ratio is disturbed—either by man through mismanagement of soil, or by climatic conditions—then a destructive tendency develops. Insecticides may momentarily halt the outbreak, but they will never solve the long-range problem because they are a further interference in the natural order and may actually encourage a renewed comeback by the "pests."

Bio-dynamic fertilizing does much to prevent pest problems because any attempt to increase insect activity at the root zone helps greatly to change the insect ratio favorably above ground. A loss of soil life may be experienced as a problem of insect pest activity above the ground. The bio-dynamic grower must be constantly aware of both spheres.

The bio-dynamic school of thought reaches beyond one's farm or garden to view the planet as a huge and complex organism of which the cultivated soil is but one living organ.

BIOLOGICAL INSECT CONTROL
See INSECT CONTROL

BIRCH   (*Betula*)

Deciduous and hardy, this striking genus of tall-growing trees is best known for its distinctive bark, which in varying species ranges from a pure white to shades of orange, red, brown, and black. Added to this is the delicate, graceful foliage, which turns gold in fall.

Most birches thrive in moist, sandy loam; they are hardy in cold climates, and generally short-lived in warm areas. Propagation is by seed, and sometimes by cuttings, budding or grafting.

The canoe or paper birch (*B. papyrifera*) has a very white bark that peels. The river or red birch (*B. nigra*), a hardy grower from Massachusetts to Florida and west to Kansas, has a red brown bark which sheds in thin flakes.

The cherry or sweet birch (*B. lenta*), found from Maine to Alabama and westward to Ohio, is characterized by a smooth, dark bark like that of the cherry tree, and has aromatic twigs from which oil of wintergreen is distilled. A tea can be made by boiling the young twigs, and this species has been tapped in spring for its moderately sweet sap. The strong wood, brown red at the heart, is used in cabinetry. When acted upon by ferrous sulfate, the bark makes a wine-colored dye.

BIRD-OF-PARADISE
(*Strelitzia reginae*)

Sometimes called crane flower, from a distance the bird-of-paradise does look like the head of a crane. The rose and green sheath that holds the blossoms juts out at an obtuse angle from its thick stalk, resembling a huge bird's beak, and the vivid orange petals and sapphire sepals stand up like a crane's crest.

Though found wild only along rivers in South Africa, bird-of-paradise thrives wherever temperatures seldom go below freezing, sending up blooms of orange and blue most of the winter and spring. In colder climates it can be raised in large pots and kept on the patio in summer and in a sunny window in winter.

In climates where there are only occasional cool spells, wrapping plants in burlap bags will insulate against light frosts. Another safeguard, where winters are on the borderline between subtropical and temperate climates, is to force the plant into dormancy well in advance of the cold season by holding back food and water at the end of the summer.

Humidity is highly desirable for most plants, and bird-of-paradise is no exception. It prefers the damp air of coastal regions but grows in more arid climes if it receives abundant water, is planted in soil that contains considerable leaf mold or humus and is shaded from direct sun. If the leaves begin to brown at the edges and become brittle, the plant is probably not getting enough water. Too much water is equally harmful. If grown outdoors in areas where rains are heavy, add sand and gravel to improve drainage.

Under cultivation bird-of-paradise sometimes reaches three feet, while the wild plant seldom attains two. One of the reasons for this is frequent fertilizer applications. Bird-of-paradise is a heavy feeder, and should be given a good application of a complete organic fertilizer in the spring followed by a second application three months later. As a potted plant, it needs a monthly application of liquid fertilizer during the spring and summer. Water thoroughly but not too often.

Outdoors, give bird-of-paradise ample room to spread lest it take the food right out from under the roots of its less hardy neighbors. Three feet between plants is the minimum; five feet is better. The exception is in planting very young plants to which you intend to give more space later on.

Blossoms seldom appear unless at least ten leaves have developed, so do not be discouraged if a small plant you have had for a year or two has not flowered. It will, as soon as it is large enough, if it has had adequate care.

The bird-of-paradise flower is seldom bothered by serious pests. The occasional invaders include aphids, scale and mealybugs.

To have new plants the fastest possible way, divide established ones. Each fan of leaves is a potential plant. The larger the clump taken, the sooner flowers will appear. Cut the fan from the parent plant carefully, taking as much of the root system as possible.

Spring is the best time of the year to divide plants. The weather is mild and humid and new growth has not yet begun, giving the newly divided plant an opportunity to become established before the dormant season arrives. It is possible to divide well-established plants as late

The bird-of-paradise is easily propagated by division, each fan of leaves being a potential plant.
(Courtesy of Longwood Gardens)

as August if you take ample roots.

Few cut flowers have better keeping qualities than bird-of-paradise. Several flowers come forth, one at a time, from each sheath. If you change the water every day and cut the base of the stem every other day, floral arrangements should last two weeks.

BIRDS

The interest in watching birds and attracting them to the garden has grown enormously in recent years. Their beauty, song and active behavior make birds the most conspicuous form of wildlife that lives in close proximity to man.

Their exuberant presence can transform the garden from a collection of plants into a lively community of interrelated life forms. They satisfy a human need for close contact with the wild things that share the planet with us. Organic gardeners value birds highly in their role as efficient predators of insects. A varied population of resident birds will help to control insect pests. Bird and insect populations tend to balance each other out, and birds will disappear from gardens that are doused with pesticides and herbicides at every appearance

The slate gray berries of the juniper will satisfy the appetites of some birds which might otherwise turn to the garden for food.

of aphid or dandelion. Organic gardeners are accustomed to thinking of pests in terms of balanced control rather than overkill, and they have taken an important first step in making their gardens attractive to birds by refusing to use these poisons. The birds will increase in number and variety if a few other requirements are met.

Birds have three basic needs for survival: food, water and cover. A well-stocked feeder can increase the garden's bird population dramatically in winter, and a birdbath can be a busy center of activity during the heat of summer. These two amenities in combination with plantings attractive to birds as nesting sites, shelter and sources of food will help to insure a year-round population of birds in the garden.

Planting for Birds: In the wild, more species of birds will be found in the brushy area where woods and fields meet than will be found in the interior of either the woods or fields themselves. Ecologists call this phenomenon "edge effect," and when it can be duplicated on the home grounds, a greater variety of birds will be encouraged to take up residence there. One way to accomplish this is by surrounding the lawn with a thick border of fruiting trees and shrubs. The wider and more varied in content the border is, the better, but even a narrow boundary hedge can make a garden more appealing to some birds. A gradation of heights in the planting will make it more aesthetically pleasing and more attractive to more species of birds. Some birds, robins among them, forage on the lawn; others like catbirds and mockingbirds prefer to nest in dense shrubbery; and still others such as orioles spend most of their time in tall trees. The outer edges of the planting might be framed by tall shade trees, grading down to small fruiting trees and tall shrubs, faced in turn by lower shrubs around the perimeter of the lawn, which should be kept as open as possible so the birds can be seen. Evergreens should be included in the border because of their value as year-round cover. Mass them where a permanent screen is wanted, or where they can serve as a windbreak for the garden and house. This kind of mass border open lawn planting will provide birds with an abundance of nesting sites, a variety of habitats, ample shelter, and food in the form of insects, seeds and fruit. It can be installed over a period of years as the budget permits, and will cause its owner little work once established.

Bird gardens are of necessity low-maintenance gardens because birds prefer things to be as natural as possible. Converting large areas of lawn into islands and borders of shrubbery cuts down on the monotonous chore of grass mowing. The shrubs and trees in the bird garden might be pruned occasionally to induce formation of forks and crotches that can support nests, but they should be allowed to grow together, thicket fashion, to some extent. Close clipping of fruiting shrubs should be avoided because it reduces berry production. Use the prunings as pea stakes in the vegetable garden, or to make a brush pile in some out-of-the-way corner. Brush piles are attractive to ground-dwelling birds as resting and feeding areas. Vine and bramble fruits can be planted around them to form dense thickets which are the preferred nesting sites of several species. Leaves which fall in the shrub borders should not be raked up. Leaf litter harbors many insects and is a rich foraging area for birds, and it will slowly decay into leaf mold, which is the only fertilizer the shrubbery will need. Many common weeds will furnish valuable seeds for birds. The common annuals lamb's-quarters (*Chenopodium*) and pigweed (*Amaranthus*) produce highly nutritious seeds favored by many species. The plants can be cut in fall, tied in shocks and placed near feeders or among shrubs so birds have access to the seeds in winter. The purple black berries of pokeweed are eaten by 28 species of birds. This plant can make a showy addition to the shrub border. Gardeners may rebel at allowing such pests as ragweed and poison ivy to get established in the garden, but both are excellent bird food plants. Garden flowers are most closely associated with hummingbirds, but many will provide food for other birds if allowed to ripen their seeds. The colorful small-seeded sunflowers, cosmos, China asters, marigolds, and zinnias are especially good.

Even though a planting devoted to birds should be kept as casual and wild as possible, it should be as carefully planned as any other major landscaping project. There are limits to the amount of actual jungle that can be tolerated, especially on small suburban properties where there are usually finicky neighbors to contend with. Make a scale drawing of the area to be planted, and lay out the planting on paper before anything is put in the ground. While it is true that a great variety of plant material means a great variety of birds, don't overdo it by planting one each of two dozen different shrubs at random around the garden. Try to group at least three shrubs of each species together, and repeat the groups at various places in the border. This will insure good cross-pollination and fruit set, and will make the border more pleasing to the eye by giving it a pattern. Choose plants that fruit at different times so food is available most of the year. A limited list of proven bird attractors follows.

Fruiting trees: cherry, crabapple, dogwood, hawthorn, Juneberry (*Amelanchier*), mountain ash, mulberry, and red cedar.

If appropriate food and shelter are provided, birds such as this black-capped chickadee and downy woodpecker will flock to the garden area.

Fruiting shrubs: autumn olive, barberry, bayberry, coralberry, elderberry, species of holly, tatarian and Amur honeysuckles, pyracantha, spicebush (*Lindera Benzoin*), many viburnums (*see also* VIBURNUM), and yew.

The following cultivated fruits can be used in both the bird garden and kitchen: blackberry, blueberry, Nanking and Hanson bush cherries, sour and sweet cherries, currant, gooseberry, persimmon, raspberry, and strawberry.

Hummingbirds will visit almost any flower, but they prefer tubular flowers in the red to orange color range. Some hummingbird magnets are: trumpet vine, trumpet honeysuckle (*Lonicera sempervirens*), red bee balm (*Monarda*), cardinal flower (*Lobelia Cardinalis*), and jewelweed or touch-me-not.

Species of birds which may be expected to nest in gardens east of the Mississippi are listed below. Residents of western states are urged to consult regional bird guides for counterpart species found in the West.

Birds which need areas of open lawn with some shade or evergreen trees for nesting include: mourning dove, starling, common grackle, American robin, house sparrow, and chipping sparrow.

Species nesting in dense shrubbery are: mockingbird, gray catbird, brown thrasher, yellow warbler, yellowthroat, cardinal, purple finch, house finch, American goldfinch, rufous-sided towhee, and song sparrow.

Rows or parklike stands of shade trees might attract: eastern kingbird, northern oriole, orchard oriole, and warbling vireo.

Gardens in suburbs with established trees or gardens adjoining woods might attract: various woodpeckers, eastern wood pewee, blue jay, white-breasted nuthatch, black-capped and Carolina chickadees, tufted titmouse, wood thrush, scarlet tanager, and rose-breasted grosbeak.

Some cavity nesters which will accept manmade birdhouses built to their individual needs and placed in the proper habitat are: American kestrel; screech owl; various woodpeckers; great crested flycatcher; tree swallow;

purple martin; the chickadees; tufted titmouse; house, Carolina and Bewick's wrens; eastern bluebird; starling; and house sparrow. The eastern phoebe and barn swallow will nest on shelves or beams inside buildings. The wrens, starling and house sparrow are the least fussy and will stuff their untidy nests into almost any cavity they can enter.

If there are no natural sources of water in the vicinity, a well-placed birdbath will add greatly to the attractiveness of the garden for birds. Almost any wide, shallow container with a rough interior surface, gradually sloping sides, and a maximum depth of three inches will do. Place the birdbath out in the open away from shrubbery which might hide lurking cats. A waterlogged bird is a clumsy flier and makes easy prey. Where cats are a problem, a ped-

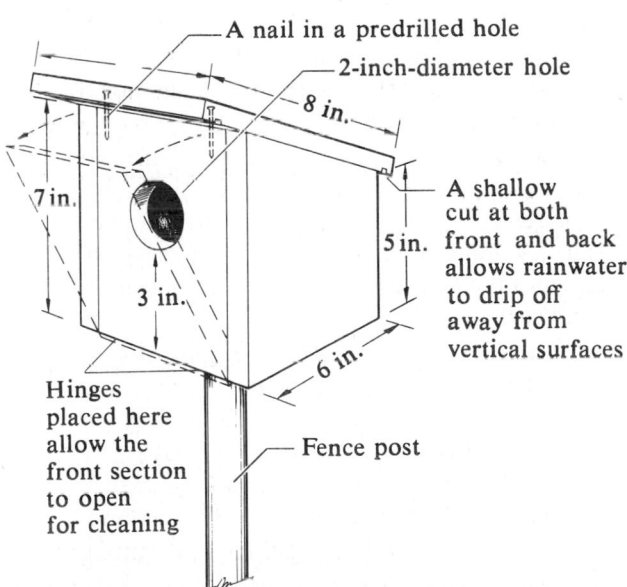

Attracted by the garden insects, eastern bluebirds will nest in the hollows of nearby trees or in homemade birdhouses nailed to fence posts.

estal-type bath is best. Otherwise, a naturalistic bath can be made by scraping a depression in the ground and lining it with concrete. The gleam and sound of dripping water will attract more birds. A hose can be suspended from overhead tree branches and turned on just enough to provide a slow, steady drip, or a bucket with a pinhole in the bottom can be hung over the bath. Make the hole very small initially; it can always be enlarged if desired. The bucket can be camouflaged with bark, and it should be covered to prevent debris and birds from falling in. During warm weather, a popular bath may need a daily refilling and a weekly scrubbing with a stiff brush to remove algae. It can be interesting to watch the elaborate preening ritual birds go through after bathing. Keep them in view while they do this by placing a few dead branches near the bath for them to perch on.

Great migrations of birds to and from their breeding grounds take place in spring and fall. The well-planted bird garden can be a welcome resting and feeding place for tired migrants during these seasons, and the sedentary gardener busy with his own seasonal routines can sense the wonder of this continent-spanning flow of life as he watches them come and go. Many northern birds looking for a good place to spend the winter appear in fall. These winter visitors together with the resident birds can make the garden a lively place all season if food is provided to keep them around. Feeder-watching can be one of the greatest pleasures of dreary winter days, and it is a good way of becoming familiar with birds. The lure of a reliable food source overcomes their instinctive wariness and brings them out in the open where they can be easily seen. The birds may become dependent on the feeder once natural food sources are used up, so if you start feeding, don't stop until winter is over. Any of the commercial wild bird feed mixes or fine cracked corn and sunflower seed will satisfy the seed eaters. Suet and peanut butter will attract additional species.

See also WILDLIFE, WINDBREAK.

BIRD'S-FOOT TREFOIL
(*Lotus corniculatus*)

Bird's-foot trefoil is a long-lasting pasture legume for the Midwest and the North. Like alsike clover, it will stand poorly drained soils and tolerate soil pH levels too low for alfalfa or sweet clover, but it prefers good soils. With good harvest and storage practices, bird's-foot trefoil makes excellent silage. It's also a good legume to use when renovating permanent grass pastures. In comparing bird's-foot trefoil/ Kentucky bluegrass pastures with grass or grass fertilized with nitrogen, most studies show higher animal production on trefoil/grass pastures and suggest it is more profitable to renovate pastures and establish bird's-foot trefoil than to invest in yearly applications of nitrogen on established grasses.

BIRD'S-NEST WEED
See QUEEN-ANNE'S-LACE

BITTER NIGHTSHADE
See BITTERSWEET

BITTERSWEET
(*Celastrus scandens*)

An ornamental vine or climbing shrub with attractive foliage and brightly colored fall fruit, bittersweet is excellent for walls, trellises or arbors. Bittersweet grows well in either shady or sunny locations, and in ordinary garden soil. It often reaches a height of 20 feet. Hardy throughout practically all of the United States, it can be propagated by root cuttings, layers or seed.

Another plant that is called bittersweet is *Solanum Dulcamara*. This is a vinelike herb, growing up to 15 feet, with poisonous scarlet fruit. It is sometimes known as climbing or bitter nightshade.

BLACKBERRY   (*Rubus*)

A very valuable member of the Rose family, blackberries grow in just about every region of the United States. In addition to its hardiness, the plant will usually do well in ordinary soil, but thrives in clay loam that is moist yet well drained.

Blackberries prefer soil that is enriched with humus. Leaves, weeds, straw, and healthy prunings from the brambles themselves work well. A continuous mulching may save the gardener the time usually dedicated to watering and weeding.

Blackberries propagate by means of suckers that arise from the underground root system. Plant the suckers in early spring two feet apart in rows spaced three feet apart. A four- to five-inch length of sucker planted in late spring will bear fruit the following year.

For large-scale propagation, root cuttings of three to four inches are preferable. Place them in sand in a cold frame over the winter, and plant them in the garden row the following spring.

New canes obtained from the nursery should be planted in the late spring or early fall. Fall plantings should be protected from frosts by a good covering of hay or leaves. Before planting, be sure to cut back the long canes.

Blackberries are great ramblers and will run rampant over a yard or meadow if not pruned properly. After harvest, the canes that have just borne and spindly new ones should be cut out. Pinched back canes usually produce strong lateral branches and do not yield to the strong winds of the winter. Canes should be pinched back in the winter before the weather becomes inclement. Spring pruning is also necessary. Cut back the laterals about

Blackberries should not be harvested until they are very dark, sweet and soft.

half the length to keep the plant in a close growth.

Berries are not ready to be plucked from the vine when they first turn black. Wait until bees start to swarm about them—a sign that the fruit is sweet and ripe and ready to eat. When fully ripe, the core of the berries is soft and almost undetectable.

Varieties: Of the bush blackberries, Darrow and Ranger are best for planting in the North. Eldorado is another variety frequently found in the colder northern climes. Early Harvest and Snyder are most often found in the Midwest. The South boasts prolific growths of Humble and Lawton. Alfred is recommended for the coldest northern states, with Raven the favorite in the middle states. Thornless and Smoothstem are two new varieties which are hardy and ouchless.

The Northwest grows trailing blackberries of the Evergreen and Himalaya varieties. Although not as hardy in winter as bush blackberries, Cascade, Brainerd, Chehalem, Marion, and Olallie are other favorites of the trailing type. Bush and trailing varieties were crossed to make Jerseyblack, an East Coast cultivar, and McDonald, usually found in Texas.

A healthy patch of blackberries produces on the average of six to eight good crops, and poorer ones afterward. The chief causes of running out are the virus diseases such as mosaic, blue stem, etc.; winterkilling in severe weather, sometimes drought; and finally, lack of proper cultural conditions in growing the plants. Most of these shortening factors can be averted or diminished by giving full attention to the plant. Blackberries, like red raspberries, may produce well for 20 years, but the average over the country seems to be ten to 12 years. Loganberries are shorter-lived than blackberries and dewberry plantings often last for 15 years and are productive all the while. In general, blackberries are the most productive bramble fruits, followed by black raspberries and red raspberries. But in all cases, good care is the most essential thing, along with the free use of compost and mulches to maintain the organic content of the soil.

Insects and Diseases: Crown borers and the red-necked cane borer are the chief pests that attack blackberries. The cane borer is infamous for cigar-shaped swellings on the canes near the base. Prune off damaged canes and burn them when you prune in the early spring. The crown borer is detectable only by observing the old canes pruned out in the spring. If the canes appear hollow at ground level, the crown borer has more than likely made a visit. It is difficult to control but fortunately rarely reaches harmful population growth.

To control orange rust, noticeable by the orange spores that appear on leaves, burn out the plants—roots and all. Double-blossom, which produces reddish, spongy buds and double flowers, should be treated in the same way.

See also BRAMBLE FRUITS.

BLACK GRAM   *See* URD

BLACK NIGHTSHADE
(*Solanum nigrum*)

An annual herb that belongs to the Potato family, black or deadly nightshade is one of the more villainous "pest plants." In July and August it produces poisonous green berries that when eaten cause paralysis and narcosis. If such poisoning is suspected and a physician is not immediately available, an emetic (anything which causes vomiting) should be given. These plants have wavy white flowers, and green berries that turn a dull, purple black as they ripen. They are found in waste areas, fields, yards, campgrounds, or open woods. Nightshade is best controlled by pulling out the roots or hoeing.

BLACK RASPBERRY
See BRAMBLE FRUITS

BLACK ROT   *See* DISEASE

BLACK WALNUT   *See* WALNUT

BLACK WIDOW SPIDER

This feared female is so-called because of her shining black body and her habit of devouring her mate. Her bite (the males are harmless) is rarely fatal to humans but causes terrific pain and violent illness. As with other animals, the widow population rises and falls in cycles. In peak years, town dumps, stone fences, woodpiles, and cluttered yards, garages and cellars may be crowded with them. Watch for a spider with a ½-inch-long shiny black body and a red hourglass-shaped mark on the underside of the abdomen.

The widow, however, is more fearing than to be feared. She is extremely timid and will only bite if irritated, as when pinched or pressed in a fold of clothing. Black widows are nocturnal in habit, but don't move around much, so there is little danger of being bitten in bed. The best way to get rid of them is to seek them out at night with a flashlight and a fly swatter. Better yet, keep the house and yard neat and free of all rubbish and clutter.

BLADDERWORT
See CARNIVOROUS PLANTS, UTRICULARIA

BLANCHING

The whitening or bleaching of various green vegetables is known as blanching. Some vegetables, celery and asparagus for example, are blanched for largely cosmetic reasons; others, like endive and cauliflower, are blanched to alter the taste or to slow down development. Inasmuch as the plant's chlorophyll content is what gives it the green color, blanching usually lowers the vegetable's food value.

To achieve a blanched effect, light must be excluded from the plants for a certain period just before ripening. This is usually done by piling up earth around them, by shading them with boards or by tying certain parts of the plant closely together.

See also entries for individual vegetables, FREEZING FOOD.

BLANKET FLOWER   (*Gaillardia*)

The cheerful colors, long stiff stems and excellent keeping quality of these red and yellow annuals and perennials make them good flowers for cutting. Blanket flowers range in height from one to three feet.

Requiring only light, friable soil and full sun, the blanket flower will volunteer annually and produce abundant flowers persistently, even on the light sands of the seashore. Primarily summer bloomers, they can be propagated by division in spring or fall, and all gaillardia can be grown very easily from seed.

G. grandiflora is a hardy perennial growing two to three feet high. Burgundy, 30 inches tall, bears wine red flowers. Goblin is a dwarf form growing to only 12 inches and bearing yellow-bordered red flowers all summer. Perennial forms grown from seed will flower the first year if seed is started early indoors.

BLAZING-STAR   *See* TRITONIA

BLEEDING

When tree limbs are pruned or wounded, the exudation of sap is known as bleeding. Ordinarily, this has no harmful effect on the tree, except in very severe cases. Maples and birches bleed profusely if pruned in spring, and should be trimmed at another time.

See also PRUNING, TREE.

BLEEDING-HEART   (*Dicentra*)

This perennial does well in average soil under part shady or sunny conditions. The American native fringed bleeding-heart (*D. eximia*), a fine rock garden plant, blooms from April to May, requiring no particular care other than watering during dry periods. *D. spectabilis* is known for its slightly larger spring flowers.

Bleeding-heart is propagated by seed, cuttings or division of the rhizomes, and is grown in any moist, shady location.

It grows from one to two feet tall. Both species have rose pink, heart-shaped flowers and finely cut foliage.

Propagation is by seed or division of clumps in spring. Transplanting can be done even when plants are in full flower.

Most *Dicentra* species do well in open borders or in rock gardens.

See also DICENTRA.

BLIGHT

The term blight is used to refer to a great number of plant diseases—usually diseases affecting a number of plants in one area, rather than isolated cases. Most blights are caused by pathogenic organisms, and are manifested by browning of foliage and reduced vigor or death of the plant.

See also DISEASE.

BLISTER BEETLE

This is a large, elongated beetle, gray or striped, that also goes by the name old-fashioned potato bug and Yankee bug. The beetles typically feed in colonies on the blossoms and foliage of a number of garden, field and ornamental plants. Control by handpicking, but wear gloves to protect your skin against the caustic fluid the beetles give off for defense.

See also INSECT CONTROL.

BLOOD, DRIED

Dried blood is a by-product of slaughterhouses that is collected, dried and ground to powder or meal. Much goes into animal feeds, only a small proportion being sold as fertilizer. For the home gardener, dried blood is an excellent source of quickly available nitrogen, which amounts to 12 to 15 percent of the material by weight. It should be used carefully around plants which might overgrow or produce excess foliage at the expense of fruit or root growth, such as tomatoes. It is an excellent side dressing for quick-growing lettuce and greens plants and for corn. Dried blood has a pungent odor that attracts dogs and carnivorous wild creatures, so it must always be dug or tilled into the soil immediately after application. Dried blood also contains approximately 1.3 percent phosphorus and less than 1 percent potash.

Sources for dried blood products are the mail-order houses, fertilizer plants and feed stores.

See also FERTILIZER.

BLOODROOT   *See* TETTERWORT

BLUEBELLS   *See* MERTENSIA

BLUEBELLS-OF-SCOTLAND
    See CAMPANULA

BLUEBERRY   (*Vaccinium*)

This popular insect-resistant shrub, growing six to ten feet high, bears plenty of fine-tasting fruit and adds beauty to the home when used as an informal hedge.

Soil: The cultivated blueberry is still

Blueberries are self-sterile and will yield best if two or more varieties are grown together.

close enough to its wild ancestors to be appreciative only of natural, organic fertilizers. They like humus and soft, woodsy soil so much that it is almost a question of growing them organically or not growing them at all.

In nature the blueberry plant displays its blossoms and tasty fruit in the seldom-frequented spots of forest and wilderness whose soil is covered with a rich blanket of decaying vegetation. It grows wild among the redwoods of California, on forest hillsides in New England and on the broad crests of the Appalachian ridges.

Soil should be of a pH from 5 to 5.6, which is quite acid. A liberal amount of peaty material is needed; a mulch of peat is fine. If additional acid is needed, use peat or compost made without lime to give the right acidity. The peat should be dug into the earth, and well intermixed with it. *See also* ACIDITY–ALKALINITY.

Despite the need for moisture, blueberries require good drainage. Water should not stand on the surface. If needed to keep the water condition right, dig an open ditch or install tile drains. Cool, moist, acid conditions are needed in the soil for the best growth of roots to support the plants.

Planting: Upon arrival of plants (rooted shrubs) for setting out, it is urgent that the roots be protected from drying. Cover them at once with soil or burlap—if unpacked. Do not expose the roots to the drying effects of sun or wind. Put the plants in a cool moist cellar or in the shade till set. Dig the hole large enough to receive roots without bending or cramping them. When the subsoil is very hard, break it up at the bottom of the hole, using a pick or crowbar if necessary. Set the plants slightly deeper than they stood in the nursery and spread all roots out naturally. Place good surface soil next to the roots and work it in with the hands. When the hole is half-filled, tamp the soil firmly. Fill the hole and tamp the soil harder. Leave loose soil on top or cover with mulch. Leave a saucerlike depression at the top to catch water. If manure is used, it should be well rotted and worked into and mixed with the soil. Manure can be used on top for a mulch. Never put fresh or unrotted manure next to the roots. It may heat or dry out and hurt the roots.

Careful planting is important and should never be hastily done. In all cases, pack the soil firmly about the roots and use moist soil for the purpose. Young plants, usually eight to 15 inches high, should be planted in early spring or late fall. Space them about five feet apart, with the rows about seven feet apart. Ten- to 15-year-old bushes usually yield about 14 quarts of berries.

Blueberries are not self-pollinating, so more than one variety should be planted. Since each of the common varieties has slightly different characteristics, it is good home-garden practice to plant a selection of different types. They ripen at different times and vary slightly in flavor.

For good pollination, encourage and protect bees wherever possible.

Preferred varieties in the two chief areas of highbush blueberry production are as follows:

Michigan–*Early:* Earliblue; *Midseason:* Blue Ray, Bluecrop; *Late:* Jersey, Coville.

New Jersey–*Early:* Earliblue, Blue Ray, Ivanhoe; *Midseason:* Bluecrop, Berkeley; *Late:* Herbert, Darrow.

Some of the older varieties like Concord, Rancocas, Weymouth, and Stanley do well in the northern and middle Atlantic states, though they usually produce smaller berries than the varieties listed above.

Pruning: In the wild, blueberry plants are pruned by the "burning over" process on the managed areas; the old stems are burned out. But in the garden the pruning shears need to be used after four or five years from set. Varieties vary greatly in growing habits. Some of the more open and flat-topped ones like Cabot, Herbert and Pioneer need very little pruning. The upright and close-growing varieties (Weymouth, Rubel and Rancocas), on the other hand, need considerable opening to prevent them from becoming too thick and bushy. A little attention to the natural degree of openness will suggest what thinning-out to do—if any is needed. It is well to compare and contrast different modes of growth before starting the pruning.

There are two types of growth to cut out in pruning—the very slender stems which may not bear much, and the oldest and largest that have borne several years and may not bear much more, except at the tips. It is well to keep the clumps fairly open to avoid crowding and shading. More than one foot asunder for all stems is too open; less than four inches is too close.

Problems: It is important to suppress all weeds. This is best done by the liberal application of acid mulches each year—peat and oak leaves are better than sawdust or pine needles. Compost is helpful. Woodland soil is often suitable for the plants.

Insect damage to blueberries is confined primarily to the blueberry fruit fly, whose eggs hatch into maggots inside the ripening berry, and the cherry fruitworm, a small red worm whose damage is usually confined to large commercial plantings. Best control of the fruit fly is rotenone dust, 25 pounds to the acre, applied five times between June and the end of harvest. Shallow cultivation also helps by exposing larvae to predator ants and birds.

The most troublesome blueberry disease is the mummy berry, which causes berries to rot and fall off. Control by collecting old mummies off the ground or turning them under when cultivating.

BLUEBONNET
See BACHELOR'S-BUTTON

BLUE-EYED GRASS
See SISYRINCHIUM

BLUEGRASS   *See* LAWN

BLUE GUM TREE
See EUCALYPTUS

BLUETS   *See* QUAKER-LADIES

BOG-ROSEMARY   *See* ANDROMEDA

BOK-CHOY   *See* CHINESE CABBAGE

BOLTONIA

Also known as false chamomile, false starwort or thousand-flowered aster, these attractive perennials of the Composite family are often grown in borders or in groups. Two native varieties—*B. asteroides* var. *decurrens* and var. *latisquama*—are both tall (five to eight feet), with small flower heads ranging from white to blue to purple. They bloom in late summer and early fall. Boltonias are very easy to raise in full sun and ordinary garden soil. Propagation is by division in spring or fall.

BONE MEAL

Rich in phosphorus and nitrogen, bones have been used for centuries as a fertilizer.

In the early days of farming in this country, great amounts of buffalo bones were collected on western plains for use as fertilizer. Now the main source of bone meal comes from slaughterhouses. Consisting mostly of calcium phosphate, the phosphorous and nitrogen content in bone fertilizers depends mainly on the kind and age of the bone. Young bones generally contain less phosphorus and more nitrogen than older bones. The percentage of fluorine in older bones is considerably higher than in younger bones.

Raw bone meal generally contains between 2 to 4 percent nitrogen and 15 to 25 percent phosphorus (P_2O_5). Because of the fatty materials found in raw bone meal, decomposition is somewhat delayed when it is applied to the soil.

Steamed bone meal is the most common of the bone meal fertilizers sold. This type is made from green bones that have been boiled or steamed at high pressure to remove the fats. Its removal causes a slight loss in nitrogen content, but a relative increase in phosphorus. When the bones are steamed, they can be ground more easily and are considered to be in better condition for the soil; steamed bone meal is almost always finer than raw bone meal. Steamed bone meal contains 1 to 2 percent nitrogen and up to 30 percent phosphorus.

Charred bone has a nitrogen content of about 1.5 percent, a phosphorous content over

30 percent and many trace elements.

Best results for bone meal are obtained when it is applied in conjunction with other organic materials. Its effectiveness is increased because of its nitrogen content. In general, bone meal acts more quickly when applied to well-aerated soils. Because of its lime content, bone meal tends to reduce soil acidity. Because of expense, it is best used on compost piles, on small gardens and around shrubs.

See also PHOSPHATE ROCK, PHOSPHORUS.

BONESET   (*Eupatorium perfoliatum*)

Boneset is a rather long-lived hardy perennial plant commonly found in low grounds throughout the eastern half of the United States. The dried leaves and flowering tops are used in medicine.

Growing to three or four feet tall with small clusters of white flowers, boneset is best taken from the root clump of a wild plant in the fall. Set the divisions a foot apart and mulch lightly for winter protection.

Plants can also be grown from seed, collected as soon as ripe, and sown in shallow drills about eight inches apart in a moist, rich seedbed, preferably in partial shade. When of sufficient size the seedlings are set in the field spaced about the same as the divided clumps.

The plants are cut when in full bloom late in summer, and the leaves and flowering tops are stripped from the stems by hand and carefully dried without exposure to the sun. Yields of 2,000 pounds or more per acre of the leaves and tops of cultivated boneset can be obtained under favorable conditions.

See also HERB.

BONSAI

This is a centuries-old method of tree dwarfing developed by the Chinese, that is fast becoming a popular hobby in the Western world. In short, it permits you to grow a tree in a flower bowl.

Bonsai isn't a difficult art. What it requires even more than skill is patience, since a fully mature specimen may take ten years or longer to produce.

Some plants are especially well adapted to bonsai dwarfing. Among these are juniper, Japanese maple, cypress, Mugho pine, and cryptomeria. In general, evergreens need less feeding, pruning and training, but deciduous varieties are sturdier and take shape faster. Deciduous kinds also show the change of seasons; their leaves turn color in the fall and, artistically trained, their bare winter form is as lovely as when they are full leaved in the summer. (One caution: use small-leaved types because the foliage is not reduced in proportion to the trunk.)

In any case, whether you choose to grow a biblical cedar-of-Lebanon, a colorful fire thorn shrub or anything from an elm or pomegranate to a yew or even a giant sequoia (scale: 1 inch to 25 feet), the method is the same.

You can start with cuttings or by layering, but experienced growers usually recommend seeds. You may be able to get very tiny seedlings from some nurseries, or dig them up while on a tramp through the woods. A flat of sandy loam is best for starting seeds. Keep them outdoors if possible, sheltered from hot sun and wind.

All seedlings should be transplanted when one year old. Use an organic soil mixture of

40 percent loam and 50 percent sand for ever-greens and 70 percent loam and 20 percent sand for deciduous plants. All mixtures should contain 10 percent leaf mold. Use two-inch pots, with a bit of moss at the bottom to prevent clogging of the drainage hole.

Before potting, gently peel the dirt from the roots—the Chinese use chopsticks for this —and cut back the taproot about one-third with sharp scissors or pruning shears. Remove all old, dead parts of roots.

Do this operation quickly, in a cool room; a damp basement is excellent.

After transplanting, keep the plants indoors for several days, then gradually expose them to outdoor conditions. Thereafter, any roots that push through the bottom of the pot should always be cut away. You can also start pruning the tops lightly at this time, to develop a pleasing shape.

After this, your evergreens will require transplanting every three to five years, broad-leaf trees every two and flowering and fruiting plants yearly. Spring is the best time for each successive transplanting. Use only a slightly larger pot each time; any container with drainage holes is suitable.

Always make up a fresh soil mixture, and prune the roots fairly vigorously. Cut back the side roots irregularly and thin out the smaller roots to encourage the forming of a dense system.

Evergeens need little branch pruning, but deciduous trees, shrubs and vines should be pinched back to two or three buds on the previous year's growth. Always transplant and prune *spring-flowering* plants immediately *after* bloom has faded.

Culture: Most bonsai experts use strictly organic fertilizers. You will probably have to work out your own fertilizing program to fit the needs of your specific plants. Most Chinese and Japanese growers advise very dilute applications of liquid fish fertilizer monthly or perhaps more often, except when the plant is dormant. But others say feeding only three or four times a year is plenty. Excessive feeding will result in too vigorous growth, and you'll have a pot-splitting giant instead of an elegant dwarf.

If a tree looks weak, a sprinkling of ⅛ teaspoon of high-nitrogen dried blood will perk it up. For regular feedings, very weak manure tea is as good as fish fertilizer. Occasional light sprinklings of manure compost are also excellent. Just enough fertilizer to keep the tree looking healthy is all that is necessary.

Water only when the soil feels dry to the touch, and don't overwater. The soil should never be either bone-dry or waterlogged. In dry, hot weather, you may have to water two or more times a day. (Some Oriental growers, incidentally, use extremely porous soil and water five or six times daily, on the theory that starving the plant by leaching out fertility elements makes for slower, more compact growth.) Syringe the foliage now and then to remove dust and soot.

Bonsai do best outdoors, although many people have had fine success raising them entirely on sunny windowsills. They need abundant light, with some protection from the hot afternoon sun. Exposure to the elements makes the strongest trees, so let them spend as much time outdoors as possible—they provide a beautiful focus of interest for a patio, balcony or walled garden. You can, however, bring them indoors for a few days at a time if you put them in a cool spot away from heat sources.

Semihardy plants should be wintered in a greenhouse, cold frame or basement. An unheated garage or lath shelter covered with burlap or tarpaulins is also satisfactory except in the coldest weather. Hardy varieties can be kept outdoors all year.

Shaping: When your trees are about four years old, start shaping them. Some look best gnarled and twisted, others stately and dignified —pattern your dwarfs' shapes after those of their prototypes in the wild. Bend the trunks and branches in natural curves, winding copper wire around them to hold the new shape. This wire must be removed in a year or so, before it can scar or strangle the tree. This is a good time, too, to thin out excessive growth, cutting on a point just above the joint.

For added interest, when your trees are growing older, you can make a complete little garden in their bowls by mulching with smooth pebbles or granite chips, and decorating with moss, small rocks or shells and figurines.

Although bonsai grow best outdoors, they need not be planted in the garden bed. Here, a striking dish garden has been made with a juniper bonsai, sedum and baby's tears.

BORAGE   (*Borago officinalis*)

Borage is a hardy annual herb, whose long flowering season makes it especially attractive to honeybees. It grows to two feet and has white woolly leaves and clusters of blue flowers.

The herb borage bears clusters of attractive blue flowers throughout the growing season.

Borage is cultivated as a potherb in Europe, the leaves tasting like cucumbers and being most palatable when young.

Plants do best in dry, sunny places. Propagation is by seed, though borage self-sows readily.

See also HERB.

BORDER

This term generally refers to a long and narrow strip in the garden, sometimes between properties, often along front walks. The actual form that the border takes depends on the general contour of the land, the architecture of the house and its proximity to the garden, walk and driveway.

Borders may be of straight or curving lines, following the boundaries of the property or the enclosures of lawns and open spaces. The planting of a general border may consist of shrubs only or a combination of shrubs and hardy flowers; or it may combine annuals and perennials. Since shaded borders are more difficult to plant if flowers are desired, the border should be located to receive several hours of sunlight a day.

The soil should be prepared on the assumption that the majority of the plants, except those which need dividing, are to remain there for a number of years without removal. In choosing plants consider carefully their cultural requirements, and then place them accordingly.

After the soil is in good general condition, bury a liberal supply of well-decayed manure to a depth of at least 18 inches. This encourages the roots to penetrate deeply—a protective measure in times of drought. Prepare the soil in the fall and let it settle over the winter. Spring planting is preferred to fall planting, in most cases. Heaving of new plants often results when they are set out in autumn, as they have no time to make new roots to anchor themselves in the ground securely before frost.

For plants that have special soil preferences, arrange a pocket in which to place the plant. This allows plants of different soil requirements to be grown as companion plants.

The distance at which plants are placed is dependent upon their habit of growth. Some of the stronger ones need as much as three or four feet—dahlias are a good example. Mat plants, such as dwarf phlox and pinks, are placed only a few inches from each other.

Crowded plants can neither be cultivated properly nor produce good flowers. The border may look skimpy the first year, but this is easily remedied by placing annuals between.

After they reach maturity, many of the plants will need staking to prevent their being toppled over by heavy winds. Provide supports that are as inconspicuous as possible and place them in such a manner that subsequent growth will cover them.

Division of the clumps will help to keep strong plants from encroaching upon their less vigorous neighbors. Some kinds will need replanting. If the shoots in the center of the plant become weak and spindly with yellowish leaves, this means they have used up the available plant food in the soil. When you reset such plants, place well-rotted manure or a balanced fertilizer in the soil.

After the border is established, proper care includes keeping down weeds, maintaining a surface mulch to conserve moisture, thinning out plants and young seedlings, providing support for top-heavy plants, watching for and destroying insects or diseases, and fertilizing and replanting the rampant growers.

Winter protection, after decaying stems and leaves are removed from the perennials, will prevent heavy losses. Partly decayed manure, two or three inches thick, will not only protect the plants from loss of moisture but will also provide a source of nourishment. Hay or cornstalks are excellent mulching materials as well. Inasmuch as you are covering the plants, not to keep them warm but to maintain even conditions around them in periods of freezes and thaws, do not cover them too early. Wait until winter has earnestly set in.

Plan your border on paper first. In this way you can get a good idea of what it will look like. Rough out approximately the amount of space given to each plant group and fill in its color with watercolors. Large plants should be figured as about three or four to a group, and of the small ones, not less than a dozen. If the border is small, try to stick to one or two dominating colors. Irregular silhouettes, rather than straight ones, are always preferable. To avoid the monotony a regular slope from front to back is apt to provide, plants of different heights should be placed near each other. Medium-sized plants can be brought toward the front of the border to form little coves in which smaller plants may be grouped and trellises, walls and shrubbery can be added for special effects.

Perennials which require several years to bloom from seed: monkshood, wild indigo, Christmas rose, peonies, and globeflower.

Perennials which bloom the first year from seed: hollyhocks, chamomile, Chinese larkspur, pinks, sweet Williams, and forget-me-nots.

Perennials to grow in the shade: monkshood, lily-of-the-valley, bleeding-heart, plantain lily, trilliums, anemones (Japanese), wild flowers, bee balm, bugloss, foxgloves, pansies, and bluebells.

Perennials with evergreen leaves: candytuft, coralbells, flax, thyme, sedums of many kinds, and yucca.

Perennials for dry soils: butterfly weed, columbine, blanket flower, cranesbill, and stonecrop.

Dwarf Borders: This group includes edgings for perennial borders, though the plants themselves may be perennials or annuals.

For a warm, sunny border, dianthus, or garden pinks, have long been a favorite in gardens. Most of them have fragrant single or double flowers and the tufty green foliage is attractive when the plants are not in flower.

In recent years many new varieties have been added to the list. *Dianthus alpinus* cv. 'Allwoodii' grows from four to six inches high and makes a compact plant. It thrives in good garden soil that has free drainage and flowers the first year from seed if sown in a greenhouse in late winter.

Candytufts are good plants for finishing off a border of mixed perennials or a group of low-growing shrubs. *Iberis sempervirens* is covered with white flowers in spring, completely hiding the dark evergreen foliage. Little Gem begins to flower in May or June, depending on the climate. Its neat habit of growth makes it valuable as an edging plant. Snowflake has flowers three times as large as *I. sempervirens.* Candytufts do best with a few hours of morning sun and a moderate amount of water. Cultivate the ground around them frequently.

A fine plant of neat habit with white flowers and rich green foliage is *Arenaria montana.* A sunny place in the garden and rather gritty soil that offers free drainage suit it very well.

The various fragrant thymes make a nice informal edging to a border that has a flagstone path along the planting. Encourage the plants to encroach on the flagstones in a natural, irregular way; this gives an artistic effect and offers a change from the well-trimmed edging. From the Azores comes *Thymus Serpyllum,* growing four inches high and covered with purple flowers in early summer. Lemon thyme is a small plant of bushy habit. *T. Serpyllum* var. *albus* forms a neat green mat only four inches high. During the summer the plants are covered with lovely white flowers.

For borders that are in light shade during the hottest hours of the day, use dwarf campanulas. They like a rich, well-drained sandy soil. Space them eight to ten inches apart.

Carpathian harebell is a neat plant, growing six to eight inches high, and has clear blue flowers that are carried well above the foliage. There is also a white variety of this plant. Cullinmore is a hybrid form with blue flowers.

Violas and pansies are popular as edging plants. They thrive in deeply dug, rich loam with plenty of compost worked into the soil. They flower for a long time in climates where the winter is mild. If planted in the early part of October, when buds have formed, they will flower during the winter and spring until May. Top-dress the ground with old manure in January and March to have the largest flowers.

Hybrid gazanias make a strong edging for a border in a warm, sunny position. These plants flower the first year from seed if sown in winter in a greenhouse. Colors vary from white

A low-growing annual that blooms continuously throughout the summer, ageratum is an excellent, attractive edging plant.

to yellow, amber, pink, and various shades of red. Gazanias require very little water and are particularly drought resistant.

Ageratums are annuals that flower over a long season. Midget Blue, four inches high, has azure blue flowers, and Blue Perfection has dark violet ones. The annual alyssums, Carpet of Snow and Little Gem, are also excellent border plants.

Phlox Drummondii is an annual easily grown from seed. Since phlox seeds sown in a flat and then transplanted to the garden do not make vigorous plants, they should be sown directly into the bed. Phlox require a sunny position in good, rich soil.

Portulaca is another annual that does well in full sun. Its seeds are sown directly in the ground and the seedlings thinned if too many come up. The varicolored flowers are either single or double.

When any of these plants needs feeding, use manure or compost tea once every two weeks during the growing season. This will build up the plants and produce larger, more numerous flowers.

See also ANNUALS, BEDDING.

BORECOLE   *See* KALE

BORERS

Borers are the larvae of many insect species that damage plants by tunneling through stems and trunks. A borer attack may be signaled by sawdustlike material at the pest's entrance hole, or by local wilting of the plant.

Generally, borers are less inclined to attack healthy, vigorously growing plants. The pests can be controlled by pruning and burning weakened, wilting branches. Tree borers can sometimes be fished out of shallow holes with a wire. Flower stems and berry canes can be slit open with a knife, the borer plucked out, and the operation sealed by binding with string.

See also BRAMBLE FRUITS, INSECT CONTROL.

BORON

Boron, though required by plants only in small amounts, is absolutely vital to plant health. It is the archetypal trace element.

Scientific experiments have demonstrated that boron plays a part in 15 different plant functions, including cell division, nitrogen and carbohydrate metabolism, flowering, and fruiting. A deficiency of boron in the soil causes such degenerative diseases as internal cork in apples, yellow of alfalfa, top rot of tobacco, cracked stem of celery, and heart rot and girdle of beets.

Soils rich in organic matter seldom are boron-deficient, indeed few soils are boron-deficient. But too much calcium in the soil can depress boron availability. Maintaining a high level of organic matter is the best method to assure the availability of boron and most other trace elements.

In a pinch household borax can be used to supply boron, if a boron deficiency is *definitely* diagnosed by a thorough soil test. Use no more than four or five ounces per 1,000 square feet of garden. Too much is just as bad as not enough.

See also SOIL DEFICIENCIES, TRACE ELEMENTS.

BOSTON FERN   *See* FERN

BOTANICAL NOMENCLATURE

In this encyclopedia, the standard binomial—two-word—system is used to classify and name plants according to the characteristics they share with other plants. All members of the vegetable kingdom, except for mosses, liverworts, fungi, and certain other primitive plants, are grouped in one of two major sections, Pteridophyta, which reproduce by spores, and Spermatophyta, which produce seeds. With the exception of ferns, most garden plants are spermatophytes. They are further classified as gymnosperms which bear cones or angiosperms which flower and produce coated seeds. The angiosperm class, in turn, is divided into subclasses which are divided into orders.

The main units of practical concern to the gardener are family, genus and species. The family name can be recognized by the ending *ceae* and refers to a group of plants sharing certain flowering or fruiting traits. There are many families in each order and each one is composed of one or more genera. Nearly all genera are then composed of several species. Genus and species names are the working units of botanists. In this book, they usually appear right at the beginning of an entry, immediately after the key word. The genus name is capitalized. The species name may or may not be capitalized but both words, being Latin, are italicized. The species name is usually a descriptive term, indicating the plant's habitat or behavior or perhaps honoring the person who discovered it. Individuals of a common species resemble each other very closely. Where distinct differences exist, plants are further distinguished by a variety name and/or, if the plant has been specially bred for traits significant in horticulture, a cultivar name. Technically, a cultivar name is very different from a formal botanical term used for variety. But, for the purposes of this book, cultivars are distinguished from regular varieties only when the full specific epithet is formally listed. In these cases, cultivars are enclosed in single quotation marks.

Thus, onion is given the botanical name *Allium Cepa* and leek, *Allium Ampeloprasum* var. *porrum*. These vegetables are generically related but, since they possess different characteristics, they are differentiated at the level of the species. A particular onion might be more specifically named *A. Cepa* cv. 'Ebenezer' and another named *A. Cepa* cv. 'Sweet Spanish Hybrid'. A leek might be named *A. Ampeloprasum* var. *porrum* cv. 'Giant Flag'. If the complete botanical names are not given, these vegetables might simply be referred to as Sweet Spanish Hybrid onion or Giant Flag leek.

BOTTLE TREE   *See* PHOENIX TREE

BOUGAINVILLEA

These vines are natives of Brazil and South America and were introduced in the United States by a French navigator, de Bougainville. The flowers are small and inconspicuous, but they are surrounded by large and showy bracts which constitute the decorative value of the plants.

There are about a dozen species and varieties, and new ones are introduced from time to time. If possible, buy this vine when in flower in order to have the color that is wanted, for different plants of the same variety sometimes vary in the color of the bracts (colored leaves directly below the petals). Those listed as Crimson Lake (*B.* x *Buttiana*) may show lighter or darker coloring.

Planting: In planting bougainvilleas, make the hole twice as deep and wide as the container. In the bottom of the hole put fully a foot or more of well-decayed compost and mix some good soil with it. These vines are difficult to transplant; they have top growth out of all proportion to the small root system. The best method is to slit down the four sides of the five-gallon container and leave the plant in it; the slit sides will allow for plenty of drainage and the roots will not be disturbed. Cut away the rim of the container so it will not show above ground and place the can with the plant in it in the middle of the hole. Then fill in with good, rich soil. When the hole is almost filled in, have water from the hose run in gently until it settles the soil thoroughly. Add more soil and finish planting by making a well around the plant to hold water. After it is established and growing well, it will need only a moderate amount of water. Good drainage is very important, so eight or nine inches of gravel or cut stone should be placed in the bottom of the hole, if there is any doubt about the drainage being good.

Bougainvilleas are easily grown from cuttings which root in a few weeks. The cuttings may be six to eight inches long, and are placed in a flat of sand or a greenhouse bench in a temperature of 65 to 75°F. (18.33 to 23.89°C.).

Bougainvilleas are injured by heavy frosts, but after being cut back, come out again with renewed vigor. They need a sunny, warm place in the garden. These plants should be given a mulch of well-rotted manure or leaf mold.

Bougainvilleas can be grown successfully in greenhouses in the North. They grow well

Bougainvillea is sensitive to prolonged periods of frost and must be grown in greenhouses in the northern regions.

and bloom profusely during the winter months. They make an excellent wall cover in greenhouses which have one end abutted against a building.

They also do well pruned to bush form and grown in pots. A good potting soil for bougainvilleas consists of two parts loam to one part leaf mold, with sand added to increase friability. Water them regularly, never allowing the roots to dry out, and feed weekly with a very dilute solution of fish emulsion. Keep the growing tips pinched to induce bushiness, and

after the winter flowering period try cutting the plants back to 12 inches to encourage new growth.

Varieties: *B. spectabilis* is the hardiest of this genus—a rapid and robust grower. During the flowering season the vine is a mass of red purple. As companion vines, it should have those with light yellow or light blue flowers, for its color is so dominant that it does not blend well with many colors.

B. x *Buttiana* cv. 'Praetoria' has beautiful bronzy bracts with apricot shading. It grows best in frostless areas or near the seacoast.

There are a few vines that may be used to ideal advantage in covering a large wall space or a high wire fence. They may be trained up either side of windows to frame them in areas free from frost. They grow up and over tall trees and will cover the branches with warm, rich color. A tree that has died and was needed in that particular position as a screen may have one or more of these vines trained up through the branches to produce almost the same effect as the live tree. They make a fine covering for an arbor that is to be an outdoor living room during the summer months, and will climb to the roof of a garage, converting it into a spectacular mass of color. *B.* x *Buttiana* cv. 'Mrs. Butt' or cv. 'Crimson Lake' is excellent for this purpose. The large crimson bracts are particularly fine and the vine makes a vigorous growth. Golden Glow has rich golden yellow bracts fading to apricot—an unusual and beautiful combination of color.

BOW-STRING HEMP
See SANSEVIERIA

BOX   *See* BOXWOOD

BOXTHORN
See MATRIMONY VINE

BOXWOOD   (*Buxus*)

Boxwood, or box, is a broad-leaved ever-green valued as hedges and as trees. There are a great number of varieties, from dwarf shrubs to 20-foot trees. The dwarf type, *B. semper-virens* cv. 'Suffruticosa', is the best for edgings.

B. microphylla var. *japonica,* which grows to about six feet, and *B. m.* var. *koreana,* grow-ing to 18 inches, are the two hardiest box-woods. The larger variety can be propagated by cuttings from mature wood in early autumn or by layers, while the dwarf forms can be in-creased by division.

Boxwood will grow well in most well-drained soils, and does best under partial shade. Some form of winter protection is necessary in the North. Boxwood is such a slow grower, and mature plantings are so valuable, that the pains of care are well worth the effort.

When transplanting, always set the plants deeper than their previous ground level, making sure that the hole is deep and large. It is best to clip boxwood in late August or early fall. Give plants an annual dressing of organic fertilizer, such as compost or composted manure; boxwood will also benefit greatly from a mulch of similar materials so long as it is not deeper than 1½ inches.

Insects and Diseases: The chief enemies of boxwood, other than severe winters, are boxwood canker (a fungus disease) and spider mites, which cause a gray mottling of leaves. In spring, go over the plantings very carefully, pruning out all dead wood and brushing out dead leaves and other debris with a whisk broom. Then apply a dormant-oil spray. Check carefully through the season for signs of disease and prune out infected wood immediately.

BOYSENBERRY   (*Rubus ursinus*)

A highly productive, easily grown bramble fruit, the boysenberry is a California cultivar of the loganberry (*Rubus ursinus* var. *logano-baccus*). Its large, dark red to black fruit is good for jams and jellies, but less distinguished than red raspberries or blackberries when eaten fresh.

Because of its woody, wandering stem, the boysenberry usually needs the support of a fence or trellis. Set sturdy posts fully five feet tall, and string two wires between them, one at a three-, the other at a five-foot level. Canes which have borne fruit are cut down immedi-ately after the harvest. Canes grow eight to ten feet high.

The root area of the boysenberry should be heavily mulched before winter sets in. Un-like other brambles, the canes should be laid on the ground and covered with a light layer of straw before there is any probability of snow flying. In spite of their apparent strength they are sensitive bushes. Culture is similar to that required by the loganberry.

See also BRAMBLE FRUITS, LOGANBERRY.

BRAMBLE FRUITS   (*Rubus*)

These fruits are of American origin from wild species, having stems that are more or less prickly. Belonging to the Rose family, they are intermediate between an herb and a shrub; that is, the root is perennial but the stems die back nearly to the crown the second season of their life after maturing a single crop of fruit. There are, however, some exceptions to bearing, as in the case of the everbearing species, which bear terminally and continuously all summer. The cultivated brambles are prickly bushes bearing berries and include the species named below:

1. The American red raspberry— *Rubus idaeus* var. *strigosus.*

2. The European red raspberry— *R. idaeus.*

3. The sow-teat blackberry— *R. allegheniensis.*

4. The blackcap raspberry— *R. occidentalis.*

5. The American dewberry— *R. flagellaris.*

Also grown for their edible fruit are dewberry, wineberry, loganberry, and its variant, boysenberry.

The canes of the first three species grow upright throughout the season; the last two grow upright the first season but later droop down near the tip and may strike root.

The red raspberry is the most important species in this group, and is an especially desirable fruit for desserts, jams, drying, and deep freezing. It has become commercialized in cultivation all over the United States and in southern Canada. With due care in selecting for hardiness, or with winter protection, it can be grown as far north as any cultivated fruits.

Propagation of Brambles: It is important to know how and when to propagate the bramble fruits. One can perpetuate his own plants if familiar with methods and devices that can be easily understood and practiced. Moreover, it is interesting to propagate and sometimes economically important to do it. Here are a few suggestions.

Tip Layering: Several species are propagated by layering the tip of the plant in late summer. Among these plants are the black and purple raspberries, dewberries, loganberries, and trailing blackberries. A few of the red raspberries will tip layer. This work is usually done by hand in the fall when growth for the season is nearly completed. There are two important factors for good rooting. The soil should be light and moist but well drained and the plant nutrients, especially organic matter, should be abundant. If the land is not fertile there will be poor rootage and inferior plants. Layers from one-year-old plants are generally better than those from new ones. Under good conditions five or more layers may be obtained from each parent plant.

It is time to layer when the tip becomes slightly thickened and snakelike or rat-tailed, and grows without leaves. Late August and early September are the best times to tip layer. On good friable soil the tip will root of itself, but a little assistance will insure it, and more will set if slightly covered with soil or partially imbedded. Pegging down the tips or placing stones over them is unnecessary except on windy sites or where the surface soil may wash. Plants thus layered in early fall should have abundant roots and a strong bud before winter.

A larger percentage of stronger, new plants may be secured from root cuttings one inch long and started under glass with mild bottom heat. Such root cuttings are made in autumn, packed in sand in shallow boxes and stored for callousing in a cool cellar until February or March when they are planted in the propagating bed from which they are set out in the garden in due time.

Good plants can be secured by using a narrow spade or heavy trowel rather than by plowing a furrow for tip layering. In any case, if the soil is hard, it should be loosened so that the tip may readily strike root. Three or four inches of earth make a good covering. A vertical placement is better than horizontal for tip-layered rooting.

In setting out the rooted plants be sure the soil is fitted for them. It should be open, deep, friable, enriched with manure or compost, and kept in good tilth. Set the plants three or four feet apart in rows six or seven feet apart. Some of the larger-growing varieties should have an extra foot each way. Care should be taken in handling not to injure the bud at the crown as growth starts from this bud. Also take care that the layered plants do not dry out in planting. Keep them moist by preparing a good, composted soil before planting and by generous mulching.

In digging the tip—best done in spring after being attached to the parent plant all winter—use a four-pronged potato hook or fork. In separating the layer plants from the parent, leave six to eight inches on the tip; these stubs may serve as handles in handling the plants but they may be shortened to four inches after being planted. It is a good idea to discard any and all unhealthy or weak plants, using only the best that are well rooted. This results in more uniform plantings.

Suckering: Red raspberries and blackberries can be propagated by suckers that grow from underground stems or roots. These suckers appear in the spring and continue to form well into the season. One can get red raspberry plants by digging up the entire plant, or just the suckers. It is best to have separate plants for propagation and for production. The suckers may be set in permanent places or, what is better, grown in temporary beds where they may build up strong root systems before being set as permanent plants. Sucker plants generally do better if held over one year before permanent setting.

Allow blackberry suckers to come up until they are spaced about one per foot. If suckers are slow in coming, try bending a low cane over and burying a portion of it about six inches back from the tip. A Y-shaped stick placed upside down over the cane will hold the sucker under the dirt. When new roots have developed and the sucker is happily growing, cut it free from the mother plant.

Root Cuttings: Many blackberry growers prefer to propagate their plants by root cuttings. These should be three to four inches long and the size of a lead pencil. The cuttings are best made in the fall and are then stratified in moist sand, or buried outdoors in a well-drained location. When set out to grow in the spring they are placed horizontally in a trench covered with several inches of soil. Better growth is secured by setting the cuttings in a frame with bottom heat supplied with manure. After one year of growth in the frame they are set out in permanent places. Discard any weak plants at this time. It is urgent that the transplanting be done while the plants are dormant and before any growth starts. Good yields can only be secured when good foundation stock is used in the plantings. Look for good fibrous root systems.

Diseases and Pests: *Mosaic:* This is the most common disease afflicting raspberries. The leaves of the plant turn a mottled yellow brown, sometimes becoming puffy or warty. Downward curling of leaves is called *leaf curl.* New canes which turn bluish are afflicted with *streak.*

Nature plays many tricks on the gardener, one of them being the "Is it a virus or just a nutritional deficiency?" ploy. When raspberry leaves turn yellow, don't despair and burn your crop. Observe them for a while, and if they continue to decline, it's a safe bet they have mosaic. Poor drainage may be the problem, so check out all alternatives before giving up on berries.

Once a plant is infected, it touches all parts of the plant. No suckers or root cuttings can be used from the plant. The best precaution against the spread of the disease to other plants is to burn the infected plant, roots and all. This way, the spread of mosaic by aphids to other plants in your garden can be controlled.

It is always advisable to buy virus-free plants from reputable nurseries. The most resistant varieties are Latham and Taylor. Other varieties which are resistant to mosaic, but not necessarily to other virus diseases, are Sumner, Fall Red, Meeker, and Indian Summer.

Crown gall: This is recognized by the presence of galls or knots on the roots and sometimes on the canes and by symptoms on the foliage much like those of mosaic. Plants are weakened by the presence of this bacterium, which invades the tissues and causes the galls to form. As the gall decays, the germ lives for some time in rotted tissue in the soil and causes reinfection under favorable conditions, such as open wounds.

Control measures are confined to the planting of gall-free stock on gall-free land, together with absolute destruction of affected plants. Select only inspected, "certified" plants that are guaranteed to be virus-free. Do not replant berries on infested land. Choose a new plot and sterilize the soil and leave idle for three years.

Anthracnose: Also known as rust, cane spot, gray bark, and scab, anthracnose is the second most serious raspberry ailment. It may be found in all small gardens. The amount of damage or the losses incurred depend on the weather, general sanitary conditions and the location of the planting. Rust is recognized by small spots unevenly distributed on the stems which at first are red brown and which are less than ¼ inch in diameter.

Later these spots have white, slightly shrunken centers surrounded by a red ring. On the leaves may be seen small yellowish spots $\frac{1}{16}$ inch in diameter which turn red as they grow and elongate and possess a light coloring. Prolonged rains, crowded plants and dense shade favor the disease. The scars on the stems are scattered over the cane and seem more abundant on the young and succulent ones. Sometime in June small whitish spots $\frac{1}{16}$ inch across appear on the leaves. These leaf spots later turn red as they enlarge. The leaf lesions are somewhat similar to those on the canes.

While leaf infections do not usually cause serious damage, under certain conditions the leaf spurs may be defoliated. Anthracnose spots on the leaves may easily be confused with septoria leaf spot; but anthracnose spot is angular and light in color, whereas septoria spot is always circular and somewhat darker.

While heavy infection on young canes can stunt them seriously, ordinarily the cane infections are not harmful but are noticeable. If the lesions develop sufficiently, the affected canes may crack open during the winter and subsequently dry out and break off during their fruiting year. It is interesting and important to be able to detect rust and deal with it.

All the brambles are subject to anthracnose, and any or all of the aboveground parts of the plants may be attacked.

As with mosaic, anthracnose is best controlled by maintaining sanitary conditions. Old canes should be cut out as soon as they are finished bearing, and the row should be kept clean of weeds and excessive cane growth. Anthracnose has a better chance of flourishing where air passage is poor.

Among the black raspberries, Black Hawk, Dundee, Allen, and Bristol are resistant varieties; among the purples—Amethyst and Sodus; the reds—Cuthbert, Indian Summer, Latham, Newburgh, Boyne, Hilton, and Haida. Along with choosing resistant varieties, it is sound practice to buy only certified disease-free plants from reputable nurseries.

Borers: Wilting tips of raspberry stalks are symptoms of this insect trouble. The creatures are slender, cylindrical, long-horned beetles ⅔ inch in length which lay eggs in canes and cut two rings around the cane near the tip. The part above the girdled ring soon wilts, and later dies. The work is done by a white grub which hatches from an inlaid egg, works down the stem sometimes boring the second year even to the crown of the plant. Control is by cutting off the cane below the lower ring and burning the pruned tip to destroy the borer and its eggs. It is important to repeat the tip pruning as long as wilting tips can be found. Begin inspecting in early July and continue each week until late summer. It will help much if attention is also paid to the neighboring plants, including the wild ones. Insects and diseases often move rapidly from garden to garden so that constant vigilance is the price of healthy, productive plants.

Leafhoppers: These creatures that, when disturbed, hop from plant to plant with the aid of strong hind legs, are properly named. They jump and hop, sometimes in groups, and there is no mistaking their identity. The rose leafhopper feeds on the older and lower leaves, causing discoloration in spots that are nearly white, but very small; sometimes there are curlings of leaves and defoliation. The species of hopper on the rose hibernates in the egg stage in little slits in the bark. There are only two broods in a season. Sticky flypaper will catch many of them.

Mildew: This makes a fine cobweblike growth of a white fungus which is common and widespread. The fuzzy growth occurs most abundantly on the top surfaces of leaves and is quite prevalent in wet seasons. Berry leaves are conspicuous sufferers from powdery mildew. The fungus is white, but the winter spores are black as seen late in the season, and show as mere black dots over the surface of the foliage. Practically the whole fungus is on the exterior, the entire body of it being superficial. Control is by the collection and destruction of affected parts—or sometimes the whole plant. Thin out the plants to let in sun and air. Keep the plants dry.

Red spider mites: The minute creatures known as red spider mites affect many herbaceous plants (e.g., phlox) as well as some woody ones (e.g., raspberries). The spiders seem to be small red dots, usually enmeshed in fine webby growth which is their nest. They assemble on the underside of leaves, rarely on top, and occur in large numbers. They are so small they can hardly be seen without a magnifying glass but their bright red color distinguishes them. They eat the skin of leaves and some of the inside tissues, and in the aggregate do much damage. They are not true insects as they have eight instead of six legs and are related to spiders.

Red spiders eat ravenously on leaves of phlox, raspberries, carnations, and many other plants. They are rarely suspected until much harm has been done. Leaves of affected plants look pale, unthrifty or undersized and are of little value to the plant because of injury. Red spiders may spread disease, hence there is need of control.

The destruction of affected parts when generally infested will suppress and control these creatures. Wetting down the plants with a forceful stream of water will wash off many of them, and they may perish before they can return to the plant. All applications of water from the hose should be made toward the under surface of the leaves. Use an angular nozzle or a curved one to get the right delivery to dislodge the creatures.

Pruning: A few small tools for pruning and thinning bush fruits and other brambles are a convenience but a strong, sharp pocket-knife will do the job. The briar hook, which is still used by some, is handy for cutting off dead canes that have fruited and do not bear again. The cutting part is made of a rod of good steel, $\frac{5}{16}$ inch in diameter, flattened and curved at the distal end with a thin edge on the concave side of the curve. The handle should be three feet long and the cutting edge placed at the base of a cane where a quick pull severs the stem. It is important to cut close to the ground, leaving no tall stubs.

The pruning knife is useful for small woody shoots and is all that some people use. The blade should be good steel and the point should be curved forward a little to prevent the edge from slipping off when the cut is made. The handle should be large to avert blistering the hand and the base of the blade should be thick to furnish support for the thumb.

In using the knife, the shoot to be cut off should generally be pressed with one hand

After the berries have been picked, thin the brambles so that only the thickest and most productive canes remain.

toward the member that supports it, and the blade should be inserted at the proximal side.

Pruning shears are commonly used but they cut less smoothly and less closely. They should be kept sharp and the blades should articulate well. Cut but do not pry with them. Lever shears with three-foot handles are excellent and enable pruning without scratching the hands. In any case, whatever tool is used, wear long-wristed gloves to protect the hands and wrists. All prunings should be gathered and burned for clearance of debris and to dispose of diseased canes and insect-infested portions of the plants.

Old dead canes and branched canes that have borne are useless and should be cut as low as possible. With these gone, there is the further job of thinning out. Most clumps send up too many canes and they are too close together. Keep only the thick, sturdy ones as they are the most productive; the slender ones are of little productive value and should be cut out. Canes should also be spaced from four to six inches apart if one can and still have enough left for good crops. Six or eight sturdy canes are enough for a clump. The yield depends more on the number of stocky canes well distributed than upon mere number of stems.

With raspberries, the only pruning that need be done is a simple pinching off of the blossoms. Pinching permits more vigorous growth the following year. Canes should be

Training bramble vines between two wires helps make a very neat, manageable row and saves a great deal of garden space.

cut back to about three feet during the first winter. When new canes start growing the second year, cut off the fruiting canes completely. Once the berries have been picked, cut out the old canes. All weak new canes should be eliminated from the row at this time. Try to keep the number of canes to about four to six spaced about six inches apart. A thin row will allow the growth of bigger berries and prevent the influx of disease to the crop. All old canes and pruned tips should be burned.

Winter Support: If it is likely that winds and snows will break down the plants, they should be supported in some inexpensive way. A simple system of support may be made by a single small fence wire with posts ten or 15 feet apart and one wire strung either side of the posts with the canes between the two wires held apart by a short crossbar. If substantial wire is used it should last for many years and be useful all the while by supporting the plants summer and winter.

Another simple way is to drive stakes in the middle of the clump and gather the canes loosely with a wire or strong string so that they may swing a little but not break down with snow and ice on them.

Mulching: Mulching in early winter before or after the ground is frozen and before the snows come is often worthwhile. An application of eight to ten inches which will press down to four or five will not be too much material. Use leaves, straw, stover, or even small evergreen boughs for holding the snow on the ground as a blanket and thereby reducing the danger of sudden deep freezing and offering protection against the drying effect of continuous cold dry winds. Mulch between the rows both fall and spring for clean cultivation. The berry grower should endeavor to steadily build up organic content of his soil to enable it to retain moisture better and to make available the necessary plant food materials in the land. Mulching is always advisable in localities subject to drought. Berry plants need plenty of water for developing the fruit so that the fruits may be large and luscious. A dry spell is likely to result in small berries that are rather dry and seedy.

See also entries for individual berries, CUTTINGS, DISEASE.

BRIDGE GRAFT   *See* GRAFTING

BROCCOLI
(*Brassica oleracea* var. *italica*)

Broccoli is a hardy, fairly quick-maturing crop which belongs to the Cabbage family.

Culture: Broccoli prefers coolness and moisture. In the regions of the country where summer arrives early, it will be most successful if planted as a fall crop. However, certain gardeners contend that it thrives best as a two-season crop for both spring and fall.

In the latter case, seeds are sown in late winter, one-half inch deep in flats and placed in a warm, sunny window or greenhouse. Seedlings can be set out early in spring, as soon as the garden soil can be worked. Later, when most danger of severe frost has passed, more seeds are sown directly in the garden. When stalks are three or four inches tall, thin the plants or transplant them so that they stand 18 to 24 inches apart in the row.

The transplanted broccoli can be harvested throughout the spring and early summer.

Broccoli that is direct-seeded in late May will mature during the cool, early autumn months. Thus, with a little planning, you can enjoy fresh-picked garden broccoli throughout the growing season.

Broccoli is not a greedy feeder. It will do best in a moderately rich soil, provided that soil is well drained and easy to work, and thrives in soils ranging from sand and clay to peat. It is a thirsty vegetable, though, and requires plenty of moisture.

The plant form of broccoli consists of a thick main stalk, at the end of which develops a central cluster of tiny, dark green flower buds. Stem, buds and leaves are edible, but the leaves are less tender than the stem and buds and are usually discarded.

Some watchfulness is necessary to see that the greenish heads are harvested well before the flower buds expand and dry out. After the main head has been cut the side shoots will continue to form smaller heads and provide a steady and heavy harvest over a considerable period. All heads should be cut off in such a manner that a fairly long stub of stem remains on the plant.

After the central head of broccoli has been cut for food, a number of small lateral roots will develop in the axils of the remaining leaves. These shoots also produce flower buds which are edible. The welcome harvest of this important, easy-to-grow vegetable will last for several weeks. From four to six cuttings of stems and buds may be expected from every stalk.

Varieties: Green Comet Hybrid is a favorite choice of gardeners due to its short growing season of 40 days. The two branching varieties, Spartan Early and De Cicco, both have a maturation of 60 days. Calabrese is prolific and hardy.

Nutrient Value: Broccoli is a good source of vitamin A (4,500 I.U. per serving) and ascorbic acid (162 I.U.). It is also rich in calcium and iron.

BROMFIELD, LOUIS

(1896–1956) The late Louis Bromfield, well known for his many fine novels, also contributed a great deal to the advancement of soil conservation methods. On his Malabar Farm in Lucas, Ohio, he demonstrated why organic matter was the foundation of any sound agricultural and gardening program. He also was one of the founders of Friends of the Land, an active conservation society of the time. His books about his farming ideas include *Pleasant Valley, Out of the Earth* and *From My Experience.*

BROWALLIA

These tropical American herbs are useful as hardy annuals and are noted for their deep blue flowers which appear over a long period. They can be grown from seeds or cuttings. Also grown as potted plants, browallias should be kept stocky by pinching and staking when necessary. Volunteers often occur. For indoor starting, plant in early spring and transplant outdoors in May.

Recommended for bedding plants, they do well in humusy soil and bloom until frost. *B. americana* grows to about 24 inches high, while *B. speciosa* reaches a top growth of five feet.

BROWN ROT

Brown rot of stone fruits is caused by a parasitic fungus which spends the winter on dead fruits and leaves on the trees, or on the ground beneath the trees.

See also FRUIT TREES.

BROWSE

Browse is the tender portion (leaves, buds, twigs, and shoots) of woody plants eaten by animals.

BRUSSELS SPROUTS
(*Brassica oleracea* [Gemmifera Group])

Brussels sprouts are readily distinguished from all other varieties of brassicas by the sprouts or buds, about the size of walnuts, which grow thickly around the stem; these sprouts are the parts used, and are equal in tenderness and flavor to cauliflower and broccoli. This vegetable has never come into general use in this country, probably because it is too tender to stand the winters of some of the northern states. Still, by sowing in April or May, and planting out in July or August, Brussels sprouts may be had in fine condition until December. In the South, they may be harvested from November to March.

Culture: In early season, Brussels sprouts are treated exactly like any late cabbage. Till ample amounts of compost into the soil about two weeks before planting. When setting out plants, pinch off a few leaves and set

Harvest lower Brussels sprouts first, always leaving a crown of leaves to produce food for the plant.

plants 16 to 20 inches apart in rows of the same distance. Break off most of the lower leaves late in summer, to concentrate the plant's energy on the immature buds. Sprouts are ready to harvest when heads are one to 1½ inches wide; begin picking the lower buds first. Shortly before the ground freezes, plants can be spaded up with some soil and transplanted in a moist greenhouse, cold frame or basement. If the soil is kept damp, sprouts will continue to mature. Brussels sprouts are a late-season crop and are improved by a few fall frosts. As with cabbage, avoid planting where a brassica was the previous crop.

Varieties: Jade Cross Hybrid produces delicious, blue green sprouts. Long Island Improved has a maturation of 90 days.

Nutrient Value: Sprouts are rich in cal-cium and iron, and contain significant quan-tities of vitamins A and C.

BRYOPHYLLUM   *See* KALANCHOE
BT   *See* BACILLUS THURINGIENSIS

BUCKWHEAT
(Fagopyrum esculentum)

Buckwheat is the tame brother of a group of weeds characteristic of poor soils. It has an amino acid composition that is nutritionally superior to other cereals, including oats, and has a very high lysine content, as well. Buck-wheat does create problems for the grower, however, and has yet to be grown successfully on a large-scale commercial level. It is a low-yielding crop (30 bushels to the acre is a good yield); the stems are brittle when mature and will break in heavy rains or wind; and the seed ripens at different times, so early-ripened seed often shatters before later maturing seeds can be harvested.

Buckwheat offers certain advantages for the homesteader, however. It matures in 70 days, so it can be planted late and still har-vested. It makes an excellent second crop in a double-cropping rotation for this reason. It also smothers weeds, is a good green manure crop and an excellent bee plant. It has the ability to produce on just about any soil, so marginal soils can be planted in buckwheat and still produce a crop.

Varieties: Researchers have just begun developing new varieties of buckwheat. Penn-quad, a new variety, has thicker stems to resist lodging and also a more uniform seed size. Common buckwheat grows best in cool weather, and most of the buckwheat crop grown in this country is grown in the Northeast and in Canada. The most commonly grown variety is Japanese buckwheat, which takes about seven weeks to reach terminal growth. The seeds of this variety are large and brown. Silverhull has smaller, less triangular seeds. Common Gray is similar, but with smaller seeds. Both varieties have a short growing season and thresh out with a low percentage of hull in the grain. Tartary or mountain buckwheat is a less commonly grown variety that also occurs as a weed.

Planting: Buckwheat will grow on just about any soil, so it is not necessary to fertilize. It can also be planted at just about any time, but spring plantings sometimes yield poorly because buckwheat, a cool-weather crop, will not flower well in hot weather. Buckwheat can be planted as late as July and still make a crop before frost. Growing thickly in midsummer to fall, it smothers weeds, but does not inhibit weed growth well if planted early.

Buckwheat can be planted as any other small grain would be, either by broadcast or with a drill. Work garden soil with a tiller, or disk and harrow fields. Seed at the rate of about 1½ bushels per acre, and, if seeded broadcast, run over the ground with a tiller or a rotary hoe to bury the seed.

Diseases and Insect Pests: Buckwheat is amazingly resistant to both diseases and insects.

Harvesting: Buckwheat is a good green manure crop, using phosphates in the soil unavailable to other grains. Plow under as you would any green manure crop—it can make *three* crops in one season.

Buckwheat is harvested with a combine using the same adjustments and screens as for oats. Wait to combine until frost has killed the plants and the mature seeds have had time to dry. Most growers harvest at about 17 percent moisture and dry the seed artificially to 12 to 13 percent for storing or milling.

Small amounts of buckwheat can be harvested by hand. Cut the plants with a scythe, tie them into bundles and allow them to dry in a sheltered spot or under cover. Thresh as for wheat. *See* WHEAT.

Using and Storing: Chickens and rabbits can be fed buckwheat, straw and all. For flour for your own use, first heat the buckwheat groats in a low oven, and then grind in a blender. Most of the hulls can be sifted out of the grain. Buckwheat flour makes good pancakes and can be used in a variety of dishes. Check a good whole-grain cookbook.

Although it yields only a small amount of grain per acre, buckwheat is an excellent green manure and honey crop.

Store small amounts of buckwheat in plastic bags in your freezer, larger amounts in tightly covered barrels.

BUDDING

Budding is perhaps the most widely used form of grafting. It is the method in which the scion, or piece inserted into another plant called the stock, is merely a short section of branch with a single bud, in contrast to the section with three or more buds on the scion as is usual in standard grafting. It is also called bud grafting, for the methods are basically similar to the standard methods, especially the so-called "bark graft" which depends, as budding methods also do, on the bark being in a condition to slip.

"Slipping bark" refers to the state which is characteristic of active growth when the bark can be easily separated from the wood, and when the cells of the cambium, the layer of living tissue between the bark and wood, are actively dividing. Both the stock and the inserted scion must be in this state. When conditions are optimum the bark will slip most of the summer, but lack of water, unusual cold or defoliation may tighten the bark earlier in the season. All methods for budding except the chip method depend on bark that is slipping.

Bud scions are vegetative, not flowering buds, cut with a quick, smooth, one-inch slice into the bark of the scion stem. Some are also cut so as to include a little wood, too. The small core of wood that runs up into the bud must not be pulled out, for that ruins the bud. Leave on the leaf stalk or petiole, but cut off the leaf blade.

T-Budding: This is the most commonly used method for cutting the stock in preparation for inserting the bud scion. The operation can be very simple and speedy. Professional rose budders and fruit-tree budders, if provided with a helper to do the tying afterwards, can insert as many as a couple of thousand buds in a day. When all goes well, the percentage of successful grafts can run between 90 and 100 percent.

Young, ¼- to one-inch-in-diameter stems are the best to use for grafting, but topworking young trees by top-budding is also often very successful, even when all the branches are grafted. The scion used for T-budding is cut in an oval or shield shape, about an inch long and less than ½ inch wide. It is inserted from above into a T-shaped cut in the stock in an area of smooth bark. The cut on the stock should be two to ten inches above ground level, the nearer the ground the better. In preparing the stock, make the vertical cut first then the horizontal cut at the top of the T, letting the cut go about a third of the distance around the stem, and giving the knife a slight flip to open the bark. The scion bud is cut off starting about ½ inch below the bud and slicing upwards to about an inch above it. With the bud pointing up, the shield piece is slipped down under the two flaps of bark on the stock until the cuts on the shield and the stock are even. Then the bud union is tied in place with nurserymen's adhesive tape, raffia or the now widely used budding rubber strips, which are self-destructive after a few weeks when they are no longer needed. After the graft heals, the top of the stock is cut off, and the new shoot grows. All buds on the stock must be rubbed off whenever they appear.

Patch Budding: This method is one in which a rectangular patch of bark is removed and replaced with a bud on a piece of bark of the same size. Though more difficult than T-budding, it is a valuable method for thick-

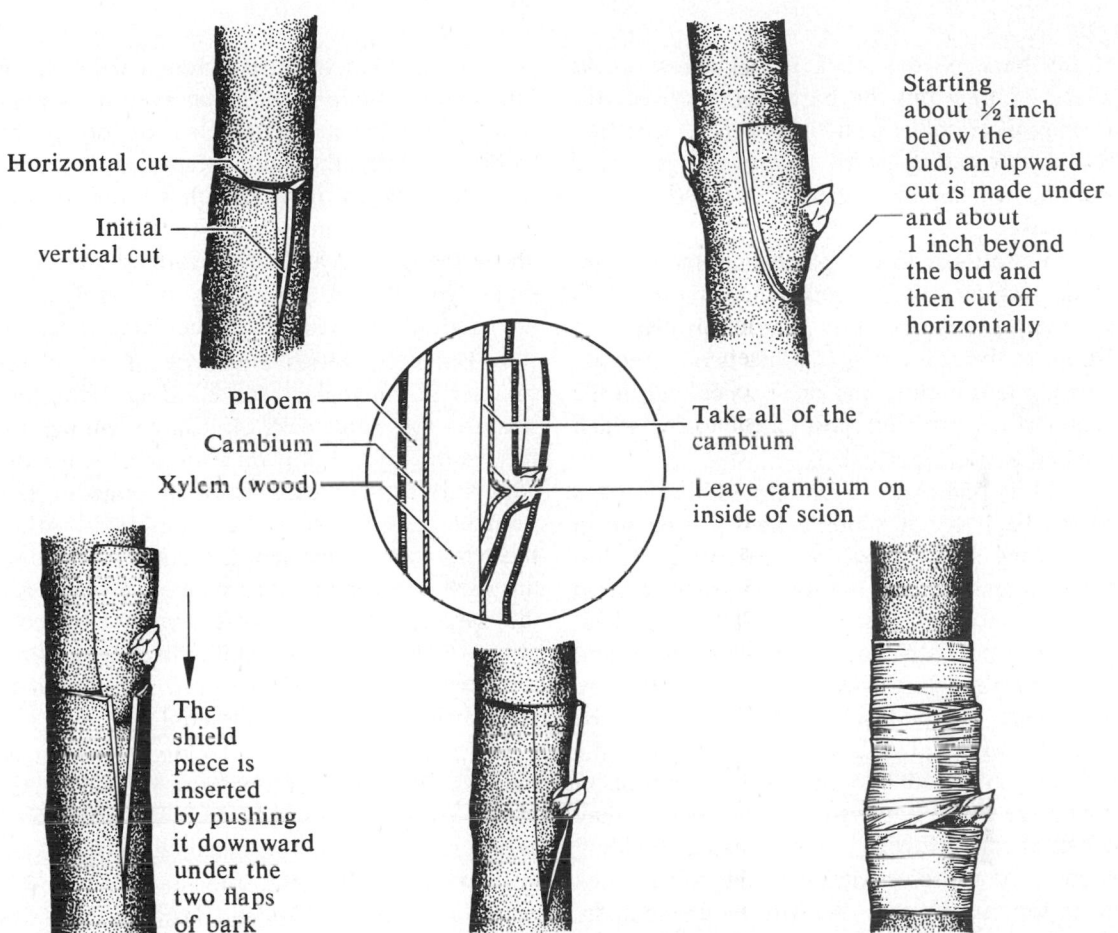

Horizontal cut

Initial vertical cut

Starting about ½ inch below the bud, an upward cut is made under and about 1 inch beyond the bud and then cut off horizontally

Phloem

Cambium

Xylem (wood)

Take all of the cambium

Leave cambium on inside of scion

The shield piece is inserted by pushing it downward under the two flaps of bark

T-budding is the simplest way to graft the bud of one plant variety (scion) to another (stock). First, a shield-shaped scion with one bud is cut from the scion branch. Then, a T-shaped incision is made in the bark of the young stock. With the bud pointing upward, the scion is slipped into this cut until the top of the scion and the stock's "T" cut are even. The union is tied in place with nursery tape, and after the graft has healed, the stock is cut off and the bud puts forth a new shoot. The result is a new plant with the fruiting and flowering characteristics of the scion parent.

barked species and tropicals like rubber trees. The diameter of the stock plant and the scion plant should be about the same size, from ½ inch to an inch. By using a double-bladed knife to make the horizontal cuts of the patch area on the stock and carefully cutting away the bark with a vertical slice, and by carefully removing the bud from the scion with a section of bark of the exact same size and shape, the method can be successful. Here, as with the cutting of the scion for T-budding, it is essential not to remove the core of wood in the bud. When the wrapping is put on, it must cover all exposed slits, but leave the bud uncovered.

If the bark on the stock is cut a few weeks ahead of time but the bark not removed, the formation of callus near the wounds, necessary for all successful grafts, will have begun and thus hasten the healing after the bud-scion is inserted.

Variations of the patch-bud method include ring or annular bud, where the stock is girdled, and where it is almost girdled. An I-bud, as the name suggests, has two horizontal cuts top and bottom and one vertical cut in the center, thus providing two flaps under which the bud scion is inserted.

Chip Budding: This is possible on trees whose bark is not slipping and is used in an emergency or very early in the spring. It has been successful, for instance, on grapes grafted onto nematode-resistant stock. A V-shaped cut is made into both stock and scion sticks and fitted together, but since there is no bark flap to protect the bud scion, the graft must be carefully wrapped with budding rubber and the union covered with fine moist soil. The rubbers may have to be removed by hand before they constrict the growing stem because budding rubbers do not disintegrate in the soil as they do in the air and sun. As with other methods, the top of the stock is not cut back until the graft union heals.

Top-Budding: Budding on the shoots of young trees of four to six feet having good vigorous shoots is a fast, reliable way to improve a tree by grafting methods. Old trees pruned back severely the year before will provide watersprouts suitable for top-budding also. Usually ten to 15 buds are put on fast-growing branches, with one on each branch saved for the new plant, even though several buds are sometimes grafted onto the branch in the first place. The proper size of the branch is ½ to ¾ inch in diameter at shoulder height. Such budding is done in midsummer as soon as well-developed buds are available. By doing the work this late, the buds often stay inactive until they begin new growth in the spring. Then the stock branches are cut back just above the grafted buds, thus forcing them into quick growth. All branches not grafted, if any, should be removed at the same time.

Times for Other Budding: Fall or late summer is convenient for budding fruit trees because the rootstocks are large enough to receive the buds, but it must be done while the bark still slips. Peach is often done in late summer. In choosing the scion buds, select those not at the succulent tip, but farther down the stick, and choose the vegetative buds, not the larger, plumper flower buds. In cold northern climates, fall budding usually requires a covering of soil over the graft union area to protect the plant during the cold.

Though called fall budding, the times when the buds will be dormant enough to use stretch over most of July and August as well as the fall. Roses, for instance, are budded in many areas between July 1 and July 15; pears between July 10 and July 30; cherries from July 15 to September 1, depending on the variety; and quince from July 15 to August 15. Peach can be budded as late as September 15. August is the best time for amateurs to practice budding.

June Budding: In California and the South it is possible to obtain a "one-year-old" budded tree within one growing season if the budding is done early and growth forced. The T-bud method is used on fruits and almonds, beginning in May or not later than early June. Use the current year's growth for the bud scion which will be in active growth at this season, and for the stock use a young plant with enough growth started so there are several leaves to be left below the bud union. To force the plant, cut back the section of stock above the union to within four or five inches above the graft within four days after grafting; and cut back entirely to the union after two weeks. After this kind of pruning the bud will shoot forth new growth quickly and vigorously. The lower leaves are removed at the time of the last pruning.

See also GRAFTING.

BUDDLEIA

These late-blooming shrubs, sometimes called butterfly bush, flower from July until frost in some varieties. The fragrant, rose purple flowers of *B. Davidii* var. *magnifica* are much loved by butterflies and hummingbirds. Growing ten to 15 feet, this shrub is not very hardy and may winter-kill north of Washington, D.C., so use a winter mulch. Many persons cut it to the ground each year, as it grows with extreme rapidity, and flowering specimens are obtained without the loss of a season. Plant them in good soil, where they will get plenty of sun.

Other varieties of orange-eye butterfly bush, *B. Davidii,* grow to just four or five feet tall if they are kept well pruned.

Also hardy in the North are the varieties of *B. alternifolia,* all gracefully fountain shaped. They flower in June, producing deep lilac blue blossoms in clusters along stems of gray green foliage.

See also SHRUBS.

BUFFALO BUR   (*Solanum rostratum*)

Buffalo bur is a noxious annual weed that frequently occurs first in field lots and then spreads to cultivated areas. A member of the Potato family, it is native to western areas. The plant generally reaches a height of one to two feet and has poisonous, prickly stems and berries. Its yellow flowers are similar to those of tomato. These pesky plants can be controlled by clean cultivation; waste places where they grow should be mowed to prevent their producing seed.

BUGBANE   *See* CIMICIFUGA

BUGLE LILY   *See* WATSONIA

BUGLEWEED   *See* AJUGA

BULB

Because of the remarkably beautiful flowers they produce, bulbs have become tremendously popular. They're versatile in the wide range of color, form and size of their flowers; they grow indoors as well as out; and in addition, they're relatively easy to grow.

Size alone does not constitute the value or quality of a bulb, but firmness, weight and condition do. If a true bulb (daffodil, lily or tulip), the layers or scales should be firmly joined, so that there is little or no feeling of looseness or squashiness when it is compressed in your hand. If a rhizome, corm or tuber (such as calla, crocus or dahlia), the flesh should be plump and fairly hard.

There are bulbs that will grow indoors or out, in water or on land and will flower in spring, summer or fall. Here are pictured the potted plant vallota, the aquatic canna, the spring-flowering narcissus, and the summer gladiolus.
(Courtesy of Longwood Gardens)

Good bulbs also present a distinct effect of being fairly heavy. It is not unusual to find bulbs of the same size and variety varying considerably in weight; those of inferior quality will tend toward lightness.

The condition of the skin or coating (as in hyacinths, tulips and others) should be smooth, bright and free of deep cuts and bruises, in particular, the disk at the base. Should this show signs of extreme injury or disease, the bulb will more than likely rot after planting.

It is best to plant bulbs soon after purchasing; however, if this is impossible, keep the bags containing them in a cool, well-ventilated place where the air is not dried out by artificial heat. Remember, any condition causing the bulbs to shrivel will injure them.

In storing, also keep in mind that squirrels, rats and mice regard all bulbs, with the exception of daffodils, as delectable dishes.

See also FORCING.

BULRUSHES   (*Scirpus*)

A grasslike plant commonly found in ponds, lakes and marshes, its spongy, leafless stems are often used in weaving strong mats, baskets and chairs. Bulrushes are also proving one valuable biological tool in the treatment of water pollution.

Both annual and perennial bulrushes grow in most wet areas. They have flat, creeping leaves usually three to six feet long, and a stem leading to a brown spike from six inches to one foot long. This spike contains the male and female flowers for reproduction. *S. fluviatilis* is prevalent in pond borders and bays; great bulrush (*S. validus*) grows in more shallow ponds. Many types of bulrushes are known to decay and produce odors.

Scientists are now experimenting with bulrushes and reeds to test their abilities to devour and repel poisonous metal ions and toxic bacteria in the water. Many believe the fish and other microorganisms clinging to bulrushes help fight water pollution today. Marsh filtration using bulrush ponds is being explored as an economical alternative to activated sludge plants presently used. In addition, after the plants have been used to absorb pollutants, bulrushes can be harvested annually for use as fish and animal food.

Enthusiasm for bulrushes as one biological tool in water pollution control is sometimes quashed by critics who charge that bulrush ponds can produce contaminated fish or plants, or that this or other biological systems are less efficient in fighting chemicals than harsher chemicals themselves. Despite these criticisms, bulrushes may become one of several biological weapons of the future in the battle against water pollution.

BURBANK, LUTHER

(1849–1926) Luther Burbank produced more new varieties of useful plants than any one person before or since, although relatively few have withstood the test of time. One of his chief desires was to make it possible to produce more food and flowers and forage crops. In order to accomplish this ambition, he developed new varieties of fruits, vegetables, nuts, forage plants, flowers, and grains to a total of about 1,000 new varieties.

BURDOCK   (*Arctium*)

Two species of burdock (*A. Lappa* and *A. minus*) are large biennial plants well known

The weed burdock is sometimes grown for its culinary and medicinal properties.

as common and troublesome weeds in the eastern, central and some western states. They are sometimes cultivated. The plant has some culinary uses, and the dried root from the first year's growth and the seed are used medicinally.

Burdock will grow in almost any soil, but the best root development is favored by a light well-drained soil rich in humus. The seed germinates readily and can be sown directly in the garden in rows 18 inches to three feet apart either late in fall or early in spring. When well up in spring, the seedlings are thinned to stand about six inches apart in the row.

The roots should be harvested at the end of the first year's growth to obtain the most acceptable drug and to prevent the plants from bearing seed and spreading as a weed. The tops of the plants can be cut with a mower and raked off, after which the roots can usually be turned out with a shovel. In a dry and very sandy soil the roots frequently extend to such depth that it is necessary to use a post-hole digger or slender spade to get them out. Burdock, however, is *cultivated* quite seldom. Those who actually use the plant or its parts may forage them in the wild.

The wild food forager relishes burdock for its root particularly, but also for its leaves and stem. The Japanese consider it a source of strength and endurance, and something of an aphrodisiac as well. The first-year roots should be peeled, sliced crosswise, cooked for about 30 minutes in water to which a bit of soda has been added, then cooked another 10 minutes or so in very little water. For the best eating, the roots should be gathered in June or early July. The flower stalks should be gathered just as the flowers are forming. These should be carefully peeled off the bitter rind and cooked as you would the roots, using two waters with a bit of soda in the first. The young leaves so cooked are a serviceable green vegetable.

Burdock is generally considered a pesty weed when occurring in neglected farmyards, fencerows or rich soils of uncultivated areas. Plants can be eliminated by cultivation, especially during the first year.

See also HERB.

BUR MARIGOLD
See BEGGAR'S TICKS

BURNET   *(Poterium Sanguisorba)*

A pretty perennial with very small white or rosy flowers, burnet grows to about one foot high. The leaves taste somewhat like cucumbers, and are used in salads and in cool drinks.

The graceful appearance and pleasant green of burnet leaves make it a useful plant near the front of a border. Many gardeners, preferring the beautiful greenery, clip its ragged flowers.

It grows in any garden soil and is easily raised from seed or propagated by division. It needs full sun and plenty of lime.

BURNING BUSH
See FRAXINELLA

BURNING FIELDS

The burning of weeds, grass or trash is a destructive practice and should always be avoided. Earthworms, bacteria, fungi, protozoa, algae, and other soil organisms are killed. Soil organic matter in the upper few inches is consumed. Moisture is dried out of the soil and the water table is lowered. The tilth of the soil is harmed because soil particles are broken down. There is always the danger of the fire spreading to nearby buildings, fields or forests.

BURN PLANT   *See* ALOE

BUSH BEAN   *See* BEANS

BUSH CHERRY
See CHERRY, BUSH

BUSH FRUITS, ORNAMENTAL

Fruit-bearing bushes can serve as ornamentals in the home landscape. Homeowners have used bush cherries as foundation plantings, dwarf trees as hedgerows, blueberries as property dividers, and even strawberries as flower borders. Such plantings provide a source of fresh fruit, while traditional choices bear poisonous fruit or none at all.

Bush Cherry—a Tame Hedge: The bush cherry is perhaps the most likely fruit to replace many small hedges and foundation plantings. This variety can be planted in close rows, and can be trimmed to almost any height desired. Blossoms are beautiful in spring, and the silvery green foliage is always attractive, but the real payoff comes when quarts of succulent cherries are picked in late summer for canning, pies and preserves. Bush cherries are also adaptable for specimen plantings. Use this just as you would any ornamental of comparable size.

Wild Hedges: The wild hedges, those which should not be trimmed, include the blueberry, raspberry and rugosa rose. They may best be used for spots where larger, rambling hedges would ordinarily be used, such as along property lines, farm pastures and along roadways. These plants generally grow with amazing speed, and are perfect for shutting out undesirable views, or for secluding a patio from a roadway or other houses. Raspberries generally grow six feet high, and should be planted about three feet apart. A trellis can be used to help train canes, prevent wind damage and keep fruit off the ground. Blueberries grow six to ten feet high, and for commercial purposes are planted five feet apart. You may, however, wish to sacrifice some of the fruit surface to gain a more dense hedge, planting three to four feet apart.

Rugosa Rose: The rugosa rose is famous for the hips, or fruits, that form on its branches after the blossoms fall. Rose hips are nature's most compact source of vitamin C. A quarter-pound of rose hips contains as much C as 120 oranges. The plant will grow to a height of five or six feet and, when planted about two feet apart, will grow into an attractive, thick hedge, with beautiful blossoms appearing all summer long.

Dwarf Trees: Full-sized fruit—apples, pears, cherries, and others—can be enjoyed all summer in the space which otherwise might have been devoted to ornamental shrubs. Most of these trees are very attractive, especially at spring blossom time, and the fruit they bear is equal in all respects to that of full-sized trees. Dwarfs usually range from six to 15 feet in height. In Europe, dwarf apples are commonly used as hedgerows.

Strawberries: These low-lying plants are useful as a border for the flower bed. They are very attractive, and provide another example of how landscaping can be combined with fruit growing. Strawberries can make an extremely attractive low hedge or border.

A variety of minor fruits are worthy of consideration. *See also* AMELANCHIER, EL-DERBERRY, GOOSEBERRY, LOQUAT, PAPAW, QUINCE.

BUTTER-AND-EGGS   *See* LINARIA

BUTTERCUP
See RANUNCULUS, TROLLIUS

BUTTERFLY BUSH   *See* BUDDLEIA

BUTTERFLY FLOWER
(*Schizanthus pinnatus*)

Sometimes called "poor-man's orchid," this delicate, graceful plant, when properly grown, is covered with tiny orchidlike blooms and always attracts a great deal of attention. Because it requires constant care and rather exacting conditions, the butterfly flower is usually grown in the house or greenhouse. For winter flowering, seeds should be sown 1/8 inch deep in August. During the growing period, temperature should remain between 45 and 55°F. (7.22 to 12.78°C.).

Grown outdoors, the plant does best in cool-weather areas of the North or those sections of the West which have cool, mostly frost-free winters. The seed, which can be slow to germinate, should be sown in a seed pan and covered lightly with germinating mix. The seed pan should then be put in a plastic bag and set on a windowsill until seedlings emerge. When large enough, they can be transplanted to the garden. Plants should bloom in six weeks from seed. Since they flower heavily for only a short time, seeds should be resown to extend the bloom period.

BUTTERNUT   (*Juglans cinerea*)

The butternut, or white walnut, was once a very familiar and pleasant sight along the

The little-known butternut or white walnut is valued for its lumber and protein-rich nuts.
(Courtesy of U.S. Forest Service)

country lanes and in woodlands, but recent years have seen it disappearing from the landscape. To blame are blight and oystershell scale.

The root system is not very sturdy, and nurserymen graft butternut to strong, vigorous walnut rootstocks. Trees with superior cracking and extraction quality are available commercially.

The butternut is hardy throughout most of the United States, reaching a height of 90 feet. After planting this tree, use a leaf mulch up to within a foot or so of the trunk, and water weekly at first.

Although not as heavy or tough as walnut, the fine wood of this tree deserves the name white walnut, and can be made into attractive paneling and furniture. The leaves, bark and unripe nuts were once used to dye woolens a

dark brown, while the roots impart a fawn color.

The tasty nuts will be easier to crack if soaked in water overnight.

See also WALNUT.

BUTTERWORT
See CARNIVOROUS PLANTS

BUTTONBUSH
(Cephalanthus occidentalis)

This is a fragrant ornamental shrub often found along the marshy ground and banks of quiet streams. From August through September, hundreds of small creamy white flowerballs dangle in clusters on long stems from the gracefully drooping branches of these low, rounded bushes. The fragrance attracts bees and butterflies.

Although this plant is at home in swamps, it does well in ordinary garden soils as long as they are not too dry. It is hardy over most of the United States.

Buttonbush is especially desirable in that it blooms in late summer when relatively few other shrubs are in flower.

BUTTON SNAKEROOT
See LIATRIS

BUTTONWOOD TREE
See PLANE TREE

CABBAGE
(*Brassica oleracea* var. *capitata*)

Cabbage grows well only where there is a good supply of moisture and the weather is cool; extremely dry spells or intense heat will kill off plant growth, unless a heavy mulch or other protective measures are used.

Cabbage can thrive in almost any kind of soil, but prefers one enriched with well-rotted animal manure. It is best to cover the entire part of the garden which is to be used for the cabbage wtih the manure. It can be spread at least three inches thick and then thoroughly plowed under. This job should be undertaken about two weeks before the cabbage plants are ready to be set out in the garden. Decayed leaves are also a good fertilizer provided they are buried deep enough in the garden.

Many gardeners prefer to grow their own cabbage plants from seed. Seeds will last four years. The early varieties grown from seed should, of course, get an early start in the greenhouse, or in a cool room or cellar. In such cases, the seed is sown in fine soil in flats or in pots. In the northern states, this can be done in February or March. Much depends upon the climate in the various states when figuring the time to sow seed. The soil in which the seeds are planted should not be too rich, or the seedlings will grow too fast and become "leggy."

The later varieties of cabbage are handled in the same way except that the flats or boxes are kept outside instead of under glass. When the seedlings reach a height of three or four inches, they should be pricked out and replanted in flats or boxes some distance farther apart. This action will assure the grower of good stocky plants. The seed-sowing should be timed six weeks or at least a month ahead of the time at which the plants are to be set out in the garden.

In setting the plants out in the garden, a good deal depends upon the variety chosen. The early varieties are best set 14 inches apart in rows 28 inches apart. Midseason varieties should be planted 16 inches apart in rows 28 inches apart; and the late varieties, 24 inches apart in rows 36 inches apart.

Set out the early varieties as soon as danger of frost is over. The late varieties should be planted not later than August 1 in the northern states. Depending on the variety, it takes up to 67 plants of the early types to fill a 100-foot row. For the later types, 40 plants are enough. A 100-foot row will produce enough cabbage for a family of five. Late varieties of cabbage can be salvaged way into the winter. Pull the entire plant and stack each one upside down in a protected corner of the yard. Cover the cabbage pile with a foot layer of leaves or straw. Perfectly good cabbage heads will then be easily available for consumption anytime during the following winter or early spring.

Varieties: Disease-resistant early varieties include Golden Acre, Marion Market, Stonehead Hybrid, and Early Jersey Wakefield. Savoy King is a heat-resistant variety which produces tender heads. Danish Ballhead is a favorite winter variety. Savoy King Hybrid is a high yielder and is heat resistant. Ruby Ball is a short-growing red cabbage variety, well known for its firm, round heads.

See also CABBAGE LOOPER, CABBAGE MAGGOT, IMPORTED CABBAGE WORM.

CABBAGE APHIDS   *See* APHIDS

CABBAGE LOOPER

The cabbage looper, a pale green worm that doubles up or loops as it crawls, eats small holes in the leaves of cabbage and other crucifers, and if not removed promptly, will prove disastrous to the crop. In the South, the harlequin cabbage bug attacks the plants by sucking the juice from them. Biological controls include the commercially available trichogramma wasp, a parasite, and *Bacillus thuringiensis,* a powdered bacterium sprayed on the crop.

See also BACILLUS THURINGIENSIS, INSECT CONTROL.

CABBAGE MAGGOT

The cabbage maggot attacks stems of early-set cabbage, other crucifers, radishes, and turnips just below the soil surface, riddling them with brown tunnels. They are white, legless and ⅓ inch long.

To control the maggots, pull dirt away from the plant where the maggots can be seen working on the stem. Place a heaping tablespoon of wood ashes around each stem, mix

Where cabbage maggots are a problem, cover seedbeds with a fine net to prevent the adult flies from laying eggs in the garden soil.
(Courtesy of U.S. Department of Agriculture)

some soil around with the ashes, firm the plants in, and water. When setting out winter cabbage in early August, mix wood ashes, lime, phosphate rock, and bone meal (four parts wood ashes to one part each of the other ingredients) and stir two cups of this mixture in a two-foot radius for every plant.

Cabbage maggots can also be controlled by prompt removal of the small white eggs, about the size of a grain of rice, that appear on the surface of the ground near the stem of the plant.

CABBAGE WORM
See IMPORTED CABBAGE WORM

CABOMBA   *See* AQUARIUM

CACTI　　(Cactaceae)

These succulents are members of the Cactaceae which contains over 2,000 species. Cacti are native to the Americas as far north as Canada and as far south as Chile. Most are found in the sunny, hot and dry regions. In their long bitter struggle for survival in these regions, they have evolved specialized forms which enable them to survive adverse conditions. Water loss was reduced by evolving smaller leaves, or no leaves, and thickened sap. Water storage capacity was increased by greatly enlarged stems in order to survive periods of drought, and strange shapes and ribs evolved so that one side was not turned constantly to the searing sun. The green stems took over the leaves' process of manufacturing food through photosynthesis, and destruction by hungry animals was discouraged by spines and thorns. Such adaptation to adverse conditions is the reason they make such good house plants.

A well-drained soil is needed for cacti. The simplest growing medium consists of one-half coarse washed sand and one-half roughly screened compost or leaf mold. The addition of one cup steamed bone meal and one cup hoof and horn meal per bushel or one tablespoon of each per two quarts of the above mix is also beneficial.

Clay pots are better than plastic ones for cacti, since air and water diffusion through the clay sidewalls causes the soil to dry quicker. For cacti, a pot with drainage holes is recommended.

During active growth in the spring, summer and fall, cacti should be watered more often than in the winter. Apply water until it flows from the drainage hole and discard the excess in the saucer. Allow the soil to dry thoroughly between each watering. At times of active growth, this can vary from three to ten days and should be increased to 21 to 30 days during the winter period of inactive growth or dormancy. If too much water is used, root rot readily results and is usually fatal. Insufficient water will cause the plant tissue to shrivel. Fertilizer should only be used during active growth. Fish emulsion diluted to one-quarter its recommended strength and applied twice as frequently as suggested gives good results.

Most desert-dwelling or xerophytic cacti need a southern exposure with full sun for best results indoors. During the summer they can be placed outdoors in semishade. Tree crotch dwellers or epiphytes such as Christmas cacti can tolerate less sun, such as that provided by an east window, or a shaded patio during the summer. During the winter, reduced water and temperatures of 45 to 50°F. (7.22 to 10°C.) are needed for resting xerophytes if they are expected to blossom during the spring. An unheated sun porch or window in a cool cellar can often be used to provide these temperatures. Some species of *Opuntia* are hardy as far north as New York City. Holiday cacti such as the Thanksgiving or Christmas cactus need short days or darkness in the fall from 6:00 P.M. to 8:00 A.M. until buds are set. Alternately, temperatures of 50 to 55°F. (10 to 12.78°C.) in the fall for four weeks can override the short day requirement and cause bud set. These temperatures can often be found outside during fall nights or at a window in an unheated cellar in the fall. Cacti blossoms are spectacular and sometimes bigger than the plant itself, well worth the effort required for their production. Best growth and blossoms occur when cacti are grown in a greenhouse kept on the cool side (45 to 50°F. [7.22 to

When it comes to choosing cacti, the selection is overwhelming. It is easy to specialize in cacti alone. Common names of various cacti include old-man, old-woman, drunkard's dream, powder-puff, bird's-nest, snowball, living-rock, bishop's cap, golden star, and many others.

See also DESERT GARDEN, HOUSE PLANTS, SUCCULENTS, WINDOW GARDENING.

Because of the succulence of their stems and their ability to withstand drought, cacti are among the easiest plants to graft. Here a slow-growing variety has been grafted onto a very different, fast-growing type.

10°C.]) in the winter. Dramatic results can also be produced indoors if the above cultural hints are followed.

Smaller globular forms are propagated by seed, which requires time and patience. Some cacti produce offsets which can be removed and rooted. Others can be propagated by cuttings taken during active growth. Any damaged area should be air-dried to form a callus prior to rooting cuttings; otherwise rot can occur. Whenever handling cacti, gloves or forceps should be used.

CACTUS, ORCHID
See EPIPHYLLUM

CACTUS DAHLIA
(Dahlia juarezii)

This is a brilliant scarlet variety of dahlia. For its cultivation, *see* DAHLIA.

CAJEPUT   *(Melaleuca Leucadendron)*

An ornamental tree closely related to myrtle and eucalyptus, this Australian native grows to 40 feet and has narrow evergreen leaves and spikes of cream-colored flowers that bloom all summer. Its flaking bark is thick and papery white on the outside and spongy or corky on the inside.

Resistant to wind, drought, saltwater, and light frosts, the cajeput is much used for binding muddy shores along the Gulf and Pacific coasts. Its aromatic leaves yield an oil valued for its antispasmodic, diaphoretic, stimulant, and pain-killing properties.

Propagation is by cuttings of ripened wood.

CALADIUM

This member of the Arum family is a striking, large-leaved foliage plant, native to tropical South America. The heart- or arrow-shaped leaves are six to 24 inches long, delicately veined and splashed with green, cream, pink, red, or white. Spathes of tiny blue flowers often hide under the leaves.

Tubers are started in late winter or spring for spring or summer color respectively. Tubers are buried ½ inch deep in a 1:1 mixture of sand and compost. Bottom temperatures of 75 to 85°F. (23.89 to 29.44°C.) should be supplied with a heating cable or by placing the container in a wet pebble tray set on top of a radiator. When they root, pot them in a humus-rich soil. If used outdoors, they require temperatures consistently above 70°F. (21.11°C.). A shady location and even soil moisture are needed. When the leaves start to die, withhold water and store the dry tubers in plastic bags at 60°F. (15.56°C.) for two or more months. Propagation is by tuber division or seed. There are over 100 beautiful cultivars from which to choose.

See also HOUSE PLANTS.

Calceolarias thrive in slightly shady gardens where temperatures are not too high.

CALCEOLARIA

Native from Mexico to Chile, these herbaceous and shrubby plants of the Snapdragon family are much valued for their pouch- or slipperlike flowers that range in color from yellow, orange and red through brown and purple. Some are even spotted.

Though most calceolarias are grown as annuals, there is one perennial species grown in the greenhouse. *C. crenatiflora,* to two feet, has yellow, red or orange flowers that bloom in April and May. Seed should be sown in summer.

Annual species can be started from seed in the greenhouse during February and March. Seed flats (holding a finely sieved mixture of sand and peat) should be covered with plastic or glass to prevent the soil from drying out. Keep them shaded until the seeds sprout, then remove the glass and give them a northern or western exposure. Plants are placed outdoors in a lightly shaded place after frost danger is past. They fare poorly when the temperatures are high. Annual species include *Calceolaria multiflora, C. mexicana, C. tigrina,* and *C. tripartita.*

CALCITE

A mineral, calcite or calcium carbonate occurs in many crystalline forms, such as chalk, marble and limestone.

CALCIUM

A relatively abundant metal in soils, about 3.6 percent of the earth's crust is composed of calcium. Calcium is usually found in combination with other elements when it occurs naturally.

Known also as one of the "alkaline earths," calcium is important agriculturally because it is the principal element concerned in soil reaction, especially in humid regions, and has a primary role in determining soil pH, availability of several nutrients and the general soil fertility. It forms a major part of limestones, marbles, corals, natural chalks, and shells.

In plants calcium is present mainly in the leaves. One of its important functions is to neutralize certain toxic acids which form in many plants as a by-product of their metabolism. It also serves in the building of plant proteins, in preventing magnesium toxicity and in aiding healthy cell structure.

Blossom-end rot in tomatoes as well as black roots and pale leaf margins in other plants are signs of calcium deficiency. The best sources for calcium are natural ground limestone, dolomite, wood ashes, bone meal, and oyster shells.

See also ACIDITY–ALKALINITY; FRUIT TREES, DEFICIENCIES; LIME; OYSTER SHELLS; SOIL DEFICIENCIES.

CALCIUM HYDROXIDE
See LIME

CALCIUM NITRATE
See FERTILIZER, CHEMICAL

CALCIUM SULFATE
See GYPSUM

CALENDAR OF GARDEN OPERATIONS
See PLANTING DATES

CALENDULA   (*Calendula officinalis*)

The commonly cultivated species of this plant are annuals that should be started each year from fresh seeds. The yellow to orange flowers will bloom most of the year in southern states if regularly picked.

Calendula prefers full sun in moderate to rich loam, although any workable garden soil is acceptable. Seeds, which vary in size and shape, should be planted in April or May for bloom in July or August. Sprouts should be kept clear of weeds and thinned to about ten inches apart. The flowers can survive a light frost and last well into fall, especially in high-phosphate soils.

The petals of the calendula are most commonly used to flavor soups, stews and salads. They can also be used as a substitute for saffron in such dishes as yellow rice or to color homemade butter. Calendula tastes pasty and sweet at first, but the aftertaste is one of saltiness.

To preserve the petals, the flower heads should be harvested on a sunny day. Pinch off each flower, strip the petals from the head and dry them on newspaper. Avoid using screens as the petals tend to stick to the mesh. Also avoid contact between the petals while drying since this causes discoloration. Because they will readily absorb moisture, the petals should be sealed in an airtight container.

Medicinally, calendula has stimulant and diaphoretic properties and is used in folk medicine to reduce the pain of sprains, cuts and insect stings. Commercial calendula salves are available for minor wounds.

CALICO BUSH
See MOUNTAIN LAUREL

CALIFORNIA HOLLY
See TOYON

CALIFORNIA LAUREL
See UMBELLULARIA

CALIFORNIA PITCHER PLANT
See DARLINGTONIA

CALIFORNIA POPPY
(*Eschscholzia californica*)

Especially effective when grown in large groups in a sunny garden, the California poppy grows one to 1½ feet tall and has large, cup-shaped flowers in pink, red, scarlet, yellow, orange, and white. The variety Mission Bells produces double and semidouble flowers. Blooming from July to early fall, the blooms are excellent as cut flowers when arranged in low containers with their own foliage, which is blue green and deeply cut. Flowers close in the evening.

California poppies do best in light, dry soils, such as those found on poor banks. They are often disappointing to gardeners in the East,

where humid, rainy summers seem to cause weak, straggly growth and few flowers.

CALLA LILY   (*Zantedeschia*)

These showy rhizomatous plants, which are winter hardy only in the warmest parts of the United States, produce flaring floral bracts and large, heart-shaped leaves.

When growing under glass, pot the rhizomes August through December for winter bloom. The tip of the rhizome should protrude from the soil surface. Water sparingly till growth starts and generously thereafter. The soil mixture should be rich in manure and leaf mold with some bone meal added. It should have some shade, and winter temperatures should range between 55 and 65°F. (12.78 to 18.33°C.). After blooming, withhold water and dry the rhizomes before repotting for the following season.

For patio container or outdoor bed culture, start the rhizomes in pots in March or April and transfer them outside after danger of frost is past. Choose a location out of direct sun. Lift plants before frost and dry them out until the following spring. *Z. aethiopica* grows to 2½ feet with white bracts; *Z. Elliottiana* is yellow with spotted leaves; *Z. Rehmannii* is smaller with pink to rose flowers. There are forms said to be winter hardy in very protected situations of some northern areas.

CALLIOPSIS   See COREOPSIS

CALOCHORTUS

Native to the western United States, this

genus of the Lily family bears showy, cup- or tulip-shaped flowers, often having darker centers. Colors range from white and yellow through pink, lilac and purple, and heights from six inches (*C. caeruleus*) to three feet (*C. clavatus*). Common names for this genus include mariposa lily and globe tulip.

These plants prefer gritty, rather poor soil, perfect drainage and full sun. Corms should be planted two inches deep in fall. North of southern Georgia, they should be mulched after the ground freezes to prevent heaving. Remove the mulch in spring before the corms sprout. Away from their native West, the corms should be dug up and stored dry after blooming until replanting time in fall.

CALYCANTHUS

These fragrant deciduous shrubs, most of them hardy in the North, prefer well-drained, rich soils, and do well in both sunny and shady locations. They bear a fruit similar to rose hips. *C. floridus* grows three to ten feet tall, has dark green leaves and red brown flowers and is the hardiest species. They can be propagated by seed, layers set down in summer or division of older plants.

See also SHRUBS.

CALYX   *See* FLOWER

CAMASSIA

Entirely hardy, camassias produce showy blue, blue white or rich purple blooms that make them a fine attraction for the border or large rock garden. They will thrive anywhere in the United States. Some varieties send up their lovely spikes of lacy florets, 18 to 36 inches high, at the same time as the daffodils. Others bloom up to three weeks later.

These members of the Lily family do equally well in sun or semishade. Plant them four inches deep in a rich, sandy loam in the fall and don't disturb them. The recommended planting distance is usually three to five inches, but their basal foliage spreads so wide it's better to space them eight or nine inches apart. Camassias will thrive for many years, and may even increase from self-sown seeds. *C. Cusickii*, to three feet, blooms with late tulips. It does well naturalized near water.

The Indians ate camassia bulbs, which they called "quamash." Camassias are not to be confused with death camass, a variety of *Zigadenus* and a plant which poisons stock in the West.

CAMBIUM

The cambium is the soft formative tissue which gives rise to new tissues (wood, bark, etc.) in the stems and roots of all shrubs and trees. This green inner bark carries the foods produced in the leaves to the roots. Therefore, when the complex ring of a tree's cambium layer is cut, the tree eventually dies.

CAMELLIA

These are broadleaf evergreen shrubs of the Tea family which flower in autumn, winter or early spring. The waxy single or double flowers can be from two to seven inches across,

Double or single, the flowers of the Camellia japonica *range in size from one to five inches and in color from deep red to white.*
(Courtesy of Longwood Gardens)

depending on the species. Foliage is glossy and handsome all season.

Camellias are shallow rooted like azaleas and require similar culture. Grow them in well-drained, acid soil enriched with humus derived from leaf mold and peat moss. Keep them mulched with leaves in summer to keep the roots cool and the soil moist. Plant them with the top of the root ball one inch under the surface in part shade, especially where summers are hot.

Most camellias are not hardy in areas having heavy frost, but they can tolerate an occasional light winter freeze. Some new hybrids can be grown along the Atlantic Seaboard north to New York City, but only in sheltered places with elaborate protection. Generally, they are not hardy north of the Delmarva Peninsula. Some hybrids make spectacular winter-flowering plants for cool greenhouses in the North.

C. japonica, which can grow to 30 feet,

has flowers to five inches across in late winter and early spring. Some named varieties are fragrant, and flower color can be white, and many shades of pink, or red. There are bi-colored or variegated flower types. Purity is a double white, Debutante is a double pink and Sara-Sa is a variegated semidouble.

C. Sasanqua is the hardiest species, growing to 12 feet with fragrant white flowers two inches across. It blooms in fall until December. There are also pink and red named varieties.

See also JAPONICA.

CAMPANULA

Also called bellflower, this large genus of flowering herbs includes many fine choices for the rock garden or border.

The popular Canterbury-bells (*C. Medium*) is a biennial growing two to four feet high, with blue, pink or white flowers. The chimney bellflower (*C. pyramidalis*) is a bushy perennial three to five feet high that has stately spires of blue or white flowers. *C. rotundifolia,* often called bluebells-of-Scotland, is a slender perennial with bright blue flowers; and *C. Trachelium,* or Coventry bells, makes a vigorous border perennial about three feet high.

Campanulas prefer a well-drained garden soil and full sun or part shade. Propagation is by seed, division or cuttings. In the North, mulch with several inches of organic material to provide winter protection.

See also PERENNIALS.

CAMPION   *See* LYCHNIS

CANADIAN THISTLE
(*Cirsium arvense*)

This is a deep-rooted, troublesome weed with purple flowers. The most economical means of eradicating them in fields is to plant alfalfa. The alfalfa shades the rosettes of thistles, and cutting the crop twice a year reduces the storage reserves of the roots so that they die in the second or third season. Use a duckfoot cultivator to cut off the shoots as soon as they appear in the spring and continue until time to plant alfalfa; this helps to deplete the underground storage reserves and will eradicate most of the plants.

CANDYTUFT   (*Iberis*)

This attractive, low-growing perennial or annual is available in white and many pastel tints. It is very easy to grow, requiring no particular soil or care. It is perfect for rock gardens and borders, and some varieties are even grown as house plants. An annual shearing should be made after the blooms have begun to fade. Seeds can be sown outdoors in mid-spring and should begin to bloom in about eight weeks.

There is a perennial candytuft, much like the annual, which can be propagated by division. *I. sempervirens* has evergreen foliage and white flowers.

CANKER WORMS

These pests, known also as inchworms or measuring worms, threaten tree fruits and shade trees. They are sometimes seen suspended below a tree on a nearly invisible filament. The worms are brown on top, green below, and show four stripes along the length of each side.

Fortunately, the female adult, a gray wingless moth, must climb trees in order to lay her eggs. She can be arrested with a sticky band about the lower trunk—commercial products are available for this. Apply the sticky material to a band of paper so that the trunk will not be damaged. As there are fall and spring species, the bands should be put to work both early and late in the season.

A spray of the bacterium *Bacillus thuringiensis* has proven effective.

See also BACILLUS THURINGIENSIS, INSECT CONTROL.

CANNA

Tall perennials producing showy spikes of red, yellow or white flowers, cannas brighten the flower bed or border from midsummer to frost. Individual flowers range from two to six inches across.

Cannas can be purchased in two- or three-eye divisions from most bulb dealers. The roots should be planted as soon as the soil has thoroughly warmed up in the spring. Set them about two inches deep and 12 to 24 inches apart. A good shovelful of compost should be mixed in the soil around each root. If you want earlier flowers, the roots may be started inside in four-inch pots early in April. Use good soil with some compost mixed in. After warm weather comes, transplant them to the garden.

Cannas need as much sunlight as they can get. They do not bloom in shade, and should have sun at least half of the day. The soil must be moist at all times, and should never be allowed to dry out. By midsummer they will make good growth and will be ready for another feeding of compost. With correct culture, each root division will have grown into a large clump by fall. On the morning you find the leaves frosted, cut off the stalks just above the soil line *before* the sun shines on them and turns them black. This improves the keeping quality of the roots. Lift each clump carefully, allowing some soil to adhere to it.

One of the best methods of storing is to put the soil-covered clumps in boxes and cover with dry sand. A temperature of about 60°F. (15.56°C.) is best for storage. Cannas will rot at a low storage temperature, and dry at a high one. The roots should be examined several times during the winter, spoiled ones removed and the temperature changed if necessary. When planting time comes again, remove all dirt from the roots and divide them into sections with two or three points, or "eyes." Each of these will grow into a stalk.

New light-colored varieties are difficult to keep successfully. If you have trouble, here is a method which may be helpful. Cover these cannas when frost is expected. After a frost, when other varieties are lifted, lift these that have not been frosted with a large ball of earth on them. Cut the stems back halfway, and pack the plants in boxes or buckets with moist soil around them. Set them in the basement near the window so they can get as much light as possible. Keep the soil just moist enough through the winter to keep the leaves green. Keep them rather cool so they will not make too much growth, at about the same temperature as for completely dormant roots. In the spring these plants can be divided and started in pots or in open ground in the usual way.

CANNING

Canning is, by far, the most widely used method of home food preservation. Recent surveys report that almost half of all American families can some of their own food every year. This is most likely because an investment in canning equipment is much cheaper than the cost of a freezer, and there are no freezer operating costs to worry about. In addition, there is practically no storage problem. You may can until your pantry bulges, whereas freezer space is limited. If you want to both can and freeze foods, it's a good idea, for economic and space reasons, to freeze those foods which are not suitable for canning.

The following listings can serve as a general guide in your choice of foods for canning and freezing. If you have gotten results contrary to these recommendations, by all means follow the wisdom of your own experience.

Best foods for canning: tomatoes, pickles and pickled relishes, relishes, peaches, apples and applesauce, pears.

Best foods for freezing: strawberries, red raspberries, cauliflower, broccoli, peas, carrots, turnip greens, spinach, Brussels sprouts, kohlrabi, cherries, all meats, dairy products, breads, grains.

Foods suited to either method: asparagus, lima beans, beets, rhubarb, squash, sweet corn, green and wax beans, green snap beans, apricots.

In simplest terms, the object of canning is to sterilize food and keep it sterile by placing it in glass or tin containers. The food is sterilized by heating it and its container sufficiently to kill all spoilage and pathogenic organisms present in the raw food.

In order to destroy botulism-causing bacteria, low-acid foods must be processed at a temperature of 240°F. (115.56°C.) in a pressure canner.

High-acid foods, such as tomatoes (except, perhaps, for new very low-acid varieties), pickled vegetables and fruits, are only vulnerable to heat-sensitive organisms. To sterilize these foods and make them safe to eat, they only have to be heated to boiling temperatures. Low-acid foods such as vegetables, dairy products and meats are susceptible to heat-sensitive organisms *and* bacteria which can stand temperatures above boiling. To kill any traces of toxic organisms that might be present, these foods must be processed at 240°F. (115.56°C.), a temperature that can only be reached in a pressure canner.

It is impossible for destructive organisms to enter just-sterilized food if the container is sealed immediately after heat processing. A vacuum is created inside the container after sealing which protects the food's flavor and color, prevents rancidity, helps retain vitamin content, and aids in retarding corrosion of tin cans and closures on glass jars.

Choosing and Preparing Food: When canning use only fresh foods in the best condition. Discoloration of the food may take place during the canning process, but a change in color won't mean the food is not safe to eat. For best results food should be canned quickly; serious deterioration in food quality may take place if the food, especially if it is starchy like peas or corn or vulnerable to spoilage like meats, has stood too long between steps. All equipment should be clean and ready before you begin.

Equipment: High-acid foods must be processed in a boiling-water canner. Any large pot can be used as long as it is deep enough, has a snug-fitting lid and a rack or some such thing to keep the jars from touching the bottom of the pot. A steam-pressure canner can be used if it is deep enough. If you're using a pressure canner, set the cover in place without fastening it and be sure the petcock is open wide or remove the weighted gauge, so that steam can escape and no pressure is built up inside.

A steam-pressure canner must be used to process low-acid foods. You must have a canner specially made for steam-pressure canning and it must be in good working condition.

Containers: Most people who can foods use jars that are made especially for this purpose. They are available in standard pint, quart and half-gallon sizes and come with replaceable bands and lids. They are heavy-duty and made to withstand extremes in temperatures.

Some home canners, though, recycle jars in which mayonnaise, instant coffee and other foods were packed and use these for canning. If you decide to use such jars, make sure that regular canning lids and bands fit them properly so that you can get a good seal. Also be careful not to subject them to temperature extremes because they crack more easily than regular canning jars. It is not advisable to use such jars for *steam-pressure canning.* All jars, no matter what kind they are, must be in good condition, hot and clean before packing food in them.

Should you choose to use tin cans (which are becoming more difficult to find for home canning), use only perfect cans, lids and gaskets. Wash the cans and if the lids need to be cleaned, simply wipe them with a damp cloth before sealing them on the cans. If you use tin cans you will need a sealer and it must be properly adjusted according to manufacturer's instructions.

Most foods may be packed either by the hot-pack or raw-pack method. The hot-pack method is best for food that discolors during canning. You can get more food in jars if you hot-pack it because food shrinks slightly when heated. However, foods may lose some heat-sensitive nutrients in the hot-packing process that they would not lose if they were packed raw.

Special Steps for Canning Fruits: During canning fruits tend to darken. To prevent this they may be placed in a solution of two tablespoons lemon juice or vinegar and two tablespoons salt to a gallon of water. After washing and slicing, the fruit should be dropped into this solution. Let them soak for 20 minutes and then rinse them in cold water before packing.

Although most people pack fruits in sweet syrup, they may be canned without sweetening or in extracted juice or in water. Sugar is not needed to prevent spoilage, but it helps the fruit hold its shape, flavor and color. Unsweetened and sweetened fruit are processed the same.

If you choose to use sweet syrup, a good syrup can be made by mixing two cups of honey with four cups of very hot water. Choose a light-flavored honey for the syrup so the honey taste will not overpower the flavor of the fruit. Pack the fruit in the hot syrup as soon as it is peeled and sliced to keep it from darkening.

Checking Seals: Check all seals on containers after processing and cooling. For glass jars, press down on the center of the lids. If they do not "give" when pressed, the jars are properly sealed. Check tin cans by examining all seals and seams to make sure they do not bulge and are smooth. If you believe a container is not sealed properly, don't take any chances. Open the container and reprocess the food or discard it.

Canned foods should be stored in a cool, dry place for best keeping. The chance of nutrient loss is greater at higher temperatures.

Spoiled Food: If you suspect a canned food has spoiled when you open it, do not taste it! If there is an unappetizing odor developing, you can be sure the food is not safe to eat. Burn the food or bury it deep so no animal can discover it and eat it.

Step-by-Step Instructions: For specific directions for canning individual vegetables and fruits as well as meats and fish check the several books and booklets available on the subject. Some of them include: *Home Canning of Fruits and Vegetables,* available from the Superintendent of Documents, U.S. Government Printing Office, Washington, DC 20402; *The Ball Blue Book,* published by Ball Corporation, Muncie, IN 47302; *Stocking Up,* by the editors of *Organic Gardening and Farming,* Rodale Press, Inc., Emmaus, PA 18049, 1977; and *Putting Food By,* by Ruth Hertberg et al., Stephen Greene Press, Brattleboro, VT 05301, 1975.

See also Freezing Food, Storage.

CANTALOUPE   *See* MELON

CANTERBURY-BELLS
See CAMPANULA

CAPE MARIGOLD
(*Dimorphotheca*)

Growing from eight to 18 inches tall, Cape marigolds produce abundant daisylike flowers in shades of white, yellow, orange, salmon, rose, and purple. They need full sun to blossom properly, and blooms will close in shade, on overcast days and in the evening.

A popular species sometimes called African daisy, *D. sinuata* is a half-hardy annual with apricot petals and deep violet centers. It is excellent for the flower garden, blooming from midsummer to frost.

Sow seeds where plants are to bloom in a light, dry soil in full sun. In areas having humid, rainy summers, the plants will tend to produce more foliage than flowers.

See also AFRICAN DAISY.

CAPSICUM   *See* PEPPER

CARAWAY   (*Carum carvi*)

An annual or biennial herb, caraway has been cultivated in many parts of the world for its seeds, which are used for bakery products, flavoring and confections. The oil distilled from the seed is used for certain medicinal purposes and for the manufacture of liqueurs.

The plant grows in a wide range of soil conditions, even ones heavy and dry. Fertilization is not critical. For a biennial crop, caraway should be seeded in early spring directly into the beds where it will grow; it does not transplant well. Plant a new crop each year for a steady supply.

Spring plantings produce bushy green plants about eight inches high with feathery leaves similar to those of coriander and fennel. The plants will remain green over winter. During the second summer, they will reach two feet in height and develop white flowers. Seed will set by midsummer and ripen by August.

Annuals may be sown in early fall and left to overwinter. They may develop flowers and set seeds the following summer.

Plants may be windrowed to dry, and the herb may be moved indoors to complete drying, or it may be placed in shocks or piled on large pieces of canvas in the field. As the seed comes to final maturity in the curing process, shattering is likely to be excessive unless the crop is handled carefully. For this reason drying on canvas or in barns or open sheds where the shattered seed can be collected has a definite advantage. Seed that does not shatter after drying can be removed by threshing as for wheat.

Pay particular attention to weed control when the crop is young. When new shoots reach two inches in height, pinch out the smaller ones and allow the remaining plants six to 12 inches of room. Some gardeners plant caraway and peas in the same row. Peas come up first and are harvested first and normal cultivation takes care of weeds between the rows.

Caraway roots can be prepared and eaten much like carrots.

See also HERB.

CARBON

Carbon is the most common component of all organic matter. The various stages that carbon undergoes in the soil are called the "carbon cycle."

In the air and the soil carbon is most important as carbon dioxide—CO_2—a gas consisting of one atom of carbon and two of oxygen. Carbon dioxide is present in the air to the extent of only .03 percent—or three parts CO_2 to 10,000 parts air—but its presence in the atmosphere is absolutely necessary for the existence of man, animals and plants.

The Carbon Plants: When organic matter decays, carbon dioxide is given off. For many years, it was believed that plants secured their carbon from the atmosphere, but Lundegard in 1924 discovered that decaying organic matter in the soil was a more important source. Some CO_2 is also available from respiring plant roots and rainfall. A small amount of CO_2 reacts with other elements in the soil to produce salts that can be utilized by plants or may be lost in drainage, but most of the gas escapes into the atmosphere to be used by plants through their leaves.

Organic Matter: Scientists have found that the amount of carbon dioxide in a soil is directly dependent on the amount of organic matter present. In fact, the amount of carbon dioxide escaping from soil has been used as a measure of the amount of organic matter present in the soil. The factors that aid in decomposition of organic matter are the same factors that are good for the production of carbon dioxide, namely, high temperature, sufficient moisture and adequate aeration. In one experiment it was shown that four times as much carbon dioxide was given off from a manured soil as compared to an unmanured one.

Composting: With regard to the production of carbon dioxide in a soil, research shows that in composting, large amounts of carbon dioxide dissipate into the atmosphere because of the heat generated. For this reason an anaerobic form of composting where as much air as possible is kept from the fermenting matter is sometimes considered the better means of conserving more of the carbon. Turning under a green manure crop is a good way of providing organic matter for use in the soil.

The use of chemical fertilizer retards the formation of carbon dioxide. Its use results in lower moisture, aeration and even temperature. (Tests have shown that a soil high in organic matter will have somewhat higher temperatures.) Certain fertilizers, like nitrate of soda, cause a severe hardening of soils, reducing their aeration, and good aeration is important so that a sufficient supply of carbon dioxide might be given off. Many farmers who use chemical fertilizers overlook the use and importance of organic matter.

Soil microorganisms require CO_2 to furnish their energy. In fact, the formation of carbon dioxide from organic matter is almost entirely due to bacterial action. Soil bacteria and other microorganisms also produce carbon dioxide as a waste product of their own metabolism. This action produces the heat in composting.

A sufficient supply of carbon dioxide in the soil will create a healthy, dark green foliage in plants. The abundance of carbon dioxide in soil varies at different seasons. In certain experiments it was found to be highest in May and in August. This may be a combination of a time when organic matter decays most readily, plus the time when organic matter is plowed under.

See also CARBON–NITROGEN RATIO.

CARBON DIOXIDE

Bacteria release carbon dioxide (CO_2) from decomposing organic matter. Combined with water, it forms a weak acid which helps to release minerals and other plant nutrients from colloidal clay, humus and minerals in the soil.

Carbon dioxide is loosed into the air where it is used by plants. An abundance of CO_2 rising from the soil insures a healthy dark green foliage color. If carbon dioxide is trapped in a compacted soil, it will kill the plants, whose roots need oxygen to live.

The same three essentials that are necessary for the proper utilization of all other vital soil components are needed for the formation and proper use of carbon dioxide: an open, friable soil structure, ample organic matter and the presence of other elements in sufficient quantities so that none may have a limiting or unbalancing effect on any of the others.

See also AERATION, CARBON.

CARBON–NITROGEN RATIO

When talking about soil, the carbon-nitrogen ratio (abbreviated as C/N ratio) is the relationship between the carbon in organic matter and the nitrogen in the soil. In general, the C/N ratio is the proportion of carbon to nitrogen anywhere in a natural material. A batch of organic matter composed of 40 percent carbon and 2 percent nitrogen has a C/N ratio of 20:1.

Examples of Ratios: The following is a list of specific materials and their carbon-nitrogen ratios as obtained from several sources; the figures vary greatly depending on conditions.

Young sweet clover	12 to 1
Alfalfa hay	13 to 1
Rotted manure	20 to 1
Clover residues	23 to 1
Green rye	36 to 1
Sugarcane trash	50 to 1
Cornstalks	60 to 1
Oat straw	74 to 1
Straw	80 to 1
Timothy	80 to 1
Sawdust	400 to 1

Generally speaking, the legumes are highest in nitrogen and have a low carbon-nitrogen ratio, a highly desirable condition. The high C/N ratio of sawdust means that it is highly carbonaceous and has a very low nitrogen content. Low nitrogen materials can tie up nitrogen in the soil.

There is a difference between the carbon-nitrogen ratio of raw organic matter and that of humus. The average nitrogen content of practically all humus is about 5 percent, but the nitrogen content of organic matter in general fluctuates considerably. With regard to carbon, a different condition exists. While decomposing organic matter loses large amounts of carbon as carbon dioxide, the percentage of carbon to the total mass does not seem to fluctuate too much. Thus, if you start with some rotted manure with a carbon-nitrogen ratio of 20:1, you may wind up with a 10:1 ratio when it turns to humus: that is, a 50 percent carbon and a 5 percent nitrogen content. The C/N ratio always decreases when organic matter decomposes, but the content of carbon in humus does not vary too much, averaging about 50 to 52 percent.

The C/N Ratio in the Soil: The carbon-nitrogen ratio of the soil is on the average much less than that of organic matter. By the time green matter is decomposed in the soil, the C/N ratio has dropped. The C/N ratio in soils declines as one goes downward through the soil. Typical carbon-nitrogen ratios for brown silt loams in Illinois are 12:1 in the topsoil, 11½:1 in the subsurface layer and 9:1 in the subsoil.

The C/N ratio of soil microorganisms is usually much lower than that of organic matter, humus or soil. The average C/N ratio of the bodies of bacteria and fungi falls between 4:1 and 10:1. It is lower than the C/N ratio of the humus because microorganisms require more protein than carbohydrates for tissue building while the carbon in carbohydrates is used for energy. Humus has more carbohydrates than the bodies of microbes, which are high in protein. Since about 16 percent of protein is nitrogen, it is apparent that the microbes' bodies will have a very high percentage of nitrogen to carbon.

When raw organic matter is applied to the soil, microorganisms will multiply rapidly, but in this process of working they have to consume nitrogen. If the material that is plowed under has a high C/N ratio, that is, it is low in nitrogen, the soil organisms in decomposing will have to look elsewhere for their nitrogen. They will deplete nitrogen in the soil with a depressing effect on the crop yield. When they die, however, future crops will benefit from the decay of their bodies, gorged in nitrogen. When plowing under a highly carbonaceous organic matter, a sufficient period of time should elapse before a crop is planted.

One investigator (Broadbalk) discovered that where the C/N ratio of added organic matter plowed under was 33:1 or more, a withdrawal of nitrogen occurred. Between 17 and 33 nothing was added or withdrawn; in other words, nitrification ceased. But if it was under 17, the nitrogen store of the soil was increased. The value of adding compost to the soil comes from a low C/N ratio.

When plowing under organic matter with a high C/N, some form of nitrogen should be added. The organic gardener can use dried blood, bone meal, hen manure, cottonseed meal, fish scraps and dried ground fish, peanut shells, silk and wool wastes, castor pomace, cotton gin wastes, cowpea and soybean hay, felt wastes, feathers, hoof or horn meal, and a number of other organic materials having a high nitrogen content for such purposes.

Russel, in *Soil Conditions and Plant Growth,* 10th ed., 1974 (Longmans), gives an interesting illustration of a comparison between the earthworm and microorganisms in reducing the C/N ratio of rye-straw. He says, "Thus, L. Meyer found that earthworms feeding on rye-straw composted with basalt meal reduced its C/N ratio from 23 to 11 during a period of two years while the soil microorganisms alone reduced it to about 18 during the same period." This means that the earthworm is a better conserver of nitrogen than microorganisms.

The Significance of the C/N Ratio: It has been shown that the C/N ratio of plowed under organic matter is important to the conservation of the soil's store of nitrogen. It is also of great significance in the general operation of soils. Mainly, it is a matter of having enough nitrogen available. There is a difference in the way a low C/N ratio works, depending on whether it is in raw organic matter or in humus. Organic matter, applied to the soil, represents nitrogen on the move. In a finished compost it is in a more static condition—less is given off. In the application of raw organic matter, the extent of nitrogen movement depends on its C/N ratio. If it is high, as in sawdust, there will be no nitrogen movement, but if it is a material like young sweet clover there will be a satisfactory rate of nitrification.

In humus, although the C/N is low, there is a resistance to rapid decomposition. The movement is slower, and will take place over a longer period of time. This is of some value as it means the nitrogen is stored for future use. In the case of fresh organic matter with a low C/N, not only is there a fast nitrogen movement, but much carbon is given off in the form of carbon dioxide.

Age of Organic Matter: The younger the plant material is, the lower the C/N ratio, which means that it will not only decompose more quickly, but will release more nitrogen and increase the yield.

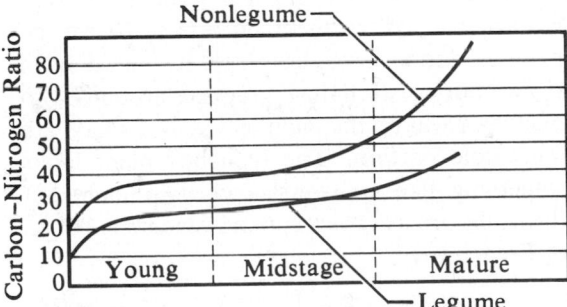

The maturity of the plants turned under determines the carbon-nitrogen ratio of the organic matter they add to the soil. Older plants have a higher proportion of carbon to nitrogen than young ones. Leguminous plant tissue is very rich in nitrogen.
(Redrawn from Nyle C. Brady, The Nature and Properties of Soils, 8th edition [New York: Macmillan Publishing Co., 1974], p. 154)

Rainfall also affects the C/N ratio. As rainfall goes down, the C/N ratio also declines. The higher the rainfall, the lower the nitrogen. The C/N ratio of arid soils is always lower than those in regions of higher precipitation. Higher temperatures also decrease the C/N and the C/N is decreased in arid conditions. It has also been found that the higher the temperature the lower the C/N.

See also CARBON, COMPOSTING.

CARDINAL CLIMBER
See STAR-GLORY

CARDINAL FLOWER
(*Lobelia Cardinalis*)

The bright scarlet spikes of the cardinal flower can be found in July and August along a brook or a sluggish stream, usually in semi-shade. Never dig up wild plants or pick flowers from them. If you wait until the seeds are ripe, you can gather them, plant them in a flat and raise excellent little plants easily. The seeds require cold to induce germination, so place the seed flats in the cold frame for about a month in February or March and then bring indoors. Small seed flats can be sealed in a plastic bag and put in the freezer for a few weeks. When they develop their first set of true leaves, transplant the seedlings to a larger flat or into individual peat pots. When they develop into rosettes of dark green leaves with sturdy roots, they are ready to be placed in their permanent setting. Although they prefer a damp soil, they may grow in an ordinary flower garden.

One good place to plant them in the garden is among azaleas in the light shade of deciduous trees. Like azaleas, they must have cool, moist humusy soil around the roots, and their brilliant flowers seem to glow when set off by the dark azalea foliage. When growing cardinal flowers in the open border, be sure to add plenty of humus to the soil, preferably in the form of leaf mold or peat moss with aged manure or compost that is not limy. Mulch and water copiously in dry periods. Even under the best conditions, they often die out in two or three years, so keep new plants coming along. Learn to recognize the seedling leaf rosette, as they often self-sow under good conditions. This is one of the favorite flowers of the ruby-throated hummingbird, and worth growing for that reason alone. The cardinal flower grows three to five feet high.

A relative of the cardinal flower is the great blue lobelia, *L. siphilitica*. The flowers are bright blue touched with white, fading to pale blue. Its requirements are much the same as the cardinal flower's, but it tends to live longer under cultivation.

The hybrid *Lobelia* x *Gerardii* (*L. Cardinalis* x *L. siphilitica*) produces three-foot spikes of brilliant purple flowers from July to September. Give it the same culture as the cardinal flower, and be sure to protect the basal leaf rosette in winter with a loose mulch like evergreen boughs. It is a good practice to protect all perennial lobelias this way.

A member of the Artichoke family, cardoon should be started in a greenhouse or hotbed and transplanted to the garden after all danger of frost has passed.

market vegetable in a few places in California. A close relative of the artichoke, cardoon grows rapidly in any rich organic soil that is moist but well drained. Plants should be raised in a hotbed, and transplanted after last frost about three feet apart. In plant and leaf structure it suggests a cross of burdock and celery. When the plant is about three feet high it should have straw, burlap or paper wrapped around it to blanch or whiten the main leaf stalks, which are the edible portion. The blanched plant looks something like an oversize celery bunch, but the stalks are used as a cooked vegetable, boiled or French fried.

CARDOON
(*Cynara cardunculus*)

An old vegetable, known to the ancient Romans, cardoon has been largely overlooked by American gardeners. Small quantities have been imported from France, and it is a minor

CARNATION
(*Dianthus Caryophyllus*)

In sweetness of perfume, beauty of color and symmetry of form, the carnation is unexcelled. These attributes, combined with the ease of culture and the certainty of flowering, give the carnation preeminence among flowering plants. It is also long lasting when cut.

These half-hardy perennials grow to two feet high; it is a nice plant for the garden where it can be used for borders as well as in beds or in simple mixed plantings. Furthermore, its adaptability to potted culture makes it possible to grow it in the house, where it may blossom much of the year. Separate pots may be made to bloom successively to prolong the peak of flowering, if preferred; or all may be grown at one time for greater abundance of flowers on special occasions.

In the greenhouse, plants are set into permanent beds, worked into strong sandy loam

that is porous in structure and possessed with a liberal organic content. House plants should not be allowed to become pot-bound by being beset with roots. It is urgent to repot the plants every six months.

Tankage is an excellent organic fertilizer for carnations; leaf mold and compost are also good and may be used as a part of the surface mulch.

New stock plants are grown from cuttings which are easy to root. Side shoots which develop along the main stem are used. Rooting takes place in about three weeks. Bottom temperatures of 60 to 65°F. (15.56 to 18.33°C.) and room temperatures of 55°F. (12.78°C.) are conducive to rapid rooting. Carnations are cool-temperature plants but need sunshine to do well. Do not try to grow them in diffused light or shade.

Grown as a house plant or in the greenhouse, the winter-flowering carnation is propagated by cuttings taken from the basal, side or main shoots.
(Courtesy of Longwood Gardens)

CARNIVOROUS PLANTS

There are a number of plants that are able to capture and devour insects and even small animals or birds. Most of them have basic physiological similarities in that they live in environments—usually bogs or marshy soils—that can't provide nitrogen in the usual sources used by plants; they must therefore obtain nitrogen from other sources. If you wish to plant these unusual and often strangely attractive plants at home, you must duplicate as closely as possible their native environments by providing a rich, moist soil, plenty of direct light (although some will tolerate slight shade) and constant moisture. They do well in terrariums, and can be fed with bits of meat or egg whites.

Drosera is a genus of carnivorous plants commonly known as sundew or dew plants.

They trap insects by secreting glistening drops of a sticky substance on their leaves. When an insect alights there, tentacles close over it, the fluid becomes acidic and the insect is digested. There are 90 to 100 species scattered throughout the world, but most grow in Australia. *D. filiformis* and *D. rotundifolia* are American varieties with small, white flowers. They grow well in a greenhouse or terrarium. Use a fine muddy loam and sphagnum moss, keep the roots wet and provide plenty of direct light.

The small shrub *Drosophyllum* grows mostly in southern Spain, Portugal and Morocco. Unlike many other carnivorous plants, the *Drosophyllum* does not respond to touch; rather, its pink, filamentous leaves secrete a sticky substance which traps insects that land on them. Subtending these are glands which secrete a sticky substance to digest the captured insect.

Pinguicula, or butterwort, is a small plant with long-stemmed flowers that resemble snapdragons, and leaves that appear in a broad, basal rosette. The upper surface of the leaves secretes a digestive fluid, and the upper margins of the leaves fold in when an insect is captured. They are rarely cultivated except in botanical gardens. A few varieties grow wild in the United States and Mexico. *P. vulgaris* is native to the United States while *P. caudata* and *P. gypsicola* grow wild in Mexico.

Bladderworts (*Utricularia*) are a genus of 200 aquatic and terrestrial plants scattered worldwide. The terrestrial plants are the most attractive, and some are even cultivated for their blooms by orchid lovers. Several of the aquatic varieties are carnivorous. Bladders growing on the leaves, branches and sometimes the roots trap small aquatic animals and insects. These enter through a valvelike door and are prevented from exiting when the valve closes.

There are other popular varieties of carnivorous plants. The Venus's-flytrap (*Dionaea muscipula*) is a wild, semiaquatic herb, that has leaves ending in two plates. When an insect alights, the trap closes and, once shut, the insect is devoured.

Another group of carnivorous or insectivorous plants is the pitcher plant. These are any one of a number of plants (either *Nepenthes* or *Sarracenia*) whose leaves are formed in the shape of a pitcher. Insects which enter the pitcher are trapped by a sticky fluid in the hollow base, where they are eventually dissolved.

See also DARLINGTONIA, PITCHER PLANT, VENUS'S-FLYTRAP.

CAROB   (*Ceratonia Siliqua*)

An evergreen plant belonging to the Legume or Bean family, carob has for centuries grown wild in the lands bordering the Mediterranean Sea and in the Near East. The carob, which resembles an apple tree with small flowers, has glossy leaves and sometimes reaches a height of 50 feet.

The carob plant produces a leathery brown pod, about four to ten inches long, which produces a sticky pulp used as a feed for livestock. John the Baptist supposedly ate carob pods when he lived in the wilderness. It is sometimes referred to as Saint-John's-bread.

Carob was introduced to the United States in 1854, when the U.S. Patent Office distributed 8,000 plants throughout the southern states. Today carob is found mostly in California and Florida.

The plant thrives in semiarid regions where there are no severe frosts. Most plants should receive at least 12 to 14 inches of rain per year, and an average of 23 inches is ideal. The plant will, however, suffer from being watered too frequently, as evidenced by the sickly condition of trees planted in wet areas.

Carob requires a near rainless autumn when the pods are approaching maturity. Ripening will occur in September or October, according to variety. The pods should be harvested in October or November.

Early fall rains of short duration do little or no harm to the plant, especially if followed by dry winds. A longer period of precipitation will, however, produce mold and fermentation on the pods once they have matured and their sugar content is high (40 percent of the pod is sugar). If the pods do get moldy, they will quickly become infested with worms. A fog belt along the coast of Southern California has this particular problem. The commercial planting of carob should be done further inland, away from damp ocean winds.

Many types of soil, from adobe to sand, are suitable for the carob. A rather deep, heavy loam with good subdrainage is recommended. The root system of the plant is very extensive with relatively few fibrous feeder roots.

Carob seeds, when collected fresh from recently ripened pods, germinate quickly. They may be planted under glass in beds or flats, and when the second set of leaves develops, transferred to small pots or paper containers. When the plants reach a foot in height, they should be planted in boxes four by 12 inches deep, or in nursery rows in open ground where there is little danger of frost. When seedlings have developed a stem 3/8 inch in diameter, they are budded in the same fashion as citrus trees. Mature trees should be spaced 40 feet apart. The budded tree, under favorable dry conditions, should begin to bear fruit in the

sixth year and produce an average yield of five pounds of pods per tree. The size of the crop will increase gradually, reaching an average yield of 100 pounds in the twelfth year. More arid land will produce greater yields.

Rabbits and gophers must be controlled until the carob tree grows beyond their reach. A good idea is to surround the seedlings with poultry netting during the first year. Other pests are negligible.

Carob pods are easily shaken down. They can be dried in the sun for a few days until they are completely dry. After drying and fumigating, the pods may be stored indefinitely if protected from mice.

While the carob makes a handsome shade tree, it can be grown commercially as an orchard crop. It is a good source of protein. Although it has been known for its use as a food for livestock, carob makes a nourishing drink for human consumption and can be used as a substitute for chocolate. Carob flour, made from the flesh of the pods, has been used with wheat flour in making bread, hotcakes and waffles. Carob flour is usually made from imported pods.

CAROTENE   *See* CARROTS

CARPETGRASS   *See* LAWN

CARPETWEED   (*Mollugo verticillata*)

This low-growing weed forms mats in gardens and on paths, and thrives on light, sandy soils. It will not resist hoeing and cultivation.

CARROTS
(*Daucus Carota* var. *sativus*)

An easily grown vegetable and important source of vitamin A, carrots should occupy a prominent place in every home garden.

Carrots require a sandy loam free from lumps and stones. Obstacles such as these found in garden soil force roots into deformities and cause them to split. If manure is going to be used in the soil, it should be dug in during the fall before planting. Fresh manure should never be used, for it makes the carrots rough-skinned and soft by stimulating root branching. A mixture of one part dried blood, one part phosphate rock and four parts wood ashes can be dug into the bed at the rate of seven pounds per 100 square feet. A two-inch layer of well-rotted humus may also be spread over the bed after it has been dug.

One ounce of carrot seed will sow 100 feet. The seeds should be sown relatively thick, about a half-a-dozen seeds to the inch. Later the plants should be thinned to stand about two inches apart in the row. Rows should be spaced 12 to 16 inches apart. Seed for late sowings will come up sooner if pregerminated. If seed is spread in a thin layer between two sheets of wet blotting paper and stored in the refrigerator, white root tips will break out when seeds are ready to be planted. The damp seed may be mixed with a little dry sand to make even sowing easier.

To insure a constant supply of carrots throughout the summer and for winter storage, seed should be sown every three weeks from early spring until 2½ months before the first fall frost.

Properly stored fresh carrots keep well, retain their flavor and have a higher food value than canned ones.

Carrots can be stored in cool, moist surroundings in baskets or barrels. Plug the mouth of the storage receptacle with straw. If indoor storage is not practical, bury the box in the ground and line the trench with straw, covering with a thin layer of earth.

Several varieties of carrot are available to growers. Early Chantenay is excellent for canning, Imperator for fresh market, and Gold Pak for processing. The Chantenay varieties are best suited to heavy clay or rocky soils because they do not grow deep. Imperator or Gold Pak will grow well in good, light, loamy soils.

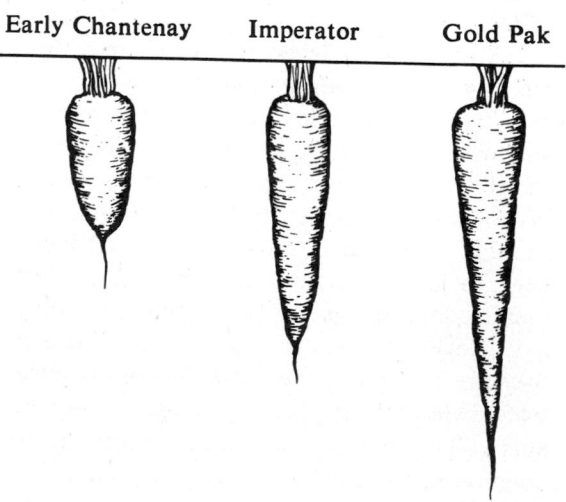

Early Chantenay   Imperator   Gold Pak

Pests: The carrot rust fly is a persistent pest that burrows tunnels in carrot roots. Crop rotation is one control often used by carrot fanciers. Wireworms can be hindered by sprinkling the carrot rows with wood ashes.

Bacterial soft rot, which turns the center of the carrot soft, may be prevented by rotation of the rows. To prevent the infestation during storage, thoroughly dry the roots in the sun before storing.

Varieties: Burpee's Goldinheart is a popular, all-purpose carrot perfect for home gardeners. Both it and the Nantes Half Long mature in 70 days and have a delicious flavor. Oxheart (75 days) and Little Finger (65 days) are small, sweet carrots and are especially tender. The Tiny Sweet Carrot (65 days) is a miniature variety reaching a length of only three inches.

Nutritional Value: One whole carrot eaten raw provides the complete RDA of vitamin A as suggested by the Food and Nutrition Board of the National Research Council. Strained carrots have been used to stop diarrhea in babies. An excess of carrot juice can create the condition carotenemia, or yellowing of the skin.

studies at Johns Hopkins University and elsewhere, Miss Carson had little time to write. It wasn't until World War II, when the government poured money into oceanographic research, that she decided to share her knowledge with the layman. A Guggenheim Fellowship gave her the necessary time away from her job as an aquatic biologist with the U.S. Bureau of Fisheries. The result was *The Sea Around Us,* published in 1951, and for which she won a National Book Award for nonfiction.

Of her four books, the most famous one, ironically, is not about the sea. Taking an early stand against pesticides and herbicides that could permanently upset the ecological balance of the earth, *Silent Spring* raised a furor of controversy when it was published in 1962. Though many considered her predictions unnecessarily gloomy, there were others who were convinced she was right, and who began demanding justification for the continued use of toxic chemicals in the land and water. Her other works include: *Under the Sea Wind* (1941) and *The Edge of the Sea* (1955).

In keeping with her love of the outdoors, Miss Carson was an avid field ornithologist. She also worked for the preservation of wilderness areas.

CARSON, RACHEL LOUISE

(1907–1964) Miss Carson's fame is due, in part, to her ability to make elegant prose out of scientific information. Her original career plan was to be a writer, but her consuming interest in the ocean and in natural history persuaded her to switch from English to zoology during her undergraduate years at the Pennsylvania College for Women in Pittsburgh. While pursuing graduate and postgraduate

CARUM   *See* CARAWAY

CASABA   *See* MELON

CASHEW   (*Anacardium occidentale*)

A native of Central and South America, this small- to medium-sized evergreen tree is grown commercially on a modest scale in

Florida. The fruit, or cashew apple, that surrounds the nut is sweet and can be eaten fresh. It is difficult to harvest the nut, as a toxic, oily fluid lies between the inner and outer shell.

See also NUT TREES.

CASSAVA   *See* MANIHOT

CAST-IRON PLANT
See ASPIDISTRA

CASTOR BEAN   (*Ricinus communis*)

The bean is the fruit of the castor-oil plant which is a robust perennial in tropical countries, but in regions subject to frost it is grown as an annual. The seeds of this plant, called castor beans, yield castor oil.

The crop is adapted to corn or cotton land, which should be prepared as for these crops. Corn planters with certain modifications can be used in seeding. The spacing of rows and of plants within the rows may be such as to permit the use of available planting and cultivation equipment. The seed should be planted 1½ to three inches deep, depending on the moisture in the soil. From seven to ten pounds of seed are required to plant an acre, depending on the variety. Weeds must be kept under control by frequent shallow cultivation early in the season.

The soil for beans requires plenty of organic matter if they are to give good yields. This can usually be supplied by crop rotation and by plowing green manure under before planting.

Besides the actual cash value of castor beans, it is the rich fertility of the castor bean pomace or residue left after the beans are hulled that is of prime interest and importance to organic-minded farmers and gardeners. Analyses show the hulls to be richer in appreciable amounts of nitrogen, phosphates, potash, and a number of other minor plant food elements than either fresh barnyard manure or cotton burrs.

In addition to the value of the hulls, the stalks are high in cellulose content and easily decomposed, and, when they and the leaves are chopped and turned under, the soil can assimilate them readily. It is estimated that from 35 to 50 percent of the gross weight of the castor beans and capsules can be returned to the soil for its improvement.

In harvesting, the beans are either hauled to the hulling plant, or a portable huller goes to the grower's field. In either case, the hulls are saved and the farmer takes his home, in most instances, to spread on his field, orchard or garden.

Many farmers find in rotating other crops with castor beans that their succeeding crops are more vigorous and productive. Potato foliage is found to be greener and healthier from the organic contribution of castor bean humus. City gardeners are seeking the hulls for mulches on rose gardens and other flowers, strawberries and asparagus and are also spreading it over lawns. The plant wastes make excellent compost.

The high-protein pomace contains ricin, a deadly poison, and should not be fed to cattle or other livestock. The seeds of beans also should be avoided.

Castor pomace is handled by fertilizer dealers in various parts of the country. Recent studies have indicated that castor pomace is fully comparable to cottonseed meal, if used on an "efficiency" basis. This means that 160 pounds of nitrogen in castor pomace will have the same crop-producing effect as 200 pounds of nitrogen in cottonseed meal. For farm practices, castor pomace may be substituted, pound for pound, for cottonseed meal.

CASUARINA

Rapid growers native to Australia and the South Pacific, these trees are often planted near the shore to hold shifting sands with their extensive root systems. Casuarinas have no leaves, having adapted themselves to the strong winds common to their native area.

The name comes from the trees' resemblance to the feathers of the *Casuarius,* or cassowary, a bird native to Australia. In the South Pacific it is sometimes called the cassowary tree.

In the United States, the tree is called Australian pine or beefwood, from its bright red color. It is sometimes planted in the extreme South for its unusual appearance.

C. equisetifolia, the best-known species in the United States, grows to 70 feet, with drooping branches. The wood is very hard and is sometimes called oak in Australia. The fruits, which it produces abundantly, resemble small pinecones.

Casuarinas do well on brackish and alkaline soils. Propagation is by seeds or cuttings of partially ripened wood.

CATALOGS

For many people the real start of the garden season is the arrival in January of the new seed and nursery catalogs. With catalogs in hand the gardener can begin to make con-

crete plans for the coming months, based not only on the results of previous gardens but also on the new seed offerings.

There is much to be gained from a careful examination of seed and nursery catalogs. In the first few pages of their catalogs companies usually offer special features. New varieties— a space-saving bush-type squash, a disease-resistant potato, a high-vitamin or low-acid tomato—often appear there and may make a worthwhile change from the standard varieties usually planted. In the beginning of the catalog, combination packages of seeds may also be offered. Such package deals, seeds for a complete family garden for example, can be especially helpful for the new gardener.

Organic gardeners can look for catalogs which offer untreated seed, organic composts, dried manures, and biological pest control products. A catalog can sometimes be judged by the quality of the garden aids offered. Sensible devices—netting to protect fruit trees from birds, strips of plastic for mulching, or well designed small greenhouses, for example— can be valuable purchases for the home gardener.

The best catalogs will give planting hints: How far apart and how deep to plant seeds, and in what kind of soil, how much a packet will plant, how to tell when the crop is ripe and ready to pick. Look for quiet claims like "heavy crop" or "bears well for several weeks if kept picked" rather than inflated promises. Read the descriptions to judge whether the seedsman is stressing qualities important to the commercial grower or to the home gardener. A thick-skinned, especially firm tomato, for example, may be designed for its shipping qualities, qualities not particularly important to the home gardener with a dozen tomato plants in his backyard.

Though many gardeners receive seed catalogs from all over the continent, it's generally a good idea to deal mainly with seedsmen in one's own zone. These seedsmen are aware of the limitations and advantages posed by their particular climate and growing season, and their seed selections will show it. Experimentation with a variety of plants exotic to the locale can be interesting and rewarding, but for the bulk of garden production rely on varieties suited to the local clime.

CATALPA

These quick-growing, handsome flowering trees are often used to ornament lawns and

Catalpas are fast-growing, hardy shade trees which provide white flowers in early summer, followed by cigar-shaped seedpods.

streets. They have relatively short lives, and aren't recommended as permanent plantings.

The showy Indian bean or southern catalpa (*C. bignonioides*) grows to a height of 50 feet and displays large clusters of white flowers in early summer. The hardy or western catalpa (*C. speciosa*) reaches a height of from 40 to 90 feet; it is hardy and well suited to hot summers and dry soil. Catalpas can be propagated by cuttings or layering.

CATCH CROP

In intercropping, a catch crop refers to a quick-maturing crop that is grown along with a major crop, but is matured and removed by the time the major crop expands to its mature size. Improving the organic matter content of soils by growing and plowing under catch crops for green manure has proven a profitable practice in many parts of the country. A rotation of corn, oats and wheat, for instance, allows a grain crop each year and a catch crop in the wheat plowed under for corn. Barley is commonly harvested before corn planting in a similar manner. Soybeans can be interseeded in still-standing wheat, and wheat can be sown in a legume field.

While the value of the catch crop varies with the cost of seed, the type of soil and the specific crop rotation in use, it is true almost without exception that legume catch crops are valuable by virtue of the increase in crop yields from the fixed nitrogen and the increased organic matter.

CATENA

Catena refers to the association between

soils on the basis of drainage or of differences in relief. Soil surveyors make use of this relationship when classifying soils in a given region.

CATNIP (*Nepeta Cataria*)

Catnip comes from a genus of aromatic annuals and perennials of the Mint family. A perennial plant from Europe, catnip is frequently seen in this country as a weed in gardens and about dwellings. It has long had a popular use as a domestic remedy. Both leaves and flowering tops are in some demand in the crude-drug trade.

Catnip grows to three feet, with downy, pale green foliage and small lavender flowers growing in spikes to five inches.

In England, catnip tea was once a popular substitute for Chinese tea, and it was brought to America by the colonists primarily for this purpose. In the past, the herb was recommended for hysteria, headaches and nightmares. An infusion of catnip was used as a tonic, nervine and antispasmodic.

Catnip does well on almost any good soil, but thrives best on a well-drained, moderately rich garden loam. It will be more fragrant, however, if grown in sandy situations rather than in heavy soils. It does well in sun or shade. The plant may be propagated by root division or from seed sown in rows either late in fall or early in spring and covered lightly. Fall-sown seed usually gives a more even stand and a heavier growth. When the plants have reached a height of four to five inches they are thinned to stand 12 to 16 inches apart in the rows. In some localities field sowing does not give good results, in which case plants may be started in a cold frame and later transplanted to the field. Shallow cultivation will favor vigorous growth.

Tea made from dried catnip leaves is a traditional remedy for headaches, hysteria and nervousness.

The flowering tops, harvested when the plants are in full bloom, are dried in the shade to preserve their green color. When larger quantities are grown, the herb may be cut with a mowing machine with the cutter bar set high. The plants should lie in the swath until partly dry, and the curing may then be finished either in the shade of small cocks in the field or in the barn, care being taken to preserve the natural green color as far as possible.

Tea is not the only end product of catnip. Candied catnip leaves make an enjoyable dessert, and the oil from its leaves is used as an antidote for nervousness and headaches. The dried leaves of this plant can amuse and excite a cat for hours on end. Put a few catnip leaves in a small pouch and watch your feline roll in it, rub it and shred it to pieces in sheer delight.

See also HERB.

CATTAIL   (*Typha latifolia*)

Sometimes referred to as reeds, flags, rushes, Cossack asparagus, or reed-mace, cattails are tall plants that grow on swamp or marshland. From three to 12 feet at maturity, cattails are topped by a cigar-shaped flower spike. The spike is a dense mass of minute one-seeded fruits, each on a long hairlike stalk and covered with long, downy hairs. The base of the long stalk is tightly sheathed by long, pale green tapelike leaves. The roots are ropelike and branch frequently.

A perennial plant, cattails spread rapidly. In a single year one rhizome may push up more than a quarter-million separate clumps of leaves spreading over three acres of marsh. Once established, they crowd out all competition, and a cultivated stand offers no weeding problem. The cattail has no natural enemies of any consequence.

Widely known only for its use in dried floral displays, the cattail can actually be a source of valuable food and other products. Acre for acre, the cattail can outproduce corn, rice, wheat, or potatoes in quantity, quality and variety of food harvested. Offering four different vegetables and two kinds of flour, cattails can be harvested from October through mid-June.

In October, yellow green sprouts begin to grow from the rhizome. These asparagus-flavored sprouts, available throughout the winter, can be severed from the rhizome and cooked as a vegetable. In spring the sprouts shoot up through the ice. When they stand 18 or more inches above the water's surface, the stalks are ready to be harvested. Edible raw or cooked, the stalks taste like cucumbers with a carrot's texture. The male flower, which matures in mid-June, can be peeled, boiled and served like corn on the cob. If allowed to ripen, the male flower produces a fine yellow pollen which can be collected and used as a flour in making pancakes and muffins. The core of the rhizome itself can be used either

Cattails spread rapidly in marshland and, once established, crowd out all competing vegetation.

as a potato substitute or to make a nutritious high-gluten flour.

Experimental studies show that cultivation will produce a larger cattail crop. They can be grown on lands unsuitable for other crops, providing the land can be irrigated. Though they need ample water, cattails do not require swamp conditions.

The cotton or down collected from ripe cattail heads is used in life rafts and life preservers. The long basal leaves furnish the material from which rush seating is made for chairs. The by-products from processing cattails for food can often be fed to livestock, and the reeds themselves can be composted or used as a mulch.

CATTLEYA

Native to the foothills and mountains of South America, these epiphytic orchids are the most popular and the easiest to grow in the greenhouse or home. Flowers, which are shades of orange and lavender, vary from 1½ to ten inches in width and normally appear once a year. Each pseudo-bulb has one to three straplike leaves that are 12 to 20 inches high.

Cattleya generally like relative humidity levels above 40 percent, moderate levels of sunshine or fluorescent light and a moisture-retaining medium such as osmunda fiber or shredded fir bark. The growing medium should dry between water applications, but must not remain dry for prolonged periods of time. An average home temperature between 68 and 70°F. (20 and 21.11°C.) in the day with a slight drop at night is suitable. Repotting is necessary when the plant begins to grow over the pot edge or drainage becomes poor.

The South American cattleya orchid can be grown under lights in the home.

This should be done in spring or early summer for best recovery. Plants must be firmly set to avoid root breakage during growth.

For beginners, *C. Trianaei* is the best choice because it is quite tolerant to abuse and grows well.

See also ORCHIDS.

CAULIFLOWER
(*Brassica oleracea* var. *botrytis*)

To produce the circular head of pure white curds that give this vegetable the deserved name of "flower," plenty of attention is needed. Of first importance is the soil. This should be deeply dug, pulverized, rich in organic fertilizer, and above all, contain a high percentage of nitrogen. A shortage of nitrogen will cause leaves to droop and die and the head to be stunted and turn yellow.

In preparing space for the cauliflower do not forget that a rapid, vigorous growth is necessary for its development. So, in addition to maintaining organic matter in the earth by plowing under green manure crops, feed the ground generously with compost. If your soil is very acid, give it a medium application of lime well in advance of planting time.

Set cauliflowers in rows of furrows dug two feet apart. Place the large, late varieties two feet apart, and early, smaller ones 15 inches from each other. Make a shallow furrow between the rows, and use this for watering when the weather is dry. Some successful gardeners run a stream of water through the planting rows, and allow it to soak in before setting the plants. Others plant them in dry soil and water them generously immediately after setting in the ground. Either method gives the added advantage of settling the soil firmly around the roots.

In most of the home gardens in the East, cauliflower is grown either in the spring or the late fall. The last few days in May will be the spring planting date, the tenth of July the approximate one for fall. The spring seeding is started in flats in the house. Sow the seeds sparsely here, so as to give the small plants plenty of room to develop. When these have four leaves apiece, thin them, leaving a full two inches between them. If the spring weather is mild enough to allow planting the seeds directly in the ground, put three or four of these in the place where one is to be left standing. In this case you will have to thin the plants as

soon as possible to avoid their crowding each other.

Only when mild weather has come to stay should the early crop be planted directly in the ground. A late frost will stunt the plants and cause a premature growth of the head bereft of all leaves.

When the head first pushes itself above the level of the ground, small incurving leaves close around it and protect it from the sun. As the head enlarges, however, these leaves

In order to produce a pure white head of cauliflower, tie the large, outer leaves in an upright position. This will shield the developing head from the sun.

are forced apart and away from it, and human hands are needed for further care. The gardener must then shield the head from the sun by bringing the largest leaves up over it and tying them in an upright position with soft tape, raffia or string.

Even after the leaves are tied watchfulness should still be the order of the day, for you must make sure that the heads do not over-develop. It will be better to cut cauliflower a little too early than too late. The weather will help you decide when to harvest. If it is warm, a cauliflower will be ready to cut in from three to five days after its leaves have been tied. If the weather is cool, as much as two weeks may pass before it reaches the accepted size for cutting.

The general rules for cutting are: Cut when the head is six inches in diameter, and while its curds are compact, not after they begin to separate and resemble grains of rice. When the time comes for harvesting, cut the plant with a sharp knife, leaving one or more whorls of leaves around the head to keep it from breaking.

Varieties: Early Snowball is a 60-day maturer, with small- to medium-sized heads. Purple Head matures in 85 days and has a taste similar to broccoli. Snow King Hybrid is hardy and heat tolerant, as is Danish Giant.

Nutrient Value: One serving of cauliflower contains 66 mg. of ascorbic acid (vitamin C), which exceeds the amount suggested as the Recommended Daily Allowance.

CAYENNE   (*Capsicum annuum*)

Cayenne and other pungent red peppers used as condiments are obtained as dried fruits from an annual herbaceous plant, *Capsicum annuum,* widely cultivated in many parts of the world and variable in the character of its fruit. They are closely related to the so-called sweet, or mild-flavored, varieties commonly grown in home gardens. The pungent varieties used in the dried form are designated in the trade as dry peppers to distinguish them from the others used in the fresh condition and classed as vegetables. Included among the dry peppers is paprika, a mild type.

The pungent red peppers vary in size, shape and degree of color and pungency. The pungency is greatest in the tissues near the seed, and the extent to which these tissues are removed determines to some degree the pungency of the finished product. The varieties of pungent peppers are known under various names, such as chili, cayenne and Tabasco.

They require a warm climate and light soil. The plants bear fruit throughout the late summer and fall and to produce a full crop must have a long growing season. The plants are propagated from seed planted under glass or in outdoor seedbeds, and the seedlings are set in the field later and cultivated like other truck crops.

See also PEPPER.

CEDAR-APPLE GALLS
See FUNGUS

CELERY   (*Apium graveolens*)

Celery is often thought to be difficult to grow. This is not especially so if a few simple precautions are taken.

Celery is an especially heavy feeder, requiring high amounts of organic nitrogen, phosphorus and potassium as well as certain key minor nutrients.

Planting: For best results, celery seeds should be started indoors in flats or trays eight to ten weeks before planting outdoors. Fall or winter crops are also started in flats or cold frames, rather than in rows where it will grow. Scatter seed in neat rows approximately one inch apart, and cover them with a fine layer of sand. Soil should be composed of a mixture of two-thirds mature compost and one-third clean, washed sand. Watering can be done from the bottom by immersing the tray in a container

of water. Good ventilation, cool temperatures and good drainage should produce healthy plants which will not succumb to damping-off.

When seedlings reach a height of three to four inches, they should be transplanted to another flat and spaced three inches apart. When approximately six inches tall, the plants are ready to be set out in the garden. Be sure all danger of frost is past before transplanting outdoors.

At least a week before setting the young plants out, the ground should be properly prepared to permit the settling of the soil. Add nitrogen, phosphate and potash fertilizers, plus lime, if necessary.

This mixture should then be deeply dug in and the soil worked to a depth of 14 inches. If you prepare the soil during very dry weather, it is advisable to follow the digging by a thorough drenching. In any event the soil should be supplied with sufficient water to penetrate several inches a couple of days before the setting out of the plants.

Celery is a heavy feeder that needs a steady and quick growth. If the supply of compost material is low, rotted poultry, stable or sheep manure comes in handy provided it is well incorporated in the soil before the setting out of the plants. Moisture is essential.

The plants should be set out in the garden six inches apart, in rows at least two feet apart. Care should be taken to see that they are not set deeper than they stood in the flat. They should be well watered during and immediately following transplanting.

Another effective method of planting celery is in circles of eight plants each. A small hole is dug in the center of the circle, into which is placed compost and manure fertilizer. As the celery stalks grow, their leaves shade the moist center hole, thereby preventing the loss of much needed moisture and plant nutrients.

Culture: A heavy mulch is needed to preserve moisture in the celery patch. Manure water should be applied liberally every ten days or so. Frequent watering is necessary for productive celery growth. Should cold weather threaten, dry straw or hay can be used to protect the plants.

To blanch celery, wrap heavy paper, such as newspaper, around the stalks when the plants are 18 inches high, allowing six inches of leaves to protrude from the top. Tie the paper securely around the stalks and bank soil around the base of the plant to exclude light from below.

Boards may be used for summer blanching, if available. Place the boards next to the plants on each side, working them into the soil. Drive stakes into the soil on the outside of the boards to prevent their falling over. Boards may also be used to blanch winter crops. However, by simply hilling soil around the celery stalks, leaving only leaves exposed, the same effect can be achieved.

Harvest: Celery which is to be used immediately should be cut below the soil surface. If you are planning to store the harvest, remove the celery and its roots and store it in a cool cellar, in boxes, covered with straw. Plants may also be stored in boxes set in deep pits in the ground. Simply cover them with a layer of straw to retain humidity.

Enemies: Damping-off is the greatest danger affecting celery plants during hot, humid weather. It is best to protect plants with some shading device to prevent this problem. Aphids can also affect crop yields of celery. Careful weeding should minimize an infestation. *See also* DISEASE, INSECT.

Varieties: Tall Fordhook Tendercrisp is great for winter storage. Burpee's Golden Self-Blanching matures in 115 days to produce a delicious, yellow vegetable.

CELERY CABBAGE
See CHINESE CABBAGE

CELLULOSE

Cellulose is an inert carbohydrate that forms the major percentage of the cell walls of plants, wood, linen, paper, etc.—in fact, it is the most abundant naturally occurring substance. The purest form of cellulose, found in purified cotton, is composed of 44.4 percent carbon, 49.4 percent oxygen and 6.2 percent hydrogen. Plants synthesize cellulose from glucose.

Although cellulose has no function in human diet except as roughage, some animals are able to digest cellulose because their stomachs retain the cellulose long enough for bacteria to digest it. Cellulose is very important to soil fungi and bacteria as it furnishes nutrients as it decays.

CELOSIA

Usually called cockscomb, these well-known tender annuals of the Amaranth family produce either crested or plumed flower heads mostly in strong colors. They are at their best in the heat of summer and can be easily grown in a light, rich soil with adequate moisture. It

Celosia plumosa *should be pinched back to encourage heavy flowering.*

is best to start seed in warmth indoors six to eight weeks before the last frost. Seeds germinate quickly, but the young plants are highly susceptible to damping-off, so be sure that air circulates freely around them. Allow the surface of the soil in the seedling flat to dry out between waterings after the plants are up. Use tepid water. Transplant seedlings to other flats or into 2¼-inch peat pots when the first set of true leaves appears. Set outside in full sun when danger of frost is well past. Water the plants in dry periods. They like moisture but resent a soggy, poorly drained soil.

Celosia argentea var. *cristata* is the true cockscomb, with fuzzy, curved flower heads resembling the pea combs of some roosters. Varieties range in height from six inches to two feet. They are so striking in form and color that they must be used carefully in the garden to avoid having them clash with other flowers.

Plants grown from seed mixtures are often best in beds by themselves. A few go a long way. Jewel Box is a dwarf mix with colors in red, pink, orange, and yellow shades. Fireglow is a 24-inch All-America winner with rich red flowers in large heads whose color combines well with those of other annuals, especially yellow ones.

C. plumosa, with its foxtail flower heads, produces a spiky, upright effect in the border. There are dwarf forms, but the tall two- or three-foot varieties are the most useful. When setting plants out in spring, pinch out the tip of each one. This will hasten development of side shoots and cause heavier flower production. The longer stemmed celosias make long-lasting cut flowers. The dwarf crested or cockscomb types do not, and should not have their tips pinched out.

It is best to buy seed of specific colored varieties and to avoid mixtures of older types since the latter will invariably produce many plants with flowers in shades of shrieking magenta that clash with everything. The yellows and golds are the best colors for use in a mixed bed. Golden Triumph, Golden Fleece and the orange gold Tango are all outstanding in August and September. Forest Fire Improved has red flower heads on two-foot stems. Foliage and stem are shaded magenta red. Red Fox has clearer red flowers and green foliage. All varieties and types of celosia are good for drying.

CENTAUREA

These summer-blooming annual and perennial herbs of the Composite family grow one to four feet tall and produce flowers in shades of blue, white, crimson, pink, and yellow. Centaureas prefer a light, well-drained garden soil and full sun, and are showy plants in the border and cutting garden, especially when crowded together. Propagation is by seed or root division.

Popular species include bachelor's-button or cornflower (*C. Cyanus*), growing to three feet, with blue, pink or white flowers; dusty-miller (*C. cineraria*), to 1½ feet, grown for its fine gray foliage; basket flower (*C. americana*), to four feet, with lavender blooms; and sweet-sultan (*C. moschata*), to two feet, with blue, pink, purple, and white flowers.

See also BACHELOR'S-BUTTON.

CENTIPEDEGRASS   *See* LAWN

CENTRANTHUS

The most popular species of this small genus of the Valerian family is *C. ruber,* often called Jupiter's beard or red valerian. A bushy perennial growing two to three feet tall, red valerian has gray green leaves and dense clusters of small, tubular red flowers that bloom in midsummer. Propagation is by seed or root division in spring.

CENTURY PLANT   *See* AGAVE

CEPHALARIA

A genus of the Teasel family that is easily grown in ordinary garden soil and full sun or partial shade, cephalarias are tall annuals and perennials that are best planted at the back of the border or in the cutting garden. *C. gigantea* is a popular species with large yellow flowers resembling those of scabiosa. It grows to six feet. Propagation is by seed or division.

CEREAL LEAF BEETLE
See INSECT CONTROL

CEREALS

Cereals are agricultural grains of the Grass family, such as barley, rye, wheat, oats, corn, rice, and sorghum. Rye is commonly used as a cover crop on sandy, rocky and poor soils. Barley is also recommended for cover cropping since it makes a heavy, quick growth. A winter cover crop of barley is often used to prepare the soil for early spring crops.

CEREUS

This genus of treelike cacti likes a light, porous soil with good drainage. It needs a reasonable amount of water during the growing season (almost as much as ordinary house plants), but while not active it should have only enough to keep it from shriveling. Feeding should be light.

Cereus are noted for their large white flowers that bloom at night. One species, *C. Jamacaru,* grows to 40 feet.

See also CACTI.

CEYLON GOOSEBERRY
See UMKOKOLO

CHAMOMILE

Chamomiles—plural is proper, for there are two main varieties and a welter of lesser ones—are among the chief beneficiaries of the revival of interest in herbal culture and lore within the last several years.

Chamomile tea, a fine aromatic delight for any tea drinker, is widely available today in gourmet and grocery shops. Chamomile has a wide range of medicinal uses depending on the variety. The two main types are, in actuality, of two separate genera. They are *Anthemis nobilis,* commonly called English or Roman chamomile, and *Matricaria recutita,* known as German or Hungarian chamomile. Part of the identity problem is the close physical resemblance of the two plants. Another is the fact that the *Matricaria* genus is botanically ill-defined and spills at times into neighboring

genera such as *Anthemis, Chrysanthemum* and possibly *Pyrethrum.*

Whatever the reason for their similarity, their chief differences are these: *A. nobilis* is a prostrate creeping perennial with very fine foliage and solid, deep yellow flower disks with creamy white rays, and is probably more aromatic. *M. recutita,* on the other hand, is an erect annual with somewhat coarser foliage and daisylike flowers and white rays.

Like all annuals, the European variety must be planted from seed each year, and that's a delicate process because of the unstable viability of *M. recutita* seed. It's one of the rare seeds that needs light to germinate. Broadcast it in August and stir the earth very lightly over it. By mid-September, plants should be well-enough established to transplant. Once established, they are exceedingly hardy and should need no winter cover. Seeds also can be started in indoor flats in March and transplanted after hardening off. Postfrost spring plantings directly in the garden usually are successful, too.

The English variety also can be started from seed, but a much easier and more successful approach to that variety is to purchase the plants and allow the runners to spread them gradually over the area of the garden you've designated for chamomile. Its root clusters, too, can be divided to propagate the plant.

Both plants are useful when their flowers are infused as a tonic, stomachic, anodyne, or antispasmodic. Chamomile tea, in addition, is sprayed by some gardeners on seed flats to prevent damping-off. German chamomile is said to aid the absorption of calcium when added to the compost heap.

Some other less common species of the *Anthemis* genus are *A. Cotula,* a wild chamomile also known as mayweed, and *A. tinctoria,*

The daisylike flowers of the chamomile are dried to make a medicinal tea.

hardy or golden marguerite, that yields a yellow dye. All the chamomiles are wild and will readily escape the garden.

See also HERB.

CHARCOAL

A black, porous form of carbon, charcoal is prepared from vegetable or animal substances, usually by charring wood in a kiln from which air is excluded.

Pieces of charcoal are often recommended as additions to potting soils, as they improve drainage.

Charcoal, and the ash left from burning charcoal in a stove or barbecue, contains valuable minerals and can be an excellent source of plant nutrients. Charcoal chunks make an unusual-appearing mulch in an ornamental garden.

CHARD   *See* SWISS CHARD

CHARITY   *See* JACOB'S-LADDER

CHASTE TREE   *See* VITEX

CHECKERBERRY
See WINTERGREEN

CHEESEWOOD   *See* VICTORIAN BOX

CHELATORS

Chelators, a term which comes from a Greek word meaning clawlike, are organic compounds which have attached molecules of inorganic metals to themselves. These are usually available in small molecules which are relatively unstable in the soil and difficult for plants to absorb. When bonded to stable organic molecules, or chelated, the metals become more available in the soil for plant use. Although the process of chelation has been demonstrated in the laboratory, it has only recently begun to receive attention as it naturally occurs in the soil.

The process called chelation is a complex one, involving several biochemical reactions and a large number of organic compounds in the soil, and is not fully understood. Humus, compost material, manure, and all organic matter applied to the soil have chelating properties. ". . . composting," wrote Dr. Albert Schatz et al. in a paper published in *Compost Science,* "may be looked upon as a process for the manufacture of natural chelating materials."

Metals in the soil, and especially trace minerals such as iron, copper, boron, manganese, cobalt, and others, have positively charged ions which can unite with negatively charged ions in organic matter compounds. They can also serve to unite molecules of organic matter at points of negative charge, often at two or more sites. Because of their chemical structure, chelates are stable and exhibit properties that neither the metal nor the original molecule of organic matter had.

Chelated minerals are water soluble, although the activity of metal ions in the solution decreases. No one yet knows how plants use metal chelates, although research indicates that soil pH may have some effect.

Many soil fungi produce a variety of compounds that behave as chelators. This may be a major function of the mycorrhiza which form a symbiotic relationship with the roots of trees and other plants. Without their fungus partners, these plants either grow poorly or are unable to develop at all.

Chemical compounds produced by lichens are powerful chelators. These creatures are able to live luxuriantly in barren places where other forms of life cannot even survive by using "built-in" chelators to dissolve rocks and provide vital trace metals. This is one of the best examples of biological weathering or the chemical breakdown of rocks and minerals by living organisms.

There are some chelators available commercially; the one most commonly used is called EDTA. However, experimenters have observed that it works no better than natural chelators. Indeed, manufactured chelators may actually be too strong, absorbing too much of the stored nutrients in soil at once, leaving little for future crops to utilize.

CHEMURGY

This branch of applied chemistry deals with industrial utilization of organic raw materials, particularly from farm products.

Chemurgists have three major aims: 1) the improvement of present crops and methods of processing them; 2) the development of new crops and uses for them; and 3) research to find new, nonfood uses for farm crops, their residues and by-products.

CHERNOZEM SOILS

Chernozem is a zonal soil group in the classification system used prior to 1965. Now called mollisols these soils are characterized by deep, dark surface horizons, rich in organic matter, which grade into lighter soil colors below the surface. At 1½- to four-foot depths, they have layers of accumulated calcium carbonate. They developed under tall and mixed grasses in a temperate to cool sub-humid climate.

CHERRY   (*Prunus*)

Sweet, sour and hybrid cherry trees have been producing valuable crops and wood for centuries.

Sour cherries are among the hardiest of fruit trees, standing up well to heat, cold, neglect, and insects. Sweet cherries are more sensitive. The young trees are susceptible to spring frosts, and hillside locations are preferable. Trees planted along ponds or lakes fare better in cold snaps because bodies of water reduce extreme changes in nearby air temperature.

Orchard soil should be well drained. A sandy loam enables trees to establish deep roots. While shallow-rooted trees may produce satisfactorily for a time, a hard winter or period of abnormal rainfall may wreak havoc with them. An indifferent soil can be improved at planting time by mixing in peat moss and compost.

The development and ripening of the fruit depend on plenty of sunlight, so allow trees sufficient space. If you have little land to work with, dwarf varieties can be set 18 or so feet apart. Large sweet cherry trees should be set 30 feet apart.

While cherry trees were customarily planted in spring, they may be set out in fall as well. If trees are to be planted in spring, plow the land the previous fall. Water the roots of young trees as soon as they arrive from the nursery, and plant them at once if possible. If planting must be delayed, prepare a trench in a sandy, well-drained spot, place the roots in it, and fill it with soil, working the soil into the roots. Before you set the trees in the ground, trim off any roots which have been broken or injured in moving, and shorten any straggling ones. Plant the trees a little deeper in the ground than they were at the nursery. A good way to settle the earth around the roots is to move the tree gently up and down as you throw the first few shovelfuls in place.

Provided the soil is deep and plentifully supplied with nitrogen, you can grow cherry trees in sod, but be sure that the sod isn't allowed to compete with the trees for moisture and nourishment. Use a mulch of hay or other suitable material, and cut the grass two or three times in May and June.

Trees not grown in sod should be treated with manure or compost and then surrounded with a cover crop. Rye is an excellent spring cover, and should be sown at the rate of 1½ bushels of seed to the acre. Sow as early in spring as possible, and turn it under before the crop matures so that it will not compete with the young trees.

A late summer cover crop is even better. Good choices are buckwheat, oats and millet; none survives the winter, and all add nitrogen to the soil as they wither on the ground. Sow these grains when the fruit is ready for harvest —sometime during the first two weeks of July. As the season advances, you will find this late crop of value in improving the soil, especially if it tends to be heavy, while it improves the wood during the late summer and fall by preventing erosion and loss of nutrients.

At the time of planting, have the main stem higher than any of the branches. Thin the others from about four to six inches apart, leaving the lowest ones about 16 inches from the ground. After that, cut only to keep the center of the tree free from sprouts, inward-growing branches and crossing branches.

Although sweet cherry trees produce good pollen, none of them are self-fruiting. Generally speaking, pollination will take place when any of these are planted together, but there are exceptions to remember, namely, the sweet cherries Bing, Emperor Francis, Lambert, and Napoleon. Duke cherries, grown primarily for home gardens because they are noted for their hardiness, are hybrids of sweet and sour varieties and will pollinate both types.

Warm, red brown heartwood from the black cherry (*P. serotina*) is prized by cabinetmakers. It can be worked well with hand tools and is a good wood for carving. The small purplish fruit can be used in jelly or to flavor cider. Cherries, wild or cultivated, can be frozen, canned or sun-dried. Pick them without the stems to avoid damaging fruiting twigs; as this will leave a break in the fruit, they should be processed at once. Netting will keep birds from harvesting the cherries before you get to them.

See also entries for individual cherries, FRUIT TREES, ORCHARD.

CHERRY, BUSH

The bush cherry makes an attractive hedge or foundation planting, and in late summer produces tart, black purple cherries suitable for pies and preserves. While the cherries are not as large as those from trees, the bush cherry is hardier, easier to grow and take care of and is rarely bothered by insects or diseases. The bush cherry will grow to a height of four or five feet in as many years, producing fruit the second year, along with two weeks of small white blossoms early in May. The attractive silvery green foliage turns red in autumn.

Originally called the sand cherry, probably because it was developed on a sandy soil, the plant will thrive on a wide variety of soils, including clay loam. However, it prefers good soil, and annual applications of compost are recommended. The bush cherry takes well to pruning, which should be done before August as the flowers are borne on both new and old wood in late summer and late pruning would remove many flower buds.

Most authorities recommend early spring as the best planting time, but many owners have successfully started plants in fall. If they are started in fall, a heavy winter mulch is a requisite.

Hansen's bush cherry is an improved form of *Prunus Besseyi,* our western species, and probably the best. The Nanking bush cherry (*P. tomentosa*) and the Japanese bush cherry (*P. japonica*) are similar. By judicious pruning, these shrubs can be kept from four to six feet, making them much easier than trees to cover against bird depredations at the crucial ripening time. These bushes are all advertised as self-fertile, which means you should get fruit even with only a single specimen. New plants are usually started from softwood cuttings.

The Nanking is one of several varieties of winter-hardy, self-fertile bush cherries.

CHERRY, FLOWERING
(*Prunus yedoensis, P. serrulata*)

Hardy throughout most of the United States, these beautiful ornamental shrubs and trees include the Japanese flowering cherries *Prunus yedoensis* and *P. serrulata.* They generally grow between 20 and 40 feet high, and are cultivated similarly to such fruit trees as cherries, plums and peaches. All of them grow well in open sunlight and well-drained soils. Mulch them during winter with compost or well-decomposed manure as this encourages early spring blooms. Plant them about 25 feet apart. *See also* CHERRY.

CHERRY, SOUR   (*Prunus Cerasus*)

The sour cherry is one of the most resistant of all fruit trees to insect damage and disease. It might well be termed the universal fruit tree, for no other fruit tree will thrive in so many different zones. Some varieties are extremely hardy, particularly the Rhex sour cherry. Generally, sour cherries are easier to grow than sweet cherries. The sour cherry is also known to grow and bear in dry and drought-affected areas where other fruit trees wither and fail to produce. Add to these the advantage of having dead-ripe fruit in early summer, and it's easy to see why the sour cherry is one of the most popular fruit trees in America today.

Not all sour cherries are tart. Some are good for eating right off the tree as well as for cooking.

The three most popular varieties are Early Richmond, Montmorency and English Morello. Early Richmond is an early producer of small fruits used almost exclusively for cooking. Trees are hardy, vigorous, very large, and productive. Montmorency produces large, tart, red cherries. It is the most popular of all varieties, thriving from Virginia all the way up into Quebec. The trees are large, very hardy, vigorous, and productive. English Morello gives a medium-sized, red black fruit, produces rather late and is excellent for cooking. The tree is small, vigorous and hardy.

Trees often suffer greatly in the transition from nursery to permanent location, so take pains in preparing the planting hole. The few pests of the tree are not likely to present serious problems. Brown rot and black knot leaf are two diseases to watch for. At the first sign of trouble, remove dead or injured wood, cankers and knots to prevent further infestation.

See also CHERRY, FRUIT TREES.

CHERVIL (*Anthriscus cerefolium*)

An annual herb used today mostly as a salad green, chervil comes in two varieties,

For a constant supply of fresh salad greens and medicinal tea leaves, plant chervil seeds in early spring and again in late summer.

plain and curly. The plants grow to about two feet high and develop small, white flowers arranged in umbels.

Chervil can be started from seed. Make a furrow about one inch deep, and scatter the seed evenly, pressing down with the tines of a rake held vertically. Do not cover with soil, as chervil needs light to germinate. Keep moist until the plants are visible. Since the plant germinates quickly and does not transplant well, it is best to sow it outdoors.

The herb is not particular about soil and does not require much in the way of fertilizer. A good, thick straw mulch will help keep the soil cool.

Chervil grows better in cool weather, and should be sown in March or early April or after July for autumn harvest. For fresh leaves throughout the winter, sow seeds in the cold frame in early autumn. For a constant supply of leaves during the summer, plant seed continuously through the summer, preferably in the shade. The older leaves are more nearly horizontal than new leaves and should be cut first.

See also HERB, PARSLEY.

CHESTNUT   (*Castanea*)

Native to the eastern and northern United States, the American chestnut (*C. dentata*) once grew to a height of 100 feet, its green leaves changing to bright yellow in autumn. Chestnut wood, both durable and versatile, was used for telephone poles, fence posts, log houses and barns, and also served the leather and paper industries.

When the fungal disease *Endothia parisitica* wiped out thousands of acres of American chestnuts, the blight-resistant Chinese chestnut (*C. mollissima*) was introduced to replace it. Today, some 50 years after the appearance of the catastrophic blight, plant breeders continue their quest for a blight-resistant sport of American chestnut. Typically, the seedlings grow up from the roots of blighted trees and then succumb after a few years.

Chinese Chestnut: This introduced tree produces a nut that is comparable in taste to, and larger than, the native American chestnut. The Chinese chestnut does well in almost any climate or soil, grows quickly (bearing after four years), produces heavily, and is practically blight-free.

Ideally, the tree should be grown in a well-drained, slightly acid soil. It will thrive from the southern temperate zone to the Great Lakes region, although it does better in southern states. Roughly, this chestnut shares the peach tree's range.

Organic matter in the soil is vital to the Chinese chestnut, providing proper nutrients for young seedlings and holding moisture in the soil. This tree is comparatively shallow rooted, and does not require as deep a soil as most nut trees. This characteristic has both advantages and disadvantages: It is not necessary to work the soil as deeply when planting seedlings, and shallow roots will absorb water more quickly than deep-rooted trees; on the other side of the ledger, roots will tend to dry out quickly in surface soil, and will be subject to surface soil temperature changes. Because roots are shallow, mulching is a necessity. The homesteader or suburban gardener who wants only a few trees for beauty, shade and food can do very well with a straw mulch of four to six inches, placed around each tree to the outer extent of its branches. To discourage field mice, keep mulch two feet away from the trunk, and lay a six-inch layer of coarse stones in this mulch-less area. The mulch should never be removed; a good mulch will break down slowly, year after year, feeding the soil and retaining a good tilth in the surface soil.

Some commercial growers use a permanent sod mulch system. The sod is cut and allowed to act as a growing mulch around each tree. This system is easier than straw mulching, but may cause a nitrogen deficiency, correctable by feeding applications of manure or cottonseed meal in late winter or early spring, before new growth starts. A word of caution here—some growers have had very unfortunate experiences with fertilizers, killing trees with heavy applications. Cultivation is unnecessary and impractical, as roots may be injured in the process.

Newly transplanted trees have begun to bear in as few as three years, with crops increasing annually until, at maturity, trees produce well over 100 pounds of nuts per season.

The best characteristic of this tree is that it bears comparatively heavy in its early years. You won't have to wait forever to enjoy the fruits of your labor.

Trees should be planted 25 to 30 feet apart. Frost pockets mean sure death and should be avoided. Air drainage must be good. After ten to 15 years, every other tree should be cut out so that the planting distance is enlarged to 50 by 50 feet. Yields will not be increased by crowding trees.

It is wise to plant several varieties in close proximity, as the Chinese chestnut is self-sterile. Trees grown alone will produce but a few nuts. Supply plenty of moisture for young trees, as it is vitally important for good spring growth and for the very life of the tree. You might form a shallow basin around the tree to catch and hold water. The mulch around trees will protect the topsoil from drying and caking, while plenty of humus will hold water in the soil. It would be a good idea to use a moisture meter to keep constant check on young trees until they are well established.

Although done successfully by some growers, grafting and layering the Chinese chestnut are rather difficult for the home gardener. Therefore, propagation is usually limited to planting seedlings. Since the career of this tree in America is still in infancy, experimenters are constantly working to improve the variety. Some experts maintain that in due time the Chinese chestnut will surpass the American variety in quality and yield.

Chestnut weevils can become a major problem, but may be controlled by gathering nuts from the ground daily to prevent the worms from entering the soil. Chickens will rid the area of worms if allowed to run under the trees.

See also Nut Trees.

CHICKEN

Chickens are probably the most popular animals on the small farm since they produce both meat and eggs and contribute a valuable manure to the compost pile. Raising chickens can be especially economical if you can raise your own grain for feeding; and if allowed enough room and access to range they seldom sicken or have the diseases that plague commercial poultry-raisers who keep thousands of birds in close confinement.

Breeds: In general, you can buy egg breeds, meat breeds and what are called general-purpose breeds. This means that the bird produces a fair number of eggs per year and also possesses a good configuration for meat production—large size, a broad breast and rapid growth.

Rhode Island Reds, and White, Barred and Plymouth Rocks are popular general-purpose breeds for the homestead. They are good layers, producing large brown eggs. Other breeds, such as Cochins, Light Brahmas and especially Araucanas, are popular because they are good setters, a trait bred out of many modern birds. These birds also tend to be seasonal layers, so you will get a large egg production in spring which will slacken off as the days get shorter and the weather gets colder.

For most efficient egg production, buy White Leghorns or Leghorn crosses. These are the breeds used by professional poultrymen and their laying ability is exceeded only by their disinterest in setting their eggs. Since they are bred for laying, cost per dozen eggs is low but Leghorns make poor meat birds. Any chicks will have to be purchased or raised from fertile eggs in an incubator or under a banty that will set them.

For meat production, Cornish and Cornish crosses are best. They reach a large size quickly, have white breasts, yellow skin and white pinfeathers which make them a good market bird. Egg production is low, however, and since they eat more, cost per dozen eggs is high.

There are numerous other fancy and unique breeds which you might like to try on your farm. You can also buy banties or bantams in many breeds. These are miniature chickens, bred for small size from larger species. They are popular on the homestead because they are good insect-catchers, don't take up much room and are fierce setters who will even set eggs from nonbroody hens.

You can usually find a local hatchery that stocks White Leghorns and perhaps some other breeds and will sell you a few chicks. Although you can occasionally buy pullet and cockerel trios (two pullets and a cock) of more exotic breeds from local poultry fanciers, the widest selection can be found in catalogs of mail-order poultry houses. Addresses of these concerns are available from most farm and poultry magazines.

Starting: Probably the best way to start is with day-old chicks, bought mail-order or locally. Chicks are sold in either straight-run or sexed batches. Straight-run means that you take your chances on how many pullets versus cockerels you will be sent; but remember that you can always slaughter extra cocks or pullets at the end of the summer when you select your layers and breeders for the next season.

The area for starting chicks should have ½ square foot of space per bird. It should be deeply littered—use a litter that will not raise a dust, such as peanut hulls, ground corncobs or peat moss. Straw is not a good litter for chicks. Cover the litter with newspaper for a few days; if you don't, the chicks will eat it.

A heat lamp should provide warmth for the chicks; the temperature two inches above the floor should be 95°F. (35°C.). Temperature can be regulated by raising and lowering the light. Provide a circular enclosure for the chicks; they will pile up in the corners of a rectangular structure and smother if frightened.

Provide starter mash in small feeders, allowing one-inch-per-chick feeding space. Keep feeders constantly three-fourths full. A constant supply of fresh water is a must; plastic chick waterers screwed on regular fruit jars are fine. Provide two one-gallon waterers for every 100 chicks.

When the chicks arrive, dip the beaks of each into the water and put them in the enclosure. Make sure they are all in good condition—hatcheries have different procedures for reporting losses and provide extra chicks to cover deaths en route.

Feeders and waterers should be washed daily. After the first few days, remove the newspaper from the litter and turn frequently. A small night-light of 15 watts should be provided. Reduce the heat in the enclosure 5F.° (2.78C.°) each week until it reaches the outside temperature.

Chicks need a constant source of grit. Feed free-choice in feeders separate from the mash.

After a month, your chicks are ready to move to larger quarters. Allow ¾ square foot of space per bird. You can move the chicks to a brooder house and can also allow them access to the outside at this time. In the brooder house, provide roosts allowing at least four inches of space per bird. A five-gallon waterer for each 100 chicks and three inches of feeding space per bird are necessary. Birds can be fed a commercial or home-compounded growing mash at this time.

At three months, move the layers and the cockerels you intend to keep into their permanent quarters. It is unprofitable to keep birds intended for meat longer than six months; the amount of feed they eat compared to weight gain is too unbalanced.

Housing: If you are building a henhouse, remember that the more room your chickens have, the healthier they will be. A dozen chickens, enough to provide the average family with eggs for a year, can be kept in a building 6 by 8 feet, but if you have thoughts about increasing the size of your flock, build larger. Choose a high spot so runoff water flows away from the building.

A henhouse does not have to be fancy. Plans for small poultry houses are available from your county agent or from the USDA.

In any case, you can also remodel an existing small building. Five-gallon buckets nailed to the wall can be used for nesting boxes —a wooden lip fastened to the front of the bucket will prevent hens from rolling out eggs or scratching out nesting material. Commercially made galvanized nesting boxes can also be used, as can homemade 12-by-12-by-12-inch nesting boxes.

A roost will also be necessary. A single 2x4, 8 feet long, nailed to braces 18 inches from one wall, should be enough for up to 20 hens.

The house should be well ventilated, but not drafty. Windows that open to the outside are better since they do not take up space inside the house.

A deep layer of bedding is necessary on the floor of the coop. Ground corncobs, leaves, straw, sawdust, or peat moss work well. Scatter whole grains on the litter and the chickens will scratch for them, turning the litter and picking up vitamins in the process. They will also eat fly eggs that might be laid in the litter.

Allow access to an outside run. Some people allow their chickens free range around the farm, but this can make egg gathering a chore since chickens will lay anywhere. Chickens will forage for insects but also like many garden crops, including lettuce, tomatoes and strawberries. You can protect these vegetables with chicken wire.

Managing Layers: Chicks started in the spring will begin laying in the fall. Chickens need 14 hours of light a day to encourage laying. As days get shorter, you can continue to stimulate their laying by lighting the henhouse artificially. Cold weather is less of a problem. Chickens are hardy and cold resistant, although they will eat more to maintain their body heat. Waterers need to be checked often so that water is never frozen. Gather eggs more frequently to make sure they don't freeze.

Commercial farms don't keep their layers a second year because it isn't profitable. You might want to keep those birds who are prolific layers. Whatever chickens you do keep must be separated from any new pullets you may order. In the spring, you should also cull any poor producers and replace them with new stock.

Feeding: You can feed commercial starter mash, growing mash and laying mash if you can't grow your own. Make sure all such feeds are compounded without medications or antibiotics. It might be cheaper for you to compound your own feed from whole grains purchased at the feed store. The formulas suggested below can be changed and altered by substituting what you have available.

A starter-growing mash should have 17 to 20 percent protein. One formula would use 50 parts corn; 20 parts soybean meal; five parts each wheat, oats, fish meal, meat scraps; three parts each alfalfa meal, dried whey, brewer's yeast; one part ground dolomitic limestone.

A layer-breeder mash for a flock with access to ranging, with 15 to 16 percent protein: 50 parts ground corn; 20 parts soybean meal; ten parts each ground wheat, ground oats, alfalfa meal. Or substitute a good alfalfa hay fed free-choice. You can use this formula as a feed for finishing.

Chickens need a constant supply of grit, and layers need ground oyster shells to produce healthy, thick shells on their eggs. Feed both free-choice.

A constant supply of fresh water is a necessity. Empty fountains every day and clean them at least weekly.

Diseases: Most books on chickens list many diseases to which the birds are prone. However, allowing plenty of room in the chicken house and access to range keeps chickens pretty healthy.

One problem you may encounter is cannibalism. This can be due to many causes—crowding, too much heat or light, boredom, bad diet. Cannibalism starts when one bird picks another and draws blood, usually in the vent region; the whole flock may join in and kill the affected bird. Some chickens are sold debeaked to prevent cannibalism, and pine tar rubbed on the affected area as soon as signs of cannibalism appear is quite effective. If you allow your chickens to range and give them plenty of room, many causes of the problem disappear.

Other diseases are common to other forms of poultry as well. *See also* POULTRY.

Slaughtering: Your flock can be managed so that unwanted hens and roosters can be slaughtered for specific purposes. Medium-heavy birds can be killed for fryers at eight to ten weeks, broilers at 12 weeks, roasters at six months. Older birds are used for stews or soups.

There are a number of ways to kill chickens. You can use an axe, chop off the chicken's head, and allow it to run around or thrash about under a bushel basket until it has bled to death. A method that uses fewer bushel baskets is recommended to those who plan on dry-picking their birds. Hang the chicken upside down by a cord attached to its legs. With a thin knife, slash the jugular vein at the side of the head just on top of the neck. Insert the blade into the mouth and thrust through the roof of the mouth to pierce the brain located in the back of the head. This method loosens the feathers on the bird and makes them easier to pick.

You can also scald the bird. After killing, dunk the bird in a large kettle of 126°F. (52.22°C.) water for about 30 seconds. Begin by pulling out wing and tail feathers, then start on the breast and finally the legs. The faster you work, the easier picking will be. You might have to dunk the bird a second time to complete the job.

Dry-picking is said to produce a better carcass, although the quality of the bird should not be affected if the scalding is done quickly.

Eviscerate, dry, chill, wrap, and freeze. *See also* BANTAMS.

CHINCH BUG

This is a very small black and white sucking insect, red when young, that causes large brown patches in lawns and sucks plant juices from corn stems. Lawns will do better on soil made up of one-third crushed rock, one-third sharp builder's sand and one-third compost. Interplanted soybeans shade the bases of corn plants and thereby discourage the bug. On the other hand, planting wheat next to corn will only encourage it.

Experiments have shown that when this insect feeds on plants grown in nitrogen-poor soil, it not only lives longer but lays more eggs. Well-fed soil and crops should discourage the bug. It can be kept from the corn patch by turning up a ridge of earth around the perimeter and pouring a line of creosote on top. Resistant varieties are also available.

See also INSECT CONTROL.

CHINESE CABBAGE
(*Brassica Rapa* [Pekinensis Group] and *B. Rapa* [Chinensis Group])

Chinese cabbage is sometimes called bok-choy, pak-choi or celery cabbage, although it does not taste too much like cabbage. It is perhaps best described as a sweetly flavored, lettucelike vegetable with large, crisp leaves. It is used fresh for salads, boiled as greens or sautéed.

Chinese cabbage is an annual requiring cool weather during the greater part of the growing season in order to develop to perfection. A continued period of heat tends to force the plant into flower before the leaves have reached any size or formed heads, at the same time giving them an undesirable taste.

Where the summers are cool you may plant early in the spring, at the time lettuce is sown. In sections of the country where the summers are hot, a fall sowing is advisable. Plant the seed in the early part of August, and keep the seedbed well cultivated from the time the rows can be recognized. Seed longevity is three years.

The best growth is made in a rich, light loam. Apply a generous amount of compost or well-rotted manure to the soil before planting. If the soil is reasonably rich, a three-inch layer of compost can be lightly dug in along the line where the rows are to stand. An application of dried cow manure during the growing period will also be beneficial. It is important to encourage a quick and fleshy growth. In soils known to be acid, lime should be raked into the soil to correct this condition.

Sow the seed in the open ground, as the plant is somewhat checked in its growth by transplanting. Plant ½ inch deep in rows about 12 to 16 inches apart. When the plants are three to four inches high, thin out to stand

Chinese cabbage needs cool temperatures during most of its growing season; where summers are hot, sow seeds in the fall, otherwise sow them in early spring.

about ten inches apart in the row. You may use the thinnings for greens or salad. This crop requires a good amount of moisture. Cultivate frequently to keep down weeds and save moisture. Water during dry spells, if possible, with a thorough drenching every evening.

Most varieties reach maturity in approximately 70 to 80 days after planting. When the heads mature, they may be cut for use as needed. The heads can be harvested after the first light frost and stored for a couple of months in a cool cellar or outdoor storage pit. In gathering, pull the plants with the roots, remove the outer leaves and store in layers protected by dry straw and cover with soil.

Varieties: Michihli is the favorite among gardeners. It is hardy and easily grown from seed. Burpee Hybrid matures in 75 days to produce a succulent vegetable. Crispy Choy, Loose-Leaved is well known for its mildly pungent flavor.

CHINESE CHESTNUT
See CHESTNUT

CHINESE DATE   *See* JUJUBE

CHINESE EVERGREEN
See LITCHI

CHINESE FAN PALM   *See* PALM

CHINESE FORGET-ME-NOT
(*Cynoglossum amabile*)

This somewhat weedy annual of the Borage family grows 1½ to two feet high and produces racemes of blue or white flowers throughout the summer. Easily grown in ordinary garden soil and full sun or part shade, the Chinese forget-me-not is a good choice for the border or cutting garden. Propagation is by seed.

CHINESE GOOSEBERRY
(*Actinidia chinensis*)

This vigorous deciduous vine produces an edible fruit, similar in taste to the gooseberry, that is known as Kiwi fruit. Growing up to 30 feet tall, with heart-shaped leaves and small white flowers, the Chinese gooseberry is most attractively displayed on a trellis or arbor. Young branches and twigs are covered with bright red hairs.

Chinese gooseberries are cultivated south of Washington, D.C., where they thrive in full sun or part shade and ordinary garden soil. They can also be grown in the North if taken down and covered with leaves for the winter. Seeds are usually sown in flats and transplanted out in rows 15 inches apart after all danger of frost is past. They can also be propagated by cuttings of half-ripened wood in summer or hardwood cuttings under glass.

Since the Chinese gooseberry is dioecious, it is necessary to have both male and female plants, though only the females bear fruit. Plant the male close to the female to insure cross-pollination. One male should be planted for every six to eight females.

CHINESE-LANTERN
See PHYSALIS

CHINESE TALLOW TREE
See VEGETABLE TALLOW

CHINKERICHEE
See ORNITHOGALUM

CHIONODOXA

Small bulbs of the Lily family, chionodoxas have grasslike leaves and starry, blue, pink or white flowers that bloom in spring. They are especially attractive when planted in masses in sunny spots in the rock garden or around such shrubs as forsythia and early magnolias. If allowed to reseed themselves from year to year, they will soon form a dense carpet. The best species are *C. Luciliae* and *C. sardensis,* both about six inches high. Plant them in October about three inches deep and three inches apart in a light and moist but well-drained soil.

See also BULB, FORCING.

CHIVES   *(Allium Schoenoprasum)*

A bright and easy-to-grow perennial, chives belong to the *Allium* genus, and so are closely related to onions, garlic and leeks. In aroma and taste, they resemble a light and delicate onion. Left to flower—which they shouldn't be, if they're being grown for the kitchen—chives develop lovely little lavender pompons at their tips. They make a charming border for a garden or a rock garden accent.

Chives can be started easily from seed that's available commercially. The seeds lose their viability fast, so plant them the year they're purchased. Chives thrive best in rich, coarse soil, ideally two parts compost with one part fine gravel or coarse sand and one part garden soil. Broadcast or sow in rows. Press the seeds lightly into the soil, and keep them moist. When they sprout, thin them to about six shoots per clump. They'll multiply rapidly, and additional plants can be made by dividing the root clumps. This should be done every two or three years to rejuvenate the plants. Keep the young shoots clipped if the crop is for the kitchen. Mature shoots tend to lack succulence. Fertilize liberally with a fish emulsion or other high-nitrogen food as repeated cuttings are made.

Because they grow easily and are a compact plant, chives make a near-ideal kitchen herb for indoor potting. They can be seeded in indoor pots or flats, or a late-summer clump can be potted and sunk into the garden soil for a few weeks to get reestablished. Bring the plant inside in early fall, and you'll have a January crop of fresh chives.

The cut tender shoots can be dried, but that must be done quickly and the dried chives sealed tightly. A better method is to cut, wash and drain a cup of chives at a time. Fill a jelly glass with the drained cuttings and freeze.

CHLORINATED HYDROCARBONS

In a manner not yet understood, chlorinated hydrocarbon insecticides act upon the central nervous system. These chemicals are stored in the fatty tissues, and are released as fat is used for energy. Some insecticides in this group are thought to be carcinogenic. Dieldrin, aldrin, heptachlor, and DDT have been taken off the market. Chlorinated hydrocarbons have come to be criticized because they do their job too well: They are broad-spectrum, persistent pesticides that are toxic to a wide range of life forms and do not break down into nontoxic materials soon after application. Therefore, these chemicals have no place in the garden.

See also INSECTICIDES.

CHLORINE

An essential trace element, extremely small amounts of chlorine must be present in soil for optimum plant growth. Chlorine deficiency is not much of a problem, however, since rainfall supplies ample amounts of chlorine to the soil.

CHOKEBERRY   (*Aronia*)

A genus of the Rose family noted for its red, fall foliage, these hardy deciduous shrubs range in height from four to 12 feet. The black chokeberry (*A. melanocarpa*) is a very showy, summer-blooming shrub with clusters of white blooms and short-lived black berries. It grows to about six feet. The red chokeberry (*A. arbutifolia*) growing to ten feet, bears white flowers and red berries.

Though chokeberries generally prefer moist garden soil, *A. melanocarpa* will tolerate a rocky, dry one. Propagation is by seed, suckers, layers, or cuttings.

CHOKECHERRY
(*Prunus virginiana*)

This is a widespread shrub or tree that bears edible, but tart, dark purple fruit. These pea-sized cherries can be made into a wine or jelly, but the pits are poisonous. An ornamental variety, *P. v. melanocarpa* cv. 'Xanthocarpa' is interesting for the early season change in foliage color from green to red purple.

CHOLLA   *See* PRICKLY PEAR
CHRISTMAS BERRY   *See* TOYON

CHRISTMAS CHERRY
(*Solanum pseudocapsicum*)

The names Christmas cherry, Jerusalem cherry and winter cherry are used interchangeably by amateurs. The plant is not really a cherry, but a decorative potted plant related to the potato, loved for its attractive, but poisonous, red to yellow cherrylike fruits. Growing to four feet tall, it has narrow leaves and clusters of small, star-shaped white flowers. It is rather fussy as a house plant.

Keep the plants in a sunny window of a fairly cool room with an even temperature of from 40 to 45°F. (4.44 to 7.22°C.). Keep the soil moderately moist at all times, using room temperature water. Do not allow water to stand in the saucer for any length of time. Protect the plant against cold drafts. Sooner or later, according to conditions, the berries will shrivel and the leaves drop off. When the plants have lost their attractiveness, prune them back severely, retaining only two or three eyes on each branch. Put the plants in a cool place (40°F. [4.44°C.]) and restrict the amount of water. To encourage development of new shoots, syringe the tops daily with water.

In May, when all danger of frost has passed, the pots may be sunk up to the rim in a sunny place in the garden. Some gardeners prefer to remove the pots and set the plants into moderately rich soil. If the plants have been hardened thoroughly before planting out, a light frost will not do much harm. Firm planting is essential, and plenty of water is needed during dry weather. By the end of June, weak liquid manure may be given once a week. By fall the plants will have made strong, rounded bushes of good appearance.

Early in September, soak the ground thoroughly and a few hours later, take up the plants and carefully repot them. (Plants sunk outdoors in pots may remain in place longer than those that need potting.) Place a piece of crock over the drainage hole and use a mixture of one part rich garden loam and one part leaf mold to which has been added a little dried sheep manure and fine sand to fill the space between the walls of the pot and the root ball. Pot firmly, but allow enough space at the top to make thorough watering possible. After watering, keep in a cold frame with the sash in place, or in a cool room without much ventilation. Avoid winds and drafts until the plants have recuperated from the ordeal of transplanting. Before frost place all plants in a greenhouse or at a sunny window, and keep them at 45 to 55°F. (7.22 to 12.78°C.). They need plenty of light, fresh air and regular watering. Weak liquid manure may be used when the plants show signs of having taken hold of the soil in the pots.

Plants can be propagated from seed saved from fully ripened berries or by cuttings. Sow the seed thinly and barely cover with fine soil. Place a pane of glass over the flat after watering and keep moderately warm (55 to 65°F. [12.78 to 18.33°C.].) When the seedlings break through the soil, remove the glass. Keep moderately moist and give as much light to the plants as possible. When the seedlings are large enough to be handled, plant them in individual small pots.

If cuttings are to be made, wait for young shoots to appear after cutting the plants back. Take these so that each new sprout has a part of the old stem attached, and insert them in small pots filled with sandy soil. Place the pot in a box covered with a tight-fitting pane of glass. Keep watered and spray the tops daily. Rooting will take place quite quickly, and a somewhat warmer temperature than that required by the old plants will be needed until the plants make an active growth. Gradually accustom them to the cooler temperature of the old plants, and from then on handle in the same manner.

CHRISTMAS ROSE
(*Helleborus niger*)

Christmas rose grows natively in the shade of trees and shrubs in northern Italy and other parts of southern Europe. It is commonly called the Christmas rose because its blooming season often begins before the holidays and extends through and beyond them, and also because the flower resembles a single rose. It grows best in a shaded place where the soil is deep and contains much humus and moisture. Plant it in deciduous shade where you might grow ferns and protect it from strong winter winds. This can be accomplished most simply by planting it on the off-wind side of evergreen shrubs and trees, and by covering the plant lightly with evergreen boughs during the months of December to March or until the snow disappears.

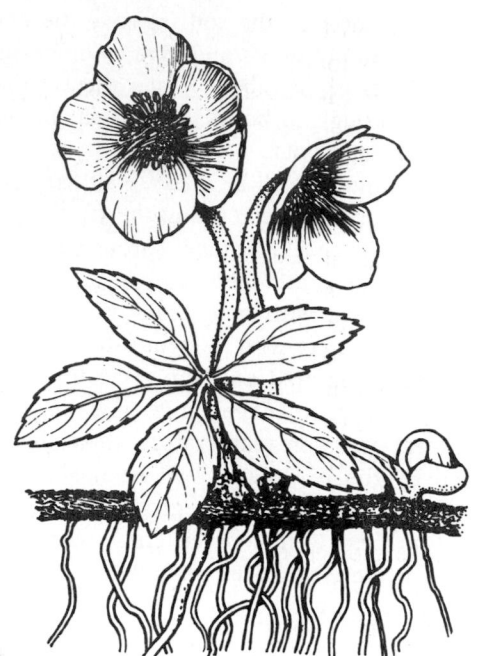

If planted early in the spring, Christmas roses will bear white flowers the following winter.

The best time to plant Christmas rose is from August until winter and in early spring before much growth has been made. A common mistake with Christmas rose is to plant it too late in the spring. Unless planted early, the plants will not build up enough reserve energy to enable them to bloom the following winter and flowers will not be formed until a year later.

Christmas roses must not be planted too deep and special care must be taken that the roots are not damaged. Plant them so the crown is no more than one inch below the soil surface. The soil should be well prepared with humus and pulverized rocks because a planting lasts for decades. Leaf mold and peat moss are good materials for further enriching the soil.

Avoid using manure less than three years old. Heavy use of organic matter will cause the soil to be moisture retentive yet well drained, a condition essential to success with these plants. Although they are woodland plants, Christmas roses do not like very acid soils. The pH should be near neutral—6.6 or 7. Add limestone if it is more acid than this.

Christmas roses can bloom anytime from November to April depending on weather conditions. It is far more likely that they will bloom during mild periods when snow has left the ground than that they will actually bloom through the snow as often claimed. It is true that they usually flower when nothing else does. For this reason, and because they require so little attention once established, they deserve a place in the garden.

The leaves are palmately divided. There usually is only one long-petioled leaf, but the flower stem may bear one or more sessile (unstalked) leaves or aborted leaves called bracts. The leaves are leathery and evergreen and quite handsome when the plant is not in flower. The plants have creeping rootstalks. The white flowers are borne on either simple or one-branched stems about 12 inches high so that the flowers are elevated a few inches above the leaves. Common cultivars of *Helleborus niger* include Praecox which blooms as early as October and continues until after the New Year, and Angustifolius which has narrower leaves and smaller flowers than the typical Christmas rose. All have white flowers which may flush pink as they age. The word *niger* in the botanical name refers to the black roots.

The Lenten rose (*H. orientalis*) is similar in foliage and cultural requirements to *H. niger*, but the two- to three-inch flowers appear sometime from March to May and can be white, chocolate, purple, or even green.

Blooming Indoors: To be absolutely sure of having plants in bloom at Christmas, one must move strong plants into the greenhouse. Or before freezing weather, entire beds can be brought into bloom for cut flowers by covering them, or plants about to bloom may be balled and placed under a protective covering. If one wishes to sell blooming plants, they should be potted in six-inch pots (or larger pots for the larger plants) in early spring, and the potted plants should then be sunk in the soil to a depth of about five inches in the shade of a high tree and provided with water during the summer. At the proper time in late autumn, the pots must be taken up and put under conditions which will bring them into bloom at the desired time.

Christmas roses do not require high temperatures for forcing. In warm weather, they should have good air circulation and be shaded. After the buds appear, the plants should be kept in the dark for a time. This will insure longer flower stems. Later, however, the plants must be given full light again but not bright sunlight. The forcing of the broad-petaled variety must be started somewhat earlier than that of *H. niger* and the early-flowering varieties.

CHRISTMAS TREE FARMING

Many landowners have found it profitable to grow evergreens as a crop.

Though it is feasible to grow Christmas trees from seed, most farmers prefer either two-year or four-year plants. Two-year seedlings come about eight inches tall, and should be planted in a replant bed until they are four years old and able to stand the rigors of life in the open.

A replant bed should have rich, well-drained, sandy loam. Plant the seedlings about six inches apart in rows about 15 inches apart. They should be set with their roots slightly deeper than they were in their original bed. Pack the soil very firmly around the roots, tamping it down with your feet—air pockets mean death to the young seedlings. Keep weeds out of the bed, and supply a three-inch mulch of straw, old hay or leaves after the first frost to protect the roots from cold.

The field in which the four-year-old trees are to be planted should be cleared of briars and brush that might compete with the crop for light and nourishment. Plowing is not necessary, but get rid of all briars—the Christmas tree farmer's worst enemy.

Spring is usually the best time to plant seedlings. Fall is equally good, provided the soil has plenty of moisture in it. The trees can be planted haphazardly, or placed in check rows. A five-by-five-foot spacing is the minimum for spruces and firs, while a six-by-six-foot spacing is best for pines. The former arrangement figures out to 1,740 trees per acre, the latter to 1,210 trees. Contour planting will help hold the soil on slopes.

With a spade or mattock dig a hole a little larger than the clump of roots. Set the tree in straight, firming the earth around it and tamping it down to eliminate air pockets. Firs and pines should be set slightly deeper than they were in the original bed, but set spruces at the same depth they were before.

Keep the roots moist while handling and planting. Most farmers carry the seedlings to be planted in a bucket of mud or water. How many can you expect to plant a day? One man alone should be able to manage 600 to 1,000.

Once established, the trees need only a few days of care a year. You'll have to grub

Christmas trees require very little yearly maintenance. Each summer, clear out all hardwood seedlings and prune the trees to insure proper development.

to see in their living rooms. Equipped with a shears, you can prune about 50 trees an hour. A light dressing of manure the year before harvest year will give the trees a better color.

Early December is the time to check the Christmas tree planting to pick out the best trees for harvesting. Don't cut the trees any sooner than necessary. You can get a higher price by digging up the trees and wrapping the ball of roots, complete with soil, in heavy burlap. Tell buyers to keep the trees well watered and to replant them as soon after Christmas as possible.

Norway spruce and Douglas pine are the most popular throughout the Midwest Christmas tree belt. Both are well formed, with short, dark needles. Balsam fir is a slower grower, taking about ten years to grow to a six-foot height, but its pleasant odor makes it a fast seller. Scotch pines take eight years to reach six feet. Blue spruce and white spruce are fairly expensive as seedlings and grow slowly, but their beautiful shape and foliage color attract many Christmas tree buyers. Both of these, as well as the Douglas fir (a very slow grower) are often sold as ornamentals.

Trees can be sold on a choose-and-cut basis, or on the stump to another retailer or Christmas tree broker. Wholesale prices typically run 50 percent less than retail.

out all hardwood seedlings once a year to give your young trees a chance to live. And weeds and brush should be kept down to a minimum, for in dry weather they can feed a brushfire that will wipe out a plantation in minutes. Keep stock fenced out from your evergreens, too—they can eat a tree to death in a short time.

A yearly pruning every June or July (cutting back half that year's new growth) will insure the full, conical shape consumers like

CHRYSANTHEMUM

This is a genus which has contributed several species to the flower garden. These include *C. coccineum*, pyrethrum or painted daisy; *C. frutescens*, marguerite; *C.* x *superbum*, Shasta daisy; and *C. Parthenium*, feverfew or matricaria. The one considered here is

C. morifolium, the hardy chrysanthemum.

Hardy chrysanthemums are among the most popular and important garden flowers because of the long, colorful show they put on in late summer and fall. By choosing carefully from the hundreds of varieties, the gardener can have mums blooming from mid-August to heavy frost. They can be grown in containers if fed and watered carefully. The dwarf cushion types can be dug with a generous earth ball when in bud or flower and moved to brighten a dull corner of the garden. Few flowers have such a variety of color and form, and all are excellent for cutting.

Hardy chrysanthemums require a great deal of maintenance to keep them in top form. Gardeners who have little time to work with their flowers should avoid having large plantings of them. While they can be propagated from cuttings and seed, most gardeners will find that division is the easiest method. Indeed, annual (or at most, biennial) division in spring is necessary to keep them flowering well. When separating the clump, you will notice many pale stolons, usually with a tuft of small leaves at the end, spreading out among the darker roots at the base of the plant. Each one of these stolons can grow into a large flowering plant by fall, so cut off as many as you will need and discard the rest of the old clump. If you should wish to start with larger divisions, use a sharp spade and cut pieces with several new crowns each from around the outside of the old clump and put the worn-out center in the compost heap. Small divisions or stolons make the best plants, and they should be set out in full sun in soil rich in compost or rotted manure, which can be supplemented with bone meal or sludge. Mums are heavy feeders and will benefit from topdressings of compost during the growing season. They must be watered carefully at all stages of growth: Drying of the soil in the heat of summer will stunt growth and diminish flowering.

When the young plants have grown six or eight inches tall, pinch out the tip of each stem to induce side-branching. Pinch again after each six inches of growth until mid-July, after which the plants should be left alone so they form flower buds. This early pinching induces heavier flowering and helps to keep tall varieties more compact. The cushion mums, which mature at 12 inches or less, are self-branching and should not be pinched. Some varieties, such as the football and spider mums which develop very large flowers, should be disbudded to make them look really spectacular. All secondary flower buds are removed, allowing each stem only one bud at the top which opens into a flower that can be five to eight inches across. Such varieties usually bloom too late to mature before frost and the flowers can't take heavy rains, so they are best left to florists and greenhouses. While sometimes advertised as being suitable for the open garden, they are really not.

Almost everyone knows of or owns chrysanthemum plants which seem to survive and bloom year after year with little or no winter protection. Even so, the term "hardy chrysanthemum" can be misleading because too often a newly bought variety which was planted in spring and bloomed in fall dies in the winter. This is often caused by poor drainage; while mums require abundant moisture during the growing season, their soil must never be soggy in winter. Try not to plant them in heavy clays if you wish to winter them in the garden. To prevent alternate freezing and thawing, cover the plants with an airy mulch such as straw, evergreen boughs or an inverted basket in winter. To be sure that choice varieties survive, dig them with earth balls after frost has killed the tops and store them under light mulch in a cold frame for the winter. In spring, plant several of the stolons and compost the old plants. Treated this way, any hardy mum will grow and bloom well each season.

There are several recognized flower types of hardy chrysanthemums of which the button, pompon, decorative, and single-flowered types are most suitable for the open border. There are many named varieties to choose from in each class, so check the catalogs for those which appeal to you most. The cushion or dwarf types might be the best for busy gardeners because they do not need pinching.

See also PYRETHRUM, SHASTA DAISY.

CHUFA   (*Cyperus esculentus* var. *sativus*)

Listed in some seed catalogs under the name "earth almond," it is sometimes grown in northern gardens as a curiosity.

The plant is a relative of the papyrus plant from which the ancient Egyptians made paper. It looks much like a coarse, heavy bunched marshgrass, but should properly be called a sedge, the edible portion being the small tubers attached to the roots. These vary greatly in size and shape, but they average the size of medium-sized beans, from ¼ to ¾ inch. They have a sweet taste, very much like that of coconut, but are not often used for human food, as when matured and dried, they become hard and woody.

Chufa tubers are grown in a bunch at the base of the plant, and as the roots do not spread or run through the ground, they can be easily dug or harvested.

This plant can well be a valuable adjunct in the reclamation of much sandy land now of low fertility and classed as submarginal.

The chufa grows well and can be easily harvested in any loose, friable soil and relatively high yields are reported, sometimes 200 bushels or more an acre.

CIDER

Apple cider made from ripe, orchard apples is a great addition to the family pantry. It isn't necessary to pick the ripe fruit from the tree; fallen fruit will do if still fresh.

Apple pressing equipment can range from hand chopping and pressing with a rolling pin, to use of a local cider mill. Two to three gallons of cider can be pressed from a bushel of apples.

Start with mildly acid apples like Winesap, Jonathan, Stayman, Northern Spy, York Imperial, Wealthy, R.I. Greening, or Pippins. Wash them well. (Do not use rotten apples; they give the cider a soapy flavor.) After the choice of variety is made, you are ready to begin pressing.

The juice can be canned or boiled down to a thick syrup to be used as toppings on pancakes, waffles or ice cream.

CIMICIFUGA   (*C. racemosa*)

Growing from two to five feet tall, these hardy ornamental perennials produce foot-long clusters of white threadlike flowers in late summer or autumn. Cimicifugas, or bugbanes as they are also called, like a soil enriched with humus and a shaded spot at the far end of the garden. Propagation is by seed or root division.

CINERARIA   *(Senecio)*

Popular daisylike florists' flowers, cinerarias grow one to three feet tall and have blossoms in shades of red, pink, blue, or white. They are suitable only as greenhouse or indoor potted plants in the North. They are not difficult to grow, but plants may be bought from the nurserymen if you do not care to go to the trouble of raising your own.

Sow seed in May for autumn blooms or in October for spring blooms. The seed is fine and may be mixed with sand to secure even distribution. Do not cover it with earth; just press down firmly with some flat surface. After transplanting, keep shifting the plants until they are in six-inch pots, which will give you large specimens. Grow them at 45 to 50°F. (7.22 to 10°C.) night temperature and 68 to 70°F. (20 to 21.11°C.) day temperature.

They require a great deal of water and light, but not enough direct sun so that the leaves wilt and are burned. After the flowers appear, fertilize with liquid fertilizer about every two weeks. Keep all the old blossoms picked off to prolong bloom and be sure they get plenty of fresh air, but avoid cold drafts. Stakes may be needed to support the flowers. They are sometimes afflicted with red spider mites. Remove all leaves which show any signs of disease.

CINNAMON FERN
See OSMUNDA

CINQUEFOIL   *See* POTENTILLA

CION   *See* SCION

CITRUS

Since the first requirement of any citrus tree is a warm climate, most citrus fruits are grown in Southern California, along the Gulf of Mexico, and in southern and central Florida. A great many gardeners in those areas use groupings of orange and grapefruit trees as shade trees around their homes.

Citrus trees are broad-leaved evergreens, varying in height from ten to 15 feet (lime), ten to 20 feet (lemon), 15 to 40 feet (orange) and 30 to 50 feet (grapefruit). There's little difference in their growth pattern. When young, the trees are upright and spreading. As they become older, they become somewhat pyramidal in shape. Generally, citrus trees are long-lived and begin bearing at four to six years.

Unlike the peach and apple, citrus trees are nonhardy, able to withstand temperatures only a few degrees below 32°F. (0°C.). For example, the critical temperature of the sweet orange is about 24°F. (−4.44°C.), while that of the lemon is about 26°F. (−3.33°C.). In the subtropical zone of the citrus-growing districts, temperatures below these critical points frequently occur; that's why the unique practice of orchard or grove heating has been developed. Oil or gas heaters, burning small piles of wood, wind machines that mix warm and cold air, protecting trunks of young trees by mounding them with soil high enough to shield the bud union—these are some methods used by growers to save trees from cold.

Soil Requirements: Citrus fruits require well-drained soils of the sandy or clay loam type. The soil should be slightly acid, with a pH of between 5 and 7. Incorporate some phosphate rock and granite dust into the soil before planting to give the planting site the nutrients the young stock will need.

Cover crops are helpful in maintaining soil fertility in sandy soil. Beggarweed, cowpeas, velvet beans, and hairy indigo are recommended for orchards. *See also* COVER CROP.

Citrus fruit can be cultivated on soil that is not well drained and tends to harbor puddles of water on the surface after a rainfall by simply planting the stock on mounds raised about 1½ feet above the surface. Keep the mound about 12 feet in diameter at the base, narrowing to eight feet at the top. Before planting, be sure the soil has been cleared of all large stones and roots, thereby keeping the soil loose and friable.

Planting: Citrus trees grow best in direct sunlight; when planted in partial shade, they tend to be weak. Most varieties are fast-growing, averaging about one foot per year growth in overall height and spread. Therefore, when choosing a location for trees, remember that distance between trees is most important. Usual spacing for most orange trees is 25 by 25 feet; grapefruit, 25 by 30 feet or 30 by 30 feet; mandarins and hybrids (as Temple), 20 by 20 feet; kumquat, lime and lemon, 15 by 15 feet.

Whenever possible, it is best for the home gardener to go directly to the nursery to buy the stock before it has been dug. In this way you can be sure of buying quality stock that has not been culled or sorted out for poor quality. A quick inspection of the plant in the nursery will reveal whether it has been grown in soil that is disease infected.

Orange trees are usually grafted. In healthy stock, the graft should appear at least six inches above soil level, with the thickness of the trunk above the joint almost equal to that below. A thinner trunk may be evidence of disease or that the root was budded twice. Check to be sure that the bark on the trunk and rootstock is smooth and clean, not rough or gray in color. The leaves should be large and healthy. A large one-year-old tree can be distinguished by the leaves that are still growing out of the trunk below the main stem. Look for this sign of a young, fast-growing tree when in the market for stock. It is better to buy a year-old tree that has attained this size than a two-year-old tree that has taken twice the time to grow to this stage.

Trees are usually obtained from nurseries in one of four conditions: 1) bare rooted; 2) balled in burlap with the soil still around the roots; 3) bare rooted and placed in sphagnum; or 4) in pots. Balled and potted trees are preferred since the roots are still protected.

A hole should be dug to accommodate the root system of the new tree. For balled trees, be sure to dig the hole a foot wider in diameter than the width of the balled roots. If the tree roots are bare, cut off any damaged roots until the cut shows live undamaged tissue. Any especially long roots should be trimmed back to the length of the other roots.

A planting board may come in handy when beginning your cultivation. Make one out of a piece of scrap wood of any width, about four feet long. Cut a notch two to four inches wide in each end and another in the center of one side. Lay the board on the ground with the center notch placed where the tree is to stand. Drive a stake into the ground in each of the end notches and remove the board. Place the stock in the hole and replace the planting board over the stakes, allowing the tree trunk to rest in the notch in the center of the board. The soil line on the trunk should now be two inches higher than the present soil line. In other words, the tree is now planted a little higher than it grew in the nursery.

Fill the space around the hole with topsoil

first. If the tree is balled, fill the hole two-thirds full with soil before untying the burlap. Then untie the burlap and fold it back as far as possible. Finish filling the hole, leaving the burlap in it to rot.

Run water into the hole when it is filled within two inches of the top. Be sure to shake the tree several times while watering to settle the soil. When the water has drained away, fill the hole to ground level. During the first two weeks after the tree has been planted, it should be kept moist. Water frequently, perhaps three or four times a week. The remainder of the first growing season, water every week or ten days. By the time the tree's second season of growth begins, the roots should have penetrated quite deeply, permitting less frequent waterings. Ten to 20 gallons of water applied to each tree every two to three weeks will suffice.

Varieties: Orange—blood orange (*C. sinensis*)—growing 15 to 25 feet with fragrant white flowers; king orange (*Citrus* x *nobilis* cv 'King')—small white flowers, large juicy fruit; mandarin or tangerine (*C. reticulata*)—small, attractive tree whose fruits have become so popular; Seville or sour orange (*C. Aurantium*)—medium-sized tree whose stock is extensively used for budding other citrus fruits since it is especially adapted for growing in a wide range of soils, even low wet areas; otaheite orange (*C.* x *limonia*)—attractive miniature orange tree, growing about two to three feet high.

Lemon (*C. Limon*)—small sensitive tree with rather large, reddish-tinted flowers.

Grapefruit (*C.* x *paradisi*)—large tree, round topped with large, white flowers.

Lime (*C. aurantiifolia*)—small tree with small white flowers, considered the most sensitive to cold of any of the citrus trees.

Pests and Predators: Ladybugs are wel-come additions to the orchard, for they prey on insects that may plague your crop. *Aschersonia* spp., beneficial fungi commonly found on citrus trees, kill immature white flies. They are pink and form pustules on the underside of leaves. The brown white fly fungus also aids in the control of white flies.

Oil sprays are effective in helping to control populations of white flies, red scale and sooty mold. For additional insect controls, *see* INSECT CONTROL.

For nutritional values, *see entries for individual fruits.*

CITRUS WASTE

Citrus wastes are most easily composted. The fact that some citrus peels may have spray residues on them need not be cause for concern, since such residues are small and likely will not harm the soil after the material is broken down into compost.

Orange skins and citrus skins of all kinds are richer in nitrogen if the skins are thick. Their phosphoric acid content is extremely high, and an ash analysis shows about 3 percent of the valuable element in orange skins, while the potash content of the ash is only surpassed by banana skins—the former analyzing about 27 percent, the latter almost 50 percent in potash. Lemons, as a rule, have a lower potash, but a higher phosphorous content than oranges; grapefruits seem to hold the middle between the extremes: 3.6 percent phosphoric acid and 30 percent potash. Whole fruits, so-called culls, are also useful, though their fertilizer value is necessarily lower than that of the skins, because they contain great amounts of water.

Some home gardeners discard citrus rinds in the mistaken belief that the sourness, acidity and oily skins are detrimental to soil or compost. This is not so. Rinds will decompose or compost more rapidly, however, if they are cut into small chunks.

CLARKIA

Native to the western United States, this annual is hardy and comparatively easy to grow in mild winter areas during the cool weather of winter and early spring. The plants attain a height of about three feet and produce spikes of single or double flowers in shades of white, pink, salmon, or red. The plants need some support. Seed should be sown before the earth freezes in November where winters are not too severe or when the snow is leaving the ground in late February. Broadcast the seed on a mild day where it is wanted, preferably in light soil in a spot where there is full sun or part shade. An early start will insure quick growth and bloom before summer heat. They flower from July to October. Clarkias grow best in areas having cool summers and should not be expected to thrive where summer days are humid and temperatures exceed 80°F. (26.67°C.) for long periods. The new F_1 hybrids are said to be more heat resistant than older forms.

CLAY SOIL

As a textural class, clay soil contains 40 percent or more of clay (a soil particle less than 0.002 millimeter in diameter), less than 45 percent of sand and less than 40 percent of silt. A typical clay soil may be composed of approximately 60 percent actual clay, 20 percent sand and 20 percent silt. Such a soil tends to compact, which makes cultivation difficult and interferes with the oxygen supply for plant roots. Water can do little to enter the impervious clay soil, and runoff is very common during rainfalls. The villain, of course, is the miniscule clay particle that, in the absence of humus, gives very poor soil structure.

See also ORGANIC MATTER, SOIL.

CLEFT GRAFT   *See* GRAFTING

CLEMATIS

During the past several decades there has been a greatly increasing interest in these ornamental vines. In this family of vines there are over 200 small- and large-flowered varieties, although many of them are not practical for the home gardener.

There are now about 90 different varieties available to those who are enthusiastic about growing clematis. Most of these are own-root plants, started from cuttings and much better than grafted stock because of their ability to start from the collar (the point where the roots branch from the stem) in cases where the stem has been injured, still maintaining their original variety. These own-root plants also produce a better root system and are more resistant to the temperature changes of our various seasons.

The Clematis family of vines is mainly divided into two general groups. The first group comprises the small-flowered varieties which range in shape from flat blooms to a variety of urn, bell, lantern, and starlike flowers. The second is made up of the larger-flowered hybrids which are available in a number of different sizes and colors and are usually platter shaped. These larger-flowered clematis will often produce blossoms up to eight or ten inches across.

By careful selection of the varieties planted, a gardener can have continuous blooms from early spring until frost. Depending upon the variety, growth in one year may be from six to 30 feet.

In general, clematis are prolific bloomers, with this condition: the larger the size of the flowers, the fewer the number of blooms. A compensating factor is that those which do not bloom so profusely generally make up in quality of bloom for what they lack in quantity.

There are a great many uses and arrangements in which the clematis excels. You can combine them with other flowers on your favorite garden arch, trellis or fence; you can grow them alone on a pillar, post, stone wall, or terrace; or you can use them to completely cover and hide an old stump. When used as a perennial border, they will make a very fine arrangement and will completely cover a surprisingly large area. A good method is to use some old branches over the bed area so that the vines can grow up on them away from the ground. It is sometimes helpful to arrange the branches so that they are lower in the front and higher at the back. In one season, the vines will completely cover the area, giving a mass of green foliage with bright accents of colored blossoms scattered about.

Culture: Some people who are not too familiar with clematis consider them difficult to grow, but clematis need nothing that the average gardener cannot provide with a little work.

Buy own-root plants, two years old. These two-year-old plants are the right age for a rapid top growth and will give you good blossoms without having to wait too long.

Planting can be done in the fall or spring. Fall-planted stock should be mulched well in order to prevent damage from frost action on the soil. Clematis start their growth early in the spring, so they should be planted as early as possible, and especially before the weather becomes hot and dry. Plants from pots can even be set out throughout the summer if kept well watered at reasonable intervals so that they do not dry out too much.

The location for planting clematis should be selected with these factors in mind: good drainage, no standing water; four or five hours of sunlight a day; and a good rich loam soil, well loosened and enriched with a little well-rotted manure if available. It is often well to select the shady side of a wall or fence where the vines can climb into the sunlight because the soil at the base of the plant should be cool and moist. A summer mulch of straw, grass clippings, peat moss, buckwheat hulls, or other material will help to retain moisture during the hot summer days. This mulch will also keep weeds under control.

North of Washington, D.C., it is very good insurance to provide a good winter mulch in November, before a heavy frost. This mulch prevents any sudden changes in temperature from causing heaving of the ground which would cause serious winter damage to the plants.

Dig a hole about 18 inches across by about 18 inches deep, and fill it with good loose soil, mixed with some well-rotted manure. If your soil is too heavy, add a little peat moss to loosen it up. About two months after planting you can add a good fertilizer once or twice, but do not work it in so deeply as to disturb the roots. In acid-soil areas add about ¼ cup of lime to the soil each fall.

Plant the clematis with the collar two to three inches below the soil level. Firm the soil well around the roots and water thoroughly after planting, but not enough to cause mud. Do not fertilize for at least two months after planting.

A support for the vines to climb should be provided right from the start. It will also prevent the wind from whipping the vine around and will help to keep the leaves off the ground. Clematis does best when its stems and leaves are able to grow up into the air and have light and air circulation around them.

For the first two years after planting, it is generally not necessary to do any pruning, as you want to give the plants plenty of time to get established. When the plant is established and the roots become large, you can thin the top growth in early spring by removing the old and dead wood. If you are trying to cover a special spot, you may prefer simply to cut out the dead wood only. The spring-flowering varieties should get their pruning in late January. These varieties bloom on last year's growth and you must, therefore, leave the old wood in order to avoid cutting off the new flowers.

Summer-flowering varieties may be cut back to two or three feet above the ground in early spring. You need have no fear in doing this as their rapid early growth will still make the tops as large as ever by blooming time, with better foliage and larger blooms.

CLEOME

The most commonly grown species of this genus of the Caper family is *C. spinosa,* some-times known as spider flower. It has small puffy flowers, long thin seedpods, spidery stamens, and sharp thorns. Flower colors include white, pink and yellow. It can grow as tall as five feet, and because of its height it is a stunning plant for the back of the border.

Cleomes prefer full sun and a well-drained soil. Though they self-sow freely, seedlings revert to type (a bland pink). Sow fresh seed indoors in April or directly into the garden after all danger of frost is past. Bloom period begins in early July and lasts until frost.

CLETHRA

The sweet pepperbush (*C. alnifolia*) is a popular species of this genus. Growing to ten feet, and flourishing in moist, slightly acid soil, this ornamental shrub bears delicate spires of fragrant white florets from July to September. These combine well with many uncultivated plants such as wild roses and grapes. Cultivar Rosea bears pale pink flowers.

Propagation is by seeds sown indoors in spring, division, layers, or cuttings.

CLEVELAND CHERRY
See CHRISTMAS CHERRY

CLIMBING NIGHTSHADE
See BITTERSWEET

CLIVIA

Also called kaffir lily, this genus of the Amaryllis family has straplike evergreen leaves and umbels of yellow, orange or red funnel-shaped flowers. *C. miniata* is a popular species, having red orange flowers that fade to light yellow in the center.

Clivias need shade, plenty of water and very crowded roots if grown in pots. In the garden, they should be grown in dense shade in rich heavy soil and never be allowed to dry out.

CLOCHE GARDENING

The underlying principle of "continuous cloches" is to take glass protection to a growing crop instead of growing the crop inside a fixed greenhouse or frame.

The continuous cloche, designed over 50 years ago by L. H. Chase of England, is intended to protect rows of growing crops at their normal field or garden spacing. Each cloche is a rigid entity, weighing about five pounds and consisting of two or four sheets of glass held

A bottomless jug makes an excellent hot cap that provides temporary cloche protection for transplants and seedlings in the home garden.

together by a galvanized wire framework. The continuous cloches fit together end to end to form long glass tunnels not more than 24 inches wide and of any required length. The ends of these tunnels are closed with sheets of glass to prevent excessive draft.

The maximum width of the cloche is important, as the method by which water reaches cloche-protected crops is unique, although similar in principle to the methods of irrigation used in tropical countries. The surface of the soil in which the crops are growing under the cloches is never wetted, as it is in the case of open-air crops, or in greenhouses or frames. According to J. L. H. Chase, son of the designer, the rain falls on the glass roofs of the cloches, runs down the sides and seeps into the soil and so laterally to the roots of the plants.

The result is that the soil never cakes under the cloches, and the original tilth is preserved. "This means that hoeing to keep the surface soil aerated is unnecessary, and it also means that the soil temperature is considerably raised, for the fine surface tilth prevents frost from penetrating, even at very low temperatures," states Mr. Chase.

Cloches offer good protection against frost, as well as against wind. Although relatively small and light, the individual cloches are not shifted by heavy gales unless the ends of the rows are not kept closed or they are put down unevenly on the soil.

Since they are constructed from glass or plastic with just a small amount of framework, cloches offer practically no obstruction to the sun's rays. In addition, light reaches the plants from the sides, signifying that growth will not be distorted vertically and there will be no "drawing" of the plants, as is effected when light is obtained only from above as in most cold frames.

Some crops are grown throughout the season under cloches, from sowing until harvesting, but the majority of crops are merely started under the glass and then allowed to finish in the open. Half-hardy crops, for example, can be sown or planted five weeks before the danger of killing frosts has passed. At the end of that period the cloches can be removed and the plants can grow in the open in the normal way.

Cloches are not used to cover just a single crop in the year, but a succession of crops. In England, during the winter and early spring, the choice lies between lettuces, carrots, asparagus, peas, and radishes. During April or May, the first crop is followed by a half-hardy crop, such as one of the following: tomatoes, French beans, runner beans, marrows, or sweet corn. The third crop is a summer crop, covering the plants from June onwards, and consisting of a late crop of tomatoes or melons, cucumbers, or onion sets.

There are also a number of profitable flower crops which are grown with cloche protection. Most important are: sweet peas, larkspur, pyrethrum, scabiosa, dahlias, zinnias, anemones, violets, daffodils, tulips, iris, and gladioli. Some need more height than is afforded by the continuous cloche in its normal position, and this is provided by using what are called elevators, which effectively raise the height of the cloches by about 12 inches.

Early in the 1940's, when the shortage of labor became an acute problem in England, a work-saving technique — "strip-cropping" — was evolved for the use of cloches commercially. Instead of using the drift of cloches in a solid block over one crop and then, when that crop reached maturity, shifting all the cloches to another part of the field to cover a second crop, "strip-cropping" was introduced. In this method crops were grown in alternate strips of the same width, and when one crop no longer needed protection, the cloches were merely moved six feet sideways onto the adjoining strip in order to cover the succeeding crop.

Cloche cultivation is most widespread in England. It has been estimated that there are about 15 million cloches in use in the United Kingdom, with about two-thirds used commercially and one-third by amateur gardeners.

In Canada, the greatest interest has been shown in British Columbia, for in eastern Canada the spring is so short that cloches only have a limited value in the production of early crops.

In the United States, continuous cloches were first marketed in 1950 and are known as "P.M.G.'s"—portable miniature greenhouses. Here experimentation has been primarily done by amateurs who like the chance to grow a greater variety of crops.

See also GREENHOUSES.

CLOVE PINK
(*Dianthus Caryophyllus*)

A perennial with jointed stems, blue green grasslike leaves and small carnationlike flowers, this flower's fragrance is penetrating and spicy, resembling cloves. Clove pink is a useful plant for a low border and can be propagated from seeds, cuttings or by layering. It is hardy but needs protection in cold climates. It should have good drainage.

CLOVER   (*Trifolium*)

For many centuries, clover has been grown for soil improvement purposes. A valuable green manure crop, the various species of clover are also prized for their ability to absorb free nitrogen from the air and store it in root nodules until it is eventually imparted to the soil. A good clover crop can fix in the soil more than 100 pounds of nitrogen and return another 100 pounds as green manure. Farmers have traditionally taken advantage of this accumulation of nitrogen by planting corn and other heavy nitrogen feeders after clover.

The amount of nitrogen any particular legume can fix in the soil depends on many factors: climatic region, soil conditions, temperature, and available moisture. A USDA bulletin lists the following amounts for various commonly grown clovers:

Clover Crop	Nitrogen Pounds per Acre
Alfalfa	194
Ladino clover	179
Alsike clover	119
Sweet clover	119
Red clover	114
Pastures with legumes	106
White clover	103
Crimson clover	94
Annual lespedeza	85
Vetch	80

Clover grown without chemicals is a good crop for increasing earthworm populations. Earthworms, in return, help the clover's soil-enriching program and aerate the soil. Soil shielded by a clover sod is protected almost 100 percent from erosion. It will soak up and store moisture for use in dry times. In fact, clover, and especially alfalfa, is an excellent drought-resistant crop.

When soil is conditioned properly for growing a good clover crop—pH nearly neutral, good drainage and vigorous microbial action in progress from the decaying organic matter—it increases activity not only of rhizobia, but also among the azotobacter, a family of bacteria that fixes nitrogen freely in the soil.

Clover roots extend deeply into the soil in search of nutrients and bring up to the root zone minerals that have leached too far down for other crops to make use of. In this way, trace minerals are returned to poor, farmed-out soils naturally.

The small leaves of some of the clovers, especially when cut young, decay readily and make excellent compost, while stalky material does not pack well enough to keep moisture uniformly. Where old clover is used, care must be taken in aerating the heap well, so that the stalky material can break down.

Red Clover: (*T. pratense*) Red clover used to be the leading forage plant in the United States. It is still widely grown and is an important hay plant and component of grass mixtures. Recently alfalfa, ladino clover and bird's-foot trefoil have become more widely used.

While red clover is actually a perennial, it acts as a biennial. It has a comparatively deep and much branched taproot system. The plant will range from one to two feet in height. It produces its greatest growth the season after planting. If allowed to produce seed during the first year of establishment it usually dies; hence, clipping or grazing in the early fall are recommended to prevent it from setting seed the year it is sown.

The diseases to which it is susceptible are mainly fusarium, anthracnose and mildew. The full-grown borer also causes serious injury to this plant.

The soil fertility requirements of red clover are lower than those for alfalfa. It is adapted to a wide range of soil conditions. It will not

As an excellent nitrogen fixer with a highly developed root system, red clover is widely used in cropping systems.

bird's-foot trefoil. It does best in regions with abundant rainfall and without extremes of either winter or summer temperatures; so it is confined to the humid, temperate regions of the United States.

Its most common use is for hay purposes. It is one of the most nutritious of forage crops.

Alsike Clover: (*T. hybridum*) Alsike clover is similar to red clover with which it is frequently confused. This legume is limited in acreage to conditions unsuited for red clover, particularly wet soils. Like red clover, it is a perennial but acts as a biennial. The plant is smooth rather than hairy and its flower heads are partially pink and white. This plant will vary in height from ½ to three feet. It has a branch taproot, but the stems are rather weak and hence the crop lodges easily.

Alsike clover is adapted to soils with poor drainage and of less fertility than required for red clover. It is not as sensitive to acidity; hence, it can be grown successfully on wet, cool and sour soils on which red clover fails. It prefers heavy silt or clay soils with plenty of moisture for best growth.

It thrives best in a cool climate but it does stand severe winters better than does red clover.

Alsike clover is used primarily for hay and makes a better quality hay than red clover but doesn't yield as well. The nutritive value of red and alsike clover hay is as follows.

Ladino Clover: (*T. repens* forma *lodigense*) Another great legume becoming ever more popular in the northeastern states is la-

thrive on thin, gravelly soils which suffer from drought. It requires soil high in organic matter and a pH of 6 or above. It is also a heavy user of phosphorus. Good corn land is considered good clover land.

It is not as tolerant of drought as such deep-rooted legumes as alfalfa, white clover or

Hay	Dry Matter %	Protein %	Carbohydrate %	Fat %	Calories
Red clover	84.7	7.38	38.15	1.81	92.32
Alsike clover	90.3	8.15	41.70	1.36	98.46

dino clover. Typical of current opinion in New England is the statement that "ladino clover has done more for Vermont dairymen than any other legume. It can be grown under such a wide range of soil conditions that there is a place for ladino on nearly every farm in the state." And, it might be added, in every state in the Northeast.

Ladino is of such great value because it lasts long under proper management, produces a heavy amount of fodder with its great size, gathers nitrogen, and creeps so that only a small amount of seed is needed. Usually a pound or two is sufficient per acre in mixture with other grasses; there are three-quarters of a million seeds per pound, so it goes a long way.

The fertilizing recommendations for alfalfa apply to ladino, too, for both are heavy feeders and the latter is especially fond of potash, supplied by greensand or granite dust. In mixture with alfalfa it would, of course, get the same food. It is unwise to use ladino alone, particularly for pasture, for it will cause severe bloat in cattle unless dry hay is fed first. Grown with bromegrass, timothy or orchardgrass, this danger is averted. It should not be grazed shorter than four inches and, as with alfalfa, should be allowed free growth for six weeks at the end of the season to build up a food supply in the crowns and roots.

Many farmers in the Northeast have wet fields they don't quite know what to do with and ladino furnishes an answer as long as the field is not swampy. Together with reed canarygrass, another moisture lover, ladino provides good hay and pasture on moist fields. In fact, it is not recommended for dry hillsides or droughty conditions.

Sweet Clover: (*Melilotus*) This biennial legume will grow in all parts of the United States. A fine bee plant, it does well in just about any soil if reasonably well supplied with lime, and will pierce tough subsoils. It is especially adept at utilizing rock fertilizers. Sow 15 pounds of scarified seed per acre, fall to early spring. Fast-growing Hubam, annual white sweet clover, can be turned under in the fall; other varieties have their biggest roots in the spring of the second year, so turn them under then.

On the basis of greening alone, especially when the legume is to be plowed down the fall of the seeding year or the following spring, sweet clover has a slight edge over alfalfa and red clover. However, sweet clover does not fix as much nitrogen nor is it nearly as palatable or nutritious.

Alyce Clover: (*Alysicarpus vaginalis*) This is a summer legume that makes a fast, lush growth, recommended for soil building, grazing and hay. It has been grown successfully primarily in the Deep South.

Crimson Clover: (*T. incarnatum*) An annual that grows two to three feet high, crimson clover has been widely used for soil building as well as a forage crop. Farmers have found it excellent as a winter legume capable of stopping erosion, enriching soil and providing good pasture. About 15 years ago the highly recommended reseeding crimson clover was developed. It resists severe cold and requires less than 35 inches of rainfall. While the seeds look like common crimson, they don't crack open but begin germination around fall, so they are not killed during summer.

As a result, farmers get five to seven months' winter grazing, a spring seed crop and plow the crimson under or mow it for hay— all without affecting the next year's crop.

Reseeding crimson is a good neighbor to other crops, too. It grows well in combination with sericea, kudzu, oats, ryegrass, vetch,

Bermudagrass, and other permanent grazing crops. With some, like Johnsongrass and sweet Sudan, it furnishes nearly year-round grazing.

After making good winter and spring pasture, crimson dies as the summer crops, of which corn, grain sorghum, cotton, and soybeans are widely used, begin their growth. And the nitrogen it has stored up stimulates the following crop like a shot of vitamins. When used for green manure, it should be turned under a few weeks before planting the next crop to allow time to decompose. Or, it will yield two tons of hay per acre, cut near the end of April. It also provides cover and organic matter when grown in combination with late fall and winter truck crops.

Livestock can start grazing crimson when it is about six inches high. Rotation grazing—allowing them to graze one clover field for a week or so, then shifting to another—will keep both pastures thick and prevent overgrazing.

It should be planted one month to six weeks before the average date of the first frost. Lightly harrow and disk the land and allow it to settle a few weeks before seeding. The best method is to plant during or after a light rain on a firm seedbed and cover the seeds lightly. Use 20 pounds per acre when broadcasting the seed, 15 if drilling (½ inch deep).

See also Crop, Forage.

COACH-WHIP   *See* Vine Cactus

COAL ASHES

Although coal ashes will lighten heavy soils, there is serious danger of adding toxic quantities of sulfur and iron from this material. Some ashes do not contain these chemicals in toxic quantities, but the coals from various sources are so different that no general recommendations can be made. The safest procedure is to regard all coal ashes as injurious to the soil.

COBALT

One of the trace mineral elements occurring in both soils and plants, cobalt has been the center of considerable research and dispute over the past several years. Originally, it was contended that cobalt had no function in the nutrition of plants, animals or man. Research has since shown, however, that it makes up 4 percent of the dried weight of crystalline vitamin B_{12}, an important part of the essential B complex.

Evidence has been established that a common wasting disease of sheep and cattle (which has a number of names in various areas throughout the world) is the result of cobalt deficiency in these animals, and can be treated successfully by overcoming this shortage in their feed. In addition, treatment of humans suffering pernicious anemia with the cobalt-containing vitamin B_{12} has brought similar success.

Agricultural science is as yet uncertain of the precise role cobalt plays in plant nutrition. The organic method's principle of incorporating natural, thoroughly balanced materials into the soil to maintain fertility assures the crops grown on that soil, and the animals and people fed by these, an ample share of all the trace elements, including cobalt.

See also Composting, Trace Elements.

COBRA ORCHID
See DARLINGTONIA

COCCINELLIDAE   *See* LADYBUG

COCKLEBUR   (*Xanthium*)

The rough, hooked burrs of this coarse annual weed often get tangled in clothing and the wool of sheep and can injure the hides of farm animals. First seed leaves are reported poisonous to some animals. Cocklebur frequently grows on lowlands, lake beaches and wastelands. It should be mowed to prevent seed formation.

COCKSCOMB   *See* CELOSIA

COCONUT   (*Cocos nucifera*)

A tropical palm tree growing over 80 feet high, the coconut grows best in areas where the annual temperature is above 70°F. (21.11°C.), and is therefore limited to southern Florida in this country. Produced only by seed, the shallow-planted nuts usually germinate in about six months and can be transplanted when six to ten inches high.

It requires seven to eight years before coconut trees reach full bearing, and annual yields are about 20 nuts per tree. Fertilizing with organic materials has been found of great importance, and cover crops that will add nitrogen to the soil are also recommended.

CODLING MOTH

The highly destructive larva of this moth is one inch long and colored pink white with a brown head. It is considered the worst apple pest and also seriously damages other fruits. The moth appears in spring; it is gray brown, with pale, fringed hind wings, and its wingspread measures up to ¾ inch. You are most likely to see them flying on warm, dry spring evenings.

If the moths can be trapped soon after their appearance, the number of eggs a generation can lay will be greatly reduced. They are attracted to blacklight traps, and can be caught in a small cup filled two-thirds full of sawdust mixed with a teaspoon of sassafras oil, a tablespoon of glacial acetic acid and enough glue to saturate the sawdust. Let it dry and then suspend it in a mason jar partly filled with water.

Dormant-oil sprays will take care of many of the eggs, and soapy-water and fish-oil sprays cause caterpillars to drop to the ground. Even a high-pressured hosing with water will dislodge many of the larvae. A heavier duty spray is made of two tablespoons of ryania per gallon of water.

Tiny trichogramma wasps, available by mail as eggs, can parasitize a significant number of codling moth eggs if released at the right time—the wasp eggs should hatch just as the moths are laying theirs.

The numbers of larvae can be reduced by carefully scraping the rough trunk and lower limb bark each spring. Larvae on the prowl for places to pupate will flock to bands of corrugated cardboard wrapped around the trees. Remove and burn the bands late in fall. Clean up drop fruit at least once a week, and see that the trees are amply fertilized.

See also INSECT CONTROL.

COFFEE WASTES

Coffee grounds can be fine additions to the fertilizer resources of the average family. They sour easily because they preserve moisture well and seem to encourage acetic-acid-forming bacteria. Being acid, they are good for blueberries, evergreens and all acid-loving plants. Mixed with lime, they can be fed to earthworm cultures or used as a mulch for plants that prefer a more basic environment. Chemical analyses show that coffee grounds contain up to 2 percent nitrogen, .0033 percent phosphoric acid, and varying amounts of potash, minerals, trace elements, carbohydrates, sugars, vitamins, and caffeine. Drip coffee grounds are generally richer than grounds that have been boiled.

Coffee chaff, a waste product from coffee manufacturing, is an excellent material for use in home gardens as well as farms as it contains over 2 percent of both nitrogen and potash. Its dark color adds to its value as a mulch material.

COLCHICUM

Commonly called autumn crocus or meadow saffron, colchicum is a bulbous plant native to the temperate parts of Europe and northern Africa, where it is found in moist pastures and meadows. The corm (usually called bulb) and the seed contain colchicine, a poisonous alkaloid used in medicine and obtained from foreign sources. In the last ten years, colchicine has also been used in increasing quantities by breeders in developing new varieties and types of plants. Colchicum is grown as an ornamental in this country.

Colchicum is best adapted to rather moist, rich, light sandy loam. It prefers partial shade but can be successfully cultivated in sunny situations. The top of the large corm should be three inches below the soil surface when planted in late summer or early fall. In cold regions some protection in winter is necessary. The new corms are formed from the old ones in much the same way as in tulip bulbs.

The plant blooms in fall without leaves, sending short flower stalks directly out of the ground, hence the name autumn crocus. The seed capsule develops underground in the corm and emerges with the leaves in spring. These leaves look yellow for a long time when ripening, so plant the corm in an inconspicuous place. Never cut off the leaves before they brown. The corms develop their maximum growth during July. *The corms and seed must be handled with much caution, because of their very poisonous nature.* Lilac Wonder produces vase-shaped lilac flowers in October, The Giant produces violet flowers in August and the variety Waterlily is a double pink.

See also CROCUS.

COLD FRAME

Even if you have a fairly large vegetable and flower garden, you may be able to grow most of your own plants. You will save money, raise superior plants, get plants that are directly acclimatized to your locality, and you can produce a far greater variety of crops.

A great advantage in growing your own

A simply built cold frame can help you start and harden off seedlings, extend the growing season and increase your root-storage capacity.

plants in hotbeds and cold frames is that you can send off for seeds from any part of the world, and thus raise and experiment with varieties and with new plants unobtainable from local seedmen.

What is the difference between a hotbed and a cold frame? A cold frame has the same construction as a hotbed, except that there is no heat used inside it. In a cold frame you can propagate such cold-loving plants as cabbage, the Broccoli family, cauliflower. Or you can use cold frames to acclimate to outdoor temperatures plants that have been started in hotbeds. Grow heat-loving plants—peppers, tomatoes,

eggplants, and others—in a hotbed.

There are two types of hotbeds. One is heated by a great deal of fermenting straw or fresh manure (preferably horse manure), which has been placed in a pit 2½ feet deep. Pack the manure down to a depth of 18 inches and water well. Then shovel in five to six inches of finely sieved composted soil or good rich topsoil to make the seedbed.

Another type is made by arranging electric heating cables five inches below the surface of the topsoil seedbed. The coils produce a steady heat day and night while the manure is only effective for a few weeks.

Building: The frame and top of both kinds of hotbeds and cold frames are constructed the same way. Use glass, Plexiglas or plastic. For permanent frame tops, use glass windows bought from a scrapyard or salvaged from an old building. Sides are made from thick planking.

The location of either hotbeds or cold frames should provide full exposure to the sun and good protection from cold winds. A southern exposure is best, providing that water from the eaves of the protecting structure does not drip onto the beds. The bed can be divided into two parts—one-half serving as a hotbed, the other as a cold frame.

The excavation or pit for a hotbed is usually dug from ten inches to three feet deep. The length is ordinarily some multiple of three feet, the width of standard hotbed sash. The width of the bed should also accommodate standard sash. Used window sash dimensions will dictate the size of the bed.

For a four-sash frame, the excavation should be laid out 6½ feet wide by 12⅔ feet long. The latter dimension allows for necessary sash supports or bars that run across the bed. Walls should be about 6 inches thick.

The bed is usually made so that the top of the south wall is about 6 to 8 inches and the north wall from 12 to 20 inches above the ground. This gives a slope of from 6 to 12 inches. As it is difficult to dig a 6-inch trench for concrete walls, it is customary to make the excavation for the bed first and to utilize the earth for the outer forms up to ground level. One-inch-wide boards are used above grade and for the inner forms. If desired, recesses may be cast in the top surfaces of the wall to receive sash.

The recommended concrete mixture for hotbeds and cold frames is 1:2¼:3—that is, one part cement by volume to 2¼ parts clean sand and three parts gravel or crushed stone. The coarse aggregate (gravel or crushed stone) should not be more than 1½ inches in diameter. These ingredients are mixed to a stiff, fairly dry consistency, and then tamped into place in the forms. Not more than five gallons of water per bag of cement should be used for this mix when the sand is in average moist condition. Good concrete is not difficult to make, but always measure ingredients carefully.

The newly placed walls should be protected from drying out too quickly. Hang moist canvas or burlap over them and wet down the covered walls with a garden hose. Do this frequently for a week or ten days after pouring. In cold weather the work should be protected, but does not have to be kept moist.

When the curing is completed and the concrete has hardened, the hotbeds are banked with earth and the embankment sometimes covered with straw in order to prevent heat loss.

The ground should slope away from the site of the bed since good surface and underground drainage is essential. Without ample drainage, water may possibly collect in the pit, delay the growth of the plants and seriously check the fermenting of the manure. Lengths of 4-inch drain tile are often placed around the perimeter of the bed and connected to a suitable outlet so that the bed will be drained in case water happens to collect. However, in well-drained soil, this is probably not necessary.

Proper Soil for Plants: Make a mixture of two parts good garden loam, one part fine, sharp sand and one part leaf mold or old, decayed compost. Mix well and put eight inches of it into the bed. You might loosen the bottom soil first to insure good drainage.

There is enough plant food in this mixture

without adding manure or organic fertilizers high in nitrogen. Used too soon, these cause the young plants to grow too rapidly, unbalancing their natural growth.

After the soil has been evenly distributed throughout the two sections of the bed, pour several pails of boiling water over it. This will sterilize the soil and prevent damping-off. Allow the ground to cool, then cover with window sashes. When the sun reheats the soil to 70°F. (21.11°C.), it is ready for planting.

When to Plant: Two separate compartments are helpful in the cold frame. All vegetables do not require the same temperature for germination. Some will sprout in the heat, but others will rot. To get the maximum number of plants from the seed, plants should be divided into two groups. Celery, cabbage, lettuce, cauliflower, and broccoli require low temperatures for germination. About the first week in April or eight weeks before transplanting time, plant these seeds together in one section of the cold frame. About the middle of April, when the sun is warmer, plant tomatoes, peppers, eggplants, muskmelons, summer squash, and cucumbers in the other half of the bed. The plants in the first half of the bed will have sprouted by that time and will require ventilation. Close the cover on the tomato bed until the plants sprout, then ventilate along with the other half.

Cucumbers, muskmelons and summer squash are grown in parts of milk cartons, and set out in the open after danger of frost. This is not absolutely necessary, but helps produce an earlier yield.

Planting the seeds: In the germinating hotbeds or cold frames, plant seeds evenly in rows one to two inches apart. An inch of fine mulch may be spread evenly over the seeded area to keep the ground moist and to discour-age early weeds. The growing plants will push their way through as they grow. Water lightly, then close the frame. Later you may thin the seedlings. In planting lots of seeds remember this: most seeds will produce sturdy plantlets, but others will be thin or weak. With plentiful planting you may pluck out all but the finest, sturdiest plants.

A must to remember: The grower must watch moisture and heat with an eagle eye. Do not allow the heat to rise above 75 or 80°F. (23.89 to 26.67°C.) while the plants are small. If unventilated growing beds get too hot, plants may easily damp-off and die. To ventilate, simply raise the lids a bit, but close them at night.

Water the beds daily after planting or when needed. Use a fine sprinkler and tepid (70°F. [21.11°C.]) water. Don't muddy the seedbed; just dampen it with one gallon of water per six-foot section of bed.

Once the plants have sprouted and are several weeks old and they begin to crowd one another lift the lids more. As the growing season progresses and the bedding plants grow faster, there will be warm days when you should remove the lids and give them full sun.

Ventilation: No matter what the germination temperatures had been, all growing plants do best around 80°F. (26.67°C.). Regulate temperature each day by slightly lifting the two sashes. On cold days, allow the beds to remain closed. Never lift covers into the wind; cold wind can damage the tender shoots. Open away from the draft, and secure the windows so they will not be broken.

Transplanting: When your plants have grown to a size large enough to be handled, they are ready to transplant over into the cold-frame beds. There they will grow rapidly and harden off so that the shock of final planting into the open garden won't hurt them.

An hour before you take up the plants, water the beds well. Next take out the little plants in clumps. When taking out plants, never yank. The tiny feeder roots are delicate, little hairs. If the plant is yanked out, these roots are torn off and the plant suffers. A ball of earth should be taken with every plant to insure an unharmed root system.

Place the seedlings in a tray or flat. Transplant these into flats or cold frames allowing room for growth. Allow plants to grow several weeks or until all danger of frost in open garden or fields is past.

Hardening Off: Your garden yield depends entirely upon how carefully you execute this step. Do it slowly. Remember, the plants are delicate. Start about 1½ weeks before transplanting time. Cut down on the water supply, and begin to expose the plants to the direct sunlight and wind. Remove the covering entirely for a half hour the first day. Increase the exposure each day. Take care not to underwater as this condition may cause the plant stems to turn woody. After the seventh day, the plants should be hardened enough to withstand a full day of sun. You may now remove the windows, and allow the plants to remain uncovered until transplanting time. Water well every night.

Final setting out of seedlings into garden or field: When you are ready to transplant the seedlings to their final places in the garden, again wet down beds or flats well. When you dig up the plants be careful to preserve the root systems with plenty of undisturbed and well-packed earth around them.

Transplant on cloudy days or during a light drizzle. This will help to prevent shock. Should a plant refuse to take, replace it with one from the bed.

When the soil has sufficiently warmed, take the young seedlings from the cold frame and transplant them to the garden bed. Firm the soil around the roots and water the plants thoroughly.

Damping-Off: About the only thing that can harm growing plants in the hotbeds or cold frames is overheating, drying out for lack of water or being attacked by the fungus disease known as damping-off. Damping-off, also called "black root" or "wire stem," is caused by about a half-dozen or more fungus parasites. They usually grow near the surface, and enter the tiny plants at the point where they emerge from the ground. All of these fungus parasites require a high moisture content of soil and air for quick growth.

To prevent trouble from damping-off, the best defense is to keep the air and surface of the seedbed as dry as is consistent with good growth of the plants. Heating the beds without proper ventilation causes damping-off.

Using the Cold Frame for Winter Vegetables: A cold frame is really a protected seedbed and can be used in the first frosty days of autumn just as advantageously as in early spring. Tender lettuce and crisp endive can be enjoyed until after Thanksgiving by properly utilizing the cold frame.

Plant seeds in early autumn. For lettuce, endive and parsley, plant seeds in one compartment in rows three inches apart and about ¼ inch deep, covering the seed with vermiculite to prevent damping-off. Water the rows with a fine spray, adjust the sash and place a covering of light boards over it. As soon as the seeds sprout, remove this cover and raise the sash several inches to allow good air circulation.

Seedlings will grow rapidly, and when they begin to crowd each other, they are ready to transplant. Set the little plants in another compartment, about three inches apart each way. Mulch again with vermiculite and keep them shaded for a few days. As plants grow, they can be thinned and the thinnings used in salads. The remaining plants will then begin to form heads.

When nights grow frosty, close the frame tightly before sundown to hold the day's heat within, opening it again each morning. If nights are very cold, cover the frame with a blanket and bank leaves around the sides. If the day remains cold, remove the blanket to allow light to enter, but keep the frame closed.

You'll be amazed at how much cold the plants can stand under glass. As the season grows late, plants may be frozen occasionally, but by sprinkling them with cold water and keeping them in the dark for a while, they will revive and come back in good condition. It is thus possible to have fresh salads until winter.

You can also use the cold frame in winter for storing vegetables. Before the ground freezes, remove about 18 inches of soil and place vegetables like turnips, rutabagas, beets, carrots, and celery on a layer of straw. Cover the vegetables with another layer of straw. If protected with sash boards, the vegetables will remain unfrozen all winter.

COLEUS

Most people are familiar with this old-fashioned plant with colorful variegated foliage containing hues of purple, red, pink, green, or yellow on velvety leaves. Stalks of blue or lilac flowers are common, but are only of secondary interest and are pinched to direct strength to the colorful leaves. The best known is *Coleus Blumei,* a native of Java.

Outdoors it can be used in borders, window boxes, containers, or as a summer filler. Indoors it makes a very colorful house plant during drab winter days. An all-purpose soil which dries between applications of water is required. Bright sun or fluorescent light is needed to bring out the best color. Propagation is easy from seed or stem tip cuttings. Seeds can be started in February or March and plants put outside after all danger of frost is past. Pinching them back will produce bushy plants. Cuttings can be taken in the fall prior to frost for indoor use. Indoors they will require ruthless pruning to prevent a "leggy" appearance.

A wide range of variegated foliage varieties exist, of which *Coleus Blumei* var. *Verschaffeltii* is well known. Most seed companies have an excellent selection. A point to keep in mind when raising seedlings is that the more vigorous ones are usually less interesting, since they tend to become tall, floppy and less colorful.

See also HOUSE PLANTS.

COLLARD
(*Brassica oleracea* var. *acephala*)

Easily cultivated and highly esteemed for its flavor, this member of the Cabbage family is of major importance in the South, where, by its hardy constitution, it can stand summer heat and winter cold. It has been described as a nonheading cabbage, resembling the tall kales in growth. Since it will stand more heat than cabbage, it is substituted for that crop in warm

An important perennial vegetable in southern gardens, collard is extremely resistant to warm as well as cool temperatures.

regions of the country. In the North where heading cabbage is successfully grown, collards have not become popular.

Culture: In general, the culture of collard and that of cabbage is similar. In the South, sowing is usually done in both the spring and the fall. In the North, collard may be planted in the summer for late greens. Some believe it to be improved by the first frosts. Plants may be started early in the spring and set out later in the same way as cabbage, or they may be sown in the garden row and later thinned to stand about two feet apart, with three feet between the rows. Seedlings may be thinned to stand six inches apart if the crop is to be used while plants are still small.

A good fertile soil will produce a more desirable growth. High quality relies on quick growth, and generous applications of rotted manure or compost are important. The soil should be worked into good tilth before planting.

Collards require full sun, and although they can withstand more drought than the cabbage, ample moisture should be supplied. No weeds should be allowed to establish themselves, so cultivation is necessary. Shallow cultivation is best to prevent cutting roots close to the surface. The hoe should be put into action about once a week until the plants are half grown, after which the shade of the plants will help to keep down the weeds.

Harvesting: Whole young plants may be cut or the tender leaves at the top stripped off. A cluster of leaves may be picked a few at a time as required and before they mature so as not to be tough. As the plants are gradually stripped of their lower leaves, they may need the assistance of a stake to support the top cluster.

Disease and Pest Control: Plants should be carefully examined for signs of wilting or curling of the leaves. Damping-off is a disease which causes the soft part of the stem to rot away between the main root and the surface of the soil. The diseased plant should be pulled up and destroyed.

Cabbage worms can be thwarted with homemade sprays. A mixture of ground pepper pods, water and ½ teaspoon of soap powder will work effectively against the worms when sprayed on the plants. Protective shields of mesh wire and a cylinder of hoops can be erected to prevent damage to growing collards.

Nutrient Value: Collards are high in vitamins A and C.

Varieties: Georgia collards are hardy and endure adverse conditions, including poor soil. It grows 30 or more inches in height and bears a loose cluster of large, cabbagelike leaves. Louisiana Sweet has compact centers and short-stemmed leaves. Cabbage collard is more resistant to warm weather and forms small, cabbagelike heads. Vates collard is widely adaptable and is hardy in the North.

See also CABBAGE.

COLLOID

Colloids are of great importance to the soil. "Colloid" is derived from the Greek word for glue, and in general refers to a state in which a finely divided material is dispersed through a second. Common examples are gelatin, blood, plant and animal cells, and soil. There are two types of soil colloids, organic—represented by humus, and inorganic—represented by clay minerals of various kinds. In temperate regions silicate clays are important agriculturally, and in the tropics iron and aluminum hydrous oxide clays are recognized.

Colloidal clay is made up of flakelike particles less than .0002 millimeter in diameter. Some clays are much more active than others. Humus has the same properties as does colloidal clay, and is much more effective, pound for pound, than any mineral colloid.

The properties of soil colloids include water-holding capacity, formation of good granulation through their swelling or shrinking upon wetting or drying, and their peculiar ability to absorb or hold on their surface, in a form available to plant roots, many of the mineral nutrients of the soil. These nutrient elements are present on the colloids as ions, or electrically charged elemental units of matter. Colloids are particularly significant in holding calcium, potassium, sodium, and magnesium in the soil in an available form. All are essential to plant growth. Hydrogen is also absorbed by colloidal clays.

To protect the colloid against an excess of hydrogen ions, it is necessary to provide a supply of basic ions to replace the acid-forming ones. The elements calcium, and less frequently magnesium, are best suited to do this. They are found in satisfactory proportions in limestone, which is about 22 percent calcium and 13 percent magnesium, or in dolomitic limestone, which is high in magnesium.

See also HUMUS, SOIL.

COLLOIDAL ROCK PHOSPHATE

Like raw rock phosphate, colloidal phosphate is an excellent natural source of phosphoric acid.

The colloidal form is a mixture of fine particles of phosphate suspended in a clay base. It has a content of 18 percent phosphorus (P_2O_5) and 15 percent calcium, as well as trace minerals. When it is applied to the land, the clay penetrates the soil and carries the residue minerals with it deep into the earth. Once in the soil, the minerals are slowly broken down for use by carbonic acid (carbon dioxide dissolved in water) and certain organic acids given off by plant roots. The phosphate not made available by this action will remain in the soil unchanged until roots develop in its vicinity and make use of it. The main source of this product is Florida, where the only natural deposit is located, and where many man-made deposits—the residues of rock phosphate mining—exist.

For years, the residues were unwanted. The rock itself was the valuable commodity. The clay sediment that accompanied a deposit of phosphate was forcibly washed away into holding pits, built up by a system of dikes. These areas were the curse of landowners in the phosphate mining region of central Florida.

In 1930, all of this changed. The colloidal clay residue of these surface mines, located near Ocala in a strip 100 miles long and 50 miles wide, was found to have value as a fertilizer and animal feed supplement. Colloidal phosphate contains about 60 percent as much of the nutrient as rock phosphate, so it is less expensive and less nourishing to plants. By 1934, active mining of this once-neglected material had begun in earnest. When World War II cut off the United States' agricultural supply of bone meal from South America, the colloidal phosphate of this narrow belt of land was in great demand. It was wanted because it was known to contain the same nutrients as bone meal, primarily calcium and phosphoric acid.

See also PHOSPHATE ROCK, PHOSPHORUS.

COLORADO FIR   *See* FIR

COLUMBINE   (*Aquilegia*)

These hardy perennials of the Buttercup family bear distinctively spurred flowers on thin, wiry stems well above the delicate, deeply lobed green or blue green basal leaves. The flowers have a row of pointed sepals surrounding a center of true petals, each of which tapers at the back into a tube or spur with a small sac containing nectar at the end. These flowers can be one to four inches across with spurs ½ to six inches long, depending on the species. They come in pastel shades of many colors, with the sepals often having a color contrasting to that of the petals.

Columbines are among the most versatile of garden flowers. Their light, airy grace and soft colors cause them to combine well with all

The popular long-spurred varieties of columbine are available in a wide range of colors, from pure white to various shades and combinations of violet, blue, red, pink, and yellow.

other flowers, so they can be used as "blenders" among coarser or more emphatic plants in the border. Plant them near daylily, iris or peonies, or use them to soften the upright effect of foxgloves. Columbines vary in height from six inches to three feet, according to species, and most do as well in sun as in partial shade, so they may be used in the rock garden, among bulbs and in the wild garden as effectively as in the border. All make good cut flowers.

The foliage of these plants is often attacked by the columbine leaf miner, which leaves white tracks as it tunnels in the leaves, feeding as it goes. Infestation is seldom severe enough to damage the plant, but the foliage becomes unsightly. The best control is to pick off infested leaves and put them in the hot part of the compost pile or burn them.

The major fault of columbines is that they tend to be short-lived plants in all but the best-drained soils, usually blooming well for only two to three years. They make up for this tendency and persist by self-sowing heavily, but the seedlings of hybrid parents tend to produce flowers of inferior color. Any given hybrid plant can be reproduced true to color only by division of the roots in spring, but this is a chancy thing because injured roots and crowns rot easily. It is often best to leave old plants in place until they run out, keeping replacements coming along by growing a few of them from purchased seed each year or two. All of the popular columbines are easily grown from seed, which can be started indoors in February or March with germination in about 12 days, or outdoors in spring in the cold frame with germination in 15 to 30 days. When growing them indoors, put the seed packet in the refrigerator for two days before sowing and grow the seedlings in a cool window. They require some cold to induce germination. When

true leaves appear, transplant seedlings to larger flats, peat pots or nursery rows. Plant in their permanent positions after frost danger is past, spacing the dwarfs eight to 12 inches apart and larger types 12 to 18 inches apart.

Columbines like to be kept moist in summer, but good drainage, especially in winter, is essential to success with them. The fleshy roots and crown will rot in heavy soils that tend to stay wet in winter. Liberal use of compost, leaf mold or peat moss will increase the moisture-retentiveness of dry soils and improve the drainage of heavy soils. Use sand as well in very heavy clay.

The most popular columbines are the long-spurred hybrids, which bloom for four to six weeks starting in late May, and are available as seed mixtures or named color types. McKana's Giants, McKana Improved and Mrs. Scott Elliott Hybrids are all good mixtures with full color range. Crimson Star has red sepals and spurs with red-tinged white petals. Copper Queen is copper red and Rose Queen is rose and white. All grow about three feet tall with spurs to four inches long. Dragonfly Hybrid is a dwarf strain 18 inches tall with large flowers. These hybrids were developed from crosses of several American species, notably:

A. chrysantha, native to the Southwest, has soft yellow flowers with long spurs on three-foot plants. It is usually the most durable of the lot, and tolerates heat and dryness better than some of its hybrid offspring.

A. caerulea, the Rocky Mountain columbine, is the state flower of Colorado. It bears blue and white flowers on 2½-foot plants, but is short-lived in areas having hot summers. It is illegal to dig up the plant or pick its flowers in Colorado. *A. c.* cv. 'Mrs. Nichols' looks like it and is easier to grow.

A. longissima, another southwestern species, is yellow and has the longest spurs of the group. It is said to be the most heat-tolerant species and blooms later than the others; it is recommended for southwestern gardens especially.

A. formosa, native coastally from California to Alaska, grows to three feet and has red and yellow long-spurred flowers.

Less popular now but frequently seen in old gardens are the short-spurred columbines derived from the European species, *A. vulgaris.* The plants grow to two feet but are often much smaller, and the flowers have spurs about one inch long which are tightly incurved at the end. There are pink and white forms, but seedlings revert to blue shades and should be controlled if the other colors are wanted.

Two species good for the rockery or wild garden are *A. flabellata* from Japan and *A. canadensis,* the wild columbine of eastern North America. *A. flabellata* grows to 15 inches with lavender and white flowers and light green leaves. The cultivar Nana Alba is a good six-inch dwarf with white flowers. *A. canadensis* grows to a foot or less, has nodding red and yellow short-spurred flowers and gray green leaves. It is most at home in the shady wild garden, where it will self-sow freely without becoming a pest. In the wild, thriving colonies are often found on hot, dry, gravelly banks, and under cultivation it adapts well to the drier parts of rockeries. It blooms in late April and May when most spring bulbs do, and it makes a beautiful companion for them. Wild plants are protected in many states and should not be collected in any case, since they are as easily grown from seed as any other columbine. Chill the seed and grow the plants in a cool place. *A. canadensis* is a special favorite of the ruby-throated hummingbird in the East because its bloom period coincides with the return of

this bird from its winter range. All other columbines are also good for attracting hummingbirds to the garden.

COMFREY   (*Symphytum officinale*)

Also known as knitbone or ass ear, comfrey is a standard herbal remedy for a number of ailments. Although many extravagant claims have been made for its abilities, it *is* high in calcium, phosphorus, potassium, and trace minerals, and in vitamins A and C. It is the

Comfrey leaves contain vitamins A, C and B$_{12}$ as well as several important minerals.

only land plant that contains vitamin B_{12} and is also a good source of allantoin, a substance useful in treating wounds, burns and ulcers. A good animal food, young comfrey leaves can also be eaten in salad or as boiled greens.

Comfrey is a member of the Borage family. Mature plants grow wild, and can be easily cultivated on a small scale; large-scale production is difficult. The plant grows two to three feet high, is erect and is rough and hairy over the stem and leaves (the hairs can cause itching if brushed). The leaves are ovate, resembling the ears of a donkey, and decrease in size as they get higher up the plant. The stem is stout and angular, the root branched and fleshy, often reaching a foot in length and less than an inch in diameter.

Creamy yellow or purple blue flowers are borne in racemes at the top of the plant, followed by four seeds in a cuplike fruit. Comfrey blooms throughout the greater portion of the summer, the first flowers appearing in late April or early May and continuing until the first frosts. Comfrey is hardy, however, and continues to produce foliage when other plants have been killed by frost.

Comfrey can be propagated from plants, crown cuttings containing eyes or buds and root cuttings. The latter is the cheapest method, and they can be easily mail ordered. Few growers have success in raising comfrey from seed.

Cuttings are planted three to six inches deep in a horizontal position in well-tilled and manured soil with a pH of 6 to 7. Space the cuttings three feet apart each way and mulch or cultivate between cuttings. Once cuttings are established, they can be divided for more plants. The best time to divide is in the spring when the leaves begin to appear above ground.

Harvest comfrey just before blooming. Cut the plants, leaving a two-inch stem stub, when they are 12 to 18 inches high.

Comfrey leaves can be dried for winter use. Dry quickly in thin layers in the sunlight. Store in boxes layered between layers of grass hay, being careful not to compress or shatter the leaves when packing. Comfrey root can also be dried for winter use. Clean carefully and dry slowly in the sun, turning often.

Comfrey is a tenacious plant, difficult to eradicate since it will reproduce from the slightest sliver of root left in the soil. Be careful where you plant it, since it can become a bothersome pest.

COMMONER STUDY
See FERTILIZER, CHEMICAL

COMMUNITY GARDEN
See URBAN GARDENING

COMPANION PLANTING

In nature, where plants grow without cultivation, there is always a mixture of plant types growing in an area. The selection of the plants living in an area depends on the soil type, local climatic conditions and horticultural history. With a few exceptions, the plants that grow together in the wild are mutually beneficial, in that they allow for maximum utilization of light, moisture and soil. Plants needing less light live in the shade of those which must have full light, while the roots of some plants live close to the surface, and others send their roots far down into the

Aromatic plants, like these marigolds, are said to deter cabbage moths.

feeders, light feeders, soil-conserving and soil-improving crops. The heavy feeders should be planted in soil that has been newly fertilized. Among the heavy-feeding vegetables are cabbage, cauliflower, all leaf vegetables as chard, head lettuce, endive, spinach, and celery, celeriac, leeks, cucumbers, squash, sweet corn, and tomatoes.

The heavy-feeding vegetables should be followed by such light feeders as pole beans, bush beans and other legumes. Light-feeding vegetables are great lovers of compost. Also, better than other kinds of plants, they seem to use the finely pulverized raw rocks and make phosphorus, potassium and many trace elements available to other plants.

Other light feeders are such root crops as carrots, beets, radishes, turnips, and rutabagas. Most herbs are light feeders.

Some plants have a beneficial effect upon the garden by virtue of some peculiar character of their growth, their scent or their root formation and soil demands. Among these plants are sunflower, hemp, blossoming hyssop, thyme, savory, borage, and other good bee-pasture plants. Odoriferous plants, including those with aromatic oils, play an important part in determining just which insects visit the garden. Hemp, for instance, is said to repel the cabbage butterfly.

However, there is more to companion planting than just arranging the physical needs of plants for optimum use of your garden space. Although the hard scientific evidence is often lacking, there is a whole host of insect repellent properties attributed to different combinations of plants. In addition, there are combinations of plants that seem to be natural enemies. When planted too close together, the result is often depressed yields of one or both plants. In most cases, plant scientists still do not know all the

subsoil. Some plants will hurry into bloom and flower early in the year before their neighbors have yet to produce leaves, which will cut off the light supply later in the year. This is known as companion planting when it is practiced in the garden. Companion planting enables the gardener to maximize use of sun, soil and moisture to grow mixed crops in one area.

In planting a vegetable garden, you should use plants that are mutually compatible and make demands on the environment at different times. Vegetables may be divided into heavy

why's of these relationships. Many theorize that it is root exudates, or leaf secretions. The odor of one plant may be desirable to an insect, but the odor of a neighboring plant may overpower the attractive scent and send the insect packing.

The listing of companion plants and antagonist plants presented below is based on scientific evidence as well as on folklore. What is reported as working in one garden may not work in yours. Then too, you may hit on a beneficial pairing not yet reported. The main thing is not to plant your garden in strict mono cropped rows. Diversity of plants is the easiest and most effective pesticide and fertilizer the garden has, so use it liberally.

Below are combinations of vegetables, herbs, flowers, and weeds that are mutually beneficial, according to reports of organic gardeners and companion planting traditions.

Plant	Companion(s) and Effects
Asparagus	Tomatoes, parsley, basil.
Basil	Tomatoes (improves growth and flavor); said to dislike rue; repels flies and mosquitoes.
Bean	Potatoes, carrots, cucumbers, cauliflower, cabbage, summer savory, most other vegetables and herbs; around house plants when set outside.
Bean (bush)	Sunflowers (beans like partial shade, sunflowers attract birds and bees), cucumbers (combination of heavy and light feeders), potatoes, corn, celery, summer savory.
Bee balm	Tomatoes (improves growth and flavor).
Beet	Onions, kohlrabi.
Borage	Tomatoes (attracts bees, deters tomato worm, improves growth and flavor), squash, strawberries.
Cabbage family (broccoli, Brussels sprouts, cabbage, cauliflower, kale, kohlrabi)	Potatoes, celery, dill, chamomile, sage, thyme, mint, pennyroyal, rosemary, lavender, beets, onions; aromatic plants deter cabbage worms.
Caraway	Loosens soil; plant here and there.
Carrot	Peas, lettuce, chives, onions, leeks, rosemary, sage, tomatoes.
Catnip	Plant in borders; protects against flea beetles.
Celery	Leeks, tomatoes, bush beans, cauliflower, cabbage.
Chamomile	Cabbage, onions.
Chervil	Radishes (improves growth and flavor).
Chive	Carrots; plant around base of fruit trees to discourage insects from climbing trunk.
Corn	Potatoes, peas, beans, cucumbers, pumpkin, squash.
Cucumber	Beans, corn, peas, radishes, sunflowers.
Dead nettle	Potatoes (deters potato bug).
Dill	Cabbage (improves growth and health), carrots.
Eggplant	Beans.

Fennel	Most plants are supposed to dislike it.	Onion	Beets, strawberries, tomato, lettuce (protects against slugs), beans (protects against ants), summer savory.
Flax	Carrots, potatoes.		
Garlic	Roses and raspberries (deters Japanese beetle); with herbs to enhance their production of essential oils; plant liberally throughout garden to deter pests.	Parsley	Tomato, asparagus.
		Pea	Squash (when squash follows peas up trellis), plus grows well with almost any vegetable; adds nitrogen to the soil.
Henbit	General insect repellent.		
		Petunia	Protects beans; beneficial throughout garden.
Horseradish	Potatoes (deters potato beetle); around plum trees to discourage curculios.	Pigweed	Brings nutrients to topsoil; beneficial growing with potatoes, onions and corn; keep well thinned.
Hyssop	Cabbage (deters cabbage moths), grapes; keep away from radishes.		
Lamb's-quarters	Nutritious edible weeds; allow to grow in modest amounts in the corn.	Potato	Horseradish, beans, corn, cabbage, marigold, limas, eggplant (as trap crop for potato beetle).
Leek	Onions, celery, carrots.	Pot marigold	Helps tomato, but plant throughout garden as deterrent to asparagus beetle, tomato worm and many other garden pests.
Lemon balm	Here and there in garden.		
Marigold	The workhorse of pest deterrents; keeps soil free of nematodes; discourages many insects; plant freely throughout garden.		
		Pumpkin	Corn.
Marjoram	Here and there in garden.	Radish	Peas, nasturtium, lettuce, cucumbers; a general aid in repelling insects.
Mint	Cabbage family; tomatoes; deters cabbage moth.	Rosemary	Carrots, beans, cabbage, sage; deters cabbage moth, bean beetles and carrot fly.
Mole plant	Deters moles and mice if planted here and there throughout the garden.	Rue	Roses and raspberries; deters Japanese beetle; keep it away from basil.
Nasturtium	Tomatoes, radishes, cabbage, cucumbers; plant under fruit trees; deters aphids and pests of cucurbits.	Sage	Rosemary, carrots, cabbage, peas, beans; deters some insects.

Southernwood	Cabbage; plant here and there in garden.
Sow thistle	This weed in modest numbers can help tomatoes, onions and corn.
Soybean	Grows with anything; helps everything.
Spinach	Strawberries.
Squash	Nasturtium, corn.
Strawberry	Bush beans, spinach, borage, lettuce (as a border).
Summer savory	Beans, onions; deters bean beetles.
Sunflower	Cucumbers.
Tansy	Plant under fruit trees; deters pests of roses and raspberries; deters flying insects, also Japanese beetles, striped cucumber beetles, squash bugs; deters ants.
Tarragon	Good throughout garden.
Thyme	Here and there in garden; deters cabbage worm.
Tomato	Chives, onion, parsley, asparagus, marigold, nasturtium, carrot, limas.
Turnip	Peas.
Valerian	Good anywhere in garden.
Wormwood	As a border, keeps animals from the garden.
Yarrow	Plant along borders, near paths, near aromatic herbs; enhances essential oil production of herbs.

COMPOST BINS

Gardeners who are not satisfied with compost heaps have come up with a great variety of bins, boxes, pits, and other containers for their compost. These structures make composting easier and improve the appearance of the compost pile. To some extent, they also protect the compost from washing rains and baking sun. The type of container you select for your home grounds depends on your personal taste, the amount of labor you want to

The removable side of this bin allows for easy turning and removal of the compost.

expend to build it and the materials you have on hand or can afford to buy.

Over the years, a number of bins have become popular. One of them is the brick or concrete block bin, which is easily constructed without mortar. Blocks are laid to permit plenty of aeration of the compost. This bin is sturdy, long lasting, easily accessible through its open end, and can be built to match a brick house. The materials are generally inexpensive and easily available.

A bin can be made from prefab picket fence or snow fence fastened in a square to four stout posts.

Compost can also be made in a steel drum. Aerate it by removing the bottom of the drum and setting it on an eight-inch cinder block. More complicated versions of the drum composter have been built by ambitious home craftspeople, including one version with a door in the bottom to clean out finished humus. Some have mounted the drum so that it can rotate, thus turning the compost.

A more primitive-looking but effective compost bin can be made from rough stones or logs, or saplings stripped of their branches. The latter are particularly effective if stacked so that air can circulate around them.

COMPOSTING

In the soft, warm bosom of a decaying compost heap, a transformation from life to death and back again is taking place. Life is leaving the living plants of yesterday, but in their death these leaves and stalks pass on their vitality to the coming generations of future seasons. Here in a dank and moldy pile the wheel of life is turning.

Compost is more than a fertilizer or a healing agent for the soil's wounds. It is a symbol of continuing life. Nature herself made compost before man first walked the earth and before the first dinosaur reared its head above a primeval swamp. Leaves falling to the forest floor and slowly moldering are composting. The dead grass of the meadow seared by winter's frost is being composted by the dampness of the earth beneath. Birds, insects and animals contribute their bodies to this vast and continuing soil rebuilding program of nature.

The compost heap in your garden is an intensified version of this process of death and rebuilding which is going on almost everywhere in nature. In the course of running a garden there is always an accumulation of organic wastes of different sorts—leaves, grass clippings, weeds, twigs—and since time immemorial gardeners have been accumulating this material in piles, eventually to spread it back on the soil as rich, dark humus.

In many parts of the world today, composting is practiced just as it was hundreds or even thousands of years ago. Farmers and householders in the less industrialized regions of Asia, Africa and Europe have no source of commercial fertilizer, and consequently make rough compost piles of cattle manure, garbage, human wastes, straw, and weeds. These piles decay into humus, which is then used as a soil conditioner for the kitchen garden and farm fields. Such compost is not very rich in plant nutrients, but it is a manageable form of humus that maintains the tilth and general condition of soil that has been used for generations.

Sir Albert Howard, an agricultural scientist who worked during the 1930's in the Indian state of Indore, was one of the first men to create a sophisticated method of composting, and out of his efforts has flowered the entire organic idea. Within the last 30 years, a great amount of progress has been made in adapting composting methods to solve various waste disposal and agricultural problems. In 1949, the Sanitary Engineering Department of the University of California started a compost research project that culminated in the first detailed scientific analysis of the phenomenon of composting. The California project concentrated mainly on compost made in heaps. An important result of the California project was the outlining of a method that home gardeners could use to make compost in as short a time as 14 days. The U.S. Government also became widely involved in research in the late 1950's and early 1960's.

The best introduction to composting is found in the book *Composting: A Study of the Process and Its Principles* by Dr. Clarence G. Golueke, a research biologist at the Sanitary Engineering Research Laboratory at the University of California, Berkeley. The book is published by Rodale Press, 1972.

The Purpose of Composting: Composting in heaps is an extension of a process that is going on almost everywhere in nature. When a lawn is mowed and the clippings are left on the ground, they compost. The straw that is left on fields by the combine decays into humus. Leaves that fall turn the forest floor into a compost area. The fertility of all the soils of the earth has been achieved and maintained principally by the decay of vegetable matter.

Gardening and farming disrupt the natural pattern of the return of plant matter to the earth. Compost is the link between modern agriculture and nature's own method of building soil fertility.

In addition to returning rotting vegetable material to the soil, there are two major reasons for making compost: to render certain materials such as manure and garbage pleasant to handle, and to increase the nitrogen content of low-nitrogen materials such as sawdust, straw and corncobs.

The high heat of composting rapidly "cooks" the smell out of manure and garbage. This is a significant gain because gardeners are often reluctant to use those materials fresh.

The composting process also increases the nitrogen content of the pile. Microorganisms "burn off" much of the carbon, reducing the cubic bulk of the heap but correspondingly increasing its nitrogen portion.

Organic matter is valuable to the soil only while it is decaying. Even finished compost is actually only partly decayed. It continues to break down in the soil, providing food for increasing populations of microorganisms. When building tilth on a farm, it is frequently more practical to spread fresh manure than make compost from it because a greater part of its decay will take place in the soil where it will do the most good.

Even though it may not be necessary to compost some materials, most organic gardeners prefer to compost almost all the organic matter they get. The compost heap is a convenient place to store leaves, weeds and grass clippings until they are needed. Pound for pound, compost is the finest soil conditioner to be had.

Bacterial Action in Compost: The microbiological processes that occur during composting are a form of rotting or decay, but without the unpleasant smell that often accompanies such decomposition. A well-made compost heap creates an environment in which decay-causing bacteria can live and reproduce at the highest rate of activity. As a result of this activity of microorganisms, fresh manure, garbage, leaves, weeds, and other compost materials are converted into dark humus.

There are two types of bacterial activity taking place in compost heaps: anaerobic breakdown (without air) and aerobic breakdown (with air). Some bacteria that cause decay function in a lack of air or oxygen. Others need plenty of air. Aerobic composting is more common and practical than anaerobic because it is faster and lacks the malodorous middle stage common in anaerobic decomposition.

The anaerobic method of composting was devised to improve upon the aerated composting of organic materials. Aerobic composting brings about an oxidation that must destroy much of the organic nitrogen and carbon dioxide. Secondly, some of the valuable juices of the materials leach downward and out of the mass into the ground underneath where they are wasted.

The purpose of keeping out the air is to prevent or reduce oxidation. Combustion of nitrogenous substances is always accompanied by the production of a great quantity of free nitrogen compounds. Manure kept efficiently in an open pit loses 40 percent of the nitrogen originally contained. This loss is relatively large in contrast to the 10 percent or less loss obtainable with the use of closed pits. In them the fermentation takes place out of contact with air, and the reduction of weight, when matured, is only one-quarter that of the original weight. In perfect anaerobic fermentation, no nitrogen losses whatsoever would occur. Research has also shown that anaerobic composting preserves more of the nutrients in compost than does aerobic composting.

One big difficulty has been finding an efficient and simple way to practice anaerobic composting. The latest technique is to enclose the compost in a polyethylene wrapping.

During aerobic composting, the micro-organisms convert the carbon in the heap materials into energy, creating heat. The temperature in an active heap can rise to 160°F. (71.11°C.). Nitrogen, phosphorus and potassium are required in the nutrition of the micro-organisms. Phosphorus and potassium are usually plentiful in all compost material, but there is quite often a lack of nitrogen. The relationship between the amount of carbon in compost material and the amount of nitrogen is called the carbon-nitrogen ratio, often stated as the C/N ratio. Raw garbage, for example, has 25 times as much carbon as it has nitrogen. Its carbon-nitrogen ratio is therefore expressed as simply the number 25. Sawdust has a C/N ratio of 400. Farmyard manure, which is much higher in nitrogen, has a C/N ratio of 14. The higher the number, the more carbon is present. It is generally stated that a carbon-nitrogen ratio of 30 is required for compost activity to take place at an optimum rate. By determining the C/N ratio of all materials placed in the heap a good balance of carbon to nitrogen can be obtained. Such care is required for commercial composting operations, but for home or farm composting, only rough estimates of the C/N ratio need be made.

A heap that does not have sufficient nitrogen will compost very slowly. It may not heat up at all. A pile of ordinary sawdust will take several years to break down into dark humus. But if an organic nitrogen supplement is added in the form of dried blood, tankage or poultry manure, the composting of the sawdust will be much more rapid. A lack of nitrogen (represented as a high C/N ratio) is probably the chief cause of composting failures—heaps that fail to heat and decay quickly.

Actually, there are many factors other than the C/N ratio which influence composting, including moisture, air temperature, pH, absorbency of the material, and mineral content of the material.

It is readily seen that since all those factors are variable, no two compost heaps will be exactly alike unless they are made in the same place at the same time of the same materials. The chief effect of this variability is to vary the type of microorganisms that multiply in the pile and effect its breakdown. If the heap is made of acid materials, types of microorganisms that can live under acid conditions will multiply. This variability in compost heaps is one factor that makes it highly unlikely that a bacterial activator preparation would be useful. A bacterial activator or starter is supposed to introduce into the heap particular strains of microorganisms that are efficient composters. Controlled experiments with activators conducted at the Sanitary Engineering Project of the University of California and at Michigan State University have shown that activators did not influence composting results. *See also* ACTIVATORS.

Moisture can have an important influence on microorganisms. A heap that is soggy can smother aerobic organisms—the type that work the fastest. The ideal heap is moist, not water-logged. Some composters cover their heaps with a plastic sheet to help keep the moisture content constant. This can be a useful technique in very dry areas, also in times of heavy rainfall.

Because aerobic microorganisms are the most efficient composters, compost heaps are turned primarily to assure a continual supply of air. Even so, parts of a heap can become sealed from the air in a short time after being turned, and anaerobic decomposition sets in. Shredding or grinding of material being put in compost heaps creates a fluffier mass and enables aerobic decomposition to take place for longer periods. Aerobic microorganisms convert the carbon in

the heap into carbon dioxide, which is passed off into the air.

Anaerobic (airless) decomposition is generally carried on in tanks, bins or silos. The chief advantages of this type of composting are that no turning of the mass is required and that the compost can produce methane gas for heating and lighting purposes.

Methane digesters have become a possible alternate energy source for the small farm and homestead.

Digester Composting: Although the methane digester works for small farms, large garbage digesters for municipal use are primarily of the aerobic type, although Verdier and Beccari anaerobic digesters have been used for garbage composting in Europe. The anaerobic digesters are large concrete tanks which are filled and emptied at intervals.

The goal of designers of aerobic digesters is to make a machine that will convert garbage into compost in a period of hours instead of days. Compost has been made in pilot plants in as short a time as 48 hours. Basically, digesters are used instead of open heaps in the design of municipal compost plants because they enclose the raw wastes, cutting down odors and reducing fly and rodent problems. They also enable decomposition to take place under any weather conditions, an important consideration in northern areas. Digesters can make compost more quickly than any method using heaps. A fast composting process requires less space for storage of garbage and compost, a very important point when the high cost of real estate near cities is considered.

The basic function of digesters is to create those ideal conditions which make for fast growth of aerobic microorganisms. For ideal composting an ample supply of warm, moist air must be able to penetrate all parts of the compost mass at all times. Digesters either provide compressors to blow warm, moist air into the compost, or they accomplish the same means through continuous agitation or mixing.

The DANO process is apparently the most successful of the digester systems. Its main feature is a long, rotating drum, called a "Bio-Stabilizer," set at an angle of five degrees from the horizontal. Garbage is fed into the upper end of the drum. Two rows of air jets on the inside of the drum provide aeration. The garbage moves so slowly through the drum that it can be retained for three to five days. No grinding of the raw material is required, as the abrasive action of the sides of the drum reduces the particle size of the garbage.

Generally, home gardeners and small farmers have found the compost pile or heap more feasible for them, and aerobic digesters have not been popular on the farm.

How to Make Compost: Making compost is not difficult, and can be done easily at home. Essentially, the basic methods call for layering natural ingredients in heaps in mixed proportions, providing necessary air and moisture and turning the heaps to provide bacterial action on all parts of the heap. Just about any organic matter can be used.

Materials to Use: Leaves are valuable fertilizer material since they are rich in minerals, and they should be chopped or finely shredded for best results—if not, they will impede aeration. Mix with weeds, lawn clippings or plant residues for best results.

Green legume hay will break down quickly in a compost heap. Any hay or straw makes a worthwhile addition to the heap. Shredding hastens decomposition.

Garden residues—dried or green tomato or squash vines, cornstalks, flower stems, and weeds can be shredded or added whole to the compost heap. Grass clippings are already shredded, and can be used dry or green. Sawdust and wood chips, nutshells, peanut hulls, coffee wastes, and dried blood are all good compostable materials.

Garbage, which is high in nitrogen, can be used for green matter in the compost heap.

Unprinted paper and cardboard are suitable for composting if shredded. Animal manures are, of course, valuable additions to the pile.

In short, any decomposable organic material can be used for composting, except human feces, diseased animals, plant debris heavily impregnated with pesticides or herbicides, and other toxic materials. For other suggestions, see chart.

Indore Method: There are several methods of composting that can be used on the small farm or in the home garden. The first scientific method of composting was the Indore method, devised by Sir Albert Howard. This method became popular in many parts of the British Commonwealth, especially with farmers in preindustrialized countries who could compost materials that they had previously burned. The 14-day method is commonly used by small gardeners, and is quicker because the material to be composted is first shredded. Sheet composting is practiced on large farms. Some people compost with earthworms. There are advantages and disadvantages to each system.

Compost can be made by the Indore method either in open piles or in bins. Piles are more satisfactory when machinery is going to be used to turn the heaps. Bins are sometimes used by gardeners who dislike the unkempt appearance of an open pile; they have the advantage of affording better moisture and temperature control.

The average pile for Indore composting is

(continued on page 243)

PERCENTAGE COMPOSITION OF VARIOUS MATERIALS

Material	Nitrogen	Phosphoric Acid	Potash
Alfalfa hay	2.45	0.50	2.10
Apple, fruit	.05	.02	.10
Apple, leaves	1.00	.15	.35
Apple pomace	.20	.02	.15
Apple skins (ash)		3.08	11.74
Banana skins (ash)		3.25	41.76
Banana stalk (ash)		2.34	49.40
Bat guano	1–12	2.5–16	
Brewer's grains (wet)	.90	.50	.05
Cantaloupe rinds (ash)		9.77	12.21
Castor bean pomace	5–6	2–2.5	1.0–1.25
Cattail reed and stems of waterlily	2.02	.81	3.43
Coal ash (anthracite)		.1–.15	.1–.15
Coal ash (bituminous)		.4–.5	.4–.5
Cocoa-shell dust	1.04	1.49	2.71
Coffee grounds	2.08	.32	.28
Coffee grounds (dried)	1.99	.36	.67
Common crab	1.95	3.60	.20
Corn (green forage)	.30	.13	.33
Corncob ash			50.00
Corncobs (ground, charred)			2.01
Cottonseed-hull ashes		7–10	15–30
Cotton waste from factory	1.32	.45	.36
Cowpeas, green forage	.45	.12	.45
Crabgrass (green)	.66	.19	.71
Cucumber skins (ash)		11.28	27.20
Dried jellyfish	4.60		
Duck manure (fresh)	1.12	1.44	.49
Eggshells	1.19	.38	.14
Eggshells (burned)		.43	.29
Feathers	15.30		
Field bean (shells)	1.70	.30	.35
Fish scrap (fresh)	2–7.5	1.5–6	
Fish scrap (red snapper and grouper)	7.76	13.00	.38
Freshwater mud	1.37	.26	.22
Garbage rubbish (New York City)	3.4–3.7	.1–1.47	2.25–4.25
Garbage tankage	1 –2	.5–1	.5 –1
Gluten feed	4– 5		
Grapefruit skins (ash)		3.58	30.60
Grapes, fruit	.15	.07	.30

Material	Nitrogen	Phosphoric Acid	Potash
Greensand		1–2	5.00
Ground bone, burned		34.70	
Hair	12–16		
Hoof meal and horn dust	10–15	1.5–2	
Incinerator ash	.24	5.15	2.33
Kentucky bluegrass (green)	.66	.19	.71
Kentucky bluegrass (hay)	1.20	.40	1.55
King crab (dried and ground)	10.00	.26	.06
King crab (fresh)	2–2.5		
Leather (acidulated)	7–8		
Leather (ground)	10–12		
Leather, scrap (ash)		2.16	.35
Lemon culls, California	.15	.06	.26
Lemon skins (ash)		6.30	31.00
Lobster refuse	4.50	3.50	
Lobster shells	4.60	3.52	
Molasses residue in manufacturing of alcohol	.70		5.32
Oak leaves	.80	.35	.15
Olive pomace	1.15	.78	1.26
Olive refuse	1.22	0.18	0.32
Orange culls	.20	.13	.21
Orange skins (ash)		2.90	27.00
Peanut shells	.80	.15	.50
Peanut shells (ash)		1.23	6.45
Pea pods (ash)		1.79	9.00
Pigeon manure (fresh)	4.19	2.24	1.41
Pigweed, rough	.60	.16	
Pine needles	.46	.12	.03
Potato skins, raw (ash)		5.18	27.50
Potatoes, leaves, and stalks	.60	.15	.45
Potatoes, tubers	.35	.15	.50
Prune refuse	.18	.07	.31
Pumpkin, flesh	.16	.07	.26
Pumpkin seeds	.87	.50	.45
Rabbit-brush ashes			13.04
Ragweed	.76	.26	
Red clover, hay	2.10	.50	2.00
Redtop hay	1.20	.35	1.00
Residuum from raw sugar	1.14	8.33	
Rhubarb, stems	.10	.04	.35
Rock and mussel deposits from sea	.22	.09	1.78

Material	Nitrogen	Phosphoric Acid	Potash
Rockweed	1.90	.25	3.68
Roses, flower	.30	.10	.40
Salt-marsh hay	1.10	.25	.75
Salt mud	.40		
Sardine scrap	7.97	7.11	
Seaweed (Atlantic City, N.J.)	1.68	.75	4.93
Sewage sludge from filter beds	.74	.33	.24
Shrimp heads (dried)	7.82	4.20	
Shrimp waste	2.87	9.95	
Siftings from oyster-shell mound	.36	10.38	.09
Silkworm cocoons	9.42	1.82	1.08
Spanish moss	.60	.10	.55
Starfish	1.80	.20	.25
String bean strings and stems (ash)		4.99	18.03
Sweet potato skins, boiled (ash)		3.29	13.89
Sweet potatoes	.25	.10	.50
Tanbark ash		.24	.38
Tanbark ash (spent)		1.5–2	1.5–2.5
Tea grounds	4.15	.62	.40
Tea-leaf ash		1.60	.44
Timothy hay	1.25	.55	1.00
Tobacco leaves	4.00	.50	6.00
Tobacco stalks	3.70	.65	4.50
Tobacco stems	2.50	.90	7.00
Tomatoes, fruit	.20	.07	.35
Tomatoes, leaves	.35	.10	.40
Tomatoes, stalks	.35	.10	.50
Waste silt	8–11		
Wheat, bran	2.65	2.90	1.60
Wheat, straw	.50	.15	.60
White clover (green)	.50	.20	.30
White sage (ashes)			13.77
Wood ashes (leached)		1–1.5	1–3
Wood ashes (unleached)		1–2	4–10

Source: U.S. Department of Agriculture.

six feet wide, three to five feet high and ten to 30 feet long. First, spread a six-inch layer of plant wastes over the area to be covered by the pile. This layer can include spoiled hay, straw, sawdust, leaves, garbage, or wood chips. Then, add a two-inch layer of manure and bedding. Follow with a layer of *topsoil* approximately ⅛ inch thick. Urine-impregnated topsoil is particularly valuable. On top of this layer of earth spread a sprinkling of lime, phosphate rock, granite dust, or wood ashes to increase the mineral content of the heap. Lime is not added if an acid compost is wanted.

Water the pile and continue the process of layering in the same manner until the desired height is reached. Do not trample on the heap; if it is matted down, aeration will be impeded. Vertical ventilator pipes made of tubes of wire netting are placed along the center of the heap approximately 3½ feet apart.

Within a few days, the heap will begin to heat up and start shrinking in size. The heap is turned with a pitchfork two or three weeks after being made, and again above five weeks after being made. Care is taken during turning to place the outer parts of the heap on the inside, so they can decay fully. The heap heats up to almost 150°F. (65.56°C.) at the outset. After the first turn the temperature will again rise, but it will then settle to a steady tempera-

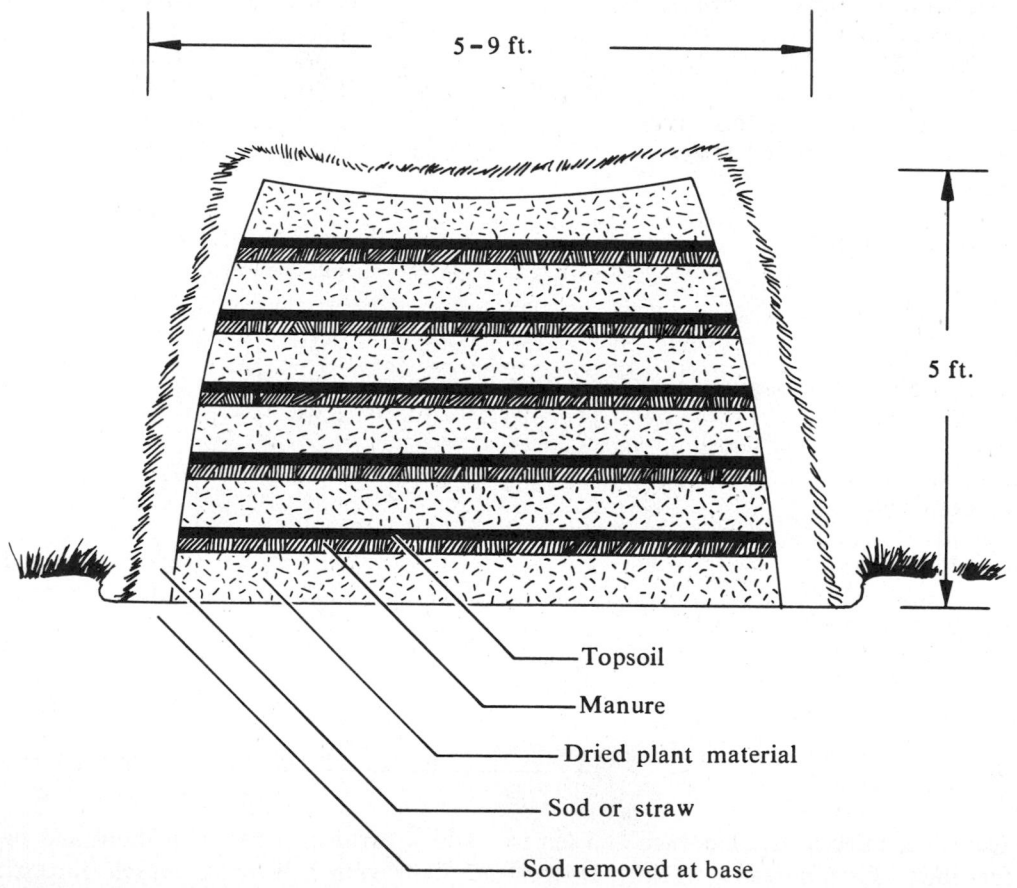

Topsoil

Manure

Dried plant material

Sod or straw

Sod removed at base

In the layered compost heap, dried plant material is sandwiched between layers of manure or other nitrogen-rich material. This arrangement not only ensures the correct ratio of carbon to nitrogen, but also distributes the materials evenly throughout the pile.

ture of about 130°F. (54.44°C.). The compost is finished after three months.

The 14-Day Method: Out of the work of scientists in the Sanitary Engineering Department of the University of California evolved the "14-day method." This technique is suitable for garden, farm and municipal use.

In the 14-day method, all material going into the compost pile is ground or shredded. Grinding has several effects on compost.

The surface area of material on which microorganisms can multiply is greatly increased, and aeration of the mass is improved because shredded material has less tendency to mat or pack down. Moisture control is improved. Turning of the heap is much easier.

No layering of material is used in the 14-day method. Material is mixed either before or after shredding, then piled in heaps no more than five feet in height. After three days, the heap is turned. Turning is continued at two- or three-day intervals. After 12 to 14 days, the heat of the pile has dropped, and the compost is sufficiently decayed to use on the soil.

If compost is being made for garden use, turning can be done easily by hand because the material is light and fluffy. For larger applications, turning is usually done by a manure loader, or a machine specially designed for turning large compost piles.

Shredding the material prior to composting presents more of a problem, especially for large composting projects. A number of shredders are available for garden use, however. Horticultural shredders made primarily for potting soil preparation can be used as compost material grinders. Small rotary lawn mowers also shred compost material efficiently and easily. Weeds, leaves, straw, or stable manure to be cut up are piled on the ground and the lawn mower is run over them. It is helpful to do this near a wall which can prevent the cuttings from spreading out too much.

Compost made by the 14-day method is often superior to compost that has been allowed to stand out in the weather for many months. Less nutrients are leached out when compost is made quickly.

Sheet Composting: In farm practice, it is often unnecessary to make compost in heaps. Raw organic materials can be spread on fields during fallow periods. The initial stages of decay will then take place before the next crop is planted.

An excellent method of sheet composting is to grow a green manure crop on the fields to be treated. Soybeans, clover, cowpeas, and many other forage plants make good green manure crops. When the green manure plants are still immature (and rich in nitrogen) the compost materials are spread over the fields with a manure spreader. Low nitrogen materials like sawdust, corncobs and wood chips can be spread over a young green manure crop without fear of causing later nitrogen shortages. After spreading, the whole mass is worked into the soil, preferably with a chisel plow that will work the organic material evenly into the top few inches of the soil, enabling plenty of air to reach the decaying material. Very often, the field is first run over with a rotary cutter to shred any long grass that might wind up on the tiller tines.

Sheet composting is not satisfactory for most garden purposes, because a gardener is seldom willing to take a section of land out of production for several months. Bacteria which break down the cellulose in sheet compost consume nitrogen which ordinarily would be contributed toward plant growth. In a few months this nitrogen is returned for plant use through the bodies of the microorganisms, but for the initial period of sheet composting a nitrogen shortage does exist. In a very rich soil this temporary nitrogen shortage is often not noticed. Also, if low nitrogen materials are just spread on the surface as a mulch they will break down very slowly and no nitrogen shortage will result.

It is a good idea to add limestone, phosphate rock, granite dust, or other natural mineral fertilizers along with the other sheet compost ingredients, because the decay of the organic matter will facilitate the release of the nutrients locked up in those relatively insoluble fertilizers.

Composting with Earthworms: Some people have had excellent results making compost with earthworms and the process is fairly simple. While earthworms breed, they work with the raw materials of their boxes and turn it into a rich, fine compost in only 60 days. In addition, earthworm compost is also rich in the castings or manure of the earthworm which is superior to animal manures.

Use wooden cases about two or three feet square and a little more than two feet high. In the boxes put a mixture of raw materials. A typical mixture would be about 70 percent weeds, leaves, grass clippings, etc., about 15 percent manure and 12 percent topsoil. If no manure is available, parts of your table wastes can be substituted. You can try almost any formula. Mix all ingredients thoroughly and place in the boxes.

It is advisable to start with purchased earthworms as they thrive best under domestic conditions. Many farm and garden publications carry ads for earthworms. Before placing them in the prepared boxes, check to see if the heaps have heated up. Don't let the heaps get too hot, or else the earthworms will either leave or perish.

The material in the boxes should be piled to a height of two feet and kept sufficiently watered, but do not add too much water or an anaerobic condition will be created. It is the combined action of the earthworms, bacteria and fungi that produces the best kind of compost.

The process takes about 60 days. Remove half a box of material and fill it with the raw materials. In 60 days the new material will be completely composted. It is advisable to feed the earthworms with something equivalent to chicken mash, but you can make your own feed, using ground corn and coffee grounds.

When to Apply Compost: The main influence on timing, rate and method of applying compost is its condition, age and degree to which the composting process is complete. Fully mature compost resembles—indeed, it *is* —supersoil, a light, rich loam. If half completed so it still contains some fibrous material, it will continue to decompose and generate heat. Such compost should be permitted to finish decomposing. Never place it near growing plants. If you have unfinished compost in the fall of the year, it is safe to apply it. It will finish up in the soil and be ready to supply growth nutrients to the first spring plantings.

The preferred time to apply fully matured compost is a month or so before planting—or, if you are a successive cropper, planting two or more crops to the same parcel of land each session, just before replanting. The closer to planting time it goes on, the finer it should be shredded or chopped, and the more thoroughly it should be hoed or tilled into your soil.

If compost is ready in the fall but not intended for use until spring, it should be kept covered and stored in a protected place. If it is kept for a long period during the summer, the finished compost should be watered from time to time.

How to Apply: For general application, the soil should be stirred or turned thoroughly. Then the compost is added to the top four inches of soil. For flower and vegetable gardening, it is best to pan the compost through a ½-inch sieve. Coarse material remaining may then be put into another compost heap.

To avoid disturbing roots of established plants, compost should be mixed with topsoil and applied as a mulch. This is often termed side dressing. It serves a double purpose, providing plant food that will gradually work itself down to the growing crop, and as a mulch giving protection from extremes of temperature, hard rains and growth of weeds.

For best results, compost should be applied liberally, from one to three inches per year. There is no danger of burning due to overuse, as happens with artificial fertilizers. Apply compost either once or twice a year. The average weight for one cubic yard of compost (27 cubic feet) is 1,000 pounds.

For the Orchard: Compost should be applied under each tree, starting about two to three feet away from the trunk, and extending about a foot beyond the dripline at the end of the branches. An annual application should be between ½ and one inch thick. The grass mat under the tree should be first worked into the soil and the compost added, keeping it in the upper two inches. Mulch with old hay or other green matter. A layer of compost about three or four inches thick would be sufficient for three or four years.

To save time, compost can be made right under the tree. This method is called the ring method because starting from about three feet away from the trunk, the material looks like a ring. Apply the raw materials under the tree as if for making compost, but make the heap two feet high instead of five.

For Grapes and Berries: Grapes and bush and cane berries have shallow root systems, so cultivating around them can be troublesome. A good application of compost three inches deep in early spring will not only kill weeds, thus reducing the necessity to cultivate, but will also feed the plants.

For Flowers: Flowers respond well to applications of compost. Compost may be safely applied even to acid-loving flowers such as the rhododendron. If a gardener has a considerable number of acid soil plantings, which include several of the berries as well as many flowers, it would be advisable that he prepare an acid compost. This is done by making the compost without lime or wood ashes.

For potted flowers, compost should not be used alone, but should be mixed with soil. Try screening and applying friction to it before using in a flowerpot. Then mix about one-third compost and two thirds rich soil. Place an inch-deep layer of compost on top of the soil in potted plants. Water leaching through the compost will fertilize the plants.

See also EARTHWORM, FERTILIZER.

COMPOSTING, VERTICAL
See MULCH

COMPOST WATER

Some of the valuable nutrients in compost dissolve in water. In solution these nutrients can be quickly distributed to needy plant roots.

Since plants drink their food rather than eat it, the use of compost water makes quite a bit of sense, particularly during dry periods when plants are starved for food and water.

Many problem plants and trees can be nursed back to health by treating them with compost water. You can use it on bare spots on your lawn and on garden plants, shrubs and trees that have been transplanted. Compost tea makes a fine fertilizer for house plants and you can even use it in the spring on vegetable seeds and young seedling plants to help them mature earlier. Compost water is also good in greenhouses where the finest soil conditions are needed for best results.

It is really no trouble to make compost water on a small scale. For treating house plants or small outdoor areas, fill a sprinkling can half full with finished compost and the rest of the way with water. Stir gently ten or 12 times and pour. The compost can be used several times, as one watering will not wash out all its soluble nutrients. The remaining compost should be dug into the soil or used as mulch. On house plants, a ½-inch layer of finely screened compost on the soil surface, replaced periodically, will provide an instant tea. When watered, nutrients in the compost will seep into the soil around the plant.

CONEFLOWER
See RATIBIDA, RUDBECKIA

CONIFER

Conifers are the most important class of naked-seed plants (Gymnospermae) and include over 500 cone-bearing trees and shrubs.

Most gymnosperms (nonflowering plants that produce naked seeds) bear their seeds in cone structures and, as such, are known as conifers.

Most are evergreen but some, such as bald cypress and larch, are deciduous.

See also CHRISTMAS TREE FARMING, FIR, PINE, SPRUCE.

CONSERVATION SERVICE
See GOVERNMENT SERVICES

CONTAINER STOCK

Container stock is a term for nursery plants that have been grown in cans, pots or other impervious containers.

CONTOUR

In contour tillage, plowing, cultivation and the direction of the rows follow the contour rather than the slope of the land. Thus instead of making straight up-and-down-hill furrows on hillsides, furrows are made to fit the slope of the land. This discourages runoff and helps the tilled soil to absorb water, thereby saving both soil and water.

See also SOIL CONSERVATION.

CONVOLVULUS   *See* BINDWEED

COPPER

Although its function is not entirely understood, copper is recognized as one of the many minor elements essential to plant growth. A component of several enzymes, it is thought to act as a catalyst for plant respiration and iron utilization. Normal levels of copper in plants range from five to 50 parts per million (ppm). Copper content in soils varies from five to over 100 ppm with the suggested analysis of a representative sample of surface soil being about 50 ppm.

In most soils, copper deficiency is rare, but where too much lime or phosphate has been applied, plants may exhibit signs of deficiency. Shoot tips die, terminal leaves turn brown and, in some cases, leaves may fail to develop.

Such fertilizers as copper sulfate and other copper salts are the traditional remedy for copper deficiency, but they are not recommended because of the danger of toxic effects on plant growth. Organic gardeners can remedy deficiency with sawdust, wood shavings or grass clippings.

See also SOIL DEFICIENCIES, TRACE ELEMENTS.

CORALBELLS   (*Heuchera*)

These perennials have shallow, fleshy roots and produce many small, bell-shaped flowers on branching, bare stems which rise 15 inches to 2½ feet above evergreen basal foliage. There are about 30 named varieties, mostly originating from crosses of *H. sanguinea* with *H. micrantha*. They are excellent garden plants, and should be used in groups at the front of the border, as their small flowers are most showy when blooming in masses. Soil should be humusy and well drained. Plant them in sun or light shade with the crown one inch below the surface, and mulch them in winter after the ground has frozen as they are highly susceptible to being heaved out of the ground during alternate periods of freezing and

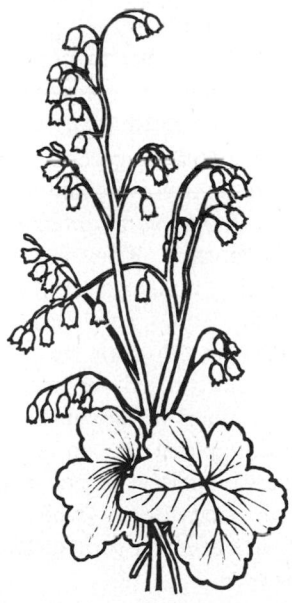

Coralbells put forth stalks of red, pink or white flowers from rosettes of evergreen foliage.

thawing. Remove the heavy mulch in spring. Once these requirements are met, the plants need very little additional maintenance and need be divided only when the clumps develop woody centers and begin to produce few flowers. The flowers appear in June and July, mostly in shades of red, pink and white. Bloom period can be extended by picking stalks that have finished flowering and keeping the plants well watered. Pluie de Feu has cherry red flowers to 18 inches, Apple Blossom has coral pink flowers, Alba has white flowers, and the showy Red Spangler is a 30-inch scarlet red. The red forms are attractive to hummingbirds.

COREOPSIS

The bright yellow or white daisylike flowers and finely cut foliage of this large genus of the Composite family make good additions to the sunny border. Easy to grow and thriving in ordinary garden soil, coreopsis also make fine plants for the cutting or wild garden.

The lance-leaved coreopsis (*C. lanceolata*), a native wild flower, and its named varieties are very good low-maintenance plants for the perennial border. They are not particular about soil, doing almost as well in heavy clay as in light, dry soil. They produce two-inch yellow flowers on two-foot stems, and clumps may be left undisturbed for years. They will bloom all summer if flower heads are kept picked. Flore pleno is an excellent semi-double, named variety. The species is very easily grown from seed, while many other named varieties are best propagated by division or by side shoots.

Golden wave (*C. basalis*) is a tender annual growing one to two feet high. Calliopsis or golden coreopsis (*C. tinctoria*) is the most popular of the annuals, growing from two to three feet tall. A hardy plant that does best when crowded, the seed should be scattered in early spring where plants are wanted. Bloom period is midsummer to frost.

CORIANDER   (*Coriandrum sativum*)

An annual herb, coriander has long been cultivated in many parts of the world. It has long stems bearing divided leaves, and grows one to three feet long. The dried fruits of coriander, known commercially as seed, are used for flavoring candies, sauces, soups, beverages, and tobacco products. The oil distilled from the seed also has a variety of uses as a flavoring agent.

The herb's generic name is derived from the Greek *koris,* meaning bug. Many people speculate the plant received this name because of its strong and sometimes offensive odor. Coriander is one of the most ancient herbs still cultivated. It was grown in Egyptian gardens and used as a funeral offering in Egyptian tombs. Hippocrates used coriander in the fifth century B.C. It was even mentioned as a food source in the Old Testament. The herb was eventually brought to the New World in the seventeenth century after widespread use in the British Isles.

The plant is indigenous to southern Europe, Asia Minor and the southern part of Russia and has been planted in most parts of the world where the climate is suitable. Although small acreages have been grown in various states from time to time, there has been no sustained commercial production in the United States.

The dried seeds of coriander are used as flavoring agents in candies, beverages and tobacco products.

Coriander will grow in a wide range of conditions but thrives best in sunny locations on rich garden loam of limestone origin with good drainage. Excessive nitrogen may delay the ripening of the seed and reduce the yield unless the growing season is long. Well-distributed moisture and fairly even temperatures throughout a growing season of 90 to 100 days are favorable for the crop. Rain or wind during the harvest period will discolor the seed and cause loss through shattering. The seed is planted as soon as the soil is warm enough for germination but after danger of frost has passed. Always plant seeds directly in the garden bed. Sow seeds thinly, one inch deep in rows about 15 inches apart. Frequent and light cultivation to keep weeds under control is recommended, and some hand weeding is usually necessary. Broadcasting the seed is not practical, because coriander does not compete successfully with weeds. Plantings made early in May will usually bloom in about nine to ten weeks and mature seed early in August. When grown in the Southwest as a winter crop the seed is sown in November and the crop matures in May.

Coriander is harvested when its seeds, or fruits, turn light brown. The small fruits, ⅛ inch in diameter, are split in half and dried. If the fruit balls are not harvested in time, the plant will reseed itself.

Coriander has medicinal and aromatic qualities in addition to its value in flavoring foods and liqueurs. Today, its main medicinal function is in disguising the tastes of active purgatives. As a food additive, crushed coriander seeds are commonly used in cakes, custards and jellies. The fruits are also used to decorate baked goods, while coriander leaves often go into soups and broths in Peru and Egypt. This herb is also a popular addition to sausage, red meats, pickles, and beet salads because of its spicy nature.

See also HERB.

CORK

Natural cork is occasionally used as a mulch. Because of the tannic acid in cork, it is of value where increased acidity is required in the soil. Cork has been used as a mulch for azaleas, laurel and other acid-loving plants.

CORK ELM   *See* ELM

CORK TREE
See PHELLODENDRON

CORM

A corm is a solid underground stem that looks very much like a true bulb. It has no scales, but nourishes the plant and bears roots at the base. It ultimately produces young cormels, which are a source of propagating material as they in time become corms. The gladiolus is a good example of a plant growing from a corm.

See also BULB.

CORN   (*Zea Mays*)

A uniquely American contribution to world agriculture, corn (originally maize) is divided into several groups depending on the ultimate use of the grain. Field corn is planted for livestock feeding. Sweet corn is used for human food when fresh, and can be frozen. Popcorn makes a nutritious natural snack and a fine baking flour. Some varieties of corn, commonly known as Indian corn, are also grown as ornamentals; when no longer wanted as decorations, the ears can be fed to cattle or chickens.

Although many home gardeners grow several varieties of sweet corn for their own use during the summer and, when frozen, over winter as well, few realize that they can raise field corn not only for animal feed, but also for cornmeal for themselves. Yellow field corn is best for livestock and also makes good cornmeal. Unlike white field corn, which can only be grown in the southern corn belt because it requires a longer growing season, varieties of yellow field corn can be grown virtually anywhere in the country. A number of hybrids are available, and generally offer the best disease resistance and higher yields. However, some people prefer open-pollinated corn because a grower can save seeds each year and will not have to depend on seed companies for his corn.

Varieties: Varieties of field corn are available from many seed companies and local seed corn salesmen. A neighbor who sells seed corn probably also raises some himself, and can give you advice on the best varieties to choose for your particular needs. He will also be able to advise you on what varieties do best on his farm, although it is likely that the two of you will be using different cultural practices.

Two specialized forms of field corn that are currently attracting attention are waxy maize and high-lysine maize. The former is a lower-yielding hybrid now grown mostly in a few counties in the Midwest. High-lysine corn, a high-protein corn, has been planted successfully overseas. Both types have caused dramatic weight gains in livestock when tested, and promise high-protein human food in the future. A present disadvantage is low yields, making both hybrids unattractive to most commercial growers. On the homestead where yields are not as important as the *quality* of the crop they might have a definite place. If you decide to try a high-lysine or a waxy maize hybrid, buy one that is resistant to corn diseases.

White field corn is commonly grown in the South or in other areas where a longer growing season allows the corn to mature fully.

Most seed companies sell a dazzling array of sweet corn varieties. Many gardeners plant early, middle and late maturing varieties so they can eat fresh corn all summer long. In addition to the standard varieties, extra sweet varieties have been developed. These promise extra sugar in the corn. This means that, theoretically, the corn should stay sweet even the day after it is picked. Sweet corn varieties include both hybrids and open-pollinated types.

Some of the popular early yellow varieties are Early Sunglow and Golden Beauty. White-yellow crosses, maturing slightly later in the season, include Honey and Cream, Butter and Sugar, and Pearls and Gold. Midseason yellow hybrids offer higher yields and are good for freezing and canning. Some popular varieties are Golden Cross Bantam, Honeycross, Carmelcross, Seneca Chief, Iochief, Illini Sweet, Stylepak, and Gold Cup. White hybrids include Silver Queen, Hybrid Stowell's Evergreen and Hybrid Country Gentleman. Open-pollinated varieties are Golden Bantam (yellow), Country Gentleman (white) and White Evergreen.

Popcorn varieties differ more in size and kernel color than other kinds of corn. White popcorn is smaller than yellow popcorn, but more tender when popped. Some hybrid varieties are White Cloud, Burpee Peppy and Hybrid White. Japanese Hull-less is a nonhybrid variety. There are many varieties of yellow popcorn; Giant Yellow, Creme-Puff and South American Mushroom are three. Strawberry Ornamental Popcorn is also used for decoration. Other novelty varieties are often listed in the seed catalogs.

Preparing the Ground: Whether you're planting a few rows of corn in your garden, or an acre of corn to feed your animals and your family during the winter, you must remember that corn is a heavy feeder and will deplete your soil if planted in the same place year after year. Even in the home garden, it makes sense to plan a crop rotation with corn always following beans or preferably clover. A rotation for a small plot of land to feed livestock might allow clover to grow as long as possible before planting corn. Just before turning this green manure crop under, spread manure or compost on the plot. Twenty tons of manure per acre is good if you have it, but any amount will help. After tilling or plowing, plant your corn. In summer, before you are ready to harvest your corn crop, sow ryegrass to plow under the next spring. Then plant soybeans or other garden beans; after harvest, plant winter wheat; plow it under and plant alfalfa in the spring. Allow the alfalfa to grow to hay the next year, and then begin the rotation again with corn.

Another rotation more adapted to the home garden would plant alfalfa for green manure, followed by sweet corn, the next year by tomatoes, then beans and peas, then spring vegetables seeded to wheat in the fall, then back to alfalfa and corn again.

When you follow one of the above rotations or plan one of your own using vegetables you are accustomed to growing, remember that corn also needs lime. Apply lime at the rate of 1,000 pounds per acre the year before you plant corn. Also spread phosphate rock at the rate of two tons per acre every four years. If your soil tests low in potash, use potash rock, greensand or an organic fertilizer high in potash.

Planting: Don't be in a big hurry to plant your corn, especially if you are planning a large crop. The proper time to plant, old people say, is when oak leaves are as big as squirrel's ears. You might want to wait a little longer, especially on a large plot, until the soil is about 62°F. (16.67°C.) about three inches down (use a soil thermometer). If you wait until the soil has warmed up, your corn gets off to a quick enough start; the warm soil hastens germination, and also cuts your chances of running into insect and weed problems brought on by rain and cold weather early in the year.

If you plant more than a quarter-acre, it would be a good idea to have a corn planter of some kind. Hand-pushed mechanical planters are available, and planters that attach to garden tractors can also be purchased. If you have a small farm, you might want to look into getting an old, two-row corn planter from a neighboring farmer.

Plant field corn in 40-inch rows with plants spaced 15 inches apart. In the garden, plant your sweet corn more thickly, with six to eight inches between plants and 30 inches between rows, closer if you plan to cultivate the corn by hand. If you want to plant pole beans with your corn, allow three feet between stalks. This is a good combination since the beans use the cornstalks as poles and fix nitrogen for the corn. When the corn reaches six inches in height, plant a bean on each side of it about eight inches away. Plant popcorn and ornamental corn as you would sweet corn.

Depth of planting depends on the time of year and moisture available. Early in the season, plant sweet corn at 1½ inches and field corn at two inches. As the soil warms up and moisture decreases, plant a little deeper; late plantings of sweet corn should be made three to four inches deep. To space sweet corn plantings for summer-long enjoyment, plant an early variety as soon as the soil warms up, a midseason variety five to ten days later and a late variety in another week.

Weeds are a problem almost immediately after planting. Mulching right after planting will help to keep weeds down, but is really only practical on a small plot. Mulch between the rows, but mulch between plants only when they reach six to eight inches in height.

If you are cultivating by hand, rake your plot about three days after planting to get weeds that might be germinating. On a larger plot, use a rotary hoe or spike-tooth harrow with the teeth set very shallow. When the corn gets high enough for you to see rows easily across the field or garden, begin cultivating with shovel cultivators or with a tiller Be careful not to bury the plants with clumps of dirt. As the corn grows higher, you can be less careful about cultivating since you won't have to worry so much about burying the plants. When the plants have reached knee height, you should have cultivated them three times. After this, stop cultivating since you won't want to destroy the spreading root systems of the corn.

Harvesting: The only way to really know if your sweet corn is ready to harvest is by pulling back part of the husk and checking the kernels. If milk spurts out of a kernel of sweet corn when you press it with your thumb, the corn is just right. If your fingernail punches into the kernel too easily, the corn is a little green yet. If you must press pretty hard to penetrate the kernel, it is too old. Older ears can be left on the stalk to dry for cornmeal; for eating fresh and freezing, though, you will probably want to pick at the milk stage.

Field corn can be left to dry on the stalk until late in the fall, harvested by hand, and stored in corncribs over winter. You won't even have to bother shelling your corn before

Yellow field corn can be left to dry on the stalk until late fall, hand-harvested and used for cornmeal or animal feed.

feeding in many cases. When the stalk is dead and brown, walk down the rows and pull off the ears, husking them and tossing them into a wagon or pickup truck alongside the row. Husking is a skill you will develop; husking pegs, once made from wood or bone, are still available from some hardware stores and through the mail, and will help you strip the husk from the ear. Once husked, the corn should be stored in a crib to dry completely. Stalks left in the field should be disked under for organic matter after shredding with a shredder or even a rotary mower.

Another method of harvesting corn by hand is cutting the whole stalk, not just the ears, and arranging them in bundles, and the bundles into shocks. To do this, you must use a corn knife and cut the stalks off with short downward strokes, leaving about four inches of the stalk in the ground. Continue down a row, gathering the stalks in your left arm. When your arm is full of stalks, drop them in a neat bundle. Later, you can tie the bundles with baler twine and shock them by leaning four of them together as if you were constructing a tepee. Arrange the rest around this central core. The size of the shock is up to you; you might want to tie several lengths of baler twine around the entire shock to keep it standing. Later in the fall when the pressing work is over and you have more time, haul the shocks in from the field and husk out the corn. You can store the corn in a crib or shed and feed the stalks and husks to cows, horses or sheep.

Popcorn can be harvested by removing the ears from the stalk but leaving the husks attached. The husks can be pulled back and used to tie several ears together, and these can be draped over a wire and hung from a rafter to dry. To keep mice from getting at the corn, poke a hole in a large tin can lid and slide it over the wire.

Controlling Insects and Diseases: The European corn borer and the earworm both threaten corn crops, but the latter is more severe in the South and central states. Where winter temperatures fall below 0°F. (−17.77°C.), most overwintering earworms die. The borer often attacks sweet corn, and can be spotted by the presence of a small pile of sawdustlike material beside a small hole beneath the tassel. Squeeze the stalk and smash the worm before it has time to crawl down and eat its way into the ear.

Corn rootworm is a serious pest to commercial growers who plant corn in the same fields year after year. The pest can be controlled by rotation of crops. They thrive particularly in poorly drained soils and during cool, wet springs.

Birds are a problem, particularly on small plots where they can wipe out the entire planting. Tar-coated seeds may save some crops, but are difficult to plant except by hand. You might want to make a scarecrow for a small plot, or try covering the corn rows with wire until the corn is too high for the birds to bother. Animal predators—particularly raccoons—usually bother the corn when it is almost mature. Organic gardeners have tried to keep raccoons out of their patches by various methods, some more successful than others. A transistor radio hung in the patch and turned on at night is supposed to keep them away. Leaving a dog tied in or near the patch might also be a good idea if you're having particular trouble.

Corn diseases and blights can be a serious problem, but they have been partially combatted by breeding more resistant varieties of corn. Some of the molds that rot corn can make you ill, however, so it is good practice never to eat moldy corn or feed it to livestock. Besides a risk of poisoning, moldy corn might be infected with aflotoxins that are carcinogenic.

The best defense against corn diseases and blights is to use resistant hybrids and to use clean culture practices. Plow under plant debris, and rotate crops. If you are having problems with an infestation of your corn crop, contact your county agent for more information.

Storing and Using: Whole corn can be stored in any number of different structures. Traditional corncribs were built at most four feet wide and out of wooden slats to allow plenty of air to circulate through the drying corn. You might build one if you grow enough corn, or perhaps you could buy a crib from a neighbor, dismantle it and reassemble it on your property. New metal cribs can also be purchased, and you might be able to build a crib from a snow fence. A few bushels of corn can be kept in steel drums. These will be ratproofed if kept tightly covered, and both traditional slatted cribs and metal ones can be ratproofed with hardware cloth. In any case, it's a good idea to have a few farm cats living near the corncrib.

Corn for table use as meal should be shelled and ground. You can feed the whole ear, ground cob and all, to cows and steers, but chickens and pigs eat shelled, coarsely ground kernels. A variety of shellers, hand-cranked and mechanical, are available, as are motor-powered gristmills. Check farm sales for used ones. Corn can also be stored and fed as silage (although not to your family)—chopped, when green, stalk and all, and stored in a tightly packed pile so air is excluded. This method of storage is not very practical for a small farm since it requires fancy equipment.

Extra sweet corn can be frozen, canned or parched—dried on the cob and popped with popcorn. Popcorn must be shelled before popping. It is best to shell all your popcorn and store the seeds in tightly closed glass jars in a cool, dry place. If the corn doesn't pop well, it might be because it is too dry. In this case, add a tablespoon of water to every quart jar of popcorn, shake well, and seal for a few days. If corn is still too dry, repeat the treatment. You know when you've added too much water if the corn pops with a relatively loud explosion and the popped corn is jagged, small and tough.

CORNCOBS

Corncobs have a nutrient value equivalent to two-thirds that of the kernels. As a consequence, it can be ground with the corn and fed to cows and steers. (*See also* CORN.) Cobs from which the corn has been shelled can still find a welcome place in the garden scheme. Ground into a spongy material, corncobs have been found to be an excellent mulch because of their moisture-holding properties.

As a mulch, corncobs should be shredded and applied to a depth of three or four inches. Because the cobs may use up soil nitrogen when decomposing, an organic fertilizer rich in nitrogen should be applied to the soil before the mulch is laid. The best ones are dried blood (15 percent nitrogen), cottonseed meal (7 percent), tankage (6 percent), bone meal (4 percent), and compost or manure.

Corncobs are also an excellent compost material, but they should first be run through a shredder; otherwise, it will take years for the material to compost.

A local mill that shells corn may have cobs free for the hauling.

See also MULCH.

CORN COCKLE
(*Agrostemma githago*)

The purple or corn cockle is a troublesome weed in the grainfield, particularly in winter grain. Its poisonous seed mixes with the grain in harvesting and threshing and spoils the grain for feeding and flour. The chaff from threshing should be checked for its presence before being fed to animals. Sheep, pigs, rabbits, geese, ducks, and poultry are particularly vulnerable to this black seed which somewhat resembles caraway seed. The rather large flowers of the corn cockle have five red purple petals that are slightly mottled on the edge with dark spots inside.

If grainfields become infested with purple cockle, hand pulling may be necessary. Do not grow grain crops on such fields for several years but plant crops requiring much cultivation, such as corn, soybeans or peas, to choke out the weeds. Though an annual, corn cockle seeds itself readily and is extremely difficult to destroy.

CORN EARWORM

The corn earworm is found almost anywhere corn is grown and is probably the most destructive pest of that crop in the United States. Also called the tomato fruitworm and cotton bollworm, it is equally destructive to the buds, fruits and foliage of many vegetable crops. The mature caterpillar is two inches long and colored yellow, green or brown, with longitudinal dark and light stripes. The adult moth is grayish with dark markings on the wings.

Earworms feed on young corn blades but do their most critical damage to the ears. Beginning on the tassels, they gradually penetrate to the center of the ears, leaving behind damp castings. Thus, pollination is hindered, kernels injured, and ears deformed and made prone to disease. As tomato fruitworms, the larvae move rapidly from one fruit to another, usually

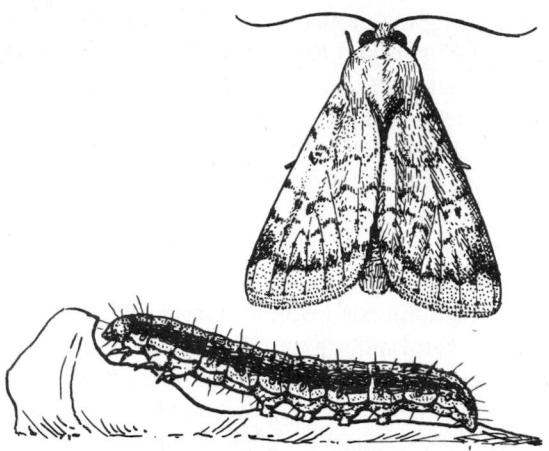

The larva of a large moth, the corn earworm attacks not only the stalks and ears of corn plants, but also feeds on the fruits and flowers of tomato, cotton, peach, pepper, rose, and many other economic crops.

burrowing through the stem end of green tomatoes. When the tomatoes have been ruined, the worms move on to beans, broccoli, cabbage, and lettuce. As cotton bollworms, they eat holes in immature bolls, leaving them ragged in appearance and possibly stunted. Other host plants include the clovers, several flowers, strawberry, grape, peach, and pear.

Home gardeners can usually control the worms on tomatoes, fruits and ornamentals by handpicking. On a larger scale, *Bacillus thuringiensis* has been proven effective, especially when applied as a dust. Rotenone is an excellent spray control, as are garlic and onion teas. Of course, all of these are most helpful when applied before the earworm has entered the fruit or boll.

Bacillus thuringiensis will also control earworms on corn, but several other, simpler remedies may be more effective. Mineral oil applied to the silk, just inside the tip of each ear, will suffocate the worms; one-half a medicine dropper's worth will do for a small ear, three-quarters for a larger one. The oil is tasteless and in no way alters the flavor of the corn. It should not be applied until the silk has wilted and begun to turn brown, however, as earlier applications may interfere with pollination and result in poorly filled ears.

The caterpillars can be removed from growing ears if one is careful not to ruin the kernels' protection. After pollination is complete, pull back the sheath a little and gouge out the feeding worm. Another, less effective control is simply to walk through the corn patch every few days and cut off the silk close to the developing ear.

Natural predators of the corn earworm, tomato fruitworm and cotton bollworm include egg parasites, beetle larvae and moles. Redwing blackbirds, certain grackles, downy woodpeckers, and English sparrows feed on the worms, but often destroy growing crops in the process. Cold, damp weather tends to reduce infestations.

See also INSECT CONTROL.

CORNELIAN CHERRY
See DOGWOOD, MOISTURE-LOVING PLANTS

CORNFLOWER
See BACHELOR'S-BUTTON

CORN SMUT   *See* FUNGUS

CORNSTALK

When green, cornstalks contain a sap that is packed with plant nutrients and is actually sweet to the taste. If possible, gardeners should pull sweet corn stalks as they harvest ears and get them immediately into the compost. Cornstalks break down in the pile very slowly, so it is desirable to chop or shred them first. For the garden any shredder-grinder will do the job. On the farm scale, an ensilage cutter is needed if large crops of whole corn plants are to be chopped to ferment into winter animal feeds. Unless stubble-cropping is being practiced, cornstalks should not stand in the field over winter. They will harbor corn borers, which will emerge in unnaturally large and harmful numbers the following spring.

To the depth of three or four inches, cornstalks provide a well-aerated winter mulch, but do not use stalks from a field which was heavily infested with borers. Lay the stalks crisscross with tops and butts alternating. Shredded, the stalks make a fine garden mulch.

See also MULCH.

COROLLA *See* FLOWER

CORSICAN MINT *See* MINT

CORYLOPSIS

These tall shrubs offer drooping clusters of yellow flowers that bloom on bare twigs before the leaves appear. Also known as winter hazel, it does best in sandy, moist soils. Although often propagated by layering, the shrubs can be grown from seeds or cuttings under glass. *C. spicata,* growing to six feet, is valued for its early, fragrant blossoms that appear in February or early March.

COSMOS

A genus of the Composite family often used as a background plant, cosmos develops as a loose bush, usually reaching a height of three to five feet. The annual species have large, wide-petaled flowers and delicate, fern-like foliage. Flower color ranges from white and yellow to pink, rose and purple, with either yellow or pink centers. Cosmos does not demand a rich soil. In fact, too rich a soil will produce leggy plants with few blooms. Plant in full sun.

COSSACK ASPARAGUS
See CATTAIL

COSTMARY
(*Chrysanthemum Balsamita*)

A perennial that may grow to as much as five to six feet with flowers like small daisies, costmary is cultivated by herbalists and gardeners for its medicinal, aromatic and culinary properties. Its leaves are used for flavoring foods and tea, and for their fragrance. They are also said to be helpful as a moth preventative.

The name of this herb comes from the Latin, *costus* (oriental plant), and the biblical figure, Mary. Costmary has a special place in Christian tradition. It was originally cultivated in the Orient, but soon spread to sixteenth century England and later to the American colonies. Colonists used the leaves as bookmarks in their Bibles and prayer books. The plant earned its name as "bible leaf" from this practice. Costmary was also used as a cure for dysentery,

Costmary will thrive wherever well-drained soil and full sun are provided.

quantities. The leaves dry quickly at 100°F. (37.78°C.) and can be stored for long periods of time.

Costmary is a most versatile herb. It was used in the United States as an astringent and antiseptic until the 1800's. It makes a minty spice for flavoring ale, salads, vegetables, and other foods. A conserve has been made from its flowers. The sweet fragrance of costmary can be used to freshen musty rooms and closets. The herb also makes a popular tea.

Even the gardener benefits from this herb. Costmary helps control weeds and gives spring flowers an attractive green background. It also forms a slow-growing edge in any garden.

See also HERB.

liver diseases, ulcers, and even consumption as late as the eighteenth century.

Costmary is best kept in the background as it grows large and is somewhat coarse. It is hardy, easily cultivated and does well in average soil, in dry sunny places.

The plant must be propagated by dividing its roots, since there is no seed. This makes costmary difficult to come by. Plants should be divided in the spring.

Harvesting is recommended before the costmary leaves turn yellow. Harvest in small

COTONEASTER

These deciduous or evergreen shrubs of the Rose family have white or pink flowers and small, ornamental, red or black fruits. Of the more than 30 species grown in the United States, several of the more common are noted here.

Rock spray species (*C. microphyllus, C. adpressus, C. Dammeri,* and *C. horizontalis*) are low shrubs useful in the rock garden, under windows or as an edging to a border of shrubs.

Tall upright shrubs in the Cotoneaster family include: *C. rotundifolius,* five to ten feet high, with white flowers and red fruit; *C. acutifolia,* same height as above, with pink to white flowers and black fruit; *C. foveolatus,* four to eight feet high, with pink flowers and black fruit; *C. hupehensis,* four to six feet high, with white flowers and deep red fruit; and *C. salicifolius,* eight to 12 feet high, with white flowers and red fruit.

Cotoneaster shrubs thrive in full sun and well-drained, slightly alkaline soils. Planting in spring is normally best; the shrubs tend to transplant poorly. Propagation is by seed, cuttings or layers.

COTTON GUM   *See* NYSSA

COTTONSEED HULLS
See COTTON WASTES

COTTONSEED MEAL

An excellent by-product organic fertilizer, cottonseed meal is made from the cotton seed which has been freed from lints and hulls and deprived of its oil. Since cottonseed cake is one of the richest protein foods for animal feeding, relatively little finds its way for use as fertilizer. A special value of cottonseed meal lies in its acid reaction which makes it a valuable fertilizer for acid-loving specialty crops. The meal is used mainly as a source of nitrogen, of which it contains varying amounts, usually around 7 percent. Phosphoric acid content is between 2 and 3 percent, while potash is usually 1.5 percent.

See also FERTILIZER.

COTTON WASTES

Often called cotton gin trash, cottonseed burrs are a source of potash, but need considerable moisture before breaking down into compost. The fine waste and the more voluminous amounts of wastes containing cotton fiber are, as a rule, rich in nitrogen because seed parts and lint are contained in them. When piled up in the open, this material will decay in a few months under southern conditions into a rich and valuable compost without further additions. These materials can also be used to activate compost heaps by covering other plant material, including cotton burrs, with them.

Cottonseed hulls and cottonseed hull ashes, especially the latter, are used as a source of quickly available potash. There is from 15 percent to 23 percent in the commercial product. Phosphoric acid content is also considerable and usually above that of other plant products, namely 7 to 9½ percent.

In recent years the cultivation of cotton has become increasingly dependent on massive applications of strong chemical pesticides. Though the cotton seed, which grows well inside the boll, is seldom contaminated, much other gin trash can contain dangerous pesticide residues. Organic growers are advised to use these materials with caution.

COTTONY CUSHION SCALE
See INSECT CONTROL

COUNTY AGENT
See GOVERNMENT SERVICES

COVENTRY BELLS
See CAMPANULA

COVER CROP

A cover crop is a crop grown primarily to prevent or reduce erosion, although such crops have other advantages in the overall farming scheme. Often they can serve as green manure crops—when turned into the soil, they will improve soil structure and build up organic matter content. (*See also* GREEN MANURE.)

Cover crops prevent erosion by binding soil but, more importantly, by reducing the impact of raindrops striking the soil in one of two ways. Raindrops strike the plant foliage instead of hitting bare soil, and leaves and stems then channel the water to the ground where it can seep into the soil. Raindrops also strike plant leaves first before striking the ground. The decrease in the velocity of the raindrops means that splash erosion is reduced.

Sheet erosion can also be reduced or prevented by the crops. Plant roots open soil channels deep into the earth, improving soil porosity, and allowing water to run slowly downward along their lengths—preventing surface water runoff.

Although it is important not to allow fall-plowed ground to overwinter without some kind of cover, cover crops planted in the fall are often not too effective in preventing erosion from winter rains because they do not develop quickly enough to provide good cover. Often crop residues alone are better at preventing erosion if left on the soil instead of being turned under, unless you can seed a cover crop without disturbing the residues. Fast-growing crops such as winter wheat or rye are best as cover crops, as are legumes which become established quickly.

In areas of high rainfall where erosion control is a primary concern, one should remember that most soil loss from cultivated land occurs during June, July and August. Therefore, if soil must be left bare during these months, spring- or summer-planted cover crops are a necessity.

Cover crops can serve the same function in the garden over winter as they do on a large field. Sow winter wheat, rye or ryegrass in autumn to protect the soil, and turn it under in spring as a green manure.

See also SOIL CONSERVATION.

COW

With feed costs as high as they are today, keeping a cow may not save you much, if any, hard cash. But, if you like cows and are willing to spend a few hours each day feeding, watering and milking one—and processing the fresh milk—then the animal will indeed "pay" with plenty of dairy products.

Proper housing is of key importance, but generally an existing outbuilding can be converted to a suitable cow barn.

Unless the cow is to be kept in a stanchion, the minimum floor area for a stable is 200 or more square feet. In northern areas, the cow stable should be windtight; all winter ventilation should be under control. An economical job can be done, when necessary, by nailing unslated roofing paper over the sides. A cow can stand more cold than generally realized. If a stable has but one window, cross-ventilation must be obtained by means of a transom over the door provided with a sliding panel or controlled through openings into other parts of the barn.

The cow may be confined by some sort of stanchion or allowed the freedom of a box stall. The box stall is recommended, since the cows can keep warmer by moving around occasionally on very cold nights. Milk production has been found to increase about 5 percent when cows are kept in a stall as opposed to a stanchion.

A calf pen is required. This should preferably be a duplicate of the cow stall since the calf may be raised through the heifer stage to a second cow or for beef. If there is visibility between the two stalls, both cow and young calf will be more content after the calf is weaned.

A cow that is four or five years old and has had her second or third calf is generally a good choice. She will be young enough to have years of production ahead of her, and old enough to have shown her milk-producing ability. There is no reason to pay the high price asked for heavy milk producers. For a family cow, the criteria should be gentleness, ease of milking and general good health.

A family milk cow will generally yield about 12 quarts daily for from eight to 12 months, consuming about 18 pounds of hay daily. Jerseys and Guernseys are most often chosen for family cows because they are smaller and do not require as much feed or give as much milk as some of the larger breeds, such as Holstein or Brown Swiss. A Jersey heifer is best bred at from 15 to 17 months; Guernseys at from 17 to 18 months; and the heavier breeds on up to 25 months. After freshening, a cow will reach maximum production during the second month. She will then decline in production at the rate of 6 to 7 percent a month. A cow that freshens in the fall or early winter will usually yield an average of 10 percent more milk and fat than one that freshens in spring or summer.

Ideally, the cow should have about two acres of pasture for summer grazing. Permanent pastures of bluegrass or mixtures of grass drop in production in the summer and may have to be supplemented to provide a uniform feed supply. The vegetable garden can furnish a bit of the animal's summer feed. Cows will eat pea vines, sweet corn stalks, cabbage leaves, and sweet potato vines.

The family cow's winter feed consists of hay and a mixture of concentrates. Alfalfa, soybean, alsike clover, or early-cut grass hay are satisfactory. A Jersey or Guernsey cow will need at least ten pounds of hay a day, and a pound of grain for each two to four pounds of milk she produces.

A mixture of ground corn and wheat bran is a good concentrate to feed with hay. Some soybean oil meal or linseed oil meal may be added to the diet of hay and grain for extra protein.

Provide a block of trace mineralized salt in a sheltered box for the cow, or add loose salt to her concentrate mix at the rate of one pound to every 100 pounds of feed.

Give the cow water at least twice daily in winter and more often in summer.

COWPEA   (*Vigna unguiculata*)

The cowpea is a multirooted legume popularly grown today for food, hay, grazing, and soil building. A native of central Africa, the cowpea spread to practically all warm, tillable areas of the earth.

Cowpeas grow wherever corn grows, but they are most widely cultivated in an area south of a line running westerly through Pennsylvania to southern Kansas, then southwesterly across the Panhandle to the Gulf. In this zone cowpeas are grown as a secondary crop with corn as a main crop, and as a soil builder in places where cotton and tobacco have depleted soil fertility.

With suitable climate, cowpeas grow on practically any type of well-drained soil, withstand drought well and make forage at a time of year when most needed. As soil conditioners, they make sandy ground more compact and heavy clays more friable through added humus. And the legume reactivates dead soil with countless bacteria from nodules supplying nitrogen.

For food, cowpeas are prepared and served like snap, shelled green or dried beans. This is the recommended method of cooking dried cowpeas:

Soak peas in lukewarm water several hours, then let simmer at low heat until tender. *Do not add soda.* Season with pork fat, onion, cheese, green pepper or celery, or a combination of all, and you have a tempting, sustaining dish. Fried cowpeas have 19.4 percent protein, 54.5 percent carbohydrates and 1.1 percent fat, being higher in protein and carbohydrates than oats but lower in fat.

Their vitamin content is high, especially B_1, and the green sprouts, ready to cook 24 hours after germination, are high in vitamin C and carry a fair amount of B vitamins.

Cowpea straw is popular as litter, mulch and feed; some growers even prefer it to cowpea hay for the latter. In protein, the straw runs 3.4 percent higher than soybean, oat, wheat, rice, or barley straw.

COWSLIP   *See* MARSH MARIGOLD

CRAB APPLE   *(Malus)*

The white, pink or red flowers of the flowering crab or crab apple trees can be favorably compared to the beauty of the Japanese flowering cherries. In addition to their beautiful blooms, these ornamental crab apples produce edible fruit suited for jelly and cider.

The showy crab (*M. floribunda*) makes a large bush-type tree with spreading branches reaching about 20 to 30 feet high. The American crab (*M. coronaria*), also known as the sweet crab, grows to about 30 feet and has rose to white flowers. The Oregon crab apple (*M. fusca*) has white flowers, grows to 30 feet, and is hardy throughout most of the United States. *M.* x *purpurea* is a medium-sized tree that shows deep red flowers. *M. Sargentii* is an ornamental shrub with white flowers.

Crab apples do best in a slightly alkaline soil.

See also APPLE, TREE.

CRABGRASS   *(Digitaria)*

Crabgrass or fingergrass is the common name for a whole genus of pesty lawn weeds. There are almost two dozen species recognized by botanists, but two of them are most common in North America. Smooth crabgrass (*D. ischaemum*) grows close to the ground and is difficult to mow; large crabgrass (*D. sanguinalis*) is more upright and has thick, hairy stems. Both spread by stolons or creeping stems, and may turn your lawn into a blotchy mass of brown weeds in dry weather instead of verdant grass.

Although crabgrass is not an easy weed to eradicate, it is possible to get rid of it once one realizes that crabgrass and good lawn grasses thrive on a different set of growing conditions. Good lawn grasses need a fertile topsoil, preferably no less than six inches deep and rich in humus; an occasional drenching; and cutting at a reasonable height. Perennial ryegrass, one of the most commonly used grasses, normally grows up to six feet high. When it is

Crabgrass is characterized by its thick, low-growing stems, its coarse leaves and stolons by which it spreads.
(Courtesy of U.S. Department of Agriculture)

kept trimmed to one or 1½ inches, it finds the growing difficult. So during the hot summer months when weeds take hold, trim grass to three or four inches high.

Crabgrass, in contrast, doesn't grow as strongly on good soil as do good lawn grasses. On good soils, it cannot stand the competition of a grass such as ryegrass or bluegrass. Since it is a low-growing plant, it is not stunted by close mowing, and in fact this gives it the room it needs to spread out and grow strongly.

Careful attention to your lawn will show good results and produce a lawn free of crab-grass. If you have a lawnsweeper, use it after several midsummer mowings to pick up crab-grass seeds that would otherwise sprout the following year. Compost the lawn clippings; the heat from the compost pile should kill the seeds. Also, aerate your soil as much as possible, using either a hand aerator or an aerating attachment for a tiller or garden tractor. Air and moisture are needed below the surface to encourage good grass roots.

Fertilization is also important. Have your soil tested and spread liberal amounts of phosphate rock, potash rock and lime if needed. For an average soil, apply ten pounds of phosphate and potash rock per 100 square feet; five to ten pounds of lime per 100 square feet, depending on soil pH; and the same amount of bone meal. These minerals should provide ample mineral food for your lawn.

Just as important is the creation of a good soil structure. The only practical way to do this is by working plenty of *shredded* compost, leaf mold, peat, or other organic material into your soil (avoid too much low-nitrogen material, such as sawdust or chopped straw). Spread these materials in installments that will give the grass a chance to grow between spreadings. Basically, what you are doing is mulching your lawn with compost, but you want to encourage the grass to grow through the mulch.

Other organic materials that will boost lawn growth include dried blood, cottonseed meal and soybean meal. These are particularly rich in nitrogen and should be applied liberally as needed, depending on availability and cost.

The result of this program will be to promote a vigorous, healthy growth of lawn grass —and, as a result, crowd out crabgrass and other lawn weeds.

See also LAWN.

CRANBERRY
(*Vaccinium macrocarpon*)

A member of the Heath family, the cranberry is native to temperate bogland from Nova Scotia to North Carolina and west to Wisconsin. The Pilgrims found cranberries growing in wild abundance when they first set foot on American soil, but no one attempted cultivation until about a hundred years ago when plantations were started on Cape Cod. Most

Native to northern and eastern boglands, the cranberry can be grown wherever the climate is moderate and the soil is wet and acid.

commercial growers are now located in Massachusetts, New Jersey, Wisconsin, Washington, and Oregon.

Culture: Cranberries demand a moderate climate with neither extreme heat in summer nor extreme cold in winter. Large plantings require a flat site which can be flooded with a dam or floodgate above and below. A small patch can be raised with sprinkler irrigation and hand weeding. Though cranberries are usually raised in acid peat bogs, the planting area is not constantly under water. The bogs are flooded to provide moisture for irrigation, insect control or frost protection, and then drained.

To prepare the site for planting, ditches must be dug for drainage, the sod over the entire bed should be inverted, and all perennial weeds destroyed. Soil pH should be between 4.5 and 5. In very early spring, just before planting, a three- to four-inch layer of sand should be applied over the entire planting area. Two or three cuttings from an established bed are then pushed into sand six to 18 inches apart. Water should be brought in to flood the bed for one or two days after planting, then drained. The bed should be flooded for two days at a time whenever the sand appears dry or when insect attack threatens. When the soil begins to freeze in the fall, the bed should be flooded deep enough to cover the plants, and the water should remain at that level through the winter. The beds are drained in the spring, though they may be reflooded if there is danger of a sudden frost.

Harvest: Though a few berries may be produced the third year, full production does not start until four years after planting. By that time, the soil should be covered with trailing vines having upright branches four inches high, about one-third of which will bear one or two berries each. Commercially, cranberries are

CRAYFISH 267

harvested by machines which pick the berry without injuring it. Berries can also be harvested by hand or with the use of a hand scoop. Under the best conditions yield may be as high as 100 barrels per acre.

Diseases: The chief enemy of the cranberry is the virus called "false blossom," which is spread by the blunt-nosed leafhopper. Flooding in late May or early June is a control measure effective against this pest as well as against the black and yellow-headed cranberry worm and the cranberry fruitworm. If the water used in flooding is warm, it cannot be left on for more than 24 hours, or fungi will set in. *See also* INSECT CONTROL.

Varieties: Cranberry types suitable for New England growing include Early Black and Howes. Stevens and Searless Jumbo are good keepers which are particularly well suited for midwestern cranberry bogs.

Nutritional Value: The cranberry is a good source of vitamin C and is believed to help clear up bladder infections.

CRANBERRY TREE
(*Viburnum trilobum*)

Also called highbush cranberry and pimbina, this beautiful shrub occurs in woods and along streams in northeastern United States and as far west as Wisconsin and Iowa. Large clusters of small white florets, red fruits and red fall foliage make this viburnum highly ornamental. The well-known snowball tree is a cultivated variety in which all the flowers are sterile and showy. The leaves have the shape and general appearance of maple leaves.

The dense and vigorous growth of the shrub makes it suitable for borders and hedges, and there are several dwarf varieties well suited to cultivation in rock gardens or as low hedges. The fruit is attractive to birds.

Viburnums are not exacting in their requirements, but seem to prefer a moist, sunny location. Propagation is by seed, cuttings, grafting, and layering.

See also SHRUBS, VIBURNUM.

CRANE FLOWER
See BIRD-OF-PARADISE

CRAPE JASMINE
See TABERNAEMONTANA

CRAPE MYRTLE
See LAGERSTROEMIA

CRAYFISH

Although crayfish closely resemble their delectable cousin, the lobster, these crustacea are seldom recognized as a protein food source themselves. Some of the 130 native American species of crayfish can be bred to yield more than 1,000 pounds of protein food per acre. They even help with aquatic weed control.

Crayfish grow from two to 12 inches long and can weigh up to eight pounds (*Astacopsis gouldi* of Tasmania). They inhabit rivers, streams, swamps, and marshland burrows. Crayfish eat a variety of water plants including water primrose and alligatorgrass, as well as insects, worms, snails, and smaller fish. In turn, they are eaten by river otters, alligators, ducks, and larger fish.

There are three crayfish families: the Astacidae and Camearidae of the Northern

Hemisphere and the Parastacidae of the Southern Hemisphere. The latter lives mainly in Victoria, Australia.

Only one state in the United States, Louisiana, taps this protein food resource. Louisiana annually consumes around 12 million pounds of crayfish in the form of gourmet bisques, "crayfish boils" and other dishes. An estimated 40 percent of all crayfish consumed there is raised on 45,000 acres of crayfish farms. "Louisiana red" (*Procambarus clarkii*) and white crayfish (*Procambarus acutus acutus*) are the most popular species for eating.

In order to construct and maintain a crayfish farm, the life cycle of crayfish must be understood. Crayfish mate in late spring and early summer when a high water level prevails in most rivers. Sperm is deposited into external pockets on the female fish, who later dig burrows near the edge of the water for mating. By the end of July, mated pairs occupy the burrows. Soon fertilized eggs are carried on the female's swimmerettes on the underside of her tail. Three weeks later, several hundred eggs will hatch.

Crayfish farms require a clean water supply kept at 70 to 85°F. (21.11 to 29.44°C.) with a pH rating of 6 to 8. They are sensitive to agricultural and industrial chemicals in water, and react adversely to creosote, nicotine, pine oil, and pyrethrum.

The crayfish farm or pond should be shallow, about 18 to 36 inches deep. Pond depths should not exceed three feet. The bottom should be relatively flat, with a drain that permits complete drainage in 30 days at most.

According to aquaculture authority Larry de la Bretonni, crayfish ponds should be dug and flooded by mid-May, so that the water distills for two weeks before crayfish stocking. The fish can be stocked at around 50 pounds per acre. In late summer, the pond should be slowly drained over a month's period, and vegetation (millet and rice) should be planted.

Reflooding should occur in September in order to free the young crayfish burrowed by the female in the summer. Pond water should remain high after reflooding until harvesttime,

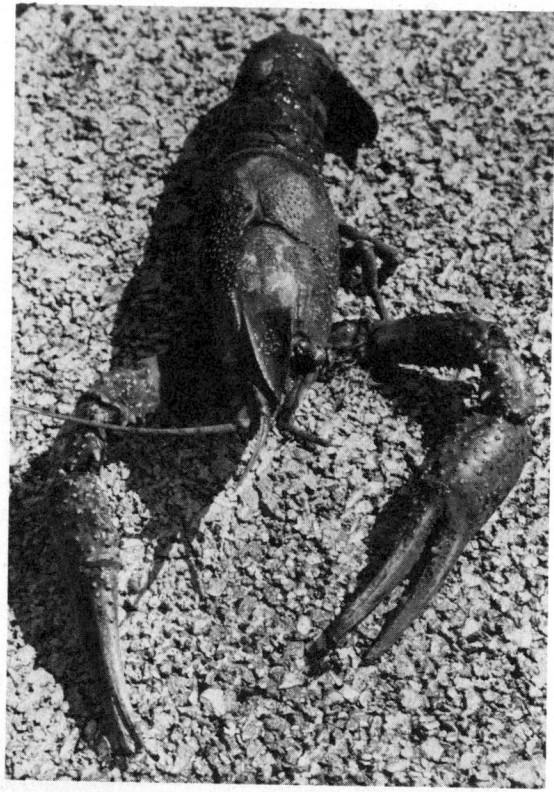

Like its saltwater relative, the lobster, the crayfish is an excellent source of protein. Some American species can be bred to yield more than 1,000 pounds of protein-rich food per acre.

usually in late November. Average harvest yields are 350 to 650 pounds per acre, with some growers boasting as much as 2,000 pounds per acre. Water quality and harvesting frequency are prime considerations for maximum production.

The crayfish industry in the United States has great potential as an organic approach to food cultivation. Scientists are researching different crayfish species and developing improved techniques of raising and harvesting crayfish crops more efficiently. Some species have even been found useful in aquatic weed control.

One major obstacle in present efforts to use this potential food source is public distaste of the thought of crayfish cuisine. Crayfish have been considered fish bait in the North rather than gourmet delights like the lobster or crab. Through the continuing development of low-cost techniques of making crayfish farming ecologically and economically sound, crayfish may become a recognized source of protein in the future.

To make a meal of boiled crayfish, simply put the live crustacea in salted, boiling water with caraway seed. Use 2 quarts of water, 1 tablespoon salt and 1 tablespoon caraway. The fish should be boiled 5 minutes, then let stand until cool. Drain and chill.

CREEPING CHARLIE
See LYSIMACHIA

CREEPING MYRTLE
See PERIWINKLE

CRENSHAW   See MELON

CREOSOTE

A widely used wood preservative, creosote is not recommended for preserving wood in seedling flats or wood for compost bins. It is highly poisonous. Linseed oil is a satisfactory substitute.

CRESS   (*Lepidium sativum*)

Sometimes called peppergrass, this easily cultivated early spring vegetable is usually grown as a salad green. It is sown thickly in early spring in rows one foot apart; as it runs quickly to seed, succession sowings should be made every eight or ten days. There are several varieties, but the kind in general use is the curled which is a good salad ingredient and garnish.

See also UPLAND CRESS, WATERCRESS.

CRIMSON CLOVER   See CLOVER

CRINUM

These tropical bulbous plants are members of the Amaryllis family.

Especially fine for southern gardens, the crinum is a very ancient plant, mentioned in the Bible, and growing throughout the subtropical world. Some of the crinums, if sufficiently mulched, are able to withstand the winters as far north as Philadelphia with occasional reports of a few farther north, though these are very rare. Many species and hybrids grow well in Texas where they are lifted each winter. Greenhouses all over the country grow many crinums.

There are two main types. In the first the flowers are salverform (the petals set flat on the tube as in the phlox). The long, narrow, erect tubes in different species have petals (limbs) long and narrow; some are lance shaped; some are white; some are faintly lined with rose down the center; some are purple or wine down the outside of the entire flower and white inside. The number of flowers varies from five to 35 on an umbel. All are variously and deliciously fragrant.

In the other group the flower has what is called the lily shape. A short or long tube broadens out in the "cup" in varying shapes. In two species the "cup" is quite open or tulip shaped. The lily-shaped crinums are far more numerous than the salverform type because it is from the lily-shaped *C. Moorei* that the wealth of crinums has descended.

Crinums grow best in the mild climate of the South, usually requiring much space. They require full sun and a rich, humusy soil mulched with compost or manure.

Planted in rich soil where they will receive sunlight part of every day, crocuses will continue to produce very early spring flowers for many years. (*Courtesy of U.S. Department of Agriculture*)

CROCUS

With the first warm rays of the spring sun the crocus pops its colorful head out of the ground to announce the coming of spring. Sometimes this little flower seems almost too impatient to wait for spring and, defying late winter snows, pushes its way through snow-covered lawns.

These spring-flowering bulbs are easy to grow even for the new gardener. Good growing conditions contribute to the best display of flowers and the continued year-after-year performance of the bulbs. The bulbs are planted in the fall any time before the ground freezes. Rich soil is not necessary but well-drained soil is. Dried sewage sludge, bone meal, or a thin coating of well-rotted manure or compost spaded into the soil will prove beneficial. Crocuses should, for showy effect, be planted in masses about two inches deep and three to four inches apart. Depth is the distance from the soil surface to the neck of the bulb.

The crocus lends itself well to many garden locations such as in the rock garden, borders, the base of trees, or informal scattering in the lawn. Crocuses must be positioned where they will get sun for part of the day. If planted in the lawn, select a southern exposure to encourage early blooms so that the foliage has matured before the grass needs to be cut. This is essential if flowers are wanted in future years.

In the lawn, plantings must be free and natural. To avoid formal arrangements scatter the bulbs and plant them where they fall. Lift the sod with a trowel, stir soil underneath and plant the bulb, right side up, and press sod back.

In localities with severe winters, a mulch of hay, straw or evergreen boughs may be used after the ground has frozen hard. This prevents the alternate freezing and thawing of the soil, and disastrous heaving of the bulbs. The mulch should be removed early in the spring.

In the spring allow the foliage to ripen. After blooming, the foliage continues to grow until it yellows and withers of its own accord (four to six weeks). Crocuses may remain in the same planting and make a splendid show for years. Do not disturb plantings unless overcrowding makes replanting necessary.

Every garden, large or small, can partake of the beauty of the crocus. The bulbs are inexpensive and with a little care will not only persist for many years but will increase considerably.

There are two types of spring crocus—the species and the hybrids. The latter are the familiar large-flowered crocuses, which are available in a good range of bright colors and many named varieties. The species crocuses are smaller, often have more flowers per corm and bloom earlier than the hybrids. Their colors are more subtle, often with unusual combinations of shades. *C. susianus* has golden orange flowers. *C. korolkowii* has widespread petals, is yellow inside and striped bronze purple outside. *C. versicolor* is white with purple stripes.

C. vernus cv. 'Vanguard' is pale blue inside and pale gray outside. *C. sieberi* cv. 'Tricolor' is lilac pink. There are many varieties of *C. chrysanthus,* which include Zwanenburg Bronze, gold buff striped brown; Bulfinch, soft blue and white; and Cream Beauty, ivory to cream with prominent orange stigmata.

Not as well known as the spring crocus are the autumn-flowering species. Most of these produce and ripen their leaves in spring and bloom in fall without foliage like colchicum. Do not plant these in the lawn. Put them around the base of trees or shrubs or plant them under vinca or pachysandra at the same depth as spring crocus. *C. latifolium* has deep blue flowers, and is very hardy. The white form, *C. l. albus*, is large and the orange stigmata prominent. The fragrant *C. longiflorus* is the showiest one, being lilac blue with orange scarlet stigmata. *C. sativus,* the famous saffron crocus, has violet blue petals and orange stigmata. Grown as a crop in parts of southern Europe and the Near East where it is native, the stigmata of this crocus are dried and sold for culinary purposes. Autumn-flowering crocuses are usually ordered in spring or summer so they can be shipped early. If they bloom before you can get them planted, cut off the flowers and plant anyway. They will bloom the following year.

See also BULB, COLCHICUM, FORCING.

CROP, FORAGE

A forage crop is a plant grown primarily for livestock feed and of which all, or nearly all, the plant parts are harvested by man. Forage crops include all grasses and legumes cut for hay or silage and also root crops such as turnips, rutabagas or sugar beets when they are fed to livestock.

See also entries for individual forages, such as ALFALFA, ORCHARDGRASS, *etc.*

CROP RESIDUES

Crop residues are the portions of plants left over after harvest—stubble, mulch, aftermath, and root residues of various kinds. Such matter is not merely waste material. In fact, it can play a significant role in maintaining soil tilth, structure and fertility, and it is an important way in which organic matter is returned to the soil.

Crop residues may be handled in two ways. They may be left on the surface to serve as a mulch. Mulches reduce the tendency of the soil to form a crust, and protect against wind and water erosion. In addition, they serve as a means of retaining soil moisture, insulating soil and lowering soil temperature. This is extremely beneficial in the summertime, but can retard plant growth in spring by keeping the soil cool.

Crop residues can also be turned into the soil; this can be done immediately after harvesting, or after they have served the purposes of a mulch. These will not only add to the organic matter of the soil, but many of the plant nutrients remaining in the residues will, as they decay, become available to succeeding crops.

Decomposition is limited, however, when the residues have a low nitrogen content, or if soil nitrogen is depleted. Decomposition of low-nitrogen residues can actually tie up soil nitrogen, making it unavailable to growing plants.

This problem can be combated in several ways. Decomposition is speeded when residues are mixed into the top layers of a warm, moist, well-aerated, fertile soil rather than plowed deeply below the surface. Crops with low-nitrogen residues (such as corn) can be seeded with a legume at the last cultivation to provide some nitrogenous residues after harvest. The residues can first be used for bedding, and, when thoroughly impregnated with urine and feces, returned to the land. Or manure can be spread over the field and turned under with the residues, providing a source of nitrogen for the crops.

See also CARBON-NITROGEN RATIO, COMPOSTING, MULCH, ORGANIC MATTER.

CROSSING

In plant propagation, this term designates the intentional combining of two different members of the same species. Frequently, it is called crossbreeding or cross-pollinating, although strictly speaking there are several methods of crossing plants. The interbred or crossbred result is known as a hybrid, and the process is also referred to as hybridizing.

Variety breeding has many important purposes. Because the crossed offspring of two plant varieties will generally retain the dominant characteristics of each parent used to produce it, improved traits can be sought and achieved through this method.

In all types of plants, such things as frost and drought hardiness, disease and insect resistance, high productivity, earlier maturing, and desirable harvesting, shipping and marketing qualities are often brought about by selective crossbreeding. In food crops, higher nutritional value, improved flavor, size, appearance, etc., have been accomplished. With flowers and other ornamentals, efforts have similarly been directed to vigorous growth, increased blossom size, lengthier blooming, soil and climate adaptability, and various other helpful characteristics.

See also PLANT BREEDING, RESISTANT VARIETIES.

CROSS-POLLINATION
See PLANT BREEDING, POLLEN

CROTALARIA

A yellow-flowering pea grown mainly in California and Florida, this is considered a valuable green manure crop in warmer sections of the country.

See also GREEN MANURE.

CROWFOOT   *See* RANUNCULUS

CROWN GRAFT   *See* GRAFTING

CROWN IMPERIAL
See FRITILLARIA

CROWN VETCH   (*Coronilla varia*)

Crown vetch is not of the genus *Vicia,* and botanically speaking, not a vetch at all. This is a point of confusion for many in seeking crown vetch seed, or rhizobium inoculant for the seed. A native of Europe, this long-lived, creeping perennial legume is often seen along interstate highways and road banks.

A hardy legume, crown vetch maintains a solid green foliage during a long growing season on raw, steep roadside banks. During the summer, it blooms into a mass of pink, rose and white flowers. The foliage provides a thick soil-protecting mat which holds the rainfall and retards runoff. The soil-conditioning action of the roots renders the soil exceedingly receptive to moisture, an important factor to good slope development.

Plants seed from mid-June to September, and spread by strong fleshy underground stems. These grow to lengths of ten feet or more and produce new plants at each node.

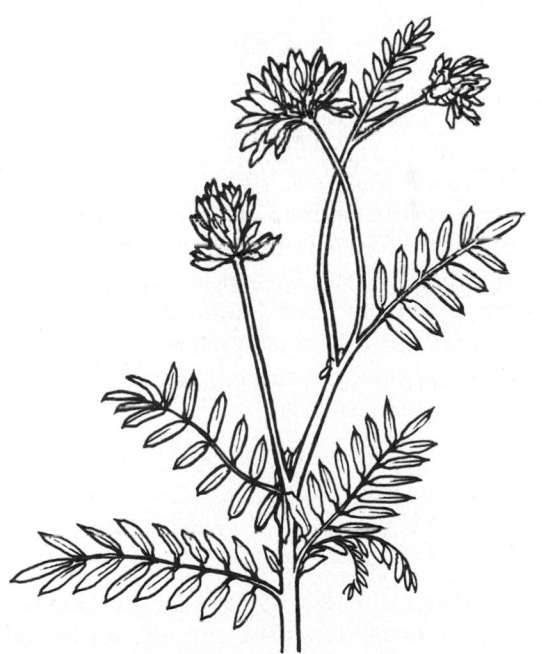

As a perennial, spreading legume that is resistant to disease, drought and freezing, crown vetch is an excellent forage and green manure crop.

Among the many advantages crown vetch seems to possess are exceptional vigor under extreme drought and cold conditions, disease resistance and a remarkable ability to grow well even on subsoils. Crown vetch is quite competitive and chokes out undesirable plants.

After mowing, crown vetch recovers very slowly, and stands have been known to be lost entirely when cut for hay. Close grazing or frequent cutting should be avoided with this legume.

CROW'S-NEST WEED
See QUEEN-ANNE'S-LACE

CUCKOOFLOWER
(*Cardamine pratensis*)

An attractive member of the Mustard family, cuckooflower or meadow cress is a leafy-stemmed perennial bearing lovely white or rose flowers in spring or early summer. It grows to 1½ feet tall, and is especially showy when double flowered. Although it tolerates a dry situation this plant prefers a moist spot, preferably along a spring or stream.

See also LYCHNIS.

CUCUMBER   (*Cucumis sativus*)

Thanks to research and the development of new strains, cucumber growing has become increasingly popular with the commercial grower and home gardener alike. The new varieties are both drought and disease resistant, which takes the risk out of their cultivation.

When choosing a field for planting cucumbers, a flat, well-drained one is preferred to a slope. A level field will retain moisture longer during the hot, dry spells. If possible, it should be a clover or bean field that had been plowed under the previous fall or in early spring.

Soil should be medium textured, neither too light and sandy, nor too heavy. The plants will grow rapidly in sandy soil but, unless irrigation is provided, they will dry up during the midsummer months. A heavy, wet soil, on the other hand, interferes with proper root development and leads to fungus and disease problems. Heavy soils also tend to produce later crops.

Cucumbers are heavy users of organic materials and produce better and more heavily when organically fed.

A balanced fertilizer should be used if the soil is deficient in the necessary elements. This should include a minimum of 5 percent nitrogen, and about 20 percent of such organic materials as ground-up cottonseed, dried blood, dehydrated manures, and bone and fish meal.

Cucumbers may be planted any time in May after danger of frost is past. About the middle of the month is best. Before plowing the field, scatter plenty of seasoned manure, aged at least four months so as not to burn the tender plants. This manure will serve two purposes in the soil: one, feeding the plants; two, helping retain moisture during the hot spells and keeping the soil porous. Adequate moisture in the soil at all times spells the difference between weak, unproductive plants, and green, robust ones.

Plant the seed just one inch below the surface to prevent damp rot in case of heavy rains.

Most cucumber rows are planted six to seven feet apart running from east to west for maximum sun. If space permits, eight feet is better. This gives the vines more room to grow without getting matted, and will make picking easier.

Space hills six feet apart in all directions. This allows for cross-cultivation which eliminates hand hoeing to keep down weeds. Plant six seeds to a mound and, when four inches high, thin out to three plants.

Start cultivating as soon as the plants are three inches high. One cultivation a week is necessary until the vines begin to creep. Since the cucumber plants grow so vigorously, the soil must be kept as loose as possible so as not to hamper their rapid growth.

When the vines have attained a length of about 18 inches, stop cultivating and apply a moderate amount of organic fertilizer along both sides of each row. A rock fertilizer, high in nitrogen, is excellent. If possible, apply during a light rain or drizzle so the water will immediately carry it down to the roots where it is needed. Then, to protect the shallow roots, mulch between and within the rows with a heavy layer of clean, dry straw, hay or sawdust.

Cucumbers can be grown on a trellis made by erecting two posts between which chicken wire is strung. Trellised cucumbers should be cultivated as described above. When the vines begin to grow, help them onto the wire to insure their fastening to the trellis.

An early cucumber crop can be grown by planting the seeds under hot caps as early as a month before normal planting. Be sure to remove the winter mulch and allow the sun to dry out the soil for a few days. Sow the seeds thickly after the ground has been heavily mulched. Gallon glass jars with their bottoms removed serve as effective hot caps for an early crop. If a frosty night should surprise your garden, simply place the lids on the jars. The bottoms of the glass jars are easily removed by setting the bottom in boiling water for a few

Start picking cucumbers six to seven weeks after planting, or as soon as two or three are found in each clump of vines.

minutes and then quickly placing it in ice water.

Harvest: Six to seven weeks after planting, small cucumbers begin to form on the vines. They bear watching because they grow into full-sized cucumbers overnight. Start picking as soon as two or three are found in a clump of vines. The first picking is usually small, but it is necessary in order to encourage the plants to produce more. For most pickles, cucumbers two to six inches long are used. For salads and larger dill pickles, wait until they are six to ten inches long. Never let cucumbers ripen and rot on the vine.

Varieties: Burpee Hybrid is a disease-resistant variety with a 60-day maturing period.

Gemini Hybrid (60 days) also has a resistance to mosaic and mildew. Poinsett is a heavy yielder, disease resistant and performs well in the South. Salty Hybrid is an early breed, maturing in only 50 days. China Long cucumbers grow to a length of two feet if properly cared for, and grow best on a trellis. Wisconsin SMR-18 is great for pickling, as is Spartan Dawn Hybrid Pickler. Marketer and Burpeeana Hybrid are hardy varieties for the home grower.

CUCUMBER BEETLE

Two species often appear in gardens, the spotted cucumber beetle and the striped. The spotted cucumber beetle is slender, ¼ inch long, black headed, and has yellow green wing covers with 11 or 12 black spots. The striped cucumber beetle is distinguished by three black stripes running down its yellowish back. The white, slender larval worms of both may damage the root system of crops, and carry bacterial wilt.

These brightly colored beetles first attack cucumbers and other vined vegetables just as the plants are pushing through the ground. They are vectors of bacterial wilt and mosaic. Late planting is an easy means of avoiding the worst beetle damage; if practical in your area, plant seed right after the beetles lay their eggs. A handful of wood ashes and an equal amount of hydrated lime can be mixed in two gallons of water to brew an effective spray. Be sure to cover both top and lower sides of the foliage. Interplanted marigolds will help keep the beetles away and the larvae can be controlled by rotating crops. Varieties resistant to mosaic and bacterial wilt are available.

See also INSECT CONTROL, RESISTANT VARIETIES.

Carriers of several bacterial and viral diseases, the striped and spotted cucumber beetles are common pests throughout the eastern United States.
(Courtesy of U.S. Department of Agriculture)

CULTIVATION

Cultivating is one of the most important tasks for the farmer, and is equally important to the large gardener as well. Although some gardeners don't cultivate on light, rich soils, and proponents of the year-round mulch system eschew cultivation of all kinds (*see also* MULCH; STOUT, RUTH), most gardens and all large fields require cultivation.

Cultivation, no matter whether done with a spading fork or tractor and plow, has primarily two purposes. The first is to prepare a firm, fine seedbed for best possible seed germination. A second important reason is for weed control. Cultivating also helps aerate the soil (*see also* AERATION), and turning under cover crops, green and animal manure and compost provides organic matter for soil organisms to live on.

There is a great deal of controversy about cultivation, and various tools all have their supporters and detractors. Edward H. Faulkner, for example, caused a mild flurry in the agricultural world in the 1940's when he decried the use of the moldboard plow in *Plowman's Folly* and several other books. Many believe the chisel plow is a better tool than the moldboard for basic soil tillage. The chisel plow has a series of curved tines that penetrate soil to a depth of 12 to 18 inches. Soil plowed with a chisel plow suffers less from wind and water erosion, and plowing is faster, but the chisel plow requires a good deal of horsepower and cannot be used with a small farm tractor. Actually, the problem in cultivation often lies in the incorrect use of a tool and even more so with the general condition of the soil. A soil with a low content of organic matter is difficult to work properly with *any* tool.

When to Cultivate: Figuring out when to cultivate is probably most difficult for the novice. Soil must be "fit" for cultivation—that is, have proper temperature and moisture content. Moisture is the most important; although any soil is difficult to handle when wet, clays can form a rock-hard surface if cultivated when too wet. On the other hand, it can be virtually impossible to plow or till soil that is too dry.

You will eventually develop a feel for when soil is fit to till. Soil is ready to work when a handful firmly compressed into a ball can be broken apart by the fingers when the pressure is released. If it remains in a wet, sticky mass, it's too wet. Sandy soils dry out more quickly and are less damaged by premature working than silty and clay soils.

Don't wait to work soil until it is too dry. Powdery, overworked soil is just about as bad

as the big clods that form in wet-worked soil. Rain on powdery clay can turn the surface into a concrete-hard crust. This can be reduced and eventually eliminated by raising the organic matter content to 5 percent or more. Anyone who insists on working clay soil too much will always have problems with crusting, and this will hamper seedling emergence.

Soil worked in the autumn and left to freeze over winter works more easily the next spring. Winter freezes and thaws mellow the ground and loosen the subsoil. In the spring, the soil surface dries out quicker than if unplowed. If you have tough clay soil, till in the fall for easier working in the spring, but keep the land rough to resist erosion. In addition, working soil in the fall enables you to spread the work of cultivating over several months, instead of making you do everything in the spring.

Tools: The cheapest tools to use for cultivating are hand tools: A good spading fork, a round-pointed spade, a garden rake, hoe, and a three- or four-prong cultivator. A good large-wheeled, hand-pushed cultivator works well for cultivating between the rows.

Use of hand tools is limited, however, by the amount of time you have to work in your garden and the size of the garden. A garden of 3,000 square feet is about the upper limit for one adult to work by hand (as a comparison, there are 5,700 square feet in 1/8 acre).

For bigger gardens, a rotary cultivator is almost a necessity, particularly if you raise most of your family's food in your plot. The best cultivators have five horsepower or more; seven or eight is better. Some European types are bigger than that, but are difficult to buy in this country. Some with both front- and rear-mounted tines are available; there are advantages and disadvantages to both. Whichever kind you choose, however, will enable you to till your soil before planting and cultivate between your rows once the plants have emerged. *See also* ROTARY TILLAGE.

Tractors for use on the small farm or large homestead come in a number of shapes and sizes. Closest to the rotary cultivators are walking garden tractors, which have hefty engines that can pull plows and cultivating equipment. Small garden tractors with a variety of attachments are also available; these offer an added advantage in that they can be used for mowing the lawn as well. The tractors with larger horsepower are generally tougher and will last longer.

A better bet, though, may well be a used farm tractor; for an old tractor and equipment to farm 15 acres you may pay less than for a new tractor and equipment that won't do half the work. If you're thinking of going this route, you'll need a tractor of from 20 to 40 horsepower, a two-bottom plow, eight-foot disk, a spike-tooth harrow about nine feet wide, and a two-row cultivator. Make sure that all your equipment has hitches compatible with your tractor.

The only trouble with old farm tractors is that they need frequent repair work. However, if you're able to do your own work, most tractor companies still in operation stock parts and maintenance manuals for their old tractors, and parts for old tractors are usually easy to come by in farming areas.

Turning the Soil: Although the mechanics of the operation are different with hand tools or power tools, the steps in cultivation are essentially the same. Although spading a garden sounds like—and is—hard work, plowing properly can be just as demanding. Both these are first steps in preparing a firm seedbed for your seeds. Turning over the soil also enables you to turn in crop residues, green manures, animal manure, and mineral rock powders to enrich your soil. *See also* COMPOSTING, FERTILIZER, GREEN MANURE, GREENSAND, PHOSPHATE ROCK, *and entries for other individual organic fertilizers.*

On the small garden, a round-pointed spade or a spading fork are the tools to use for this initial task. A spading fork is lighter to use than a spade and breaks up clods with less effort. There is a science to spading a garden so that the soil is all turned over, and plant residues are partially buried.

First, dig a trench about as deep as you can easily plunge your spade. The dirt you remove from this first trench is put in a wheelbarrow and wheeled to the other end of the plot you are going to spade to fill your last trench. Next, dig a trench next to the first one, turning each spadeful of dirt upside down into that first trench. Bury the plant residues that were on top of the soil, especially if spading sod. If you tip each spadeful of dirt on its side rather than completely upside down, plant residues and other organic matter that were on the soil surface are buried at all depths rather than at the bottom of the trench.

Proceed across the garden in the same fashion. Don't hurry and take too big a bite; you will only tire faster. Keep the spading side of your trench straight up and down. In sod, use a round-pointed shovel rather than a fork because the shovel will cleave the roots better. At the edges of the plot, mark a line and go along the length of that line jamming the shovel down about four inches to slice through the grass roots. While you're spading, the shovelful along the edge will lift out easily.

When you turn the soil over, give each

spadeful a whack to crumble it or stick your shovel or fork into it and twist. Either maneuver breaks the clod a little and leaves the surface loose and friable.

Plowing: Although plowing is done by machine, it can be difficult to plow *properly* at first. First of all, set your plow to the correct depth. Cutting depth of a plow should be limited to about half the cutting width. An eight-inch plow should be adjusted to cut no more than four inches deep, for example. It is better to buy a larger plow and vary the cutting depth from year to year between four and six inches to avoid hardpanning. In heavy clay soils, plowing year after year at the same depth forms a somewhat impermeable layer of clay at plow depth. That's a hardpan. If you're gardening organically, you shouldn't have to worry about hardpans.

A plow lifts the soil from one place and deposits it eight to 12 inches to the side. The resulting ditch is called a furrow. The first time you plow across a field the dirt turned over by the plow blade falls on the normal surface of the ground, leaving a ridge of dirt called a headland. The first furrow will have dirt from the second furrow thrown into it, the second from the third, and so forth. When you are finished plowing, at least one furrow will be left over. This is called a dead furrow. In subsequent years you make your headlands fall where last year's dead furrows were and last year's headlands become this year's dead furrows. If you don't do that, your field will become less level every year.

The most efficient shape to plow is a rectangle twice as long as it is wide and not more than 100 feet wide if you're using a small plow. If your plot is too large, make two plots from it. Leave room at each end for convenient turning, lifting the plow as you do. When the plowed section gets as close to the sides of the field as the furrows are to the ends of the field, then plow around the whole field, including the turning area, until you are finished.

The next year, begin plowing in the opposite direction on the outsides of the field. Start at H, go to I, lift the plow and go to K, drop the plow and go to J, and so forth. You are now "throwing the ground out," whereas the previous year, you "threw the ground in." If you do not alternate in this fashion at each plowing, the dead furrows on the edges of the field would get deeper at each plowing, and the headland in the middle would get higher. Plowing properly, your dead furrow the second year will come in the middle of the field where your headland is the first year.

Whether spading or plowing, remember to

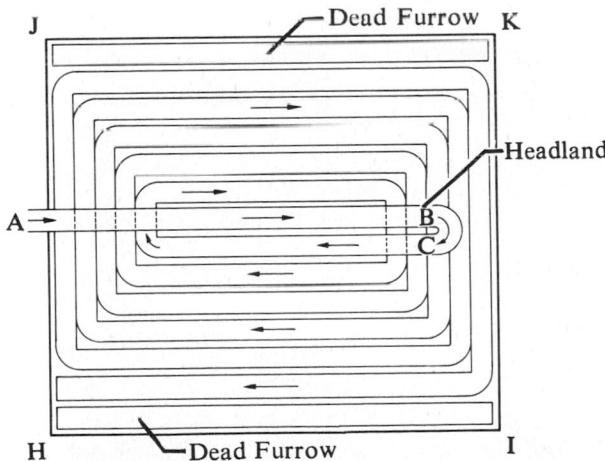

Next year, if this field is properly plowed, the dead furrow will fall in the middle of the field, where the headland is this year. In this manner, the field is kept level.

leave the surface of fall-plowed ground rough after working. The rough surface will absorb and hold more water and will mellow better in freezing. If turning over ground in the spring or early summer, you should work it as quickly as possible afterwards, however, so that the finer surface soil will hold soil moisture in.

Preparing a Seedbed: If you are using hand tools, the hoe is the best tool to begin preparing a fall-spaded seedbed. On a farm, a disk does the same job after plowing and in a large garden, the rotary cultivator.

Hoeing can be hard work, but you can halve the effort with the right technique: Do not chop with the hoe. Never raise it any higher than your knees and rarely higher than the top of your ankle. Hoeing should be a *pulling* effort rather than a pounding or chopping action. The slant of blade to handle on a good hoe is designed so that if you set the blade on the ground in front of you and pull the hoe towards you with a little downward pressure on the middle of the hoe handle, the hoe blade will go into the soil, breaking a two- or three-inch furrow as you pull. Slice up a strip no more than 12 inches. On the backswing keep the hoe blade a couple inches above the ground, letting the blade bite into the soil a foot in front of you. Pulling it towards your toe, lift again, slicing up another swath of soil the width of the hoe. This technique, when mastered, makes hoeing easier.

Once the soil surface has been loosened by the hoe, go to work with the steel rake, smoothing and leveling the ground for planting. Stand on the edge of the garden plot, pushing and pulling the rake as far as you can reach. Rake off rocks, bits of wood or sod chunks to the garden's edge. The rake will break up any clods that remain and leave the soil ready to

plant. When you have finished raking, the bed should be level, and free of all debris.

Disking: If you're using machinery for cultivation, a disk and harrow will do the jobs described above. In fact, the tandem disk is one of the best cultivating tools at your disposal. In good organic soil, a disk can work the ground sufficiently without plowing at all, unless the field is covered with tough sod. Since tandem disks may need extra weight, they are equipped with carrying frames above each gang (or double set of disks). A cement block in each frame is plenty of extra weight, and sacks of dirt make good weights, too.

Small disks cut a swath about 32 inches wide. You can vary the cutting depth of the blades by adjusting the slant of the gangs. It is

In good organic soil, a disk can sufficiently prepare the ground without plowing at all.

important that the disk leaves a level swath of worked dirt. The back two gangs must be set to level the middle and side ruts which the front two gangs make. Don't be discouraged, on hard ground or ground covered with some plant residue or mulch, if the disk doesn't work up the ground well the first time over. On each additional trip, the tool will cut increasingly better. It's important not to overwork a piece of ground. On clay soils, the disk would eventually break down the soil structure to a fine powder which would crust badly if a hard rain subsequently should fall.

No matter how well you adjust your disk, it will leave a sort of rolling surface. To solve what may be a possible problem, farmers usually pull some kind of "drag" behind the disk to smooth out highs and lows. Usually this is a spike-tooth harrow. A spring-tooth harrow is a problem because, on soils with a large content of vegetable matter, the teeth act like a rake and plug up with the mulch, straw, cornstalks, grass, or whatever you are trying to mix into your soil. Unless you shred all your old plant residues, the spring-tooth harrow won't work to your satisfaction. If, after harrowing with either tool, the ground is still rough, drag it with a heavy roller and harrow again.

Weed Control: Cultivation for weed control should begin three days after planting, before your seeds come up. Many gardeners do not understand the effectiveness of pre-emergent cultivation and don't know how to do it.

Watch the soil surface very closely after you have planted your seed. In about three days, you will notice many tiny weeds beginning to sprout. In the garden, a cursory cultivation with the steel rake will kill them without the expenditure of much muscle power. Just rake gently over the whole planted space including the rows to about an inch depth. You won't hurt your seeds if you don't rake as deeply as you planted. You can rake across corn rows even when the plants are coming up if you are gentle about it. You may break off a spear or two of corn, but the amount of weeds you kill more than makes up for that.

In the field, the same type of cultivation is important. The tool to use can be the spike-tooth harrow, with the teeth set very shallow so as not to dig your seed out. A better tool is the rotary hoe—a set of curved-spike wheels that, when pulled over the ground, disturbs sprouting weed seeds just enough to kill them without hurting your crops. In fact, the rotary hoe can be used to kill weeds even when corn and beans are an inch above the soil.

After seedlings have emerged and are making good growth, you have to be more careful when cultivating. If using a rake, continue cultivation between the rows after your plants emerge, and you can probably get by with no other cultivation at all. With a rake, you can weed very close to plants without harming them. Moreover, rake cultivation is much faster than a hoe or push cultivator.

However, you can't rake wet soil. If rain falls after planting and the weather continues to be wet for long, the weeds grow. After they reach an inch in height, they can't be killed effectively with the rake or rotary hoe. You must use your hoe or a good wheel-type push cultivator. Not only will the cultivator effectively control weeds between the rows, but, used intelligently, will throw enough dirt into the row of growing vegetables (after they are three inches or more above ground) to bury small germinating weeds there. That reduces the amount of hand weeding you have to do.

Generally, the larger the wheel on the push cultivator, the easier it is to push. This is the more commonly available type. If you have machinery, all kinds of cultivator sets are made for power garden tractors. They're just like the ones on push-wheel cultivators only much larger. They come equipped with wide shovels (sweeps) or narrow shovels (diggers) and can be adjusted to straddle a row or cultivate between rows. Some cultivators can be used also as chisel plows.

An old farm tractor will need a two-row cultivator to cultivate weeds. This will be compatible with the two-row planter and can be the most difficult tool to find. Many old tractors are sold with a mounted cultivator. Get it if you can, or buy one that fits the tractor. The other alternative is to find a two-row cultivator that you simply pull with your tractor. If you can't find a cultivator that mounts easily and solely to the rear of your tractor, look for a four-row cultivator of this type. They are more common, but are already obsolete for commercial farms, so can be purchased reasonably. Cut off the two outside gangs with a welding torch to make yourself a two-row cultivator. A four-row cultivator shouldn't be used to cultivate rows planted with a two-row planter. The cultivator will not allow for variables in row spacing and you'll probably rip up two rows with each pass.

CUMIN   (*Cuminum cyminum*)

A small, slender, herbaceous annual widely cultivated in India and the Mediterranean region of Europe, cumin's aromatic fruit (known as seed) is used as a condiment. When pepper was scarce and expensive, the ancient Romans substituted cumin in their cooking. In biblical days, cumin was said to be considered so valuable that it was used by many citizens to pay personal taxes.

Cumin requires four months for its seeds to mature. Seedlings should be planted outside, 16 to 20 seeds to the foot. The plant thrives best on a well-drained, rich sandy loam in regions where temperatures are mild and even during a growing season of about three or four months. In the Mediterranean region the seed is frequently broadcast after winter crops of cereals, potatoes or cabbage. Complete control of weeds is necessary because the plant is small and tender. Planting the seed in rows spaced to permit maximum use of cultivators would be preferable in regions where hand labor is costly.

The crop is ready for harvest when the plants wither and the seed loses its dark green color.

Large quantities are used in the preparation of curry and in combination with other aromatic seeds in flavoring sausages, cheese and numerous other food products. Ground cumin is also found in chili powders. The seed has not been produced commercially in the United States.

See also HERB.

CUPFLOWER   (*Nierembergia*)

Small annuals and perennials of the Nightshade family, cupflowers have cup-shaped flowers in white, blue and violet. The small leaves, wiry stems and closely packed blossoms combine to make the cupflower a popular edging plant, potted plant or window box subject.

Cupflowers prefer a moist soil and a sunny location. In the North, propagation is by seed planted indoors in February and set out after all danger of frost is past. In the South, propagation is by direct-seeding.

See also NIEREMBERGIA.

CURCULIO

Curculio is a name given to any snout beetle, especially one which attacks fruit. Eggs are usually laid in young fruit, and the grub that hatches feeds within; when the fruit falls, it leaves to pupate in the ground. The adult beetle emerges about a month later.

The grubs stay in the drops for awhile before burrowing underground, and it is therefore good practice to gather up drops daily. This fruit should be buried in the warm depths of the compost pile.

Any curculios that have made it to the pupal stage can be dealt with by disking under the trees. The adult beetles play possum when frightened, and will drop from trees if the trunk is jarred with a padded board. Lay out sheets below to catch the falling pests. Chickens, geese and ducks will help to catch any you miss.

See also INSECT CONTROL, PLUM CURCULIO.

CURLY PALM　　*See* PALM

CURRANT　　(*Ribes*)

Currants merit cultivation in the home garden because the fruits are rich sources of vitamin C and the plants yield dependably with a minimum of fuss.

Currants will live almost anywhere, doing best in a relatively cool, moist climate and well-drained soil. Plant growth and fruitfulness are most satisfactory on soils well supplied with organic matter. Stable manure or its equivalent in humus-making medium is important. Mulches of leaves and litter can be worked into the soil after being used on the surface.

Planting: Prepare soil for currants in the same way that it would be prepared for a vegetable crop; that is, dig in a supply of organic fertilizer and humus to a depth of six to eight inches. If the site has previously been cultivated for another crop, there will be less trouble with perennial weeds near the bushes.

Currant buds start their growth very early in spring. The bushes should be set before this growth starts. If the winters are not too severe, set the bushes in fall after they have become dormant, giving the roots a chance to make some growth and establish themselves as a protection against heaving. Where winters are very cold the plants may be set in spring before growth starts.

Bushes are set four to six feet apart, depending upon variety. If the roots are dry when the plants are received they may be soaked in water for a few hours before they are planted. Trim off any broken or damaged roots and cut back any that are too long. Set them slightly lower than they were set in the nursery. If they tend to have a trunk, set them deep enough so that the bottom branches are covered with soil at their bases. Cut the top back to six to 12 inches, depending upon the strength of the root system. Firm the soil well around the roots and spread a mulch in a three-foot circle around each bush, leaving the canes bare where they emerge from the soil. Mice like the tender shoots on currant bushes and must not be encouraged by a mulch too close to the canes.

Currants are among the fruits which show a decided preference for organic rather than chemical fertilizers. Even gardeners who pour on the chemicals through most of their garden find that manure, wood ashes and bone meal are the only nutrients on which currant bushes thrive. Fertilizer should be applied in late winter, just before growth starts. Since the roots are near the surface they will be able to use the nutrients with a minimum of leaching. Rotted manure or compost should be spread in a layer an inch deep over a three-foot circle around each bush and one ounce of wood ashes and two ounces of bone meal should be raked into the same space.

Pruning: Currants are borne in greatest profusion on wood that is two or three years old. After that age the size and quantity of the fruit declines. During the first year, a cane should make a strong, straight, unbranched growth. In the second year, it sends out three or four lateral branches which are six to 12 inches long. In the third year, more numerous and shorter laterals grow from the main cane and from one or two laterals.

Ideal pruning limits the bush to three or four canes of each age. Older canes are cut out when they reach four years old. A two-year-old bush, when pruned for the first time, will be permitted to keep no more than six to eight shoots, half new growth and half those that it had when it was planted. Each year thereafter the new shoots are cut out to leave no more than three or four strong ones which add six inches new growth each year and have a desirable growth habit. On spreading bushes, the more upright canes should be selected. On upright bushes, the canes which

spread slightly to open up the top would be preferred. Beginning in the second or third year in the garden, the oldest canes are also cut out each year. All canes removed are cut back as far as possible into the ground, to keep the base of the bush clean and free of stumps. Canes are almost never headed back, unless they are injured. The best time for pruning is in early winter.

Old bushes may be renovated by cutting back all except three or four strong canes the first year. This will force the growth of many new shoots from which a selection of a half dozen the second year will make it possible to cut out the remaining old canes. By the third year the bushes will be filled out and will be ready for the regular pruning schedule. Some authorities recommend lifting the bushes after eight to ten years and dividing them to prevent the canes from growing too close together.

New Plants: Small plants for setting out can be secured by cuttings from old ones. This is the usual way to propagate. These are short stems eight to ten inches long taken from year-old growth. They are cut in the fall from medium-sized canes after growth has ceased and when the wood is mature. They are called hardwood cuttings. The cuttings are tied in bundles of a dozen or more and stored in cool sand or sawdust and kept moist enough so they will not dry out, and cool enough so the buds will not swell. In the spring the cuttings which have now callused at the cut ends are set in a garden row with severed end down to root and grow for one year. Soil should be packed about the cuttings which are set four to six inches deep and three to 12 inches apart. When they are well rooted they may be set out in permanent places in the fall or the following spring. Fall planting is often practiced. It requires from two to three years to get plants built up to bearing age. It is well to space the permanent plants four feet apart in rows six feet apart. As currant and gooseberry plants have many shallow roots, the soil should not be worked deeply enough to injure the roots. Special care is needed the first year after setting in order not to harm the roots. Suppress weeds by mulches; add manure generously each year.

New plants can also be secured by a process known as mound layering at the base of a clump of plants. The first step is to cut back the stems severely—two-thirds to three-quarters of their length—to stimulate numerous new side shoots. In midsummer, about July or soon after, earth is mounded halfway up the cutoff shoots. By fall or the next spring many shoots will have rooted and these can be dug away with stems and roots attached and set out for new plants. If any variety has not rooted well by fall, leave it undisturbed for another year. Mound layering is more work than cuttage but also more certain of good results. Some varieties do not set well by cuttings but only a few are eccentric in that way.

Harvest: Do not harvest currants until their color is deep and they have begun to soften slightly. The longer they hang, the sweeter they become. At the same time, however, they lose their pectin content. If they are to be used for jelly, they should be picked a little green.

Pick the berries when they are dry. Grasp the stems, not the berries and pull each cluster off the bush. Berries may also be stripped from the stems as they hang, but the job becomes a messy one and the fruit will not keep long when it is picked that way.

Varieties: Red Lake and Wilder are suited to the Northeast and Great Lakes regions. These fruits are hardy and produce large red berries. Perfection is ideal for the mountain and Pacific states.

Insect and Disease Problems: Insect and disease problems are real and recurring ones unless one is familiar with the means of control. There are six troublesome insects and three harmful diseases that need attention.

Currant aphid: This damaging creature often called the leaf louse, stands at the head of the list of injurious insects because it is likely to occur anywhere and everywhere, but indirectly the creature harms the whole plant by dwarfing and starving it and diminishing fruit production. The foliage of the currant is commonly distorted and discolored, being pale or yellowish and rolled and wrinkled by yellow green plant lice on the undersides of the leaves. Later in the season the seriously injured leaves drop, and defoliation hinders the full development of the fruit. The eggs of this insect are shiny black, cucumber shaped and are attached to the bark of the new growth near the nodes. The eggs hatch soon after the leaves open in spring. The young lice crawl to the leaves and feed on the undersurfaces by sucking the juice of the foliage. This causes curling. Toward the end of summer true males and females develop, copulate and winter eggs are deposited on the twigs in October. The eggs can be washed off with water sprayed on the canes.

Currant plant louse: The currant plant louse is not easy to control, which is the reason why this creature is a major insect. The eggs may be transported on nursery stock, if infested and uncertified, so that new plants may be the source of the louse on newly planted stock. The sprocketlike cavities of curled leaves give some protection to the lice and hinder control. Plucking of affected foliage where too much curling of leaves has occurred is important.

Sharp eyes will detect the shiny black eggs on the canes and they can be rubbed off and destroyed before hatching in the spring.

Currant worm: The green as well as the imported currant worms are often destructive to foliage. They can be shaken off the bushes and stepped on.

Berry worm: The berry worm is a small white worm, a sort of maggot, that sometimes infests the fruit of currant and gooseberry. It is believed that the eggs are laid in the fruit and the worms from them feed inside the immature berry and damage it, leaving it unfit for use. For control, pick and destroy all affected fruit, leaving no berries on the bushes or on the ground.

San Jose scale: This pernicious and inconspicuous scale insect often damages many plants. It forms an ashen gray coating in mass on the canes and sucks the juice and life out of them. It is a common garden insect on ornamental shrubs. Set out only clean healthy plants, and use clean cuttings as helpful preventive measures.

Cane borer: Cane borers can become serious if they are not sought out and destroyed. Whenever a cane shows wilting leaves at its tip, cut it back until the borer is discovered, and destroy him before he emerges.

Among diseases there are several of economic importance such as rust, mildew and cane blight. Plants prone to any of these should be routinely inspected so that any disease can be stopped early.

Rust: The red rust on currant leaves is often the most evasive disease of currants. It is intimately associated with blister rust of white pine as an alternating host for the disease. The red blister rust of pine and leaf spot of currant are one and the same disease with different manifestations on each. Both alternate from one species of plant to the other with the change of seasons. Black varieties of currant and the *monticola* and *strobus* species of white pines arc the most susceptible, and should not be planted nearer than a half-mile apart. Many states have strict rules regarding this.

The symptoms of rust on each host species are easy to recognize. On the trunks of affected pines there are in midsummer red rusty eruptions of yellow dust which are the spores. On the underleaf surfaces of the currant there are spots with small, curved, pointed projections, manifesting the growth of the fungus. If only an occasional pine is affected, it can be cut and the spread of the disease forestalled.

Mildew: This very common disease of cultivated plants often occurs on currants and gooseberries. The symptoms on these plants are fine, tender, white cobwebby growths on the top surfaces of the leaves. It often occurs in patches not far away and is most prevalent in wet seasons or in moist areas. It is urgent to give the plants full exposure to sun and provide good air circulation to keep the plants dry. One should remove all incipient cases of mildew as soon as detected to prevent its spread. These preventive practices are of much importance.

Cane blight: A fungus invades the canes and causes them to wilt. The canes die suddenly while loaded with fruit and nonbearing canes contract the disease. Small black cushions on the canes indicate the presence of the fungus. It is best to examine all plants during the summer and remove all affected stalks and burn them. General sanitation is important, as refuse is often a menace to healthy plants.

In the home garden currants are often grown in the partial shade of trees, buildings or fences, an unwise practice which makes them more liable to disease, if not to insect damage, than if grown in full sun and in free ventilation.

Hence there is a need for more frequent attention to keep them healthy. Flowering and ornamental species of these plants are subject to the same enemies as are those grown for edible fruits.

See also BRAMBLE FRUITS.

CUT FLOWERS

Giving cut flowers the proper care prolongs the length of time you'll enjoy them.

One suggestion is to cut the stems at a long slant. They'll absorb more water and stay fresh longer. Another authority recommends adding a lump of sugar to the water to keep cut flowers fresh. Flower stems should never be cut with scissors, which crush the stem tissues, but with a sharp knife. The stems should also be cut every day. Never let any of the foliage come below the water level. Also, never let flowers lie around out of the water, as the stems seal themselves, thus interfering with their water absorption.

Always keep vases and flower containers immaculately clean. A dirty bacteria-laden container will shorten the lives of the flowers. Another rule is not to crowd too many flowers into one container; this crowding could cause crushed stems. A cool temperature will also keep blooms longer.

Roses need careful handling. Cut at least an inch from the stem with a sharp knife. Roses have a very porous stem which takes up water. If this becomes clogged, the flowers will wilt. It may be necessary to cut the stem back several inches if clogging occurs.

Carnations are long-lasting flowers which can stand a great deal of handling. All one needs to do to keep them looking their best is to cut an inch off the stem each day and place them in fresh water.

Chrysanthemums require care much like roses, but they last longer. Care should be taken to support the head of a large mum as bumping will cause the petals to fall. Mums need not be cut every day; the method is to break a little off and pound the end so it will take up water.

Poinsettias when used as cut flowers are sealed before delivery, so if it becomes necessary to cut the stems again, the flowers can be resealed by placing the stems in boiling water for five or ten minutes, or they may be singed over a flame. This is done because poinsettias are full of a white, milky fluid, and would bleed to death unless the ends were quickly sealed.

CUTTINGS

Cuttings is the name given to parts of plants cut from a parent plant and inserted to root in a moist, well-drained and well-aired rooting medium, such as damp, sharp sand or a combination of sharp sand, peat moss, sterilized soil, perlite, or vermiculite. Some plants will even send out roots in plain water.

By this easy method of propagation the new plants which develop from the cuttings are identical with the parent. Therefore, it is a method widely used by horticulturists to increase stock of good varieties, and is also widely used by amateur gardeners to increase their house plants, garden shrubs, perennials, and sometimes trees.

Cuttings are most often taken from stems, and they are usually referred to as softwood and herbaceous, hardwood, and semihardwood. But cuttings can also be made from roots and leaves as well as from tubers, rhizomes and stolons.

Softwood Cuttings: These cuttings, also called "slips" or "greenwood cuttings," are taken from vigorous, growing plants at a stage when the stem breaks with a snap when it is bent. If it merely crushes between the fingers, it is too young to use; if it bends without breaking, it is too woody and old. With a little practice a gardener can learn to tell at a glance which stem is appropriate to use. Most perennials, some annuals and many house plants may be increased by softwood cuttings, either in spring or fall, but not when dormant. Bedding plants are usually propagated this way. The tender growing tips of shrubs and other hardwood plants may also be used if taken during the rapid growing season in spring or summer, or from the fresh growth soon after pruning. The tops of leggy plants may be cut off and rooted, thus rejuvenating the plant and improving its appearance.

The length of a cutting depends on the plant, but it is usually two to six inches, and it usually includes at least two nodes or joints, and often the tip. The cut should be made with a sharp knife just below a node because that's where roots usually form. If no terminal tip is included, the top cut should be slanting, with a bud or node just below the cut. Remove the lower leaves from the piece of stem and insert it in the rooting medium nearly up to the lowest leaf or pair of leaves. If the leaves are very large, transpiration can be reduced by cutting back some of each leaf, but not too much because the plant must have enough leaf surface left on it to carry on photosynthesis and to make the sugars needed to feed the new growth. Do not remove any buds, for they are needed to produce the auxins or growth-promoting substances and enzymes which stim-

ulate the new roots and shoots. The younger the shoot taken for a softwood cutting, the better. In fact, some gardeners cut back plants on purpose to promote new young shoots to use for cuttings of such plants as chrysanthemums, fuchsias, dahlias, geraniums, and penstemons, as well as ornamental shrubs.

When the cutting is inserted, firm the soil well, and water it thoroughly to help establish the maximum contact possible between the stem and the rooting medium. Work rapidly and in the shade to protect the leaves from wilting.

Though moist, sharp sand is an old favorite for the rooting medium, modern gardeners are likely to use a mixture that includes sterile vermiculite (made from mica) or perlite (a silica derivative) or both. These, along with the sterile sphagnum moss or peat moss also often used, hold moisture and help to control disease, especially damping-off. Soil of a light sandy quality is also used as about a third of the mixture. A thin layer of dry sand or vermiculite on the surface of the rooting medium helps to keep the cuttings healthy, and the bit of sand which clings to the base of the cuttings when it is inserted helps aeration at the bottom of the hole and makes it easier for some cuttings to take root. Those cuttings which are planted in light sandy loam outdoors are not so much in need of protection from damping-off.

Cuttings, like seedlings, do better when they are grown in groups, perhaps because of their sharing hormones and antibiotics. The preferred way to insert them in a pot is around the rim of a clay pot, for then they are aired somewhat through the porous clay, thus helping to keep the cuttings in a moist, but never wet, growing medium. A little bottom heat will also help to get rooting started, though it is more important for hardwood cuttings planted indoors or in the greenhouse than for softwood ones. A glass or polyethylene covering is important, for it creates a small humid greenhouse atmosphere for the cutting while it is rooting.

As soon as rooting is established, perhaps as soon as two weeks, the covering should be removed. However, if the air around the plants gets muggy before that time, the covering should be taken off to let the air dry out. After rooting, the leaves will perk up and need more air and more light. Though at first cuttings are kept in semishade, such as in a north window, once they have rooted, full sun is needed. A

A humid atmosphere encourages rapid root formation in the cuttings of nonwaxy plants.

shaded cold frame is also very satisfactory for starting softwood cuttings; the shade should be removed as soon as roots are established. Once roots are growing well, each cutting can be moved to a three-inch pot and watered.

The new tissues that form a new plant from a piece of an old one are preceded by a callus which grows from the wound of the cut. It is necessary to favor this callus, especially with the slips of some herbaceous plants such as geranium (*Pelargonium*). To do this, allow the cut stems of the geranium to rest on the table for 24 hours before inserting them in the rooting medium.

Herbaceous Cuttings: Not only geraniums but many other house plants and perennials as well as some annuals are propagated by cuttings. Most are cut in spring, such as delphiniums, phlox and chrysanthemums, using a young shoot for a basal cutting, but others are cut in June or July, such as violas, candytuft and rock garden phlox. Two-inch cuttings are long enough for most rock garden plants, but four-inch cuttings are preferred for geraniums and other larger plants. It is customary to cut diagonally a little below a node or joint, and to plunge the cutting in cold water for half an hour or so, unless it is a milky-juiced plant or a geranium. The flower buds and the lower leaves should be removed, and then the stem inserted in the rooting medium so that two nodes are buried. The medium used is often one part sterilized loam, two parts peat moss and three parts sharp sand. Add enough water to hold the cutting firmly, put under glass or a plastic cap, and keep shaded until the roots form. Then reduce the humidity and move into the sun. As with other cuttings, a thin layer of dry, sharp sand over the medium is a precaution against fungus growth. Spring cuttings of this sort are planted in the fall in pots or in the garden. Some, such as coleus, chrysanthemum and some of the campanulas and rock garden plants, are started directly in the growing medium, with bottom heat and high humidity.

Leaf Cuttings: Quite a few house plants can be propagated by merely starting leaves (with or without the leafstalk) or leaf buds, in cuttings that include some of the stem as well as the buds below the leaves. Leaf cuttings are commonly made from African violets, gloxinia, snake plant, and rex begonias, the latter by simply slicing through the midrib veins of a leaf and laying it on moist sand so it will absorb more moisture than if left up in the air.

Begonias can be propagated from leaf cuttings. Here, slits have been cut in the major veins and toothpicks used to pin the leaf firmly against the rooting medium.

Leaves so started should be pinned down with a bit of wire, like a hairpin, to help keep them in contact with the moist rooting medium. New plants will grow from the points where the leaf was wounded. Gloxinias form little tubers, and the leaves of hyacinths will form little bulblets. Leaf cuttings are also best propagated in a moist, warm atmosphere, preferably under glass or plastic. Leaf bud cuttings, often used for camellias, blackberries and rhododendrons, consist of a bud sliced from a stem ½ inch below and ½ inch above the bud, in a very shallow slice. These, too, are grown in a moist, warm, humid medium.

Hardwood Cuttings: The same is true of hardwood cuttings, from deciduous woody plants, which are sometimes almost impossible to root unless they are more or less continually under a mist spray. They are made during the dormant period from the ripe wood of the past season's growth or from two- and sometimes even three-year growth. The pieces taken vary from four (for most shrubs) to 30 inches long (for grafting stock) and should contain at least two nodes. They are buried well into the rooting medium, sometimes in bundles and sometimes in lines in a trench. They are also sometimes stored in moist peat moss or sand for the winter to promote a good callus before planting.

Best results can be expected from cuttings taken from the outside branches or shoots of plants grown in the full sun; from pieces of stem near the basal part of the branch where most food is stored; from shoots not in flower or nonflowering shoots; and from those with internode lengths of average size, not too long or too short. The plant should of course be disease-free, never have been injured by frost or drought and never defoliated by insects. The basal cut is made just below a node and

To root hardwood cuttings, tie them in bundles and store them at 45°F. (7.22°C.) in a rooting medium of sand or peat moss.

the top cut about ½ to one inch above a node, and the diameter of the stem can be anywhere from ¼ inch to one or even two inches.

Three types of hardwood cuts are made: a straight cut, of the chosen stem with no old wood attached; a heel cut, with only a small piece of the older wood attached to the cutting; and a mallet cut, with a short section of old wood taken on either side of the stem.

Sometimes to help promote callus, hardwood cuttings are buried horizontally or even upside down, especially if stored over the winter not in soil but in peat moss or sand or sawdust. But whichever way hardwood cuttings are handled, they must produce roots before leaves, or they will die. The buds are held back by cool temperatures and reduced moisture. Some plants, such as apple and pear, may benefit from bottom heat (65 to 70°F. [18.33

to 21.11°C.]) for about one month before they are set out. If the tops are kept in cool air, the cuttings will develop more callus and, hence, more roots.

Hardwood cuttings from conifers such as tall junipers, spruce and hemlocks are cut from the previous year's growth in the straight, heel or mallet form, and put at once in a greenhouse or other humid enclosure with bright light and heat of at least 60°F. (15.56°C.). These cuttings should be four to eight inches long and stripped of all lower needles. Yews and false cypress may be started from cuttings of the current year's growth, but with a heel of older wood.

Semihardwood Cuttings: These are taken from branches or shoots that are almost, but not quite, ripe. They are best cut in July, August or September, and are especially successful for such plants as hydrangeas, spireas, roses, cotoneasters, and evergreen azaleas as well as some conifers. These cuttings usually root in from five to 25 weeks (as compared to two to six weeks for softwood cuttings). Semihardwood cuttings are often potted up so they can be forced in the greenhouse.

Root Cuttings: Pieces of root taken from young stock in late winter or early spring, or from house plants at the time of repotting, are used to propagate plants at a time when roots are still well supplied with food before the new growth starts in the spring. Oriental poppies, however, are propagated this way in midsummer while they are still dormant. The pieces can be as small as three inches long, but should be from the larger roots of the plant. When putting the cut pieces in the ground, place the end up which was nearest the plant, and place it so that it is almost up to the soil surface. Especially successful as root cuttings are those plants which have adventitious buds appearing

Root cuttings should be taken from young stock in late winter or early spring. Here, pieces are being cut from the largest roots of a French tarragon plant.

naturally on them, such as raspberries. Bundles of root pieces of some fruit trees are laid horizontally in damp sand, and held over to be planted in the spring, but the shoots that arise should be cut back to one. Root cuttings of various perennials and alpines are started in sandy compost, covered with ½ inch of the soil and grown in greenhouses until the shoots are large enough to be transplanted to the garden. Most plants will come true from root cuttings and be like the parent plant, though a few variegated ones, such as variegated geraniums, will come green and not variegated.

See also DIVISION, LAYERING, PROPAGATION.

CUTWORM

These plump, smooth, variously colored worms attack a number of garden plants.

Young crops may be eaten off at the soil line, while larger plants suffer from serious losses of foliage area. Cutworms burrow down several inches into the soil to pupate, and grow to be night-flying moths. When disturbed, they typically coil themselves up.

To discourage moths from laying eggs in the garden, see that it is kept free of weeds and grass, especially in the fall months. A three-inch-high collar of cardboard or tar paper is an effective barrier; it should be pushed an inch into the ground. A ring of wood ashes should work, too. If you tie the stems of wild onions around vegetables, cutworms should be no problem. Sunflowers serve as a trap crop, and tansy repels the worms. Toads and chickens are partial to cutworms.

See also INSECT CONTROL.

CYCLAMEN

These are southern European (France to Greece and Syria) members of the Primrose family. Florists' cyclamen (*Cyclamen persicum giganteum*) is well known for its succulent, heart-shaped, bluish leaves traced with silver and elegant, nodding flowers in hues of white, salmon, rose, and red. There are also hardier species which deserve to be better known in the outdoor garden.

Because of its requirements for cool temperatures (45°F. [7.22°C.] at night and 55 to 60°F. [12.78 to 15.56°C.] days) and high humidity, the florists' cyclamen is not a good plant for most homes. A cool greenhouse or partially heated breezeway or sunroom is needed. Soil should be rich in humus and kept evenly moist. Avoid splashing water in the crown, since this can cause rot. An eastern, western or lightly shaded southern exposure is

Although several hardy and half-hardy varieties exist, the most common cyclamen in this country is Cyclamen persicum, *a florists' species which is grown from seed in warm, moist greenhouses.*

good. If conditions are optimal, flowers will continue for three months or longer. Spent flowers should be removed. If conditions are poor, yellow leaves and withered buds will result. When flowers are finished, reduce water and store the plant in a cool place (cellar or north side of the house outdoors) until late summer. At that time repot it and resume watering. Beware of frosts, since these plants

are susceptible. If placed in a cool greenhouse in early October, Christmas floral displays are possible. Cyclamens are propagated from seed and require about 18 months until they reach blooming size.

Good varieties of the florists' cyclamen include Bonfire, Candlestick, Pearl of Zehlendorf, Rococo, and Rose of Marienthal. Some hardy species for the outdoor garden are Sicily cyclamen (*C. cilicium*), European cyclamen (*C. europaeum*), Neapolitan cyclamen (*C. neapolitanum*), *C. coum,* and *C. c. alba.*

See also HOUSE PLANTS.

CYMBIDIUM

Among the most decorative of epiphytic orchids, these produce slender, straplike leaves and long-lasting sprays of flowers that are often two to three feet long. Cymbidiums prefer a soil composed of osmunda fiber, peat moss and leaf mold and a minimum temperature of about 50°F. (10°C.) during the winter. The roots should never be dry, and the plant should not receive strong sunlight after early spring.

See also ORCHIDS.

CYPRESS VINE *See* STAR-GLORY

D

DAFFODIL (*Narcissus*)

Daffodils, as well as all of the hardy bulbs, require an interval of low temperature during their dormant period before they will flower properly. That is why they must be planted in late September or October.

Daffodils are hungry plants and thus fast growers. Before planting, spade the soil to about 12 to 18 inches and incorporate generous amounts of compost and well-rotted manure. Peat moss or leaf mold may be applied liberally in sandy soil, and heavy clay soils should be loosened by working in sand and humus material, such as compost. These bulbs are very intolerant of raw manure, so be sure it is well composted.

Set the bulbs about six inches deep and six to eight inches apart. It is better to plant deep than too shallow, since the latter results in dwarfed plants. Be sure to press the flattened base of the bulb firmly into contact with the soil beneath it as air spaces will delay the formation of roots or may allow rotting of the bulb to take place. The roots must be well established before hard frost.

Most bulb plantings do not require a winter cover, but in areas where winters are severe it is wise to mulch with straw, leaves, grass clippings, or pine boughs. Remove the cover early in the spring so you'll let the small plants poking through have a breath of spring air. As with all the spring bulbs, let the foliage ripen naturally. They need to store energy for next year's array of bloom.

Location: Scatter the bulbs at random and plant them where they fall. Of course they look lovely in more formal beds, too, but keep them in clumps or groups, not in rows. Once planted, daffodils may remain four to five years before you need to replant them. Be sure they get a topdressing of compost each year to insure a good display of flowers. When the

To insure an excellent display of large, spring flowers, plant daffodil bulbs deeply and dress them with compost every year.

plantings become too crowded and blooms are small, it is time to dig up the bulbs, separate them, enrich the soil, and replant.

Varieties: The type and forms available are varied and numerous. If you are interested in the double-flowered varieties, try planting Mary Copeland or Texas. Some of the single-flowered varieties are King Alfred, Golden Harvest and Carlton. There are also bicolor varieties which are very attractive, such as Spring Glory, Geranium and Dick Wellband.

See also BULB, FORCING, NARCISSUS.

DAHLIA

Tuberous perennials of the Compositae, dahlias bloom in autumn and come in a vast range of colors and forms. They make excellent cut flowers.

Dahlias do best in a sunny spot sheltered from the wind with rich, well-drained loam.

Plant tubers outdoors in the spring after danger of frost has passed. In most sections of the country this will be early May. Allow 2½ feet of space each way between the large flowering varieties and about two feet between the Pompons. If the tubers are large, dig a hole, ten inches deep; for smaller tubers, six inches is enough. Make the hole wide enough so that the tuber can be placed in it in a horizontal position. Never place the root on end. If the soil is dry at planting time, it must be well watered. The roots should then be covered with a few inches of fine soil, so that the crown is just below the soil surface.

The small dahlias can be grown as annuals, easily producing masses of brilliantly colored single and double flowers in one season. Plant seed outdoors within a week or two of the last frost. The seed will not germinate well if the weather is cool, but if you delay planting too long, you will also delay flowering. In the garden, sow seeds thinly in rows 12 inches apart. When the seeds germinate, they should be thinned to stand ten to 12 inches apart. For the longest possible blooming season, start seed indoors at a constant temperature of 70 to 75°F. (21.11 to 23.89°C.) six to eight weeks before the last frost. Transplant the seedlings to three-inch peat pots when they develop their first set of true leaves. Do not discard the smaller seedlings, as these often produce the best-colored flowers. You can dig the tubers of the best plants after frost and save them for the next year. Dahlia seed sown in December in the greenhouse can produce flowering plants in time for Mother's Day.

Dahlias should grow and branch naturally, but one main stem is likely to branch and provide enough of the best-quality flowers. When additional sprouts come from the root they should be eliminated by pinching. Pinch out the top two pairs of leaves as soon as four pairs are formed and allow three or four stalks to develop. Staking will be necessary when the stems are ten to 12 inches high. Use a soft but strong string—binder twine is good—tying tightly to the stake and loosely around the plant. Further support should be given to every 18 inches of growth.

Disbudding should begin July 10 to 20. Best flowers result when side branches and flower buds are removed, leaving only the strongest terminal bud and perhaps a branch at the lower end of the stem. Never disbud every branch of a plant at one time, but stagger the operation by stretching it over two or three weeks. Small bedding dahlias do not need disbudding.

Mulching will provide the even temperature at the roots that dahlias enjoy. A mulch three inches deep will also keep weeds in check

Whether grown from seed as an annual or from tubers as a perennial, dahlias furnish a vast array of colorful cut flowers throughout the summer and early fall.

healthier, more vigorous growth. Five pounds of bone meal mixed with ten of wood ashes may be raked deeply into the surface after spring spading or plowing. Top-dress in summer with rich compost and, in dry regions, apply a three-inch mulch.

After the tops are killed by the first heavy frost, the clumps should be dug. Cut the tops off three or four inches above the ground level. Let the tubers ripen in the ground for about one week. When you are ready to lift them, loosen the soil all around and under the clumps so that it may be lifted without breaking off any of the tubers. A tuber with a broken neck is useless for planting again and should be discarded.

Let the clump dry in the sun and air for a few days. Place under cover for continued drying. There is no need to remove any adhering soil as this will help to keep the roots plump. Spread a two-inch layer of dry sand in the bottom of a box, place the roots on top and then fill with sand until at least three inches cover the clumps. Store the boxes in a cool, frostproof cellar. Examine the roots from time to time to check for shriveling; any shriveled clumps should be placed in moist peat moss or between layers of wet newspapers for a few days to restore moisture. Repack as before.

Two or three weeks before your outdoor planting time, put the roots on damp paper, moss, sand, or soil in the light. If no shoots appear, sprinkle every day with water to encourage the eyes to swell. Separate the clumps so that each piece of crown has an eye on it. A root without an eye will not grow.

There are several types and many colors of dahlias to choose from and growers' catalogs should be consulted for specific varieties. Popular choices are Cactus, Decorative, Peony, and Pompon. Those varieties commonly

and help preserve needed moisture. An occasional thorough soaking is important during extended dry periods, because once dahlias dry out it is very difficult to bring them back into growth and flowering. As soon as terminal buds are set, give each plant about three gallons of diluted compost tea, applied when the soil is wet.

Bone meal is valuable for its phosphorous compounds and can be recommended as safe and effective. While most soils are rated as well supplied with potash, it has been found that applications of wood ashes bring a

planted from seed are Unwins Dwarf Hybrid, Coltness Hybrid and Mignon Mixed. The new variety Redskin, an All-America winner, produces plants with bronze foliage which contrasts beautifully with the single and double flowers in all dahlia colors. This is an outstanding bedding variety.

See also PERENNIALS.

DAISY

Λ common term for members of the Compositae, the word daisy was originally

One of the most popular daisies, Chrysanthemum frutescens *is extremely valuable as a perpetually blooming potted or garden plant.*

applied only to *Bellis perennis,* the English daisy of literature and poetry fame. Today the term has come to be applied to many other plants, including the chrysanthemum, arctotis, aster, rudbeckia, and townsendia.

Some daisies are favorites in the garden, while others are perennial weeds. They do best in cool, moist locations when used as borders or edging plants.

See also ASTER, CHRYSANTHEMUM, ENGLISH DAISY, RUDBECKIA.

DALEA

Daleas are relatively little-known perennials with flowers ranging in color from white to purple. Though they grow mostly in the dry soils of prairie lands, some species have been grown as border plants or cultivated in greenhouses as house plants.

DAMPING-OFF

Damping-off describes the wilting and early death of young seedlings; it is caused by parasitic fungi living in or near the surface of the soil. Crowding of seedlings, high humidity and lack of sufficient aeration all favor damping-off. Remedial measures include ensuring proper ventilation, drying the soil in which the seedlings are growing, and sprinkling powdered charcoal or finely pulverized clay on the ground.

Damping-off can be prevented by providing seed flats with proper drainage, sowing the seeds in equal parts of compost and sand, covering the seeds with pulverized, heated clay, and keeping the young seedlings in a cool, well-ventilated, well-lighted place.

DANDELION   (*Taraxacum officinale*)

Well known as a yellow, toothy-leaved perennial weed, dandelion is seldom recognized as a nutritional foodstuff or medicinal herb. Its shiny green leaves form a puffy rosette mounted on a short stem. The long taproot makes eradication difficult. The main flower stalks are hollow and smooth, and flower heads are yellow and one to two inches wide. Dandelion fruits are olive or yellow and placed on a long beak which holds a cluster of white hairs. These hairs disperse the fruit in the breeze, each fruit containing one seed. All parts of the plant contain a milky juice.

The name dandelion stems from the French *dent de lion* (lion's tooth). The jagged leaves or gold hue of the plant may have led to this name. The wide distribution of the herb was once considered a sign—in keeping with the ancient Doctrine of Signatures—that dandelion was a panacea for most illnesses. The plants have long been cultivated and processed in Europe and Asia as a digestive aid, blood cleanser, treatment for dropsy, and even an aid in liver ailments. Chinese medicine today uses the plant as a tonic and digestive aid. It was commonly ground up and applied to snakebites. While the medicinal properties of dandelion go unnoticed by most Americans, recent herbals do recommend it as a mild laxative.

Few gardeners or herbalists cultivate dandelions, since the weed is commonly found growing wild among grasses and fields throughout the country. Dandelions grow well in any good soil. The seed is planted in spring in rows 18 inches apart and covered ½ inch deep. The seedlings are thinned to stand one foot apart in the row. The crop should be well cultivated and kept free from weeds. The roots are dug in the fall of the second season. They are washed and dried whole, or cut into pieces three to six inches long and the larger portions sliced. A serious objection of growing this crop is the danger of seeding adjacent land with an undesirable weed. Best control is digging out and cultivating regularly.

Aside from its medicinal properties already described, the dandelion is also a nutritial plant. It is higher in vitamin A than most herbs, and at least four times higher in vitamin C than lettuce. Dandelion has more iron than spinach, and is rich in potassium. Its bitter leaves can be cooked as a potherb, boiled or steamed like spinach or served in a salad. Dandelion roots can be roasted and made into a coffeelike beverage, and dandelion wine is still a favorite in many parts of the country.

See also HERB, LAWN, WEEDS.

DAPHNE

A genus of small evergreen and deciduous shrubs, daphnes have handsome foliage and numerous white, rose or lilac purple flowers that bloom in spring. Berries can be white or red.

Daphnes should be planted in partial shade, in a moist well-drained loam enriched with leaf mold. Propagation is by layers, cuttings or seed sown in summer.

The rose daphne (*D. Cneorum*), sometimes known as the garland flower, is one of the best-known varieties. It is a low, bushy, evergreen shrub which produces masses of rose-colored flowers in May. Propagation is easily accomplished through cuttings taken in mid-autumn, by simply layering trailing branches, or by mound-layering the ascending stems.

The upright *D. odora* is a highly fragrant evergreen bearing clusters of red purple flowers. It grows to six feet but is sometimes kept to pot size.

DARLING PEA   *See* SWAINSONIA

DARLINGTONIA

Often referred to as the cobra orchid and as *Chrysamphora,* the darlingtonia is an insectivorous plant that reaches a height of between one and three feet. It appears as a group of erect, tubular leaves ranging from ½ inch at the base to four inches at the spotted hood, which very much resembles the head of a cobra. The perennial root produces from five to nine tubes every year.

Underneath this hooded head is a rounded opening or small mouth, about ¾ inch in diameter, from which hangs a pair of tentacles similar to a moustache. Each tentacle is about three inches long. They sit at the entrance to the mouth and move with the slightest breeze. As the plant matures, this appendage becomes bright red. It seems to attract insects by its shimmering, iridescent glow and perhaps by some odor.

Insects in large numbers enter the opening, the inside of which is smooth and offers no foothold. Slipping into the plant's tube, the insect's descent is hastened by very fine hairs along the walls. These hairs all run downward, making escape impossible.

To grow darlingtonias, seeds should be sown in April or May on fresh sphagnum moss scattered over a mixture of sharp sand and peat. This seed-starting medium should be set where it will be partly in water all the time and covered with a bell jar or glass. It is important that it be maintained at a cool, moist, even temperature—at 50 to 60°F. (10 to 15.56°C.) for best results. Adding a bit of finely ground charcoal to the medium will prevent souring of the soil. The seed is not hard-coated but soft and fluffy, and germination should take place in 14 to 21 days. Plants can also be started from divisions or side shoots inserted in small pots at almost any time of the year.

Keep the plants away from the direct sun and simulate their native habitat as much as possible. *D. californica,* known as the California pitcher plant, grows in an acid moss with a pH of 5 or lower and needs a great deal of water. To supply the necessary moisture during the hot summer months, daily syringing will probably be necessary from March through September.

DATE   (*Phoenix dactylifera*)

The delicious fruit of the date palm has been a source of nutrition for desert peoples for thousands of years. In the United States, dates flourish in Arizona and California, where the temperatures are high and the climate is arid. Although the first plantations in this country were attempted in Florida, they were less successful than the plantings in the Southwest.

Culture: The suckers which form at the base of the palm tree are the source of new plantings. These suckers should be removed gradually. Only three, three- to six-year-old suckers are taken from one plant in a season.

Dates are dioecious and require a planting of a male tree for every 100 females. Pollination must be performed by hand. One method of pollinating is to make a hole in the female bud and insert a piece of the pollen-producing inflorescence in it. Another common way is to tie a piece of the male inflorescence beside the female cluster. Pollination takes from four to six days after the female flower opens.

Suckers should be set out 30 feet apart in their permanent positions and should be well headed back. Female plants begin to bear in five or six years and will bear up to 200 pounds of fruit after they are ten to 15 years old.

To enrich the sandy soil preferred by dates, a cover crop of clover can be planted and turned under. Channels can be dug between the rows of the palms and filled with the big date leaves and other trimmings. The rich organic compost helps the plants produce large, healthy fruit. Dates require frequent and plentiful waterings (every seven to ten days) until they begin to approach maturity, when water should be applied less frequently.

Harvest: When the fruit reaches ½ to ¾ inch long, they are thinned out for better size and quality. Each cluster should then be covered with paper protectors to spare the fruit from inclement weather.

The three cultivars of dates grown in the United States are the Deglet Noor, Khadrawy and Halawy. The Khadrawy is the earliest, bearing from September to January.

Dates are high in calcium, 105 mg., and vitamin A, 90 mg.

DATE PALM   *See* PALM

DAVIS, ADELLE

(1904–1974) Best known for her attempts to educate the layman in the ways of nutrition, Adelle Davis is also remembered for her aggressive and often controversial stands against the refined food industry, the medical profession, food additives, pesticides, and a host of other agents she felt were undermining the health of the American people. Though often criticized for printing theories of nutrition that were yet unproven, her four best-selling books (*Let's Cook It Right, Let's Have Healthy Children, Let's Eat Right to Keep Fit,* and *Let's Get Well*) are generally considered authoritative and straightforward.

Formally trained as a dietician, Davis spent the early years of her career planning corrective diets for the patients of physicians with whom she worked in New York and California. She later opened her own consulting practice, devising diets for over 20,000 persons with all kinds of ailments. Though recognizing the necessity of occasional medical treatment, Davis believed that many diseases and common complaints were the result of poor dietary habits, and could therefore be cured or alleviated by correcting the diet rather than resorting to pharmaceutical drugs. These, she felt, too often robbed the body of vitamins and minerals essential to full recuperation.

DAYLILY   (*Hemerocallis*)

Daylilies are perennial plants belonging to the genus *Hemerocallis,* which is a Greek word meaning "beautiful for a day." Each blossom stays open only one day before fading, but because each plant can produce many flowers, there is a long blooming season. By selecting early, midseason and late-blooming varieties, the gardener can have daylilies in bloom from spring until frost.

Daylilies have long, leafless flower stems and narrow, grasslike basal leaves, which are attractive all season. Flowers range from solid colors of yellow, melon, orange, pink, red, and purple to those with two contrasting colors and to those called "diamond dusted." The petals of these are covered with minute particles which reflect light and give the flowers a faint glitter. Flower size ranges from less than three inches across in the miniatures to more than eight inches across in the spider types with their widely flaring petals. The plants vary in height from 15 inches to four feet. Daylilies with evergreen foliage are hardy in northern states only with elaborate protection; with so many reliably hardy varieties to choose from, northern gardeners might do well to ignore these.

Daylilies require far less care and feeding than most other flowers. All soils suit them except those that are extremely dry. They do best in well-drained soils enriched with organic matter. Dig in one or two inches of compost or leaf mold when preparing new beds, and top-dress old plants with an inch of the same material every year or two. This will keep them blooming well indefinitely. Unless the plants are in competition with shallow-rooted trees, avoid heavy or supplemental feedings, as very rich soil induces lush foliage growth at the expense of flowers. Daylilies do as well in full sun as in light shade. In hot summer areas, part shade may be preferable, especially for pastel varieties whose color can burn out in full sun. Daylilies will not bloom in full shade, but the foliage will endure.

Spacing of plants can vary under different conditions. If they are set one foot apart in beds by themselves, the clumps will quickly grow together and suppress all weeds. Give them two feet of space in a mixed border or they will soon begin to crowd their neighbors.

It is usually not necessary to lift and divide daylilies for at least five years. Beds that still bloom well after 15 years are not uncommon, but if flower production falls off or the daylilies begin to crowd out other plants, they should be dug up and divided. This should be done in spring. Lift a clump and drive two spading forks first toward each other, then away from each other, continuing this motion until the clump has been pried in two. The tightly entangled roots sustain less damage this way than if the clumps are cut apart with a spade. The subdivisions can be further divided using a hand fork. Dig in plenty of organic matter to recondition the soil before replanting, and set the crowns one inch below the surface.

About the only annual maintenance chore involved in growing daylilies is cutting off the stems after the flowers have faded. This improves the appearance of the plants for the rest of the season. Because they require so little maintenance to produce such a long show in the garden, daylilies are all but indispensable to gardeners who have little time to spend caring for their flowers. Those varieties which open or stay open in the evening are especially valuable to gardeners who must be away from home all day. Many of the hybrid cultivars bloom in spring and again in fall months, which can be colorless months in the perennial garden. These versatile plants may be naturalized on dry rocky slopes and banks of streams or ponds, or they can be used as accent plants in shrub borders or hedgerows.

Most nurseries offer a large selection of daylilies, and many specialize in them. They can usually be bought most inexpensively direct from the hybridizer or specialist. Because of the great number of named varieties available, it can be difficult to choose those which are most appealing or superior. The American Hemerocallis Society makes this often pleasant chore easier by publishing the results of their Popularity Poll each year. Daylily fanciers across the country send in lists of their favorite varieties, and the results are tabulated according to region. Write the American Hemerocallis Society, Signal Mountain, TN 37377, for more information. A variety which has won the society's Stout Medal can be recommended for any garden. Sizable collections can be built up using only Stout Medal winners from previous years. Many older varieties are just as satisfactory as new introductions, and far less expensive.

DDT
See CHLORINATED HYDROCARBONS

DEATH CAMAS
See ZIGADENUS

DELPHINIUM

Widely distributed throughout the Northern Hemisphere, this genus of annual, biennial and perennial herbs of the Buttercup family has palmately lobed or divided leaves and spikes of showy flowers that are long lasting when cut.

They are closely related to the annual larkspur (*Consolida*) and are often classified as such.

The pioneer work in the development of the garden delphinium was done in England during the first quarter of this century. In that country's climate, delphiniums are hardy, long-lived perennials which are not especially difficult to grow. They prefer pleasantly warm summer days and cool, humid summer nights. In areas of the United States with that sort of climate—notably the cool northern Pacific coast and parts of New England—delphiniums are reliably perennial. In some parts of the U.S., especially those areas having long periods in summer when both days and nights stay hot, they may produce too many flowers each season, and thereby exhaust themselves in a short time. In these regions plants may be especially susceptible to such diseases as black spot and crown rot. Consequently, they require special care. Their spectacular bloom makes them worth the effort. Delphiniums usually bloom well for only two or three years, so it is wise to grow some new replacement plants each year from seed. Many gardeners in hot-summer areas grow delphiniums as annuals and sow fresh seed each year. Delphiniums do not always breed true to type, so buy seed from a seedsman and don't bother sowing any from homegrown plants if you wish to duplicate a particular color.

Seeding: Seed may be sown indoors in January or February or outdoors in May or June. In areas having long, mild autumns, the most successful sowings are those made outdoors or in cold frames in late summer. Delphinium seed loses its viability very soon and most authorities recommend storing it at extremely low temperatures. Keep the seed flat at about 50°F. (10°C.) until germination occurs. Some home gardeners find that seed germinates well at temperatures ranging from 60 to 70°F. (15.56 to 21.11°C.). The germinating medium should be porous and well drained. Vermiculite or fine sphagnum moss can be mixed with soil, which must be sterilized as a precaution.

Indoors, seed may be planted either in flats or directly into three-inch peat pots. Germination can take from ten to 20 days. Seedlings grown in flats should be transplanted to stand at least three inches apart when true leaves appear, and set out in the border after the last frost. Some gardeners assert that frequent transplanting insures a stronger root system. Seedlings grown in peat pots can be set directly in their permanent places after frost without intermediate transplanting. Plants started early indoors often bloom in fall of the same year.

When sowing outdoors in May or June, use a cold frame or a protected, raised seedbed containing finely prepared soil. Good drainage is essential, but do not allow the seed to dry out. To maintain proper moisture, a piece of damp burlap can be laid on the seedbed until germination occurs. Slugs and snails are major enemies of delphiniums at all stages of growth. Surround the seedling rows with wood ashes or sharp sand, or sow in a flat which can be placed on inverted flowerpots surrounded with ashes. Thin or transplant the seedlings to nursery rows and protect them from hot, drying sun for several days. They can be wintered in the rows protected by an airy mulch like hay and transplanted to the border in early spring of the following year, or they can be moved to their permanent places in very early fall if there is enough time for them to get established before heavy frost. Seed can also be sown in early fall for blossoms the following season.

Asexual Propagation: Because delphiniums are so short-lived in most of the United States, it is most practical to propagate them from seed. Gardeners who are able to grow them as true perennials may wish to increase their stock of a favored plant. This can be done only by taking cuttings or dividing the roots. Old plants may need dividing after four years to rejuvenate them.

The best cuttings consist of young shoots severed from the crown of the plant in the spring. These cuttings should be taken when the shoots are about three inches long, taking care to get a small piece of the crown with each piece. As a rooting medium, use clean sand or vermiculite. Put the flats or pots of cuttings in plastic bags and keep them out of direct sun. Use short stakes to prevent the plastic from touching the leaves. Try to maintain an even temperature of 65 to 70°F. (18.33 to 21.11°C.). Rooting requires from four to eight weeks. Rooted cuttings should be transplanted in much the same way as seedlings.

Division is best done in autumn or early spring. Lift the old plant from the ground, remove all old and decayed parts, and divide the plant into a number of parts, each having one or two strong crowns and an ample supply of healthy roots. Replant at the same depth the plant grew before.

Planting: Delphiniums require extremely high fertility to produce the best flowers. When starting a new bed, dig or till-in four inches of well-rotted compost or manure supplemented with bone meal, phosphate rock and granite dust or greensand at the rate of about one pound each per 100 square feet. Do this several months before planting to give the soil a

Immediately after delphiniums complete their first flowering, cut back the blooming stalks to the first major leaves. Fertilize the plants and, in six to eight weeks, they will bloom again.
(*Courtesy of Jackson & Perkins Co.*)

them with clean, sharp sand. The sand will help discourage slugs and snails, and either method helps to prevent crown rot by insuring good drainage. It is a good idea to put ashes around the crowns in winter as a further deterrent to slugs, which may start to feed on them earlier in the year than the gardener realizes. Protect delphiniums in winter by covering them with an airy mulch like evergreen boughs or coarse hay after the ground has frozen solid. This is only really necessary with young plants. Established plants are tougher—delphiniums are more intolerant of summer heat than of winter cold.

When growth resumes in spring, feed each plant a handful of any balanced organic fertilizer, and give additional feedings of compost tea each week until they bloom. Avoid high nitrogen fertilizers like blood meal and leather dust and emphasize those high in phosphate and potassium. Add limestone to maintain a moderately high pH. When the plants have finished blooming, cut them back to within 12 inches of the ground to induce new growth for the fall flowering. Plug the cut ends of the hollow stems with clay, wax or mud to prevent water getting in and rotting the crowns. (There is no cure for crown rot, only prevention. Once it starts, destroy the plant and begin again.) When new growth is six inches high, cut all old stems off at the ground.

Black spot may infect the leaves in summer. Good air circulation helps control it, but in problem areas the plants may have to be dusted with sulfur.

Varieties: The most spectacular and popular delphiniums are tall sorts like the Pacific Giant hybrids, the Blackmore and Langdon hybrids and the Wrexham hybrids. They grow four to six feet tall and have single or double flowers closely spaced on long spikes.

chance to settle and assimilate these ingredients. When planting them in an established flower bed, dig a generous hole and mix the fertilizers in the bottom where the roots can reach for them and put ordinary topsoil around the crown. It should be neutral to slightly acid (pH 6.5). The site should be in full sun (except in southern zones), have protection from wind and be well drained. Either place the crowns at the soil surface and mound two inches of soil over them, or place them two inches below ground level and fill in around

Colors include all shades of blue, the favorite delphinium color, as well as white and shades of lavender to pink. Many have a center or "bee" of a contrasting color. These plants should be spaced two or three feet apart in groups of three, and all must be staked to prevent the hollow stems from breaking in wind or rain. Use six-foot stakes and push them at least a foot into the ground. Either use one per stem or set three stakes around each plant and wind string around them. Begin tying when growth reaches 12 inches, and tie again with each subsequent foot of growth. To get the largest flower spikes, thin each plant to three stems. The fewer stems, the fewer stakes will have to be set.

D. x *belladonna* types are shorter than the giants and branch freely. They grow three or four feet tall with many short flower spikes. They also need staking, but are said to be easier to grow than their taller relatives. *D.* x *belladonna* cv. 'Cliveden Beauty' is sky blue and three feet tall. Bellamosum is dark blue and Casa Blanca is all white. Space them two feet apart.

The new Connecticut Yankee delphiniums are among the easiest to grow. They reach 2½ feet and branch heavily. Staking is not essential. The many flower spikes have loosely spaced, mostly single blooms in several shades of blue and white. Mass them for best effect, and space 18 to 24 inches apart.

D. grandiflorum is the shortest of the group, growing 1½ to three feet tall and branching lightly. Blue Mirror is deep blue, Cambridge Blue is light blue and *D. g.* cv. 'Album' is white. Grown as perennials, many varieties will bloom continuously from June through August. Space 12 to 18 inches apart in the border.

DEPARTMENT OF AGRICULTURE
See GOVERNMENT SERVICES

DERRIS   *See* ROTENONE

DESERT GARDEN

Desert conditions are all extremes: dry air, temperatures which may fluctuate 50 degrees in 24 hours, and an almost continuous growing season with little moisture except during the brief rainy spell, when rain is likely to be measured in inches daily. Despite these adverse conditions, many plants can be grown in the desert, with the exception of shade- and moisture-lovers like begonias. Desert gardeners have to work harder than those on the coast; special preparation is essential to overcome desert conditions. The most basic prerequisites are windbreaks, water and soil building.

Windbreaks: For most desert gardens a windbreak of some sort is a must as protection against the hot, drying summer winds. A hedge, fence or building can serve as a windbreak and may also offer some protection against the searing sun. Take care not to rely on a building for wind and sun protection when in actuality the structure reflects heat and sun onto the garden.

Water: Water is the most essential element of growth. If possible, an irrigation system should be planned along with the garden. Use of both mulch and windbreaks will help to conserve precious moisture. Desert gardeners should mulch with whatever material is available—grass clippings, weeds, straw, hay, coffee grounds, wood chips, newspaper, corn husks, aged sawdust, even stones. Try to have four or more inches of mulch on the garden by the time the plants mature. If the wind disturbs the mulch too much, weight it down with boards or rocks. In addition to conserving moisture and cutting down on the water bill, the mulch will constantly add much needed humus to the soil as it gradually decays. It will also serve to insulate plant roots from the tremendous fluctuations of heat and cold.

Soil Improvement: As a general rule, desert soils are sandy and gravelly with an organic matter content between ½ and 1½ percent. In some places the blowing of the wind clears off the topsoil to leave an accumulation of pebbles and stones which is known as the desert pavement. Humus is sorely needed by desert soils, and it's advisable to start a compost pile along with a garden, if not before, and to use all organic matter available to enrich the soil.

Dig a few test holes to check the depth of the buried stones and pebbles. Sometimes desert soils contain too many stones to be power-tilled and must be spaded or plowed. Just before the rainy season begins cover the desert pavement with manure, compost, partially decayed leaves, straw, and other organic materials. After four or five inches of strong rain most of the organic matter should be working itself down into the soil. Add more organic matter as this material decays in order to build up a deep mulch.

In working with desert soils, assume they are alkaline. The soil may be so alkaline that its surface has powderings of white. If so, it may be advisable to scrape away the top inch or two and replace it with a soil hauled in from higher elevations, preferably an acid soil. Since alkaline soils tend to be light and loose, try to incorporate a heavier soil. A certain amount of light gravel in the top few inches would help to stabilize the soil and inhibit its crusting characteristics.

The best way to lower alkaline pH is to work in as much green matter as can be found. If possible, grow a cover crop and turn it under. Use every possible resource to find more organic material. To decay, organic materials require nitrogen and nitrogen-fixing bacteria. Therefore, work in generous amounts of cottonseed meal or manure, especially chicken manure. Blood meal or fish meal would also be very helpful. If these applications are timed to take advantage of the rainy season, all the better. Organic matter cannot decay without moisture.

If starting a new garden, get as much information from local sources as possible. Become acquainted with the advantages and disadvantages of the area. With plenty of work and organic matter, desert gardens can produce many vegetables and fruits abundantly, including cool-weather lovers like broccoli. But, desert dwellers should not overlook the variety of edibles native to the desert. There are roots growing in the desert that can be cooked like potatoes, fruits that can be eaten raw or in jams and jellies, plants that can be served like spinach greens, and cacti that can be used in a number of ways.

Though desert gardeners can produce a magnificent succession of ornamental blooms with the care and techniques outlined above, the desert itself boasts a multitude of plants of unsurpassed beauty. By capitalizing on the use of plants already adapted to the area's growing conditions, the gardener can have a magnificent show of plants with little more work than is required by gardens in more temperate areas. Desert trees, flowering plants and shrubs, as well as cacti, will respond well to being planted in soil mixed with some humus and an annual application of bone meal, dried manure and compost.

See also ARID CLIMATE, CACTI.

DESIGN, GARDEN
See LANDSCAPING

DEUTZIA

These ornamental deciduous shrubs of the Saxifrage family form clumps of slender, gracefully arching branches that are covered with serrated leaves and panicles of white or pinkish flowers in spring or early summer. Species range in height from three feet (*D. reflexa*) to nine feet (*D. corymbosa*).

Deutzias grow in any well-drained soil, and are easily propagated by cuttings or layers. If potted and brought indoors in late fall, they can be forced into bloom without difficulty.

DEVIL'S CLAW
See UNICORN PLANT

DEVIL'S PITCHFORK
See BEGGAR'S TICKS

DEVIL'S PLAGUE
See QUEEN-ANNE'S-LACE

DEWBERRY
See BLACKBERRY, BRAMBLE FRUITS

DIABASE

Diabase rock is equivalent to basalt and can be used in the same manner.

See also BASALT.

DIANTHUS

A large genus of the Pink family (Caryophyllaceae) which contains many popular garden flowers, dianthus may be divided into three groups: sweet Williams, pinks and carnations. All require full sun and a sharply drained, not too rich soil that has a neutral or slightly alkaline pH.

Sweet William (*D. barbatus*) is an annual or biennial growing to two feet tall with large flower clusters in shades of red, pink or white or combinations of these. The flowers can be single, double or fringed. They bloom heavily in May and June and sometimes intermittently through summer. Though the plants often self-sow, fresh seed should be sown each year to keep new plants coming. Indoors, germination takes four or five days in February; in the cold frame in spring, ten to 15 days. New varieties such as Orchid Lace, Bright Eyes and Red Monarch. Newport Pink, Scarlet Beauty and Wee Willi flower the first year.

Garden pinks are the most cold-hardy perennial forms of dianthus. They will not tolerate very hot summers, so grow them as biennials in the South. The clove-scented flowers can be single, double, fringed, or laciniated and the gray blue, grasslike foliage is occasionally evergreen. These low-growing mats are good choices for the front of the sunny, well-drained border, in the rock garden or on dry slopes. Avoid mulching them, even in winter, as the plants rot easily. An inverted basket may be used in severe winter areas. Propagate from seed sown indoors in February or March, or from cuttings. The following species are most often used: *D. plumarius,* the grass or cottage pink, has red, pink or white flowers rising from almost a foot above a grassy, gray mat.

The small red or pink flowers of *D. deltoides,* the maiden pink, rise nine to 18 inches above low, thick mats.

D. gratianopolitanus, cheddar pink, has gray foliage and pink flowers.

A hybrid between the carnation and the cottage pink, *D. x Allwoodii* retains the dwarf characteristics of the pink and has, under good conditions, the all-summer bloom period of the carnation. It grows to 12 inches and has sweet-scented flowers that are mostly double. *D. alpinus* cv. 'Allwoodii', a six-inch dwarf with single flowers, is fine for the rockery or cascading over low garden walls. Grow these where the carnation is not hardy, since they look like miniature carnations. Propagate from seed or cuttings of favored colors.

The border and florist carnations are different strains of the same species, *D. Caryophyllus.* The hardy border carnation can be grown outdoors as a perennial only in limited areas of the country, as it cannot tolerate extreme cold or humid heat. Propagate by seed sown early indoors so as to get bloom the first year. In fall in the North, pot it up and winter it in the cold frame or take cuttings and root these under glass at 65°F. (18.33°C.), planting them outdoors in spring. These plants are short-lived under the best conditions, so keep new seedlings coming along. Flowers are the familiar sweet-scented double carnations in

red, pink, orange, yellow, lavender, and white on plants growing about a foot tall.

There are many varieties of *D. deltoides* and other perennial pinks which may be grown as annuals, but the most often used annual is *D. chinensis,* rainbow pink. Sow seed indoors in March or outdoors in May. These flower in winter in frost-free areas.

See also CARNATION.

DIATOMACEOUS EARTH

Diatomaceous earth consists of the sedimentary deposits formed from the skeletal remains of a class of algae (Bacillariophyceae) that occur in both salt and fresh water and in soil. These remains form diatomite, an almost pure silica, which is ground into an abrasive dust. When the tiny, razor-sharp particles come in contact with an insect, they cause many tiny abrasions, resulting in loss of body water and death by dehydration.

Diatomaceous earth is the prime ingredient in a variety of insecticide products sold under the name of Perma Guard. It is claimed to be 98 percent repellent to insects, yet free of dangerous residues. It is digestible by earthworms and harmless to mammals and birds.

Application is most effective after a light rain or after plants have been sprayed with a fine mist of water. Dusting should progress upward from the ground, covering all stems and leaves, especially the undersides.

Besides being an effective insecticide, the dust contains 14 beneficial trace minerals in chelated (readily available) form. When the dust is washed off by heavy rains, the minerals are carried down into the soil, where they continue to be effective.

Diatomaceous earth is also a good lawn

fertilizer and insecticide. Applied four times annually at a rate of 25 pounds per 1,500 square feet, it is a potent deterrent to grubs, chinch bugs, cutworms, and other soil insects.

Diatomaceous earth is also the basis of a fossil flower product fed to animals (especially fowl) to control internal parasites and to be applied externally for the control of fleas and other external parasites. Other products for use around the homestead include a septic system activator and a deodorizer used to control odor from fecal and other wastes in barns, kennels, garbage cans, etc. The Agricultural Research Service of the USDA has produced a favorable research report (#1038) on the use of diatomaceous earth in conjunction with grain and seed storage.

DICENTRA

The best known of this plant group is bleeding-heart, *D. spectabilis,* which grows 2½ feet tall and three feet wide, producing pendent pink valentine-shaped flowers along arching stems in May and June. It should be planted in light shade in rich, humusy soil and left undisturbed for many years. The brittle, fleshy roots break easily and divisions may have difficulty reestablishing themselves. The ferny foliage tends to die down in mid- to late summer, especially if the plant is in full sun. Locate it near other plants which will mask the gap left in the border when this happens such as gypsophila, hosta, daylilies, ferns, or annuals. Once established, the bleeding-heart needs no maintenance other than an annual topdressing of compost. Plant in spring.

D. eximia, the wild bleeding-heart, has gray green, finely cut foliage and grows 12 to 18 inches tall. The elongated heart-shaped pink flowers are produced in clusters from May to August. The foliage does not die back early, but the plant is not hardy as far north as *D. spectabilis.* It should be left undisturbed for several years once planted. Give it a rich, well-drained soil in full sun or partial shade and water in dry periods. Bloom period of named varieties of *D. spectabilis* can be extended by picking off the faded flowers. Bountiful has fine blue green leaves and deep pink flowers that bloom heavily in May and autumn and intermittently through the summer. Valentine has near-red flowers with a bloom peak in April or May and intermittent flowering in summer. Zestful has gray green leaves and rose flowers which appear off and on through the summer.

See also BLEEDING-HEART.

DICHONDRA
See GROUND COVERS, LAWN

DIEFFENBACHIA

This genus is commonly called dumb cane, because chewing on it will produce swelling and irritation of the mouth and tongue. Death is possible if swellings cause blockage of the throat air passages. These tropical American members of the Aroid family are very tolerant of average home conditions. Most have attractive large leaves which have speckles or stripes of green, yellow or white.

An all-purpose soil, which is kept evenly moist (not soggy), and an east or west window are fine. Dieffenbachias will occasionally produce flowers similar to those of the wild Jack-in-the-pulpit. Propagation is by air-layering and the remaining stem can be cut into sections to be propagated as bud or eye cuttings in moist sand.

Many fine species are available and include *Dieffenbachia amoena, D. Bowmannii, D. manuculata,* and *D. Seguine.*

DIELDRIN
See Chlorinated Hydrocarbons

DIGITALIS   *See* Foxglove

DILL   (*Anethum graveolens*)

An annual or biennial herb cultivated for the leaves and seeds which are used for flavoring pickles and other foods, dill grows two to three feet tall and has feathery foliage branching off a shiny green main stem. Small clusters of yellow flowers that later develop into seeds form at the tips.

A hardy plant, easily grown from seed in any good garden soil and full sun, dill may be planted in either fall or spring. If planted early in spring, dill will produce seed the same season, but if conditions do not permit prompt germination and rapid early growth, the plants may not reach full development and will produce only a small seed crop. Good results have been obtained by late fall sowing so the seed can germinate in spring as soon as conditions become favorable. The seed is drilled in rows usually one to three feet apart, depending on the method of cultivation to be followed for weed control. The plants must be thinned to between six and 15 inches apart when three inches high. A better seed crop results when the plants are not too crowded.

The progressive ripening of the seed and the tendency of fully ripe seed to shatter present the same difficulties for machine harvesting as in other aromatic seed crops. The best practice seems to be to mow the plants when the earliest seed is ripe. In very dry weather this is preferably done early in the morning when the plants are damp with dew.

In the home garden, dillweed (leaves) should be snipped and frozen in bags. To harvest the seeds, the branches of the plant should be cut before the seeds are completely ripe, tied together and hung indoors upside down until thoroughly dry. They should then be shaken over paper, so the seeds can fall out of their casings. Foreign matter should be

To insure the full development of large seed heads, dill can be planted in late fall for early germination the following spring.

removed, and the seeds stored in airtight containers.

The generic name for this herb was derived from the old Norse *dilla,* to lull, referring to the carminative qualities of dill. In the Middle Ages, dill was believed to protect people from the evils of witchcraft. The herb was most commonly used to ease swellings and pains, digestive gas, and to increase milk in nursing mothers.

Dill is still recognized for its medicinal and culinary qualities. It is used to treat flatulence in infants. Its other medicinal uses are similar to those of fennel. Dill vinegar can be prepared by soaking a few leaves in vinegar for three to four days. Dill is commonly used to flavor cakes and other pastries in many European countries, especially France. In addition, dill leaves can be chopped to mix into soups, salads, cottage cheese, and other dishes.

See also HERB.

DIOECIOUS   *See* UNISEXUAL

DISBUD

In the cultivation of several flowers, especially roses, peonies and dahlias, disbudding means cutting or pinching off the side buds when these first appear, in order to allow all the strength to go to the terminal or main bud so that a larger flower is produced.

DISEASE

A plant disease may be defined as any abnormality in a plant produced by some causative agent. The causative agent may be a bacterium, fungus or other parasitic organism, or it may be some unfavorable environmental condition, such as hail or a deficiency of a nutrient. Nematodes (tiny parasitic worms) are sometimes classified as disease pathogens.

It isn't easy to identify diseases, since the results of infection are more visible than the agents themselves. This makes it easy to confuse the effects of a disease with those brought about by insects or weather.

Viruses cause small yields of poor quality, and some strains can bring a quick death. Mosaic viruses are so called because chlorophyll is destroyed, causing areas of yellowing on leaves. Chlorophyll is needed to manufacture the plant's food. Another kind of virus blocks up a plant's vascular system, restricting the flow of water and nutrients. Conditions known as leaf curl and yellows result, and symptoms may include dwarfing or excessive branching. Methods of control usually involve eliminating the factors that permit viruses to spread. There is little that can be done to restore the health of an afflicted plant.

Bacteria are tiny plants that cause three identifiable sorts of damage: Rots involve the decay of leaves, stems, branches, and tubers; blockage of a plant's vascular system may cause wilting; and galls are the result of an overgrowth of the affected plant's cells. Bacterial problems are encouraged by wet soil, high humidity and high temperatures. Feeding plants with slow-release nutrients will help guard them from disease. Trouble can also be avoided by using disease-free seed and resistant varieties, and by crop rotation. Rogue out infected plants promptly.

Fungi are often visible to the unassisted eye, and fungal diseases are known and named for their appearance. Downy mildew grows from within a plant and sends out branches through the victim's stomata to create pale patches on leaves. Powdery mildews live on the surface, and send hollow tubes into the plant to suck out nutrients. Rust fungi are named for the color their pustules impart to leaves. Leaf spot fungi cause yellow green spots. Soil-inhabiting fungi cause damping-off. Sanitation, roguing of diseased plants and the use of resistant varieties help to prevent fungus diseases from ruining crops. It is often wise to allow space between plants to allow air to circulate between them, as some fungi are encouraged by moisture on foliage.

Nematodes are tiny parasitic worms that effect a slow decline in vigor by sucking plant juices. Control measures involve crop rotation, enriching the soil with humus and planting pest-free stock. Interplanted marigolds exude an underground substance that keeps nematodes away.

Environmental troubles are behind many diseases that growers attribute to pathogens. The vagaries of wind, rain, sunlight, and temperature combine to create such conditions as dieback, blasting, leaf scorch, hollow heart, and sunscald.

Preventing Disease, Organically: For each kind of plant, learn whether it prefers an acid or slightly alkaline soil, a northern or southern exposure, a heavy or light soil, a well-drained or wet soil, a long or short day, a dry or humid atmosphere.

A garden planted to one kind of vegetable and a field planted to one kind of crop are examples of monoculture, a practice which usually is avoided by nature. Out of cultivation, plants grow in mixed cultures—that is, they grow together to form a more or less complex plant society. Our grandmothers' gardens contained vegetables, flowers, herbs, and small fruits, and perhaps, they were damaged less by pests than present-day vegetable gardens in which are grown only a few kinds of plants and no flowers and herbs.

Sanitation is of the utmost importance in the prevention of plant diseases. Diseased plant parts, including stems, leaves and fruits, should be put in the compost heap to be converted into compost.

Crop rotation has been advised for the prevention and control of many plant diseases. If the same crop is grown in the same soil year after year, parasites are likely to accumulate to the point that the crop can no longer be grown successfully. Rotation of crops and change of location are helpful in all cases and indispensable where root knot and root rots are concerned. Tomatoes, melons, okra, and other summer-growing crops should not be grown on the same land more often than once in three years. The land should be devoted to other crops such as corn, grains and early vegetables that are harvested by June. The small garden can be divided into thirds, with summer vegetables susceptible to root diseases grown on a different plot each year.

A soil rich in soil organisms is the best kind of insurance against plant diseases, as it provides conditions favorable to a vigorous growth. Antibiotics produced in living soils help keep crop plants free from disease. A great variety of diseases, such as the root rots of cereals, are more destructive in sterilized soil than in comparable nonsterilized soil, both being equally inoculated with the pathogens. In such experiments, if bits of the original soil are introduced into the sterilized soil, the microflora is quickly reestablished, the pathogen checked and the disease controlled.

The physical condition of the soil has an important bearing on the prevention and control of diseases. Important are such factors as temperature, aeration, moisture, and soil reaction. Some disease-producing organisms attack their host plants in soils of certain temperatures, but not when soils have a different and, apparently for the pathogen, unfavorable temperature. For instance, fusarium yellows typically attacks crucifers in a warm soil only. An entire tomato crop may be destroyed by verticillium wilt in wet soil, while nearby plants grown in well-drained soil are often entirely immune. It has long been recognized that potato scab is less prevalent in soils that have a reaction below 5.2 than in soils with a higher pH value.

Use healthy plants. Many diseases start in young seedlings in greenhouses or plant beds and later cause heavy losses in gardens. One can rarely detect disease at transplanting time. Either grow your own plants, or purchase them from a grower in whom you have complete confidence.

Many vegetable diseases spread from weeds to nearby gardens. Cucumber and muskmelon mosaic may spread from milkweed, pokeweed, ground cherry, and catnip. Tomato mosaic may come from ground cherries, horse nettle, Jimsonweed, nightshade, bittersweet, and matrimony vine. Many cabbage diseases come from wild members of the Cabbage family, such as wild mustard and shepherd's purse.

Cultivate, weed and harvest vegetables when foliage is dry; most disease-causing fungi and bacteria require moisture for their spread from plant to plant. For example, bean blight and anthracnose are easily spread by picking beans when the vines are wet. Any movement of animal or man through wet plants is likely to spread the causal organisms to healthy plants, so it is best not to go to work until well after a rain.

Practice fall cleanup. Most disease-causing organisms can live in the old diseased refuse through winter. When plowed under, they rarely cause disease unless brought to the surface through cultivation. If plowing under is not feasible, rake up old plant parts and discard them well away from the garden.

Control of Some Common Plant Diseases: The actual occurrence of a plant disease is a sure sign that one or more requirements for normal health and growth has not been met completely. The trouble, as a rule, is in the soil and can be corrected, but sometimes the difficulty is environmental.

Asparagus: Remove all badly infested plants to the compost heap to discourage rust. Use rust-resistant varieties.

Bean: Compost all plant material soon after harvest. Select varieties resistant to rust and use a long crop rotation.

Cabbage: Many diseases of cabbage can be avoided by purchasing seed from the Pacific Coast region, where black rot and blackleg are rare. Practice a two- or three-year crop rotation.

Grape: Inspect the vines often and remove any spotted grapes. Discolored or mined leaves should also be removed. Fungi are discouraged by ample air circulation, so prune back excess growth as soon as the fruit has set. Air circulation is also improved by growing vines on a slope.

Pepper: Mosaic is often spread by aphids, so these insects should be controlled. Do not plant peppers next to tomatoes, cucumbers, tobacco, alfalfa, or clover, and pull up and destroy any plants that show signs of the disease. Before transplanting, peppers can be sprayed with milk to prevent spreading this virus.

Potato: Potato scab can be inhibited by keeping the soil pH low. Avoid using lime, wood ashes or fresh barnyard manure on infested soil, as these will increase the alkalinity. Land should grow potatoes but once every three to five years. A number of resistant varieties are available.

Early and late blight are best discouraged by the use of clean tubers. Either remove culls far from the garden, or burn them, as volunteer plants are likely to spread disease to the next year's crop. Resistant varieties are available.

Raspberry (*and blackberry*):   To avoid virus diseases, berries should be planted 500 to 1,000 feet from wild or old domestic berries. Keep the berry patch free of weeds, remove old canes after harvest, rogue out sick plants, and keep plants well mulched.

Anthracnose is a common fungus disease of berries. Cut plants low when planting, and discard any showing gray bark lesions. Improve air circulation by eliminating weeds and thinning out weak and spindly canes; this will speed drying of moisture on the leaves and thereby discourage spore germination and infection.

Squash: A serious disease of squash is bacterial wilt, spread by striped or spotted cucumber beetles. Juice from the end of a severed stem is sticky and stringy. Control cucumber beetles, and take out wilted plants (once a plant contracts bacterial wilt, it is beyond help). Acorn and butternut squashes are resistant.

Tomato: Large-scale plantings should be rotated every three years; note, however, that it is not a good idea to grow tomatoes in rotation with potatoes, eggplant, okra, or peppers, as these crops are susceptible to many of the diseases that hit tomatoes. Diseases such as leaf spots and blights spread readily when plants are wet, so keep out of the tomato patch after rains and heavy dews. Tomatoes are very

sensitive to deficiencies or excesses of nutrients. Use well-composted manure to avoid burning the plants. To control late blight in the field, destroy affected plants, and be sure to start off with healthy seedlings. Smokers should not handle plants without first washing their hands at the risk of spreading tobacco mosaic. To protect tomatoes from viruses, it is best to isolate them from potatoes, cucumbers and tobacco. Aphids spread viruses, so their control is important to a healthy tomato patch. Rogue out infected plants as early as they are noticed, and burn them.

Resistant Varieties: The threat of many potentially serious diseases can be minimized by selecting resistant varieties—those specially bred strains that diseases don't attack and those which are attacked but can tolerate the damage. New strains continually appear on the market, as the diseases themselves evolve into new strains.

A list of resistant varieties becomes dated in time, but you should be aware of some of the diseases for which varieties have been developed. Your state agricultural experiment station can provide up-to-date listings of resistant varieties.

So, if you have been troubled by the above-named diseases, rest assured that there will soon be a resistant strain which you can try next season.

See also APHIDS, FRUIT TREES, LAWN, RESISTANT VARIETIES.

DISH GARDENS

One of the most popular forms of exotic indoor planting is the dish garden, an outgrowth of the Japanese miniature garden. Pottery, bronze, brass, or wooden bowls that have received several coats of spar varnish may be used as long as they are adequately drained. If they are without drainage holes, sphagnum moss or bits of broken pots and pebbles covered with sand or pieces of charcoal should be placed at the bottom. Care should be exercised when watering these arrangements because most plants quickly die in waterlogged soil. A small bulb sprayer is probably the safest way to water them. Be sure to choose plants with similar water, soil and light requirements.

Imagination in selection and arrangement is the only other requirement for a successful dish garden. Besides the standard fillers such as prayer plants and vinca, don't overlook tree seedlings and dwarf forms of outdoor plants.

DIVISION

Division is a method of propagation by which new plants are made by separating rooted sections of parent plants. It includes 1) breaking or cutting large clumps of plants or the removal of new crowns growing up around old ones; 2) the division of plants growing from runners, rhizomes, root buds, or suckers; and 3) the dividing of plants with proliferating bulbs, tubers, corms, or rootstocks.

Certain perennials such as asters and phlox die out in the center of the old crown and send up new shoots around the periphery. These must be separated to avoid crowding and to rejuvenate the plant. Cut the outside crown into several pieces and discard the dead or dying center. Phlox, especially, must be divided every few years to keep it blooming true to type; otherwise, the invading seedlings in the crown will cause the plant to revert to magenta bloom and will eventually choke out the original plant. The whole plant can be lifted and divided with a sharp knife, being careful to discard any seedlings you discover.

Runners and suckers of such plants as strawberries and blackberries, when they root themselves at the nodes, can be divided from the old plant for new plants. Suckers which form on red raspberries and snowberries can also be cut away from the parent plant and transplanted. Crowns that develop from the tips of rhizomes, such as those "pips" which grow from lilies-of-the-valley, can be taken up to make separate new plants, and even potted up and forced, as many nurseries do each year.

Plants like irises, with big, sturdy rhizomes, should be divided every few years by cutting the rhizomes into pieces, each with an eye or some stem, and replanting with the stems facing out and away from each other. Tuberous plants, like dahlias, are broken apart very carefully, also with a piece of stem or growing bud attached to each piece. Most bulbs can be separated when they have divided themselves or grown bulblets or scales. Corms of plants like gladioli develop new corms and also little cormels which can be taken off when the corms are lifted for winter storage.

Most division is done in the autumn for spring- and summer-blooming plants, and the following spring for autumn-blooming plants such as the asters and other late perennials. Prepare the soil carefully, handle the divisions gently and replant them promptly. They need good watering until they get established, as well as mulch the first winter and a good treatment with compost or other organic fertilizer in the spring.

See also CUTTINGS, LAYERING, PROPAGATION.

DOGWOOD   (*Cornus*)

This is a large family of hardy, ornamental small trees or woody shrubs. Desirable for many decorative purposes, and especially effective in winter because of their colored twigs, dogwoods are considered among our loveliest and most popular plants.

A spring blaze of highly attractive flowers plus colorful autumn leaves and fruit make the native flowering dogwood (*C. florida*) a beautiful landscaping feature along the Atlantic coast and mid-Eastern states, as well as a garden favorite.

Many "improved" varieties have been developed, but the common dogwood remains a favorite among country gardeners who seek a graceful, spring-flowering tree.
(*Courtesy of U.S. Forest Service*)

General recommendations for soil preparation, planting, transplanting, and care of trees and shrubs pertain to the dogwoods. They typically thrive in ordinary soil, different types preferring wet or dry areas, and some favoring acid soil.

For most species, propagation is by fresh seed, sown in a cold frame in the fall and usually germinating the following spring. Others are increased by cuttings, suckers, grafting, or budding. Generally, home gardeners seek established nursery stock to start their own plantings.

Flowering dogwood, the prized native, ranges from central New England south to Florida and west to Texas and Ontario. Growing from ten to 30 feet high, it is characterized by a low, spreading head of horizontal-tiered branches, and small green yellow blossoms surrounded by blunt-ended white bracts, which team to make the species one of spring's most beautiful small trees. Then, in autumn, this dogwood displays bright red leaves and showy red fruits in dense clusters.

Pacific dogwood (*C. Nuttallii*) is the 75-foot giant of the family, common in western North America and hardy in colder regions. With white or pinkish bracts spreading six inches across and bright red orange fruits, it is a striking species which in Oregon frequently blooms in spring and again in fall.

Panicled dogwood (*C. racemosa*) is a dense, spreading shrub, native from Maine to Georgia, which grows to heights ranging from three to 15 feet. It is highlighted by handsome gray branches, long sharp-pointed leaves that vary from autumn red to purple, white spring flowers and white fall fruits on red stems. This variety is well suited to banks and roadsides.

Blood-twig dogwood (*C. sanguinea*) is a low-growing (ten feet or less), upright shrub noted for its dark red branches which retain their attractive color through the winter, deep red fall leaves, green white flowers, and black fruit.

Cornelian cherry (*C. mas*) has large cornelian red, edible fruits. An attractive, good-sized shrub, it is one of the prettiest dogwoods in early spring, with clusters of green yellow blooms and yellowish leaves that last until late fall. This native of Europe grows slowly, but is long-lived and hardy. It stands smoky conditions extremely well and is valuable for city planting.

Other species include: the pagoda dogwood (*C. alternifolia*), a 20-foot native shrub or small tree noted for its whorled, spreading green branches, white May flowers and deep blue fruit; the red-osier dogwood (*C. sericea*), a liberally spreading shrub with dark green foliage, large clusters of white blossoms with a red center and white fruit, and suited to shade and wet soil; bunchberry (*C. canadensis*), a spreading, herbaceous shrub which grows just a few inches high and requires cool, shaded, woodland soil; and an evergreen dogwood (*C. capitata*), which is one of the best for use in the Deep South.

DOLOMITE

Dolomite is a type of limestone rich in magnesium. Specifically, it is a mineral, calcium magnesium carbonate $[CaMg(CO_3)_2]$. Beds of dolomite are quarried, the stone pulverized and the resulting powder sold as an agricultural lime. It is valued by organic gardeners since it adds the trace mineral magnesium to the soil as it neutralizes soil acidity.

See also ACIDITY–ALKALINITY, LIME, TRACE ELEMENTS.

DORMANT-OIL SPRAY

Dormant-oil sprays are recommended for insect control in the orchard. Oil is suspended in an emulsion and, if used without additives, the spray is nontoxic. The spray suffocates practically all the common sucking insects such as aphids, red bug, scales, red spider, thrips, and many others. The orchard is normally sprayed with a 7 percent oil solution early in the spring before any of the buds open. Sometimes spraying is repeated in late fall.

See also INSECTICIDES.

DOWSING

Dowsing is the art of water divining—locating water—using a forked twig, brass rod or other object. Dowsers use willow, hazel, peach, apple, horse chestnut, and beech twigs. Some prefer only twigs with bitter bark, others say any green wood will do. Modern dowsers are proficient with brass or steel rods, and Henry Gross, a famous Maine dowser who once accurately located water sources in Bermuda while in his home 800 miles away, claimed he could use anything from grass to wire.

The dowser grasps a forked twig firmly at the outer ends of the fork, thumbs out. If he or she possesses true divining power, it will bend down sharply as it passes over a water vein—sometimes strongly enough to tear off the bark where the dowser is holding it. Some dowsers can even figure the depth and rate of flow of the underground water by the rod's movements.

What makes dowsing work? Not even practitioners seem to know, although the art has been practiced since the fifteenth century.

Estimates of the number of people with dowsing ability range from seven out of ten to one in 12. As one might expect, the art of dowsing has been the subject of a great deal of scientific controversy, and scientists are not yet convinced that dowsing really works.

DRAINAGE

Adequate drainage and aeration are vital to the health of soil and directly affect its fertility index.

Inadequate or defective drainage can take either of two extreme forms: the land drains too rapidly and does not hold moisture for its plant life, or the land drains too slowly and degenerates into a bog or swamp. *See also* AERATION.

Severe boglike conditions can best be relieved by a thorough drainage system, including laying of pipes or drains and the digging of drainage ditches. State or county farm agents can be consulted for detailed advice. *See also* SOIL CONSERVATION.

DRAINAGE, HOUSE PLANTS

Drainage is very important in the successful cultivation of house plants. The best pots for house plants are those that have one or more small drainage holes in the bottom to allow excess water to escape. A piece of arched crock or broken pot may be laid over the hole of small pots. Large pots, say ten-inch size, require two or three inches of drainage material. This may be broken crock in the bottom layer, with gravel, cinders, carpenter's sand, or pebbles placed over it. Sphagnum moss may be laid over the drainage material, if desired, to keep the soil from washing through it, but it is not essential. To insure good drainage in pots without holes, line the bottoms with a layer of broken crockery or pebbles and then a layer of a finer drainage material like carpenter's sand, perlite or small stones before adding the potting soil.
See also HOUSE PLANTS.

DRIED BLOOD   *See* BLOOD, DRIED

DROUGHT
See DRY WEATHER GARDENING

DROUGHT-RESISTANT PLANTS
See DRY WEATHER GARDENING

DRYING FOOD

The oldest known method for preserving food is drying. Drying is also the simplest system for keeping highly nutritious, fine-tasting foods on hand for the winter and nongrowing months.

Drying food holds certain advantages over the more contemporary means of food preservation, canning and freezing. The most obvious one is the saving of space. Since 75 to 95 percent of vegetables and fruits is water, drying food reduces the major part of their mass. Five pounds of fresh fruit will yield about one pound of dried fruit, without any appreciable loss of vitamins and minerals. There is some sacrifice of vitamins C and A from most produce.

Dried goods also save on often-scarce

special canning materials. After fruits and vegetables have been thoroughly dried, they can be stored in sealed regular glassware, coffee cans or plastic bags, twisted tightly closed.

Drying also has the advantage of being an easily adaptable form of storage. Though there are several forms of drying, such as sun drying, air drying and oven drying, the basic principle is the same; that is, to remove 80 to 90 percent of the water content, enabling the dried foods to store without spoilage. The specific method of drying depends upon the needs of the gardener.

One primary rule of drying is that only fresh, fully ripe produce should be used. Since blemished foods might affect the rest of the good produce, use only the best vegetables and fruits for drying storage.

Air Drying: In air drying, fruits and vegetables are spread out on a flat surface so that they can dry in the open. The produce is prepared, according to respective requirements (see chart, pages 324–25), and then spread in single layers on any number of "trays," such as clean brown paper, wooden trays, stainless steel cookie sheets, paper-covered boards, or drying trays constructed for this purpose. The produce-laden trays are placed in an area protected from high humidity and insects, ideally, a screened porch. If a screened porch is unavailable, netting should be used to protect the vegetables and fruits from insects. Cheesecloth serves very well. The protective cover should be suspended above the food on blocks or bricks so that a greater surface area of the drying goods is exposed to the air. As the produce begins to shrivel, it should be turned over to complete the process on the other side.

A more sophisticated arrangement for air drying is to construct special drying trays. The construction is relatively simple, and utilizes wood scraps to make a framework 34 by 34 inches. Cheesecloth or wire mesh serves as both base and protective cover, with string drawn diagonally across the bottom to lend support. The drying trays can be stacked on top of each other, with wooden blocks between to allow for complete airing and to save space. Air drying requires more time than sun drying.

Solar Drying: The sun acts as a perfect natural drying agent in low humidity areas. The fruit and vegetables must be protected from insects and dew. To avoid dew, the produce can be placed outside after the dew has evaporated in the morning, and be taken indoors before the arrival of the night's moisture. Sheets of thin polyethylene or glass used to cover the top of the trays eliminate the labor involved in transporting food daily. The polyethylene will also protect against dust, which should be avoided in drying.

A solar cabinet dryer can be constructed to facilitate drying, using almost any materials on hand, such as plywood, concrete, metal, hardboard, or bricks. The cabinet should be three times as long as it is wide to minimize shading from the side, and ventilation holes should be provided, so that when the sun raises the temperature a natural convection current is generated. The hot air flows out of upper holes while fresh air is drawn through the lower area. The sides and bottom of the cabinet should be insulated to maintain a 125 to 150°F. (51.67 to 65.56°C.) temperature, a range which will also discourage insects and rodents. Mesh coverings over the holes will complete this protection.

The cabinet should be sloped 55 degrees at top, so that an optimum area facing the sun is provided for drying. Thin glass, about two millimeters thick, serves as the cover. The interior should be painted black, to absorb more of the

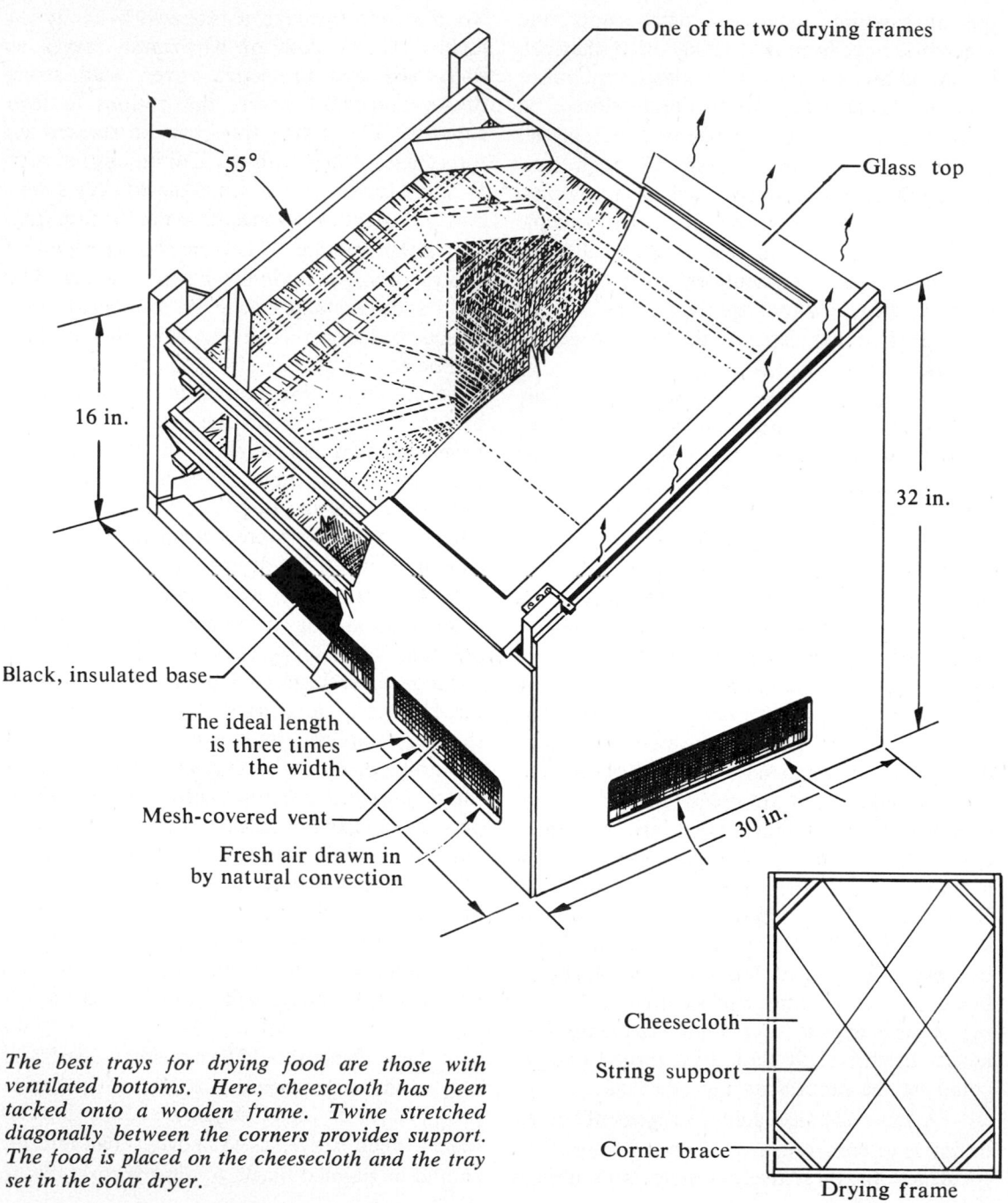

One of the two drying frames

Glass top

55°

16 in.

32 in.

Black, insulated base

The ideal length is three times the width

Mesh-covered vent

Fresh air drawn in by natural convection

30 in.

Cheesecloth

String support

Corner brace

Drying frame

The best trays for drying food are those with ventilated bottoms. Here, cheesecloth has been tacked onto a wooden frame. Twine stretched diagonally between the corners provides support. The food is placed on the cheesecloth and the tray set in the solar dryer.

sun's rays, while a white surface on the exterior will absorb less, thus directing the sunlight to the proper place.

Indoor Drying: Drying indoors is the same as outdoor drying, with a few additions. Again, the produce must be layered thinly on the trays, with as complete exposure as possible to the air. Indoor drying possesses an advantage over outdoor drying, however, in being unaffected by the weather.

Indoor drying can be done in spare rooms, attics, ovens, or in a special dryer. A simple indoor dryer can be made out of a cardboard box lined with aluminum foil (polished side up), and a small light fixture within to act as the heat source. A tray painted black on the bottom and fitted to the top of the box will dry great amounts of food at very little expense.

To dry in an oven, place the fruit within, directly on the rack or on wire mesh if the slats are spaced too far apart. At 200°F. (93.33°C.), with the door partially open, an oven will dry food quickly (in about one to three hours), though possibly with a greater loss of nutrients than through other methods.

Steam drying also dries food rapidly. A stove-top dryer with a lower section for holding water is required. A small hole in the corner allows access for more water and egress for steam. The upper container holds the food to be dried, which does so through the heat generated by the rising steam.

Electric hydrators are also available, with large-capacity sliding trays for volume drying of food.

String drying is the final variation, combining sun, air and oven drying. The food is sliced, strung and suspended in a warm, insect-free porch, attic or above a cookstove. A popular product of string drying is leather breeches. Leather breeches are made of string beans, strung as a necklace and hung in a warm, dry place, often an attic. The string beans are not strung closely together in order to circulate air around them freely. After the beans have become brittle, they are ready to store until use.

Vegetables can be dried upon a variety of different devices, such as nails in the roof beams, old window screens, chicken wire, anything that will serve to keep the slices of food surrounded by flowing air. Dust can be kept off of the produce by draping paper bags around the food.

Drying Fruit: Dried fruit is sweeter than a proportionate amount of fresh fruit, due to the high concentration of fruit sugar. Apples, pears, apricots, cherries, berries, grapes, plums, and pineapples are all fine fruits to dry. Small berries, cherries, plums, and grapes can be left whole to dry, or may be halved. Apples and pears are often pared and cut into slices or rings to expedite drying, while apricots and peaches are usually halved with their pits removed.

Generally it takes from three to four days in the sun and six hours in an oven to dry fruit sufficiently for winter storage. The fruit is finished when it feels dry and leathery on the outside, but slightly moist inside. (Test the fruit dried in an oven by taking it out and cooling it, as it will seem to be moister when hot.) An extended drying period at a lower temperature will assure complete drying. Smaller pieces dry more quickly than larger ones, so they should be removed first. If the fruit is not sufficiently dry, it will mold in storage, while overdried fruit becomes hard and brittle and loses flavor.

The fruit can be stored in plastic bags or tightly sealed jars. To evenly dry fruit, it should be stirred in these containers for four consecutive days. After drying, store fruit in a cool, dry basement or pantry.

Fruit leather, or jerky, is a common product made from the pulp of apples, peaches, apricots, and plums. Fruit leather is made by steaming fruit pulp over low heat until soft, and then pouring it ¼ inch thick onto wax paper. After a day or two, the pulp begins to harden and can be turned over to dry on the opposite side. Two weeks of drying should suffice. Various recipes can be used, and honey, pineapple juice and other ingredients can be added. The leather forms faster if juice is drained off before drying. When finished drying, the leather can be rolled and stored for future use for more than a year.

If bugs or worms are discovered in dried fruit during the winter, the fruit can be spread in shallow pans, and heated at 300°F. (148.89°C.) for 20 to 25 minutes in the oven. This process will destroy vermin and sterilize the food and eliminate any extraneous moisture acquired during storage.

Drying Vegetables: The difference between vegetable drying and fruit drying is the condition of the different foods after having been dried. Whereas fruit is leathery and somewhat moist inside when dried, vegetables are brittle and dry after complete drying. Vegetables also, on the whole, require blanching by hot water or steam before they can be dried. Blanching by steam is accomplished by using a pressure cooker, with a shallow layer of vegetables, not over 2½ inches deep, in a basket suspended over the steaming cooker or pot. Boiling water is second best, since blanching times are increased by boiling and there is a greater loss of nutrients. Blanching or precooking is necessary to maintain color, soften tissue to hasten drying, stem the ripening process, and preserve the flavor of the vegetables.

Corn, for example, should be blanched for ten minutes before drying. The corn is husked when mature, blanched and then drained. A sharp knife is used to remove the kernels, which are placed in a single layer in the oven at 140°F. (60°C.). The corn becomes transparent and hard when dry. Corn can also be dried on a stove-top dryer, and can be hung in bunches in the attic. To remove kernels dried in this fashion, put on a pair of gloves and rub hard against the cob to loosen the kernels.

Beans are dried in three different ways. Beans can be left on the plant to dry, or the entire plant can be pulled when mature and bunched to be hung to dry. Finally, the pods can be picked and spread out in shallow layers in an attic. Limas and soybeans tend to split their shells and drop on the ground when mature. Pinto beans cannot be hung, since they cling to poles in the garden. Beans being dried in trays in rooms should be turned often to dry them evenly. Dried beans and peas can be shelled by placing them in cloth sacks and beating them with a mallet. Green beans can be blanched and hung to dry. Soybeans and chick-peas must be shelled by hand, however, due to their tougher pods.

After drying and shelling, beans should be placed on shallow trays and heated in an oven at about 135°F. (57.22°C.) for an hour, or for ten to 15 minutes at 180°F. (82.22°C.). This process will kill any weevils and insect eggs which the beans may contain.

Tomatoes are first cooked and then run through a mill, discarding the skin and seeds. The pulp is boiled down to a thick paste and spread on a wooden board. Set in the sun under glass and scored several times with a

Most herbs are best preserved by drying. Cut the stalks in early morning, gather them in small bunches and hang them in a cool, dry place for several weeks.

knife, it should be dry enough to roll up after a few days. The roll should be placed in a stone jar and covered for four days. After this period, the roll is taken out, rolled into small balls, rubbed with olive oil, covered with oiled paper, and returned to the stone jar to await use.

Rehydration: Rehydration is the term for revitalizing dried fruits and vegetables with water. The process is simple, calling for three cups of water for each cup of dried food. The food is allowed to soak for several hours or longer, until the food is swollen again with liquid. After rehydration, the foods can be cooked according to the regular instructions of any recipe.

Herbs: Herbs can be dried to add flavor to winter meals. Herbs should be harvested in dry weather, after the dew has evaporated. Reap herbs just before flowering, for this is the time when there is the most aromatic and flavorful oil in the leaves. Roots should be gathered when dormant, in the fall and winter months. Herb seeds should be gathered when the pods have changed color, but have yet to shatter.

Dry herbs in hanging bunches, in dark, dry storage areas. Those herbs which cannot be suspended can be dried in shallow boxes stacked vertically. One to two weeks later, the leaves should be dry to crumbling. If not, the herbs should be allowed to dry for several more days. After drying, the herbs should be stored in jars for two weeks. If moisture appears on the top of the jar, the herbs should

(continued on page 326)

Food	Preparation
Beans, lima	Shell
Beans, snap	Wash and cut in 1-inch lengths or Shred French style (cut diagonally or lengthwise)
Beets	Wash
Carrots	Wash, peel or scrape. Cut in slices either lengthwise or crosswise, not more than ⅛ inch thick
Corn, sweet	Husk
Herbs and celery leaves	Wash, trim and drain
Onions and garlic	Trim, then slice or shred
Peas, green	Shell and discard any starchy peas
Peppers	Wash, remove the seeds, shred if desired
Pumpkin and winter squash	Cut, remove the seeds, cut in 1- to 2-inch strips, then in slices not more than ¼ inch thick
Soybeans, green	Blanch the pods in steam for from 5 to 7 minutes, shell
Spinach and other greens	Trim, discarding coarse stems and ribs, wash and drain
Turnips and rutabagas	Wash, trim and slice about ⅛ to ¼ inch thick

DRYING VEGETABLES

Treatment before drying *	Maximum tray loading per square foot	Maximum temperature in Fahrenheit degrees	Characteristics when dried
Steam for from 8 to 10 minutes	1 pound	150 (66°C.)	Hard and wrinkled
Steam for from 8 to 10 minutes if in 1-inch lengths or Steam for from 3 to 5 minutes if French style	1 pound	155 (68°C.)	Brittle, green black
Cook until done, for from 45 minutes to 2 hours, depending on size. Slip off the skins and cut the beets in ⅛-inch slices or ⅜-inch cubes	1.5 pounds	150 (66°C.)	Brittle
Steam for from 5 to 7 minutes	1.5 pounds	160 (71°C.)	Brittle
Precook in steam for from 15 to 20 minutes, then cut the corn from the cob	1.5 pounds	150 (66°C.)	Dry and brittle
None or steam for from ½ to 1 minute	.5 pound	150 (66°C.)	Crisp
None or steam for from 1 to 2 minutes	1 pound	160 (71°C.)	Brittle, light color
Steam for from 3 to 5 minutes	1 pound	150 (66°C.)	Hard, wrinkled, green
None or steam for from 1 to 2 minutes	1 pound	160 (71°C.)	Leathery to brittle
Steam for from 5 to 7 minutes	1.5 pounds	160 (71°C.)	Tough to brittle
Blanching before shelling is sufficient	1 pound	150 (66°C.)	Hard and wrinkled
Steam for from 2 to 5 minutes. Pile the leaves loosely in a basket so that steam can reach the center of the mass immediately	.5 pound	150 (66°C.)	Crisp
Steam for from 6 to 10 minutes	1 pound	150 (66°C.)	Brittle

* Blanch vegetables in hot water two-thirds as long as in steam.
   Source: Cornell Extension Service.

be removed, spread out and dried again. Herbs can also be dried in the oven at 100°F. (37.78°C.) until crumbling.

Herbs can be crushed to store in jars, but they preserve their oils and fragrance better if allowed to remain whole and crushed right before use. Herbs should be stored in non-absorbent containers, such as tins and glass jars.

Best for their leaves are: basil, savory, chervil, marjoram, lemon balm, parsley, rosemary, sage, and thyme. For seed: anise, coriander, cumin, caraway, dill, and fennel. For roots: angelica, burdock, comfrey, ginseng, ginger, and sassafras.

DRY WEATHER GARDENING

While the gardener cannot control the amount of rain that falls, he or she *can* control the soil's ability to retain the water it receives and even increase the amount of water the soil can retain. In doing so, one must realize that the type of soil determines how often and how much it needs water.

There is a wide variation in water-holding capacity of soils. Soils composed of coarse particles hold less water than those with fine particles; for example, extremely sandy soils hold only about ¼-inch equivalent water per foot of depth, while a silt loam may hold 2.5 to three inches of water per foot of depth. But you aren't stuck with the soil you've got. Poor soils can be improved. Add large amounts of organic matter to increase the water-holding capacity of sandy soils and sandy loams. Organic matter will also make it easier for water to soak into heavier soils such as loams, silt loams and clays. Sheet composting, green manuring and applying organic fertilizers are the best and fastest ways to increase the garden's humus content.

Subsoil conditions also influence the plant-water relationship. In some soils, a few inches of good topsoil cover a hard, tight layer that it is practically impossible for roots or water to enter. The result is a shallow zone for root development, preventing a normal root system from growing. The limited amount of water held by such a shallow topsoil is soon exhausted in dry weather. In addition, plants suffer for water relatively soon after a rain or irrigation.

A heavy organic mulch should be part of any garden irrigation system.

Rock which is close to the soil surface is even worse. Under such conditions water must be supplied frequently in moderate to small amounts. Heavy watering may virtually drown the plants by overfilling the soil pores and preventing proper aeration of the root zone.

On a farm, the best and most universally used method of breaking up a hardpan is by subsoiling, using a heavy-duty rotary tillage tool. However, if the hardpan is located more than ten inches below the surface, it will require too much power to eliminate. Such soils can be loosened by using small, slow-detonating explosive charges. A rather slow way of loosening a hardpan is through sheet composting and green manuring; it will take at least several years to do the job. *See also* SUBSOILING.

At the other extreme are surface soils underlain by deep deposits of sand or gravel. Roots can pass readily into these coarse layers but may obtain little water. Crops on soils having such open subsoils suffer quickly for the lack of water and heavy watering of subsoil not only wastes water but leaches plant nutrients down to levels where the roots fail to reach them. Here again, the best solution is to incorporate large amounts of organic matter into the soil.

Mulching: The best way to protect the plants from drought on ordinary soil is by using a good mulch. Mulch not only helps soil retain water, but also keeps the soil temperature more even.

Mulch should be applied thickly for best results in dry weather. Place six to eight inches of mulch around spinach, lettuce and peas. Shade the lettuce if possible. For beets, carrots, parsnips, and kohlrabi, first thin plants. Then water thoroughly and put mulch all around them at once, six inches deep and between rows. If the mulch is wet, so much the better.

The same can be done for bush beans if they're already planted. If not, make a drill four inches deep, plant the beans sparsely, cover with two inches of soil, water, cover with a board or cardboard and mulch. Remove board as soon as beans sprout.

If corn is already planted, thin to two plants in a hill. Water and mulch with six inches of material.

Late cabbage, broccoli, cauliflower, peppers, and tomatoes, if not planted, can be planted four feet apart and mulched heavily. Flowers can also be mulched deeply and carried through dry periods. *See also* MULCH.

Garden Irrigation: Many gardeners may also be interested in setting up a small irrigation system for use in dry periods. However, irrigating a large backyard garden may require enormous amounts of water. Before going ahead with any irrigation setup, check whether an ample water supply will be available at reasonable cost. (Remember that many communities place restrictions on the use of water during dry spells.)

The USDA's Yearbook of Agriculture for 1955 gives the following estimate of what is necessary:

"Consider a garden 60 by 70 feet, approximately one-tenth of an acre. Suppose this garden is in a district that normally depends on rainfall but still needs additional water from time to time during the summer and early fall— a good watering during a half-dozen short dry spells. Under average conditions the equivalent of an inch of rain may be considered an adequate single application."

If a large supply of water is available, the next question is *how much* water is needed. Briefly stated, the amount of irrigation water a plant requires during any season is the difference between the use of water by the plant and the effective rainfalls received. However, this is complicated by the variations in *intensity* of rainfall. For example, five inches of water received in a month may be far less effective when it falls as one five-inch rain than when it falls in five one-inch rains.

Average amounts of water used by vegetable crops vary as well. Potatoes, tomatoes, beans, and sweet corn are reported to have higher water requirements than many other vegetables, but in the home vegetable garden, where many different vegetables are grown close together, it is obviously impractical to attempt irrigating with different and specific amounts of water for each kind of crop.

The best results will be obtained by applying a good average amount based on soil and plant conditions and the weather. Plants will need less water when small and when the weather is damp than they will when large and the weather is dry. Experience will be the best guide for judging when and how much to irrigate.

Irrigation can be accomplished by a number of methods, but sprinkling and surface application through a perforated hose are best for the home. A sprinkler can be moved from place to place or mounted in a fixed location and provides a fine "rain" that will not pack or erode the soil. On the other hand, perforated hose provides water directly to plant roots and keeps leaves dry, preventing some leaf diseases. *See also* IRRIGATION.

The difficulties in setting up an irrigation system for the home garden clearly emphasize that the most practical, inexpensive and efficient way of conserving or even *adding* water is via a mulch.

Fertility and Water: Regardless of the extra water supply, bear in mind that plants need plenty of fertility to be able to use water.

While irrigation does supply water it will not make up for deficiencies in organic matter, mineral nutrients or other essential features of a good garden. This brings up two other suggestions.

Although irrigating an entire garden area is not practical in most cases, try compost irrigating on a limited basis. Very often, some of the valuable nutrients in compost dissolve quite readily, and in solution these nutrients can be quickly distributed to needy plant roots.

Since plants "drink" their food rather than eat it, the use of compost water makes good sense, particularly during dry periods when plants are starved both for food and water.

It is no trouble making compost water on a small scale. For treating small outdoor areas, fill a sprinkling can half with finished compost and half with water, stir gently ten or 12 times, and pour. The compost can be used several times, as one watering will not wash out all its soluble nutrients. The remaining compost should be dug into the soil or used as a mulch.

Deep fertilizing is another technique that will aid plants in dry periods. When drought strikes, the top layer of soil dries out first. A week of dry weather will probably dry out the top two inches of soil. It takes a severe and prolonged drought to dry things up to a depth of a foot to 18 inches. Therefore, a key way to protect the garden from drought damage is to build fertility deep down in the soil, where plant food will stay moist longer. This can be done by drilling in granular organic fertilizers with a fertilizer drill attached to a garden tractor. Or, spread fertilizer on the surface—and then work it in as deeply as possible with the plow or tiller.

Drought-Resistant Plants: Another way of combating dry periods is by growing plants that are specially bred to be resistant to drought.

Some good plants for dry conditions are listed below. Seed catalogs should be consulted for a more complete list.

Annuals:

Annual phlox (*Phlox Drummondii*)
Calliopsis (*Coreopsis tinctoria*)
Cape marigold (*Dimorphotheca*)
Convolvulus, dwarf (*Convolvulus tricolor*)
Cornflower (*Centaurea cyanus*)
Four-o'clock (*Mirabilis Jalapa*)
Ice plant (*Mesembryanthemum crystallinum*)
Larkspur, rocket (*Delphinium ajacis*)
Love-lies-bleeding (*Amaranthus caudatas*)
Morning-glory (*Ipomoea purpurea*)
Perilla, green (*Perilla frutescens*)
Prickly poppy (*Argemone grandiflora*)
Rose moss (*Portulaca grandiflora*)
Sanvitalia (*Sanvitalia procumbens*)
Scarlet sage (*Salvia splendens*)
Snow-on-the-mountain (*Euphorbia marginata*)
Summer cypress (*Kochia scoparia*)
Sunflower (*Helianthus annuus*)
Zinnia (*Zinnia elegans*)

Shrubs:

Barberry (*Berberis vulgaris*)
Bayberry (*Myrica pensylvanica*)
Beach plum (*Prunus maritima*)
Black haw (*Viburnum prunifolium*)
Burnet rose (*Rosa spinosissima*)
Bush clover (*Lespedeza Thunbergii*)
Fragrant sumac (*Rhus aromatica*)
Indian currant (*Symphoricarpos orbiculatus*)
Juniper (*Juniperus Sabina*)

Panicled dogwood (*Cornus racemosa*)
Pentaphyllum (*Acanthopanax Sieboldianus*)
Prairie rose (*Rosa setigera*)
Rose acacia (*Robinia hispida*)
Rugosa rose (*Rosa rugosa*)
Saint-John's-wort (*Hypericum frondosum*)
Staghorn sumac (*Rhus typhina*)
Wayfaring tree (*Viburnum Lantana*)

Trees—Deciduous:

Amur maple (*Acer Ginnala*)
Black cherry (*Prunus serotina*)
Black locust (*Robinia pseudoacacia*)
Box elder (*Acer Negundo*)
European white birch (*Betula pendula*)
Filbert (*Corylus* species)
Gray birch (*Betula populifolia*)
Hawthorn (*Crataegus* species and varieties)
Hedge maple (*Acer campestre*)
Honey locust (*Gleditsia triacanthos*)
Large-toothed aspen (*Populus grandidentata*)
Monarch birch (*Betula maximowicziana*)
Mulberry (*Morus* species and varieties)
Osage orange (*Maclura pomifera*)

Bulbs:

Brodiaea (*Brodiaea*)
Bugle lily (*Watsonia*)
Climbing onion (*Bowiea volubilis*)
Corn lily (*Ixia*)
Flag (*Iris*), bearded varieties
Star lily (*Leucocrinum montanum*)
Sword lily (*Gladiolus*)
Tiger flower (*Tigridia Pavonia*)
Tulip (*Tulipa*)

Ferns:

Bracken (*Pteridium aquilinum*)
Cliff brake (*Pellaea*)
Hart's tongue fern (*Phyllitis Scolopendrium*)
Interrupted fern (*Osmunda Claytoniana*)
Lip fern (*Cheilanthes*)
Walking fern (*Camptosorus rhizophyllus*)
Woodsia (*Woodsia*)

Perennials:

Adam's-needle (*Yucca filamentosa*)
Asphodel (*Asphodelus*)
Baby's-breath (*Gypsophila paniculata*)
Blackberry lily (*Belamcanda*)
Blanketflower (*Gaillardia aristata*)
Blazing-star (*Liatris*)
Butterfly weed (*Asclepias tuberosa*)
Carolina lupine (*Thermopsis caroliniana*)
Chamomile (*Anthemis nobilis*)

Columbine (*Aquilegia*)
Cushion euphorbia (*Euphorbia epithymoides;* also *E. mammillaris* and *E. polygona*)
Elecampane (*Inula Helenium*)
False indigo (*Baptisia*)
Great bellflower (*Campanula latifolia*)
Ground ivy (*Glechoma hederacea*)
Iceland poppy (*Papaver nudicaule*)
Madwort (*Alyssum*)
Michaelmas daisy (*Aster laevis;* also *A. linariifolius*)
Pearly everlasting (*Anaphalis margaritacea*)
Poppy mallow (*Callirhoe* species and varieties)
Red-hot-poker (*Kniphofia Uvaria*)
Red valerian (*Centranthus ruber*)
Rock cress (*Arabis*)
Snow-in-summer (*Cerastium tomentosum*)
Sunflower (*Helianthus Maximilianii;* also *H. mollis*)

DUCK

Ducks are very easy to handle, taking less time and work than other fowl. Also, their housing needs no insulation and less heat than chicken housing.

One of the big dividends of duck raising is the manure. It is twice as rich in nitrogen, and contains approximately six times the phosphorus and the same amount of potash as average farm manure.

Breeds: There are egg breeds, meat breeds and ornamental breeds of ducks, and the breed you grow depends on what you expect from your birds. For eggs, the Khaki Campbells and Indian Runners are both good. Although neither breed produces a good meat bird, Khaki Campbells have averaged close to 365 eggs per year per bird as opposed to 300 per year for many chickens.

There are three primary meat breeds. The Pekin is the bird raised commercially in the United States for meat production. The meat is a good quality, the birds reach market weight in eight weeks, and they are white feathered, a big advantage in the market. However, the ducks are poor sitters and very nervous, so flocks have to be handled with care. Aylesburys are popular in England for meat production and, like the Pekins, mature in eight weeks. Although they are not as nervous, they are poor

While the Aylesbury (foreground) and Muscovy (background) are equally popular meat breeds of duck, the Muscovy has the extra advantage of being a good sitter.

sitters. Rouens, another breed that is sometimes raised for meat, is less popular because it has dark feathers.

Muscovies, another meat breed, take longer to mature—about ten weeks—but the carcass is larger than a Pekin carcass and has less fat. In addition, Muscovies, though only fair layers, are good sitters.

Ornamental breeds include Cayugas, Oriental Mandarins and Blue Swedish.

Starting: It is best to start with day-old ducklings rather than try to incubate fertile eggs. A 10-by-12-foot brooder house will accommodate 200 to 300 ducklings, or a temporary pen may be built in a laying house. Quarters should be cleaned and aired thoroughly before the ducks arrive.

Put the day-old ducklings immediately under the brooder set at 90°F. (32.22°C.). Reduce the temperature five degrees (F.) a week until they are let out. After the first few days, ventilation is vital; ventilate enough to keep dampness down, but avoid drafts.

During their first two weeks, the ducks should get starter pellets or a starter mash thoroughly wetted; only mix as much mash as the birds will eat—extra will sour and ducklings will not eat it. After two weeks, switch to growing pellets or growing mash with about a 15 percent protein content; you can use the same mixture you're feeding your chickens. At eight weeks, switch to fattening pellets.

Ample fresh, clean water is a necessity. Running water in shallow, narrow troughs will allow baby ducks to submerge their bills and eyes without getting their bodies wet.

Ducklings need a constant supply of fine grit. Feed separately from the mash.

If ducks are to be raised entirely in confinement, they will need three square feet per bird by the time they are six weeks old. They will also require deep litter; straw makes good bedding material. If ranged in warm weather they can be let out after the first three weeks. Ducklings are much hardier than baby chicks. Cool temperatures make them feather out faster and eat better for smooth, plump flesh, but it's a good idea to harden off the ducklings by admitting increasing amounts of cool air for a week prior to ranging.

On range, tall weeds or trees, or frames covered with boards and building paper, are sufficient protection from sun and rain.

Move mash hoppers and water fountains frequently to avoid bare spots.

On small farms try to locate duck yards on gently sloping land with light sandy soil. Manure should be scraped up regularly, or a couple of inches of gravel laid down to make the yards self-cleaning when it rains. A yard 50 by 75 feet will hold 100 ducklings.

A pond or brook will reduce the amount of water hauled to your flock. The ducks don't need a particularly large or deep pond, just one big enough to clean themselves. It should be shallow and flowing. Some farmers dam a stream and periodically flush out the resulting pond to remove manure. A settling basin is an excellent way to catch the sludge after flushing, which can then be used on your garden. Some farmers provide shallow splash pans of water which they clean frequently. This is particularly necessary during breeding season, when moisture is essential for proper hatching of the eggs.

Breeding Ducks: For a steady supply of ducks throughout the year, a breeding flock is a necessity. Select ducks for breeding carefully; ducks should come from early hatches, have good weight, conformation and feathering. Allow approximately one drake to six ducks.

Separate your breeders from the rest of the flock, and check for general health and vitality. Ducks need about five square feet of housing space per bird, outdoor exercise in all but the worst winter weather, and swimming water to keep in top condition.

Duck eggs are incubated four weeks before they hatch (Muscovy eggs take five weeks). They require a lot more moisture than hens' eggs and must be turned three or four times a day. Since ducks lay at night, gather eggs in the morning for best results in the mechanical breeder. Wash carefully. Have eggs at room temperature before incubating. Candle eggs at seven or eight days, and discard those with dead embryos or infertile eggs; living embryos have the appearance of a spider floating inside the eggs.

When hatched, put the baby ducklings in the brooder as soon as they are dry and fluffy. See that ample food and water are available.

Diseases: Ducks raised in relative isolation and in small numbers suffer little from diseases. Muscovies appear to be more resistant than Pekins or Runners. If you have a large flock and suspect disease, don't waste time; call a vet.

Slaughtering: Properly grown Pekins weigh between five and six pounds at nine to 11 weeks. After 12 weeks or so, they won't grow larger without considerable extra feeding, and the meat is tough and stringy. Muscovies should not be slaughtered after 17 weeks of age for the same reason.

Dry-picking birds is best, although many commercial concerns dip the ducks in boiling water or in wax which, when cooled, peels off quite easily bringing feathers with it. If dry-picked, the birds hold their flavor better. Duck down can also be a valuable by-product for the homestead. It should be treated in the same way as goose down. *See also* GEESE.

Duck eggs sometimes find a good market, and duck is a popular entree in many restaurants.

DUMB CANE   *See* DIEFFENBACHIA

DUSTY-MILLER   *See* CENTAUREA

DUTCH ELM DISEASE

This blight, transmitted by bark beetles, is extremely hard to control, and as yet, no remedy for checking it has been found. Imported into this country from abroad, blight diseases wreak havoc on indigenous vegetation which apparently requires exposure to the disease for many centuries before developing resistance. Symptoms of Dutch elm disease include foliar wilting, yellowing, curling, and dropping.

Keep trees healthy by proper feeding and watering, and by pruning dead or dying twigs and branches in winter. Burn the resulting debris. If elm logs are to be used for firewood, the bark should first be removed and burned.

See also ELM, ORCHARD.

DUTCHMAN'S-PIPE
See PIPE VINE

DWARF FRUIT TREES
See FRUIT TREES, DWARF

DWARFING TREES
See BONSAI, GRAFTING

DWARF PLANTS *See* BORDER

E

EARTH ALMOND   *See* CHUFA

EARTHWORM

The earthworm is extremely valuable in creating topsoil and maintaining soil fertility. Earthworm castings, or excrement, are far richer in minerals than the soil which they ingest, and it is said that an average earthworm will produce its weight in castings every 24 hours. Earthworms burrow as far as six feet into the ground aerating the soil, making holes for the rain to penetrate and breaking up hardpans. Each year their castings furnish a considerable amount of valuable nitrogenous fertilizer which may amount to more than 50 tons per acre in a rich organic soil.

Members of the Annelida, a phylum containing over 6,000 species, earthworms are found everywhere on the earth's surface except in extremely cold northern and southern latitudes. They may range in length from microscopic sizes to several feet long. Some common names familiar in different areas of the United States are orchard worm, rain worm, angleworm, brandling, night crawler, and field worm. Hybrids have been developed by crossbreeding.

All earthworms are headless, eyeless, toothless, and without antennae. From tip to tail the body is composed of ringlike segments. A short distance from the anterior end is a swollen band, lighter in color than the rest of the body.

Earthworms are bisexual—that is, they have both male and female reproductive organs. Each earthworm is capable of producing egg capsules, but must first have contact with another worm to be fertilized. Each capsule contains several worms. Three to four weeks after a capsule has been deposited (usually near the soil surface) wormlets emerge as minute white threads about $\frac{1}{16}$ inch in length. They are self-sufficient from this time on.

Worms begin to mate two to three months from birth depending upon the richness or poorness of the soil in which they live and upon the temperature. Though mating can occur once a month in some species, it generally occurs once or twice a year.

Certain species of earthworms, particularly those that surface and crawl about during wet or rainy weather, are chiefly active at night. Other species are active throughout most of the day and night and seldom, if ever, surface, remaining from six to 30 inches beneath the surface depending on the porosity of the soil.

Every morsel of soil and decayed vegetable matter taken in by the earthworm passes through a digestive system equipped with a gizzardlike organ. Food value in the swallowed matter is extracted for use by the worm and the balance is excreted.

Breeding: Earthworms can be easily raised on the homestead, small farm or even in a suburban basement or garage. The easiest method for beginners is the culture box method, although earthworms can be raised in pits outdoors or in the field or garden.

Any good-sized *wooden* box will serve for

box culture (avoid boxes with cardboard components). Fruit or vegetable lug boxes, approximately 17 by 14 by 6 inches, are fine and can occasionally be obtained free or for a small fee. Larger boxes or packing crates will also work and can be purchased, made specially or salvaged. Some growers use specially constructed outdoor pits for worm culture. In any case, the bottoms of boxes must be well drained; if they are tight, bore ¼-inch holes for drainage.

A fruit or vegetable box will take about 500 full-grown breeders or half a pound of pit-run stock which ordinarily amounts to about 800 worms from babies to breeders. Since the usual earthworm order is for either 1,000 breeders or one pound of pit-run worms, you'll need two of these size boxes to start off with.

Mixing the Compost: Compost for a 17-by-14-by-6-inch box, can be compounded as follows. Quantities can be increased for a larger box or a bed.

Spread 12 quarts of finely screened topsoil on a flat surface and level to a layer three inches high; on this spread 12 quarts of finely ground peat moss that has been thoroughly soaked in water for 24 hours and drained of dripping water; spread over this 12 quarts of crumbled horse, cow, sheep, or rabbit manure. Sprinkle the surface with a cupful of dry cornmeal thoroughly mixed with one or two pounds of coffee grounds. Mix all ingredients well.

The ideal moisture content for the compost is reached when you can squeeze a handful of compost in your fist and have it hold together in a wet but not dripping ball. If it needs more

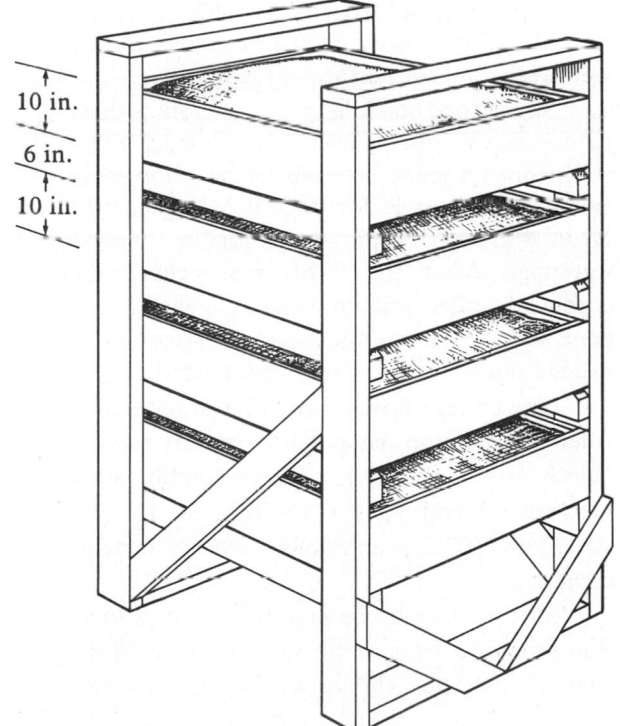

10 in.
6 in.
10 in.

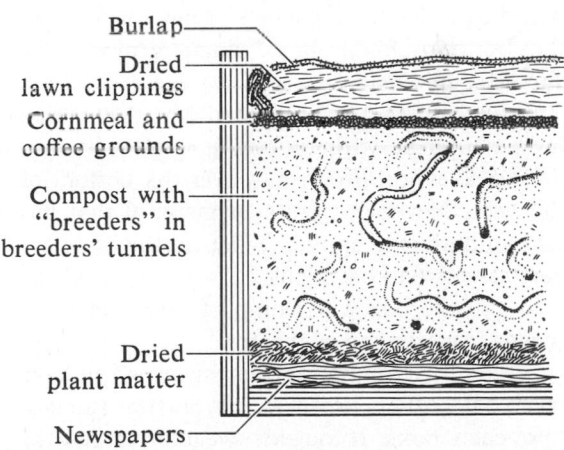

Burlap
Dried lawn clippings
Cornmeal and coffee grounds
Compost with "breeders" in breeders' tunnels
Dried plant matter
Newspapers

The culture box provides earthworms with the ideal breeding environment. The worms tunnel into the warm, moist compost and come to the surface to feed on dry cornmeal and coffee grounds. Several of these boxes can be stacked on top of one another with about six inches of ventilation space between.

moisture, sprinkle some water over it gently and evenly and let it penetrate through the loose pile. Continue tossing, mixing and turning once a day for five days.

On the fifth day, stick your hand into the center of the pile and test it for heat. If it is cool to the touch, your work is done. If there is the slightest warmth, keep mixing and moistening once a day until it is thoroughly cooled. Earthworms will crawl out en masse if your compost is warm; if they can't escape, they will burn up from too much heat.

Filling and Stocking the Culture Box: It usually takes the average earthworm hatchery from one to three weeks to fill and ship your order, so get your compost ready ahead of time. When your worms arrive, prepare the culture boxes as follows.

Toss the compost again in case it got lumpy or packed while waiting for the worms. Test for moisture and remoisten if necessary.

Lay a piece of burlap, corrugated cardboard or a few folded sheets of newspaper over the bottom of the box. Some growers use shredded newspaper.

Spread about a ½-inch layer of dried lawn clippings, withered small weeds, crushed dried leaves, or alfalfa hay over the bottom of the box. Never use grass or material that has had an herbicide applied, since earthworms are very sensitive to chemicals.

Fill the box with compost to within three inches from the top of the box.

Dump about half the earthworms you have received—either breeders or pit-run stock—into each box. If outside weather is raw or dark, do this job inside; cold worms scarcely move. Since worms don't like being exposed to strong light, you can encourage them to burrow into the compost indoors by hanging a 100-watt light bulb a foot from the box. This

should take from five to 30 minutes.

Fill the box with compost up to within an inch from the top. This gives the worms a depth of six inches of compost to work—their minimum requirement.

Mix a handful of dry cornmeal with three handfuls of coffee grounds (this will be enough for two boxes). Sprinkle two handfuls of this mixture on top of the compost in each box, keeping the food two inches away from both the sides and the ends of the box. This will give the worms a chance to escape to the edges of the box in case their feed heats up temporarily.

Fill the box to the rim with dried lawn clippings or similar material. Press these into a mat by using a light board, being careful to tuck all the grass inside the walls of the box. Lay a piece of well-soaked burlap over the grass, and sprinkle evenly with a quart of water (improvise a sprinkler from a coffee can with several holes punched in the bottom). Avoid wetting the outside surface of the box.

Storing and Stacking: You can stack these culture boxes four to five high, allowing about six inches of space between boxes. Improvise a right-angle nozzle for your hose so that the boxes won't have to be moved for their weekly watering. After the third week, check the cornmeal/coffee mixture, and if most of it is gone, add more. Otherwise no attention is needed until the boxes must be divided.

The culture boxes should be stored somewhere where the temperature never reaches below 50°F. (10°C.), and preferably stays between 60 and 70°F. (15.56 to 21.11°C.). At 32°F. (0°C.) and lower worms become dormant.

The boxes may be kept outside in a location protected from wind, rain and heat in the summertime, but should be brought indoors in the winter if you live in a cold climate.

Dividing Boxes: Eventually your culture boxes must be subdivided as the worms breed and increase. Boxes stocked originally with breeders can be divided after 30 days, boxes stocked with pit-run worms after 40 days, and boxes stocked with eggs and spawn after 90 days.

During the week when you are planning to divide the boxes, don't water them. When handling worms, keep a can of dry soil at hand and keep rubbing your palm and fingers in it to keep them from getting gummy.

Dividing a culture box is about a 15-minute job. It should be done in strong sunlight or under a 100-watt bulb hung a foot above the box.

Prepare a new culture box similar to the one first described. Put in an inch layer of compost. Remove the burlap, grass mat and uneaten cornmeal/coffee ground mixture from the top of the original culture box and lay these materials over the compost in the new box.

Expose the surface of the original box to the light for a few minutes until the larger worms have had a chance to go back down to their channels in the lower three inches of the box. Try not to disturb this area. The spawn and capsules are to be transferred and they are in the upper three inches of the box.

Prop one end of the box on a table. Quickly and gently start scraping out the compost from the lower end of the box with your fingers. Do not use a solid-edged tool which will cut into your worms. Let these scrapings fall in a pile and empty it into the new box. Keep scraping this end of the box, taking about ½ inch at a time until you begin to see the heads of your breeders sticking out of their channels. Turn your box around, propping up the other end, and work on the other half of

the box until you come to the breeders there. Empty your remaining scrapings into the new box and level them out gently.

Set your original box level on the table again and sprinkle the whole surface lightly with the cornmeal/coffee grounds mix. Fill the box to one inch from the top with new compost, top with a grass mat and new burlap, gently water, and store. Divide this box again in about 30 days, feeding and watering as before.

Harvesting the Castings: About the fourth month after starting your original boxes you will notice that the bottom four inches of material is getting blacker and finely granulated. These are the castings. They can be removed and dug into your flower beds or garden to enrich the soil.

Don't water the culture box for a week before you do this job. After scraping down to the breeders, as per above, turn the box upside down onto cardboard under a strong light. Pile the castings up in a tall, tight cone, and give the worms time to get down to the bottom center of the cone. This should not take more than 20 minutes. Then go back and start taking double handfuls of castings off the top of the pile and collecting the same in a bucket. Start cutting in around the base of the cone until you can see the mass of worms at the bottom. Place them in a newly prepared culture box.

Introducing Outdoors: After you have ten or 15 culture boxes full of worms, you can introduce them into outdoor pits. Remember that the worm works best in the upper six to ten inches, so it is unnecessary to place the worms into a pile three feet deep. Make your pit long and shallow.

Plan to plant 500 breeders or 1,000 mixed sizes per cubic foot of compost and the worms will work quickly and well. Be sure to have a solid or wire net bottom on the pit or moles will ravage it. Planking, shiplap or a thin concrete slab will do. The sides can be wood, concrete or concrete block. An overall height of two feet provides room for ten to 12 inches of compost on the bottom and protective layers of dry leaves, wilted grass, weeds, green garbage, or hay to shield the worms from the elements.

EARWIG

Both adult and nymph are red brown, beetlelike insects with sharp pinchers at the tail end. The pinchers are formidable in ap-

Although hideous in appearance, earwigs are usually beneficial in habit, acting as scavengers and predators of various insect larvae.
(*Courtesy of U.S. Department of Agriculture*)

pearance, but do no harm to humans. These insects forage by night, and hide during the day. They occasionally feed on vegetables and flowers, and may enter the house to eat stored food. Earwigs may give off an unpleasant odor.

Traps have been found very effective in controlling earwigs. A simple trap can be made by laying sections of bamboo, open at the ends, throughout the garden or flower bed. Check the traps early in the morning, and dump the captives in a container of water topped with kerosene.

ECHINACEA

A genus of the Composite family, this native perennial plant found on the prairies of the Middle West is closely related to the rudbeckia. The large, daisylike flowers, which range in color from pink through purple and crimson, have conelike centers and are long-lasting when cut. Bloom period is from July to September. Echinaceas, also called purple coneflower or hedgehog coneflower, grow three to four feet tall.

Preferring a rich, well-drained loam and full sun, echinaceas can be easily propagated by seed or root division.

The most popular species for the wild garden or perennial border is *E. purpurea.* The black roots of purple daisy (*E. angustifolia*) are used medicinally in the treatment of ulcers and boils.

EDELWEISS   (*Leontopodium alpinum*)

An emblem of purity, this lovely alpine perennial herb grows four to 12 inches high and

If seeds of the edelweiss are sown in late winter, the plant can be set outdoors in the rock garden the following April or May.
(Courtesy of Longwood Gardens)

is covered with a whitish wool and small yellow flowers surrounded by star-shaped, woolly bracts. It is a recommended rock garden plant, preferring light, well-drained soil and full sun. Seeds are sown indoors in early February and transplanted out in May.

During the winter, edelweiss often appears to have died away completely, but as soon as the soil is warmed by the first spring sunshine, its silvery leaves peep through once more.

EDGING   *See* BORDER

EELWORM   *See* NEMATODE

EGGPLANT   (*Solanum Melongena*)

This purple black glossy vegetable of the Nightshade family has a mild flavor similar to that of fried oysters and is often substituted for meat. A warm-season crop that produces best in hot, sunny weather, the eggplant is grown from seed as a tender annual. Eggplants can be cultivated in northern areas if started indoors and set out after danger of frost is past and protected when autumnal frosts are imminent.

Six to eight weeks before the frost-free date, seeds to be started indoors should be sown in flats and covered with ½ inch of mellow, well-pulverized soil kept at a temperature of 70 to 75°F. (21.11 to 23.89°C.). When the seedlings are about two weeks old, or about three inches high, they should be transplanted singly to three-inch clay pots or to flats and beds where they can stand four to five inches apart. The soil for this first transplanting should be particularly rich. A good mixture would consist of two parts rotted sod to one part compost mixed with a small amount of sand. The daytime temperature should be 65 to 70°F. (18.33 to 21.11°C.), the nighttime 50 to 55°F. (10 to 12.78°C.). Water carefully and check for insects.

Two weeks after the frost-free date, those seedlings growing in flats or beds should be blocked out; that is, a knife should be run through the soil midway between the plants, cutting the roots, and leaving each plant with its own block of soil. Keep these young plants lightly shaded and well watered until it is time to set them outdoors, about a week later. Mean daily temperatures for outdoor planting should

Use kitchen shears or a sharp knife to harvest eggplant while the skin is still glossy and the fruit is two-thirds its full size.

must never be allowed to dry out, especially while fruit is setting, as this produces inferior fruits or none at all.

One packet of seed will start 40 to 60 plants, each bearing three to eight fruits. Seed longevity is four years.

Eggplants should be harvested when young, as soon as the skin has attained a high gloss. Not only is the flesh more tender and the seeds smaller, but the plant will produce more fruits if kept picked.

Good varieties include Black Beauty, which matures in 85 to 90 days, and Burpee Hybrid, which is more resistant to drought and disease than any other variety. Early Long Purple and Stokes Hybrid are smaller varieties that require less garden space.

Eggplant should be peeled, cut into ¼-inch slices, dipped either in flour or an egg batter, and sautéed in olive oil.

be around 65 to 70°F. (18.33 to 21.11°C.) unless some protective covering (paper cones, cloches, plastic containers, etc.) is given the plants. Such protection allows the plants to be set out one to two weeks earlier.

Eggplants should be spaced 2½ feet apart in rows set three feet apart and grown in a deep, rich soil that is moist but well drained. To conserve moisture and to protect the young seedlings from wind damage, a deep mulch of straw or hay should be applied in the spring. Beginning four weeks after they are set out, the plants should be fertilized with a manure/water tea once every two weeks. Eggplants

EGGSHELLS

Added regularly to the compost heap, eggshells will supply a considerable amount of lime to the soil over a period of years. They contain a good deal of calcium, over 1 percent nitrogen and about .4 percent phosphoric acid.

ELDERBERRY   (*Sambucus*)

Often called elder, this plant is a widely found member of the Honeysuckle family. There are five or more principal species, but the American or sweet elder (*S. canadensis*) is most recommended, since it produces abundant purple black berries.

Often found growing wild, elderberries are easy to cultivate. The fruit requires a moist, fertile soil, and plenty of room to spread. A humus or mulch may be applied, but avoid sawdust or other material with a high acid content.

A new plant will bear fruit one to three years after planting. At the end of the first year, canes should be tipped back approximately one foot. In the winter following a fruit-producing summer, cut back and remove old and dead canes.

More than one elderberry plant can be cultivated by digging up the original and dividing the root mass into as many parts as you want plants. Suckers growing from roots can be dug and transplanted too.

Elderberries are popularly used in jams and pies. Delectable wines are produced from the plant's fruits and flowers. The blossoms are also sometimes fried in batter and eaten like fritters, and the berries are used to make a deep red dye. An elderberry hedge will grow up to ten feet tall and produce showy and fragrant white blossoms; it is most attractive both to the property owner and to birds.

Flies are said to be repelled by the elderberry's odor. The major known nuisance to the berry is the currant borer, which will burrow into the hollow stems of the plant and cause some damage.

Adams #2 produces large fruit clusters and berries. Johns ripens in early August and yields vigorous growth.

In midsummer, elderberry shrubs put forth clusters of fruit which can be used in jams, pies and wines.

ELECAMPANE   (*Inula Helenium*)

A beautiful European perennial herb now growing wild along roadsides and in fields throughout the northeastern United States, elecampane grows up to six feet tall and has large, toothed leaves and daisylike yellow flowers.

It prefers full sun and a sandy loam well supplied with moisture, and is best propagated by division of old roots, which are set out in fall about 18 inches apart in rows three feet apart. It can also be propagated by seed sown in spring. Cultivation should be sufficient to keep the soil in good condition and free of weeds.

The beautiful, perennial elecampane or horseheal grows wild throughout the northeastern United States.

Also called horseheal and scabwort, elecampane has long been known as a medicinal herb. It was used to treat cutaneous horse diseases (horseheal) and to heal scabs on sheep (scabwort). American Indian herbalists used this herb to treat bronchial and lung disorders by mashing the roots and boiling them in water, alcohol and honey. Today the herb is grown for the insulin contained in its roots.

See also HERB.

ELECTROCULTURE

Electroculture is a method of setting up an electrical field to influence the growth of plants. The word *electrical* in this sense does not mean a conventional electric current, but atmospheric, magnetic and terrestrial electricity. According to research, this electricity has been found to have some beneficial properties for plant growth and germination.

The basic principle is that wherever there is cellular activity there is electrical energy developed, and conversely, wherever electrical energy is applied, cellular activity is increased and better growth obtained. Electroculture is the science of securing this growth through the application of electricity by using suitable techniques.

Probably the first electroculture investigator was a Frenchman, M. Bertholon, whose "electro-vegetometer" supposedly collected atmospheric electricity by means of an antenna, and passed it through plants growing in the field. He found an acceleration of growth in treated plants as compared to untreated and reported these results in his treatise entitled *On the Electricity of Vegetables,* published in 1783.

About 50 years later, in 1844, W. Ross, an American, applied for a patent for a device or system using large zinc and copper plates which he buried in the ground about 200 feet apart. The plates were connected above ground by wire, thus forming a galvanic cell, and potatoes were planted in the rows between the plates. It was believed that larger-than-ordinary potatoes were obtained this way. But total yields were not given and Ross reportedly did not specify that soil of a uniform quality and texture was used.

From about 1900 to 1920, numerous experiments with atmospheric electricity were conducted by horticultural researchers. Usually wire nets were used, suspended at varying distances above the experimental field and held there by insulated supports. One terminal of the voltage source was attached to the net and the other was grounded.

Research continued through the first half of the twentieth century and into the 1960's. Tests were carried out at the Massachusetts Experiment Station and, as recently as 1962, E. G. McKibben, director of the Agricultural Engineering Research Division of the USDA, presented a paper before the American Society of Agricultural Engineers entitled "A Look Ahead at Farm Electrification Research." In this paper McKibben spoke highly of the many possibilities of the application of electromagnetic energy in its many forms to agriculture. And up until 1967, Rodale Press was conducting successful electroculture experiments at its Experimental Organic Farm and reporting on them in *Organic Gardening and Farming* magazine.

Electroculture Technique: The following methods have been used by experimenters in electroculture:

1. *Radiomagnetic,* in which the seed is sown in a bed provided with a sheet of ½-inch iron-wire netting. For a plant or tree a jacket or apron is formed, one inch to one foot wide, depending on the girth, and placed around the stem or trunk. For individual branches of a tree a collar of the same wire netting is formed.

2. *Treatment of seed before sowing,* either by spreading it out in a thin layer on an insulated metal plate and then giving the plate a high-tension spark of 2,000 volts for one minute or by soaking the seed in electrified water in an insulated vessel for one or two hours. In both methods, the seed is sown without being touched.

3. *Giving the plant electrified water.* Whenever a growing part is given such a mantle of electrified water, its growth is increased. This is much more than irrigation, which is watering the roots.

Water is electrified by taking it in an earthenware container, placing it on a rubber mat, dipping one end of a high-tension cable into the water while the other is hooked onto the ignition plug of a car and the engine run for a minute.

4. *Interculture* of the growing plant with other suitable plants such as are rich in M rays or gurwitsch rays or ultraviolet rays—like onions and other root crops.

Other radiations are also effective, such as X rays, ultraviolet rays, violet rays, etc., but the exposure should not, as a rule, exceed one minute.

ELM   (*Ulmus*)

These hardy deciduous trees are widely planted as shade and street trees. Before the widespread depredations of Dutch elm disease, they were the most commonly planted ornamental tree in the Northeast.

The American elm (*U. americana*), growing to a height of 120 feet, has a wide-spreading head on a wide trunk.

The English elm (*U. procera*) is a more compact tree, growing to 90 feet. The leaves stay green longer in the fall than those of the American elm.

The red-barked slippery elm (*U. rubra*), suited to most eastern regions, rarely grows over 60 feet.

The rock or cork elm (*U. Thomasii*) does not have the elegance of the American elm, being a large, stiff-looking tree, but it can be planted as far north as Quebec. It is named for the corky ridges on most of its branches. The tree grows up to 90 feet, and the foliage turns yellow in fall.

The charming, wide-spreading Scotch or wych elm (*U. glabra*) produces large rosettes of flowers that can almost be mistaken for leaves.

The wahoo or winged elm (*U. alata*), one of the smallest of the genus, is hardy south of Virginia and west to Arkansas and Texas. It is usually grown on upland soil near streams and lakes.

Culture: Mulching with leaves or sawdust is helpful if grass won't be grown under the tree. If the soil is acid, correct the pH to about neutral.

The dread Dutch elm disease is first observed as a wilting or yellowing of the leaves. In severe cases trees suddenly wilt and die without excessive yellowing of leaves. The fungus mycelium gets into the water passages so that the sap supply from the roots is cut off.

See also DUTCH ELM DISEASE.

ENDIVE (*Cichorium Endivia*)

Often called escarole (which has wider leaves), this salad plant will succeed in any ordinary garden soil not deficient in humus and normal moisture. Like lettuce, its succulent growth must be rather rapid to enable it to form tender leaves. On poor, dry, exposed soil its growth will be slowed up so that its leaves, if they form in quantity, will be tough and unnecessarily pungent.

For success in growing endive, use the same area where lettuce succeeded early in the spring, and add a thin layer of compost between the rows.

Planting: Seed should be thinly sown, covered with not more than ⅓ inch of finely sifted, mature compost humus, clean sand, or a mixture of the two. To make the job easier, seed, sand and humus may be well mixed in a container and then spread along the bottom of a shallow trench. The rows should be placed about one foot apart and the plants thinned to stand one foot apart in the row. For a fall crop, seed must be sown in late summer.

You may find it best to raise endive in a flat or similar container set in a partly shaded spot, or by using a shaded seedbed. Flats and seedbeds may be protected from excessive summer heat by stretching cheesecloth over them. When transplanting the young plants to the garden, be sure they are set slightly deeper than they were in the flat and are well firmed. A little work with the hoe to keep down weeds, or a light mulching of straw or rough compost, is about all the cultivation the plants need.

Blanching: The slightly bitter, unappetizing flavor of the leaves can be eliminated by blanching. This may be accomplished by inverting flowerpots over the plants, by placing foot-wide planks on edge so that they cover the row with a light-tight miniature roof, or by tying up the heads when the plant is about half-grown and the head fairly well formed. To do this, draw together the long outer leaves and tie them with soft string or a strip of muslin. The plants should remain covered or tied for about three weeks.

Plants that reach maturity in late fall should be gently dug up with a good ball of earth around their roots and set in a dark corner of a cool, unheated cellar. Here the heads will soon blanch without the necessity of tying.

Although blanching reduces the bitterness natural to the leaf, it also reduces its food value. The green, unblanched outer leaves are rich in vitamins A, B₁ and C. The bitterness of these outer leaves can become a savory asset when cooked in soups with a flavor and with greens. They can also be used to add distinction to the salad bowl.

Varieties: Green Curled and Broad Leaved Batavian both reach maturity at 90 days. Each has rich green, firm leaves that are excellent in salads. Salad King (98 days) has bright green leaves that blanch to creamy white.

ENDRIN
See CHLORINATED HYDROCARBONS

ENGLISH DAISY   (*Bellis perennis*)

Sometimes cultivated in pots in the greenhouse, this perennial English native grows to six inches and has white, pink or red, single or double flowers that bloom in spring. In cool, damp areas of the West Coast it may flower all summer as it does in England. It is a good choice for edgings and rock gardens or for massing with spring bulbs.

Start seed indoors in March and transplant out when several inches tall. English daisy prefers moist, rich soil and full sun, but will not tolerate excessive heat. Protect it in New England and other cold winter areas with a mulch, or dig plants and winter them in a cold frame.
See also DAISY.

ENGLISH ELM   *See* ELM

ENGLISH IVY   (*Hedera helix*)

Usually climbing more than 15 feet and covering walls and trellises, this evergreen vine is also useful for outdoor boxes and baskets and as a ground cover under shade trees.

It prefers a sheltered, shady location and a moist, rich soil. Propagation is by cuttings.
See also IVY.

An easy-to-grow house plant, English ivy is also a fine evergreen ground cover for shady banks with northern exposures.

ENTOMOLOGY

Entomology is the branch of zoology that deals with insects.

See also INSECT, INSECT CONTROL.

ENZYME

Enzymes are complex organic substances, such as amylase or pepsin, that accelerate, or catalyze, specific chemical transformations, as in the digestion of foods in plants and animals. Without enzymes, plants would not grow, seeds would not germinate, organic matter would remain unchanged on a compost pile, microbes would not function, and there would be no soil.

EPIPHYLLUM

A genus of the Cactus family often called orchid cactus, epiphyllums originated in the Central American jungles and the northern parts of South America and Mexico. The showy flowers, which grow directly off the leaf-like stems, come in all colors except a real blue and vary in size from two to ten inches across. Their large size tends to make them more suitable for greenhouse cultivation.

The orchid cactus requires a moister and richer soil than is needed by desert types of cacti. An ideal composition would consist of three parts leaf mold and two parts sharp sand. A tablespoon of steamed bone meal and one of hoof and horn meal are added to two quarts of the soil mix.

Though the California climate is especially favorable to growing orchid cactus under lath or in the open, they are easily grown anywhere outdoors in the summer. During active growth the soil should be kept evenly moist. They should be kept indoors in the winter months, preferably in a sunny eastern exposure or lightly shaded southern one. During this rest period, they should be kept as dry as possible without allowing the leaflike stems to shrivel. The winter rest is necessary to assure satisfactory summer blooming from April through June.

Growing epiphyllum from seed is a long process and they do not always come true to the parent plant, as they do if propagated a-sexually. This is done by taking a cutting from the main branch. A ten- to 16-inch cutting gives quick bloom, but it takes two years for the plant to bloom from seeds.

When taking cuttings, allow them to cure for five to ten days before replanting in a dry soil mixed with equal parts leaf mold or good compost material and building sand. Withhold water for at least three days, and then water sparingly until reestablished. Plants that are damp or watered at once after transplanting may rot off at the base. Be sure the containers have good drainage. The more crowded the plant, the better the blooms.

After the first year some feeding is necessary. Compost or manure tea or fish emulsion during active growth will supply the necessary nutrients.

See also CACTI.

EPIPHYTE

Plants that grow on other plants but are not parasitic upon them are called epiphytes, air plants or tree perchers. They derive nourishment from the organic matter around them. Extracting their food by means of aerial roots, epiphytes will even grow on telephone wires and buildings.

EROSION

Erosion is the wearing away of the earth's surface by a variety of natural forces—most commonly water and wind. Each year millions of tons of topsoil are lost through erosion; both good and poor land suffer the loss. Erosion can be averted or halted by proper agricultural and soil conservation practices.

See also SOIL CONSERVATION.

ERYNGIUM

These summer-blooming perennials, also known as sea holly, have globular white or blue flowers, prickly foliage and steely blue stems. Good plants for the rock garden or border, eryngiums need full sun and a moist, fairly rich soil. Varieties include button snakeroot (*E. yuccifolium*), four to six feet; *E. Bourgatii,* 1½ feet or less; and *E. giganteum,* over six feet.

ESCAROLE   *See* ENDIVE

ESPALIER

Coming from the French word, *epaulet,* which refers to a shoulder strap, espalier got its name because of the way shoulderlike limbs branch at a right angle to the trunk. The system is based on the principle of sap flow con-

trol. In practice, this means that you may have to severely prune or kill off stronger branches in order to help along weaker ones to give the tree a more even shape.

The objective in espalier is to train trees in a manner similar to vines or grapes so that the branches grow flat along a wall or trellis. Therefore, an espalier tree becomes a two-dimensional growth; it grows up and across the wall but not out from it.

Planting: Follow the same planting suggestions as for dwarf fruit trees. It is best to begin with an unbranched whip. Plant as early in spring as your region will allow, or in fall if in a warmer area. Plant the trees one or two feet apart.

The soil should be moderately open and well drained; the hole should be big enough to take the tree roots without bending them. Cultivate the soil deeply, making certain to loosen the soil at the bottom of the hole.

If you plant trees close to the foundation of your house, you may run up against a heavy, hardpan subsoil left by the builders. Break up and work in compost, peat or other humus material so that the roots of your tree won't be cut off from water, air and nutrients.

Both tree roots and top should be pruned before planting. Fill the hole to within a few inches of the top with good-quality topsoil, and leave a slight depression around the tree so rainwater can collect there. Tamp the earth gently but firmly around the roots leaving no air pockets; next, water and mulch two to three feet around the tree and several inches deep.

Keep in mind that dwarf fruit trees should always be planted with the graft-union an inch above ground. (The graft-union is an onion-shaped knob at the base of the trunk and can be recognized by a change in the color of the bark.) If planted below ground, the part above the graft will put out roots, resulting in a standard-size tree and slower-maturing fruit.

Training Trees: The final shape of the tree depends on the equal flow of sap throughout the branches. You may have to hold back certain portions that are naturally stronger and faster growing and encourage the slower and weaker branches. There are several ways to do this:

1. Prune the strong branches short but allow the weaker to grow long; all pruning of side branches should be done in the summer.

2. Kill off the useless buds on the strong

parts as soon as possible. Do this as late as possible with the weaker parts.

3. Tie up the stronger branches very early and close to the wall, but delay doing this to the weaker branches.

4. Pick off some of the leaves on the stronger side.

5. Leave as much fruit as possible on the stronger branches but pick all fruit off the weaker one; by thinning out to four fruits to a foot or branch, larger fruits will appear the following year.

6. Keep the strong side close to the wall and keep the weak part away.

7. If necessary, even place a covering over the strong side to deprive it of light.

Varieties: Apples: McIntosh, Winesap, Baldwin; Pears: Flemish Beauty, Bartlett, Anjou; Plums: Burbank, Italian; Peaches: Elberta, Champion. A tree that does not self-pollinate should be planted near a tree of the same variety.

Espaliered trees are the result of radical pruning and careful training along horizontal wires, pipes or trellises.

EUCALYPTUS

Handsome foliage and flowers in addition to varied, interesting bark, make these fragrant broad-leaved evergreens popular ornamental trees for streets and lawns. Native to Australia and growing in warm or semitropical areas, the eucalyptus or gum tree is also valued for its timber, the oil distilled from its leaves and its use as a windbreak and fuel tree. There are also attractive dwarf forms, suitable for gardens.

The blue gum (*E. Globulus*) is a tall tree widely grown in California and the Southwest. It is quite sensitive to abrupt weather changes and freezing temperatures, but also adapts very well to the dry soils of this region. Murray red gum (*E. camaldulensis*) resists both drought and flooding, withstands extreme heat and thrives in alkaline soil. Red ironbark (*E. fibrosa*), growing to 40 feet, has blue or gray green leaves, dark-hued bark and a profusion of rose-colored blossoms. Red mahogany (*E. resinifera*) has small flowers and grows to 100 feet.

Grown mostly in California, the eucalyptus tolerates a variety of soil types, but does best in a rich loam. It should not be grown too close to other plants because of its tendency to feed heavily on soil nutrients. It is propagated by seed sown under screens.

Medicinal uses of this herb range from antiseptic to antispasmodic. The powdered leaves were once inhaled to treat bronchial disorders. Oils from eucalyptus leaves have been used for fevers, croup and spasmodic throat disorders. Large doses of this herb can cause vomiting and muscular weakness.

Eucalyptus oil and leaves also make a potent insecticide.

See also HERB.

Oil from the eucalyptus leaves is used in cough medicines and insect repellents; full grown, the trees are excellent ornamentals and windbreaks.

EUONYMUS

Also spelled *Evonymus,* this genus includes a large number of deciduous and evergreen vines, shrubs and small trees that are popular for many garden and landscaping uses. Propagated by seeds, layers or cuttings, they do well in any soil and in sun or partial shade. Although generally found in warmer areas, most deciduous and a few of the evergreen types are hardy in the North, where they thrive in city and seashore environments.

Some of the popular species in the genus include: running strawberry bush (*E. obovata*), spindle tree (*E. europaea*) and burning bush or wahoo (*E. atropurpurea*), growing respectively 1½, 15 and 25 feet high. Burning bush, which is found from New York to Montana and southward, produces handsome red leaves and seeded fruits in October. Another popular species, cultivated in warmer parts of the country, is *E. japonica,* an evergreen hedge plant growing ten to 15 feet tall.

All are spring flowering and have bright seeded berries that ripen from July to frost.

See also EVERGREEN, SHRUBS.

EUPHORBIA

This diverse genus has about 2,000 species, which come mostly from Africa and the East Indies. Considering the arid regions of origination, they are the equivalent of the American cacti. Unlike cacti, their flowers are small and insignificant, but their bracts can be highly colorful, like the red ones of the poinsettia. Some species are spiny like cacti, while others have strange, exotic, tortured shapes. All have a milky sap, whose toxicity can vary from an irritant to a deadly poison. Watch children around these plants and avoid getting the sap in cuts or your eyes.

Many of these plants succeed well in greenhouses and homes. A few hardy species can be used in the garden. Soil should be well drained like that used for cacti. A sunny southern exposure is best and the soil should dry between waterings. These dry periods should be longer in the winter. Propagation is by offsets (if produced) or cuttings, which have dried until the wound forms a callus.

A few species are native or naturalized in the United States. Those found in gardens include flowering spurge (*Euphorbia corollata*), cypress spurge (*E. Cyparissias*), cushion euphorbia (*E. epithymoides*), painted spurge (*E. heterophylla*), snow-on-the-mountain (*E. marginata*), and myrtle euphorbia (*E. Myrsinites*). Those from Africa make interesting house plants. A few of the better known include poinsettia (*E. pulcherrima*), crown-of-thorns (*E. Milii*), Medusa's-head (*E. caput-Medusae*), milkbush (*E. Tirucalli*), and living-baseball (*E. obesa*).

Balsam spurge (*E. balsamifera*) is grown in the Canary Islands where a thickened jelly made from the juice is eaten.

See also CACTI, SUCCULENTS.

EUROPEAN CORN BORER
See INSECT CONTROL

EVENING PRIMROSE   (*Oenothera*)

These showy night-blooming plants are easily grown in full sun and light, well-drained soil. Blooming in summer, they are good plants for the border or the wild or rock garden. *O. biennis,* the familiar evening primrose of roadsides and waste places, grows two to four feet tall and has yellow flowers. Sundrop (*O. fruticosa*), the day-blooming counterpart of the evening primrose, grows two feet high, has long red stems and bears clusters of lemon yellow flowers in June and July. Two cultivars are Major and Yellow River. Sundrops do best if given a little shade. *O. missourensis,* the Ozark or Missouri primrose, is a 15-inch sprawling plant with deep yellow flowers five inches in diameter. This American native will thrive for years with little attention, blooming through most of the summer.

EVERGREEN

Evergreen shrubs and trees lend an air of permanence to the home grounds and gardens. Used with restraint, the practice of planting evergreens around the base of a house is both aesthetically pleasing and practical. Tall-growing specimens are useful and necessary to emphasize a corner or to break the lines of a long, low house. Many evergreen shrubs have showy flowers and are attractive additions to the garden. Such shrubs include mountain laurel, rhododendron, azalea, and trailing arbutus, all members of the acid-loving Heath family.

Evergeens, both broad- and narrow-leaved, truly come into their own with winter. Practical evergreens for the northern states are pines, spruces, cedar, hemlock, yews, and juniper. The bright, shiny foliage of many of the broad-leaved kinds contrasts well with the dense growth of the conifers. In the North, various laurels, bog rosemary (*Andromeda Polifolia*), fetterbush (*Leucothoe Catesbaei*), and many hollies are hardy. Nandinas, cherry laurel, crape myrtle, rhododendrons, and the evergreen privets can be used for winter gardens in the South.

Dividing evergreens into two categories, mass plantings and accent plantings, makes it easier to secure successful arrangements. Small trees used in a limited area, such as the vast spaces below windows or to hide a high foundation, are mass plantings, and include the low, spreading evergreens such as yews, dwarf junipers, and such shrubs as rhododendron, privet or boxwood.

Accent plants are important trees on a large lawn, or those placed near the entrance or corners of a house. They serve to blend the house into the surrounding landscape, providing an interesting frame. Accent plants typically are tall, pointed, large limbed, and have generous foliage. Arborvitae, upright junipers and cedars are good choices. Remember you want to achieve a pleasing frame and not a screen for your home.

If you keep in mind that the shrubbery and house should have equal prominence, you'll find it simple to work out the best informal planting for your home. You won't grow many types of evergreens clustered in tight little bunches. Neither do you want to obscure your second-story windows with an overgrown forest. Consider the future growth of the plants you choose.

Color is important, too. Select plants of a uniform tone. Brightly colored, exotic specimens might be fine in a large garden or estate, but stand out like sore thumbs by the average-sized home.

Always buy stock that is fully guaranteed. Be especially careful to get plants at least three years old, as they will have vigorous root systems and top growth. They can be expected to survive the shock of transplanting and adapt to new conditions rapidly.

Planting Evergreens: The shock of moving either conifers or broad-leaved evergreens is greater than with other woody plants. Evergreens are never entirely dormant. They should be dug with a large ball of soil and then tied up at once in burlap or canvas. Burlap generally finds use on small plants and is not removed when they are planted. Just slit it in a few places. Canvas is used for large, heavy trees and must be removed before planting, as it rots very slowly.

Drainage is particularly important. Excessive moisture can kill the tree, especially if the soil is naturally heavy. Even if there is good soil as deep as two feet, check to see that there is no layer of hard gravel or rock below. Dig the planting holes deeper and wider than the roots require. A hole two to three feet wide is right for a small tree if the soil is of good quality, but should be wider if the soil is poor. Pile the topsoil to one side, and dig out and discard the poorer subsoil to a depth of about two feet.

Always handle the tree by the burlap-covered root ball. Branches can be tied to prevent breakage. Above all, avoid deep planting—the cause of ill health and early death of many trees. Place the tree at the ground level it had originally.

Don't cut back the roots of an evergreen at planting time, and never cut off the tops of any trees, as either will stunt its growth. If it is necessary to remove any of the lower branches, cut them off individually. Remember to turn the best side towards the direction from which it will be seen.

If you are unable to plant the specimens immediately, place them in the shade with the ball and burlap on and water them thoroughly. The wrappings keep the roots from drying wind. Plant early in the spring or in late August or early September. If you set them out too late in the fall, the roots do not have an opportunity to get a fresh start. Keep them well watered.

Feeding and Trimming: Many plants thrive best in an acid soil. The soil should also be rich in humus and have good drainage.

An occasional topdressing of well-rotted manure can be given, but if the soil is well supplied with humus and if a plentiful leaf mulch is maintained, any special feeding is best done with fertilizers of an acid-forming nature.

After the plants have become established, the soil surrounding them should be disturbed as little as possible, for the roots are very near the surface. It is known that there is a definite mycorrhizal association between the feeder roots of most of the evergreen plants and shrubs and certain fungi. Sometimes a balanced organic food or one rich in nitrogen is given to stimulate growth. This should be dug into the soil, and the area well watered; or it may be applied in solution or in crowbar holes driven at two-foot intervals down to the feeding roots, starting the holes at least 18 inches from the trunk.

Excellent materials for mulching are evergreen boughs, threshed rye straw, salt hay, oak leaves, peat moss, and grass cuttings. They should be applied in a layer not in excess of three inches and extending a little beyond the natural spread of the roots.

Evergreen shrubs can be trimmed any time during the growing season, but early flowering evergreen shrubs are best pruned after they have flowered. For each branch you snip off, you will get four or five in the spring growth, giving the shrub the solid, compact appearance so necessary to its beauty. This close trimming will also prevent the leggy and somewhat unhealthy appearance found so often in uncared-for shrubs.

Loss of Moisture: Since evergreens can't protect themselves during the winter by dropping their leaves, water continues to evaporate through them. Too much wind and winter sun may cause an extra loss of moisture, and this common drying injury is known as winter burn. Excellent means of protection are either a covering of burlap, stretched on a wire frame over the entire plant, or a screen (made from laths, straw mats or burlap) set up on the east and south sides of the plant. Both are recommended for the small conifers, especially if the trees are in an exposed position. Well-ventilated boxes can be used, too, but remember that all protectors should be kept beyond reach of the branches.

Slender evergreens with long, erect branches, such as the Irish junipers, often suffer in winter gales. The dwarf evergreens, used in foundation plantings, also suffer—but windbreakers made from slatted fencing and held in place by steel posts will protect them. Breakers made of lath and wire, like highway snow fences, will also work well. If grown in extremely exposed areas, it may be necessary to wrap foundation conifers in burlap. Start at the bottom and tie a stout cord to one of the branches, and then walk around the specimen, lifting each branch and holding it in place with the cord until the top is reached. Tie the end of the cord to the next lower stand. Next, apply three-inch strips of cloth (preferably burlap), starting at the bottom. Fasten the end to the first round of cord with wire nails used like pins, and walk around the specimen as before, winding the burlap spirally upward and fastening each lap in several places with the nails. If desired, the top may be covered with a square of burlap pinned in place or with any other cap that will shed the snow.

When staking, arrange three stakes in a triangle with the tree trunk held centrally by means of wires or stout, nonstretching cords which pass between the stakes and around the trunk. Protect the bark from being cut by applying pieces of rubber hose, automobile tire or even a thick wrapping of several layers of burlap.

Heavy Snow and Sleet on the Branches: As soon as a storm stops and while the snow is soft and fluffy, heavy snow loads should be jarred from the branches. This should not be done by striking them from above, because such blows only increase the strain and often break the branches.

Keep the snow and ice off foundation shrubs such as the yew. This conifer, unlike most evergreens, has several main stems that are easily damaged by a heavy snow blanket. The remedy is either to shake the snow off or else tie the entire plant together. Props placed under heavy branches of old conifers will prevent breakage from heavy snow and ice loads, but be careful to avoid tearing the bark.

See also ACIDITY–ALKALINITY.

EVERLASTINGS
See XERANTHEMUM

EXOCHORDA

A member of the Rose family, the pearlbush is a slender-branched, deciduous shrub with bright green foliage and showy clusters of pure white flowers that bloom in late April or May. It is an excellent shrub for forcing blooms in water indoors, and receives its name from the unopened flower buds which resemble large pearls. This bush is easy to cultivate in sun and well-drained, loamy soil, and can be propagated by seeds, softwood cuttings or layers. *E. racemosa,* growing to 12 feet, is one of the most popular species.

EXTENSION SERVICES, COOPERATIVE

The Cooperative Extension Service System in this country operates under the combined funding of federal, state and county governments. It is administered by the land-grant university as designated by each state's legislature. Volunteers, county agents and the extension specialist work together to provide educational materials on forest management, crop production, horticulture, and poultry, livestock and dairy production to farmers involved in these projects. 4-H programs, nutrition programs and a myriad of family-oriented services including health and safety programs, family housing, food and nutrition, and family resource management are available to the community through the extension service.

What follows on the next page is a list of the State Cooperative Extension Service Offices and their addresses.

Auburn University
Auburn, AL 36830

University of Alaska
Fairbanks, AK 99701

University of Arizona
Tucson, AZ 85721

University of Arkansas at Little Rock
PO Box 391
Little Rock, AR 72204

University of California
2200 University Avenue
Berkeley, CA 94720

Colorado State University
Fort Collins, CO 80521

University of Connecticut
Storrs, CT 06268

University of Delaware
Newark, DE 19711

Federal City College
1424 K Street, NW
Washington, DC 20001

University of Florida
Gainesville, FL 32601

University of Georgia
Athens, GA 30601

University of Hawaii
Honolulu, HI 96822

University of Idaho
Moscow, ID 83843

University of Illinois
Urbana, IL 61801

Purdue University
Lafayette, IN 47907

Iowa State University of Science and
Technology
Ames, IA 50010

Kansas State University of Agriculture and
Applied Science
Manhattan, KS 66502

University of Kentucky
Lexington, KY 40506

Louisiana State University and Agricultural
and Mechanical College
Baton Rouge, LA 70803

University of Maine at Orono
Orono, ME 04473

University of Maryland at College Park
College Park, MD 20742

University of Massachusetts at Amherst
Amherst, MA 01002

Michigan State University
East Lansing, MI 48823

University of Minnesota
Minneapolis, MN 55455

Mississippi State University
Mississippi State, MS 39762

University of Missouri
309 University Hall
Columbia, MO 65201

Montana State University
Bozeman, MT 59715

University of Nebraska at Lincoln
Lincoln, NB 68504

University of Nevada at Reno
Reno, NV 89507

University of New Hampshire
Taylor Hall
Durham, NH 03824

Rutgers, the State University
PO Box 231
New Brunswick, NJ 08903

New Mexico State University
Las Cruces, NM 88001

Cornell University
Ithaca, NY 14850

North Carolina State University at Raleigh
Raleigh, NC 27607

North Dakota State University
Fargo, ND 58102

Ohio State University
2120 Fyffe Road
Columbus, OH 43210

Oklahoma State University of Agriculture
and Applied Science
Stillwater, OK 74074

Oregon State University
Corvallis, OR 97331

Pennsylvania State University
University Park, PA 16802

University of Puerto Rico
Río Piedras, PR 00931

University of Rhode Island
Kingston, RI 02881

Clemson University
Clemson, SC 29631

South Dakota State University
Brookings, SD 57006

University of Tennessee at Knoxville
PO Box 1071
Knoxville, TN 37916

Texas A. & M. University
College Station, TX 77843

Utah State University
Logan, UT 84321

University of Vermont
Burlington, VT 05401

Virginia Polytechnic Institute and State
University
Blacksburg, VA 24601

College of the Virgin Islands
PO Box 166
Kingshill
Saint Croix, VI 00801

Washington State University
Pullman, WA 99163

West Virginia University
294 Coliseum
Morgantown, WV 26506

University of Wisconsin-Madison
432 North Lake Street
Madison, WI 53706

University of Wyoming
University Station
Box 3354
Laramie, WY 82070

F

FAIRY LILIES   *See* ZEPHYRANTHES

FALLOW

In a rotation schedule, this term refers to the practice of keeping a portion of land bare of vegetation for a season. Its major benefit is the conservation of soil water and, if used wisely, it can be an effective farming technique. However, it relies on the use of harmful chemical herbicides and results in a devastating loss of soil organic matter through erosion and even in an eventual depletion of soil minerals.

Organic farmers who want to practice fallowing should use a modified system. Rather than plowing under all of the plant residues after harvest, conscientious growers should allow a stubble to remain on the soil surface. This, combined with a heavy mulch, eliminates the erosion problem and tends to encourage snow and rain to filter into the ground.

Even more beneficial is the practice of planting a green manure crop on the field that would normally be left fallow. This is especially good for soils with a low humus content. By growing the leguminous plants, such as vetch, soybeans or sweet clover, on a fallow field and then plowing it under as green manure, the soil will be greatly improved. Sweet clover is recommended for a green manure fallow since it turns a considerable amount of organic matter into the soil, and does an excellent job of making the phosphorus in phosphate rock available to crops following in the rotation.

FALSE CHAMOMILE
See BOLTONIA

FALSE DRAGONHEAD
See PHYSOSTEGIA

FALSE HELLEBORE
See VERATRUM

FALSE INDIGO
See AMORPHA, BAPTISIA

FALSE MALLOW   *See* SIDALCEA

FALSE SOLOMON'S-SEAL
See SMILACINA, VAGNERA

FALSE STARWORT
See BOLTONIA

FAREWELL-TO-SPRING
See GODETIA

FAULKNER, EDWARD H.

(1886–   ) A noted agricultural writer, Faulkner is best known for his unorthodox book, *Plowman's Folly,* published in 1943. Faulkner advanced the concept that plowing is not only unnecessary, but actually harmful to the soil. He stressed the importance of returning humus to the soil and using rock fertilizers. In 1947, *A Second Look,* a sequel to *Plowman's Folly,* was published. Faulkner's earlier background included work as a county agent, agricultural teacher, field tester of soil-management theories, and farm editor for a Cleveland radio station.

FAUNA

The fauna of the living soil is one of the most valuable assets that the gardener has.

As soon as the leaves fall to the ground, decay sets in by way of molds, fungi, bacteria, and other minute soil faunas such as springtails, mites, various grubs of small flies, and worms. These in turn are devoured by other animals, such as beetle grubs and centipedes. Woody material is chewed up and eaten by wood lice, the grubs of various species of flies, beetles, and moths.

One feeds upon another, and eventually they are, in turn, attacked. The waste products of each are again consumed, first as before by the bacteria and molds, then again by the organisms that feed on these. And the leaf that fell in autumn is passed through the bodies of many living things, one consuming another, forming a continuous living chain, reducing the leaf, link by link, until, still a living thing, it is in such a state that the new plant can absorb it and become a real living thing in its turn.

The living soil faunas are instrumental in conditioning the soil by their biting, chewing, tunneling, and crawling through the mass of material. They loosen the soil, thoroughly mix the mineral with the organic matter, and by the very nature of the physical structure of their excrement, create that valuable crumb structure which is so desirable.

Where there is an abundance of organic matter there is also a diversity of soil animals. *See also* MICROORGANISM.

FEATHERED COCKSCOMB
See CELOSIA

FEATHER PALM
See QUEEN PALM

FEATHERS

Feathers are a good addition to a compost heap since they contain 15.3 percent nitrogen and decay rapidly if kept sufficiently moist.

Feather meal, made from poultry feathers, has also been made into a valuable fertilizer by a process developed by the USDA Western Regional Research Laboratory. The feathers are pressure-cooked with steam for 30 to 60 minutes, then dried to an 8 to 12 percent moisture content and ground. This yields a dry, friable meal or powder. There is no appreciable loss of nutrients during the steam treatment. The finished product weighs about 50 to 60 pounds per cubic foot. Its total nitrogen content averages between 12 and 13.5 percent, of which 10 to 13 percent is water insoluble.

The slow release of nitrogen makes feathers and feather meal valuable for all crops requiring a steady, long-lasting supply of that element. Put on the cover or green manure crop late in the fall, it will release nitrogen slowly all winter and spring, and prevent a nitrogen shortage caused by bacteria attacking the green matter of the crop when plowed under.

All home poultry raisers should add their slaughtered birds' feathers to the compost heap. Gardeners near poultry-processing plants may be able to obtain large quantities of feathers for little or no charge.

FEIJOA   *See* GUAVA

FELDSPAR

Feldspar is a closely related group of minerals that are silicates of aluminum, with potassium, sodium or calcium.

See also MINERAL ROCKS.

FELT WASTES

The nitrogen content of felt wastes has been found to be as high as 14 percent, making it an excellent compost material. Moisture and bacteria are necessary for the decomposition of these materials and the process is hastened if manure or some other high-protein material is added to increase the amount of bacteria.

FENNEL   (*Foeniculum vulgare*)

Occasionally cultivated in the United States as a garden herb, fennel is an herbaceous perennial whose dried aromatic fruits, commonly referred to as seed, are used for flavoring liqueurs and in medicine. A volatile oil is present in the seed and may be obtained by steam distillation. It possesses the characteristic flavor of the seed and is also used for flavoring and medicinal purposes. The several varieties of fennel are quite different in growth habit. The Indian fennel matures at about 3½ to four feet in height when grown under favorable conditions. The Moroccan variety requires about three weeks longer to mature and grows about six feet tall.

The plant has a main taproot which is generally fleshy and white with smaller horizontal roots attached. The main root leads to a central main stem and a cluster of yellow umbels. Large, feathery leaves are attached to the nodes. The plant has a strong, pleasing odor.

This herb's botanical name was derived from the Latin word *fenum,* meaning hay. It is similar to hay in appearance. The Greeks used fennel to treat more than 20 illnesses and to reduce appetites. Ancient Romans ate fennel roots, leaves and seeds in their salads, breads and cakes, and enjoyed its aromatic fruits and edible shoots. Later, in the Middle Ages, fennel was recognized as a favorite strewing herb that offered a pleasant scent and repelled insects. In the kitchen, it was used to flavor spoiling foods. Fennel, like dill, was also believed to be a safeguard against witchcraft.

Fennel grows well in a fairly mild climate and on almost any good soil but thrives best on nonacid, well-drained loams. It is readily grown from seed but can also be propagated by root and crown division. The seed is sown thickly directly in the garden late in fall or early in spring, in rows three or four feet apart and covered lightly. When well established the plants are thinned to stand eight to

12 inches apart in the row. The plants can also be started in a seedbed and transplanted to the field when three or four inches high. The cultivation required is the same as for ordinary garden crops. If the plants are grown as a winter crop in the warmer valleys of the southwestern states, the tops can be injured by winter freezing, but they will make a good growth under favorable conditions early in spring.

Fennel is believed to be adapted to the central and northern states and probably to some sections of California, where it has escaped from cultivation in some places and grows to large size.

Fennel leaves are harvested during the first year and, to some extent, during the second. Harvest when seeds turn light brown. Morning hours are best for cutting ripe umbels with minimal seed loss. Leaves should dry in warm shade until they break when pressed. Harvested seeds should dry in the sun.

In addition to its sweet and fragrant aroma, fennel has a variety of uses to gardeners, cooks and physicians. The herb demands special attention from the gardener who uses it as a background plant or for future flower arrangements. It must be separated from bush beans, tomatoes and caraway; there are other plants it will harm if planted near them. Fennel flowers attract pollinating insects, and powdered fennel plant will repel fleas around kennels and stables.

For the kitchen, fennel leaves serve as a garnish for salads, stews and vegetables. Fennel can be boiled with salmon and mackerel to lessen fish-oil indigestibility. Fennel stalks can be skinned and soaked with vinegar and pepper for a salad. Dried fruits are used to enhance the flavor of pastries and candies.

The plant has also been known for its ability to help treat digestive gas, gallstones and

The large yellow flowers of the fennel plant bear seeds that can be harvested for use in baked goods.

dozens of other ailments. Fennel juice syrup was once even thought to be a cure for chronic coughs and lung diseases.

Even young mothers have found fennel useful. It is said that a mixture of leaves and seeds boiled in barley water may increase the quality and quantity of milk a mother produces.

See also HERB.

FENUGREEK
(*Trigonella Foenum-graecum*)

A stemmy annual legume native to the Mediterranean region, and closely related to sweet clover, fenugreek is grown mainly for its medicinal and culinary value. In 1859 the "seeds of helbeh" were introduced to the United States through the Patent Office of Palestine. A *helbeh* conserve was later exported to Britain.

The plant is erect, more or less branched and attains a height of over two feet. It has three leaflets and small axillary flowers that are white with dark markings. The long, needlelike pods bear several small, yellow to brown seeds. The whole plant has a pronounced odor and taste, and is not relished by livestock.

Fenugreek fruits are picked when ripe, before the seeds shatter. Seeds are shelled from the pods and dried by artificial heat.

Fenugreek seeds are used in folk medicine externally to treat boils, carbuncles and abscesses, and internally to help cure digestive tract disorders. The seeds can be eaten raw, boiled or as part of curry powder. In India, the plant is used as a potherb. The leaves of this herb are often used to make a pleasant-tasting tea.

A small acreage of fenugreek is cultivated today as a green manure crop in California.

FERN

Perennial, flowerless plants, ferns are the "old men" of the plant kingdom. Long before the appearance of man, great forests of giant ferns covered the earth. Today all that remains of these dense jungles are vast beds of coal, formed by the decay of the plants when they were submerged by floodwaters.

However, quite a few of the descendants of these prehistoric ferns still thrive and over 10,000 species have been identified.

Ferns are ideal for damp, low spots by fences, shady areas under trees, on the north side of houses, and indoors where light is filtered and temperatures fairly low. Some, of course, are strictly tropical and must be grown in the greenhouse in temperate climates. But many of them will thrive in cool, shady, moist spots, even swampy areas. Some hardy types, such as the resurrection fern, seem to die under hot, dry conditions but spring into life as soon as water is supplied.

Ferns make a fine background for many flowering plants. The deciduous types are especially valuable in filling the empty spaces after spring-flowering bulbs have bloomed. Their leaves, or fronds, hide the untidy brown bulbs and continue to look good even after the shrubs and trees have put forth leaves and made dense shade.

The ferns that stay green all year, like the leather wood fern (*Dryopteris marginalis*) and the Christmas fern (*Polystichum acrostichoides*), can be a garden mainstay right up until snow blankets them. The larger ferns are excellent for filling in around newly planted shrubs and supplying height in good landscape design.

They also cool the ground and moisten the atmosphere, shading the plants beneath them like a lacy parasol. They are very helpful in protecting young or delicate plants.

Planting: Spring and fall are the best times to plant or move ferns. Those with running rootstocks will send up new fronds if transplanted in any season but they tend to overrun their sites. Use running rootstock ferns such as hay-scented, bracken and ostrich only where a large, mass planting is desired. If you are hesitant about moving ferns from the wild, you can purchase them from a wild flower nursery.

Planting directions vary according to

species but, in general, ferns with spreading roots prefer to have their roots barely covered, while central-crown types like the crown exposed or just above the soil surface.

A woodsy location, with shade, moisture and an organic soil high in leaf mold, is perfect for the majority of ferns. Dig a fairly deep hole and put in a mixture of leaf mold, sand and loam. Oak leaves and compost are good substitutes for the leaf mold. If the soil is acid, limestone may be needed, and a mulch of organic materials is always recommended.

Rock-growing ferns are hard to establish directly on the rocks. But plant them alongside and they will quickly spread over the rocks. For sunny rock gardens the best varieties are hay-scented, woodsia, ebony spleenwort, bracken, and cliff brake. You can use these ferns to blend in a big boulder that would be hard to remove, or to soften the outlines of a rock ledge.

The fragrant hay-scented fern also thrives in shady rock gardens as do hart's-tongue, royal, northern lady, New York, maidenhair, and the evergreen and marginal wood ferns. The smaller kinds among these and the polypodies look very pretty planted in soil placed in the crevices of fieldstone fences.

For massing in low shady spots, you'll like the handsome cinnamon or the interrupted fern. Like its cousin, the royal fern, cinnamon has colorful fruiting fronds that resemble flower heads. The leathery fronds of sword ferns are also eye-catching planted thickly under dense shade trees.

Some ferns, like hay-scented and lady fern, are tolerant of many different conditions. They will flourish almost anywhere. But for dry, shady places, Christmas fern is your best choice. And for boggy spots, try marsh fern, sensitive fern or the lovely pale green New York fern. Royal fern prefers full sunlight but will tolerate very wet conditions like lakeshores, even growing in shallow water if its crowns are above the high waterline. Crested wood fern is another that likes damp sites, but with much shade.

The popular maidenhair is easy to establish in any well-drained soil. The hardy climbing fern, however, likes acid soil and grows well among mountain laurel and blueberry bushes. A heavy mulch of oak leaves will keep it thriving. For limestone sites, walking fern (its threadlike frond tips "walk" to root and form new plants) spreads to a tangled mat over mossy rocks in the shade.

You may find that you have a perfect spot for a fern garden. A brookside, a damp rocky slope or even an old garage or barn foundation might be an ideal place to establish dozens of varieties in a natural setting.

Indoor Planting: How about indoors? Here, too, ferns are highly valuable. Provided with dim light, a large number of ferns will thrive indoors. A northern window or any window which has little or no direct sunlight will suit ferns since the sun injures the delicate fronds. Potting soils should be rich in organic matter and well drained, and temperatures should be kept from 50 to 70°F. (10 to 21.11°C.). Only a few species can stand temperatures above 70°F. (21.11°C.) during the day.

Ferns do not like a heavy soil. One composed of four parts sandy loam, one part sand and one part manure will give good results. For most of the ferns a little leaf mold may be added. Pack the soil firmly about the roots but do not make it hard. While the soil in which ferns are growing must never become dry, neither must it become waterlogged. It is a common assumption that, because ferns grow wild in damp places, they cannot be overwatered, but while that soil may be very damp it is always well drained and aerated.

Keep the roots cool. This can be easily done by placing the pots in jardinieres or vases and packing damp sphagnum moss around them. If you want to use the plant for table or other decoration it can be removed from the receptacle, used in the decoration and returned later.

Keep the leaves of the ferns clean. This is best done by syringing them with clear water on all bright days when the sun can dry them.

Thrips and red spiders are troublesome, especially in dry atmospheres. The two can be kept in check by spraying water on the plants, especially on the underside of the fronds.

Annual repotting is necessary only for young ferns, and monthly feedings of dilute manure tea will keep all of them healthy and vigorous for years. Never use chemical fertilizer—ferns are extremely sensitive to its unbalanced formulations. Give them plenty of water: only the leaf-losing kinds should be allowed to dry out during their resting season.

Small ferns or young plants of the larger varieties that require lots of humidity are perfect for terrariums. For a lovely conversation piece, put some humusy soil in any good-sized glass container and plant polypodies, rattlesnake and grape ferns, oak and beech ferns, small spleenworts, maidenhair and walking ferns, along with other wild plants you pick up in the woods and fields. Be careful never to overwater. A glass cover over the top will conserve humidity.

You can propagate ferns by division of the crown or rootstock, but the most fascinating way is with spores, those tiny dustlike "seeds" clustering on the backs or edges of the leaves.

Brush them off into a paper bag, let them dry for a week or two, then shake them onto a pot of moist leaf mold and sand. Set the pot in a saucer of water and cover it with glass to retain humidity.

Sword ferns: A popular fern is the common sword fern (*Nephrolepis exaltata*). This type is rarely seen in the florists' shops, having been superseded by the Boston fern (*N. e.* cv. 'Bostoniensis').

This is the best of all the sword ferns. Even when young in small pots the plants are attractive, but as they make a fairly rapid growth one does not have to wait long to

A special cultivar of **Nephrolepis exaltata,** *Fluffy Ruffles fern is best propagated by division of its roots or runners.*

obtain a large plant. The fronds of the Boston fern are two to three feet long, two to three inches across and of a rich green color. Unlike most ferns it will stand some abuse. With all the other ferns, if the soil once becomes dry the plant is ruined for the season at least, if not absolutely killed; but this sword fern can usually be revived even if its soil has dried out for a few days.

Another fern of the *Nephrolepis* genus which has given satisfaction in many window gardens is known as *N. e.* cv. 'Philippinensis'. The fronds are smaller than the Boston fern, being only about 18 inches long and 1½ to two inches wide. They are very dark green. The cultivar Scottii is a miniature Boston fern, the fronds being shorter and narrower, thus making a denser, more compact plant.

There are several plumose cultivars of *Nephrolepis* in which the "leaflets" or pinnae are much divided. The fronds are usually a foot or so long and quite broad. They are known under such trade names as Pierson, Barrows and Whitman. These do well in the house, but with the exception of Whitman, the fronds are more or less liable to revert to the type. This is caused by a dry heat and insufficient light.

The sword ferns will grow in almost any soil, but a well-drained sandy loam is best.

Holly ferns: The glossy, dark green foliage of the holly fern (*Cyrtomium falcatum*) always attracts attention. The upper side of the pinna is very dark green, the underside is somewhat lighter green and studded with brown spots—the spores. The pinnae are large, four to six inches long and one to two inches broad, and the fronds about two feet long and very stiff.

Maidenhair ferns: The graceful, feathery fronds of the maidenhair ferns always excite

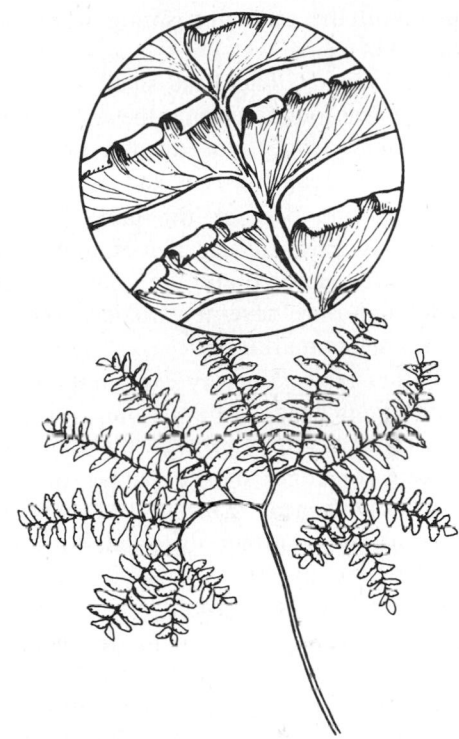

The delicate maidenhair ferns are among the easiest to grow indoors, requiring only adequate moisture and sunlight.

interest. The most beautiful one, *Adiantum tenerum* cv. 'Farleyense', often seen in the florists' shops, cannot be grown in the window garden, but there is a good substitute for it in the so-called Venus's-hair fern (*A. Capillus-Veneris*). This will withstand the trying conditions of the house just as well as will the Boston fern.

The soil in which maidenhair ferns are growing must never be allowed to dry out since the fronds immediately wither and may even die before you realize the problem. Should such an accident happen, remove the injured fronds and keep the plant in as good a condition as possible until the following spring when new growth will be made.

Table ferns: The best small ferns for the home are found among the table ferns (*Pteris*). The fronds are divided once, the divisions being long, narrow and pointed.

One of the best of the table ferns is *P. cretica*. It grows nearly a foot high. The stalks are straw colored and the foliage is dark green but there are several varieties, some of which have white markings.

Another table fern very commonly grown is *P. multifida,* which differs from *cretica* in not being such a strong grower, the stalks are brown and the edges of the pinnae of each frond are saw edged. Like *cretica,* this has many forms, some rather distorted, to which such descriptive names as cristata, variegata and angustata have been given.

The best variegated fern for the window garden is *P. quadriaurita* cv. 'Argyraea'. This is somewhat stronger growing than those already mentioned, but its chief feature is a broad, white band down the middle of each division of the frond.

All the table ferns are used more for dish gardens than for specimen plants, to which they are, however, admirably suited.

Miscellaneous ferns: One of the shield ferns (*Polystichum setiferum*) somewhat resembles the sword ferns. The fronds are from one to two feet long and rather narrow. The pinnae differ from those of the sword ferns in that they are triangular rather than oblong. This fern seems to withstand the unfavorable conditions of the house well.

The hare's-foot fern (*Polypodium aureum*) and rabbit's-foot fern (*Davallia fejeensis*) are always interesting because of their rhizomes. These rest on the ground and are densely covered with long, coarse, yellow hairs. Sooner or later these hang over the edge of the pot and bear a strong resemblance to a rabbit's foot.

Staghorn fern (*Platycerium bifurcatum*) is an exotic epiphytic fern with handsome fronds that grow up to two feet long. It requires more care than many plants and should be kept in a cool, humid, and moderately sunny place.

Another interesting fern is the Japanese climbing fern (*Lygodium japonicum*) and related species. This fern has twining fronds that often grow several yards long. Although delicate and feathery in appearance, it is very house hardy and will thrive under conditions suitable for other indoor ferns. Provided with a wire support, it will form a lacey screen.

Stenochlaena palustris, an epiphytic type, is also a vigorous climber. It is sometimes grown in a very warm greenhouse where it is made to climb the stems of various tree ferns.

FERTILITY

A fertile soil is one which produces satisfactory yields of crops and, because of the incorporation of plant and animal residues, contains an abundance of organic matter or humus. It has a favorable texture, not too loose and light nor too heavy and stiff, is well drained and has a proper pH for best plant growth. Finally, a fertile soil has an abundance of available plant food.

How to Increase Soil Fertility: There are many ways to increase and maintain the valuable nutrients of your soil which contribute to its fertility. The best way is to set up and follow an organic program that fits your particular garden needs. Some plants need a rather acid soil, while others need a more alkaline soil. They also need different nitrogen, phosphorous and potash ratios.

Each plant brings about changes in the soil and has soil needs different from other plants. You won't have to worry much about having *exactly* the right amount of each element for each plant you grow, however. As long as your soil is well balanced and rich in organic matter, your plants will not suffer.

See also COMPOSTING, COVER CROP, FERTILIZER, ORGANIC MATTER.

FERTILIZER

Fertilizer is a substance added to the soil to improve its fertility. Since a variety of elements contribute to the fertility of the soil, many individual elements and combinations of elements can be considered fertilizers.

In brief, a fertile soil has good amounts of the major plant nutrients—nitrogen, phosphorus and potassium; a sufficiency of the micronutrients (sometimes called trace minerals)—zinc, manganese, boron, iron, sulfur, copper, magnesium, molybdenum, and chlorine; an abundance of organic matter; and humus. To be fertile, the soil must also have a nearly neutral soil pH as well as good structure and drainage.

In the organic garden, natural fertilizers maintain and contribute to the improvement of all these necessary elements. Although the vocabulary of chemical agriculture dictates that fertilizers are only those substances that have measurable quantities of at least one of the major plant nutrients, organic growers hold to a much broader, more complex interpretation of soil fertility that recognizes the roles of organic matter and soil structure. Unlike those farmers who rely on chemical fertilizers to supply crops with specific nutrients in forms that are immediately available, they use many different, natural materials to maintain overall fertility. In this way, soil fertility and soil health are improved even as plant yields increase.

The organic approach eschews chemicals for a variety of reasons (*see also* FERTILIZER, CHEMICAL). Its practitioner uses a wide variety of natural materials and substances derived from natural materials to boost and maintain the soil's fertility. The most basic are animal manures and green manures, composts, and rock powders—substances that provide the soil with not only the major nutrients, but with trace minerals and organic matter as well. As nonchemical farming has gained credence during the 1970's, more and more fertilizers derived from natural materials have come on the market. Many of these products have definite value, but none should take the place of the basic organic fertilizers: organic matter and rock powders.

Organic gardeners and farmers believe balanced, fertile soil, rich in organic matter, will consistently yield healthy plants in abundance. Their soil-building techniques basically resemble those practiced by their chemical-oriented counterparts. They test their soil so they know its nutrient levels, organic matter content and pH. They develop a long-range soil-management program based on the soil test results. They seek to maintain major nutrient levels consistent with good plant yields.

But they don't ignore the value of organic matter in all areas of soil fertility.

Organic matter has aptly been referred to as the storehouse of the soil's nutrients. Briefly, the reasons it is so vital to soils are that it 1) improves tilth and structure, 2) improves water-holding capacity, 3) aids in nitrogen fixation, and 4) makes nutrients available to plants.

Soils differ widely in their content of plant nutrients, depending on the minerals from which they were formed and on the extent to which these original nutrients have been lost through erosion, leaching and crop harvesting. Some of these losses are made up by the weathering of minerals, rainfall, the action of earthworms and bacteria in the soil, and other natural soil phenomena. But serious deficiencies must be corrected if the soil is to produce adequate and healthy crops. This is the reason why organic fertilizers and mineral nutrients should be added—to maintain crop yields and to produce crops with the proper nutrients.

One of the best ways to gain an understanding of the major nutrient problems of soil is to have it tested—either with your own soil test kit or by your state experiment station or a commercial laboratory. Generally a test of this kind will tell you whether or not your soil has a sufficient amount of the major nutrients—nitrogen (N), phosphorus (P) and potassium (K). Often, it will also indicate whether your soil is acid or alkaline.

While most state experiment station laboratories still interpret soil tests and make recommendations in terms of excesses or deficiencies of chemical NPK, a growing number are prepared to provide organic equivalents on request. Be sure to state this preference when you submit your sample.

The basic objective of natural soil fertility management is to feed the soil, not necessarily the plant. This approach entails a long-range commitment to building the overall fertility of the soil, as contrasted with merely supplying the minimum amount of nutrients to produce a single crop in one season.

The chemical fertilizer user has long made use of special proportions of fertilizers, such as 5-10-10 or 4-8-4. Such fertilizer formulas are merely simple ways to show the amounts of nitrogen, phosphorus and potash in the mixture of fertilizer. For example, in the combination 2-4-2, 2 percent is nitrogen, 4 percent is phosphorus and 2 percent is potash. The remaining 92 percent of the fertilizer is "inert" matter.

The Value of Nitrogen: Nitrogen is a major element in plant nutrition. It is responsible for producing leaf growth and greener leaves. A deficiency causes yellow leaves and stunted growth. An excess produces an overabundant growth of foliage with delayed flowering; the plant is more subject to disease and its fruit is of a reduced quality.

If you believe your soil is deficient in nitrogen, you can correct it by adding compost, manure or other nitrogen-rich fertilizers such as dried blood, tankage, cottonseed meal, cocoa bean and peanut shells, bone meal, or sewage sludge. Returning weeds, grass clippings and other garden wastes to the soil will add to its humus content and improve its nitrogen content at the same time. *See also* MANURE, NITROGEN, SEWAGE SLUDGE.

The Value of Phosphorus: All growing plants need phosphorus. It is a constituent of genetic materials and is important for proper seed development. Although the specific properties of phosphorus are not completely understood, a deficiency seems to cause stunted growth and seed sterility. Phosphorus is said to hasten maturity, increase seed yield, increase fruit development, increase resistance to winterkill and diseases, and increase vitamin content of plants.

Phosphate rock, a natural rock product containing from 28 to 30 percent phosphorus, is the organic gardener's best source of phosphorus. When the rock is finely ground, the phosphate is available to the plant as it needs it. Phosphate rock is especially effective in minerally balanced soils containing plenty of organic matter. The bacteria that thrive in humusy soils secrete organic acids that promote the breakdown and availability of the phosphorus. Humus forms its acids slowly, releasing nutrients to the plants as they need them rather than in a single massive dose, as is the case with highly soluble chemical fertilizers.

Besides phosphate rock, other phosphorous sources are basic slag, bone meal, dried blood, cottonseed meal, and activated sludge. In most areas, barring any great deficiencies or excesses, a pound of phosphate rock for every ten square feet of garden space (two tons per acre) is a good amount to use once every three or four years. Dried blood, containing approximately 3 percent phosphorus, may be applied at the same rate, although allowance must be made for its substantial content (15 percent) of rather highly available nitrogen at the same time.

Phosphate rock is most effective when applied in combination with manure—about 25 pounds of manure for every ten pounds of phosphate. Put the manure on first, work the ground, then add the phosphate rock a month or two later. Sprinkle the ground phosphate on the soil just as you would lime, then work it into the top inch of soil. Spread on lawns the same way, one pound per ten square feet.

Bone meal is another source of phosphorus that makes sense on a small garden. Bone fertilizers have a phosphorous content of over 20 percent, but are slow to decompose and release their nutrients. *See also* PHOSPHATE ROCK.

The Value of Potassium: Potassium, the third major nutrient, is equally important to the strength of the plant. Often referred to as potash or potassium oxide (K_2O), it helps in the formation of carbohydrates and is necessary for protein synthesis. In addition, it promotes early growth, improves stem strength and contributes to cold hardiness. It is also known to improve the keeping quality, color and flavor of fruit. Plants deficient in potassium are usually stunted and have poorly developed root systems. Their leaves, particularly the older ones, are usually spotted, curled or mottled and may even appear "burned" around the edges. Even before these symptoms appear, they produce low yields of crops.

Mineral fertilizers supply virtually insoluble potassium, which takes a very long time to dissolve into forms available to plants. Highly soluble sources of potash like muriate of potash (KCl) and potassium nitrate (KNO_3) may cause the plant to take up an excess of the element, which can restrict its ability to assimilate other essential nutrients. Since the natural mineral fertilizers become available more slowly, there is no chance of this occurring.

The organic grower has three sources of potassium at his disposal: (a) plant residues; (b) manures and compost; and (c) natural mineral sources, like granite dust, greensand and basalt rock.

Included in the first category are wood ashes (6 to 10 percent potash), hay (1.2 to 2.3 percent) and leaves (.4 to .7 percent). The best approach is to combine both organic and mineral potash fertilizer—organic for short-term potash release and mineral for the longer period.

Many organic gardeners are turning to seaweed and seaweed extract to raise their potash levels, especially on porous, sandy soils. Seaweed also contains a moderate percentage of nitrogen. Since it is in organic form, it is not available to plants until decomposition has

PERCENTAGE COMPOSITION OF COMMON ORGANIC MATERIALS

	Nitrogen	Phosphorus	Potash
Activated sludge	5.00	3.00	
Alfalfa hay	2.45	.50	2.10
Animal tankage	8.00	20.00	
Apple leaves	1.00	.15	.35
Basic slag		.80	
Blood meal	15.00	1.30	.70
Bone meal	4.00	21.00	.20
Brewers' grains (wet)	.90	.50	.05
Castor pomace	5.50	1.50	1.25
Cattle manure (fresh)	.29	.17	.35
Cocoa shell dust	1.04	1.49	2.71
Coffee grounds (dried)	1.99	.36	.67
Colloidal phosphate		18–24	
Cornstalks	.75	.40	.90
Cottonseed	3.15	1.25	1.15
Cottonseed hull ash		8.70	24.00
Cottonseed meal	7.00	2.50	1.50
Dried blood	12–15	3.00	
Feather meal	12.00		
Fish scrap (red snapper)	7.76	13.00	3.80
Granite dust			5.00
Greensand		1.50	5.00
Guano	12.00	8.00	3.00
Hoof meal and horn dust	12.50	1.75	
Horse manure (fresh)	.44	.17	.35
Incinerator ash	.24	5.15	2.33
Leather dust	5.5–12		
Oak leaves	.80	.35	.15
Peach leaves	.90	.15	.60
Phosphate rock		30–32	
Poultry manure (fresh)	2.00	1.88	1.85
Rabbit manure (fresh)	2.40	.62	.05
Red clover	.55	.13	.50
Seaweed	1.68	.75	5.00
Sheep manure (fresh)	.55	.31	.15
Swine manure (fresh)	.60	.41	.13
Tankage	6.00	8.00	
Tobacco stems	2.00		7.00
Wood ashes		1.50	7.00

taken place. With the majority of seaweeds, however, this occurs rapidly in the soil, and it is not generally necessary to compost seaweed before adding it to the soil.

Granite dust is an excellent source of organic, slow-working potash. Its potash content varies from 3 to 5 percent. Granite dust should be applied at a rate of two tons to the acre. Ideally the granite dust should be mixed with phosphate rock and manure and turned under in the spring, before planting. Smaller applications call for 20 pounds to 100 square feet.

Greensand or greensand marl typically contains about 5 percent potash, although that extracted from especially rich deposits may average 1 or 2 percent higher. Being an undersea deposit, greensand contains most of the elements found in the ocean and is an excellent soil builder. Superior deposits of greensand contain 50 percent silica, 18 to 23 percent iron oxide, 3 to 7 percent magnesia, and small amounts of lime and phosphoric acid.

Greensand has the ability to absorb large amounts of water and provides an abundant source of available potash. Its minerals or trace elements are also essential to plant growth. Traditional recommendations call for an application rate of 25 pounds per 100 square feet but, since it is so slow to dissolve, it is best to combine it with manure and phosphate rock. *See also* POTASH.

Other plant foods needed by crops in lesser amounts include calcium, magnesium, sulfur, iron, zinc, molybdenum, tin, and iodine. These trace elements are very important to proper growth of plants even though they are only needed in small amounts. Some, in fact, have been found to serve as partial substitutes for other nutrients and to increase disease resistance in certain plants. For details on how to detect deficiencies of these elements and to supply them to the soil, *see also* TRACE ELEMENTS.

Mixing Organic Fertilizers: The fertilizer listing at the end of this entry presents some typical blends of organic materials. Despite the serious shortcomings of listing organic fertilizer recommendations in terms of NPK formulas, these combinations have been included to help the beginning gardener develop a feel for blending his own formulas. The nutrient preferences of an individual plant can be found in the entry for that plant.

To make up, for example, a 2-4-2 mixture, the proportions of one part leather dust (10 percent N), one part bone meal (21 percent P) and two parts granite dust (5 percent K) are needed. If you want four pounds of it, weigh out and combine one pound of leather dust, one pound of bone meal and two pounds granite dust.

Remember, however, the NPK percentages listed here are for total available nutrients, not immediately available nutrients. Rock powders and organic materials release their nutrients to the soil over an extended period of time, depending on soil type, bacterial conditions, moisture conditions, and acidity. This is why the percentages are generally lower than their highly soluble chemical counterparts, and it also points up the limitations of getting involved in the fertilizer "numbers game" when what is really desired is a long-range soil fertility program. Phosphate rock, for example, provides only about 1.5 percent available P the first year, even though it has a total P of 28 to 30 percent which it releases gradually over three or four years. Superphosphate, on the other hand, with a P rating of 19 to 21 percent, is highly available for a very brief period of time before it leaches out of the soil, leaving behind salt

ORGANIC FERTILIZER FORMULAS

1–4–3

1 part basic slag
1 part tankage
4 parts greensand

1–5–5

1 part tankage
3 parts wood ashes
2 parts basic slag

2–3½–2½

1 part bone meal
3 parts alfalfa hay
2 parts greensand

2–4–2

4 parts coffee grounds
1 part bone meal
1 part wood ashes

2–4–2

1 part leather dust
1 part bone meal
3 parts granite dust

2–4–5

1 part tankage
1 part wood ashes
1 part granite dust

2–5–2

2 parts coffee grounds
1 part tankage
1 part bone meal

2–5–2

5 parts basic slag
2 parts wood ashes
2 parts leather dust

2–8–3

3 parts greensand
2 parts seaweed
1 part dried blood
2 parts phosphate rock

2–13–2½

1 part cottonseed meal
2 parts phosphate rock
2 parts seaweed

3½–5½–3½

2 parts cottonseed meal
1 part colloidal phosphate
2 parts granite dust

2½–6–5

1 part dried blood
1 part phosphate rock
4 parts wood ashes

3–4–3

3 parts basic slag
2 parts wood ashes
2 parts leather dust

0–5–4

1 part phosphate rock
3 parts greensand
2 parts wood ashes

3–6–3

1 part leather dust
1 part phosphate rock
3 parts seaweed

3–7–5

1 part dried blood
1 part phosphate rock
3 parts wood ashes

3–4–3

3 parts wood ashes
5 parts basic slag
2 parts dried blood

3–8–5

1 part leather dust
1 part phosphate rock
1 part fish scrap
4 parts wood ashes

2½–2½–4

3 parts granite dust
1 part dried blood
1 part bone meal
5 parts seaweed

4–5–4

2 parts dried blood
1 part phosphate rock
4 parts wood ashes

6–8–3

2 parts fish scrap
2 parts dried blood
1 part cottonseed meal
1 part wood ashes
1 part phosphate rock
1 part granite dust

3–6–2½

2 parts tankage
1 part colloidal phosphate
3 parts seaweed

deposits which inhibit soil bacteria.

Don't worry about getting precise proportions when mixing organic fertilizers. If you have cottonseed meal on hand, for instance, but no blood meal, don't hesitate to substitute. According to the "Percentage Composition of Common Organic Materials" chart (see page 368), cottonseed meal contains half the nitrogen content of blood meal, so you would double the amount in your mixture. Since the P and K values are higher for the cottonseed, you should make a corresponding reduction in these elements when combining them with other materials. One reason that the organic method of fertilizing is so successful is its flexibility.

In mixing organic fertilizers, an attempt should be made to combine quick- and slow-release ingredients. This keeps plants growing well throughout the season and leaves something in the ground for the following season. The combination of bone meal and phosphate rock, for instance, provides for quick- and slow-release sources of phosphorus. Kelp and granite dust in combination give quick and slow potash. Blood meal and cottonseed meal do the same for nitrogen.

If a fertilizer formula contains raw organic matter, try to turn it under at least several weeks before planting. Even more time may be needed if the bacterial population of the soil is low from past use of chemical fertilizers. If you can grind up organic matter such as leaves, alfalfa or straw, they will decay much quicker.

This list of organic fertilizers is far from complete. These have been selected simply to serve as guidelines for formulating some typical combinations. There are also many commercial preparations of rock powders and organic matter that can be used. Care should be taken, however, not to be deluded by commercial fertilizers listed as being "Organic Base." These are not genuine organics, but rather chemical preparations mixed with a dry manure base. Read the labels carefully.

Commercial organic mixtures typically consist of composted animal manure, minerals (phosphate rock, granite dust, greensand), plant residues (leaves and hay), and seaweed products. Like all natural fertilizers, they should be used in conjunction with a balanced soil-building program, including routine crop rotation and green manuring.

Converting Fertilizer Recommendations: Generally speaking, bagged fertilizers weigh about a pound to the pint. Some are slightly heavier; others that are bulky weigh less.

AMOUNT OF FERTILIZER PER ROW
FOR VARIOUS RATES OF APPLICATION

Approximate amount per 100 feet, for rows different distances apart

Rate per acre	12 in.	15 in.	18 in.	24 in.	30 in.	36 in.
250 pounds	9 oz.	12 oz.	14 oz.	1 lb.	1¼ lbs.	1½ lbs.
500 pounds	1 lb.	1¼ lbs.	1½ lbs.	2 lbs.	2½ lbs.	3½ lbs.
750 pounds	1½ lbs.	2 lbs.	2½ lbs.	3 lbs.	3¾ lbs.	4½ lbs.
1,000 pounds	2¼ lbs.	2½ lbs.	3 lbs.	4½ lbs.	5¾ lbs.	7 lbs.
1,500 pounds	3½ lbs.	4 lbs.	5 lbs.	6½ lbs.	8½ lbs.	10½ lbs.
2,000 pounds	4½ lbs.	5 lbs.	6½ lbs.	9 lbs.	11 lbs.	13½ lbs.

Source: Pennsylvania Agricultural Extension Service.

One pint is equal to two cups, 32 level tablespoons, 96 teaspoons, or slightly less than one-half liter.

One acre contains 43,560 square feet (4,047 square meters), but for most purposes, the figure 40,000 is more convenient and yet is accurate enough in determining amounts of fertilizer for small areas.

Using these figures, you can figure fertilizer applications for small areas from given rates per acre. For each 100 pounds per acre, equal rates for small areas would be as follows:

for 1,000 square feet —2½ pounds or 2½ pints
  100 square feet —¼ pound or ½ cup
    1 square yard—½ ounce or
            2½ teaspoons

For each 2,000 pounds or one ton per acre, equal rates for small areas would be:

for 1,000 square feet —50 pounds
  100 square feet — 5 pounds or 5 pints
    1 square yard —½ pound or 1 cup

FERTILIZER, CHEMICAL

Any inorganic material of wholly or partially synthetic origin that is added to the soil to supply certain elements essential to the growth of plants is a chemical fertilizer. Organic gardeners choose not to employ such harsh means to achieve soil fertility. Indeed, providing alternatives to chemical fertilizers is a basic feature of the organic method. *See also* FERTILIZER.

Although man has been fertilizing his gardens and fields for at least as long as he has been keeping agricultural records, it is only recently—within the last century—that he has been using mineral salts to promote increased plant growth. The use of these fertilizers in commercial agriculture has reached the point that most agricultural experts regard them as essential.

There are many reasons historically and practically for the development, promotion and use of chemical fertilizers. Mechanized transportation replaced the horse and, at the same time, many farmers turned away from livestock-oriented operations. Something was needed to replace animal manures as fertilizer. At about the same time, scientists became convinced that nitrogen, phosphorus and potassium were the principal plant nutrients, and that by charging the soil with these elements in some form usable by plants, crop yields could be increased and maintained at high levels year after year. Moreover, chemical technology developed sufficiently to make it feasible to manufacture easily applied materials containing nitrogen, phosphorus and potassium, the three chief fertilizer elements.

Advances in chemistry have refined both soil testing and chemical fertilizer manufacture to the point that supplying the fertilizer elements in specific rates has become a very sophisticated process. Because chemicals can be applied at *exact* rates, the recommendations of soil testers to farmers may call for a certain number of pounds per acre of, say, a 20–36–18 fertilizer broadcast ahead of planting, followed by so many pounds per acre of a 6–14–8 directly beside the seed in a row. The numbers refer to the percentages of NPK in the fertilizer mix. With bulk blending, farmers can order any combination of chemicals they want, no matter how exotic.

Chemical fertilizer materials are generally classified according to the particular fertilizer element it supplies, although a number of them supply more than one. Among the major types of chemical fertilizers are the following:

Ammonium chloride: 26 percent nitrogen, 66 percent chlorine. Seed germination is reduced as chlorine is built up in the soil.

Ammonium nitrate: 32½ percent nitrogen. It is manufactured by passing ammonia gas through nitric acid.

Ammonium sulfate: 21 percent nitrogen, 24 percent sulfur. Ammonium sulfate is strongly acid in the soil and is death to certain beneficial bacteria.

Ammo-Phos: Grade A, 11 percent nitrogen, 15 percent available phosphorus; Grade B, 16 percent nitrogen, 6½ percent available phosphorus.

Anhydrous ammonia: 82 percent nitrogen, containing more nitrogen than any other fertilizer. Farmers force it into the ground as a gas.

Calcium nitrate: 24 percent calcium, 15 percent nitrogen.

Magnesium sulfate: 20 percent magnesium, 26½ percent sulfur.

Manganese sulfate: 27 percent manganese, 24 percent sulfur.

Muriate of potash: 53 percent potash, 47 percent chlorine. Continued use lowers the protein content of certain food crops, particularly potatoes, and damages their quality.

Potassium nitrate: 39 percent potash, 13 percent nitrogen. Continued use ruins soil structure by separating clay particles. Then the land is no longer granulated and porous.

Potassium sulfate: 48 percent potash, 16 percent sulfur in the form of gypsum. Sulfate can build up in inorganic soils and may become a problem.

Superphosphate: raw ground phosphate rock treated with sulfuric acid. A ton of the acid is generally used to treat each ton of phosphate rock.

Urea: 42 percent nitrogen.

The sophistication of the soil testing and fertilizer blending processes tends to imply that farmers apply only what is absolutely necessary, but the impulse on the part of farmers to apply excessive amounts in the hope of boosting yields is commonplace. As a result, millions of tons of chemicals are pumped, spread, sprayed, or turned into the soil yearly. In 1967 alone approximately 14 million tons of nitrogen, more than four million tons of phosphorus and nearly four million tons of potassium—almost all in highly soluble form—were applied to the American countryside.

Where does it all come from? A variety of places. The phosphorus is stripped from the few deposits on earth, then treated in a highly energy-consumptive process with acid to yield superphosphate or triple superphosphate.

Almost all of the nitrogen comes from the air. There are three basic reactions by which nitrogen is taken from the air. One uses too much power to be commercially feasible and directly oxidizes nitrogen into nitrous oxide. Another reacts nitrogen with calcium carbide. Another is the Claude-Haber process by which nitrogen and hydrogen are combined into ammonia. The last two processes are in commercial use today. And although 14 million tons of this factory-produced nitrogen are used, a lot of it is wasted.

According to Fred Adams and A. E. Hiltbolt of the Department of Agronomy and Soils at Alabama Polytechnic Institute, "only 50 pounds will be used when a crop is fertilized with 100 pounds of nitrogen per acre." Nitrogen not used by growing plants leaches into the groundwater quickly when it is in nitrate form. When ammonia is used on soils, much nitrogen goes up into the air as ammonia gas or is liberated by bacteria as elemental nitrogen gas.

In 1971, a research team—Barry Commoner, Daniel Kohl and Georgia Shearer—published the results of a study in which they examined the buildup of nitrates in water supplies and its relationship to the use of nitrogen fertilizers. The research was conducted in the area of Lake Decatur, the drinking water reservoir for Decatur, Illinois. The lake is fed by the Sangamon River watershed which drains a large farming area. Neither the river nor the reservoir receives any significant amounts of nitrogen-carrying sewage from industrial or municipal sources. Their conclusions were that approximately 55 percent of the nitrogen chemicals showing up in Lake Decatur in the spring of 1970 (the period when fertilizers are laid down on crops) came from fertilizers being washed into the watershed.

The effects of that chemical runoff were discussed in a report conducted at Massachusetts Institute of Technology. Four researchers at MIT's Department of Nutrition and Food Science said the excessive use of nitrates as fertilizers can lead to high accumulated levels in water supplies and plant tissue. Bacteria can then convert the nitrates into nitrites—the raw material for a group of chemicals known as nitrosamines. Those nitrosamines have been known to cause cancer in animals, and the question is whether animals will take the nitrates and convert them into nitrosamines. In the test tube, at least, the MIT researchers have found that this could happen.

The Commoner research warned that the runoff of nitrates into ponds and streams causes a buildup of algae and other aquatic vegetation. As this decomposes, the water's oxygen supply is depleted and the body of water is unable to support animal life.

The health problems associated with nitrate and nitrite compounds are manifold. It has been pointed out, for instance, that plant proteins formed on soil too rich in nitrogen are less complete than those formed on soil with the right amount. Nitrates from food plants can convert blood hemoglobin to methemoglobin, especially in youngsters, causing sickness and death.

A study by W. M. Beeson of the Department of Animal Sciences at Purdue in 1964 pointed out that excess nitrates cause both death and toxicity in animals (including man) as well as interfere with the body's ability to convert carotene to vitamin A.

Excess nitrates in the soil, it almost goes without saying, generally result from the use of chemical fertilizers, rather than from the use of organic fertilizers. These health problems, however, are not the only strikes against chemical fertilizers.

The organic school does not approve of chemical fertilizers for a variety of reasons. Chemical fertilizers are quick-acting, short-term plant boosters and are responsible for:

—deterioration of soil friability.
—destruction of beneficial soil life.
—the alteration of vitamin and protein content of some crops.
—increasing the vulnerability of certain crops to disease.
—preventing some plants from taking up minerals they need.

Moreover, chemical fertilizers are responsible for pollution of surface and ground waters as noted, since they are water soluble and leach readily from the soil. And finally, the manufacture of chemical fertilizers requires lavish quantities of energy, a fact of increasing significance.

The soil must be regarded as a living organism. An acid fertilizer, because of its acids, dissolves the cementing material made from the dead bodies of soil organisms, which holds the rock particles together to form soil crumbs. On the surface of the soil such cement-free particles settle to form a compact, more or less water-impervious layer. This compact surface layer of rock particles encourages rainwater to run off rather than to enter the soil.

For example: A highly soluble fertilizer, such as 5–10–5, goes into solution in the soil water rapidly so that much of it may be leached away without benefiting the plants at all. But the sodium in a fertilizer like sodium nitrate tends to accumulate in the soil where it combines with carbonic acid to form washing soda, sodium carbonate. This chemical causes the soil to assume a cementlike hardness. Other minerals, when present in large concentrations, percolate into the subsoil where they interact with the clay to form impervious layers of precipitates called hardpans.

Hardpans seal the topsoil off from the subsoil. Water cannot pass downward into the subsoil, and water from the water table cannot rise to the topsoil in which the plants are growing. Many plants cannot live when their roots are kept too wet. Then too, the subsoil below the hardpans is anaerobic and rapidly becomes acid. In such anaerobic acid soils, the soil organism population changes radically and in ways which are unfavorable to crop plants.

In turn, the changes that affect drainage and friability also affect aeration.

Such highly soluble chemicals as chlorides and sulfates are poisonous to the beneficial soil organisms, but in small amounts act as stimulants. These chemicals stimulate the beneficial soil bacteria to such increased growth and reproduction that they use up the organic matter in the soil as food faster than it can be returned by present agricultural practices. When chemical residues accumulate in the soil, the microorganisms may be killed off by hydrolysis (water-removing). The high salt concentration in the soil water will pull water from the bacterial or fungal cells, causing them to collapse and die.

Many artificial fertilizers contain acids, such as sulfuric acid and hydrochloric acid, which tend to increase the acidity of the soil. Changes in the soil acidity (pH) are accompanied by changes in the kinds of organisms which can live in the soil. Such changes often are sufficient to interfere greatly with the profitable growth of crop plants. The maintenance of a high organic matter content and of a balanced pH can offset this effect of chemical fertilizers, but only if the gardener or farmer is diligent, and many who rely on chemicals are not.

As noted above, many chemical fertilizers kill off beneficial soil organisms. Among those killed off by high-nitrogen fertilizers are the nitrogen-fixing bacteria that inhabit a healthy soil naturally. About 78 percent of the atmosphere is made up of gaseous nitrogen. Living soil contains enough nitrogen-fixing bacteria to fix enough atmospheric nitrogen to supply abundantly the needs of crop plants. In the presence of soluble nitrates, these bacteria use the nitrogen which man has provided in his artificial fertilizers and fix less from the atmosphere.

Chemical fertilizers may even have deleterious effects on plants. Several experiment stations, for example, have found evidence that citrus trees supplied with lots of nitrogen tend to yield fruits with lower vitamin C contents than trees supplied with lesser amounts of nitrogen. Similarly, it has been found that highly soluble nitrogen fertilizers depress the protein content on some hybrid corns.

Over applied, chemical fertilizers may make plants more susceptible to disease. The fertilizers do this in part by killing off microorganisms that protect plants from certain diseases. Many plant diseases are kept under control by antibiotic-producing bacteria or fungi thriving around the plant roots.

When plants are supplied with too much nitrogen and only a medium amount of phosphate, plants may contract mosaic infections also. Most resistance is obtained if there is a small supply of nitrogen and plenty of phosphate. Fungus and bacterial diseases have then been related to high nitrogen fertilization, as well as to a lack of trace elements.

The lack of trace elements in soil regularly dosed with chemical fertilizers is not uncommon, and again, the lack of availability of these vital micronutrients to plants is a consequence of the use of the chemical fertilizers. The colloidal humus particles are the convoys that transfer most of the minerals from the soil solution to the root hairs. Each humus particle is negatively charged and will, of course, attract the positive elements such as potassium, sodium, calcium, magnesium, manganese, aluminum, boron, iron, copper, and other metals. When sodium nitrate, for instance, is dumped into the soil year after year in large doses, a radical change takes place on the humus particles. The very numerous sodium ions (atomic particles) will eventually crowd out the other ions, making them practically unavailable for plant use. The humus becomes coated with sodium, glutting the root hairs with the excess. Finally the plant is unable to pick up some of the minerals that it really needs.

Not all of these objections are fully accepted by the experts of conventional agriculture, of course. In some cases, the contentions of organic agriculturalists are rejected, in other cases the significance of the charges against chemical fertilizers are rejected. In most cases, the conventional wisdom is that the people of the world will starve without the continued use of chemical fertilizers.

But among the data collected during a 1974 study of 32 corn belt farms, were definite indications that crop yields on well-managed organic farms are comparable to those on similar but chemically oriented farms. The study was conducted by the Center for the Biology of Natural Systems at Washington University in Saint Louis, Missouri. The researchers collected information from 16 organic farmers in Iowa, Nebraska, Minnesota, Missouri, and Illinois, as well as 16 conventional farmers operating in the same states. The farm sizes were comparable, and averaged 476 acres.

One of the most important findings of the study was that yields per acre for major crops were about equal. Conventional farmers averaged five bushels per acre more for corn, for example, and organic growers produced three bushels per acre more wheat.

Thus, if the world's masses starve, it won't necessarily be because farmers don't (or can't) use chemical fertilizers. With the increasing cost of fossil-fuel energy and the consequent increasing cost of highly energy-consumptive fertilizer manufacture, the nation's farmers may have to do without, or at least with less.

In 1972, for example, production of nitrogen fertilizers used up about 15 million cubic feet of natural gas annually. The manufacturing process involves reacting natural gas with steam to get pure hydrogen and carbon dioxide,

FIG 377

then reacting the hydrogen with nitrogen from the air to force ammonia. The steps in this process gulp great amounts of energy. Nature does it better at a fraction of the cost in dollars and resources.

The upshot of it all, of course, is the organic gardener's warning: "Beware of fast-acting fertilizers." Repeated tests by organic gardeners have shown that they are short-term feeders and that they can't build up soil to virgin goodness. Only 10 to 15 percent of their nutrients are used by plants. The rest is washed out or locked up chemically in the soil.

Extremely few fertilizers are complete plant foods—despite what you read in advertisements for chemicals. No man yet knows all the nutrients that a plant needs. The only way to be sure of putting into your soil a complete plant food is to reproduce as closely as possible the way the soil was built originally. Add the mineral-bearing rock fertilizers and trace elements, along with liberal doses of compost, manure and other organic matter, to build and maintain a rich, humusy soil that is the key to organic soil fertility.

FESCUE *See* LAWN

FEVERWORT *See* TRIOSTEUM

FIELD BINDWEED *See* BINDWEED

FIELD DODDER *See* BINDWEED

FIG (*Ficus carica*)

This tree (more like a bush in appearance) is seldom found in commercial orchards, and when it is, the fruits are almost always either preserved or dried. The reason is that the fig does not continue to ripen after being picked, and by the time it reaches its peak, it is too perishable to ship without expensive precautions. Therefore, to enjoy delicious fresh figs, your own "dooryard" tree is a requisite.

Fig Propagation: New trees are usually started from cuttings, or by layering. The cuttings should be about ⅜ inch in diameter, ten to 12 inches long and from one- or two-year-old wood. It may be rooted where the tree is desired, set six to seven inches deep with only one bud left above ground.

Like all fast-growing semitropical plants, the fig responds quickly to fertilizer. There is danger in overfeeding, however, as lush tender growth is easily damaged by cold. A slow, mature growth is preferred to a fast one. A heavy mulch in the summer to retain moisture, and in the winter to protect against the weather, plus a spring application of good compost, will usually guarantee even growth. A tree treated like this needs no cultivation.

Different varieties thrive in different localities, according to their resistance to cold weather. The fig requires warm summers, mild winters, ample moisture, and excellent drainage. It thrives when planted next to a house, for the building offers some winter protection. If the trees are protected by heavy mulch, or by about 15 inches of soil over the roots during winter, they will come out from the root and produce fruit that year, although the top may be killed back by severe cold. Older trees are usually more resistant to cold. Young trees are sometimes pulled over and are covered with soil during the winter.

One good method to prevent loss of trees to severe cold is to cut out superfluous branches, wrap layers of burlap around the others and tie them in a bundle without breaking them. Tar paper or oilcloth may be applied for extra security against the cold.

When fully ripe, figs will drop from the tree; then they can be eaten fresh, canned, or sun-dried and stored for later use.

Harvest: Figs should be allowed to remain on the trees until they ripen sufficiently to drop from their own weight. Then they can be dried on large wooden trays placed in the sun. Drying will decrease their weight by about two-thirds and should only take about two days, since the figs are already partially dried when harvested.

Insect and Disease Problems: The fig meets with little trouble from insects or diseases. It is an ancient tree, popular for thousands of years, and has survived the test of time. In the Gulf Coast area, the most common insect pests are nematodes and tree borers. To discourage nematodes, the tree should be planted in deeply cultivated heavy soil and encouraged to root deeply. Shallow-rooted trees in sandy soil are more susceptible to nematodes. Planting near a building also discourages nematodes, which do not infest the roots under the structure.

Tree borers are discouraged by good housekeeping in the garden. Any dead or broken limbs should be pruned immediately, and the scars and any other breaks in the bark should be promptly painted with tar or some other healing aid.

Rust and cotton root rot are the most common diseases in the South. The rust, like the tree borer, is prevented by careful housekeeping. Strong, healthy trees are seldom attacked. Cotton root rot can be prevented only by not planting the tree in soil where cotton has been grown.

Paper bags tied around the fruit will prevent the predation of birds, who seem to enjoy the fig almost as much as do humans.

Cultivars: In the Southwest, Mission, Kadota and Genoa are popular. Southern climes are most successful with Celeste, Hunt and Verdone. Hardy cultivars for the North include Brown Turkey, Magnolia and DiRedo.

FIG MARIGOLD

The name fig marigold refers to several different flowering succulents including *Carpobrotus edulis, C. acinaciformis* and *Glottiphyllum depressum*. Some of the fig marigolds were once classified as members of the genus *Mesembryanthemum* and many seed catalogs continue to list them as such. They are closely related to ice plant (*M. crystallinum*) and bear brightly colored daisylike flowers and small fruits like miniature figs. Most species are perennial and can be grown outdoors only in dry areas of California and the Deep South.

However, given full sun and a mixture of heavy soil and sand, these succulent shrubs and carpetweeds will thrive year-round in the greenhouse. Like other succulents, they require very little water and do not need a very fertile soil. Keep the temperature around 55 to 60°F. (12.78 to 15.56°C.) in winter and, in summer, place the pots outdoors in a bed of sand. A few days of cool, dry weather will usually force them into bloom. To propagate fig marigolds, root cuttings in a light, sandy medium and transplant them to the garden after the soil has warmed.

There are many species from which to choose. One of the most widely cultivated in this country is *C. acinaciformis* or Hottentot fig. A low-growing perennial, it has long, vining stems with triangular-shaped fleshy leaves and bright pink flowers. It thrives in hot places and is an excellent choice for dry rock gardens where it will bloom continuously throughout the summer. *C. edulis* has slightly shorter stems and bright yellow or pink flowers. *G. depressum* also has large yellow flowers but it blooms only in the spring and early summer.

FIGWORT   *See* SCROPHULARIACEAE

FILBERT   (*Corylus*)

The filbert, or hazelnut, is native to much of the United States. The principal species, *Corylus americana,* grows in thickets and produces a ripe nut by August. The nuts are small, and the tree is usually grown only where the European filbert (*C. Avellana*) is not hardy. The European species does best in the Pacific Northwest, and is extensively cultivated in an area west of the Cascade Mountains. In the East, it suffers somewhat from winters and disease. A single-trunked filbert tree is about the size of a thrifty plum tree. Set out in orchard form, the trees should not be closer than 25 feet apart. If you grow the filbert for nuts, you will prefer it as a single-stemmed plant, and will find it bears more prolifically that way. If you have an orchard of filberts, the single-stemmed trees will probably be a trifle easier to handle.

In the West, however, where the commercial crop of filberts is grown, many orchardists let their filberts have three or four main stems. The plant will send up innumerable shoots, so that the grower can train it with as many heavy branches as desired. Grown in this manner, the filbert can be highly ornamental. The tree can also be grown as a bushy shrub. Several stems are allowed to come up, and then are pruned to outside buds to spread out the growth. Shrubby filberts can thus be formed into a hedge.

The leaves of the filbert are large and lovely. Although the female blossom is so inconspicuous that one can hardly find it, the catkins, or buds, stretch out at the first touch of warmth in the spring.

Blooming Period: A weakness of the filbert is its tendency to bloom too soon. Forced out by a prematurely warm day, the catkins may be frozen stiff by the frosty night that follows. This doesn't harm the tree, but it can ruin the nut crop. Of course, the same is often true of other nut trees and of the apple and the peach; the difference is that the filbert comes out much earlier in the year and so is more likely to suffer. Don't plant in a southern exposure as the warmth would be apt to force the flowers. The cooler the site the better.

An attractive feature of the filbert is the involucre, or husk, that encases the nut. "Encases" is exactly the right word, for the involucre grows out around the nut much like a pillowcase about a pillow. The difference in length of involucres is a matter of interest. Some of these vegetable pillow slips are not as long as the nut to be enclosed (hazelnuts). Some fit the nut very nicely. Others extend well beyond the nut, the outer ends of the husks being more or less wrapped together (filberts). All these husks are beautifully fringed or pinked at the ends.

Furthermore, filberts are borne singly, in pairs, as triplets, or in groups of four or five, depending probably upon how well pollination was effected. As the nut ripens, the husk fades in color from a vivid green to a yellow and then a brown. Now the nuts are ripe. They will rattle out of their little cases, although some varieties retain the nuts within the husks. After they have been gathered, the nuts should be immersed in water and floaters discarded. Dry the crop by spreading it out in a dry room, no more than three nuts deep, and stirring occasionally. When all excess moisture is gone, store the nuts in rodentproof containers at a temperature of 55 to 65°F. (12.78 to 18.33°C.).

Filberts will grow almost anywhere in the country, and are easy to grow. Being propagated almost exclusively by layering, they come to the purchaser with a generous growth of roots and begin to grow promptly and vigorously. They will not stand wet feet, so make sure drainage is good.

A most striking characteristic is their tendency to "sucker up." The nurseryman will send you a plant with a single stem, but in no time there are many more shooting up from the roots. So you must decide promptly what sort of filbert you want to grow. If you want a bush, let the suckers come. If you want a tree with a single trunk, remove all volunteers.

Then be watchful, for the plant will continue from year to year to send up suckers.

This, however, is not an undesirable trait. If the main stem is injured or diseased, you can remove it and soon you will have a good substitute. You can't do that with a peach or apple tree; they are grafted, and shoots from the roots would probably be from inferior and undesirable stock.

The filbert is one of those plants that must have cross-pollination. If you want nuts, you will be wasting time by planting a single filbert plant. Buy two or three varieties. Local nurserymen will tell you what to use in your locality. Many varieties of filberts have now been developed. Some are excellent pollinators. Some are not so good. All are practically self-sterile. So be sure to secure at least two varieties that work well together.

See also NUT TREES.

FILBERTWORM

The filbertworm cannot enter nuts until after the husks have begun to crack, so the nut crop should be harvested at the earliest possible date. Furthermore, the worm is unable to complete its development on dried nutmeats. Therefore, the crop should be dried thoroughly as soon as it is harvested.

FINGERGRASS   *See* CRABGRASS

FIR   (*Abies*)

A handsome tree that thrives in cooler climate areas, this hardy member of the Pine family is one of the most beautiful evergreens. Tall and stately, firs form pyramids of stiff branches with upright cones and bristly, blunt-tipped leaves arranged in flat, spiraled sprays. The new cones appear in a variety of bright colors—everything from blue to red, green, purple, and brown, depending on the particular species.

In the northern latitudes, firs are deservingly popular for the home grounds, serving attractively in landscaping designs, providing desirable winter color and acting as a windbreak.

Firs prefer a moist soil, shade and cool, humid air free of dirt and city smoke. Although some types may become spindly when mature, most will keep their fine form under favorable conditions and with care. As with many evergreens, they require little pruning, although removing the terminal buds (of all but the main shoot) will develop side branches and add to the tree's foliage and compactness.

Young firs are especially suitable and pleasing in the home garden. Careful placement is important when first planting if the trees are not to be moved later. However, their fibrous root system allows even large trees to be transplanted.

As for difficulties and precautions, the root and wood diseases which generally afflict conifers in a forest setting are seldom noted or serious in ornamental plantings. Several rust diseases, though, are often troublesome, including witches'-broom. This dwarfs young twig growth and causes a broomlike effect on upright branches. Any infected branches should be carefully cut out, and weeds which host the disease should be destroyed. Most fir species are relatively free from insect pests. The spruce budworm feeds on the needles of new growth,

The white fir is a native of the American West but will flourish in most areas south of Massachusetts, Nebraska and Iowa.
(*Courtesy of U.S. Forest Service*)

usually webbing them together. These caterpillars are dark brown with cream-colored tubercules, and measure about ¾ inch in length. Mixed stands fare better than solid plots of fir. Cut off and destroy infested tips.

Among the best-known fir varieties is the Colorado or white fir (*A. concolor*), the most adaptable and widely used species. It is a fast grower, reaching 120 feet at a rate of about 18 inches a year. A native of the West, this tree is hardy north to Massachusetts, Nebraska and Iowa. It tolerates heat and dry weather and prefers a rich, well-mulched and moderately moist soil, which helps it keep its lower branches well into maturity. A smooth, light gray trunk and branches, gray green cones from three to five inches long, and bluish needles are features which make this fir attractive and popular.

Other species include the balsam fir (*A. balsamea*), common in wet soils and hardy in the northeastern states, and the nikko fir (*A. homolepis*), a very hardy, popular native of Japan which is found throughout the eastern United States, Minnesota, Montana, and North Dakota, and grows to a 90-foot symmetrical pyramid with dark green foliage and purple cones. The alpine or Rocky Mountain fir (*A. lasiocarpa*) thrives in Canada and the Northwest, has a silver gray bark and serves well in group plantings. The silver fir (*A. alba*) is a graceful native of China and southern Europe, reaches heights up to 150 feet, features dark green leaves with whitish undersides, is not hardy in colder sections, and requires protected locations. The Himalayan fir (*A. spectabilis*) displays large purple cones and is a good species for the south central states.

See also CHRISTMAS TREE FARMING.

FIRE BLIGHT

This serious bacterial disease of pear, apple, quince, and a number of ornamentals causes blossoms to blacken and shrivel as though burned. Cankers appear on twigs and the trunk.

A number of steps can help prevent fire blight from ruining a crop. Avoid sudden increases in nitrogen supply, being particularly careful to give no more manure than needed. Do not encourage late growth; cover crops of grass or alfalfa should be mowed early in the season and allowed to grow in midsummer in order to help check late growth. Check the soil for a deficiency of potash, and add lime as necessary to bring the pH up to 5.5 or 5.6.

Dormant-oil sprays will help to keep down numbers of aphids and leafhoppers, two sucking insects that may inoculate trees with fire blight. A single site of infection can destroy an entire tree, so it is important to cut off infected twigs, including at least a foot of healthy-looking bark.

Resistant varieties offer an effective means of minimizing losses from fire blight.

FIREFLY

One of nature's most fascinating wonders is the firefly's blinking beacon. It is light without heat, made by a mysterious substance called luciferin contained within the firefly's abdomen. By opening a special tube, the bug exposes the luciferin to oxygen, which causes luminescence. When temperature, moisture and light conditions are just right, the male flashes his light every six seconds, to be answered two seconds later by the female. Thus they seek each other out in the soft summer dusk.

In the tropics, fireflies grow considerably larger, and their light rivals the stars. Some varieties truly deserve the name of lightning bug, for when a number of them flash simultaneously, the whole landscape is brilliantly illuminated.

The firefly larva feeds on snails and slugs, as well as small insects and cutworms underground and in rotting wood. These larvae are flat worms with a toothed outline and long jaws.

FIRETHORN   *See* PYRACANTHA

FISH, DRIED

Mainly used for feed mixtures, but also available for fertilizer needs, dried fish analyzes around 8 percent nitrogen and 7 percent phosphoric acid; these analyses are so high that such material can be handled like dried blood when composted. Fish meal or dried ground fish is very malodorous, and one must be careful to comply with health department regulations and to protect escape of the nitrogen into the air. The best method is to cover the compost pile with heavier layers of earth and to keep the heap evenly moist so that bacterial action is not interrupted. One hundred pounds of dried ground fish should be composted with several hundred pounds of plant matter. If sawdust is added, the amount of wilted plant matter can be somewhat reduced, because sawdust is highly absorbent and requires more nitrogen for complete composting.

FISH FARMING
See AQUACULTURE, PONDS

FISH, ORNAMENTAL
See LILY POND

FIVE-FINGER   *See* POTENTILLA

FLAG   *See* CATTAIL

FLAMBOYANT TREE
(*Delonix regia*)

Also known as the royal poinciana or peacock flower, this summer-blooming tree grows to about 40 feet and produces clusters of bright scarlet flowers. It is generally restricted to California and Florida.

See also POINCIANA.

FLAME FLOWER   *See* KNIPHOFIA

FLATS
See COLD FRAME, GERMINATION, SEEDS AND SEEDLINGS

FLAX   (*Linum usitatissimum*)

The history of this plant in the United States goes back to the seventeenth century when thrifty New Englanders grew small plots of fiber flax to provide linens for family clothing. The invention of the cotton gin in 1792 reduced the demand for the fiber flax. Today, the growing of flax for fiber has virtually ceased in this country and is only a minor industry in Asia and the Far East.

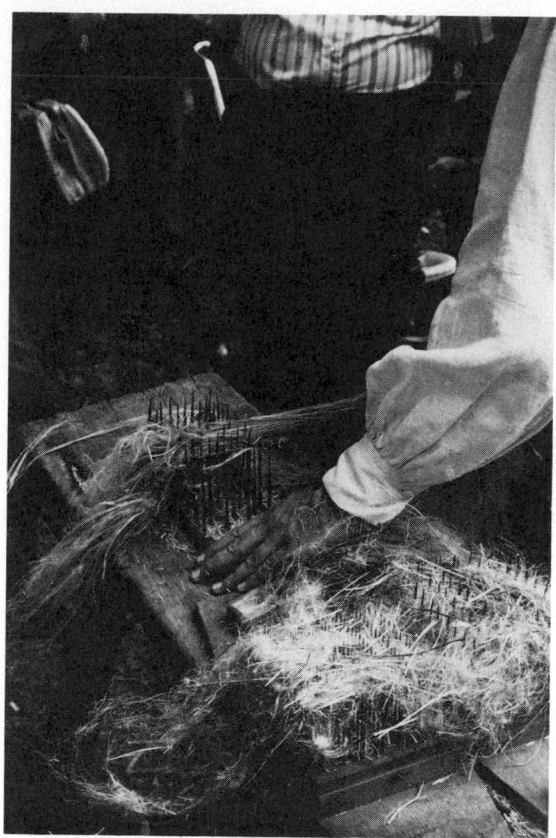

An acre of flax produces about one ton of straw from which fiber is combed, carded and eventually spun.

Flax production in the United States is concentrated in the Dakotas, Minnesota, Montana, Iowa, and Wisconsin. A considerable acreage is grown in Texas as a fall-sown crop. Flax is also grown in California and Arizona as a fall-sown crop under irrigation.

Flax is grown much like wheat, drilled (or broadcast) about an inch deep, two to three pecks per acre. A thick stand will discourage branching and therefore make longer, smoother stalks for longer fibers. It is planted early in the season, and good soils should not need fertilizer. Flax competes poorly with the weeds which extra nitrogen fertilizer could encourage. Do not plant after sorghum, millet or Sudangrass, whose rotting roots may be harmful to the growing flax. Culbert is a variety of flax outstanding for wilt and rust resistance, and bred mainly for seed production. For fiber production, Argentine might be a better variety to try. You can expect at least a ton of straw per acre from which to extract fiber. A tenth of an acre would give a hobbyist about all the fiber he or she would want to spin the first time.

Instead, most of the flax grown in this country today is for the production of linseed. The seed flax varieties have shorter stems than the fiber varieties. Linseed cake, a by-product left after extraction of the oil from the seed, is a valuable concentrated-protein feed for animals. Some of the flax straw is used in industry, particularly for making high-grade papers, while linseed oil is used a great deal in manufacturing paint, varnish and lacquer.

FLAX DODDER   *See* BINDWEED

FLEA BEETLE

The several species of flea beetle likely to raid the garden from time to time are typically dark, $\frac{1}{16}$ inch long and very jumpy. They are most often eating shot holes in the leaves of potatoes, tomatoes, peppers, beets, and related crops.

A weed-free garden shouldn't be overwhelmed by flea beetles. The pests shy away

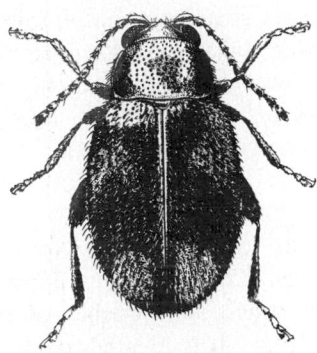

The several species of flea beetle are best controlled by frequent cultivations which eliminate overwintering eggs.
(Courtesy of U.S. Department of Agriculture)

from shade, and it therefore often helps to sow seed thickly, thinning later in the season when the danger of attack has passed. A spray made by mincing garlic in a blender is very effective in repelling flea beetles.

See also INSECT CONTROL.

FLEECEFLOWER   *See* POLYGONUM

FLOODS

Suppose it were possible to trace the whereabouts of a soil particle for about ten years. This piece of soil starts out on a sloping bit of land that is being farmed up and down hill, rather than on the contour.

Then when the rains come, the water turns the steep rows into a little canal taking the soil particle along. Its temporary destination is a roadside ditch.

Again the rains begin. This time the particle reaches a mud bar on a small stream. After resting there for several years, more rain disengages the particle and carries it downstream to a large river.

Dikes of earth along the river could not hold back the water—and the particle plus others like it overflow the banks, leaving a muddy trail on highways, in factories and homes.

This is not a false dramatization of how floods can arise. Millions of particles just like the one described are being taken off fields —leaving behind a bare, hard surface that has little capacity to absorb water. Rains and melting snow, that should have supplied needed moisture to growing plants, instead mass up as they rush downhill and never slow down until they have inundated everything in their path.

Flood damage can be controlled by following several effective techniques against soil erosion. By increasing the moisture-retaining capacity of the soil, runoff is reduced, thereby making more water available to crops and plants. Good vegetative cover, fertile topsoil and high organic matter content enable the soil to retain rainfall and water already present.

Terrace farming, or farming by the contour of the land, helps in water retention and acts as a deterrent against runoff. Reservoirs situated at points of high watershed can protect against erosion.

By controlling erosion, damage caused by sedimentation is decreased. Soil washed away by erosion fills lakes and rivers, thus reducing the capacity to hold water.

A combination of these control methods, coupled with accurate forecasting of floods, would greatly decrease the damage resulting from this natural disaster.

See also SOIL CONSERVATION.

FLOPPER   *See* KALANCHOE

FLOSSFLOWER   *See* AGERATUM

FLOWER

"Flower" is a term properly used for the blossom of a plant, characteristic of the highest group of plants, the Spermatophyta. Flowers come in a wide variety of colors, shapes and sizes, borne singly and in clusters. But no matter how showy or how drab a flower may be, the primary function of all flowers is sexual reproduction.

The swollen point at which the flower and stem join is called the receptacle. The sepals,

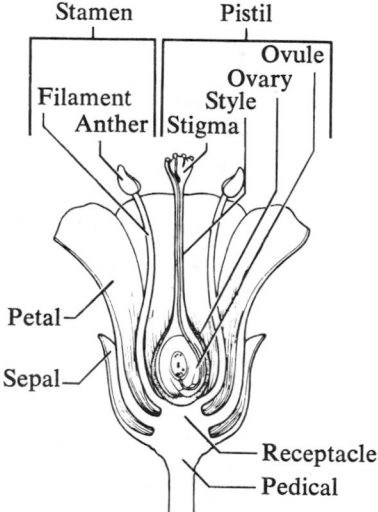

Perfect flowers contain both male and female reproductive structures. Pollination occurs when the pollen from the male organ (anther) is transferred to the female part (stigma). The pollen grains form tubes and travel down the style. One male cell eventually reaches the ovary where it fertilizes the ovule.

petal-like green structures that enfold and protect the flower bud rise from the stem. Collectively, they are called the calyx. Inside the calyx are the petals, which may number in the hundreds or may be united in a single cup or tube. The sepals and petals together are called the corolla.

Inside the petals are the flower's reproductive organs. The pistil is the flower's female reproductive organ and consists of the ovary, style and stigma. It is located at the center of the flower, at the end of the floral axis. A flower may have more than one pistil, in which case the group of pistils is called the gynoecium.

The small, hollow ovary contains a number of ovules which, after fertilization by pollen, become seeds. The stigma, which may be located on the surface of the ovary or separated from it by a long style, is a moist hairy area that receives the pollen.

Surrounding the pistils are the stamens, the male organs. Each one consists of a slender, stubby stalk (the filament) topped by an oval or oblong enlarged part called an anther, which forms the pollen. A group of stamens is called the androecium. When the pollen is ripe, it drops on the stigma and fertilizes the ovules; it may be carried there by the wind, by insects such as bees or by other animals.

Some of these parts are occasionally absent on flowers; if so, the flowers are called incomplete. At least one set of organs is necessary for a functional flower. Flowers are called perfect if they have both stamens and pistils in the same flower, and are thus capable of self-fertilization. If the sex organs are borne on different flowers, the flowers are called imperfect, and individual flowers are either staminate (if they have stamens) or pistillate (if they have pistils). If staminate and pistillate flowers are borne on the same plant, the plant is monoecious. If they are borne on different plants, the plants are dioecious, each one being either "male" or "female."

FLOWERING CHERRY
See CHERRY, FLOWERING

FLOWERING CRAB
See CRAB APPLE, TREE

FLOWERING MAPLE (*Abutilon*)

Also known as parlor maple, this tropical shrub makes a fine indoor plant. Its blossoms are papery bells, somewhat resembling those of the hollyhock. Colors range from shades of pink and rose to red, and there is also a yellow-flowered variety.

Plants are usually large and bushy. Established plants should be cut back sharply once a year in order to promote best flowering; young plants normally tend to flower well without cutting back. Temperatures should be about 65 to 70°F. (18.33 to 21.11°C.) during the day and 55 to 60°F. (12.78 to 15.56°C.) at night. Plants can be started from seed or from cuttings about four inches long.

Two species of parlor maple are widely grown in the greenhouse and, less frequently, in the warm garden: Chinese lantern (*A. hybridium*) and trailing abutilon (*A. megapotamicum*). The former is a bushy type that is usually about two feet tall with white, yellow, pink, or lavender pendent flowers. Trailing abutilon is an excellent choice for hanging baskets since it has stems up to five feet in length. Its flowers are red and orange with brown anthers.

Flowering maple requires plenty of moisture, bright exposure with some sun and rich, humusy soil.

FLOWERING QUINCE
See QUINCE

FLOWERING TOBACCO
See NICOTIANA

FLUORESCENT LIGHT

In growing house plants, light, along with temperature and humidity, can be controlled and thus become a tool for producing luxuriant healthy growth. With fluorescent light you can give plants just the illumination they need all the time, no matter what the weather outside.

Plants grown under two 40-watt, 48-inch fluorescent bulbs with a reflector may receive up to 1,000 footcandles of light, depending upon their distance from the source.

Distance from source (inches)	Intensity (footcandles)
1	1,000
2	950
3	750
4	650
5	560
6	460
7	430
8	370
9	360
10	350

Fluorescent bulbs produce blue, short-waved light that encourages the growth of the leaves and reproductive parts in plants.

These rays are good for top growth and seed germination. Fluorescent lights are predominately blue which helps produce flowers, develop roots and deepen color of the leaves. They are cool and can't overheat plants.

Among fluorescent lights, some types are better than others for specific purposes. The Gro-Lux wide-spectrum fluorescent combines some of the good characteristics of incandescent with the best light ranges of fluorescents, and is probably the most satisfactory single light to use for foliage plants, vegetables and flowering plants. However, a combination of the standard Gro-Lux and the wide-spectrum Gro-Lux is better for raising seedlings, propagating cuttings and forcing bulbs. Seedlings should be placed with a distance of about three inches between the tubes and the seedling tops as soon as the green sprouts have broken through the soil.

It's not hard to learn at which distance from the lights your plants do best. Just watch them. If the leaves turn brown or bleach out, and if the plant tends to hug the sides of the pot, there is too much light. If plants grow tall and willowy with little or no bloom, there is too little. Generally, plants that don't bloom need much less light than plants that do.

As a humidity control, put a plastic curtain around shelves; just a strip of clear plastic thumbtacked to the top and bottom shelves gives plants their own little greenhouse. Plants grown in this plastic enclosure seldom need watering, and they have that shining-with-health look that goes with plenty of humidity. Open the curtain every day to give them a change of air.

Here is another way in which plants benefit from controlled light. There are three kinds of plants growing in most homes: short-day plants, like poinsettias, gardenias and chrysanthemums, which start to form buds only

Keep in mind that light intensity is not the same all along the tube. The most light is right in the middle, the least at the ends. Therefore, a light-loving plant, like the geranium, can be placed on a little block if necessary to make its tip just clear the light in the middle of the tube. Start cuttings, which are satisfied with little light, right in the peat moss at the ends of the tubes.

Fluorescent lights are better for growing plants than the incandescent ones, which give out a light in which red rays predominate.

when days become shorter; tuberous begonias, calceolaria and other plants that need long days to flower; and a third group, of which African violets and roses are members, which doesn't seem to care what the day length is. Florists use this knowledge to control the light their plants receive and to produce flowers when they are most easily marketable.

To find out just how much light each specific plant should get, use the chart on light requirements. The list of plants serves only as a guide; if your favorite plant is not there, try it anyway!

Plants growing under lights need not be left there continuously in order to stay healthy. Plants can come and go without apparent bad effects. You can put them under the lights until they attain desired growth and luxurious foliage or bloom, then take them out and place them where they show to best advantage.

Feeding: The more nearly perfect growing conditions are, the faster plants will grow, the healthier they will be, and the more food they will need. That is another way of saying that the plants close to the lights, which are the substitutes for the sun, need more food than

DISTANCE OF HOUSE PLANTS FROM LIGHT SOURCE

African violets (8–12 inches)
Aluminum plant (8–12 inches)
Asparagus fern (below 8 inches)
Begonia, metallic-leaf or rex (8–12 inches)
Begonias, other (below 8 inches)
Bromeliads (8–12 inches)
Bulbs (8–12 inches)
Cacti (below 8 inches)
Cast-iron plant (12–18 inches)
Chinese evergreen (12–18 inches)
Citrus (below 8 inches)
Coleus (below 8 inches)
Croton (below 8 inches)
Dieffenbachia (8–12 inches)
Dracaena (8–12 inches)
Ferns (12–18 inches)
Fig, banyan (8–12 inches)
Fig, fiddleleaf (below 8 inches)
Flowering annuals (below 8 inches)
Generiads (below 8 inches)
Geraniums (8–12 inches)
Grape ivy (8–12 inches)
Ivy (below 8 inches)
Kalanchoe (below 8 inches)
Medicine plant (below 8 inches)
Moses-in-the-cradle (below 8 inches)
Nephthytis (12–18 inches)

Norfolk Island pine (8–12 inches)
Orchids (shade-loving types: *Cypripedium, Phalaenopsis*) (8–12 inches)
Orchids (sun-loving types: *Cattleya, Cymbidium, Dendrobium, Epidendrum, Oncedium* and *Vanda*) (below 8 inches)
Palms (8–12 inches)
Parlor ivy (12–18 inches)
Patience plant (below 8 inches)
Peperomia (8–12 inches)
Philodendrons (other than parlor ivy) (8–12 inches)
Pothos (8–12 inches)
Prayer plant (8–12 inches)
Rubber plant (8–12 inches)
Screw pine (12–18 inches)
Shrimp plant (below 8 inches)
Snake plant (12–18 inches)
Spider plant (8–12 inches)
Succulents (below 8 inches)
Tree ivy (below 8 inches)
Umbrella tree (8–12 inches)
Vegetables (below 8 inches)
Velvet plant (below 8 inches)
Wandering Jew (8–12 inches)
Wax plant (below 8 inches)
Zebra plant (below 8 inches)

plants farther away. Watch for new growth; it is lighter and thinner than the old. If they are growing fast, feed them well.

Fluorescent Fixtures and Bulbs: The two basic types of fluorescent lamp fixtures are the industrial type, which has a built-in reflector, and the strip (or channel) type, usually used under shelves or cabinets, with a supporting background painted with flat white paint which acts as a reflector. The industrial type can be hung in the open, raised and lowered with adjustable chains that hook into the fixture; however, it is normally painted with glossy white paint which reflects less light than flat white. If you choose the industrial type for its flexibility of height, it would be best to remove the glossy enamel with paint remover and repaint it with flat white, in order to get the maximum light reflection. Both fixtures are available in models which hold from one to four tubes and which can take various watt-size lamps. The most readily available replacement bulbs are the 40-watt (48-inch) and 72-watt (96-inch) sizes. The 40-watt size will light a growing area of 48 by 6 inches, and the 72 watt a space of 96 by 6 inches; two bulbs would double the available growing area.

Your next problem is to choose the type of bulb: the preheat lamp, the rapid-start lamp and the slimline instant-start lamp. If you use the four-foot-size fixture, a preheat lamp starter is good for the sake of economy and good performance in high humidity. The eight-foot fixtures are most often available only in slimline instant-start types. Do not assume that two short bulbs will give the same light as one long one—light intensity is reduced at the ends of the tubes and more tubes naturally will have more ends! However, two shorter tubes might give greater flexibility by letting you adjust them to different heights for different growing needs.
See also HOUSE PLANTS.

FODDER

Fodder is a coarse food fed to livestock. Usually, it consists of corn and sorghum forage (including leaves, stems and grain) which has been cut and dried.

FOOD PRESERVATION
See CANNING, DRYING FOOD, FREEZING FOOD, STORAGE

FORAGE

Forage is any plant or plant part used as feed for livestock, especially when it is obtained by grazing.

Forage crops come from two great botanical families—the grasses (Gramineae) and the legumes (Leguminosae). Here are some of the factors that influence the choice of a forage crop:

Soil conservation and improvement: Deep-rooted legumes are generally selected for their ability to hold down the soil; they also increase its nitrogen content.

Long-lived meadows for hay: Good choices are alfalfa and bird's-foot trefoil.

Short-lived meadows for hay: A mixture of red clover and timothy is a good example of a short-lived meadow which is used for hay purposes.

Annual hays: Millets, Sudangrass, rye, and wheat, grown alone or in combination, fall in the category of annual hays.

Coarse grasses for silage or fodder: Examples of coarse grasses for silage or fodder are corn, sorghum and pearl millet.

DISTRIBUTION OF FORAGE CROPS

Crop	Distribution in North America
Alfalfa	Widespread, especially suited to southern and Gulf regions of U.S.
Alsike clover	Southern Midwest regions of U.S.
Bermudagrass	Southern and southwestern U.S.
Bird's-foot trefoil	Great Plains
Black medic	Throughout U.S. and Canada
Bromegrass	Southern and southwestern U.S.
Corn	Throughout U.S. and Canada, especially in central regions
Cowpea	Southern U.S.
Crimson clover	Southeastern U.S.
Fescues	Central and southern parts of U.S., western Canada
Field peas	Northeastern, central and Pacific regions of U.S.
Hop clover	Southern U.S.
Kentucky bluegrass	Northern and eastern regions of U.S. and Canada
Kudzu	Central and southern U.S.
Ladino clover	Throughout U.S. and Canada
Lespedezas	Southern U.S.
Millet	Eastern U.S. and Great Plains
Oatgrass	Eastern and central U.S. and Canada
Orchardgrass	Eastern and central regions of U.S. and Canada
Peanut	Southern U.S.
Red clover	North central and northeastern U.S. and parts of Canada
Redtop grass	Throughout U.S. and Canada, except in Deep South
Reed canarygrass	Northern U.S. and parts of Canada
Rye	Throughout U.S. and Canada, especially in southern regions
Sorghum	Throughout U.S. and Canada, especially in the Great Plains
Soybean	Throughout U.S. and parts of Canada, especially in the corn belt
Sudangrass	Widespread, except in extreme northern and southern regions
Sweet clover	Throughout U.S., especially on the Pacific coast
Timothy	Eastern corn belt
Vetches	Throughout U.S. and Canada, especially in the South
Wheat grasses	Northern Great Plains
White clover	Throughout eastern U.S. and Canada

Permanent pastures: Species for permanent pastures are Kentucky bluegrass and white clover in various more or less complex mixtures.

Semipermanent pastures: Species particularly adapted for semipermanent pastures are orchardgrass/ladino, bromegrass/ladino, reed canarygrass/ladino, orchardgrass/alfalfa, bromegrass/alfalfa, timothy/bird's-foot trefoil as well as other tall-growing grasses and legumes.

Supplementary pastures: Species adapted for supplementary pastures are the small grains, Sudangrass, domestic ryegrass, and field bromegrass.

Soiling crops: Soiling crops, such as corn which has been thickly planted, sweet sorghum and soybeans, are cut and fed to cattle green.

Adaptability to environment: Different forage crops are adapted to widely different climatic conditions, as climatic conditions frequently limit the area in which each species can profitably be grown. See "Distribution of Forage Crops" on page 391.

Yielding ability and feeding value: The yielding ability and feeding value of forage crops are very important. Unless high yields are obtained and the forage is highly valuable nutritionally, it doesn't pay to grow it.

Length of life: Species are classified as annuals, biennials and perennials. In the long run, perennials are preferred because they yield more and last longer, making their production much cheaper.

Cost of seed is sometimes a factor: One of the limitations to the expansion of the bird's-foot trefoil acreage in the Northeast is its high seed cost.

Versatility of species: The more uses a species can be put to, the greater is its forage value. It is highly desirable that a species be used interchangeably for pasture, grass silage, hay, or seed as needs dictate.

Ease of harvesting and curing: In order for forage to have maximum value it should be comparatively easy to harvest and to cure for later feeding. Many species fail to satisfy this requirement and are less useful to the small farmer. For example, sweet clover is sometimes so coarse that it is difficult to handle and cure. Kudzu, with its very prostrate, viny habit of growth, is also a poor choice.

See also COVER CROP, LEGUME.

FORCING

The growing and blooming of plants outside their usual season is known as forcing. Flowering branches that are most commonly brought into the house for forcing include forsythia, pussy willow, winter hazel, hardy jasmine, flowering quince, red maple, magnolia, flowering crab apple, native white and pink dogwoods, spring-blooming spireas, all kinds of cherries and other fruits, rhododendron, mountain laurel, wintersweet, and andromeda.

Hardy bulbs suitable for indoor flowering include snowdrops, crocus, grape hyacinths, daffodils, hyacinths, and early tulips. Tender bulbs recommended for forcing include amaryllis and paper-white narcissus, both of which require special treatment.

Forcing Branches: The forcing of branches takes less time and preparation than does the forcing of bulbs. Some branches, those of the pussy willow for example, will force in ten days or less. Others, like apple and peach which are woodier and also naturally later blooming, may take as long as three to four weeks. For a continuous supply of blooms, cut a fresh lot of branches every week or so from early February to the end of March. Of course, branches cut closer to their usual outdoor blooming date will flower sooner indoors.

Branches two to three feet long and heavily laden with flower buds will make the most impressive display. On fruit trees flower buds can be distinguished from leaf buds by the short gnarled spurs that hold the flower buds in position. Remember to leave the best branches on the tree or bush so that it blooms attractively at the normal flowering time, and be careful not to destroy the symmetry of the plant by injudicious cutting.

The middle of a mild day, when the temperature is above freezing, is the best time to cut. Using a sharp knife or shears make a clean diagonal cut. If the branch is hard and woody, crush the end of the cutting with a few strokes of a hammer or make a one- or two-inch slit in the stem. This will help it absorb water easily.

The branches should be completely submerged in a tub of water for three or four hours to soften the hard outer covering of the buds and encourage movement of sap in the stems. After soaking, put the branches in deep containers of water and keep them in a cool, dim place until the buds start to show color. The more gradually heat and light are increased, the longer the blooms will last. If the water in the containers is not changed daily, a piece of charcoal will help keep it fresh.

Misting the buds daily will further soften the hard bracts which protected them during the winter. As soon as they start to open, bring the branches into your living area. The blooms should last a week or more. Pussy willows, if removed from water after the fuzzy flowers are fully developed, will keep in a dry vase for months.

By experimenting with the branches of other trees and shrubs, many interesting effects can be produced. The buds of birch and alder produce novel catkins, and oak and maple also provide unusual materials for arrangements.

Forcing Bulbs: If planning to force bulbs for early spring display, purchase only firm heavy bulbs. Tulips should have their brown skins intact. Larger bulbs will provide stronger bloom stalks, though small bulbs can also be forced and will take less time to bloom. Store the bulbs carefully in a cool, dry, airy spot until mid-October or mid-November.

Plant bulbs in regular flowerpots or the more shallow bulb pans. Other containers may also be used, but they should have a drainage hole. Bulbs will rot if left standing in water. Place a handful of broken pottery or small stones over the drainage hole. Four parts rich garden soil mixed with one part peat moss will make a suitable potting soil. Add a small handful of bone meal, and mix it in well.

For the best display, plant three to five bulbs of the same variety in one pot, thus assuring that all bulbs will mature at the same time. Place enough potting soil in the pot to permit the bulbs to sit one inch below the surface rim of the pot. Fill with soil until the tips of the bulbs just show at the soil surface. Water the pot until water begins to seep out of the drainage hole.

All hardy bulbs need prolonged periods of dark, cool, damp conditions to form sufficient root growth and produce good tops. Tulips force best if stored ten to 12 weeks. Eight weeks is enough for most other hardy bulbs, but they too could benefit from a longer storage period. Temperatures during storage should range from 40 to 50°F. (4.44 to 10°C.). An unheated basement or dark garage may supply the proper conditions, but an outdoor trench or pit 12 to 15 inches deep is the pre-

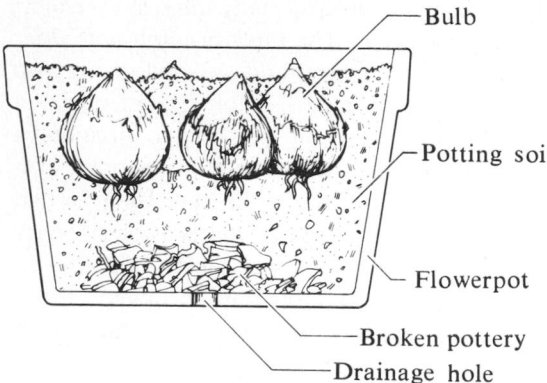

Bulb

Potting soil

Flowerpot

Broken pottery

Drainage hole

To force bulbs, plant them in a well-drained mixture of soil, peat moss and bone meal.

ferred storage place of many home gardeners. Place the pots close together in the pit. For protection against mice and other predators cover the pots with screening. Mulch the trench with a thick layer of pine needles, straw or other material which will not mat down.

Begin checking the bulbs after eight weeks. When they are ready to be forced, the bottom of the pot should contain a mass of roots and new roots should be pushing out of the drainage hole. There may be a yellow sprout or two peeking out from the soil surface.

By bringing in only a few pots at a time a succession of blooms can be had. Allow an adjustment period of about two weeks for the soil to slowly thaw. During this time store the pots in a semidark place where the temperature stays around 60°F. (15.56°C.). Water them well. When the sprouts are three to five inches high, begin moving them closer to direct sunlight. Rotate the pot for even growth. When the shoots are a healthy green, the pots should be in full sunlight, though they do prefer cool temperatures. Keep the rooting medium moist, but not soggy.

Once blooming begins, move the pots out of direct sunlight and water frequently. Gradually dry the bulb out as foliage starts to dry. When the pots are dry, move them to a very cool room (40°F. [4.44°C.]). Plant the bulbs outside as soon as the ground can be worked. Allow them to fatten up for a year in the garden, and they'll be ready to replant.

To force paper-white narcissus, place bulbs in a supporting medium—sand, gravel, pebbles—and add water until it just touches the base of the bulb. Set in a cool room (60°F. [15.56°C.]) to develop roots. Move into a warmer room as buds have formed, usually within three to five weeks.

Amaryllis bulbs can be potted in the winter. Allow one inch of space around each bulb, and leave the upper third of the bulb above the soil. Give the plants good light and a cool (60°F. [15.56°C.]) room. Water lightly. They will flower in six to eight weeks. Continue to water the bulbs after they flower. Amaryllis can be allowed to grow the year round.

See also BULB.

FOREST SERVICE
See GOVERNMENT SERVICES

FORGET-ME-NOT   *(Myosotis)*

A large group of annual, biennial or perennial, low-growing herbs that are hardy in the North, these plants produce small flowers that are usually blue, though there are pink and white forms. Generally, forget-me-nots prefer moist, partially shady locations, but some also grow satisfactorily in open sunny borders.

Seed can be sown from spring through summer for bloom the following year. Perennials can be propagated by cuttings or division.

Forget-me-nots make excellent bedding plants, especially under bulbs like tulips, and should be massed together for best effect. *M. alpestris* and *M. sylvatica* are biennials, usually under a foot tall, producing masses of little blue flowers in April and May. They do best in moist places under deciduous trees where they should be naturalized with other early-flowering plants like arabis, primroses and small bulbs. They self-sow freely in such locations and persist for years. *M. scorpioides,* the true forget-me-not, is a common plant along small streams. Its flowers can be pink or white as well as blue, and it often blooms well into summer. The biennial Chinese forget-me-not, *Cynoglossum amabile,* is grown as an annual for blue summer flowers. This one will do very well in dry soil in full sun. It blooms quickly from seed, and it is often best to make successive sowings to keep flowers coming along. Plants grow 12 to 18 inches tall.

FORMALDEHYDE   *See* FUNGICIDE

FORMAL GARDEN

Contrasted to the unconstrained design of the informal garden, which generally aims to imitate nature, the formal garden is a precise study in layout and arrangement. Everything is planned and kept in exact geometric balance and symmetry. Trees and shrubs are clipped uniformly. Color is kept restrained and in a single scheme. Ornaments and accessories are chosen in discreet scale to maintain the balance and style. Frequently, one major feature, such as a fountain, birdbath, figure, or pool, is centered as a highlight.

The formal garden is not necessarily forbidding. It can often lend a feeling of spaciousness and charm where these characteristics are difficult to achieve, such as in a small urban garden. Formal gardens require a great deal of maintenance to keep them at their best. Any small imperfection or asymmetrical feature will be noticed immediately and detract from the design.

FORSYTHIA

These especially attractive, spring-blooming shrubs are also called golden-bells. The flowers are yellow and very profuse. Of all the upright forms of this shrub, the nine-foot *F. x intermedia* cv. 'Spectabilis' is by far the best cultivar. *F. x i.* cv. 'Primulina' has pale yellow flowers more numerous at the tips of the branches. *F. suspensa* is the old weeping golden-bells and, if left untrimmed, may be trained as a vine over a wall. All the forsythias are rapid growers, so you can save money by buying small plants a foot to 18 inches high. Give them plenty of space, at least six feet apart, and even then they will have to be thinned when they reach maturity. They grow readily in any good garden soil and are easily propagated from cuttings in midsummer or from the new shoots, which root as easily as privet.

Forsythias flower in April and May and can grow eight feet high with a ten-foot spread. The large types should not be used in small gardens or limited spaces where heavy pruning would be necessary, as this destroys the natural arching shape of the plants. Prune by removing old canes at the ground; avoid giving the bushes a crew cut as you might privet or yew. Newer cultivars are Lynwood Gold, Beatrix Farrand and Spring Glory. They are hardy, but in extreme winters they are sometimes partially winter-killed, especially the tips of the branches and the flower buds. *F. ovata,* a five-foot species from Korea, is extremely hardy and blooms earlier than any of the others, producing amber yellow flowers occasionally even in late March. This is an excellent shrub for places with severe winters, such as Maine and the other northeastern states. Do not prune any early spring-blooming shrub until just after it has flowered, as the blossoms are borne on last year's wood.

See also SHRUBS.

FOUNDATION PLANTING

The foundation planting is largely an American invention, developed at the time when high houses were commonly built with two or more feet of foundation showing between the walls and the ground. It was to conceal this ugly feature that shrubbery was planted around the base of the house. Many of the houses being built nowadays have their foundations architecturally concealed, which means that a foundation planting is not always necessary or even desirable.

Where such a planting is called for, it should be designed to harmonize with and enhance the architectural design of the house. Each house must be treated individually, so there are no set rules. An effective foundation planting blends the house into its surroundings by softening the hard angles of corners and the abrupt meeting of house and ground. Plant as sparingly as possible to achieve this effect—

the most common mistake is to overplant a foundation with shrubbery that grows up to smother the house.

The entrance is the focal point of the house and should be planted so its importance is emphasized. A good basic design would call for using medium-height shrubs here, grading down to lower ones along the sides of the house, with the tallest reserved for the corners. The soil next to foundations tends to dry out quickly, so it is best to keep the plants at least two feet in front of the wall. Where space is limited, an espaliered shrub or a light vine might be trained up the wall.

When selecting plants for the foundation, several important points should be considered. In landscapes, horizontal lines and rounded forms are most pleasing to the eye and are most effective for blending purposes, whereas strong verticals have a dramatic agitating effect. Botanical exclamation points such as arborvitae and certain junipers are useful where an upright accent is needed, but they should be used with discretion around foundations because their strong upright shape might contrast too strongly with the lines of the house. Their effect can be toned down by planting low, rounded shrubs in front of them.

Color and texture of foliage are also important considerations. Plants having variegated or otherwise highly colored foliage should generally not be used around foundations. By drawing attention to themselves, these standouts compete with other plants and the house and disrupt the harmonious effect desirable in foundation plantings. By the same token, compact shrubs having small- or medium-sized leaves are more likely to complement the house than coarse, large-leaved kinds.

The height of the fully grown plant is another factor determining its usefulness. Avoid using trees or shrubs that will require frequent trimming to keep them at a size in scale with the house. Plants such as hemlocks, spruces and pines which reach forest-tree size under normal conditions are inappropriate for use along foundations. The heavy manicuring they need to keep them in bounds is a tedious chore, but if it is not done, these trees quickly outgrow their space and become eyesores or hazards. Most large, spreading shrubs are also inappropriate, especially under windows or along walks, which they will quickly block unless kept tightly trimmed. Many species of trees and shrubs have dwarf forms which are naturally slow growing and mature at appropriate and manageable heights. These are ideal for foundation plantings because of the comparatively low maintenance they require. Though usually costlier and harder to find than taller forms of the species, they are well worth searching out.

FOUR-O'CLOCK   (*Mirabilis*)

These are popularly grown tender annuals, though *M. longiflora* is often treated as a perennial in the southern half of the country. It grows two to three feet high and produces flowers that open after sunset. *M. Jalapa*, known commonly as marvel-of-Peru, grows one to 2½ feet high and produces one-inch white, red or yellow flowers that open in late afternoon.

FOXGLOVE   (*Digitalis purpurea*)

Foxglove, also known as digitalis, is a fairly hardy European biennial plant that has long been grown as an ornamental in flower gardens in this country. In addition to being an important source of the medicine, digitalis, it is one of the handsomest garden herbs. Foxglove leaves and their products are heart-ailment medicines, and no satisfactory substitute for them has been introduced. The numerous horticultural forms developed differ principally in the size and color of the flowers. All are known to be medicinally potent, and their leaves are therefore acceptable for drug purposes. The species also grows wild in the

Available with flowers of pink, purple, yellow, or white, the old-fashioned foxglove is a favorite country garden perennial or biennial.

coastal mountain ranges in the northern Pacific Coast states.

Foxglove flowers in long, racemose, one-sided clusters of showy purples, yellows or white. The flowers develop on a three-foot stalk surrounded by plant leaves.

Ancient herbalists chose foxglove for external use at first, ignoring its value as a blood circulation stimulant and aid in the treatment of heart diseases. Not until 1755 did an English physician tap this medically valuable plant. Since that time, the herb has been used as a drug in many heart-related treatments.

The plant thrives in ordinary well-drained soils of open texture and reasonable fertility. Propagation is by seed. Direct field sowing is not usually successful, because the seed is exceedingly small and does not germinate well except under favorable conditions. To facilitate even distribution it may be mixed with sand and sown early in February in flats in a greenhouse or in a hotbed. When danger of frost is over, the plants are hardened off and transplanted to the field. Plant them one foot apart in rows conveniently spaced for cultivation. They do not bloom until the second season. Mulching for winter protection is advisable where very low temperatures prevail. The plant is usually cultivated as an annual or biennial crop although it also grows sometimes as a perennial.

See also HERB.

FRANKLINIA   (*Franklinia Alatamaha*)

In the autumn of 1765, John Bartram of Philadelphia was making an exploration of southern Georgia, following generally the course of the Altamaha River. Few settlers had come inland as yet in the new colony, and the country was thoroughly wild. But the high point of interest on that trip was not Indians or strange animals. It was the discovery of a small shrubby tree that looked a little like a stewartia. Though its leaves blazed with autumn red and gold, the tree was still covered with large white flowers. A thrilling sight, for Bartram was a botanist.

When he got back to Philadelphia he checked it carefully against his herbarium specimens and all the books he could find. It was unknown to botany and he named it franklinia, after his friend Benjamin Franklin, the well-known printer of that day.

Nine years later, in 1774, Bartram's son William introduced this fall-blooming tree into England (where Franklin was also at the time, endeavoring to persuade the home government not to drive the colonists to open rebellion). There it was renamed Gordonia, the earlier naming of Franklinia being unknown. (Franklinia is now the recognized name, however.)

In 1778 Bartram went back to Georgia and collected all the good plants he could find. These came back to his gardens in Philadelphia and were propagated and distributed (as soon as the War of Independence permitted) through America and England. Twelve years later a search along the Altamaha River located just one living tree. Since that time the plant has never again been seen growing wild. Possibly within the enormous Okefenokee Swamp some plants may still survive, hidden on some islet, but all the plants now in the world's gardens—and there are many highly prized specimens—are descended from those collected in the second expedition in 1778.

Franklinia likes moist, peaty soil. It is hardy north to Boston, Rochester (New York) and Chicago. Full sun is best.

It can be propagated by seed but is usually grown from hardwood cuttings, since this is quicker. They root in sand, with bottom heat, in a few weeks. If taken in late autumn, fewer than 50 percent will succeed. But if not taken from the plant until after January 1, they root much better, close to 90 percent rooted being the usual crop.

In transplanting plants under five feet, no earth ball is needed in late fall or early spring. However, a certain amount of the top is likely to die back on transplanting, and it is important to prune down to living wood. Once the new leaves start to come out late that spring, your new franklinia can usually be depended on for many years of beauty.

FRAXINELLA (*Dictamnus ablus*)

An ornamental perennial native to Europe and Asia, fraxinella is called burning bush and gas plant, since the strong-smelling vapor given off by its foliage will sometimes ignite if a match is placed to it.

This is one plant that is difficult to propagate. The seeds should be planted as soon as they are ripe, since they can take as long as one year to germinate.

Fraxinella prefers a deep, rich soil and a sunny well-drained location. Because its foliage is as attractive as its blossom, the plant is often grown singly. Plant in the spring, at least 12 inches apart; once established, transplanting is not recommended. Fraxinella roots are winter-hardy and require no special maintenance in cold weather.

The leaves are harvested and dried to prepare a strong but tasty tea. The dried root was once used to remedy hysteria and fever.

FRAXINUS   *See* ASH

FREESIA

Freesias are beautiful, fragrant South African herbs with yellow or white flowers that bloom in winter.

Since the introduction of hybrid varieties with large flowers in many lovely and delicate shades, freesias have further gained in popularity. These hybrids are the results of crosses made between the white *F. refracta* varieties and the colored *F.* x *hybrida*. Flowers bloom in salmon orange, buff, lovely lavender pink, golden yellow with an orange blotch, rosy salmon with a golden yellow throat, light purple, and many other fine shades. The old white freesia, *F. alba,* is still most desirable. It bears its snow white blooms on stems ten inches long; colored hybrids grow a few inches taller. Under proper conditions the plants remain in bloom for about two weeks, and through successive plantings made two weeks apart, a continuous supply of blooms may be obtained in the greenhouse or house.

Freesia corms, usually but incorrectly called bulbs, should be planted indoors in August. The large corms, measuring ¾ inch in diameter, are the first ones to bloom; smaller ones, ½ inch in diameter, require a longer time and are likely not to bloom until April.

The culture of freesias is quite simple. The corms and plants are tender and must never be subjected to freezing temperatures. They are suited to house culture exclusively. Success depends primarily upon correct temperature. Prepare a special soil mixture composed of one-third each of leaf mold or shredded peat moss, good rich garden soil and fine clean sand. Moisten the mixture moderately and place it in pots or deep bulb pans, first covering the drainage hole with a few pieces of broken flowerpot. Five or six corms can be planted in a five-inch pot, from eight to ten in a six-inch pot. Some gardeners have found that freesia corms are surer to bloom if they are dried thoroughly for about two weeks on a sunny windowsill. When planting, space the corms about two inches apart and press them into the loose soil mixture so that the tips are covered with from ½ to one inch of soil. Next, place the pots or pans, without watering them, in the shaded window of a cool room where the temperature remains between 45 and 55°F. (7.22 to 12.78°C.). Under such conditions root growth will commence promptly. When the sprouts break through, place in a south window. It seems that the colored varieties do better if the temperature is kept at 55 to 60°F. (12.78 to 15.56°C.).

When the surface soil shows signs of drying out, give a light sprinkling of tepid water with a fine spray. Excessive watering and cold water are harmful. Repeated sprinkling with small quantities of water must be continued so that the soil will never be water-soaked. After the flower buds begin to form, raise nighttime temperatures to 60 to 65°F. (15.56 to 18.33°C.). Place a thermometer near the plants to be sure of the temperature.

Always keep the plants as close to the window as possible, but beware that they are not harmed by the frost during cold nights. The foliage must never be allowed to touch the glass of the window. A few thicknesses of paper placed between the plants and the glass during extra-cold nights will be an added protection. Water moderately, but never let the soil dry out. When the buds begin to open,

very weak liquid manure may be substituted for the water to encourage long flower spikes set with larger blooms. Support flower stems with four or five short, thin stakes stuck around the edge of the pot and connected with thin twine. For cutting, remove each spray when the first two blooms have opened.

When the blooming season is over, gradually withhold water and dry off in a cool room. The process of ripening the corms requires about a month or so. When perfectly dry, shake the soil from the corms and store in a dry place until next fall or early winter, when they may be replanted. Corms which started into growth during storage fail to bloom in most cases. The new growth during storage consists of the formation of a new, small corm at the growing tip of the old corm hidden beneath the fibrous skin. Most gardeners will not bother to save old corms, as they require exacting storage conditions in order to do well the following year. Another problem to the gardener saving his corms is the fact that they remain dormant for a set period of time, after which they will commence growing no matter what the conditions are.

FREESTONE

This refers to varieties of peaches and nectarines in which the flesh of the fruit easily separates from the stone. The fruit of other varieties, known as clingstone, sticks more to the stone.

FREEZING   *See* FROST

FREEZING FOOD

If prepared correctly and stored no longer than recommended, many foods come out of the freezer almost as nutritious and fresh-tasting as they went in.

Freezing Vegetables: An intelligent approach to the subject of vegetables for freezing is to determine which are the most nutritious and the tops in family popularity. Then, plan your garden accordingly, not only for serving produce directly from the garden but for freezer storage so that it will be available in off-seasons.

Vegetables for freezing should be tender, succulent, fully colored, and free from wilting; try not to freeze old, tough vegetables. An important tip to remember is that the quicker you prepare and freeze vegetables after picking, the more flavorful—and nutritious—they will be when served.

Usually vegetables should be blanched (scalded) before freezing, as blanching inactivates the enzymes which would otherwise produce unpalatable flavors and disagreeable odors, and cause an unnecessary loss of vitamin C.

Put the vegetables to be blanched in a wire-mesh basket and drop it into boiling or near-boiling water, or, better yet, suspend it above steam for the best results. Blanch for a few minutes (see chart), and then remove the wire basket from the boiling water or steam, and cool the contents as quickly as possible, either by plunging the basket in ice water to which ice cubes may be added as necessary, or under very cold running water. Vegetables should be completely cooled before freezing; if not, there will be a loss in color, texture, flavor, and nutrients.

Fortunately, properly frozen, thawed and served vegetables lose little of their basic nutrient value. It's only if they're allowed to thaw and the juices leak away that they begin to lose food value. Some of the vitamins are water soluble, others are destroyed by the action of air—a process which is hastened by a combination of light, warm room temperature and by oxidative enzymes acting within the plant tissue. Freezing aids in retaining vitamin value and retarding enzyme activity if vegetables are properly blanched beforehand. Blanching in water causes some loss, 10 to 30 percent of vitamin C, but more of this vitamin would be lost during freezing if the food were not blanched first. Less loss takes place when the vegetables are subjected to blanching over steam. There is a 10 to 50 percent loss of vitamin B_1, depending on the variety of vegetable, and the blanching time involved. There is a very slight loss of vitamin A.

RECOMMENDED BLANCHING TIME FOR SOME COMMON VEGETABLES

Vegetable	Minutes
Asparagus	2 to 4
Beet	until tender
Broccoli, split	4
Brussels sprouts	3 to 5
Carrot (small, whole)	5
Corn (on the cob)	4
Eggplant (peeled and sliced)	4
Green bean (whole)	3
Green bean (cut)	2
Green pea, shelled	1½
Green pepper, seeded, cut in strips	2
Spinach greens, trimmed	2
Summer squash	3

Freezing Fruits: Fruits are even easier to freeze than vegetables, since they need not be blanched before they are frozen. Changes in the texture of the frozen fruits are like those produced by canning, but they retain more nutritive value and flavor under freezing than by any other preserving method. Freezing fruits requires far less labor than canning. One year is the safe limit to keep frozen fruits.

Two methods—the dry pack and syrup pack—are used for packing fruits. Fruits packed without a sweetener of any kind may lose some of their flavor, texture and color; however, in cases where you plan to use the fruits in recipes where sweetener will be added later in the cooking process, such a completely dry pack is simplest. Small berries, whole strawberries, currants, rhubarb (cut into one-inch pieces), and plums (halved and pitted) can be put right into plastic containers or freezer bags and frozen. A handy trick with plums or apricots is to halve and pit them, place them on a cookie sheet directly on the freezer shelf, and as soon as they are frozen hard, bag or box them. They will stay loose in their container for use in small quantities, as they are needed. Whole berries may also be frozen this way, for use as garnishes.

Instead of using sugar, you can sweeten your fruits with honey, either with the dry pack (½ cup honey per pint of dry fruit), or by adding a thin-to-medium honey syrup. Thin syrup is made by mixing 1 cup of honey with 3 cups of very hot water; medium syrup is made by mixing 2 cups of honey to 2 cups of very hot water. Use mild, light honeys for freezing so that they don't overpower the flavor of the fruit. Chill all syrups before adding enough to completely cover the fruit. For the dry pack, trickle the honey over the packed fruit, shaking slightly. If you pack the fruit tightly in the container, you should need about ½ cup syrup per pint container and 1 cup syrup per quart.

Darkening of the fruit tissues in thawed fruit due to oxidation can be avoided by the use of vitamin C (ascorbic acid). Add 1 to 2 tablespoons of liquid or powdered rose hip concentrate or ascorbic acid to pure honey or honey syrup before it is poured over the fruit. However, since ascorbic acid has a bitter taste, try a few test batches of fruit before tackling a major operation, to see if you need to adjust quantities of either ascorbic acid or honey. Using only mature fruits will also improve the quality and lessen browning. Handle fruits quickly, and cut directly into the syrup any fruit likely to discolor. To maintain best quality, thaw fruits at a low temperature and use while they still contain some ice crystals.

Freezing Meats: Almost all types of meat can be frozen, with the exceptions of processed, spiced, cured, and smoked products. Luncheon meats should not be frozen at all, but cured and seasoned meats like ham, bacon and sausage may be kept for periods up to two months. Seasonings shorten freezer life, so that home-made fresh sausage, meat loaf and similar mixes can be kept longer if they are seasoned after thawing.

It is important to wrap meat as soon as possible after cutting. Triple-layer freezer paper, heavy-duty plastic wrap and aluminum foil are all adequate to protect frozen meats, if wrapped so that moisture cannot escape. "Freezer burn" is really a description of meat dehydration, caused by the escape of the meat's moisture into the dry atmosphere of the freezer. The wrap needs to be pliable, to fit the irregular shapes of meats in order to avoid air pockets within packages which can speed up the rate of rancidity in the food. Strength in the wrap is also important to avoid tears around sharp corners or exposed bones; padding such sharp places with extra plastic wrap or even waxed paper can save you disappointment later. The longer the meat is to be kept, the more imperative it is to use a double wrap or some other special care in wrapping. Another good idea for ease in the thawing procedure is to separate individual chops, steaks, hamburgers, and so on with a piece of waxed paper or plastic.

Always be sure to label each package with the weight, type of cut (or number of pieces) and the date frozen. Use earliest freezing dates first. Try to freeze meat as quickly as possible; if your freezer has no quick-freeze compartments or plates, a trip to a butcher's flash-freeze unit may turn out to be economical in the long run. Do not place more than two to three pounds of fresh meat per cubic foot of freezer space in a 24-hour period; always place it in the coldest parts of your freezer, on the bottom or freezer plates and along the walls. Pack it loosely while freezing to allow the air to circulate freely; then when it is hard it may be packed tightly to conserve space. Freezing units within regular refrigerators are seldom cold enough for long-time storage of meats, so use a separate freezer or rent a freezer locker.

RECOMMENDED MAXIMUM STORAGE TIME FOR MEATS

Meat	Months
Beef	6–12
Veal	6–9
Pork	3–6
Lamb	6–9
Ground beef, veal and lamb	3–4
Ground pork	1–3
Variety meats	3–4
Poultry	6–7
Leftover cooked meat	2–3
Prepared casseroles, stews, meat pies, etc.	3–4

Freezing Dairy Products: Freezing is a very simple way to preserve milk and cream. Use glass or plastic containers, and be sure to allow two inches at the top for expansion. Freeze quickly after sealing the container tightly. Thaw for two hours at room temperature before using. Thawed cream is not satisfactory to use as is over cereal or in coffee, nor is it always possible to whip it, but for cooking or baking it is quite adequate. Just make sure to beat it a little to mix in the butterfat which may have separated during freezing.

RECOMMENDED STORAGE TIME FOR DAIRY PRODUCTS

Dairy Product	Months
Milk	4–5
Cream	2–3
Butter (unsalted keeps longer)	3–6
Cottage cheese	3–4
Semihard and hard cheese	6

Butter may also be frozen, after wrapping tightly as you would meat. It should thaw for three hours in the refrigerator before use.

Cheese, both soft like cottage cheese, and hard like cheddar, can be frozen. If you make your own cottage cheese, freeze it in airtight containers without rinsing out the remaining whey. Then when it thaws it can be rinsed and seasoned. When freezing harder cheeses, cut them into smaller pieces of not more than ½ pound and wrap them tightly. This will let them freeze and thaw quickly and reduce damage to the cheese's texture and flavor.

Freezer Containers and Wraps: Any containers that will prevent contamination and loss of moisture can be used for freezing. Ice cream containers, waxed inside, are ideal for fruits and vegetables. If glass jars are used, don't fill them to within more than an inch of the top, as that space would allow room for the normal expansion of the food without accidents. Fruits and vegetables which are to be packaged loose and meats can be packed in heavy-duty plastic bags, heat-sealed with a hot iron or closed with a wire twist at a point as close to the food as possible so that there's a minimum of air in the package. It's advisable to overwrap thin plastic bags with another plastic bag to prevent the plastic material from either breaking or tearing.

Types of Freezers: There are three types of freezers: uprights, chests and no-frosts. Upright freezers take up less floor space than chests and the food is more accessible since it's easier for most people to reach in than bend over and dig around. However, since cold air is heavier than room-temperature air it spills out of an opened upright easily, whereas a chest-type freezer contains the cold air and doesn't let it spill out. Over a period of time an upright freezer can mean shorter food storage life and higher electrical bills. No-frost freezers, because the inside temperature periodically rises slightly to melt frost, will cost 50 to 60 percent more in electric bills to operate. This variance in temperature may also shorten the storage life of your frozen foods.

Freezers, no matter what kind, should obviously be placed in the most convenient, coolest, driest and best ventilated place, whether that be in the cellar, kitchen or garage.

For more information check: *The Ball Blue Book,* published by Ball Corporation, Muncie, IN 47302; *Stocking Up,* by the editors of *Organic Gardening and Farming,* Rodale Press, Inc., Emmaus, PA 18049, 1977; and *Putting Food By,* by Ruth Hertzberg et al., Stephen Greene Press, Brattleboro, VT 05301, 1975.

FRENCH-INTENSIVE METHOD
See INTENSIVE GARDENING

FRINGED GENTIAN
See GENTIAN

FRINGE TREE
(*Chionanthus virginicus*)

The ornamental fringe tree can be grown in all but the extreme northern and arid southern parts of North America. It has hanging clusters of fleecy white flowers, long leaves that turn yellow in the fall and small blue berries. It is one of the last trees to put forth leaves in spring with the flowers following in early summer. The fringe tree is closely related to the lilac and should be given much the same care. Do not prune the trees unless winter injuries make it necessary.

See also LILAC, OLD-MAN'S-BEARD.

FRIT   *See* TRACE ELEMENTS

FRITILLARIA

Mostly bulbous, spring-blooming, hardy plants, fritillarias resemble lilies in the shape of their drooping flowers. Most popular kinds are crown-imperial (*F. imperialis*) and checkered lily or guinea-hen tulip (*F. Meleagris*). The checkered lily has nodding, pendulous flowers on nine- to 12-inch stems. Flowers are not conspicuous and can be colored bronze, gray, purple, and white with a checkered pattern of different shades. Plant bulbs four inches deep in very well-drained soil and protect in north-ernmost areas. This species is good for sunny rock gardens.

Crown-imperial blooms in early spring. Often growing to three feet, its bell-shaped blooms are yellow, orange or red. After the foliage ripens, the plant goes dormant.

Soil should be rich and friable, neither too moist nor too dry. Use compost or well-rotted manure. Plant the large bulbs, ones that are three to four inches in diameter, about eight to 12 inches deep. These large-size bulbs should be spaced about six to 12 inches apart, depending on when you want to dig them for transplanting. Deep, far-apart planting permits you to leave them alone for as long as ten years.

Tiny bulbs, ½ inch or less in diameter, need not be planted more than an inch deep, but make sure they are well mulched. Crown-imperial should always be planted in a pro-tected location in colder parts of New England.

Transplant when the bulbs are dormant, shortly after the foliage has died. Plant where they do not get hot afternoon sun. They should not be crowded by other plants, shrubs or trees, either above or below the soil. Mulch when the plants die down. Bulbs can be multiplied rapidly if transplanted every year or two.

FROG

A number of tailless, leaping amphibians (genus *Rana* and allied genera of the family Ranidae) are commonly known as frogs. Among the best-known American species are the bullfrog (generally applied to any large frog, especially *R. catesbeiana, R. grylio* and *R. aurora*), leopard frog (*R. pipiens*) and pickerel frog (*R. palustris*). Some species are permanently aquatic and have fully webbed toes, while others are more land oriented, ex-cept during mating season in spring when frogs breed in the water.

The terrestrial frog species are often a farmer's best friend. They will live in moist spots of a small farm or garden, provided pond or stream water is nearby. Tree or cricket frogs are most valuable to farmers and gardeners, since they keep insects in check on the ground and in trees.

Like toads, frogs will quickly devour anything moving close by. However, since frogs generally inhabit ponds instead of gardens, their food consists mainly of pond life, including minnows, crayfish, water bugs, and smaller frogs. Frogs which live in marshes thrive on spiders, beetles, crickets, grasshoppers, and other small ground creatures. The toad is more of a land lover, and thus is more valuable to the gardener.

Gray tree frogs eat large insects, such as katydids and grasshoppers. Other species feed on mealworms, crickets and dragonfly nymphs. Some types of frogs and toads also eat algae growing on nearby rocks and in ponds.

A few species of frogs are tasty to man, especially the legs of the bullfrog. Bullfrog farming for this gourmet market is not very widespread, however, due to the high cost of labor and low output in harvesting the frogs. Therefore, most bullfrogs for the market are still hunted in wildlife ponds, marshes and lakes, drastically reducing the overall frog population.

Frog legs are commonly breaded and fried. One recipe recommends scalding the frog legs for a minute, then draining and drying them. Next, coat the legs with salt and pepper, dip in beaten egg, then in crackers. Fry the legs in deep, hot fat. The taste of frog legs resembles that of fried chicken.

See also TOAD.

FROST

The term "frost" or "hoarfrost" is used to designate the deposit of feathery ice crystals on the ground or other exposed surfaces, the temperature of which has fallen to 32°F. (0°C.) or lower. It is customary, however, when such a temperature occurs to say there has been a frost even if it was not accompanied by a deposit of ice crystals.

In order to understand the underlying principles of frost protection, it is necessary to know something of the processes through which the ground surface and the air at lower levels cool during the night.

How Frost Is Formed: Whenever two adjacent objects have unequal temperatures, the colder always gains heat at the expense of the warmer. During the night, when the earth receives no radiation from the sun, it loses heat to the atmosphere. If enough heat is lost, the surface temperature drops to below freezing. When the humidity is high and the night air temperature is below the dew point (the temperature at which the relative humidity equals 100 percent), but above freezing, moisture condenses and forms dew. If the air temperature drops below freezing and below the dew point, a "white frost" occurs. If the air temperature is above the dew point, but below freezing, a "black frost" occurs.

When to Expect Frost: Frosts or freezes may follow almost any type of local weather, and predictions based on local indications alone are likely to prove disappointing. However, there are a few local indications that may prove to be of some value.

The weather of the United States is largely governed by the movement of, and interaction between, great moving masses of air which originate in different regions and have different characteristics of temperature, moisture and wind; these air masses may be divided broadly into two main types—polar, or cold, originating in the North, and tropical, or warm, originating in southerly latitudes. Each air mass carries with it its own particular type of weather. The most changeable weather, accompanied by cloudiness, wind, and often by rain or snow, normally is found near the boundaries between two air masses of differing characteristics, called fronts. A boundary at which warm, moist air is overrunning relatively cold air is known as a "warm front"; while a front at which cold air is pushing under and lifting a warm air mass is known as a "cold front." Speaking very generally, the passage of a warm front is accompanied by a blanket of heavy low clouds and more or less continuous precipitation, while a cold front passage is characterized by intermittent precipitation, followed by broken cloudiness and clearing skies.

Practically all freezes and a large proportion of local frosts follow the passage of a cold front and the subsequent influx of polar air. Cold rain or sleet is followed by intermittent showers or thunderstorms, then clearing skies and falling humidity. At times, however, frost does not immediately follow the cold front passage because of wind conditions. Relatively cold polar air masses usually move southward in the westerly portion of a cyclone, or low-pressure area, and in the eastern portion of an anticyclone, or high-pressure area.

Although moisture in the ground after a rain tends to prevent warming of the ground during the day, it also tends to prevent a large fall in temperatures during the night. When the dew point is reached, the latent heat given up checks the rate of cooling, and when the abundant surface ground moisture freezes, the liberated heat also aids in checking the rate of fall in temperature.

As the humidity decreases, the surface of the ground usually dries out considerably. The dew point is likely to be lower, and there is more danger of a damaging frost, especially a "black frost" in which vegetation turns very dark.

By the third night after a rainstorm, the day temperature usually has risen high enough to make a heavy local frost unlikely, although there are exceptions to this rule. In California, heavy frosts sometimes occur following a strong influx of polar air without any local indications of the passage of a cold front. Low night temperatures occur immediately following the cessation of strong, dry north to east winds.

Large bodies of water exert a modifying influence on the climate of nearby localities, and such localities are less liable to damage by frost. A light wind blowing from a large body of water is generally more or less laden with water vapor, which retards the rate of surface cooling; and as the temperature of the water is usually considerably above freezing, that of the air passing from it to the land is often high enough to prevent the formation of frost.

Rivers often give up a large amount of moisture to the surface air, so that when the temperature falls to the dew point a surface fog forms which covers a part or all of the lower land in the valley, absorbing and returning radiation and preventing a further fall in temperature. In valleys near the ocean, fog sometimes drifts in from the water toward morning and prevents a damaging frost. On nights with ground fog, the hillsides are practically always colder than the lowlands unless the fog extends high enough to cover both hillsides and valley floor.

Protecting Plants: Much damage may be wrought in the garden by the unexpected late spring frosts which sometimes follow a period of warm growing weather. Removal of the protecting evergreen boughs and leaves from the perennial beds will have been necessary in most sections, as an extended delay yellows the growth beneath the cover and causes it to be weak and lanky. Keep this material handy in an out-of-the-way place. Native plants are less likely to be caught by late frosts than those that are acclimated to other zones.

It is remarkable to see the resistance the early-spring-flowering bulbs show to cold. Snowdrops will push through the soil while the ground is still covered with snow. Crocus, scilla and glory-of-the-snow are almost equally resistant to cold weather and need no emergency protection if they have not been coddled by a winter cover. Narcissus and hyacinths also are endowed by nature to withstand a cold snap after they have made quite some top growth. But a light protection of evergreen boughs will be of aid. Particular care must be given to the tender bulbs like species of *Brodiaea, Camassia* and *Calochortus,* which are easily injured by late frost. Early-blooming bushes, like Japanese quince, are sometimes caught unawares, and large sheets placed over them will usually save the display of flowers.

Seedlings coming along in the cold frame need particular watching. Close the sash upon the approach of freezing temperature, and if the drop is severe, bank the outside of the frame with soil or litter and place burlap bags over the glass panes. These keep the cold out during the night, and the shade prevents an undue rise of temperature during the day. When the temperatures rises above 32°F. (0°C.), give air by raising the sash with a brick or block on the side of the frame opposite to the direction of the wind.

Young plants of hardy annual flowers sown outdoors early in the spring are sometimes affected by late frosts. Individual plants may be covered with berry boxes held in place by stones or earth placed upon them. Where they are planted in rows, the boxes may be placed a foot or two apart with sheets of paper placed over them like a tent. Cover the sides of the paper with soil.

Perennials that have early growth should be covered with berry boxes, wooden boxes, flats, flowerpots, pails, and even cardboard boxes. One of the finest lilies, *Lilium Hansonii,* needs particular attention, as it starts growth early, yet is quite easily injured by late frosts. Often the young shoots of this lily are quite tall and require a taller basket to cover them. Line the inside of the basket with a couple of thicknesses of newspaper as a further protection and place a heavy stone on the top. Where dry leaves are still at hand, cover the perennial plants with them before using the inverted boxes.

The purpose of all coverings is first to keep the severe cold off as much as possible and then to accomplish a gradual warming up afterwards. Use good judgment as to the length of time it is kept on, as the young plants or shoots beneath it need light as well as air to make a normal growth. Fortunately these late cold spells do not last long enough to necessitate protection for more than a few days; usually they are just harmful for a night or two. That, however, may be enough to do severe damage.

Plantings close to the foundation of the house deserve special attention, as the proximity to a heated cellar or a chimney wall warms the soil in such positions and causes an advance in growth. As plants in such locations are usually well established, they can stand a cover of double-thickness mulch (even newspaper held in place by stones or soil). A light covering of leaves below the paper serves as an additional protection.

The work of protecting plants against frost injury extends also into the house. Though there may be little danger of the temperature on the enclosed porch falling below the freezing point, be sure that none of the plants touch any of the windowpanes. Move the plants a few inches from the windows, or if this is cumbersome, place three or four layers of newspaper between them and the glass pane.

FRUIT FLIES   *See* INSECT CONTROL

FRUITS FOR DRYING
See DRYING FOOD

FRUITS, GROWING INDOORS

House plants which produce edible fruits have always been of great interest to home gardeners and house-plant fanciers. Although such plants may not significantly decrease grocery bills as will an outdoor garden and small orchard, many people like growing fruits indoors simply for their attractive foliage—with fresh fruit as an added bonus.

Culture: Since potted plants cannot send their roots very far in search of food, it must be brought to them. This is done by potting in compost-enriched soil and fertilizing frequently. A soil made from two parts garden loam, one part compost and one part sharp sand with one cup of bone meal added per peck of mixture is fine for most fruiting plants. To fertilize, water bimonthly or at least once a month with manure tea or fish emulsion, or place a one-inch layer of compost on top of the soil. When you water, nutrients will leach into the soil from this layer. Replace the compost monthly.

· Proper exposure is important. All plants need good light for best growth, and flowering and fruiting plants need all the sun they can get. Heaviest bearing will result from exposure to full sun, preferably in a southern window. Fluorescent bulbs may also be used in addition to sunlight. Temperature is also important. A daytime temperature of 65 to 75°F. (18.33 to 23.89°C.) with a nighttime temperature of 60 to 70°F. (15.56 to 21.11°C.) is sufficient.

Watering can literally kill a plant if overdone. Water whenever the soil is dry to one inch below the surface. It is best to keep the air around the plants as humid as possible; spray the top growth at regular intervals to increase humidity. In addition, placing the plants where there is movement of people will help increase the amount of carbon dioxide available to them.

Fruiting house plants can be planted in large tubs and carried outside in the summertime. Remember when taking the plants outdoors that they have to be exposed gradually to the sun.

Fruits and Varieties for Indoor Growth: Citrus fruits are commonly grown house plants and are good choices since they are both ornamental and edible. The plants can be placed outdoors in the summer and will continue fruiting, but hand-pollination indoors is necessary. Citrus does best in acid soil so water monthly with ½ teaspoon of vinegar diluted in one quart of water. Propagate by cuttings.

The Ponderosa lemon is a favorite species and produces a large, sour fruit. The Meyer lemon produces a smaller fruit of better quality. Otaheite orange (*Citrus* x *limonia*), myrtle-leaf orange (*C. Aurantium myrtifolia*) and calamondin orange (x *Citrofortunella mitis*) are good dwarf species of oranges for indoor growth, although their small, bitter fruits are better suited to marmalades than to eating raw. Not very many varieties of limes (*C. aurantii-folia*) are well adapted for growing at home, but the Tahiti and Bears varieties of key lime may succeed.

Kumquats, a relative of the citrus fruits, are similarly grown. *Fortunella margarita,* the nagami kumquat, is best because it has fewer spines than the standard round kumquat (*F. japonica*).

Figs are no novelty in the indoor garden. Select cultivars of the species *Ficus carica* which set fruit without the aid of the small gall wasp. Adriatic sets excellent fruits that dry well and Brown Turkey is hardy in the North and does well in pots. It is a good idea to rest fig trees after picking the fruits by forcing dormancy. Decrease water and set the tree in a cool (35°F. [1.67°C.]) place for several months. Leaves will fall off the tree and it will remain dormant. After three or four months, bring the tree back into the warmth and begin to water again.

If you want to grow strawberries indoors, try alpine strawberry, a hardy perennial six to eight inches high. The plants do well in humusy soil and can be propagated by seed or crown division. Fertilize every two weeks and do not allow the soil to dry. Cultivars include Baron Solemacher, Alpine, Everbearing, and Perpetual.

Banana plants can be grown indoors and are another example of a plant with unusual foliage and edible fruits. The red purple bud which appears at the top of the trunk bears many flowers and bends downward. *Musa nana* or the Dwarf Cavendish cultivar of *M. acuminata* is well suited to culture in a two-foot-diameter tub. It prefers a humusy, alkaline soil. Only one sucker should be allowed to grow and bear fruits, but while the fruits on that sucker are maturing, another can be allowed to grow. The plant will require much water and weekly fertilizing at this stage. No hand-pollination is necessary, but once fruit is set other blossoms should be removed.

Although tomatoes and peppers are classified as vegetables by many people, they are in fact fruits. In their native tropical habitat they are both perennials. You can grow ordinary bell peppers indoors for years in eight-inch pots and have them remain in good health. They take longer to mature than tomatoes.

Tomato plants for indoor growing can be propagated from seed, from a branch rooted in water, or by bending a branch from a plant in your garden, covering it with soil and allowing it to root. After roots form, the new plant can be severed from the parent. Tomatoes will have to be staked and require a great deal of light and heavy feeding. Fertilize biweekly with fish emulsion or manure tea and water when the top inch of soil dries out. Prune back top growth. Hand-pollination will be necessary.

Tomato varieties for indoor growing need be chosen with some care. Generally, smaller-sized tomatoes are better. Pixie, Small Fry, Tiny Tim, Red Cherry, Stakeless, and Dwarf Champion are good varieties. For slicing, try one of the varieties bred for greenhouse culture, such as Tuckcross 533, Michigan or Michigan Ohio.

Another relative of the tomato is the tomato tree (*Cyphomandra betacea*), a woody shrub which must be pruned to prevent a scraggly appearance. Fruits are egg shaped and similar to a tomato in taste. The plants are propagated from seed and do well in a humusy soil, and, once they begin bearing fruit, they will bear for several years.

Apricots (*Prunus Armeniaca*) can also be grown indoors with judicious top and root pruning. The tree may be set outside after all danger of frost is past. Because it is self-fertile, it may produce too many fruits; if this should happen, thin to four inches apart when the apricots are marble sized. The tree should be forced into dormancy when the fruit has been picked but never subjected to severe cold. Although the commercially grown California cultivars may do well in warm regions, hardier cultivars do better in colder regions. These include Manchu, Sungold, Zard, August, and Kok-pshar.

Acerola cherries (*Malpighia glabra*), famous sources of vitamin C for vitamin supplements, can be grown indoors with little trouble, and will grow to a height of eight feet. The plants can be placed outside when the nighttime temperature reaches a constant 60°F. (15.56°C.) or higher. Water freely during spring and summer, but only moderately in the rest of the year.

The Brazilian cherry (*Eugenia uniflora*), also called the Pitanga cherry or Surinam cherry, is an evergreen shrub which tolerates pruning well and is therefore a good subject for tub culture. It can be propagated from seed or cuttings. Move outdoors when evening temperatures reach 50°F. (10°C.) or above.

The ground cherry or cape gooseberry (*Physalis* species) grows wild and can also be grown indoors. They are treated in the same manner as tomatoes and, like the tomato, may be grown outdoors and brought indoors to continue blooming in cold weather. Strawberry tomato (*Physalis pruinosa*) generally reaches two feet in height and bears prolifically. Jamberry or tomatillo (*P. ixocarpa*) is somewhat taller. Peruvian cherry, or the true cape gooseberry (*P. peruviana*) has slightly larger, golden fruit.

Casimiroa (*Casimiroa edulis*) is an evergreen adapted to tub culture by top and root pruning. Its fruits are yellow green and peach-like in flavor and about the size of an orange. They are high in vitamins A and C. The plant can be moved outside when the average temperature reaches above 65°F. (18.33°C.), but must be wintered indoors in places other than Florida or Southern California.

Pineapples (*Ananas comosus*) can be easily obtained by cutting off the crown of a grocery-store pineapple, leaving one inch of fruit attached. Dry for 36 hours and root in sand or perlite and spray the leaves twice a month with fish emulsion. Keep soil evenly moist, never soggy, place in full sun, and keep in a 72°F. (22.22°C.) location. You may move the plant outdoors when the temperature reaches above 65°F. (18.33°C.) at night. Fruit will develop atop a stem which may have to be supported when the fruit gets large. If no fruit develops, enclose the plant with an apple in a plastic bag. Ethylene gas produced by the apple will help stimulate fruiting.

FRUIT TREES

Growing fruit trees is one of the most challenging activities for the home gardener, and it can be one of the most rewarding as well. According to his climate and soil types the gardener can choose from among the pome fruits (apples and pears), the drupe fruits (cherry, peach and plum) and the citrus fruits (grapefruit, orange, lemon, and lime).

Choosing Trees: Buy first-class trees as a rule. Select those which are medium size for their age, shapely in body and head, and stocky, with straight, clean trunks and abundant roots. Reject stunted trees and those showing injuries from rough handling or borers. If choosing a budded tree, look for a union close to the ground.

Vigor, cleanness, stockiness, and firm hard growth are more important than mere size. The toughest and best trees are usually medium in size. In dollars and cents, the difference between first- and second-class trees is small compared to the return you will get from each tree.

Age of the tree is also important. The proper planting age varies, depending on varieties and other circumstances. In general, younger trees better withstand the shock of transplanting. There will be exceptions to this, and planting an older tree with a good background may be a worthwhile experiment in some cases.

The state experiment station should be able to offer advice on varieties suitable for the area's climate and soil conditions and resistant to local insect and disease problems. Some temperature moderation can be expected from the construction of windbreaks or a particularly favorable planting site, but the tree's need for a growing season of a certain length or for a cold winter to break its dormancy cannot be adjusted.

If planting a single tree, the gardener must make sure that it is self-fertilizing. If it is not, it will depend on the presence of other trees for propagation. *See also* ORCHARD for a discussion of self-sterile and self-fertile trees.

If space is limited, the gardener should consider planting dwarf trees. In contrast to the 40-by-40-foot space usually considered necessary for a single standard-sized apple tree, a mere ten-by-ten-foot plot will suffice for the dwarf varieties. A single dwarf will produce three to four bushels of fruit equal in quality and size to that of the standard-size tree, and a dwarf is easier to maintain as well. *See also* FRUIT TREES, DWARF. Other space-saving possibilities include espaliering and container planting. *See also* ESPALIER.

The orchardist may want to consider planning for a succession of harvests during the growing season through the choice of early- and late-bearing tree varieties. His choices may also be influenced by the number of years it takes a tree to enter full production. Some apple varieties may not bear a full harvest for ten years; a peach may reach full production after only two. Dwarf varieties usually bear one to three years earlier than standard varieties, but are not normally as long-lived.

BEARING TIME FOR FRUIT TREES

	Years Start	Years Bear
Apple	3–10	50–100
Apricot	3–4	10–25
Cherry, sour	3–4	15–25
Cherry, sweet	4–5	25–75
Peach	2–3	5–15
Pear	3–5	25–75
Plum	3–4	10–20
Quince	3–4	10–20

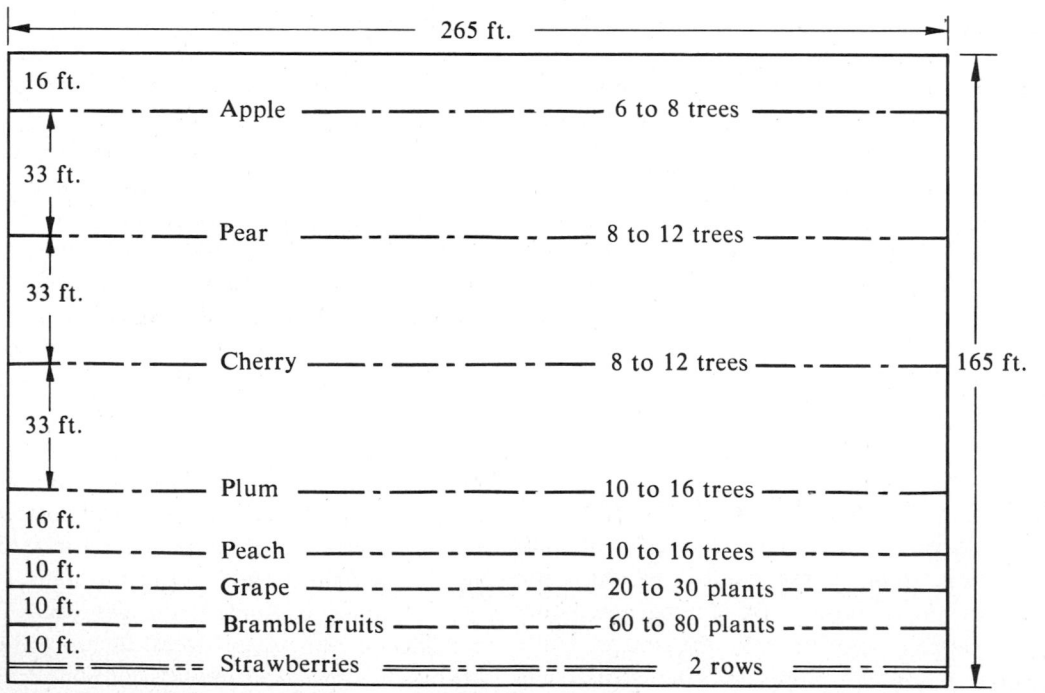

One acre of ground devoted to fruit trees and berry bushes can easily supply a family with most of the fruit they can eat.

Where to Plant Trees: An anticipated landscaping effect should not be the determining factor in choosing a tree site. The most important considerations are soil quality, soil drainage, exposure to sun, and exposure to prevailing winds.

Whether you plant one tree or 100, select a fertile, well-drained soil. Don't plant trees in a swampy, low-lying spot where the frosts come early in the day and stay late. Give each tree a good home with plenty of humus and a good supply of organic nutrients.

Plant your trees where there is good circulation of air. A north or northeast slope is ideal. Don't plant on a sunny slope, where the sun might blister trees during the day and winter frosts might chill them at night.

Planting Distances: Trees are wide feeders; the root system of the average tree just about equals the extent and volume of its system of branches. The distances given below are recommended as safe. Where the soil is particularly fertile and a good organic groundwork has been established, the distances may be pared a trifle.

PLANTING DISTANCES

Apple, standard	40 ft. each way
Apple, dwarf	10–15 ft. each way
Apricot	20 ft. each way
Cherry, sour	20 ft. each way
Cherry, sweet	30 ft. each way
Peach, standard	18–24 ft. each way
Peach, dwarf	10–15 ft. each way
Pear, standard	20–25 ft. each way
Pear, dwarf	12–16 ft. each way
Plum, standard	18–24 ft. each way
Plum, dwarf	10–15 ft. each way
Quince	16 ft. each way

When to Plant: Where the temperature does not drop below 0°F. (-17.78°C.), fall planting is generally considered preferable to spring planting, particularly for hardy tree fruits. Fall-planted trees can take hold in their new sites during the benevolent Indian summer weather. By the following spring, they are already making an early start in ground which is still too hard to permit spring planting. This early start not only means a better growth during the vital first season, but ensures that the trees are in good shape to meet the dry midsummer weather. Some growers consider fall planting to be risky, especially in the North. Tender fruits may suffer considerable winter injury in severe climates and should therefore be planted as early in the spring as the ground will permit.

Soil Preparation with Cover Crops: On larger plots, a cover crop will pay dividends far beyond the time and trouble invested. It serves a double purpose, both protecting the soil from the elements and improving its fertility. The various covers include clovers, vetches and leguminous crops such as mixed beans. When turned back into the soil, all of these add valuable nutrients and promote better soil structure through the addition of humus.

Cover cropping helps prevent hard soil from puddling or cementing, holds rain and snow until they have had time to soak into the land, serves as an added protection against frost, holds some of the nitrates which might otherwise leach away, and renders plant foods more readily available.

If possible, plant a cover crop a full year before fruit trees go in, in order to prepare the soil. For example, put in a winter cover of vetch or clover and turn it under in spring; let the vegetation age in the soil until the fall. *See also* COVER CROP, GREEN MANURE.

How to Plant: Holes for fruit trees must be broad and ample. In hard soils make the hole a little larger and break up the ground a bit

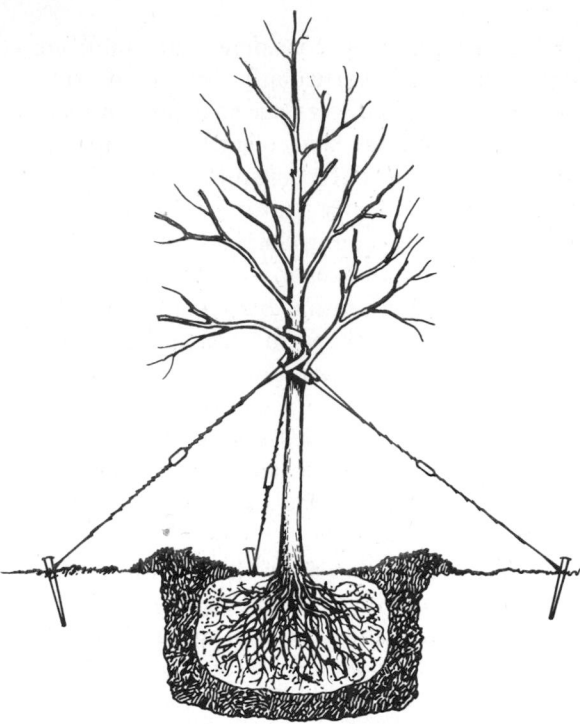

Plant bare-rooted trees in a hole generously filled with topsoil. Cut away about one-third of the top growth and stake the tree to hold it steady until the roots have become established.

To set the tree well and firmly into the hole, make a small mound of topsoil and place the young tree on it gently, keeping the roots in their natural position as much as possible. Fill with more topsoil, working it gently around the roots to avoid air pockets. When the hole is partly filled, tamp the earth down as firmly as possible. Carefully repeat this operation several times.

To get air holes out from around the roots, fill the half-filled hole with water and then gently rock the tree on its mound. As the water settles, it carries soil with it into the air pockets. It is good practice to leave a depression to catch water around the base of the tree. Water the tree immediately after planting, giving it a thorough soaking. Fill the depression with water and allow it to soak into the ground slowly. Thereafter, water once a week only. A good soaking rain can take the place of one week's watering, but a brief sprinkle or shower will not meet the tree's needs.

Use decomposed compost or straw or hay as a first-season mulch. Mulching with compost will stimulate feeder root growth and ensure that the tree takes hold rapidly. Cover the ground around the tree up to the dripline but keep a few inches to a foot of clear space around the tree to keep mice and rodents away from the tender bark. A protective bank of wire mesh around the tree will also deter rodents. Make it 18 inches high and no less than nine inches across. Press it firmly and deeply into the ground so that rodents cannot burrow under it.

As soon as the tree is firmly in place, it should be pruned back to keep the branch and root systems in balance.

Failure to Bear Fruit: While the reason for a tree's failure to bear may sometimes be obscure and difficult to explain, unfruitfulness

more to give the roots a better chance to spread out. While standard trees may be planted a little deeper than they stood in the nursery, they must not be planted too deep. Properly planted trees develop a strong feeder root system which takes firm hold of the ground close to the surface. This series of spreading tenacious roots provides the tree with a firm, sure base.

If planting a dwarf tree take care not to bury the lower graft union. If the scion finds its lower parts underground, it may send out its own roots, canceling out the dwarf root system. *See also* FRUIT TREES, DWARF.

in the majority of cases is due to one or several well-recognized factors.

Weather conditions: If a frost occurs when fruit trees are in bloom, injury frequently results, ranging from the killing of a few weak or tender blossoms to the complete destruction of the entire anticipated crop.

Frequently fruit does not set well, even though the trees blossom abundantly and no killing frost occurs. There is probably little pollen germination if the temperature during blossoming falls for long below 40 to 42°F. (4.44 to 5.56°C.). Other essential parts of the blossom, including the pistil and the ovules, may be adversely affected by low temperatures, so that should pollen germinate, fertilization may not take place even though no actual freezing of the flower parts occurs. Sometimes the blossoms open during a warm period which is immediately followed by a cold spell that continues during the remainder of the blossoming period. Under such conditions, a very poor set of fruit will result. An exceedingly heavy June drop commonly follows such a blossoming period, continuing sometimes until practically the whole set of fruit is gone.

If a very heavy rain occurs immediately after the blossoms open, much of the pollen may be washed away. If the blossoming period is cold or windy, bees, the principal agent in carrying the pollen from one tree to another, may be inactive, and self-sterile varieties are likely to pass through the blossoming period without cross-pollination.

Extremely cold winters can kill or injure peaches and some of the other more tender fruits. The most tender part of the blossom is the ovule or the small embryo fruit, which occupies the center of the flower. The temperature may be low enough during the winter to destroy these central parts in many of the buds.

Such buds may open normally, and unless the blossoms are carefully examined, injury may not be suspected until it is noticed that the trees are setting few if any fruit.

Self-sterility: Self-sterility occurs in many varieties of apples, most varieties of pears, probably in all varieties of sweet cherries, in most if not all varieties of the native and Japanese plums, and in some varieties of the European or domestic plum. Sour cherries are considered largely self-fertile, although there is some evidence of partial self-sterility. Most peach varieties are self-fertile. Sterility in plums, cherries, and perhaps other fruits, may sometimes be due to deformed or imperfect pistils.

Every conceivable degree of self-sterility exists, from one extreme where no fruit sets without cross-pollination to the opposite extreme where a tree's self-sterility is not a serious factor in fruit production. Even varieties considered highly self-fertile will set a better crop if cross-pollination occurs. Since self-sterility is so common, the importance of weather conditions favorable to the activity of honeybees is apparent. The fruit grower actually depends on them for the cross-pollination of his fruits.

When choosing varieties the gardener should be aware of those varieties which are self-sterile and should be careful when planting to ensure cross-pollination. Every third tree in every third row is usually regarded as a safe proportion for a minimum number of pollinizer trees. When self-sterile varieties are planted around the house and there are no others of the same kind growing near enough to ensure the passing of bees from one to the other, the trees will blossom but not set fruit.

Under such conditions, the permanent remedy is to topwork a certain number of trees or branches to a variety that blossoms at the same time as the trees themselves and is known to be an effective cross-pollinizer of the variety. This remedy, however, requires several years. Fortunately, a temporary expedient frequently proves quite effective. When the tree to be cross-pollinated is in bloom, secure some blossoming branches from a tree of another variety of the same kind of fruit and place them in a pail or other water container at the top of the tree. Bees will transfer the pollen as they revisit the blossoms on the tree.

Nutritional conditions: The nutritional reasons for failure to fruit are somewhat complicated. In general, trees that are overvigorous and those that are lacking in vigor are not in shape for the formation of fruit buds. Those that have been overfertilized devote their energy to vegetative, not reproductive (flowering and fruiting) growth. Trees that have not been adequately fertilized lack the energy to produce either type of growth. They need fertilizing in order to be fruitful. The most commonly limiting nutrient is nitrogen. This deficiency can be corrected by applying generous amounts of compost, cottonseed meal, soya meal, or dried blood. Fertilizer may be applied anytime, but preferably it is done in early spring. *See also* FRUIT TREES, DEFICIENCIES.

The blossom buds of the common deciduous fruit trees form during the season preceding the spring when they open. Conditions in any season that affect the vitality or nutrition of a tree may correspondingly affect the next season's crop of fruit by influencing fruit-bud differentiation. Examples of such conditions include: excessive shading by nearby buildings or large trees; uncontrolled diseases or insects which may destroy or greatly reduce the normal functioning of the foliage; and the production of an excessively heavy crop of fruit, which affects the storing up of plant foods in the tree tissues.

Pruning: Though old trees which are somewhat lacking in vigor may be stimulated into better fruit production by judicious pruning, young trees are often overpruned, thus causing a delay in their bearing. This effect is especially marked with apple trees, but it is true for other fruits as well. In some cases, apple trees 12 or 15 years old and bearing satisfactory harvests have been pruned so heavily that their nutritional condition is thrown out of balance and the trees have borne little or no fruit for several years thereafter. Only experience can guide the orchardist in pruning judiciously.

See also entries for individual fruits, FERTILIZER, INSECT CONTROL, ORCHARD, PRUNING, TREE.

FRUIT TREES, DEFICIENCIES

Deficiencies in all deciduous trees have the same symptoms and can cause dieback of new growth, abnormally twisted leaves and blotchy fruit. It is not enough for the necessary elements to be present in the soil; they must also be in usable form. Some factors that affect their availability are pH of the soil, soil aeration, soil moisture, and organic matter content.

Nitrogen deficiency often shows up in the discoloration of leaves. Leaves on older branches turn yellow green, working from the stem to the tip. There may also be a red or red purple discoloration. If nothing is done to relieve this deficiency, leaves become very small, and the twigs become slender and hard. Nitrogen deficiency can be corrected by adding cottonseed meal, dried blood, tankage, raw bone meal, fish wastes, legume hay, or one of the organic nitrogen products now on the market.

Phosphorous deficiency is evinced by discoloration of twigs, stems and leaves. The young twigs develop a ghostlike hue, the stems show purple coloring and the leaves are abnormally small and dark green. Old leaves become mottled with light and dark green areas. Bronzed leaves will occasionally show up on mature branches. To correct a phosphorous deficiency, add raw or colloidal phosphate rock, bone meal, fish wastes, guano, and raw sugar wastes.

Signs of *potash deficiency* include purplish discoloration and scorching of leaf edges. Dead spots are found on mature leaves, and if the deficiency is not corrected even very young leaves are affected. Peach foliage often becomes crinkled and twigs are unusually slender. Add granite dust, glauconite marl (greensand), wood ashes, seaweed, and orange rinds.

If *magnesium deficiency* is present, the large old leaves will display flesh-colored patches of dead tissue, not restricted to leaf edges. Watch for dropping of leaves, first on old branches and then on twigs of the current season. Defoliation may be so severe that only tufts or "rosettes" of thin, small leaves are left. Add dolomitic limestone or raw phosphate rock.

Zinc deficiency is very similar to magnesium deficiency. Either can cause rosetting of leaves in the advanced stage. But without zinc, crinkled leaves are common and leaves are often chlorotic (washed out in color). On citrus trees, the fruit is apt to be very small and the leaves pointed; there may also be a striking contrast between dark green veins and yellow leaf tissue. Add raw phosphate rock.

Calcium deficiency, like boron deficiency, will show up first on young twigs rather than on mature branches. Dead areas appear on the young, tender leaves at the tips and edges. If this deficiency is not corrected, the twigs will die back and the roots will be injured. Treat by applying raw pulverized limestone.

The most common symptom of *boron deficiency* is internal cork of apples. Early in the season, hard brown spots with definite margins form inside the fruit. As the season progresses, the spots soften, become larger and lose their definite outline. The leaves may be entirely unaffected. In other cases, the young leaves become very thick and brittle, and the twigs die back. Some trees may also form wrinkled, chlorotic leaves. Add phosphate rock, manure and acidic organic matter such as peat moss, sawdust and ground oak leaves.

Iron and aluminum deficiencies may be caused by an overdose of lime. The minerals may be right in the soil, but are held insoluble when soil acidity is low. Look for yellow leaves with brown patches and loss of flavor in the fruit. Add glauconite marl, avoid lime and use the organic acid matter recommended for boron deficiency.

See also entries for individual fruits, FERTILIZER, FRUIT TREES, INSECT CONTROL, ORCHARD, PRUNING, RESISTANT VARIETIES.

FRUIT TREES, DWARF

Dwarf fruit trees, usually from six to ten feet tall, are easier to plant, fertilize, mulch, and harvest than are standard-sized fruit trees. They usually begin fruiting far sooner, often by their second year and sometimes the same year they are planted. Standard trees usually take five years to begin bearing and sometimes as long as ten.

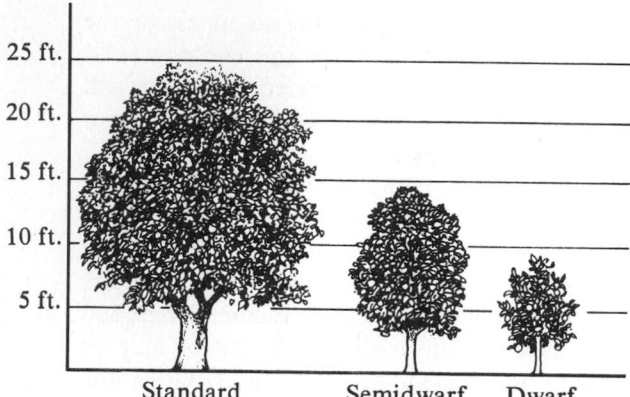

25 ft.
20 ft.
15 ft.
10 ft.
5 ft.

Standard   Semidwarf   Dwarf

Standard fruit trees bear most of their fruit on the outer rather than inner branches. Semidwarf varieties produce fruit on inner as well as outer branches and tend to give very high yields, while dwarf varieties are only moderate producers.

A mature dwarf apple or pear can produce two or three bushels of quality fruit per season. Semidwarf varieties, growing from 12 to 15 feet tall, are also available. These produce more than twice as much fruit per season in a quarter of the space necessary for the standard tree. The fruit from dwarf trees is equal in size and quality to that of the standards, and is often larger and of better quality because of the individual care the growers lavish on their trees.

Dwarf trees allow the homeowner with a small plot of land to have a variety of fruits in a succession of harvests. For example, the 40-by-40-foot space usually deemed necessary for the standard 25-foot apple tree could accommodate 16 dwarfs, each of which requires a 10-by-10-foot space.

How Trees Are Dwarfed: Though there are natural dwarfs, trees which intrinsically have a compact growth habit, dwarf trees offered today are usually the product of grafting a desired variety onto a dwarfing rootstock. The rootstock restricts the growth of the scion (shoot or bud) grafted onto it. Some nurseries now combine one or two especially vigorous rootstocks with a piece of trunk for its dwarfing properties and a top known for desirable fruiting qualities.

Most apples are dwarfed by being grafted onto Malling or Malling-Merton rootstocks, varieties which were developed at the East Malling Research Station in Kent, England. Pear trees are grafted onto roots from quinces which are, by nature, compact trees. Peaches, apricots, nectarines, and plums are dwarfed by being grown on rootstocks of the western sand cherry and the Nanking cherry, though some nurseries are now developing a dwarf peach. A variety of sour cherry, North Star, is a natural dwarf and has been used as a rootstock for some varieties of sweet cherries. The ground cherry has been used as a rootstock for both sweet and sour cherries, and there are several good natural semidwarf cherries.

Planting and Culture: Though the planting and culture of dwarf trees are much the same as that of standard trees, a few special considerations should be mentioned. It is vital to plant a dwarf with the graft-union above ground. If the lower portion of the scion is buried, it will form its own roots, thus canceling out the dwarfing rootstock. The graft-union usually appears as a knob at the base of the trunk above which the bark will be a lighter color. Plant dwarfs ten to 12 feet apart each way, or six to eight feet apart in rows 15 feet apart. *See also* FRUIT TREES.

Because a stand of dwarf trees will be planted much more densely than a standard orchard, and because the branches will be close to the ground, a site with good air circulation is recommended to prevent the spread of mildew and other plant diseases. However, the site must also be protected from heavy winds which could damage tender young branches, strip off fragile blossoms and overturn dwarf trees, whose root systems are shallower and less extensive than those of standard trees.

Prune a newly planted dwarf to keep the top in balance with the roots. All undesirably spaced branches and those less than six to 12 inches above the ground should be removed. Thereafter, remove water sprouts and suckers, and trim off broken ends. Though a few centrally positioned fruits can be allowed to ripen the first year, all other blossoms or fruits should be removed so their weight doesn't damage tender new growth and so that the tree's strength goes into vigorous root and top growth. In later years, excess fruits, more than one fruit per six inches of branch, should be thinned. Otherwise, dwarfs may set more fruit than they can carry.

Dwarf trees are often used in container plantings and as espaliers, serving a double purpose of ornamentation and food production. Espaliers are trained by pruning, bending and tying the trees to conform to different shapes.

See also entries for individual fruits, Es-PALIER, FERTILIZER, FRUIT TREES, INSECT CONTROL, ORCHARD, PRUNING.

FUCHSIA

Fuchsias are graceful, shrubby plants producing many pendent single or double flowers on long, arching stems. In the United States, they are hardy only in a few areas, doing best in mild parts of California. Fuchsias are, to a great extent, shade-loving plants. A few varieties will stand full sun, but their roots must be shaded or well mulched. Fuchsias will not do well in areas where both days and nights stay hot for long periods. They like warm days and cool nights coupled with high humidity. As potted plants they should be grown in filtered light only, and the foliage should be frequently misted in hot, dry periods. They will need copious watering, but the soil should always drain well.

Fuchsias are started by both seed and cuttings but the average grower should propagate them from cuttings. In February cut or prune back to hard wood, leaving two nodes or buds on each stem. Soon the new green growth comes out; these new shoots may be used as softwood cuttings when about three inches long. Insert the cuttings about one-half their length in a box of thoroughly moistened half coarse sand and half peat moss, having removed all leaves where they would be below the soil surface. Cover with plastic and keep at 70 to 75°F. (21.11 to 23.89°C.) out of direct sun. In about 14 days, try to lift the cuttings out of the soil. If you feel a pull, they are rooted; if not, wait a few days more to lift and plant in three-inch pots. The soil for growing fuchsias is composed of one part leaf mold, one part compost or sand, one part well-rotted cow manure, and one part peat moss.

Keep plants moist at all times. A cutting started in spring will be a beautiful blooming plant by August.

Fuchsias are fast growers and will require supplemental feeding to replace nutrients leached out by the heavy watering they require, so twice a month give them a feeding of manure tea. Put five pounds of rotted cow manure in two gallons of water. Keep well stirred for two or three days. Then take a quart of the liquid

The brightly colored pendent flowers of the Ladies'-Eardrops fuchsia make it a splendid choice for hanging baskets.

and add to two gallons of water and stir.

Whether you have propagated plants yourself or bought them from a nursery, you will have to winter fuchsias over indoors in most of the United States. To do this, put the plants in a 40°F. (4.44°C.) cellar before frost. Water them only enough to keep the hardwood supple —perhaps once a month. The foliage will drop. In February, bring them to a sunny window and water thoroughly. When they sprout, cut back drastically to hard wood. They will bloom on new stem growth. Repot to the next-sized container. Pinch the tips to induce bushiness.

You will find almost any variety you wish in both hanging types and uprights. You can espalier fuchsias to create a beautiful effect. They can also be trained as a tree. The basic colors are red and purple; however, the newer varieties are red and white, pink and white, all white, all red, all pink, and some so deep a purple they look almost blue. Some named cultivars are Swingtime, a red and white bicolor; Ting-a-Ling, a white single; and Voodoo, a double royal purple.

FUMIGATION, SOIL

Fumigation is a standard commercial greenhouse practice used to combat insects and diseases. Chemicals usually used are carbon disulfide, hydrocyanic acid, calcium cyanide, paradichlorobenzene, and nicotine preparations. Fumigation is not a recommended practice in the organic program because of its harmful effect on beneficial soil life, and greenhouse owners who use soil fumigation have found it increasingly ineffective because insects develop a resistance to the fumigants. If you have soil that contains nematodes or disease-causing organisms, pasteurization is recommended.

See also SOIL PASTEURIZATION.

FUNGICIDE

A fungicide is a preparation used to destroy fungi or inhibit the growth of the spores or hyphae. Among chemicals used in the preparation of fungicides are various forms of sulfur, copper, mercury, formaldehyde, and minor elements—none of which is recommended in the organic method. Sulfur finds the least objection with organic gardeners, and it has found favor with fruit and grape growers.

The best alternative to fungicides is sanitation, eradication of diseased plants and the use of resistant varieties.

See also FUNGUS, RESISTANT VARIETIES, SULFUR.

FUNGUS

A fungus (fungi, plural) is a plant that takes its energy entirely from organic matter. If a fungus feeds on live matter, it is classified as parasitic; if the matter is not alive, the fungus is called saprophytic.

The common names for fungi often describe their appearance. Downy and powdery mildew are well known to gardeners. Rust, leaf spotting and gray mold are also common.

While some fungi are of the pesty sort, others are essential to the processes of life. For example, saprophytic fungi work in the compost pile to break down wastes into valuable

Morels

Inky caps

Among the edible fungi that can be easily recognized are the inky cap and morel mushrooms.

plant food. Others, such as certain bracket fungi and mushrooms, are edible.

See also DISEASE, MUSHROOM, SULFUR.

FUNKIA   *See* HOSTA

G

GAILLARDIA   *See* BLANKET FLOWER

GARBAGE FOR COMPOST

Garbage is a neglected source of compost which is particularly rich in nitrogen and other nutrients essential to soil building and plant growth.

The individual gardener should compost his kitchen wastes whether he lives in a rural area or a suburb. In either case, insect- and animal-proof bins should be used. If the gardener lives in a densely settled community, local statutes should be consulted. Meat, dairy and poultry product wastes are the garbage ingredients that attract scavengers and vermin. In urban areas it may be best to compost only the vegetable portion of kitchen wastes.

Commercially built anaerobic bins are available to the suburban gardener. These are moderate in cost and are designed to hold several months' garbage.

If the local situation permits, the gardener can build his own garbage composting bin. It need not be anaerobic but it should be insect and animal proof. To start his joint garbage disposal-composting program he merely dumps his garbage in it daily. It is important to add a layer of soil, preferably mixed with leaves or old hay, over each day's kitchen wastes.

Some gardeners bury their garbage on next year's planting sites, thus rotating their garden and leaving some land "resting" in anticipation of next year's crop. They take the precaution of burying the material deep enough to escape detection by scavenging animals.

Still another course is open to the farmer or homesteader. He can build an enclosure of cement blocks, high and strong enough to be animal proof. Here he can dump his garbage, permitting it to break down partially. From time to time he removes some of this highly nitrogenous material, adding it to new compost heaps composed mostly of plant matter. In this way he is assured of a steady supply of activating material for his composting program.

See also COMPOSTING.

GARDEN HELIOTROPE
See VALERIAN

GARDENIA

Belonging to the Madder family this genus includes about 200 evergreen shrubs and rarely small trees. Best-known representatives are *G. jasminoides,* or cape jasmine, and *G. Veitchii,* the florists' gardenia, with its waxy, fragrant white flowers and glossy foliage.

G. jasminoides is a summer-blooming variety, with flowers slightly smaller than those of *G. Veitchii.* It is grown in pots or tubs as a house plant, being summered in the garden in a shady place, and wintered in the house in a relatively cool room. During its blooming season, *G. jasminoides* must be kept thoroughly wet, and not allowed to dry out, but in winter it is kept fairly dry.

G. Veitchii is an everblooming gardenia, the most popular hothouse or house plant variety. It is also summered outside, in a shaded moist location, and kept wet summer and winter. It must be returned to its partly sunny window indoors before frost. Gardenias do best indoors in a cool room. If this is not available, see that the temperature drops at night and keep the plants near a window where the temperature is normally lower than in the rest of the room.

Gardenias demand a very acid soil, with a pH of 4.5 to 5. This may be supplied by well-composted sawdust or oak leaves. Leaves that fall from the plant, as well as its own faded flowers, may be placed on top of the soil to form a self-mulch. If the foliage shows a tendency to turn yellow, a handful of rotted manure or cottonseed meal may be mixed with the top layer of soil.

An abundance of moisture is the most important factor in successful gardenia culture. Plant containers may be placed in trays or bowls in which water is allowed to stand to a depth equal to the depth of gravel or rubble in the bottom of the flowerpot. If sufficient water is supplied, the plants will be free of bud rot, which causes the buds to drop before flowering. Humidity around the leaves can be kept high by putting a plastic bag over the plant.

Insects which trouble gardenias are thrips, red spider mites and mealybugs. Mites may be combated by a daily spraying of the foliage with clear water. Thrips and mealybugs may be handpicked, but will trouble the plant little if it is in robust health.

See also HOUSE PLANTS.

GARDEN PLANNING
See LANDSCAPING, VEGETABLE GARDENING

GARLAND FLOWER
See DAPHNE

GARLIC (*Allium sativum*)

Garlic is a valuable tool of the gardener, providing a safe but effective means of dealing

Like onions, garlic chives can be propagated by means of the small black seeds that are exposed when the fruits open.

with pests and some plant diseases.

Garlic can be interplanted with susceptible crops to repel a number of important pests. A spray made by mincing garlic with water in a blender will discourage most pests from taking a bite out of treated crops. It has been found that a garlic spray has antibiotic powers, controlling downy mildew, cucumber and bean rust, bean anthracnose, early blight of tomato, brown rot of stone fruit, angular leaf spot of cucumber, and bacterial blight of beans.

GAS PLANT   *See* Fraxinella

GAZANIA

Also called treasure flower, gazanias grow as perennials in the Southwest, in southern California and in other mild climates. They are treated as annuals in the rest of the United States. The petals of the daisylike flowers close at night; they are usually ringed and banded with contrasting colors—red, orange and yellow predominating.

G. linearis makes an excellent summer-blooming perennial that is used as an annual. *G. ringens* grows to about 1½ feet. Both are very low-growing, spreading plants that thrive in dry rock gardens. The Sunshine mixture is dazzling.

In the hot, dry areas of the Southwest, gazanias are used as ground covers that flower all year. In the North, plant them in dry soil in full sun for summer flowers. In humid, rainy summers they may be disappointing.

See also African Daisy, Border.

GEESE

Many rural families have found that it is worthwhile to include a few geese among their farm animals since they require little attention, virtually no housing and find their own feed. Besides, roast goose is a delicious and different Christmas or Thanksgiving treat.

Breeds: The Toulouse goose has a broad, deep body, is a fair layer averaging about 25 to 40 or more eggs a year, grows rapidly, and is a good market bird. However, its dark pinfeathers make it less attractive on the market than the Emden. Emdens grow well, are fairly good layers, producing 35 to 40 or more eggs a year, and are better sitters than Toulouse geese.

Chinese geese come in white and brown and are better layers, averaging 40 to 65 or more eggs. They are also good weeders. Chinese geese are smaller than either Toulouse or Emden and make an ideal bird for home use. While the Toulouse or Emden commonly weighs 12 to 20 pounds, Chinese geese average eight to 12 pounds. Crosses with the Emden and Toulouse are also available.

Other varieties of geese include Pilgrims, which have the advantage of being naturally sexed—the adult gander is white and the goose is gray; African geese, attractive gray birds with a brown shade; Canadian geese—the American wild goose; and Buff, Egyptian and Sebastapol.

Housing: Except in extremely cold weather, mature geese need no shelter and will hardly ever use a house. Open shelters or shades are provided on range to give protection from the sun. In the North, a barn door can be left open for the geese so they can go inside in cold weather.

Starting with Geese: The best way to start is to buy day-old goslings from a hatchery. Goose eggs do not incubate as well as hen's eggs, so it is inadvisable to begin with fertile eggs.

Don't order goslings until the weather is warm; if the outside temperatures are low, the goslings must be kept warm. Start them inside under a brooder of 90°F. (32.22°C.) and gradually reduce the heat over a period of ten days to three weeks, depending on outside temperature.

Goslings can be fed wetted regular chick starter, whole-grain bread soaked in milk or water, or cooked oatmeal covered with water. Supply tender, chopped greens at all meals. Feed the goslings three to four times a day what they can clean up in 15 minutes. After a week, reduce the grain supplement to only two meals a day and offer more greens. At three or four weeks of age, cut the geese down to one feeding of grain per day and provide greens at the other feedings.

Water and fine grit should be available at all times. Provide water in a chick feeder and jar with pebbles in the trough so that the geese cannot get their whole bodies into the water.

At four weeks of age the goslings can be put outside and will support themselves well on range. Provide a shelter in case of rain and a run enclosed on the sides and top with chicken wire. After a few days they can be allowed several hours of freedom a day, and lured back to their coop at night by a late afternoon feeding of grain. Be sure that litter in the coop is clean and dry. At six weeks they can sleep outside at night except during lengthy periods of chilling rain, and by eight weeks they can take care of themselves.

Feeding: After goslings are six weeks old they can be raised on pasture alone, but enough growing mash may be provided to keep them steadily growing. Pasture grasses, clover and alfalfa make fine pasture, and an acre of good pasture can support 15 to 25 geese. Poor pasture can be supplemented by cut fresh greens.

Geese may be used to weed strawberry beds until the plants are nearly ripe. Feed a pound of grain per five geese daily, and change location of this feeding and their waterers every few days so the geese range over the entire patch. After the strawberries are picked, geese can be turned back into the patch to handle late summer and fall weeding. In the garden, however, geese will supplement their pasture by feeding on your ripening vegetables, even onions. If you have a roaming flock of geese, keep them out of your garden with a heavy wire fence.

Geese need a constant supply of fresh, clean water. A waterer such as a hog fountain is excellent since geese cannot get into the water container. Like all poultry, they need a constant source of oyster shell or other insoluble grit.

Geese should be fattened before slaughtering. This is best done in cool weather. Geese are ready to fatten when fully feathered or when the long wing feathers reach the tail when folded. They are usually five to six months old and weigh from 11 to 15 pounds, depending on breed.

Feed birds a crumbly mash three times daily, or twice daily with a feeding of whole grain. They should be allowed little exercise and confined or permitted limited range. Unlimited water should be provided, but the geese should not be able to fit into their water dispensers. If confined, plenty of clean, dry bedding should be available.

Geese must be starved for 12 hours before slaughtering, but should have water available.

Breeding geese kept over winter should have grain, laying mash and roughage. Oats mixed with corn, wheat or barley are a good feed. Geese can be fed whole corn, and should be given clover or alfalfa hay as roughage.

Breeding: Geese mate permanently in pairs. Breeders should be selected from medium-sized, vigorous and well-developed birds that grow rapidly and have compact, meaty bodies. A gander may be mated with up to five geese, but pair and trio matings are most common. Mature ganders have a longer neck and head than females and have a higher pitched voice; the female is smaller, less coarse and has a deeper cry.

Most breeds lay in the early spring, the Chinese somewhat earlier. Laying mash is fed once a day in December or January to encourage egg production. Farmers with just a few geese can use regular hen laying mashes. Broodiness in geese can be checked by confining the broody goose in sight of but away from the gander. Geese will continue to lay until mid-June if not allowed to set, so collect the eggs regularly to encourage egg production. Geese kept outside can use nesting boxes made of old packing crates inverted on the ground and with a hole cut in one end. Fill the boxes with clean straw.

Eggs for hatching should be collected twice daily until March 1. Geese eggs do not hatch as well as hen's eggs in an incubator, so you may want to use a hen or a Muscovy duck to set the eggs. Hens must be watched, however, since the goose eggs hatch a week later than hen's eggs. Eggs should be turned once a day, and should be sprinkled with lukewarm water daily during the last two weeks of hatching.

Newly hatched goslings should be given to the geese to mother, if possible, and should be confined indoors until they are two weeks old. Even at that age, goslings should not be allowed to get wet—even by walking through wet grass. Goslings are commonly not allowed to swim until they have begun to feather.

Slaughtering: Kill geese the same way other poultry is killed. *See also* CHICKEN. Goose down is a valuable by-product of goose raising and if down is desired, the bird should be dry-picked. Since geese have tender skin, be careful not to bruise the bird if you plan to market it. Semiscalding makes picking easier. Dip the goose into almost-boiling water for two to 2½ minutes until feathers pull easily. If desired, detergent may be added to the water. After picking, geese should be cooled in cold water or in the refrigerator, and then packed for shipping or storage, or bagged and frozen.

Feathers can be saved from dry-picked geese. Flesh should be cleaned from feathers if any remains after picking and the feathers placed in a burlap or cheesecloth bag. Wash with soap and warm water and allow to dry in the shade or in a well-ventilated room.

GENTIAN   (*Gentiana*)

Gentian is an herb native to the mountainous regions of Europe and now cultivated for use in rock gardens and woodland settings. Gentians are frost germinators and require a cool situation with good drainage and ample amounts of humus and compost. The very small seed are slow to germinate and should be as fresh as possible.

Gentiana lutea, the recognized medicinal species, has a stem three to four feet tall, with oblong bright green leaves and large yellow flowers that have a faint aromatic fragrance. An American gentian, *G. Saponaria,* or soapwort gentian, inhabits swampy areas from Virginia to Florida. It grows between one and two feet tall and has a blue club-shaped blossom. *G. Andrewsii,* the bottle gentian, grows throughout eastern North America. The fringed gentian (*Gentianopsis* spp.), a biennial with bright blue flowers, and *G. acaulis,* a perennial, are especially well suited for rock gardens.

GENUS

A genus is a major classified group of plants, actually a category between family and species. Genus (the plural is genera) includes one or more species which have structural or floral characteristics in common. A species is a subdivision of a genus which differs too slightly to be classed as a separate genus. Subdivided types within species are termed varieties. In the scientific (formal or Latin) name of a plant, the first word (capitalized) is the genus, the second the species.

GEOLOGY

This is a science which deals with the history and life of the earth as indicated by rocks.

See also MINERAL ROCKS.

GERANIUM

A large genus of popular, cultivated flowering ornamentals, geraniums are usually perennial or biennial, but there are a few annual varieties. The common florists' geranium is not a true geranium at all, but is a member of the genus *Pelargonium.*

Culture: Geraniums are not difficult to raise. They need only a moderate amount of water, a fairly cool, well-drained, moderately rich (but not too rich) soil and plenty of sunshine. In the northern regions of the country, they should be planted in full sun, but in the South and Southwest, half-a-day's exposure

The popular P. x hortorum *geranium can be raised indoors as a potted plant or outside in window boxes or border plantings.*

should be enough to make the plants bloom freely without burning. An annual topdressing of decayed manure or rich compost should be ample stimulation for geraniums. The fact that geraniums are fairly drought resistant makes them a popular cultivated plant of the Southwest.

Potting: A recommended mixture for potting geraniums is two parts garden loam, one part leaf mold or compost and one part sharp sand. Some gardeners recommend including one part well-rotted manure, and some add a teaspoon of bone meal to a five-inch pot when planting. If the soil in your outdoor beds is heavy, it should be lightened with leaf mold and sand. And although geraniums may be planted directly in the earth, it is sometimes better to sink them in clay pots for easier removal. If you do this, water them more frequently.

Propagating: The average home gardener is going to be most successful by propagating from cuttings. This is particularly so in reference to *P.* x *domesticum,* the Martha Washington geranium. As early as the first week in September, take three- or four-inch cuttings of leaf bud—not flower bud—material. Use a very sharp knife and make a cut straight across, just below the bud. Never use pruning shears for there is a danger of crushing the delicate tissue. Do not allow your cuttings to get dry, but set them in moist sharp sand immediately. If you start several cuttings in a flat, avoid watering from above and wetting the leaves, as this might cause rot. Water from below by setting the flat in a larger pan with water in it. Protect with a muslin shade, and do not allow them to dry out. Pot up as soon as the roots are well started (about three to six weeks), using a potting soil that is not too highly fertilized.

Cuttings: Cuttings are best made in late summer or early fall from new tip growth taken from earlier flowering plants that have been cut back a month or so before. Select stems about three or four inches long with two or three leaf nodes, remove the lower leaves and any flower buds, and allow the cuttings to dry several hours before sinking them in damp sharp sand. Some gardeners have success rooting geranium cuttings in water, and some merely plunge them into the soil near the mother plant.

The length of time required for the roots to form seems to vary from as little as two weeks to as long as six or eight. The usual procedure is to plant the rooted cuttings first in 2½-inch pots, later transferring them to progressively larger ones. If you start directly in four-inch pots, as do some commercial growers, be sure that your soil is light and well drained. As the new cuttings grow, pinch the tips every once in a while to keep the plants from getting leggy, and don't allow them to bloom until they are well grown. Wait until all danger of frost is over before taking the new plants outside.

Seed: Plant seed in late winter for blooms about four to six months later. Sow seed about ⅛ inch deep in very warm soil. Keep moist by watering with a fine spray or by setting containers in a pan of water until soil surface is moist. Some seed may germinate in several days, but sprouting usually continues for two to three weeks. When seedlings have their first pair of true leaves, transplant to individual pots; when plants have several leaves, pinch out growing tips to encourage bushier growth. Keep them in a sunny, cool window (55 to 60°F. [12.78 to 15.56°C.]). Slightly pot-bound plants often give better results than those with a lot of room for roots.

Diseases and Insects: If the leaves of your potted specimens begin to turn yellow, they are receiving too little sun or too much water.

Once in a while indoor geraniums may develop leaf spot, particularly if you have been wetting the foliage when you water. If you find evidence of this disease, isolate the sick plants from healthy ones, place them where they will get plenty of light and fresh air and where the humidity is low, and remove the affected leaves and flowers.

For mealybugs, which seem to favor geraniums, particularly the scented varieties, isolation is also recommended. Often mealybugs can be eliminated by cleaning the infested parts with swabs of cotton dipped in alcohol. The same treatment may prove effective for onslaughts of aphids. Also try rinsing these pests off with water, but keep the plants away from the sun until foliage is dry.

Landscaping Beauty: Geraniums present a rich and varied diversity, not only in the foliage, but the abundance of brilliant flowers. Many of the zonal geraniums (*P. zonale*) can be used for hedges, and when you want a brilliant splash of color, the vivid orange scarlet Paul Crampel variety can be planted for it is seldom out of bloom.

The versatile trailing ivy-leaved geraniums are more and more being employed for the planting of baskets and window boxes of lasting and colorful beauty. You can combine them with harmonizing colors of the zonals for upright accent. Many of the scented-leaved geraniums have finely cut foliage. Combine them with other geraniums to add textural interest, or mass them in a bed along a path where they can be touched. Brushing against the leaves releases the scent.

Perennial or Hardy Geranium: The true geraniums are hardy perennials of spreading, moundlike growth with attractive, finely divided leaves and one- to two-inch flowers borne singly. They vary in height from four to 18 inches. Several species make excellent, trouble-free border plants. The dwarf species are equally effective in the rock garden or as edging plants for the perennial border. They can be grown in full sun or partial shade in average, well-drained soil. Rich soil will cause some of them to spread rapidly, necessitating frequent division of the clumps, but under average conditions they will not outgrow their space or need dividing for four years or more. Give them enough room to start with; plant the dwarfs at least 12 inches from other plants and the taller kinds 18 inches from their neighbors. Divide in spring when this becomes necessary.

G. dalmaticum grows to four inches and has pink flowers with deeper veins in May and June. *G. Endressii* cv. 'Johnson's Blue' has masses of light blue flowers on 15- to 18-inch plants. Another *G. Endressii* produces pink flowers most of the summer. The Iberian cranesbill, *G. ibericum,* has violet blue flowers in June and July. It grows to 18 inches.

The larger *G. himalayense* can form a clump a foot wide and 18 inches high. It bears large two-inch magenta flowers June until July. *G. Regelii* is 12 inches high with blue flowers. The bloody cranesbill, *G. sanguineum,* is the one most likely to spread out of bounds. Its clumps are often two feet across and one foot high with purple red flowers May to August. It will persist for years in dry soil on the sunny side of a shrub border if grass is kept out of it. This species and its varieties have red foliage in autumn. *G. sanguineum* var. *prostratum* (or *G. lancastrense*) is a dwarf, less-spreading form to six inches high with red-veined pink flowers all summer.

GERBERA

Gerbera Jamesonii varieties, also known as Transvaal daisies, are choice perennials flowering from May till November. Natives of South Africa, they can be grown year-round outdoors only in warmer parts of the South. In the North, plants should be dug and potted up for wintering in the greenhouse. Permanent plantings in the North are usually found only in large greenhouses or conservatories.

Gerberas should be planted in a sunny position in well-drained soil that is slightly alkaline. A sandy loam suits them very well, so that in a season of excessive rains the water will not stand around the crowns and roots, causing them to rot. If the soil is heavy, add sand and well-decayed compost, leaf mold or old manure, well worked into the ground. This will lighten it and add humus to the soil.

Some gardeners consider these plants hard to grow. The culture is not difficult if a few essentials are observed. The plants may be grown from seed or by taking cuttings from side shoots and rooting them in sand like any other cutting. In August, seed may be sown in flats in light, sandy soil, and the seed should be sown in rows or broadcast over the soil and lightly covered. When the seedlings are large enough to handle, transplant to flats filled with rich, sandy loam in which a little old manure is mixed. They are spaced two inches apart in the rows and the rows two inches apart. They are grown until they are large enough to set out in the ground, where they are to grow and flower.

In planting, make the holes deep enough so the roots will go straight down. They must never be doubled up. Always firm the soil around the plants in planting. The crown of the plant is kept a little above ground level, not below it. Too frequent watering or sprinkling is not desirable. Irrigate deeply so the water will last for a week or ten days, depending on how hot the weather is. One must use judgment in watering.

After several years in the ground the clumps should be lifted and divided. The long roots can usually be pulled apart in late summer; each division should have two buds. Trim old leaves away before resetting the plants.

Gerberas appear to greatest advantage when planted in a bed by themselves. When grouped in a border of mixed perennials they generally get too much water.

They look well in a narrow bed along a garden walk in a sunny position, and shades of yellow and orange may be used, or terra cotta and reds.

The plants are long-lived if their growing conditions are congenial, and considering their long season of bloom, gerberas are well worth growing.

The daisy-shaped flowers of the new hybrid strains are graceful and may be had in the following colors: white, yellow, orange, terra cotta, pink, salmon, and red.

There are single and double flowers. The flower stems of well-established plants grow from 18 to 20 inches high. They make a very satisfactory cut flower, with long-lasting qualities, and group well with other flowers.

GERMAN CATCHFLY
See LYCHNIS

GERMAN CHAMOMILE
See CHAMOMILE

GERMANDER   *See* TEUCRIUM

GERMINATION

Seed with the power to grow—viability—are said to germinate when they break their dormancy and begin growth. It is usually a combination of water, warmth and air which makes this germination take place. The viability of seed varies greatly, some being ready for germination as soon as they are ripe, some not until they have been through a dormancy period, some with viability lasting for a few months, many for at least a year, and some for over a century.

Though germination is thought of as beginning when the seedlings first appear at the surface of the soil, it actually happens as soon as the first tiny root, the radicle, and the first tiny shoot, the plumule or epicotyl, begin to grow. After water is taken up, food in the endosperm or storage part of the seed is drawn on for the energy needed for growth. Stored starches, proteins and fats are converted into soluble materials needed by the developing tissues, and the respiration of the seed, very low during dormancy, speeds up greatly. This is why germinating seed must have access to air.

Soon the radicle produces the primary root and then root hairs and lateral roots; later, the green part of the plant develops in one of several ways. Flowering plants are divided into two groups, according to whether they have one or two seed leaves, or cotyledons: those with one being monocots, short for monocotyledons; those with two, dicots or dicotyledons. In beans and peas, for instance, the seed leaves are the storage areas, and as the plants grow up through the soil, these cotyledons come up through, too.

The same is true of the radish, squash, sunflower, maple, and other plants. Corn and

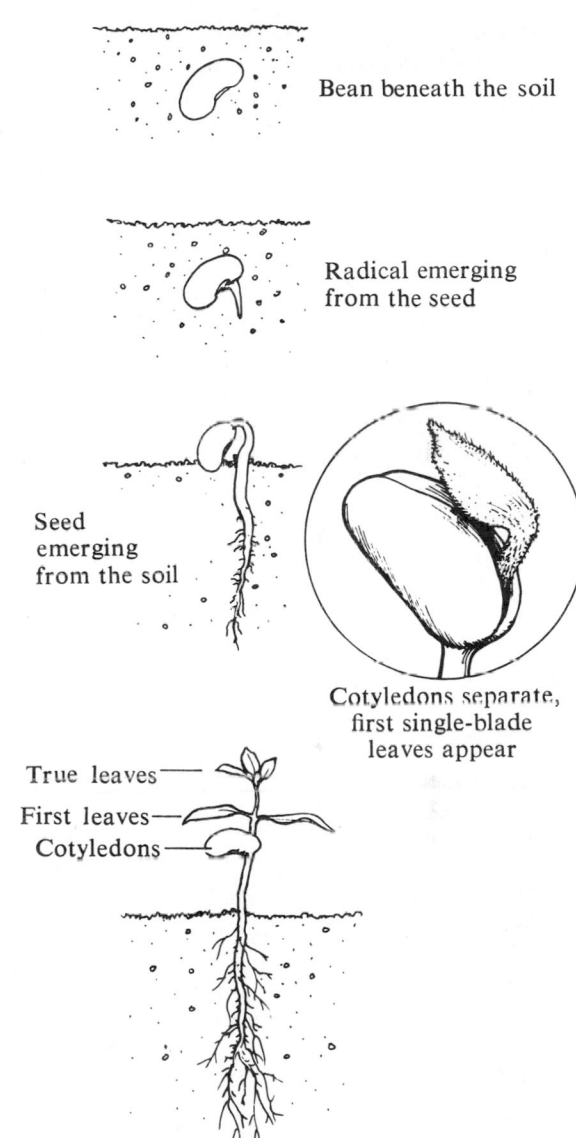

Bean beneath the soil

Radical emerging from the seed

Seed emerging from the soil

Cotyledons separate, first single-blade leaves appear

True leaves
First leaves
Cotyledons

As the bean seed absorbs water, the young root or radical within begins to penetrate the seed coat. Several days later, the radical emerges, side roots form and the cotyledons or seed leaves are pushed up through the soil surface. The stem straightens and, as the cotyledons separate, the plant's first true leaves appear.

grains, which are monocots, do not send their one cotyledon above ground. It stays below with the grain, but sends out enzymes to digest the stored food and initiate growth of the plumule or epicotyl. An onion's cotyledon does emerge and carries the seed with it, still absorbing food from the seed's endosperm storage area.

Orchid seed, so small that there may be several hundred thousand or even a million seeds in one pod, have no endosperm. They usually have to rely on the fungi on the forest floor to supply their food while germinating, and the appearance of the first green leaf ca-

pable of making food for the plant may take months or up to a year or so. Nurseries now grow them on agar in flasks, with sugar and minerals added.

Conditions for germination include the proper proportions of moisture, air, heat and, for many seed, darkness. Once moisture has been added, it should never be cut off. The growing medium should not be too wet, however, for a supply of oxygen is also needed as well as an outlet for transpiring carbon dioxide. Most crop plants prefer a temperature between 68 and 86°F. (20 and 30°C.) for germination, but seeds of peas, lettuce, radish, and wheat,

FLOWERS

Plant	Days	Plant	Days
Ageratum	5– 8	Heliotrope	15–18
Alyssum	4– 5	Hollyhock	15–18
Anchusa	18–20	Larkspur (annual)	15–18
Arctotis	12–15	Lobelia	8–10
Baby's-breath	18–20	Love-in-a-mist	8–10
Balsam	5– 8	Marigold	5– 8
Butterfly weed	10–12	Mignonette	8–10
Calendula	8–10	Morning-glory	8–10
Candytuft	5– 8	Nasturtium	8–10
Canterbury-bells	12–15	Nicotiana	18–20
Clarkia	7–10	Nigella	8–10
Cockscomb	5– 8	Pansy	10–12
Columbine	15–18	Pea, sweet	15–18
Coreopsis	15–20	Penstemon	18–20
Cornflower	5– 8	Periwinkle	15–18
Cosmos	5– 8	Petunia	10–18
Dahlia	8–10	Phlox (annual)	15–18
Delphinium	10–15	Poppies (Iceland)	18–20
Dianthus	8–10	Portulaca	15–18
English daisy	5– 8	Rose mallow	15–18
Forget-me-not	12–15	Sage, blue	12–15
Four-o'clock	5– 8	Shasta daisy	18–21
Gaillardia	15–20	Strawflower	5– 8
Godetia	12–15	Zinnia	5– 8

VEGETABLES

Plant	Days	Plant	Days
Beans, lima	7–10	Leek	8–10
Beans, snap	7–10	Lettuce	6– 8
Beet	8–10	Mustard	6– 8
Broccoli	6–10	Okra	8–10
Brussels sprouts	6–10	Onion	8–10
Cabbage	6–10	Parsley	8–10
Cabbage, Chinese	4– 5	Parsnip	12–18
Carrot	10–15	Pea	7–10
Cauliflower	5–10	Peppers	12–18
Celery	5–14	Potato (sprouting)	21–28
Chard, Swiss	8–10	Pumpkin	8–10
Chive	5–10	Radish	4– 6
Collard	5–10	Rutabaga	4– 7
Corn, sweet	5– 8	Spinach	5– 9
Cucumber	8–10	Squash	8–10
Eggplant	10–12	Tomato	8–10
Endive	8–10	Turnip	4– 7
Kale	6–10	Watermelon	8–10
Kohlrabi	7–10		

for example, will germinate readily at 50°F. (10°C.). The depth of sowing depends on the size of the seed, with good germination expected from large seeds such as those of lupines, peas and sweet peas needing ¾ inch, but smaller ones such as zinnias and marigolds or radishes and lettuce needing ¼ to ½ inch. Tiny seeds like those of petunia and nicotiana need only to be mixed with sand and sprinkled on the soil. Some seeds need winter freezing before they will germinate.

Germination Tests: All reliable seedsmen put their seed through germination tests and print the results on the packets in terms of percentages. In order to do such a test on a small scale on seed you yourself have saved, put 20 to 40 on a moist blotter or cotton with a layer of the same material on top. Keep these warm and moist but not wet, and lift the upper layer once a day to give air to the seed. As each seed germinates, remove it if you wish, but be sure to keep count of how many germinate. After the usual term for germination of that particular variety of seed, allow another week before you terminate the test. Then count the number of seed germinated out of the total and figure out the percentage. Any in the 90's or 80's is good, and a percentage in the 70's is considered quite adequate. If you know the percentage, of course, it will guide you in deciding how much of any one variety to plant.

Rate of Germination: The tables presented here give approximate times required for the germination of some of the more popular flower and vegetable seeds.

See also SEED, SEEDS AND SEEDLINGS.

GEUM

Also known as avens, these perennials of the Rose family are often recommended for use as border or rock garden plants. *G. triflorum* grows to 1½ feet; the popular summer-blooming *G. Quellyon,* including Lady Strathedon and Mrs. Bradshaw, grows to two feet and is a fine choice for the perennial border. These plants do well in average garden soils and can be propagated by division.

See also PERENNIALS.

GHENT AZALEA   *See* AZALEA

GIANT REED
See GRASS, ORNAMENTAL

GIBBONS, EUELL THEOPHILUS

(1911-1975) Born of poor parents, Euell Gibbons learned to forage for wild foods as a child. He received his training from his mother and maternal grandmother, both self-taught naturalists with a special interest in wild foods.

Though he had no formal high school training (he left home at age 15 to become a jack-of-all-trades and general hobo), he eagerly pursued his interests in ethnobotany and aboriginal cultures by reading everything he could find in universities and libraries across the country.

In 1960, after a long and varied career as a carpenter, beachcomber, laborer, boat builder, harvest hand, grounds keeper, cowboy, trapper, farmer, and teacher, Gibbons devoted himself full time to writing. His books on foraging for wild foods were published in quick succession: *Stalking the Wild Asparagus* (1962), *Stalking the Blue-Eyed Scallop* (1964), *Stalking the Healthful Herbs* (1966), *Euell Gibbons' Beachcomber's Handbook* (1967), and *Feast on a Diabetic Diet* (1969; with brother, Joe Gibbons). For several years he was the nature editor and a monthly columnist for *Organic Gardening and Farming®*. He also contributed poems to the *Friends Journal*.

GILIA

Hardy annuals, perennials or biennials with lacy, fernlike foliage, gilias produce abundant varicolored flowers that are generally one inch in diameter. Most species are dwarfish and well suited for edgings and rockeries. As soon as the soil can be worked in the spring, sow seed in average but well-drained soil in an open, sunny location.

Species of *Ipomopsis* and *Leptodactylon* are closely related to this genus. *I. aggregata,* known as scarlet gilia or skyrocket, grows wild throughout the mountainous regions of the West. It can be raised from seed in any cool zone. *I. rubra,* also known as standing cypress and trailing fire, makes an attractive three- to five-foot annual or biennial with finely cut foliage. Grow it as a biennial in the North, sowing seed indoors in March with germination in about seven days. Transplant outdoors when all danger of frost is past. It should produce scarlet, tubular-shaped flowers the following June. It does well on average soil and self-sows. *L. pungens,* granite gilia, is a slightly taller, denser shrub which blooms throughout the summer in the Southwest.

GILLYFLOWERS   *See* STOCK

GINGER   (*Zingiber officinalis*)

Ginger is a biennial or perennial herb native to the tropics and cultivated in tropical countries in both hemispheres. The plant rarely flowers or produces fruit. The rhizome (the underground stem often referred to as the root), which has a characteristic, pungent taste, is used to some extent in medicine, but its prin-

The tropical herb ginger produces the familiar rhizome commonly referred to as ginger root, which is used medicinally and as a flavoring for foods and beverages.

cipal commercial use is in flavoring foods, confections and carbonated beverages.

Ginger is believed to be native to the warmer parts of Asia, where it has been cultivated from early times. The plant rapidly spread to the West Indies, South America, Australia, and Africa. Ginger has been recognized as a spice for thousands of years. Ancient Greeks and Romans welcomed the flavoring agent from southern Arabia, by way of the Red Sea. It has also been savored through history in India. Long ago, this herb was considered medicinally valuable in treatment of digestive disorders, although most growers value it today for its use as a condiment.

Ginger is an exhaustive crop and requires fertile soil with good drainage. The rhizomes are likely to rot in poorly drained soil, and the plant will not thrive in gravel or sand. For maximum growth, much rain and high temperatures during the growing season are required, and it is therefore best grown in tropical and subtropical regions.

The rhizomes are harvested early in winter, and the crop should not be replanted until early in spring. Ginger is readily propagated from small divisions of the rhizomes, each division containing at least one bud or "eye." In Florida, these may be planted in February or early March about three inches deep and about 16 inches apart in rows two feet apart. The plants come up slowly and in the early stage of growth are much benefited by some protection from the sun. Cultivation and hoeing sufficient to control weeds are necessary. As the season advances and the rhizomes enlarge, the plant develops numerous leafstalks, followed in fall by flower stalks.

In Florida the roots may be harvested early in December. This is readily accomplished with a garden fork. The soil is shaken off, the top cut off close to the rhizomes and the fibrous roots removed. To facilitate removal of the soil, it is advisable to break the rhizomes into several branches, or "hands."

Ginger grows well in a greenhouse with a 75°F. (23.89°C.) temperature. It needs a large pot and a lot of water and responds well to applications of liquid compost or manure.

The rhizomes, collected when young and green, are washed and scraped before being preserved in syrup or as a tasty preserve which is exported mainly from the West Indies and China. Ginger candy, made from sliced sections of ginger preserved in sugar, is a favorite among children and adults alike.

See also HERB.

GINSENG   (*Panax quinquefolius*)

A fleshy-rooted herbaceous plant native to this country, ginseng was at one time of frequent occurrence in shady, well-drained sites in hardwood forests from Maine to Minnesota and southward to the Carolinas and Georgia.

Mature ginseng plants are between ten and 20 inches high, with five-fingered leaves and small yellow green flowers that develop over a three-year maturation cycle.

Although most claims of the medicinal properties of ginseng roots are not widely accepted in this country, the herb has become a popular item in health food stores today, and is commonly consumed in teas and as a food flavoring.

Ginseng takes its name from the Chinese word, *schinseng,* meaning man shaped. This refers to the form ginseng roots often assume.

Ancient Chinese medicine regarded ginseng as a tonic, stimulant, carminative, and demulcent. It was even considered a powerful aphrodisiac.

First cultivated in America in the eighteenth century, the herb was valued as a commodity sought by Indians and white settlers alike. Today, the wild ginseng trade has declined, but domestic cultivation has increased, and many by-products are commonly found in gourmet shops and health food stores throughout the country.

One serious problem in cultivating ginseng is the length of time it takes to grow into a marketable root. The seed may take anywhere from 18 to 24 months to germinate and even longer for the plant to mature. Even those gardeners who start with mature plants must often wait four to six years for a harvest.

Another consideration is the quality of soil required to successfully cultivate ginseng. The soil must be fairly light and well fertilized with woods earth, rotted leaves or fine raw bone meal, with the bone meal applied at the rate of one pound to each square yard. Seed is planted in spring as early as the soil can be worked to advantage. It is placed six inches apart each way in the permanent beds or two by six inches in seedbeds, and the seedlings are transplanted to stand six to eight inches apart when two years old. The roots of ginseng plants, especially in woodland, are sometimes damaged by mice. Protection from these rodents may be necessary. The beds should at all times be kept free from weeds and grass and the surface of the soil slightly stirred whenever it shows signs of caking. A winter mulch should be applied when freezing weather begins and removed early in spring.

The root should be collected only in

Valuable ginseng roots are harvested in autumn, dried and scoured in hot water before being sold abroad.

autumn, when it will be plumpest after drying. Often the roots are plunged into hot water, scoured and steamed. This makes them appear yellow and semitransparent, enhancing their market value for exportation.

Most people consider the Chinese claims of ginseng's medicinal value to be mythological. In the United States, the herb is still cultivated mainly for export to China. Russian scientists, however, are trying to verify Chinese beliefs through research and promotion of their own herb—*Eleuth erococcas*—which they claim possesses medicinal qualities similar to ginseng, particularly as a relaxant.

See also HERB.

GIRASOLE
See ARTICHOKE, JERUSALEM

GLADIOLUS

Gladiolus bring beauty and color to gardens and flower beds throughout the summer. They are tender and prefer long, warm summers though some hardier varieties have been developed.

Their brilliant florets, crisp and full, adorn spikes that attain a height of five feet in the giant glads, which are the most familiar form. These are so large that they do not fit the scale of any but the most spacious rooms when used as cut flowers. The miniature and the butterfly gladiolus are more useful for indoor arrangements. The butterfly hybrids such as Toytown, Chinatown and Vivaldi have more deeply colored markings resembling spread butterfly wings in the throat of the flowers. These smaller types are usually available from the better mail-order nurseries. The giants can be bought at any garden center or market. Older varieties are generally cheaper and may be just as good as new ones. Each individual bloom is a delicate blend of pastel shades. The varieties of gladiolus that boast heavier and deeper tones of red, blue and purple have a texture of pure velvet.

Many years ago, this summer-blooming member of the Iris family was first discovered growing among the tall grass along riverbanks in Africa. At that time the florets were small compared to the hybrids of today. Through cross-pollination, a multitude of colors has been created to bring greater beauty to the glads and more buds and better height to the spikes.

Increasing Corms: If you are interested in raising giant flowers, select large corms, about four or five inches wide. In order to force plants to concentrate all of their energy into single spikes, all "eyes," except the main one located near the center, should be removed from the corms. With the tip of a knife, cut deeply to remove all of the surrounding tissue. Allow wounds to heal for a few days and then plant the corms in a well-fertilized, sunny situation.

A good way to increase your bulb supply is to cut each large bulb in half. Those corms that have sprouted are best to work on. Cut right down through the corm between two sprouts. Each half will then produce a large spike. This dividing will in no way affect the size of the flower or dwarf the new bulb in fall. When divided, the corms often produce lovelier and more robust florets.

The bulblets, or cormels, can be saved from year to year, and, in time, you will have large numbers of each color at no additional cost. Save all cormels over ¼ inch in diameter. In spring, break the hard shell and peel each clean. Plant as you would peas. Within three years these tiny bulblets will reach blooming size.

When to Plant: The best rule to follow is to make the first planting just as the leaves are unfolding on the trees in your area. For a succession of bloom make plantings every ten days for about ten weeks. Allow enough time for the last planting to flower before frost in your area.

These plantings may create problems, for no sooner does the weather turn warm than corms in storage sprout and grow. Pick out the sprouted ones and plant them first. The others are divided into the number of intended plantings and stored in paper bags where temperatures are around 45°F. (7.22°C.).

How to Plant: Well-drained garden soil rich in organic matter is excellent for gladiolus culture. Plant the corms in beds among other flowers for summer color, or plant in rows in the garden for a steady supply of cut flowers. The latter produces the largest cut flowers.

When planting in beds, dig a round hole eight inches deep and 12 inches across. Loosen soil in the bottom, add one quart old manure or a pint of dehydrated manure, about ½ cup balanced organic fertilizer and enough lime to bring the soil to a pH of 6 to 7. Work the fertilizer well into the soil, cover with an inch of dirt and set in six large corms spaced two inches apart in all directions.

Refill the hole, leaving a slight depression to catch water. The earth should be firmed only enough to eliminate air pockets.

If planting in rows in the garden, work the soil well to a depth of 12 inches. Turn in any organic matter you have on hand such as compost, aged manure, leaf mold, or green manures. Rake the area smooth and make trenches eight inches deep about two feet apart.

Since gladiolus are such heavy feeders, some compost should also be incorporated into the bottom of each trench for immediate use. Mix old manure equally with compost, and apply two inches deep in each trench. Then give each furrow a good dusting of bone meal. Work into the soil, and cover with an inch of dirt.

The larger corms are then set individually six to eight inches apart. The smaller ones are planted alternately two to four inches apart. Gladiolus that are planted six inches or deeper will require no staking when spikes appear. If spikes should become quite large, however, staking would be wise to prevent breakage.

When choosing a planting location, select one that receives full sun all day. The shorter the photoperiod, the shorter the flower heads. Under ordinary conditions, glads bloom within

70 to 90 days. In Southern California, they'll bloom twice if the first spike is cut off immediately after blooming.

Summer Care: Unless rains are extremely heavy, water gladiolus at least once a week. These flowers require an inch or more of water a week. Most failures are due to insufficient watering. Even those glads that are not well fed thrive when watered adequately. You can solve the problem of watering by allowing an overhead sprinkler to run all night every seven days. The earth around the bulbs should be damp at all times, but no puddles should be allowed to remain.

When plants are eight inches tall, loosen the soil between rows, and apply an organic fertilizer high in phosphorus. This early feeding increases the bud count on each spike and its final length. Water the fertilizer with a fine spray. When ground has dried sufficiently, hill each row to a height of six inches for later support.

To cut down on weeds and to keep the soil constantly moist, mulch heavily with at least eight inches of hay, straw or grass clippings.

Cut Flowers: There is a slight disagreement among professional gladiolus growers as to the best time to cut spikes. Some believe it is wise to gather them after sundown when the spikes are fortified with extra food. Others prefer to cut them in the early morning.

When gathering spikes, use a sharp knife and cut on a long slant to expose as many cells as possible. More water will be absorbed if cut this way, resulting in crisper flowers. Do not take any leaves if possible, as they are needed to mature the corm properly. Cut when two lower buds show color.

Spikes cut in this early stage bloom more beautifully, and last much longer. However, if

As cut flowers, gladiolus will retain their beauty and freshness when stems are cut on a long slant and many cells are exposed to the water.

you prefer to gather your spikes after half of the florets have opened, do so in the middle of the day. Allow to wilt for an hour, then rearrange the florets into a more clustered group.

Fall Care: Right after all blooms have faded, rake away the mulch and give the plants another feeding of organic fertilizer rich in potassium. This feeding produces massive corms which, in turn, will bring forth larger and more beautiful glads each year. Soak the ground, then replace the mulch.

Allow bulbs to remain in the ground until the foliage has died, then take them up with a garden fork. If you have large numbers of bulbs, break them off immediately and place in open trays in some outdoor building to dry. Smaller amounts may be tied together like onions and hung in a well-ventilated room until dry.

After three weeks, husk the corms by completely removing the paperlike covering. Gather all suitable cormels and place in a shoe box. Return the peeled corms to their trays and allow them to cure for two or three weeks. When dry, place in a carton with peat moss or in strong paper bags into which a few mothballs have been dropped to discourage mice and thrips. Store in a cool, dry place until spring.

GLAUCONITE

Glauconite is an iron potassium silicate that imparts a green color to the minerals in which it occurs. It is a rounded, soft but stable aggregate of finely divided clay. The most common and best known glauconite mineral is the greensand of New Jersey which was deposited near the "mud line" surrounding the continental shores many millions of years ago. *See also* GREENSAND.

GLAUCOUS WILLOW
See PUSSY WILLOW

GLOBE ARTICHOKE
See ARTICHOKE, GLOBE

GLOBEFLOWER   *See* TROLLIUS

GLOXINIA   (*Sinningia speciosa*)

Not to be confused with *Gloxinia perennis* (Canterbury-bells gloxinia), these are second in popularity in the Gesneria family only to African violets. Native to Brazil, gloxinias have been extensively hybridized and are not too difficult to grow. Flowers are trumpetlike, three inches long and up to five inches across, in colors of red, blue, white, or purple. Some are speckled, and blossoms can be single or double. *S. pusilla* has tiny, nodding slipperlike flowers.

A soil rich in humus and kept evenly moist is ideal. Light from an eastern or lightly shaded southern window is sufficient for

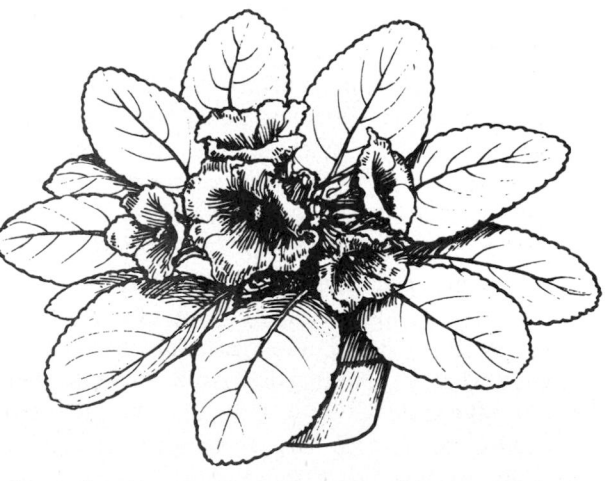

Sow gloxinia seed in the warm (70 to 80°F. [21.11 to 26.67°C.]) greenhouse in late winter for blooming the following spring and summer.

flowers. Temperatures should be about 70°F. (21.11°C.) during the day and 65°F. (18.33°C.) at night, and a relative humidity of 40 to 50 percent will produce good growth. When watering, avoid splashing cold water on the leaves, since it can cause spots.

Plants are most readily propagated from 1½-inch tubers in five-inch pots covered with ½ inch of soil. Propagation from seed or leaf cuttings is also possible.

After flowering has finished, decrease water until the leaves dry. Store the pots in a dark, cool cellar at 50 to 60°F. (10 to 15.56°C.) for six to ten weeks, watering only two or three times. At the end of this rest, put the pots in the sun and resume watering. Blossoms should be produced in six months.

For large flowering types, the florists' gloxinia hybrids offer a wide choice. For small plants two inches or less, try *S. concinna*. Emperor Frederick, Prince Albert, Etoile de Feu, and Princess Elizabeth are slightly larger and are excellent choices for terrariums.

See also HOUSE PLANTS.

GNEISS   *See* MINERAL ROCKS

GOATS

Goatkeeping is one of the simplest livestock operations, and the equipment for the "backyard dairy" is just as simple: A homemade stanchion and a manger for feeding are the basic requirements. You may wish to add a folding milking stand, attached to the wall, to ease the milking task a bit.

By their nature, goats are affectionate and gentle. They are highly intelligent and can be taught almost any trick that can be taught a dog. The milk they give is easier to digest than cow's milk. Also, goats are easier to handle and less expensive than cows.

Breeds: There are five principal breeds of dairy goats in America.

Nubians are of English, African and Oriental origin. They are characterized by large size, long drooping ears, arched nose, and any color or combination.

French Alpines range from white to black spotted. Ears are upright, face dished, eyes prominent.

Saanens are of Swiss origin. They are white, of good size, with short, erect ears, and dished or straight faces.

Toggenburgs are a Swiss breed. They are medium-large; brown in color with light markings down the face, on legs and under body; ears short and erect; face dished.

La Manchas are very calm goats and excellent milk producers. They have small, almost unnoticeable external ears and long, straight faces.

Within each of these breeds there are grade classifications such as purebred, recorded grade, American, and crossbred. A purebred goat is one whose parents are registered as the same breed. A recorded grade goat has only one registered parent with the other one being of mixed or even unknown breed. American goats are the result of three successive crossings of a grade goat with a purebred. When two purebred goats of different breeds are mated, the result is a crossbreed. In addition to these types, there is the unrecorded grade goat whose parentage is unknown.

As with any animal, the purebred type is the most valuable goat though it will not always produce more milk than an unrecorded or crossed type. The main advantage to any of the graded goats over the unrecorded ones is that you have proof of the goat's age, records of its parentage, and perhaps even some information on the dame's milk production. A purebred, grade, American, or crossbred goat costs a bit more than one that has no papers, but at least you know what you are getting.

Buying horned goats is usually ill-advised, because of the harm they can cause. Horn growth can be stopped when the kids are tiny by applying dehorning paste or cauterizing the small horn buds.

Milk: Goat's milk is more easily digested than cow's milk because of its smaller, more easily assimilated fat globules. For the same reason, it is also more nourishing, for people are nourished not by what they swallow but by what they digest. Tuberculosis does not exist among goats, so their milk needs no pasteurization and runs no danger of losing its vitamins or having its calcium salts altered by heat.

Many people start to use goat's milk to help them through an illness, and then develop a taste for it. Goat's milk is sweet and pleasant to the taste. Goats are particularly discriminating in their feeding habits. The doe is odorless and clean and nearly always produces high-quality milk.

A good doe will give three to four quarts of milk a day—plenty for most families' needs. To produce this amount of milk about four pounds of hay and two pounds of grain daily are required. You should purchase two or more goats, however, and by having them freshen (produce milk) at different times of the year, a reasonably constant milk flow can be maintained throughout the entire year.

Breeding: Young females may be bred

to freshen at 14 or 15 months of age if they are well developed. The gestation period is five months, and the usual practice is to have the does freshen once a year. Fine, purebred males are available within driving distance of most communities and it is seldom necessary or advisable for the small owner to maintain a male for breeding.

The average suburban lot can provide much of the maintenance for goats, and the unsprayed leaves and trimmings from the family garden will go far to meet the feed requirements. Add alfalfa hay, or any good leguminous hay, with a light grain ration and the goats will thrive at nominal cost.

Feed represents the major portion of the goat-raising budget. Goats, like cattle and sheep, are ruminants. They have a second stomach that lets them store large amounts of roughage in one compartment while "chewing their cud" (breaking down plant fibers and adding the enzymes needed to extract nutrients). For this reason, goats should have regular access to hay, grass, bark, and other roughages.

There are various commercial rations prepared specifically to insure proper nutrition for goats. Hay and grain make good feed, with the proper protein and mineral (especially calcium) supplements. Organic gardeners can add kelp, molasses, cider vinegar, comfrey, and other nutrients to their feed.

Manure: The goat also converts feed into high-grade manure. The goat's digestive system is such that few if any weed seeds pass through her undigested. The composition of goat manure is about the same as that of sheep manure, but of course varies depending upon the kind and quality of feed she receives. The goat is, by nature, a browser rather than a grazer; she utilizes leaves and twigs of deep-rooted plants to good advantage. Disregarding trace minerals and some other similar ingredients, goat manure will contain about:

Water	64 percent
Nitrogen	1.44 percent
Potassium	1 percent
Phosphorus	.22 percent

The manure of the goat, being dry and in pellets, is clean and odorless. In fact, the modern dairy doe is perhaps the most nearly odorless and the cleanest of any animal, and your premises can be absolutely free of any odor, if reasonably sanitary conditions are maintained.

Housing: Goats do not require costly or elaborate housing. Only a few essentials must be remembered: House them in a clean, dry place, free from drafts but well ventilated. This way, they will stand almost unlimited cold or heat in any climate.

Minimum space requirements for goats are approximately 20 square feet per animal. Earth, sand or gravel floors are desirable since they remain dry and are easy to clean when the goat house or pen is scoured each spring and fall.

Bedding can be made from sawdust, straw or even ground cornstalks. Old bedding makes an excellent contribution to the compost heap.

Stock fencing is often preferred over wood in manger construction. A keyhole-shaped manger is one way to minimize hay waste, since the shape discourages goats from spilling uneaten hay.

Goats require a constant supply of clean, fresh water. Salt and mineral blocks are also essential.

GODETIA   (*Clarkia*)

Also known as farewell-to-spring, the open, primroselike flowers of white, rose or red are borne on spikes about 18 inches long above a mound of foliage. The plants should be massed for best effect. *Godetia* is sometimes listed as a separate genus but most books consider godetias members of the genus *Clarkia*. *See also* CLARKIA.

GOLDEN-BELLS
See FORSYTHIA *or* WHISPERING-BELLS

GOLDEN-RAIN TREE
See VARNISH TREE

GOLDENROD   (*Solidago*)

These are any plants of a widespread genus of summer- and fall-blooming perennials of the Compositae family native to North America. They have wandlike stems, variously shaped leaves and heads of small yellow, or occasionally white, flowers. Species from this group have been adopted as state flowers by Alabama, Kentucky and Nebraska.

Most of these plants are striking in appearance. One that appeals to both sight and smell is the sweet or anise-scented goldenrod (*S. odora*), named for the aroma of its crushed leaves.

Sweet goldenrod ranges from Maine and Vermont south to Florida and west to Missouri and Texas. It grows in fertile but sandy or dry soil along thicket borders, in open woods or on sunny hillsides. Often reclining, it is a slender species that reaches only two to three feet high, and blooms from July to September. The leaves have many small, clear dots which secrete an aniselike scent. It is also a good honey plant.

These fragrant leaves, when dried and steeped in water, make a very pleasing drink. The plant is sometimes called Blue Mountain tea, and the beverage is regarded as a tasty and wholesome tea substitute.

Because they are such common plants in rural areas, most people think of goldenrods as weedy and unsuitable for the flower garden. There are, however, certain hybrids developed in England which make beautiful garden plants. These low-maintenance, pest-free plants deserve a place in the garden.

Goldenrods do not cause hay fever. Their pollen is too heavy to be carried about by the wind. Ragweed, which inconspicuously blooms at the same time, is the culprit.

GOLDENSEAL   (*Hydrastis canadensis*)

One of the most well known, wild medicinal herbs in America, goldenseal grows to one foot high, and supports one main leaf and multi-lobed secondary leaves. Its seed are grown in clusters of fruits. This native perennial was formerly abundant in open woodlands having good natural drainage and an abundance of leaf mold. Its range is from southern New York and Ontario, west to Minnesota, and south to Kentucky and Georgia.

Goldenseal took its name from the golden stain its roots emit. American Indians used the plant to dye their clothing and skin, and as an insect repellent. The herb's generic name, *Hydrastis,* comes from two Greek words meaning "water" and "to accomplish" referring to its medicinal value, especially its past use in treating mucous membranes. By the 1800's, goldenseal was included in medical lists of drug plants in America. The plant was used to treat dyspepsia, inflammations and other illnesses. It was an official drug plant until 1936, when it almost became extinct because of its great popularity.

Like ginseng, goldenseal must be grown in the shade of a woodland or a lathhouse. The soil should be well fertilized, preferably with decaying vegetable matter. Raw bone meal and cottonseed meal can also be used to advantage. In October, seed may be broadcast or planted ½ inch apart in rows six inches apart in a well-prepared seedbed. Cover seed with fine leaf mold to the depth of one inch. In winter, the seedbed should be protected with burlap or fertilizer sacks. At the end of the second season the seedlings are usually large enough to be transplanted to their permanent beds six to eight inches apart each way, with the rootstocks covered to a depth of about two inches. The soil should be kept free from weeds and the plants liberally watered throughout the growing season. For satisfactory growth the plant requires about 75 percent shade during the summer.

Under favorable conditions, goldenseal roots achieve full size in about five years from seed, or in three or four years when grown from root buds or by division of the rootstocks. The roots are dug in fall after the tops have withered. They are washed clean of all soil and dried on screens in an airy, partly sunny place, or indoors on a clean dry floor. When dried in the open they should be protected from rain and dew.

Goldenseal still has many medicinal values. When combined with bicarbonate of soda, it can be used to treat sore throats and inflammations of the mouth. It is sometimes used in eyewash applications as well. Goldenseal is still a home remedy for upset stomachs and is used as a laxative.

See also HERB.

GOOSEBERRY   (*Ribes*)

Gooseberries are fine fruits for home growing. Although more popular in Europe, good, cold-resistant American varieties have been developed. In addition to their intolerance to heat, European varieties of gooseberry are also more susceptible to mildew than American types.

Culture: Gooseberries can be propagated by cuttings or layering. One-year-old dormant stock should be planted either in late fall or early spring. Gooseberries will tolerate heavy soil and cold winters better than other berries. Too much nitrogen in the soil promotes heavy green growth which in turn exhausts the plant. For this reason, when manure is used as fertilizer in the fall, it is better to use stable manure than poultry manure.

Plant bushes four to six feet apart in rows about eight feet apart. Trim the tops back to within six inches of the ground. A thick straw mulch will protect the planting through the winter.

Gooseberry bushes can also be increased by ground layering—bending a low-hanging branch to the ground and covering a length of it with about three inches of soil. Allow the tip of the branch with at least three buds to stick out. The covered portion will set down roots; a year later the branch can be cut and transplanted.

Approximately nine canes should be maintained per bush. Allow three of a three-

Widely cultivated in Europe, several winter-hardy varieties of green and white gooseberries are also available to the American gardener.

year growth, three of a two-year growth and three of a one-year growth. Bushes which are shaded need more severe pruning than those in direct sunlight. Mildew is a constant threat.

Gooseberries are a potential threat to white pines because of the white pine blister rust which they may carry. In areas where white pines are important and grow profusely, the propagation of currants and gooseberries is prohibited or controlled.

Harvest: Gooseberry picking traditionally calls for heavy leather gloves or other protection against the prickly thorns. Run your hand along the length of the branch and catch the crop in a container placed below the branch. Leaves and other extraneous debris can be removed by winnowing later.

Pests: Mildew is the most serious disease affecting gooseberries. Bushes planted where there is good air circulation will be less susceptible to infection. Anthracnose is also a gooseberry enemy.

Varieties: Welcome is a hardy variety which is resistant to anthracnose. Pixwell is easy to harvest because the fruit hangs away from thorns. Old favorites include Downing, Oregon Champion, Red Jacket, and Poorman.

See also Bramble Fruits, Currant.

GOPHER

Gophers are small rodents that dig tunnels with their front feet and their two long projecting front teeth. These tunnels seem to follow no pattern, usually running from a few inches to two feet beneath the soil surface. At intervals gophers throw out lateral tunnels to the surface, push freshly dug soil out into their telltale mounds, plug up the tunnel mouth, and go on their way.

Gophers eat all sorts of plants, vegetables, flower bulbs, and weeds, and chew the bark from tree roots, often girdling and killing them. Masses of roots, plant crowns and grass are stored in underground pockets for future meals.

Gophers have from one to five litters of five to eight youngsters each year. They appear on the grounds of small homes and estates, wastelands, and even in town and city lawns and gardens. Their tunneling and mound making can ruin lawns, create havoc among flower gardens and wipe out a young orchard in weeks.

Control Methods: First, encourage the natural enemies of gophers: pet cats and dogs, gopher and king snakes, skunks, and particularly barn owls. A pair of breeding barn owls do no harm to poultry or other birds and can eat from three to six gophers every few nights.

Cats will take care of many gophers, but cats and dogs cannot kill them when they are underground. So you must trap or flood out the pests, or deter them with a one-inch mesh fence sunk underground. Specially designed gopher traps are available.

GOPHERWOOD   *See* Yellowwood

GOURDS   (Cucurbitaceae)

Gourds will thrive anywhere pumpkins and squash do well. A deep, well-drained soil of good fertility is best. Some growers add a handful or two of compost per plant. Too much fertilizer will produce a lot of foliage and not much fruit.

Culture: Plant five seeds an inch deep in each hill. A shovelful of compost and manure helps retain water and deter spotting of the gourds. Trellised plants need a concave depression in the soil around them to further aid in water retention.

Some gardeners like to shape their gourds to make them even more interesting. Soft tape works well with the smaller varieties, while the long kinds can be bent gently and frequently with your hands. One fancier succeeded in actually tying a knot in the four-foot-long handle of a Knob-kerrie gourd! Growing gourds are sometimes encased in bottles or jugs. Later, the glass is broken and the gourd holds its new shape as it matures.

Harvest: Gourds can be harvested when they are very hard to the touch, or at the first sign of frost. Cut them with a sharp knife, leaving on several inches of stem. Handle them very carefully to avoid bruising.

Wipe off any moisture, and never wash or disinfect gourds. Any mold that appears on the hard-shelled gourds such as lagenarias can be scraped off with a knife.

The hard-shelled gourds are put on a rack or indoor clothes dryer in a cool, dry place where air can circulate around them. The thinner-shelled ornamental varieties are waxed, shellacked or varnished immediately. They will rot if cut or carved, and only last several months, unlike the lagenarias which will last for many years if properly treated.

Lagenarias may require a month to six months to dry. Others, such as species of *Luffa* or *Trichosanthes,* may dry sufficiently on the vine. They are cured when the seeds rattle inside upon shaking. Scrubbing with steel wool will remove the thin outer skin of hard-shelled gourds, leaving a surface which will take a beautiful polish.

When the gourd is completely dry, it may be cut for whatever use you may wish to make of it. The shells can be carved or designs burnt in with an electric needle, and if hollowed out, gourds serve as comfortable homes for wayfaring birds.

You can use feathers to paint the gourds with a quick-drying enamel. Lacquer or varnish are equally good.

Many craftsmen prefer several coats of high-grade wax to give a natural, mellow glow. The Indians accomplished the same thing by rubbing the gourds for hours with the natural oils on their skins.

Varieties: Of the small varieties, the Striped Pear, yellow and green in color, makes an attractive decoration. Miniature Bottle and Bicolor are both varied in color and shape.

Bottle gourd (*Lagenaria siceraria*) is suitable for birdhouses and dippers. The outer shell of Dishcloth or Luffa gourd makes excellent sponges for housework or personal hygiene. The Long Green Snake and Serpent (*Trichosanthes* spp.) are excellent long-necked choices.

GOVERNMENT SERVICES

In 1862, the United States Department of Agriculture was established. Its purpose: "To acquire and diffuse useful information on agricultural subjects in the most general and comprehensive sense." Today, the department dispenses a wide range of advice and aid of interest to farmers and gardeners.

Through its Cooperative State Research Service, the Department of Agriculture conducts and coordinates far-ranging research activities at the state agricultural experiment stations, land-grant colleges and schools of forestry throughout the country. The findings of this huge research complex are made available to the public through the agricultural experiment station offices of the individual states.

The Agricultural Research Service, with its main headquarters in Beltsville, Maryland, conducts research on improving nutrition, conserving natural resources, managing the environment, and improving yield and disease resistance of crops. The ARS also has responsibility for helping developing nations with nutrition and food technology programs. Inquiries should be directed to the ARS, Information Division, USDA, Washington, DC 20250.

The Agricultural Marketing Service conducts marketing research, makes crop and livestock estimates, and sets the standards for farm products. Most of its information is sent out through its press service to newspapers, farm magazines and radio stations.

The Forest Service conducts research in woodland and range management. In particular, it distributes planting stock for woodlots and shelterbelts, and aids in the conservation of water and other wildland natural resources.

The Farmers Home Administration makes or insures loans to buy or improve family farms, to install conservation measures and, through its Production Credit Association, to purchase equipment, seed, fertilizer and other farm inputs. The administration also has broad authority for improving housing, water supply, sewer and other community facilities in rural areas. There are over 1,500 local offices.

The Soil Conservation Service acts as a technical service agency in the conservation of soil and water, flood prevention and resource development. Through its many local offices, the SCS offers planning assistance to individual farmers and homesteaders.

The Watershed Program deals with the protection of watersheds and the utilization and disposal of upstream water areas.

Detailed information on USDA activities and publications may be obtained from the Information Office, 14th Street and Independence Avenue, SW, Washington, DC 20250.

See also EXTENSION SERVICES, COOPERATIVE.

GRAFTING

A graft is a successful union of two diverse but related living plant pieces in such a way that the cambium or living conductor of nutrients and food of the lower piece or stock will connect with the cambium of the upper piece or scion. Then when the two match up, they can grow together and make one healthy living plant. Both the stock and scion are wounded before they are matched, and from the wounds of each a callus forms. The two calluses interweave in a successful graft even before the matching of cambiums takes place.

Grafting is most successful when the stock and scion are young, and some very satisfactory grafts are made from a single bud with its adjacent tissues used as the scion.

Grafting has been practiced for three thousand years, especially on fruit and olive trees, with many of the early grafts made to repair injuries from storm or other attacks on the trees. Methods proliferated so much that by 1821, well over a hundred methods of grafting were in use. Today, grafting is mostly used to propagate desirable varieties of fruits, nuts and flowering shrubs.

Grafting is usually done to reproduce variations in the stock, which may be a large plant, a seedling, a rooted cutting, the roots themselves, a layered plant, or the top part of the plant in a method called top-grafting or top-working. One important method is that of dwarfing, in which the stock so affects the scion that it never grows tall, and turns into an early-bearing, sturdy, small tree very suitable for home gardens.

Methods of using scions include those for short pieces of detached shoot with several buds on them, and cut as wedges, arrows or clefts. They also include a method called approach grafting, which is a graft between two rooted plants wounded in strips on their near surfaces, and pulled over to be bound together until they grow into a close enough bond so that one may be severed from its base.

One aim of grafting, aside from dwarfing and the creation of sturdy, healthy plants, is to adapt plants to adverse soils and varying climatic conditions. Peach stock, for example, is used in the South to adapt plum grafts to sandy soil; and plum stocks in the North help adapt peach grafts to wet, cool soil.

Compatibility is an essential for successful grafting. It may be due to the close genetic relationship of two plants, their similarity in vigor, their particular physiological or biochemical makeup, or the dates when vegetative growth starts in the stock and scion plants each year. Incompatibility may come from very delicate maladjustments. For instance, one plant may have too much of some kind of acid to go well with the other and may injure it when circulation of nutrients and foods is established in the new continuous conducting vessels.

Aside from compatibility and an intimate connection between the two cambiums and related vessels, a graft needs protection of all cut surfaces with wax or tape, good strapping to hold the parts together, plenty of water for the stock, and the right humidity if a good callus and successful graft are to form. Both the scion and stock should be in dormancy, though scions can sometimes be successful on stocks that are in active growth, such as in bridge grafting done in the spring. All suckers must be removed so they do not choke the graft, and any tendency to wobble must be stopped by staking.

More on Dwarfing: Studies in England have shown that the best vigor in dwarfing stock occurs where there is a high proportion of bark to wood in the lateral roots, with much of the wood tissue consisting of living cells, in places where nondwarfing stocks have few. As noted above, dwarfing stocks bring on early fruiting, perhaps as a result of wounding or girdling before the graft, perhaps because of the increased concentration of carbohydrates, especially in the roots, or even in the shoots early in the season, favoring early flowering and thus early fruiting. Though dwarf plants have fewer growing points and less sugar in their leaves, the effect of dwarfing evidently causes increased uptake of nutrients and resulting beneficial concentration of both organic and mineral nutrients. These dwarfing stocks, being basically somewhat weak, promote early storage of starch, which aids early flowers and fruits.

Equipment Needed: The basic needs for grafting are a grafting knife and a budding knife, some grafting wax, and tape or twine to tie the two parts of the graft together. The wax may be made of resin, beeswax, raw linseed oil or tallow, and some lampblack or powdered charcoal.

A typical recipe for wax is five pounds resin, ¾ pound beeswax, ½ pint linseed oil, one ounce lampblack plus 1½ ounces fish glue. The glue is heated in a double boiler with just enough water to dissolve it. The other ingredients are melted in another container and cooled only to the point where they are still liquid. The glue is then stirred very slowly and continuously into the other ingredients. Then this material can be cooled entirely, hardened and chipped into lumps to store. At the time of grafting, reheat the mixture until it barely begins to bubble and apply it to the grafted plant pieces with a small new paintbrush. Besides this old-fashioned grafting wax, you can get modern commercial mixtures of asphalt and water which can be used. These may have to be applied again if it rains soon after application—before the mixture has had a chance to evaporate and harden.

Tie the graft before waxing with twine, raffia or an adhesive tape which will adhere to itself, such as nurserymen's adhesive tape, often used on whip grafts.

Types of Grafting: These include whip or tongue, splice, side, cleft, notch and wedge, bark, approach, bridge, inarching, double grafting, top-grafting, herbaceous, nurse-seed, and cutting.

Whip or tongue: This common grafting method is especially good to use for small, young ¼- to ½-inch material, and is often very successful because of the considerable extent of cambium contact—especially when the diameter of the stock and scion are just about equal. Two cuts are made. The first is a long, smooth diagonal cut from below to above, of one to 2½ inches in length. The second cut, almost parallel to the first, and again cut from below to above, ends at a point about one-third the distance down from the tip of the first cut. The scion is usually prepared beforehand with cuts of exactly the same size and shape, in a piece between four and six inches long, with at least three eyes or buds for best results—though scions with two or even one eye have been known to take. Do not let the lower end of the scion overlap the top of the stock too much, or there may be a big callus growth which hampers final healing. The same may happen if the stock is too big for the scion. The two pieces must be held together unless there is an absolutely perfect fit. Use twine or tape, and wax or one of the other materials suggested above to keep the graft from drying out. If, however, the grafted pieces are to be planted soon with the graft area below the ground, protection from drying is not needed. Grafts above ground that are taped should have the tape cut off as soon as the graft has taken. If there is a chance that the graft will get too dry, peat moss, moist sand or moist sawdust should be added to protect the grafted area. Tongue grafts used in topworking young trees (to put scions on branches at intervals around the trees) are usually tied with adhesive tapes, later cut off when the new growth commences.

Splice: This is a variation limited to just one smooth slice at the top and bottom of the two pieces to be grafted. It is good for herbaceous plants and for those with lots of pith, or with wood so stiff you cannot make a flexible tongue.

Side: This method may be of several sorts: side-tongue, side-veneer and spliced side graft. The first is used for branches of trees too large for a whip graft, and is characterized by an oblique cut into the stock at a 30 degree angle and the much smaller scion cut at a wedge which will fit into the side of the cut branch. For example, a three-inch, three-budded scion will fit about an inch down into the side of the cut branch. Best fit with the cambium of the stock is often attained by insertion of the scion at an angle. A spliced side graft or veneer graft is often used on seedling evergreens. A smooth downward and inward cut of one to 1½ inches is made beginning just above the crown of the stock plant, and ending a few inches below where a short second inward cut makes a notch of wood and bark to take out. The scion is given two similar cuts, made so that the cambium layers of the two pieces may be matched. When the graft is fitted, it may or may not be waxed, may or may not be wrapped in damp peat moss and may or may not be put under mist or in a high humidity case, depending on conditions. Whatever method is used, when the union is healed, the stock must be cut back to let the scion take over.

Cleft: For larger plants, the cleft graft is more often used. After a limb is cut, the stub is divided by chopping or slicing into it to make an opening of just the right size so that small scions may be inserted in the cambium

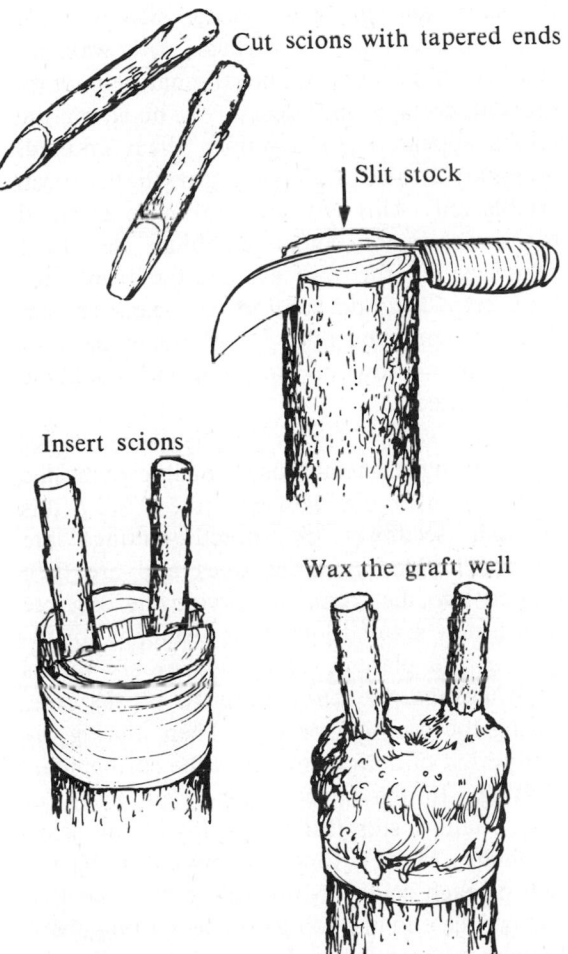

Cut scions with tapered ends

Slit stock

Insert scions

Wax the graft well

In cleft grafting, two scions are sharpened and inserted into the spliced rootstock so that the cambion layers of the two pieces meet. A coating of wax holds the scions in place until the union has formed. Later one of the scions is cut away and the other, superior one is left to develop.

area when the cleft is held open with a wedge. Several scions are inserted, and each must be tapered carefully without splitting the wood. Two are set at first to keep the cleft balanced, but afterwards, when the grafts take, the better one is kept and the lesser one cut away. It is important to wax the entire exposed surface of stock and scion in this kind of grafting. Scions for cleft grafting are prepared when the wood is dormant, but the best union is if the graft is made on the stock in early spring when the sap begins to flow.

Notch and wedge: When the branches are two to four inches in diameter, a more shallow split may be made. With a thin-bladed saw, make three cuts almost to the center of the stub, and then widen these cuts as much as necessary to make perfect fits with the scions. The scions for this method are usually four to five inches long with two buds, and are prepared with a long, tapering end to be inserted to match the cambium of the stub of the branch. No tying is necessary, but all exposed surfaces must be waxed. V-cut wedges can also be made and the scions cut to fit.

Bark: This is a much simpler method, causing little damage to the plants and healing quickly because of the excellent cambium contact that is possible. Begin by cutting off a limb, then below the cut merely slit two pieces of bark, about two inches long and a distance apart that will suit exactly the size of the scion. Lift up and cut back about two-thirds the piece of bark between the long cuts. The scion, with a smooth, slanting cut along one side and on the other side a less slanting cut of about ½ inch, will fit snugly into the opening in the bark. After fitting it in, nail down the flap of bark, or tie it in position and cover the whole area with wax.

Another method of bark grafting, used in

the spring when the bark will slip easily, is to cut into the bark deeply so that a section can be lifted up enough to slip in the scion. One advantage of this kind of bark grafting is that you need make only one cut in the bark, and if the branch is over two inches in diameter, there will be room to slip in two scions on the two sides of the branch.

Approach: In this method two independent, living plants are pulled together and grafted, after sections of bark have been removed so the branches can make contact. Usually one or both of the plants so grafted can be grown in a container. The rootstock plant is placed near and tied to the scion plant, preferably in the spring when growth is active, though it can be done at any time. Sometimes, in order to attain a very tight fit, the tongue or whip cuts are used for approach grafting. At other times, a slot in a thick-barked stock plant is cut just the width of the small scion, and the scion tied into the slot, then nailed down and waxed.

Bridge: This is a method very useful for trees that have been injured or girdled by rodents, disease or winter storms. To keep the trees from dying, cut scions an inch or two longer than the damaged area to be bridged, allowing four to a limb or one to every two to three inches in the limb's circumference. Allow more for a girdled trunk. Both ends of each scion are cut to a wedge-shaped taper and fitted exactly into two-inch slits in the bark above and below the damaged area. Leave ½-inch flaps which can be nailed down and waxed after the scions are inserted. Take the scions from dormant, healthy, one-year-old growth with a diameter of from ¼ to ½ inch. For best results, the bark on the damaged tree must be trimmed back to undamaged tissue, eliminating all jagged pieces. It should be done in the spring, fairly late so that the scion wood will have buds that have already started to grow. Nevertheless, these buds must be removed. The scion lengths should bow out from the branch or trunk, for this position helps to insure good, firm contacts between the stock and the new scions. Secure them well and cover all cut surfaces with wax, including all surfaces of the original wounds to prevent disease and decay. If buds on the scions appear, keep removing them until all areas are healed and good growth has been established. This type of grafting is essential for saving trees whose cambium has been destroyed all the way around the trunk, for these trees have no continuous means to conduct nutrients and food to the upper parts of the plant and down to the roots, and would die if not grafted.

Inarching: This is another form of repair grafting, especially used for improving the root system of old damaged trees. With this method, seedlings or rooted cuttings are planted beside the older trees and are then grafted into the trunk to provide the old tree with a new set of roots. The seedlings for inarching are planted about five or six inches apart around the circumference of the tree, during the dormant period. Then, during the first period of active growth in the spring, start grafting. In the bark of the stock tree, cut long, shallow slits just the width of the scion seedlings. Make a long shallow cut along the side of each scion on the side facing the tree and cut the end in a wedge shape, cutting about ½ inch on both sides. Insert the tip under the bark. When in place, wax the whole area thoroughly.

Double grafting: Because some varieties of apple, for instance, are incompatible for single grafting, the method of double grafting has been devised. In the first year, a compatible scion is grafted onto the apple rootstock (usually by whip grafting or budding). Then, after a season's growth, a second graft is added to the first to resolve the incompatibility. This method can be used to provide a cold-resistant or disease-resistant stock for a desired tree, to get strong trunks or strong, wide crotches, or to obtain dwarf trees. When quince stock is used to dwarf Bartlett pears, an interstock is needed (because of incompatibility) in the form of another pear.

Top-grafting: This method is considered most appropriate for long-lived trees that have attained mature growth. Start with three or four small, secondary scaffold branches of three to four inches in diameter, well spaced around the tree and up and down the main trunk. After the branches are properly pruned, insert two to four scions in each. If the bark, whip, side, cleft, or notch and wedge graft method is used for insertion, the top-grafting should be done in the spring when the bark slips easily. The severe pruning involved in top-grafting may induce leaf burn and even death of the tree, but injury is less likely to happen if the work is done while the tree is still dormant and the weather is cool. Sometimes trees have been totally cut back, but then the scions are likely to become so succulent that they winterkill the following winter. Less drastic pruning is advised, especially on the south and west sides of the trees that are subject to sunburn. These would include the citrus fruits and olives, where spacing the pruning over two or three years will help, and also top-grafting on younger rather than older trees. This is the method that is also called top-working.

Herbaceous: Though used more by professional horticulturists than by amateurs, the grafting of herbaceous plants in the seedling stage is another possibility for practicing grafting. Since the material is very soft, only a simple splice graft is used, and for support and protection a small piece of thin polyethylene tubing is slipped over the stock and the scion fitted into it. Both stock and scion are given diagonal cuts at similar angles so they will fit well together. Healing is rapid, usually within about 12 days after the graft was made.

If slightly larger plants are used, a few leaves may be left on the stock in order to support its life systems. A cleft graft is used on a single scion, with a cut similar to that on the stock. The scion should have only one bud, and should be of exactly the same diameter as the stock. The union area is then bound with budding rubbers, raffia, or special adhesive latex tape called nurserymen's tape. It is best to stake such fragile materials. The graft usually heals in about 14 days.

Nurse-seed: This is the method frequently used to graft nut trees at experiment stations and in some nurseries. A scion is chosen from the previous year's growth in a dormant state. The petioles or leafstalks of the seed leaves or cotyledons, which in nut species such as chestnut and walnut or avocados are still inside the seed at the time of the grafting, serve as the stock. Insert the scion in a slit between the cotyledons so that it comes in contact with them, and place the plant in a rooting medium to grow. Camellias grafted this way achieve transplanting size as rapidly as those grafted by other methods.

Cutting: A final method of grafting is to choose as stock a cutting of the desired stock. The scion is inserted with a simple splice, on a slope of 30 degrees, and the union is tied with a rubber band. Cuttings are placed in a rooting medium, and stored in a humid

place. This method is used to propagate difficult conifers and rhododendrons as well as
to dwarf citrus trees. After about eight weeks,
when the graft union has healed, the top of the
stock is cut off and the grafted plant put in the
soil.

See also BUDDING, CUTTINGS, PRUNING.

GRAIN CROP

A grain crop is any cereal grain, including
barley, buckwheat, corn, rye, sorghums, and
wheat.

GRANITE DUST

Granite dust or granite stone meal is a
highly recommended natural source of potash.
Its potash content varies between 3 and 5 percent and sometimes more.

One of the first researches showing the
value of granite dust to plants took place at
the Connecticut Experimental Station. Tests
carried out there showed that the potash in
granite rock is available to a growing crop of
tobacco.

Potash rock is cheaper than chemical
potash fertilizers and leaves no harmful chemical residues. It also contains valuable trace
mineral elements. The common sources of
commercially available potash, such as sulfate,
nitrate, carbonate of potash, and ashes, all
have limitations in their usage.

Sulfate may cause a sulfur buildup in the
soil. In some areas, carbonate of potash and
ashes are unsatisfactory because of their alkaline effect on the soil. Granite dust, on the
other hand, causes no changes in soil pH and

releases its potash very slowly over a long
period of time.

Granite dust can be used as a topdressing,
worked directly into the soil or used when
establishing a cover crop. In the garden, suggested rates of application are ten pounds per
100 square feet; on the farm, two tons per
acre.

See also FERTILIZER, MINERAL ROCKS,
POTASH.

GRAPE   (*Vitis*)

Of all the fruits grown in America, grapes
are the most widely adapted to varying soils
and climates. Our first settlers found grapes
growing from the coast of Maine to Florida
and inland to the Rockies. Besides growing
over a wide area, no fruit offers so many different flavors or is more delicious. Grapes are
one of nature's oldest and most healthful fruits,
and, being easy to grow, should be included in
every home planting.

Location: Almost any garden can produce good grapes. Selection of a favorite site
for planting is important and the best is one
that has a gentle slope to provide good air circulation. Low frosty pockets should be avoided
because of the danger of injury from spring
frosts. Plant where the vines will receive full
sun and away from trees so that they will not
have to compete for moisture and other elements necessary for growth. Where growing
seasons are very short, ripening can be hastened by planting on the south side of a building and training the vine against it. Heat
radiation from reflected sunlight will make the
fruit ripen as much as a week earlier than those
planted in the open.

Grapes are not particular as to soils. As long as they are well drained and fairly deep, they grow well on both heavy and light soils. A soil of average fertility is best because too rich soils stimulate cane growth causing poorly formed clusters. A slightly acid soil is best but good growth and production are possible on neutral soils.

Since grape roots grow deeply into the soil, they are able to find moisture even in dry weather. The best insurance against a dry soil is a long-range program of nutrients released from manures, mulches and rock phosphate. Waste hay, straw, sawdust, wood chips, and other organic materials should be applied every other year.

Green manure crops such as buckwheat and clover planted between rows will aid the organic fertility program.

Planting: Planting can be done either in spring or fall. Spring planting can be done from March through May, but it is better to plant as early in spring as the ground can be worked. Late October or early November is the best time for fall planting.

Usual spacing is eight by eight feet, but if space is limited a seven-foot spacing will do. Holes should be dug 12 to 14 inches deep and 16 inches in diameter. To prevent drying of the roots, leave a slight depression around the stalk to hold rainwater. Before planting, the top should be pruned back to a single cane and this cut back so two buds remain. Delay pruning the top until spring. Instead, simply cut away any broken roots and those that are too long to fit in the hole.

First-year growth can be allowed to trail over the ground. In the winter, however, place posts about every 15 feet along the row, with two wires, one about two feet off the ground, the other 5½ feet above ground. Train the vines to these wires.

Pruning: Grapes develop on the growth of the current year. Buds left on the vine at pruning time will produce fruit in summer. Year-old wood is the best yielder of fruit. If you keep these ideas in mind, pruning will be simple.

Each fall, cut out the branch that produced fruit last year, thereby leaving a new, year-old arm near the main trunk. This cane will provide the fruit for the following year. Cut back the branching vines at every node to about one or two buds. Also leave a vine that has been cut back to one or two buds near the base of the arm. From this vine will grow the cane that will be saved next year for the following season. New vines will begin bearing fruit five to six years after being set.

Propagation: Layering is a simple way of producing new vines for the home vineyard. Simply bury a portion of a low-growing vine about two inches beneath the soil surface. After that piece roots, cut it from the mother vine and transplant it.

Cuttings from year-old wood should be about a foot long, with two nodes on the ends and one in the middle. The cutting may be transplanted immediately after it is taken from the mother plant. Plant the cutting in the ground leaving two of the nodes subsurface. From these two nodes new roots will form.

It is important to plant the cutting right side up, i.e., the part toward the base of the vine should be planted in the ground, while the part near the end of the vine should remain above ground. To avoid confusion when planting, cut the basal end at a slant below the node, and the top end straight across, or vice versa, whichever you prefer. Should moisture

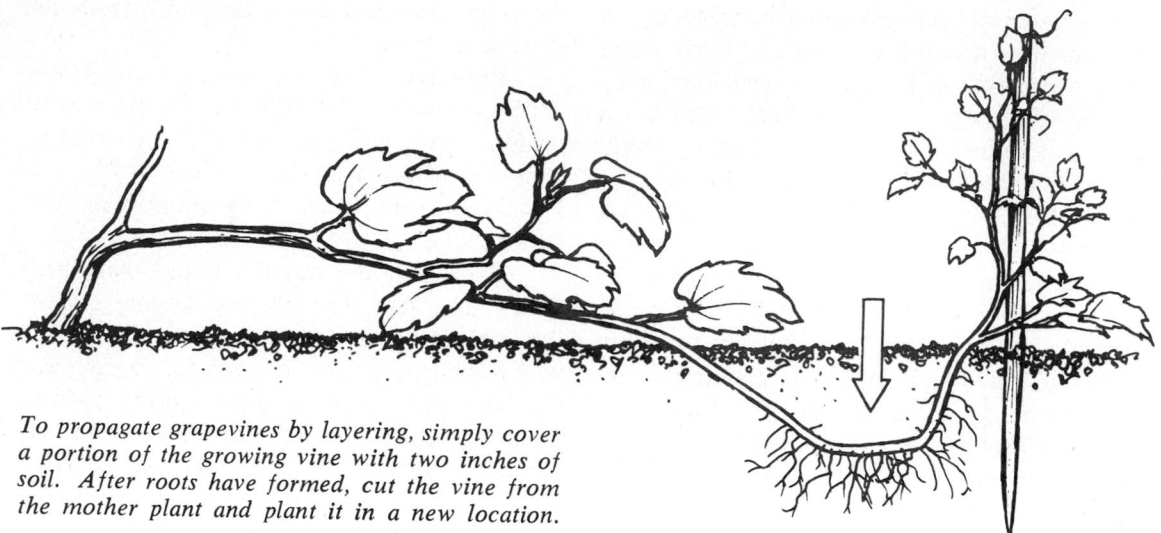

To propagate grapevines by layering, simply cover a portion of the growing vine with two inches of soil. After roots have formed, cut the vine from the mother plant and plant it in a new location.

be at a premium during warm weather, supply your own with mulch and watering.

Harvest: Grapes should be harvested only when ripe. They will keep well on the vine if not picked immediately. Beware of hungry bees which may be lunching on the inside of a grape. Indication of ripe fruit is a browning of the stem of the bunch.

Fresh grapes can be stored on trays and kept in humid, cool cellars for several months. Be sure to use only firm fruit and store in an area that will maintain an optimum temperature of 40°F. (4.44°C.).

Varieties: Of the slip-skin types, Concord is the most famous. Other blue black grapes include Fredonia, Wordon, Beta, Van Buren, and Steuben. These are adaptable varieties and productive in northern climates.

Delaware is a favorite red. The Caco, an amber red, is suitable to northern climates. Catawba is another red used frequently for wines.

Niagara is a popular white variety. Seedless white varieties include Interlaken, Himrod, Lakemont, and Romulus. These types are more susceptible to mildew than Concord Seeders.

For wine makers, Cascade is a variety that rates high in mildew resistance. For Burgundy wines, Foch and Baco Noir are both hardy and mildew resistant. Aurora and Villard Blanc are recommended for white wine making.

Diseases and Pests: Grapes are much less subject to attacks of insects and diseases than most other fruits, though birds can be a major nuisance. By placing paper bags over the clusters when they have developed and rubber-banding the free end, pecking birds will be discouraged. On a larger scale, it is often necessary to cover the vineyard with netting. Some growers use loud clackers, shotgun blanks rigged to detonate periodically, and recordings of distress calls to keep birds at bay. Outdoor cats can also help.

The Japanese beetle can be controlled by

brushing the pests into jars and disposing of them. Milky spore disease, a beneficial fungus disease that attacks the beetle in its grub stage, is also effective.

Black rot, visible as tiny spots appearing on green grapes, can be controlled only by effective pruning, which permits good aeration. Resistant varieties are always indicated to combat mildews and rot. Pick off dried fruit in which the disease overwinters and add it to the compost heap. Compost made from the diseased fruit will aid the vines in resisting black rot fungus.

The grape berry moth moves through the cluster by consuming the inside of one berry, then moving on to the next. A dusting of rotenone provides effective control.

GRAPE ARBOR   *See* ARBOR

GRAPE BERRY MOTH
See INSECT CONTROL

GRAPEFRUIT   (*Citrus* x *paradisi*)

Largest of the Citrus family both in tree and fruit size, the grapefruit is not especially suited to the small home garden—although it may be successfully grown in favorable climate and soil areas. Like the orange, lemon and lime, the tree is an evergreen, has dark green glossy-topped leaves, large white flowers and fruit up to six inches or more in diameter. Also termed a pomelo, this fruit is generally round, with a thick, smooth peel and juicy flesh divided into many segments.

Originating in the West Indies, the grapefruit was introduced here first in Florida. California, Texas and Arizona also produce a share of the nation's supply.

Grapefruit trees grow vigorously, and when mature are better able to withstand cold than other citrus types. Their care and culture are similar to that of the citrus fruits in general.

Grapefruits have been grown successfully as house plants. Seed should be soaked in a cup of water overnight and then planted in pots of compost-rich soil. Do not plant the seed too deeply, for grapefruit roots are long and need the space available to them in the pot.

Cultivars include the Marsh, which has a less acid pulp and juice than others, although its fruit size is smaller; Duncan, Ellen, Innman, and McCarty, which are better sized but contain many seeds; and Foster, Thompson and Redblush which are popular pink-fleshed varieties.

See also CITRUS.

GRAPEFRUIT WASTE
See CITRUS WASTE

GRAPE HYACINTH   (*Muscari*)

This hardy, spring-flowering perennial of the Lily family is easy to grow if given a loose, deep rich soil and a sunny location. Bulbs should be planted in early fall about three inches deep and apart. Common grape hyacinth (*M. botryoides*) grows to about ten inches and has white flowers. *M. armeniacum* has dark purple flowers. Tassel hyacinth, *M. comosum,* is somewhat taller with spikes of brown to blue flowers. *M. Tubergenianum* is a Persian species in which the clear blue flowers at the top of the spike contrast pleasantly with the deeper blue flowers at the bottom.

GRAPE POMACE

Grape pomace is the leftovers from wine making. Besides the pressed parts of the grape, pomace contains a varied bacterial flora, especially yeasts; about 1 percent nitrogen; and smaller amounts of phosphorus and potassium. Such material should be treated like other green matter in the composting process. The seed of grapes contain valuable stored elements that will break down without much trouble through the action of fungi. It is heir to the same disadvantages as apple pomace. *See also* APPLE POMACE.

GRASS   *See* LAWN

GRASS CLIPPINGS

Almost everyone who has a garden also has a lawn and therefore a regular supply of grass clippings. If the grass is cut once a week it is sound practice to leave the clippings right on the lawn so that they may become natural humus as they would under field conditions; but sometimes, the growth is heavy or rain prevents regular cutting, so that leaving a heavy crop of clippings would lead to wads of yellow hay covering parts of the lawn. In that case, rake the material up and add it to the compost heap as part of the green matter. By the time the lawn is cut and the grass is raked it is sufficiently wilted to start heating soon. Don't remove all grass clippings. Some can and should be left as occasional replenishment for the lawn itself.

Grass clippings are no different from hay except in the matter of curing. The quality of the soil and the maturity of the growth have much to do with the nutritive content of the residues. A fertile soil rich in nitrogen and phosphorus produces a grass richer in nitrogen than a poor light soil. Grass cut before blooming is richer in nutrients than grass that has grown long stalks with flower heads or, worse still, that has set seed and turned into straw.

Dried green grass has a higher phosphorous and potash content than hay if the latter has been weathered long. Kentucky bluegrass hay, for example, analyzes at 1.2 percent nitrogen, .3 percent phosphoric acid and 2 percent potash. Timothy is a bit lower, perennial ryegrass often noticeably higher. Redtop analyses show a relatively high percentage of phosphorus. A mixed lawn, composed of several grasses, represents over a pound of nitrogen and two pounds of potash for every 100 pounds of clippings in the dry state.

Uses for Clippings: Grass clippings can play an important role in soil improvement. First of all, a good lawn doesn't need as much enrichment, added organic matter or mulching as do more heavily cropped plots. As a rich source of nitrogen, the clippings should be utilized to the utmost. There are three excellent ways in which they can be put to work in the garden and flower beds: They may be used as a mulch; they may be turned in as green manure; and they may be used in the compost heap to create the heat necessary for good decomposition.

Mulch: As a mulch, lawn clippings surpass most materials. They are easy to handle, will remain in place nicely, will fit in the smallest spaces with no trouble, and when dried, will give your rows and beds a neat appearance. Of course you will not have enough mulch for your entire garden from the first cutting, but mulch as much as you can each week. It is a good idea to mulch first those vegetables that mature early, then work on the others. Because they are so finely chopped, the clippings disappear completely into the soil by fall.

Green mulch may temporarily rob the soil of available nitrogen, including both ammonia and nitrates. But this condition is so short-lived that it will not stunt the rapid growth of the plants. *See also* MULCH.

Green manure: Late in the season, you may have a surplus of grass clippings on your hands. If you have empty space in the garden, scatter a few inches of green clippings over the entire area. Turn these in immediately as green manure along with the previously applied mulch. Work a small plot at a time, depending upon the amount of excess clippings on hand. Later, you may remulch the entire area and allow it to remain until the following spring.

If you wish, you can turn in green grass clippings as green manure before planting a second crop in a vacant plot. Give the section a week or ten days to return to normal, then plant as before. Many times, the second crop surpasses the first.

When used as green manure, grass clippings greatly improve the physical condition of heavy-textured soils. They also provide much-needed humus and nitrogen. If acidity is a factor, a small amount of limestone may be applied with the clippings. *See also* GREEN MANURE.

Compost: A third use of grass clippings is to incorporate them into the compost pile to give necessary heat for proper decomposition.

Use two-thirds grass clippings and one-third stable manure or other high-nitrogen material. *See also* COMPOSTING.

GRASSHOPPER

A number of species of grasshopper are found in the United States but not all of them are of economic importance. Those that are, cause a problem that goes beyond the actual amount of greenery they eat, as they chew through stems and leaves to cause large portions of plants to fall to the ground.

Fall tillage, right after harvest, makes the ground unattractive to egg-laying hoppers and exposes eggs already deposited. Plow under weedy margins of fields or garden, and replace the wild growth with a perennial grass. A good layer of compost or mulch will keep many of the newly hatched from surfacing in spring. Seedlings can be protected by laying cheesecloth over the rows.

Good field sanitation practices, fall tillage, cover cropping, and mulching can help to avoid an infestation of grasshoppers.

If your crops are in trouble right now, try a hot pepper spray; use hot pepper pods, pure soap and water. A simple trap can be made by half filling two-quart mason jars with one part molasses in ten parts water.

Grasshoppers are vulnerable to a great number of natural enemies, from birds, snakes and skunks to certain fly maggots, beetles and red mites.

GRASSLAND FARMING

Grassland farming is an agricultural system which emphasizes the importance of grasses and legumes as livestock feed and in land management. Of course, grassland farming differs in different parts of the country because climate and soil differ, necessitating different crops and different methods of growing them, but the principles are the same. Grassland farming is understood as a long-term program aimed at increased production from improved grasslands and more efficient use of a high-quality forage, rich in all food values.

At the same time, the grassland farming system de-emphasizes the use of cash crops, preferring forage production and utilization with livestock. This requires different skills and a higher level of management on the part of the farmer, but can result in higher profits and more benefits to the land.

Grassland farming is based primarily on legumes and grasses: alfalfa, timothy, red clover, fescue, wheatgrass, bird's-foot trefoil, ladino clover, lespedeza, vetch, smooth bromegrass, and orchardgrass are quite important. Such crops generally conserve and improve soil structure, acting as a primary means of controlling erosion. They improve both soil tilth and fertility, and increase the water-ab-sorbing and water-holding capacity of the soil, both while growing and after harvest, when used as mulch or turned under as a green manure. In addition, grassland agriculture is beneficial because it is adaptable to a wide variety of soils and climates, providing a more comprehensive use of land resources.

See also entries for individual grasses and legumes.

GRASS-OF-PARNASSUS
See PARNASSIA

GRASS, ORNAMENTAL

Ornamental grasses range in height from short, tufted varieties to grasses that grow to ten feet or more. Ornamental grasses are chosen for their beautiful forms; their waving feathery plumes and soft pastel colors are ideal with the bolder colors grown in the garden. When cut and dried, many of them are suitable for winter decorations in the home.

Seed for the perennial varieties are readily available. They are easily grown, and develop rapidly. Others may be increased by division—one large clump of grasses can be cut into three or four pieces. When planted, these will soon grow to make nice-sized clumps. Divide the clumps in early spring as soon as the soil can be worked. This method works best with the variegated varieties since most of them will not come true from seed.

When planting clumps of grasses, allow at least a foot between plants. The clumps will rapidly fill the intervening spaces. As the perennials grow they will either require more space, or will have to be thinned regularly.

Annual varieties are easily raised from seed sown in early spring where plants are to stand. Thin to about ten inches apart when plants are quite small, allowing plenty of room to grow. A common mistake in growing ornamental grasses is not to allot enough room for growth.

Some ornamental grasses do well in a dry location; others love water and cast beautiful reflections in pools or brooks. These grasses generally do well in any good soil with plenty of humus worked in around the roots in both spring and fall. Most of the grasses will adapt themselves to the soil condition and, given all the room they need, will grow into their full grace of height and form.

Popular Varieties: Beachgrass (*Ammophila*) is a genus of tall-growing perennial grasses suited for the edge of pools or along streams. It is a good sand binder. Sow seed where plants are to stand. When the plants attain the height of four to five inches, thin to eight inches apart. *A. arenaria* (marramgrass, sand reed or psamma) grows to three feet and has panicled flowers growing to one foot, with long branching rootstocks.

Blue fescue (*Festuca ovina* var. *glauca*) provides fine blue gray foliage about nine inches high, and does well in a dry location. Sandy soil and moderate shade are needed for this beautiful little edging plant.

Cloudgrass (*Agrostis nebulosa*) is like a soft, fine hair. It grows to 18 inches tall and likes a dry situation. Quakinggrass (*Briza*), growing to one foot, has spikelets that are flat and tremble in the slightest breeze. Bromegrass (*Bromus*) is distinguished by drooping spikelets that resemble those of the quakinggrass. It grows to two feet, and is often a biennial.

Eulalia (*Miscanthus sinenis*) is the best ornamental grass for northern regions. Once established, it will remain for years. Good soil and enough moisture will develop this grass into attractive clumps for border or around the lawn. The leaves are three feet long and one inch wide, and have a large central vein which is a ridgelike extension of the petiole or main ridge on the leaflike part. The panicles of silky plumes grow as long as two feet. The leaves of variety Variegatus have white or yellow stripes. Zebragrass (*M. s.* cv. 'Zebrinus') has yellow-banded leaves.

The giant reed (*Arundo Donax*) is the largest of the grasses, excepting the bamboos. It is a perennial but will need some protection in the North. The plant grows from eight to 20 feet and is the source of reeds for woodwind instruments. It bears loose, feathery flower spikes one to two feet long, creating a handsome border.

Hare's-tail grass (*Lagurus ovatus*), also called rabbit-tail grass, is an excellent edging plant, doing especially well in a sunny location having well-drained soil. It grows to a height of one foot, with leaves two inches long and less than ½ inch wide. The flower clusters or spikelets are two inches long, rather broad, and have dense woolly heads or panicles. The plants are attractive in the garden and also make very attractive bouquets.

Lovegrasses (*Eragrostis*)—some annual, some perennial—are valued for their ornamental sprays of delicate beauty. The small panicles are carried in open spikelets, growing four to 15 inches long. *E. elegans, E. interrupta* and *E. tenella* all grow to three feet and are very useful in dried bouquets.

Pampasgrass (*Cortaderia*) grows in thick tussocks with slender basal leaves. It sends up stalks six to 12 feet high crowned with ample, silky flower heads. Easy to raise from seed, pampasgrass is especially practical and attractive for unsightly areas because it grows high enough to serve as an effective screen. Moreover, it serves handsomely as a decorative accent plant anywhere in the garden.

Although actually a perennial, pampasgrass is not reliably hardy in severe climates, and so must be treated as an annual in these regions. Sow seed as early as possible in the spring and then place the seedlings in a sunny, well-drained location.

The beautiful silky plumes of pampasgrass reach full maturity in August (even in Maine where seasons are short) and remain lovely for weeks. They may be either white or pink, and make perfect additions to dried collections.

In warmer climes where pampasgrass remains a perennial, it may be used in small clumps for permanent screens or unique lawn accents.

The genus *Pennisetum* includes grasses native to the tropics and subtropics, that are grown for their ornamental foliage. There are both annual and perennial varieties and both are good garden subjects. Seed started indoors or in the hotbed will get an earlier start than those planted out-of-doors. They prefer a sandy loam in a well-drained soil and a sheltered site. In the fall the plants may be lifted and placed in the cellar or under glass. *P. alopecuroides* has dark brown foxtail plumes tipped white. *P. setaceum* grows to four feet and has narrow leaves one foot long. The flower spikes, a foot or more in length, are purple, coppery red and rose.

Plumegrass (*Erianthus*) is hardy from southern New York south. This genus of the perennial grasses is tall, attaining the height of ten to 12 feet in a single season. Ravenna-grass (*E. ravennae*) is the tallest, has leaves three feet long and about ½ inch wide, and displays a plumelike flower which grows to about three feet long.

Ribbongrass (*Phalaris arundinacea* var. *picta*), striped green and white, grows to about five feet tall and forms thick clumps in the border.

Another popular ornamental grass is the silvery beardgrass (*Andropogon saccharoides*), growing to about three feet. It bears silver plumes which are good for drying, and offers an effective contrast in the winter bouquet.

Spearneedle or feathergrass (*Stipa* spp.) grows from two to seven feet, having rolling leaves at the edges, while the spikelets are borne in clusters. Australian stipa, *S. elegantissima,* bears purple bearded spikelets in loose clusters half the height of the plant. Most species are perennials.

Spikegrasses (*Uniola latifolia* and *U. paniculata*) are native perennial grasses. The former, a native of America, grows to five feet in height. Planted for landscape effects, it is ideal as a background for a border planting, and is hardy from Pennsylvania to Texas. The latter species is often called sea oats and is native to the warmer, coastal regions of the southern United States. It grows four to eight feet high and thrives in sandy soils.

GRASS PINK   *See* DIANTHUS

GREENHOUSES

Traditionally defined as any glass-roofed building or adjoining structure whose purpose is to contain plants, today's greenhouse comes in a variety of sizes, shapes and compositions.

There are several advantages that all-year gardening greenhouses afford. Summer and fall crop yields can be stretched one season longer, often through the otherwise deadly winter season. Gardeners also use their greenhouses to gain a head start on springtime planting.

Another important plus to greenhouse gardening comes with the opportunity to control the growing environment. Frosts, blizzards, rainstorms, heat waves, and other weather nuisances can be virtually ignored behind the protection of greenhouse windows and walls.

Further, there is the therapeutic value of home gardening. Tending fresh fruits, vegetables and ornamental flowers throughout the year is considered by many doctors to be a tranquilizer for daily stress and work tension.

Greenhouses today fall into several general categories: *attached* (units adjoining the house, including window box, basement, patio, or sunporch greenhouses) or *freestanding* (full-sized units separate from the house, either above or partially below grade).

The Attached Greenhouse: The gardener seeking to minimize construction and maintenance expenses, and possibly even capture some heat for the house, may find that an attached greenhouse is more suitable than a freestanding one.

To be most effective, a south wall of the house should be chosen for this type of greenhouse. The spot should not be heavily shaded by trees or other buildings, but it should be protected from strong winds that could chill the greenhouse and possibly weaken it structurally. Greenhouse designers and builders

agree that the most efficient use of space and solar heat gain can be obtained by making the length of an attached house about twice as great as its width.

Supplemental heating can be minimized—or eliminated entirely—by taking advantage of some features that are being incorporated into new solar and energy-efficient houses, namely, the use of multiple-layer glazing; nighttime insulating shutters, curtains and shades; and the addition of thermal mass, such as concrete, stone, or brick floors and house walls and

With a few small heating cables, an extended southeastern window can be converted into an inexpensive, year-round greenhouse.

water- or rock-filled containers to store solar heat during the night and on cloudy days.

A truly efficient attached greenhouse can actually provide heat for the house in winter. Vents near the floor allow cool house air to enter the greenhouse, where it is warmed and then circulated back into the house by means of another vent near the ceiling of the greenhouse. Since warm air naturally rises, no fan is necessary in many instances to move this air. Such venting not only helps to warm the house, but it also permits good air flow throughout the greenhouse, raises the humidity of the house and distributes plant-loving carbon dioxide from the house to the greenhouse. Of course, vents to the house should be closed during the summer months, and vents from the greenhouse to the outdoors should be opened during this time so that neither the house nor the greenhouse gets overheated.

Although space in the attached greenhouse is limited by the upright building wall, every inch can be put to work by the use of plant benches, ground beds, eave shelves, ledges, and hanging baskets. The straight-sided lean-to makes it possible to grow tall plants close to the glass. Straight sides accommodate eave shelves better too, and they provide better ventilation and temperature control. The straight-sided houses are somewhat more expensive, however, because there is more glass area. On the other hand, slanting sides capture more sunshine.

Window greenhouse: This variety is one of several "mini-greenhouses" designed to produce healthy flowers and herbs at a low cost. Window greenhouses are also used for starting seed in winter and spring before transplanting into the outdoor garden.

Almost any window opening into the house can be used for these small conservatories attached to a windowsill and framing. For gardeners planning to use the window greenhouse year-round, a southeast-facing window is recommended. This direction will obtain ample sunlight even in winter. Small heating units which fit into the window extension, or heating cables, may be used to keep the greenhouse sufficiently warm, and insulating shutters or shades can be pulled over the glass at night.

Galvanized trays one inch deep are recommended for the window unit. These trays can be filled with gravel and kept moist in order to maintain adequate humidity.

Basement greenhouse: From the outside, a basement greenhouse looks like a sloping cold frame built against the foundation. Inside, it is an alcove in the cellar wall, with a concrete floor raised above the basement floor. Like the foundation, it is built of concrete blocks.

The floor should be at least 3½ feet above the basement floor because of the sharp angle of the midwinter sun. The foundation wall in front should be about two inches higher than the greenhouse floor to prevent water from running out on the cellar floor. This front wall should be finished with a neat concrete cap that makes an attractive shelf or parapet for displaying plants in the foreground.

A shelf placed beneath the glass at one end is used for sun-loving plants and can be duplicated at the other end. The greenhouse should face south, southeast or southwest. With only one hot air vent in the basement, the temperature should stay between 55 and 60°F. (12.78 and 15.56°C.).

The Freestanding Greenhouse: To many people, freestanding greenhouses offer distinct advantages. Although their typically all-glass composition often translates into a 25 percent hike in heating bills, and they require extra expenditures for wire and pipes, the estimated 50 percent addition of plant-growing space over attached greenhouses is ample compensation. Other advantages are that most of these greenhouses can catch sunlight from every direction, and they are more adaptable for ground beds. The more energy-efficient freestanding greenhouses have north walls built

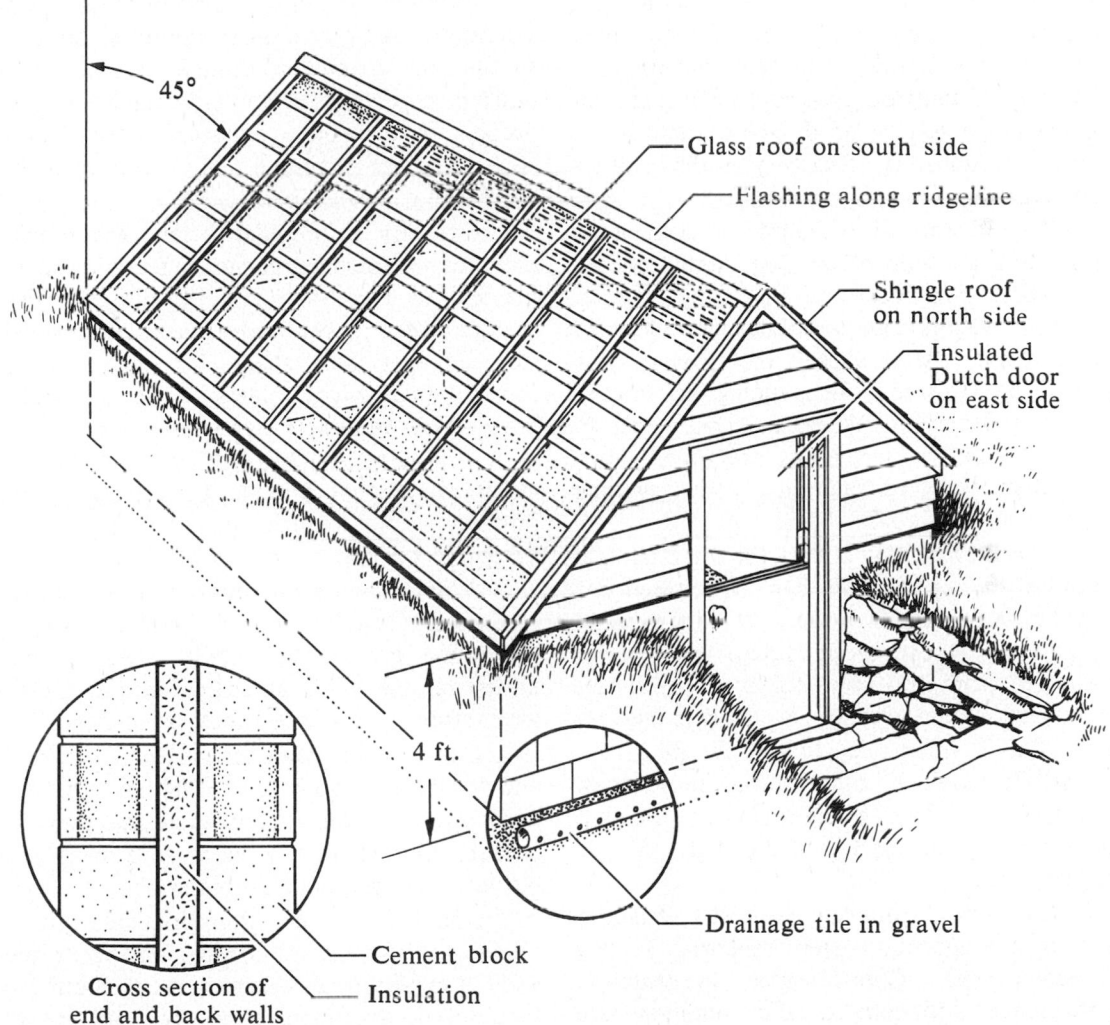

45°

Glass roof on south side

Flashing along ridgeline

Shingle roof on north side

Insulated Dutch door on east side

4 ft.

Drainage tile in gravel

Cement block

Insulation

Cross section of end and back walls

Unless winter temperatures fall well below zero, the pit-type greenhouse needs only the sun for heat. Double walls provide adequate insulation. After sunset, the glass roof can be covered with thick pads and tarpaulins for further protection.

into a hillside or have floors which are a few feet below ground level. Many people refer to these as pit greenhouses.

The pit-type house, except for severe sub-zero (F.) weather, is sun heated. The only additional heat needed under conditions of extreme cold is usually a 200-watt electric light bulb or a small electric heater. Temperatures in the pit-type house make daily watering unnecessary. Usually only the south side is glassed in, and this is set at a 45-degree angle to admit the most sunshine. Ordinary hotbed sashes can be used.

To add warmth to the pit house, the ends and unglassed side should be double walled with about 3½ inches of insulating material between. Doors and ventilators should also be insulated. After sunset, the glassed areas should be covered with padding or another insulated covering. When pads are used to cover the sashes, tarpaulins are rolled down over them to keep them dry. Wet padding makes poor insulation.

The Dutch door is best for the pit house because the upper half can be opened for ventilation during the winter. The door should be at the east end of the house to be better protected from prevailing cold westerly winds. A ventilating window can be placed at the west end. This is most important in the pit greenhouse. It should be open during the warmest hours of every day. Some pit houses use sky-light openings on the top of the unglassed side for ventilation.

Location: Choosing the best greenhouse site is an important step requiring several considerations. Convenience, accessibility, yard space, and general land conditions are variables to consider. Attached greenhouses enable the gardener to enter the greenhouse quickly and easily through adjoining, enclosed entrances. They best suit gardeners with little yard space, but with sunlit basements, large windows and sills suitable for a small green-house "box," or enclosed porches. Freestanding greenhouses should be located in more spacious environments, and where they can be exposed to ample sunlight.

Exposure to sunlight is an important consideration. All greenhouses should be situated so that the maximum dosage of sunlight is utilized, especially in winter when it is most needed. A three-hour exposure of sunlight is considered the minimum daily requirement for most plants during winter.

Contrary to popular belief, the precise direction in which a greenhouse faces is usually not a crucial consideration. If the ends face east and west, plants on the greenhouse's north side may get more shade, but this is not a shortcoming. Many plants thrive on shade. Some plants in attached greenhouses grow best in a southern, southeastern or southwestern exposure, in that order. Western exposures provide ample sunlight but lack the shade needed in summer.

A more important consideration is the direction of prevailing winds. Hinged doors of the home greenhouse should always swing away from the wind, rather than into it. Otherwise, strong gusts will knock them down.

Construction Materials: Once the style and location of your future greenhouse have been selected, construction materials must be chosen. Gardeners can select from many film plastic, fiberglass and glass materials.

Above ground: Prefabricated green-houses are usually about nine, ten or 13 feet wide. Lengths are in sash sections of about 2½ feet, so the greenhouses can be built in any length. They come with slanted or straight sides. These greenhouses are made in sash panels that can be put together with a screw-driver, wrench and hammer. All the parts are furnished, cut to fit in place. The glass is cut to size and is not putty glazed. It goes into glass grooves in the sash and is held weathertight with a special caulking rope.

While the prices for the materials for a prefabricated greenhouse are higher than parts such as glazing bars, sills, eaves, ridge and fittings of a conventional-type greenhouse, the time they save in labor greatly offsets the difference.

Greenhouses with polyethylene film or plastic instead of glass are becoming popular for reasons of economy. They are light, so require less rigid supports, but they can rip in heavy winds and the constant exposure to strong sunlight causes them to deteriorate in as short a period as six months. Thin, flexible films are best used as inner glazing only under thicker plastics or glass. More information about plastic greenhouses is available in USDA Bulletin #357. Write Superintendent of Documents, U.S. Government Printing Office, North Capitol and H Sts. NW, Washington, DC 20402.

Fiberglass is another popular alternative in greenhouse construction. It is a sturdy and transparent material, especially when coated with Tedlar. Fiberglass also makes a good heat insulator, retaining up to 70.8 times more heat than polyethylene film and some plastics. Fiberglass houses provide natural shade, even during intense sun exposure. Fiberglass has its shortcomings as well, however. It is highly flammable and often wears down, reducing light transmission and increasing dust and dirt accumulation.

Rigid acrylics come closest to resembling glass, but they are easier to work with because they are five times lighter than glass and don't break as easily.

Glass has a tendency to turn brittle and crack, and while it is good-looking when clean,

it is a difficult material for do-it-yourselfers to work with.

For many homemade greenhouses, a suitable aluminum or wooden frame must be selected. Although redwood frames are less expensive than aluminum, they require treating every few years. Aluminum frames, however, are virtually maintenance-free.

Foundation: The walls below the sills of the greenhouse are the hardest part to build. Masonry walls are best because they are more permanent than those of wood. They also offer some thermal mass for heat retention. Poured concrete, brick, cut stone, or cinder blocks may be used. Cinder blocks provide the easiest means of building a wall. For appearance's sake, the outside can be coated with stucco and painted. The attractiveness of a greenhouse depends a great deal upon its walls, for this is the largest solid area.

If you live in the northern United States, the walls of a prefabricated greenhouse should extend below the freezing line. This would be about 2½ feet in most areas but may be less in the southern states and more in the far North. The footings below the ground can be of poured concrete and gravel. A conventional-type greenhouse is built with steel posts set on footings and encased in piers that extend below grade. The side walls need only go down to solid ground, a few inches below the grade.

After the greenhouse has been selected, located and constructed, the continual task of greenhouse management begins. Managing the greenhouse can be divided into two categories: controlling of the greenhouse climate and handling of the plants.

Heating and Cooling: The key to controlling the climate indoors is regulating the temperature to simulate the outdoors. Heartier plants grow best when temperatures tend toward cool. In excessively warm environments, greenhouse plants grow rapidly, but become vulnerable to mildew and insect infestation.

The proper heating system for your greenhouse depends largely upon the climate and temperature range. Solar greenhouses that are double- or triple-glazed, built on the south wall of a building or earth bermed on the north side, fitted with insulating shutters for use at night and on cloudy days, and designed to include as much concrete or brick as possible for thermal mass, may need no supplemental heat at all. Other solar greenhouses may be fitted with solar collectors that warm water or air for supplemental heat.

In areas that seldom get colder than 20°F. (-6.67°C.), more traditional greenhouses may need only an electric heater. The heater is inexpensive and can come equipped with an automatic thermostat to turn on the heating element and fan.

For colder environments, gas or hot-water heating systems are necessary in traditional greenhouses. A no-vent gas unit for heating is highly recommended by many gardeners, since it creates no noxious fumes and costs a few hundred dollars. Coal or wood-burning furnaces can also be used to heat greenhouses.

Some suggestions for conserving fuel include keeping the greenhouse as airtight as possible; using two outside doors and having one serve as a storm door; using mulch to insulate and retain heat; installing heavy-gauge aluminum foil between the heat source and the outside wall to reflect and retain heat; and planting a windbreak of trees and shrubs nearby to retain heat and protect against wind turbulence.

The most important companion to any greenhouse heating system is ventilation. Without fans to circulate air, the greenhouse temperature can vary from 45°F. (7.22°C.) on the ground, to over 90°F. (32.22°C.) near the roof in winter. Mount the fan so that it will blow away from the heat source to the floor and sides of the greenhouse. This way, warmer air will mix with cool air and pick up needed moisture in the process. Proper air circulation is an important safeguard against plant disease and infections, since it reduces excess condensation, fungus and mildew buildup.

Never build a greenhouse too small. In a small area, it is impossible to maintain an even temperature and a healthy atmospheric condition. On sunny days, even in the winter, the temperature in a four-by-six-foot greenhouse would run over 100°F. (37.78°C.) in a matter of a few minutes. Then at night when the sun goes down, it would cool off just as rapidly. Plants will not grow under such conditions.

There are several ways to save room when planning your home greenhouse. Installing shelf hangers on sash bars or gable ends is one space saver. Double-deck benches work well for greenhouses containing at least three benches, where the upper deck covers the middle bench. Shade-loving plants such as coleus, begonias and impatiens grow well under these decks or under any benches in the greenhouse.

Shade must be provided during summer months in the greenhouse, in order to protect plants which cannot be set outside. Bamboo or slatted matting may be spread over the roof, or the glass may be whitewashed. By autumn, most of the whitewash will have flaked off, and the balance can be removed with a brush.

Finally, maintain a humid atmosphere for greenhouse plants. Relative humidity should be about 60 percent. Excessive humidity invites plant diseases and decreased fruit and flower production. Insufficient humidity in the green-

Suspended from the greenhouse roof, plants such as this ivy geranium benefit from the increased air circulation and exposure to sunlight.
(*Courtesy of Longwood Gardens*)

house hastens development of flowers and fruit at the expense of leaf growth. To increase humidity, the gardener can install mist systems, plastic sheets or glass panes over seed flats or benches.

Handling of Greenhouse Plants: In caring for your plants, try to simulate all conditions favorable to the plants' growth and development needs. If this demands a period of rest in the garden, a period should be allowed in the greenhouse. Sun, shade and soil requirements outdoors should be duplicated as much as possible in the greenhouse.

Soil: Concocting the proper soil mixtures is another important requirement for the successful greenhouse gardener. Good soil is an investment in the well-being of greenhouse crops, and it should be well fertilized and cultivated for that reason. Rich topsoil with living organisms, dead organic matter and a porous texture is best for hardy plant growth. Medium-texture soils, rather than fine or coarse compositions, are best for holding moisture, air and soil nutrients. Adding organic matter to sandy soils improves water and mineral retention, as well as helping loosen clay soils.

For most greenhouses, a loam soil is recommended, because of its good drainage and aeration. Greenhouse soils today are often mixes, high in organic matter content. A good mix for bench or potted plants is two parts topsoil, one part sphagnum peat moss and one part sand or horticultural perlite. Another common soil mixture is one part soil, one part peat moss and one part vermiculite, coarse sand or perlite. Whichever soil mixture is selected, it always should be kept fairly moist, in order to sustain the living organisms inside.

Many fertilizers and additives offer vital nutrition to organic matter in greenhouse soils. Poultry and rabbit manures are packed with nitrogen, phosphorus and humus. Both are applied at the rate of eight to ten pounds per 100 square feet of bench planting space. Sheep, cow and horse manures are organic fertilizers which add humus and make good soil conditioners.

Bone meal is a slow-releasing plant fertilizer. The steamed variety breaks down quicker for plant nutrition than raw bone meal.

Lime and wood ashes help neutralize highly acidic soils. Sawdust and wood chips complement successful potted plant propagation. The chips repel snails and provide good drainage.

PLANTING PLAN FOR YEAR-ROUND GREENHOUSE BLOOM

Flower	Seeding Dates	Blooming Period
Arctotis stoechadifolia	April	July-October
Begonia, fibrous rooted	February	January-March
Begonia, tuberous rooted	January and February	August-October
Browallia speciosa cv. 'Major'	February Cuttings—March	October-May
Calceolaria	May	May and June
Calendula	August	February-April
Campanula isophylla	July and August	July-September
Campanula Medium	May	February-April
Celosia	March	August-October
Chrysanthemum	Cuttings—December- March	November-January
Clarkia	August	March-May
Cyclamen, triumph hybrids	August or February	November-March
Dianthus Caryophyllus, perpetual flowering	Cuttings—December- March	October-March
Francoa ramosa	March-May	April-July
Gardenia	Cuttings—March	November- February
Geranium, winter flowering	Cuttings—March	November-March
Gesneria	February	September and October
Gloxinia	February	June-August
Helipterum Manglesii	January	April and May

Peat moss, which puts humus into the soil and holds nutrients particularly well, makes a fine soil conditioner, rather than a fertilizer. Moisten peat thoroughly before mixing into the soil. (Dry peat often resists water absorption.)

Gypsum conditions and alkalizes greenhouse soils. It also offers calcium to plants and indirectly to gardeners who harvest and eat them.

Vermiculite and perlite lighten dense soils and help start plant cuttings or seed. Fertil-izers and plant nutrients are added after roots are established in either medium.

The salt concentration and pH level of soils must be watched carefully in the greenhouse. The state agricultural extension service will check field soil for high salt or pH levels, which can damage plant roots, cause wilting, or slow plant cutting or seedling growth. Loosening the soil and thorough watering help dissolve high concentrations.

Watering: Greenhouse gardens should be watered in the mornings of sunny days, if

PLANTING PLAN FOR YEAR-ROUND GREENHOUSE BLOOM

Flower	Seeding Dates	Blooming Period
Impatiens Balsimina	January and February	April and May
Lathyrus odoratus	October	April and May
Matthiola, winter flowering	June	November–April
Poinsettia	Cuttings—March and April	December and January
Primula x *kewensis*	February	December–March
Primula malacoides	August	February–April
Primula obconica hybrids	February–May	March–July
Primula sinensis	February–May	November–March
Saintpaulia	March	September March
Salpiglossis	October	May and June
Salvia splendens	February Cuttings—January	October–January
Schizanthus hybrids	August	March–May
Senecio x *hybridus,* large flowered and stellata	June or July	March–May
Streptocarpus hybrids	April or May	April–July
Torenia Fournieri	March	June–August
Trachelium	February Cuttings—August	June–August
Trachymene coerulea	February	May and June

possible. Water should be supplied sparingly in order to minimize the dangers of fungus disease. Watering should be thorough, but plants should be permitted to show signs of thirst before watering is repeated. Watering should be withheld, if possible, in cloudy weather, since these conditions make evaporation slow, and fungus spores cannot be destroyed as well as they can by hot sun rays.

Here are still more tips on proper watering in the greenhouse:

1. Try to avoid ice-cold water. Room temperature water is preferred by most greenhouse plants.

2. Water can run freely over the bench or tub, but be sure that roots are not left soaking.

3. Keep soil loose for good drainage. Organic matter and sandy loam make the soil healthy and properly drained.

4. Water plants less in winter, especially those that go into dormancy during cool weather. Their need for water decreases at these times.

5. Avoid water softened with a commercial water softener. This water contains chemicals harmful to plants. Flushing salty or hard water usually prevents salt buildup.

Insect and disease control: In handling plant life in the greenhouse, special care and attention must be given to prevention of pest and disease infestation. Insects and diseases which commonly plague greenhouse crops are easy to control through the use of good-quality, clean seed and plants, in addition to the maintenance of an overall sanitary growing environment. Insects, bacteria, viruses, and fungi which thrive in "hothouse climates" can be battled by following these simple sanitation tips:

1. Remove diseased and dead plants; keep them far from the greenhouse.

2. Prevent wild weed growth near the greenhouse. Such growth attracts insects and promotes disease.

3. Keep the greenhouse neat and free of plant clutter.

4. Be certain that new plants introduced into the greenhouse don't harbor new germs and pests.

5. Start seed, roots and cuttings in soilless mediums. Sterile perlite, vermiculite and peat moss are commended for controlling seedling and cutting diseases.

6. Provide proper greenhouse ventilation.

7. Finally, avoid soaking foliage when watering. Also avoid overwatering or overfertilizing greenhouse plants.

The organic greenhouse gardener can turn to several safe insect controls, dusts and sprays for disease outbreaks, especially those in the beginning stages. Commercially available controls include sabadilla, rotenone, pyrethrum, and nicotine sulfate. Many gardeners develop their own recipes for homemade pest or disease control.

Not all greenhouse or garden insects are enemies to the propagation of healthy plants, however. Ladybugs, praying mantis, lacewings, spiders, and horse hair snakes are among the many winged or crawling "comrades" in the garden who eat harmful insects.

If helpful insects are not enough, plant companion herbs in the greenhouse, such as tansy, sage and rosemary, mints, basil, parsley, valerian, marigolds, and pyrethrum. Well-composted soil or plentiful humus, and the removal of rotting leaves and plants, always help in the battle against plant diseases and pests.

Cool Greenhouse: Since fuel cost practically doubles with every five-degree (F.) rise in temperature, a cool greenhouse with a night temperature of 50°F. (10°C.) is best for the gardener. Plants needing higher temperatures can be grown in the cool greenhouse if they are placed high on shelves where it is several degrees warmer. Practically all the popular annuals and perennials do well in the cool greenhouse: asters, pansies, stock, carnations, sweet peas, marguerites, chrysanthemums, winter-flowering marigolds, calendulas, alyssum, candytuft, schizanthus, snapdragons, Boston yellow daisies—the list is endless.

Hanging-basket plants like oxalis, miniature ivy, browallia, strawberry begonia, trailing fuchsia, and periwinkle grow well in a moderately cool greenhouse.

In cool temperature and organic soil, bulbs such as tulips, Dutch iris, lilies, daffodils, hyacinths, ranunculus, and anemones are easy to grow and give fine blooms. Lettuce, radishes, Swiss chard, kale, and scallions do very well as do carrots, cauliflower, peas, red and green cabbage, and beets, if you have the extra space they require. Many herbs thrive in the cool greenhouse. A few pots or boxes of rue, sage, mint, marjoram, parsley, chives, and the like will provide garnishes for winter meals.

One of the most profitable ways to use a cool greenhouse is to raise plants for transplanting in the summer garden. They can be grown by the thousands in a home greenhouse. Husky plants for cabbage, cauliflower, lettuce, broccoli, and celery, as well as all of the bedding plants for the flower garden are commonly cultivated. Seed is inexpensive and the plants are finer than those on sale. Also, they can be raised in strains not available on the market.

Warm Greenhouse: While it costs almost twice as much to bring the home greenhouse up to moderate or warm temperatures in comparison with a cool house, many exciting plants can be grown that make it worthwhile. Orchids are among them. With a collection of 50 to 75 plants of different varieties, it is possible to have something in bloom every day of the year. Cymbidiums will keep as long as three months. Any orchidist will tell you the plants are not difficult to grow. In fact, they will stand more abuse than most of the annuals previously mentioned. Insects are not a serious problem. Orchids can be grown in any greenhouse where it is possible to maintain an even temperature and keep the atmosphere fresh and healthy. High humidity is essential and this is usually provided by placing a tray of coke underneath slat plant benches. This coke holds tremendous quantities of moisture and gives it off slowly.

Other flowers and plants that do well in the moderate to warm greenhouse include amaryllis, azaleas, begonias, ferns and tropical foliage plants, bougainvillea, cactus, gardenias, gloxinias, poinsettias, potted roses, *Saintpaulia,* and lantana. Tomatoes, cucumbers and melons can also be grown in the warm greenhouse where temperatures are at least 60°F. (15.56°C.) at night. Those who enjoy growing unusual things will include such plants as *Tacca Chantrieri,* the devil flower, *Columnea gloriosa* with its fleshy leaves on long trailing stems that make it excellent for hanging baskets, and *Rondeletia odorata* that blooms more or less continually with bright coral red flowers.

GREEN MANURE

One of the most important aids in organic gardening is the cultivation of green manure cover crops. Green manure crops provide inexpensive, convenient sources of organic matter, which increase the soil's absorptive and biochemical processes. These crops also provide a vegetative cover which protects valuable topsoil from wind and water erosion. That is how many green manures earned the name "cover crops."

Green manure crops are commonly cultivated to be later plowed or tilled into the soil, adding soil nutrients which enhance fertility. As commercial chemical fertilizers become more costly and scarce, farmers and gardeners are increasingly turning to cover crop cultivation.

There are two types of green manures, legumes and nonlegumes. Legumes, mostly clovers and vegetables, are valued because they help fix large quantities of nitrogen from the air, making it available to plant roots. Many common vegetables are legumes, providing food and green manure from the same crops. Examples of legumes include peas, beans, alfalfa, and clovers. Nonlegumes, mostly grasses, are favored for short-term production of organic matter for the garden. Nonlegumes such as rye are sown in late summer or fall and plowed under the next spring, so as not to occupy the land during growing season.

There are several general advantages to green manure cover crops. The crops help cut expenses for fertilizers and soil nutrients. They also protect soil in harsh weather, and use solar energy to provide winter crops which replenish the soil after harvests. Green manure crops are also the answer to gardeners who cannot compost enough material for larger areas. Another advantage comes with the protection from plant disease and insects which green manure crops offer after seasonal rotation.

Advantages unique to legumes include their abilities to find and store plant food and moisture, deep root growth that helps tap soil minerals, soil aeration and drainage services, and their use as honey plants for bees. Some cover crops add as much as 150 pounds of nitrogen to garden soil per acre, equivalent to approximately five tons of manure.

Many varieties of green manure cover crops provide the advantage of convenient organic mulch matter. Mulches such as long ryegrass offer nutrition for the soil and attract earthworms by keeping soil moist, dark and cool. As the mulch decomposes, necessary soil nutrients are released, remaining available for hungry plant roots longer than fast-dissolving chemical fertilizers.

Even the quality of ailing garden soils can be improved with cover crops. Sandy soils are provided needed moisture by green manures, which absorb and save water underground. Crops such as alfalfa help clay soils with long roots which soften the tough ground. Weedy soils can be cleaned up with fast-growing grasses which choke out unwanted weeds and restore soil minerals they extract. Gardeners plagued by erosion and water buildup also benefit from cover crops which provide erosion barriers by holding topsoil and absorbing excess moisture. Green manuring has a certain advantage over usual composting methods in that it supplies the soil with suc-

culent organic matter at the peak of its nutritional benefit. Compost, no matter how carefully tended, will lose some of its nutrients due to leaching and other actions of the elements. But, by careful treatment of green manure, the soil will hold its nutrients (especially the minerals found only deep in the subsoil) until they may be assimilated by the stands which follow.

Despite all these other advantages, green manures are most commonly recognized as garden fertilizers. The most important source of organic matter is plant roots. These roots, penetrating often to great depths and continually decaying, leave great quantities of organic matter to be broken down into humus. Fertilization this deep cannot be duplicated in any other form so easily and inexpensively.

This decay occurs quickly in garden soils, so the added soil fertility should be used by growing crops as early as possible after manure crop tilling. In warm humid weather, decomposition occurs in less than six weeks. Young, succulent material decomposes more readily than older plants.

Organic gardeners can choose from a wide variety of green manure cover crops. A good crop should grow the maximum amount in the minimum amount of time. Most crops will thrive in temperate climates and soils.

Green Manure Crops: Here are some of the more common green manure crops.

Alfalfa: deep-rooted legume, grown throughout the United States. This crop does well in all but very sandy, clay, acid, or poorly drained soils. Apply lime if the pH is 6 or below, and add phosphate rock. Inoculate the seed when growing alfalfa for the first time. Sow seed in spring in the North and East, and in late summer elsewhere. Eighteen to 20 pounds of seed will plant one well-prepared acre. Favored for its high protein and high nitrogen content, it also contains calcium, magnesium and potassium.

Alsike clover: legume, grown mostly in the northern states. Alsike prefers fairly heavy, fertile loams, but does better on wet, sour soil than most clovers. Sow six to ten pounds of seed per acre in the spring, or in the early fall in the South.

Alyce clover: legume, grown in the extreme southern regions. This clover prefers sandy or clay loams with good drainage. Sow in late spring, 15 to 20 pounds of scarified seed per acre.

Barley: nonlegume, grown in the North. Barley requires rich, loamy soil and does not perform well on acid or sandy soil. In colder climates, sow winter varieties, elsewhere spring varieties, two to 2½ bushels per acre.

Beggarweed: legume, grown primarily in the South and sometimes north to the Great Lakes. Beggarweed thrives on rich sandy soil, but is not exacting and will grow on moderately acid soils. Inoculate the seed if you have not grown the crop before. Sow 15 pounds of hulled and scarified seed or 30 pounds of unhulled seed when all danger of frost is past. If seed is allowed to mature, you may have trouble getting rid of this crop.

Black medic: legume, grown throughout United States. Very closely related to alfalfa, black medic is a vigorous grower on reasonably fertile nonacid soils. Sow seven to 15 pounds of scarified, inoculated seed. In the North, sow seed in spring; in the South, plant in the fall. Black medic needs ample lime.

Buckwheat: nonlegume, grown mostly in the Northeast. Buckwheat is one of the best choices for rebuilding poor or acid soils. It has an enormous, vigorous root system and is a fine bee plant. Plant seed when the ground is warmed in midsummer, after peas and other early crops have been harvested. Sow about two bushels to the acre. It is possible to grow three crops, 40 tons of green matter per acre, in a season.

In late summer, use a rotary tiller to chop and turn under waist-high buckwheat. Or, to get two manure crops in one sowing, mow the growth and let the seed to settle in the soil. Then, replant the crop the following spring.

Cowpea: legume, widely grown throughout the United States. It is a fine soil builder since its powerful roots crack hardpans. Inoculate the seed when planting it the first time. Sow seed as soon as the soil is well warmed, broadcasting 80 to 100 pounds or sowing 20 pounds in three-foot rows. This legume grows very quickly.

Crimson clover: winter legume, grown from New Jersey southward. Crimson clover does well on almost any fairly good soil. On poor soil, grow cowpeas first for a preliminary buildup. Sow 30 to 40 pounds of unhulled seed or 15 to 20 pounds of hulled, about 60 days before the first killing frost. Hard-seeded strains volunteer from year to year in the South.

Crotalaria: legume, grown in very poor soil in the South and as far north as Maryland. Sow scarified seed in the spring, ten to 30 pounds, depending on the variety. Plowed under in the fall, crotalaria makes sandy soil like loam.

Domestic ryegrass and Italian ryegrass: nonlegumes, grown in many areas. These grasses tolerate a wide range of soils. For one acre, sow 20 to 25 pounds of seed in the spring in the North, fall in the South.

Fenugreek: winter legume, grown in the Southwest. Fenugreek needs a fairly rich loam soil. Sow 35 to 40 pounds of seed in the fall.

Field bromegrass: nonlegume, grown in the northern half of United States. It is widely adapted to many soils. It is a good winter cover, hardier than rye. Sow seed in early spring or late summer, ten to 15 pounds per acre.

Field peas: legume, grown throughout North America. Well-drained sandy to heavy loams are preferred. Sow 1½ to three bushels, depending on the variety, in early spring in the North, late fall in the South. Inoculate seed the first time the plants are grown.

Hairy indigo: summer legume, grown in the Deep South. This plant will tolerate a moderately poor sandy soil and will make a very tall, thick stand. Sow in early spring six to ten pounds broadcast, three to five drilled.

Lespedeza: legume, grown in the South and as far north as Michigan. All types of soil can support lespedeza. The northern species *L. cuneata* is particularly good for poor, sour soils—for these, it's one of the best fertility builders available. In the spring, sow 30 to 40 pounds of seed per acre. Fertilize the soil with plenty of phosphate rock.

Lupine: legume, grown throughout the East. Sour, sandy soils can support lupine. Blue lupine is a fine winter legume in the South; white and yellow are most often grown in the North. Sow in spring in the North, late fall in the South, 50 to 150 pounds per acre, depending on the variety. Always inoculate the seed.

Millet: nonlegume, grown in arid regions of the South and Southwest. Millet does better on poor soil than many forage or green manure crops. It is usually planted thickly, about 35 pounds of seed broadcast over the acre.

Oats: nonlegume, widely grown through-out North America. Oats can be grown on almost any soil provided the climate is cool and moist. Winter oats are only suited to very mild winters. In the spring, sow two bushels of seed per acre.

Persian clover: winter legume, grown in southern and Pacific states. This clover prefers heavy, moist soils. In the fall, sow five to eight pounds of seed per acre.

Red clover: legume, grown in practically all areas, but is most useful in the North. This clover will thrive in any well-drained soil rich in phosphorus. Its decay is of exceptional benefit to crops that succeed it. Sow seed early in the spring to allow time for two stands. For one acre, 15 pounds of seed is adequate.

Rye: nonlegume, widely grown in the Northeast. Rye tolerates many soil types, even very poor ones. It is easily cultivated and adaptable to any cool, dry climate. The annual variety which lasts until winter frosts is ideal for areas planted in early spring. The perennial variety, winter rye, endures the winter and can be plowed under in late spring.

Soybeans: summer legume, grown throughout North America. Soybeans thrive in nearly all kinds of soil, including sour soils where other legumes fail. They can stand considerable drought. Use late-maturing varieties for best green manure results. Sow 60 to 100 pounds per acre, spring to midsummer. For best results, inoculate the seed.

Sudangrass: nonlegume, grown in all parts of United States. Sudangrass tolerates any soil except very wet ones. It is a very rapid grower and therefore excellent for quick organic matter production. In late spring, broadcast 20 to 25 pounds of seed per acre.

Sweet clover: legume, grown in all parts of United States. Just about any soil, if reasonably well supplied with lime, will support sweet clover. Plants are especially adept at utilizing rock fertilizers and are excellent honey plants. Sow 15 pounds of scarified seed to the acre, fall or early spring. Fast-growing annual white sweet clover can be turned under in the fall; other varieties have their biggest roots in the spring of the second year, so turn them under then.

Velvet beans: legume, grown in the South. This is one of the best crops for sandy, poor soils. Plants produce roots 30 feet long, vines up to 50 feet long. Sow seed when the soil is well warmed, 100 pounds broadcast, or 25 to 30 pounds in wide rows.

Vetches: legumes, varieties for all areas. Vetches grow in any reasonably fertile soil with ample moisture. Hairy vetch does well on sandy or sour soils and is the most winter-hardy variety. Hungarian is good for wet soils in areas having mild winters. In the North, sow seed in spring, elsewhere in the fall. Depending on the variety, 30 to 60 pounds will plant one acre.

Weeds: Whenever weeds will not be stealing needed plant food and moisture, they can be used as green manures. Some produce creditable amounts of humus, as well as helping make minerals available and conserving nitrogen.

Wheat: nonlegume, grown throughout North America. Wheat prefers a fairly fertile soil with a pH of about 6.4. Broadcast five to six pecks of seed per acre.

Winter Cover Crops: The best winter cover crops are rye, wheat and ryegrass. All may be sown from mid-August to mid-September, so they are well established before the frosts begin. During winter they hold the soil in place and prevent erosion. Winter cover crops usually feature large fibrous root systems which add organic matter to garden soil when plowed or spaded under. Plowing or spading is done in the spring.

Spring Cover Crops: Green manure crops planted in early spring help improve garden soil for planting later in the season. Garden peas are one variety of legume that is planted in spring.

Summer Cover Crops: Summer cover crops are particularly suitable for areas to be made into lawn. Soybeans, oats, millet, and Sudangrass are useful for this purpose, and may be sown in the spring and plowed under in late summer or fall. These plants are ready to be turned under by mid-August or early September, in time for fall lawn making.

Buckwheat is another crop sometimes used to provide organic matter. It may be sown any time from June to late summer and is usually plowed under while it is in bloom. It is killed by cold weather, but it may be left on the ground all winter and plowed under in the spring. It returns to the soil the least amount of organic matter of all the crops mentioned here, but it has the advantage of being able to grow on rather poor soil. It shades out weeds as successfully as any of the prelawn crops and is easily spaded under.

Fall Cover Crops: Rye is also a suitable fall cover crop, noted for its hardiness. It can be started as late as mid-October, to provide green cover growth to protect garden soils.

Sowing the Green Manure Cover Crop: Just when you begin your green manure crop cultivation depends on a number of variables, including soil quality, sun exposure and drainage. With poor soil, begin cultivation as soon as the ground can be worked. Many gardeners prefer to experiment with green manures and particular fruits and vegetables, so they prefer summer or fall cultivation, after harvest. Other organic gardeners grow food crops on half of their land, while enriching the other half with green manure crops, rotating halves every few years.

To prepare the soil for a green manure crop, begin by chopping and turning under residues soon after harvest, when they are still green and tender. With a tiller, residues such as tomato and pea vines, thick roots and cornstalks can be turned under for soil decomposition. Some gardeners even reduce garden residues in a separate compost pile.

With the garden free of crop residues, you are ready to prepare a fine seedbed. Lime and fertilizer can be added to stimulate growth.

Crop seed can be sown by hand broadcasting and then lightly covered with a fine soil. In a few weeks, your crop should be growing well, ready to protect and enrich the soil. In the spring, the cover crop can be chopped or tilled under. With perennial crops that survive winter, let the plants grow in again before tilling.

Working in Cover Crop: If the crop is heavy, it's best to chop the growth before working it into the soil. Farmers can do this with a heavy crop disk. Often two or three diskings are needed to work in a heavy crop. As a result, it decomposes quickly enough so that a crop can be planted in only a few weeks. In orchards, the usual method is to disk only to kill the growing plants.

For the gardener, often a rotary mower is used to cut up the growth into smaller pieces; then several passes are made with a rotary tiller to work the material into the soil. Some rotary tillers that have a cutting action as well as a digging one are especially effective for this job.

The time to work in a cover crop is usually determined by the time a crop in that section is to be grown. Since so much of the value of cover crops depends upon the quantity of organic matter produced, many growers postpone working them in for as long as planting schedules permit, allowing them to get increased growth from early spring warmth.

Plant Nutrients in Cover Crops: The amount of plant food in a well-grown cover crop is equivalent per acre to a ton of high-grade fertilizer. The availability of plant food from such a crop depends upon the type of crop grown, the time it is plowed under, and the moisture, temperature and fertility of the soil. Properly grown green manure crops will contain, by dry weight, approximately 2 percent nitrogen, .5 to .8 percent phosphorus and from 3 to 6 percent potassium.

Much of this plant food can be obtained from the residues left from the cash crop. For legumes, the nitrogen is obtained from symbiotic action. Tilth and porosity are greatly influenced by the type of root system of the cover crop selected. For soil aeration, this is quite important.

See also CITRUS, CLOVER, LEGUME INOCULATION, SCARIFICATION, SOIL CONSERVATION.

GREEN PEPPER   *See* PEPPER

GREENSAND

Glauconite greensand or greensand marl is an iron potassium silicate that imparts a green color to the minerals in which it occurs.

Being an undersea deposit, greensand contains traces of many if not all the elements which occur in seawater. It has been used successfully for soil building for more than a hundred years and is a fine source of potash.

Greensand is commonly called a glauconite potash mineral, because it contains from 5 to 6 percent of available potash. The best deposits contain, in addition to the potash, 50 percent silica, 18 to 23 percent magnesia, small amounts of lime and phosphoric acid, and traces of 30 or more other elements, most of which are important in the nutrition of the higher plants.

Factors underlying the immediate response of grasses to greensand seem to be greensand's ability to absorb and hold large amounts of water in the surface layer of the soil where the plant roots feed and to slowly release, over a long period of time, the potassium necessary to stimulate photosynthesis. In addition, it contains the trace elements which may be deficient in the soil or in the surface layer of the soil in which the grass roots feed.

Greensand is so fine that it may be used in its natural form with no processing except drying if the material is to pass through a fertilizer drill. An application consists of about ¼ pound of greensand per square foot of soil, but you may want to spread it thinner. It may be applied at any time spring or fall without danger of injuring plants, but, since greensand contains aluminum, do not overapply. It may be applied on the surface in sheet composting, or used in the compost heap to stimulate bacterial action and enrich the compost.

GREYWATER   *See* IRRIGATION

GROUND BEETLES
See INSECT CONTROL

GROUND CHERRY   *See* PHYSALIS

GROUND COVERS

These practical plants should be considered as an important asset to your landscaping scheme, especially if you've had trouble growing other plants under shady trees or on banks.

Of course, not all ground covers will grow on a windswept or rainwashed slope. Tough specimens like crown vetch or goutweed could be planted in such spots, but they grow with such abandon you'd have a hard time holding them in check.

Requiring less than half the soil preparation necessary for a lawn, ajuga makes an attractive, nontraditional ground cover.

Types of Ground Cover: What height should your ground cover be? Should it be trailing or compact? What color should it be? Vines and shrubs up to two feet tall are suitable for large open areas and some slopes, while small areas, like the flower garden borders or odd corners which the lawn mower can't cut, call for something low with delicate foliage. There are many ground covers from which you can choose and each one offers certain special qualities.

The evergreen varieties of ground covers are quite popular in the North, but very few provide any blossom color. Brighten up green beds by underplanting with spring-flowering bulbs. Crocuses, hyacinths or daffodils peeking up through the leaves add a colorful accent. Strengthen the bulbs that are in competition with the ground cover's roots by applications of a good organic fertilizer.

Creeping lilyturf (*Liriope spicata*) is unsurpassed for planting under trees or shrubs. Very hardy, it withstands extreme heat, drought and poor soil, in full sun to deep shade. In the South, it is often preferred to grass, as it has a coarse, dark green foliage and attractive lilac-colored blooms in summer. Growing to a height of 15 inches, it tolerates salt spray. Dwarf lilyturf (*Ophiopogon japonicus*) grows to a maximum of 12 inches.

Dichondra (*D. carolinensis*) is a round-leaved herb that grows to a height of two inches. Because of its very low growth, it is widely used as a lawn substitute. Dichondra prefers moist soil, full sun to deep shade. Native to California and the South, it thrives in warm climates. Used extensively in Palm Beach as a covering material, it can be walked upon or mowed without harm.

English ivy (*Hedera helix*) makes a beautiful, rapidly spreading cover in shade or sun and moist soil. In many parts of the North where this plant doesn't do well trained upright, it will thrive when grown on the ground. Its creeping foliage thrives under maples and beeches, where few other plants survive. The leaves remain green in winter, though they usually develop a purplish tinge.

Japanese spurge (*Pachysandra terminalis*) has turned many an eyesore into something pleasant to look at. This hardy evergreen grows two inches high and endures shade, but grows equally well in sunshine. It needs slightly moist soil. The cuttings root easily if planted in rich soil. Plants spread easily if the tops are cut back occasionally. The lovely dark green foliage has a neat appearance which makes it excellent for use as a border for walks. It is a really vigorous plant; try it where everything else fails.

Partridgeberry (*Mitchella repens*) adapts itself readily to a woodland garden. The trailing vines with their oval evergreen leaves bear small flowers of a creamy white to pink color. This plant takes root along its stem as it creeps over the ground; it blossoms in April, May or June, and later develops red berries. It is one of the finest ground covers for densely shaded spots. It does well in acid soil, but needs humus and moisture. Partridgeberry has been grown with success in both northern and southern sections of the country. Birds love the red berries, so planting partridgeberry is an ideal way to attract them.

Periwinkle or myrtle (*Vinca minor*) is a very successful glossy-leaved evergreen ground cover that develops cheerful violet blue blossoms from early spring until late in the season. It grows to a height of four to six inches in sun or shade and in ordinary soil, if not too dry. Periwinkle holds banks well.

Nonevergreen ground covers of merit include varieties of Adriatic bellflower (*Campanula Elatines*) which put forth blue, star-shaped flowers throughout the summer and autumn, common violet (*Viola sororia*) and lily-of-the-valley (*Convallaria majalis*).

Ground ivy (*Glechoma hederacea*) bears small blue flowers throughout the summer. Adaptable to any type soil, it thrives in sun or shade. Ground ivy is so sturdy you can run a lawn mower over it without doing any damage.

A trek in the woods can pay off with wild strawberry plants. This plant, with its white flowers and delicious berries, thrives in any soil, but does need some sun. Another woodland plant, moneywort (*Lysimachia Nummularia*), so named because of its bright "gold piece" flowers, requires light shade and dry or moist soil. Since these are wild-growing plants, they are apt to be just as wild in the garden. Keep them in check by cutting.

Planting and Culture: Perhaps the most important factor in establishing a ground cover is the soil. It is very important that the ground be fertile and, for most plants, fairly moist. Soil rich in organic matter holds moisture and prevents leaching on slopes, besides aiding a quick, dense plant growth that refuses to give weeds a chance.

Dig to a depth of at least eight inches, removing all weeds and foreign material. Mix in a two- to three-inch layer of organic material such as compost, peat moss, rotted manure, or aged sawdust and soak well for a few hours.

Since ground covers are higher in initial cost than seeding a lawn, there are many schools of thought on how to economize. Some gardeners prefer to set plants a good distance apart, using a smaller number of plants and battling weeds until the plants establish themselves. Others buy seed, seedlings or rooted cuttings from nurseries in order to produce the ground cover more cheaply at home. But if these are planted directly outdoors, many will die, giving a ragged effect to the bed. It's better to start them in your "home nursery" or in pots, carefully shading and watering before setting them out. Some economy-minded gardeners transplant wild plants from nearby fields and woods.

The ideal method is to set small plants close together. The proper distance between seedlings depends on the rate of growth and size of the plants at planting time. Three to

One of the perennial sedums is often the perfect choice for ground cover in a sunny, sloping area.

A SELECTED LIST OF GROUND COVER PLANTS

Botanical Name	Common Name	Evergreen	How it spreads	Rate of spread
ANNUALS				
Sanvitalia procumbens ‡	Common sanvitalia		T	Fast
Verbena tenuisecta †	Moss vervain		T	Fast
PERENNIALS				
Ajuga reptans †	Bugleweed		R	Fast
Arabis procurrens †	Rockcress	Yes	T	Fast
Arenaria verna †	Sandwort		U	Slow
Asarum canadense *	Wild ginger		R	Slow
Campanula †	Bellflower		R	Medium
Convallaria majalis †	Lily-of-the-valley		U	Fast
Coronilla varia ‡	Crown vetch		T	Medium
Dianthus deltoides †	Maiden pink	Yes	T	Fast
Dichondra carolinensis †	Lawn leaf		R	Medium
Euphorbia Cyparissias †	Cypress spurge		U	Medium
Galium odoratum *	Sweet woodruff		U	Fast
Iberis sempervirens †	Candytuft	Yes	T	Slow
Liriope spicata †	Creeping lilyturf	Yes	U	Fast
Mitchella repens *	Partridgeberry	Yes	T	Medium
Myosotis scorpioides †	Forget-me-not		T	Medium
Pachysandra terminalis o	Japanese spurge	Yes	UT	Slow
Phlox subulata ‡	Moss pink	Yes	T	Fast
Ranunculus repens and *R. acris* †	Buttercup		T	Fast
Sedum album ‡	Stonecrop	Yes	T	Fast
Sedum reflexum ‡	Stonecrop	Yes	T	Fast
Sedum sexangulare ‡	Stonecrop	Yes	T	Fast
Sedum spurium ‡	Stonecrop		T	Fast
Sedum ternatum *	Stonecrop		T	Fast
Teucrium Chamaedrys †	Germander	Yes	U	Medium
Thymus pulegioides cv. 'Alba' ‡	Thyme	Yes	T	Fast
Thymus pulegioides cv. 'Coccineus' ‡	Thyme	Yes	T	Fast
Verbena canadensis ‡	Hardy verbena		T	Fast
Veronica filiformis *	Speedwell		T	Fast
Veronica prostrata †	Speedwell		T	Fast
Vinca minor †	Periwinkle (myrtle)	Yes	TU	Fast
Viola canadensis †	Canada violet		S	Fast
Viola sororia †	Common violet		S	Fast
WOODY PLANTS				
Akebia quinata †	Akebia	Yes	T	Medium
Euonymus Fortunei forma *colorata* †	Winter creeper	Yes	T	Medium
Euonymus Fortunei var. *radicans* †	Winter creeper	Yes	T	Fast
Euonymus obovata †	Running strawberry bush		T	Medium
Hedera helix *	English ivy	Yes	T	Fast
Hedera helix cv. 'Baltica' *	Baltic English ivy	Yes	T	Fast
Lonicera japonica cv. 'Halliana' †	Japanese honeysuckle		T	Fast
Parthenocissus quinquefolia †	Virginia creeper		T	Fast
Rosa Wichuraiana ‡	Memorial rose		T	Fast
Xanthorhiza simlicissima †	Yellow-root		U	Slow

* Shade only   † Sun or shade   ‡ Sun only

R Runners; roots   S Seed   T Trailing   U Underground stem

Source: Victor H. Ries, Ohio State University.

eight inches apart is correct for most ground covers, while some vines can be placed up to three feet apart.

When planting on banks or slopes, cut pockets into the bank at different heights along its length, and wedge stones deeply into these holes. Then cover with a good rich soil and plant the ground cover.

Once established, ground covers need no coddling, but while they are getting started they do deserve some care. Water occasionally during the first season. Top-dressing with compost, humus or well-rotted manure will supply the nitrogen needed for dense growth, to cover the ground without any "holes." As the plants grow, they will strangle any crabgrass or plantain.

GROUND IVY
See GROUND COVERS, NEPETA

GROUND LAUREL
See TRAILING ARBUTUS

GROUND RATTAN   *See* PALM

GROUNDSEL   *See* RAGWORT

GUANO

The droppings, dead bodies and other residues from bird and bat colonies in regions without rain or in caves are a rich source of nitrogen. Rain would leach this important plant food out, but, protected by the cave, it remains in a good state of preservation. Some guano is imported from the coastal islands of the Southern Pacific west of the Andes; some is mined in caves of the Southwest. The nitrogen varies from 1 to 10 percent and the phosphorous content may go as high as 25 percent. When available, guano can be substituted for manure, dried blood, hoof and horn dust, and similar sources of nitrogen. In the earlier history of bagged fertilizers, guano was most popular with gardeners and even farmers, but today the supply is limited.

See also MANURE.

GUAVA   (*Psidium*)

The guava is a small, tropical tree which grows about 15 feet in height and is valued for its fruit as well as for its landscaping quality. The tree has a smooth bark, green brown in color, smooth, oval light green leaves, and white flowers. Its round or pear-shaped fruit, up to four inches long when mature, is usually yellow, has a number of hard, small seeds, and a sweet, musklike taste and aroma. Fully ripe, it is rich in vitamin C. In addition to being eaten raw, it is often used in preserves and jams.

The guava is grown principally in Florida and Southern California. It is easily propagated from seed and increased by budding or cuttings, and has no special soil preferences as long as good drainage is provided. Left to itself, the plant spreads rapidly and may become a nuisance.

Culture: Guavas can be grown wherever the temperature does not go much below 15°F. (−9.44°C.), although they can tolerate 10°F. (−12.22°C.) for short spells. Most nurseries carry them in one- and five-gallon cans all year-round and they may be planted at any time. They are partial to heavy loam if the drainage is good. All varieties do best in full sun. Allow 12 to 15 feet between plants.

To get them off to a good start, dig a hole about two feet in diameter and depth; replace the soil with a mixture of loam, compost and well-rotted manure. It will help to mix in a cup of bone meal or ground phosphate rock.

Set the plant about an inch or so higher than it was in the can to allow for settling and pack the earth firmly for good root contact. Around the tree make an irrigation basin about 18 to 24 inches in diameter and four to six inches deep. Fill it two or three times and then mulch it well, keeping the trunk clear. Water about once a week until it shows new green growth; then increase the time between waterings to two weeks, or water when the soil is dry four to six inches below the surface. If you live where it rains in the summer, treat it as you would any of your other shrubs. As it grows, increase the size of the basin out to the tips of the branches. Keep soil heavily mulched.

No pruning is needed except to keep it in bounds. Home garden plantings are seldom bothered by insects; an occasional attack by whiteflies or scale can be easily controlled by weak dormant-oil sprays.

Varieties: Guavas bear fruit when quite young, often the second season after planting. Best varieties are Andre, Coolidge, Superba, and Choiceana. Coolidge will fruit when planted alone; the rest need another variety planted close by for pollination.

The strawberry guava (*P. Littorale*) is hardy and has a dark, maroon fruit with a delicate flavor. The lemon guava is extremely tender and is not regarded as suitable for home gardens. Pineapple guava (*Feijoa Sellowiana*) is not really a guava at all. The "pineapple guava" term is simply a popular name—the plant and fruit are completely distinct from the common guava.

GUINEA FOWL

Popular homestead birds, guinea hens provide eggs as well as a delicious, slightly gamey meat. They are excellent foragers if allowed to run wild, and don't scratch for feed, so they are less destructive in the garden than chickens. They can also be raised in the henhouse.

Breeds and Varieties: There are three varieties of guinea fowl available—Pearl, Lavender and White. There is little apparent difference among them except in color. The Pearl variety has purple gray plumage, dotted with white. Lavender guineas are similar but their plumage is light grey or lavender regularly dotted with white. Whites have pure white plumage and a lighter skin.

Starting: Guinea chicks, called keets, can be mail-ordered. Brooding procedures are the same as with chickens. *See also* CHICKEN.

If you wish to raise keets from your own guineas, it is best to incubate the eggs yourself or give them to a domestic chicken hen to raise since guinea hens are poor mothers. The hens lay seasonally, and will wander off with their mates at midday to lay. Hens usually lay one egg a day, and will lay 30 to 40 eggs before becoming broody. Often several hens will lay in the same nest.

To keep the hen laying throughout the season, remove eggs from the nest when she is absent. Leave half-a-dozen marked eggs to encourage laying.

If you are incubating the eggs, treat them like chicken eggs. If one of your hens is setting on guinea eggs, keep her lice-free and change the nesting material regularly. The incubation period for guinea eggs is 28 days. During the last week, keep the eggs lightly sprinkled with water to aid the keets in breaking their shells.

Housing: A few guineas can be kept on any farm with hens or allowed to go wild. They will do very well if left by themselves, or they can be fed twice a day to encourage them to come home to roost.

If you want to raise more than a few in captivity, provide them with a coop. Guineas will require a run, the larger the better, with five- or six-foot-high walls of poultry fencing with a tight covering of the same material. Roosting facilities should also be provided in the run.

Guineas raised on range should be provided with shelters like chickens on range. A good stout fence will help to keep marauders out. Stand warned, however, that unless the

Guinea fowl provide meat as well as eggs and, because they do not scratch for feed, are less destructive in the garden than chickens.

birds are pinioned or the six primaries of one wing removed, guineas will quickly fly out of their range enclosure and live in the wild.

Feeding: Guineas will feed themselves if allowed to run wild, eating grubs and insects. If kept inside, the birds are fed the same as turkeys. On range the birds can also be fed similarly to turkeys, but should be fed twice a day. Feed in the late afternoon if you want them to return to their shelters for the night.

The first feed for keets may be turkey starting mash. When you are going to put the keets in your brooder, dip their beaks in turkey starting mash and then in water. Starter mash should contain 25 percent protein, and may include oatmeal or finely chopped green feed.

Growing mash and grain should be fed to the keets after they are about six weeks old. After the first ten days, keep mash constantly in front of the keets or feed four or five times daily.

Guineas in captivity need a constant source of fresh water. For keets, a chick waterer with jar is fine; put pebbles in the trough so the keets will not drown themselves in their drinking water.

Sexing: Guinea hens and cocks resemble each other, and sexing is often difficult. General advice for sexing is that the female guinea emits a cry that sounds like "buckwheat, buckwheat," while the cry of the male is monosyllabic. Males have higher and darker combs, longer wattles, and the white, skinlike covering of the head extends farther down the neck than on the female. If a pair is disturbed during laying season, the male will utter a shrill cry and fly away while the female remains on the nest.

Slaughtering and Using: Young birds are usually marketed when they reach 1½ to two pounds live weight. At this stage the meat is tender and resembles the flesh of quail or partridge. At six to ten months the flesh closely resembles that of pheasant and is slightly gamey. Guineas may be prepared for the table as are other poultry of a corresponding size or age, and may also be prepared as game birds. Indeed, in England and Europe guinea fowl are often hunted as game birds.

The easiest way to slaughter domestic guineas is to take a sharp knife, sever the artery in the roof of the mouth, and pierce the brain by pushing the knife into the skull cavity. Birds should be hung upside down to drain. Piercing the brain this way aids in loosening the feathers, and guineas then can be dry-plucked. Never scald the birds. After they have been plucked, chill them quickly.

Guinea eggs are smaller than chicken eggs, and can be fried, scrambled or hard-boiled. The whites are lighter when whipped than the whites of hens' eggs and are therefore good for cake baking. Sixteen whites from guinea eggs equal 11 whites from chicken eggs. Be sure the birds do not see you gathering the eggs, or they are likely to move their nests.

GULLY

The severely eroded condition of gullies sometimes appears on neglected areas of the farm. If ignored, such conditions result in rapidly increasing loss of soil. Gullied areas can be corrected by sloping with a bulldozer, and planting with soil-binding crops.

See also COVER CROP, SOIL CONSERVATION.

GUMBO   *See* OKRA

GUMMOSIS

Gummosis, the formation of amber gum on the bark of fruit trees, may be caused by soil fungi, peach tree borers or too much ground moisture.

To avoid gummosis, plant trees high enough so that, after settling, the point at which the first lateral roots branch out will be at ground level. In heavy soils, use resistant stocks. With older trees, all soil should be removed from around the trunk, down to or a bit below the first lateral roots. Never apply water around the base of the tree.

Treat affected trees by exposing the crown roots and cutting away the dead bark and about ½ inch of the live bark. Cover the wound with a tree surgeon's solution.

GUM MYRTLE   *See* ORANGE GUM

GUM TREE   *See* EUCALYPTUS

GYMNOGRAMMA
See PITYROGRAMMA

GYPSOPHILA

Also called baby's-breath, this mistlike pink or white flowering perennial is especially useful for cutting and drying. *G. paniculata,* single or double, has gray green foliage and masses of tiny white flowers which are very attractive in the border.

Baby's-breath must have a neutral to alkaline soil of at least pH 7 to do well. Have the soil tested and add ground limestone accordingly. It is also essential that drainage be excellent, but that the soil be fairly moist. Set the crown of new plants one inch below the soil surface in full sun. Once these requirements are met and the plant is established, do not move it, as digging will destroy the taproots. To prevent the long, weak stems from flopping, surround the plant closely in spring with six or eight stakes pushed deep in the ground and weave them tightly together with twine. The resulting cage or corset will hold the stems upright. Bristol Fairy is the most popular double variety.

See also BABY'S-BREATH.

GYPSUM

The use of gypsum for agricultural purposes is a controversial subject. A hydrated calcium sulfate, gypsum is often used to reclaim alkali beds. For this purpose, it is finely ground and is generally applied with a lime spreader. It is claimed that gypsum replaces the sodium of alkali soils with calcium and improves drainage and aeration.

Gypsum effectively conserves the nitrogen in manures or other types of rapidly decomposing organic matter. When it is applied to these materials, the escaping ammonium (NH_4) is changed to ammonium sulfate ($N_2H_8SO_4$), in which form the ammonia is stable. Used in the gutters in dairy barns, gypsum not only saves ammonia, but virtually eliminates objectionable odors. Since it is white, it gives the stable a cleaner appearance.

But many farmers question its efficiency, and some organic gardeners question whether or not it is "organic." Test the soil before going ahead with any large-scale application of gypsum to increase soil acidity or improve drainage.

See also FERTILIZER, CHEMICAL.

GYPSY MOTH

The larval worm of the gypsy moth is responsible for the defoliation of numerous fruit, ornamental and shade trees in the Northeast. The brown and hairy caterpillar grows to two inches in length, and feeds nocturnally through June and July. The adult moths are brown and yellow (male), or beige (female).

Although infestations cover large areas, you can have some control over the gypsy moths in your immediate locale. To trap them, wrap several lengths of burlap around a tree trunk and fold the top over to form a shelter. Worms will be attracted to the burlap when they instinctively feel it is time to pupate. Crush the caterpillars inside the band, or remove the band and shake the pests into a container of water topped with kerosene. The tan egg clusters, arranged in one-inch ovals, can be scraped from the hard surfaces on which they are usually laid. A *Bacillus thuringiensis* spray is effective. Be sure to observe federal quarantine regulations and prevent the spread of these pests.

See also BACILLUS THURINGIENSIS, INSECT CONTROL.

H

HACKBERRY (*Celtis*)

Related to the elms, the common hackberry tree (*C. occidentalis*) grows as high as 100 feet and is hardy throughout most of the United States. It is also known as the nettle tree. The sugarberry (*C. laevigata*) grows mostly in the southern states, has red fruit changing to dark purple and grows 60 to 80 feet high. Both trees generally do well in ordinary soil.

Hackberries are considered valuable as shade trees; their wide-spreading head and light green foliage are very attractive in lawn plantings. Rarely susceptible to insect or disease damage, they even do well in dry areas.

Hackberry wood is handsome and easily worked, and is suited for cabinetry and furniture. Many birds feed on the dark, cherrylike fruits; humans can also eat the sweet fruits of some species.

In the northernmost part of its range, the hackberry should be propagated from the seed of trees native to the region's climate, as the resulting trees will likely be hardier than those grown from southern seed. The seed should be stratified for 60 to 90 days, and may take as long as two years to germinate.

HAIR

Hair, like wool and feathers, has a high nitrogen content. If the sweepings from a barbershop were regularly applied to a compost heap, an enormous amount of nitrogen could be saved, since six to seven pounds of hair contain a pound of nitrogen or as much as 100 to 200 pounds of manure. If kept in a well-moistened heap, hair will disintegrate as easily as feathers.

HAIRY INDIGO
See GREEN MANURE

HANSEN'S BUSH CHERRY
See CHERRY, BUSH

HARDINESS

Hardiness is the quality which enables plants to survive the climatic conditions of the particular area where they are to be placed. When gardeners speak of a "hardy" plant, they usually mean one which will survive the winter. But the term can also be applied to plants native to a cold climate which will survive the heat of a more temperate climate. Gardeners quickly learn from experience that the degree of hardiness of a given plant can vary greatly according to local conditions. There are, for example, many plants considered tender in the North which survive winters in city gardens that they could not endure a few miles away in the country. There are many variables, and because of them, hardiness can be defined only in very general terms. Under these circumstances, terms like "half-hardy" can have no precise definition at all. If a plant is listed as half-hardy for your locality, assume that it is tender and winter it in a cold frame or indoors.

HARDPAN

Hardpans are impervious horizontal layers in the soil that may lie anywhere from six inches to about two feet below the surface. They are usually $\frac{1}{16}$ to $\frac{1}{2}$ inch thick. A true hardpan is formed by the cementing together of the soil grains into a hard stonelike mass which is impervious to water. A more common condition is an impervious layer in the subsoil caused by the pore spaces becoming filled with fine clay particles. Such "tight clay" subsoils, called claypans, are generally associated with an extremely acid condition, so that from both the physical and chemical standpoint they are objectionable.

When hard- or claypans exist, the surface soil is cut off from the subsoil; no new minerals are added to the lower part of the soil; plant roots often are unable to penetrate these layers. Plant roots usually grow down to this hard layer and then extend horizontally over the top of it. This results in shallow-rooted plants which may suffer from lack of nutrient elements otherwise available in the subsoil. Often such shallow-rooted plants die out completely from lack of water during dry periods, while plants growing where there is no hardpan flourish.

If land is characterized by poor drainage and extensive runoff or puddling after a rain, there is good reason to suspect the presence of a hardpan. Experiment station agents test for a suspected hardpan by thrusting a blunt-pointed steel rod, attached to a handle, down through the soil profile. If an obstruction is hit, its depth is noted, and further borings are made. If the obstruction crops up at the same depth in each boring, a hardpan is probably present.

A further check would be to dig several small holes in scattered places to a depth greater than that at which the hardpan was detected. Observe the soil profile and gently scratch the soil at the depth of the suspected hardpan with a knife. If it crumbles easily and falls away loosely the layer is not an impervious one, but if the layer is hard and compact it is.

The best and most universally used method of breaking up hardpans is by subsoiling. Subsoiling consists of cutting 16 to 30 inches deep into the ground with a subsoil chisel. In exceptional cases, the chisel may penetrate to a depth of over five feet.

See also AERATION, SUBSOILING.

HARDWOOD CUTTINGS
See CUTTINGS

HARDY *See* HARDINESS

HARE'S-FOOT FERN *See* FERN

HARE'S-TAIL GRASS
See GRASS, ORNAMENTAL

HARLEQUIN BUG
See INSECT CONTROL

HARROWING

This farming operation usually follows plowing. Its objective is to break up the clods in a field just as the rake does in the home garden. Harrowing is done immediately prior to seeding a crop.

See also CULTIVATION.

HARTFORD FERN
See LYGODIUM

HAUGHLEY EXPERIMENT

The Haughley Experiment was conceived in 1938 by a number of individuals who were concerned with trends that were appearing in modern farming and felt that too little was known about the long-term effect of these trends and that too little research was being undertaken to monitor these effects.

Lady Eve Balfour, who had farmed since 1919 at New Bells Farm, in Suffolk, England, and her neighbor, Miss Alice Debenham, decided to amalgamate their two farms and use them as the basis for a long-term investigation into the effects of different farming systems on soil fertility, the nutritional quality of produce and the health of livestock.

The farms were divided into three sections. The first control section was called "Organic," or simply "O." The plan was to farm these 75 acres organically, without the use of artificial fertilizers or synthetic pesticides. This farm was to carry livestock and to feed them. For its fertility it was to depend on the composted wastes produced by the section. Over the years the idea crept in that this organic section should be a "closed cycle," with no importation of nutrients from outside.

The second, "Mixed" or "M" section, was to be farmed with a similar rotation and similar livestock to the O section but fertilizers and pesticides were to be used in amounts recommended commercially. It, too, occupied 75 acres.

The third, "Stockless" or "S" section, a smaller one of 32 acres, was to carry no livestock and thus would be more dependent than the M section on the use of fertilizers.

After a number of experiments the rotation for the O and M sections was established in 1950. It was a ten-year rotation of winter wheat, roots and forage, barley, winter beans and spring peas, oats, silage (oats and peas), and four years ley (temporary pasture). Four fields are in permanent pasture. The rotation for the S section was established in 1952. It was a five-year rotation of wheat, sugar beet, barley, barley undersown to clover, beans, clover, fallow. The O section received ten to 12 tons of compost per acre in the second and sixth years, the M section 12 to 15 tons of compost per acre in the second and sixth years and fertilizers in varying amounts every year, and the S section fertilizers every year. The stock consisted of cows, sheep and poultry.

Yields were constant on the O section, but rose on the other sections. There were significant differences in the soils. While the humus content rose on all sections over the ten years from 1953 to 1963 the rise was most marked on the O section. The structure of the O soil showed improvement while that of the S section deteriorated. The fields on the O section were said to be easier to work and less tractor fuel was consumed in working them than in working the fields of either of the other sections. The O section appeared to miss insect and fungal attacks from which other sections suffered, although the wheat on the O section was badly affected by blight in several years when the M and S crops escaped. Weeds appeared to increase where herbicides had been used; in general, weeds were not a severe problem on the O section. For many years the cattle on the O section yielded more milk than those on the M section for the same amount of feed.

Since 1971, the farms involved in the Haughley Experiment have formed the nucleus of the J. A. Pye Research Centre, which has continued experimentation in organic agriculture.

HAWKWEED
(Hieracium aurantiacum)

Hawkweed is a low-growing weed whose attractive flowers are readily worked by bees, producing an amber honey. In northeastern wasteland areas where it is especially abundant, hawkweed is considered a troublesome pest.

HAWTHORN   *(Crataegus)*

The hawthorn is a medium-sized tree, that can be recognized by its long, sharply pointed thorns, which really are modified branches. It is desirable on the lawn for its form, bloom, autumn leaf colors, and showy red fruit. The flowers are white, pink or red. The hawthorns comprise a large genus of thorny shrubs and trees belonging to the Rose family, and are found throughout the eastern United States. Some of the hawthorns are very hardy and seem to enjoy the wind-beaten environment along the seashore.

The hawthorn is native to England, and is the plant for which the ship *Mayflower* was named. It is known for its use as a hedge, and often grows wild in untilled fields. It is widely cultivated as an ornamental and, in the past,

has been used as a heart tonic and as a treatment for rheumatism, arthritis, emotional stress, and nervous conditions.

Because of their thorns, hawthorns can form impenetrable barriers, although they may suffer when pruned back for hedges.

Most hawthorns breed true to type from seed. Before sowing, it is advisable to soak the fruit in water until the flesh has decayed and then rub the seeds free of the pulp. Sow the seed in flats and keep in a cool cellar, basement or lathhouse for two years, watering them occasionally. Germination will not occur until the second spring, and possibly not until the third.

Transplant the seedlings in the first year to encourage the formation of a fibrous root system. Rare varieties are obtained by grafting on seedling stock of the English hawthorn (*C. laevigata*) or other species. Hawthorns prefer a loamy soil and sun.

The English hawthorn grows to 15 feet, forming a small tree or bush. The white flowers are followed by bright red fruit. Variety Pauli puts out bright scarlet, double flowers and is the most popular variety in this country.

C. mollis is native to the Midwest and is the state flower of Missouri. It is an attractive species with glossy leaves, short thorns and small, scarlet, pear-shaped fruits which drop shortly after ripening.

Cockspur thorn (*C. crus-galli*) has widespread, often drooping branches, frequently covered with long thorns. This variety frequently attains a height of 30 feet but can be kept dense and short by careful pruning.

The Washington hawthorn (*C. Phaenopyrum*) grows to 30 feet, is a native of the South and makes an excellent hedge with pruning. It puts forth white flowers in dense clusters which are followed by lustrous fruits that remain until midwinter.

The fruits of the hawthorn tree attract several kinds of birds and can be used in jellies and preserves.

Contemporary uses of hawthorn include its role in modern medicine and horticulture. Promising scientific findings have been made in connection with hawthorn and treatment of various heart ailments, including angina pectoris and abnormal heart actions. Hawthorn is also believed an effective aid for arteriosclerosis (hardening of the arteries). The berries are used in a dry powder, or in a tincture with grain alcohol for medicinal purposes. It should be noted that if taken in a large dose, hawthorn can cause dizziness.

Fruits from several of the hawthorns can be used to make fine jellies and preserves.

See also HERB.

HAY

The top growth of green forage crops dried to a moisture content of 25 percent or less is called hay. It is a good, cheap livestock feed when pasture or silage is not available. The chief reason for including hay in the diets of ruminants and horses is to provide energy for work or for the production of milk, and not as a source of vitamins and minerals. However, hay *is* important to pigs or chickens as a source of vitamins and proteins.

Cows and other ruminants are biologically equipped to consume large quantities of roughage. A cow has four stomachs and a long intestinal tract. The main center of bacterial action, the rumen, is located near the front of the tract. Since most digestion occurs here, products of digestion are absorbed directly into the blood.

The hay must be of the best quality to do its job well. For satisfactory digestion of poor roughage, a cow needs supplementary protein and minerals. But when an adequate amount of good roughage is present in the ration, no extra supplementation is needed.

High-Quality Hay: Good-quality hay is grown on well-limed, fertile soils, cut in the early-bloom stage and cured rapidly with a minimum loss of nutrients and minerals. It is green in color, the leaves are intact and the stems are soft and pliable. It has a pleasant aroma, and is free from dust, moisture, mold, and foreign matter such as stubble and weeds.

Such hay will produce most of the protein and energy needed for high milk production. Very good alfalfa hay contains 18 percent protein; a poor alfalfa hay may only contain 10 percent. Even more important, the protein in good hay is more digestible than that in poor hay. A brown, leafless timothy hay will have less than half as much digestible protein as a rich green timothy hay.

What does this mean to the farmer who feeds hay? If one acre produces four tons of alfalfa which is properly cured into hay, it will yield 1,440 pounds of protein. An acre of poorly cured alfalfa hay grown in infertile soil will yield only about 800 pounds of protein of poor digestibility. To make up the difference in the ration, 118 bushels of corn or 28 bushels of soybeans would be necessary.

Poor-quality hay is one of the main reasons for sickness, breeding troubles and lack of thrift in livestock. An animal's health depends on the food it eats. Improperly cured hay, low in vitamins, minerals and trace elements, if not supplemented, may be responsible for a variety of deficiency diseases. It makes sound economic sense to feed good hay rather than risk disease and unthriftiness.

Low soil fertility is one of the important factors that result in a poor-quality hay. A soil that is poorly structured and low in nutrients, trace minerals and organic matter content will not produce plants of good food value.

Acid soils or those low in calcium will grow calcium-deficient plants. The animals eating these plants will not have strong bones or teeth, and will suffer from generally poor health. A lack of phosphorus causes a craving for unnatural foods and creates other eating troubles. In addition, the organic matter content of the soil is definitely related to the carotene and protein content of the hay. Little carotene (pro-vitamin A) is found in plants grown on soil low in nitrogen.

Trace minerals are equally vital, although scientists are not always sure how they function. Copper, cobalt, manganese, iron, magnesium, and iodine have all been proven important to the health of livestock.

In short, well-cared-for soil will produce better hay. Test your soil and adjust soil pH if necessary. Lime added to acid soils will make them more alkaline; alfalfa, for example, prefers a pH as near to 7 as possible. Phosphate rock will provide necessary phosphorus as well as trace minerals. Stable manure and green manure crops will improve soil structure and increase organic matter content.

Proper Handling: Improving soil to grow highly nutritious plants is not all there is to the job. Experiments show it is possible to increase the value of a hay crop one-third by earlier cutting and better curing, handling and storage methods.

The stage of maturity at harvest *is* very significant. Carotene reaches its maximum just before or right at the early-bloom stage in nearly all hay plants. Digestible matter is also the greatest at prebloom stage. Practically all the valuable constituents of a hay plant— carotene, sugars, ascorbic acid, vitamins B_1 and B_2 decrease as the plants mature, while crude fiber increases, making the hay far less palatable to animals.

Although late cutting usually gives the highest tonnage per acre, it yields the least digestible protein and feed values. Stalks and leaves are tougher. Good hay has plenty of leaves since they contain two-thirds of the plant's protein and most of its minerals. Natural green color indicates good curing, palatability and plenty of the vitamin A necessary for normal reproduction and growth.

Average methods of haying fall miserably short of accomplishing their purpose of retaining the best feeding qualities. Poor curing and storing can make a hay worthless. Late cutting or excessive handling causes shattering of the leaves. Overcuring in the swath and windrow causes bleaching (sunlight destroys carotene), rain leaches nutrients from the hay and heating and fermentation result from the action of enzymes and bacteria. These can destroy from 20 to 50 percent of the nutritional value of the hay.

Nutrient losses begin the minute hay is cut. The sooner it is cured and stored the better.

Hay is best cut as early in the day as possible, even if there is a dew. On a good day, hay cut early in the morning will be drier by afternoon than hay cut later in the morning. No more hay should be mowed than can easily be handled under the prevailing weather conditions.

Once it has been mowed, allow the hay to lie in the swath for a few hours until partly cured. Before the leaves are dry enough to shatter, rake the hay, preferably with a side-delivery rake, into loose windrows. If favorable weather continues, the hay can be allowed to cure in the windrow and hauled to the stack or barn or baled when cured. To avoid excess shattering of the leaves during dry weather, it may be necessary to handle the hay only in the early morning before it has become too dry. If the weather is damp and the hay cures slowly, or if it has been rained on, it may be necessary to turn it in the field so that it will cure properly.

The object of curing is to reduce the water content in the hay. For freshly cut forage to store safely, the water content should be lower than 25 percent. Hay that contains too much moisture when stored is liable to ferment, or worse, to ignite through spontaneous combustion. One practical method of testing whether hay is sufficiently cured is to twist a wisp of it in your hands. If the stems are slightly brittle and there is no evidence of moisture when twisted, the hay can be stored safely. In dry, sunny weather, the hay may appear to be drier than it is because the leaves may be dry and brittle while the stems still retain a high moisture content.

If rain threatens, you may want to haul the hay into the barn to finish the curing. Spread it out to a depth of three to five feet—no deeper. Ventilate well by keeping barn doors open, and do not cover with other hay until thoroughly dry.

There are a number of methods of dealing with the hay once it is cured. Hay may be stored loose in the mow (the part of the barn where it is to be stored); the simplest way of doing this—and the most time-consuming—is to fork the hay onto a wagon or pickup, and unload it into the mow. Machines have been developed for storing loose hay, but they are expensive and next to impossible to pick up used.

Most commonly, hay is baled in the field and then transported to the barn. Balers, which are available to process a wide range of bale sizes, take the hay from the windrows, compress it into (usually) rectangular parcels and tie it together. Bales are usually dropped on the ground behind the baler, and can be picked up and loaded on a pickup or wagon. Some balers have chutes that propel the bale upward into a trailing wagon, where the bales can be stacked until they are taken to the barn and unloaded. Bulk handling systems for hay, which are capable of baling and handling large acreages, are not really practical for use on the small farm.

Once hay is baled, it should be taken to the barn and stored according to grades. For example, store early-cut hay in one place for feeding sheep and cows (early-cut hay should not be fed to workhorses, however, since they will do better on hay cut when in bloom), and store hay of lesser quality separately.

You may also be interested in investigating barn drying systems for your hay. In some of these systems, forage is mowed and raked into windrows, where it dries to about 40 to 50 percent moisture content in four to eight hours. It is then hauled to the barn and stored in the mow. Forced air keeps it cool while more water evaporates, until the hay reaches about 20 percent moisture. Oftentimes supplementary heat is used so that the hay dries faster.

Although barn drying produces a good-quality hay and preserves protein content by avoiding shattering, bleaching and leaching out of nutrients, the systems are expensive to buy and operate. Another major drawback is that they are very costly in the amount of irreplaceable fossil fuel they use.

See also entries for individual hay crops, GREEN MANURE.

HAYFEVER PLANTS
See RAGWEED

HAZEL   *See* FILBERT

HEALTH AND SOIL

The idea that health can possibly be related to the soil was—and in many cases, unfortunately, still is—considered an extremely radical one. The fact that there is a direct, strong relationship between health and soil is an integral concept of the organic method. In short, better soils produce better-fed and healthier people. More and more researchers—both agricultural and medical—are coming to agree with this concept.

But for many years, the conventional wisdom was to reject any connection between soil fertility and human health. "Soil fertility will determine how many plants will grow, but for all practical purposes of human nutrition, the content of the soil will have little if any effect on the composition of plant food grown on that soil," was the way one establishmentarian writer expressed it. Invariably, such statements were and are intended to discredit the organic method. By the mid-1970's, however, the wording of these statements changed to reflect the difficulty of defending the basic contention.

In September 1976, for example, the Committee on Nutritional Misinformation of the National Academy of Sciences prepared a statement on "Soil Fertility and the Nutritive Value of Crops" that was clearly aimed at discrediting the organic method. Yet the statement conceded that the type of soil in which the plants are grown and the type and quantity of fertilizer applied to the growing plants play a role in plant composition.

"The evidence is clear," says Dr. Mark Schwartz, *Prevention* magazine's director of research and development. "The soil serves as more than a medium of physical support for plants. Our well-being depends on the growth of nutritionally balanced crops."

In a carefully documented report, Dr. Schwartz showed the definite connection between the fertility of the soil and the nutrient content of produce. "Intensively farmed land just can't keep on supplying the amounts of zinc, manganese, iron, copper, and other trace minerals necessary to prevent dietary deficiencies," he said.

Recent years have witnessed an increased awareness of the indispensability of micronutrients to the maintenance of health in man, animal and plant. Overcultivation of the land along with modern agricultural practices, such as double cropping, using high-yielding hybrids and concentrated chemical fertilizers have reduced the supply of many of these elements.

There are even instances of reduced yield traceable to these missing micronutrients.

Scientists generally agree that the mineral balance of foods is determined by the mineral quality of the soil on which they're grown. Thus, corn from fertile soil has a higher protein content and is a better hog feed than corn raised on poor, though highly fertilized, soil.

In 1965, Dr. Homer T. Hopkins of the U.S. Food and Drug Administration reported on the relation of soils and fertilizers to the quantity and chemical composition of foods of plant origin to Dr. Phillip L. Harris, director of the division of nutrition. While working for the U.S. Department of Agriculture previously, Dr. Hopkins had studied the mineral elements in fresh vegetables from different geographic areas and found a considerable divergence. He reviewed the literature on this subject for Dr. Harris and concluded that the statement that "the nutritional values of our crops are not significantly affected by either the soil or kind of fertilizer used" could not be defended.

Dr. Hopkins cited the following as the basis for his conclusions: Application of 40 tons of barnyard manure to potato soils on Long Island, New York, resulted in doubling the iron content of potatoes grown there. Composition of roughages may be affected greatly by the amount of plant food in the soil. Hypomagnesemia, or grass tetany, occurred in animals fed on grasslands heavily fertilized with potassium fertilizer. The chemical composition of forages may be altered by fertilization of soil. Application of a plant nutrient to soils in quantities greater than those required for maximum yield response usually resulted in luxury (excessive) consumption of the nutrient by the plant. Biological assays showed that forages grown on sandy soils, when fed to guinea pigs, had lower biological value than forages grown on clay soils. Further, it has been demonstrated that the amounts of trace elements added to the soil as "contaminants" in chemical fertilizer supplying nitrogen, phosphorus and potassium are inconsequential.

Scientific effort in the study of soil quality's effect on nutrition has been given a very low priority. Neither has there been much research into methods of producing food of better-than-normal nutritional value. The genetic makeup of plants is a very significant factor in the nutritional value of the food those plants produce. Genetic factors, however, have been manipulated primarily to produce plants of uniform size, uniform date of ripening and other benefits to mechanized agriculture. Nutritional factors have been sacrificed as a result.

That the addition of organic matter to the soil improves its water-holding capacity, increases its drought resistance and reduces the activity and movement of pesticides is well known. The effect of organic matter in the soil serves as an important reserve source of certain nutrients for plants, and in many cases it helps to keep important nutrients available to the plant. The importance of organic matter and its effect on available nutrients has been demonstrated. There is a highly significant positive relationship between soil organic matter and iron content of vegetables. A 1971 report by the USDA indicated that the highest death rate areas in the United States generally corresponded to those where agriculturalists have recognized the soil as being depleted for several years.

The obvious, perhaps unscientific conclusion of these various findings is that there is some connection between soil and health. The conclusion is neither new nor unscientific, however, for a number of pioneering scientists, including Sir Albert Howard, Sir Robert McCarrison and Dr. William Albrecht, pursued the connection throughout their scientific careers.

Sir Albert Howard is generally regarded as the founder of the organic method of agriculture. He developed the Indore process of composting and did the essential practical research basic to the organic method. Over a period of 30 years in India, Sir Albert determined that the use of chemical fertilizers was devitalizing the soil and the food that was grown in it.

As a mycologist in the West Indies, Sir Albert had an opportunity to study the diseases of sugar cane. He came to the conclusion that the existing methods of scientific research would never solve the problem of plant disease. In 1905, he was appointed Imperial Economic Botanist to the Government of India.

Around his farm, Sir Albert kept a close watch on the methods of the natives and saw how careful they were that all animal and plant residues were returned to the soil. Every blade of grass that could be salvaged, all leaves that fell, all weeds that were cut down found their way back into the soil, there to decompose and take their proper place in the natural cycle. The crops in the region surrounding Sir Albert's experimental farm were practically immune from disease.

Sir Albert also observed a gradual lessening of animal disease. When his oxen rubbed noses with other cattle that had the dreaded hoof-and-mouth disease they did not contract it; they had become strengthened and could fight off dangerous disease organisms because their food came from a soil rich in living humus matter, that had not been defiled with harmful chemicals. Sir Albert sums up his work with the classic statement, "Artificial fertilizers lead to artificial nutrition, artificial animals and finally to artificial men and women." Another author put it in a different way. He said: "The only crop that can be raised on poor land is poor people."

Sir Robert McCarrison was another pioneer of the organic method. His most familiar work centered on the ten years he spent with the Hunzukuts of northern India around the second decade of this century. When he discovered that the people of Hunza had an excellent diet which made them extremely healthy, he decided to find out if rats would experience the same good health if fed a similar diet. He worked with three groups of rats—one group fed on the same diet as the Hunzas; a second group on the diet of the southern India rice-eaters; and a third group that was subjected to the diet of the lower classes of England, containing white bread, margarine, sugar-sweetened tea, a little boiled milk, cabbage, potatoes, canned meats, and sugared jam.

McCarrison found the Hunza group quite healthy, but group number two suffered from a wide variety of diseases.

The third group, the British rats, not only developed these diseases, but were nervous and apt to bite their attendants. They were hostile to one another and by the sixtieth day of the experiment began to kill and eat the weaker ones amongst them. McCarrison's evidence, like that of many researchers since, seemed to indicate clearly that diet is associated with health.

The most prominent American student of the connection between soil and health was Dr. William Albrecht, head of the soils department of the University of Missouri for many years. Albrecht used knowledge from basic and applied research to promote human health.

His underlying interest was preventive medicine.

In this respect, Albrecht was far ahead of his time. He believed that human health is determined to a large extent by proper nutrition; and that the nutritional quality of food depends, in turn, on the fertility of the soil which produces that food. Aware of the value of soil organic matter, he looked upon agriculture, the care of domestic animals and the maintenance of personal health, not as examples of laboratory experiments carried out on a larger scale, but as complex biological processes that follow certain laws which must be obeyed. He made it clear that the primary health concern of every individual should be the use to which the world's topsoil is put.

HEART NUT   (*Juglans ailanthifolia*)

Introduced into this country from Japan almost 100 years ago, the heart nut is now recognized as one of the best ornamental nut trees. With its luxurious, almost tropical foliage, the heart nut provides a dense shade, yet grass grows well under it.

Heart nut trees seldom grow larger than apple trees, as they have a tendency to grow rather low and very spreading. Because of this tendency, it's necessary to "fight" it for the first few years to get the tree headed high enough. Do this by cutting off one or two of the lower limbs each year and cutting back some of the longer laterals. Any of the new growth that threatens to compete with the leader should also be cut back. Sometimes growers find it necessary to place a high post beside the tree, to which they can tie one of the most vigorous branches in an upright position to form a leader.

The heart nut—along with other members of the Japanese walnut species—thrives in both clay and sandy soils. J. Russell Smith, nut tree expert, describes it as "a veritable goat in its feeding habit," making it a very rapid grower, "and in rich soils a single leaf is sometimes a yard long."

In form, the nut is distinctly heart shaped with a short, flat base and sharply pointed tip. Produced in clusters—sometimes of ten or more—their flavor is mild, except with the choicest varieties, which taste much like the butternut. Generally the tree tends to bear annually, though not as heavily as the black or Persian walnut.

Because of its many good features, the heart nut and other Japanese walnut trees should receive more attention from plant breeders in the future. In its native home, the trees grow throughout the climatic range of Japan, a range as wide as that from Nova Scotia to Georgia.

At the present time, the heart nut's average life span in America seldom exceeds 30 years.

See also NUT TREES.

HEATH; HEATHER   (*Erica*)

This large genus of woody perennial shrubs is noted for its small white or brightly colored flowers and its compact habit of growth. Many species are grown in California and a few hardy types can be grown in the North. There are many popular greenhouse heaths, or heathers, which can be set outdoors during summer months.

All heaths prefer an acid soil, but one species, winter or spring heath (*E. carnea*), tolerates some lime. Plant low-growing types in the rock garden or perennial border where the soil is light and sandy. Supply potted specimens with plenty of peat and coarse sand. Watering is necessary only during severe droughts. Prune the plants immediately after flowering to prevent them from becoming straggly. They are easily propagated from cuttings of young wood, taken in early summer and planted in moist sand.

The most common species in this country are Cornish heath (*E. vagans*), cross-leaved heath (*E. Tetralix*), Irish heath (*E. mediterranea*), Scotch heather (*E. cinerea*), and winter heath (*E. carnea*).

Cornish heath is a dwarf, spreading shrub that is usually less than two feet tall. Flowers are white or deep pink and appear in late summer. The plant is one of the hardiest heaths and will survive the winters of central New England.

Cross-leaved heath is somewhat less hardy. Also known as bog heather, it bears rose flowers throughout the summer and early fall.

Irish heath is a tall species that reaches heights of ten feet. It can be grown as far north as Kentucky where it blooms in late spring.

Scotch heather is found growing wild on Nantucket. It grows to two feet, has deep purple to blue flowers, and blossoms in summer and early autumn. Many cultivars are available.

Winter heath, also known as spring or snow heather, is a very hardy species that blooms in early spring or, in some regions, throughout the winter. It is one foot high with red flowers.

HEAVING

Heaving refers to a type of winter injury in which plants are loosened and frequently lifted from the soil as a result of successive freezing and thawing. Soils with a considerable clay or silt content, which alternately freeze and thaw in the spring, are most prone to heaving. To prevent such injury, the gardener can protect his plantings with a heavy mulch cover and can add humus in the form of compost to improve his soil and proportionately reduce its clay content.

HEAVY SOIL

Heavy soil is soil that contains a high percentage of clay and/or silt. It generally holds too much moisture and has poor drainage. The term originated from the heavy draft on horses when plowing such soils.

See also AERATION, CLAY SOIL, SOIL.

HEDERA
See ENGLISH IVY, HOUSE PLANTS, IVY

HEDGE

A hedge is a row of plants, generally woody, used as a border, fence, screen, or windbreak. It is usually trimmed to a more or less formal shape. Plants used for hedging are chosen for their capacity to hold a shape, and to form a thick intertangled growth from the ground up. Hedges, though sometimes used as borders around formal gardens, are to be distinguished from edgings, which are mostly temporary borders along walks or enclosing flower beds.

Along property lines, where it is desirable to screen in the property or provide a wind-break, hedges may be as high as a line of poplars or a row of evergreen trees. Where a lower wall or fence would be used, the hedge may be equally low. In formal European gardens dating back to the seventeenth and eighteenth centuries, six- to 12-inch hedges were used to outline flower beds of fancy shapes. In Europe, hedges are often used in place of fences around fields and pastures.

Either evergreen or deciduous plants may be used for hedging. Evergreen hedges are usually slower growing, and are preferred for that reason. But any shrub which makes a dense growth may be trimmed to perform the function of a fence.

Planting and Maintenance: To grow a good hedge, it is necessary to prepare the soil deeply, set the plants close and shear them at least twice each year. Distance between plants will be determined by the plant and by the proposed height of the hedge. Privet, planted for quick effects, is spaced about nine inches apart. Most evergreens are best planted at least 18 inches, and some 24 inches apart. Arborvitae may even be set as far as three feet apart.

To insure a dense growth, deciduous plants are usually cut back almost to the ground when planted. Plants grown especially for hedges may not need such drastic pruning, but it is advisable to cut back top growth by at least 30 percent.

Shaping should begin the year after the hedge is planted, though for the first few years pruning should be light until the desired height and general shape are attained. Deciduous hedges should be pruned after the first strong growth of the spring has slowed down, typically in May or June, and again in midsummer when the secondary growth may need to be shaped. Evergreens grow more slowly, and should never be severely pruned. Shaping once each year in midsummer should be sufficient.

For densest growth to the ground, hedges should be kept narrower at the top than they are at the bottom, shaped in cross section like a truncated pyramid. This shape will permit the lower branches to get enough light to keep them healthy and thickly foliated. When permitted to broaden at the top, a hedge will lose its lower leaves and become leggy. This effect is also sometimes the result of pruning neglect. When a hedge has not been pruned for several years, it becomes thin at the bottom. The only remedy is frequent and careful pruning for a year or two.

To maintain its health, a hedge should be kept clean at its base, particularly in wet seasons when fungus diseases may attack. Because the foliage protects the soil under it from the rays of the sun, mulching is usually unnecessary, and leaves that blow under the hedge from neighboring trees should be removed.

Deciduous plants recommended for low hedges (under 18 inches) are: dwarf cranberry-bush, *Viburnum Opulus* cv. 'Nanum'; *Spiraea* cv. 'Anthony Waterer' and *Spiraea* x *Bumalda;* box barberry, *Berberis Thunbergii* cv. 'Atropurpurea'; privet, *Ligustrum* spp. Low-growing evergreens include: box, *Buxus sempervirens* cv. 'Suffruticosa'; pygmy Hinoki cypress, *Chamaecyparis obtusa* cv. 'Pygmaea'; common thyme, *Thymus vulgaris*. Evergreens which will not grow to a height of more than two feet are:

Thuja occidentalis cv. 'Globosa' and other dwarf arborvitae; Hinoki cypress, *Chamaecyparis obtusa;* Japanese yew, *Taxus cuspidata;* Japanese holly, *Ilex crenata;* inkberry, *Ilex glabra.*

Deciduous shrubs which can be grown for medium-height hedges are: California privet, *Ligustrum ovalifolium;* Ibota privet, *L. ibota;* Amur privet, *L. amurense;* Japanese barberry, *Berberis Thunbergi;* flowering or Japanese quince, *Chaenomeles speciosa;* rugosa rose, *Rosa rugosa;* Vanhoutte spirea, *Spiraea vanhouttei;* arrowwood, *Viburnum dentatum;* Peking cotoneaster, *Cotoneaster acutifolius.*

Evergreen trees which make a close growth for good hedges are: tall varieties of *Thuja occidentalis;* hemlock, *Tsuga canadensis;* Irish juniper, *Juniperus communis* cv. 'Hibernica'; Norway spruce, *Picea Abies.* Deciduous trees that make good hedges are: European beech, *Fagus sylvatica;* English hawthorn, *Crataegus laevigata;* cockspur-thorn, *C. crusgalli;* and hornbeam, *Carpinus Betulus.*

Formal or Informal: There are two types of hedges—formal and informal. The formal hedge has definite lines and clean-cut surfaces. The informal hedge is allowed to grow freely, and is not clipped close. The only trimming needed is an occasional pruning to keep it within bounds. Trimmed hedges are often used in landscape design as horizontal lines and to tie buildings and formal gardens together.

Plants for formal hedges include the privets, boxwoods, yews, and arborvitae. Some plants for informal hedges are the barberries, mock orange, lilac, spirea, viburnum, and dwarf deutzia.

Aside from the beauty they contribute to a landscape, informal hedges are valued around pastures and fields for the shelter they provide.

Sometimes called shelterbelts, these hedges encourage earlier grass growth and greater total production, and reduce wind erosion of soil. Shelter trees can also help sustain livestock through the winter season and neutralize turbulent winds that reduce crop yields. Shelterbelts also supply cheap timber for farm use.

Wild fencerows are often the centers of abundant wildlife, including pheasants, squirrels, mice, and wild bird species. The winter snow and chill protection they provide sustain many wildlife species.

Favored plants for fencerows include apple, grape, cherry, plum, and honey locust.

See also EVERGREEN, SHRUBS, WINDBREAK.

HEDGEHOG CONEFLOWER
See ECHINACEA

HEEL-IN

The practice of covering plants temporarily with soil before planting them is called heeling-in.

Plants set out in the spring require little attention before planting. Simply unpack them in a cool, shady place and examine them for any signs of damage. If they are to be planted at once, cut off any broken or ragged roots with a sharp knife or shears so as to make a clean cut. If the stock is received too late for planting, or for some reason cannot be cared for at once, heel-in as follows: Dig a shallow trench in a well-drained spot with one side vertical and the other sloping. Lay the plants

To store plants before placing them in a permanent location, "heel" them in by putting them in a shallow trench in a well-drained location. Cover the roots, tamp the earth and water thoroughly.

close together in the trench with the roots against the vertical side and the stems resting on the slope. Cover the roots completely and water them thoroughly. If the plants are to stay heeled-in all winter, tamp the earth firmly around the roots and cover the trunks and lower branches as well. Heeled-in material can be pulled out and permanently planted at a later date.

HELENIUM

Known as sneeze-weed, these are mostly hardy yellow-flowering perennials that bloom from summer to fall. Yellow star (*H. autumnale*) grows about five feet and is usually placed toward the rear of flower borders. They do best in a moist, rich soil in a sunny location.

HELIANTHEMUM

Belonging to the Cistaceae family, these are low-growing woody plants often used in the rock garden. Known as rockroses and sunroses, helianthemums are native to North and South America. *H. nummularium* is the commonest sunrose, having yellow flowers and generally growing less than 18 inches tall. They are especially adapted to the California climate, where they are well suited to dry, sunny rock gardens and are propagated by seed, cuttings or division.

HELIANTHUS   *See* SUNFLOWER

HELIOPSIS

Heliopsises are summer-blooming perennials that in many ways resemble the sunflower. Orange sunflower (*H. helianthoides* subsp. *scabra*) grows to about three feet with a strong stem that does not require staking. The variety *incomparabilis* produces deep yellow semidouble flowers three to four inches across. Summer Sun has completely double yellow flowers and blooms readily the first season.

Soil should be moderately rich and not dry. Heliopsises are usually trouble-free plants requiring little maintenance to keep them in top form. Propagate by division in spring.

HELIOTROPE   (*Heliotropium*)

Temperate and tropical plants popular for their large fragrant flower heads, heliotropes range in height from one to four feet. The common heliotrope (*H. arborescens*) is generally cultivated as an annual, growing two to four feet tall. The plant is appreciated for its scent and beauty in the garden.

Heliotrope was brought from Peru to Paris in the eighteenth century, and has since become popular in England and America. English gardens often displayed these ornamental plants, and they were also favored by Victorians for their scent. They were used in sachets and toilet waters. The name "heliotrope" means "turning to the sun," and supposedly refers to the tendency this plant shares with most others to grow towards the sun.

The old-fashioned, very fragrant heliotrope is perhaps most familiar as a spring potted plant but can be grown in garden beds and borders as well.

Requiring a light, rich soil and much warmth, heliotrope is started indoors late in spring. After the soil has warmed and all danger of frost has passed, set the plants about one foot apart in the garden rows.

A small tree for window gardens can be cultivated by persistently clipping side shoots as they appear and applying good fertilizer. The potting soil must be rich but well drained. Standards need a firm stake for support. The tops can be trimmed and the flowers pinched off until a trunk, three to five feet high, is grown. This process requires perseverance and takes about four years.

Today, heliotrope is valued mainly by the gardener who wants a fragrant, flowering plant or small tree in his garden. The Harkness Garden, near New London, Connecticut, is known for its fine collection of heliotrope trees.

See also HERB.

HELIOTROPISM

Heliotropism, or phototropism, is the tendency for plants to "grow towards" sunlight. For reasons which are not entirely understood, growth hormones (auxins) build up in the shaded side of a plant's growing tip. The cells on this side elongate more rapidly than those on the side facing the light source and so the stem begins to curve toward the light. This phenomenon can be observed in house plants placed on a sunny windowsill or in garden plants that grow away from the shade of large shrubs and toward the open space.

Sunflower heads, for example, seem to follow the sun's movements across the sky, and then—during the evening—they slowly return to the east.

HELLEBORUS   *See* CHRISTMAS ROSE

HEMLOCK   (*Tsuga*)

This very popular evergreen tree of the Pine family is often seen in the garden landscape. It is a graceful tree, with fanlike sprays of green blue foliage and quantities of small cones. The cones are somewhat woody but not stiff, and are generally borne on the twig ends.

The small, flat needles, ¼ to ½ inch long, are arranged in rows on each side of the twig, and drop off quickly when dry.

The two most common species are the Canada (*T. canadensis*) and Carolina (*T. caroliniana*) hemlocks. The Canada hemlock (often called hemlock spruce or eastern hemlock) is the one best known in the northeastern section of the country. It is conical, tapering evenly from a broad base to a long, straight head. Capable of reaching almost 100 feet, it usually grows much shorter. It is commonly used as a hedge.

The Carolina hemlock is often called spruce pine, and has dark, dense foliage with sweeping branches.

Although very hardy trees, hemlocks do best in a rich, moist soil, and like a somewhat wind-sheltered location. They do not stand up well to intense summer heat or periods of drought.

Other varieties include the pyramid-shaped Japanese hemlock (*T. diversifolia*); western hemlock (*T. heterophylla*), adapted mostly to the West Coast; and mountain hemlock (*T. Mertensiana*), also restricted mostly to the western part of the country.

See also EVERGREEN.

HENBANE   (*Hyoscyamus niger*)

A poisonous annual or biennial herb of the Potato family introduced into this country from Europe, henbane is occasionally found as a weed in some of the northern and Great Plains states. The herb (leaves, flowers and small stems) contains several poisonous alkaloids used in the preparation of important medicines.

This herb was known to the ancient Greeks. Henbane is believed to be the soporific sponge used as an anesthetic from the ancient

All parts of the annual henbane weed are poisonous but scientists have successfully extracted certain valuable medicines from the leaves.

Greek civilization until the Middle Ages. Henbane is also said to have been mixed with tobacco to produce a narcotic effect. Witches of the period were supposed to have included henbane in their rituals.

The soil and climatic requirements of henbane are very similar to those of belladonna, but the plant is less subject to root decay under poor drainage conditions. The seed germinates uniformly in about two weeks.

If the annual type is grown, the crop is harvested when the plants are in full bloom. The biennial type makes a large rosettelike growth the first year and blooms early in the second season.

Today, henbane is used less than in past centuries. It is still recognized for its abilities to relieve pain, induce sleep and relieve nervous irritations. Authorities note the use of this herb to treat mercury poisoning and morphine addictions.

Henbane is the source of the hypnotic poison, hyoscyanin, whose effects resemble those of atropin. If accidentally eaten, a strong purgative and medical attention is imperative. Henbane is rarely eaten, even by mistake, because of its unpleasant odor. There have been cases recorded, however, of people mistaking the herb roots for salsify or chicory.

See also HERB.

HENSEL, JULIUS

(1833–1903) Hensel's concept of mineral nutrition is extremely different from the more traditional theories of Justus von Liebig. Von Liebig, the founder of agricultural chemistry, believed that the only major mineral nutrients in soil were potassium, nitrogen and phosphorus. The entire synthetic fertilizer industry is based on his original tenets.

Hensel, however, believed that the use of potassium, nitrates and phosphates alone does not replenish the soil. A soil analysis reveals the truth of this position as well as the existence of calcium, magnesium, manganese, silicium oxide, aluminum oxide, and the many trace elements.

Hensel observed that plants grown in mountain valleys and on virgin soils are always healthy, vigorous and almost disease-free. He thought that the strength of these plants must lie in fertile bottomland, which had been enriched by the minerals washed down the mountainsides by rains and natural streams. In the plains, where no new alluvial soil is added, the land gradually becomes exhausted. This simple observation was the basis of his plan to powder mountain rock and apply it where nature herself could no longer do it. He then analyzed plants and found that different plants vary widely in their mineral constituents.

With the addition of finely ground stonemeal, Hensel obtained positive results. He observed that plants not only grew in quantity but were also healthy and free of parasites. Another important observation was that roots grew particularly well in soils thus treated. According to Hensel's book, *Bread from Stones* (published in translation by Charles L. Davidson, Sr., P.O. Box 527, Lithonia, GA 30058), "If we desire normal and *healthy* crops, and that men and animals living on them should find in them *all* that is necessary for their bodily sustenance . . . (phosphate and fluorate of lime and magnesia for the formation of the bones and teeth, potassa, iron and manganese for the muscles, chloride of sodium for the serum of the blood, sulfur for the albumen of the blood, hydrocarbons for the nerve-fat), it will not suffice to merely restore the *potassium, phosphoric acid* and *nitrogen.* Other things are imperatively demanded."

HEPATICA

Also known as the mayflower and liverleaf, hepatica is a low-growing, perennial native wild flower that blooms in early spring. It does best in the partial shade of open woods or forest edges. The soil should be rich and well drained. Propagation is usually by root division in the fall. Seed can be sown in fall or very early spring for blossoming the following year. Common hepatica (*H. americana*), also known as blue anemone, grows to six inches high and has mostly blue, but sometimes white or pink, flowers. Similar in appearance is the sharp-lobed hepatica, *H. acutiloba,* named for its pointed three-lobed leaves. Both are good subjects for the wild flower garden.

Hepatica leaves can be infused and made into a tea that soothes colds and sore throats. It has long been recognized as an astringent and cold treatment.

HEPTACHLOR
See CHLORINATED HYDROCARBONS

HERALD'S-TRUMPET
(*Beaumontia grandiflora*)

This is a tall, woody vine or small tree of the Dogbane family. Its leaves are six to nine inches long, and the tree's fragrant, white flower trumpets measure four inches long and four inches across. The fruit is a long cylinder lined with a silky material. Native to India and grown outside only in frost-free climates, the tree may also be grown in a warm, moist greenhouse, but it should not be confined to a pot. Beaumontia prefers a rich, loamy soil and full sun.

HERB

The primary definition given the word "herb" by the dictionary is: "A seed-producing annual, biennial or perennial that does not develop persistent woody tissue but dies down at the end of a growing season." This is the botanical definition of the word. But it eliminates many plants that are traditionally regarded as herbs.

The definition most accepted as *the* definition of "herb" is: "A plant or plant part valued for its medicinal, savory, or aromatic qualities." Or, as the Herb Society of America, as good an arbiter of such things as any, puts it: "Any plant that may be used for pleasure, fragrance or physic." Thus defined, herb includes a broad spectrum of plants—trees, shrubs and herbage.

Historically, most plants that can be categorized as herbs contain some substance in the root, leaf, bark, flower, or fruit that, at one time, has been used in medicines. Paging through any old herbal—and most new ones— one will find the names of hundreds of plants, some still popularly considered herbs (rosemary and thyme), others commonly viewed as weeds (purslane and dandelion), and still others considered only trees or shrubs (poplar). But beyond the old herbals, one finds the marketplace flooded with books on herb cookery, on using plants for making fragrant potions, lotions and objects, on dyeing and decorating with plants, and on landscaping and gardening with plants. All involve using plants for pleasure, fragrance or physic; all are herbs.

Medicinal Herbs: The oldest and probably the most interesting use of herbs is for healing. In every age, some writer recorded the medicinal uses of herbs. Herbals survive from the earliest Chinese civilizations, from the ancient Greeks and Romans, from the Elizabethan English, and from the earliest settlers in the New World. Even today, modern herbalists and students of folk medicine are collecting and spreading the lore of medicinal herbs.

The healing value of herbs, of course, is not simply folklore. For centuries, the established medical authorities prescribed particular plant parts and combinations thereof for the remedy of illnesses. In relatively recent years, pharmacy has advanced to the point where scientists now analyze plant tissue in order to extract the chemical constituents and isolate the plants' healing factor. Once pinpointed, the factor is synthesized. This enables physicians to prescribe specific doses of an accurately measurable size and consistent quality. The number of pharmaceutical firms that package and sell botanicals has dwindled, and the pharmacists that do more than count out pills are few and far between.

In modern China, however, the situation is very different. There herbs are widely cultivated, chiefly for their medicinal qualities. Even military installations have their prominent herb gardens, with each plant carefully labeled. Soldiers are taught to identify medicinal plants, to enable them to forage for healing plants in field situations. Paramedical personnel work closely with the people, using herbal remedies to a great extent. As one Western observer put it: "Everyone in China is a little bit of an herbalist. The housewives, the farmers, and even the school children grow herbs and learn to recognize them. Furthermore, herbs are easily available at stores, are extremely cheap, and are reasonably safe to use."

There is, perhaps, a tendency to expect more of medicinal plants than they can deliver. But if you are looking for a refreshing beverage when you have a scratchy throat, try some horehound tea. Or to settle a touch of indigestion, try chamomile tea.

A word of caution is in order here. There are any number of plants—medicinal herbs, in fact—that can make you sick or even kill you. If you are prompted to seek out more information on herbal medicine and especially to try it, avoid the dangerous herbs. Many of the available herb books fail to make clear the potential dangers of the following plants: jimsonweed, daffodil, spurge, arnica, wormwood, mandrake, hellebore, squill, poison hemlock, tobacco, tonka bean, aconite, white bryony, nux vomica, calabar bean, camphor, ergot, bittersweet, gelsemium, henbane, celandine, belladonna (deadly nightshade), foxglove, and mayflower. Others that should be dealt with cautiously include tansy, valerian, rue, lobelia, goldenseal, and bloodroot.

Don't feel that you'll be missing much if you don't try the above plants. There are plenty of other plants with reputed medicinal values that are in no way dangerous, and that have fragrant and visual values as well. For example, according to Mark Bricklin, executive editor of *Prevention* magazine, writing in *The Practical Encyclopedia of Natural Healing* (Emmaus, PA: Rodale Press, Inc., 1976), the ten most practical medicinal herbs are: comfrey, garlic, chamomile, peppermint, cayenne, sage, horseradish, catnip, rosemary, and coltsfoot. The herbs selected were those that

(continued on page 514)

Name	Type Height Flowers	Distance apart	Suggested methods of propagation
ANISE *Pimpinella Anisum*	annual 18 in. white	6 in.	seed (self-sows)
BASIL *Ocimum Basilicum*	annual 24 in. white	10 in.	seed
BORAGE *Borago officinalis*	annual 36 in. white, blue	15 in.	seed (self-sows)
BURNET *Poterium Sanguisorba*	perennial 12–18 in. white, rose	12 in.	seed
CARAWAY *Carum Carvi*	biennial (treat as annual) 24–36 in. white	6 in.	seed (self-sows)
CHERVIL *Anthriscus cerefolium*	annual 18 in. white	6 in.	seed (self-sows)
CHIVE *Allium Schoenoprasum*	perennial 18 in. lavender	6 in.	seed division

GARDEN HERBS

Cultural Directions	Culinary Uses
Full sun, fairly dry, rich soil.	Leaves for salad, seeds for garnish, cakes and cookies. In Holland, seeds are steeped in hot milk to induce sleep.
Full sun, rich soil; needs some protection from wind. Several cuttings of the top three to four inches can be made in a season.	Superb for tomatoes and tomato dishes. In soups, and with meat, fish and vegetables. Place in water when boiling shellfish. Use in salads and in egg, cheese and spaghetti dishes.
Full sun, average garden soil. Make two sowings.	Adds piquant cucumberlike flavor to salads and drinks. Blossoms used as garnish for drinks.
Full sun, poor dry soil. Sow seed in early spring or fall.	Cucumber flavor for salads. Good for tea and vinegar.
Full sun, average garden soil.	Seeds with bread, cookies, baked apples, ragouts, cheese.
Semishade, rich, moist soil. Likes humus (best plants often come from old seed heads thrown on compost pile). Sow seed in early spring and late summer.	Fish, soups, salads, omelets. Combine with butter sauce when basting chicken for broiling. Flavor is best preserved by freezing herb rather than drying.
Full sun, richer soil than most herbs. Sow seed thickly. Dress with compost or manure. Divide every year.	Gives zip and color cut fine into cream soups, salads, omelets, scrambled eggs, cheese dishes, potato soup.

Name	Type Height Flowers	Distance apart	Suggested methods of propagation
COSTMARY *Chrysanthemum* *Balsamita*	perennial 60 in. yellow	12 in.	division
DILL *Anethum* *graveolens*	annual 36 in. yellow	sow in clumps	seed (self-sows)
FENNEL *Foeniculum* *vulgare*	perennial (treat as annual) 60 in. yellow	18 in.	seed
HYSSOP *Hyssopus* *officinalis*	perennial 12–18 in. blue, pink	10 in.	seed (self-sows) cuttings division
LEMON BALM *Melissa* *officinalis*	perennial 24 in. white	18 in.	seed (self-sows) division
MARJORAM *Origanum* *Majorana*	perennial (treat as annual) 12 in. white	6 in.	seed
MINT *Mentha* spp.	perennial 12 in. purple	12 in.	cuttings division
OREGANO *Origanum vulgare*	perennial 20 in. pink	12 in.	seed cuttings division

Cultural Directions	Culinary Uses
Sun or semishade, rich soil.	Strong anise flavor. Use sparingly in green salads, poultry dishes, some jellies. Used for tea.
Full sun, good soil. Sow seed in clumps so plants can lean against one other.	Seeds for vinegar and pickling, in seed cakes and bread. Leaves to flavor soups, sauces, fish, lamb. Cook with beans, sauerkraut, cabbage, cauliflower. Mix into potato salad, macaroni, coleslaw.
Full sun, good soil. Sow early spring and fall. Has heavy flower heads and should be supported against a fence.	Stems used like celery. Seeds and leaves impart licorice tang to fish sauces, chowders, soups, pickles. Seeds for bread, tea.
Full sun, limey soil.	Very strong. A few leaves give an interesting flavor to green salads and beef soups. Dried flowers sometimes used in soups. Leaves, shoots and tops for tea.
Partial shade, moist soil.	With fish, lamb, beef, and in salads. Used like mint in beverages. Dried leaves for tea.
Full sun, dry soil.	In stews, meat loaf, green salads, poultry stuffing. Cook with beans, peas, carrots. Rub on meats before roasting.
Part shade, moist, slightly acid soil. Avoid manure since it causes fungus disease. In late fall, cut plants to ground level, mulch with compost.	Sprinkle on fresh fruits, peas or squash. Use in salads, drinks, make tea. Combine with lemon balm for delightful herb vinegar. Mint sauce.
Full sun, fairly dry soil.	In Spanish, Mexican and Italian dishes. Rub on veal and lamb before roasting. In goulash, stew, sauces, soups.

Name	Type Height Flowers	Distance apart	Suggested methods of propagation
PARSLEY *Petroselinum crispum*	biennial (treat as annual) 10–15 in. yellow	6 in.	seed
ROSEMARY *Rosmarinus officinalis*	tender perennial 36 in. blue	18 in.	seed cuttings layering
SAGE *Salvia officinalis*	perennial 24 in. blue	15 in.	seed cuttings division
SAVORY *Satureja hortensis*	annual 12–18 in. pink	5 in.	seed
SESAME *Sesamum indicum*	annual 18 in. lavender	6 in.	seed
SHALLOT *Allium Cepa*	perennial 24 in.	4 in.	cloves
SWEET CICELY *Myrrhis odorata*	perennial 24–36 in. white	18 in.	seed (self-sows) division

Cultural Directions	Culinary Uses
Partial shade, average garden soil. Seeds are slow to germinate and should be soaked overnight.	With all vegetables, salads, soups, stews, omelets. One tablespoon equals adult daily requirements of vitamins A and C.
Full sun, poor light soil with ample lime. Bring indoors in winter or store dormant in cool cellar.	In chicken dishes, soups, stews, gravies, muffin batter. Add to water when cooking peas, potatoes, turnips. Sprinkle on meats before roasting or broiling.
Full sun, sandy soil. Soak seed a few hours to aid germination.	With meats and fish. In dressing, stuffing, egg and cheese dishes. Leaves for tea to relieve colds, sore throats.
Full sun, rich and fairly dry soil. Does not transplant well.	In meat loaf, hamburger, beef stew. Biscuit and dumpling batters, egg dishes, pea and bean soup. On fish and pork, and in cooking beans, peas, cabbage, sauerkraut.
Full sun, average garden soil.	Seeds in bread and cake. Grind and mix with nuts, figs, poppy seed, or honey to make a healthful candy.
Full sun, average garden soil. Bulb breaks up into many cloves.	Good with any dish calling for onions. Wonderful with steaks, roast beef, game. Use four or five cloves when recipe calls for one shallot.
Partial shade, acid, moist soil. Sow seed in July, for germination the following spring.	Leaves add anise flavor to green salads. Seeds good with cabbage and many other foods.

Name	Type Height Flowers	Distance apart	Suggested methods of propagation
TARRAGON *Artemisia* *Dracunculus*	perennial 24 in. yellow	12 in.	cuttings division
THYME *Thymus vulgaris*	perennial 12 in. lavender	8 in.	seed cuttings division

"are not only famed for their medicinal properties (and often, good taste) but are also used frequently enough throughout the year to make it worthwhile cultivating them yourself." More information about them is found under the plant names.

Herbs in Cooking: One doesn't need to be sick to find herbs useful. Indeed, herbs are undeniably used more in cooking today than in medicine.

To most people just the mention of the word herb cultivates interesting culinary ideas. Experimenting with different combinations of herbs can change ordinary cuts of meat, vegetables or desserts into different and unusual dishes. They can also improve bland recipes for people on restricted diets. Oregano can replace salt, and sweet cicely can replace sugar, for example.

Using fresh herbs when they are available for cooking is preferable, but the dried herbs work nearly as well. The rule of thumb is to use twice the amount of fresh herbs to the dried. Be careful not to overdo either the fresh or the dried until you have tested your family's preference.

When entertaining, be sure to try out a new recipe before serving it to your guests. Sometimes a few sprigs more or less can make a world of difference. Another caution is to limit the number of dishes containing herbs. Two or three unusual flavors are enough for your guest at one meal. Plan your menu with a basic idea in mind and work around it. It is usually easier to decide on the main dish first, then your other foods will fall into place.

The accompanying chart lists 24 common garden herbs, suggesting culinary uses for them. These suggestions should be sufficient to start any cook off on herbal experiments in the kitchen. Beyond this, there are a number of herb-oriented cookbooks available.

Aromatic Herbs: Since ancient times, herbs have been valued for their fragrance. This valuation isn't far removed from medicinal uses, since the original aromatic uses involved

Cultural Directions	Culinary Uses
Full sun, average garden soil, some protection from wind.	Poultry, steak, fish, and egg and cheese dishes. In green salad and salad dressing, and tartar and lemon butter sauces. Rub roasting bird inside and outside for taste treat.
Full sun, sandy soil. This herb will layer if mulched with earth in fall.	A universal herb—use with meat, fish, vegetables, egg dishes, soups, stuffing, chowders. Tops with tomatoes, cheese canapes.

the masking of unpleasant odors which were believed unhealthful. The least contrived such use was to strew plants on floors, where the foliage would be crushed under foot to release the herb's fragrance. Sachets and potpourris, pomanders, aromatic waters, and herbal oils all involve some kind of processing.

These herbal aromatics have both tangible and intangible benefits. A cloth bag of dried herbs hung in the bath water will yield tonic effects comparable to a cup of herb tea; but instead of drinking the tea, you bathe in it. An herb sachet stored with sweaters will not only imbue them with a lovely fragrance, but can repel moths as well.

Herbs in the Garden: There are a lot of reasons for including herbs in your garden. Having plants to put to the traditional herbal uses noted above is not the least of them. Herbs are also a pleasure to include in the garden simply for their beauty and fragrance. There are so many herbs, that it is inconceivable that you won't find dozens to suit your fancy. They can be used as accents in the vegetable or flower garden, or they can be arranged in a special garden of their own.

Lots of gardeners plan and plant a special little herb garden near the kitchen door, where favorite culinary herbs are handy. Others prefer to plant elaborate traditional herb gardens, including as many different kinds and varieties of herbs as they can find. Formal herb gardens can be a pleasure to maintain.

But herbs also have a place in the vegetable garden. As companion plants, many herbs have the power to repel or destroy insect pests. No one has yet sufficiently documented and stringently tested this part of the design to suit the scientists and academicians in the field.

Companion planting is explained in detail elsewhere in this book. Suffice it to say here that herbs are important in any companion-planted garden. Plants that help control insect pests tend to have a strong scent and this strong scent is the key to their effectiveness. Most repellents do not actually "repel" insects so much as they mask, absorb or deodorize the attracting scent of the plants being protected.

Growing Herbs: The best herbs are those that are grown organically, on a small scale, and carefully harvested and dried. Throughout the centuries herbs have changed very little. Unlike vegetables they have not been selectively bred for quantitative growth, and hybridization is very rare. A visitor from ancient Egypt would still recognize a coriander plant.

In order to give an herb plant the proper garden environment, it is necessary to understand its native habitat. Since most herbs originate in the areas around the Mediterranean, they do best when grown in sunny regions where humidity is low and rainfall moderate but evenly distributed. Most perennial herbs are only semihardy and do not survive extremely cold winters unless provided with adequate protection.

Soils found around the Mediterranean are not the most fertile and productive. Therefore, herbs often thrive in soils that offer even the smallest amounts of nutrients. Lavender, for example, or chamomile and thyme are able to flourish where other plants would make a very poor showing. Though there are exceptions to this rule, the majority of herbs feel comfortable in a well-drained soil of sandy, even gravelly, structure. This does not mean, however, that they would not do well on other soils, but drainage remains always an important factor. For the purpose of a home gardener every type of soil can actually be prepared without great effort to accommodate any herb that he or she desires to grow.

Obviously, different herbs prefer different types of soil and soil conditions and consequently need specific soil preparation. Particulars are discussed with individual herbs.

There are, however, some initial requirements for successful herb growing that apply to all herb plants.

The first is that nearly all herbs require well-drained soil. This is, of course, desirable for all types of gardening, but herbs seem particularly finicky about drainage. If your garden plot is poorly drained for whatever reason, an effort must be made to correct this defect.

Another requirement should be kept in mind as an important part of soil preparation. Quite a number of herb seeds are small and slow to germinate, while another group of herbs, especially all the thymes, grow close to the ground and rarely reach a height of more than two inches. For both groups it is mandatory to grow them in soil that is as weed-free as possible. Weeds should be discouraged by an early working of the soil. Prior to planting, the soil can be hoed, raked, rototilled, or cultivated at weekly intervals, thus preventing the sprouting weed seeds from getting established. Plowing or spading the garden in late fall aids in weed control and prepares a fine seedbed for spring planting. Frosts help to pulverize the soil and thus benefit the fine seeds of thyme, marjoram and others that can be seeded outside if soil preparation allows it.

Herbs have kept their natural taste for manures and composts and do not benefit from treatments with water-soluble chemical fertilizers. The amounts of concentrated essential oils in most herbs determine the quality. The formation of these oils is not as dependent upon the earth as upon the cosmic factors of light and the heat intensities. All animal manures, used as fertilizing agents, support rather than inhibit the gradual buildup of oils and other ingredients in the herb plants.

Herb plants also respond well to fertilization with compost; in fact, long experience has shown that compost is the ideal fertilizing agent for all herbs, though the stage of breakdown in the compost pile at time of application can vary with the specific plants. For the home gardener's all-purpose use, the compost should be made from a variety of materials (manures, leaves, weeds, kitchen garbage) and should be well decomposed at the time of application.

Apply compost in spring, after spading or plowing the ground. Within a day, work it into the soil by cultivating or hoeing. If planting does not immediately follow, it is advisable to work the soil once more before setting out the seedlings. This destroys young weeds that have germinated in the meantime and at the same time helps to distribute the compost more uniformly throughout the soil.

There is no question that most herbs should be mulched. The first and foremost reason is to keep the leaves of the herb plants clean in case of heavy rains. Parsley and oregano, for example, grow so low that whole plants can be blown over in a strong storm and pushed into the soil. A mulch prevents this from happening by providing a protective layer between the plant roots within the soil and the elements.

Another main reason for mulching, of course, is weed control. In stands of vegetables or flowers, weeds can become a real nuisance as many gardeners will readily admit. In herb gardens, weeds can be even more of a problem since they are much higher and faster growing than the low herb plants and actually would choke the herbs out if not controlled. Herbs need sun and light and moving air around them, all things that weeds selfishly deny them.

As far as materials for mulching go, each herb grower has his own favorite, partly chosen on the basis of availability. Among the most popular herb mulches for home garden use are cocoa hulls, freshly cut grass, chopped hay, chopped straw, and chopped seaweeds.

Cocoa hulls are ideal because they are dark brown in color, keep little water for themselves and are high in nitrogen. A mulch material influences soil temperature to a great degree by shading the soil and keeping it cooler than it would be without a mulch. However, a dark mulch material, like the cocoa hulls, absorbs rather than reflects the sun's warmth, and in a way resembles soil in this respect, or if the soil is of sandy texture and light color, even improves it. Herb plants, especially thymes and rosemary, like warm soils. Keep this in mind when selecting a mulch material.

The other above-mentioned materials are well known to the organic grower and are generally easier to get. They are handled the same way vegetables are handled, except the thickness of application should be less for herbs. Chopped material is preferred because it settles better, looks neater and is less likely to interfere with harvesting.

After these preparations and considerations are completed, the next step for the practical herb grower is planting. Like all other plants, herbs can be propagated from seed, cuttings, division and to a lesser degree, layering. *See also entries for individual herbs for specifics on propagating them.*

Most individual species of herb plants have strong genetic resistance to insects; the less the variety has been bred, the less prone it is to insect attack.

In growing herbs for culinary or beverage purposes, it should be remembered that any substance which would cause a residue on the leaves will alter the flavor of the finished product and diminish its purity. It is best to avoid even rotenone and pyrethrum.

The above applies in a similar way to the

treatment of plant diseases that are rare to begin with, in organic herb-growing that is. Timely harvest is very important in order to avoid overaging of leaves. As the leaves grow older, they show less resistance to disease and occasionally become host to mildew, especially if cloudy moist weather persists for more than three days. For a small area it is preventive disease control to pick up yellow leaves from the ground after harvest or to cover them with an inch of good compost. Furthermore, it is important to plant sun-loving herbs in a sunny spot and, above all, to keep good drainage in mind.

Harvest and Storage: There are several ways to preserve herbs, but you'll want to take into account what you want to use them for and when they'll be ready for harvest. Most herbs you'll want to dry, but some you'll freeze or refrigerate. And if you move your favorite culinary herbs to the windowsill in winter, you'll use them fresh all year.

Most herbs for culinary use are ready to harvest just before the flowers appear on the plant. At this time, the plant contains the most oils and therefore the greatest flavor and fragrance.

The herbs for drying should be harvested early in the season so that successive cuttings can be made. Harvesting perennial herbs late in the season not only causes a lessening of flavor, but the possibility of plant loss as well. Plants need the chance for regrowth in order to survive the winter. Another caution is to not cut annuals such as basil and borage too close to the ground. This lower foliage is necessary for continued plant growth. At the end of the growing season, annual herbs can be harvested entirely.

The best time of day to harvest herbs is in the early morning of a clear day, just as the sun dries the dew from the leaves, since the oils are the strongest in the plants at this time. As the sun becomes more intense, a chemical change takes place in the plants and the oils diminish.

As soon as the herbs have been cut, waste no time in getting them ready for drying. If the foliage is dirty, wash the leaves, then shake off the excess water. If the plants have been mulched, it is usually unnecessary to wash the plants before drying. This is especially important for basil which bruises easily from too much handling. The tops and leaves can be picked off the heavier-stemmed herbs such as lovage and basil. The reason for removing the leaves from the stems is to shorten the drying time—thus getting better flavor and color. For herbs like parsley, leave most of the stems on until after drying.

To air-dry herbs, simply gather the herbs and tie them in small bunches. These bunches are then hung in a warm, dark place for about two weeks until they are dry. To keep dust off the foliage and to dry seed heads without losing the seeds, place the plants in paper bags before hanging them up. Allow the plants several weeks longer to dry.

Another variation on the air-drying theme is to disassemble the herb plants and spread the parts on screens to dry. You can use a window screen or one constructed especially for the task. Prop it up in some way to permit the air to freely circulate through the screen. Place it neither in the direct sun nor in some damp spot.

The fastest drying method is oven drying. The oven temperature should be 150°F. (65.56°C.) or lower. Herbs are placed on sheets of brown paper. The paper should have slits cut in it to allow for the passage of air. The oven door is left ajar to allow the moisture to escape. With this method it takes from three to six hours to dry the foliage. After a few

Store the dried leaves and flowers of herbs in clean, airtight glass jars.

ture present on the inside of the bottle. The moisture indicates that there is still water present in the herb. If not dry, remove from the bottle and redry. The herb should crumble easily and be crisp when it is dry.

Leave the herb foliage whole when storing. The flavor is retained longer when whole leaves are stored. Crumble the leaves as you use them. Keep the dried herbs in a dark place to preserve the natural color. Sunlight will fade the leaves and destroy some of the flavor. Label all containers before storage to prevent later confusion.

Freezing is a very simple way to store the culinary herbs for winter use. Gather the herbs at the specific times previously mentioned for drying, wash them if necessary, and shake dry, and then place in plastic boxes or bags, properly labeled. Place these immediately in the freezer. The herbs can be chopped or left whole.

The herbs can also be blanched before freezing, although it is not necessary.

Do not defrost the frozen herbs before using. If the recipe calls for minced herbs, it is easier to chop them while they are still frozen, since they break apart so readily. Chives, sorrel, parsley, dill, oregano, sweet marjoram, lovage, tarragon, and mint leaves freeze well.

Another method to freeze herbs is to place the chopped herbs into ice cube trays filled with water. After freezing, place the cubes in a plastic bag, label and store in the freezer. When needed, just pop an ice cube with herbs into soup, stew or casserole.

When storing the fresh herbs in the refrigerator, harvest them as usual, place in plastic bags or special crisper boxes and refrigerate. Herb foliage lasts longer if washed just prior to use rather than before it is stored. This method is especially suitable in the late fall, just before frost. This way fresh herbs

hours the leaves can be easily removed from the stems, then dried further if necessary to ensure complete drying before storing. Basil and chervil are very sensitive to heat and a temperature of about 90°F. (32.22°C.) is best if they are to retain their color without browning.

In storing the herbs dried by either of these two methods, an airtight container such as a glass jar should be used. The herb must be thoroughly dry before sealing in your jars. Check after a few hours and then again after a few days to make sure that there is no mois-

are available for Thanksgiving and sometimes even for Christmas.

Herbs can be your year-round companions. Get to know them; use them for their fragrance, their color and their flavor. Travel the road to herbal delights in your own garden and home.

See also entries for individual herbs.

HERBIVORE

Those animals which habitually rely upon plants and plant products for their food, as contrasted with carnivorous animals which live primarily on meat, are known as herbivores.

HIBISCUS

A genus of more than 200 species of trees, shrubs and herbs of the Mallow family, the hibiscus is of great horticultural interest because of its wide variety of garden annuals, perfume and food plants, decorative perennials, and beautifully colored tropical trees and shrubs.

The leaves are alternate, sometimes lobed or parted, with veins that fan out from the petiole or leaf stem. Its flowers are generally large, usually bell shaped, with five petals and sepals. They range in color from white or yellow to deep purple, almost always with a maroon center.

The plants are most popularly known as mallow, rose mallow or giant mallow. They can be propagated by seed or, in the case of perennial species, by division as well. The diversity of hibiscus is great; those annuals mentioned below may be treated as hardy plants and the seed sown directly into the planting site. Most are late summer and fall bloomers in the temperate regions, but they may thrive better if mulched during the winter. Most species require deep, rich soil.

Abelmosk: (*Abelmoschus moschatus*) Often included in the hibiscus genus, this is a tropical Asiatic annual or biennial herb two to six feet high. A native of India, it is grown mostly for its seeds which give a musky perfume. It needs more summer heat than is found in most parts of this country, but will thrive in greenhouses in the northern sections.

China Rose: (*H. Rosa-sinensis*) Also called blacking plant because its flowers are used in the tropics to polish shoes, rose-of-China is a beautiful Asiatic shrub which frequently attains a height of 15 to 20 feet in the tropics. It cannot endure frost and is grown in this country chiefly in Florida and California. The leaves are broadly oval, three to four inches long and tapering. The flowers are mostly solitary, four to six inches long, and spectacularly showy because of the rose red petals and long columns of stamens. It can be grown in warm, moist greenhouses where it requires rich feeding with liquid manures and potting mixture.

Cotton Rose: (*H. mutabilis*) A native of China, this shrub is sometimes called Confederate rose. The leaves are broad and oval, four inches wide, three to five lobed. The flowers, three to four inches wide, open white or pink and later change to deep red. The fruit is globe shaped.

Flower-of-an-Hour: (*H. Trionum*) A garden annual, this flower grows up to four feet high and produces yellow or cream-colored flowers.

Many other species of hibiscus are widely

grown for economic rather than ornamental value. Among those cultivated for the food and fiber which they yield are *H. tiliaceus,* a fibrous tropical plant, and *H. Sabdariffa,* a southern species whose flowers are cooked and used in many dishes.

Great Rose Mallow: (*H. grandiflorus*) This southern species resembles *H. Moscheutos* but is taller and has broader leaves. Flowers are white or pinkish, usually with a darker red center.

Okra: (*Abelmoschus esculentus*) This plant is another one improperly called hibiscus. It reaches from two to six feet, and puts forth edible beaked pods four to 12 inches long.

Roselle: (*H. Sabdariffa*) A tropical annual whose culture here is confined to the warmest parts of the country, it is also known as Indian sorrel or Jamaica sorrel. The plant, which is grown very much like eggplant, is cultivated for the calyx which contains an acid that may be used as a substitute for the cranberry in the making of drinks, sauces and jelly. The calyx must be harvested while immature. Attaining a height of four to seven feet, the roselle displays stalkless and solitary yellow flowers that are twice as long as the thick, red calyx and bracts.

Rose Mallow: (*H. Moscheutos*) Variously called swamp rose mallow and sea hollyhock, the rose mallow is a salt-marsh plant native to the eastern United States. It can be dug out of its wild habitat and transplanted into the garden with complete success. This is rarely done today, however, because of the improved domestic varieties now available as a result of selection and crossbreeding. These improved mallows are at home in any rich garden soil but need plenty of room.

Growing to a height of three to seven feet, the rose mallow is a strong-growing,

hardy perennial. Its leaves are three to seven inches long and generally ovate, though they can be angled or lobed. The white to pink flowers, four to seven inches wide, appear in August and September. They are not recommended for bouquets, however, since they wilt almost immediately.

Rose-of-Sharon: (*H. syriacus*) Highly valued for its late bloom, this is the only hardy shrub in this genus. It grows five to 15 feet high with unlobed, sharply toothed oval leaves two to five inches long. The flowers are solitary, short stalked, three to five inches long,

Hibiscus syriacus *can be grown in all but the coldest regions and, although it benefits from full sun, does well in partial shade.*

red, purple, violet, or white in color, broadly bell shaped and most showy on dark days. It is generally hardy south of the bluegrass line and offered there in many forms.

See also HERB, MALLOW, OKRA.

HICKORY   (*Carya*)

The hickories are tall trees, valued for their timber and nut crops. Leaves are alternate and compound and both male and female flowers appear on the same tree, in separate clusters.

The fruit is a fleshy drupe that hardens with age and separates into four sections, revealing a nut within. Nuts of many wild species are bitter and inedible, but several hickories produce nuts that are not only edible, but delicious. The most important member of the genus is the pecan (*C. ilinoinensis*), widely grown throughout the South. Other species of hickory are not as widely cultivated but are nevertheless valuable as hardy, nut-producing shade trees. Shellbark hickory (*C. laciniosa*) grows wild in the Middle West and shagbark hickory (*C. ovata*) can be found throughout the eastern and central woodland regions of the country. The nuts of both species are tasty but generally hard shelled and rather small. Crosses between *C. illinoinensis* and these species have resulted in hardy varieties of hickory that produce nuts which are thin shelled and large, like those of the pecan. These hybrid types, or "hicans," thrive in most temperate regions and are worthwhile choices for the homesteading orchardist. The varieties listed below are the most popular hicans.

Burton: the most reliable and productive variety; thin-shelled nuts.

Henke: fairly productive; sweet, medium-shelled nuts.

Pixley: not very productive; very cold-hardy; medium-shelled nuts.

Since the species are being improved steadily, it is advisable to check recent catalogs before ordering. On the whole, it is best to favor varieties recommended for the region where they will be planted.

In harvesting hickory nuts, pick them up soon after they fall and lay them on screens to dry in the shade. When the kernels have become crisp, place them in a mesh bag in a cool, well-ventilated place.

Hickories have deep taproots and much care must be taken not to injure them when planting or setting the young tree. The hole

Like other hickories, the shagbark is slow growing and needs very deep, fertile loam in order to attain full production.

should be large enough to accommodate the roots with ease and filled only with topsoil; put no manure in the hole. Do not allow the roots to become dry for even a short while. Heel-in all young trees waiting to be planted.

After planting cut back the growth one-third and stake carefully. Water thoroughly if it has not rained in some time. After the trees are established this should be no longer necessary. In general, cultivate and mulch the trees as for most fruit trees, giving them the same seasonal care.

Hickory is among the strongest and toughest of woods. It has a very high fuel value.

See also NUT TREES, PECAN.

HIGHBUSH CRANBERRY
See CRANBERRY TREE

HIMALAYAN FIR   *See* FIR

HIP   *See* ROSE HIPS

HOARFROST   *See* FROST

HOARHOUND   *See* HOREHOUND

HOG   *See* PIG

HOLLY

Two genera of the family Aquifoliaceae, *Ilex* and *Nemopanthus,* are commonly known as hollies. Species number more than 400, mostly evergreen shrubs and trees. The most popular garden varieties are English holly, *I. Aquifolium;* American holly, *I. opaca;* Chinese holly, *I. cornuta;* and Japanese holly, *I. crenata.*

It is usually best to buy potted or basketed hollies, especially if they must be shipped any distance. Few hollies are grown from seed or collected from the wild. Propagation is by cuttings from named varieties; grafting does not work well because grafted hollies often sprout from the understock.

Hollies grown from rooted cuttings will often form berries when small, although they will not berry every year. Holly grows swiftly but needs judicious pruning. Left to grow without much pruning, hollies will reach eight feet and higher at 15 years of age, but will be less broad and dense. They should be pruned freely to maintain a dense, bushy growth.

Planting: Holly should be planted either in early spring or early fall, after the season's growth has begun to ripen. Foliage should be stripped from the plants to avoid moisture loss. If dug with a ball of earth and severely pruned, plants may be moved without stripping. Plants should be sprayed with water daily for several weeks after planting.

Dig a hole at least twice as big as the ball of the holly to be planted. Fill with oak leaf mold, placing the holly so that the top of the root ball is level with the surface of the surrounding earth. A thick mulch of leaf mold, two or more inches deep, is placed over the top of the roots and the surrounding area. Hollies should be soaked thoroughly with water when planting to compact and settle the leaf mold around the roots so that no air spaces remain. Potted hollies should have the pot removed when planting. Burlapped hollies should be planted in the burlap; the burlap will hold the root mass together until the tree has settled in.

Hollies require a well-drained location. Some American hollies are quite hardy and will tolerate temperatures as low as −30°F.

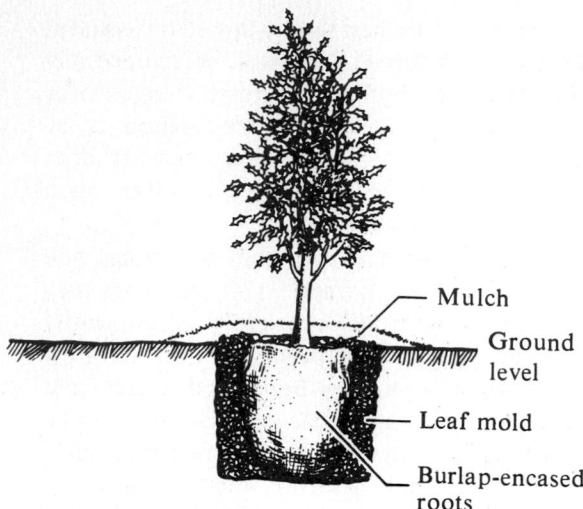

- Mulch
- Ground level
- Leaf mold
- Burlap-encased roots

Do not remove the burlap when planting a holly tree, for it protects the root mass until the tree has established itself. Instead, place the covered root ball in a hole twice its size and fill with oak leaf mold.

(−34.44°C.), but in colder climates hollies should be planted out of winter winds as much as possible. As long as there is plenty of oak leaf mold around plant roots, hollies are not fussy about soil requirements.

Holly plants are either male or female. The male is necessary for berry formation and must be planted nearby if the female is to have berries. One male plant is sufficient for ten females.

Holly is easy to care for. It loves water and should be thoroughly soaked once every week or two during the growing season; summer rains are rarely heavy enough to please a holly. Yearly mulch the ground around the tree as far out as the branches spread with a well-rotted leaf mold. A mulch of tobacco stems is also especially good for holly.

Pruning not only shapes the trees, but also furnishes branches and berries for Christmastime show. Unusually long twigs or leaders should be cut back to the general pattern or shape of tree desired. Hollies can stand heavy pruning.

Varieties: English holly grows up to 40 feet. Although it does best in the Pacific Northwest, it can also be grown in the East in sheltered locations along bays and in some river valleys. It is occasionally successful inland if given excellent wind protection and plenty of shade.

Dahoon (*I. Cassine*) and yaupon (*I. vomitoria*) are small trees attaining heights of 40 feet and 24 feet respectively. They are strictly southern plants ranging from North Carolina to Florida.

Japanese holly is an extremely handsome evergreen shrub, hardy and similar to American holly in its cultural requirements. It has small, rounded, smooth leaves and purple black berries. Convexa is a popular variety, and dwarf varieties include Helleri and Mariesii. Rotundifolia is slightly larger. Most varieties require full sun for best growth and berry formation.

Inkberry (*I. glabra*), also called winterberry and gallberry, is evergreen in the South. Farther north, it turns a rusty green in the autumn. It bears wedge-shaped berries and grows no higher than six feet. The plant does well in sandy garden loam and favors a leaf mulch.

Smooth winterberry (*I. laevigata*) grows up to 12 feet high and is primarily cultivated for its reddish fruits. Although a southern plant, it can grow as far north as Maine.

American holly is one of the hardiest of the cultivated hollies, but is less colorful than either the English or Japanese species. Preferred varieties include Foster and Hume. These will survive an occasional hard winter if planted in wind-sheltered locations such as on the east side of sheltering evergreens or on the east side of a house. They do best in full sun.

Chinese holly is more sensitive to temperature and will stand dry air better than other types, which makes it practical for home plantings in the Southwest. It seldom produces berries in climates where winter temperatures are 0°F. (-17.78°C.) or below.

HOLLY FERN   *See* FERN

HOLLYHOCK   (*Alcea*)

This garden favorite is a member of the Mallow family. It is closely related to the genus *Althaea* which includes marsh mallow and to the genus *Hibiscus*.

Hollyhocks are noted for hairy alternate leaves and terminal racemelike clusters of attractive flowers. Each flower has five red or white petals.

The hollyhock is native to China and was imported to England about 400 years ago. It attained popularity in early American colonial gardens. Planted under windows and along fences, it brings a fresh, bright note of color to these places.

Culture: Almost any suitable garden soil will do. If grown as biennials, sow the seed in frames or flats outdoors in July or August for next year's blooming. Grow the seedlings until the first frost when they should be mulched lightly and left in the frame or flat but without any added heat.

Move them to their final site in the spring. Take care to keep the roots pointing down because they are susceptible to frost heaving; also plant a little deeper than before. This safeguards the roots and permits the plant to secure a firm hold.

Varieties: Due to constant hybridization, the varieties are quite unstable. This pertains particularly to annuals which will run not much better than 50 percent true from seed. Biennials are somewhat more reliable, although instability will be noted. The following colors can be relied on: crimson, pink, rose, salmon pink, scarlet, yellow, and white. Forms are single-flower, double and semidouble. The first is still most popular, possibly because simplicity constitutes the essential appeal of this flower.

The following varieties enjoy considerable popularity and may be grown with common-sense precautions in almost any garden.

Antwerp Hollyhock: (*A. ficifolia*) This biennial herb is not often grown, although it can be a valuable addition to wild gardens. Formerly grouped in the genus *Althaea*, it resembles the common hollyhock and grows very slowly.

Common Garden Hollyhock: (*A. rosea*) Originally a tall, perennial Mediterranean herb, it is grown today mostly as a biennial. It is erect, five to nine feet high, with a leafy, spire-like stem. The red or white single flowers are stalkless in terminal clusters. A good double-flowered hybrid is Majorette, producing ruffled pompon flowers of scarlet, rose, pink, yellow, and white.

Marsh Mallow, or Sweatweed: (*Althaea officinalis*) A perennial herb which grows three to four feet high, its leaves may be unlobed but are generally three lobed, ovalish, with the mid-lobe largest. It grows wild in the salt marshes of the eastern seaboard.

See also MALLOW.

HOLY CLOVER   *See* ONOBRYCHIS

HONESTY   (*Lunaria*)

Also known as moonwort and the money plant because the seedpods are round and flat, lunarias are easy to grow in ordinary garden soil. The showy purple flowers are most attractive in June, and the seedpods add much to winter bouquets of dried flowers. *L. annua,* known also as silver-dollar, is a biennial that reaches 1½ to 2½ feet. It will grow in sandy damp places that are somewhat shady. The less showy perennial honesty (*L. rediviva*) grows best in partial shade and can be increased by division. Most lunarias, however, are best propagated by seed. They will reseed themselves each year.

HONEY

Honey is the material formed in bees' honey sacs from the nectar produced by flowering plants. It is composed of 33 to 40 percent fruit sugar; 32 to 39 percent grape sugar; 1 to 4 percent saccharose; minute amounts of iron, calcium, manganese, potassium, sulfur, and phosphorus; and water. According to U.S. standards, no honey can be sold as "pure honey" if its water content is more than 25 percent.

For every pound of honey, it is said that a bee makes from 40,000 to 80,000 trips, collecting from many times this number of flowers. From one to 1½ miles are covered in each trip.

With her ligula, the worker bee extracts the nectar from flowers, which after being held in the mouth for a while passes into the honey sac, or honey stomach. Upon filling her honey sac, the bee returns to the hive and regurgitates the juices into a cell of the honeycomb. She departs at once for more nectar, while other bees add an enzyme which converts the nectar into honey. Each cell is hermetically sealed and the ripening process continues until the substance completely ripens and is ready for consumption.

One pound of honey contains 1,300 calories, and since it is predigested in the honey sac, it is easily assimilated. Often it is given as supplementary food to small children and elderly people.

Honey is germfree and has long been successfully used for dressing stubborn old sores or fresh wounds. Because it is water-absorbing, honey acts as a disinfectant on infected mucous membranes and is especially recommended in the case of a cough. Honey has also been effectively used to treat a number of illnesses including kidney diseases, liver trouble, bad complexions, poor circulation, respiratory and digestive track disorders, and inflammation. Prescriptions calling for honey have been found in ancient papyri in Egypt.

Of course, honey is most often used as a sweetener and is valued for its distinctive taste. Beekeepers interested in selling their honey to the commercial trade must blend various kinds of honey in order to produce a good-quality standard product. Most honey consumers become accustomed to a particular taste in the honey they buy.

Honeys do not always have the same taste. Different honey plants produce different honeys. Those derived from flowering plants and leaf trees are considered better than those gained from coniferous trees, though some favor the latter. There are numerous types of regional honeys, depending on the prevalent honey plants in the region, and flavors vary from pungent to mild and colors from clear white to wine red or even black. The mild, light-colored honeys include alfalfa, aster and basswood. Clover, the largest single source of honey in the United States, yields a light, amber-colored honey. So do locust flowers, citrus blossoms, goldenrod, and tulip trees. Wild thyme and buckwheat produce the darker and stronger tasting honeys.

Bees collect over half their nectar from wild flowers growing where no man-made fertilizers are used. This guarantees that honey is a natural food and free from chemical residues. Bees have low resistance to insecticides, and some carelessly used sprays have decimated entire apiaries. Bees are often killed in the field, and if they die outside the hive it is possible that the hive can be saved. However, if many return to the hive they may kill the entire hive population. As insect pollination becomes more crucial to crop production, growers will begin to realize the value of the honeybee and curtail spraying or perform it at hours when bees are inactive.

The quality and purity of raw honey can be affected by chemical repellents used to drive bees from the extracting supers and by improper extraction and processing. Overheating also greatly destroys the flavor and biotic material in natural honey.

Honey should be stored where it is dry and warm. If it is kept for a long time, particularly in an area of cold temperatures, it granulates; this does not mean spoilage but is not liked by the consumer. To reliquefy, set the jar of honey in warm water. Quick granulating honeys, such as aster or goldenrod, should be extracted immediately because if they are left on the hive they will granulate in the comb.

See also BEEKEEPING, BEES, HONEY PLANTS.

HONEYDEW   *See* MELON

HONEY MESQUITE
See MESQUITE

HONEY PLANTS

Not even the hardest working bee can produce an appreciable amount of honey or do a good job of pollination without a plentiful supply of rich blossoms on which to forage.

For better pollination and larger and more active hive populations, one must improve the range over which workers can forage for nectar. A succession of nectar-rich plants should mature throughout the growing season, one this month and a different one the next. The greater the succession of nectar plants present throughout the season the more bees will be present to pollinate field and garden crops and produce honey.

In view of the pressing need for more and better honey and pollen plants, a honey plant testing ground was established at Pellett Gardens, Atlantic, Iowa, and maintained for some years in cooperation with *The American Bee Journal.*

There, hundreds of plants have been tested for their value as honey plants and for other possible uses. Native plants, foreign plants, trees, shrubs, mints, oil plants, common plants, and uncommon plants all have been tested. Of the hundreds tried, a number appear promising. If you are a beekeeper or want to attract bees and wild pollinating insects to your land, you may be interested in planting some of these crops.

For honey plants to be of any great value they must be sufficiently hardy to withstand competition and must be able to take care of themselves or else have some other use to encourage their cultivation. Naturally the most important honey plants are those which are forage crops or others which are grown extensively in large acreage, like alfalfa and clover. But also important are the smaller areas of some plants which bloom at the off-season. In so many cases plants can be used which will serve the original purpose and at the same time be good honey plants. This factor may well be considered when making selections for conservation programs as erosion control and wildlife conservation. Plantings of trees and shrubs can usually be those which also will furnish some bee pasture.

A number of easily grown annual flowers and herbs are among the best of honey plants. They are worthy of a place in the flower garden with the dividend of bringing honeybees and other pollinating insects. Among the annuals noted for flowers attractive to bees are the spider plant (*Cleome*), *Salvia farinacea*

and annual dragonhead (*Dracocephalum Moldavica*). These annuals can be expected to furnish blooms within a few weeks from the time the seed is sown in spring or early summer.

Bees don't seem to be attracted to many flowering shrubs, but there are two perennials that attract honeybees and are in bloom all summer. The first of these is lythrum or loosestrife, which comes in five colors including white. The other is a ground cover called dropmore purple. The gray green foliage has a pleasant, pungent odor. Bees are especially attracted to dropmore purple and are there as long as it is in bloom, which is quite late.

Vitex Negundo var. *heterophylla* is a shrub or small tree which originally came from Africa and India. This plant is gaining favor among beekeepers in this country because its flowers have a long blooming period and freely yield nectar.

It begins blooming at an early age, sometimes the first year from seed. The first blooms appear in midsummer and sometimes continue in bloom until late fall. Reports indicate *Vitex Negundo* var. *heterophylla* will grow in a wide variety of soils and situations. It is also among the best of honey plants almost anywhere it grows.

As a flowering shrub it makes a good screening hedge growing from 12 to 20 feet high, or it can be trimmed to a small tree. *Vitex Negundo* var. *heterophylla* is not sufficiently winter-hardy to stand the coldest climates of the country. It appears best adapted to climates southward from areas such as central Missouri and southern New England.

Purple loosestrife (*Lythrum Salicaria*) is an Old World plant which has become naturalized in some parts of this country. It blooms over a long period, in late summer and fall, with purple flowers on long spikes freely visited by bees. A perennial growing to three or more feet tall, it is a good plant for flower gardens and will grow well in most places.

Purple loosestrife is especially adapted to moist or boggy land. Under these conditions it spreads extensively by self-seeding in many situations. From New England to Iowa it has demonstrated its ability to spread on wet land, along streams and lake edges where the seed is carried by the water. The acres of bloom are a pretty sight and many times reported as a major source of nectar.

Mountain mint (*Pycnanthemum pilosum*) is a native plant which holds promise as a source of essential oils. Tests indicate that it is capable of yielding a much heavier amount of oil than most mints now in cultivation. It blooms very heavily over a long period in late summer and fall and seldom fails to find the bees working it. An attractive plant with a very pronounced minty flavor, mountain mint is suited to garden cultivation.

Anise hyssop (*Agastache Foeniculum*) reportedly attracts the bees most consistently over the longest blooming period of any honey plant, though attraction can vary according to locale. This attractive herb begins blooming in June, blooms heavily through most of the summer and usually continues with some bloom until frost. Bees work the flowers from daylight until dark. A native plant of pioneer times which has since almost entirely disappeared, it was estimated in the old days that an acre of anise hyssop might be sufficient pasture for 100 hives of bees. Thus it is sometimes termed "wonder honey plant."

Other very good perennial honey plants which are worthy of a place in the flower garden or border include butterfly weed (*Asclepias tuberosa*), New England aster, wild marjoram (*Origanum vulgare*), wild indigo (*Baptisia*), *Nepeta Mussinii,* and others belonging to the Catnip family.

Some very good honey plants may be growing wild in waste places and fencerows. In many localities wild asters and goldenrod give a good fall honeyflow, though honey from these plants is quick to granulate. Catnip and motherwort, often thought of as weeds, are among the best of honey plants. When the "weeds" are good honey plants and doing no harm it is well to leave them. More honey

One of the country's major honey crops, white clover puts forth masses of white flowers throughout the season.

plants make for a better beekeeping location—more bees and better pollination.

The most widely distributed major honey plants—alfalfa, alsike clover, sweet clover, and white clover—with the states in which the reporters gave them first or second place as honey producers, are as follows:

Alfalfa
First: Idaho, Nevada, Oregon, Utah.
Second: California, Colorado, Kansas, Montana, Nebraska, Oklahoma, South Dakota, Wyoming.

Alsike Clover
First: Indiana, Maine, Maryland, Massachusetts, New York, Ohio, Pennsylvania.

Sweet Clover
First: Alabama, Colorado, Connecticut, Illinois, Iowa, Kansas, Michigan, Minnesota, Montana, Nebraska, North Dakota, Oklahoma, South Dakota, Wyoming.
Second: Idaho, Indiana, Nevada, New Jersey, Oregon, Utah, Wisconsin.

White Clover
First: Arkansas, Connecticut, Indiana, Louisiana, Missouri, New Jersey, Tennessee, Vermont, Virginia, West Virginia, Wisconsin.
Second: Illinois, Iowa, Maryland, Massachusetts, Michigan, Minnesota, New York, Ohio, Pennsylvania, Washington.

See also BEEKEEPING, BEES, HONEY.

HONEYSUCKLE   (*Lonicera*)

The honeysuckles make up a large group of shrubs and woody vines, all of which are fine garden plants. The taller shrubs are used in hedges, borders and single specimens, while many of the lower-growing forms appear in rock gardens. The showy fruits range in color from white to black, and are popular with birds. Honeysuckles prefer a moist loam soil, and thrive in almost any location, whether shady or open.

Varieties include the common or Italian woodbine (*L. Caprifolium*), a climbing type often reaching 20 feet, with yellow white flowers and orange fruit; like many other varieties,

The climbing Japanese honeysuckle is a superior wall and ground cover for shady spots.
(*Courtesy of U.S. Forest Service*)

it's hardy in the central and southern states. The yellow honeysuckle (*L. flava*) is more of a spreading vine, considered by many as the most attractive of the Honeysuckle family.

Japanese honeysuckle (*L. japonica*) is a strong-growing climbing vine, reaching as high as 30 feet and featuring white flowers and black fruit. Woodbine (*L. Periclymenum*) is another woody climber that grows to 20 feet; it has red fruit. Trumpet honeysuckle (*L. sempervirens*), also known as coral honeysuckle, is an evergreen climbing vine bearing showy orange flowers. European fly honeysuckle (*L. Xylosteum*) is a bushy shrub that reaches about ten feet high, and has yellow flowers and red fruit.

Most honeysuckles are spring and summer bloomers, producing a great quantity of showy fragrant flowers.

HOOF AND HORN MEAL

There are many grades of hoof and horn meal for garden fertilizer use. The granular material breaks down with some difficulty unless kept moist and well covered; it also tends to encourage the growth of maggots because it attracts flies. The finely ground horn dust which gardeners use for potting mixtures is, on the other hand, quite easily dissolved. The nitrogen content is from ten to 16 pounds per hundred-pound bag or as much as a ton of manure or more, while the phosphoric acid value is usually around 2 percent. If available, this is a very handy source of nitrogen for flower growers and gardeners with small compost heaps because it can be easily stored, is pleasant to handle and relatively less costly than other forms of bagged organic nitrogen.

HOPS   (*Humulus*)

Hops are hardy, viny plants sometimes grown as ornamentals but, more often used in the production of beer. The "spent hops," or residue of beer-making, are extremely valuable as a garden fertilizer. Dried, they contain from 2.5 to 3.5 percent nitrogen. In many areas, gardeners and farmers have been successfully using the hops in their wet, natural condition, spreading them in the same way as farmyard manure. Many other growers have been composting the hops before applying to the soil.

Spent hops have been used as a mulch with excellent success. They have a very strong odor, but this disappears very quickly. Because of their high water content, they heat up and decompose readily when applied in the summer months. Keep them at least six inches away from young stems to prevent plant injury. A six-inch application around a plant will last at least three years and sometimes longer.

Another brewery waste available is the grain parts left over from the mashing process. This wet brewer's grain decays readily and has been found to contain almost 1 percent nitrogen. Unfortunately, it is harder to find spent brewery wastes because small breweries have been going out of business.

HOREHOUND   (*Marrubium vulgare*)

A perennial herb one to two feet high with branching stems and whitish flowers, horehound is commonly found as a weed, especially on the Pacific coast. The plant has a musky odor and woolish appearance. Horehound is valued for medicinal and culinary properties; its leaves and flowering tops are in demand as a crude drug.

There are many theories about the origin of this herb's Latin name. Egyptians called it the seed of Horus. Scholars often claim it was named after *Maria urbs,* an ancient Italian villa, but most attribute it to the Hebrew *marrob,* a bitter juice. Ancient Hebrews and Egyptians used horehound as an antidote for poisons and a cure for respiratory illnesses,

The leaves of the perennial horehound can be chopped, dried and stored in a tightly sealed jar for use in medicinal teas and candies.

ulcers and even snakebite poisoning.

The plant grows well in almost any soil and thrives in those that are light, dry and rather poor. It grows readily from seed, which is usually sown early in spring and covered with about one inch of soil. Plants can be started in cold frames from seed, cuttings or divisions of old plants and later transplanted to the field. Plants may stand six, 12 or 18 inches apart in the row; those standing close together have small stems and hence yield a crop of finer quality.

Horehound is harvested by cutting all growth three inches above the ground. In the northern United States, two or more cuttings per year are possible. The plant remains productive for several years.

To store horehound, chop and dry, then seal tightly in a jar.

The most common use of horehound is in the manufacture of syrups, teas and lozenges to treat colds and sore throats. An effective cough or cold syrup can be made by mixing ½ ounce each of horehound, rue, hyssop, licorice root, and marsh mallow root with one quart of water. The mixture is boiled down to 1½ pints, strained and portioned out in ½-cup doses.

See also HERB.

HORMONE

A dictionary definition states that a hormone is "any of various chemical substances formed in the endocrine organs (that is, ductless glands that secrete internally) which activate specifically receptive organs when transported to them by the body fluids." Named from the Greek verb *hormanein,* meaning "to arouse or excite," the principal hormones are the secretions of the pituitary, thyroid and adrenal glands and pancreas and reproductive organs.

Natural hormones in humans function in the control, coordination and stimulation of all vital body activities, including secretion, metabolism, growth, and reproduction. Needless to say, it is impossible to have good health if the body's hormones are not working properly.

Synthetic hormones are manufactured from a variety of chemicals by a complex process. Recent years have seen an increase in the use of synthetic hormones in animal feed and insect control.

Hormonal Feed Supplements: Synthetic hormones are being used a great deal in today's livestock programs. The object is to speed up the rate at which cattle put on weight. One such synthetic hormone, stilbestrol, is being used by almost 50 percent of the cattle growers, even though little is actually known about how the hormone works.

Stilbestrol, for example, has all the properties of an estrogen, a type of female sex hormone. For some years, a synthetic estrogen has been used by doctors for the treatment of disturbances in women during their menopause. However, the *Journal of the American Medical Association* has frequently warned that estrogen should only be administered when symptoms are very severe and even then not over an extended period of time.

A look at stilbestrol's history offers insight into its potential dangers. Some years ago, stilbestrol made its first appearance in poultry houses. The general idea was to inject a pellet of stilbestrol under the skin near the top of the chicken's head.

The purpose of using stilbestrol was to produce a bird which was essentially a capon. Here is what happened to the bird: externally it showed up in the shrinking and paling of comb and wattles; the bird became sluggish and tame and had no desire to fight; internally the sex organs shrank; the final result—and most important to commercial growers—was that the bird took on flesh and fat at a rapid rate.

The hormonized bird was ready for market in 20 weeks from hatching and possessed a size and quality comparable to that of an eight-month-old true capon. Stilbestrol cut the poultryman's costs.

During the last few years, however, poultrymen have been warned about using stilbestrol pellets because residual pellets have been found in the birds. In one case, an official of the Food and Drug Administration bought a drawn chicken which had four pellets in its neck, one of them three inches down from the skull.

Farmers have also been warned against giving stilbestrol feeds to dairy cattle, beef bulls, suckling calves or female beef to be kept for breeding purposes, or to steers being fed for shows. This is because the hormone tends to cause such animals to develop unwanted sexual characteristics.

Dairy cattle would go off milk production, beef bulls can become too female and not sire calves, and female beef breeders might not conceive, or would abort, or in different ways not produce a good calf crop.

It has been stated by research agencies that stilbestrol fed to cattle never lodges in the meat, and that it is only in the blood and passes through the animal very quickly. The Food and Drug Administration has made a ruling that cattle should be taken off stilbestrol feeding 14 days before slaughter as a precautionary measure.

Hormonal Insect Control: Just as hormonal imbalances can trigger bizarre bodily changes in humans, livestock and poultry, so do they alter the normal metamorphosis and molting habits of insects. One of the most active areas of insect control research in recent years has focused on the technique of synthesizing hormone "mimics" that can be used to play tricks with a pest's development, rendering it harmless.

At first glance, hormonal controls look good. Unlike conventional pesticides, they are not toxic to pests, but instead lead to control indirectly, either by death or by interfering with reproductive capability. Neither have they been found toxic to man and other vertebrates. Another point in their favor is their potential host specificity. While it was thought at first that the chemical hormones would be highly *species* specific, researchers now believe that they are *order* specific—which is less desirable, but still superior to most insecticides. A third consideration is that most growth-regulating chemicals degrade rapidly in the environment.

Two kinds of hormones are of interest: juvenile hormones and molting hormones. Harvard biologist Dr. Carrol Williams found that juvenile hormone (JH) is needed to stimulate an immature worm to grow larger, but that it must be absent if the worm is ever to become a sexually mature adult. So, a larva treated with synthesized JH will continue to molt into progressively larger worms instead of becoming an adult. In other cases, a half-pupa, half-adult monster is the result. If administered to an adult female during the reproductive cycle, the hormones disturb development of the sex apparatus, formation of the yolk and maturation of the eggs within the female. Fiddling with an insect's hormones can also undo its ability to go into a resting phase (diapause), or wake it from diapause when the habitat is unfavorable.

While JH can only determine what sort of molt will take place, molting hormones (MH) actually cause the molt, disrupting insect development at any larval or nymphal stage. JH is the slower of the two, as it allows insects to continue to feed until their terminal molt. Thus, development is reflected in less mating and a lower population density. Another disadvantage is that JH compounds must be applied during certain susceptible periods in an insect's development in order to take effect. Coupled with the fact that JH is unstable in the field, this means an application may miss an insect's vulnerable period.

For organic growers the initial enthusiasm for hormonal control has been tempered by the realization that this method might share the problems inherent in traditional chemical control. "There is danger that developments in this field could follow the pattern resulting from the almost exclusive reliance on conventional insecticides, with similar attendant ills," stated a background paper prepared for a 1973 conference on integrated pest management held in Berkeley, California. And one by one, the unique aspects of hormonal control that supposedly set it apart from conventional chemical control have been critically examined.

1. Although hormonal chemicals may disrupt processes peculiar only to insects, vertebrates are not necessarily immune to their effects. The Berkeley paper states, "Effects on vertebrates or other nontarget species could arise through processes other than those with which they are associated in insects." While it's true that the compounds appear safe to vertebrates even when ingested in huge amounts, it comes to mind that developers and manufacturers of chemical products have been incredi-

bly lax in the past in testing for long-term effects. If scientists had known as much in 1945 about DDT as is known today, the earth would not be covered with a layer of the stuff.

2. It had been thought that insects could not develop resistance to hormonal controls, as these chemicals mimic compounds in the insects' own bodies. But William E. Robbins suggests in *Pest Control: Strategies for the Future* (published in 1972 by the National Academy of Sciences) that the chemicals likely differ structurally from the insects' own hormones. This means that the chemicals may well be handled by the insect as foreign compounds rather than its own metabolic juices.

3. To make their product more marketable, companies are coming up with new formulas that will last longer in the field and will knock out a bigger number of species. This undoes two advantages that hormonal controls could have, and to organic growers who believe that persistent, wide-spectrum chemicals wreak environmental havoc, the new formulas should be anything but attractive.

The use of hormonal controls, as envisioned by the firms now developing them, conflicts with organic practice in a number of other ways. As is true with conventional pesticides, broad-spectrum hormones can eliminate both the target pest and its natural enemies, paving the way for a resurgence of the pest and according to Dr. Barry M. Trost, a University of Wisconsin scientist doing research on such compounds, the result could be "an ecological disaster."

Researcher Francis Lawson sees broad-spectrum hormonal controls as just another chemical. "Any broad-spectrum chemical is going to kill pests and their natural enemies. . . . Who knows what effects you may get? The real problem is that for thirty to forty years we have sought only chemical solutions to insect control." Just as hormones seem to be the answer today, DDT was once looked upon as the perfect control.

4. Other concerns stem from the impressive power of hormonal chemicals. For one thing, their use could not very well be restricted to the area of application, as minute amounts might easily get carried by wind and water and end up biologically bombing a grower down the road.

5. Any control that works too well poses a threat both to your plot and potentially to the earth around it. If this seems an overstatement, consider human nature for a moment. Hormones are a threat because their magical expediency is so appealing. They would make it possible to ignore the processes of biological control by encouraging monocropping (thereby undoing the diversity of insects that keep each other in line) and by encouraging growers to bypass the organic approach to insect control (through growing healthy plants from a healthy soil). "Hormones oversimplify the system," warns Everett Dietrick, head of Rincon-Vitova Insectaries. "They are a short-sighted answer."

In sum, hormonal control denies the interrelatedness of all the parts of our ecosystem, and appears at this time to be little more than the newest in a succession of increasingly sophisticated chemicals in man's arsenal.

HORNBEAM (*Carpinus*)

Belonging to the Birch family, these slow-growing trees or shrubs are fairly hardy. The American hornbeam (*C. caroliniana*), also known as blue beech, prefers a shady, wind-

As an ornamental, the low, spreading American hornbeam is best suited for shady areas.

raciously until they reach a length of four inches. The worms are green, marked with white diagonal bars along each side and a prominent horn at the back end—green and black on the tomato species, and red on the tobacco hornworm.

Because they are so easy to see, hornworms can be controlled by handpicking in modest-sized plantings. Dill can be interplanted as a trap crop. Hornworms are vulnerable to a *Bacillus thuringiensis* spray—a bacterial control available commercially. Blacklight traps have proven effective in reducing populations of the adult moths.

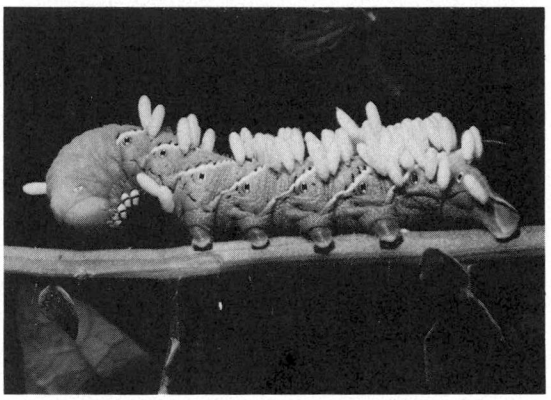

The braconid wasp has injected its eggs into the body of this hornworm; upon hatching the larvae feed on the caterpillar, gradually eating their way out of its body.

protected location, and grows to about 30 feet. The European hornbeam (*C. Betulus*) grows to about 50 feet high, but is usually kept much lower when cultivated in the garden. The variety Columnaris is often used as a hedge, growing straight and slender.

HORNWORM, TOMATO (TOBACCO)

These two similar worms are among the largest of insect garden pests, feeding vo-

HORSE CHESTNUT　　(*Aesculus*)

Often used as a street tree because of its dense shade, the horse chestnut is especially attractive when in flower. The Ohio buckeye

The first shade tree to burst into leaf, the common horse chestnut is particularly suited for bowers as the tops head-in for very dense shade.
(Courtesy of U.S. Forest Service)

HORSE GENTIAN   *See* TRIOSTEUM

HORSEHEAL   *See* ELECAMPANE

HORSEMINT   *See* BEE BALM

HORSE NETTLE
(Solanum carolinense)

An erect perennial growing from one to four feet tall, the horse nettle has sharp yellow thorns, large leaves, blue or white flowers, and conspicuous orange yellow berries. The leaves and berries are poisonous when eaten.

A close relative of the buffalo bur, this plant is a troublesome perennial weed which spreads by seed and by underground rootstocks up to three feet long with vertical taproots penetrating to depths of eight feet. Its susceptibility to tomato mosaic makes it particularly objectionable near tomato fields. It can be controlled by clean cultivation, and can be choked out in recreational areas by establishing a good sod of bluegrass. Patches of this weed in uncultivated areas should be mowed to prevent seed formation.

HORSERADISH
(Armoracia rusticana)

A perennial herb of the Mustard family, horseradish has a very thick, fleshy taproot system. The taproot gives rise to many fleshy lateral roots in the surface foot of soil, where frequently the main root divides into several rather equally prominent branches. It is con-

(*A. glabra*) grows to 30 feet, and is hardy in central to southern states. The common horse chestnut (*A. Hippocastanum*) reaches as high as 100 feet, producing its white showy flowers in spring. The red buckeye (*A. Pavia*) is usually a shrub, growing ten to 12 feet tall and producing egg-shaped fruit. The sweet buckeye (*A. octandra*) and Japanese horse chestnut (*A. turbinata*) grow around 60 feet high, and have yellow flowers.

Horse chestnuts do well in ordinary garden soil and sun.

sidered an herb because of its use as a condiment, cosmetic and medicine.

The herb took its name in order to be distinguished from the edible radish. Ancient Greeks knew horseradish as *Raphanos agrios* (wild radish). It was one of the five bitter herbs the ancient Hebrews were commanded to eat at the Passover meal, with cooked lamb and unleavened bread. Throughout history, horseradish has been used as a stimulant, laxative, diuretic, cure for scurvy, and a source of vitamin C. A more common use has been as a condiment for fish and meats.

The great extent and rapid development of the horseradish roots explain why the plant grows best in a very deep, moist, fertile loam soil; why deep cultivation is beneficial; and why a good soil structure is an important environmental factor for growth.

In planting, the roots are placed with the upper end of the cutting two to five inches below the soil surface. The soil should be packed firmly about them to insure good contact and prompt growth. Weeds should be kept out so that sufficient water and nutrients will be available late in the season when the plants make their best growth. On hard, dry or shallow soil the roots are very likely to be crooked, unshapely and scarcely fit for use. The growth of long, straight roots of more uniform size is promoted by preparing and maintaining a deep, moist, mellow soil. The usual distance between plants is ten to 18 inches, in rows three to four feet apart.

Horseradish grows best in the cool months of autumn, steadily improving after September. Many gardeners dig a few roots at a time, allowing the remainder to stay in the soil, since the root is hardy.

Although most medicinal use of horseradish ended in this century, it is still recog-

Although young horseradish leaves can be harvested in the early spring for use in salads, the main culinary portion of the plant is the long, white taproot which is lifted in late fall.

nized as a quality source of vitamin C, and an herb that can stimulate the nervous system or even remedy hoarseness. As a cosmetic, horseradish is applied in a milk solution to restore color to pale skin. The juice of this herb is even mixed with white vinegar to lighten freckles.

Horseradish is still most popular as a spicy condiment. Grate one cup horseradish root in a blender with ¼ cup vinegar. Other herbs can go into this hot spice, including dill and mustard. Because of its tanginess, this is one herb that often brings tears to the eyes of unwary overindulgers.

See also HERB.

HOSTA

Also called funkia and plantain lily, these very hardy perennials of the Lily family, native to China and Japan, are grown mainly for their striking foliage. Hostas rank among the few ornamentals which approach the ideal of a no-maintenance perennial. Average, reasonably moist soil is all they require, but they do best if a generous amount of leaf mold or compost has been dug in. Wet soils are unsuitable. They prefer partial shade and will thrive in full shade in competition with tree roots if enough moisture is available. Some species can be massed as a ground cover in shady locations. They will quickly grow together and form a cover too dense for weeds to penetrate. In such locations, the leaves which fall on them in autumn should be left in place to act as mulch and fertilizer. Since there is much variation among hosta species in the size, form and color of the leaves, visually interesting effects are easily achieved by grouping plants of the different types together. The largest species make outstanding specimen plants.

Once established in a suitable location, most hostas can be left undisturbed indefinitely if the clumps show no sign of losing vigor. However, the gardener can easily and quickly increase his stock by lifting and dividing them in spring every three or four years and replanting each of the many divisions separately. Set the crown one inch below the soil surface. A thin layer of compost or leaf mold applied every year or two will insure good growth.

Most species bear their flowers on long stalks well above the foliage. They are usually small, lilylike and white, deep blue or vaguely blue; few are truly showy. The stalks should be cut off after the blooms fade to improve appearance and to keep the plants from self-sowing. Hostas do not come true from seed, and the seedlings can grow up to crowd favored varieties. Cutting off the flower stalks is the only real chore involved in growing these tough plants.

Hostas are widely available, but any one variety may appear under different names in different catalogs because classification of species is confused. Pay careful attention to written descriptions in catalogs to avoid buying varieties you already have.

Two very large hostas good for accent plants are *H. elata* and *H. Sieboldiana* (or *H. glauca*). The former grows into clumps five feet in diameter with glaucous green leaves up to 12 inches long. The latter grows to three feet across with heavy-textured blue green leaves to 12 inches long; flower stalks stay hidden in the foliage.

H. Sieboldii and *H. decorata* cv. 'Thomas Hogg' are similar in color and size. Both grow two feet across and have green leaves with a prominent white margin and occasional white streaks running to the center. Lilac flowers bloom in August on two-foot stems. *H. Fortunei* cv. 'Marginata-aurea' has yellow-bordered leaves. The most familiar white-leafed form is *H. undulata* (or *H. u.* cv. 'Medio-picta', or *H. u.* cv. 'Variegata'). It has wavy lance-shaped leaves heavily marked white on green, and is often seen as an edging to walks in full sun. Flowers are washy lilac on short stalks in July.

Three hostas are worth growing for both flowers and foliage. *H. plantaginea* (*H. subcordata*, *H. p.* cv. 'Grandiflora') has very fragrant white trumpet-shaped flowers four inches long on two-foot stems in August. Honeybells has fragrant lilac flowers streaked blue at the same time. Royal Standard has scented white flowers into September.

See also LILY.

HOTBED

A hotbed is nothing more than a heated cold frame. It is especially valuable for starting heat-loving plants such as tomatoes, peppers and eggplants, or for raising them in cold regions.

See also COLD FRAME.

HOUSELEEK   *(Sempervivum)*

Often used in wall and rock gardens, these evergreen foliage plants prefer a rather dry, poor soil in a sunny location. Mostly summer bloomers, houseleeks frequently appear in the open border. Common houseleek (*S. tectorum*), also known as hen-and-chickens and as old-man-and-woman, is a low, spreading, succulent plant. It has rosettes of thick, fleshy wedge-shaped leaves. White, pink, yellow, and purple flowers grow in clusters on stems that grow out of the centers of the leaf rosettes. Cobweb houseleek (*S. arachnoideum*) is lower and produces prolific cobwebbed leaves, with dense clusters of red flowers. There are many other species and varieties of sempervivum to choose from, most of which make fine ground covers under unpromising conditions.

HOUSE PLANTS

Any plant which will grow under the adverse conditions of aridity, temperature and light encountered in an ordinary house may be a house plant. If special conditions not normal to ordinary house environment must be supplied to a potted plant to ensure its survival indoors, the plant is more properly considered a greenhouse plant.

Special equipment which supplies greater humidity, additional light or temperature control has been designed to enlarge the range of plants which may be brought inside. This equipment may be as simple as a tray for holding water under plant containers or as elaborate as a special window attachment that converts the window into a small greenhouse.

Some plants may be grown indoors with no special provision for light or moisture, and with little sunlight. These are mostly foliage plants whose native habitat is tropical or desert. Generally speaking, any flowering plant will need plenty of sun or artificial light, while many foliage plants thrive with little or no sun. Some desert plants, such as the many varieties of cactus, need sun but little humidity. In contrast, many deep woods plants, like several varieties of fern, need almost no direct sun but must be surrounded by moist air.

Outdoor garden plants will thrive as house plants if given the same cultural environment they would find outdoors. Impatiens, petunias, dwarf marigolds, wild violets, morning-glories, and miniature roses are easy to grow and provide excellent indoor color.

Flowering House Plants: If you're interested in flowering house plants, it is helpful to know which bloom readily and which do not. Wax begonias (*Begonia semperflorens*), African violets (*Saintpaulia ionantha*), flame violets (*Episcia cupreata*), citrus, amaryllis, and forced bulbs (hyacinths, daffodils, crocus) are relatively easy to grow. Other more difficult plants include gloxinias (*Sinningia speciosa*), bromeliads, Christmas cactus (*Schlumbergera Bridgesii*), Thanksgiving cactus (*S. truncata*), kalanchoe, poinsettia (*Euphorbia pulcherrima*), primrose (*Primula*), cyclamen, geraniums

Shrimp plants need frequent pruning to prevent straggly growth.

(*Pelargonium*), crown-of-thorns (*Euphorbia Milii*), zebra plant (*Aphelandra squarrosa*), coralberry (*Ardisia crenata*), azalea, gardenia, shrimp plant (*Justicia Brandegeana*), orchids, wood sorrel (*Oxalis*), bird-of-paradise (*Strelitzia reginae*), Cape primrose (*Streptocarpus*), flowering maple (*Abutilon*), fuchsia, columnea, kaffir lily (*Clivia miniata*), oleander (*Nerium Oleander*), passion flower (*Passiflora*), powderpuff plant (*Calliandra*), sweet olive (*Osmanthus fragrans*), and wax plant (*Hoya carnosa*). Flowering house plants will often rest after their blooming period. Some will drop leaves and others will require pruning or even repotting. A summer's rest outdoors in semishade is often beneficial. Be aware of your plant's cultural needs afterwards if you expect it to bloom again.

Moisture Control: All house plants, except cacti, need more humidity than is available to them in an artificially heated house. Water constantly evaporates from all foliage, though the rate of evaporation differs according to leaf structure. Usually plants with smooth, leathery foliage will lose less water through their leaves than those with hairy or spongy textured leaves. The former are easier to accommodate in the house, and the latter will need special handling.

Because of water expired by each plant, a group of plants in a small area will be surrounded by a moister atmosphere than one plant by itself. Any plant stand designed to hold a number of plants, or a window with shelf-room for more than one plant will improve the atmospheric conditions for all the plants.

A bulb spray syringe or mister may be used to spray water over house plants daily, if their surroundings will not be damaged by the moisture. Or they may be moved to sink or tub weekly for a spray bath of all foliage. Flowers are sometimes damaged by strong streams of water, so apply it gently.

Most house plants benefit from a weekly soaking in a tub with water up to the pot rim. After it has absorbed enough water to make the surface moist, the plant should be thoroughly drained before being returned to its window. The amount of water given between soakings will differ according to the plant, the size pot and the accidental clogging or opening of the drainage hole in the bottom of each pot that takes place after it is filled.

Most plants should not be allowed to stand in saucers filled with the water that has drained after their watering. However, if their need for moisture is greater than can be supplied in any other way, the plant saucer may be filled with pebbles which are kept moist, and the plant will stand on the pebbles above the waterline.

This treatment may be given to individual plants, or a tray large enough to hold many plants may be constructed of waterproofed wood or metal. If the planter is deep enough, the pots may be set into it, and the space between them filled with damp sphagnum moss. Or a shallower tray may be filled with water and covered with heavy wire screening on which the plants may be set. If the plant window is over a radiator, a tank-shape humidifier may be made to cover the top of the radiator, with shelves for plants built above it.

For special moisture-lovers, like orchids, it may be necessary to build a special glass case to contain their own atmosphere. A glass cabinet like an old china cupboard with its wooden back replaced by glass makes an ideal miniature hothouse for these prima donnas.

Or a case may be specially constructed of Plexiglas using the window itself for one wall. Supplemental daily spraying with a bulb syringe will keep the humidity high enough in such a case for the most demanding plants. Thermometers with humidity gauges are available and should show a humidity of 60 to 80 percent for orchids.

Temperature: Conditions ideal for house plants are almost the same as those best for human beings. Temperatures of 65 to 70°F. (18.33 to 21.11°C.) in the daytime, and 50 to 55°F. (10 to 12.78°C.) at night are optimum.

Temperatures in a plant window may fluctuate much more than this, especially if curtains or dividers behind the plants prevent circulation of air from the room. During the day the sun will quickly heat a small enclosed space to shoot the mercury up ten to 25 degrees (F.). Window glass should be doubled to protect plants on very cold nights.

Circulation of air near the plants is not necessary to provide them with oxygen, which they manufacture themselves during the day, but to moderate the temperature. Changes in temperature are achieved more slowly in a large than in a small space. If the air circulating through an entire room flows around the plants, or around the case or glass jar containing them, they will suffer less from abrupt temperature changes than if they are isolated in too small a space.

Specially constructed plant windows, described below, must be built with air vents in the roof to allow the escape of hot air on sunny days. A small electric fan kept running during hours when temperatures in the window may be expected to reach extremes can also help to circulate air from the room into the window enclosure.

When plants grow in too hot an atmosphere, even though they are given plenty of moisture and food, the growth is too soft, the plant is easily injured and is easy prey for insects.

Light: Light, but not necessarily sun, is important to almost all plant life. Just as some plants thrive outdoors in the shade or half-shade, so some house plants may not want more than a small amount of sun, filtered through a thin curtain or screen.

Ideally, house plants should be supplied with light on all sides. A bow window or specially constructed plant window may permit almost as much all-around light as if the plant were outside. If such conditions are not possible, however, the plants must be turned often to prevent their reaching toward the light supply and becoming lopsided.

African violets, gloxinias and gardenias are among the flowers which prosper with something less than direct sun, but all three need bright situations, possibly in north or northeast windows. Ferns usually like the same light conditions—the more delicate ones are dried up by direct sun. Other plants that will flourish with no sun are ivy, philodendron, rubber plant, sansevieria, strawberry geranium, caladium, and dracaena.

African violets will also grow in windows that can catch only one to three hours sun each day, provided the sunny hours are in the morning. Some of the other plants that need only a small amount of sun for bloom are azalea, begonia, the bromeliads, cyclamen, spring-flowering bulbs, ivy geranium, and scented geranium.

Although many flowers can be brought to bloom in windows with a few hours' sun, most will be improved if they get all the sun

short winter days provide. For these a glass case with three glass sides and a glass roof may be built outside an ordinary window frame to form a miniature greenhouse. Several prefabricated types are offered on the market. They are equipped with vents at the top to let out hot air, and are often made with double glass to protect against cold. *See also* GREENHOUSE.

A miniature landscape can be created in almost any glass container, from a sherbet glass to an aquarium.

Terrarium: A Lilliputian garden with its own moisture control may be built in almost any glass container. Select compatible slow-growing plants that require similar growing conditions.

In a covered terrarium the water transpired by the plants condenses and is recycled by the plants. The plants maintain themselves for long periods of time and they should be watered infrequently.

Plants suitable for a woodland terrarium are tiny ferns, like ebony spleenwort, baby maidenhair, and rock fern; rattlesnake plantain, partridgeberry, wintergreen, or pipsissewa for bright berries; various sedums and mosses; ground pine, or seedlings of evergreen trees, such as white pine.

For a desert terrarium you can choose from many small cacti and succulents such as leafy stonecrop, English sedum, spiderweb houseleek, painted-lady, and Mexican snowball.

Plants good for a tropical terrarium include African violets, episcia, dracaena, baby's-tears, and creeping fig.

Pots: Traditional plant pots are made of clay. The natural appearance and porosity of clay, allowing air and water to pass through its walls, give the clay pot a few advantages over other types. Since roots require an interaction between oxygen and water, the porosity of clay benefits the house plant. One disadvantage of clay pots is that they are fragile and heavier than plastic ones.

When buying clay pots, choose the heavier ones, because thin ones dry out too quickly. Soak new clay pots in water until they stop "bubbling." Otherwise, the soil of the newly potted plants will dry out too quickly as the dry clay absorbs water from the soil.

After you remove a plant from a clay pot, be sure to clean the pot before the soil in it dries and becomes hard. To clean the pot use cleanser and steel wool. Be sure to rinse it thoroughly with hot water and let it dry before using it again. If pots are old and green with algae, clean them by scrubbing them with sand and water, for the "green" makes them less porous, and old earth dried on the inside surface interferes with the new root growth.

Plastic pots can also be used for house plants. They are lightweight, easy to stack, resistant to breakage, easy to clean, and inexpensive. However, they lack porosity; air and water can enter through the soil surface, but not through the sides. This does not mean clay pots are better, simply less water will be evaporated and less air will enter a plastic pot. Since the soil is not aerated as often in a plastic pot, root rot may take place. To avoid this, reduce the amount of water used and the frequency of watering. The amount of fertilizer should also be reduced, for an excess can build up more quickly in a plastic pot than in a clay one.

Decorative pots can also be used for your house plants, but can be costly if you have a great number of plants. Decorative pots come in glazed, unglazed and enameled clay.

Be sure the pots you buy have adequate drainage holes. Do not buy a pot that has no drainage holes, for this will only cause problems for your house plant. Clean all pots between plantings to prevent plant diseases and to make it easier to remove plants when it comes time to transplant.

Soil: The window box and flowerpot must be regarded as miniature, portable gardens. In addition to holding the soil, these containers ought to provide adequate drainage and aeration so that the soil becomes a favorable environment for the plant roots and the microorganisms which live in the soil and play important roles in the plant's nutrition.

Some house plants, such as bromeliads and cacti, thrive in soils that are inadequate for most other plants. Others, like the Chinese evergreen, can get along very well for long periods on just plain water and air. However, most of them require a soil high in humus and rich in minerals.

Soils for the indoor garden are formulated by mixing suitable proportions of such ingredients as loam, sand, pulverized rocks, and organic matter in the form of compost, leaf mold, muck, and peat. These materials can be kept in containers and mixed together as needed. Some suggested potting mixtures are given below:

1. General Potting Mixture

   2 parts good garden loam
   1 part compost, leaf mold, or other decomposed organic matter
   1 part clean, coarse sand

To the above mixture, add pulverized phosphate rock and potash rock (granite dust or greensand), each at the rate of a tablespoon for each pot of mixture.

2. Potting Mixture for Seedlings

   1 part good garden loam
   1 part compost, leaf mold, peat, or other form of humus
   2 parts clean, coarse sand

3. Potting Mixture for Humus-loving Plants

   1 part good garden loam
   2 parts compost, leaf mold, peat, or other form of humus
   1 part clean, coarse sand

To this mixture add pulverized phosphate rock and granite dust or greensand at the rate of one tablespoon for each six-inch pot of mixture.

4. Potting Mixture for Cacti

   1 part good garden loam
   2 parts clean, coarse sand
   1 part broken pots, coarse gravel or small stones

To this mixture add pulverized phosphate rock and potash rock (granite dust or greensand) at the rate of one tablespoon for each six-inch pot of mixture.

These potting mixtures represent four different soil types which are useful in the indoor garden. Potting mixture 1 will meet the requirements of most house plants, particularly those which prefer mineral rather than organic soils. For woodland plants, such as ferns, African violets, primroses, and azaleas, use potting mixture 3. The potting mixtures given above may be modified in one way or another to still better meet the requirements of special plants. In the case of acid-loving plants, for instance, acid peat may be added to give the soil an acid reaction, and lime may be added to make a soil mixture neutral or slightly alkaline.

The added compost and slow-release minerals such as phosphate rock and potash rock supply essential plant nutrients for a relatively long period of time, or until the plant needs to be repotted. This makes it unnecessary to feed plants in the indoor garden with manure water or with soluble chemicals.

The best forms of humus to use in potting mixtures are compost and leaf mold. Leaf mold can be collected in almost any woodland,

Before choosing a rooting medium, consider its water-holding capacity, porosity, ease of handling, and cost.

or it can be made from autumn leaves. If the leaves are shredded and then put in heaps mixed with a small amount of soil, leaf mold can be made in a few months.

Drainage: One of the most important characteristics of a good soil is drainage. This is best secured by adding sand. Use a clean, sharp sand such as a mason would use for making mortar; this is salt-free and very rough and coarse. If sand from the seashore must be used, get it from the shore side of the sand hills, and wash it thoroughly before using in order to remove any salt. If the plants are to stay for a year or so in single pots without repotting (as is the case with palms), charcoal is a distinct advantage, not only because of the better drainage it affords, but also because it prevents the soil from souring.

Before mixing the soil, determine its moisture content. You can tell if it's moist enough by taking a handful of the soil and pressing it firmly in the hand. If water can be squeezed out, the soil is too damp. If it will not remain in a lump but breaks up immediately as pressure is released, it needs more water. Ideal soil forms a cast, but crumbles easily when touched.

Pasteurization: Soil for house plants must be free of disease and harmful insects, but it should not be absolutely sterile. In most cases, pasteurization is sufficient.

To pasteurize your potting soil, place it in a tray and moisten it thoroughly so heat can be uniformly conducted through it. Preheat the oven to a temperature of 130°F. (54.44°C.). Plant disease pathogens or microorganisms will be killed at a temperature of 180°F. (82.22°C.) for 30 minutes. Fungi and bacteria which aid the plant will quickly be reintroduced from the air, plant root hairs and organic fertilizers.

Potting and Repotting: The best time of year to repot most house plants is the spring (April or May) when new growth starts. Only in very exceptional cases do house plants need repotting during the winter. Plants are then resting or are making very little growth, and meddling is positively dangerous to their lives. When a plant is resting it is unable to make a new root system rapidly and take hold of the new soil, so it may become sickly or die of shock.

To remove the plant from its pot, take the pot in the right hand and place the stem of the plant between the index and middle fingers of the left hand; then invert it and strike the edge of the pot sharply against the edge of a bench. The ball of earth and roots will slide out easily, unless the earth is dry. In that case, immerse it in water until the earth has become damp.

Now, with the right hand, disentangle and spread out the lower half of the mass of roots. If part of the ball of earth crumbles away, it does not matter. Then place enough soil in the new pot so that the surface of the old ball is about ½ to one inch below the rim of the pot.

The roots of palms, rubber plants and other large-rooted plants may be matted to-gether in circles. If possible, without injuring the roots, remove the old drainage. This will leave a large hole in the ball. Before putting the plant in the new pot, fill up this hole with soil; otherwise, the water will drain away too rapidly, and the interior of the ball will become too dry. Sometimes the roots are so matted that it is impossible to remove the drainage. When this is the case it's better to leave the drainage material where it is rather than risk injuring the roots.

Usually cuttings and seedlings are potted up in thumb pots (two-inch) and shifted to larger ones as soon as they become root-bound. The soil used in filling these small pots must be free from all lumps. The best way to pot these small plants is to hold the cutting just beneath a leaf node while covering the roots with soil. When the pot is full, firm the soil with the thumbs and then give the pot a sharp rap on the bench to settle the soil. This will prevent any air pockets from forming.

Transplanting Indoors: When potting plants which have been outdoors in the flower beds all summer, select only stocky, healthy ones. Dig them carefully so as to secure as many roots as possible. If the soil contains a great deal of clay, it must be neither so wet that it is muddy and the roots cling together, nor so dry that the dirt crumbles entirely away from them. The right soil condition can be obtained by a thorough watering at least five hours before potting.

If the plants are growing in sandy soil, it is better to have it rather dry, for then more of the working roots can be separated from the sand and be saved.

After potting, thoroughly water the plants and set them in a shaded place. Syringe the foliage several times a day until the roots have

Most plants should be repotted when a great many roots begin to appear around the perimeter of the soil ball.

stick with moderation, and be careful not to strike the roots.

If the soil contains many lumps or coarse pieces of sod (as sometimes happens when the sod is not completely rotted), screen them out before potting. This will be necessary if the pots are less than six inches. With larger pots it will make little difference. Save the coarse material. It will be useful when potting.

In the bottom of each pot put some coarse drainage material. Broken pots are usually used for this, but coal clinkers or stones are just as good. Broken charcoal is also very good. Large pots need from ¼ inch to two inches of drainage material according to the size of the pot. Pieces of broken pottery will fit best if placed convex side up. Over this drainage put some of the coarse screenings to keep the finer soil from washing down. If there are no coarse screenings, use sphagnum moss.

Any pot which seems to be in proportion to the plant, holding soil enough to keep it from being top-heavy, is sufficiently large. House plant growers often make the mistake of using a pot a size or two too large. It is very easy to overpot and few things in the plant's life can be more disastrous than an oversized pot. The plants will be overwatered and the soil will sour.

Mulching: Plants may be mulched to prevent rapid drying from the surface, if desired. Sheet moss, commonly used to line hanging baskets, is recommended for the job.

Moss should be soaked 15 or 20 minutes in water before being placed on top of the soil. It does not pack down over the surface of the soil, but remains fluffy, allowing sufficient aeration of the soil beneath. The moss is alive, and will turn green and provide a growing cover for the soil. Water may be poured

taken hold of the new soil. However, under ordinary conditions, the soil will not require more water until the new roots have been made. As soon as the plants have rooted, gradually get them accustomed to direct sunlight.

The best way to work the soil into the root mass is to hold the plant with the left hand, put a little soil around the roots and work the plant up and down a little. Put in some more soil, and tamp it down with a stick. It is possible to get the soil too firm, so use the

through it, or plants may be watered by plunging pots in a tub of water.

When used on African violets, gloxinias or other flowers with succulent petioles, the moss may be permitted to extend over the rim of the pot. This will prevent petiole rot, which can severely injure or kill these flowering plants.

Plants may also be mulched with sphagnum or peat moss, though these are more likely to cause rot in certain soft plants.

Raising Plants from Seeds: A house plant is propagated in two basic ways: sexually (seeds) and asexually (vegetative). Seeds are usually inexpensive and create new hybrids. They do require care and patience, however, since they often need special conditions and a long time to germinate and grow into full plants.

Seeds can be started in almost any container. For a few plants, use an unglazed pot or an egg carton. For larger plantings, try a plastic "seed pan" purchased from a garden supplier, or a wooden "flat" made from slats of soft lumber. These shallow, large (about ten by 15 inches) trays are convenient, space saving and efficient.

Over the holes or cracks in the flats put a damp paper towel. This will keep the soil from washing away each time the plants are watered. Sieve part of the special seed-starting mix so that you have two lots of soil, one coarse, the other fine. Spread a ½-inch layer of the coarse material over the damp paper towel and fill the flat to within ½ inch of the top with the fine, screened soil. Level the soil and tamp it gently with a board. If the soil has not been pasteurized, pour boiling water on it. When it is damp, but not soggy, seeds can be planted.

Mark drills about two inches apart by pressing a piece of narrow board lightly into the soil. Sow the seed thinly and evenly in the drills, and cover lightly with screened soils. Use a screen which has a mesh about the size of that in mosquito netting and simply sift the soil over the seed. A good rule to follow when covering seeds is to put on a layer of soil which is as deep as the diameter of the seeds. Sand, dry sphagnum, peat moss, or leaf mold which has been rubbed through a fine screen make very good coverings. They are very light, have a high water-holding capacity and are easily penetrated by the tender seed-shoots.

Water the soil thoroughly after sowing. The best way is to set the flat in a large pan partly filled with water, allowing it to soak up from below. This is better than overhead watering because no matter how fine a spray is used it may wash away some of the soil and finer seeds. Another way is to water through a sheet of blotting paper. Place the blotting paper on top of the seedbed and slowly apply the water, allowing it to soak through the paper.

Cover the box with pane of glass. This encourages a more humid atmosphere, and reduces evaporation from the soil. Every day remove the glass and wipe off any condensation which may be on it. Place the flat in a position where it will receive all the light possible, but shade it from direct sunlight.

Pricking out is the first transplanting of the seedlings, and it needs to be done tenderly. As a rule, as soon as the seedlings have made their first two real leaves it is time to transplant them to other flats prepared similarly to the seed flat.

Do not try to take each single seedling from the seedbed. Take out a portion of soil which has a number of seedlings in it, lay it on its side and gently separate the soil.

The dibble is a very useful tool for this purpose. It is a small wooden dowel, about ¼ or ⅜ inch in diameter and about four inches long. One end is tapered to a long point and the other is drawn down to a spatula shape. This end is very useful in separating the plants and firming the soil about the seedling after it has been set in the new soil.

Do not delay the pricking out. Do it just as soon as the little seedlings can be handled, for they may all be lost by "damping-off." Should the seedlings begin to damp-off, apply some hot sand, sprinkling it on with a fine-meshed sieve.

Put the little plants in rows an inch or two apart, water thoroughly and shade them for several days with newspapers or inverted baskets. Do not water again until the surface begins to dry.

As soon as the plants need still more room remove them singly and transplant to thumb pots. When transplanting, insert the plantlet a little deeper than it was in the old bed.

Vegetative Propagation: Vegetative propagation does not involve the reproductive organs, but is done with parts of the stems, leaves and roots of the plant. This method is a quick and usually fairly simple way to reproduce the parent plant and its characteristics. This method of propagation can usually be performed at any time of the year, but the best times are early spring or late summer. Best results are achieved with a healthy plant about to start its growth activity.

One of the easiest and most reliable means of vegetative propagation is division of older plants. Plants are divided by severing or breaking apart the plant and separating the multiple crown or roots. Each part is potted and grown as a new plant. For a few weeks afterward give the plant little sunlight and water. Keep wounds small and do not over-water to insure against fungal disease.

Various types of cuttings—stem, bud or eye, leaf-bud, leaf, and root—can be used to propagate house plants. Stem cuttings are made with softwood or hardwood plant parts. Hardwood cuttings, taken from dormant wood, are only rarely used in propagating house plants. In softwood propagation, the young stem tips of healthy plants are removed with a sharp knife. Take a cutting by making a diagonal cut on a main or side stem piece, and plant ⅓ deep in a moist rooting medium, such as sharp sand, vermiculite or perlite. Increase the humidity around the plants by covering them with an inverted glass jar or enclose the whole container in a plastic bag.

Waxy plants, such as begonias, peperomia, ivy, pothos, and jointed cacti will not need extra humidity. Keep the rooting material moist, but not soggy, and put it under reduced light the first week. Within four to ten weeks the plant will root and you should increase the light, decrease humidity and provide a weak fertilizer. The plant is rooted when it resists a gentle tug. Pinch out the growing tip and transplant the cutting in a pot. Ivy, geranium, wax begonia, fuchsia, impatiens, coleus, dracaena, gardenia, wandering Jew, grape ivy, and philodendron can be rooted in water from stem cuttings and do not require extra humidity.

Bud cuttings are taken from the part of the stem which contains growth buds or eyes. Strip the woody stem of its leaves, and cut it into two- to four-inch pieces, making sure each piece contains an eye. Dust the ends with charcoal to prevent decay. Half bury the piece in a horizontal position in moist sand. Enclose the container to increase the humidity and leave it in a cool place. When a callus forms in six to eight weeks move the container to a warm place, 70 to 80°F. (21.11 to 26.67°C.), and keep it enclosed and out of the direct sun. After it sprouts, cut the slip on either side of the new growth and pot the new plant.

Leaf-bud cuttings can be used for propagating some plants. This cut consists of a leaf and part of the stem. The method is the same as for stem cuttings, but takes longer.

Leaf cuttings can be made in two ways. In the first way, a mature leaf with two inches of leaf stalk is inserted in the rooting medium so it almost touches the medium. The second consists of taking only the leaf or piece of leaf containing ribs or veins. After severing the vein junctions with a razor blade, triangular leaf pieces containing a portion of the main vein and the junction with a lesser vein are inserted halfway into the rooting medium. Both of these procedures require a great deal of humidity for success. Keep the cuttings lightly shaded and warm.

Some plants can be propagated by root cuttings. They are successful with plants prone to have root suckers, such as geranium, leopard plant and plumbago. A one-inch piece of main root containing a bud or eye is removed during transplanting.

Some plants can be propagated through offsets, stolons, runners, and suckers. Runners can be rooted by pinning down the plantlet at the end with a wire loop or hairpin in a separate pot. You can sever the new plant from the main stem after it roots. Offsets and runners may be cut and rooted like a stem cutting. Stolons may be severed from the mother plant and potted directly in separate containers. Suckers and offshoots are cut to include some mother plant roots and are then potted.

To propagate by air layering, take a sharp knife and cut an upward slant into the stem eight to 14 inches below the growing tip. Soak up any milky sap with a paper towel. Hold the cut open with a toothpick. Wrap a moistened handful of sphagnum moss around the cut area and hold it in place with twine. Cover this with plastic film, closed at both ends with twine. If the moss dries, loosen the top and add water. Roots will form in two months. Then you can sever the stem and plant the rooted tip.

Gift Plants: Because most gift plants get their start in life in the close-to-ideal environment of a greenhouse, they must be pampered more than plants raised from seed or cuttings in a house. New flowering house plants should be acquired in any season other than winter unless greenhouse conditions can be duplicated in the home. The shock of adapting to the average home environment is most severe in the winter when many houses are too hot and dry. A plastic dry cleaning bag should be placed around any arrival which shows signs of yellowing or dropping leaves. This can be opened gradually, thus aiding the acclimatization of sensitive plants. Immature plants will adapt more readily than mature ones.

Equally fatal are chilling drafts. The ideal place for most gift plants is in a large picture window or an enclosed, heated porch. In an apartment, the best choice is a window with morning or afternoon sun. It's generally quite a bit cooler near a window than in the rest of a room. They must not be put anywhere near a radiator.

Enemies: Perhaps the greatest enemy of plants grown in houses heated by hot air furnaces or coal stoves is coal gas. An otherwise imperceptible trace of it in the air will cause the leaves of some plants (such as Jerusalem cherry) to drop off promptly. If you heat with coal, make sure your chimney has a good draft and the damper is working properly.

Illuminating gas is almost as bad as coal gas. The slightest trace will retard the development of new leaves on all but the toughest textured plants, like rubbers and palms. Such thin-leaved plants as geranium, coleus, heliotrope, and begonia succumb quickly. When gas is present in a very small quantity the plants do not necessarily die, but growth is stunted and the flower buds wither when beginning to show color, looking much as though they had been chilled.

The most common insect enemies of house plants are plant lice or aphids. Look for these pests on the underside of the leaves where they suck the sap. To combat them use tobacco water or soapsuds. Tobacco water can be made from cigar or cigarette butts, or from tobacco "stems," which can be bought from almost any florist or seedsman. Put a large handful into a gallon of warm water and let it stand for 24 hours, then dilute it to the color of weak tea and syringe the foliage, being careful to hit the underside of the leaves. A simpler way is to buy a tobacco extract and follow the directions on the package.

If you wish to use soapsuds, use only a pure soap (like Ivory or Fels Naphtha). Never use a detergent, as it can do your plants more harm than good. Be sure to rinse the plants with clear water afterwards.

Aphids sometimes attack the roots, causing the plants to take on a sickly or yellow color. They are easily found by digging down near the base of the stem and can be controlled by watering with the tobacco water already described.

Next to the aphids in destructiveness are red spiders, very small red mites which can scarcely be seen by the naked eye. They live on the underside of the leaves, but their presence can be readily discovered by numerous minute yellow spots on the upper side. Like the aphid, the red spider subsists on the plant's juices. It thrives in a hot, dry atmosphere, and its presence is a sure sign of insufficient moisture. The conditions ordinarily found in living rooms are very favorable for this pest. The remedy is obvious: syringe the plants with water, applying it on the underside of the leaves, and with considerable force because the spider is protected behind a web.

Mealybugs, which are almost always present in the greenhouse, sometimes infest house plants, too. This insect looks like a small tuft of white cotton and is found on the underside of the leaves and in the joints. A strong stream of water will usually wash it off, but if that fails, use kerosene emulsion or fir tree oil, which must be diluted according to the directions on the package, and applied as a spray or with a feather. Rubbing alcohol has also been used when there are only a few mealybugs. With a feather or small stick put one drop on the bugs and they will immediately succumb.

Very often scale insects will be found on the leaves of palms, ferns, rubber plants, and cycads. The most common one is the brown scale. It is ¼ to ⅜ inch long, and nearly as wide. Its hard, convexed shell is dark brown. The other scale commonly found on greenhouse plants is white, and about the size of the head of a pin. Both these scales can be removed easily by spraying with whale oil soap, kerosene emulsion or fir tree oil.

Sometimes plants are infected with thrips, which eat the epidermis of the leaves. They are small, slender, brown or black insects, about ¼ inch long, and are easily controlled by any of the remedies already mentioned.

Here are some general rules for protecting house plants from insects: New plants you bring home or ones that have been outside should be checked for insects before placing them with your other plants. If you suspect even a few unwanted insects on such plants, give them a good rinsing with soapsuds (discussed above) or a fine spray from the hose. Each month dust plants with a soft cloth, as dust cuts down on light that the plants receive. Clean leaves with warm water also, supporting the leaves from the bottom as you work. Bathing leaves in warm, soapy water is effective in protecting plants from red spiders and mealybugs. Make a regular practice of turning the leaves over and checking underneath, since that's where most insects do their work.

Summer Care: When the sun first becomes warm, plants must be moved from their customary windows either back into the room, or into another window, where they receive less sunlight. An east or west window in summer is equal in sunlight to a south window in winter, while a north window in summer is equivalent in sunshine to an east or west window in winter.

Give the plants plenty of fresh air, but keep them out of drafts. Plants dry out more quickly in summer and require more frequent watering. A mulch of grass clippings, peat moss, leaves, hay, or buckwheat hulls will help keep moisture in the soil and keep the roots cool.

Very few house plants can take the full sun of a south window in summer. An ideal location in summer would be an east or west window. If you cannot move them, a shade or tinted glass curtain will give some protection from burning. The following plants will grow in such windows:

African violet	Grape ivy
Amaryllis	Lantana
Artillery plant	Oxalis
Asparagus fern	Patience plant
Begonia	Pothos
Caladium	Prayer plant
Christmas cactus	Screw pine
Coleus	Shrimp plant
Coralberry	Strawberry begonia
Corn plant	Succulents
Croton	Sweet olive
Crown-of-thorns	Wandering Jew
Flowering maple	Wax begonia
Geranium	Wax plant

Some plants do not need very much light in order to thrive. A north window or a location near the source of light will do. The following plants can be used to decorate summer living quarters.

African evergreen	Jade plant
Apostle plant	Philodendron
Cast-iron plant	Pickaback plant
Chinese evergreen	Snake plant
Dumb cane	Spider plant
Ferns	Swiss-cheese plant
Fig family	Watermelon begonia
Ivy	

Moving Outdoors: Indoor plants are too tender to be placed out in the garden until all danger of frost is past. A few very delicate ones should, even then, go no farther than a sheltered porch. But the majority of them will enjoy being out. First, select a sheltered place receiving only filtered sunlight or perhaps just early morning sun. This spot may be under a low, spreading bush, in the lee of a hedge, or perhaps between bushes close to the house.

If the ground is hard, dig it over and incorporate some compost into it, removing all grass, weeds and large roots as you work it. It is sometimes recommended that the plunge bed be dug out to a depth greater than that of the tallest pot, and a layer of cinders or gravel be placed in the bottom for drainage. But unless drainage is a real problem in your area, this is not necessary.

Be sure that the plunge bed is well protected from children and dogs. A few small barberry bushes set in front of it or a low picket fence will usually suffice. Even a few lengths of cord strung between stakes may be enough to deflect the "traffic" from your prized plants. If your section of the country is apt to have summer hailstorms or extremely heavy rains, it is wise to guard against possible damage from these by making a cloth-covered frame to set over the plants on stakes when necessary.

Before taking the plants outdoors, knock them out of their pots to see if they are root-bound. Plants "on vacation" will grow at a great rate, and will derive the most benefit from their summer out if they have ample root-room. Repot those that need room in a mixture of sand, humus or leaf mold, and compost. Water thoroughly and keep sheltered for a day or two before setting out.

When placing the plants, put them into the soil up to the pot rims. Then mulch thoroughly around each plant and between the pots with dried grass clippings, until nothing can be seen but the plant tops. The grass clippings will conserve moisture and, as they break down, will add nutrients to the soil.

During the summer, replenish the mulch as necessary. Even with such a mulch, it is doubtful that the normal rainfall will be adequate for your potted plants, so check them at intervals to determine their need for an extra soaking.

Herbs: A sunny kitchen windowsill may contain pots of herbs which are used in cookery throughout the winter. Most herbs are very hardy, and like fresh air directly from the outside on warm winter days. But at night they should be protected from cold drafts through window chinks. Most herbs do best in glazed pots or metal containers. Tops should be sprayed frequently with tepid water. Generally, leaves should be picked from the outside of the plant to encourage the inner leaves to grow and make the plants bushy.

Herbs may be potted and brought in from the garden in the fall. Seeds of the annual varieties may be sown indoors and started directly in the window.

Especially recommended for window gardens are parsley, chives, basil, summer savory, and rosemary. Perennial herbs which may be brought in from the garden include sage, thyme and mints.

See also entries for individual house plants and herbs, BULB, FLUORESCENT LIGHT, FORCING.

HOWARD, SIR ALBERT

(1873–1947) Sir Albert Howard was the pioneer of organic farming methods. Although he was not the earliest critic of modern agriculture, he was the first popular champion of practical organic alternatives. His genius lay in his constructive approach. He saw the solution to the problem in the thorough study and application of the methods evolved by nature.

The most fruitful phase of Sir Albert's life was spent in India. His exacting scientific research in that country stands as his monument.

Albert Howard (knighthood was not conferred until later in England) went to India in 1905. He had already achieved recognition for work in the West Indies on sugarcane, hops and cacao. With him came his first wife, Gabrielle. Together they made a remarkable team: he had an "instinctive awareness of the importance of natural principles," and she "an enormous capacity for patient detail." The *London Times* paid tribute to their partnership by saying that "seldom in the sphere of economic investigation has there been a more fruitful collaboration between husband and wife."

They spent nearly 30 years in India. In all their work, the Howards never lost sight of one fundamental principle: agricultural research must solve the problems of both the land and the people. Their investigations were always practical, always keyed to an overall picture that gradually evolved into a system of farming. Sir Albert's most biting criticism was directed against "fragmentation"—the unnatural separation between the soil, crops, livestock, and humans. He believed these all were part of a natural complex, and research on each one without reference to the others was highly dangerous. In fact, he believed the dependence on chemical fertilizers, insecticides and drugs for human ills was directly caused by this fragmentation.

This was a novel approach. Abstract research, technical, hard to apply and generally confusing to the average farmer, was the order of the day. Sir Albert, however, had faith in the innate wisdom of the peasant and strove for a sincere relationship between experimenter and farmer. Only when an improvement was thoroughly integrated and adapted to the tools and ability of the Indian farmer did he release his findings.

India was probably the finest testing ground he could have had for his ideas. The rigorous climate exacts a terrific toll on faulty practices, making it far more instructive than temperate zones.

Despite the low yields, Sir Albert found many commendable practices, particularly in the field of fertility maintenance. Rotations were widely used so that wheat, rotated with barley, peas, mustard, rape, and linseed, and some leguminous weeds, could be grown continuously without manure fertilizers.

Sir Albert spent 12 years breeding varieties of wheat, during which time the significant problem of plant disease arose. Indian wheats, even the new varieties the Howards developed, were very susceptible to rusts. Sir Albert saw that poor tilth, water-logging, packing, and surface crusting went along with the disease, and he embarked on a long and fruitful study of soil aeration. To better control the monsoon rains, he developed a system of contouring and terracing the fields; but the real answer, he found, lay in using native, deep-rooted plants to let air into the soil.

This led him to his first conclusions on soil fertilization. Sufficient air in the soil, he discovered, permits myriad organisms to release plant foods like the nitrogen supplied by the green manures. Therefore nitrates and phosphates are unnecessary, natural forces doing the job much better.

This was his first clue to the value of the soil's microbial life. Thereafter in all his work with tobacco, fruits, fodder crops, vegetables, and the rest, he followed up his theory that organic matter, the prime raw material with which these organisms worked, is the most important factor in crop success. A soil well supplied with organic matter grows bigger yields of healthier crops.

This, of course, is only the broadest outline of the evolvement of Sir Albert's system. Hundreds of acute observations, backed up by thousands of field trials, went into this work. Only the most open-minded investigator, one who was willing at all times to regard nature as an infallible teacher, could have accomplished it.

More than anything else, his personality led him to success. He could be, when necessary, an awe-inspiring antagonist. When appointed to the botanical section of the then new Pusa Experiment Station, he found no land appropriated for his work. He was deputed to work with plants, not with the soil, so his superiors considered only a laboratory necessary. His long fight for 75 acres for his experiments was characterized by a fierce obstinacy and an "amiable brutality."

On the other hand, his great honesty, cheerfulness and sincerity opened many doors to him. In the words of his widow, "It was because he was honest enough and humble-minded enough to note what the Bihar peasants were doing, what the Baluchistan tribesmen grew and how they grew it, because he loved talking to West Indian planters and Kentish hop growers . . . that all who cultivated the earth's surface, of whatever calibre, or education, or station, became his instructors: he was able to learn from all because he wanted to learn from all." Moreover, he had great "respect for the empiric knowledge of cultivation methods accumulated in the course of several thousand years of tradition and experience." (Howard, Louise E. *Sir Albert Howard in India*. London: Faber and Faber, 1953).

This marriage of Eastern wisdom and Western science led to a new concept of agriculture. Like much of their work, the Howards' earliest project, improving the Indian wheats, had to be started at the very bottom. They found practically no work had been done in classifying the many varieties of tropical crops. Plant breeding thus became the first consideration.

But Sir Albert was not content with this. He assigned himself the added task of growing all the crops to be studied on a field scale. The practical difficulties of large-scale cultivation brought up virtually every crop-growing problem including poor drainage, and disease and insect infestations.

Here the Howards were breaking new ground. Their work on irrigation alone was monumental. They developed a system of field contouring and drainage, all to be done by hand labor, that proved of enormous value to Indian farmers.

This led them directly into the question of poor soil aeration, a leading cause of low yields in tropical elimes. From these studies their theory of soil conditions and disease resistance was formed. And by 1912, they were deep into a study of green manuring, which paved the way for the investigations of soil fertility. Each new problem led them to another. Up to that time, agricultural botanists had studied only the flowers, fruits and foliage of a plant, ignoring the roots. Sir Albert spent ten years, using equipment he made himself, examining the roots of several fruit trees as deep as 40 feet below ground.

This integration of research and the results it produced have had, and are still having, a profound effect upon agricultural experimentation. The research station which Sir Albert later designed and built at Indore has become a model for present-day stations. He brought to agriculture a fresh outlook, saving it from the increasing stagnation that threatened to leave an ever-growing world population with ever-decreasing food resources.

Following his return to England, he devoted the remainder of his life to perfecting and publicizing his ideas of good agriculture which were founded on his belief that the only real basis of fertility was the return of all wastes to the soil and that plant, animal and human health were directly dependent on this regenerative cycle.

HUBBARD SQUASH   *See* SQUASH

HUCKLEBERRY   (*Gaylussacia*)

Frequently mistaken for the wild blueberry, a huckleberry has ten large seeds, while a blueberry has many very small, soft seeds. Huckleberry shrubs include both fruit-bearing and ornamental varieties.

Highbush or black huckleberry (*G. baccata*) is hardy throughout most of the United States. It grows to a height of about three feet. Juniper berry (*G. brachycera*), also known as box huckleberry, is a low-growing ever-green, reaching about 1½ feet, and producing white or pink flowers. Dangleberry (*G. frondosa*) often grows to six feet, and is a spreading bush. Most huckleberries prefer partial shade. Their culture is similar to that required for blueberries.

Plants can be started inside about six weeks before the last frost date. Transplant them while still quite small—as soon as they acquire three sets of leaves—and cover each plant with a glass jar to create a small, moist greenhouse. By lifting each jar whenever checked, the plants get enough ventilation. Remove the jars at first just at night or on cloudy days, then completely when the plants have developed enough roots to prevent daytime wilting.

Huckleberries started in the warm, low-light conditions of the house are apt to be weak. It is important to harden them off gradually, especially in windy regions. Keeping them slightly on the dry side helps to toughen the tissues, but never let them wilt. Leave them outside in a protected spot for increasingly longer periods each day and bring them in or cover them well at night.

Harvest huckleberries seven to eight weeks after berry clusters turn dark. When the five-point foliage above the berry turns brown and curls to the stem, the berry is ripe and ready to be picked. Huckleberries will be soft to the touch when ripe.

Be sure to pick all the berries after the first light frost—a hard freeze will leave them soft and mushy. If you pull up the plants and rip off the clusters outside, then sit in comfort to pull off the individual stems, it is an easy job. Just wash in a colander and freeze.

Given plenty of room and unstunted growth for a full season, a single plant will give up to two quarts of berries and contribute both distinction and nutrition to your desserts. *See also* BLUEBERRY.

HULLS

Hulls, the outer coverings of cereal grains, are rich in potash and can be used for either mulches or compost. They decay readily and may even be spaded into the ground directly before the rainy season. Whether you prefer to apply the material in compost or as mulch will depend on the site of your garden. If it lacks water-retentiveness, it may be wise to use the hulls for mulches. Hulls of rice, cottonseed, buckwheat, cocoa bean, and oats are most often used.

HUMIFICATION   *See* HUMUS

HUMMINGBIRD'S TRUMPET
See ZAUSCHNERIA

HUMUS

Building the soil's humus content is the very heart of the organic method. When organic matter is incorporated into warm, moist soil, soil microorganisms immediately begin to work on the plant tissues. As decomposition occurs, plant tissues break down into a number of substances. Some of the resulting products, like carbon dioxide, are released into the air and others are absorbed by plant roots. Even-

tually, the easily decomposed food is exhausted, and more resistant compounds remain. This includes both compounds of higher plant origin such as fats, oils, waxes, and lignin, and new compounds that are synthesized by microorganisms and held as part of their tissue. These materials form the basis for humus; the process by which organic matter turns into humus is called *humification.*

Humus is a complex mixture of dark-colored, amorphous, colloidal substances containing approximately 30 percent each of lignin, protein and polyuronides (complex sugars plus uronic acid). It is nearly insoluble in water, but does dissolve in dilute alkali solutions. Humus contains about 5 percent nitrogen and 60 percent carbon. It is not a specific compound, nor does it have a single structural makeup. During humification, reactions occur that permit nitrogen to become an integral part of humus; these reactions are not completely understood, but they function to make the resulting compounds stable and fairly resistant to further decomposition.

The most noticeable difference between humus and organic matter is that the latter is a coarsely textured, rough-looking material. Its parent tissues are quite evident. Humus, on the other hand, is fine, more uniform in texture, not fibrous, of no definite shape, and of an unspecified character.

The microorganisms in actively decomposing humus are beneficial, and there are such great numbers of them that they prevent plant-destroying fungi and other pathogens from establishing themselves in humusy soil. Thus, humus helps protect plants from diseases. Because it also enhances plant health, it helps protect plants from insect damage, too.

A garden soil does not begin to realize its

potential productivity until it contains a humus content of at least 5 percent. In actual practice, it is all but impossible for gardeners to use too much humus from their compost heaps. Two pounds for every 4½ square feet (ten tons per acre) is an adequate treatment, though one could double that rate before there need be any concern for nitrate toxicity. Legume crops, which seem to require less nitrogen, in tests have increased in yield as the application of humus was raised from none to five tons per acre. Beyond that, increased humus applications did not increase yields. But on grasses and grains, leafy vegetables and root crops, the more humus the better, within reason.

Humus from finished compost has a carbon to nitrogen ratio of about ten to one. It will contain approximately two parts nitrogen, one part phosphorus and one part potash, with a pH of about 7 or nearly neutral. Though low in nitrogen, phosphorus and potash when compared to chemical fertilizers, compost seems to produce tremendous growth response in plants, estimated at about eight times more than its mathematical formula would indicate. One reason for such a response is the slow release characteristic. Another is the fact that nitrogen in humus does not readily leach away in periods of high moisture. None is wasted, whereas applications of chemical nitrogen that bring the carbon-nitrogen ratio below 25 to one can result in a 50 percent loss of nitrogen. Furthermore, humus is generally well endowed with almost all the known trace elements plants need—and perhaps some not yet known to be essential.

Apart from its fertility value, actively decomposing humus is most beneficial as a soil amendment. You can make topsoil with it where you have only denuded subsoil or hard clay. Apply a three-inch layer of humus, digging it in to a depth of six inches with spading fork or rotary tiller. Repeat three years in a row and you'll accomplish what it takes nature at least 100 years to do.

Specific uses for compost take advantage of both its fertility and tilth-restoring values. Humus seems to produce healthy germination and to invigorate seedling growth, so a liberal application in the planting row is most beneficial. Humus applied liberally around roots of transplants (vegetables, bushes, trees) increases the rate of survival and growth response after the shock of transplanting.

Mulch gardeners often observe how easily seeds from trees root and take hold in rotting mulch. In fact, almost any kind of garden seed, like those from last year's residue of rotted tomatoes or squash, will spring to life no matter how carelessly scattered on rotting mulch. There just has to be some very special life-enhancing property to humus. It is quite evident when humus is mixed into a rooting medium.

For cold frame and hotbed soil, compost is beneficial too. Mix two parts fertile loam, one part sand and one part compost.

A couple of tablespoons of compost in potted plants is a good practice. A "tea" made from steeping compost in water is also a good mild fertilizer for house plants.

Colloidal Quality: Humus is colloidal to a certain extent. Its fine particles (micelles) are negatively charged and very reactive. Cations (positively charged ions) are attracted to the particles and are absorbed under normal conditions.

This process, called cation exchange, is a very important reaction in the soil. Research has shown that the capacity of a soil to exchange cations is the single best index of soil fertility. The rate of this exchange is directly related to the organic matter content of the soil: the more soil organic matter present, the higher the cation exchange rate, and the higher soil fertility.

Color of Humus: Humus is usually dark in color, although in soils heavily fertilized with artificial fertilizer it may be bleached to a light gray in the surface layer. One cannot always tell the quality of the soil by its color, however.

Some soils are dark colored because they may be oversupplied with manganese; others may have originated from black rocks, and their dark color may be partly due to weathered rock fragments in the soil. A dark color may also indicate the presence of old humus in an advanced stage of decomposition. Such soil has lost most of its fertility and is normally not as productive as one that is supplied with fresh organic matter. In general, yellow and gray topsoils are indicative of soils deficient in humus. Red soils are more productive; the red coloring indicates iron oxide, a good source of iron.

Dark peat and muck soils may be deficient in certain important elements. Such soils can be made productive if the deficiencies are corrected.

See also COMPOSTING, FERTILIZER, ORGANIC MATTER.

HUNNEMANNIA   *(H. fumariifolia)*

Sometimes called Mexican tulip poppy, hunnemannia resembles a sulfur yellow California poppy of giant size, though coarser and of greater substance. The plants, about two feet in height, are very prolific, hardy and easy to grow once seeds have germinated. Like the poppies, they require a warm, sunny spot. Seedlings may not transplant readily so the seed should be sown in the permanent bed. Hunnemannia excels as a cut flower.

HYACINTH
(Hyacinthus orientalis)

The fragrant and colorful hyacinth is an important early spring flower, often blooming before the daffodils are under way. The hya-

Hyacinths are among the earliest spring-blooming perennials, often putting forth their pink, purple, rose, or yellow flowers long before the daffodils are under way.
(Courtesy of U.S. Department of Agriculture)

cinth comes in several shades of purple, blue, pink, rose, yellow, and salmon, and there are both single- and double-flowered forms.

Many gardeners are under the impression that hyacinths must be planted in formal beds, but they are equally attractive when planted informally throughout perennial beds, along a picket fence or by a stone wall. They can be planted in a single line or massed in groups in front of low shrubbery. You may even wish to force them for indoor flowers during the winter months.

Hyacinths prefer light, sandy soils which drain easily and warm quickly in the spring. Because they root deeply, the soil should be cultivated and fertilized at least eight inches deep. Thoroughly incorporate a generous amount of compost, very well-rotted manure and bone meal or dried sludge.

The bulbs should be planted four to six inches deep and six to eight inches apart. Be sure to plant the bulbs at a uniform depth so that they bloom at the same time. The actual depths depend on soil conditions. In light soil plant deeper than in heavy clay. The planting period starts about September 1 and extends until the ground freezes hard, but best results are obtained from late September or October.

In sections of the country with severe winters, mulch the bulb plantings with a loose covering of hay, straw, leaves, or evergreen boughs. Remove this covering early in the spring after the ground begins to thaw and there is no danger of refreezing.

After blooming is over, let the foliage continue growing until it turns yellow and withers of its own accord. Good leaf growth is important for the development of the bulbs for the next spring's performance. Begin to plant annuals as soon as the hyacinths stop

blooming, and by the time their foliage becomes unsightly the annuals will take their place. The leaves of the hyacinth may be bunched together and tied loosely to allow more room between the bulbs for planting annuals.

Hyacinths tend to "run out" and have to be replaced more often than other spring bulbs, but they will bloom several years if fertilized each season and divided and reset every two to three years as foliage withers.

For blue and purple shades try planting Ostara, King of the Blues or Grand Maitre. For pinks and reds try Pink Pearl, Marconi, Amsterdam, or Princess Irene. Among the desirable white varieties are Edelweiss and Innocence. Orange Boven or Salmonetta is a soft salmon orange.

See also BULB.

HYBRID

Plants which result from the crossing (cross-fertilization) of species or varieties are called hybrids. Crossbreeding has become a basic means of causing slight variations and a way of improving a type. One disadvantage is that hybrids often do not breed true and in some cases are sterile. In many cases, however, crossing has improved the yield, nutritive quality and disease resistance of a number of species and their varieties.

HYDRANGEA

This highly ornamental shrub of the Saxifrage family produces showy pink, blue or white flowers. More than 20 species of hydrangea grow as natives in the central and southern areas of the United States but cannot thrive in colder temperature zones. The shrub usually grows between four and ten feet high, with heart-shaped leaves and flowers that appear in June and July.

Hydrangea is sometimes called "sevenbark," a name which refers to the shrub's stem bark, which peels off in seven thin layers of different colors. These shrubs were used by the Cherokee Indians who believed in their medicinal value. Hydrangea has also been used as a diuretic, cathartic and treatment for gallstones.

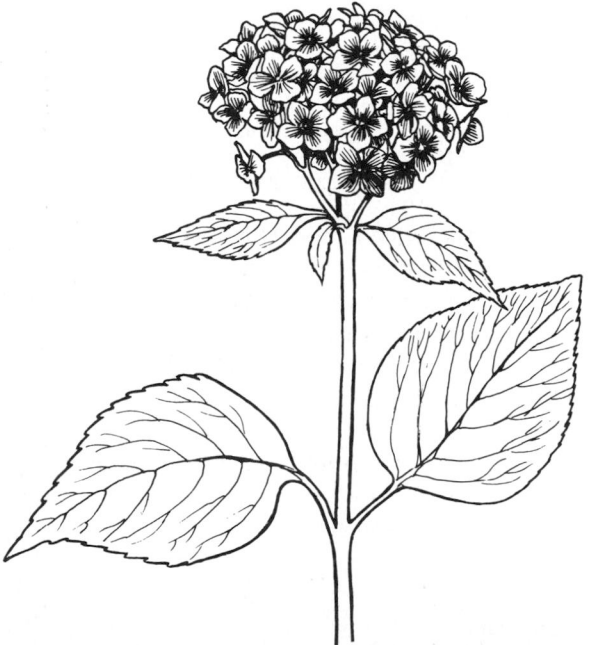

A dense shrub or tree, growing to five feet in height, the arborescens *hydrangea produces highly ornamental fragrant flowers from midsummer through early fall.*

Good plants for the shrub border, hydrangeas grow best in rich, well-drained soil. They bloom most abundantly if placed in full sun and given sufficient moisture. Pruning is generally done in fall or early spring, the branches of the previous year's growth cut back to a single pair of buds. Weaker branches are always cut off, and the less hardy varieties should be given protection during winter. Hydrangeas can be propagated by cuttings of fairly ripe wood, by layering or by division.

Common hydrangea (*H. paniculata*) is hardy throughout the United States and is rarely troubled by insects and diseases. It is a dense shrub or tree growing from six to 25 feet high, and has off-white flowers that bloom in August and September. Hortensia (*H. macrophylla*), much grown in the South as a tub plant and in greenhouses, has been tried successfully outdoors in northern gardens. It usually grows to ten feet. Give it winter protection by mounding the soil about the stems in the same way as roses. A slightly acid soil is recommended.

Since flower heads are quite heavy, it is often necessary to support the plants. This should be done in early spring before buds swell.

Wild hydrangea (*H. arborescens*) reaches three to five feet; the variety Grandiflora is called hills-of-snow. Climbing hydrangea (*H. anomala* subsp. *petiolaris*) is a woody vine sometimes going up as high as 50 feet. Tea-of-heaven (*H. macrophylla* subsp. *serrata*) grows to five feet and is also relatively tender.

See also HERB.

HYDRATED LIME   *See* LIME

HYDROPONICS

From the Greek roots *hydro,* water, and *ponos,* meaning work, hydroponics is the science of growing plants in water, without soil. The plants are supported in an inert, non-organic medium such as sand, fine gravel or mica compositions, which are saturated with prepared nutrient solutions for short periods of time. These solutions typically contain nitrogen, phosphorus, potassium, calcium, magnesium, sulfur, iron, manganese, boron, zinc, and copper. All of the essential inorganic plant foods are available to plant roots in great quantities.

Hydroponic gardening requires a trough or container for the plants, an aggregate such as sand, gravel or vermiculite for root support and a water supply with a pH rating of between 5 and 7. Needed nutrient solutions are added to the water regularly.

Vegetables such as lettuce, tomatoes and spinach can be cultivated in hydroponic gardens, as well as strawberries, grapes, various herbs, and flowers.

Hydroponics has intrigued scientists and agriculturists because it eliminates the need for soil in ordinary cultivation. Its main advantage is in the labor saved by automatic watering and fertilizing, although installation costs are higher than costs for plants using soil. No greater crop yields result from hydroponic gardens. Until very recently, commercial acceptance and implementation of hydroponic methods have been impeded by high costs, the reliance on chemical nutrient solutions and frequent testings, and the greater familiarity with soil cultivation by most growers.

With mounting interest in urban agriculture and rooftop food production, however, hydroponics seems destined to assume greater significance. The organic grower can either use a tea made from high-quality compost, or can mix a basic solution of one tablespoon fish emulsion, one tablespoon liquid seaweed, and a teaspoon of blood meal to each gallon of water. The mix varies, depending on the type of plant to be grown. Less blood meal should be used with flowering and fruiting produce than with leafy crops. Other nutrients can also be added: blended eggshells, for example, might be helpful when added to a cabbage crop. Organic hydroponics is very much in a developing stage, and a taste for experimentation is essential.

While soil is cheaper than perlite or vermiculite, it is significantly more difficult to cart up to a rooftop in bulk. Moreover, container soil is prone to rapid leaching and usually requires repeated fertilization, so the actual cost of organic fertilizers for hydroponically grown plants is comparable with that for conventionally grown plants. Hydroponics advocates also point out that since hydroponic roots do not need to grow as far in search of nourishment as the roots of soil-grown plants, planting densities can be more intensive and higher yields can be achieved.

The equipment for hydroponic production can be constructed simply and inexpensively. The container must be elevated slightly at one end and have drainage holes at the opposite end. One-inch plastic pipes with holes drilled every three inches are laid about an inch below the medium and raised at both ends of the box. Smaller rubber hoses coming from the nutrient supply are inserted into the pipe at one end; the upward bend in the pipe at the opposite end stops the flow of the solution. A gravity system for controlling nutrient flow, composed of two five-gallon buckets elevated on boxes and standing two feet above the top of the growing container, makes it easy to add nutrients and care for the hydroponic plants.

HYMENOCALLIS

Also called spider lily and Peruvian daffodil, these members of the Amaryllis family produce large trumpet-shaped, usually fringed white flowers and long, straplike leaves resembling those of amaryllis. The flowers are exceptionally fragrant, especially in the evening. They are not hardy in the North, but are easily grown there in summer beds or containers.

In open beds, plant the bulbs three inches deep in a rich acid soil in full sun and provide plenty of water. Take them up before frost and allow them to dry off, storing at no less than 60°F. (15.56°C.) in a dry place for the winter. They are perhaps better suited to container culture because these can be put out of the way when the relatively short bloom period is over. Use pots eight inches or larger for big bulbs, and plant with the top of the bulb just under the surface of a rich, acid potting mix. Water heavily and feed every two weeks during the summer. Repot in fresh acid soil and remove offset bulbs at the end of the winter storage period. Flowers of *H. calathina* come in early summer.

HYPERICUM
See SAINT-JOHN'S-WORT

HYSSOP   (*Hyssopus officinalis*)

A fragrant, hardy plant growing up to three feet high, hyssop has long, thin leaves, a strong scent and blue, pink or white flowers. Blue-flowered hyssops are used in medicine, while the other species are valued by gardeners, perfume manufacturers, housekeepers, and cooks.

Hyssop has a long, versatile background. It earned its name, adopted from the Greek

Hyssop should be harvested when the flowers are just ready to open, before the stem and leaves become woody.

azob (holy herb), because it was used to clean temples and other sacred places. Egyptians used it to cleanse lepers. Native to Europe and Asia, it spread quickly to America and now grows wild in many places. The herb was used in teas to treat coughs, jaundice and throat inflammations.

Hyssop is a slow grower, and should be started indoors from seed for best results. Older plants can be divided early in spring and replanted at least one foot apart.

The plant needs dry, sunny areas with calcium-rich soil. During the first few weeks, hoe, weed and thin thoroughly. Mulching is recommended once the plants are six inches high.

Harvesting should be done when the flowers are ready to open. It must not be delayed beyond this stage since hyssop will quickly turn woody, reducing the yield of leaves and stems that produce its valuable oils and flavors. The leaves can be chopped, dried and stored for many months.

As a companion plant, hyssop is known to hike the crop yield of grapevines. It also deters the cabbage butterfly and several bacterial diseases of plants. It should never be planted near radishes, however.

As an herb for cooking, hyssop is included in recipes for soups, stews, fruit cocktails, and pies. It is valued as a grease-cutter and is often served with pork or fat fish. Hyssop teas are still used to treat coughs, colds and sore throats, and to loosen phlegm.

The oils extracted from hyssop make the English eau de cologne and other popular perfumes used today.

See also HERB.

IBERIS   *See* CANDYTUFT

ICELAND POPPY
See PERENNIALS, POPPY

ICE PLANT
(Mesembryanthemum crystallinum)

Ice plant is a low, spreading annual that grows in dry regions. It has daisylike white, pink or red flowers and thin, succulent leaves that are covered with small raised dots like bits of frost or ice. Native to South Africa and naturalized in parts of California, the plant grows best in a poor sandy soil in a sunny position. It is an excellent choice for desert and rock gardens.

Propagation is by cuttings rooted in a sandy soil or, more commonly, by seed sown in a warm greenhouse or outdoors in late spring. Avoid overwatering.

IGNEOUS

Igneous rock is a "fire formed" mineral, the result of the cooling of molten rock below the earth's crust.

See also MINERAL ROCKS.

ILANG-ILANG   *(Cananga odorata)*

This pretty evergreen tree grows about 80 feet in the southernmost parts of Florida and is hardy nowhere else in this country. It bears yellow green flowers which are highly fragrant and used to make perfume in some tropical lands.

Another plant called ilang-ilang is *Artabotrys hexapetalus,* a woody vine with the same hardiness range, but which is also suitable for growing in the warm greenhouse. The flowers are similarly colored and fragrant, and it bears yellow, fragrant fruits that resemble grape clusters. Outdoors it needs full sun, very fertile soil, and a mulch of rotted manure or rich compost.

ILEX   *See* HOLLY

IMPATIENS

Comprising both tender annuals and perennials, this genus of plants includes some very popular garden and greenhouse flowers. The plant gets its name from the Latin, which refers to the tendency of the ripe pods to burst open at the slightest pressure.

The wild Impatiens pallida *or jewelweed can be found growing wherever poison ivy flourishes. The juice of its leaves is a natural remedy for poison ivy rash.*

Patient Lucy or sultana (*I. Wallerana*) is an orange-flowered annual that requires moist, shady areas. Hybrids of this and other species have become some of the most useful of bedding annuals because they are one of the few flowers capable of producing heavy bloom in deep shade. Most cultivated varieties range in height from six inches to two feet, in single- and double-flowered forms, with foliage shiny green to reddish or variegated green and yellow green. The flowers come in white, purple and various shades of red. Bicolor forms are also available.

Seed should be started indoors in February or early March. A shallow layer of vermiculite, perlite or milled sphagnum moss placed on top of the soil mix will help to maintain even moisture and prevent damping-off. Do not cover the seed; sow it on top of the germinating medium, water well and place the flat in a plastic bag out of direct sun or cover with a pane of glass. Keep the flat at a constant temperature of 75°F. (23.89°C.), using bottom heat until seed germinates in about 14 days. Some seed may take longer. Do not transplant to the garden until frost danger is well past, as the plants are quite susceptible to cold.

They are remarkably pest-free, and require little maintenance to produce masses of bloom. The Imp series grows to 12 inches; the Elfin series matures at six inches. Garden balsam (*I. Balsamina*) is an excellent, large potted plant with brilliant-colored flowers. Growing two feet high, it prefers a mostly sunny spot. Seed should be sown in May and plants spaced about 1½ feet apart. Flowers appear in mid-summer and continue through early autumn.

The pale touch-me-not (*I. pallida*), called jewelweed, has light yellow to orange pendent flowers and likes moist, shady locations. This is the plant whose juices so effectively relieve the itch of poison ivy rash. It is also a favorite food plant of the ruby-throated hummingbird, which will visit the flowers for nectar all during the late summer bloom period. For these two reasons, it is well worth establishing a colony of the plants, which will grow readily in any shady, reasonably moist location. Gather seed in fall for a wild colony and scatter them in lightly prepared soil. Once established, a colony will self-sow indefinitely.

IMPORTED CABBAGE WORM

The imported cabbage worm is undoubtedly familiar to every vegetable gardener in the eastern part of the United States and Canada. The adult is the cabbage butterfly whose white wings are marked with three or four black spots and tipped with gray. Throughout the spring, these butterflies deposit eggs at the base of broccoli, Brussels sprouts, cabbage, cauliflower, collards, kale, and kohlrabi plants. About one week later, caterpillars emerge and begin feeding. They eat huge, ragged holes in foliage, leaving behind bits of green excrement. Later in the season, they bore into the developing cabbage heads.

Companion planting is one of the best defenses against these pests. Plant all crucifers in one bed and surround with tansy, tomatoes, sage, rosemary, nasturtium, catnip, or hyssop. The old standbys, onion and garlic, may also serve as repellent plants.

The predators of cabbage worms include cowbirds, song sparrows and redwing blackbirds. Yellow jackets and hornets also prey on the worms and should be encouraged in the garden.

Where the worms are an especially serious problem, a number of homemade sprays may be used to supplement the work of repellent plantings and natural predators. A little sour milk spooned into the center of cabbage heads works for some gardeners. Others swear by a mixture of ground mint, onion, garlic, hot peppers, and peppercorns with a little soap and water. Or try dusting plants with a mixture of salt and flour; the worms will eat it, become bloated and die.

See also INSECT CONTROL.

INCHWORM   *See* CANKER WORMS

INDIAN BEAN   *See* CATALPA

INDOOR GARDENING
See FRUITS, GROWING INDOORS;
HOUSE PLANTS

INFECTION   *See* DISEASE

INFORMAL GARDEN

This term refers to a more natural, irregular form of garden landscaping, where the objective is to achieve the free-flowing lines of nature. Many organic gardeners, trying to capture the spirit of nature in their own plantings, maintain the original landscaping features of their grounds as they first found them. Their goal is to accentuate the most beautiful elements in this setting, rather than to introduce a new design. Paradoxically, to obtain this effect, often as much time is spent in careful study as is spent on many formal gardens. However, the final effect should be one that is almost completely devoid of artificiality and intrusion by man.

See also LANDSCAPING.

INKBERRY   *See* POKEWEED

INNOCENCE   *See* QUAKER-LADIES

INOCULANT   *See* ACTIVATORS

INSECT

All insects belong to the large phyllum Arthropoda, which is broken down into five classes: Insecta (insects), Crustacea (including crayfish, sowbugs, fairy shrimp, lobsters, crabs), Arachnida (spiders, ticks, mites, scorpions), Diplopoda (millipedes), and Chilopoda (centipedes). The adult members of these five classes are alike in certain ways—they have segmented bodies, jointed legs, antennae, and other appendages, and a hardened covering over their bodies called an exoskeleton.

General Characteristics: The body of all insects consists of three main parts—head, thorax and abdomen, although these parts are not always clearly visible. At some time during their development, insects have six legs and, usually, two or four wings. The legs and wings sprout from the middle section, the thorax.

The design of an insect's mouthparts determines how it will go about eating plants or how it will go about attacking insect pests. Chewing insects have mandibles (or jaws) that move sideways to bite off and chew food. Sucking insects are equipped with a beak through which liquid food is drawn.

Respiration takes place by a network of tiny tubes, or tracheae, that connect with openings (spiracles) in the exoskeleton. Blood flows freely throughout the body cavity, and is not confined to veins and arteries. Insect blood is usually colorless or tinted pale yellow or green.

Life Cycle: Most insects start life as eggs laid by the female. In general, the insects develop from the egg stage in either of two ways. One group, which is said to have a complete life cycle, goes through four stages of development—egg, larva, pupa, and adult. The larva is a tiny worm which hatches from the egg. It grows until it enters into a motionless resting stage, the pupa. In this stage an insect is best able to resist an adverse environment. The adult insect emerges by splitting the pupal skin. Beetles, flies, bees, butterflies, and moths are examples of insects which have a complete life cycle.

The other group has an incomplete life cycle, and goes through just three stages of development. When the young hatch from the eggs, they look like small versions of the adults. They are called nymphs, and shed their skins as they grow larger, finally developing wings and reaching adult size. Grasshoppers, crickets, roaches, and the so-called "true bugs" are examples of this group.

See also INSECT CONTROL.

INSECT CONTROL

Gardening organically depends on creating a balance of life on the plot of earth you till. Ideally, sprays, dusts and traps become unnecessary as beneficial predators and parasites reach the point where they can keep the numbers of potential pests at a low, tolerable level. The key word here is "tolerable." It describes a peaceful state of garden activity in which the bugs keep themselves in line, with the only price to the gardener being occasional nibbles taken out of a few crops. If you can tolerate the minor losses necessary to keep a few plant-eaters around, you should always have a supply of beneficial insects at hand.

Obviously, chemicals are inimical to this delicate balance of life. But many organic gardeners don't realize that nontoxic homemade sprays can also upset the balance and pave the way for a pest infestation. So the best advice for pulling any crops through the season can be expressed in a short sentence: Don't interfere until the bug damage becomes intolerable.

Preventing Trouble: There is much you can do to avoid insect troubles. As many gardeners have found, healthy plants are more able to withstand infestations than are weak plants. Perhaps this is nature's way of censoring inferior strains of life. Whatever the reason, examples occur throughout the homestead. It is the weak, underfed, rough-coated calves—and not the suckling, fat, smooth-coated ones—that are eaten up with lice. A sickly hen in the flock will always carry most of the lice. Trees weakened by drought, leaky gas mains, or loss of roots due to excavation are more heavily attacked by borers than are nearby healthy trees of the same species.

A fundamental way to maintain healthy plants is to make sure they get a balance of nutrients, and this can only be brought about with a healthy soil. Plants need nitrogen, but an overdose has been found to make the plants overly succulent and to encourage various sucking insects. It is best to make nitrogen available to plants slowly, by using natural fertilizers. *See also* SOIL DEFICIENCIES.

Flat-headed apple tree borers usually attack only weak, improperly pruned trees.
(Courtesy of U.S. Department of Agriculture)

Another important strategy of prevention is protecting plants with other plants. This can be accomplished in several ways. First of all, plants fare better if not grown in monoculture, that is, in a field or plot given to just one crop. Growing row after row of a pest's favorite food is asking for trouble, and the chances of an infestation are reduced if a different vegetable is grown every two or three rows. A pest can be further discouraged by planting crops it likes next to plants it can't stand—companion planting.

The following list suggests repellent planting for some of the more notable garden pests:

Aphids: mints, garlic, chives, coriander, anise, and nasturtium or petunia around fruit trees.

Cabbage maggot: mints, tomato, rosemary, sage.

Cabbage moth: mints, hyssop, rosemary, thyme, sage, celery, catnip, nasturtium.

Colorado potato beetle: snap bean, horseradish.

Cucumber beetle: tansy, radish.

Cutworms: tansy.

Flea beetles: mints, tomato interplanted with cole crops.

Japanese beetle: garlic, tansy, rue, geranium.

Leafhoppers: petunia, geranium.

Mexican bean beetle: marigold, potato, rosemary, summer savory, petunia.

Mites: onion, garlic, chives.

Mole cricket: spurge, castor bean, mole plant, squill.

Nematodes: marigold, salvia, dahlia, calendula.

Slugs (snails): prostrate rosemary, wormwood.

Squash bug: tansy, nasturtium.

Tomato hornworm: borage, marigold.

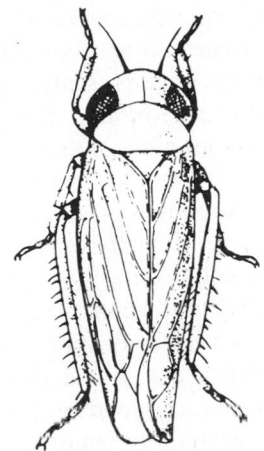

Control the disease-carrying beet leafhopper by eliminating garden weeds and removing plants that are stunted or have curled, brittle leaves.
(Courtesy of U.S. Department of Agriculture)

Whiteflies: nasturtium, marigold, nicandra.

Wireworms: white mustard, buckwheat, woad.

Another way of protecting plants with other plants is trap cropping—growing a bug's

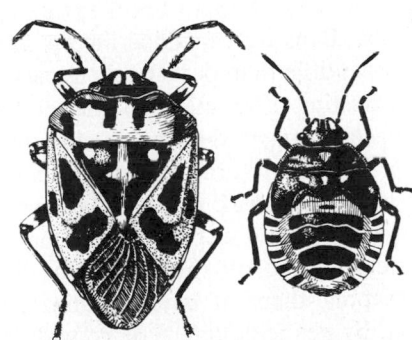

Both nymph (right) and adult (left) harlequin bugs feed heavily on all members of the Cabbage family. To keep them away from their favorite foods, grow "trap" crops of mustard or turnip greens nearby.
(Courtesy of U.S. Department of Agriculture)

favorite next to a crop you wish to protect. Japanese beetles might be lured from valued crops with plantings of white or pastel zinnias, white roses, soybeans, or odorless marigolds. Dill seems to draw the tomato hornworm from tomatoes. Careful observation in the garden should suggest other trap crops. *See also* COMPANION PLANTING.

Resistant varieties offer a sure and easy way to prevent much damage. Because of fortuitous mutations, some crop strains do better than others; these strains are developed and marketed as resistant to one or more particular pests. *See also* RESISTANT VARIETIES.

A last method of preventing bug problems is to take advantage of their natural cycles. If you have gardened for a few seasons you no doubt have noticed that insects usually appear at about the same time every year, live their short active lives and disappear until the next year or until a second generation is spawned. In many cases, this leaves plenty of time to sneak in a crop, either before or after the bugs go through their hunger stage. Although timing a planting is very dependent on the vicissitudes of local weather, a couple of examples should be instructive. Cabbage may escape the ravages of the cabbage worm, looper and aphid if planted as early as possible. Near New York City, snap beans planted early in June should miss the Mexican bean beetle. This season, log the kinds of pests that cause trouble, when they appear, and when they disappear. Your garden records should suggest several possibilities for timed planting.

Biological Controls: If a crop is endangered despite your precautions, you should first consider biological controls. While most gardeners are familiar with the predaceous ladybug and praying mantis, many lesser known bene-

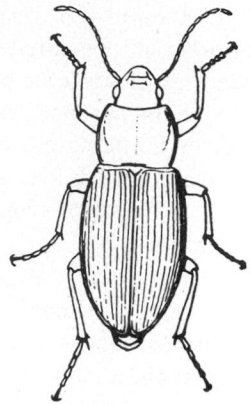

Most species of ground beetles are excellent predators of plant-eating insects such as tent caterpillars, webworms and canker worms.
(Courtesy of U.S. Department of Agriculture)

ficial insects and even pathogens deserve recognition as effective natural controls. The parasitic tachinid flies resemble ordinary houseflies and as maggots they feed on caterpillars. Ambush, assassin and damsel bugs are fierce predators of many insects, including various caterpillars and grubs. There are also many helpful beetles, including large, dark ground beetles, checkered beetles, soldier beetles, and the larvae of lightning bugs. Several species of

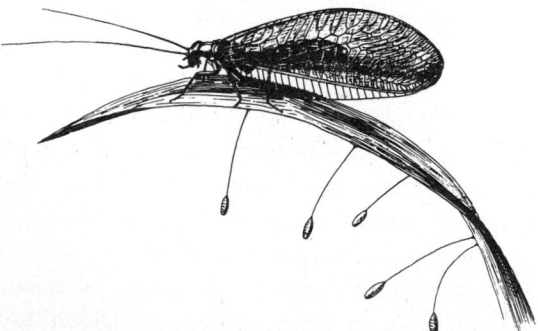

Most of the beautiful lacewings are invaluable predators of aphids, mites, mealybugs, certain scales, and other soft-bodied insects.
(Courtesy of U.S. Department of Agriculture)

lacewings eat significant numbers of mealybugs and aphids. Braconid and chalcid wasps parasitize mealybugs, aphids, scale, and the larvae of many beetles and moths. One egg parasite, known as trichogramma, is commercially available. *See also* TRICHOGRAMMA.

In addition to these insect predators, there are several types of pathogens at work in the garden: bacteria, viruses, fungi, rickettsia, nematodes, and protozoans. The bacterial diseases are most numerous; they usually work by entering insects through the mouth and then multiplying in the bloodstream. Two such diseases are available commercially. *Bacillus thuringiensis* is effective against an impressive number of common pests, most of which are moth and butterfly larvae. *Bacillus popilliae* is used to combat the grubs of the Japanese beetle. The spores that form within infected grubs lend a whitish cast to the victims, explaining the pathogen's common name, milky spore or milky disease. *See also* BACILLUS THURINGIENSIS.

All of these controls are working in the well-tended garden, but there are several things you can do to increase their populations and effectiveness. Most important is excluding toxic chemicals. Because beneficial insects are often more susceptible than pests to chemicals, spraying and dusting often allow the target insect to come back stronger than ever. Another malfunction of the natural clockwork caused by toxins is the outbreak of secondary pests that were innocuous and went unnoticed until doses of pesticide killed off the beneficials that had been keeping them at bay. A third problem spawned by pesticide interference with biological control is pesticide resistance. Because of their greater reproductive powers and better chances for adaptation, plant-eating bugs are able to build up resistance faster than their natural enemies, and successively larger doses only serve to set back these enemies. Well over 200 pests are known to be resistant to one or more pesicides.

You can encourage beneficial insects by interplanting with the favorite crops of those species you wish to attract. For instance, the adult forms of some beneficial species are not carnivorous and rely on high-protein foods such as nectar and pollen to sustain themselves. Some ladybugs will turn to pollen if the aphid population drops off, and this suggests the importance of growing pollen-producing plants near crops of trees vulnerable to aphids.

Traps and Barriers: After biological controls have failed to stem an insect attack, and before turning to sprays and dusts, consider trapping the enemy. One of the most popular traps is nothing more than a shallow dish or jar lid containing a bit of stale beer. Snails and slugs will drown in the stuff at night. Earwigs can be trapped by setting out one-foot-long sections of bamboo pole on the ground; come morning, the poles are shaken out over a bucket of water topped with kerosene. Grasshoppers are drawn to molasses and citrus fruit, ants to sugar water, Japanese beetles to geranium oil, and male fruit flies to citronella oil. A trap for codling moths is made by hanging cups full of molasses and water on the upwind side of the tree.

Sticky substances for trapping insects are commercially available. They can be applied in bands around tree trunks to stop crawling insects, and you might try smearing the stuff on red or orange plastic fruit to catch fruit flies. The traps should be hung two or three to a tree.

Light traps are valuable tools for large-scale pest problems. The traps involve a sticky surface, a fan to suck bugs into a collecting container, or an electric grid. Black light draws the most pests. Light traps may also attract

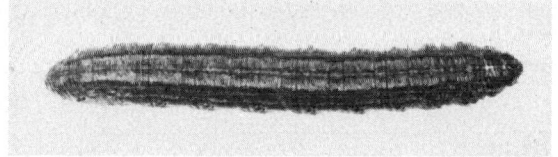

The larvae of gray or brown moths, cutworms feed on the roots of almost all kinds of plants. To protect seedlings, and transplants, place a stiff paper collar around the stems and upper roots.

harmless or beneficial insects, and if the pests collected are few in comparison, the trap is doing more harm than good.

A perimeter of wood ashes scattered around the bases of plants will block many crawling and walking insects. You can also sprinkle lines of bone meal, lime, powdered charcoal, coal ashes, diatomaceous earth, or vegetative dusts such as sabadilla and pyrethrum. Aerial fruit tree pests can be kept away by hanging mothballs in mesh bags from branches. If birds rob all the fruit and berries each season, it may pay to invest in a roll of mesh.

Controls from the Laboratory—Pheromones and Hormones: While they can't be brewed in the kitchen like most organic nostrums, pheromones and hormones are nontoxic and can be highly effective—so effective. in fact, that some entomologists are led to wonder if man has enough knowledge at this point to use their power without causing serious ecological upsets.

Pheromones are odorous secretions of an animal or insect that are emitted for the purpose of communicating with other creatures of the same species. These are complex compounds, and can signal danger warnings, discovery of food, mating calls, and so on. Many have been isolated, and certain of them are synthesized for use as attractants. Species of pests can be drawn selectively to traps or to poisonous baits. Pheromone traps are marketed to monitor the emergence and flights of adult orchard pests, the idea being that the more a grower knows about the enemy's activity, the fewer the sprayings. And fewer sprayings mean less money invested in a crop, as well as a better chance for predators and parasites. The traps do not snare enough pests to significantly lower their population, however.

Like pheromones, hormones are compounds that occur naturally in the insect. Hor-

Insect	Hosts / Injury / Range	Control
ANTS	Rarely pests, mostly a concern to gardeners because of their relationship with aphids. Aphids secrete excess plant sugars that are lapped up by the ants. In return, ants take aphids to new feeding sites. Widespread throughout North America.	Repellent plantings of mint or anise help somewhat. A sticky substance such as roofing tar can be wrapped around tree trunks to prevent ants from climbing trees. *See also separate entry.*
APHIDS Small, green, gray, violet, red, yellow, or brown insects that suck plant sap. Soft bodied, pear shaped, with long antennae and tubelike projections on the abdomen.	Congregate on the leaves of many different plants to suck juices. Cause leaves to curl and pucker; eventually deform and stunt flowers and buds. Act as vectors of mosaic and other virus diseases. Widespread throughout North America.	Gently rub leaves between thumb and forefinger. Interplant with aromatics such as garlic, chives, petunia, or anise. Spray with soap and water, tobacco tea, or lime water. Even a strong spray of water will wash them from the leaves, at least temporarily. *See also separate entry.*
BEETLES Order of insects distinguished by a tough wing cover that acts as first set of wings. At rest, the wing sheaths meet in a straight line down the middle of the back. When most beetles fly, the coverings are held straight out to the sides. Mouth parts variable.		

monal compounds trigger bodily changes, namely metamorphosis and molting. Researchers have learned to synthesize hormone "mimics" that can be used to affect a pest's development, rendering it harmless. And like pheromones, hormones are nontoxic but nevertheless not necessarily a friend to the ecosystem. One by one, the aspects of hormonal control that supposedly set it apart from conventional chemical control have been critically examined. It is not certain that vertebrates would be immune to the effects of hormones.

In short, their power and expediency invite misuse. Hormones would enable us to ignore the interrelatedness of all the parts of our ecosystem, and appear at this time to be little more than the newest in a succession of increasingly sophisticated chemicals in man's arsenal.

Specific Insect Problems: Presented here is a very partial listing of common garden pests, the damage they cause to plants, and a few of the organic measures that can be used to combat and control them.

Insect	Hosts / Injury / Range	Control
Asparagus Beetle Metallic blue black with three yellow to orange squares along each wing cover. One-quarter inch long. Larva longer, olive green or gray with black legs and head.	Both adult and larva eat foliage and disfigure shoots. Beetle hibernates in garden trash, then emerges in spring to feed on shoots. Distributed throughout North America.	Frequent cultivation, sanitation. Interplant with tomato, nasturtium, calendula. Poultry will clean an infested patch. Or dust with phosphate rock or bone meal.
Bark Beetles See Native Elm Bark Beetle		
Blister Beetles Long, slender, soft-bodied beetles with large heads. Antennae fairly short. Discharge a caustic fluid.	Some species are beneficial, preying on eggs of grasshoppers. Others are damaging as plant-eating adults. Feed on many kinds of flowers and foliage. Widely distributed.	Handpick, wearing gloves to avoid irritation. Dust with sabadilla or with equal parts of lime and flour. *See also separate entry.*
Cereal Leaf Beetle One-quarter inch long with dark head, red brown thorax and legs, and a metallic blue back. Larva dark brown. Small yellow eggs are laid on the underside of leaves.	Feeds heavily on cereal crops and corn. Occurs from Wisconsin and Illinois east to the Middle Atlantic states.	Early planting helps to some extent.

In its larval state, the blister beetle is a helpful destroyer of grasshopper eggs, but as an adult, it feeds heavily on many flowers, vegetables and young trees.
(Courtesy of U.S. Department of Agriculture)

Gardeners and farmers should be wary of the cereal leaf beetle which has been known to destroy up to 50 percent of European corn crops and is now present in certain eastern and middle western American states.
(Courtesy of U.S. Department of Agriculture)

Insect	Hosts / Injury / Range	Control
Colorado Potato Beetle Yellow with a broad, convex back. One-quarter inch long with fine black lines running lengthwise down wing covers. Thorax is covered with black dots. Larva is dark red grub with two rows of black spots on each side and a black head. Yellow eggs laid on underside of leaves.	Feeds on potato, but also attacks eggplant, tomato, pepper, and petunia. Can easily defoliate a potato patch. A pest in all the continental states except California and Nevada and in parts of Canada.	To avoid a beetle problem, grow potatoes on top of the ground with a heavy straw mulch. Flax, horseradish, garlic, marigold, and green beans can be intercropped as repellent plants. Handpick yellow eggs and adults. Spray with extract of basil, or dust plants with wheat bran. Select resistant varieties.
Cucumber Beetle See Spotted Cucumber Beetle or Striped Cucumber Beetle		

Insect	Hosts / Injury / Range	Control

Flea Beetles
Color and pattern vary according to species, but flea beetles can be recognized by their habit of jumping when disturbed. Very tiny, usually not more than $\frac{1}{16}$ inch long. Eggs deposited in soil.

Attack corn, eggplant, horseradish, potato, spinach, strawberry, sweet potato, tomato, and several ornamentals. Especially injurious to seedlings set out from the greenhouse. Great numbers of them may infest a single plant, leaving behind a shot-hole pattern in the leaves. Adults feed early in the season. Various species found in all parts of North America.

Frequent cultivation and garden sanitation. Flea beetles tend to avoid shade so plant seed thickly and thin only after danger of infestation has passed. Interplant with garlic. Wood ashes or a garlic spray discourages them.

Japanese Beetle
About $\frac{1}{2}$ inch long, shiny, metallic green. Wings copper brown. Six small patches of white hair along the sides and back of body, under the edges of the wings. Grub, about an inch long, lies in a curled position in the soil.

Grub feeds on roots and rhizomes of many plants, particularly grasses. Adult attacks birch, chestnut, elm, marigold, zinnia, rose, plum, peach, apple, quince and cherry, to name a few. Distributed throughout the eastern United States as far west as Missouri.

Handpick the beetles, dropping them into kerosene. Or shake them from the tree or shrub early in the morning and let them fall on a sheet. Repeat this every day. Larkspur planted nearby may attract and poison the beetles. Geraniums repel them.

June Beetle
Also known as june bug, and the larva as white grub. Adult is large, robust, brown beetle. Larva is somewhat larger than the white Japanese beetle grub.

Adult may damage the leaves of berry fruits. Larva feeds on the roots of bluegrass, corn, soybean, and timothy, as well as on several other crops and decaying vegetation. Distributed throughout North America.

Bacillus popilliae combats the grub. Rotation of crops susceptible to june beetle damage with deep-rooted legumes helps some. Plant legumes in the years of major beetle flights. Damaged grasslands can be rejuvenated by turning up the sod in spring or late fall and treating with organic fertilizer. Clean cultural practices and weed control help. Where adults are a problem, control as for Japanese beetle.

Insect	Hosts / Injury / Range	Control
Long-horned Beetles Adults are cylindrical, over ½ inch long, with long, thin antennae.	Adults feed on foliage and bark, larvae bore through the wood. See Borers, Round-headed Wood Borers in this chart.	
Mexican Bean Beetle So-called "black sheep" of the lady beetle family. Adult is copper colored with a very round back. Marked with 16 black spots arranged in three rows down the back. No markings between the body and head. Larva is fuzzy, lemon colored, covered by spines.	Infests all sorts of beans and cowpeas. Larva and adult attack pods, stems and foliage. Overwinters in garden trash. Found in all states east of the Mississippi.	Handpick the beetles. Eliminate debris after harvest and plant early to avoid infestations. Destroy any yellow eggs found on the leaves. Interplant with potato, nasturtium, savory, or garlic. Spray with concoction of turnips and corn oil, or, dust with rotenone or derris for serious infestations.
Native Elm Bark Beetle Small, blackish beetle with a stout body and wing covers coarsely punctured with small depressions. Eggs laid in galleries that run across the grain of the wood.	Serious pest because it carries Dutch elm disease fungus, as does a larger variety, the European bark beetle. Distributed throughout North America.	Remove dead and dying trees before the beetles emerge in the spring. Do not trim heavily or cut off too many healthy branches as this encourages the beetles, and hence the disease.
Pine Beetles Various beetles attack pine, fir, and spruce trees. Range in color from red brown to black and in length from ⅛ to ½ inch. Most are hard bodied, with short legs.	Most adults are attracted to weakened trees. They bore through outer bark then tunnel into inner bark, girdling the tree and introducing a fatal fungus. Infested trees marked by whitish, red or yellow pitch tubes scattered over the tree's bark. Widespread throughout North America.	Remove infested trees before the weather becomes warm and the beetles attack new trees. Keep pine stands properly thinned. Remove all injured and unhealthy wood as it appears.
Scarab Beetles See Japanese Beetle and June Beetle		

Insect	Hosts / Injury / Range	Control

Spotted Cucumber Beetle
Also known as the southern corn rootworm. Adult is ¼ inch long, with a black head, yellow green body. There are 12 spots on the back.

Does not defoliate the plant to any great extent but does carry and spread several bacterial diseases including cucumber wilt. Infests early bean, cucumber, melon, squash, gourd, asparagus, tomato, beet, cabbage, pea, potato and eggplant. Also feeds on blossoms of chrysanthemum, cosmos, dahlia, daisy, rose, sweet pea, and zinnia. Larva attacks roots of corn plants. Found in most eastern states; especially destructive in the South.

Rotation of crops will prevent a problem with larvae. Cultivate fields thoroughly and plant crops a bit later in the season. Mulch heavily. Adults controlled by spraying or dusting with rotenone.

Striped Cucumber Beetle
Yellow wing covers with three black longitudinal stripes. One-quarter inch long with a black head. Larva is larger and whitish.

Same as above.

Same as above.

Proper pruning and removal of dead and diseased branches are the best ways to eliminate native elm bark beetles and hence, control the Dutch elm disease which they carry.
(Courtesy of U.S. Department of Agriculture)

The European corn borer not only attacks corn, but is also a serious pest of many flower and vegetable plants.
(Courtesy of U.S. Department of Agriculture)

Insect	Hosts / Injury / Range	Control

BORERS

Listed here are the caterpillars and grubs that bore into plant stems and tree trunks and branches.

Many different borers attack various shade, fruit and ornamental trees as well as some flowers and shrubs. Young trees are especially vulnerable; also injured, defoliated, or in any way weakened plants.

Preventive measures against borers include planting uninfested trees; fertilizing, watering and wrapping young trees, and properly pruning them to maintain a low profile. If borers appear, handpick where possible by splitting stalk or branch and plucking out the worm. Dig out the worms from infested tree trunks and branches by thrusting a wire into the holes. Treat exposed wood with tree-wound paint. *See also separate entry.*

European Corn Borer

Flesh-colored caterpillar with brown spots and a dark brown head. One inch long.

Attacks the stalk not only of corn, but also of some flowers such as aster, cosmos, dahlia, hollyhock, and chrysanthemum, and such vegetables as bean, beet and potato. Mostly found in the eastern and central states.

Shred and plow under cornstalks where borers may overwinter. Advisable to plant as late as possible, still avoiding vulnerability to corn earworm and keeping within the growing period of the area. Plant resistant or tolerant varieties. To control, handpick where possible by splitting stalk. *Bacillus thuringiensis* is an effective control for serious cases.

Flat-headed Apple Tree Borer

Larva of a green blue beetle with punctured, coppery spaces. Borer is pale yellow with an enlarged and flattened thorax.

Larva bores into the inner bark not only of apple trees, but also ash, mountain ash, beech, cherry, chestnut, dogwood, hickory, linden, maple, oak, poplar, sycamore, and willow. Also attacks most orchard fruits, rose and raspberry. Favors injured trees in need of water. Makes a U-shaped mark in the bark as it feeds. Occurs throughout North America.

Beetles are drawn to sun-warmed trunks, so shade trunks of young trees in early spring and summer. Follow other controls and treatment as for borers.

Insect	Hosts / Injury / Range	Control
Flat-headed Wood Borers A large family of which the flat-headed apple tree borer is perhaps the most common member. Others share the characteristic enlarged, flattened thoracic segments.	Various species attack fir, pines, hemlock, orchard fruits, and many ornamentals. Widespread throughout North America.	Same as above.
Peach Tree Borer White, 1¼ inches long. Adult is a blue black, wasp-like moth with clear wings.	Larva feeds beneath the bark, at or below the soil surface. Girdles young trees, often kills them. Productivity reduced, trees generally weakened. Widespread throughout the United States.	To prevent infestations, encircle base of tree trunk with a band of tin, leaving a two-inch space that is filled with tobacco dust. Repeat each May for several years. Young trees can be swabbed with Tanglefoot or Stikem that ensnares moths and larvae before damage can be done. Garlic planted around the tree trunk repels them as does a ring of mothballs.
Round-headed Apple Tree Borer Young grub is brown red or whitish with a round, thick area just behind the head. Adult is slender, long-horned beetle, colored gray and marked with two longitudinal white stripes.	Prefers apple trees but may also attack quince, peach, plum, pear, hawthorn, mountain ash. Infestations can weaken or girdle a tree. Adult can be seen feeding on leaves and fruit, laying its eggs in the bark near ground level. Rusty brown material shows at borer's hole, also brown castings above and below soil level. Occurs in eastern North America.	Examine trees closely for first sign of borer's presence. Boiling water can be poured directly into the borer's hole or chamber. Follow general borer controls.
Round-headed Wood Borers Larvae of long-horned beetles. Adults are long, cylindrical and have very delicate antennae. Most are over 1½ inches in length.	Various species attack evergreens and firs, orchard fruit trees, and ornamentals. Adult beetles feed on flowers, foliage or bark, and larvae mine into the wood. Widely distributed.	See above.

 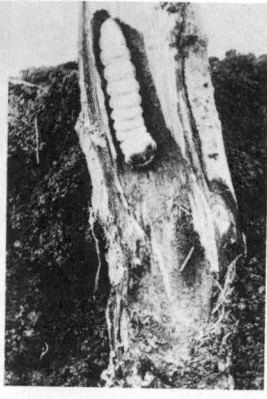

Like most borers, the round-headed apple tree borer lays eggs in the bark near the base of trees. Upon hatching, the larva (right) begins feeding on the inner bark and tissue of the tree.
(Courtesy of U.S. Department of Agriculture)

The first sign of squash vine borers is a sudden wilting of the vine, followed by the appearance of a yellowish sawdust material protruding from holes in the stems.
(Courtesy of U.S. Department of Agriculture)

Insect	Hosts / Injury / Range	Control
Squash Vine Borer Inch-long caterpillar, white with a brown head and small brown legs. Adult is a moth with clear wings and an orange and black abdomen.	Newly hatched larva tunnels into the stems of most cucurbits. Sudden wilting may be a sign of squash vine borers. Also, presence of yellow, sawdustlike deposits at the stem base. Distributed east of the Rocky Mountains.	Slit the stem and pluck out the larva within. Plant late to avoid feeding time. Or plant early so that the plants are well established before eggs are laid in July. Choose resistant varieties.
Stalk Borer Thin, striped caterpillar about one or 1½ inches long. Adult moth is gray with white spots on the wings.	Feeds on practically anything. A frequent pest of aster, dahlia, iris, rhubarb, pepper, tomato, and many weeds and grasses. Stems break and leaves wilt. Small round hole appears in stem where the caterpillar has entered. Found everywhere east of the Rocky Mountains.	Sprays of little use. Handpick or, better, remove infested stems altogether. Clean cultivation and weed control are good preventive measures.

Insect	Hosts / Injury / Range	Control
Strawberry Crown Borer Small, yellow or pinkish grub. Adult is a brown beetle, 1/5 inch long with red patches on the wings. Adults cannot fly.	Borer overwinters under leaves or soil surface. Lays eggs in crowns in late March through August. Adult feeds on foliage. Distributed throughout the eastern United States and Canada.	Only remedy for serious infestations is to plow plants under after harvest and set a new bed at a new site that is at least 300 yards away. Avoid setting infested plants; dig transplants in February before the eggs have been laid.

BUGS

True bugs belonging to the family Hemiptera are included below. Mostly large, easily recognized by their dissimilar wings, the front pair having a coarse base and membranous tips, the hind pair being completely membranous. When folded, the membranous part of both front wings overlaps to form an X on the back. Many members of this group emit a strong odor.	The garden pests of this family pierce plant stems and leaves and suck the juices.	
Chinch Bug Small, black bug with white wings that have a triangular black patch on them. Nymphs minute. Reddish with a white band across the middle, changing to black with a white band. Have an offensive odor.	Injurious to corn and grain crops. The bugs and their nymphs climb corn plants and suck the juices from the stems. Distributed throughout the country, especially widespread in the Middle West.	Keep garden area weed-free. Plant crop early in well-fertilized soil. Interplant corn with soybeans as the bean leaves will shade the base of the corn plant. Some resistant varieties are available. *See also separate entry.*
Hairy Chinch Bug Very similar in appearance to chinch bug but adults are short winged.	Infested lawns may show irregular brown patches where the bugs have destroyed plant tissue. Serious lawn pest throughout the eastern United States.	Shade discourages them. Also a lawn soil of builder's sand, crushed rock and compost is not likely to invite them. Well-fed lawns withstand attacks better than underfed ones.

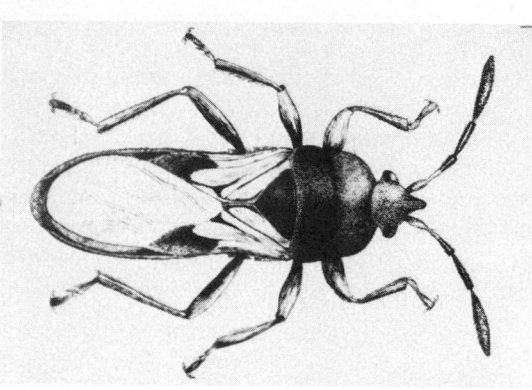

Well-fertilized soil and early planting are the best defenses against the tiny, tremendously destructive chinch bug.
(Courtesy of U.S. Department of Agriculture)

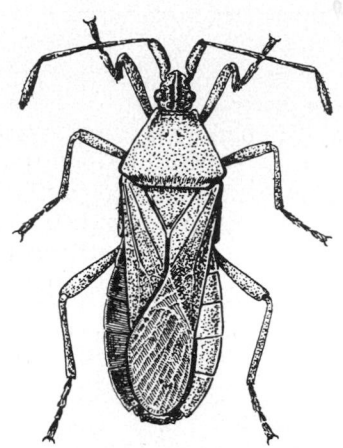

Like many true bugs, the squash bug injects a toxic substance into vines, causing them to wilt, blacken and eventually die. Weeding and proper sanitation are the basic control measures.
(Courtesy of U.S. Department of Agriculture)

Insect	Hosts / Injury / Range	Control
Harlequin Bug Black with orange to red markings. Shield shaped, flat, and ⅜ inch long. Disagreeable odor. Eggs look like small white pegs with black hoops, lined up in two neat rows.	A most important pest of the Cabbage family. Also feeds on lettuce, corn, eggplant, grape, potato, plum, rose, and squash. Mostly found in the South.	Plant a trap of turnips or mustard greens near the cabbage patch. Patrol trap area, gathering and killing the bugs. Keep garden well weeded. Sabadilla and pyrethrum will control them, as will soap and nicotine sprays.
Lygus Bug Adults are small, flat, football shaped. Greenish or brown in color. Nymphs resemble aphids when young.	Russian thistle, mullein, horseweed, and sweet clover are favorite reservoir hosts. Adult feeds on legumes, ornamentals, peach, and apricot. Most serious infestations occur in the South and West.	Because the bugs overwinter as adults, clean cultivation should reduce their population sufficiently. A trap crop of alfalfa can help keep the bugs away from garden plants.

Insect	Hosts / Injury / Range	Control
Squash Bug Brown black, about ¾ to one inch long. Commonly called a stink bug because of its odor. Nymph has reddish head and legs, and green to brown body. Eggs are brick red, laid in clusters on the leaves.	Feeds on plant tissue of all vine crops, especially squash, pumpkin and melon. Causes plant to wilt and eventually to die. Widely distributed.	Can be repelled by plantings of radish, nasturtium and marigold. Garden sanitation is important, as is weed control. Rotate crops. Handpick the insects and eggs.
Tarnished Plant Bug Related to lygus bug. Adult small, roundish, brassy brown or greenish with black spots on the thorax and abdomen. Nymph smaller, but similar.	Bug injects a poison into plant while feeding. Attacks many flowers, especially aster and dahlia. Bean, beet, cabbage, cucumber, potato, and some orchard fruits are susceptible. Eggs are laid on tree trunks. Widely distributed.	Spray of little use unless applied in early morning before bugs are at their most active. Sabadilla dust may check large populations. *See also separate entry.*
CANKER WORMS Also called measuring worms and inchworms. Small, striped, black or green larvae of small moths. Two species that gardeners must deal with are the fall and spring canker worms.	Pests of fruit and shade trees in spring and fall. Feed on unfolding foliage in spring or on the ripening fruits of all orchard trees, especially apple. Eggs laid on the trunk. Widely distributed.	Sticky material applied to a band of cotton batting wrapped around the trunk prevents the females from laying eggs. Apply in October for fall species; in February for spring. Also may spray with *Bacillus thuringiensis* in April or May. *See also separate entry.*
CATERPILLARS AND HORNWORMS Included here are the larvae of moths and butterflies that are not canker worms, leaf miners, or wood and stalk borers. Fairly large; surface leaf feeders.	Generally eat holes in the leaves of plants.	On the garden scale, most of these pests can be handpicked.

Insect	Hosts / Injury / Range	Control
Cabbage Looper Large, 1½-inch-long, pale green worm with light stripes down its back. It loops or doubles up as it crawls. Eggs are green white, laid on the surface of the leaves.	Attacks all members of the Cabbage family as well as tomato, potato, parsley, pea, lettuce, and celery. Some flowers are bothered by them. Widely distributed.	*Bacillus thuringiensis* will infect and kill the looper. *See also separate entry.*
Corn Earworm Striped, light yellow, green or brown caterpillar with yellow head. Up to two inches long. Also known as tomato fruitworm and cotton bollworm. Adult is a moth with gray brown front wings marked with dark lines.	Feeds on the buds and unfolding leaves of young plants. Eats the tassels and ears of corn. Feeding on silk prevents pollination, on the kernels it causes several fungi to appear. Eats holes in the fruits and buds of tomato, bean, cabbage, broccoli, and lettuce. Also attacks clover, grape, gladiolus, okra, peach, pear, pepper, pumpkin, rose, squash, strawberry, and vetch. Occurs everywhere corn is grown.	On corn ears, control by applying mineral oil into the silk just inside the tip of each ear, a half medicine dropper's worth for a small ear. Do not apply until the silk has wilted, as earlier treatment will interfere with pollination and ear formation. Or, after the tassel has begun to wilt, simply cut off the silk close to the ear. Marigold might serve as a repellent plant. *Bacillus thuringiensis* is effective as a dust. On tomato and other garden plants, control larvae with garlic and onion sprays, or rotenone. *See also separate entry.*
Fall Webworm Fully grown caterpillar is about 1¼ inches long and is marked with a broad, dark brown stripe along the back with parallel yellow stripes on either side. Eggs laid in white masses on underside of leaves. Larvae make white webs or nests on the ends of branches.	Caterpillar strips and even kills orchard trees and several nut, shade, and woodland trees. Larva spins a layer of "silk" over leaves as it begins feeding. Widely distributed.	Cut off nests as they appear. Burn them. Clean up debris around trees.

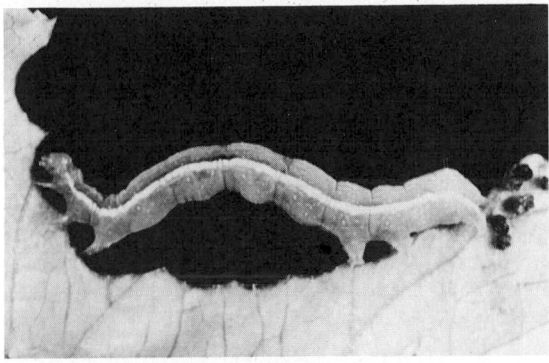

After two weeks of feeding on lettuce, cabbage, parsley, pea, potato, or tomato, this cabbage looper will spin a cocoon and produce another generation of destructive larvae.
(Courtesy of U.S. Department of Agriculture)

Larvae of the fall webworm begin spinning layers of silk as soon as they begin feeding. Left unchecked, they form large, unsightly nests at the ends of tree branches.
(Courtesy of U.S. Department of Agriculture)

Insect	Hosts / Injury / Range	Control
Filbertworm Small, pinkish caterpillar, about ¾ inch long. Adult moth has a wingspread of ½ inch and is marked by two golden bands across each fore wing. Eggs laid singly on leaves' upper surfaces.	Larva bores into various fruits and nuts, including acorn, hazelnut, chestnut, and walnut. Widely distributed.	To avoid the problem, harvest nuts as early as possible and dry immediately.
Hornworms Tomato hornworm is green with diagonal white bars on each side and a distinctive horn on the back end. Reaches a length of four inches. Adult moth resembles a small hummingbird. Known as sphinx moth, has wingspan of four or five inches. Tobacco hornworm very similar but with a red horn.	Larvae feed on leaves and sometimes on the fruit. Attack tomato, tobacco, dill, eggplant, pepper, and potato. Widespread throughout North America.	Easily controlled by handpicking. Hot pepper dust may discourage them. *Bacillus thuringiensis* eliminates them. Natural predators and parasites include the brachonid wasp which lays eggs on the worm's back; if an infested worm is spotted, leave it to nurture a new brood of the wasps.

Insect	Hosts / Injury / Range	Control
Imported Cabbage Worm Adult is the well-known white cabbage butterfly that has three black spots on the wings and a wingspread of about two inches. The caterpillar is about one inch long, bright green and covered with fine, closely set hairs. Eggs are yellow and slightly ridged; they are laid at the base of leaves in early spring.	Feeds on all members of the Cabbage family as well as lettuce and nasturtium. Sea kale is rarely bothered. The caterpillar eats holes in the leaves and drops bits of green excrement on the surface. Found throughout eastern North America.	*Bacillus thuringiensis* is a safe, effective control. Rotenone can also be used with equally favorable results. Interplantings of tansy, rosemary and other aromatics may repel them, as will tomato. Protective veils of cheesecloth or netting prevent moths from laying eggs on the plants. Clean cultivation and postharvest cleanup eliminate the hiding places of pupae.
Parsleyworm Also known as the carrot worm and celery worm. Larva is two inches long, green with a yellow-dotted black band across each segment. Disturbed, the caterpillar emits a strong, sweet odor and projects two orange horns from its head. Adult is the black swallowtail butterfly.	Feeds on celery, carrot, dill, parsley. Occurs all over the eastern part of the country with similar species distributed in the West.	Population rarely very great. Handpick the caterpillars early in the morning or, in serious cases, dust with rotenone or derris.
Pickleworm Mature caterpillar is ¾ inch long, colored green or copperish. Younger, it is pale yellow with black spots. Adult moth is yellowish, night flying.	Caterpillar bores into buds, blossoms, vines, and fruits of most cucurbits. Especially damaging late in the season. Serious problem in the Gulf states, but also found as far north as New York and Michigan.	Very early crops are seldom damaged. Hibernating pupae killed by plowing early in the fall. Clean up plant refuse after harvest. Squash can be planted as a trap crop. Select resistant varieties.
Spring Webworm See Fall Webworm		

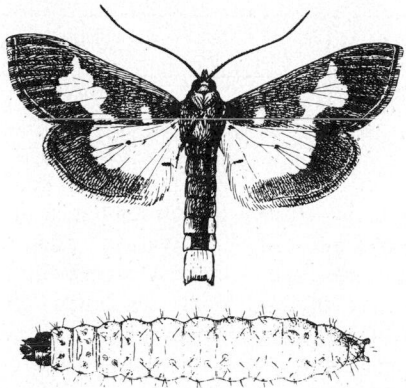

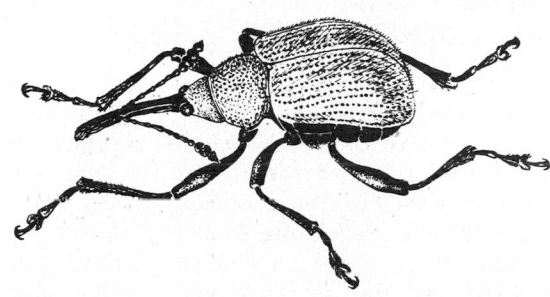

The pickleworm is the larva of a yellow white moth which emerges in late spring to lay eggs. First generations are often destructive to developing stems and leaves, but the real damage occurs in August when pickleworms begin boring into fruits. Since each worm may enter and ruin several fruits, the damage can be very extensive. (Courtesy of U.S. Department of Agriculture)

The adult rose curculio drills holes in the buds of all types of roses, riddling young flower petals with holes. Frequent cultivation and removal of ruined buds help eliminate the larvae before they mature and begin laying eggs. (Courtesy of U.S. Department of Agriculture)

Insect	Hosts / Injury / Range	Control
Tent Caterpillars Name especially applied to eastern or apple tent caterpillar. Larger than webworm with white stripe down the back. Two parallel yellow lines and a row of bluish spots mark the sides. Young larvae spin large nests in forks of tree limbs. At maturity, they leave nest and spin cocoons on buildings, fences or tree bark. Cocoons are one inch long, white or yellowish.	Young caterpillars feed on the foliage of many deciduous trees and shrubs. Wild cherry and apple trees most often attacked. Peach, pear, plum, rose, hawthorn, and some shade trees occasionally infested. Abundant and troublesome for several years in a row. Feeding occurs in spring. Widespread throughout the East and in some midwestern and Rocky Mountain states.	Tear nests out by hand or with a pole and crush or burn the caterpillars. In winter, egg masses can be destroyed by cutting off infested branches and burning them. Keep wild cherry trees away from orchards, if possible. Spray with *Bacillus thuringiensis*. Baltimore orioles are excellent effective natural predators.

Insect	Hosts / Injury / Range	Control

CRICKETS AND GRASSHOPPERS

A number of species in the country; few of economic significance. Among crickets, the Mormon and northern mole are the most common pests. Mormon cricket is about one inch long, small winged with large antennae. Problem in the western and Great Plains states. Northern mole and southern mole crickets are large, brownish and covered with velvety hairs. Frequent damp, muddy places of the South.

Not all harm crops or rangelands, but those that do chew through stems and leaves and kill plants. Grasshoppers are especially serious pests in drought-stricken areas. Various species attack grain and forage crops as well as some vegetables.

Grasshoppers and crickets can be somewhat controlled by clean cultivation and elimination of nearby weeds and grasses. Protect seedlings with a veil of cheesecloth. To eliminate the insects, spray with a concoction of hot pepper pods, pure soap and water, but sprays generally of little use. A few well-placed traps may work. Try filling mason jars with a few cups of molasses and water and setting them in the garden.

CURCULIOS, SNOUT BEETLES, WEEVILS

The head of these beetles is lengthened into a protruding snout which varies in size and shape according to species. Antennae arising from the snout are elbowed and clubbed.

Adult snout beetles generally make holes in fruits and nuts; larvae feed on the inside of seeds, flower buds, fruits, and stems.

Carrot Weevil

Coppery colored, about ⅛ inch long. Larva is small, whitish grub with white head.

Adult overwinters in garden debris and weeds. Migrates only a short distance. Feeds on celery, parsnip, parsley, carrot, and several types of weeds. Distributed from Colorado east to Georgia and New England.

Clean out debris, high grass and fallow fields to eliminate overwintering areas. In spring, destroy grubs by deep cultivation.

Insect	Hosts / Injury / Range	Control
Plum Curculio Brown, mottled with gray, and distinguished by four humps on its back; ¼ inch long. Apple curculio is very similar but smaller.	Beetle appears about the time trees blossom in spring. Feeds on fruit, leaving crescent-shaped cuts in the skin. A pest of most stone fruits and apple. Apple curculio produces many, closely spaced punctures in the fruit skin. Occurs in eastern states.	Gather dropped fruit where the grubs may stay. Bury the fruit in a deep hole or deep in the compost pile. Knock or shake tree branches, catching the beetles in a sheet. Poultry will help pick them up. Control for apple curculio is the same. *See also separate entry.*
Rose Curculio Reddish with a long, black snout. Larva is small, white. Eggs laid in the rose hips.	Adult feeds on the buds of both wild and cultivated roses. Buds either fail to open or produce flowers that are ruined by holes. Found throughout the country, especially in colder regions.	Handpick. Collect ruined buds before the larvae have the opportunity to mature. Control larvae in soil as for Japanese and june beetles.
Vegetable Weevil Adult is dull buff in color with a pale V on the wing covers. Head has a short, broad snout. Larva is green or cream colored with yellow head patterned with brown dotted lines.	Adult feeds on foliage at night and hides close to ground by day. It begins feeding on the crown, then often defoliates a whole plant, leaving only the stems and midribs of the leaves. It attacks beet, cabbage, cauliflower, lettuce, onion, potato, tomato, and turnip, among others. Widely distributed.	Rotation is the best control. Destroy underground pupae by cultivating. Keep garden clear of weeds and trash.
White Pine Weevil Brownish and mottled with light and dark scales; ¼ inch long. Grub is yellow, ⅓ inch long.	Prefers white pine, but will also attack jack, red, and Scotch pine, and Norway spruce. First sign of damage is the appearance of tiny drops of resin on the bark. In feeding, the larva girdles the growing terminal which then withers and dies. Found throughout eastern North America.	Remove and burn tips below the dead bud-end that grubs have fed upon. Pine grown in shady spots will suffer less weevil damage. Thick-barked varieties are more able to withstand the insect infestations.

Insect	Hosts / Injury / Range	Control

CUTWORMS

Plump, soft-bodied larvae, dull in color with a few bristly hairs. Found in the soil at the base of plants. Disturbed, they coil their bodies. Overwinter in cells several inches below ground surface.

Feed on plants near the soil surface. Some species climb up stems to feed on fruits, flowers and leaves. Prefer the stems of Cabbage family members, bean and tomato, but may destroy just about any vegetable. Various species occur throughout North America.

Keep garden weed- and grass-free, especially during fall months when cutworm moths are laying eggs. Cultivate around plant base to find and destroy the worm. When setting out transplants, place a stiff paper collar around the stems, burying it at least one inch deep in the ground. Chicken manure, oak-leaf mulch, damp wood ashes, crushed eggshells, or sharp builder's sand can be scattered around plants as preventives.

EARWIGS

Brown with short, leathery front wings and membranous hind wings that fold beneath front wings when insect is at rest. Distinguished by a pair of "pincers" on the abdomen.

Rarely pests. Feed on decayed plant material and other insects. Occasionally feed on lettuce, sweet corn and potato. Widely distributed.

Trap earwigs in a section of bamboo set in the garden, collect and destroy the insects.

EARWORMS

See Caterpillars and Hornworms

FLIES AND MIDGES

One- and two-winged insects varying in size and feeding habits. Midges are very small, delicate members of the Diptera order. Flies are usually larger. In many the second pair of wings is reduced to a very small flap.

Insect	Hosts / Injury / Range	Control
Cherry Fruit Fly Resembles a small housefly but with dark bands on the wings and yellow on the margin of the thorax. Eggs are laid in fruit.	Limited mostly to cherry, pear and plum. Damage done in early June when the flies emerge and lay eggs on the young fruit. Maggots develop within the fruit, gradually consuming it. The result is deformed, wormy fruit. Found in northern United States and parts of Canada.	Spray trees with rotenone as soon as flies appear in spring.
Rose Midge Minute yellow or reddish fly that lays tiny yellow eggs on leaves and below flower buds.	Limited to roses. As eggs hatch, larvae start to feed on leaf stems and flower buds, deforming and killing them. Very brief life cycle; new generations develop in a matter of weeks. In greenhouses, most injury occurs between May and November. Widely distributed.	Control by mixing tobacco dust into the soil. Cut off and destroy all infested buds.
Whitefly See Whiteflies		

LEAFHOPPERS

Mostly small insects that hold their wings in a rooflike position when resting. Wedge shaped.	Pierce plant tissue and suck sap, causing host plant to gradually lose color in the leaves and generally weaken. Carry many viruses.	Pyrethrum is effective on many species. Weed control often eliminates the problem.
Aster Leafhopper Also called six-spotted leafhopper. Green yellow with six black spots and grows to a length of ⅛ inch. Nymph is gray.	Causes leaves of aster to turn brown and die. Carries the disease, aster yellows. A pest to many annual and perennial flowers as well as lettuce, celery, carrot, and grain crops. All of these crops are susceptible to aster yellows. Widely distributed.	Insect prefers open areas so plants grown near a building or wall are less likely to be attacked. Growers with large areas of asters, burn surrounding weeds in early spring to destroy overwintering hoppers. Only way to fully protect flowers is to grow them under a veil of netting.

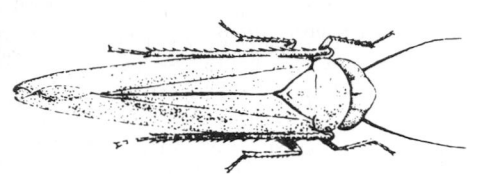

Potato leafhoppers cause hopperburn to potatoes, peanuts and bean plants as well as certain flowers. (Courtesy of U.S. Department of Agriculture)

Since leaf miners spend most of their destructive lives feeding between the two surfaces of plant leaves, they are virtually unaffected by sprays or dusts. Infested foliage should be removed and burned or buried deep in the compost heap. (Courtesy of U.S. Department of Agriculture)

Insect	Hosts / Injury / Range	Control
Beet Leafhopper Called whitefly in the West. Pale yellow or green, ⅛ inch long, wedge shaped.	Vector of curly top disease that affects beet, bean, tomato, cucumber, spinach, squash, and many flowers. Symptoms of curly top are pronounced leaf veins, curled brittle leaves and stunted growth. Can result in the death of plant. Found west from Illinois and Missouri.	Eliminate weeds around the garden. Remove afflicted plants as soon as symptoms appear. Use resistant varieties.
Potato Leafhopper Wedge-shaped green insect. White spots on the head and thorax.	Attacks bean, dahlia, potato, peanut, and lettuce. Causes hopperburn, a condition in which the tips and sides of leaves curl up, yellow and become brittle. Potato yields are reduced; fruits and flowers of other plants may be stunted. Especially serious pest in the eastern United States, though similar species found in West.	Grow potatoes in a sheltered area if the insects are a problem in your region. Or, cover plants with netting during the first month or so of growth. Potato leafhoppers can be trapped with black fluorescent lamps. Select resistant varieties.

Insect	Hosts / Injury / Range	Control

LEAF MINERS

These are insect larvae that tunnel between the upper and lower leaf surfaces.

Leaf miners remove tissue from the leaves, cause foliage to yellow. Often the tunnel can be seen traced on the leaf surface. At other times, infested leaves appear blotched and yellowed. Various miners attack apple, birch, blackberry, boxwood, elm, and holly. Among flowers, chrysanthemum, columbine, larkspur, and rose may be affected. Also spinach, beet, potato, pepper, and cabbage. Widely distributed.

Remove and burn infested leaves of the plants, trees or shrubs. Vegetables and flowers should be well cultivated and kept weed-free. Many leaf miners are controlled by naturally occurring parasites. When possible, choose resistant varieties.

LEAF ROLLERS

Included below are those caterpillars that cause leaves to roll up as they feed.

Damage fruit clusters, leaves and buds of many trees, flowers and vegetables.

Many leaf rollers are controlled by *Bacillus thuringiensis*.

Fruit Tree Leaf Roller

Green caterpillar about ¾ inch long when full grown. Head is black. Adult moth is brown and gold. Very similar to red-banded leaf roller which is slightly smaller and tends to infest more ornamentals than the fruit tree leaf roller.

Prefers fruits such as apple, apricot, blackberry, cherry, gooseberry, pear, plum, raspberry and, to some extent, citrus. May also attack shade trees. Caterpillars appear in the spring and feed on fruit. Light webs are spun together, the caterpillars often feeding within. A common and serious destroyer of apple crops. Widespread throughout the country.

Spray trees with dormant-oil spray just before the buds break. *Bacillus thuringiensis* may prove helpful.

Insect	Hosts / Injury / Range	Control

Oblique-banded Leaf Roller

Green caterpillar with black head. Eggs laid on branches of the host plant.

Young larva mines leaves. Older caterpillar rolls and webs leaves together and feeds within. Eats rose, aster, geranium, and carnation. A serious pest of many ornamental and orchard fruit trees. Widely distributed.

If only a few plants are infested, remove the affected parts and destroy them. A dust of tobacco dust and pyrethrum powder checks heavy populations. Or spray with a mixture of rotenone and pyrethrum. Dust or spray in two applications, 30 minutes apart.

Strawberry Leaf Roller

Mature larva is ½ inch long, yellow green or green brown caterpillar. Adult moth is red or brown with a ½-inch wingspan. Eggs laid on underside of leaves.

Causes folded, webbed leaves on strawberry, raspberry, dewberry, and blackberry. Found in the northern portions of the United States.

Natural parasites usually prevent serious damage. If problem is very serious, dust rotenone onto the underside of the leaves.

MAGGOTS

Fly larvae that tend to feed on fruits, nuts and on some vegetables.

Apple Maggot

Also known as apple fruit fly and railroad worm. Legless whitish maggot develops into small, black fly.

Causes brown tunnels in apples, sometimes causing the whole fruit to rot. Attacks blueberry, plum, cherry, as well as apple. In northeastern orchards, most serious infestations occur in July. Occurs in northern United States and southern Canada.

Collect dropped apples before the maggots leave them. For summer apple varieties, collect twice a week; for later types, only once is sufficient. To trap them in the fly stage, hang jars of fermented molasses and yeast from tree limbs. If flies are a serious problem, select a later-maturing variety.

Female apple maggots lay their eggs through punctures in the fruit's skin. If the infested apples are destroyed before the maggots emerge, the pest population can be checked.

A northern pest, the adult onion maggot emerges in early spring to lay eggs at the base of plants. The three generations of maggots destroy both young and mature bulbs.
(Courtesy of U.S. Department of Agriculture)

Insect	Hosts / Injury / Range	Control
Cabbage Maggot White maggot, ⅓ inch wide, with one tapered end. Adult fly is small, dark gray with black stripes on the thorax.	Carries bacterial soft rot and blackleg. Attacks stems just below the soil surface, producing brown tunnels in the plant tissue. Seedlings yellow, wilt and eventually die. Most serious problem with early cabbage and broccoli, transplants, and direct-seeded radish, cabbage and turnip. Cauliflower, cress, celery, and Brussels sprouts may also be damaged. Generally limited to northern and central states.	Plant seed and set out transplants as early as possible to avoid egg-laying flies. Tar paper next to the stem may discourage the flies from laying eggs at the plant base. Or, cover rows with cheesecloth or netting.

Insect	Hosts / Injury / Range	Control
Onion Maggot Maggot is white, legless, about ⅓ inch long. Adult fly is brownish, hairy and about ¼ inch long. It can be recognized by its humped back and large wings. Cylindrical eggs laid along the base of plants or even in bulbs.	Maggot feeds on the lower part of the stem or developing bulb. Onions are susceptible at all stages of growth. Serious in northern states.	Onions planted for sets are more likely to suffer than the larger table onions. Also white are more susceptible than yellow, and red varieties the most resistant. Avoid planting onions in rows. Rather, scatter plants throughout the garden so as to discourage or at least limit the maggots' feeding. Or, try covering row with a layer of sand or wood ashes. Do not place damaged onions in storage for they will decay and cause other, healthy bulbs to rot.
MEALYBUGS Soft-bodied scale insects. Most common mealybugs resemble cotton tufts on the underside of leaves. Secrete excess plant sugars and so attract ants.	Feed by sucking the sap from the leaves, bark or buds of house plants, vegetables and fruit trees. Some species cause plant diseases; the presence of others encourages the growth of certain fungi. Widely distributed.	Where possible, spray underside of leaves with a strong stream of water. In the house or greenhouse, kill them with a drop of alcohol. Fruit trees may be sprayed with soapy water or kerosene and water. *See also separate entry.*

MEASURING WORMS

See Canker Worms

MITES

Relatives of the spider. Minute, lacking antennae and having only two segments of the body.

Insect	Hosts / Injury / Range	Control
Cyclamen Mite Microscopic. Also called strawberry crown mite.	Often infests new leaf and blossom tissue, causing them to swell and become distorted. Infests not only cyclamen, but also other greenhouse plants and garden strawberries, pepper and tomatoes. Reddish larvae burrow into crowns of plants to cause stunting and general weakening. In flowers, blossoms are often blotchy and fall prematurely. Present in greenhouses and gardens throughout the country.	In the garden bed, the best control is crop sanitation and rotation. In the greenhouse and home, be certain to provide ample space between plants. Lightly infested plants in house and garden can be treated with a very warm water bath.
European Red Mite Can be seen with a hand lens. Adult mite is dark red with white spots. When young it ranges in color from red to green.	A serious pest of apple, pear and plum trees. Feeds on leaves and causes foliage to become bronze colored. Feeds throughout the summer, but peak populations are reached in July or August. Fruit from infested trees may be small. Serious in northern states.	Apply dormant-oil spray early in the spring to kill overwintering eggs. Fertilize apple trees adequately.
Spider Mites Appear as tiny red dots on the underside of foliage. Very common. Many of these mites typically called red spider mites; others of special importance are the spruce spider mite and the two-spotted spider mite.	Leaves become discolored and tiny webs appear on leaf surface. Gradually, leaves turn brown and drop. Attack roses, evergreens, shrubs, ivy, and many different vegetables. Warm, dry weather favors the development of the spider mites. Widespread throughout the country.	Hose off plants to wash away the mites and break down the webs. Spray seriously infested gardens with a sticky slurry of flour and buttermilk. Or, mix phosphate rock or ground limestone with a sticky liquid and spray on plants. Spray after leaves have matured and mite population reaches a level of about three mites per leaf. Certain crop rotation systems may lessen mite problems. *See also separate entry.*

Insect	Hosts / Injury / Range	Control

MOTHS

Wings are covered with scales and antennae usually feathery. Typically night fliers.

Codling Moth

Larva is white, tinged with pink, one inch long, with a darker, brown head. Adult moth is gray brown with fringed hind wings.

Among the most serious of apple pests. Also infests peat, cherry, peach, and plum, and certain nuts. Eggs are laid on the blossom end of fruit in June. Larva develops, eats its way through the fruit, then spins cocoon in the bark where it overwinters. Found wherever apples are grown.

In spring, wrap a band of corrugated cardboard around each tree trunk. Keep the bands on until September, then remove and burn them together with the cocoons that have been spun on them. Or, scrape the bark each spring and spray with a high-pressure stream of water to dislodge the larvae. Soapy-water and fish-oil sprays may destroy caterpillars. Nasturtium repels them. Woodpeckers attracted to the orchard will pick out and consume many of the caterpillars and younger larvae.

Grape Berry Moth

Young larva is white or cream, gradually becoming green or purple as it ages. Adult moth is tan with dark markings on the fore wings.

As larva feeds, it encases berries and flowers and foliage in a silken web. Red spots appear where larva enters berry; later, spots turn purple and berries split. Often green berries of blue varieties will redden prematurely. Distributed in the eastern United States, especially common and injurious in New England.

Early cultivation will bury the pupae and prevent the development of first generation larvae. Clean up all fallen leaves and plant debris in the autumn.

Insect	Hosts / Injury / Range	Control
Gypsy Moth Larva is really the damager, though the pest is known and recognized best in its moth stage. Adult moth is brownish or buff with dark markings. Larva is two or three inches long, brown and very hairy.	A serious pest to many shade, woodland and fruit trees. Evergreens may be killed the first year, deciduous trees in two or three seasons. Larva feeds at night, gradually defoliating the tree. Mostly limited to New England and the eastern regions of New York and Pennsylvania.	*Bacillus thuringiensis* is the only effective natural insecticide presently available. Quarantine controls must be strictly regarded to avoid the further spread of the insect. Destroy any egg clusters and caterpillars. Some natural parasites have been released by the Department of Agriculture.
Oriental Fruit Moth Moth is gray with brown markings. Flat white eggs laid on leaves or twigs of the tree. Larva hatches in late spring and is pinkish with brown head.	Larva is serious pest to peach but also attacks other stone fruits. First sign of infestation is wilting of the terminal growing points. Later broods more harmful to fruit. Worm enters fruit and feeds on flesh next to pit. Found throughout the country.	Grow early-ripening peaches. Parasites available such as *Macrocentrus ancylicorus* wasp and *Trichogramma minutum*. Practice clean cultivation.
NEMATODES Also called eelworms. Nematodes are not insects but are included here as common garden pests. They are microscopic round worms. Many are parasites of plant tissue, but not all.	Some are ectoparasites, spending their lives on the surface of plants and feeding through the cell walls; others are endoparasites that enter plant tissue and feed within. Symptoms of nematode injury include malformation of flowers, leaves, stems, and root structure, chlorosis of the foliage and dieback. Some nematodes cause galls or root knots that clog the plant's nutrient flow. Feeding wounds invite many disease organisms. Widely distributed.	If evidence of nematode damage appears, take a soil sample to the extension service for analysis. Standard controls are sterilizing soil, encouraging natural predators and rotating crops. Some growers claim success with interplanting marigolds with the susceptible crop. Nematodes can also be starved by growing an immune crop for two or more years in the infested field, or by fallow cultivation during May and June. *See also separate entry.*

Insect	Hosts / Injury / Range	Control

SAWFLIES

Relatives of wasps and bees. They have two sets of wings that are transparent and overlap. Larvae resemble caterpillars but with more legs.

Feed on plants in the larval stage. Females cut leaves in order to lay eggs in the plant tissue.

Some can be controlled with rotenone. Clean culture and the removal of infested branches or fruits are important at early stages.

European Apple Sawfly

Adult "fly" is brown and yellow with many transverse lines.

Larva feeds inside the fruit just below the skin, then begins to attack the center of the fruit. It leaves a chocolate-colored, sawdustlike substance on the surface. Occurs in eastern states.

Spray trees with rotenone when petals fall, then again one week later.

Pine Sawflies

Various species of sawflies infest pine, fir and spruce trees. Larvae are very tiny.

Larvae devour needles and often defoliate the whole tree. Widely distributed.

Control is best through natural parasites and enemies. Raking plant debris from beneath trees helps eliminate the pupating regions. Rotenone controls serious infestations.

SCALE INSECTS

Minute, one-segmented insects, often legless.

Most are serious garden pests, feeding on many kinds of plant tissue. Like mealybugs and aphids, they secrete excess plant sugars which attract ants to them and create a perfect medium for certain molds.

Often controlled by dormant-oil spray.

Black Scale

Most easily recognized is the female which is dark brown or black, hemispherical and about ⅛ inch long. A ridge on the back forms the letter H.

Feeds on all citrus trees as well as certain nuts, flowers, and ornamental trees and shrubs. Found on leaves, twigs and sometimes even fruit. Mold that grows as a result reduces the leaves' capacity to gather light. Found in all citrus-growing regions.

Some biological controls have been discovered and released to control the insects in citrus-growing regions. On a small area, scales can be scraped off or brushed with turpentine or soapy water.

Insect	Hosts / Injury / Range	Control
Oystershell Scale Scales resemble small oysters on the trunk, stems and branches of trees and shrubs. Range in color from gray to brown to black.	Widely distributed on deciduous trees and shrubs. Gray scales on lilac, beech, willow, and maple. Brown oystershell scales on fruits, especially apple. The very dark encrust other ornamental trees. A yellow brown scale sometimes infests birch and poplar. Found throughout the country.	Scrape the bark to remove the eggs beneath the scale. Dormant-oil sprays suffocate the pests.
Purple Scale Narrow, oyster shell-shaped female is about ⅛ inch long and purplish.	Found on twigs, leaves and fruits of all citrus. Also infests tropical fruit trees, dogwood, eucalyptus, oak, plum, and walnut, among others. Produces a toxic substance that kills parts of the tree. Found in all citrus-growing regions.	Some parasites have been released. Dormant-oil spray is effective if applied in midsummer.
SLUGS AND SNAILS Unrelated to insects, but serious plant pests in some gardens. Snails and slugs both have soft bodies covered by a thick mucous membrane. Most are brown or grayish with various darker markings.	Silvery trails show where they have traveled on garden foliage, ground and walkways. Primarily night feeders, they feed on many plants in both the garden and greenhouse. Dry, cold weather sends them to shelter beneath boards, large plant leaves or other garden trash. Widely distributed.	To keep them from the greenhouse, surround the building with a border free from grass and weeds. Store pots away from plant debris. In cold and dry weather, try trapping them beneath boards. Handpick or sprinkle with salt. Use a mulch of oak leaves, tobacco stem meal and wormwood tea. Stale beer will attract them if set out in saucers in the garden; the slugs drown in it. *See also separate entry.*

Insect	Hosts / Injury / Range	Control

THRIPS

Small, slender insects that are barely visible. Have two pairs of long, fringed wings.

Thrips damage plants by sucking out juices of leaves, fruit and flowers. Often found on flowers. Foliage becomes bleached or slightly silvered and eventually withers. Flowers and fruits may be scarred. A number of different hosts, including beans, citrus fruits, many flowers, fruits, and weeds. Widely distributed.

Weed control most important. Area of clean culture should extend some distance. Aluminum mulch is effective in keeping thrips off of low-growing crops. Sprays of oil and water or tobacco may work. Rotenone is also effective.

WEBWORMS

See Caterpillars and Hornworms

WEEVILS

See Curculios, Snout Beetles, Weevils

WHITEFLIES

Adults are about $\frac{1}{16}$ inch long with powdery white wings. Eggs laid on the underside of leaves. Eggs are yellow, turning gray as they mature.

Feed on plant juices causing leaves to lose vigor, yellow and eventually die. As with spider mites, a mold or fungus often grows where whiteflies feed. Universal pests of both greenhouse and garden.

Small wasps known as *Encarsia formosa* are available to greenhouse growers as natural parasites of whiteflies. Any nicotine spray will help control whiteflies. Also some oil sprays. *See also separate entry.*

WHITE GRUBS

See Japanese Beetle and June Beetle

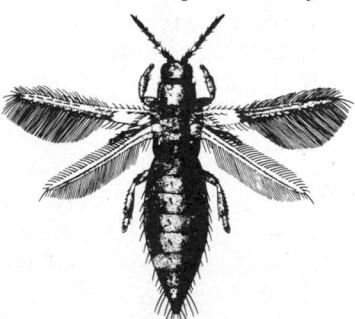

San Jose scale is a serious pest of deciduous fruit trees. To control, spray trees early in spring with an oil emulsion.

Viewed beneath a hand lens, thrips can be recognized by their fringed wings and short antennae.
(Courtesy of U.S. Department of Agriculture)

INSECTICIDES

Insecticides are substances toxic to insects, and have been used by farmers and gardeners for centuries. The oldest of insecticides are still with us: pyrethrum, derris, and rotenone are plant-derived poisons that are toxic to insects but safe for humans and other warm-blooded animals. Other early insecticides such as mercury, arsenic and nicotine are poisonous to men and animals. The introduction of DDT during World War II provided a much more potent weapon against many insects than had previously been available, and opened the door to a whole family of new insecticides based on German nerve gases and organic phosphates.

Despite the fact that DDT and many newer insecticides are many times more toxic than older materials, farmers and gardeners are still not able to attain a satisfactory degree of insect control. There are several difficult problems that complicate the use of insecticides, no matter how powerful they may be.

1. Because insects multiply rapidly and mutate freely, new generations may become immune to the powerful new poisons within a few years of the insecticide's introduction. Some species, such as mosquitoes and houseflies, develop immunity quicker than others.

2. Insecticides usually kill insects indiscriminately, destroying both the harmful and the harmless species. Even birds may be killed. This mass execution of animal life upsets the balance of nature—and it is this delicate balance that is the grower's best pest control. Garden-size ecological holocausts are encouraged by the fact that beneficial bugs typically take longer to build up their population, and harmful insects are thus free to multiply even more rapidly than before. Also, insects that formerly were not troublesome multiply quickly without natural checks and move into pest status.

3. Insecticides impart toxic residues to treated plants and the soil. There is much concern that sprayed and dusted foods are harmful to human health. DDT, for example, accumulates in the fatty tissue of the human body and can gain strength to the point where it may cause cell degeneration. Newer chemicals continue to show up in drinking water samples, including dieldrin, endrin, chlordane, aldrin, and lindane. Of these toxins, dieldrin, DDT and aldrin have been taken off the market after the danger they presented to human life was belatedly admitted.

Despite the costs and hazards, insecticides are used freely by many farmers and gardeners. The farmer who sees his crops being attacked, his yields reduced, and his profits eliminated by insects wants an immediate weapon of retaliation. Increasingly, however, gardeners and farmers are switching over to methods—some modern, some centuries old—that do not harshly damage the environment.

Safer Methods: What are those safer insect control methods? First, there is the selection of plants that have greater resistance to insect attack. It is a fact that some varieties of plants are better able to resist insect attack than others. The techniques they use to fight off insects are sometimes quite unusual. Some years back it was found that certain types of wheat actually kill the Hessian fly because their stalks suddenly stiffen and the flies, which puncture the stalks with their probosci, are unable to extricate themselves.

Another constructive method of fighting insects is biological control—usually involving the introduction of natural enemies of troublesome insects. Crop rotation, proper tillage and the addition of humus to the soil are other effective ways to control insect populations.

Organic gardeners and farmers have long noticed that humus-rich soil with an ample supply of minerals grows plants that are so healthy they are either unattractive to insects or are better able to withstand insect attack.

Mass Spraying: Much public concern about the harm insecticides can do was engendered by the campaigns to attempt to eradicate the gypsy moth in New England and the imported fire ant in the South with aerial sprays of DDT and dieldrin. Both of these insects were introduced into the United States from foreign countries, and because they had no natural enemies in this country, multiplied rapidly and became pests. The U.S. Department of Agriculture attempted to eradicate them by spraying whole counties and even states from the air. As a result, almost all insect life in the sprayed areas was killed—both good insects and bad ones. Birds, small animals, bees, and even deer were killed in large numbers. Crops meant for human consumption were tainted by insecticide residues above the legal tolerances. In short, the balance of nature was disrupted and harm was done to human and animal life. The irony of the situation is the fact that the massive sprayings did not really eradicate the pests. In fact, man has never succeeded in eradicating any insect.

Systemic insecticides—those that are absorbed into the sap stream of the plants—also created public health concern. Peeling or washing food treated with systemic insecticides does not reduce the poison concentration, as the poison is absorbed into every cell of the plant.

Rachel Carson's *Silent Spring* did much to bring these dangers to the public's attention. Nevertheless, the amount of insecticides used for agricultural purposes has continued to increase since the book's publication in 1962.

The USDA sets tolerance levels for insecticide residues, and sometimes shipments of foods with excess residues are seized. However, there is much doubt that the USDA tolerance levels adequately protect the public's health. First, the government is not able to test more than a minute percentage of all food shipments. Second, even farmers who mean well are unable to follow the complex instructions for application of the poisons. They may apply the correct dose to an average of all plants, but some sections of a field may get many times as heavy an application as others. Third, residue tolerance levels cannot take into consideration the fact that the consumer ingests pesticide poisons from many different foods, thereby increasing greatly the total that is consumed. Some of these poisons may potentiate, or react together in such a way as to multiply their poisonous effect many times. Fourth, the chemicals unleashed on the countryside often produce carcinogenic effects for many years before the danger is recognized and they are banned.

Many people become organic gardeners and farmers because they want food that is not contaminated with insecticides or poisons of any kind. For them, producing food that has *any* insecticide residue is a compromise. Fortunately, much work is being done by public and private researchers in the areas of biological control, resistant varieties, interplanting, and other poisonless alternatives.

See also CHLORINATED HYDROCARBONS, INSECT CONTROL, ORGANIC PHOSPHATES.

INSECTIVOROUS PLANTS
See CARNIVOROUS PLANTS

INTENSIVE GARDENING

Although ideal for pocket-sized gardens, intensive gardening was not originally designed for that purpose. Instead, it was designed to increase yields and improve their quality without a large capital investment. No farm machinery is needed to raise and harvest crops that produce up to four times as much as crops grown under conventional methods.

Though intensive gardening has been practiced in one form or another for many centuries, the basic methods remain the same: the use of raised beds; double digging; organic fertilizers and compost; nonlinear, intensive planting; and companion planting.

The key to the whole system is the raised bed. By separating the garden from the path, there is no problem with soil compaction, since no one ever walks on the beds. Water, fertilizer and labor aren't wasted on paths either. The soil in raised beds warms quickly, drains well and is well aerated.

The beds should be laid out for maximum sun exposure. They are generally three to five feet wide so the gardener can easily weed, water and harvest crops from the sides, though it may

The traditional Chinese method of gardening involves a system of interplanted, slightly raised garden beds. Trellising and staking help to conserve space and maintain an ordered appearance.

The raised bed is the key to most intensive-gardening systems. Curving the beds creates sheltered pockets for shade-loving plants as well as more open areas for flowers and vegetables that require full sun.

be more convenient to have narrower beds (1½ to two feet wide) for staked crops such as tomatoes.

The primary method for preparing a raised bed is a technique known as double digging. Dig a trench (12 inches wide and 12 inches deep) the width of the bed. Set the soil aside, outside the bed. Use a spade or pitchfork to break up the soil in the trench until it is loose and crumbly to a depth of 12 inches. Move the top layer of soil (12 inches wide and 12 inches deep) from the next trench into the first trench and spade the lower level of the second trench to a depth of 12 inches. Repeat this process until the entire bed is dug to a total depth of 24 inches. The soil removed from the first trench is used to fill the last trench.

Let the bed rest for a few days before working it again. This time, again remove the top layer of soil and loosen the bottom layer. As the topsoil is returned to each trench, nutrients are added at different levels. The *Postage Stamp Garden Book* (Los Angeles: J. P. Tarcher, Inc., 1975) recommends adding bone meal first (four pounds per 50 square feet), a little topsoil, a four-inch layer of compost, some more topsoil, about two inches of rotted manure, some more topsoil, and a small amount of wood ashes (three pounds per 50 square feet). Cover with soil and rake the top surface well. Soil conditioners are added to the upper layers of the bed only, as is done in nature. By working manure and compost into the topsoil layers you protect these layers from nutrient leaching, drying and other ills they are exposed to at the surface. The top of the bed should be raised some four to eight inches above ground level when everything has been added. This raised form will allow adequate ventilation for young roots and stimulate growth. With no one walking on it, the soil will remain light and easy to work throughout the growing season. The high amount of organic matter will hold moisture and provide adequate nutrition for the large number of plants the bed must support.

Nonlinear, intensive planting means that plants are spaced as closely as possible in triangular patterns covering an entire bed. When the plants are mature, their leaves should barely touch each other. Such spacing encourages improved growth, conserves moisture and greatly helps to control weeds. Row planting, by the way, is an invention designed to facilitate cultivation of large areas; plants do not grow in rows in nature.

Once the basics are mastered, the intensive gardener is ready for interplanting, a technique which calls for planting crops that mature at different rates. A fast-growing crop could be planted at six-inch intervals around the perimeter of the bed, with a later-maturing crop planted at 12-inch intervals in the center. Some intensive gardeners have harvested four different crops from the same bed using this technique.

When you interplant long-season and short-season plants, however, it is difficult to prepare the beds for the next short-season crop. When redigging parts of the bed to be replanted, care must be taken not to disturb the roots of the later-maturing crops. The old French market gardeners strove to have an entire bed of plants ready to be harvested at the same time, and this seems to be the most efficient use of the intensive method. Herbs and flowers can be companion planted at the ends of the beds to help ward off insects and other garden pests. If you do interplant different crops, be sure they are companions.

See also COMPANION PLANTING, INTERPLANTING, SUCCESSION PLANTING, VEGETABLE GARDENING.

INTERCROPPING
See INTERPLANTING

INTERCULTURE
See ELECTROCULTURE

INTERPLANTING

Interplanting, also called intercropping, is nothing more than growing more than one crop simultaneously on a piece of ground. The advantage is that the technique will increase the land's total harvest. Scientists have found that a field planted to the highest yielding density for one type of plant can still produce a significantly higher total harvest if plants of another kind are grown among the first.

To a farmer used to acre upon acre devoted to just one productive cash crop, this idea will seem revolutionary if not impossible to imagine. But it is important to recognize that any strangeness in the idea of intercropping has its roots in the mass production techniques and equipment, especially for harvesting, which have come to dominate our agriculture. These practices associated with monoculture were developed to reap the benefits of mechanization rather than to utilize the full potential of the land.

Today, agricultural research is beginning to take a harder look at mixing the kinds of plants put into a field. Intercropping represents a feasible way to increase production. Modern pasture systems involve pairings of grasses and legumes which are complementary in habit of growth and season of harvest. The legumes are doubly valuable because over the seasons they enrich the soil's nitrogen content while boosting the protein in each crop of hay.

This kind of compound advantage seems to be a fairly regular effect in a wide variety of crop combinations. The extent of this fortunate and remarkable feature is just now being explored. And of course the way it works varies widely with the crop plants involved. Here are a few examples of the commonly reported bonuses.

Besides increasing the productivity of soil, water and solar inputs, interplanting frequently provides a certain amount of pest control. Insect pests seem to be discouraged by several factors. The varied environment encourages more predators for one thing, and companion plants form natural barriers to epidemic spreading of both insects and diseases.

Denser stands of crop plants mean less place for weeds to grow. Weeds tend to be shaded out earlier in the season, which means less need for cultivation.

The farmer, in turn, spends significantly less time maintaining the fields. And planting two or more crops where there might be just one staggers the expenditure of labor over a longer period which means steadier, more efficient work for people. Then too, when one crop does not yield well a particular season, the companion plant evens out the deficit in the harvest.

The CGIAR (Consultative Group on International Agricultural Research), sponsored by the FAO and the Development Programme of the United Nations and the World Bank, maintains large research centers around the world. Scientists based at these institutions have most often been the source of the reports on well-established systems of intercropping. Many of their researchers have begun systematic studies to explain intercropping's success. Some are working out ways to increase its efficiency.

At ICRISAT (International Crops Research Institute for the Semi-Arid Tropics), in Hyderabad, India, interplanting has been found to open a new dimension for native farming by stretching the growing season. Late-maturing pigeon peas cropped with a variety of other legumes, sunflowers or millets, produce two crops a year. Planted at the normal time, the peas would be forced to develop in the middle of the drought. The established system of fallowing the land over the dry season produced no measurable benefit over interplanting to the crops the following year. So not only is a larger crop harvested, but the season of useful employment is also lengthened and the food supply enriched.

Based in the Philippines, IRRI (International Rice Research Institute) has sponsored extensive research on intercropping systems in Southeast Asia. Their scientists report high increases in productivity. Corn intercropped with rice yields about 80 percent more than either component monocropped. On Java various local cropping systems range from 30 to 60 percent more productive than sole cropping. IRRI researchers have also demonstrated that intercropping can simplify pest management, for example, by shading out weeds. Mixtures of corn with peanuts and soybeans somehow encourage predatory spiders to move into fields, keeping corn borers in check.

At CIAT (International Center for Tropical Agriculture), in Colombia, the reports again indicate the importance and suitability of beans in intercropping systems. An interesting principle their research turned up is that different varieties of a single type of bean can respond differently to intercropping systems. For example, the yields of a climbing bean grown with corn were reduced far more than the yields of the same variety but of a bush habit. Researchers there are collecting seed from many different sources to use in breeding programs. They plan to develop plant types well suited to intercropping over a range of growing conditions.

Agricultural researchers in the United States are just beginning to turn their attention to intercropping. Interest is especially strong among entomologists seeking better biological alternatives to chemical insect controls.

INTERRUPTED FERN
See OSMUNDA

IODINE

This element is a trace mineral in animal nutrition, but it isn't necessarily vital to plant health. Because it is present in many soils, and because plants grown on those soils will take it up, the animal need for iodine is satisfied by eating those plants.

Curiously enough, it was the soils deficient in iodine that brought iodine's critical role in animal nutrition to light. An iodine deficiency causes goiters. Goiters were prevalent in a particular region of the country that came to be known as "the goiter belt." The goiter belt was eventually proven to be a region of iodine-deficient soils. The region extended from the northern Appalachians and Great Lakes west across the northern Great Plains and the Rocky Mountains to the Oregon and Washington coasts.

The iodine-deficient diets were corrected in large measure by the introduction and widespread use of iodized salt. But they could also have been corrected by eliminating iodine deficiencies in soil using such ocean-derived organic fertilizers as seaweed and fish products.

IPOMOEA
See MORNING-GLORY, SWEET POTATO

IRIS

A perennial herb, the iris is native to the North Temperate Zone. Its lovely flowers spring from two types of rooting systems—the bulbous and the nonbulbous or rhizomatous.

Bulbous irises are native to southern Europe, Africa and Asia Minor. They have particularly large, showy blossoms that appear early in the season. Although these types require winter protection, they do well in most northeastern states and in northern California. Florists force the Spanish and Dutch bulbous irises, *I. xiphium,* for early spring flowers.

The rhizomatous irises are more widely cultivated in this country. Each type is classified as bearded, beardless, or crested. Bearded

Most of the 200 species of iris are hardy or half-hardy perennials which produce lovely purple to yellow flowers for about a month in early summer.

or German irises such as *I. germanica, I. fulva*
and *I. pumila* are characterized by a tuft of
"hair" on the flower's lower petals or falls. Old-
fashioned beardless or flag types native to North
America have perfectly smooth falls and the
crested species has a ridge along the lower part
of each fall.

Most of the hybrid irises offered in catalogs are dwarf, intermediate or tall bearded
varieties. Tall beardeds growing from two to
four feet are the most common. They usually
bloom from late spring to early summer, though
some "reblooming bearded" types that flower
in spring and then again in midsummer or early
fall are available.

Cultivated forms of beardless iris include
Louisiana hybrids (two to three feet), Japanese
irises (three to four feet), Siberian irises (three
feet), and Spuria iris hybrids (three to four
feet). Louisiana hybrids put forth three- to
four-inch flowers in mid to late spring or, in
northern states, in early summer. Japanese
irises have very large (up to eight inches in
diameter), flat-topped flowers that appear in
early or midsummer. The long-lasting flowers
of the Siberian hybrids are three to four inches
across and occur in early summer. Spuria hybrids, which bloom in early summer, are the
best cutting variety. All of these types come in
a variety of shades, from white to yellows,
pinks, purples, and browns. Often the standard
or upright petals and the falls are of different
colors.

All species of iris require a very sunny position. Bearded forms will grow in most parts
of the United States and in all but the coldest
regions of Canada. Spuria and Japanese hybrids prefer areas south of New York, but they
will blossom in New England and certain northwestern regions as well. Louisiana hybrids are
unable to withstand severe winter temperatures
and are best grown in the Deep South. Soil requirements vary according to species. The old-
fashioned yellow flag prefers a moist, even
boggy soil, while the Japanese, Siberian and
Louisiana hybrids require damp, slightly acid
soils well supplied with organic matter. Bearded
irises grow best in well-drained, neutral soils,
with some varieties able to withstand periods of
drought.

Planting: Plant bulbous irises in late autumn. Since many kinds are not cold-hardy,
they must be planted very late so that they do
not begin to grow until the warm, spring
months. Plant the bulbs in masses, three to six
inches deep in the garden bed.

The rhizome-rooted irises are planted in
mid or late summer. Set them in the soil one
foot apart, with barely an inch-thick covering of
earth. In heavy soil, some experts feel that the
rhizome, or swollen rootstem, may be left
slightly exposed. Since irises are not replanted
more than once every four years, prime the
planting hole with compost about one foot below the rhizome. Avoid fresh manure near the
root. Water thoroughly. Planting time for tall
beardeds is late June or July; for Japanese and
Siberian varieties it is early spring and September or October.

Dividing and Maintaining: It is a good
idea to dig up rhizomatous irises every four or
five years so that weak rhizomes can be removed and the soil reworked and fertilized.
After the plants have bloomed, lift the entire
clump with a spade and separate it into small
clusters of rhizomes. Choose only the largest
and healthiest-looking ones for transplanting.
Let the hose run gently over these while you
spade the soil deeply for the new plantings.
Sprinkle bone meal over the spots and spade in.

Irises demand plenty of rich soil, so mix in a generous portion of rotted manure or compost. Good drainage is a must and will prevent borers and root rot.

Place one or several of the divisions into the prepared soil. If several are planted together, space them in a circle, leaves turned outward. If leaves turn inward, the growth will soon center and become crowded. Make each hole deep and broad enough to take the roots without crowding and adjust the height of the plant so that the rhizomes are barely covered. Tamp the soil firmly.

During the blooming season in April, May or June, pick the faded flowers from their stems every day and guard against other plants in the bed or border pushing up too closely. This is especially important for the bearded species—they need all the sunlight they can get.

As soon as all the blossoms on the stems have faded, cut the flower stalks halfway down leaving foliage to hide the stumps. If cut too close to the rhizomes, the stems may rot.

During July the first dying leaves of the bearded iris will droop. Remove these. They will be a good addition to the compost pile, while if left on the plant they will shut out the sunlight from the rhizomes, and give the plant an unkempt appearance too. However, do not cut off the leaves until they have obviously wilted. Many gardeners make the mistake of cutting down all the leaves as soon as the blooms have faded. The leaves must be allowed to grow and produce food for the rhizomes to store for the following season.

During the rest of the year there is little to do for these hardy perennials. In January and February it is sometimes necessary to tramp over an old iris bed to push down the rhizomes which have been pushed up during a thaw. In the middle of March give the beds a dressing of bone meal and lime, using equal parts of each. This mixture should be distributed evenly and thickly. The heavy spring rains—or melting snow—will carry the nutrients down to the plant roots.

Insects and Diseases: The following rules may be of help in maintaining healthy irises:

1. Plant on a slope with good drainage, or supply necessary drainage material.

2. Avoid excess watering and rich nitrogen fertilizers for the tall beardeds. Lush growth encourages disease and borers.

3. When replanting, examine each plant carefully, throwing diseased specimens and leaves into the compost heap. Constantly pick off diseased foliage. Cut away any borers or rot found.

4. Handle plants very carefully. Each wound may provide an entrance for the iris borer.

5. Keep the soil supplied with compost. *See also* BULB, PERENNIALS.

IRON

This element has long been recognized as important to proper plant growth. Iron is a major factor in chlorophyll and carbohydrate production. A deficiency of iron in plants causes chlorosis, resulting in the same symptoms as those for nitrogen or magnesium deficiency—namely, sickly yellow color.

Soils generally contain sufficient iron, but most of it is in an insoluble form. Deficiencies often occur in alkali soils. Iron deficiency is particularly common in the major fruit-growing districts of the country, such as Florida and California. In many cases, the spraying of solutions of iron sulfate, iron oxide or iron chloride on iron-deficient citrus trees has resulted in the formation of soluble salts like ferrous sulfate, which are toxic to many plants. Therefore, the use of these materials to correct an iron shortage is not recommended.

Application of glauconite or greensand can supply iron, but the best solution is to add organic matter to iron-deficient soils.

Most of the soil iron is in the form of rather insoluble rocks and minerals, and as such, it is unavailable to plants. Some of this iron may be brought into solution by the carbonic acid that is given off as an end product of respiration by plant roots and microorganisms. But most of the iron that dissolves in the soil solution is probably made to do so by the action of organic chelating or compounding agents. Humus is very likely the most abundant chelating substance found in nature. In addition to humus, many organisms bring iron and other important trace metals into solution where they can satisfy the nutrient needs of growing plants. Microbial cells, many organic products, bacteria, actinomycetes, fungi in the soil, and fresh and decomposing organic matter all are important chelators.

As a general rule, then, the small amount of iron needed by plants is made available by the action of humus.

See also CHELATORS, SOIL DEFICIENCIES, TRACE ELEMENTS.

IRON SULFATE
See FERTILIZER, CHEMICAL

IRONWEED   (*Vernonia*)

Ironweed is of a genus of shrubs, trees and perennial herbs from all over the world, belonging to the Composite family. Its characteristics include simple alternate leaves and pink, purple or white flower clusters composed of disk flowers only and sometimes surrounded by bristly bracts. Fall bloom makes some species valuable in the border. *V. noveboracensis,* New York ironweed, grows to about seven feet, though usually shorter, with bristles surrounding purple flower heads. This is a tall wild flower common in wet meadows and along open streams in the East. Its large royal purple flower heads and purple-tinged leaves are very showy. Its bloom period overlaps that of Joe-Pye weed (*Eupatorium maculatum*), which produces large pinkish flower heads and occupies the same habitat. A spectacular effect can be achieved by naturalizing these two in a damp meadow or pondside with New England asters. The bloom period of such a planting will extend from August to October and require little maintenance.

See also VERNONIA.

IRRIGATION

The objective of irrigation is to keep a readily available supply of moisture in contact with plants' roots at all times. But all too often farmers and some gardeners depend on irrigation to the exclusion of soil-building and management practices. Their soil is not in condition to receive and properly utilize the water falling upon it as rain or applied by irrigation.

Experts say the correct treatment of land will insure that 90 to 95 percent of irrigation and rain water will be used for crop benefit. The average in both irrigated and nonirrigated areas is under 50 percent.

In New Mexico, for instance, only three of the average 12 inches of rain soak in. The soil is rich in minerals from centuries of weathering, but there is almost no organic matter. The lack of water, however, is much more obvious, so the farmer is led to believe that all he has to do is apply water to get good crops. But the water runs off or leaches away—taking huge amounts of minerals with it—and the soil becomes packed.

Cultural Practices: The first thing a farmer should do when bringing semiarid land under cultivation is to institute practices— green manuring and the like—to build up its organic matter content. Irrigation should be held to a minimum necessary to grow the green manure. Too much water can make machinery contribute to soil compacting.

A soil rich in organic matter will catch and hold nearly all the rain falling on it. Thus, much less irrigation water will be needed, and what is applied will be held better, too. Mulching, green manuring, strip-cropping, contour plowing and terracing help to cut irrigation costs and save the underground sources from going dry.

The farmer with an irrigation system is often tempted to use it more than necessary. A heavy supply of water when crops are establishing their roots, for instance, will tend to make the roots stay in the upper layer of soil, instead of reaching downward. Thus the plant becomes dependent on irrigation, for when drought hits, it has no deep roots to seek out subsoil moisture. Thin, surface roots mean the plant can't pick up rich subsoil minerals for optimum growth. Experts say that rainwater that has been in the soil for months will be laden with more minerals than irrigation water. And if irrigation water is applied constantly, it will prevent nutrient-laden capillary water from rising to the root zone.

Like the drip system, sprinkler irrigation applies water precisely and uniformly to all kinds of crops and soils. However, the initial costs are high and, in arid regions, evaporation may consume most of the water before it reaches the soil.

Better management practices to build the soil and hold rainwater are a lot less costly than irrigation. Properly used, however, irrigation can be a valuable tool. Water is often a limiting factor in crop growth. In very dry seasons, irrigation may make the difference between crop success and failure.

Light irrigation at planting time on many crops will give earlier starting, more even growth and earlier maturity and harvest.

In the orchard, irrigation can be an adequate standby measure if done correctly. Don't spread out the water; it's better to water a few trees with 1,000 gallons each than to "tease" many trees with 100. Sods or mulches are vital to prevent runoff when these large amounts are applied.

Drip Irrigation: Even the best of conventional furrow-and-flood-type irrigation systems makes heavy demands on limited labor and water resources. Drip irrigation avoids these shortcomings by stretching the water supply as far as possible and reducing maintenance to a minimum. Drip irrigation is simply putting small amounts of water on or near plants at more frequent intervals than with conventional systems. When you cut down on the total amount of water applied to the garden at any one time, you simultaneously reduce the rate of runoff and nutrient leaching, so the efficiency of the drip system is further enhanced.

A typical drip system consists of a small plastic pipe placed along the rows of the garden. Tiny holes are punched in it wherever plants are to grow, allowing water to drip slowly into the ground in the immediate vicinity of the roots. The pinpoint holes, called emitters, allow water to escape at a rate of about a gallon per hour per emitter. Depending on the weather and soil conditions, the gardener might let the system run all night once or twice a week, or he might run it for an hour or two every day.

When 100 gallons of water are applied down a furrow in a conventional irrigation system, only about half of it gets to the plants' root zone. Sprinklers rate slightly better, delivering about 75 out of every 100 gallons to the target area. A properly installed drip system, however, can direct 90 to 95 gallons of the 100 to precisely the right place.

Compost Irrigation: Some farmers have successfully coupled irrigation with organic fertilizing. They run their irrigation water through compost piles, where it picks up billions of tiny particles of rich, bacteria-laden compost and carries them to the fields. The soil stays friable and highly fertile, always loaded with earthworms. Irrigation farmers in the West are increasingly turning to this practice. Many of them use no other fertilizers.

In some areas, sludge from canneries as well as municipalities is being piped directly onto farm fields, and results have been very good.

Land-leveling is another practice that goes hand-in-hand with irrigation. It can save 50 percent of the water formerly used, and insure so much better utilization of the water applied that crop yields are often doubled. Where the subsoil is exposed by the leveler blades, using feedlot manure and working with a chisel or Graham plow have made it produce a good crop the first year. Leveling is expensive, but it can pay for itself quickly in lowered water costs.

Installation: Here are a few tips if you are thinking of installing an irrigation system:

Get competent help from an equipment company. One farmer who worked out his own system found he would have to keep it going day and night for two weeks to apply an inch of water on ten acres.

Check your water source first. A good-sized pond or a stream that won't run dry is best—infinitely cheaper than digging a well. When buying equipment, look for simplicity, portability and coverage to fit the land and crops.

Water should be applied at the time when the crop normally makes its most rapid growth, if the soil moisture is low then. Check with a soil corer to a depth of eight inches. Don't apply water faster than the soil can absorb it, but be sure to wet it to the lower levels. Watch the weather forecasts—a heavy rain following irrigation can drown out the crop.

Irrigation can be worthwhile, if it is not used as a substitute for rain wasted through a lack of soil-building practices. It is most successful when installed after a complete organic program has been put into practice.

Reusing Household Wastewater: The potential for reuse of household water for garden irrigation is great. Of all the water used in an average home, 55 to 60 percent is classified as greywater, while 40 to 45 percent is listed as blackwater. Blackwater is any water that has been used in a toilet. While there are a great many ways to cut down on the amount of blackwater generated, at this time home treatment and reuse of blackwater is best left alone. However, home treatment and reuse of greywater is possible at this time without large capital investment or technical know-how.

Greywater comes from the kitchen, laundry, shower/bath and bathroom sink. It contains grease, food particles, soaps, detergents, hair, dead skin, bacteria and viruses, and anything else that gets thrown or dropped down the drain. The main concern about using greywater on the garden is its effect on plants and any possible health effects on humans or animals eating those plants. The average volume of greywater for a house of four people is 150 gallons a day. It is possible to reduce that figure, and studies have shown a conscientious home, with water-saving devices, can average as low as 20 gallons per person.

For the drought-stricken gardener, immediate use of greywater during the growing season is the goal. Of the four sources of greywater—kitchen, laundry, bathroom sink, and bathtub—the kitchen accounts for about 17 percent of the volume. The kitchen is also the source of the most potential garden pollutants, including cleaners, ammonia, dishwashing liquids, and other harsh chemicals. Rather than risk using kitchen water in the garden, save it and pour it into toilets for flushing.

This still puts more than 80 percent (or 120 gallons a day for the average family of four) of your greywater in the reusable category. The trick will be to find a way to collect it, and to learn not to pollute it with chemicals or cleaners that will harm your garden.

Dr. John H. Timothy Winneberger, editor of *Manual of Grey Water Treatment Practice* (Ann Arbor Science), recommends the use of biodegradable detergents and soaps to the greatest extent possible. The one item not recommended is any soap or detergent containing borax. The borax contains boron, and that is fatal to plants.

"Detergents don't kill plants, they depress their growth due to an unbalanced supply of nutrients," Winneberger explains. "When you also supply a balanced supply of nutrients, like sewage sludge, the plants love the combination."

In Winneberger's view, "it's safe to use anything on the garden that you can use on your skin. Any cleaners of the sort you have to use rubber gloves with, don't put on the garden."

Greywater should always be applied to the soil, not the leaves, as it could cause leaves to burn, especially when exposed to hot summer sun. If possible, use a trickle irrigation system that uses batches of water, and use the greywater promptly to prevent odors and to keep grease in the wastewater from congealing.

The best way to collect greywater for garden irrigation is simply to undo your drainpipes, and let the sinks drain straight into buckets. If you unhook the kitchen sink and catch that water for use in toilets, you can interrupt the bath and bathroom sinks at the junction before they join the toilet, and connect them directly to a soaker hose in the garden. A direct connection of the washer to a soaker hose will also work quite well, although if you have a large collection tank, it is best to mix the rinse water with the wash water to dilute the detergent content before applying on the garden.

ISMENE   *See* HYMENOCALLIS

ITALIAN RYEGRASS
(*Lolium multiflorum*)

This member of the Ryegrass family, sometimes known as Australian rye, is a perennial that grows 12 to 30 inches high. Seldom grown in gardens, its flower clusters are most often seen in fields.

See also RYE.

IVY

This name alone usually is used to signify *Hedera helix,* though any member of the genus *Hedera* of the Ginseng family may be called ivy. Other ivies not *Hedera* are: Virginia creeper, *Parthenocissus quinquefolia;* Boston or Japanese ivy, *P. tricuspidata;* Cape ivy, *Senecio macroglossus;* German ivy, *S. mikanioides;* ground ivy, *Glecoma hederacea;* Kenilworth ivy, *Cymbalaria muralis;* marine ivy, *Cissus incisa;* poison ivy, *Rhus Toxicodendron;* and ivy geranium, *Pelargonium peltatum.*

Species of *Hedera,* or ivy, are evergreen shrubs that climb by rootlets which fix themselves in cracks in the support over which they form a cover. They are planted as wall cover, ground cover, or sometimes against buildings, and are grown as house plants.

Ivy thrives in rich, moist soil containing plenty of humus. It is propagated by cuttings which easily root at the leaf nodes where its climbing roots are already formed.

Hedera helix, English ivy, is the species most often grown as a climber. It is hardy to New England. It clothes its support in a thick cover of green which, in some varieties, becomes scarlet to rusty red in autumn. Its drawback is that the small rootlets may hasten deterioration of brick or masonry walls.

Some outstanding varieties are Eva and Little Eva, Jubilee, and Little Diamond.

See also HOUSE PLANTS.

J

JACK-IN-THE-PULPIT

See ARACEAE

JACOB'S-LADDER

(*Polemonium caeruleum*)

Jacob's-ladder is a hardy perennial herb whose main value is as an ornamental border plant. The plant gets its unusual name from the ladderlike arrangement of its alternating leaves. Growing up to three feet tall, Jacob's-ladder has feather-shaped leaves and bright blue flowers with yellow stamens.

Seed should be planted in a loamy mixture in a cold frame in early spring. When several inches high, the seedlings can be transplanted to a moist spot and set about ten inches apart.

Jacob's-ladder, sometimes called charity, is not widely recognized as a medicinal plant, though other members of the genus are. Abscess root (*P. reptans*) has been used to treat fever, inflammations, pleurisy, coughs, colds, and bronchial disorders.

See also HERB.

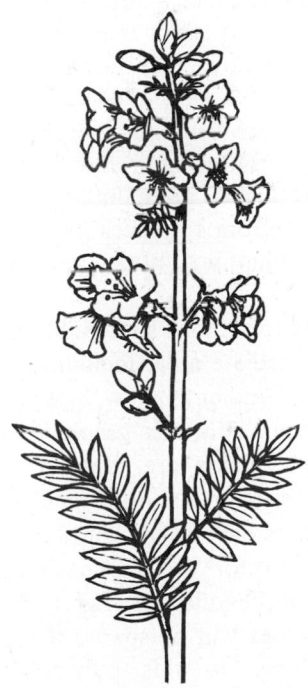

The blue-flowering Jacob's-ladder is rather short-lived but nevertheless makes an excellent summer border plant.

JAPANESE BEETLE

The beautifully iridescent Japanese beetle was accidentally introduced into this country in 1916. From that time, the beetle flourished until it became a prime garden pest.

In 1933, government entomologists fortunately isolated a bacterial organism that produces a fatal blood disease in the grub. Since it brings about an abnormal white coloring in the infected insects, it was dubbed milkly spore disease. It is present naturally throughout the soils of Japan, and is the main reason that Japanese beetles are kept in check in their native territory. Like scores of other de-

Adult Japanese beetles feed on several hundred varieties of fruits, trees and garden flowers, reaching their peak population in midsummer.

structive pests, the beetle became a problem only when brought accidentally to areas lacking the predators, parasites and insect diseases designed by nature as an ever-present, effective counterbalance.

Milky Spore: The commercial spore powder—a standard mixture of the germ spores, chalk and filler—is produced under a process patent owned and licensed by the USDA. Since its introduction, communities as well as individual gardeners have joined forces to control the beetle in their regions.

Grubs of the Japanese beetle are hatched and live in the ground—frequently in lawn turf —until they pupate into mature, winged beetles.

When treated grubs die, the spores which fill the body cavity are left in the soil to be taken up by other grubs as they feed. As the cycle goes on, the number of spores in the soil increases, more and more grubs are killed and fewer beetles emerge. Ordinarily, only a single application is required for lasting control and protection; however, it takes a few years for the disease to have a profound effect on the grub population.

The disease powder kills only Japanese beetles and a few of their close beetle relatives. It is totally harmless to the soil and to beneficial insects, bees, earthworms, all plants, animals, and humans.

Application is simple: apply a teaspoonful of the spore-disease powder on the grass or sod in spots three to four feet apart and in rows the same distance apart. It can be applied at any time except when the ground is frozen or when it is windy. Only mowed or cropped grass areas are recommended for treatment.

Other Controls: Many problems can be prevented by following a few basic cultural controls. Remove prematurely ripening or diseased fruit from the trees or ground. Delayed corn plantings often get by without damage.

It's best to remove susceptible wild plants from the immediate area, including elder, evening primrose, Indian mallow, sassafras, poison ivy, smartweed, wild fox grape, and summer grape. These plants are often a continuous source of infestation for other plants.

Gardeners have found that larkspur has a fatal attraction for the Japanese beetle; the pests nibble at the foliage and keel over. Others report that roses will be spared if interplanted with geraniums, as this pungent flower is noxious to the beetle. Garlic, tansy and rue repel the beetles.

See also INSECT CONTROL.

JAPANESE CHERRY
See CHERRY, FLOWERING; TREE

JAPANESE PAGODA TREE
See SOPHORA

JAPANESE QUINCE   *See* QUINCE

JAPANESE VARNISH TREE
See PHOENIX TREE

JAPONICA

Many genera of plants have species listed as *japonica,* and the word is often used as a common name for those species. Most often, however, it refers to *Camellia japonica,* a very showy evergreen shrub that grows to 30 feet or to the dwarf Japanese quince (*Chaenomeles japonica* or *C. speciosa*), an early-blooming shrub that grows to three feet.

See also CAMELLIA.

JASMINE   (*Jasminum*)

Popular outdoors in the South and in the greenhouse elsewhere, these fragrant, flowering shrubs, often called jessamine, are easy to grow if given a sunny location and well-drained loam. Propagation is by layers or cuttings of nearly ripe wood.

Spanish jasmine (*J. grandiflorum*), also known as Catalonian and royal jasmine, is a white-flowering, nearly erect shrub, reaching a height of four feet.

Italian jasmine (*J. humile* cv. 'Revolutum') is evergreen or half-evergreen and hardy as far north as Maryland. It grows to a height of 20 feet, with yellow flowers blooming in summer and fall.

Primrose jasmine (*J. Mesnyi*) is another evergreen type, growing five to ten feet high. Its yellow flowers bloom in spring. The common white variety (*J. officinale*) or poet's jasmine is a tall, 30-foot, summer-flowering, deciduous shrub. Winter jasmine (*J. nudiflorum*) has yellow axillary flowers that often bloom all winter in mild climates.

JERUSALEM ARTICHOKE
See ARTICHOKE, JERUSALEM

JERUSALEM CHERRY
(*Solanum Pseudocapsicum*)

This shrubby plant, a native of Madeira, has a dense cover of pointed, oval leaves and starlike white flowers. These produce orange scarlet, cherrylike fruit. A yellow-fruited strain also exists. Florists usually time them to pro duce fruit at Christmas, hence, their secondary common name, Christmas cherry. The fruits are about ½ inch in diameter, and remain in good condition for months. Because they are poisonous, these plants should be kept away from children.

An all-purpose soil which is allowed to dry between waterings is best. Somewhat fussy, this plant needs a sunny southern exposure which can drop to 55°F. (12.78°C.) at night. A partially heated sun-room is ideal. Propagation is by seed or cuttings. Seed started in March will result in the late fall fruit. After fruits have dropped, the plants are heavily pruned back and repotted. A summer rest in partial shade will produce a larger, heavier-fruited plant in the fall. Bring it in before frost occurs. From seed, the best variety is the spreading dwarf, *S. P.* cv. 'Pattersonii'.

JESSAMINE   *See* JASMINE

JEWELWEED   *See* IMPATIENS

JIMSONWEED
(*Datura Stramonium*)

An ill-scented, dangerous weed, this plant is a rank-growing annual. All daturas are strong narcotics; large doses are poisonous. Smaller doses are hallucinogenic and jimsonweed is sometimes used by shamans and medicine men to achieve mystic insights.

A bushy weed, jimsonweed can grow six feet tall with smooth green or purple stems. Leaves are alternate, unevenly toothed and strong scented. The large, trumpet-shaped flowers are white on the green-stemmed variety, violet or purplish on the purple-stemmed type. Fruit consists of a hard, prickly, four-part capsule containing many large, flat, dark brown or black seeds. At maturity, the capsule splits open into four parts.

Jimsonweed grows in fields or waste places, mostly on rich, gravelly soils. It should be mowed before seed is produced, but if mowed after fruits are ripe, the plants should be burned. Jimsonweed is poisonous to cattle, who can die from eating the tops of the plants. In humans, the nervous form of poisoning is most common, with symptoms including head-ache, nausea, thirst, a burning sensation of the skin, dilated pupils, and loss of sight and control of limbs.

See also WEEDS.

JOE-PYE WEED
(*Eupatorium purpureum, E. maculatum*)

Also known as purple boneset, this perennial herb of the Composite family grows three to eight feet tall and has large, flat clusters of purple florets that bloom in late summer or early fall. Of some value as a honey plant, Joe-Pye weed is common in low, damp ground in the eastern states during late summer, and is found in most parts of North America. A common roadside plant, named for an Indian doctor who used its roots and leaves as an astringent for diarrhea, and as a diuretic and tonic, Joe-Pye weed can be grown from seed, cuttings or root division in the spring.

See also HERB.

JOHNSONGRASS
(*Sorghum halepense*)

Native to Southern Asia and Europe, Johnsongrass was introduced into the United States from Turkey about 1830. Ten years later, Col. William Johnson of Selma, Alabama, introduced it to that state.

Johnsongrass has long been considered one of the biggest plant pests in the southern half of the United States. Although introduced as a forage plant, Johnsongrass is best known as a tenacious weed. The grass presents a particularly serious hazard in areas subject to

Johnsongrass is an especially serious pest in corn-fields where it acts as a carrier of maize dwarf mosaic virus.

Johnsongrass needs a fairly rich soil, but it also grows well on fine sandy loams. It will grow as far north as central Illinois, but agronomists do not recommend it as a perennial north of southern Tennessee. It spreads by vigorous underground rootstocks as well as by seed.

It is a good ground cover, growing thickly three to seven feet high. The grass grows well along basins and terraces, on steep slopes and in waterways. It can be started where it is difficult to get a stand of other grasses.

Plant Johnsongrass any time after the soil gets warm until the end of June. Early plantings yield the most. Thorough disking well in advance of planting will provide a firm seedbed. A legume planted with the grass will supply nitrogen, and phosphate rock and potash can be applied as dictated by a soil test. Three to five tons per acre of manure are good, too, if available.

The seed may be broadcast at the rate of 20 to 30 pounds per acre, or drilled in four to six pounds per acre. Always drill it in one to two inches deep, on the contour. When mixed with legumes, 15 to 20 pounds of grass seed are usually used, but some farmers recommend more.

flooding. In river and creek bottomlands throughout the South, farmers have fought its encroachment into their good cropland—often losing the battle to its rugged persistence.

But many farmers have found that the properties they once despised make it a dependable, profitable crop. Johnsongrass is hardy, grows fast, resists drought, and yields well with little attention. In addition, it is high in protein and so palatable that all livestock relish it.

JONQUIL   *See* NARCISSUS

JUGLANS
See BUTTERNUT, HEART NUT, WALNUT

JUJUBE   (*Zizyphus*)

Belonging to the Buckthorn family, jujubes are evergreen or deciduous shrubs grown mostly in California and the Southwest for their egg-shaped fruits, which are generally sold candied. Jujubes prosper in well-drained garden soil, tolerate heat and drought, and are resistant to insects and disease. They grow up to 35 feet tall, and should be planted 20 feet apart. Also called Chinese date, jujubes are about an inch long and turn dark red or brown when ripe.

JUNE BEETLE
See INSECT CONTROL

JUNEBERRY   *See* AMELANCHIER

JUNIPER   (*Juniperus*)

Unlike most of the varieties cultivated for home gardens the Sierra juniper is a true tree, often reaching a height of 60 feet.
(Courtesy of U.S. Forest Service)

A large genus of evergreen trees and shrubs belonging to the Pine family, junipers are excellent choices for hedges and windbreaks, often making the most outstanding plants in the formal garden. The tall, pyramidal types are conspicuous planted singly or in groups, while the low, spreading forms are excellent for foundation plantings and in rock gardens. Certain varieties are well adapted to sandy banks along seaside locations.

Junipers have needle-shaped or scalelike foliage, inconspicuous flowers and small round fruits. They do best on a sandy loam with sufficient moisture, but grow satisfactorily on slightly dry, gravelly soil. They need a sunny, open location. Propagation is by seed, or more commonly, by cuttings of nearly ripe wood in autumn.

Common juniper (*J. communis*) grows to 12 feet, and sometimes as high as 40 feet. A fine upright shrub hardy throughout the United States, it has needlelike leaves and black fruit. The gray green dwarf or ground variety (*J. c.*

var. *depressa*), known as the prostrate juniper, can grow well in poor soil and any exposure. Although it reaches a height of only two or three feet, this wide-spreading form may exceed five feet in width. It is excellent as a low wall plant. One variation of the dwarf form, the Irish juniper (*J. c.* var. *communis* cv. 'Hibernica'), is often recommended as an accent plant.

Creeping juniper (*J. horizontalis*) is another low-growing type, hardy throughout the United States. It does best in a sandy, rocky soil.

Sierra juniper or California juniper (*J. occidentalis*) is a true tree, growing 40 to 60 feet high, with needlelike leaves and black fruit. Red cedar (*J. virginiana* cv. 'Burkii') grows as high as 100 feet, although usually about 50 feet. Its varieties have foliage varying from dark green and gray to ones with branches that have yellow tips.

See also EVERGREEN.

JUPITER'S BEARD
See CENTRANTHUS

JUTE   (*Corchorus capsularis*)

A member of the Basswood or Linden family, jute is a fast-growing plant grown in the Gulf states for its fiber, which is made into strong, bulky fabrics and twines.

Jute needs a rich, well-drained soil and a hot, humid climate. Pakistan and India are the world's largest producers of jute.

K

KAFFIR-LILY   *See* CLIVIA

KAKI   *See* PERSIMMON

KALANCHOE

Originally from Africa and Asia, these tender succulents of the Stonecrop family are good subjects for indoor planting. Christmas-tree (*K. laciniata*), a particularly fragrant species, will produce light rose or pink flowers at Christmastime if its seed is sown in spring. Tom Thumb (*K. Blossfeldiana*) will also bloom at Christmas if given 13 hours of darkness a day starting in September. It is a dwarf species with waxy, toothed leaves and clusters of vivid red flowers. Other species of kalanchoe produce yellow, orange, scarlet, and purple flowers. Many are noted for the formation of plantlets on the leaf margins.

Kalanchoes require a well-drained soil that should be allowed to dry between waterings. They should also be given a sunny southern or eastern exposure. Propagation is by seed, leaf plantlet or cuttings air-dried for 24 hours prior to rooting.

Interesting species suitable for potted culture include *K. Daigremontiana,* which has brown green, tricornered arching leaves with many plantlets at the serrated leaf margins; the air plant or flopper (*K. pinnata*) whose leaf plantlets root in moist air; and panda plant (*K. tomentosa*) with white and brown fuzzy leaves.

Some species of kalanchoe are classified as *Bryophyllum,* but *Kalanchoe* is the preferred genus name.

See also HOUSE PLANTS, SUCCULENTS.

KALE   (*Brassica oleracea*)

Kale, or borecole, is hardy and lives over winter in latitudes as far north as Pennsylvania. It is an all-year plant since it is also resistant to heat and may be grown in summer, but its real merit is as a cool-weather green. In northern regions where it lives over winter, the last sowing should be about six weeks before frost so that the plants may become well established. It can follow any vegetable other than a cabbage or brassica crop.

Planting and Culture: Like all brassicas, kale is a heavy feeder and likes fertile, fine-textured soil. The quality of the entire cabbage group is closely associated with quick growth. For this they need both rotted manure or compost at planting time, and a side-dressing of organic nitrogen—about ⅓ ounce to a foot of ground—at intervals of three weeks during the summer. Lime is essential for all members of the Cabbage family. A liberal application of crushed calcium limestone or shell limestone should be applied to the area at the time of preparing the ground to assure good growth and make the plant food supplied by the previously applied compost readily available.

Kale develops best in deeply prepared,

loamy soil. It will have neither good flavor nor texture if grown in either light, sandy or heavy, clayey soils.

The best garden varieties of kale are low-growing, spreading plants with thick, crinkled, curly leaves. They may be sown in the central states from early spring on until a few weeks before the first hard frost. When sown in the fall, the seed may be broadcast like those of turnips. If sown in the spring, when weeds are especially active, plant the seed in rows 30 inches apart and later thin plants to 16 inches apart. One packet of seed will be enough for a family of four or five persons.

Dwarf, curly-leaved varieties of kale can be direct-seeded for an attractive, edible border.

In preparing the seedbed, dig in small amounts of lime and liberal amounts of well-decomposed manure or other types of organic matter. Broadcast or plant the seed, and cover them lightly by raking the soil over them. When the sprouts are two or more inches high, scatter humus lightly along the sides of the row, and around the individual plants, but do not allow it to go nearer than three inches from the stems of the plants.

It will bear repeating that, like all other members of this Cabbage family, one cannot expect to obtain top-quality kale if the growth of the plants is hindered by lack of nutrients and water, and so is unable to make the rapid growth necessary for its highest development. If this growth appears to be slow, side-dress the plants with the following application: Dissolve two cups of stable manure in 12 quarts of water and let the solution stand for 24 hours. At the end of this time, make a narrow furrow three inches away from the plants, and pour into it one cup of the liquid for each foot of the row. Two weeks later, make a similar application, this time placing the solution six inches away from the plants.

Mulches are especially valuable in growing kale, for a large part of the root system develops near the surface and runs through the soil almost horizontally across the rows. For this reason cultivation should be shallow. A mulch will not only conserve moisture and keep the soil cool in the heat of summer, but will also make it possible for the kale roots to feed on the topmost two or three inches of soil. Place your mulch during the latter part of May or early in June.

Kale may be harvested either by cutting the entire plant, or by taking the larger leaves while they are still young. Old kale is stringy and tough and of little use in the diet. Harvesting from the first planting in the spring can usually begin the first week in June. A crop planted near the middle of August should be ready for cutting by the middle of October.

Insect and Disease Control: The worst enemies of kale are the flea beetles, which eat holes in the leaves; aphids, which suck the juice of the plant on the undersides of the leaves and stems; and the Herculean beetle which, with its masses of eggs, is easily seen and picked off by hand. For control of flea beetles and aphids, *see* INSECT CONTROL. Like all garden vegetables, kale is least vulnerable to pests when quality seed is used, when the soil is periodically enriched with organic matter and when careful mulching is employed.

Kale is valuable for its vitamin C content and, though it is rather coarse, it can be combined with other greens in a salad or used as a garnish. Its best table use, however, will be to boil it as one would spinach. The cooking liquid when mixed with others makes a good soup stock and healthful drink. Popular varieties include Blue Scotch or Dwarf Curled, Dwarf Blue Curled Vates, Dwarf Scotch, and Siberian. The latter is the most tender and of the most delicate flavor.

See also COLLARD.

KALMIA

This genus of evergreen shrubs includes mountain laurel (*K. latifolia*), pale laurel (*K. poliifolia*) and sheep laurel (*K. angustifolia*). Kalmias have showy pink, white or purple flowers, and prefer a shady location in a humus-rich, moist, acid soil. If planted in a dry or wind-exposed location, be sure to use a mulch of oak leaves or a similar acid organic material. Sheep laurel, also known as dwarf laurel,

grows two to three feet high, and is hardy throughout the country. This species is best suited for mass plantings, though its leaves are considered poisonous to animals. Pale laurel is a two-foot-high shrub that grows mostly in meadows and bogs in the North only. It produces rose-colored flowers.

See also MOUNTAIN LAUREL.

KEI APPLE   *See* UMKOKOLO

KELP

A loosely defined group of large brown seaweeds, especially the families Laminariaceae and Fucaceae, kelp has been found valuable as a soil conditioner. It is rich in potash, 2.25 to 6.25 percent, and nitrogen, 1.7 to 2.5 percent; and has about .5 percent phosphoric acid.

See also SEAWEED.

KENTUCKY BLUEGRASS
See LAWN

KIDNEY BEAN
(*Phaseolus vulgaris*)

Kidney bean is a bushy variety of shell bean, usually red, favored for stewing, baking and salad making.

See also BEANS.

KINNIKINICK   *See* UVA-URSI

KITCHEN WASTES

Kitchen wastes represent a tremendous potential of organic matter which ought to be returned to the soil. Reports indicate that the average United States citizen is responsible for creating from 150 to 300 pounds of garbage a year. At present, most cities destroy garbage, burning it, burying it or dumping it into the sea. With the environmental and economic impact of sea dumping and landfilling becoming increasingly untenable in recent years, some cities have been adopting various methods of municipal composting, whereby all the city's garbage is composted and reduced to a fine material suitable for garden and agricultural use.

Almost all kitchen refuse is excellent compost material, the only exceptions being grease, oil and animal fats.

Some gardeners make a successful practice of burying kitchen wastes directly in the garden. This can be done either in long trenches, with the vegetable plantings eventually made on top of the covered trench, or in a pit, which allows you to put everything out of sight, eliminate any chance of odor and still make use of the decayed wastes in the spring. When the garbage is placed in trenches as described above, it is well to rotate the position of the trenches on a three-year rotation.

See also COMPOSTING, GARBAGE FOR COMPOST, MUNICIPAL COMPOSTING.

KNIPHOFIA

Often called torch lily and flame flower, these perennial plants of the Lily family begin growing in early spring, and by June make thick clumps of long grassy leaves. From these arise bare slender stems topped by long clusters of tiny tube-shaped flowers. The flowers at the bottom of the cluster open first. Sometimes they fade to a lighter color so that the cluster has a two-tone effect. Kniphofias are good for cutting and come in shades of red, orange, yellow, and white.

Easily grown in moist, rich soil and full sun, the only care kniphofias need is an annual feeding of manure and a straw mulch for the winter. They are best planted in spring and given a lot of room. All kniphofias grow from two to four feet tall.

KNITBONE   *See* COMFREY

KNOTWEED   *See* POLYGONUM

KOHLRABI   (*Brassica oleracea*)

It must be admitted that nobody seems to know where the kohlrabi comes from and how it got to be the way it is today. It has been called "the mongrel of the vegetable kingdom" because it is like a "turnip growing on a cabbage root."

Culture: Though kohlrabi grows equally well in hot or cold weather, for best results it should be grown in the cool days of spring or fall. The species is naturally a cool-weather plant which matures rapidly within 12 weeks. It will grow well at high altitudes, provided it has a growing period of at least 80 days.

Soil should be rich, well-drained loam enriched with plenty of humus. Green manure previously turned under gives good results. Compost, barnyard manures and old mulches are also very satisfactory.

Make sure the soil is not too acid. Lime, in the form of fine-ground limestone, should be added when the pH falls below 5.5.

Planting: Because kohlrabi is a very hardy and fast-growing vegetable, three sowings can be made in temperate zones—in April, toward the end of May and in early July. Plants can also be started in the house or cold frame and later transplanted, but better results will be obtained if the seeds are sown directly into the garden.

Make a shallow furrow and drop about ten seeds to one foot of row, or about ⅛ ounce of seed to 100 feet. Cover the seed with almost an inch of soil. Firm with your foot and mark the row, which should be 15 to 18 inches apart from its neighbor.

When thinned, the plants should stand about four inches apart. The culls can be transplanted in another section of the garden, thus extending your harvest season. The shock of transplanting retards the growth process and the thinned-out plants come to maturity later than the original stand of kohlrabi.

Rapid growth is a must. Slow-growing plants are tough and the flesh is strong. Kohlrabi should grow in soil that is always moderately moist. Shallow cultivation is also important because the young roots spread out just under the soil surface. Until the plants are tall enough for mulching, just scrape between the rows with a sharp hoe.

If you want to give the plants a booster feeding, side-dress them with an organic fertilizer after they have been thinned. Loosen the soil between the plants and in the rows before putting on a thick mulch, making sure to keep the cultivation shallow.

Harvesting: Harvest the plants while they are young and tender, about 80 days after sowing. Kohlrabi tastes best when the

A moist soil that is rich in humus and weed-free will encourage rapid growth of kohlrabi and make for tender, mild-flavored stems.

bulb is small and tender, about 1½ to two inches in diameter.

If they're growing faster than you can use them, harvest the bulbs and store them in a cool basement. Or bury them deep in the soil and cover them with straw or hay. They will keep crisp and fresh well into the winter.

Kohlrabi should always be cooked in its skin to preserve flavor. The sliced root may be simmered and the bulb steamed or boiled for winter meals. Kohlrabi can also be eaten raw or sliced into midsummer salads.

It's a good practice to keep the ground working and improving after you have gathered kohlrabi. Plant snap beans and turn them under when they begin to form pods. They will release plenty of nitrogen right into the soil as they decay. In this way you will fertilize your garden and get it ready for the following year with very little extra effort.

Varieties: Early White Vienna is a good variety for freezing. Early Purple Vienna is a popular type known for its tenderness.

KOLKWITZIA

K. amabilis is the only species of this particularly beautiful flowering shrub, sometimes known as beauty bush. A slender shrub with a graceful, arching, elegant habit of growth, kolkwitzia reaches a height and spread of six to eight feet when fully matured. It is not a rampant grower and takes about three years in the nursery to become a decent-sized plant. The very fragrant flowers that cover the plant in early June are tubular and have a white to pinkish cast.

KUDZU   (*Pueraria lobata*)

Though originally thought of as drought insurance for farmers in the Southeast, kudzu is now recognized as a pest. Its rank growth is difficult to contain and nearly impossible to eradicate. Once started, it has been known to take over entire buildings, kill trees and choke out woodland. Anyone comtemplating planting kudzu is warned to consider carefully its drawbacks. The deep roots must be completely dug out to ensure its removal. Often this process takes several years. It grows well in Pennsylvania, New York, Illinois, Ohio, and Nova Scotia, according to reports from those areas. Its uses in agriculture are many, including erosion control, permanent pasture, hay, and as a soil improver in rotations. Kudzu hay makes a mulch equal in value to alfalfa; it could be used in orchards, spread over fields in sheet composting or mixed in the compost pile.

Propagation is by seed, cuttings, and root division. It shows large, three-part, lobed leaves, spikes of fragrant, purple flowers and large, flat, hairy seedpods.

Kudzu is a legume, a member of the Bean family, with all the desirable qualities of that plant group, including the tendency to serve as a host for nitrogen-fixing bacteria. A deep-rooted perennial, its roots go beyond the farmed-out top inches of soil to eight feet and more to utilize minerals previously of no value to the farmer. It does have limitations of climate—a severe winter of temperatures of $-20°F.$ ($-28.89°C.$) will probably kill the roots—and it needs irrigation where rainfall is under 20 inches a year.

Kudzu resembles a grapevine; its large leaves protect the soil from torrential rains during the growing season, and after frost has killed the tops, these leaves form so perfect a mulch that water loss on the steepest slopes where it has been grown is only 2 percent. Kudzu is well liked by all forms of livestock, including cattle, horses, sheep, hogs, goats, rabbits, and poultry. Kudzu is a high-protein feed, testing as high as 18 percent and comparing favorably with alfalfa in every respect, except that it is lower in calcium when grown on acid soils.

The Georgia Experiment Station gives this analysis of cured kudzu hay: protein, 11.3 per-

Once planted as a drought-resistant, protein-rich forage crop, kudzu is now recognized as a tenacious pest that is almost impossible to control.

cent; crude fat, 2.2 percent; crude fiber, 35.1 percent; nitrogen-free extract, 39.2 percent; calcium, 1.4 percent; phosphorus, .2 percent; other minerals, 5.3 percent; and moisture, 5.3 percent.

KUMQUAT   (*Fortunella*)

A dwarf evergreen citrus tree grown extensively throughout China and Japan, this hardy relative of the orange is grown as a prized ornamental in the warmer regions of this country. It can tolerate temperatures as low as 15°F. (−9.44°C.) while dormant, though not for prolonged periods.

Dense and shrubby, kumquats generally reach a height and spread of ten to 15 feet. They have narrow, dark green leaves and small, fragrant, white flowers that bloom in spring. Thorns are either very small or absent. The fruit of the kumquat is small, oval or round, and golden orange. When well ripened, the fruit's outer rind is spicy, the inner, sweet, and the juice, acidic. Kumquats can be eaten raw or made into marmalade, jelly or crystallized fruit.

Though usually grown outdoors in orchards and hedges, most varieties of kumquat are suitable for potted culture. *Fortunella margarita* is a dwarf species often grown as a house plant. The season for kumquat production begins in October and extends through winter.

Heavy pruning, which should be done during the winter after the fruit is harvested, increases the size and quantity of fruit. Kumquats may have one or two crops of bloom and settings of fruit.

See also CITRUS, ORANGE.

L

LABURNUM

This is a genus of small ornamental trees of the Pea family. Flowers, borne in May or June, are long hanging clusters of yellow pealike blossoms, which give the trees their common name of golden-chain tree. Leaves are light green to yellow.

The trees thrive in any soil if it is well drained, and may be planted in full sun or partial shade. They may be successfully used in city plantings. Propagation is by seed (which germinates easily), by layering or by grafting. Fruits of all species are poisonous.

Common laburnum (*L. anagyroides* or *L. vulgare*) is the less hardy of the two principal species, but it can be grown in central New York State, in the southern New England states, and along the Pacific Coast. In the colder regions, its flower buds are damaged by spring frosts. Its flower clusters are about eight inches long and open in May. Two interesting varieties are Aureum, which has yellow leaves, and Autumnale, which flowers a second time in September.

Scotch laburnum (*L. alpinum*) is a more hardy species, and, because it blooms two weeks later, its buds are not so likely to be frost-killed. It is stiffer and more upright than the common species, which has a tendency to droop, and its flower clusters are longer. Scotch laburnum is hardy as far north as Massachusetts.

LACEWING
(*Chrysopa californica*)

The lacewing is an insect enemy of many garden pests. Egg cases can be purchased commercially.

See also INSECT CONTROL.

LACINARIA   See LIATRIS

LADDER FERN   See NEPHROLEPIS

LADINO CLOVER   See CLOVER

LADYBUG

The familiar ladybug is probably the best-known beneficial insect in the garden. Both the cherry-colored adults and lizardlike larvae are important in making poison-free gardening as easy as it is. Larvae have the best appetites, consuming aphids, asparagus beetle eggs, Colorado potato beetles, grape rootworm, bean thrips, alfalfa weevils, and chinch bugs. The beetles specialize on aphids, scale, mealybugs, whiteflies, and spider mites.

Ladybugs are commercially available, shipped to the consumer in a dormant state. But before you place an order, make sure that a good number of beetles aren't already at

The several species of lady beetles are some of the most valuable garden insects, for they feed on aphids, scales and mealybugs.

hibernate in the refrigerator for several more weeks.

After you have received your order, mulch and lightly water the garden. Then, in the late afternoon or early evening, carefully place the beetles about 15 to 20 paces apart at the base of plants. Do not scatter them as you would sow grain, since rough handling, especially in warm weather, may cause them to fly away. As night approaches, the beetles will seek protection in the cool, moist mulch and, the next morning, they will climb the nearest plant and begin feeding.

About 30,000 individuals are considered adequate for protecting ten acres of crops. To bring this number into perspective, recall that the beetles are so tiny that it takes 1,500 of them to make an ounce. If the weather is warm and sunny, your stocked beetles will mate and lay eggs in a day or two. In 15 more days you should already have a second generation of larvae hard at work.

work. The naturally occurring population typically keeps pace with the insect meals at hand, but if you feel your supply of ladybugs is deficient, take a few precautions to ensure that they get off to a good start.

Don't stock too early. If there are not enough pests in your garden patch to sustain them, they will either feed on what is there and then fly away in search of more insect food, or else starve to death. If pests are evident but not plentiful, place some ladybugs in the garden and store the rest in the refrigerator (not in the freezer) until needed. They will

LAGERSTROEMIA

This is a genus of shrubs and small trees of the Loosestrife family. Flowers with fringed petals grow in loose terminal clusters, and may be white, pink, red, or purple, depending on variety. The blooming period lasts for several months in summer. Propagation is by seed or cuttings, which are easily rooted. Seedlings often produce bloom the first year, and cuttings either the first or second year.

Crape myrtle (*L. indica*) is the principal species grown in the United States. It is hardy only in the South and north to seaboard Maryland. This myrtle is root-hardy to Massachusetts if the roots are protected, but the tops will die back each year. Vigorous growth and bloom will follow the next spring. When grown indoors in a pot or tub, it is cut back severely each fall, and will bloom several times during the year. Young plants grown outdoors in the South must also be cut back almost to the ground after blooming, or growth the following year will go into foliage and the bloom will be sparse. A dressing of manure or compost should be spread around plants in spring. After root systems have become large enough to supply food for both foliage and flowers, heavy pruning may be continued if a shrub is desired or lighter pruning done if it is to be allowed to become a flowering tree. Trees attain a height of about 20 feet.

Queen's crape myrtle (*L. speciosa*) is a tropical tree growing to 50 feet that is suited only to southern Florida and southern California. Its mauve to purple flowers grow to three inches in diameter, and its leathery leaves to one foot long. It is extremely showy when in bloom.

LAMB'S-QUARTERS
See WILD PLANTS, EDIBLE

LAND CLEARING

Land clearing was perhaps the most fundamental of all farming work at one time. The pioneers had to clear the forests before they could plant crops to sustain themselves. All too often, they farmed out the land within a few years, and then moved on.

Although woodland is still an important resource on the small farm or homestead, today many farms have one or more patches of land overgrown with scrub timber and brush that could be put into pasture or crop production if cleared. Homesteaders often settle on properties that haven't been farmed in years. Such land must be cleared before crop production can begin.

If the land has a good production potential and can be cleared at reasonable cost, it's worth the time and work. Land clearing can be done at any time of the year when other work is not pressing. Winter is the traditional time of year for this job for a number of reasons, but farmers and homesteaders today can fit land clearing into their spare time. New tools have made the job of clearing land easier, and chain saws, especially, have cut the labor and time in clearing land to a fraction of what it once was. Others find a workout with the axe and machete enjoyable.

At one time, brush, branches and leaves from land clearing had to be disposed of by burning. Modern machines like wood chippers and shredders make valuable soil-building material from the brush. Such machines can be purchased cooperatively with other farmers, or, if privately owned, can be leased to others for use on their farms.

Primary Considerations: Two things have to be considered before attacking any overgrown land.

First, decide to what use the land can be put when cleared. Many a farmer has regretted letting a high-priced, poorly trained custom operator talk him into having land cleared haphazardly. Some wooded land, for instance, with careful thinning and selective cutting could be built up into a fine woodlot that would yield steady income for decades. Other land, because of its steepness, stoniness or poor drainage, would be best left merely as a wildlife refuge. Put into pasture or crops, it might well deteriorate to desert conditions in a very short time.

If you have doubts as to the advisability of clearing any land for production, let an expert decide. Your county agent will help you figure out whether a given piece of land is suitable for cropping without requiring stringent conservation measures, intricate drainage systems or other practices that might be costly. The soil surveyor who draws up a soil map of your farm, or the Soil Conservation Service technician who makes up a complete conservation plan for the farm, are excellent persons to consult. You may find that some overgrown land you had thought practically worthless can grow crops with a suitable rotation, or will make permanent pastures as good as any you already have.

A second consideration involves fertility and its maintenance. The soil of the overgrown land may be deep and rich or thin and infertile. To the expense of clearing must be added the cost of whatever may be needed to bring the soil up to satisfactory fertility. Even if you plan to grow legumes, it will probably require some lime, phosphate rock and manure to establish them, and soil tests may even show trace element deficiencies.

Have the soil tested before clearing, and use a soil corer to study its depth, structure and subsoil characteristics. Knowing about these and about the degree of slope will help you make a rough estimate of the total cost of conservation and fertility measures necessary to put the land into production. If the profit from the crop you intend to grow pays back the cost of clearing and fertilizing within a reasonable time, lay out a plan for clearing the land.

Clearing Costs: The costs of clearing may vary greatly for different types of land

and different methods. You may find, for example, that there are enough large trees on the area to pay for clearing if they are cut and sold as cord or pulpwood.

A self-propelled circular saw or a one-man chain saw can be used for many other jobs around the farm. Many modern saws are light enough to be held over your head to get high branches. Some circular saws have their own wheels, others are hand carried and some work from the power takeoff of a tractor. Some people prefer to work with hand tools, which do not make a noise or smell as power tools do. Certainly, the very best axe, machete, grubbing hoe, or bush axe is just as useful, will last longer and is less expensive than a power tool.

A couple of swipes with an axe may be the most practical way to take out saplings and scrubby brush—and it's certainly the cheapest. However, sometimes a patch is totally overgrown with briars and saplings, and the land is needed in a hurry. In this case, it's probably better to hire someone to go over the land with a bulldozer. Costs for this work vary depending on how thick the growth is and on the type of equipment on the bulldozer. To make sure you are getting someone who is qualified to do the job, check around with others in your area before hiring a bulldozer operator. You don't want your topsoil ripped up and left to wash away with the first rain.

After the land is cleared, cover the soil as soon as possible so erosion cannot steal your newly won topsoil. Mulch the land with organic materials or plant a green manure crop on it until you're ready to seed it to pasture or row crops.

Disposing of the Brush: Don't burn the brush! Use a wood chipper or shredder to chew it up for mulch. The plant food and organic matter in an acre of brush and branches can be worth much if used for soil building and protection. Brush can also be used, along with corncobs and other organic material, to fill gullies—it will catch eroding soil, and rot, gradually sealing the gully.

Wood chips make fine bedding—in some respects better than straw—for animals and poultry. You may find a ready market for wood chips if you live in a dairy- or poultry-raising area. Deep mulches of wood chips are fine for orchards and berry bushes as well as for vegetables and other crops. Don't work the material into the soil unless it is well rotted, or it will temporarily tie up the nitrogen needed by crops. *See also* MULCH.

Depending on the kind and size of growth, some brush waste may be used for kindling or stove wood when cut to length and dried. If there are large stumps in the field, they may be left to rot, or chopped out and pulled from the ground. Large stumps can be dragged to the edge of the field, and if pulled close together can serve as a stump fence. Such a fence will not foil goats, but it may discourage cattle from wandering.

LANDSCAPING

Landscape design is primarily the arrangement of outside spaces for use. The charming and peaceful gardens which appear so delightfully natural and uncontrived seldom, if ever, just happen. They are generally the result of a great deal of planning and good basic design. It is of fundamental importance, therefore, that the landscape pattern is designed before the planting design is even considered. No amount of planting can cover up a lack of planning.

While there are many things to consider in the planning of a garden, a good design is by no means beyond the amateur if he adheres to the basic design principles. But even before these principles are considered, he must decide what he wants from his garden. What activities are to take place there? Who will be using the garden? How much time and money does he wish to spend there?

Secondly, consider what is already growing in the area. Each site will have its own built-in character which may be emphasized or altered. What is the existing topography of the site? If there is a definite slope, the design of the garden will have to be adapted to it. Are there any large or interesting specimens worth preserving? What are the ecological conditions of the site? You will want to encourage plants that are right for the soil type and climate. Are there any views you wish to emphasize or camouflage?

With these considerations in mind, you are ready to begin planning the landscape design. The established facts of the site should be accurately put down on paper. Graph paper and use of a simple scale will increase the accuracy. The boundary of the site and the existing features should be noted, as well as anything worth keeping. Views you wish to emphasize can be indicated by arrows. Roughly outline the areas you wish to designate to your various activities.

Next, using tracing paper laid over the plan, begin to evolve a pattern which will be pleasing in itself. The basic pattern of the garden should combine the site functions and natural features in one overall design.

The designer must keep in mind the overall scene while creating a series of small pictures which relate to each other within the landscape. The fewer individual eye-catchers the better.

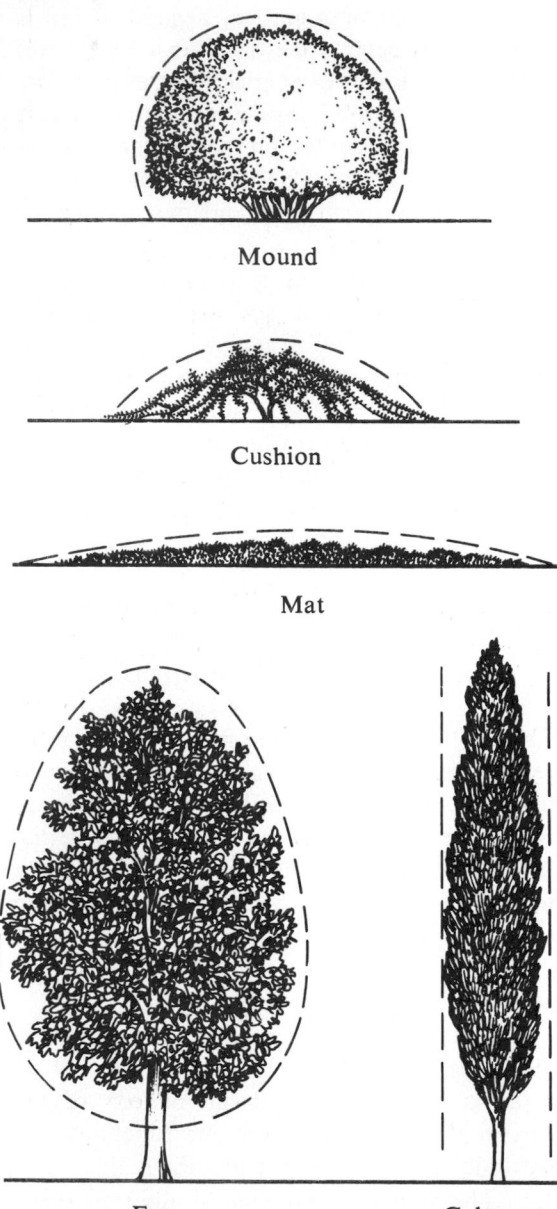

Mound

Cushion

Mat

Egg   Columnar

Shown here are just a few of the typical form characters which should be considered, along with texture and color, when selecting plants for a landscape composition.

The final plan requires a knowledge of soil types, weather and levels. It will take into consideration types of surfaces, necessary drainage and structures. The planting design, which will include plant varieties used structurally in the composition as well as those of horticultural interest, will evolve from this final plan.

Of fundamental importance is the definite and concrete recognition of form, scale, accent, color and texture. By following these principles of design, you will ensure that your planting effectively carries out the landscape plan.

Form: The form, which has already been determined in your plan, must be created by the planting design. This will include the form type of the various plants that make up the composition, as well as the resulting effect when these plants are built into particular groups and masses. To develop a satisfying effect in the landscape one should not have dissimilar collections of flowers or plant forms, but should use a repetition of form character with just enough contrast introduced to lend variety and offer subdued points of interest.

One should know what form character to choose for any composition to be designed. Among the most common are: cushion form—an effect obtained by using the prostrate junipers; mound form—obtained by using boxwood or the barberry or privet; egg form—obtained by using the maples; mat form—by using creeping myrtle; and columnar form—by using poplar.

Plant forms are indicative of character, moods and personalities, and should be chosen for a particular location with this in mind. Take, for instance, the delicacy of the birch tree. Its graceful lines indicate a gay personality which will create a mood of cheerfulness in any composition. Then there is the quiescent personality of the weeping willow. The rugged individualism of the sturdy oak gives an air of towering strength. Compare a group of birch trees with an oak grove and you will discover the importance of character forms. Airiness, grace, delicacy, trimness, power, strength: these traits are the outcome of line and shadow in the plants and they give the entire composition personality and character.

Vertical and horizontal elements have dominant and recessive characters, and work to determine the effectiveness of the plan.

Vertical-lined forms (such as hollyhock, delphinium and foxglove) contribute to development of vertical effects made in the garden. They are at their best when planted in groups located at the back margin and occasionally allowed to extend toward the front.

Horizontal-lined forms which are not defined sharply produce a restful and quiet effect. Sweet William, iris and peony are representative of these, and should be planted in masses which are longer than wide, rather than in groups or as single specimens.

By studying various deciduous trees and shrubs in the winter, you can gain a better idea of their shape and lines. Still, one must imagine how the trees will look when they are clothed with summer foliage. Evergreens, of course, can be studied for their form at any time.

The contour of the land where the planting is to be made will have a modifying effect on the forms of plants and trees, and will control the direction in which they are laid out.

Departing from the dominant forms— those basic plants used in largest amounts—is necessary to prevent the planting from becoming monotonous as well as to create an accent. Go about this slowly, however; if the dominant forms are varied to create an accent, it must be remembered that the more sudden the variation, the stronger the contrast.

Scale: Scale is another important factor to consider. By scale is meant the apparent size of trees in comparison to the size of the landscape to be used.

Height should also be given consideration in a landscape composition for the relationship between height and area determines the scale with which you must work. If all plants are of similar height, the result is flat, uninteresting and out of proportion.

In expanded estate-type plantings, the larger forms such as elm, red oak, black ash, and hickory can be used effectively to obtain a desired result or to frame a smaller scaled perspective.

Examples among the larger trees include: cylinder type—tulip tree; pear type—hickory (both pignut and shagbark); vase type— Chinese elm and hackberry; spiral type—all larger conifers.

If you are working with a small confined site, be sure to select plant varieties which are fitting in size and proportion. The pattern of your planting should break up the space so that the whole is not visible at one glance. This will make the area appear larger and offer surprise. It is also possible to use shadow and perspective to increase the apparent size of your garden.

Accent: An accent is a point of attention that catches the eye momentarily, then allows it to pass over the remainder of the picture. An important location or object can be accented by a change of line, a change of position, a contrast of foliage textures, or a contrast of color.

The important aspects of the garden should be accented so as to avoid monotony. On the other hand, too many accents, a very common fault with amateurs, can make the landscape wearisome. If accents are not placed properly, they will destroy the balance of the landscape, and ruin the desired harmonizing effect.

Color: Because the effect of color is largely psychological, and because it is influenced, as it appears in the garden, by light, shadow, climate, and humidity, it is nearly impossible to lay down rules for its use. Using one of the standard color charts it is comparatively simple to determine what plants to use and where to place them in order to obtain proper color balance in the garden.

While color is not the most important thing in gardening, it does affect form and texture and, hence, is a means of creating fine composition. Good color harmony must not be considered to the exclusion of other, more important principles of artistic expression. Use color for accents and emphasis, balance, repetition, and sequence.

Texture: Some trees, shrubs and flowers have a smooth appearance, while others have a rough one. These smooth and rough appearances directly result from variations of size, appearance and shape among the parts of the plants.

Texture can mean more than just smooth and rough appearance. These two qualities are the basic ones, but there are others such as: fineness and coarseness, lightness and heaviness, denseness and thinness, flexibility and stiffness.

Many of these factors change with the seasons. Take, for instance, the dogwoods. In the spring their red, yellow and gray bark makes a beautiful background, and as the summer brings on the green foliage there is still a hint of these shades of bark showing through the green leaves, providing another type of texture.

Remember to avoid too great a contrast as well as too great a variety of textures, or you may end up with a discordant result. Also, in using the various textures in landscape design, strive for a simple effect, one that involves scale relationship, sequence and balance.

If you keep these in mind you will be able to design a garden that is pleasing.

LANGBEINITE

Langbeinite is a naturally occurring mined substance used primarily as a source of potash. Because it is a soluble salt, some organic agriculturalists do not consider it to be a bona fide organic amendment in the same sense as lime or phosphate rock. Langbeinite contains 22 percent potash, 11 percent magnesium and 22 percent sulfur, all in soluble form. Applications vary according to soil tests, but 300 to 600 pounds to the acre is average for row crops where potash or sulfur are low.

LANTANA

This tropical shrub is often grown as a potted plant indoors. Red or yellow sage (*L. Camara*) is a very popular showy shrub in the South. In the northern parts of the country, it is usually grown as a cool greenhouse plant. It grows to about four feet high and has yellow flowers that change to red. *L. montevidensis* or *L. Sellowiana* has a trailing, vinelike habit of growth.

LANTERN PLANT
See PHYSALIS

LARCH   (*Larix*)

Larch is the common name for any tree of the genus *Larix* of the Pine family. Larches are deciduous conifers which shed their needle-like leaves each year. The American or eastern larch (*L. laricina*) is also known as the tamarack. It is the only pine native to the Northeast that loses its leaves each fall. This larch grows best in low, wet places, and is often found along the boggy banks of a lake or stream. It is occasionally planted as an ornamental.

The European larch (*L. decidua*) is a tall and graceful species introduced from Europe for its ornamental value. It is also of value for its lumber, which is tough, elastic and extremely durable. The tree yields Venetian turpentine, and its bark is used in tanning.

Leaves of the larch are narrow, one to 1½ inches long, growing in pinelike tufts on short spurs, or distributed spirally on rapidly growing branches. When the young growth appears in spring, it is misty green in color. Leaves are yellow green while those of *L. laricina* are a pale blue green. Male and female flowers grow on the same tree, and cones grow to one or 1½ inches, with woody persistent scales. The European larch will grow in almost any soil in an open situation, with sufficient moisture.

The principal enemy of the larch is the larch sawfly, whose black-headed larva attacks the leaves. The fly hibernates over the winter in surface litter, and lays its eggs in spring on new shoots. The best preventive is to remove all litter from below the trees in the fall.

Often planted as an ornamental is the Japanese larch (*L. leptolepis*), a fast-growing species which grows farther south than the European or American larches. It will grow to 90 feet, has a scaly reddish bark and produces oval cones.

The Dahurian larch (*L. Gmelinii*), a northern species, attains a wider spread than the other species. Its shoots are brown, and its small pink cones grow no more than an inch long.

The only northeastern deciduous pine, the eastern larch prefers a swampy area but will also do well on dry land.
(*Courtesy of U.S. Forest Service*)

LARKSPUR   *See* DELPHINIUM

LARVA

The larval stage is the second stage in complete metamorphosis. It is followed by the pupa, a resting period in which the insect becomes an adult. Larvae of butterfly are caterpillars, maggots and grubs.

See also INSECT.

LATANIA

This genus of fan palms is native to the Mascarene Islands in the Indian Ocean. As tropical plants, they are seldom grown outdoors in this country. One species (*L. lontaroides*), however, can sometimes be found growing in southern Florida where the night temperatures remain above 60°F. (15.56°C.). *L. Loddigesii* is strictly a greenhouse specimen. Unlike *L. lontaroides* which has red or purple leaves, this species has attractive blue green fans whose individual segments measure two feet at maturity. Young leafstalks are barbed and are red, fading to green as they get older. The barbs become hairy bristles. Both latanias have stout, ringed trunks.

Like all palms, the latanias need manure or leaf mold-enriched soil, whether they are planted indoors or out. They want a reasonable amount of moisture during their growing periods, April to October, after which they are practically dormant, especially when grown indoors. At this time the potted specimens should be allowed to become almost dry.

·After nights have become warm, potted latanias may be placed in the border, with their pots sunk deep in the earth. They should be given a protected position, with partial shade. A feeding of manure water about every second week during the growing season will promote general health. Before the nights turn cool in September, the pots should be returned to indoor positions. Gradually withhold water so that the plants can enter dormancy.

LATHHOUSE

A wooden framed structure made primarily of slats spaced so as to reduce excessive sunlight is called a lathhouse. Used in both private gardening and commercial cultivation, lathhouses provide plants with shade and protection from arid, moisture-sapping winds. A lathhouse has been described as a greenhouse without glass since humidity tends to increase within the structure. In much the same way as mulch protects a plant's roots and keeps the ground cool, a lathhouse provides protection for the entire plant.

Although the laths can be either horizontal or vertical, the former is preferred because it provides a better distribution of sunlight. The laths are normally ¾ inch thick and spaced one inch apart. Redwood is a good construction material since it weathers well, requires no paint and is resistant to termites.

A typical lathhouse is 20 feet long and 10 feet wide. Sills are 2-by-6 inches and rest on standard-sized cinder blocks. Wall studs and rafters should be 2x4s on 4-foot centers. Smaller lathhouses, even 4-by-6-foot structures, have been built. A lathhouse may be built adjacent to an existing structure such as a garage, greenhouse, shed, or barn.

The protective environment inside a lathhouse is particularly suited to growing tuberous begonias, African violets, achimenes, fuchsias, gloxinias, azaleas, camellias, summering Christmas cactus, and other plants that require filtered sunlight.

A "house" constructed of ¾-inch-thick laths spaced about one inch apart, creates a shady, protected spot where house plants will thrive during summer months.

LATHYRUS

A large genus of plants of the Pea family, lathyrus is found throughout the world, but occurs most often in the North Temperate Zone. Annuals and perennials growing erect or in vines are included in the genus. Some climb by means of tendrils which are extensions of the main leafstalk. Showy flowers of the cultivated species come in colors ranging from white through yellow, pink, blue, purple, and red. Most species are cultivated for their flowers, but several are grown in the south of Europe for fodder and for their edible lentillike seed.

The most important species is *L. odoratus* or sweet pea, an annual flowering vine climbing to six feet, but some dwarf or bush types are available. There are as many as six showy fragrant flowers to a stalk. Some of the hybrids have beautiful ruffled flowers. Propagated by seed sown in early spring, sweet peas require full sun, deeply prepared rich moist soil and cool temperatures.

The everlasting pea, *L. grandiflorus,* is a perennial which bears two or three rose lavender flowers on a stalk. It blooms continuously throughout most of the summer. It can be propagated from either seed or cuttings, and grows luxuriously once established in good garden loam and partial shade.

Also known as everlasting peas are *L. latifolius* and *L. sylvestris,* both perennials with habits similar to that of *grandiflorus.* Flowers are rose pink to white and a few cultivated forms are dark red. Vines grow somewhat taller than *grandiflorus,* and may be trained to cover porches or to trail over banks.

Two species of perennial peas used to bind sand in seaside gardens are *L. littoralis* on the Pacific coast, and *L. japonicus* on the Atlantic coast. The plants, which are both called beach pea, are quite similar, except that flower clusters of *japonicus* are usually larger and darker.

The edible grass pea, *L. sativus,* also called chickling vetch, is an annual which grows no more than two feet high. Flowers are white tinged with blue.

See also PEA, SWEET PEA.

LATOSOLS

The latosols form a group of zonal soils in the classification system used prior to 1965. These soils, and the laterites, which are similar, formed under hot, humid, forested conditions. They are characterized by their red color, low mineral content, low content of soluble constituents, high aggregate stability, and a number of other, more arcane properties. Modern classification systems call these soils oxisols.

LAUREL

The true laurel or bay tree (*Laurus nobilis*) is commonly grown as a large potted plant, pruned and trained for use as ornamental accent. It is also grown as a tree of up to 60 feet in height. The dark green glossy leaves

The native mountain laurel bears showy blossoms in early summer and presents a strong, dense foliage year-round.
(Courtesy of U.S. Forest Service)

are much used by florists in foliage arrangements. The laurel is propagated either by cuttings or seed. It thrives in humus-rich soil if given sufficient moisture. Wind-free, partially shaded sites are best.

Other plants called laurels include Alexandrian laurel (*Danae racemosa*), California laurel (*Umbellularia californica*), cherry laurel or laurel cherry (*Prunus caroliniana* and *P. Laurocerasus*), ground laurel or trailing arbutus (*Epigaea repens*), laurel oak (*Quercus Laurifolia*), laurel willow (*Salix pentandra*), laurelwood (*Calophyllum inophyllum*), mountain laurel (*Kalmia latifolia*), Portugal laurel (*Prunus lusitanica*), sheep laurel (*Kalmia angustifolia*), and spurge laurel (*Daphne laureola*).

See also MOUNTAIN LAUREL.

LAVATERA

Also known as tree mallow, this genus includes annuals, biennials and perennials that produce showy pink or purple flowers. *L. trimestris* is a hardy, summer-blooming annual that grows to six feet. *L. assurgentiflora*, a perennial that reaches more than ten feet high, is often used for a temporary screen in warmer climates. *L. arborea* is a biennial growing to ten feet.

LAVENDER   (*Lavandula*)

The true lavender is a small shrubby herb native to southern Europe and widely cultivated for its fragrant flowers and the valuable oils distilled from them.

Lavender is a many-branched, somewhat woody perennial that grows from 1½ to three feet high. Its narrow, gray green leaves are about two inches long, and small flowers are borne on stemmed, slender spikes. Smaller varieties are often used in the border, while the taller ones are recommended for informal hedges.

Known as common or English lavender, it is listed as both *L. officinalis* and *L. angustifolia,* sometimes called *L. Spica.* French lavender, a similar plant, is *L. dentata.* Lavender was a popular bath oil or soap scent for pre-Christian Greeks and Romans. This may have led to its generic name *Lavandula,* from the Latin *lavare,* meaning to wash. Lavender was eventually recognized for its medicinal value in Tudor England, where it served as a nerve stimulant, stomach settler and reliever of minor aches and pains. Lavender never gained the reputation as a panacea that other herbs did, however. Today, this herb's fragrance is its main attraction and makes it a principal in the English and French perfume industry.

Planting and Culture: The plant thrives best in light and rather dry soils well supplied with lime, but can be grown in almost any well-drained loam. On low or wet land it is almost certain to winter-kill. The plant can be grown from seed, but is more readily propagated from cuttings or by division. In cold climates, the plants must be mulched well for winter protection. Early in spring the seedlings or rooted cuttings are set in the bed, 12 to 15 inches apart in rows spaced to suit the cultivation intended. Frequent and thorough cultivation is desirable.

Growth is slow, and the plants do not produce any considerable quantity of flowers for several years, but full crops may be expected some time thereafter if the plants are given proper care. The flowering tops are harvested when in full bloom, and if used for

True lavender is a fairly tender aromatic herb that requires well-drained soil, full sun, and in cold regions, good winter protection.

the production of oil, are distilled at once without drying. If the dry flowers are wanted, the tops are carefully dried in the shade at 90 to 100°F. (32.22 to 37.78°C.) and the flowers later stripped from the stems by hand.

Using: Lavender has many aromatic, medicinal and culinary qualities. It is often used in sachets and pillows to perfume linens, and in commercial colognes and scents, supporting a substantial perfume industry throughout Europe and America.

The scent is also used to repel moths, flies and mosquitoes when lavender oil is soaked in cotton balls and suspended from room ceilings.

The herb has also been considered an aid in treating nerve disorders, hoarseness, sore joints, and even toothaches. Lavender was employed as a vermifuge or antiseptic for wounds as late as World War I.

Finally, lavender has found its place in many American kitchens as a flavor enhancer. Lavender vinegar, which can be used in any way vinegar is used, can be made by mixing two parts vinegar, six parts rose water and one part spirits of lavender.

See also HERB.

LAVENDER COTTON
(*Santolina Chamaecyparissus*)

Lavender cotton is an evergreen shrubby perennial wtih spreading branches, blue gray leaves and a texture that makes it useful in knot and other formal herb gardens. It grows to a height of two feet and is used as a colorful accent plant in flower gardens as well. Lavender cotton is not consistently hardy in northern states. Green santolina (*S. virens*) is similar.

The plants are propagated from seed or, more commonly, from root cuttings. Santolinas grow best in full sun and medium-to-poor soil. Protection from snow is required.

The plant should be clipped, and can be used as a border or low-growing hedge. Santolina is valued for the moth-repelling properties of its leaves. Oil of santolina is used in the manufacture of perfumes.

LAWN

It isn't difficult to have a healthy, lush lawn without chemical fertilizers, toxins and herbicides, providing you pick a suitable variety of grass and take care of seasonal chores.

Which grass is best for you? The accompanying map sections the country into four regions—areas derived from the more than two dozen climatic zones that can be defined. These regions serve to simplify the process of deciding which grasses you should consider.

Region A: Region A is in two pieces, one in the Northeast and the other occupying the Pacific Northwest. Homeowners in both locations typically use a variety of Kentucky bluegrass. Merion has been called the superior variety, but it has several disadvantages. It is susceptible to striped smut fungus and to rust;

it is not cheap; and it requires a good deal of potash to offset nitrogen in the soil. Fylking is an alternative bluegrass variety, offering resistance to rust and striped smut, and needing less care than Merion. Baron, Park and Newport are being used as successors to Merion.

It should be kept in mind that bluegrass is dormant during the summer, which is the way it weathers the heat. It appears a dry, rather brown, wiry turf. But with the cool days it resumes its normal green, holding its verdure until the ground freezes.

Bluegrass does not grow well in shade or on infertile, dry, or poorly drained land. It does not fight weeds very well at the beginning,

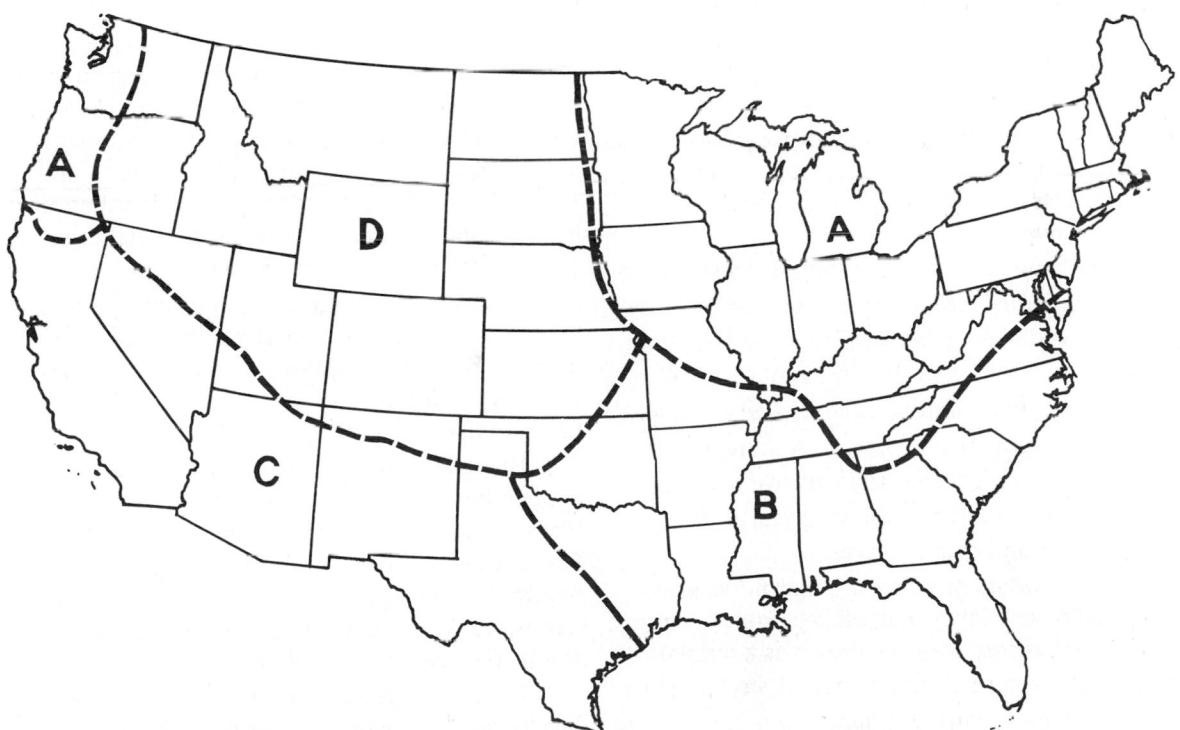

(Redrawn from R. Milton Carleton, Your Lawn: How to Make It and Keep It *[New York: Van Nostrand Reinhold Co., 1971], p. 34)*

as its turf is not as dense as a lawn of bent-grasses, but with time and proper management it will build up a healthy green carpet that will keep the weeds down.

This calls for high mowing—between 2½ and three inches, particularly in June, July and August—but the grass shouldn't go into the winter season more than two inches high. Fertilize in the spring and fall and soak the soil to a depth of six inches when watering.

Clover mixed with bluegrass will shade the lawn, keeping it green longer into the summer. Clover also fixes nitrogen from the air, feeding it to the soil.

Shady lawns in Region A should do well with a seed mixture such as Pennlawn or various fine-leaved fescue varieties. Mow these grasses at a height of from 1½ to two inches.

Tall fescues are not often recommended, as they have a coarse growth and must be heavily seeded. Bentgrasses, which are susceptible to many diseases, are not suited for most sites. They do find some use on shady lawns, taking frequent waterings and mowing to less than ¾ inch.

Redtop is a popular "nurse grass," used as a temporary ground cover until the more desirable varieties in the seed mixture take hold. It is very resistant to drought and does well on acid soil, but, unless planted very heavily, makes a poor-quality lawn. Although during its first season it forms an attractive fine-bladed light green cover, the following year it develops long stems and coarse leaves.

Ryegrasses are also popular nurse grasses that help new lawns get off to a quick, strong start. Sometimes they are grown as a temporary cover to be turned under several weeks before the permanent lawn is planted.

In Region A, *Zoysia japonica* is planted as plugs, ideally spaced on one-foot centers. In time it forms a dense green turf that excludes weeds. A drawback is that it turns brown each winter. This variety is very resistant to drought in the North.

Should you sow a mixture of seeds? Yes, for several reasons. First, a lawn composed of different varieties will not be wiped out by a disease fatal to a particular variety. And because varieties are at their best over different periods of the year, mixtures can assure a good color from spring until fall. Common Kentucky bluegrass is in itself a mixture of a great number of varieties, and the weaker ones will, over a period of several years, die off in favor of the stronger ones.

Regions B and C: The Bermudagrasses are to the South (and Southwest) what the bluegrasses are to the North. There are many varieties, each suited to a particular region or purpose. Bermudas with fine-textured leaves are available from local nurseries as sprigs. They require a good deal of nitrogen, and should have frequent watering, but are superior to common Bermuda. Mow at the height recommended for the variety you select.

Tiflawn is a deep green variety, finer in texture than the common Bermuda. It is very disease resistant, a vigorous grower which must be mowed closely and often or it will form a heavy mat.

Everglades No. 1 is finer and greener than Tiflawn but tends to grow prostrate. Ormond is coarser and more upright than Everglades. Three other varieties, Tiffine, Tifgreen and Bayshore, are used in fine lawns and golf greens. All require much maintenance, and are fine in texture and a medium green.

Recently, special zoysia grasses have been developed that equal or surpass the performance of these Bermudas. Lawns in some parts of Region B can be sown with Korean or Japanese lawn grass. *Zoysia tenuifolia* is suited to Florida only; it never needs mowing and does well in shade. Hardiest of the zoysias for this region is *Z. japonica,* which forms a fine-textured turf but undergoes a long brown dormant spell. It can be grown from seed, unlike others of the species. *Z. Matrella,* also known as Manilagrass, has the texture of Kentucky bluegrass, requires close mowing and is suited for the middle of Region B. Irrigated California lawns often are of this variety. It browns in the winter, and spreads rather slowly into a good turf. Emerald zoysia is an attractive green, with fine texture.

Bluegrasses may work in cool highlands and along the northern border of Region B. Some newer varieties can be grown in California.

Carpetgrass does well on moist, sandy and poor soils. It has some tolerance for shade but winter-kills north of Augusta, Georgia. This grass requires frequent mowing to keep it no more than one inch high, but otherwise needs little care.

Centipedegrass is considered the best low-maintenance lawn grass in the South. It requires less mowing, watering and fertilizing than other southern grasses. It resists insects and disease well but is vulnerable to saltwater spray and sensitive to a lack of iron.

While drought resistant, centipedegrass should be watered during dry periods. Do not plant it on a farm lawn, as it may escape into nearby pastures and destroy their grazing value. This variety spreads rapidly by short, creeping stems that form new plants at each node. It is established mostly with sod, but some seed is available.

If you must have a green winter lawn, ryegrasses can be sown over the existing lawn, but you run the risk that this grass will give serious competition to the standard variety. Fine-leaved fescues are a better choice for overseeding, as they are less apt to give warm-season grasses a tough time come spring.

Saint Augustine grass is rated the number one shade grass of the southernmost states. A creeping perennial, it spreads by long runners that produce short, leafy branches. It does well south of Augusta and Birmingham and westward to coastal Texas. It is propagated from sprigs, plugs or sod.

Saint Augustine grass withstands saltwater spray but is vulnerable to the chinch bug and armyworm. It grows best in moist soils of high fertility and produces good dark green turf in the muck soils of Florida. It needs a lot of nitrogen, particularly in sandy soils, and should be mowed one inch high.

Region D: Unless irrigation is available, only gramagrass, buffalograss and certain other desert species can be grown. With sufficient water, all of the species listed for Region A may survive.

Starting a New Lawn: The best time to start a new lawn is from the middle of August to the middle of September. At this time, the weather tends to be settled, so the ground will be at its best for planting and the new grass will have only moderate competition from weeds.

In the case of a new home where the building crew has just left, the first job is cleanup. Gather all the trash left by the builders. If any is buried in the soil, dig it up.

Hard, packed soil that does not let water through and restricts root growth is probably the most common cause of lawn failure. To aerate the soil and improve drainage, work in organic materials as you break up the clods of earth. This will also speed and ease the job

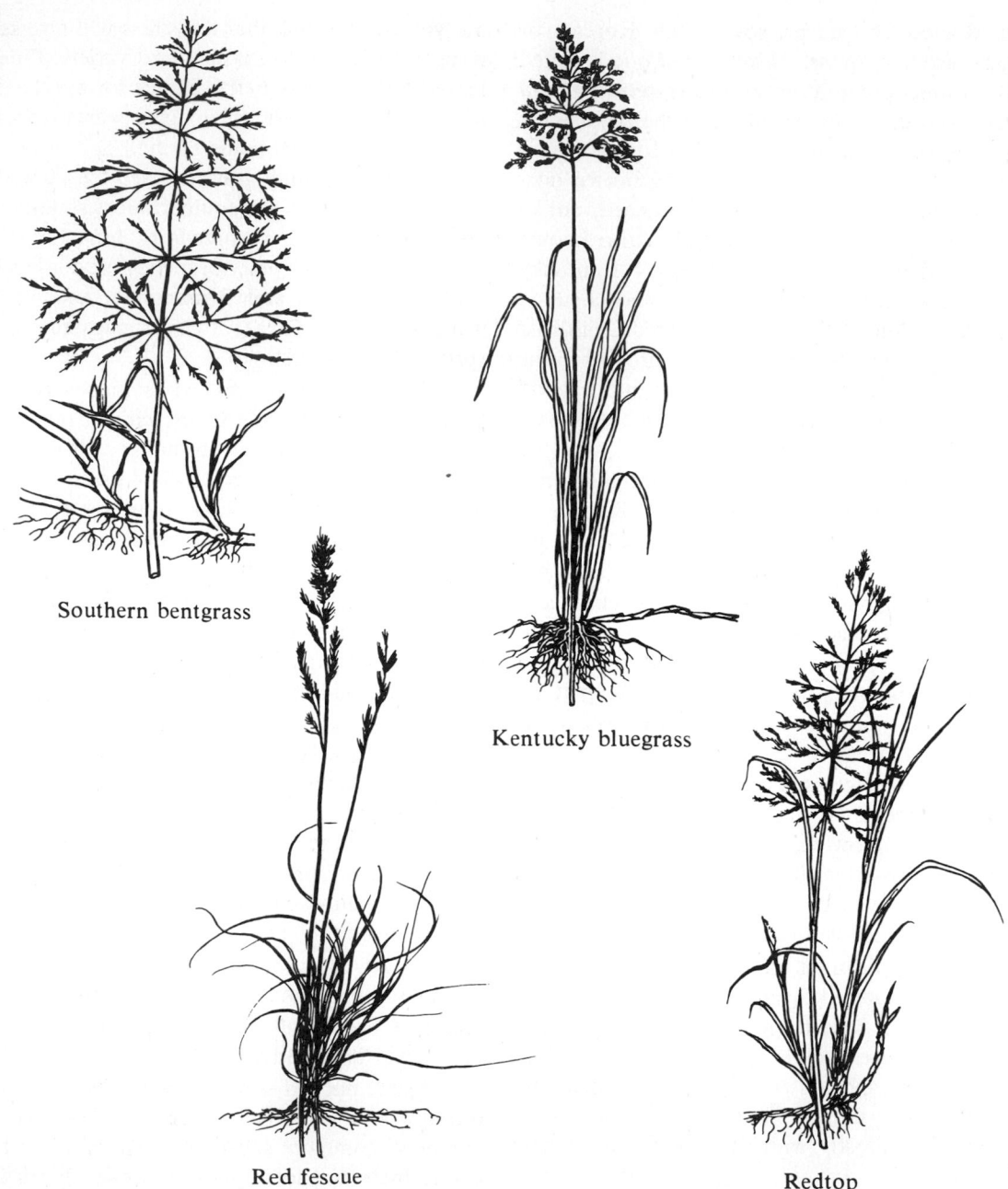

Southern bentgrass

Kentucky bluegrass

Red fescue

Redtop

Among the most common lawn grasses in this country are southern bentgrass, Kentucky bluegrass, red fescue, and redtop.

of making a proper grade. A rotary tiller renders the job much easier.

At this stage, if it is evident that the land will not drain adequately, seriously consider putting in underground drains. Don't do this without professional advice. Check with your local county agricultural agent before calling a tile dealer to supply the pipes and drains.

Grading: Try to avoid steep grades. A drop of more than 25 percent (one foot in four) will be hard on future lawn maintenance—the soil will simply wash away. If faced with this problem, try terracing or breaking the slope with retaining walls.

If the land is almost dead level around the house, make a slight grade away from it so that water will tend to flow from the foundation. The ideal lawn grade is ⅛ inch to the linear foot.

Liming: Most of the grasses do best on very slightly acid, almost neutral soil. Use very finely ground limestone, which is long lasting. Ground limestone does not destroy the humus and does not cake on top of the soil when used as a topdressing. Overly acid soil impedes the growth and activity of bacteria necessary to convert raw fertilizing substances into forms the grass can absorb.

If the bacteria do not function, the grass can starve in the proverbial land of plenty. More fertilizing will not correct this the way it does in a soil with a pH of 6 or better. The situation worsens in really acid soils because organic matter does not decay at a normal rate and roots tend to congest the turf. This prevents air and water from getting into the topsoil, which further aggravates the acid condition.

To find the acidity–alkalinity of lawn soil, either send a soil sample to the state experiment station or make the test yourself. All you need

is some litmus paper, generally available at a drugstore. After a rain, take a piece of litmus paper and press it with the thumb down into the moist soil. If the test paper doesn't change color, except to darken from wetness, the soil's pH is approximately 7. If it turns pink, the soil is acid. Blue means that the soil is alkaline. It's best to test the soil in several places.

If tests show soil that is quite acid, you can raise it one full unit (from pH 5.5 to 6.5) by adding the following amounts of lime per 1,000 square feet:

Sandy soil	35 lbs.
Sandy loam	45 lbs.
Medium loam	70 lbs.
Silt or clay	75 lbs.

Sprinkle the lime either by hand or with a cart spreader, but be sure to work from two different directions, at right angles to each other. This is also the way to seed and spread fertilizer, because it guarantees even distribution. It is wise to do these operations on comparatively windless days. Do not spread lime when the grass is wet and be sure to water the ground immediately after the lime has been spread.

Fertilizing: Mix organic fertilizers right into the topsoil while it is in the topping-off phase. Again, spread and mix at right angles to ensure uniformity.

Processed sewage sludge is an excellent fertilizer, providing two pounds of nitrogen for each 34 pounds spread to 1,000 square feet.

Sludge should be mixed in with the soil several months before seed are sown. If the soil is heavy clay, mix in one part sludge to two parts soil. Spade down to at least six inches and make sure the sludge is thoroughly mixed in with the soil—avoid having layers of sludge and layers of soil.

Sludge should be applied to the well-established lawn in the winter and early spring months when the ground is frozen. The lawn may be covered with a layer of sludge ½ inch deep during December, January and February. This cover will provide insulation to protect the grass roots from alternate thaws and freezes.

Sludge can also be a help in reconditioning a tired old lawn by spading down six inches and thoroughly mixing the sludge into the soil.

When using manure, compost or bone meal, 100 pounds per 1,000 square feet will add two pounds of nitrogen to the soil.

Cottonseed meal is recommended for its high nitrogen count. It is available from the local feed mill, but is comparatively expensive. Tobacco stems are excellent for potash as well as nitrogen, while bone meal provides phosphorus and nitrogen. Be guided by what you can get locally at good prices. Don't hesitate to substitute.

Lawns without topsoil: Perhaps the builders took away the topsoil or buried it too deeply. If so, resist the temptation to buy a truckload of topsoil. Such soils may be full of seeds and perhaps even infertile. Instead, start a lawn and build topsoil as you go. It's not too difficult, but it takes time—at least a year—and involves sowing a green manure cover crop right into the subsoil after you have enriched it with sludge, cottonseed meal, tobacco stems, and bone meal.

In the South, crimson clover and hairy vetch can be used as green manure crops. Elsewhere, rye and winter rye or field peas are used. After liming and fertilizing the subsoil, sow the green manure crop and let it reach a height of six to 12 inches before tilling it under. Six weeks later, you can sow the permanent grass seed.

Sowing the seed: The seeds of some grasses, such as bluegrass, have a water-soluble acid coating that inhibits germination. For best results, you should place these seeds in a cheesecloth bag and soak them in a tub of water for 12 to 24 hours. Then, rinse the seeds under the faucet and spread them on newspapers. Let them remain in a dry, shaded place for at least two hours. If necessary, they can be kept in the drying place for several days until sowing conditions are right.

The rate of seeding varies according to the type of grass you selected. In most cases, four pounds of seed will adequately cover 1,000 square feet of ground, but specialty grasses such as Bermuda may require only one or two pounds. A mechanical seeder can help you spread the seed evenly and smoothly.

After sowing, roll the ground lightly or, if you prefer, gently rake the area so that the seed are barely covered with soil. Some gardeners simply scatter dry peat moss or straw over the seed. If you have seeded on a steep embankment, pin cheesecloth or burlap over the ground. Left in place as the blades emerge, it will gradually rot and break down into compost. Water the area liberally and, unless it rains overnight, continue to water each evening until the turf becomes established. Seed that have been presoaked should germinate in one to two weeks.

Many grass varieties, particularly those flourishing south of the bluegrass line, are best propagated by vegetative methods than by seeding. This is done by planting units of the mature grass or by planting the underground shoots known as stolons. Grasses propagated by "plugs" include zoysias, Bermudagrasses, Saint Augustine grass, centipedegrass, creeping bentgrass, and velvet bentgrass. Of these varieties, only the last two should be propagated in autumn. Creeping bentgrass and velvet bentgrass can be stolonized. This method calls for ten bushels of stolons to plant 1,000 square feet of ground. Top-dress with ½ inch of soil and roll the area.

Soil Fertility: Inadequate fertility is responsible for more lawn problems than any other factor. If the lawn cover is thin or yellow or if it is filled with weeds, then chances are, the soil should be improved. Of the three major nutrients—nitrogen, phosphorus and potassium—nitrogen is the most important. You can apply plenty of organic lawn fertilizer without burning the lawn because it is slow acting. Good sources of nitrogen are cottonseed meal and sewage sludge. Cottonseed meal is excellent lawn topdressing, containing 7 to 8 percent nitrogen, 3 percent phosphoric acid and 2 percent potash. Top-dress 12 pounds per 1,000 square feet right on the grass, and then water it in with a hose. Bone meal is a very good source of phosphorus, a nutrient that makes good stiff growth. Top-dress five pounds to 1,000 square feet. Apply any of these each spring.

The pH is also important. A low pH, or excessive acidity, discourages desirable bacteria and gives rise to toxic quantities of iron and aluminum. A high pH, or excessive alkalinity, also interferes with natural functions of the soil. In heavy rainfall areas in the East and other locations, it may be necessary to use ground limestone. In northeastern United States, 50 pounds of ground limestone per 1,000 square feet are usually required every two or three years. If you are in a region of excessive alkalinity, careful measures must be taken upon advice of turf specialists.

Mowing: Do not cut newly planted grass until the blades have reached a height of at least three inches. Set the mower at 1½ or two inches and do not reset it to the height recommended for your variety until the lawn is a tight sod. Young lawns do best under the blades of a reel mower, but cutting a hilly lawn is easier with a rotary type.

Once the lawn is established and growing vigorously, as many as two mowings per week may be necessary. Kentucky bluegrass and zoysia are more drought tolerant and weed-free if cut to 1½ or two inches. Bentgrass and Bermudagrass lawns can be cut closer than one inch. Merion Kentucky bluegrass can be cut as closely as one inch if conditions are favorable.

Excessive growth between clippings makes for more open, stemmy turf, and you may have to rake up the clippings to avoid smothering the grass. It's best to leave the clippings, if not too dense, right where they are, as they provide the lawn with food and help control weeds such as crabgrass.

Either a reel or a rotary mower can be used satisfactorily for most lawns. However, the reel type is better adapted to closer mowing, while the blade type is better for the higher cuts.

Weed Control: A dense turf is recommended universally as the all-around weed control measure. Grass is very aggressive when fertilized generously. If weeds continually trouble the lawn, increase the use of fertilizer. Factors that can contribute to weeds include insect damage, disease, excessive watering, and mowing too closely.

The secret of controlling annual lawn weeds is to prevent seed development. Crabgrass is no exception. Prevent seed set for several seasons and simultaneously develop a dense turf, and this weed should cease to be a bother.

Persistence is necessary in eliminating weeds from the lawn. If the lawn is not too big, hand weeding can be the answer. It may be a tremendous job at first; however, use of fertilizer in conjunction with weeding will thicken the turf and greatly reduce the amount of weeding required the next season.

Nimble-Will (*Muhlenbergia Schreberi*) is the number one lawn weed in some areas. Rid your yard of it the hard way, by hand weeding or vigorous raking. This weed is often confused with Bermudagrass and crabgrass.

Clumps of fescue can be killed by severing the center of the crown.

Insects and Diseases: The white grub larvae of the Japanese beetle and june bug and the hairy chinch bug harm lawns by cutting off grass roots. Should your lawn show brown patches and loose sod in late spring or late summer, rake off the loose turf and turn over the soil beneath. Do this every few days, until late fall. Birds will pick up the exposed pests.

Lawn diseases are difficult to recognize. If you suspect trouble, contact your extension agency. The turf specialist there will supply you with color photographs of the common diseases. Most problems can be avoided by heeding the following points:

1. Plant a mixture of grasses, rather than one variety, so that the lawn cannot be wiped out by a single disease.
2. Fertilize in early spring and fall, rather than in midsummer.
3. Close mowing of bluegrass weakens the grass and leads to the tender leaf growth that encourages fungus.
4. Watering late in the evening renders lawns susceptible to fungal diseases.
5. Heeding the lawn's nutritional requirements, much as you would those of other valuable plants, can prevent most lawn diseases.

Excessive nitrogen, coupled with too little phosphorus and potassium, may lead to brown patch. Chlorosis, or yellowing of turf, is often caused by a deficiency of iron. Get around this trouble by avoiding overfertilization, by watering during dry fall periods and by applying no more lime than necessary to keep from raising the soil pH.

Watering: The well-managed lawn will stand the midsummer strain of great midday heat and little water with surprising success. Again, it is a matter of having a lawn with deep roots.

During periods of drought, it is better to not water at all than to sprinkle lightly. Water once a week, soaking the soil to a minimum depth of four inches. If you don't have enough water to maintain this program, it is better not to water at all.

The deeper the water penetrates, the better the root development. A healthy, sturdy system of roots gets full food value from the surrounding soil by penetrating as deeply as possible. Shallow sprinkling forces the roots to spread out near the top of the soil where they will later be baked by the hot summer sun and rendered unable to withstand drought.

Soil with plentiful organic humus will hold water in suspension so that it can be readily absorbed by the grass. A lawn with plenty of organic humus that is thoroughly watered at regular intervals will stay sound and drought-resistant during the summer.

Watering should be planned according to the type of soil. Light soils need more water because they drain readily. Heavy, clay soils obviously need less water.

Rebuilding Bare Spots: Rake out all dead grass and break up the surface thoroughly, even though some good grass plants may be dislodged in the process. Reestablish the even contour of the surface by careful raking, then follow the instructions given for starting a new lawn. In small areas, even seeding can be accomplished with the use of a flour sifter. In larger areas, use a standard grass seeder.

Turf Substitutes: Dichondra, or lawn leaf, is a very satisfactory substitute for lawn grass. It requires no mowing or reseeding, thrives in either sun or shade, is tolerant to a wide variety of soil conditions, and is very resistant to rough usage. Moths and beetle larvae do not injure it. Best of all, particularly in arid regions, it remains vigorously fresh during dry spells that ordinarily kill grass.

ORGANIC LAWN FOODS

Bone meal: a stockyard by-product particularly rich in nitrogen, phosphoric acid and calcium. It is excellent for preparing land for a new lawn or for top-dressing old turf. The coarser ground meal is slower acting while the finer grinds are quick to act, often producing greener grass within two weeks. A mixture of coarse and fine is recommended for all-round performance.

Castor pomace: the ground remains of castor beans after oil has been squeezed out. An excellent and slow-acting plant food, castor pomace should be used in combination with other organic soil nutrients.

Cattle manure: cleanings from cattle pens. It is good to work into the soil a season before planting if fresh, but must be weathered before being applied as a fertilizer. Dehydrated manures can be applied directly to the soil.

Cottonseed meal: the squeezed fibrous residue of the seed of the cotton plant. It is slow acting but an excellent source of nitrogen. Cottonseed meal should be applied with other foods.

Sheep manure, pulverized: suitable for mixing as topdressing with other foods. It is dried to destroy most weed seeds; this tends to keep down the amount of weed growth on lawns top-dressed with pulverized manure.

Tobacco scrap: stem and leaf fragments from tobacco factories. Excellent, long-acting source of potash and other nutrients because stems and leaf veins decay slowly. Also wards off many insects.

Dichondra is popular in California and elsewhere in the Southwest.

To prepare a dichondra lawn, work up the soil thoroughly with well-rotted compost. Chicken droppings, bone meal and dried blood are excellent ingredients. After mixing, rake the earth level and smooth.

Don't broadcast the seed too thickly, as each plant will spread over about four square inches. Cover seed with a thin layer of finely screened compost mixed wtih ground phosphate rock, and water liberally during the first week. Germination takes about ten days.

Sometimes dichondra seed is mixed with white clover or a short-lived grass. When mixes are planted the new lawn will need mowing, and it is necessary to rake off all the clippings as these will harm the dichondra seedlings. The young plants gradually replace the clover or grass.

Although grown mainly for lawns, dichondra makes an excellent ground cover around shrubs and between flagstones. When allowed to spread, it chokes out noxious weeds and covers unattractive bare places. Dichondra can even be used in rock gardens, where its gay patches of green produce a decidedly ornamental effect.

See also CRABGRASS, FERTILIZER, GRASS CLIPPINGS, GROUND COVERS.

SOIL CONDITION AS INDICATED BY WEED GROWTHS

Condition	Weeds	Remedy
Wet	Ferns, horsetail, sedge, rush, cattail, buttercup, pennywort	The surface may be dry but these weeds are a sure indication that the land is wet below. Drainage may be necessary.
Acid	Sorrel, dock, wild strawberry, bramble	The soil should be limed.
Poor, dry	Devil's paint brush, spurge	Manure and sludge are needed.
Tight, compressed	Knotwood, poa annua	Perforate surface, work in sand and peat moss dust.
Deep clay	Self-heal, wild onion	Break up the soil and add organic matter.
Limestone	Chicory, teasel	Manure and other organic matter are needed.

LAYERING

This is a very easy method of vegetative or asexual propagation, in which an attached stem of a shrub or other plant is put into the ground in early spring and allowed to root. In order for the roots to form, a cut must be made in the stem on the part to be laid in the soil. This cut is sometimes treated with a root-promoting hormone such as indoleacetic acid, a natural substance found in living plants.

For best results the soil should be warm and always moist, not only while the roots are forming but also afterwards, and the branch or shoot used should be in active growth.

Simple Layering: Early spring is the best time not only for simple layering, but also for other methods, because at that time there are flexible young branches just starting into active growth. Choose those the size of a large pencil and gently bend them down, after making the cut on the slant, halfway through the stem. Make it just where the branch will touch the soil, and when you bend the branch down, leave only a small part of the end above the soil to form the shoot of the new plant.

It is generally advisable to put a V-shaped stake or hairpin over the buried part of the branch to hold it firmly, and also to stake the tip of the shoot if it seems likely to wobble. Use fine, rich topsoil over the buried part of the stem. Instead of a cut, it is possible to girdle the stem or to put a wire constriction around it to obstruct the movement of nutrients and food up and down the stem and thus to promote root growth.

Amateur gardeners using this method for propagation should select a moist, shady area of the yard. They should use plenty of mulch and be constantly watchful to see when watering is needed. Large-scale commercial layering is usually most successful where the climate is damp and misty, or where, as in Holland, the water table is only ten or 12 inches below the soil surface.

After rooting woody plants, it is customary to wait until the late fall or early spring to sever the new plant from the parent and then to leave it one more year before trying to move it to another location. If more bushiness is desired, top growth can be cut back.

The plants easiest to layer are the same ones which propagate readily from cuttings: bittersweet, carnation, deutzia, euonymus, forsythia, honeysuckle, and privet. Though rhododendron is difficult to layer, this is the usual method of propagation because cuttings tend to dry out rapidly.

Nurserymen do not allow their stock plants to form a trunk. By mound or stool layering, they keep cutting back the plants to 12 inches to keep young shoots coming up so they can use the same plants year after year. The soil they prefer is well drained and light, and they add peat and sand if necessary, because adequate aeration and continuous moisture are important. Compaction or heat can injure the new roots, so mounding the cutting with moist peat moss is sometimes necessary.

Tip Layering: Some plants, such as black raspberry, currant, dewberry, and gooseberry, layer themselves naturally. They just bend down the tips of their branches until they touch the ground and take root. To propagate these plants, bury the tips four or five inches deep. Sometimes this is done right in a pot where they can be left and easily transported after rooting. It is best to make a cut in the stem, to retain the leaves of the parent stem so the layers can continue to make food. If the hole is made with one side sloping and one side vertical—and the slope toward the parent plant—the angle will stop tip growth and promote good root growth.

Serpentine Layering: This variation involves the use of long supple branches which are put into the ground and removed several times at appropriate intervals.   It can be used for muscadine grapes, wisteria, clematis, and other ornamental vines.

Air Layering: With this method the new roots form on a growing stem after it has been slit with an upward slice or partially girdled. The slit stem is wrapped in moist sphagnum moss, which in turn is wrapped tightly to keep it continuously moist, but not wet, during the rooting process.   The outer wrapping can be of paper, aluminum foil or polyethylene plastic which lets oxygen and carbon dioxide in and out, but keeps in moisture.

Make air layers in the spring on wood of the previous year's growth, or in late summer on partially hardened shoots that have plenty of active leaves.   House plants which have long, leggy stalks can be shortened and made into stocky, good-looking plants by air layering.

A rubber plant, for example, can be prepared first by girdling the bark about ten or 12 inches below the tip, scraping the area to make sure the cambium is removed, adding indoleacetic acid if desired, and then wrapping the wounded area with slightly dampened sphagnum moss to extend about an inch above and below the cut bark.   If the stem is frail, a splint may be inserted or a stake put up to hold the plant.   Wrap the moss in polyethylene, tied at both ends.   Within a few months, or perhaps later, the roots will be visible through the plastic film, and then you can remove the top

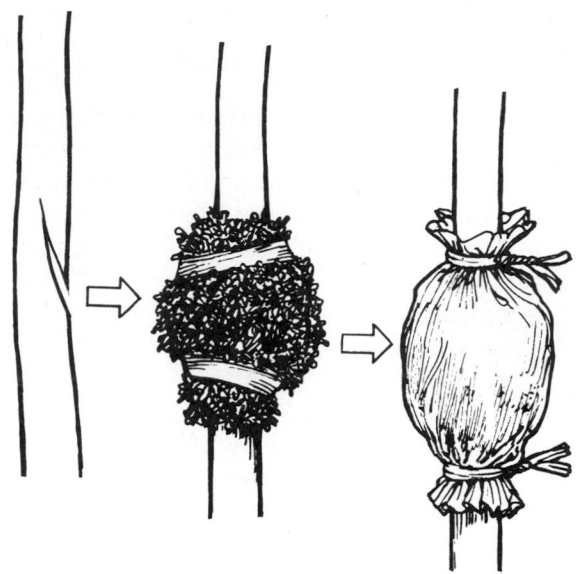

Rubber plants are usually propagated by air layering. First, girdle the bark about ten inches below the tip and scrape the area to remove the inner bark. Wrap the wound with damp sphagnum moss and cover with plastic. After several months, the roots will appear beneath the plastic. The top part can be cut off and this new, little plant potted in a fresh container.

part with its roots and pot it in a freshly prepared container.

One variation of air layering, called pot layering, is done by using a bottomless clay pot instead of polyethylene to hold the sphagnum moss.   With this method it is best to cut a two-inch slice into the stem and to prop it open with a small stick.   Keep the moss moist, and when roots have formed, transfer the entire top growth to equal parts of peat moss, sand and leaf mold.

See also CUTTINGS, DIVISION, PROPAGATION.

LEACHING

Rainwater and irrigation are known to dissolve a certain amount of valuable nutrients from the soil, carrying them down to greater depths where they cannot be reached by roots. This leaching is inevitable and should be remembered when fertilizing. The problem is particularly acute where water-soluble chemical fertilizers are used. In the surface of some rural areas, ground and water supplies have been contaminated by the leaching of nitrogen-rich chemical fertilizers.

Leaching also occurs in house plants, but this kind of leaching can be avoided by not overwatering plants. Remember that every time water runs out of the drainage hole and is thrown away as excess, it carries with it some soil nutrients.

There has been relatively little research on the exact amount of nutrients lost by leaching. In experiments at Michigan State University, however, it was found that the nutrient content of the plant, the plant species, sunlight, maturity, and the amount and duration of rainfall are among factors which determine loss.

LEADWORT   *See* PLUMBAGO

LEAFHOPPERS
See INSECT CONTROL

LEAF MINERS
See INSECT CONTROL

LEAF MOLD   *See* LEAVES

LEAF ROLLERS
See INSECT CONTROL

LEATHER DUST

Leather dust makes an excellent fertilizer. The material contains between 5.5 and 12 percent nitrogen. It is not rich in any other major nutrients.

LEATHERWOOD
(*Dirca palustris*)

A choice native shrub which blooms before leafing out in the early spring, leatherwood is reported hardy as far north as Minnesota. It grows to about five feet and remains shapely at all times.

Its great number of small yellow blossoms makes it showy and beautiful when there is little or no other color in the border, and its light yellow autumn foliage gives a second bonus of color towards the end of the year. It is wild in the eastern parts of the country, where it grows in moist places, but it can be cultivated in ordinary garden soil. It does best in shade.

LEAVES

Each leaf on a plant functions as a factory, where sunlight, carbon dioxide from the air, and minerals and water from the earth are converted into carbohydrates—food for the plant and for animals who eat it.

All living things are composed of carbon compounds. These compounds are in a constant process of breaking down, yielding heat and energy. They are also used to make more complex compounds in the form of fats and proteins. Each change requires energy when it occurs, and carbohydrates are burned to provide this energy. When a carbon compound is burned, carbon dioxide is produced as a by-product. Thus, carbon is returned to the atmosphere in the form of carbon dioxide.

Green leaves are the only known organs that can take mineral carbon from the carbon dioxide in the air and in the presence of light combine it with water and other minerals to build carbohydrates. Without photosynthesis, the carbohydrate supply would soon run down and life could not continue.

When they die, leaves replenish the layer of organic matter on the earth's surface. Microorganisms break down this layer into its component minerals and gases. The latter escape into the air or are washed by rain into the earth. Plant roots recover minerals from the soil. Minerals are carried in solution in water up into the leaves through the trunks of trees or stems of plants. Water is then transpired through the leaves. The more water the tree uses, the more is transpired and the more minerals the leaves will contain. Leaves of ash, willow or other trees growing in wet places may contain up to 7 percent minerals, while pines, which transpire little, contain no more than 2.5 percent.

Leaf Structure: Cells of a typical leaf are arranged in specialized layers. The thin layer of cells that makes up the upper and lower surfaces of the leaf is called the epidermis and is coated with a waxy substance known as cutin. It protects the tender cells and keeps the tissue from drying out. Between the two epidermal layers are the regular leaf cells collectively referred to as the mesophyll. The cells closest to the upper epidermis tend to be long and narrow and arranged closely together in columns. These cells make up the palisade layer and contain most of the plant's chlorophyll (the substance that absorbs light energy necessary for photosynthesis). Beneath them, the leaf cells are more loosely arranged with large air pockets between them. Most of the actual food making takes place in these cells where there is free access to oxygen and carbon dioxide.

Veins passing through this spongy layer carry water and food to other plant parts. During the day, water and nutrients are transferred to the cells and, when there is no light, the manufactured foods are carried to the roots for storage. The stored food is necessary for growth, flower production and fruit production.

Garden Uses: When perennials enter their winter rest period, leaves fall to the ground, retaining remnants of the products they have manufactured through the year. In

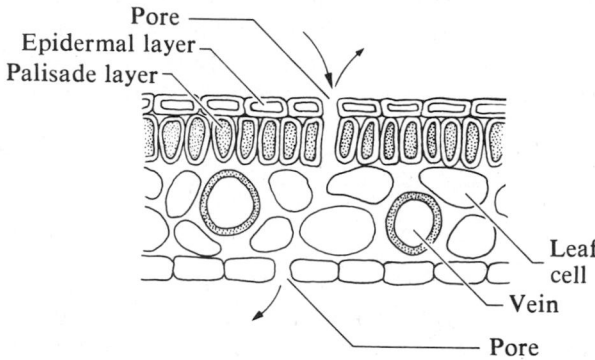

The upper layer of leaf cells, just beneath the "skin" or epidermal layer, is particularly rich in chloroplasts. The spongy region below provides the air space necessary for gas exchange and transpiration. Depending upon the species of plant, pores may occur in the upper, lower or both upper and lower epidermal layers.

the forest, the leaves lie on top of others that fell in previous years. Beneath the surface, microorganisms of all kinds are at work making the leaf mold usable by the roots of smaller forest plants. Nothing is wasted. Plants and fallen leaves become food for next year's growth.

Pound for pound, the leaves of most trees contain twice as many minerals as does manure. For example, the mineral content of a sugar maple leaf is over 5 percent; even common pine needles have 2.5 percent of their weight in calcium, magnesium, nitrogen, and phosphorus, plus other trace elements.

Mulching: Leaves may be used as a winter mulch. They may be stored and dug into the soil in preparation for the spring garden, made into leaf mold which will be used as a summer mulch and fertilizer or, when shredded, used to make compost.

Actually, leaves are most valuable for the large amounts of fibrous organic matter they supply. Their humus-building qualities mean improved structure for all soil types. They aerate heavy clay soils, and, in sandy soils, soak up water and check evaporation.

Dry leaves are excellent winter protection for perennials, provided that matting can be avoided. They may be spread over strawberry beds if coarse material such as cornstalks, bean plants or tomato stalks are first scattered over the bed to hold leaves away from the plants and prevent smothering. When the stalks are removed in spring, the leaves may be worked into the soil to add to its humus content.

Plants which require acid soil—azaleas, rhododendrons, holly, and magnolia—will welcome a mulch of acid leaves such as oak leaves or pine needles. *See also* MULCH.

Leaves may be used as mulch just as they fall from the tree, or they may be shredded first. Shredded leaves break down more quickly than those that are left whole. They are less apt to scatter in the wind and do not form such compact mats when wet.

There are a number of shredders on the market which will shred leaves (*see also* SHREDDER). A rotary mower may also be used if run over the leaves when they are dry and crisp. If the mower has a special leaf-mulching attachment, the leaves will be ground to a powder.

Leaf mold: Leaf mold is not as rich in plant foods as composted leaves, but it is easier to make, and is especially useful as a summer mulch. A bin of snow fencing, wood or stone may be made to contain the leaves. As the leaves, shredded, if possible, are placed in the enclosure, they are dampened and tamped to pack them. If intended for any except acid-loving plants, they will probably need an application of ground limestone, since most leaves are somewhat acid.

Leaves in a bin will not break down in the course of one winter into the fine black leaf mold found on forest floors. Such black mold is the result of several years' decomposition. But if shredded, the leaves will break down enough to make excellent mulch. The ability of such leaf mold to hold moisture is five to ten times that of ordinary topsoil. Leaf mold from deciduous trees is somewhat richer in such mineral foods as potash and phosphorus than that from conifers. The nitrogen content varies from .2 to .5 percent.

Two steps are necessary to assure success in composting leaves.

1. Extra nitrogen must be added. Nitrogen added to the heap will speed the heating process, because leaves alone do not contain enough nitrogen to supply food to bacteria.

Manure is the best nitrogen supplement. A mixture of five parts leaves to one part manure will break down quickly. Nitrogen supplements like dried blood, or cottonseed meal, will work almost as well. Use two cups of such supplements to a wheelbarrow of unshredded dried leaves.

2. Grind or shred leaves for composting. This makes the material easier to handle, prevents matting and helps to start the process of decomposition. *See also* COMPOSTING.

If leaves are not needed to produce compost for the flower or vegetable garden, they may be shredded where they fall on the lawn when the mower is run for the last time in autumn. A rotary mower will make leaves disappear quickly with half the work needed to rake them. The shredded leaves will enrich the lawn, and the humus sifted over grass roots will hold moisture against the next summer's drought.

Low spots in the lawn may be successfully corrected by spading under as much leaf mold or compost as is needed. Cut the sod with a sharp spade, fold it back gently, work the leaf compost into the soil thoroughly until the desired level is attained, return the sod, pack, and water freely.

LEECHEE   *See* LITCHI

LEEK   (*Allium porrum*)

Leek is an onionlike plant used in cooking and recognized by its distinct odor. Leek is a relative of the onion, chives and garlic.

The plant has long, quill-like leaves and a bulb which contains the fruit.

Leek is believed to be native either to Algiers or to Switzerland. The herb was first grown by ancient Greek and Roman civilizations. In Europe, leek was cultivated during the Middle Ages as a savored vegetable and a flavoring agent.

Planting and Culture: Leeks like a rich, deep loam, but are not too particular about soil requirements. They respond readily to heavy

Leeks benefit from generous applications of organic matter and repeated mulchings.

applications of mature compost. Well-rotted manure may be substituted if necessary, but avoid the use of raw manure. Leeks will tolerate a moderately acid soil, but it must be one rich in nitrogen.

Seed is planted thickly, ½ inch deep. When the seedlings are eight inches high they should be carefully dug up. Remove half the tops and replant the seedlings six inches apart in trenches six inches deep and three or four inches wide. A heavy supply of sifted compost humus should be incorporated with the soil in the bottoms of the trenches. As the plants grow, the sides of the trenches should be broken down to blanch the edible stems. During the early stages of their growth, leeks require an abundance of plant food. A plentiful supply of moisture is necessary to make this available to them.

Varieties: Broad London and Elefant are very popular. Other hardy varieties are Giant Flag, Carentan Winter, and Italian Winter.

See also ONION.

LEGGY

Leggy is a term used to describe a plant, usually a seedling, which has grown a long stem out of proportion with its foliage. In seedlings, this results from having the seed flats too crowded, from giving the plants too little sun, or from making the soil in the seed germinating flat too rich. In older plants, it is usually a result of crowding or of lack of proper pinching back or pruning. Zinnias may become leggy, or grow one long central stem if not pinched back early. Forsythia may grow to 12 feet, with bare leggy wood at the base, through lack of pruning.

LEGUME

Pod-bearing plants such as peas, beans and clovers are called legumes. They are characterized by their fruits which have a single-cavity ovary. This ovary splits along two seams when dry. Leguminous plants are also unique in harboring nitrogen-fixing bacteria in their root nodules. These fix nitrogen from the air for plant use. Legumes in a mixed pasture stand can "fix" 100 pounds or more of atmospheric nitrogen per acre.

Legumes are the best soil-building and forage crops. Properly grown, they supply more protein, calcium and vitamins A and D per acre than any other roughage. Alfalfa, for instance, can yield a ton of crude protein per acre year after year without nitrogen fertilization. Legume feed, as hay, pasture or silage, is the cheapest source of total digestible nutrients and protein you can grow.

The ability of legumes to improve fertility and soil structure is rightly famous. With deep, probing roots—alfalfa often goes down over 30 feet—they facilitate drainage and bring up nutrients from the subsoil's hidden storehouse. Plowed down, a good legume stand adds all this plant food, plus tons of organic matter, to the soil.

Nitrogen Production: It's in nitrogen production, however, that legumes really excel. An acre of inoculated legumes will take as much nitrogen from the air as is contained in ten tons of manure. Much of this is stored in the soil, and much or all of the rest is returned to the soil when the plants or their residues are plowed down.

Leguminous crops are active nitrogen gatherers—so active, in fact, that legumes furnish far more nitrogen to our crops than do farm manures and fertilizers combined. This nitrogen comes largely from the air, mainly through the action of a group of bacteria called rhizobia. The rhizobia infect the roots of legumes and form nodules. Inside these, the rhizobia draw energy from the plant and in return supply it with nitrogen fixed from the air. Some strains of rhizobia are more effective at this than others. Since fixation slows down or stops in the presence of nitrogen fertilizer, most legumes do not respond to nitrogen fertilizer.

Because of the high nitrogen content, plowing under legume crops is no shock to the soil. The best time for incorporating them in the soil is before blooming time, because then the plants are most leafy and richest in nitrogen. It is usually most economical to cut established legume fields for hay and to let the plants become well established. As they sink their roots down, they not only aerate the soil, but add valuable organic matter to it and bring minerals to the surface.

Culture: With all legumes, adaptation to soil, moisture and temperature conditions is essential, and the origin of the seed may furthermore seriously affect their success, especially with alfalfa. Crimson clover, for example, is a winter annual and will not do well in cold, water-logged soils. It must be cut young but does not develop an extended root system and is therefore not as valuable for its residues. Lespedeza is grown in the warmer regions, both for hay and for pasture. It has deep roots but is not as nutritious as the clovers. It is an annual. So is bur clover, another warm-weather crop suited mainly to green manuring. The vetches are also warm region plants, though the hairy vetch extends farther north

than the common vetch. Soybeans and cowpeas, velvet beans and field peas, field beans and peanuts are rarely grown for manuring purposes, because their seed is valuable and because they are annuals and therefore do not develop deep root systems.

A few typical analyses follow:

Legume	Nitrogen	Phosphoric Acid	Potash
Cowpea forage	.4	.1	.4
Cowpea hay	3.0	.3	2.8
Pea forage		.3	1.4
Pea hay	1.5–2.5		
Soybean hay	1.5–3.0	.3–.5	1.2–2.3

In addition to soil builders, legumes also include edible plants such as peanuts, lentils and carob; shrubs and trees such as the locust, mesquite and broom; flowers such as baptisia, anthyllis and lathyrus; and tropical plants such as acacia, derris and mimosa.

Rebuilding pastures: The best time to renovate your grass pasture is in the late winter, but you can start anytime. You'll need to apply limestone and phosphate rock. Apply enough lime to bring the soil pH to at least 6, and add enough phosphate rock to increase soil phosphorus by 50 pounds per acre. (Caution: Be sure the phosphate you use is low in fluoride. Fluoride can build up to toxic levels in soil.) You can apply the lime and phosphate any time the weather will let you get on your fields.

During winter, graze or mow the grass to about four inches high. You want to weaken the grass, but not kill it, before you seed the legume. In February or March, when weather permits, use a disk or field cultivator to disturb the grass sod. For smaller pastures, you can do the job with a light once-over with a rotary tiller. You don't need to do a thorough tilling; merely expose soil so that the legumes can get started. This light tilling also helps work the limestone and phosphate rock into the top layer of soil and leaves the trash on top as a mulch.

Keep seeding mixtures simple, whether you're renovating an existing grass stand or establishing a new pasture. One legume and one grass species ordinarily do the trick.

You'll want to use a legume that fits well with your grass variety. Alfalfa complements orchardgrass and bromegrass, particularly if you're after high-quality hay. Fescue and ladino clover work well together in pastures, if you keep the clover to about 25 percent of the stand.

Alfalfa and the clovers are the most efficient nitrogen fixers, with good management fixing 100 pounds or more of actual nitrogen per acre. There is some hazard of bloat when cattle graze either alfalfa or clover. The bloat danger is reduced when cattle have access to high-quality graze year-round, however. Bloat commonly occurs when cattle move from sparse pasture to lush pasture, where they overeat.

Other legumes—such as lespedeza or trefoil—are safe for grazing, but do not fix as much nitrogen as alfalfa or clover. The choice of grasses and legumes to include in your pasture will depend on varieties adapted to your soil type and annual rainfall.

If you're seeding alfalfa or red clover, use ten to 12 pounds per acre. One pound of ladino clover per acre should be sufficient. You can drill or broadcast the legume seed into the grass sod. Be sure to inoculate the seed with the proper culture for the variety you plant.

Later in the spring, as soon as the sod will support the traffic, graze the pasture until the animals begin to bite off the young legumes. Then, remove the cattle and apply fertilizer materials high in phosphate and potash. Don't apply manures or other high-nitrogen fertilizers in large amounts. These nitrogen-rich fertilizers will stimulate the grass to overcompete with the fledgling legume seedlings.

After fertilizing, let the pasture rest for six weeks or so. Thereafter, manage the mixture for the legumes—and the legumes will take care of the grasses.

See also entries for individual legumes.

LEGUME INOCULATION

Legumes are actually nitrogen factories, and growing legumes inoculated with nitrogen-fixing bacteria is the simplest and most economical way to put this vital plant food into your soil. As the seed sprout, these bacteria enter the root hairs, forming nodules in which they live. There they take nitrogen from the air and make it into compounds the plant can use.

Just how these species of bacteria fix nitrogen is not known, but their activities show up in increased crop yield and quality. Inoculated alfalfa, for example, may contain over 16 percent protein, as against 10 percent for noninoculated (which has had to depend on the soil supply for the nitrogen with which to manufacture its protein). Soybeans when inoculated have raised their yields by more than 12 bushels per acre, with 9 percent more protein and a comparable rise in oil content.

Often the difference between inoculating and not inoculating is the difference between getting a healthy profit from a crop and not getting enough to bother harvesting. Given good weather, organic soil and proper fertilization, legume seed that is inoculated by the particular strain of bacteria that lives on that legume, will outyield uninoculated seed, by 15 to 25 percent.

In addition, root growth is more vigorous and extensive. This is an advantage that is invaluable. Good tilth, produced by strong roots breaking up the soil deep down then adding organic matter to it when they decay, is something no chemical fertilizers or soil conditioners can bring about. The soil's physical condition determines the amount of water it can hold to keep plants growing well in dry weather. It also insures the aeration necessary for plant roots and for the bacteria that work to make nutrients available to them.

Sometimes a farmer will show you a clover plant from a fine stand that has plenty of nodules on its roots, and tell you that he has never inoculated his seed. This is more often the exception than the rule. There are always some of the right bacteria in the soil, of course, but their numbers are rarely sufficient to do the job well. Even when the same legume was grown on the field the previous year, most bacteria will have died out or lost their efficiency in the intervening time. Also, the inoculants sold commercially contain improved strains of bacteria that do a better job than those occurring normally in most soils—and this shows up in better yields.

Inoculants are very inexpensive and easy to use. Be sure to buy the right inoculant for the seed you are planting. Most states have laws regulating the quality of inoculants on the market, so you can be sure of getting one that will perform as expected. Use it fresh, however; the bacteria may become inactive if kept from year to year. Cold has no effect on inocu-

lant bacteria, but never store them in the sun or near a hot stove.

Legume bacteria come packaged in moist humus or in bottles of a nutrient breeding solution called agar. Add a little water to the inoculant and pour it over the seed which have been moistened slightly. Mix it in well. With a special attachment, soybeans can be inoculated right in the drill. If you're planting a meadow mixture that calls for several types of inoculants, mix them all together and apply them the same as you would a single inoculant.

Plant the seed immediately after inoculating, as any long exposure may reduce the efficiency of the bacteria. The bacteria are completely harmless even if you have open cuts in your skin. Reinoculate any seed kept overnight.

If you want your bacteria to live to do the job you bought them for, don't use any chemical fertilizers or other seed treatments when planting. Like nearly all beneficial soil organisms, they are sensitive to these foreign substances.

A very acid soil will not support the growth of most legume bacteria. A pH of 6.5 is best for them, so lime the soil as needed. Both the bacteria and the legumes themselves will benefit from the calcium, which they need in large amount for growth.

Humus provides the ideal living conditions for all beneficial bacteria, and the nitrogen-fixing species are no exception. Soil with plenty of organic matter suffers less from moisture loss, hot sun, lack of aeration, and all the other organism-killing ills that chemically fertilized or worn-out soil is heir to. Don't expect even the best inoculated seed to "catch" on severely eroded, badly packed or dried-out soil. Work in some manure or organic materials first, well in advance of planting. Subsoiling with machinery may be necessary if the soil is extremely packed.

Legumes are topsoil builders, but like any crop they require plant food to grow. Soil tests and applications of rock fertilizers are just as necessary to them as to corn or cabbage. Liberal applications of phosphate rock, in particular, produce strong, vigorous growth in legumes.

LEMON   (*Citrus Limon*)

Originally from Asia, the lemon spread west to Europe and then to America about the time of Columbus. During the seventeenth century, the first extensive plantings were made in Florida. Today, California is the center of lemon growing in this country.

Planting and Culture: Lemon trees respond well to heavy soils, and can tolerate the occasional light frosts that hit the regions in which they are usually grown. For planting, it is best to use rootstocks particularly adapted to the local soil, although seedling trees may also be planted. The lemon is usually grafted to the stock of the sour orange.

Potted, indoor varieties require compost-rich soil and a humid atmosphere. Setting the pot in a shallow container with an inch of small stones, partially covered with water, adds the needed humidity. Plenty of sunlight is required to insure growth. Do not overwater lemon plants, for too much water can be as detrimental to plant growth as too little.

Varieties: Perhaps the best variety for home planting is the Meyer, which is hardy, disease resistant and vigorous. It can withstand temperatures down to 10 to 15°F. (−12.22 to −9.44°C.) without being killed. Propagated by cuttings, the mature tree reaches a six- to ten-foot height and prolifically bears a fruit with a very thin skin and lots of juice. Also adaptable are the Eureka, Ponderosa and Lisbon.

See also CITRUS.

LEMON BALM
See BALM, MELISSA

LEMON MINT   *See* BERGAMOT

LEMON VERBENA
(*Aloysia triphylla*)

Once classified as *Lippia citriodora,* lemon verbena is native to Chile, Peru and Guatemala. In this country it is grown mostly as a potted plant, and kept pruned to small size. Its foliage has a strong scent, which made it an old-time bouquet favorite. Flowers are small white spikes. Leaves are long and narrow, and grow in whorls.

When grown as a greenhouse subject, it should be wintered at cool temperatures of about 55°F. (12.78°C.). In summer it may be planted in the garden or placed in a protected position in its pot. Potting soil should be a mixture of sand, loam and leaf mold, with additions of a small amount of manure and bone meal. Propagation is by greenwood cuttings rooted in sand. In frost-free climates, it may be grown outside year-round, and pruned to a small standard tree shape.

Harvesting lemon verbena can be done anytime, although if the herb's fragrance is to be preserved, late summer is best. Strip the leaves from the shoots or cut the shoots and chop them with the leaves. Let dry in the shade.

Lemon verbena was once used to treat stomach disorders and served as a skin stimulant. Its most popular contemporary use is in cooking, where its lemony flavor is used in preparing poultry, fish and stuffings. A minty tea can be made from this herb, also.

Besides lemon verbena, the only other cultivated variety is the carpetgrass or frogfruit (*Phyla nodiflora* var. *canescens*) of southern California, a creeping form used on dry, poor soils as a ground cover. Also from South America, it spreads from creeping stems, and can be kept mowed. Mowing to remove seed heads prevents it from becoming a pest. Flowers are small, lilac-colored heads. Leaves are long and slender. The best means of planting is by clumps spotted at intervals. It will spread rapidly to cover an entire area.

See also HERB.

LEMON WASTE
See CITRUS WASTE

LENTEN ROSE
See CHRISTMAS ROSE

LENTIL   *(Lens culinaris)*

Since antiquity, lentils have been used as food in Mediterranean countries. An annual of the Pea family, the lentil grows on a straggling 12- to 18-inch vine, and produces inconspicuous whitish to lavender pealike flowers, which are a good source of honey. These are followed by flat, two-seeded pods. Lentils vary in size, and in color of leaves, flowers and seeds. There are three varieties of seed: small, flat brown ones, small yellow ones, or larger, pea-shaped ones. Seed is sown in early spring in sandy soil, with rows 18 to 30 inches apart. Seed keeps best when left in the pod.

LEOPARD PLANT   *See* LIGULARIA

LEPTOSPERMUM

This is a genus of about 25 species of evergreen shrubs and trees of the Myrtle family. The best-known common names are tea tree, because the leaves can be used as a substitute for tea, and sand stay, because the plants are used in Australia and California to bind loose, sandy soils. They are warm-climate plants native to Australia and New Zealand, and can be grown only in the southernmost portions of the United States. Several of the most freely blooming species have been developed as greenhouse plants. They are kept in a cool house throughout the winter and gradually brought up to 60°F. (15.56°C.) in February or March, when they will bloom.

Leaves of *Leptospermum* are stiff and small, growing ½ to one inch long. The white, pink or red flowers grow in the leaf axils and produce quantities of bloom in the spring. Propagation is by seed in spring, greenwood cuttings under glass early in spring, or mature cuttings in sand in the fall.

Most commonly planted in California is *L. laevigatum,* sand stay. It will grow to 30 feet, but is also pruned to a shrub. Leaves are one inch, flowers white and ¾ inch. With similar flowers but much shorter, silkier leaves is *L. scoparium,* also called tea tree.

Some varieties of *L. scoparium* are grown in this country as greenhouse plants, but not many are cultivated outdoors. They are shrubs or small trees 12 to 25 feet tall, but may also be found in dwarf forms of one to two feet, and are more acceptable for indoor culture. Flowers of this species are usually white, but some varieties have colored blossoms—Chapmann, bright rose; Nicholls, carmine; Rose, rose pink; and Red Damask, dark red.

LESPEDEZA

Lespedeza is a legume widely grown for pasture, hay and soil conservation, especially in the Southeast. There are three species of lespedeza grown for forage: Korean, striate and sericea (perennial). Korean is an earlier and larger variety than the striate.

Lespedeza is very hardy and drought resistant and will flourish on poor soils. Seed should be broadcast in early spring. It reseeds itself and is best maintained in permanent pasture when grown with timothy, orchardgrass or other non-sod-forming grass. It makes a good hay—almost the equivalent of alfalfa in feeding value—when cut early.

A well-balanced pasture and forage system can be achieved from lespedeza in combination with winter wheat. Both crops can be grown on the same land every year, and good returns can be obtained even on soils of marginal fertility.

Some members of the family are grown as ornamentals or as food and shelter for wildlife. *L. bicolor* and *L. Thunbergii* are late-blooming shrubs with purple flowers. They do best in sandy soil and an open location, and are propagated by cuttings. *L. bicolor* grows six to ten feet high and *L. Thunbergii* grows three to eight feet.

See also COVER CROP, GREEN MANURE, LEGUME, SERICEA.

LETTUCE   (*Lactuca sativa*)

Few salad vegetables exceed lettuce in popularity, and you should have little difficulty in growing it. Success in producing a steady supply of fresh, crisp leaves, rich in vitamin A, depends to a great extent upon an understanding of the habits of this plant.

Lettuce grows readily because all cultivated strains were obtained originally from the prickly lettuce (*L. Serriola*), an Asiatic weed. Prominent among other wild forms are sleepwort (*L. virosa*) and the familiar wild lettuce (*L. canadensis*), a tall, yellow-flowered herb which is often a troublesome weed.

Planting and Culture: Almost any fairly good garden soil that is well drained and not excessively acid is suitable for lettuce. The only real secret about growing fine plants is to keep them uncrowded and growing rapidly. Rapid growth demands an abundance of moisture plus an abundance of natural plant nutrients. Mature compost humus or well-rotted manure should be dug in along the row before the seed is sown. In transplanting, a generous amount of organic humus should be worked into the hole before the plant is set out.

Wild lettuce prefers a temperate climate and its cultivated descendants naturally thrive best during cool weather, although some loose-leafed strains are valued for their ability to grow during summer heat.

Heading lettuce may be planted to head-up either during the early summer or the fall. For the early crop the seed should be sown about ¼ inch deep in flats or similar containers and placed in a sunny window or a cold frame about the beginning of March. The young plants should be ready to set out early in April. In the flats, the seed should be thinly sown and the seedlings thinned just as soon as the leaves touch. Probably no fault is more universal than sowing lettuce seed too thickly.

For the spring crop, start seed indoors in flats or pots in a sunny, cool (50 to 60°F. [10 to 15.56°C.]) location. Or, sow seed outside in a hotbed or cold frame, about four to six weeks before the last severe frost. One seed packet will sow a 100-foot row. For a good potting mixture, sift together one part sand, one part good loam and one part compost. Keep moist and, when the seedlings have at least their first set of true leaves, transplant to plant bands or flats. Gradually harden off the plants by setting them outdoors during the sunny part of the day.

Transplanting: Setting the transplants out very early is essential. In fact, some gardeners make a practice of sowing their lettuce seed in the fall in a carefully prepared area. The seedlings become fairly large before severe frost. As cold weather approaches, the seedlings are covered with a gradually deepened layer of loose straw, leaves, twigs, or other materials. Under this, the small plants survive the winter easily and the gardener has a heavy supply of sturdy, very early seedlings upon which to draw.

In setting out the transplants, put them about 15 inches apart in the row in rows about two feet apart. When seed is sown directly into the garden, the seedlings should be ruthlessly thinned to stand at least a foot apart to prevent overcrowding.

Care: In the early stages of growth the plant has a cluster of shallow feeding rootlets. This condition makes it ideal for transplanting but, while small, makes it an easy victim of weeds. A light mulching of compost sifted around the plants will do much to keep down weedy growth and later will supply easily available plant nutrients.

Lettuce plants will not do their best unless they have a very liberal supply of moisture. Normally the supply of rainwater is insufficient and unreliable. It will aid your plants to continue rapid growth during dry weather if you water them with rainwater which has filtered through a container holding a quantity of fertile compost.

It may be that for one of many reasons your plants do not reach the heading stage before the arrival of hot weather. Many gardeners have had this experience. The most popular solution to the problem consists in covering the plants so as to give them partial shade. A few stakes driven into the ground along the sides of the rows may be used to support a length of cheesecloth stretched upon them. A slightly heavier framework may be made to support a thin layer of brush, or a slat roof in which the slats are alternated with spaces about equal to the width of the slats. Any such arrangement which excludes excessive sunlight will usually produce the coolness necessary to the plants if they are to form satisfactory heads. Some gardeners make good use of a partially shaded spot in the garden as a favored site for lettuce.

Diseases and Pests: Lettuce rot, which first affects the lowest leaves in contact with the soil and then spreads through the plant, can be avoided by spreading clean sand over the surface of the soil. Fungus and bacterial diseases are best avoided by rotating the crop. Do not plant lettuce in the same rows two years in

Crisphead

Loose-leaf

Romaine

Butterhead

Although crisphead lettuce is the best-selling type of lettuce, loose-leaf, romaine and butterhead are considered superior in flavor and quality.

succession and do not plant where endive, chicory or dandelion have just grown. These are all subject to the same diseases.

Insects which cause the greatest damage in new lettuce plantings are cutworms and slugs. Cutworms may be outwitted if loose collars of stiff paper are put on the seedlings when they are planted. The collars are made about one to 1½ inches in diameter and are wide enough so that when ½ inch is buried in the soil an inch or more remains as a barricade above ground.

If slugs are a problem, limestone or wood ashes may be sprinkled over the soil around the plants to discourage them. In a wet season when slugs are very bad, do not use small baskets or boxes to cover newly planted seedlings. These only act as shelters during the hot part of the day and slugs may sometimes be found by the dozens inside inverted berry boxes. Instead, shade seedlings with a canopy held a foot or more above the bed.

Harvesting: Pick lettuce in the early morning hours to preserve the crispness it acquired during the cool of the night. Immediately after being picked, it should be washed thoroughly but as briefly as possible and dried immediately to prevent loss of vitamins. If stored in a closed container in the refrigerator, it will retain its crispness for days.

Loose-leaf types should be cut off at ground level and the roots left in the soil. Later in the season the roots will send up new leaves for a second crop.

Varieties: Cultivated lettuce may be divided into five main types:

Butterhead: These form a soft head, yellow almost to the center with dark outer leaves. Most varieties of Bibb lettuce mature in 60 to 70 days and have loosely folded leaves. Fordhook and Dark Green Boston mature in 80 days and are known for their excellent flavor.

Cabbagehead: This type is slightly more heat resistant than the butterhead varieties. Premier Great Lakes is resistant to heat and tip burn. Great Lakes stands up well in hot weather.

Celtuce: This lettuce is grown for its thick stem rather than the leaves. Celtuce matures in 80 days, producing a vegetable with two or three times the vitamin C content of normal lettuce.

Cos or Romaine: These form a tall, elongated head and have a leaf shaped somewhat like the bowl of a spoon. Paris White is the favorite of this type. It matures in 80 days.

Loose-leaf, nonheading: This type is best for home gardens since it can be grown where temperatures are too high for heading types. Grand Rapids is a crisp variety maturing in 45 days. Black-seeded Simpson is a brittle, crisp variety with a delicate flavor. Oak Leaf matures in about 40 days.

LEUCOJUM   *See* SNOWFLAKE

LEUCOTHOE

This fairly small ornamental shrub, known as fetterbush, produces white, bell-shaped flowers in dense clusters. Varieties of leucothoe are grown mainly in the South and along the East Coast and bloom in April or May. They have attractive foliage and flowers and make good foundation and border plantings. They grow best in humus-rich moist soil that is fairly sandy. *L. Fontanesiana* is an evergreen shrub that grows to about six feet and is the hardiest of the leucothoes. *L. racemosa,* also known as sweetbells, is deciduous and sometimes reaches a height of 12 feet.

LEVISTICUM OFFICINALE
See LOVAGE

LEWISIA

A genus of the Portulaca family, lewisias are native to the Northwest. They are low-growing evergreen and deciduous perennial herbs with starchy, fleshy roots which (in

L. rediviva) are used as food by Oregon Indians. The genus was named for the explorer Meriwether Lewis. Most species are hardy throughout the United States.

The plants grow close to the ground, forming rosettes of leaves one to three inches long. Satiny cactuslike flowers grow singly or in loose clusters on short stems seldom more than eight inches high. Flowers are about two inches across and come in shades of pink, lavender, orange, red, and in white tinged with these colors.

Planting and Culture: Lewisias are suited to the rock garden, rather than to the open border. All varieties must have well-drained soil for their fleshy roots, most preferring abundant moisture early in spring, when leaf and flower growth is made, and dryness during the summer. Partial shade is preferred by most species except in damp regions where full sun is advised. Evergreen ones need more moisture.

Soil for both types of lewisias should be composed of at least half coarse, gritty sand, and half leaf mold or compost. The soil should be deeply prepared. Seed germinates best if sown very early in spring, or in fall. If it must be sown in warm weather, it should be refrigerated for several weeks first. Evergreen species should be grown in a bed mulched on the top with an inch of fine gravel, to permit water to drain easily from the axils of the leaves.

Types: One of the most common lewisias is bitterroot (*L. rediviva*), the state flower of Montana. In the spring, it covers acres of that state with its white to rose flowers. It does well in dry rock gardens and can be grown in most parts of North America.

Two species that thrive in moist, rocky areas are *L. oppositifolia* and *L. nevadensis*. The former has few leaves and medium-sized rose-colored flowers that stand six to 12 inches from the ground. It blossoms from late winter to early spring. *L. nevadensis* has white flowers with a slight lavender tinge. It blooms during the summer months and grows wild throughout the West.

Of the evergreen types, *L. columbiana* and *L. Cotyledon* are most common. The former species has clusters of deep pink flowers on stems that rise about six inches above a dense rosette of green leaves. The variety Rupicola is widely available from seedsmen. Several varieties of *L. Cotyledon* have been developed. Howell has wavy-margined leaves and numerous clusters of pink flowers striped with violet and white. It grows about six inches high. Heckner has slightly smaller pink flowers. Both varieties blossom early spring to summer.

One other species sometimes grown in the garden is *L. Tweedyi* which blooms throughout the summer. Its flowers are much larger than other types and come in various shades of salmon and pink.

LEY

The English use this term to refer to arable land that is planted with grasses and clover, harvested for hay, and then plowed under for other crops. The use of a ley, or lea, is a good land management practice. English farmers refer to four-year leys and two-year leys, for example, to designate different kinds of rotation.

LIATRIS

This genus of the Composite family contains about 20 flowering perennials native to

North America. Sometimes called lacinarias, they are characterized by stiff narrow leaves and spikes of flowers that bloom from the top of the spike down, rather than blooming from the lowest buds and continuing toward the top. They resemble soft pink brushes. Blossoming time is late summer and early fall. The flowers attract many butterflies and bees.

Though liatris will thrive in almost any soil and in full shade, they prefer a light soil with a good amount of humus. Most species prefer full sun. They are easily propagated by seed sown in the fall, by division of the tuberous roots, or in some species by offsets. They are good subjects for the wild garden, since some species are difficult to combine with other colors in the flower border. The flowers are excellent for drying.

The most decorative and widely grown species is *L. spicata,* the blazing star or gay-feather. It grows wild throughout the eastern and southern United States and can be grown in most mild areas. It does very well in poor soil but prefers a moist situation. Flower stems are up to three feet high with compact, purple to red blossoms. They appear in late summer and continue through early fall. For cut flowers or for mass plantings, this species is by far the best of the liatris.

LICHEN

A lichen consists of two separate and different plant forms, an alga and a fungus, teamed together in a symbiotic or mutually beneficial relationship. The fungus's role is to absorb and conserve moisture and provide shelter, without which the alga, a water plant, cannot live. The alga, in turn, shares with the fungus the food products which it fabricates from the raw materials around it. The fungus has no such food-producing ability.

Some lichens are instrumental in dissolving rock particles and helping in soil formation. By secreting acids, these lichens break up rock and other hard surfaces. Other types act to remove some of the mineral binding of the particles and thus free them to the soil. Some species help bind soil against wind erosion.

Types: The first lichen to appear on a bare surface is usually a crust form, the later ones being leafy or even shrublike, growing with a tiny "trunk" and branches. Their one absolute requirement is pure air—a smoky or chemical-laden atmosphere spells death.

A wide variety of lichens—some 6,000 different kinds—is found throughout the world. California's oaks are famed for their "old man's beard," a blue green epiphyte that hangs from their trunks and branches in rich profusion. The lichens on rocks and walls are usually bright orange, while "cup" or "trumpet" lichens are a lively red and often have a shrubby growth. Flint pebbles are covered with a black crust form.

Brown "Iceland moss" has long provided both animal fodder and food for the Lapps and other Northern peoples. Eskimos have winter pastures; their reindeer fatten on field and rock lichens, and especially prize the bearded forms on trees. Raked up during wet weather, Iceland moss can be dried and fed to all kinds of animals. Containing 5 percent protein, it gives a marvelous richness to the milk of northern Scandinavia. Powdered, it is made into excellent breads, cereals, jelly, and salads. A similar variety is believed to be the "manna" that fed the starving Israelites in the wilderness.

In the Garden: You can have a lot of fun with lichens in both indoor and outdoor gardening. Lichen-covered twigs and pebbles dress up an aquarium, and you'll find the brilliant red-crested lichen, or "British soldier," which grows on sterile soil, a delightful decoration for dish gardens.

Collect some lichens in the country. Look for old rocks and tree trunks overgrown with them. A knife can be used to scrape them off. After a few hours drying in the sun, they can be crumbled and rubbed into the surface of a rock freshly sprinkled with water. Moisture is very important—sprinkle the rock two or three times a day. In a few days, a gentle green will appear, gradually deepening until the whole surface is carpeted. Granite is slower to respond than sandstone, shale or limestone, but the result is equally pleasing.

LIEBIG, JUSTUS VON

(1803–1873) Von Liebig was a German-born chemist and biochemist known to many as the pioneering influence in the development of chemical fertilizers. He was the originator of the laboratory method of teaching chemistry, the discoverer of chloroform and other chemicals, the first to isolate the amino acid, tyrosine, and the developer of baking powder.

For 28 years von Liebig taught at the University of Giessen, in Germany, where his innovative theories and methods of teaching won him acclaim. He was the first professor of chemistry to open his laboratory to all his students, allowing them to obtain a practical knowledge of the chemicals they were working with. From the interaction with his students, von Liebig developed the first textbook on qualitative analysis, which enabled students to analyze minerals and to determine their chemi-

cal composition. This textbook became a landmark in the development of the study of geology.

The predominant theory in the study of agriculture at this time was the "humus theory." Agriculturalists were certain that plants "ate" humus, but when von Liebig published his *Chemistry of Agriculture and Physiology* in 1840 he attempted to dispel this theory. His book set the standard for the beginning of modern agricultural science. "If plants get all their food from humus," von Liebig asked in his classic text, "then where did the first plant get its food—since humus is composed of decayed plants?"

But von Liebig overlooked the fact that the first plant was only a moss or lichen that grew on rocks, and that at the beginning of the world, nothing grew but this moss which received its nourishment from the air and the rock. The decaying lichen, plus admixtures of rock pulverized by the elements, made the soil in which plants began to grow—first ferns, then the higher developed ones. The original lichen could not produce seed but reproduced by spores flying in the air.

Sir Albert Howard in his *Agricultural Testament* (Emmaus, Pa.: Rodale Press, Inc., 1973) criticized von Liebig, stating, ". . . he followed the science of the moment. In his onslaught on the humus theory he was so sure of his ground that he did not call in Nature to verify his conclusions. It did not occur to him that while the humus theory, as then expressed, might be wrong, humus itself might be right. . . . He was unable to visualize his problem from two very different points of view at one and the same moment—the scientific and the practical. His failure has cast its shadow on much of the scientific investigation of the next hundred years. . . . During [the] period (1840–

1900) . . . the use of artificial manures became firmly welded into the work and outlook of the Experiment Stations; the great importance of nitrogen (N), phosphorus (P), and potash (K) in the soil solution was established; what may briefly be described as the NPK mentality was born."

LIGHT

Light affects plant life in many ways. The scientific name for the process by which green plants use light energy to synthesize carbohydrates (foods) from carbon dioxide and water is "photosynthesis," from the Greek words *photos,* meaning light, and *synthesis,* meaning putting together. Light supplies the energy needed to transform carbon dioxide absorbed from the air, water, and certain inorganic minerals into organic matter and into the oxygen, which the plants give off as long as light is present. Where light is absent, photosynthesis stops, and the plants absorb oxygen and give off carbon dioxide.

Growth Responses: Science has shown that not all of the light reaching plants is used in the photosynthetic process. Natural daylight, white light, is actually composed of different wavelengths each with a different color—red, orange, yellow, green, blue, violet, and ultra-violet. Chlorophyll in plants' leaves absorbs essentially the wavelengths comprising the blue and red ranges, and reflects the green wavelengths, thus making plants appear green. Red energy triggers growth but too much red light can cause plants to grow tall and leggy. Blue light used alone causes short, stocky growth with few or no blooms. Accordingly, when choosing artificial light sources to encourage plant growth, the ideal lamps would be richest in both blue and red areas of the spectrum.

Phototropism: Phototropism is a growth movement in response to one-sided illumination. The bending of sunflowers toward the sun and the leaning of house plant stems, leaves and flowers toward windows are common examples of phototropism. Growth regulators or hormones build up on the darker side of the stem and decrease on the light side. The extra dose of hormones on the darkened side of the plant causes the stem to elongate faster on that side than it does on the lighter side.

Photonasty: Photonasty is the oriented movement and disproportionate growth of flat plant parts in respect to the plant itself and not to an external stimulus like light. An example of photonasty is the sleep movement of beans: during the day the first pair of leaves above the cotyledons is horizontal; at night they fold down alongside the stems.

Phototropism is the process by which plants grow towards the available light source. Hormones build up in the dark side of the growing plant, causing the stem cells to elongate more rapidly than those on the lighter side.

Photoperiodism: About 50 years ago two USDA scientists discovered the phenomenon of photoperiodism, the response of plants to length of the daily period of illumination. The light–dark rhythm influences the timing of maturity and blossoming, tuber and bulb formation, seed germination and root formation, the color and formation of leaves, and the branching of stems.

Research into photoperiodism has resulted in the classification of plants according to their day-length characteristics. One group, "short-day plants," flowers when days are short and nights are long. "Long-day plants" flower when days are long and nights are short. Still others are unaffected by day lengths and are called "light neutral" or "indifferent." The following list includes the common flower and vegetable plants according to their light requirements.

Short-day plants (10 to 12 light hours)

Asparagus	Dahlia
Aster	Gardenia
Beans	Kalanchoe
Carrot	Poinsettia
Cattleya orchid	Potato (tuber de-
Christmas begonia	velopment)
Chrysanthemum	Strawberry gera-
Cocklebur	nium
Corn	Sweet potato

Long-day plants (14 to 18 light hours)

Most annuals	Hibiscus
Beet	Onion
Chicory	Pea
Chinese cabbage	Radish
Dill	Spinach
Grains	Tuberous begonia

Indifferent plants

African violets and other gesnerads	Kale
	Kohlrabi

Broccoli	Lettuce
Brussels sprouts	Marigold
Cabbage	New Zealand
Cauliflower	spinach
Celery	Okra
Coleus	Pepper
Collard	Rose
Cress	Semperflorens
Cucurbits	begonia
Endive	Tomato
Geranium	Turnip

Regulating Light in the Garden: Outdoor gardeners can improve their results by increasing the amount and the consecutive hours of light their plants get. A white mulch (such as light stones), a white painted building or fence or strips of aluminum foil placed in the garden will reflect more light energy onto plants, spurring them to greater growth. Fruit growers can prune out the center of their trees to increase flower bud formation by getting more light to the center of their trees.

Light also affects the germination of seed. Some seed germinate more readily when exposed to light than when buried in the earth. Grasses, lettuce, celery, snapdragon, petunia, and flowering tobacco will all be more successful if seed are merely pressed down or gently watered down into the growing medium.

See also FLUORESCENT LIGHT, HOUSE PLANTS.

LIGHTNING

Nearly half of all farm fires occur during July and August—and over two-thirds of these are caused by lightning.

To a great extent, man has himself to blame for these fires. He builds structures of concrete, wood, brick, and glass—all poor conductors of electricity. When an electrical charge hits one of these materials, it has so much trouble going through it that terrific quantities of heat are generated. Result: explosion and fire.

Metal is a good electrical conductor; so, if a path of metal is made from a high point on a building to the ground where the lightning can release its energy harmlessly, no destructive heat will be built up. Hence, the need for lightning rods.

Lightning Rods: Statistics show that a properly installed and maintained lightning protection system is an absolute guarantee against damage from lightning. Insurance companies, checking on reported "failures" of rod systems, find that in nearly every case the damage is the result of carelessness in installing the system or of failure to maintain it or extend it when changes are made to the building.

Lightning protection, incidentally, is good business. Besides the safety it affords, a good protection system on farm buildings often means reduced insurance premiums on those buildings.

It's a good idea to check your system and make sure it's doing the job it was meant to do. Old, unlabeled systems may need to be checked by a reliable installer.

Lightning rods, or air terminals, must be at least ten inches higher than the elevation they protect. They should be placed not more than 20 feet apart (25 if they are more than 30 inches high), and at or within two feet of the ends of all ridges, gables, chimneys, or large dormers. Terminals higher than two feet should be braced halfway up. Every farm building 12 by 14 feet or larger should be rodded, unless directly attached to a rodded structure.

Many lightning systems use a compact ⅜-inch solid copper rod ten to 15 inches high, and

have all conducting cables on the inside of the building to give a neat, efficient appearance.

An improperly grounded system won't stop any lightning bolts. Make sure your ground connections are tight in the earth; they should go down at least ten feet to permanently moist earth. Then follow the conductors over the building. There should be at least two grounded conductors for a building 80 feet long or under, and one more for each additional 60 feet.

Check the conducting cables to see that they are continuous, and that all connections to parts of the building are tight and made with clamps or cleats of the same metal as the conductor. If a down conductor is torn away from the side of a building, put copper clamps over it every few feet and nail them down with copper nails.

Safety Precautions: All metal objects in the building—ventilators, door or hay carrier tracks, eave troughs, stanchions, water pipes—should be bonded to the roof or to down conductors.

Buildings with metal roofs or siding, contrary to general thought, are not invulnerable to lightning bolts. They need a full protection system just like wooden or concrete structures. Use conductors of the same kind of metal as the roof or walls.

Cattle often seek shelter under isolated trees during storms. To protect them, wire a copper down-lead from an underground rod at the tree's base, through a brass or copper-coated pipe, to an electrode driven at least six feet into the ground. All wire fences should be grounded. Those attached to buildings should be grounded at the post nearest the building.

LIGHTNING BUG   *See* FIREFLY

LIGNIN

A major constituent of wood, lignin has been classed as the major waste in industry. Pulp and paper mills alone discharge two million tons annually. Sawmills and other woodworking plants scattered throughout the nation can readily make available another ten million tons of wood waste, while potential forest and agricultural wastes are many times that amount.

Lignin is slow to decompose but eventually supplies a great deal of energy. In a partially decomposed state, lignin supplies a basic material for humus. Where available, it should be used for compost making and in mulches, but, since it is high in carbon, it should be used with a high-nitrogen material such as manure or sludge. The lignin content of cornstalks is 11 percent, that of oak leaves 30 percent, of old pine needles 23 percent, and of dry alfalfa plants 11 percent. A forest humus has about 48 percent lignin in it.

LIGULARIA

A genus of hardy and half-hardy perennials of the Composite family, ligularias were formerly included in the genus *Senecio* and came originally from Europe and Asia. Some species may be grown outdoors only south of Washington, D.C., and many are grown exclusively indoors. Others make good summer bedding plants and can be grown in the flower border in ordinary soil from seed planted in April. They may also be propagated by root division or cuttings.

Ligularias can grow up to six feet tall and are noted for their showy flower heads and interesting foliage. The broad leaves and large yellow orange flowers are supported by long, slender stems. Leaves can be palmate, kidney shaped or orbicular. The summer flowers are generally nodding.

L. dentata cv. 'Desdemona' is a 3½-foot cultivar with basal leaves that sometimes grow as much as 12 inches across and have a purple tint. The flowers have yellow orange rays and brown disks, in heads four inches across. This variety, along with other forms of this species, is the hardy ligularia often found in nurseries. Plant at least 2½ feet from other plants, as it grows quite large. Water well in dry weather and use plenty of compost in the soil. It can be left for five years before dividing, and becomes a striking specimen in the border.

Another striking species is *L. japonica*. Growing to five feet and displaying huge leaves and orange flowers, this ligularia should be planted in a moist spot where a bold effect is wanted. The palmate leaves, often a foot across, are usually divided into seven to 11 narrow lobes. It is hardy to New York.

Leopard plant, *L. tussilaginea* cv. 'Aureo-maculata', grown mostly as a house plant, is one of the more tender species. Leaves are up to ten inches across and blotched with yellow, white or light rose. In the variety Argentea, markings are cream colored on green leaves which show a whitish bloom. Flowers are light yellow, in heads two inches across.

LIGUSTRUM   *See* PRIVET

LILAC   (*Syringa*)

A group of ornamental shrubs and small trees belonging to the Olive family, lilacs are cultivated for their showy and often fragrant flowers.

Planting and Culture: There is an old saying about lilacs: "A little sun, a little soil, a little rain, and little toil." Lilacs are hardy and can withstand all sorts of ill treatment, but the prize blooms will be picked from the shrubs that have had a little care.

Lilacs mildew easily in a shady site and, although this unsightly affliction does not seem to do the plant permanent harm, they fare better if planted in a sunny location. The soil

Lilac flowers arise on last year's wood so picking should be done with care.

should be loamy and well drained.

Since it is a heavy feeder, fertilizing is called for at least every other year. In the spring, side-dress with a six-inch layer of well-rotted compost placed out far enough to take in most of the branch spread. Dig this in well, being careful not to injure the roots. Lilacs, like most shrubs, grow best in slightly acid soil. A mulch of hay or leaves, wood ashes, or pine needles will increase soil acidity. If the soil is too acid, an application of agricultural lime is recommended. In the late fall, work this mulch into the soil, and remulch with leaves or grass clippings for the winter to prevent heaving of roots as the ground freezes and thaws.

Lilacs bloom on last year's wood, so spare as much new wood as possible when gathering the flowers. One should pick off faded blooms to conserve the energy of the shrub, but on a tall specimen this can be a chore. Healthy plants seem to produce blooms year after year, nevertheless, but if your lilac is not flowering well, take the trouble to cut off each faded flower cluster.

Pruning is mostly a matter of removing weak, ungainly branches and overabundant sucker growth. It is best to loosen the soil and pull up these unwanted sprouts, because if cut off at ground level, the roots may send up new growth.

Propagation and Transplanting: Perhaps you will wish to begin a new plant from one of the suckers. This is a simple process, but one to be used only if the lilac is one of the common, or New England, species (*S. vulgaris*). Select the shoot farthest from the parent bush. Dig it out gently, with the root, and plant it in a hole wide enough to take the root without cramping. Fill the hole with a mixture of topsoil and well-rotted compost, adding a few cups of bone meal. Water generously throughout the first season. When the shoot has made some growth, lay a mulch of finely chopped grass clippings around it.

The propagation of the hybrid lilac is a bit more complicated, but the results are as successful. In late June, take cuttings or slips from the soft new growth of a mature shrub and set in sand. Keep under glass until they have taken root. In September plant them in their permanent position, and in November mulch them heavily for the winter.

Unless your winters are very severe, it is best to transplant a well-started shrub in the fall. Dig a hole two feet deep. Layer the hole with a mixture of compost, topsoil, and bone meal, and set the roots on this. Fill in the hole with the same mixture and water generously.

Types: There are over 500 varieties of lilacs which are classified in about 30 species. There are single florets with simple charm or opulent double ones; drooping sprays or upright panicles; the tiny lacelike florets of the Persian lilac or the long narrow trusses of *S. Sweginzowii.*

Some early-blooming lilacs are *S. oblata,* a compact shrub with lilac-colored blooms; *S.* x *persica* (Persian), with graceful, slender branches and pale lilac flowers; and *S. vulgaris,* usually with lilac-colored blooms. The hybrids of this species, called French lilacs, are the most widely planted lilacs so there are many named varieties to choose from.

S. x *chinensis* (Chinese), with its red purple flowers and wine-colored foliage in fall, is an early bloomer, and so are *S. Josikaea* (Hungarian), a dense shrub with deep lilac flowers, and *S. pubescens,* whose blooms are especially fragrant.

S. amurensis, a treelike shrub with yellow white flowers, and *S. reticulata* (Japanese), which is similarly colored, are both midseason bloomers.

Late bloomers include *S. pekinensis,* with yellow white flowers in flat clusters; *S. reflexa* (nodding), usually scentless, with red buds opening into white flowers; *S. Sweginzowii,* with long, narrow, pale pink clusters of flowers; and *S. villosa,* a hardy, dense shrub with profuse clusters of lilac-colored flowers.

Several species are double bloomers. *S. microphylla* cv. 'Daphne', a graceful spreading shrub with small, pink, fragrant flowers, blooms in May and again in late summer. *S. Meyeri* has magenta flowers and blooms in May and late summer.

LILY

Many plants have the name lily, but not all of them are members of the Lily family. Calla lilies belong to the Arum family, kaffir-lily (*Clivia*) to the Amaryllis family, the water lilies to the Water Lily family, and the blackberry lily (*Belamcanda*) to the Iris family.

There are over 200 genera which do belong to the Lily family, and they are, for the most part, native to the Northern Hemisphere. Besides the true lilies, which belong to the genus *Lilium,* there are several other well-known members of the family. Of great horticultural interest are the tulips (*Tulipa*), hyacinths (*Hyacinthus*), the daylilies (*Hemerocallis*), the checkered lilies (*Fritillaria*), lily-of-the-valley (*Convallaria*), plantain lilies (*Hosta*), and the trout lilies (*Erythronium*).

Many members of the Lily family are bulbous plants. It is interesting to note that while this family contains many plants of outstanding beauty, this beauty is not coupled with difficulty of culture or with tenderness; indeed, the members of the true lily genus are hardy in North America, with the possible exception of the Madonna lily (*L. candidum*).

Daylilies: There are some 12 species of *Hemerocallis,* most of them native to temperate eastern Asia. The flowers produced are very numerous, and even though the individual flowers last only a day, sometimes two, the plants are rarely out of flower.

In recent years many new hybrids have been introduced. The colors range from yellow to red with many shades of orange and pink. All are hardy and will grow well in most garden soils. They take a year to settle in and once established should not be disturbed until the clumps become untidy and the vigor of the plants begins to diminish. They should then be lifted and divided: replant only the clean, healthy roots. Divisions can be made in the fall or spring. If done in the fall the roots should be replanted so that they are well established before the winter cold weather sets in. If you live in a very cold area it is best to wait until the spring before lifting and dividing.

The flowering time varies according to species and parentage. The first to flower are hybrids of *H. Dumortieri,* the species itself flowering in May or June.

The common daylily found in the northeastern states is *H. fulva.* This seldom sets seed, being self-sterile, although it has been used with other varieties for hybridizing. It flowers from June through August.

H. Lilioasphodelus is the lemon, custard, or yellow daylily. It is somewhat smaller than the orange daylily, but it does have an advantage in being fragrant. The time of flowering is April or May, and it reaches a height of 2½ feet, about a foot less than *H. fulva.*

The Japanese daylily (*H. Thunbergii*) flowers in the later summer. This is a vigorous species with flower spikes three feet long, branched near the top. Its flowers are sulfur apricot with a deeper-colored throat.

Daylilies are fine flowers for the garden. With the right selection of hybrids it is possible to have varieties in flower for much of the summer and into the fall. Each year new varieties are being introduced, and deep-colored reds and shades of pink and rose, as well as the more traditional orange and yellow shades, make it possible to have a very colorful border.

In the very hottest areas some shade will bring out the shades of the flowers, and if the plants are grown near a stream or with adequate summer moisture a vast array of flowers can be expected. The plants are strong feeders, and when planting it is recommended that well-

Daylilies, like the ones shown here, make excellent, dramatic additions to the flower garden because they are so colorful and multiply so readily.

rotted compost or well-rotted manure be incorporated. Because of their vigor, plant the new roots some 18 inches apart.

Lily-of-the-Valley: Lily-of-the-valley (*Convallaria majalis*) is native to Europe, temperate Asia, and North America. This legendary bridal bouquet flower has a well-known fragrance which is, like the flowers themselves, unique. It is an easy plant to grow but does not do well where the winters are mild since it prefers to go through a dormant stage. If it likes its location it can become a pest because it will spread rapidly. Grow in shade and, if possible, on the north side of a home.

The plants are purchased in the fall or spring and are known in the trade as "pips." The roots are light yellowish brown and support a distinct bud which is purple blue in color. The buds which are fat are pregnant with the future flowers; those that are thinner will just produce foliage.

Lily-of-the-valley can be forced into flower. Either buy the plants in the fall, or dig them from the border. Wrap them in sphagnum moss, and place them in a very cold place or in the freezer. This is essential if they are to bloom well. When you wish to start them into growth, thaw them from the ice which will surround them, and place them in a porous potting mix. Give them a temperature of 55 to 60° F. (12.78 to 15.56° C.) at night and higher during the day. Do not let them dry out. They can also be forced at a lower temperature, but this will take longer. If you wish, they can be grown in sand or in a bowl with sphagnum moss and adequate moisture. With this method the plant will utilize its food reserves, and the plants will take a while to recover and flower again.

Plantain Lilies: The botanical name for these handsome plants, grown mainly for their attractive foliage, is *Hosta*. They are native to eastern Asia, especially Japan. They are herbaceous perennials and are at home in a border with shrubs such as rhododendrons. They prefer light shade, adequate summer moisture, and a soil with a high humus content. The flowers, while an attractive bonus to the foliage, are not as striking as the fantastic colorings of the leaves.

Plantain lilies are hardy, and will increase each year, so if additional plants are needed they can be lifted and divided in the fall or early spring.

The shorter-leaved species can be used for edging a border, but the greatest value lies with the larger-leaved species. These make ideal companion plants in woodlands where they are attractive throughout the summer until the advent of the first frosts.

H. Fortunei is a good plant for the edge of a border; the leaves are up to eight inches long and almost as wide. The grayish green leaves are excellent for use in flower arrangements. There is a variety, *H. Fortunei* var. *gigantea,* which has leaves some three times as large. The cultivar Marginato-alba has white-margined leaves and pale lilac midsummer flowers. *H. Sieboldiana* has probably the most outstanding leaves. They are blue green and up to 12 inches long and nine inches wide. *H. undulata* has four-inch-wide green leaves that are splashed with white.

The nomenclature of the plantain lilies is somewhat confusing. If you wish to grow these marvelous plants be guided more by the descriptions of the different varieties in the catalogs than by the actual names given to them.

Remember that the plantain lilies are grown mainly for their foliage and that the flowers are of secondary importance; however, there is a fragrant species worthy of note—*H. plantaginea*. The flowers are white and are produced in late summer. They form a fine combination with the medium-green leaves which are often up to 24 inches long and eight inches or more wide. The flowers are carried above the foliage to a height of some three feet.

True lilies: True lilies are members of the genus *Lilium*. There are approximately 80 species of lilies and many more hybrids. The species are found only in the Northern Hemisphere, and the majority are in the temperate zone. They have an underground bulb which is composed of scales; it does not have a protective outer coating. The modified leaves are fleshy. The flowers of lilies vary greatly in size, from quite small to very large, and are composed of six petals which in botanical language are called tepals. Each flower has six stamens, and the flowers come in all colors except true blue.

The majority of lilies are hardy in North America. All are perennials, and most will die down in the winter to reappear in the spring. They are among the most beautiful of bulbs, and by the correct selection of varieties and species they can be in flower from spring till fall.

Planting and Culture: Lilies like to have their heads in the sun and their feet in the shade. In very hot areas they prefer light shade. This is especially important when the more delicate pastel shades are desired. The light colors can sometimes be blanched by strong, full sun. Lilies can be grown in containers. They are also ideal plants for the shrub border, adding late spring and summer color when many of the shrubs have finished flowering.

Lilies like moisture during the growing season, but they must have good drainage; they do not like to have their roots in standing water. The soil should be rich in humus, and if they are being grown in containers the bulbs benefit from fertilization with fish-oil emulsions. A mulch of leaf mold is most beneficial, as it will control weeds and keep the bulbs from drying out in the summer.

Lily bulbs should be planted with twice as much soil over the top of the bulb as the bulb is high. This means that a bulb standing three inches high should have six inches of soil over the top of it; one four inches high should be covered with eight inches of soil. Well-rotted compost should be incorporated into the soil around the hole before the bulb is planted.

Plant either in the fall or spring, when the bulbs are dormant, or rather not in active growth, as the bulbs are never completely dormant. If at all possible, planting should be done some three or four weeks before the first severe frosts arrive in the fall. If this is not possible, the bulbs should be planted as soon as the ground can be worked in the spring. The only exception to fall or spring planting is the Madonna lily, which should be planted in August. Many lilies will produce stem roots which are those portions of the stem that emerge from the bulb below the ground. These, in turn, will produce roots which help feed the bulb during the growing season.

Once planted, the bulbs should be left undisturbed for years, to be lifted only when it is apparent that they are not as hearty as they were the previous year. This obvious loss of vigor will most likely be due to overcrowding. The bulbs should be lifted in the fall when the stalks have ripened. The larger bulbs should be selected for replanting and the smaller bulbs planted in nursery rows. These smaller bulbs can be planted one or two seasons later when they are a good size.

In cold areas it pays to protect the bulbs from the thawing and freezing routine by covering the area with a thick mulch of straw, salt hay, leaves, or grass. The mulch will also help protect the young shoots in the spring from a late frost which can damage them as they emerge.

The actual size of the bulbs will vary. Many species, being quite small, have bulbs only three to five inches in circumference, while some of the more vigorous hybrids will have bulbs eight to ten inches in circumference. The health of the bulb is more important than the size. The scales should be firm and plump, not cut or bruised. There should be a certain number of roots attached to the bulb, and these should be thick and fleshy.

Propagation: Certain varieties and species can be propagated by seed, scales, and bulblets produced in the underground portion of the stems. Other varieties are propagated by bulbils which are produced in the axils of the leaves.

Seed can be sown outdoors, but most gardeners will prefer to sow in boxes filled with light soil mix, milled sphagnum moss, vermiculite, or a combination of these ingredients. Space the seeds ½ inch apart, and cover lightly with soil. Keep soil moist, and as soon as they are large enough to handle, move the seedlings on to a larger flat or container.

The bulbils found along the stem on such lilies as the tiger lily can be sown in the same way as the seed; these are miniature bulbs and, as they are produced asexually, they will not differ from the parent.

Scales are the individual parts that make up the bulb; they are removed one by one when the bulbs are lifted or purchased in the fall and placed in a plastic bag in vermiculite, damp peat moss, or sphagnum moss. Seal the bag and store the scales at 70° F. (21.11° C.) for several weeks. Soon little plantlets will be formed at the base of each scale. When they are of fair size—about the size of a large pea—remove and store them in the refrigerator until the weather warms up in the spring. In the spring, plant the scales in well-prepared trenches, planting them some 1½ inches deep and spaced four to six inches apart. Cover and keep moist during the growing season. Many types will flower the second season after being scaled; others will take three to four seasons.

Cutting: If the flowers are being cut for the home, care should be taken to cut only the flowers; the stems are needed to manufacture food for the bulbs for the following year. The weakening of the bulb will be in direct proportion to the amount of stem removed. In the fall the stems should be left until the leaves turn brown, then removed completely by cutting at the base, taking care not to jerk or pull the stems, which can damage the bulb.

Varieties: The popular Easter lily (*L. longiflorum* var. *eximium*) is normally forced into flower for Easter. After it has finished flowering, the flower head should be removed and the lily planted in the garden. In colder areas wait until the danger of frost has passed.

One of the most popular lilies is the tiger lily (*L. lancifolium*). This late-summer-flowering species, with its distinctive pendent orange flowers, is a fine species. But don't overlook the modern hybrids. Enchantment, the first lily to receive a plant patent, flowers in June or July and has vigorous, upright flowers of nasturtium red. It is ideal for container growing as well as being a great garden plant. There are thousands

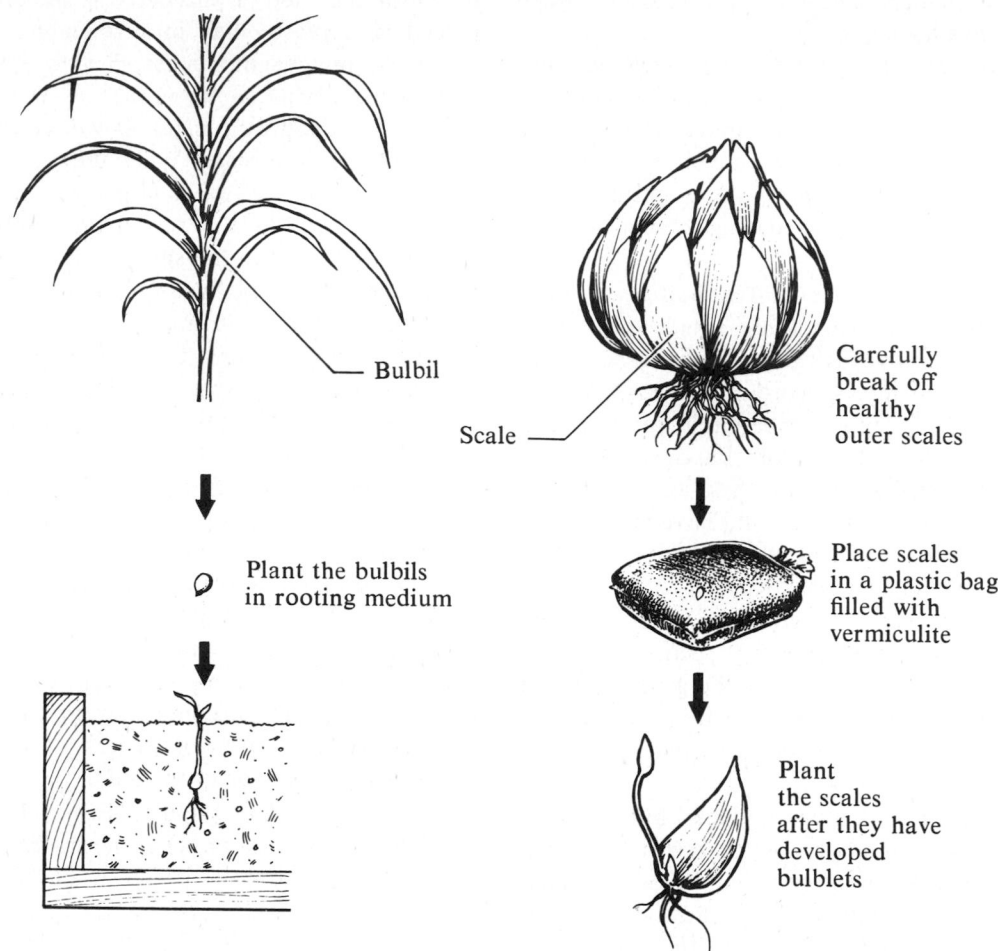

Bulbil

Plant the bulbils
in rooting medium

Scale

Carefully
break off
healthy
outer scales

Place scales
in a plastic bag
filled with
vermiculite

Plant
the scales
after they have
developed
bulblets

Propagation of true lilies differs according to species. Tiger lilies, for instance, bear tiny, black seedlike structures which, when planted in a fairly light medium, will form new bulbs. Other lilies are best propagated by the bulb scales. Either method will produce flowering plants in a few years.

of this variety grown as cut flowers, because it can be easily forced. For a change in color and form of flower try the hybrid Hornback's Gold. The flowers, which appear in July, are shaped like a Turk's cap and are five to six inches in diameter. The stems are often four to five feet high with as many as 15 flowers per stem.

The trumpet lilies (*L. longiflorum*) can be found in July. For many years the regal lily (*L. regale*) was the great summer lily, and now its form is captured in Golden Splendor, Pink Perfection, and Black Dragon, the latter being pure white on the inside with dark reverse to the petals. These trumpet lilies grow to four or five feet in height and are fully hardy.

In the late summer the gold band lily from Japan (*L. auratum* var. *platyphyllum*) comes into its glory with its fragant flowers. Its fragrant offsprings, the Imperial hybrids, are available in Imperial Gold, Silver, Crimson, and Pink.

See also BORDER, DAYLILY, HOSTA, HYACINTH, PERENNIALS, TULIP.

LILY-OF-THE-FIELD
See STERNBERGIA

LILY-OF-THE-VALLEY
See LILY

LILY POND

The garden landscape is often enhanced by a lily pond. If you have limited space for your project, perhaps the tub pond will be most suitable. It is the easiest method of creating a small pond and requires practically no maintenance once constructed.

Construction: Sink a wooden tub halfway into the ground. Then fill it about halfway with good, rich soil. Put about six inches of water over the soil. Plant a hardy water lily horizontally, about one inch deep, with the crown exposed. After planting, add a one-inch layer of sand in order to keep the water clear. Next, gradually fill the tub with cool water. At first, some water will be lost due to leakage, but in a few hours, the tub boards will be swollen and permanently watertight.

A few rocks, boulders or plants placed around the pond will add interest and beauty. Various bog and floating water plants will help give the pond a natural appearance.

Larger concrete pools are also used in lily pond construction. Select a sunny location if possible, although many lilies will bloom in partial shade. Build your pool with sloping sides. No special form is required. Use a 3–2–1 concrete mixture (three parts gravel, two parts sand, one part cement). The pool should be six inches thick, two feet deep, and should be reinforced near the top with a few strands of heavy, smooth wire placed in the center of the concrete. Pockets can be built along the sides for shallow water plants by pressing bricks into soft concrete. Fill with water and drain twice before planting lilies or adding fish. When dry, paint with underwater enamel if desired.

Fertilizing: Rotted cow manure placed near the bottom of the tub is a good fertilizer for water lilies. Place it near the bottom to prevent the manure from turning the water green. A ratio of three parts soil to one part manure is recommended. Fertilize every spring and again in July. In the spring, add dried blood to each tub. Small pots require one tablespoon, while large three-foot tubs require one pint. Chemical fertilizers are especially dangerous to fish and other water life in your pond.

Fish: Graceful goldfish, darting back and forth beneath the lily pads, add the finishing touch to the pond. The fish will earn their keep by eating mosquito larvae and insects. For this reason, they are an absolute necessity in the pond.

Water scavengers are the housekeepers of the pond. They keep plants free from disease and clean the pond. Snails eat green scum and algae; tadpoles live on decaying lily leaves and fish excrements; frogs live on mosquitoes, flies and other insects; even salamanders aid in the pool janitorial work. Every pond should have two scavengers for every square foot of pool surface.

Oxygenating plants are absolutely essential for fish life. These plants absorb the carbon dioxide which the fish give off and liberate oxygen which the fish must have to live. Fish need oxygenating plants in which to spawn and lay their eggs. Baby fish need them to hide in, lest they be devoured by their own parents. These plants and other pond materials can be obtained at pet stores or may be ordered by mail from firms specializing in pond supplies.

Winter Care: Cover the pool or tub with boards and leaves, hay or straw. Hardies can survive in the pool over winter. Tropical plants, however, should be replaced each spring, unless a greenhouse is available. Goldfish may be left in the pool, provided the water is about two feet deep. Otherwise, transfer them to the house until the freezing weather is past.

See also WATER GARDEN.

LIMA BEAN   *(Phaseolus limensis)*

The lima bean is a perennial vine in its native tropics, but it is grown as an annual in gardens of the temperate regions. Flowers are yellow to white, growing in loose spikes or clusters. Leaves have three leaflets and pods are flat and up to five inches long, with two to six seeds. Many bush varieties of lima beans are available.

Planting and Culture: Soil for lima beans should be well-drained loam, with a moderate amount of ground limestone and some compost added. Plant the beans in a sunny spot where there is no shade during any part of the day. To protect the garden from winds and to avoid shading lower growing plants, pole limas may be trained along a fence on the north side.

Seed should be planted after the soil is thoroughly warmed, late in May in most temperate regions or about two weeks after the first string beans are planted. Seed planted in cold soil will rot. After compost has been tilled into the soil, dig a trench two inches deep and place the seeds, eye down, about four inches apart. A fine sifting of soil is used to cover the seed and is firmed down.

Unless beans or peas have recently been grown in the same soil, it is advisable to inoculate the seed with an appropriate strain of nitrogen-fixing bacteria, which may be purchased from seed houses. The seed is dampened, and the black powdery inoculant stirred into it before sowing. After germination, bush limas may be thinned to stand eight inches apart in the rows. Rows should be spaced 24 to 30 inches apart.

Pole limas are planted around rough ten-foot poles which have been sunk three feet into the ground before the beans are planted. Or, three poles may be sunk one foot into the ground and tied together at the top to form a tripod. Six or eight seeds are placed around each pole and the seedlings are thinned to leave the three or four strongest to climb the poles.

In order to produce large, tender beans, limas need plenty of moisture after the blossoms have fallen. A heavy straw mulch is helpful and, in a severe drought, irrigate along the roots of the plants. If watered too heavily, the roots may rot.

Harvesting: When the beans plump up

in the pods, it is time to pick them. Leave flat pods for a later picking. If you pick the pods very gently, the limas may produce new blossoms in a few days.

Limas freeze well if blanched in boiling water for three minutes, and then cooled with ice, packaged, and frozen. Lima beans also dry well. Blanch for 15 to 20 minutes in boiling water, drain, place on trays and dry. Dried limas can be used in soups or cooked with bacon or ham.

See also DRYING FOOD.

LIME

Lime is seldom thought of as a fertilizer, since most soils contain enough calcium in one compound or another to supply all that plants need. The primary use for lime in the garden or farm is as an alkalizer, to raise the pH factor and thereby lower the acidity of the soil. *See also* pH.

Chemically, it is the oxide of calcium, with the formula CaO. It occurs in limestone, marble and chalk as calcium carbonate, $CaCO_3$. If these substances are heated, carbon dioxide, CO_2, escapes as a gas and CaO, or quicklime, remains. Quicklime combined with the correct amount of water yields slaked lime or hydrate of lime, $Ca(OH)_2$.

Any of these substances may be used to alkalize soil, and at various times each of the three has had a vogue. The difference in their action relates to the organic life of the soil.

Quicklime, CaO, will unite with water in the soil to form a hydrate. If enough free water is not available, as it seldom is, the quicklime wrenches water from living organisms in the soil, such as bacteria, fungi or plant roots, usually burning them enough to bring about their death. If manure or other nitrogenous fertilizers are present, the quicklime will unite with the nitrogen compounds they contain to rob them of their water, and will free the nitrogen as a gas, lowering the amount of nitrogen present in the soil in compounds which can be used by plants.

Hydrate of lime has already united its calcium with water, so it will not have the burning effect of quicklime. However, hydrate of lime does dissolve quickly in the soil. Rainwater washing through the soil dissolves the hydrate of lime, and leaches it down where it cannot be reached by plant roots. It may burn plant roots if applied to soil where plants are growing.

Ground limestone is the best form in which to provide lime so that it will be available to plants over a long period of time. There are two kinds of limestone available, calcic and dolomitic. The latter is particularly valuable because it contains magnesium, a trace element important to plant growth. In order to be of use immediately and to continue to break down gradually, it should be ground fine enough to sift through a 100-mesh sieve. In this form, the lime will be exposed to water in the soil in sufficient quantities to dissolve slowly over several years.

Physical Effect: Lime has a physical, as well as a chemical, effect upon soil. When spread upon clay soils, lime flocculates the clay; that is, it causes particles to gather in groups to make larger physical units in the soil. Water and air more easily penetrate such a soil than a soil composed of fine clay particles. On the other hand, in a sandy soil lime has the effect of holding the particles more closely together, so that water is held for a longer period.

One other function of lime in the soil is to release some of the phosphorus and potash from their insoluble compounds, making them available for plant use. Thus, though lime is not itself a fertilizer, it has the effect of increasing the fertility of the soil.

Application: To increase the pH of the soil by one unit, apply 30 pounds of ground limestone to every 1,000 square feet of soil if the soil is very sandy; if it is a sandy loam, spread 50 pounds; on loam, spread 70 pounds; and on a heavy clay, 80 pounds. Repeat the application every three to four years.

Fall or spring applications well in advance of planting are best. Liming is done on freshly cultivated soil. Make sure that the lime is spread evenly and thoroughly to avoid skipping areas. Unlike fertilizer, lime does not spread over adjacent areas, but works itself into the soil.

Sources: In addition to the common sources of lime, there are many other materials that can be used to lower soil acidity. Gypsum, sometimes called sulfate of lime, contains about 23 percent calcium oxide. It helps liberate potash for plant use, but its sulfur content tends to make the soil acid, so its effect is opposite to that of lime. It has special uses, such as in reclamation of alkaline soil. Gypsum forms up to 50 percent of superphosphate fertilizers. *See also* GYPSUM.

Marble is a crystallized form of limestone. If it has not been burned to form quicklime, it is as satisfactory as limestone. Like limestone, it must be finely pulverized.

Marl is a crumbly lime-clay deposit found under the organic deposits in the beds of streams and other bodies of water. It can be used to supply lime to soil, but it is more slowly available than limestone.

Oyster shells have, in addition to a large percentage of calcium carbonate, about 8 percent phosphoric acid, which makes them valuable sources of both lime and phosphorus. They should be used, in ground form, whenever available.

Wood ashes, especially hardwood ashes, are a rich source of potash and lime. Percentages of each vary with the kind of wood that was burned to make the ash. In addition, phosphoric acid and magnesium are found in wood ashes. Rain quickly leaches all the nutrients from ash and makes them available to plants. Store ashes in a dry place, as rain will destroy nutrients before they are applied to garden soil. Wood ash should never be used on soil in which acid-loving plants are grown.

Other ashes—from paper, leaves or coal —are not particularly useful and may be harmful to soil and plants. Paper ash contains much acid residue from acid used in the manufacture of the paper; leaf ash contains mostly charcoal and carbon; and coal ash contains no valuable nutrients and may contain harmful sulfur compounds.

Some gardeners add pulverized limestone to the compost heap or manure pile to help speed the bacterial process. However, the alkalizing action of the lime burns up valuable nitrogen which is then lost to the atmosphere in the form of vapor.

See also ACIDITY–ALKALINITY, BASIC SLAG.

LIMEBERRY   *See* ORANGEBERRY

LIMEQUAT   (x *Citrofortunella*)

These hybrids resulted from crossing the lime with the kumquat. All limequats produce fruit resembling the lime in appearance and character. In general, they should be considered as substitutes for that fruit. They are more hardy than the lime and probably more resistant to certain diseases. They can be recommended for cultivation only in regions too cold for the lime. There are several named varieties of the limequat, Eustis and Lakeland (x *C. floridana*) and Tavares (x *C. Swinglei*) being the most common.

See also CITRUS.

LIMESTONE
See ACIDITY–ALKALINITY, DOLOMITE, LIME, MINERAL ROCKS

LIME TREE   *See* LINDEN

LINARIA

A genus of the Figwort family, linarias are annual and perennial plants that resemble miniature snapdragons. The most common species is *L. vulgaris,* toadflax or butter-and-eggs. It is a native of Europe and Asia and may be found on every roadside in America.

Annual species are usually started early indoors. Perennials may also be started from seed, but will usually not produce flowers the first year. They may also be propagated by division. They prefer a light soil.

Toadflax, the common roadside variety, has been improved and is now sold as a garden annual. *L. maroccanna,* another annual, grows to about 15 inches and produces flowers in orange, blue and crimson. It is also offered by seedsmen in a large variety of colors in a compact variety, called Fairy Bouquet or Northern Lights. It tends to stop flowering early in hot summer areas, but can be useful planted in drifts to cover bulb beds or set among later-flowering chrysanthemums.

L. alpina is a perennial dwarf rock plant, growing six inches high, with blue violet flowers with an orange palate. There is also a rose variety. *L. anticaria* is a low-branching plant with blue and white lilac-spurred flowers. It is a good rock garden subject that does well in part shade.

L. genistifolia is a yellow and orange perennial species similar to butter-and-eggs, but it grows taller and is showier.

LINDEN   (*Tilia*)

The linden tree is also called lime tree or basswood or bastwood because of the bast fiber obtained from inside the bark. About 30 species of linden are native to the North Temperate Zone. They are deciduous trees grown for timber, ornament, bast fiber, and an oil extracted from the flowers for use in manufacture of perfumes. Their numerous clustered yellow blossoms attract bees in June.

Lindens thrive in a rich, moist soil, which must be well drained. A heavy mulch over the roots in hot dry weather will help protect the tree from drought, which affects it adversely.

Lindens are used extensively in formal plantings because their regular pyramidal shape adapts itself well to driveway borders. They are also used extensively here and abroad in city street plantings. Their dense foliage gives good shade.

Propagation may be from seed, which requires two years to germinate, and from layers, cuttings, and grafting. Young trees are best set out in early spring rather than in fall.

American linden (*T. americana*) is one of the most stately lindens, growing to 120 feet. Leaves are heart shaped, toothed and four to eight inches long. Variety Dentata has irregularly toothed leaves, and variety Macrophylla has larger leaves.

The common linden (*T.* x *europaea*) does well along city streets. A hybrid of *T. cordata* and *T. platyphyllos,* it has dull green, four-inch leaves. The cultivar Wratislaviensis has golden leaves.

Crimean linden (*T.* x *euchlora*) is one of the handsomest lindens, a hybrid of *T. cordata* and *T. dasystyla*. It grows to about 50 feet, and its four-inch leaves are glossy dark green above, paler green below, heart shaped and sharply toothed. Flowers hang in pendulous clusters in June.

Japanese linden (*T. japonica*) grows to 65 feet, with three-inch leaves that are blue green beneath when young.

The large-leaved linden (*T. platyphyllos*) which grows as large as the American linden, has light green, four-inch leaves that are heart shaped at the base. A cluster of three whitish flowers blooms in June. In variety Aurea, the branches are yellow when young; in Rubra they are red. Variety Lacinia has more deeply toothed leaves.

The Mongolian linden (*T. mongolica*) is a comparatively short linden, growing to only about 30 feet. Its 2½-inch leaves are glossy, coarsely toothed and three lobed.

The small-leafed European linden (*T. cordata*) has leaves less than 2½ inches long. It holds its shape well as it grows to 90 or 100 feet. Clusters of fragrant yellow blossoms appear in early summer.

White or silver linden (*T. tomentosa*) is also a tall pyramidal tree, growing to 90 feet. Leaves are broad, to five inches long, dark green above and slightly downy below, and the bases are either heart shaped or straight.

LINNAEA   *See* TWINFLOWER

LINNAEUS, CAROLUS

(1707–1778) The Swedish botanist and author of the first practical classification of the plant kingdom was born Carl Linne and known as Carl von Linne after being granted a patent of nobility in 1761. His name was latinized as Carolus Linnaeus on the books which he published, all of which were in Latin.

Linnaeus's most important books on the classification of plants were his *Systema Naturae, Fundamenta Botanica, Genera Plantarum, Classes Plantarum,* and *Species Plantarum.* The last named was published in Stockholm in 1753, setting forth for the first time specific names for all the plants known at that time.

Linnaeus's system of classification was based upon the sexual characteristics of plants. It is a fundamental system which is used to the present time, although many of its classifications have been rearranged. His first work in the field was inspired by a review of Sebastien Vaillant's *Sermo de Structura Florum,* which set him to examining the structure of flowers.

Though much of Linnaeus's work has been modified and changed, his system of defining genera and species, and his uniform use of descriptive terminology is retained in modern classification.

See also BOTANICAL NOMENCLATURE.

LINUM

With only one exception, all species of this genus of the Flax family are cultivated as ornamentals. *L. usitatissimum* is the species grown commercially for flax, from which linen and linseed oil are derived. *See also* FLAX.

Most species have small, narrow leaves and red, blue, yellow, or white flowers. Blooms are profuse but short-lived, usually lasting one day.

Flax likes full sun and average garden soil. Annuals may be planted where they are to stand, or started early under glass and transplanted when danger of frost is past.

L. grandiflorum, called flowering flax, is the species most often grown. An annual, it grows to two feet, with red to purple blue flowers 1½ inches across. Varieties have scarlet, pink or red blooms.

Golden flax, *L. flavum*, is a two-foot perennial, half-hardy, with bright yellow flowers. Variety Compactum is recommended as a dwarf form.

L. monogynum and *L. suffruticosum* are hardy showy forms not generally grown. Both grow to two feet, with large white or white-tinted flowers.

The most dependable perennial is *L. perenne*, with panicles of bright blue flowers. A white variety is also available.

For rock gardens, the perennial *L. narbonense* is recommended. Its flowers are azure blue with white eyes.

LIPPIA   *See* LEMON VERBENA

LIQUID MANURE
See MANURE TEA

LIRIOPE SPICATA
See GROUND COVERS

LITCHI   (*Litchi chinensis*)

The litchi, or leechee, is a 40-foot Chinese evergreen tree. It is popular in warm Oriental countries where it is grown for its fruit which is eaten fresh or dried. When fresh, it has a red skin and sweet white flesh. When dried, the fruit of the litchi is prunelike and surrounded by a thin, papery shell.

In this country, litchi trees can be grown only in the warmest sections of Florida and California where frosts seldom occur. For best growth, it needs a fertile acid soil with plenty of moisture and organic matter. For fruit production, plant trees about 35 feet apart. Because of its bright red fruit, yellow flowers and leathery green leaves, the trees can be planted singly as landscape ornamentals.

LITHOSOL   *See* AZONAL SOIL

LIVE FOREVER   *See* SEDUM

LIVERLEAF   *See* HEPATICA

LIVESTOCK
See entries for individual animals

LOAM

Soil which is composed of a friable mixture of clay, silt, sand, and organic matter is called loam. The mixture of mineral and organic material in a good loam should be of such a proportion as to provide 50 percent solid matter and 50 percent space, about half of which should be filled with water and half with air for optimum plant growth.

Clay, silt and sand are particles of rock, usually of the rock which underlies the field on which they are found. Silt is composed of rock particles of less than $\frac{1}{16}$ millimeter in diameter which have been deposited on the bed of a body of water. Sand is coarser rock material, clay is finer.

If the mineral content of a loam is composed of more than half sand, it is said to be a sand loam. If clay predominates, it is a clay loam; or if it is mostly silt, it is a silt loam.

If the rock underlying the soil is limestone, the soil above will probably have a neutral or slightly alkaline pH. If the mineral content of the soil does not come from limestone, the pH will probably be acid, except under unusual conditions.

Amounts of organic matter in loam vary from a trace to about 15 percent. Good loam contains at least 5 percent organic matter, which helps the soil to retain its moisture, and contributes to the never-ending process of decomposition and growth which goes on in the soil.

See also HUMUS, SOIL.

LOBELIA

Perennial or annual members of the Bellflower family, lobelias make excellent border and bedding plants. The showy flowers are usually blue or red, and are formed in long, spikelike clusters.

Edging lobelia (*L. Erinus*) has small flowers in shades of blue and lavender, and varieties come in red and white as well. Edging lobelias are either compact, under six inches tall, or spreading, up to ten inches tall. The charming much-branched dwarf plants are covered with tiny blue flowers throughout the blooming season. Unfortunately, these annuals demand cool weather but cannot stand freezing, so they must be grown during the winter in frost-free sections and receive protection on cold nights. In areas having hot, humid summers these plants bloom well only until about midsummer, when they begin to burn out. For a good early show, start seed indoors in March or April so you will have strong plants to set out after frosts are over. Light shade from the afternoon sun will help to prolong the blooming season. Edging lobelia prefers a moist, light loam.

See also CARDINAL FLOWER.

LOCOWEED   *See* WEEDS

LOCUST

Locust is a common name applied to a family of insects closely allied to grasshoppers and sometimes called short-horn grasshoppers. They are eaten in many countries—roasted, fried, preserved in lime, or dried in the sun. In this country, they are known as pests of grain and vegetable crops. One of the most destructive forms is the Rocky Mountain locust. In 1931, thousands of square miles of the midwestern states were ravaged by locusts.

See also GRASSHOPPER.

LOCUST   (*Robinia*)

Not to be confused with the honey or moraine locusts (*Gleditsia*) which grow throughout the eastern and southern United States and are valued as timber trees, these locusts are hardy ornamentals. They are among the most widely distributed deciduous trees and shrubs native to North and Central America. They have feathery foliage and in spring the blossoms are in long drooping clusters of pink, white or

Black locust is one of the hardiest and most common Robinia.
(Courtesy of U.S. Forest Service)

purple pealike flowers. Flowers are fragrant and attract bees. Seedpods are brown and leathery. Some persist through the winter and make a dry, rustling noise in the winter winds.

Locusts thrive in any soil, even sand. They transplant well, and may be propagated by root cuttings, suckers, division, and cuttings, as well as by seed.

The most common species is the black locust (*R. Pseudoacacia*), a tree which grows to 70 or 80 feet. Leaves are compound with from nine to 17 leaflets in each one. Fragrant white flowers hang in pendulous clusters of up to five inches. The bark is brown and furrowed, and the wood is strong and resists decay from moisture.

The clammy locust (*R. viscosa*) is grown as an ornamental in the South and in some intermediate areas. It has feathery foliage and pink flowers. It grows from 30 to 40 feet tall, but seldom attains that height because it is usually attacked and killed by borers. This species and the black locust should be watched for signs of sawdust around their trunks. When sawdust is found, the hole of the borer must be sought somewhere above, and the borer dug out and destroyed. If the borer is inaccessible, plug the hole with putty.

Rose acacia (*R. hispida*), also called moss locust, is a shrub growing to nine feet. It is hardy only in the South, where it is sometimes trained as a standard. Drooping clusters of pink or rose flowers in May or June are followed by two- to three-inch pods covered with red bristles. This species suckers freely, and may be propagated by severing and transplanting suckers.

The thorny locust (*R. neomexicana*) is a native of the Southwest, and is not hardy in northern regions. It grows as a spiny shrub or small tree not over 30 feet and has rose-colored flowers from June through August. Leaves are feathery, and the smooth seedpod measures four inches long.

See also MORAINE LOCUST.

LOESS

A fine-grained, erosional sediment deposited by wind, loess covers vast areas in Asia, Europe, and North and South America. The largest deposit in the United States is in the drainage basin of the Mississippi River. Loess has given rise to soils of considerable diversity.

LOGANBERRY   (*Rubus ursinus*)

A popular cultivar that resembles the blackberry and the boysenberry, the loganberry is a red-fruited form of a trailing blackberry that was discovered in southern California. It is not hardy in the Northeast, but can be grown with winter protection in places where temperatures do not drop to 0°F. (−17.78°C.). Ninety percent of the fruit is grown on the West Coast. The loganberry is self-fertile and does not require a pollenizer.

See also BOYSENBERRY, BRAMBLE FRUITS.

LOMBARDY POPLAR
See POPLAR

LONG-LEAVED MINT
See MINT

LONICERA   *See* HONEYSUCKLE

LOOSESTRIFE
See LYSIMACHIA, LYTHRUM

LOQUAT   (*Eriobotrya japonica*)

The loquat is an evergreen fruit tree of the Rose family widely grown in China and Japan, and occasionally in the warmer sections of California. It bears apple- or pear-shaped small fruits that are also called Japanese medlar, biwa, lukwati, and pipa. The tree, which will not be killed by occasional drops to 10 to 15°F. (−12.22 to −9.44°C.), is sometimes grown as an ornamental in the less tropical areas of the southern states. One or two degrees of frost are sufficient to kill blossoms or fruit, and since the tree blooms in fall and ripens its fruit through the winter, it does not make a dependable crop in this country.

Soil requirements are not rigid, though the loquat seems to prefer well-drained clay and appreciates mulch. A small amount of compost or well-rotted manure applied every other year in the fall may help to produce larger fruit. In orchards loquats are planted 20 to 25 feet apart, or may be somewhat crowded to increase fruit size. Propagation is by seed, grafting, cuttings, or shield budding. Ornamentals are usually grown from seed.

The tree grows to 25 feet, but usually not to more than 15 feet when grown as an ornamental. It may also be grown as a greenhouse subject. Leaves are stiff and shiny, to one foot long; flowers are white, fragrant, ½ inch across, and borne in six-inch clusters. Fruits are yellow to orange, one to three inches long, and a good source of vitamin C. Fruit will appear when the tree is about three years old.

The loquat is hardy and resistant to disease. Because it tolerates any amount of pruning, damaged areas may be pruned down to the healthy branch. Be sure to burn the diseased parts as soon as they are removed.

LOTEBUSH   *See* LOTI-BUSH

LOTI-BUSH   (*Ziziphus obtusifolia*)

Sometimes known as Texas buckthorn or lotebush, this thorny shrub with greenish flowers is found from southern Texas to Mexico and Arizona. Its roots yield a substitute for soap. The berrylike fruits are edible but not very tasty.

LOTUS

The term lotus can be used as a common name for water lilies of the genera *Nelumbo* and *Nymphaea* and as the name of a genus of leguminous shrubs and herbs of the Pea family.

Nelumbo: These are large water lilies with shield-shaped leaves standing above the water. Flowers usually rise several feet above the surface, opening three successive days before fading. Native to southeastern Asia, they can grow in any climate where roots will not freeze and in this country are usually grown in the South.

The large and very tough seeds are sometimes filed or bored to aid germination. Plant in shallow pans outside, or roll them in clay and drop them into ponds. When grown in pans, roots are not planted in ponds until well developed. They require a rich bed and full sun.

East Indian lotus (*N. nucifera*) is popularly but incorrectly known as the sacred flower of the Egyptians, and the long fleshy rootstocks were used in some countries for food. Its leaves are one to three feet in diameter and rise above the water three to six feet. The fragrant pink or rose flowers range from four to ten inches wide. Varieties include white and red, dwarfs and doubles.

American lotus or water chinquapin (*N. lutea*) has smaller and lower, cup-shaped leaves, one or two feet in diameter. The ten-inch flowers are yellow.

Nymphaea: Flowers and leaves of these water lilies stand or float on the surface of the water. Of all the aquatic lilies, these are considered the most showy and spectacular. Included in the genus are three species known as lotus.

Blue lotus of Egypt (*N. caerulea*) is tender, with leaves 12 to 16 inches wide. The flowers are light blue with white centers and measure three to six inches wide. This lotus was probably the Egyptian's sacred lotus.

White lotus of Egypt (*N. Lotus*) is also tender and has leaves 12 to 20 inches across. The white flowers have pinkish outer petals and are five to ten inches wide. They open in the evening and remain open until nearly noon the next day.

The blue lotus of India (*N. stellata*) is a smaller variety than either of the two above. It usually has pale blue petals with white bases, though in some varieties the petals are pink.

Lotus: Also called lotus is the genus of the Pea family composed of herbs and prostrate shrubs of little horticultural importance, except for those few species which are cultivated as ornamentals, fodder or edible peas.

L. Berthelotii is a small shrub grown outdoors in California and sometimes under glass for its odd scarlet flowers.

Bird's-foot trefoil (*L. corniculatus*) is a perennial which is sometimes grown for forage. It is a sprawling plant, but can grow to two feet, bearing small yellow flowers from red buds.

Winged pea (*L. tetragonolobus*) is a trailing annual grown for the seed and pods, which are edible when young.

See also AMERICAN LOTUS, BIRD'S-FOOT TREFOIL, NYMPHAEA.

LOUSEWORT   *See* PEDICULARIS

LOVAGE   (*Levisticum officinale*)

A perennial plant introduced from the mountains of France, Greece and the Balkan states, lovage is one of many herbs that now finds use in the kitchen. The root has long been supposed to have medicinal properties and is in some demand in the drug trade. The yellow flowering tops yield a volatile oil, but there is little demand for it. The seed, leaves and roots are also used for flavoring foods.

Ancient Greeks and Romans used lovage, especially the roots and seed, as a medicine. Home winegrowers used it to produce lovage wine and a cordial which included tansy and yarrow. In the Middle Ages it was considered a panacea for many digestive and nervous disorders, as well as jaundice and colic. The fragrant plant was even used as a deodorant. Lovage might have earned its name because of its use by European women in luring men— they commonly wore the herb around their necks to spread its pleasant aroma.

Planting and Culture: Lovage grows well in almost any deep, well-drained soil. It is benefited by the liberal use of fertilizer, although heavy applications of manure tend to produce excessive top growth. It is propagated from

Once valued as a medicine and perfume, today lovage is grown for its culinary qualities.

seed or by root division. Seed may be planted in the garden in fall and lightly covered in rows 18 inches apart, or sown in early spring in a hotbed, greenhouse, or well-prepared seedbed in a sheltered part of the garden, and covered very lightly with sand or finely sifted soil. It is advisable to spread old burlap or other sacking over the bed and sprinkle it occasionally in dry weather. When the first seedlings break the soil the cover should be removed. The plants reach a size suitable for transplanting by the end of May, when they are set eight inches apart in rows spaced for convenient cultivation.

Harvesting: The roots may be dug in October of the second or third year after setting the plants. Numerous offsets will generally be found, and if these have good roots they may be reset at once to renew the planting without recourse to seed. The freshly dug roots are washed, cut into slices about ½ inch thick, and carefully dried. Artificial heat, not to exceed 125°F. (51.67°C.), may be used to hasten the drying.

Today, lovage is most commonly used in the kitchen, especially as a condiment on salads and vegetables. Oil from this herb is sometimes used to enhance tobacco flavors. Some countries, especially England, make tasty candies flavored with lovage.

See also HERB.

LOVEGRASS
See GRASS, ORNAMENTAL

LOVE-IN-A-MIST   *See* NIGELLA

LUDWIGIA   *See* AQUARIUM

LUFFA

This genus of tropical gourds belonging to the Cucumber family contains two species— *L. acutangula,* with fruits which grow to 12 inches, and the more popular *L. aegyptiaca* with fruits which grow to 20 inches.

Inside the luffa is a mass of spongy tissue which, when processed, makes excellent pot holders, door mats, table mats, bathroom rugs, gloves, sandals, and sun helmets, and is also used for stuffing pillows and mattresses. In fact, luffa makes such good towels and sponges that it has been named "towel gourd" and "vegetable sponge." Although luffa is a tropical plant, it grows well in temperate climates, growing as far north as Connecticut. During World War II, the U.S. Navy used luffa for filters in steam engines in preference to any other material, and the army used it for wiping the windshields of jeeps. It was even used in surgical operations.

In many parts of the world, luffa is considered a medicine. It has been used for treating every ailment from intestinal worms to hemorrhage including hernia, scarlet fever, smallpox, aching teeth, and parasitic infections, and it has been used as a tonic for the genital organs.

The fresh fruits of the sweet variety are sliced and eaten like cucumbers. They may also be cooked and used in any way that squash is used. The pure seed oil has been suggested as a substitute for olive oil.

The Japanese slice the young fruits and dry them in the sun, like apples. The Malayans relish the young leaves, while the Annamites like the male flowers and flower buds.

The usual practice is to start luffa in March or April in a hotbed or indoors in pots placed in a warm, sunny window. About three seeds to a pot is plenty. The started plants are transplanted to the garden on a cloudy day after all danger of frost is past. This is usually about the time the sweet corn starts coming up.

A good organic soil with plenty of humus and well-rotted manure is best for growing luffa. The plants should be set out about four feet apart, with four feet between rows.

The young leaves may be eaten at any time, and the young fruit is used until it gets as large as cucumbers. If grown on a good soil the fruits will grow to be over two feet long and will mature before frost. The mature fruits are

If allowed to ripen on the vine, the spongy, gourd-like fruits of the luffa plant can be processed and used as scrubbing sponges.

the ones used for mats, sponges and sandals since they have developed the desired coarse fiber.

Many gourds may grow on a single vine, and the gourds may weigh as much as five pounds each. Better fruits can be had if care is taken in pruning off all of the first flowers and any newly formed gourds which are deformed, pear shaped, or coarse. Also, fruits should be kept off the ground by placing a flat

stone under the fruit or providing a trellis for the vines to climb.

See also GOURDS.

LUNARIA   *See* HONESTY

LUNGWORT
See MERTENSIA, PULMONARIA

LUPINE   (*Lupinus*)

A member of the Pea family containing mostly perennial species, lupines bear varicolored, pea-shaped flowers closely placed on long, hollow, stiff spikes. They are tall plants, generally reaching a height of three to five feet, with the bloom spikes often over a foot long. Because all the flowers in each spike are open at one time, lupines make a gorgeous showing, especially when planted in masses. They bloom in early and midsummer and some species make good cut flowers.

Planting and Culture: The general soil recommendation calls for a sandy or light soil that is slightly acid. In heavy clay the roots frequently rot. Lupines like full or partial sun and plenty of moisture with good drainage.

Since lupines resent transplanting when once established, seed should be sown outdoors in place in early spring, or indoors in February or March, and transplanted while still small, leaving plenty of earth around the roots.

There are several ways to prepare the seed before planting. Some people chill it in the refrigerator for several days; others nick the seed coat; and still others soak the seed in water. Germination can take as much as 20 days. Hybrid plants will sometimes self-sow, often producing flowers of duller color than the parents. The perennial lupines can be either seeded in summer for flowering the following year or divided in very early spring.

Types: The Russell hybrids of the native *L. polyphyllus* are the most spectacular lupines but they tend to die out in two to four years, so it is wise to grow a few new plants each year. They produce flowers from mid-spring to mid-summer.

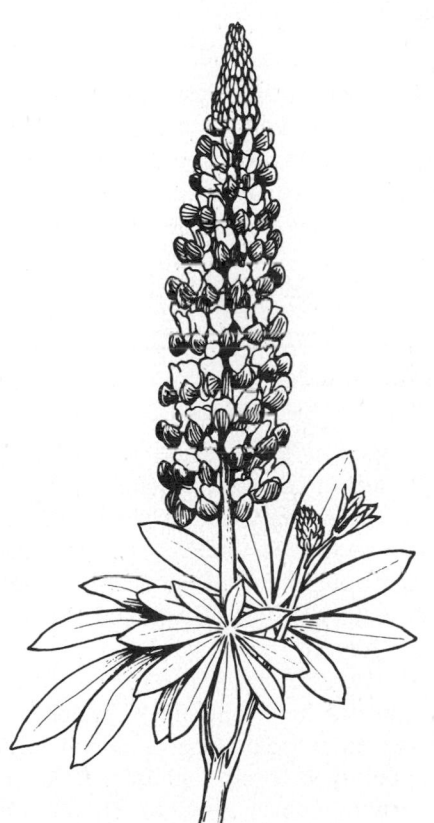

Like certain other flowering plants, lupines turn their leaves constantly toward the sun so that, by observing their position, one can tell the time.

Quaker bonnet (*L. perennis*) is the common wild lupine prevalent in the eastern states. It prefers a sandy soil, grows one to two feet and has blue or white flowers. Tree lupine (*L. arboreus*) grows four to eight feet and has fragrant yellow flowers. Bluebonnet (*L. subcarnosus*) makes an attractive spring-blooming annual, growing to about a foot high. It is the state flower of Texas.

LYCHNIS

Lychnis is a genus of the Pink family comprising a large number of annual, biennial and perennial flowers, most of which have been cultivated in their present form for many years. All are in shades of white, pink, rose, scarlet, or magenta and many have woolly or hirsute foliage. In most species, the flowers are densely clustered and have five notched or centrally divided petals radiating from a tubular compartment which contains the seeds. Several species are commonly called campions, a name also applied to some closely related species of the genus *Silene*.

Planting and Culture: Most species like full sun, and will do well in any good garden soil, even if it is somewhat sandy. Seeds of all are easily germinated, the perennials giving a light bloom the first year if sown indoors very early. Perennials may also be propagated by division of clumps early in spring or, in mild areas, in late fall. Bloom starts in June and lasts through August.

Species: Arctic campion (*L. alpina*) grows only one foot high, and makes a good rock garden plant. The type has dense heads of rose pink flowers, but there are varieties in white and red.

Rose campion (*L. Coronaria*), also called mullein-pink or dusty-miller, has woolly gray white leaves on woolly branched stems, each tipped with a magenta flower one inch across. White varieties, as well as bicolors, are also known.

Perhaps the most showy lychnis is *L. chalcedonica,* called Maltese cross, Jerusalem cross and scarlet lightning. It is a two- to three-foot perennial with somewhat coarse, hairy foliage, and large umbels of scarlet flowers raised above the foliage in spring, followed by smaller heads from lower leaf axils later in summer. There are also varieties in white, pink and salmon, and doubles.

Rose-of-heaven (*L. Coeli-rosa,* formerly *Agrostemma Coeli-rosa*) is a one-foot annual with solitary one-inch rose flowers at the top of each stem. White, red, purple-eyed, and toothed-petal varieties have also been listed.

L. coronata is an annual, or a tender biennial blooming the first year from seed sown early. It bears loose clusters of salmon pink, brick red or cinnabar flowers early in summer.

Cuckooflower (*L. Flos-cuculi*) is a hardy, rapid-spreading perennial with loose panicles of pink, red, or white, and some double one-inch flowers. This flower should not be confused with the rock garden or bog plant, *Cardamine pratensis,* which is listed as cuckooflower in the seed catalogs.

Flower-of-Jove (*L. Flos-jovis*) is a low-growing perennial with dense umbel heads of rose pink blossoms. It blooms in early summer, sometimes continuing until July.

German catchfly (*L. Viscaria*) has sticky patches below the red or purple clusters of flowers. Varieties are Alba, Nana, Rosea, and Splendens.

A delicate rock plant, *Silene colorata* was once classified as *L. pyrenaica* and may still be found under that name in some catalogs. It is about four inches high, with a basal rosette of club-shaped leaves from which rise stems with heart-shaped leaves terminating in single ¼-inch solitary pink flowers.

LYCIUM   *See* MATRIMONY VINE

LYE

Lye, which is crude sodium hydroxide, should not be used in the compost heap to speed decay as it will kill soil organisms. If put with refuse it would dissolve all the tin cans, but the resulting product would not be biologically sound.

LYGODIUM

Lygodium is a genus of climbing ferns mostly native to tropical climates, with only one species (*L. palmatum*) native to the United States. This species, the Hartford fern, has been so much sought for ornamentation that it is almost extinct in New Jersey and Connecticut, where it formerly grew along riverbanks.

Most species are grown in greenhouses for their graceful habit and finely segmented and resegmented fronds, some of which terminate in palmate-type forms. Some species in their native surroundings grow to 30 feet, but in greenhouses seldom attain more than eight. Fronds grow at intervals from creeping stems.

Lygodiums grow best in very acid soil, and prefer a mixture of loam, peat moss and leaf mold. They climb best on other plants, or on twigs, rather than on artificial supports. Culture is the same as that of most common ferns.

L. japonicum is the most popular greenhouse species, having pale green, finely divided, pinnate foliage.

Hartford fern grows to three or four feet and needs the support of other plants. The palmate fronds are about four inches wide with five equal radial lobes.

LYONIA

Lyonia is a genus comprising about 30 shrubs of the Heath family. Most are not hardy in the North, and only a few are cultivated as ornamental shrubs.

Mostly deciduous, with only one, the tetterbush, an evergreen, they have small alternate leaves and small white or pink flowers borne in clusters either from the leaf axil or from the ends of branches.

Lyonias are usually propagated from cuttings, and are grown in rather sandy soil with a pH around 5. They need a heavy mulch, preferably of oak or other acid leaves, and do not like to be disturbed.

Maleberry (*L. ligustrina*), also called male blueberry and he-huckleberry, is a hardy deciduous shrub growing to 12 feet. Spring flowers are in six-inch racemes, and the foliage changes color in fall.

Tetterbush (*L. lucida*) is found only south of Washington, D.C. It grows to six feet, with shining leaves and spring flowers growing in branched clusters.

Staggerbush (*L. mariana*) is hardy to Rhode Island. It grows six feet tall, and has pink or white nodding clusters of flowers in May and June. The staggerbush needs an acid sandy loam to do its best.

LYSIMACHIA

Though commonly called loosestrife, lysimachia is not a genus of the Loosestrife family, but rather of the Primrose. Very few have been cultivated, though one species, moneywort, is used as ground cover. Lysimachias are hardy perennials that need a moist, partially shaded spot in the garden. Propagation is by division.

Moneywort (*L. Nummularia*), also called creeping Charlie and creeping Jennie, spreads by trailing stems that send out roots from the joints. Small yellow flowers bloom profusely in midsummer above round, dark green leaves. The variety Aurea has golden leaves and makes a stunning ground cover. Moneywort will grow in sun, but prefers shade.

Garden loosestrife (*L. punctata*) produces yellow flowers with brown basal markings in the leaf axils all along the stem. It grows to about three feet and prefers moist soil in partial shade, flowering in June and early July. The plants quickly form large clumps and should be given ample space, but they do not need dividing or much other attention for several years once established.

LYTHRUM

Lythrum is a genus of herbs and subshrubs that includes the true loosestrifes. Na-

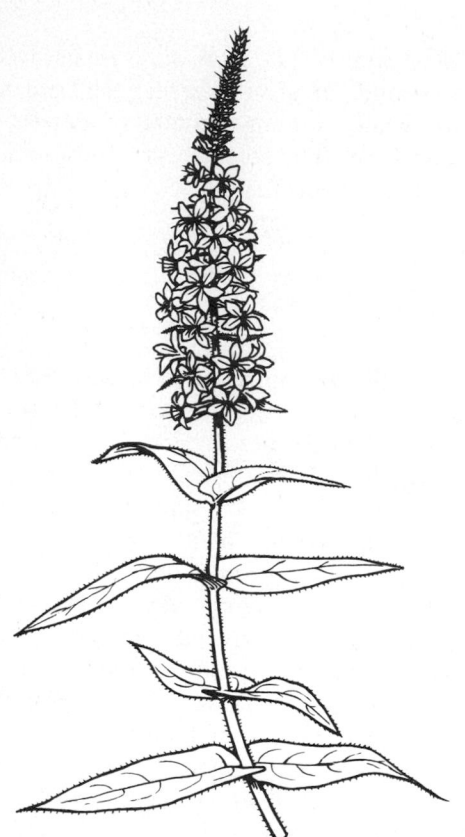

A European introduction, purple loosestrife has become naturalized throughout the marshes and moist fields of the eastern United States.

tives of northeastern America and Eurasia, they are mostly marsh plants that do well in cultivation when planted in moist soil. Lythrums attain a height of two to three feet in the wild, and four to five feet in cultivation. The genus contains both annual and perennial species, the latter being propagated by division in spring.

Purple loosestrife (*L. Salicaria*), sometimes known as the willow-herb because of its willowlike foliage, is a perennial that grows to four or five feet. Originally introduced from Europe, it has naturalized in marshes throughout the East where it blooms in late summer. A rose purple variety is Superb. Cultivars make excellent border plants, but can become invasive if not divided about every two years. *L. virgatum* is similar, but has smaller flowers in leafy racemes.

M

MACADAMIA
(*Macadamia ternifolia*)

This handsome evergreen tree, native to Australia, does well in Hawaii and the southern and warmer central states. The nuts are of excellent quality, about an inch in diameter, hard-shelled and with a mild, delicate flavor resembling that of Brazil nuts.

The macadamia does best in well-drained, slightly acid soil, although it will tolerate soils ranging from fairly heavy to quite sandy. In general, it prospers under the same water, climate and cultivation conditions that favor avocados. Trees should not be planted in areas known to be too frosty for avocados, lemons or sumac.

Even if the tree did not bear valuable nuts, its beauty would warrant more extensive plantings. The leaves are a deep, lustrous green with spiny margins, looking much like a big holly leaf. These contrast interestingly with the smooth, gray trunk and lovely foot-long racemes of white flowers.

In farm woodlots and on land not needed for other purposes, macadamia can be cultivated for its reddish, close-grained wood, which is in demand for cabinetmaking.

Macadamia trees grow rather slowly, at about the same rate as orange trees, but they are easily propagated by stratifying the nuts over the winter in sand, then planting them in separate pots of humusy soil with bottom heat. These will germinate in about a month, whereas those planted outdoors will sprout much more slowly. Water the seedlings sparingly to prevent damping-off and transplant them outdoors when they are about 18 inches tall. Try to disturb the roots as little as possible when transplanting.

Mature trees may attain a height of 40 feet with a canopy of 25 feet in diameter. Tree spacing of 20 feet by 25 feet is recommended. Young trees are very susceptible to fertilizer burn and require little or no fertilizer up to three years. Well-rotted manure forms a beneficial mulch, but should not contact the trunk. Trees over ten years old may receive up to two pounds of nitrogen per year in three or four doses.

See also NUT TREES.

MACHINERY, CARE OF

The general rule is: follow the manufacturer's instructions. These come, or should come, with every piece of equipment sold. Look for them when making any purchase and keep them handy in a place where they can be readily consulted.

Power tools range from one-cylinder mowers, tillers and shredders, to four-cylinder tractors. Principles of good care and management are practically identical for any powered metal tool whose moving parts operate at high speed and depend on proper lubrication to overcome heat and friction.

Cleanliness is the first order. After a machine has been used in the field, it should be cleaned and inspected before being put away. Before a machine is taken out of the shed or barn to be used it should be checked for overall tightness and for proper lubrication.

In addition to the daily or weekly inspection-plus-cleaning, seasonal checkup in the spring and late fall can prevent much trouble. Following these principles should keep breakdowns and poor performance to a minimum:

1. Using a kerosene-soaked rag, wipe off excess grease and oil from drive chain, flywheel, axle, wheels, and other moving parts.

2. Drain dirty oil from engine.

3. Add clean oil of proper consistency for warm weather operation.

4. Put a few drops of light machine oil on all drive chains.

5. Using a grease gun, grease all lubrication points on the power appliance with heavy lubricating grease.

6. Tighten all nuts, bolts and screws.

7. Clean off rust spots with emery cloth and touch up with good-quality paint.

8. Sharpen and clean all cutting edges of the attachments; lubricate moving parts where specified.

9. Check rubber tires on power units for cuts, nicks and proper air pressure. The proper pressure is usually listed by the manufacturer.

10. Fuel the appliance with regular gas and the equipment is ready to operate. High-test gas is not recommended.

To these can be added the cautionary admonition to run the machine in the way it was intended. Don't overload it, and don't give the tool tasks it was not designed to do, thus inviting the grave danger of a serious breakdown ending in an accident.

A good operator knows when a machine is running well from the way it sounds and its general "feel" and vibrations. An immediate check is called for if the machine does not sound or "feel" right.

Winter Storage: Common-sense practices of cleaning and checking for excessive wear and tear must be followed. Before starting out, disconnect the spark plug lead-in wire to avoid the danger of any unintentional starts.

Give the undercarriage of the machine and all joints an extra-special cleaning. Lubricate with the proper oil. Repaint parts when the manufacturer advises. Coat all machined parts that are not otherwise covered or protected with heavy oil.

Drain oil from the crankcase and replace with clean oil. If possible, flush interior with clean gasoline and rinse before filling with fresh oil. Remove the air filter over the carburetor, wash the mesh screening in clean gasoline, drain the oil out of the cup, refill with fresh oil and reassemble.

Remove the spark plug and clean the terminals with emery cloth. Check the gap and reset for correct aperture if necessary. Replace the plug if it appears badly pitted or damaged.

Drain the gas tank to prevent the gasoline from forming lead deposits. Pull the starter rope a few times to empty the carburetor and exhaust. The extra meticulous will also cork the exhaust and fill the cylinder with light machine oil for the winter. This should keep rust out of the interior and effectively seal out dampness. To fill the cylinder it will be necessary to remove the spark plug, pour in the light oil and then replace the plug. The cylinder will have to be emptied in the spring and flushed with clean gasoline and the plug terminals cleaned and dried.

It should be stressed that farm and garden equipment is called upon to work in a hard terrain under conditions which frequently are far from ideal. Unlike the automobile which operates on a smooth surface, agricultural tools literally work in dirt, mud and mire.

MADAGASCAR JASMINE
(Stephanotis floribunda)

This twining, vigorous vine of the Milkweed family is native to Madagascar and Malaya and is often grown in a cool greenhouse as a specimen plant. Characteristic markings include thick leathery leaves four inches long and white, waxy, fragrant flowers which appear in umbels from spring to fall. The plants are propagated by cuttings of half-ripened wood. These root easily under glass or in a pot covered with a plastic bag kept at 70°F. (21.11°C.) out of direct sun. They must be kept moist and shaded in a greenhouse between 60 and 65°F. (15.56 and 18.33°C.) in winter and 70 to 90°F. (21.11 to 32.22°C.) in summer and should be cut back and repotted each year after flowering.

See also WAX FLOWER.

MADONNA LILY   *See* LILY

MAGGOT   *See* INSECT CONTROL

MAGNESIUM

Magnesium, a vital plant and animal nutrient, is variously listed as a micronutrient and a major nutrient. Since it is critical to plant development and it is used in relatively large quantities, it should be categorized a major nutrient.

Without magnesium, there would be no green plants. Each particle of chlorophyll—the "green" in green plants—contains one molecule of magnesium. Furthermore, magnesium is essential for plant utilization of nitrogen, phosphorus and sulfur; it aids in protein formation and is capable of correcting acidity in plants and soils.

A magnesium deficiency will cause lower leaves to turn yellow between the veins, which remain green. Leaf edges turn first; the color changes to orange and brown in later stages, after which the leaf soon dies. An excess of magnesium is rarely encountered but can cause calcium deficiency.

Generally, the magnesium content of soils equals the calcium content of soils. But there *are* magnesium-deficient soils, mostly in the Northeast. Magnesium occurs in all plants and farm crops in somewhat smaller amounts than calcium, but in the seeds of grains it is stored up three times more than calcium. Magnesium is assimilated more slowly than calcium; in fact, it is as a rule assimilated more slowly than any other ash element. The plant does not require magnesium until the approach of seed formation, although a small amount is necessary for perfect leaf action, since it enters into the chemical composition of chlorophyll.

The best cure—and preventive—for magnesium deficiency is the use of dolomitic limestone in any soil-liming program. Dolomitic limestone, or dolomite, is a mixture of magnesium and calcium carbonate.

MAGNESIUM SULFATE
See FERTILIZER, CHEMICAL

MAGNOLIA

Magnolias are among the most beautiful trees and shrubs for the garden. They fit into formal and informal plantings and dominate their surroundings when in flower.

Diversity and delicacy of color, range of flowering seasons and adaptability to landscaping arrangements for gardens and lawns have made magnolias a gardening favorite across the country.

There are 35 American and Asiatic species as well as many hybrids of the magnolia, a tree named in honor of Pierre Magnol, an eminent seventeenth-century French botanist.

The Chinese magnolias bloom before the leaves appear, and the flowers show to great advantage if given a background of evergreen trees. They are not difficult to grow, but prefer a sunny location, and like a rich, deep, sandy loam with plenty of humus to hold moisture around the roots. The roots must not be waterlogged, and good drainage is essential to carry off any excess moisture. During the active growing season in spring, water them once a week if the weather is hot.

Magnolias rarely require pruning, but if it is necessary at any time, prune immediately after the shrubs have finished flowering. Buds are usually formed for next year's flowering by July, and cutting of the branches must not be done after this date.

Propagation: Stock is increased by cuttings made from mature wood and by layering. Set the branches for layering in June and July. After the layered branch has rooted it may be cut from the parent stock and grown on its own roots. When the layered branch is cut from the shrub, do not move it until the following spring. Allow the layered branch to become well established on its own roots before lifting it to plant in some other section of the garden. A mulch of manure or compost is beneficial for magnolias during hot weather.

Varieties: There are many outstanding species and hybrids. The lovely *M. heptapeta,* also known as the Yulan and Conspicua, bears large white, cup-shaped flowers that have made it a universal favorite.

M. quinquepeta has a large, purple, lily-formed flower. It is sometimes sold as *M. hypoleuca* and *M. purpurea* and has several hybrids.

The magnolia most generally grown is *M.* x *Soulangiana;* although shrublike, it will form a tree if grown to one stem. The flowers are white with pink and lilac shading.

The southern magnolia has fragrant, white flowers and heavy, dark foliage. It grows to a height of 100 feet.

M. x *Soulangiana* cv. 'Lennei' is a hybrid with large, dark, red purple flowers and is one of the last of the Chinese magnolias to bloom.

M. stellata, the star magnolia, is the first of the deciduous magnolias to bloom, and the pure white flowers are delightfully fragrant. The starry white buds open in early spring and continue to flower for a long time. Each flower is about three inches across and composed of many petals. *M. stellata* cv. 'Rosea' is the pink form and makes a good companion to the white one. In growing magnolias, plant the tall-growing ones behind *stellata,* as this shrub ultimately grows wider than it is high.

Among the Indian species are *M. globosa* and the magnificent *M. Campbellii* of the Himalayas. The latter is a large forest tree which grows 80 to 100 feet high. The rose-colored, spring flowers are six to ten inches across.

Culture: Species and varieties may be chosen to provide colorful blooms from March until July or even August, because certain members of the genus produce flowers before the foliage is fully developed.

Earliest to show color is *M. stellata,* a shrubby plant, hardy north of Boston, which blooms in early spring. It is followed by *M. salicifolia, M. Kobus, M. heptapeta, M.* x *Soulangiana,* and *M. quinquepeta,* all of which produce flowers before leaves.

About mid-June the following species come into bloom: *M. acuminata, M. hypoleuca, M. Fraseri, M. macrophylla, M. Sieboldii* and *M. tripetala.* The evergreen species, *M. grandiflora,* is hardy throughout the country, but retains its foliage only in the warmer regions.

Good drainage is more essential than a rich soil to successful cultivation. For best results, apply a natural fertilizer or compost such as well-rotted stable or cow manure around the plant's base every two or three years. Whenever possible, magnolias should not be transplanted but left where they are. If moving is imperative, ball and burlap the roots with great care and do not permit them to dry out.

Magnolias can be grown from seed, but more frequently the hybrids and varieties are veneer-grafted on *M. Kobus.* This is done in the greenhouse during January, and is recommended to the enthusiast. Vigorous shoots are pegged into the ground (after the bark is scarred with a knife to stimulate new growth) and covered with a few inches of soil. After one to two seasons, those shoots which have taken good hold are severed from the parent plants and set out in good soil. When budding is practiced, *M. Kobus* is used for the stock and the buds are tied from the tops down, a reversal of the usual procedure.

MAHOGANY   (*Swietenia*)

The true mahogany is a tall, slender, tropical evergreen tree grown in extreme southern Florida as an ornamental and shade tree. In the West Indies and Central and South America, it is a valuable timber tree and the world's foremost cabinetwood. Philippine mahogany is generally coarser than the wood of African and American trees. The mountain mahogany (*Cercocarpus*) and varieties of eucalyptus called red, swamp or bastard mahogany are not related to the true mahogany.

MAHONIA

These spring-blooming shrubs bear fragrant yellow blooms in pretty racemes and are fine specimens for foundation plantings and shrub borders. They like shelter from the winter sun and wind, and a medium-fertile soil. *M. lomariifolia,* the tallest of the mahonias, reaches 12 feet. The Oregon grape (*M. Aquifolium*) grows up to three feet or so in height, is quite hardy, and has small, blue, edible berries. *M. nervosa* is sometimes called Oregon grape and bears similar edible berries, but it rarely grows over two feet high. Blue barberry (*M. pinnata*) grows about ten feet tall, and creeping barberry (*M. repens*) is a ground cover under a foot in height, with creeping roots. Agarita (*M. trifoliolata*), a six-foot shrub, is grown occasionally in the Southwest and is not hardy north of that area. All the mahonias can be propagated by seed and suckers, as well as by layers and cuttings of half-ripened wood under glass.

MAIDENHAIR FERN   *See* FERN

MAIDEN PINK   *See* DIANTHUS

MALABAR

The well-known farm of the late Louis Bromfield, Malabar, is located in Pleasant Valley near Mansfield, Ohio. The thousand-acre expanse of worked-out soil was chosen by Bromfield in 1939 when he returned to the United States after nearly 20 years in India and France.

He did not believe in the use of agricultural chemicals; but believed in using grasses and legumes, soil-building crops, rotation, return of organic matter, and other natural farming and conservation practices. In this way, he rebuilt a topsoil three to seven inches deeper than the original, virgin soil had been.

Bromfield himself said of Malabar: "It might be described as a gigantic test plot in soil and water management. . . . We are primarily interested in what works and what is permanently good for the farmer, his soils, his crops and his animals and what gives him the highest production and the best nutritional quality."

MALLOW   (*Malva*)

These annual or perennial herbs are easily grown in ordinary garden soil. The annuals are hardy and can be sown where they are to grow, and the perennials are easily divided in spring or fall. Mallows are related to *Hibiscus* but are not nearly as popular. *M. moschata,* musk rose or musk mallow, and *M. Alcea* grow up to two feet tall and have white or pink flowers. Curled mallow, *M. verticillata* var. *crispa,* may grow up to six feet high, with thick clusters of white blooms. Another variety, high mallow, *M. sylvestris,* sometimes called cheeses because of the shape of its fruit, is one of our worst garden weeds and must be cultivated out strenuously. There is danger that other species of mallow will spread into adjacent areas of the garden, but they are not as difficult to eradicate.

See also HIBISCUS.

MALTESE CROSS   *See* LYCHNIS

MAMMILLARIA
See PINCUSHION CACTUS

MANDARIN   *See* CITRUS, ORANGE

MANDIOCA   *See* MANIHOT

MANGANESE

One of the micronutrients, manganese serves as a catalyst in the process of plant nutrition, encouraging the growth and the maturation of plants. Only a very small amount of manganese is necessary, but it *is* necessary.

Manganese is one of the few micronutrients whose availability is not assured by high organic matter content in the soil. An alkaline condition may depress or halt the availability of the element, even though it is present in the soil. Omitting lime and working to acidify the soil can cure the problem.

In practice, a manganese deficiency is very difficult to diagnose, since the symptoms resemble those of several other deficiencies.

The condition on oats known as "gray speck" is due to manganese deficiency or unavailability in the soil. When different species of plants are grown on the same type of soil they show a considerable range in manganese content. The leguminous plants usually contain the least amount of manganese, and the grasses the greatest amount.

See also SOIL DEFICIENCIES, TRACE ELEMENTS.

MANGANESE SULFATE
See FERTILIZER, CHEMICAL

MANGO   (*Mangifera*)

Mangoes are fruit trees of great antiquity from Southeast Asia, comprising approximately 30 species of the Sumac family. Of these, the common mango (*M. indica*) is cultivated throughout the tropics in both the Eastern and Western hemispheres.

Attaining a height of 90 feet, it is a handsome, round-topped tree with lance-shaped, alternate leaves, eight to 14 inches long. The flowers are small, pink white and usually in terminal clusters. The large, red or yellow orange fruit is drupelike, fleshy and aromatic. It is very juicy but extremely perishable.

Culture: Mangoes are propagated either by seed or grafting. Grafting is preferred because when used the new planting will be true to type. With seed planting, an entirely different type may grow. *See* GRAFTING.

When planting, be sure the soil is rich in compost and manure. Dig a large hole to accommodate the new tree. Irrigate the new planting at least twice a week in dry areas. When mature, the trees require wide spacing, at least 30 by 30 feet. Bearing of fruit takes at least five to seven years.

Varieties: Haden and Paíri are the most common varieties. Others are Irwin, Kent, Borsha, Mulgoba, Sundersha, Zill, and Palmer.

Diseases and Pests: The ambrosia beetle is a cylindrical insect which bores in the limbs and trunk of mango trees and spreads a fungal infection. The best prevention against fungal spread is to prune the diseased portions and burn them.

The red-banded thrip feeds on mango leaves and turns them dark or russet. An oil-emulsion spray is the most effective deterrent.

Red, mango, wax, and shield types of scale insects spread fungal diseases that may kill off the planting. A dormant-oil spray and the introduction of ladybugs to the orchard are good precautions against disease.

Anthracnose, a fungal disease evidenced by spots on flowers and fruits, can be controlled by cutting out the infected branches and burning them. Stem rot, believed to be caused by a lack of moisture, will disappear if trees are kept well ventilated and watered. Dry, light brown leaf tips, caused by tip burn, are best controlled by proper watering, mulching and application of potash.

MANIHOT

Cassava or manihot, occasionally called manioc or mandioca, is a shrub whose edible rootstock yields a nutritious starch. Cultivated throughout the tropics, it is a source of tapioca. The huge roots, often weighing more than 20 pounds, are poisonous until the juice is extracted by pressing and heating. *M. esculenta* grows about eight feet tall, with yellow green flowers. In Florida, it is grown as a food for livestock, and in the North it does well in a dry, warm greenhouse. Sweet cassava, *M. dulcis,* is a similar plant, but its roots are not poisonous when young. Other varieties are trees that yield a poor kind of rubber. *M. carthaginensis* is a tree found growing wild in the desert of the Southwest. All varieties can be increased by cuttings rooted over bottom heat.

MANIOC   *See* MANIHOT

MANTIS, PRAYING

Praying mantises are odd-looking relatives of the grasshoppers. Their name stems from the way they hold up the stout front legs as if in prayer. This stance, however, is hardly one of pious reverence; "preying" would be more descriptive. Actually, the mantis is poised to capture and consume insects. This is accomplished by a lightning-fast movement of the forelegs, which are equipped with rows of sharp teeth for holding victims.

These devout-looking benefactors are valuable in keeping pests down to manageable levels. However, their appetites are not as selective as once thought, and they are known to eat beneficial and harmless bugs. Mantises aren't even above sharing an occasional small frog or bird.

The eggs are laid in tan foamlike masses in fall, and little mantises hatch out in spring. You should have little trouble introducing praying mantises to the garden, but there's no guarantee that they will stay put. Enough hatch from a single egg case, however (anywhere from 100 to 300 or more), so that several cases placed in strategic spots around the yard will provide enough for both you and the neighbors.

There are several commercial sources of praying mantis egg cases in the United States, but anyone with an observant eye should be able to gather an ample supply of cases between late fall and early spring. Look for them wherever plants grow in clumps a few feet high. Goldenrod clusters, hedgerows between fields and roadside borders may all yield egg cases for your garden. When gathering your own cases, leave them attached to a section of twig. They can then be stored in the refrigerator or, better yet, immediately placed in the garden area.

Lash the egg-bearing sticks to plant branches or to sticks set firmly in the ground. If you store the cases over winter, keep them cold. More than one schoolchild has found that a dormant egg case can fill a warm bed-

Praying mantises will patrol the garden for aphids, caterpillars and other insect pests.

room full of tiny mantises, so keep them in the refrigerator or outdoors. They're very winter hardy, able to stand subfreezing temperatures. How many cases are needed for adequate protection? A general rule is one egg case for each major shrub or tree, and four cases per ¼ acre without shrubbery. It should be noted that egg cases can be sent by mail only during the dormant period—approximately November 1 to May 15. Since the mantis is recognized as a beneficial insect, there are no restrictions on its eggs being sent through the mails and it is exempt from insect control laws.

See also INSECT CONTROL.

MANURE

The excreta of agricultural animals, along with stable litter, constitutes one of the oldest and most effective fertilizers known to man. The rise of chemical fertilizers in the twentieth century has led to a decrease in the amount of manure utilized by world agriculturists.

It has been calculated that a farmer by wise management of his animal manures can return to the soil 70 percent of the nitrogen, 75 percent of the phosphorus and 80 percent of the potash which was taken out by the homegrown plants his animals eat. This is a considerable saving when it is realized that a dairy cow gives 27,000 pounds of manure annually and a horse, 18,000.

Actually only a small fraction of the potential crop-producing and soil-conserving value of manure is used. Approximately half of the excrement from farm stock is dropped on pastures and uncultivated ground. Vast amounts of manure in stockyards, poultry farms and other animal industries are considered worthless wastes and are dumped on uncultivated lands. On most farms manure is so badly handled that it suffers enormous losses of nutrients.

Nutrient losses also result from the inefficient use of manure; for instance, when it is not applied at the season, in the manner, at the rate, or to the crop which would give the greatest return. It is safe to assume that only from a third to a quarter of the potential value of the manure resource of this country is now realized. The present wasteful and inefficient methods of using manure, seen in all sections of the country, are sufficient evidence that many farmers do not understand the true nature of manure, the perishable character of its most valuable constituents and the direct money loss incurred through its improper treatment. This situation is doubtlessly due in large part to the increased use of artificial fertilizers.

Content and Value of Manure: The most common domestic animals which are a source of manure are horses, cattle, goats, sheep, pigs, rabbits, and poultry. The dung consists of the undigested portions of foods which have been ground into fine bits and saturated with digestive juices in the alimentary tract. It also contains a large population of bacteria, composing as much as 30 percent of its mass. The urine contains compounds from the digested portion of the foods and secretions from the animal's body. Because they are in solution, the elements in the urine are more quickly made available as plant nutrients than the constituents found in the dung.

The value of animal manure varies with the food eaten by the animal, the age of the animal, and the physical condition and health of the animal. The richer in essential elements the animal's food is, the more valuable will be the manure. The manure of animals fed on wheat bran, gluten meal and cottonseed meal, for instance, will be much richer in nutrients than that of animals fed with straw or hay without grains. The manure of young animals who are forming bones and muscles from their foods will be poorer in nutrient elements than the manure of mature animals.

As a rule, horse manure is more valuable than the manure of other farm animals. This doubtlessly varies with the amount of grain which is included in the diet. Grains are relatively high in all plant nutrients. Horse manure is richer in nitrogen than either cow or hog manure and is much more subject to fermentation. For this reason it is frequently referred to as a hot manure. Another hot manure

is that of sheep, which is generally quite dry and rich. Cow manure and hog manure are relatively wet and correspondingly low in nitrogen. Because of their high water and low nitrogen content, these manures ferment slowly and are commonly regarded as cold manures.

It is worth noting that the urine of most animals contains more nitrogen and more potash than the solid excreta. Unfortunately, farm manures are handled in such ways that most of the urine is carelessly allowed to escape into drains which lead it off the farm. Urines are especially valuable as activators in converting crop residues into humus.

The amounts of fresh excrement produced by farm animals are subject to wide variations, being governed by the kind of animal, its age, the amounts of food it eats, its activity, and other factors. The amount produced annually per 1,000 pounds of live weight is given in the following table:

Source	Fresh Excrement (tons)	Liquid (%)
Cattle	12.6	85
Horse	5.8	66
Poultry	5.6	62
Sheep	5.9	66
Swine	13.2	85

Source: Nyle C. Brady, *The Nature and Properties of Soils,* 8th edition (New York: Macmillan Publishing Co., 1974).

Unfortunately, the value of manure and fertilizers in general has been based on the relative amount of nitrogen, phosphoric acid and potash which they contain. It is misleading to make a direct comparison between farm manures and artificial chemical fertilizers on the basis of the relative amounts of N, P and K alone. Manure has value that far exceeds its NPK value alone. For example, soil needs organic matter to keep it alive. Organic matter in the soil is converted into humus, and humus plays an important role in making the nutrient elements in the soil available to the higher plants. Manure, unlike chemical fertilizers, provides organic matter to the soil, and supplies trace minerals as well.

It has been estimated that 80 percent of the nutrients found in the diet of milk cows are voided in the excrement. In fattening cattle and hogs, as much as 90 percent of the nutrient elements in the food are voided. By keeping these percentages in mind, it is not difficult to calculate the amount of nitrogen, phosphoric acid, potash, and other elements in the manure when the composition of the feeds is known.

On the average, a ton of cow manure has NPK values equivalent to 100 pounds of a 12–3–9 chemical fertilizer. Similarly, horse manure averages 14–5–11, sheep and goat manure 19–7–20, hog manure 10–7–8, and chicken manure about 20–16–9. In addition, these manures will supply organic matter and trace elements.

Handling Manure: Manure can be handled in several ways. It can be hauled out directly to the fields as it accumulates, or it can be stored or composted. When spread directly from the barn, it should normally be disked or plowed under as soon as possible. However, a thin layer of manure spread over your fields in spring or summer can greatly benefit pastures, lawns and growing hay crops.

Some farmers haul their manure to the fields each day and, during the winter, put it on top of snow. There can be disastrous losses of the vital nutrients if the manure is applied to hilly land using this method. In fact, nutrients can be washed off land with a considerable slope in the wintertime even if there is no snow on the ground.

Fresh manure should never be applied directly to the garden in spring or summer unless it is tilled in four weeks before planting.

The method by which manures are stored and kept affects their value to a greater degree than any other single factor. It is almost impossible to prevent loss of nutrients entirely. Sources of loss are escape of the natural drainage occurring in manure, leaching caused by soaking of water through the manure and volatilization into the air. Perhaps the best storage is in watertight, covered pits.

If stored in the open, manure should be heaped on a level or slightly concave place with a clay base to prevent seepage of the juices into the soil. The heap should be made so high that rain will not soak through from top to bottom, and the top of the heap should be slightly concave to catch rainwater. It is also well to cover the heap with a thin covering of topsoil if it must stand for a long time.

In the enclosed pit, the manure soon becomes impregnated and completely enclosed by an atmosphere of carbon dioxide in combination with a relatively high humidity. Under these conditions manure breaks down semi-anaerobically to form a product that is rich in important nutrients. There is little or no loss of nitrogen or other elements when manures are fermented in a properly constructed enclosed pit. The conditions which affect the fermentation of manures are temperature, degree of compaction, degree of moisture, and the composition of the manure. It is especially important to prevent the manure from drying out. When manure dries to the point of turning white, it has lost a considerable portion of its nitrogen and some of its organic matter, which has escaped into the air as carbon dioxide.

Manure can also be composted. *See also* COMPOSTING.

Decomposition Changes: Manure changes in several ways as it decomposes: The first change is the formation of ammonia in urine as the urinary nitrogen decomposes; this is lost unless the manure is kept moist and compact. Next, the insoluble nitrogen contained in the solid parts of the excrement undergoes putrefactive changes with the formation of ammonia. The ammonia and other soluble compounds of nitrogen are used in considerable amounts as food for the bacteria in the manure and are stored in their bodily substance in insoluble form. This nitrogen becomes available when the bacteria die and undergo decomposition. Stored manure is unlike fresh manure, where the nitrogen is mostly soluble.

Under certain conditions ammonia and nitrates are decomposed with the formation of free nitrogen which escapes into the atmosphere and is thus lost permanently. The fibrous parts of the manure which are made up largely of cellulose, lignin and other complex carbohydrates are eventually broken down with the escape of the carbon into the atmosphere in the form of carbon dioxide, and hydrogen in the form of water. These elements, carbon and hydrogen, escape in such amounts that from one quarter to one half the original dry matter in the manure is lost. This is the reason for the great shrinkage in bulk during decomposition. Because of the weight loss, composted manure is richer in plant nutrients pound-for-pound than fresh manure.

Benefit to Crops: Some crops benefit from the application of barnyard manure, while others are damaged or produce crops of poor quality. Fresh manure, rich in nitrogen, may burn plant tissues if applied to some plants. Other crops, however, are not harmed by fresh manure. Grasslands are generally much benefited by top-dressing with farm manure, either fresh or fermented.

POUNDS OF NITROGEN, PHOSPHATE AND POTASH PER TON OF ANIMAL MANURE

Source	Nitrogen	Phosphate	Potash
Cattle	10.0	2.7	7.5
Horse	14.9	4.5	13.2
Poultry	29.9	14.3	7.0
Sheep	23.0	7.0	21.7
Swine	12.9	7.1	10.9

Source: Nyle C. Brady, *The Nature and Properties of Soils,* 8th edition (New York: Macmillan Publishing Co., 1974).

Root crops usually respond most satisfactorily to generous applications of stable manure. Some precautions, however, must be taken in the case of potatoes and sugar beets. Excessive amounts of fresh manure on light soils and loams cause the beets to become very large but with a low sugar content. Fresh manure can result in leggy plants.

Corn, millet and leafy crops in general respond favorably to manure, either fresh or decomposed.

Garden crops in general respond quite favorably to generous applications of manure. Approximately 25 pounds of manure, to which has been added ten pounds of phosphate rock for every 100 square feet of garden, will enrich and condition soils. If it is not well rotted, apply the manure and incorporate it into the soil at least four weeks before planting.

Young deciduous trees and shrubs respond favorably to manure, but prefer it decomposed.

Cereals are injured by large applications of manure. The straw of wheat and barley, in particular, grows very large at the expense of the grain—a condition that favors lodging.

See also COMPOSTING, FERTILIZER, MANURE TEA.

MANURE, GREEN
See GREEN MANURE

MANURE TEA

Manure tea is often recommended for fertilizing house plants as well as outside plantings.

There are several ways of making manure tea. For an easy tea for house plants, place an inch of finely sieved compost on the soil. When you water the plant, water soaking through this layer will make its own tea. The following method is easy, economical and not a bit messy for a larger application.

As soon as the weather is warm enough to keep water from freezing, fill three 100-pound sacks with a mixture of fresh cow, horse and chicken manure in equal parts. Suspend these in 60-gallon steel drums, one to each drum, and fill the drums with warm water. Be sure the sacks of manure are underwater.

Cover the drums and let the manure steep in the water for 30 to 45 days. At the end of this time, remove the sacks of manure and add enough water so that the mixture is about the

Made by steeping fresh manure in water, manure tea is useful in establishing transplants and in fertilizing older plants just before they bloom.

color of weak tea, or fill the drum to within one inch of the top.

The manure tea is used to give plants a boost just before they start to bloom. The liquid can be made at any time so that it is ready when flowers and shrubs bloom.

This "liquid manure" should be applied to the ground around the particular plants which are to receive it and then washed in with water. You can save labor if you apply the manure just before a good rain.

Many gardeners give plants three applications a year in the proportion of one gallon to five square feet of plant bed. For shrub groups use the same proportion.

See also COMPOST WATER, MANURE.

MAPLE   (*Acer*)

There are well over 100 different species of maples, almost all of which make handsome ornamental, shade or street trees. They range in height from ten to 120 feet. Many of them are prized for the magnificent coloring of their leaves in autumn. They also have interesting winged seeds, known as keys.

Maple wood is fine in texture, strong, and offers a variety of grains: bird's-eye, blister and curly maple are used for ornamental effect in furniture and musical instruments.

The red maple (*A. rubrum*) is one of the tallest maples and is so named because the twigs, stems, blossoms, and fall foliage are all a brilliant red. Although the trees are occasionally sapped, they yield far less sugar than *A. saccharum,* the sugar maple. The sugar maple also offers an especially strong and valuable wood. It is a tall and stately tree, turning scarlet or orange in the fall, and is popularly used for lawn and street planting.

The leaves of the silver maple (*A. saccharinum*) turn an uninteresting yellow in fall. It is an extremely hardy tree, growing from Canada to Florida and west to Nebraska. The Norway maple (*A. platanoides*) offers red foliage in spring that later turns green.

Among the medium-sized maples are the box-elder (*A. Negundo*), a rapid grower reaching 60 feet, and very good for shelterbelts; the vine maple (*A. circinatum*), a handsome large shrub or small tree; *A. Ginnala* and *A. tataricum,* both 20 feet high; the striped maple or moosewood (*A. pensylvanicum*), an acid lover reaching about 40 feet; and *A. cappadocicum,* which grows to 70 feet but is not as hardy as the others.

The Japanese maple, *A. palmatum,* grows as shrubs or 25-foot trees and can be grown as a potted plant. The mountain maple (*A. spicatum*) is a dwarf about ten feet tall; it does well in rather dry, acidic soil and has showy yellow blooms borne in spikes in early spring, followed by drooping reddish seed clusters.

The vast variety of maples makes it easy to find ones to fit any particular situation. Most species suffer from few diseases when grown in good organic soil, and are seldom bothered by insect pests.

See also MAPLE SUGAR, TREE.

MAPLE SUGAR

Hundreds of years ago, the American Indian taught the white man how to boil down maple sap into a sweet syrup. Since that time, sugaring has become a big business in the Northeast.

The materials needed for boiling sap down to a few gallons of syrup are few and fairly cheap. Still, it takes time and care to evaporate most of the water from the sap.

The average sugar maple tree produces sap with a 2 to 3 percent sugar content. However, sap may contain as little as 1 percent sugar, in which case it takes 86 gallons of sap to make one gallon of syrup. At the other extreme, excellent trees in favorable seasons may give as high as 9 percent sugar. The soil's condition affects production. In Ohio tests, deep, moist soil, loose and mellow with abundant leaf litter and organic matter, produced the most and richest sap. Even red, silver and Oregon maples, generally poor yielders, gave better-than-average sap under these conditions.

You should have at least 30 to 40 mature maples. Sometimes woodlots can be thinned out, cutting some of the other species to make room. Uncrowded maples develop thick crowns that keep down the growth of useless briars and weeds by excluding sunlight. Any grazing on the woodlot should be light.

Cold, brisk nights, with unusually warm days, are "sap weather." Prompt gathering and boiling, plus clean equipment, will insure light-colored, high-quality syrup with fine flavor. Boiling, filtering and packaging all require care, but they can be as much fun as gathering the buckets on a brisk end-of-winter day.

While several trees should provide enough syrup for the table, commercial-scale production demands a thousand or more tap holes. A tree with a chest-high diameter of ten to 15 inches should have only one tap hole, a tree measuring 15 to 25 inches can have two or three, and a tree over 25 inches in diameter can have four.

The maples are drilled with a bit approximately ½ inch in diameter, and the sap channeled through a manufactured or home-made sumac-branch spile. Gallon jugs or large, clean tin cans will suffice as collectors but should be checked often, as some trees may put out two or more gallons a day. Large operations dispense with bucket collecting by connecting trees to a central tank with capillaries of plastic tubing. Prior to boiling, sap can be held in metal or plastic trash cans. A washboiler or washtub will make a good evaporator. Set the container up on concrete blocks and build a fire below. Small batches can be boiled off on the stove, but it is best to evaporate outdoors, as the steam deposits sugar on the walls and ceiling.

The easiest way to determine when the sap has boiled down enough is to take the boiling liquid's temperature. The boiling point of syrup is 219°F. (103.89°C.) at sea level; the

Tapping maple trees does not require fancy or expensive equipment.

boiling point is lowered one degree (F.) for each 550 feet of elevation. Or, the boiling point of finished syrup is always seven degrees (F.) above that of water or fresh sap.

The boiling hot syrup should be poured into clean jars or bottles, sealed, and turned upside down immediately to sterilize the top. Properly sealed syrup can be stored at room temperature indefinitely.

The USDA offers a detailed maple sugaring manual.

MARANTA

The fleshy rootstock of *M. arundinacea,* grown in the tropics, yields arrowroot, a nourishing starch. It survives outdoors only in Florida, but elsewhere it is a handsome subject for greenhouse cultivation, sometimes having variegated leaves. Other beautiful species are *M. bicolor* and *M. leuconeura,* both of which have purple, red-spotted or white-banded leaves and do not grow over a foot tall. They are sometimes sold by florists as calathea. In the greenhouse, marantas need very rich organic soil, biweekly feedings of liquid manure, and ample moisture both in the soil and in the air. A constant temperature of 75°F. (23.89°C.) or more, and some shading from the hottest sun, are also recommended. *Maranta leuconeura* is often called the prayer plant because its leaves turn up at night like praying hands.

MARGUERITE
See CHRYSANTHEMUM

MARIGOLD   (*Tagetes*)

One of the most easily grown and popular annuals, the marigold comes in varieties from six inches to four feet tall. The colors range from bright yellow through orange and red. Most varieties have strongly scented foliage. All of them flower freely from mid-June until frost and are excellent for cutting.

The half-hardy African marigolds bear enormous yellow to orange flowers all summer; in the fall they can be potted and brought indoors where they will continue to bloom for a few weeks.

The French marigolds are the lowest growing and feature single- and double-flowered types. They are fine for bedding. The dwarf forms make good edgings and window box subjects. The taller African marigolds are less bushy and suit the open border. There are chrysanthemum-flowered and carnation-flowered varieties. In addition, many new types appear every season, like the semidwarf hybrids which produce large flowers on bushy plants just over a foot tall and bloom so profusely that the foliage is hidden. Hawaii is a tall odorless form, and a white-flowered type recently appeared on the market.

Culture: The heaviest bloom is achieved in hot, sunny, southern exposures. Treat marigolds as a tender annual and sow the seed indoors early to get bloom several weeks in advance of outdoor-planted seed. Set the young plants out when the soil is thoroughly warmed up. Marigolds will give more and better bloom in poor soil than in rich.

Marigolds should be freely interplanted with vegetables because of their pest-repellent properties. Certain forms exude substances from the roots which will rid the garden of nematodes if planted each year. Those forms with the strongest odor are the most effective and have been reported to repel pests as diverse as bean beetles and rabbits. The dwarf French types are the most versatile as they take up little space and can be planted right at the base of staked tomatoes, bell peppers and trellised cucumbers, or simply scattered here and there in the garden.

MARINE PLANTS
See AQUARIUM

MARJORAM, SWEET
(*Origanum Majorana*)

Sweet marjoram is a widely cultivated perennial herb native to the Mediterranean region. It can be distinguished from 30 related species of marjoram by its characteristic pleasant, fragrant, spicy odor and by the flavor that makes the plant very popular for seasoning soups, stews, dressings, and similar dishes.

Traditionally, sweet marjoram has symbolized youth, beauty and happiness. According to one legend, a handsome youth was transfigured into the herb after displeasing King Cinyrus of Cyprus. The herb was mentioned by Virgil and Shakespeare, and the French have long been familiar with its culinary uses. They even used its fragrance to freshen hope chests and linen drawers. The English used the oil of marjoram for furniture polishes and in washing water. The herb's leaves have long been used to prepare a sweet-flavored tea. History also records the medicinal uses of marjoram. Herbalist Gerard prescribed marjoram for colds, sinus problems and convulsions.

The plant grows well in any well-drained fertile garden loam. Although primarily a warm-climate plant, it makes good growth in cooler regions but is very subject to winterkill unless well mulched with straw or leaves. For this reason it is often grown as an annual. The seed is small and is best started in the greenhouse, the seedlings being transplanted to the field after all danger of frost has passed. Outside, space plants six to eight inches apart, or in three-plant clumps if shoots are still small. Propagation by cuttings is also practical.

Use well-rotted compost rather than fresh manure. Regular hoeing is necessary to check weeds. Delay mulching until two weeks before the first harvest.

Harvest when green tips appear at the end of the stems. The leaves can be dried and their flavor stored.

Pot marjoram differs from sweet marjoram in being hardier, and in having slightly larger leaves without stalks. The scent and flavor are somewhat more thymelike than those of sweet marjoram. It grows best in a light limestone soil. Hardy north to New York City,

it should be taken indoors where winters are very severe. Propagation is from seed or by division.

Marjoram is still recognized for its medicinal value, as well as its use in cooking and as an aromatic. When mixed with sage, catnip and peppermint and boiled in hot water, this herbal ingredient is believed to help treat headache and nervousness. Wild marjoram is a stimulant, carminative and diaphoretic.

For use in the kitchen, the leaves of this herb are cut from the top to prevent blossoming, then used in soups, in stuffings, with lamb, and with vegetables, eggs, pork, and duck.

The pleasant scent of sweet marjoram sprigs is still enjoyed today, and so marjoram is also used as an air freshener and strewing herb in many homes.

See also HERB.

After the small, round flowers appear in mid-summer, sweet marjoram should be cut back to an inch above the ground. Within several weeks, a lusher second growth will appear.

MARJORAM, WILD
(*Origanum vulgare*)

A hardy perennial native to Europe and Asia and now naturalized in the eastern United States, wild marjoram has sprawling stems which can grow to two feet. It has small pink or white flowers.

Much coarser than sweet marjoram, it smells more like thyme. Its leaves are used as a flavoring in cooking, but most people do not consider them as good as sweet marjoram leaves. Other than for flavoring, wild marjoram is of little horticultural value, except perhaps that its flowers are pleasantly fragrant, making it an attractive honey plant.

Historically, wild marjoram has played more of a medicinal than culinary role. It has been used to relieve nervous headaches when its leaves were infused, and its oils have been applied to sore gums and teeth. The herb has also been used as an emmenagogue, mild tonic, stimulant, and even a diaphoretic.

Wild marjoram grows well in poor soil and can be propagated by seed or root division.

See also HERB.

MARKET DISEASES

Market diseases of fruits and vegetables are those that develop during the process of the harvesting, grading, and packing of the crop, its transportation to market, its storage at shipping point or at the market, and the various handling operations required to move it from the wholesale dealer to the retail store and the ultimate consumer. During any of these operations the product may be subjected to conditions that impair its appearance and food value, and render it subject to attack by decay-producing organisms.

Fruits and vegetables are susceptible to invasion by bacteria and fungi at bruises and skin breaks. Hence, it is of prime importance that they be handled as carefully as possible at all times.

Temperature and humidity have a direct effect on the development of decay in fruits. They should have the critical attention of those who wish to ship or store fruits, and of those who attempt to determine why a given lot, at any stage in the marketing process, shows decay or other deterioration. Too low temperature may freeze the fruit, or it may cause only chilling injury; subtropical fruits are particularly susceptible to such injury. Too high temperature encourages decay and may cause undesirable color changes. High humidity favors the growth of fungi, and low humidity causes loss in weight and possibly shriveling, especially if combined with high temperature.

See also DISEASE.

MARL

An oceanic deposit, marl is usually a mixture of lime and fine clay. Greensand marl, for example, is found in New Jersey and is an excellent soil builder. Marl is used as a liming material.

See also GREENSAND, LIME, MINERAL ROCKS.

MARSH MARIGOLD
(*Caltha palustris*)

Popping up brightly in swampy areas and along brooks all over the country, marsh marigold provides fresh green food for health-conscious people in the spring. Often called cowslip, it is a member of the Buttercup family and one of the tastiest of all the spring greens. Marsh marigold is a strong-growing perennial that thrives in wet spots and will do well in the wild garden, to which it is easily transplanted. It will grow nicely in the border if the soil is moist and rich and partial shade is provided. Other suitable growing spots are along shallow streams, around springs and even in roadside ditches. For cooking use, pick it just as the first flower buds begin to burst into golden bloom. Marsh marigold grows up to two feet tall and is easily propagated by seed and division of roots.

MARSILEA   *See* PEPPERWORT

MAST

Forage derived from the fruits of oaks, beeches and some other trees is known as mast.

MATRIMONY VINE   (*Lycium*)

These deciduous or evergreen shrubs of the warmer regions of both hemispheres are also known as boxthorn. They are often spiny and tend to become rampant. Most may be propagated from suckers, which grow so profusely as to be a nuisance; they also are propagated from seed and by layering and cuttings. The shrubs thrive everywhere, even in sandy soil.

L. chinense is not evergreen but holds its leaves until late fall. It is a shrub with branches often spreading to 12 feet. The many small purple flowers are followed by one-inch, orange red berries.

L. halimifolium is upright with curving spiny branches spreading to ten feet. Flowers are dull lilac and the fruit is a red orange berry, about ¾ inch long.

MATTHIOLA   *See* STOCK

MAYAPPLE   (*Podophyllum peltatum*)

A plant belonging to the Barberry family (Berberidaceae), it is commonly termed the

Mayapples should be planted in association with later-growing perennials, as their lovely green foliage dies down in midsummer.

American mandrake. It is native to low woods, from Quebec to Manitoba and southward to Florida and Texas. In some areas, mayapple is a common wild flower; in others it is cultivated for its beauty in wild gardens. It has been used as a medicinal plant. The yellow "apples" are edible only when fully ripe. This woodland perennial has a creeping rootstock and is easily propagated by division. Its green leaves are often a foot wide; and in May it bears pinkish or white, waxy, cup-shaped flowers, which have a somewhat unpleasant odor.

The root yields the drug podophyllin, which, useful in stimulating the glands, is purgative when taken in large doses.

Mayapple is an interesting plant for the wild garden, growing about 18 inches high in rich, well-drained woods soil. It will do well in full or partial shade and appreciates an annual feeding of bone meal. A winter mulch of hardwood leaves is recommended to prevent root damage from heaving.

MAYFLOWER

See HEPATICA, TRAILING ARBUTUS

MAYWEED   *See* CHAMOMILE

MEADOW

A field or area covered with finely stemmed forage plants, wholly or mainly perennial, and used to produce hay is called a meadow.

See also FORAGE, HAY.

MEADOW-BEAUTY   (*Rhexia*)

These pretty little perennial wild flowers need wet, acid, sandy soil. The two common varieties, *R. mariana* and *R. virginica* (also called deer grass and handsome Harry), grow from one to two feet high, with purple flowers in clusters. They are found in sandy or pine-barren bogs along the East Coast and west to Texas.

Meadow-beauty is transplanted fairly easily from the wild into boggy sites along the edges of ponds or streams. Naturally boggy soil usually contains large amounts of humus and fiber. Acid peat, decayed hardwood leaves or sawdust are excellent for filling this requirement when making an artificial bog garden. Dig them in or use them as a mulch.

MEADOW CRESS
See CUCKOOFLOWER

MEADOW RUE   *See* THALICTRUM

MEADOW SAFFRON
See COLCHICUM

MEALYBUG
(*Pseudococcus maritimus*)

These horticultural pests are particularly damaging to house plants. They are oval with many fine leglike filaments. They often look like bits of cotton fluff because their eggs are carried in a cottony sac. Mealybugs are sluggish and do not move much, feeding by sucking plant juices. Bud drop and sickly foliage result.

See also HOUSE PLANTS.

MEASURING WORM
See CANKER WORMS

MEDICINAL PLANTS   *See* HERB

MELISSA   (*Melissa officinalis*)

Also known as lemon balm, melissa is a hardy perennial herb native to southern Europe and has long been cultivated in gardens in this

Lemon balm is one of the sweet perennial herbs which has escaped cultivation and grows wild in hedgerows and along the edge of forests.

country. In many places in the eastern states, it has escaped and is now growing wild. The fragrant leaves are widely used for culinary flavoring, and the leaves and flowering tops are used in medicine. The flowers, which are grouped in small clusters, are off-white to yellow, and bloom from May to October.

Balm grows readily in any good garden soil where full sun is provided. It is easily propagated from seed or cuttings or by division. The seed is small and is best sown thinly in shallow flats in a greenhouse or hotbed. The seedlings should be transferred to deeper flats as soon as their first true leaves appear and

set outside when four to five inches high. Space about a foot apart to allow cultivation between the plants. In colder climates it may be wiser to treat balm as an annual to be wintered indoors in the form of slips taken from the summer garden.

MELON   (*Cucumis melo*)

Members of the species *Cucumis melo* of the Cucurbitaceae include both cantaloupe and winter melon varieties. Though their cultural requirements are similar, watermelons are classified as *Citrullus lanatus*. All varieties of *Cucumis melo* are also known as muskmelons, even though not all are musk-scented. Botanically speaking, the term "cantaloupe" should be applied only to melons with a rough, warty surface and hard rind. This type is classified *C. m.* var. *cantalupensis* and is not grown in the United States. The green- and yellow green-skinned, netted melons, classified as *C. m.* var. *reticulatus,* are called cantaloupes in this country.

The winter melons (*C. m.* var. *inodorus*) are late-maturing types grown in California. They will keep well into winter if stored in a cool dry place. They include the following melons: the Honey Dew, with smooth ivory white or greenish skin and firm green flesh; the Casaba, globular fruits with pointed stem ends which have golden yellow skins when ripe, and thick white flesh; and the Crenshaw, pear-shaped fruits with pale yellow tan skins which may be thinly netted, and thick, light salmon-colored flesh with a delicate flavor.

Culture: The culture for all melons is very similar. They will not do well in heavy clay soils and will do nothing at all until the weather warms. Cool temperatures and prolonged cloudiness, even where no freezing occurs, are hard on these sensitive plants. In warm areas they can be started in the garden from seed; in colder areas they should be started indoors in individual peat pots or other containers which can go directly into the garden. They transplant badly and will not thrive if their roots are disturbed.

Slopes and south-facing hills are ideal sites for planting melons. They are heavy feeders, so an application of well-rotted manure to the planting site is advisable. They

Place a board or clay tile beneath the developing melon to prevent rotting.

prefer a humus-rich soil which is sandy, light and friable.

Melons are usually grown in hills spaced about four feet apart each way. Plant about six to eight seeds in each 12-inch hill, to which has been added a shovelful of rich compost or manure. One ounce of seed will plant about 20 hills. In about two weeks the seed should germinate and plants appear. When four inches high, they should be thinned to three plants per hill. If seedlings are used, plant three or four per hill.

The cucurbits require lots of moisture, so mulch each hill well. Water thoroughly at least once each week as fruits begin to form, but allow the ground to dry out a bit as they approach maturity.

Pests and Diseases: The most serious threats to the melon family are the striped and spotted cucumber beetles. In addition to feeding on the plant's leaves, stems and roots, the beetles carry the fungus which causes fusarium wilt. If infected by the wilt, the plants may suddenly wither away even if they appeared, up to that time, to be flourishing. The beetles have less opportunity to damage young plants when seedlings are used than when seeds are planted, and further protection can be gained by covering the young plants with glass jars. As the plants outgrow the jars, screen boxes or tents of mosquito netting or cheesecloth can be substituted. A mixture of 75 percent colloidal phosphate and 25 percent wood ashes may also deter the cucumber beetle. To be effective, this mixture should be applied frequently— two or three times a week and after heavy rains. *See also* INSECT CONTROL.

Harvest: Each melon vine usually produces three or four fruits. The size of the melon is some indication of its maturity, and many people are able to detect the ripe melon by its characteristic aroma. However, the stems are the surest indicators. As the fruit matures small cracks appear in the stem where it joins the fruit. When the cracks circle the stem, and the stem itself looks shriveled, the melon will break off with a light twist. If more than light pressure is necessary to pick the fruit, it's not ripe and should be left on the vine. For peak flavor allow the melon to rest a day or two before serving.

Though melons have been hybridized to produce fruits which ripen earlier and are able to develop in the shorter growing season of the North, early frosts frequently catch a portion of the crop still on the vine. Beginning in early September, gardeners threatened by early frost should cover their melons with bushel baskets at night.

Varieties: Proven, dependable varieties include Burpee Hybrid, Hearts of Gold, Hale's Best, Fordhook Gem, and Mainerock Hybrid.

Compost Value: Cantaloupe rinds are quite valuable in the compost heap. Their ash contains almost 10 percent phosphoric acid and over 12 percent potash. They decay readily and help activate decomposition.

MENDEL, GREGOR JOHANN

(1822–1884) Mendel, an Austrian botanist and monk, is recognized as the father of genetics, the modern science of heredity. His work with peas, conducted over eight years in an Augustine monastery, resulted in what we call Mendel's laws.

Mendel discovered that plants transmit their characteristics to their offspring in a predictable, mathematical way. He found that crossing a purebred red-flowered pea, for example, with a purebred one with white flowers produced seeds that all grew into red-flowered plants (F_1). He called red-floweredness the "dominant" characteristic. The white-floweredness, however, was still there and so was called "recessive." (Dominance is rarely total, the recessive trait expressing itself to some degree, usually in a modification of the dominant.) This, he concluded, was due to a special factor—now known as genes—in the reproductive cells of the plants.

Mendel then followed up by self-pollinating the red-flowered hybrids and obtained seed that gave three red-flowered plants to one white-flowered one (F_2). When these in turn were self-pollinated, the white-flowered peas were seen to give only white-flowered plants; while of the red-flowered varieties, one out of three bred true, and the other two produced three red-flowered varieties to one white-flowered variety (F_3).

Mendel's work thus proved that a minute mechanism within the cells of plants regulates the traits of their descendants in accordance with precise mathematical laws. All further work on heredity has been based on the solid foundation of his discoveries.

MENTHA   *See* MINT

MERCURY   *See* FUNGICIDE

MERRYBELLS   *See* UVULARIA

MERTENSIA

Sometimes called lungwort or bluebells, mertensia is a handsome perennial that grows about two feet tall. Its two common varieties are suited to the wild garden and can be easily transplanted there from the wild. *M. ciliata* is found mostly in the Rocky Mountain region, while *M. virginica* is a native of the East from Tennessee northward into New England. The latter is often known as Virginia cowslip. Both have loose spikes of brilliant blue flowers although a variety of *M. virginica* has white blooms.

Mertensias like a moist, rich, humusy soil and semishade, imitating the conditions in the woodlands where they are found. Some species do well in the rock garden; *M. virginica* thrives in the open border if mulched. Because they are hard to divide successfully, new plants should be grown from seed sown immediately after they have matured.

The leaves of mertensia disappear soon after the plant has finished flowering in late spring to early summer, and gardeners should take care not to injure the roots by accidentally digging into them during the long dormant period. Interplant mertensia with ferns or other plants whose foliage will hide the bare spots left after their leaves have withered.

MESCAL BEAN   *See* SOPHORA

MESEMBRYANTHEMUM
See FIG MARIGOLD *or* ICE PLANT

MESQUITE   (*Prosopis glandulosa*)

The mesquite is a thorn-studded tree averaging 12 to 30 feet high that grows abundantly on southwestern prairie lands. Considered a pest by some ranchers, the tree nevertheless is an inexpensive and nutritious feed for livestock.

Mesquite beans are similar to those of carob in analysis and often have served as a human as well as animal food. When fresh, the beans are red brown or straw colored and have the smell of cereal.

The pods can be crushed manually or with a hammermill to extract seeds, which may be ground into a nutritious meal or flour and used as a cereal similar to cornmeal. At one time, American natives made the meal into bread. Today, seeds from one of the *Prosopis* species grown in northern Nigeria are consumed as food and seeds ground into powder are an important part of the diet of people in certain areas of Brazil. In Argentina and Hawaii, there are many plantations where algarroba beans (*P. chilensis*) are grown as cattle fodders.

In this country, mesquite is grown primarily as a honey plant and cattle food. Honey mesquite (*P. g.* var. *glandulosa*) is an important honey plant in parts of the Southwest and in the Great Plains states. Western honey mesquite (*P. g.* var. *Torreyana*) is important in Southern California and northern Texas.

MEXICAN BEAN BEETLE
See INSECT CONTROL

MEXICAN SUNFLOWER
See TITHONIA

MICHAELMAS DAISY
See ASTER

MICHIHLI   *See* CHINESE CABBAGE

MICROBES   *See* MICROORGANISM

MICROMERIA

The common name for members of this genus is "savory," but they should not be confused with the sweet savories or calamints that belong to the genus *Satureja* and are cultivated as condiments. These plants are grown as fragrant rock garden ornamentals and shrubby border plants. *M. piperella* and *M. rupestris* are low-growing tender perennials. They are worth featuring for their fragrant foliage, which smells something like pennyroyal. The tiny flowers that appear from July to frost are red purple in the first variety and white and lavender-spotted in the second. Micromerias like a well-drained, not very rich, nearly neutral soil. Propagate them by division of the roots in spring.

See also SAVORY.

MICROORGANISM

There are large numbers of microorganisms in the surface foot of soil and each kind plays some significant role in the decomposition of plant and animal residues, liberation of plant nutrients or in the development of soil structure. Many groups are dependent on each other; consequently development of one kind may tend to follow development of another.

Types of Microorganisms: Microorganisms set up a series of reactions in the soil that follow one another in an organized sequence. In size the organisms range from those that are visible only with the aid of an electron microscope to those that can be seen with the naked eye. In shape they vary from tiny dots to weird twisted forms.

With enzymes, these diverse organisms digest soil materials and, in so doing, form gigantic, complex enzymatic systems that extend throughout the soil. There are few things in the soil that escape digestion.

Actinomycetes: Closely related to the bacteria, these organisms are more complicated in structure than bacteria. The musty odor that is evident in newly plowed soil in the spring is due to substances produced by the actinomycetes. Some of the organisms belonging to this group produce plant diseases, such as potato scab. Many carry on the essential activities of decomposing organic matter and making mineral nutrients available for higher plants.

Algae: These are microscopic plants that form chlorophyll in the presence of sunlight. Most obvious in bodies of water, they are

QUANTITY AND WEIGHT OF MICROORGANISMS IN SOIL

Kind	Population (per gm.)	Weight (lbs. per acre-ft.)
Actinomycetes	10–20,000,000	800–1,500
Algae	100,000	200– 300
Bacteria	1,000,000,000	500–1,000
Fungi	1,000,000	1,500–2,000
Protozoa	1,000,000	200– 400
Yeasts	1,000	

also found in surface layers of moist soil. Where light is available, they grow as green plants but, in the absence of light, they grow as other soil microorganisms. Algae change carbon dioxide from the air into organic matter in the presence of sunlight. They take their nitrogen and mineral nutrients from the soil. In moist, shady areas, algae may give the soil surface a green film. This is not injurious to plants.

Bacteria: These microorganisms account for the largest number of organisms in the soil, some of which resemble balls or cylinders, and others which are shaped like corkscrews. Bacteria in the resting stage are resistant to heat, dryness and other adverse environmental conditions. Spore-forming bacteria, which constitute about 10 percent of the soil bacteria, are highly resistant when in the spore or resting stage. Higher plants can combine carbon dioxide and water in the presence of sunlight and chlorophyll to make their own food, but bacteria are much like animals in that most of them must get their energy from carbohydrates, fats, proteins, or other compounds synthesized in plants or bodies. In the process of obtaining their food from plant and animal residues, bacteria in the soil bring about the decomposition of these materials.

Some of the important soil bacteria are the ones that convert unavailable nitrogen of the soil organic matter to ammonia, and those that convert ammonia to nitrites and then to nitrates. Others fix nitrogen in the root nodules of legumes. Many other bacteria make nutrients available or unavailable, modify soil structure and change the air relations of the soil.

Bacteriophages and viruses: Bacteriophages and viruses are the smallest forms of living matter in the soil and are classified as falling somewhere between living organisms and the nonliving materials. The phages cause diseases of higher plants.

Fungi: The fungi are an essential part of the soil microbial flora. Although fungi may be outnumbered by bacteria per gram of soil, they have a greater mass of growth. These organisms form a maze of tiny threads called mycelium that may enmesh soil particles into granules. Fungi grow best in an aerated soil. Many of them cause plant diseases, but most are beneficial since they decompose organic matter and, during the decomposition of plant and animal residues, synthesize organic matter into cell tissue.

Protozoa: These organisms are the simplest form of animal life. Although they are unicellular and microscopic in size, they are larger than most bacteria and more complex in their activities. Protozoa obtain their food from organic matter in the same way as bacteria.

Yeasts: These single-celled organisms are like bacteria except they are larger and their structure is more highly developed. The yeasts make up only a small percentage of the total organism population in the soil. Their role in the ecology of the soil is not known.

Soil Environment: Many factors in the soil environment influence the number and activity of soil microorganisms. Factors of considerable importance are temperature, moisture, aeration, and acidity or alkalinity.

Acidity or Alkalinity: Certain organisms such as the bacteria that occur in the root nodules of legumes and the azotobacter which fix nitrogen in an acid soil become inactive in acid soils. Where lime is deficient, legumes tend to have fewer root nodules. In general, fungi are more active in acid soils than are bacteria. In more alkaline soils the actino-mycetes become active. Soils that are excessively alkaline may be devoid of the proper kinds of microorganisms or the activity of the microorganisms may be limited or directed along lines that are unfavorable for plant growth.

Aeration: Too much moisture may also intensify the shortage of oxygen by slowing down the movement of air through the soil. Generally, a well-ventilated soil supports the growth of beneficial microorganisms that convert nutrients to available forms essential for high crop productivity. Soils possessing good structure are usually well aerated. Soil aeration may be improved by good tillage practices. In a soil not adequately aerated, microorganisms compete with each other for the oxygen and some may convert oxidized compounds such as nitrates into a form not available to plants. Sulfates may be converted to hydrogen sulfide, and iron may be converted to a reduced form.

Moisture: Moisture influences the decomposition of plant and animal residues. When the soil is too dry there is little or no microbial activity. When the soil has the optimum level of moisture the beneficial groups of microorganisms are most active. If too much moisture is present, the organisms may convert nitrates to gaseous nitrogen sulfates and then to sulfides, thereby depleting all the oxygen in the soil. Because of this undesirable microbial activity, wet soils are often unfavorable for certain plants.

Temperature: In most regions, microbial activity in the soil is at a standstill during the winter. In the spring, after temperatures reach 50 to 60°F. (10 to 15.56°C.) microbial activity begins to pick up. The optimum temperature for a high state of activity is about 85 to 90°F. (29.44 to 32.22°C.). In order for

microorganisms to decay plant material and develop nitrates at a rapid rate the soil must be warm. Microbial growth is retarded at high as well as at low soil temperatures. Temperatures higher than 100°F. (37.78°C.) retard or stop the activity of many soil microorganisms.

See also Actinomycetes, Algae, Azotobacter, Fungus, Soil.

MIDGES   *See* Insect Control

MIGNONETTE   (*Reseda*)

Because of its delightful fragrance, the chief value of mignonette is as an addition to bouquets of flowers which have no odor of their own. But, since the plants are difficult to grow, they are seldom found in homegrown arrangements.

Mignonette transplants poorly, so seeds are always direct-seeded in a rich, partly shady spot. Seed may be sown in the cold frame in late April or started indoors in peat pots. When seedlings show their first true leaves, pull out the weaker plants. Plant, pot and all, outside in May after danger of frost is past.

To extend the blooming period, many people make subsequent sowings until midsummer. When flower shoots are well set, an application of liquid manure may be applied.

There are many species of mignonette; *R. odorata,* with yellow white flowers, is the common one. One of its many varieties, Grandiflora, is quite large and is often grown as an annual. *R. alba* is somewhat hardier and grows wild in parts of the eastern United States and Canada as does *R. lutea.*

MILDEW

Mildew is a fungus that often appears as a fine cobweblike growth produced on plant surfaces, especially in wet seasons.

See also DISEASE, FUNGUS.

MILKWEED
See WILD PLANTS, EDIBLE

MILKY SPORE DISEASE

This bacterial disease is artificially spread to control the Japanese beetle. Applied to the ground in powder form, it is then ingested by beetle grubs.

The disease is called "milky spore" because the normally clear blood of the grubs turns white as the spores grow. The grubs eventually die, and the bacteria from their bodies are ingested by other organisms.

See also JAPANESE BEETLE.

MILLET

Although used since ancient times for grain and flour for humans, most of the millet grown in the United States is used for pasture or hay, and the mature seeds for birdseed. Millet is a nutritious grain, containing more essential amino acids than wheat, oats, barley, rye, or rice, and it forms a complete amino acid when combined with buckwheat or another food high in lysine. It can be fed to chickens, stalk and all. Millet also has a high alkaline mineral content and is easily digested. Few diseases bother millet and it is relatively insect-resistant.

Varieties: There are three different families of millets and a fourth kind which, although called African millet, is really a sorghum. This type, also known as orange sorghum, or even sumac, is grown for hay and pasture in Texas and surrounding states.

Broomcorn millet (*Panicum miliaceum*) or proso millet, so called because the spread-

The Proso or Broomcorn family of millet is especially suited for human consumption.

ing seed heads resemble small broomcorn heads, is widely grown in the Orient. Seeds are red, yellow or white. Early Fortune and Turghai are older red varieties, White is a white variety, and Crown is off-white.

Foxtail millets (*Setaria italica*) are grown primarily for emergency hay, silage and pasture throughout the United States because they are finer stemmed and not hairy like proso, and mature later. Hungarian, Siberian and Manta are the more northerly varieties. Empire, White Wonder and German mature later and are grown in the South. Japanese millet, grown in the North, and Browntop, grown in the South, are sometimes included with foxtail and are sometimes listed as separate varieties. Japanese millet makes almost as much silage as does corn. It will regrow after cutting, and dries faster than Sudangrass. It is also best for hay.

Pearl millets (*Pennisetum americanum*) resemble cattail seed heads and are grown almost totally in the South. They thresh free from the hulls, making them more desirable for the homesteader who wants millet for table use.

A variety of hybrids are available. Millex and Pearlex are forage varieties available in the North. In the South, Bahi, Starr and Southgraze hybrids would be good seed investments.

Planting: Plant seed by broadcast or drill one to three inches deep. Like buckwheat, millet can be planted late. It does better than most grains on poor soil, and it sometimes smothers weeds better than buckwheat. You can begin using the plants 30 days after planting.

Harvesting: As hay, millet can produce over five tons per acre. Cut, cure, and bale or bundle the crop just as you would alfalfa hay.

For table use, millet can be planted rather thickly in regular garden rows. Allow stalks to stand until they are almost ripe, then cut, bundle, and allow them to dry in a dry place. Later they can be threshed.

MIMOSA   (*Albizzia Julibrissin*)

Not to be confused with the fragrant, flowering mimosa sold by florists (*Acacia dealbata*), this mimosa is actually a tree grown and even naturalized throughout the south-

The familiar sensitive plant is but one species of mimosa; others are woody and, in the South, can be grown outdoors as shade trees.

eastern United States. Known also as the silk tree, it is a quick-growing tree with fragrant white or pink blossoms. Given ordinary care, it is quite hardy from Maryland south. It makes fine shade and has the added advantage of shedding leaves so tiny and brittle that they disintegrate into the ground and do not have to be raked.

If you are planting the seed or seedpods, they should be given the same care and rich soil that you give any vegetable or flower grown for transplanting. When the plants come up, transplant them to the garden until they grow a little larger. You can also put them out in their permanent place by following the procedure for larger plants, being sure to fill in with rich soil and watering and mulching well.

Setting out large plants necessitates a hole from one to two feet deep, depending on the length of the root. The roots of a mimosa generally grow almost straight until they are older and begin to branch. When transplanting, be sure to get all of the taproot or the main stem. The smaller roots are not as important. Be sure the hole is several inches deeper than the length of the root, and that the root is planted straight down. If the subsoil is very hard and dry, fill in the hole with richer soil and compost.

While the plants are young, and until they get a good start (a year or two), they should be mulched and kept watered. In selecting plants, you will find that the small ones, one to two feet high, may grow faster than the taller ones. If you find it necessary to brace them to straighten them, you can do that much more easily when they are small. After they get a good firm root and are a few feet tall, you can forget them. They will require nothing more than an occasional pruning.

If you plan to have several mimosas in your yard, set them out about ten or 15 feet apart. Even at that distance, they will probably touch each other after several years, making a good shade but still letting in plenty of light and air.

The growth of the tree depends a lot on the moisture and mulching you give it for the first two or three years. Under normal conditions, it will grow about two to four feet a year in height, and bloom about four years after it is set out. Of course, some trees bloom much earlier than others. To ensure blooms, you will need two or more mimosa trees, though sometimes single trees bloom.

After a few years, the branches will begin to grow so thick and fast you will have to trim them back to keep your tree growing upward instead of outward and downward. If the lower branches are not kept trimmed off, they hang too close to the ground and break off. When trimmed properly, the trees will be shaped something like an inverted umbrella, being widest across the top, which is where most of the blooms are.

MIMULUS   *See* MONKEY FLOWER

MINERAL ROCKS

Every alert farmer and gardener is a practical geologist, even without formal study. Most of them have discovered through close observation of the earth many of the principles of geology. Every grower should be interested in the geology of his own farm and soil.

The popular idea of geology is that it is a science of rocks, but in fact the study of rocks and soil is only one segment of a broad field.

Equally important are such topics as land and soil erosion, the occurrence of artesian and spring water, the formation of coal, oil, and metallic ore deposits.

Geologists also study the rise of mountain ranges and their reduction by wind, water, and glacial ice; caves; dunes; river floodplains; wind and glacial deposits; geysers; earthquakes; and volcanoes. Even the principles involved in the artificial terracing of fields are geological.

Mantle Rock: Beneath the earth's surface lies a hard covering, a layer of rock known as *bedrock*. This is covered by loose and unintegrated material called *mantle rock* and found almost everywhere. The part of this *mantle rock* that sustains the growth of plants is, of course, the soil, also called the soil mantle.

Mantle rock, a term which includes soft masses such as sand and clay, as well as harder substances such as granite, is classifiable into three divisions, based on origin. *Igneous* rocks are cooled from a molten condition and constitute the primary sources of phosphorus, potash, lime, and soda. *Sedimentary* rocks are produced by the debris of other rocks and are called fragmentary or clastic. From the viewpoint of soils, they comprise the great soil-building formations, and contain a very high percentage of silica. They are moved from elsewhere and deposited in new deposits by wind, water or the action of glacial ice. *Metamorphic* rocks are rocks that have undergone a physical change. The process sometimes strengthens rather than weakens the rocks; for example, marble is much harder than the more friable limestone from which it was derived. Gneiss, schists, slates, quartzite, and marble are the more common types of metamorphic rocks. Besides their different origins, certain differences of mineral and chemical composition characterize each group. Because the different compositions influence soil types, erosion and economic products, these differences are of practical importance.

Igneous Rocks: Igneous rocks (they have also been called the primary rocks) are those that solidified from hot, molten rock material. Lava flows that emerge from volcanoes, and volcanic cones that rise as mountains are composed of igneous rock. Much of Oregon and Washington in the Columbia River region are surfaced by huge black lava flows that have solidified outside or on top of the earth's surface. The igneous rock called basalt is common in flows.

Long after solidification is complete, the original, subsurface igneous body may be exposed by prolonged erosion and removal of the rock cover. Alternatively, earth movements or earthquakes may break the earth's outer crust and push the solidified igneous mass outward. Large parts of the Appalachian Mountain chain, the eastern Ozarks, cores of the Rocky Mountain ranges, parts of the Great Lakes region, and the central portion of the Sierra Nevada range are examples of raised and exposed intrusive igneous rocks.

If closely examined, the igneous rocks of these mountain cores are mostly granites, or granitelike rocks. Granites are composed of grains coarse enough to be distinguishable with the unaided eye. They are hard and glassy in luster. Usually they are gray, pink or red and contain at least two different kinds of mineral grains, relatively constant in composition, which are intergrown.

The Minerals in Granite: One variety of the mineral grains in granite is white or pink, semiopaque, and breaks so as to leave tiny flat-surfaced faces. This is potash feldspar. Other feldspars contain calcium and sodium, but the feldspar of granite characteristically contains about 16 percent potash. Upon weathering, if pulverized, it will release potassium somewhat grudgingly. It is recommended to organic farmers.

Granite also contains clearer, harder and more glassy mineral grains. These are quartz, composed of silicon dioxide. Quartz when reduced comprises most of the sand in soil, and in bars, beaches, dunes, and sandstones. Quartz has no nutrient value to plants. Granites commonly contain tiny flakes of mica, usually green to black, colorless or water-white. Mica can be identified by its habit of flaking off, or cleaving, and because it is relatively soft.

Soils derived from the weathered products of granite are usually gravelly or sandy because of the abundance of quartz. Pulverized granite when used as a mineral fertilizer carries an excessively high content of silica, and weathers slowly. Usually, volcanic ash or leucite-containing igneous rocks, higher in potash and lower in silica than granite, decompose more readily.

Basalt and Its Minerals: Basalt is fine-grained, dark-colored and has a different chemical composition from granite. Its fine grain is due to rapid cooling and solidification on the earth's surface. Where basaltic lava has solidified more slowly underground, it gives rise to a coarse-grained, dark-colored rock called diabase.

Basalts are more susceptible to weathering than are granites. They contain less silica and more calcium and magnesium. Hence, pulverized basalt is preferred to granite as a mineral fertilizer. Soils derived from basalts are rich in clay and iron oxides. Where abundant organic matter is present, iron oxides are reduced to compounds which are on the dark gray to green black side. Soils from basalt may be rich in inorganic elements. *See* BASALT.

Weathering: The next logical step in the geological story of the rock cycle is that of weathering, followed by the eventual formation of sedimentary rocks. Weathering, slowly but surely, attacks and reduces even the hardest of igneous rocks. Without weathering there would be no soil. The agents or forces of weathering include rain and groundwater, acid clays, soil humic acids, plant roots, bacteria, oxygen, carbon dioxide, the atmosphere, freezing and thawing, glaciers, and others.

The net result of weathering is the conversion of rocks into insoluble soil material and soluble substances that are leached away in spring or stream water.

Clay minerals are developed from weathered feldspars and minerals present in basalt. Red and brown iron oxides result from the weathering of iron-containing minerals. Clay, quartz sand and iron oxides are insoluble and remain as a soil-forming mantle, or may be eroded or washed away in suspension in stream water.

Calcium, magnesium and sodium are easily dissolved in groundwater during weathering and are quickly leached away. That explains why the calcium of a soil derived from limestone may be entirely leached out in a humid region. Water containing calcium and magnesium in solution is hard water. Potassium may be only partly leached. Because of its ionic size and chemical properties it may be semipermanently fixed in the clay.

The residuum of weathered rock products which accumulate as soil represents only a temporary halt in its march to eventual deposition in the sea as sedimentary rock. Its stay as soil is prolonged by terracing and by controlling erosion. Nutrients are removed by the crops grown on that soil and new reserves in the form of pulverized rock fertilizers are added.

Sedimentary Rocks: From the viewpoint of the geological process, the fate of weathered products is movement toward a lower resting place on the sea floor. Suspended sand and mud, and dissolved calcium, sodium, and magnesium are poured out into the ocean. Gravel, sand, silt, and clay mud progressively settle out in the quiet water. They are imperfectly sorted as to particle size, the coarser being deposited first. The finer mud is deposited in quieter water to become sedimentary rocks.

Sodium remains in solution in ocean brine as sodium chloride. Calcium does not long remain in solution, but ends up as deposits of limestone on the sea floor.

The sediments brought to the ocean by freshwater streams are consolidated as more and more sediment is piled upon them. Eventually they become layered or stratified rocks. Strata, or layers, distinguish sedimentary rocks.

Wide deposits of sand, as on beaches, dunes, riverbars, or in important offshore sand deposits in the ocean, will become formations of sandstone upon consolidation. Indeed, most of the sandstones now found on land were once sand deposits beneath the sea. The hard, relatively insoluble quartz grains predominant in sandstones originally derived from granite. The purer the sandstone, the richer it will be in quartz, but the leaner in nutrient elements. Fertility in a sandstone-derived soil arises only from nonquartz "impurities" and organic matter.

Mud which settles to the bottom of the near-shore ocean floor gives rise to rocks called shale, containing accessory amounts of sand, lime, iron oxides, organic matter, and a wide variety of chemical compounds and mud. Shales, after being raised above sea level, weather to a clay-rich soil. The soil is relatively heavy if the shale source is rich in clay, but a sandy shale weathers to a sandy soil.

The calcium deposited from seawater evaporation, and from the addition of the shells of marine animals that extract calcium from the water, becomes layers of limestone (calcium carbonate). Dolomitic limestones contain magnesium in varying quantities. A few limestones are slightly phosphatic. Some limestones in Arkansas contain "impurities" of manganese carbonate which is readily soluble and is an available source of the trace element manganese. Some limestones and dolomites carry potassium-rich green glauconite, the mineral of greensand. Limestones may be sandy, or clayey, if sand or clay were mixed with the lime on the ocean floor. The accessories of limestone provide a source of trace elements in limestone when it is used as a mineral supplement. *See also* LIME.

Besides sandstone, shale, limestone and several other sedimentary rocks are interesting to farmers because of their special compositions and potential uses.

Phosphate Rock: Raw phosphate rock is a sedimentary deposit that may represent either an accumulation of phosphatic organic residues, or replacement of an earlier calcium limestone by phosphate. It may originate also as a direct precipitate in the ocean. Besides the phosphate deposits rich enough to be exploited at a profit, there are countless tons of lean phosphatic limestones and phosphatic shales that would be most valuable as soil replenishers. Besides their phosphate, they contain many other naturally deposited trace elements.

Farmers should be strongly urged to make intensive inquiry from their local geologists and state geological surveys as to the location of accessible phosphate-bearing rocks that have been too low in phosphate to attract commercial production. Many of these can be worked locally and during spare times by farmers to their own benefit. *See also* PHOSPHATE ROCK.

Potash Rocks: Beds of rock salt and potash minerals like those in the New Mexico-Texas region represent mineral residues of evaporated salt lakes and cutoff arms of the sea.

Glauconite, a soft green mineral composed of potassium, iron and silica, forms under special sedimentary conditions in the ocean. The New Jersey greensands contain mainly glauconite. Trace elements are also associated with the glauconites. Fortunately, dolomites and limestones which contain sparse to rich streaks of glauconite occur in many states in our Union. A glauconite dolomite will contribute calcium, magnesium, potassium, and trace elements to the soil when used agriculturally. *See also* GREENSAND, POTASH ROCK.

Flint or chert pebbles and gravel are abundant and common over many miles of land. This rock is a solid variety of silica. Chert originates from the small amount of soluble silica which is liberated during the weathering of feldspars, and which later is deposited in solid form. It does not contain usable plant nutrients.

Sedimentary rocks cover about 75 percent of the land surface of our earth.

Metamorphic Rocks: Rocks whose characteristics show them to have been later impressed with a secondary origin are the metamorphic rocks. As their name indicates, they are changed from the original. Sedimentary rocks may be piled up thickly so that the lowest ones become deeply buried and heavily weighted. Igneous rocks may solidify beneath the earth's surface.

Under the stress of mountain-making, and the high temperature due to deep burial or frictional movements, conditions augmented by the heat of igneous action, rocks may be changed. The detailed mineralogical and chemical changes which rocks undergo during metamorphism are highly technical. The broad changes are easily recognized and understood, and will be described below. Preexisting igneous, sedimentary or metamorphic rocks may be metamorphosed to produce thick or coarsely banded, or thinly banded to slaty rocks, including marbles, as well as less well-defined varieties.

Gneiss: Coarsely banded metamorphic rocks usually appear like banded granites, and are called gneiss (pronounced "nice"). The minerals in gneiss are usually feldspar and quartz, with dark minerals like those that occur in basalt. Their response to weathering and erosion is similar to that of granite.

Thinly banded metamorphic rocks may be of parallel aggregates of mica, or of microscopic, parallel bundles of dark hornblende needles (like the hornblende in basalt). These thickly banded metamorphic rocks are called schists: mica schists or hornblende schists. Mica schists are resistant to weathering and exceedingly scanty in their delivery of nutrients. Hornblende schists weather to form clay and iron oxides, and liberate calcium and magnesium compounds.

Slate is the metamorphosed product of shale. The clay minerals in shale have been converted during metamorphism into tiny parallel mica flakes that shed rain or snow without slaking as shale would. Because of this ability to shed water well-metamorphosed slate is not readily converted into fertile soil. Weakly metamorphosed slate, however, may be decomposed and weathered similarly to shale.

Metamorphic rocks tend to respond to geologic process in much the same way that their igneous and sedimentary heredity would suggest. Gneisses and schists, because they contain igneous-type minerals, behave like igneous rocks.

Evolution of Rocks: All three types of rocks may undergo more weathering and then become new sedimentary rocks, or all three may be further metamorphosed. Furthermore, under certain conditions, they may be redissolved by the action of hot mineralizing solutions and revert to an igneous state. Rock changes are potentially cyclic, and geologists regularly refer to the entire series of changes as the "Rock Cycle."

MINIATURE PLANTS

In recent years, botanists have discovered and plant breeders have developed numerous smaller varieties of favorite garden plants. These can be used to advantage in many situations, for special effects or to make the most of cramped space.

Ornamentals: The miniature flowers are especially enchanting. In form and flower type, many are perfect replicas of their bigger prototypes. Among the most delightful are the miniature daylilies (some of which grow only eight inches tall), the English lilliput chrysanthemums, dwarf dahlias, miniature gladioli and dwarf Oregon asters. The tiny irises, *Iris pumila* and *I. Chamaeiris,* are miniatures of bearded iris. Dwarf bleeding-heart is another favorite. As with all classes of plants, the list of miniature varieties—of which we can name here only a few—grows longer every season.

Some of the best new varieties of flowering shrubs might be loosely called dwarfs. Among these are Gold Drop potentilla and Dwarf Snowflake mock orange. Several of these stay under three feet, while their relatives are double that. Little Gem arborvitae and Crimson Pygmy barberry, for instance, never grow over a foot tall.

Edibles: The dwarf fruit trees that so often serve as the backbone of the organic gardener's food production scheme are, of course, well known. But there are also many valuable miniature vegetables. Many of them grow less than half the size of the standard species. Golden Midget sweet corn, for example, is only two feet tall, but the ears have delicious, full-sized kernels. Some other miniatures are Tiny Tim tomatoes, Tom Thumb lettuce, Tiny Dill cucumbers, New Hampshire Midget watermelon, Little Marvel peas, and Minnesota Midget muskmelon. You can get sweet potatoes with vines that spread only three feet, bush squashes with short runners, or peas which grow only 15 inches high. There is even a miniature popcorn! All of these space savers are valuable to the organic gardener who aims to get the biggest possible yields from his vegetable plot.

These, of course, are only a few of the new plants that can be called miniatures. Hunting through the catalogs will produce a much more comprehensive list. Such a hunt can be fun and rewarding, particularly if your garden is small. But even in the larger garden, miniature plants used with ingenuity can produce interesting effects not possible with their bigger relatives.

MINT

The term "mint" is most often used for

the genus *Mentha,* but several others including *Monarda* and *Pycnanthemum* also use the term. Many herbs such as thymes, sages and marjorams are also related.

Mints are outstanding for the fragrance of their foliage. Volatile oils produced in tiny glands on the leaves' surface give off an odor when brushed.

Peppermint (*Mentha* x *piperita*) is a hybrid—a cross between spearmint (*M. spicata*) and water mint (*M. aquatica*). Even spearmint itself is thought to be the result of a cross between apple mint (*M.* x *rotundifolia*) and long-leaved mint (*M. longifolia*). There are many other hybrid mints, and even the true species are highly variable, so the naming of the many kinds of mints has become involved and uncertain.

The four most commonly grown mints are peppermint, spearmint, apple mint, and long-leaved mint. Peppermint can be distinguished from the other three because its leaves are on small stalks; the leaves of the others have very short stalks or none at all. Of these, spearmint can be recognized by its almost hairless leaves. Apple mint and long-leaved mint have hairy leaves. Those of apple mint are quite rounded, while the leaves of the others are longer and narrower.

Spearmint is the mint most often used in making mint jelly, sauce, juleps, and so on. Apple mint and long-leaved mint are probably just as useful, but their wooliness has kept them from becoming as popular.

Water mint (*M. aquatica*) bears its flowers in little rounded balls at the tips of the stems and in the axils of the uppermost leaves. The leaves are stalked, egg shaped and are somewhat hairy. The varieties Crispa and Citrata have crisped, crinkled leaves.

Bergamot or lemon mint (*M.* x *piperita* var. *citrata*) is very likely also a form of water mint with smooth, hairless leaves.

Pennyroyal (*M. Pulegium*) is quite different in appearance from the other mints. It is a much-branched, protrate perennial with its flower heads in the axils of rather long leafy stalks. Its delightful fragrance was believed to drive away fleas.

Corsican mint (*M. Requienii*) is a delightful little creeping plant with minute, rounded leaves, forming an almost mosslike mat. It is sprinkled in late summer with little lavender blossoms and is delightful as a ground cover for small spots. It thrives in moist shade but will also grow in sun. As it does not survive cold winters, it is better to keep it indoors in pots.

M. viridis, known simply as mint, is a hardy perennial plant found growing in abundance along the roadsides in many places. It is sometimes grown in gardens, however, and is used in soups, sauces and salads.

See also entries for individual mints, HERB.

MIRABILIS   *See* FOUR-O'CLOCK

MIST   *See* GYPSOPHILA, NIGELLA

MISTLETOE

The pretty mistletoe that brightens our Christmas season is not strictly a garden plant, but a parasite that grows on trees. Common mistletoe (*Phoradendron serotinum*) grows from New Jersey southward.

Western dwarf mistletoes (*Arceuthobium*)

are called "slow killers" because their roots invade the bark and wood of the host tree, stealing water and nutrients and eventually destroying it. The plant can be removed by cutting the branch on which it is growing 18 inches behind the shoots. Where the shoots are closer than this to the trunk, it has usually already invaded the trunk and nothing can be done.

Unlike common mistletoe which is spread only by birds, dwarf mistletoe has an "explosive" seed which can be shot out of its casing as far as 60 feet. If it lands on a young, healthy branch of a suitable host, a new plant soon appears. Dwarf mistletoe's leaves are too small to have any decorative value.

The common mistletoe is less damaging, and is generally found on deciduous trees, particularly the oaks and junipers. Contrary to common belief, it can be cultivated.

Save holiday mistletoe or gather fresh berries (which will germinate better) in the spring. Squeeze the berry until it bursts, then simply stick the seed to the underside of a young twig by means of its gummy coating. Sometimes it helps to scrape the twig lightly first, or make a cut in the bark. To be sure of getting more than one plant, since this is necessary for germination, stick on at least half-a-dozen seeds. It takes about a year before the first leaves appear, but thereafter growth is rapid. Apple, poplar and hawthorn are among the best host trees. An enterprising homesteader or farmer can make extra income by seeding an old orchard.

MITES
See INSECT CONTROL, SPIDER MITES

MOCK ORANGE   (*Philadelphus*)

Shrubs of the Mock orange family are among the most desirable flowering shrubs for the garden. They are easily grown and maintained, and in recent years many new hybrids have been introduced. Some of these are not as tall growing as the older varieties and are useful in many positions in the garden.

The philadelphus is one of the oldest shrubs in cultivation, having been grown in gardens for the past three or four hundred years.

P. coronarius, the common mock orange, is an old garden favorite. It forms a ten-foot, large, dense shrub with fragrant white flowers. There are a number of hybrids of this and other species. A shubbery might be composed entirely of mock oranges, using several of a kind, the tall ones at the back, and the lower ones in front.

P. x virginalis presents a fine display of flowers in late spring or early summer and is a popular shrub with large semidouble flowers. It is often used for forcing.

P. mexicanus, the evergreen Mexican mock orange, may be grown as a shrub, or treated like a vine and trained against a building, garden wall or fence. The double white flowers are very fragrant.

P. x Lemoinei is a popular hybrid, growing four to six feet high. Its attractive clusters of flowers are considered the most fragrant of all mock orange blooms. The variety Virginal has graceful, arching branches, covered with delightfully fragrant, single white flowers. Stock may be increased by cuttings or layering.

P. x cymosus is a hybrid with especially large blossoms, measuring 2½ inches wide.

The variety Snow Velvet grows upright to a height of four or five feet and has crisp white flowers. *P. inodorus* is an odorless mock orange and finds favor with those who object to the characteristic philadelphus fragrance.

Dig the hole three times as deep and as wide as the ball of roots. Mock orange thrives in a sandy loam. In the bottom of the hole place some well-pulverized compost and mix it with good soil. Set the shrub in the center of the hole and be sure it is straight. Fill in around the ball of roots and when the hole is three-quarters full of soil, run water in to settle it, being sure to give enough water to reach down below the roots. Fill in with more soil and make a basin around the shrub to hold water.

Shrubs should be pruned immediately after the flowering season is over. The new shoots produced during the summer will carry the flowering wood for next year. If the shrubs are not pruned till autumn or winter, there will be few if any flowers, for the flowering shoots will have been cut off.

To keep mock orange bushes in good condition and flowering freely, some of the old wood should be thinned out when the main stems become congested, as they usually do on old specimens. Cut them at ground level. This should be done immediately after the flowering season is over so that new growth may be produced while the weather is warm and growth is active. The flowering branches for the following year will have more space in which to develop.

Newly planted shrubs have to be watered regularly until they are established. Deep watering keeps the roots down; otherwise, they come up near the surface of the ground in search of water and may be baked by the sun.

During the hot days of summer, it may help to add three or four inches of mulch, especially after a thorough watering. Suitable materials include well-decomposed vegetable matter, manure and leaf mold.

MOISTURE-LOVING PLANTS

Although most garden plants like a well-drained soil, there are many attractive varieties that will do well in damp soil. Included in this list of moisture-loving plants are the primroses, polyanthus (*Primula* x *polyantha*), oxlip (*P. elatior*), marsh marigold (*Caltha palustris*), meadow-beauty (*Rhexia virginica*), umbrella plant (*Peltiphyllum peltatum*), sweet flag (*Acorus calamus*), grass-leaved sweet flag (*A. gramineus*), stargrass (*Aletris*), swamp-pink (*Helonias bullata*), purple loosestrife (*Lythrum Salicaria*), cardinal flower (*Lobelia Cardinalis*), Carolina grass-of-Parnassus (*Parnassia caroliniana*), the various astilbes (*Astilbe*), red chokeberry (*Aronia arbutifolia*), black chokeberry (*A. melonocarpa*), spicebush (*Lindera Benzoin*), and cornelian cherry (*Cornus mas*).

Most of these plants actually like very damp soil but will not tolerate a heavy clay, because it drains poorly. A sound organic program of soil building will cure most heavy soils through the incorporation of organic matter.

MOISTURE, SOIL
See AERATION, MULCH, SOIL

MOLD *See* FUNGUS

MOLE

The presence of moles is often an indication that your soil is good and that you have plenty of earthworms present because earthworms are the favorite food of moles.

The best solution to a mole problem is to kill the moles in a way that won't kill earthworms—with a mole trap, instead of with poisons.

Moles live underground, building vast networks of tunnels out from their nests. You never see their permanent "galleries," but you do see the runs just under the surface of the ground. They use these tunnels for hunting food, principally earthworms and white grubs, and the larvae of ground-inhabiting insects. In fact, a mole will often eat more than its own weight in a day. It is no wonder they can destroy lawns so quickly.

Moles breed in the spring and usually produce four young sometime late in March or early in April. The youngsters grow rapidly, spend only about a month in the nest, and by early June are practically as large as their parents.

Damage to Avoid: Although examination of the stomach-content of hundreds of moles clearly indicates that earthworms and insects are their natural food, moles are also known to cause serious damage to cornfields, gardens and flower beds by damaging roots, or carrying disease organisms from one plant to the others. Of course, shrews, meadow mice, house mice, rats, and pocket gophers often use mole runways to do more damage than the moles themselves, particularly in orchards and large fields.

Control: The most effective means of controlling these pests is to plant traps in the moles' main runs. To determine which runs are the main arteries of mole traffic, smash down the earth in several runs. Those which are later reopened by burrowing moles are the ones in which to set the traps. Traps should be set at a 90 degree angle to the axis of the tunnel. After the trap is set, it should be covered with a box to exclude light.

If you prefer not to kill the moles, a sprinkling of tobacco or red pepper may deter their action. Another method is to set a toy windmill, stick and all, into the tunnel. The vibrations of the rotating pinwheel are said to repel the moles. Castor oil is also repulsive to moles, and an emulsion of the oil and soap, diluted with water, can be sprinkled over vulnerable areas.

MOLYBDENUM

Molybdenum is an important trace element. Deficiencies of it rarely occur, but when they do, it is most often in plants grown on soils below a pH of 5.2. Applications of ground limestone will often alleviate the deficiency.

Molybdenum excesses are more often a problem. As a pollutant in industrial smoke, molybdenum is believed to be the culprit in some cases of plant and animal poisoning.

Tests indicate that of all the trace elements, molybdenum is taken up by plants in the smallest amounts. It is believed to be closely associated with the nitrogen cycle and acts as a catalyst in the reduction of nitrates to ammonia in nonlegumes. It is also used by legume bacteria to reduce atmospheric nitrogen to ammonia.

See also SOIL DEFICIENCIES, TRACE ELEMENTS.

MONEY PLANT   *See* HONESTY

MONEYWORT   *See* AQUARIUM

MONKEY FLOWER   (*Mimulus*)

Monkey flowers are perennial herbs or subshrubs of the Figwort family. Only one variety, *M. ringens,* is found in the East. It is an easily grown wild garden plant one to four feet high, thriving only in moist places. The other varieties are garden plants in the West, usually treated as annuals, or grown in the greenhouse from seed sown in January in a general-purpose soil mixture.

Outdoors, they need decidedly moist, cool conditions in semishade. They can also be propagated by division and cuttings. Most of them have yellow flowers, sometimes spotted red or brown, but there are some with white, red or violet blooms. *M. cardinalis* and *M. Lewisii* have hairy, sticky foliage.

MONKSHOOD   *See* ACONITUM

MONOECIOUS   *See* UNISEXUAL

MONTBRETIA   *See* TRITONIA

MOON PLANTING

Some gardeners believe that the moon, in its monthly revolution around the earth, exerts a significant influence on the activities of growing plants. These gardeners schedule crop plantings for times when the moon is in a "favorable" position in relation to the signs of the zodiac.

The belief in moon planting or planting by the signs is an ancient one alluded to by Greek and Roman agricultural writers, and has remained a standard method for planting crops even in this century. Although many scientists scoff at the notion of planting by the signs, it is widely accepted that there exist land tides as well as tides in the ocean—proof that the moon *does* influence the earth in at least some respects.

The two main tenets of moon planting are that plants that produce the eaten or desired part above ground should be planted in the waxing moon (the period of increasing light between a new and full moon), and that plants which produce the eaten or desired part below ground (root crops, flowers grown especially for bulbs or tubers) should be planted in the waning moon (the period of decreasing light after the full moon and before the next new moon). However, one should also consider the phase of the moon in terms of the 12 signs of the zodiac. There are several astrological planting charts designed specifically for this purpose and show what signs rule each day of the month.

Astrologers speak of the various zodiac signs in terms of their fertility. For example, Leo is considered a barren sign, and plantings made on a day governed by Leo, even if the moon is in a good phase, would not do well. On the other hand, Cancer is a very fruitful sign, and plantings made on a day ruled by Cancer should do well. In addition, the positions of the planets also affect the way plants are set out, through their influence on the zodiac. Other gardening operations such as spraying, weeding and grafting are also governed by the moon and planets.

For the best modern treatment of moon planting, see *Planetary Planting* by Louise Riotte (New York: Simon & Schuster, 1975).

MORAEA   *See* PEACOCK IRIS

MORAINE LOCUST
(Gleditsia triacanthos)

This variety of honey locust has two advantages: it stands city smoke and dust very well, and it has no thorns. Its hardiness range is the same as that of the common honey locust, but it is somewhat more tolerant of alkaline soils. A rapid grower, the moraine locust attains 50 to 75 feet and is a vigorous, wide-branched tree. It is often used for street planting, as well as for fast-growing shade trees for yards.

MORNING-GLORY   *(Ipomoea)*

The annual morning-glories are popular both for their beauty and for their ability to clamber quickly over porches, fences and such unsightly objects as stumps. Some varieties grow to a height of 25 feet. They bloom from early summer until frost and self-sow readily. Give them full sun, but plant them in soil low in nitrogen or few flowers will develop. Small amounts of bone meal and manure are helpful, and so is a mulch of several inches of peat moss or similar material. The seed are hard and should be soaked overnight or notched with a file to aid germination.

The most common species is *I. purpurea,* which is often seen growing wild in fields and roadsides. It has large, heart-shaped leaves and big, delicate pink, blue or purple flowers. There are other varieties with double flowers and white or red flowers. Dwarf morning-glory, usually sold as *Convolvulus tricolor,* grows only one foot tall and has bright blue flowers. It is very resistant to sun and heat. The spectacular Heavenly Blue morning-glory is a favorite variety.

Heavenly Blue morning-glories thrive in most soils and grow easily over railings and fences.

The morning-glories make attractive house plants for sunny windows. Soak or notch the seed, and plant five to a six-inch pot. When they come up, pull out all but the three strongest plants, and provide supports. The dwarf morning-glory is especially good for hanging baskets and window boxes. It blooms in ten weeks from seed and should be pinched once to make the plants bushier.

There are perennial species of morning-glory that are not always hardy in the North. Their roots should be dug up before frost and stored in a cool cellar for replanting the following spring.

MOROCCAN TOADFLAX
(*Linaria maroccana*)

A dwarf grower of exceeding hardiness, toadflax bears its spikes of tiny snapdragonlike flowers throughout the winter and early spring. The small dark green leaves are narrow and delicate in texture; the flowers are white, lemon, pink, blue, and purple. Since toadflax self-sows and volunteers most readily, seedlings may be used as planting stock year after year.

It blooms profusely in poor sandy soil even during frosts and is recommended for edgings, borders and rock gardens in southern regions.

MORUS   *See* MULBERRY

MOSAIC   *See* BRAMBLE FRUITS, DISEASE

MOSQUITO-TRAP
See VINCETOXICUM

MOSS

There are about 1,000 species of moss in North America, distributed in various families. Moss thrives in a very moist, acidic soil, in heavy shade. In some places in the garden—particularly in rock gardens—moss is very attractive. In spots where it is undesirable, it may be prevented by incorporating dry, bulky organic material in the soil, along with heavy additions of lime.

See also SPHAGNUM MOSS.

MOSS VERBENA
(*Verbena tenuisecta*)

This perennial plant for the rock garden has a somewhat woody base and is procumbent or sprawling in habit. The hairy to nearly smooth stems are sometimes 20 inches long and strike root readily where they come in contact with the soil. The leaves are small and finely dissected into linear, acute lobes giving a mossy appearance. The flowers are a solid blue or lilac, borne in terminal, dense, conspicuous heads that elongate when in fruit. The species is native to southern South America but now is becoming widely naturalized.

Propagation is not considered easy; thus it is a challenge to an enthusiastic gardener. Moss verbena is grown from seed and treated like an annual although it is a perennial. The seed should be sown in flats in light sandy soil about March 1. The flat should be set out in a cool greenhouse or in a cold frame with a temperature of 60°F. (15.56°C.) at night and

70 to 75°F. (21.11 to 23.89°C.) during the day. When the seedlings are large enough to handle they should be transplanted into flats or small pots and kept in the same temperature until growth starts, which is normally in about ten days. After danger of frost is past the plants may be set into their permanent beds in the garden.

Cuttings may also be made in early September when young shoots develop in the established summer growth. These young shoots can be easily rooted under glass and then kept in protected cold frames or in cool greenhouses over winter.

MOTHS   *See* INSECT CONTROL

MOUND LAYERING
See LAYERING

MOUNTAIN ASH   *(Sorbus)*

Mountain ash isn't really an ash, although its leaves, like those of the true ash, are made up of long stems with leaflets strung along both sides of them, giving the tree a feathery appearance. The true ash, however, has winged seed, not berries.

Its dense clusters of showy white blooms in spring and its bright red berries make the mountain ash a favorite tree for the home grounds. It is quite hardy and many beautiful specimens are seen in New England; these are mostly the European mountain ash, or rowan tree, *S. aucuparia,*

which reaches a height of 50 feet and was brought here in colonial days. The American species (*S. americana*) grows 30 feet tall and is commonly seen growing wild in the woods. Both have a somewhat open to round-topped crown, grow fairly slowly, and are comparatively short-lived. Their chief value lies in the

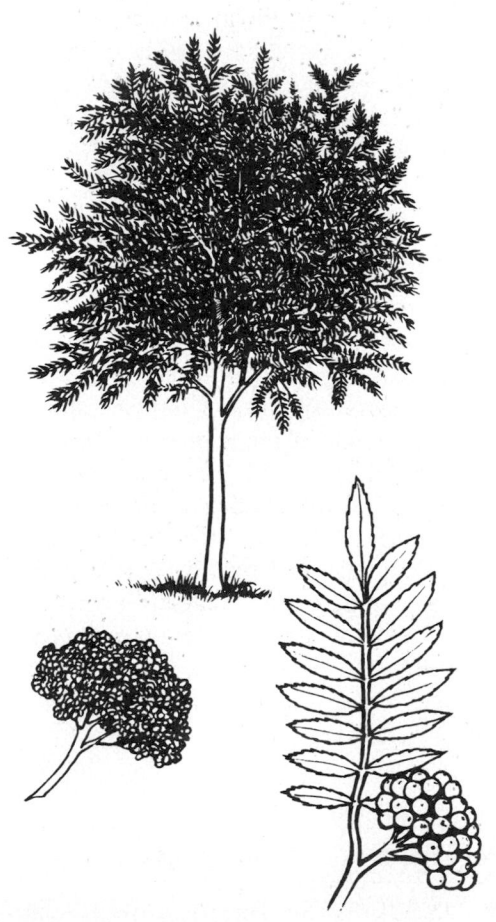

The European mountain ash or rowan tree has feathery leaves and clusters of bright red berries which are enjoyed by birds and which may be harvested for use in jams and jellies.

large clusters of berries, which remain over the winter and provide food for the birds when other supplies are short.

There are several other species: the white-beam (*S. Aria*), which grows 50 feet tall but tends to remain a shrub on poor soil; *S. decora,* a 30-foot shrubby tree; the service tree (*S. domestica*), 60 feet tall, not so hardy as the others, and having pear-shaped yellow green or brown fruits; and *S. hybrida,* a 40-foot tree.

Mountain ash is easily grown even in dry soils. It is propagated by seed and layering. The berries, incidentally, can be made into preserves and were once used to treat scurvy.

MOUNTAIN FETTERBUSH
(*Pieris floribunda*)

Fetterbush is native to the moist hillsides and mountains of Virginia and Georgia. It is a slow-growing evergreen shrub with dull green leaves and nodding white flowers borne on dense upward pointing panicles. The flower buds remain conspicuous all winter.

This shrub belongs to the Heath family and thrives best in a sheltered position in a rather moist sandy soil with plenty of peat or leaf mold. It blooms very early in the spring and is an excellent shrub for planting with azalea, laurel and rhododendron. It reaches an ultimate height of about six feet.

Mountain fetterbush is adapted for many uses in the garden. It is fine for gateway plantings, as accent plants in the shrubbery, and for the rock garden. It may be propagated by layers or by seed and should be kept mulched with shredded leaves at all times.

MOUNTAIN LAUREL
(*Kalmia latifolia*)

This native, also known as the calico bush, is often seen growing in the wild, favoring rocky hillsides and acid swamps. It is extensively planted in gardens from Maine through the central states and in elevated sections of the South. The leaves are thick and evergreen. The flowers are white to rose pink and are borne in large clusters in May and June. Each flower has ten explosive stamens that shower bees with pollen. Mountain laurel is one of the finest shrubs for specimen planting or massing. It is sometimes forced.

Either sun or shade will suit it, although it does best in partial shade. Plant it on the northern side of the house, or in a spot where the hot summer sun will be tempered by the open branches of nearby trees or shrubs. Ordinary garden soil, if not too clayey, is satisfactory, but for finest growth give it a moist, peaty, humus-rich loam. The soil should be definitely acidic. Mountain laurel requires plenty of moisture and will do well even in marshy soil. If grown in comparatively dry, exposed places, it will need heavy watering and a permanent mulch, preferably of oak or beech leaves. Propagation is generally by seed.

A popular species is *K. microphylla,* a charming dwarf less than a foot high, with pretty rose lilac flowers. *K. polifolia,* the swamp laurel, is a low shrub about two feet high, useful in the wild garden in moist or wet, acidic ground. *K. hirsuta* and *K. cuneata* are deciduous species grown mostly from North Carolina southward. Sheep laurel (*K. angustifolia*) is sometimes called lambkill because its leaves poison grazing animals. Mountain laurel honey, incidentally, may contain this poison, andromedotoxin, which can cause a person to become numb and even lose consciousness for several hours.

See also SHRUBS.

MOUNTAIN MINT
(*Pycnanthemum*)

Growing wild from Pennsylvania to Kansas and Arkansas, mountain mint grows in half-shady locations in woodland borders, usually near the tops of rather poor hills on northern or western exposures.

The plant comes into bloom in late July and lasts over a period of several weeks. The bees work the flowers eagerly and in favored localities get a fair crop of rather strong, amber honey. A single clump when well grown will have about a dozen stems with dozens of heads on each stem.

See also HONEY PLANTS.

MOURNING BRIDE   *See* SCABIOSA

MOUSE

Moles often literally pave the way for mouse troubles in the garden by providing tunnels through which the mice gain access to plant roots and bulbs.

Mice that nibble at orchard trees are usually either field mice or pine mice. The former are rather thickset, short-legged, short-eared, and usually blackish, grizzled with gray.

Pine mice are generally much smaller in size and have very short tails. Their fur is uniformly dull chestnut and of very soft texture.

Field mice are not difficult to control in the orchard. They rarely burrow below the ground and typically feed on the trunk but not on the roots. If mulch is used in the orchard, leave a gap of a couple of inches, and be sure to pull it at least three feet away from the trunk in the fall. Field mice often build nests in mulch but are rather hesitant about running around in the open once cold weather sets in. A wire cylinder around trunks will give added protection.

Pine mice are often very difficult to control. One method is to dig some of the soil away from the base of the tree in the fall and fill it in with cinders. It also helps to spread cinders in a circle out to at least three feet from the trunk. Since cinders are sharp they help prevent the rodents from tunneling in the soil. Regular, snap-back mousetraps can be effective if set in the runs.

See also MOLE.

MUCK SOILS

Muck lands have been called our "last virgin agricultural frontier." Potentially high producers, they were long ignored and the few in production yielded poorly and wore out quickly. In relatively recent years, however, the mucks have proven their potential under proper management.

Properly managed muck soils will grow practically any crop. Truck crops, sweet corn, raspberries, soybeans, and grasses of all kinds are grown with outstanding success.

Muck lands are vast natural compost heaps. Over the ages, they were formed by the decomposition of aquatic plants growing in poorly drained areas. First peat formed, then as the amount of material increased and rose above the water, aeration and drainage improved and the deposit changed to muck, a more completely decomposed organic material. In a few states, muck occupies one out of every eight acres of total land area. Muck deposits range from three to 90 feet in depth.

Drainage is the muck farmer's biggest problem. Dams and ditching are necessary to lower the water table so crops won't be drowned out. The ideal water table is about 2½ feet below the soil surface. If it is lowered beyond that point the muck will dry out and become powdery.

Some muck soils are highly acidic, others are nearly neutral, and a few are alkaline. Acid muck soils can be corrected by the application of two to three tons of dolomitic limestone every four to six years.

Because it is very high in organic matter, muck contains abundant nitrogen—generally 2 to 4 percent. For the same reason, it is also highly workable and has good structure and aeration. However, the organic matter of muck decays slowly. Therefore it is very beneficial to add fresh green material regularly. This is best done with a readily decomposed legume. Rotations, while not needed to maintain good tilth, are necessary to hold down plant disease, insects and weeds. Muck, like any other soil, should not be "mined." Onion farmers who farm muck have found that continuous cropping exhausts some ingredients that no amount of fertilizer can replace. Diversification produces the greatest long-run profit.

Muck soils are low in minerals. A newly broken muck may have a phosphorous content adequate for several years. However, organic muck farmers have found a program of phosphorous buildup pays off very well. Potash is needed, too. Most farmers use 1,500 pounds a year of phosphate rock and at least as much granite dust or greensand. *High fertilization rates mean high production on muck.* If your soil tests show deficiencies of trace elements, these should be applied as needed.

Green manuring is a vital part of muck farming. Record crops follow heavy crops of rye, vetch or oats. The more powdery and decomposed the muck, the more green manures are needed. On newer mucks, fibrous, woody organic materials bind the particles together, preventing powdering and blowing. Cover crops of oats, corn or soybeans yield considerable woody straw. Mulching is also good where practicable. Rotary tilling is usually preferable to plowing, due to the sponginess of the soil.

Windbreaks of blueberry hedges, sunflowers or trees like willows or pines, aided by strip crops of rye, barley or corn, will prevent muck from blowing, which can be highly damaging to crops. Water erosion is usually negligible, although older mucks may need some sodded waterways or diversion ditches for protection.

If spring in your area is usually wet, the muck may be cold, and should not be planted to crops like beans, eggplant, peppers, melons and tomatoes, which need a long, warm growing season. In wet spring weather, tillage implements should be kept off the muck until they can be used without clogging up with soggy soil.

One way to tell if muck is worth putting into production is to observe what is already growing on it. If there are no trees, or only a few black spruces, arborvitae and tamarisks, it may not pay to reclaim it, but if there are hardwood trees, it will pay.

Sometimes muck areas can be made into wild gardens. Many shrubs, ferns and trees will do well there. Common garden asters and sweet peas do well on muck, and many wild plants can be taken from nearby areas that are similarly swampy. Drainage should be fairly good and the muck nearly neutral in reaction.

MULBERRY   (*Morus*)

While most people think of the mulberry as a bush, usually not very good-looking and troublesome to prune, these shrubs are actually a very small part of the Mulberry family, a family of hardy, useful trees.

Full-sized mulberry trees attract birds. In turn, the birds patrol the orchard, consume thousands of insects and help maintain a desirable natural balance. Mulberries afford nutritious food for chickens or hogs. Trees planted next to pens drop their fruits on the ground where the animals can eat it.

Trees in an orchard should be spaced approximately 30 feet apart. The culture of the mulberry tree is similar to that of apple, peach and cherry trees. Mulberries can be effectively harvested by placing a clean, white sheet under the tree and shaking the branches. Ripened fruits will fall to the ground then and can be gathered for eating.

Red spiders and the spruce bagworm often take their toll on mulberry plantings. A dusting with diatomaceous earth will help control these two marauders. The bagworm cocoons can be handpicked to hinder the growth of the population.

To control the fall webworm, prune away the branch tips infected by the webworm colonies. Canker disease infection should be treated during the winter months by cutting out branches a foot below infected spots.

Types of Mulberries: Downing and Russian mulberry are the two varieties most widely sold.

The white mulberry and the black mulberry are both edible although the main purpose of planting them is so birds will eat them instead of your other kinds of berries. Poultry enjoy munching on these berries, too.

The paper mulberry is popular in the South where its abnormal trunk growth is a landscape marvel. The red mulberry produces dark red fruits and is an excellent source of shade. The weeping mulberry can be trained in a variety of ways and starts setting fruits two years after planting.

The enormous red mulberry is an effective shade tree but its fruit is considered inferior to that of the black mulberry.
(*Courtesy of U.S. Forest Service*)

MULCH

A mulch is a layer of material placed on the soil surface to conserve moisture, hold down weeds and ultimately improve soil structure and fertility. Mulching protects plants during winter by reducing the dangers of freezing and heaving. Mulching, like composting, is a basic practice of organic gardeners. It has proven quite effective in the orchard as well.

Mulching offers several advantages. For example, a mulched plant is not subjected to the extremes of temperatures that affect an exposed plant. The roots of unmulched plants can be damaged by the heaving of soil brought on by sudden thaws and freezes, but a mulch acts as an insulating blanket, keeping the soil warmer in winter and cooler in summer.

Mulch that has been applied to the soil during the spring and summer can be turned under in fall, thereby enriching the garden soil. Moreover, certain materials used for mulch contain rich minerals. These break down gradually and work into the soil to feed the roots of plants, soaking into the ground during the first heavy rain. Therefore, mulch fertilizes the soil while it remains on the soil surface, as well as after it decays.

For the busy gardener, mulching is a boon indeed. Many backbreaking hours of weeding and hoeing are practically eliminated and machine cultivation is not necessary. Weeds do not have the chance to get a foothold, and the few that do can be hoed out in a jiffy. Since the mulch helps keep the soil loose, there is no need to cultivate.

The mulch also keeps the wind and the hot, drying sun from evaporating soil moisture. A few good soakings during the long growing season will tide the plants over a long dry spell, and mulched plants often endure a long dry season with little watering. Soil underneath the mulch remains cool and damp to the touch. *See also* DRY WEATHER GARDENING.

At harvesttime, vegetables that sprawl on the ground—cucumbers, squash, strawberries, unstaked tomatoes—often become mildewed or moldy or develop rot. A mulch prevents this damage by keeping the vegetables clean and dry. In addition, mulched rows are easier to walk on and low-growing flowers and vegetables are not splashed with mud.

Despite the advantages that mulch offers, there are some potential problems. Most of these occur when mulches are incorrectly used or used in areas not suited for them. Seedlings planted in very moist soil should not be mulched immediately. The addition of any organic matter that keeps the soil very moist encourages damping-off of young plants. Damping-off, a disease caused by a fungus inhabiting moist, poorly ventilated soil, can be 90 percent fatal to seedlings. Allow seedlings to become established before mulching.

Crown rot is another fungus-caused disease that attacks perennials. To prevent it, postpone mulching, especially after heavy rains, until the soil is no longer waterlogged. Do not allow mulches composed of peat moss, manure, compost, or corncobs to touch the base of any perennial. Leave a circle several inches in diameter around the base of the plant so that the soil remains dry and open to the air.

Do not mulch a wet, low-lying area, or use only a light, dry type of material such as salt hay or buckwheat hulls. Avoid leaves; they may mat down and add to the sogginess.

Mulching Materials: Practically any organic material can be used for mulching. However, since different materials have different textures and other properties, they differ in suitability.

Materials for mulching are easy to find and often can be obtained for free or next to nothing. Many gardeners page through the Yellow Pages and make a list of promising firms from whom they can obtain materials for mulching (lumber companies, mills, meat packing houses, quarries, dairies, leather tanneries, city park departments, riding stables, wholesale food companies). Then they visit them to see what is available. Don't forget to ask park and street maintenance departments for leaves, hedge trimmings and grass clippings. The following are some commonly available mulching materials:

Alfalfa hay: Coarse and ragged in appearance, alfalfa is most easily handled when green and freshly cut. It has a high nitrogen content and will supply the nitrogen requirements of fruit trees. Rain-spoiled hay can be used as a mulch and it should be less costly than fresh hay.

Buckwheat hulls: Buckwheat hulls make a clean and attractive mulch, but they are expensive and hard to obtain. They can be spread one or two inches deep in summer, and deeper in winter.

Cocoa bean hulls or shells: Excellent as a mulch, they absorb 2½ times their weight in water.

Corncobs: Ground into one-inch pieces, corncobs have many uses. Their sugar content will help increase the microorganisms in the soil, and the material itself will give a better soil granulation. When using cobs as a mulch, use a layer at least six inches deep, and apply a nitrogenous material—blood meal, cottonseed meal, bone meal, or compost—to the soil first. *See also* CORNCOBS.

Cornstalks: When shredded, cornstalks make an excellent mulch. *See also* CORN-STALK.

Grass clippings: Among the most commonly available and inexpensive materials, grass clippings make an excellent mulch. *See also* GRASS CLIPPINGS.

Leaves: An excellent mulch, shredded leaves do not mat down, and they enrich the soil more quickly than whole leaves. There is rarely any nitrogen deficiency in leaves, so it is not necessary to apply nitrogen to the soil before mulching. If unshredded, leaves should be mixed with straw or some other light material so that they do not become a soggy mass. The mixed mulch can be applied eight to 12 inches deep for winter. *See also* LEAVES.

Nonorganic mulches: A great many nonorganic materials have been used as mulches with varying degrees of success. The main disadvantage of many is that they will not decompose to help increase soil fertility; conversely, of course, these materials offer the advantage of long useful life. Aluminum foil can be spread out under growing plants and will increase received sunlight because it reflects light up to the leaves. It can be used for years, and at the end of its useful life it can be recycled. Plastic films are especially useful in growing melons. Black plastic film is used most often since it increases soil temperature and keeps weeds from germinating.

Many gardeners have successfully used household discards as mulches. Wool or cotton cloth will last through several seasons. Newspaper is a good mulch. Newsprint ink does not contain any harmful chemicals but the coated paper of glossy magazines may contain agents that are harmful to soil organisms. Do not use these for mulching.

Peat moss: Peat moss is an old standby for mulchers. It is excavated from natural peat bogs, compressed into bales and marketed commercially. It has tremendous moisture retention characteristics, but if it forms a crust over the beds, break it up with a rake.

Pine needles: Good for strawberries year-round, pine needles can be a fire hazard when dry. Use a two- to four-inch mulch and renew yearly.

Rotted pinewood: Like pine needles, this material is excellent for mulching acid-loving plants. Compost before using for plants that require a neutral or slightly alkaline soil.

Salt hay: Salt hay grows in meadows and lowlands near bodies of saltwater. It is a good source of trace minerals and sometimes is free for the taking. It does not mat down but remains stiff and firm throughout the season. If used as a winter mulch, it can be taken off in the spring and stacked in a corner of the plot to be used again the following winter. However, it is recommended for use year-round. A good mulch for strawberries, salt hay should be applied in a 1½- to two-inch layer on strawberry beds and a three-inch layer elsewhere.

Sawdust: Sawdust makes a very good mulch. For blueberries, use a sawdust from softwoods as a mulch. There will be less packing down and better aeration, and the blueberries prefer an acidic soil. Try banking hardwood sawdust around the base of old apple trees as a means of rejuvenating them. To counteract the nitrogen deficiency inherent in sawdust, add soybean meal, cottonseed meal or compost to the soil *before* mulching. *See also* SAWDUST.

Straw: Clean and readily available straw contains no weed seeds, is quick and easy to

For winter protection, straw can be placed completely over strawberry plants then raked back the following spring for a mulch that conserves moisture, controls weeds and protects the fruits from soil pests.

lay down, and looks presentable. Once applied, it remains in place for an entire season and can be tilled into the soil in fall. By spring, it will have decomposed and become an indistinguishable part of the soil. It should have a nitrogenous substance turned under with it for best results. *See also* STRAW.

Weeds and native grasses: Although rather unsightly in the garden, these make an excellent mulch for trees where it is important to use a deep covering and where this sort of mulch does not look out of place. Expose the plants to air so they do not root under the trees, or shred and mix with grass clippings.

Wood chips and wood wastes: A good source of mulch, wood chips are sometimes available from electric and telephone companies. Chipped bark also makes an attractive mulch. *See also* BARK, WOOD CHIPS.

How to Mulch: After the soil is prepared and planted, level it with a rake. Apply the mulch on top of the soil. The thickness of the mulch should be sufficient to prevent the growth of weeds. A thin layer of finely shredded plant materials is more effective than a similar layer of unshredded, loose material.

In some crops, at least, the mulch may be applied after planting the seed. This is especially true of potatoes. Research at Rodale's New Organic Gardening Experimental Farm in Maxatawney, Pennsylvania, showed that the best way to grow potatoes under mulch was to plant the eyes a foot apart in shallow trenches. Sprinkle with just enough earth to cover the eyes and cover with six inches of hay or grass clippings.

Some gardeners have reported successfully mulching other crops right after seeding. If beans, corn, peas, carrots, beets, and similar vegetables are to be mulched immediately after the seed is planted, the mulch over the row should be loose and not thicker than from four to six inches; the mulch between rows can and should be more dense.

Transplanted tomatoes, cabbages, cauliflower, peppers, and other vegetables may be mulched immediately after the plants are set out. A circular area around each plant should be kept unmulched until the plant is well started. At that time, the mulch can be pulled up close to the stem of the plant.

Permanent Mulching: In 1955, Ruth Stout of West Redding, Connecticut, wrote a book, *How to Have a Green Thumb without an Aching Back* (New York: Cornerstone Library, Inc.), describing her own personal method of mulch gardening, which, according to Miss Stout, completely eliminated spading, hoeing and weeding. What Miss Stout did, essentially, was to carry the logic of the mulch to its fullest extent.

The practice of constant, heavy mulching has been used by some gardeners for many years. Year-round mulching can work well in fertile, well-aerated soils.

Before applying a permanent mulch, plow and harrow the garden thoroughly. As much organic material as is available—manure, leaf mold, compost—should be turned into the top layer of soil. Test the soil and add phosphate rock and potash, ground limestone, bone meal, or other needed supplements before the mulch is applied.

A six-inch layer of straw or hay will protect soil moisture and prevent weeds from growing during a period of about three months. Additional mulch may be spread whenever it is needed, but the mulch should not be allowed to disintegrate entirely, at this or any other time, because it is excellent protection against drying fall winds and heavy fall and spring rain erosion.

To plant, rake back the mulch and seed the rows. After the plants have sprouted, pull the mulch around them to keep the ground moist and to prevent weeds from taking over.

A combination of permanent mulch and tillage has been used successfully on some gardens where the soil was too heavy for the mulch alone. The mulch is spread and separated in spring where rows are to be planted. The soil is then stirred with a fork, and compost or manure is dug in on a foot-wide strip along the planting line. Where single plants such as tomatoes or peppers are to be set, or where squash, melon or cucumber hills are to be planted, push back the mulch and prepare a circular area a foot wider than the planting site. *See also* STOUT, RUTH.

Stone Mulching: Stone mulching is very similar to permanent mulching with hay or straw except that stones are placed between the rows. The stones have all the advantages of other types of mulches and also do some things better. For instance, they are particularly good for conserving soil moisture and maintaining soil structure. They allow the soil to heat up quickly in the spring, and because they absorb heat, help to protect tender plants during cool nights. They are also permanent; come in a vast variety of colors, sizes and textures; and can often be had for nothing.

The bed to be stone mulched must be cultivated deeply, just like any permanently mulched plot. Organic matter should be disked or tilled into the soil along with any supplements necessary (test soil thoroughly first). If leaves are available, spread a thick layer over the soil and place the stones on top of the leaves.

The stones are set in rows two feet wide, leaving a foot between stone paths for planting. If you are using flat stones, place them with their flat surfaces up, and level them. Spaces between the stones can be filled with compost or garden loam, and the rows can be mulched with compost, straw or other mulches if you wish. One advantage of using stone mulches is that you will be able to turn the soil in the rows easily.

Stone mulches are particularly good for orchard trees and ornamentals, although they can be used successfully for many other plants. You can use natural stones or make your own "stones" in whatever shapes strike your fancy by using wooden or metal forms and filling them with a mixture of one part cement, 1½ parts sand, 1½ parts stone, ½ part dolomite, and ½ part phosphate rock. As the concrete "stone" gradually weathers, these latter elements will slowly become available to the surrounding soil.

See also ORCHARD.

A permanent stone mulch helps to conserve soil moisture, maintain soil structure and temper the extremes in soil temperature.

MULDER, GERARDUS JOHANNES

(1802–1880) Mulder was a Dutch professor of chemistry who was opposed to Justus von Liebig's chemical conception of agriculture. He is famous for his protein theory. It was Mulder who gave the name *protein* to the albuminous substances he had isolated. He was of the opinion that protein was the foster substance of the entire animal kingdom.

It was Mulder's work with protein that caused scientists to consider the nitrogen content of farm feeds as the basis of the ration's nutritional value. Mulder had discovered that in all protein compounds, nitrogen makes up 16 percent. This is a figure still used by scientists today for calculating the protein content of a substance when its nitrogen content is known.

In 1846 Justus von Liebig began to question the exactness of Mulder's analyses. Von Liebig was probably the better chemist as far as techniques and knowledge of the exact methods of making analyses were concerned. After a stormy dispute the scientific world lost faith in the protein theory.

MULLEIN   (*Verbascum Thapsus*)

Biennial and perennial herbs of the Snapdragon family, mulleins are native around the Mediterranean but naturalized all through the Northern Hemisphere. Some species are used as ornamentals, but many are weeds which spread rapidly and may become a nuisance.

The foliage is gray green, with large basal leaves and smaller ones ascending the main stalk, which is topped by a columnar yellow, red, purple, or white flower spike.

Moth mullein (*V. Blattaria*) is a six-foot species with smooth, dark green leaves, and yellow flowers in a loose cluster. Purple mullein (*V. phoeniceum*) has dark green, wrinkled leaves in its basal rosette, and woolly purplish flowers in a branched cluster. Common mullein (*V. Thapsus*), which is also called velvet plant, candlewick, and flannel plant, is a six-foot perennial, covered with a yellowish felt. It also has yellow flower spikes.

Mullein was brought to the United States from the Mediterranean because of its medicinal values, but it spread quickly, acquiring a reputation as a garden plant. Grown easily in any soil that is not cold or wet, it is propagated by cuttings, division or seed. The seeds take about ten days to germinate. In the border, mullein is usually treated as a biennial.

Mullein is still regarded by some as a valuable medicinal herb. When infused as a

Mullein was first grown in the United States as a medicinal herb, but has since been cultivated as an ornamental border plant.

tea, it is used to remedy coughs, diarrhea and constipation. The bruised flowers can be steeped in olive oil for several weeks to make an ointment used to treat bruises, hemorrhoids and even earaches. Dried leaves have been smoked to ease congested throats and remedy various lung ailments.

This plant is most commonly cultivated as a garden plant and is valued for its ornamental yellow blossoms and long, tall stalks.

See also HERB, VERBASCUM.

MULTIFLORA ROSE
(*Rosa multiflora*)

Multiflora is a fast-growing rose variety which will reach a height of five to seven feet in three or four years. At one time, the Soil Conservation Service promoted multiflora to farmers as a low-cost conservation measure. More recently, its use has been discouraged in many areas, especially in the South, because it has proved to be extremely invasive. When planting, you should select a site where there is plenty of room for this ambitious hedge. The multiflora will grow into a dense thicket sprinkled with a profusion of small, white flowers in June and July. Late on, it will provide thousands of red, pea-sized berries, on which birds and other wildlife will feast throughout the winter.

The canes grow very rapidly and tend to tip. Ends of the canes root in the ground and start new plants. In this way, the multiflora will propagate itself until you decide to halt its progress. Control is easy, however. The tipping canes will not root well in sod, and those that do root may be mowed down right along with the grass.

Soil for multiflora roses should be well drained. Fertilizing will give plants a good start, but little extra fertilizer is necessary for normal growth. If your soil is very poor, dig in plenty of compost—or another balanced organic fertilizer—before planting. Multiflora will grow even on deficient soils, unless there is much competition from other plants. To plant the row, dig a furrow or make individual holes one foot apart, and deep enough to accommodate the roots. There should be no sod or other growth within a foot of each plant. Working the soil deeply before planting will help plants but, again, is not necessary for normal growth.

To transplant the plants, begin by placing about a dozen at a time in a bucket of water. Plants are small and resemble twigs with short roots. Set them into the soil at the level at which they were planted in the nursery and firm the soil around each one. After all are set in, pour the remaining water over the plants.

MUM   *See* CHRYSANTHEMUM

MUNICIPAL COMPOSTING

Municipal-scale composting is an increasingly promising alternative to the incineration and ocean dumping which now claim the more than 300 million tons of wet sewage sludge that are produced in and around American towns and cities every year. The practical potential of municipal composting has been clearly established by the success of pilot projects at various sites throughout the country, as well as by the numerous European cities that have been routinely turning municipal wastes into public wealth via large-scale composting.

The acceptance of municipal composting seems destined to gain pace now that society places increasing emphasis on social and environmental consequences in evaluating the appropriateness of various waste technologies. Besides its value as a soil amendment, compost has other, untapped benefits. Perhaps most important is its potential use in reclaiming damaged lands. Strip mining has destroyed many acres of land in terms of both food production and public recreation potential. The application of compost is an obvious solution to land reclamation in areas where the topsoil has been lost. In other areas, large expanses of land have been rendered useless because they serve as receptacles for chemical sludges which respond to no manner of treatment. Where compost has been tried as a means of stabilizing these sludges, the results have been favorable.

Much of the most important current research in the field of municipal composting is being done by Drs. Eliot Epstein and Rufus Chaney and their colleagues at the U.S. Department of Agriculture's Biological Waste Management Project, based at Beltsville, Maryland. In 1976, the USDA's Agricultural Research Service issued a comprehensive report, *Compost: From Waste to Resource,* based on the research done at Beltsville and at a second site at Bangor, Maine.

The report concluded that "New applications of an old principle—composting of sewage sludge—score an E for excellence in preliminary tests for efficiency, economy, environmental soundness, and aesthetic quality. Composting was once considered out of the question as a solution for the pressing needs for better waste disposal methods. Current research, however, is answering troublesome questions about the practicality of municipal composting, including the question of whether composting can be conducted successfully during the cold, wet, winter weather experienced by many American cities."

The U.S. Environmental Protection Agency is supporting the project at Bangor, Maine (population about 35,000). The EPA concludes that most cities around the country have the principal equipment necessary to adopt this relatively inexpensive process. City officials in Bangor estimate that they will save in excess of 50 percent of their annual expenditures for the loam and mulch materials, which will be replaced by the compost. In addition, they are avoiding the expense of disposing of their sludge by incineration or landfill. Projects like the one at Bangor, as well as those underway in Durham, New Hampshire, and Beltsville, Maryland, seem to indicate that compost costs will range from $20 to $50 per ton of dry sludge. In contrast, incineration costs range between $100 and $150 per dry ton.

The Beltsville system handles 50 tons of filter cake sludge (23 percent solids) daily—a rate capable of serving a city of 200,000 to 400,000 people. Outdoor temperatures as low as 20°F. (-6.67°C.) and rain totaling seven inches per week failed to interfere with the experimental composting system.

Both the Bangor and Beltsville projects employ the same experimental approach. Sludge from the Blue Plains primary and secondary treatment plant, Washington, D.C., and sludge from Bangor's primary treatment plant, undergo a seven-week composting process that reduces each 50-ton input to 20 tons of agriculturally valuable compost. Wood chips or bark are mixed with the sludge at a

3:1 ratio. The mixture is then piled to a height of 8 feet over a 12-inch base of wood chips. Under the base lies 70 feet of 4-inch diameter perforated pipe of use in aeration. The sludge-chip mixture forms a pile 40 by 20 feet. Capping the pile and extending down its sides is a 12-inch layer of finished compost that has been screened to remove the wood chips. It filters out malodorous gases that might escape into the atmosphere.

Air is pulled through the pile by a blower connected to the pipes under the pile. The blower operates automatically at various intervals depending on the temperature. Airflow through the blower inlet is about 200 cubic feet per minute, which is sufficient to provide a 5 to 15 percent oxygen concentration throughout the pile.

Bacteria responsible for the composting process are stimulated by the oxygen concentration and airflow to complete the process within three weeks. Temperatures produced in the pile are above 140°F. (60°C.) and often exceed 175°F. (79.44°C.). Such temperatures, with time, are sufficient to kill disease agents such as viruses, bacteria, protozoan cysts, and eggs of intestinal worms.

The aeration system also acts to draw gases from the pile, deodorizing them as they pass through a pile of screened compost at the pipe outlet.

After three weeks, the compost is moved to a stockpile for a four-week curing period. Then it is screened and the wood chips or other bulking agents are recovered for reuse. The compost, almost as light as sawdust, is an odorless, aesthetically attractive material suitable for use on crops, lawns, potted plants, and other ornamentals.

Compost nutrients useful for plant growth are principally nitrogen (1.6 percent), phos-phorus (1 percent), and potassium (.16 percent). The nitrogen is mostly in an organic form and thus is released slowly. Up to 20 dry tons of compost per acre can be applied to the soil without overfertilizing plants or releasing nitrates into the groundwater.

The USDA concludes its report on the practicality of composting as a solution to the pressing and expensive problem of waste disposal by stating, "the biggest benefit from composting is its value as a much-needed soil conditioner. The report praises compost for significantly increasing the water-holding capacity of soils, and thereby reducing the need to water crops or lawns. Sandy and clay soils in particular are improved by compost.

A widely held attitude that has plagued municipal composting from the start, however, is the tendency to judge a composting operation solely on its profitability. From this point of view, if the product cannot be sold, and failure to meet operational and capital costs results in deficit, the entire enterprise is regarded as a failure, regardless of how well the plant may be operating. Yet, no one ever expects an incineration operation to make money. Composting is more than just a means of treating wastes, and its success should be judged on the basis of its total performance and contribution, not strictly on its profit returns.

Many resource economists and sanitary engineers believe that composting will truly come into its own when regional waste management becomes the order of the day. When this happens, agricultural and municipal waste disposal will have become a public responsibility. Fortunately, most agricultural wastes are readily composted with municipal sludge. Furthermore, available land for landfill is diminishing, and new air quality standards are causing the costs of incineration to rise substantially. Soon the only technology available for solid wastes processing will be composting. *See also* COMPOSTING, SEWAGE SLUDGE.

MURIATE OF POTASH
See POTASH

MUSA

These giant tropical herbs include the banana and several other edible and ornamental plants. *M. x paradisiaca,* the plantain, closely resembles the common banana. It grows up to 30 feet tall, with leaves as long as ten feet. Its fruit, cooked, is a staple food for millions in the tropics. The Abyssinian banana tree, *Ensete ventricosum,* is even bigger, but its fruits are inedible. A much smaller species, the dwarf or Chinese banana, *M. acuminata,* grows about six feet tall with four-foot-long leaves. It is the most tolerant of cold and wind of all the bananas and produces good-quality fruit, but it is most often grown solely for ornament in Florida, parts of the Gulf Coast and Southern California. The fruits are fragrant and numerous, often 200 in a cluster. It likes a friable, loose and fertile soil, with full sun and plenty of moisture and benefits from heavy mulching. Another species, the abaca, *M. textilis,* has stalks that yield the strong cordage fiber, Manila hemp. Its fruit is not edible, and it is rarely grown outside of the Philippines.
See also BANANA.

MUSCARI   *See* GRAPE HYACINTH

MUSHROOM   *(Agaricus)*

The common mushroom is the only cultivated fungus commonly used as food. Although it grows wild in many places, it is safer for most people to purchase or raise the mushroom than to try to differentiate edible species such as the white mushroom (*A. bisporus*) from poisonous ones.

There are more than 50 types of edible mushrooms growing wild in this country, including the puffball, morel and chanterelle. Although they grow wild, puffballs can be cultivated for domestic use by spore planting from dead-ripe specimens in the fall. They often appear in lawns, golf courses or even cow pastures after late summer or early fall rains. Puffballs make good side dishes, gravies or salad or soup additives, as do morels. Morels (*Morchella esculenta*) resemble small sponges or honeycomb tripe, and range in color from dark honey to olive gray. Chanterelle mushrooms grow in clusters of thousands under shaded rocks or in forests. They are usually two to three inches high and yellow or red.

Poisonous Mushrooms: Gathering wild mushrooms is an interesting hobby. However, it takes an experienced mushroom hunter to be able to recognize absolutely the many poisonous species. The genus *Amanita* includes several of the most deadly kinds. This type is characterized by gills that are "free," that is, they come up close to the stem, but are not attached to it. Spores and gills are white, and a ring is present and usually prominent on the stem just below the expanding cap. This ring later shrinks and becomes inconspicuous. The base of the stem is enlarged into a cuplike sheath or bulb often hidden in the soil and easily missed unless one looks for it.

Mushrooms can be grown at home in a dark, cool (55 to 60°F. [12.78 to 15.56°C.]) and humid (80 to 85 percent) room.

A number of other mushrooms are known to be toxic in varying degrees. *One should not eat wild mushrooms without knowing which are edible.* Learn to recognize some of the edible kinds and eat only those you know well.

Growing Mushrooms at Home: For your wintertime gardening pleasure, you'll find mushroom growing just the thing. All you need is a small, dark, moist, and cool setting. For most homeowners, that place will be in the basement; even the area under the kitchen sink might do.

A certain amount of light will not hurt mushrooms, but they do need controlled humidity at 80 to 85 percent and temperature from 55 to 60°F. (12.78 to 15.56°C.). Strong drafts and dry air are fatal.

In order to find a place that maintains the proper temperature range both day and night, make some tests by placing a few thermometers in various spots of your basement. Since temperatures can vary as much as ten Fahrenheit degrees (5.6 Celsius degrees) at different levels in the same location, make certain you put the thermometer at about the level where the mushrooms will be growing.

Once you've selected the spot for your mushroom garden, the next step is to decide how you're going to grow them. If you use the tray method, a bench or hanging shelves on tiers will do the job. Generally, you can estimate that the trays will weigh about 25 pounds when ready for growth.

Prepared trays and small kits, already filled with the growing medium and inoculated with the mushroom spawn, can be purchased. They contain everything needed for growing mushrooms. Spawn is already planted in the trays, so all you have to do is remove the paper, add an inch of topsoil, and water thoroughly. If the conditions are right, you'll be harvesting your crop in about four weeks. These kits are generally available only from October to April.

Growing Medium: Mushrooms grow in organic material containing nitrogen and carbohydrates such as sugar, starch, cellulose, or lignin. However, mushrooms cannot manufacture these products the way other plants do because they have no chlorophyll in their tissues. They develop their full root system, a network of fine white threads called mycelium, before any part of the plant appears above the soil. Fresh strawy horse manure is excellent for mushroom growing. It should be composted by turning it every four or five days, shaking thoroughly and watering well each time. Keep it moist, but not saturated. After three or four turnings, it should be a rich dark brown and have no odor. It can then be put in trays of any convenient size and heated to 140°F. (60°C.). After about a week, the compost should be ready for planting.

Many growers use materials other than horse manure to make compost. To make one kind, mix together about 100 pounds of corn fodder or finely ground corncobs and an equal amount of straw. Water and firm this well and let it stand a few days. Then mix in 20 pounds each of leaf mold or peat moss, tankage, and either greensand or granite dust. Some well-rotted compost can be added to aid decomposition. About 30 pounds of whole grains completes the mixture.

After a good watering, let the mixture stand five or six days before turning. A second turning a week or so later should be enough. Then set it in the trays. Plant the spawn as soon as the temperature of the medium reaches about 75°F. (23.89°C.).

Spawn: You can purchase spawn, which is much like a cheese or bread mold, from most seed companies. Bottle spawn is the purest form of culture. Break it into pieces a little smaller than a golf ball and plant eight to ten inches apart, about two inches deep.

To get a good run of spawn, keep the room as dark as possible and the temperature at about 70°F. (21.11°C.) for the next 21 days. At the end of that time, the threadlike filaments (mycelium) from adjacent plantings should meet. The temperature should then be dropped to about 60°F. (15.56°C.) and the beds "cased"—covered with a one-inch layer of good, pasteurized garden soil. (Many home growers keep their beds near the heating plant for the sweating out and spawning periods, then move them to the 60°F. spot at casing time.)

Water well with a gentle spray; the medium should be moist and crumbly, but not so moist that water can be readily squeezed out of it. Most mushroom diseases and pests— fogging off, sow bugs and black spot—will never make their appearance if moisture and temperature conditions are carefully tended. Any snails and slugs can be trapped with lettuce or cabbage leaves. If the air in your cellar is on the dry side, a layer or two of

moist burlap over the trays will maintain the proper humidity. Water whenever the topsoil feels powdery.

In approximately three weeks, tiny white dots will appear. You'll find these clustered together in groups, called "flushes" or "breaks." In another ten days, the largest will be ready for picking, but don't rush the harvest.

Pest Control: Until recently, chemical sprays were considered the best weapon against pests that plague mushroom crops. A few years ago, a commercial California mushroom grower discovered that the phorid fly, a tiny gnat that ovulates every 72 hours, can be stopped by hanging a fine-meshed screen door on the mushroom enclosure. This prevents the flies from laying eggs on the compost pile and thereby disrupts their life cycle. Turning the heated compost pile every 68 to 70 hours also helps bury and smother any remaining eggs. These insects should not be a serious problem to the home mushroom grower.

Another threat to mushroom crops is mold. Although traditionally controlled with chemicals, the two main molds, mycogyne and verticillium, can be combated through clean compost production and inoculation with spawn raised organically.

Harvesting: Mushrooms can be picked as buttons or when fully ripe. Button mushrooms are familiar as the mushrooms sold in cans in supermarkets; they are picked before the cap has expanded and the thin membrane or "veil" covering the gills has broken. Later, the cap expands and the gills are exposed and turn a slight pink in color. At this stage, the mushrooms are more robust in flavor but bruise more easily and cannot be shipped.

Careful harvesting is necessary. Cut off the mushrooms at soil level; never pull them out of the ground.

Practice selective harvesting, picking every day if possible, and your beds will bear crops up to six months. After each "flush" is completely picked, clean out the remaining ends and diseased or underdeveloped mushrooms.

When the entire bed is cropped out, the compost will make a fine soil conditioner. Most gardeners don't try to grow mushrooms during the summer—it's too hard to maintain a 60°F. (15.56°C.) temperature—so you can set up a profitable schedule: fall preparation of compost, winter cropping and spring fertilizing of your garden with the used compost.

The wonderful flavor of cultivated mushrooms and their ability to elevate any dish from the mediocre are enough to make them a valuable part of the diet. But cultivated mushrooms also contain valuable nutritive elements. Nutritionists have found them to be a good source of extra protein, iron, vitamin C, riboflavin, and niacin.

MUSKMELON   *See* MELON

MUSTARD   *(Brassica)*

A weedy annual herb belonging to the Cruciferae family, mustard is related to a number of vegetables, such as cabbage, cauliflower and Brussels sprouts. The plant has large, thick, jagged leaves of a dark green color and is found in most temperate regions of the world.

There are many species of mustard plants, but the three best known for their commercial uses are black (*B. nigra*), grown for the production of table mustard, white (*B. hirta*), grown for its pungent seed, and brown (*B. juncea*), grown for use as a potherb.

The plant has been used in condiments for centuries. It is mentioned in the New Testament scriptures. The ancient Greeks and Romans employed it for many of the purposes for which it is still used. The oldest known recipe for preparing mustard was written by Columella, a native of Gades in the first century A.D. The English herbalist Parkinson described the grinding of mustard seed using a quern "with some good vinegar to make it liquid and running."

Mustard is an easy crop to grow. All the common varieties are annuals and will grow from seed. White mustard (also referred to as yellow mustard) is best adapted to a rather heavy type of sandy loam and light adobe soil. The darker variety requires an even lighter, more sandy loam. The crop needs only limited rainfall, preferably distributed so that the seed can mature during a period of dry weather.

Seed should be sown two weeks before the last spring frost. Seed for a fall crop should be sown at least six weeks before the first autumn frost. An alfalfa or grain seeder can be used for planting larger crops once the ground is harrowed. About three pounds of the darker seed or four pounds of the lighter seed are required per acre.

In most areas, the first planting will be ready for harvesting about August. The crop must be harvested while the seedpods are fully grown, yet closed, because the pod will shatter when it is fully ripe. The crop may be cut with mowers and dried in the sun. It can then be threshed with a pickup harvester when dry; or it can be cut and bound with a grain binder, cured in the field and then threshed with a modified grain thresher.

The taller, black mustard plant seeds are smaller than those of the white mustard plant. Average yields per acre range from 115

Although grown commercially for its seed, mustard is valued by home gardeners for its pungent green leaves.

to 548 pounds. Individual growers, however, have reported yields as high as 1,500 pounds. Mustard is grown most successfully for commercial purposes in the western United States, since it is an annual crop that yields early returns and can be easily handled by equipment available on larger farms. In other localities, it is advisable to grow a small trial acreage.

For home gardeners, it would be inadvisable to plant mustard in the garden or flower border. It self-sows very easily and might become a pest.

Besides the commercial value of mustard seed, the plant's leaves, which are an excellent source of A and C vitamins, can be used as salad greens. In addition, their bulk and fiber tend to produce a mild laxative effect.

Powder made from the seed is used as a salad dressing, for flavoring meat and in preparing pickles and certain kinds of fish. The darker seeds are known for their aroma, the lighter for pungency. In making table mustard, tumeric can be added to heighten color and add aroma.

Medicinally, mustard has been used in many ways as an oil, a tincture, a poultice and a plaster. It has been used as a relief for headaches, fevers, whooping cough, asthma, and also for liver, stomach and throat problems. Mustard liniment consists of camphor, castor oil and a volatile mustard-seed oil in a solution of alcohol.

MUTATION

Any change in the character of a plant not brought about by crossing it with another plant is called a mutation. Sometimes only a part of the plant, such as a single branch, may show the new trait. This happens often with roses and fruits. Cuttings of these branches will produce new plants having the alteration throughout, but generally, mutations appear most often among plants reproduced by seed.

Mutations are the variations plant breeders spend their lives searching for, the off-types whose new characteristics may be valuable. When reproduced, a new variety joins the ranks of useful plants. Mutations are the source of disease-resistant varieties, higher-yielding crops, and hardier and more beautiful plants, and thus are of great interest to the gardener and farmer. Natural mutations are worth watching for in your plants. Plant breeders sometimes produce them artificially by means of chemicals or radiation, or by changing environmental factors.

MYCELIUM

Mycelium is the collective term which designates mold tissue or the mass of growth of filamentous (thread) fungi. Yeasts are, in general, unicellular fungi; that is, each individual yeast organism, as a rule, consists of a single cell. The molds, also called filamentous fungi, usually are made up of branched, multicellular threads, each of which consists of a chain of cells attached end to end. These threads or filaments (hence, the name filamentous fungi) are known as hyphae. Each individual thread is a hypha; the mass of hyphae is the mycelium.

In industrial processes which employ mold fermentations, mycelium is a by-product or a waste product. In large-scale industrial processes, such as the production of penicillin and various acids, tanks or vats containing thousands of gallons of corn mash, or some other suitable raw material, are inoculated with mycelium or spores. As the mold grows and produces whatever product the fermentation is designed to produce, the mycelium increases in mass.

These products (with the exception of some fats) are, as a rule, soluble in water. The recovery procedure therefore usually begins by a separation of the mycelium from the liquid in which it has grown. However, in some cases the entire contents of the tank (mycelium and liquid) are treated without preliminary separation. This mycelium has a rather high water content (it may be 90 percent), although of course it can be dried. It may run about 2 to 3 percent ash (mineral constituents), 2½ to 5 percent nitrogen, and 40 to 50 percent carbon. There would also undoubtedly be a number of vitamins present in the mycelium. Some "ligninlike" material (perhaps 10 to 20 percent) and around 3 to 5 percent fats would also be expected to be present.

As far as its stability in the soil is concerned, it would no doubt be quickly decomposed. Mushrooms and toadstools (which are very close in biochemical composition to mycelium) seem to rot overnight. Mold mycelium would behave in a very similar manner.

In the process of growth, molds respire; they derive their energy by oxidizing a large amount of whatever they are growing on to carbon dioxide, which of course is lost as a volatile gas. There is always, therefore, much less organic matter in mold mycelium than was originally present in the organic matter on which the mold grew. This decrease is the result of the loss of some organic matter as carbon dioxide.

See also MICROORGANISM.

MYCORRHIZA

Mycorrhiza is a structure composed of a fungus and the roots of a plant. Mycorrhizae are called ectotrophic if the mycelium of the fungus occurs outside of the root, and endotrophic if the fungus occurs inside the root. They are extremely widespread and are associated with every group of cholorophyll-bearing plants except algae. Mycorrhizae are particularly abundant in forest mold and rare in water and wet soil except in logs rich in organic matter. It is generally believed that the mycorrhizae exist in a symbiotic relationship with higher plants. In acidic humusy soils, mycorrhizae help make nitrogen available to the plants and make salts more readily available to the roots. In turn, the fungus takes up carbon compounds and phosphorus from tree roots.

Ectotrophic mycorrhizae are caused by many kinds of fungi; generally, those on forest trees are caused by the Basidiomycetes. Trees may be infected by several different species of mycorrhizae, ranging in color from white to red and from yellow to deep brown, and differing in form, size and texture, because each is due to a different fungus. If trees have a well-developed mycorrhiza infection, roots are generally short, thick and have a corallike appearance.

Endotrophic mycorrhizae occur most commonly in the Heath, Orchid and Gentian families. The fungi form a close symbiotic relationship with members of the Orchid family, and the seed of several species cannot germinate unless infected by mycorrhizae. Other species show poor development unless infected.

When mycorrhizae are destroyed by soil fumigants used to control nematodes and pathogenic fungi, plants do poorly and show nutrient deficiencies.

See also MICROORGANISM.

evergreen shrub, three to eight feet tall, with the aromatic, waxy gray berries used to make bayberry candles. *M. cerifera,* the wax myrtle, is a large evergreen shrub or small tree about 30 feet in height. It also bears waxy, scented fruit and is grown from New Jersey southward. Both of these species thrive in sandy, very dry places. A third type, the sweet gale or bog myrtle, *M. gale,* is deciduous, about three feet tall, and carries its fruits in heavy catkins. It likes acidic, boggy situations from Virginia to the far North, and is a good subject for the bog garden.

Myrica is propagated by seed, layering and suckers. Some species grow well in poor, sandy soil but most thrive in moist, peaty environments. Leaf mold added to the soil helps growth.

When the root is harvested for medicinal use, it is stripped from the bark, dried then pulverized. It should be stored in dark, sealed containers.

Myrica is often used in gardens for its attractive and aromatic foliage and fruits. The bark and roots of some species are also used as astringents, tonics and stimulants. A tea which eases sore throats and jaundice can be made from myrica.

See also HERB.

MYOSOTIS   *See* FORGET-ME-NOT

MYRICA

These shrubs are often called bayberry, but they are no relation to the true bays (*Laurus nobilis*). *M. pensylvanica* is a semi-

MYROBALAN   *See* TERMINALIA

MYRTLE   (*Myrtus*)

The true myrtle (*M. communis*) is an evergreen shrub that grows to a maximum height of ten feet. It is widely grown for ornament in the South and on the West Coast. Above Richmond, Virginia, it is a popular potted plant for the cool greenhouse. Myrtle has bright green, scented leaves, and creamy white or pink flowers in July, followed by purple black berries. There are smaller varieties and ones with double flowers and variegated leaves. In Greek festivals, myrtle was used as a symbol of youth and beauty. The leaves and berries are still used in some parts of southern Europe as a medicine. Myrtle prefers a light, sandy, humusy soil and is propagated by seed or by cuttings of half-ripened wood under glass. Other plants sometimes called myrtle include a tall shrub or small tree, the luma (*Amomyrtus Luma*) and the Chilean guava (*Ugni Molinae*). Both are grown in South America and occasionally in California for their sweet, edible fruits, which taste like wild strawberries.

NAEGELIA   *See* SMITHIANTHA

NARCISSUS

The bulbous plants of the Amaryllidaceae family, including the daffodil, jonquil, paperwhite, Chinese sacred lily and poet's narcissus, can be easily grown by any gardener. Many landowners with acres of rolling hills scatter the bulbs on hillsides, planting them about six inches deep and leaving them to grow and reproduce by themselves. In this way each spring will be greeted by a greater profusion of bloom than the previous spring.

September or October is about the best time to plant narcissus bulbs, although they may be planted as late as December 1. An early planting makes for early blooming the following spring (about the latter part of April).

When planting in groups, spade the soil deeply to allow for plenty of root growth in the spring. Work in plenty of rotted manure throughout the planting area until the soil assumes a good, crumbly structure. Dig a trench six inches in depth and mix bone meal and wood ashes with the soil you removed. Set the bulbs in a one-inch layer of sand. Apply more sand until the bulbs are covered up to their necks. Then fill-in the trench with the soil you removed. The bulbs should be about three inches below the surface and at least six inches apart.

Once planted, narcissuses may remain several years before you need to replant them.

In order to develop a root system, paper-white narcissus bulbs require about two weeks in a cool, dark place; then they can be forced to bloom on a sunny windowsill.

770

Be sure they get a topdressing of compost each year to insure a good display of flowers. When the plantings become too crowded and blooms are small, it is time to dig up the bulbs, separate them, enrich the soil, and replant.

If you live in the North, use a winter mulch to protect the bulbs from alternate freezing and thawing which can heave the soil and harm the bulbs. A layer of straw, hay or evergreen boughs will serve the purpose adequately. Let the mulch remain on the bed until the plants push through the soil in spring. Then, uncover, unless you expect more frosts.

When the flowers begin to wither, pinch them off at the base to preserve nutrients which would otherwise be wasted on developing seedpods. The plants should be allowed to die down before they are cut off at their bases.

See also BULB, DAFFODIL.

NASTURTIUM   (*Tropaeolum*)

Including about 50 annual or perennial varieties, mostly climbing, nasturtiums are useful herbs in the kitchen and companion plants well known to many organic vegetable gardeners. The plants attract aphids away from susceptible fruits and vegetables in the garden. They also repel whiteflies and squash bugs when used as a repellent spray.

Common nasturtium (*T. majus*), also called Indian cress, is a tender annual with climbing stems and round, green leaves. It is one of the most popular annuals because of its showy flowers in many shades of yellow, orange and red. Large varieties climb as high as ten to 12 feet. Dwarf varieties include Tom Thumb types which grow in low, compact,

rounded bushes slightly less than one foot high and about a foot in diameter. These forms are excellent for bedding.

Nasturtiums do best in a sunny, well-drained location. When planted in a shady site or in wet ground, they tend to produce a large amount of foliage with relatively few flowers. Cultivate soil well before planting seed in spring after danger of frost is over. Cover seed with about one inch of soil, and firm well. Thin plants to about one foot apart. If soil is poor and hard, spade deeply and add several inches of finished compost to the soil surface.

The entire nasturtium plant—both flowers and young tender leaves—has a spicy, yet delicately pungent flavor similar to cress. It, like lettuce, is fine for salads and sandwiches. The seeds also make a fine snack in winter. Gather seed clusters when about half grown with some of the stem still attached. Clean,

When planted in a well-drained and very sunny spot, nasturtiums put forth plenty of bright yellow, orange or pink flowers.

and put them in a jar, covering with freshly boiled cider vinegar. Close lids tightly and store in a cool place.

Other varieties include the canary-bird flower (*T. peregrinum*), a tall-climbing annual with light yellow flowers, and dwarf nasturtium (*T. minus*), useful as a border plant.

NAVELWORT   (*Omphalodes*)

One annual species of navelwort (*O. linifolia*) grows about a foot tall and has white flowers, which resemble the forget-me-not. It thrives in moist, fertile soil in sun or partial shade. Full shade supports foliage but not flowers. For summer bloom, the seed should be sown in spring, about ⅛ inch deep, in the place where the plants are to grow. If sown in the fall, they will bloom early the following spring.

There are also two perennial species that grow eight inches high, with bright blue flowers. *O. cappodocica* is a fine subject for a shady spot in the rock garden, while *O. verna*, the creeping forget-me-not, is grown most often as a ground cover. Sow the seed in the spring, or divide the roots in spring or fall.

NEARING, SCOTT and HELEN

Scott (1883–   ) Helen (1904–   ) Because of his radical pacifist opinions and his outspoken criticism of American capitalist society, Scott Nearing was forced to give up his means of livelihood as a professor. With his wife, Helen, he moved to Vermont in 1932 to take up self-subsistent organic farming. The Nearings farmed there successfully for 19 years until encroaching ski resorts led them to abandon that farm and move to one in Harborside, Maine.

During those years in Vermont, Nearing and his wife, without the aid of machinery, built their own home of stone, revitalized the impoverished and eroded soil by organic means, and supported themselves by maple sugaring. They wrote about their experiences in *The Maple Sugar Book; Together with Remarks on Pioneering as a Way of Living in the Twentieth Century* (New York: Schocken Books, Inc., 1971).

Nearing and his wife, both vegetarians, grow vegetables and blueberries on five of their 100 acres in Maine for their own consumption as well as for sale or barter. They have no telephone or television, preferring to spend their time walking, reading or conversing with friends. Both enjoy music, and Mrs. Nearing plays the violin, organ and block flute. Winters are generally spent traveling.

Nearing is the author or coauthor with his wife of numerous books and articles, many of which are published by the Social Science Institute, an organization he founded.

Probably the most influential of the Nearings' books is *Living the Good Life: How to Live Sanely and Simply in a Troubled World* (New York: Schocken Books, Inc., 1971).

As much as any other single volume, this work gave impetus to and provided a focus for the back-to-the-land, homesteading movement of the early 1970's.

NECROSIS

Necrosis is the death of plant tissue and a common sign of disease. The condition is associated with rot, canker, blight, and wilt. *See also* DISEASE.

NECTAR

Nectar is the sweet secretion of plants which is collected and partially digested by bees to form honey. Nectaries, or plant glands that produce nectar, are usually located deep in the center of flowers, where the bees will be forced to brush past stamens and come in contact with the pistils, thus cross-pollinating as they move from flower to flower.

The nectary can be located in the calyx as in nasturtiums, deep in the spurs as in columbine, in furrows in the petals as in lilies, or in scales in petals as in ranunculus. Occasionally nectaries are found in leaf axils, or in parts of the plant not associated with fertilization. In this case, they may attract insects which will protect the plant in some way.

See also POLLINATION.

NECTARINE
(Prunus persica var. *Nectarina)*

Smooth-skinned, firm fruits, nectarines are usually slightly smaller than peaches and richer in flavor and aroma. They may be freestone or cling. Their culture is the same as that of peaches. They are grown more in California than in the East, and seem to do somewhat better west of the Rocky Mountains.

Nectarines may be grown from seed or from buds, though nectarine seed sometimes produces peaches. Sometimes both fruits are found on one tree, without cross-pollination, a phenomenon which has mystified growers for hundreds of years. Darwin called this strange, unpredictable behavior a bud mutation. It is also known as a bud sport.

Cherokee and Garden State are excellent varieties for the home orchardist in eastern states. In the West, gardeners can try Red Grand, Independence and Fantasia. Surecrop and Golden Prolific are good dwarf varieties.

See also FRUIT TREES, ORCHARD, PEACH.

NELUMBO   *See* LOTUS

NEMATODE

Nematodes or eelworms are quite tiny, sometimes as small as $\frac{1}{125}$ inch in length. Although most abundant in tropical areas, they occur in sizable numbers in all other parts of the world. Research has shown that almost every acre of land in the United States is infested with nematodes.

Without brains or eyesight, the nematodes move around in the soil in what appears to be an aimless pattern. The pattern, however, does have a direction, for they will head straight toward any root that is near them. Once they arrive, they pierce the root and feed on it, or lay their eggs in it, causing knots to form. A plant attacked by parasitic nematodes loses nourishment and becomes stunted, or dies.

Since there are also a number of free-living, nonparasitic nematodes associated with root systems of many plants, the finding of root knots is not always an indication that plants are suffering from nematode injury. Many other microorganisms, especially fungi, can cause serious root injury.

Nematodes cause their greatest damage when conditions of moisture and temperature are favorable. They are most active in soil suitable for germination and growth of plants, and considerable numbers may be killed by flooding the soil for extended periods or by permitting the soil to dry out completely.

Nematode activity diminishes rapidly as temperatures are lowered. Although cold will not destroy the nematodes, high temperatures can damage them. The sun often plays an important role in eliminating nematodes by baking the upper soil layer. Some nematodes, however, survive in protective egg shells, and when conditions again become favorable, these will multiply rapidly.

Methods of controlling parasitic nematodes are constantly being improved. Crop rotation

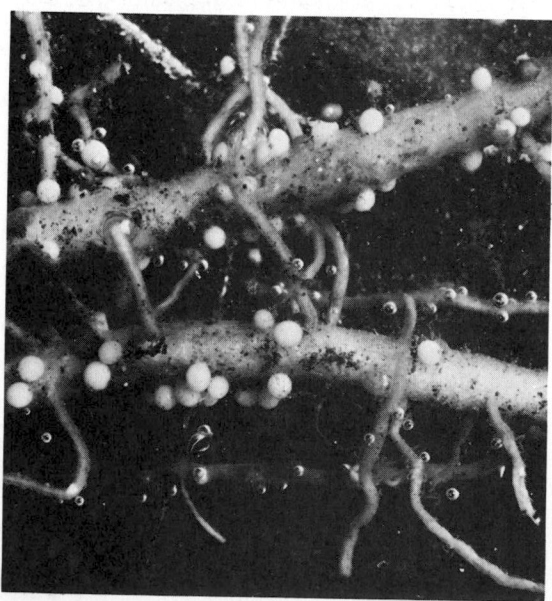

Nematodes have pierced these potato roots, fed on them and laid their eggs, causing knots to form.

is perhaps one of the most inexpensive, yet effective, measures. Nematodes, like other parasites, prefer certain types of plants to others. If a crop which is undesirable is planted, the parasites starve and their populations in the soil are reduced. Since some nematodes thrive on several different crops, the grower should be certain that the substitute crop is not one on which the nematodes can feed.

Fertilization of infected plants induces the formation of roots and improves plant vigor, thus compensating for nematode damage. Such improvements in plant growth are relatively short-lived, however.

When quantities of organic fertilizers are added to the soil around plants with roots parasitized by nematodes, the growth of organisms which prey on nematodes is encouraged. These organisms include bacteria, sporozoa, fungi, viruses, protozoa, predatory nematodes, tardigrades, enchytraeid worms, mites, and springtails.

The man most responsible for this research finding, Dr. C. L. Duddington, was a senior lecturer in botany at the Regent Street Polytechnic in London. In 1951, he made his first experiments, conducted in flowerpots on a roof in central London, to learn the value of a combination of organic materials and fungus cultures to stop nematode destruction. Later he made field tests with farm crops (mostly cereals and potatoes).

All experiments clearly showed that nematodes could be controlled by building up concentrations of beneficial fungi and organic matter in the soil.

Predaceous nematodes and nematode-trapping fungi are the two chief antagonists to plant-eating nematodes. Scientists have found that adding organic matter increases the numbers of the beneficial predators. Fungi proliferate on the organic matter, free-living nematodes feed on the fungi and increase in numbers, and predaceous nematodes increase at the expense of the free-living nematodes and indiscriminately attack larvae of root-knot nematodes.

Nematode-trapping fungi are also favored by organic amendments. There is much evidence that increasing organic matter content of the soil reduces crop loss from nematodes. These fungi are closely related to the blue mold penicillium but are invisible to the naked eye, so microscopically small are their threads. They achieve their results by virtually eating nematodes alive. Botanists refer to them as "predaceous fungi."

In their natural state, these fungi grow in decomposing vegetable matter and farmyard manure—and wherever there are nematodes. They are extremely widespread, easily isolated and harmless to crops, animals and human beings.

The fungi do their work of destruction in a number of ways. In some cases, the fine threads of the fungus have branches which form loops, and these loops in turn form three-dimensional networks something like crumpled wire netting.

The networks secrete a sticky fluid when they come into contact with the nematode, and the nematodes are caught as effectively as a fly by flypaper. After the fungus catches the nematode, it then sends branches into its body, and simply absorbs its contents.

Another way in which fungi trap nematodes is by sticky branches which reproduce rapidly and form little circular loops in which the worm is trapped.

These predaceous fungi can be encouraged by mulching. Plants such as bean, cantaloupe, celery, eggplant, lettuce, okra, pepper, squash, tomato, and watermelon are very susceptible to nematode injury and should be protected by a thick organic mulch piled around them. As the vegetable matter decays, fungi develop and begin to enter the bodies of nematodes.

NEMESIA

Half-hardy annuals of the Figwort family, nemesias are grown successfully as annuals in England and in parts of this country where the summers are very cool. Where summers are hot, they are started indoors in January or February and transplanted to the flower border by April 1. They will bloom through May and June, and then succumb to the summer heat.

Flowers somewhat resemble snapdragons in white, yellow or purple, with improved varieties of pink and orange. Leaves are small and opposite. The stems are not very strong, so the plants should stand about six inches apart for mutual support.

The most frequently grown species is *N. strumosa,* growing to two feet, with slender three-inch leaves and flowers in clusters to four inches in size. Flowers are white, yellow or purple with spotted throats and an orange or white beard. Variety Grandiflora has larger flowers; Nana-compacta is dwarfed; and Sutton has flowers in yellow, rose pink, orange, crimson, and scarlet.

NEMOPHILA

A genus of small, exquisite and hardy annuals of the Hydrophyllaceae that are native to California, nemophilas make good choices for beds, borders and low masses. The leaves are hairy, narrow and squarely notched on each side almost to midrib. The widely bell-shaped, usually single flowers bloom profusely from early spring to late summer. They are colored white, blue or purple and can be margined, veined or blotched.

Seed may be sown early in spring where plants are to stand. Nemophilas prefer partial shade, low ground and soil that has plenty of humus but is not necessarily rich.

Cultivated species include baby-blue-eyes, *N. Menziesii,* a low sprawling plant whose prostrate stems may grow to 20 inches. Its white-margined blue flowers rise six inches above the ground. *N. maculata,* another low-growing species, has white flowers with a deep purple spot at the tip of each petal. *N. aurita* climbs three to six feet over twigs or other plants by means of prickles at the base of its leaves. The blue or pale violet flowers are light around the edges with darker markings in the throat.

NEPENTHES   *See* PITCHER PLANT

NEPETA

Nepeta is a genus of aromatic annuals and perennials of the Mint family, Labiatea. The best-known species is catnip, *N. Cataria.*

Catnip, or catmint, is a sweet perennial growing to three feet. Its small white or pale lavender flowers grow in spikes to five inches and bloom from July to November. Propagate it by division in the spring or late fall.

It prefers light soil and full sun.

See also CATNIP.

NEPHROLEPIS

Called sword or ladder ferns, plants belonging to this genus are widely grown in the home. They can withstand poor conditions but will grow best in a rich mixture of sand, leaf mold and loam, and are propagated by

The most important species of Nephrolepis *is the* Boston fern *(*N. exaltata*) which thrives in the greenhouse or window garden and, in southern climates, can be planted outdoors.*

division or runners. Cultivated species seldom produce spores.

Tuber fern, *N. cordifolia,* grows from a rhizome bearing tubers, and has erect fronds up to two feet, with bright green, sharply toothed segments.

Basket fern, *N. pectinata,* is named because it is well adapted to culture in hanging baskets. Fronds are about 1½ feet long and one inch wide, with fine, toothed segments. Growth is compact.

Horticulturally, the most important species of *Nephrolepis* is the Boston fern, a variety of *N. exaltata.* Developed from a single plant in Boston sometime in the 1890's, it has been the source of many new varieties. Fronds of the species grow long and graceful, to five or six feet, with segments to three inches. An easily grown plant that will tolerate some neglect, the Boston fern is a good subject for the greenhouse or window garden. It is sometimes planted outdoors in the South. Propagation is by runners.

See also FERN.

NERIUM   *See* OLEANDER

NETTLES

Most nettles have stinging hairs on their leaves and stems. Many of them are part of the genus *Urtica,* which comprises 35 widely distributed varieties.

There are two principal kinds of nettles. One is false nettle (*Boehmeria cylindrica*) which grows mostly in rich, moist woods in deep shade or in shade along streams or lakes. The other is the stinging nettle (*Urtica dioica*), which is common on higher ground and often grows in full sunlight. The stinging nettle is a perennial plant and is usually found in dense patches.

Nettles are not generally poisonous, but they are irritating. The leaves are covered with hairs, which have broad bases, tapering toward the tip. At the slightest touch, the globular tip is knocked off, leaving a sharp point that easily penetrates the skin. At the same time, a noxious liquid oozes out of the hair into the skin, causing a burning sensation of short duration.

The wood nettle, also a perennial, produces itching similar to that caused by stinging nettles.

Both kinds have strongly developed root systems and a network of underground creeping rootstocks. One visible difference is in leaf arrangement, the wood nettle having alternate leaves and the stinging nettle opposite ones. Leaves of the wood nettle are also more often heart shaped.

Old herbalists viewed nettles as an effective weight-reducer. Nettle water made from the roots or seed was said to make a good hair tonic or cologne supplement. Medicinal qualities were also attributed to this perennial. Nettle was believed to be antiasthmatic and a treatment for consumption. Its seeds were used to counteract venomous bites. Nettle was even used to treat rheumatism.

Nettle is rarely cultivated, but more often it is found along roadsides, in empty lots and at dump sites. Nettles can be controlled by grubbing out the rootstocks and killed, where feasible, by drying. Mowing frequently, close to the ground, will prevent seed formation and exhaust the food reserves stored in the roots and rootstocks. Nettles are used today by wild food enthusiasts as a flavoring agent or vegetable. Boiled or steamed nettle foliage is a tasty vegetable, light and low in calories. The plant can also be added to salads and other dishes.

NEUTRAL

Neutral soils are ones that are neither acidic nor basic (alkaline). A pH of 7 indicates a completely neutral soil reaction.

See also ACIDITY–ALKALINITY, LIME.

NICOTIANA

Nicotiana is a genus of mostly native American annuals, perennials, and shrubby perennials of the Nightshade family, Solanaceae. Most are tropical plants. They are grown as annuals throughout the United States because they bloom freely the first year from seed. Included in the genus are commercially grown tobacco (*N. Tabacum*), Indian tobacco (*N. Bigelovii*), and several species called flowering tobacco which are used for ornament. The fragrant, tubular flowers are white, yellow, red, or purple and generally open at night. Leaves are usually large, hairy, and poisonous or narcotic. Flowers of potted nicotiana plants will stay open all day.

Though the ornamentals will self-seed, they are usually started indoors in flats or planted directly into the garden. Nicotianas prefer rich, moist loam in full sun, but will tolerate acid soil and partial shade.

Commercially grown tobacco is a striking annual growing to six feet. Its thin leaves are a foot long and the rose or red flowers, which open at night, are woolly and funnel shaped. Variety Macrophylla has larger leaves and is called Maryland tobacco. Virginia tobacco is variety Angustifolia. Indian tobacco grows to two feet and has white flowers and leaves seven inches long.

Flowering tobacco or jasmine tobacco (*N. alata*) is an ornamental growing to five feet. The tubular white flowers open at night. The rose or crimson flowers of *N. sylvestris* stay open all day but are not so fragrant. It is a shorter species, growing only to three feet.

An ornamental tree, tree tobacco (*N. glauca*) grows to 20 feet, with soft blue green foliage and yellowish flowers. It is naturalized in Texas and California, but is not hardy in the North.

NICOTINE

An extract of tobacco, nicotine can be used as a poison contact spray for sucking insects such as aphids. In the concentrated form in which it is sold, it is highly dangerous to human beings; even physical contact is dangerous. Nicotine in a sulfate solution is sometimes used to control serious insect infestations.

NIEREMBERGIA

The small plants of this half-hardy perennial (commonly called cupflower) bear showy white or pale lavender cup-shaped flowers that have purple centers. The small leaves, wiry stems and closely packed blossoms combine to make this a plant of fine texture that is good for edging, pots or window boxes. Nierembergia can be grown as an annual in the North if seeds are started in February or March. It does best in cool areas, and gardeners who live in regions having hot summers are apt to find it disappointing because it may produce good foliage but few flowers. It will not survive northern winters. The popular variety is Purple Robe.

NIGELLA

A genus of hardy annual herbs of the Buttercup family, Ranunculaceae, nigellas have blue or white flowers and misty-fine foliage with pinnate leaves. The seeds, which are enclosed in attractive horned pods, may be planted in fall for early bloom, and again in spring to prolong the blooming period. They are best sown where they are to grow, as they do not transplant readily. Nigellas prefer an open, sunny spot in the border but are not particular about soil. Their best use is in dried arrangements.

Love-in-a-mist (*N. damascena*) is the airiest species, the blue flowers blossoming separately in a cloud of fine green foliage. Plants grow 12 to 18 inches high but tend to have a short bloom period in warm areas.

Nutmeg flower (*N. sativa*) has less finely divided leaves which are slender but not threadlike, and do not surround the flowers. The flowers are blue, and the seeds, which are used like pepper, are enclosed in inflated pods.

NIGHT-BLOOMING CEREUS
See SELENICEREUS

NIGHT-BLOOMING FLOWERS

A garden of night-blooming flowers could be planted, composed of some flowers that open when the sun leaves them, some that open at midnight and others that are open on any cloudy day. Though many of the night-bloomers are tropical, and possibly open late in the day to escape a searing sun, there are enough temperate zone natives to fill a border for the pleasure of sunset gardeners.

Most night-blooming flowers are very fragrant, and many of them are white. Such exotics as night-blooming cereus, a lotus which opens at dusk and closes the next noon, or night-blooming jasmine must be grown in the greenhouse in the North. Lady-of-the-night and false aloe are also very tender night-bloomers.

Northern gardens may contain the following, which are all night-blooming and mostly fragrant: evening campion, evening stock, flowering tobacco, four-o'clock, gillyflower, *Gladiolus tristis,* honeysuckles of the *Heckrotti* species, night-blooming silene, night phlox, soapwort, and Thunberg daylily.

NIGHT PHLOX   *See* ZALUZIANSKYA
NIKKO FIR   *See* FIR

NINEBARK   (*Physocarpus*)

There are several species of ninebark, each one a hardy shrub with peeling bark and, in the spring, clusters of small white or pink flowers. *P. opulifolius* is widely cultivated in eastern gardens and is valued for its hardiness. It grows to nine feet with long, rounded leaves and a profusion of white blossoms. The variety Luteus has yellow or bronze foliage and Nana, a dwarf form, is an excellent hedge or border plant.

P. monogynus is grown in the West. Its flowers are pinkish and less showy than those of the eastern species.

Both ninebarks are quick-growing shrubs. They thrive in ordinary garden soil and enjoy sun or shade. As with any shrubs, prune them frequently to encourage dense growth.

See also SHRUBS.

stead of stiff. As a result, the plants are easily broken off or lodged by wind gusts. They are more susceptible to frost damage and to many diseases.

Nitrogen Availability: There are three basic sources of nitrogen in mineral soils. Most of the nitrogen in soils is associated with the organic matter, although varying amounts of nitrogen can be fixed by clay minerals in surface and topsoils. Soluble ammonium and nitrate compounds provide 1 to 2 percent of the total nitrogen present, except in soils where large amounts of chemical fertilizers are applied. These forms are particularly subject to volatilization and leaching.

NITROGEN

Nitrogen is one of the elements necessary for plant growth. Too much or too little nitrogen in the soil results in productivity decline. It must be constantly renewed and replaced in the soil.

Effects of Nitrogen: Nitrogen is directly responsible for the vegetative growth of plants above ground. With a good supply, plants grow sturdily and mature rapidly, their foliage a rich, dark green. In cereals, nitrogen is responsible for increasing the percentage of protein. Nitrogen also produces succulent crops.

Nitrogen deficiency is indicated by leaves which are yellowish or light green and often very small. The lower leaves are the first to show discoloration and they may even fall off before the problem is remedied.

Excesses of nitrogen can be more harmful than deficiencies. When crops take up too much of the element, they tend to rapidly develop tissues that are watery and weak in-

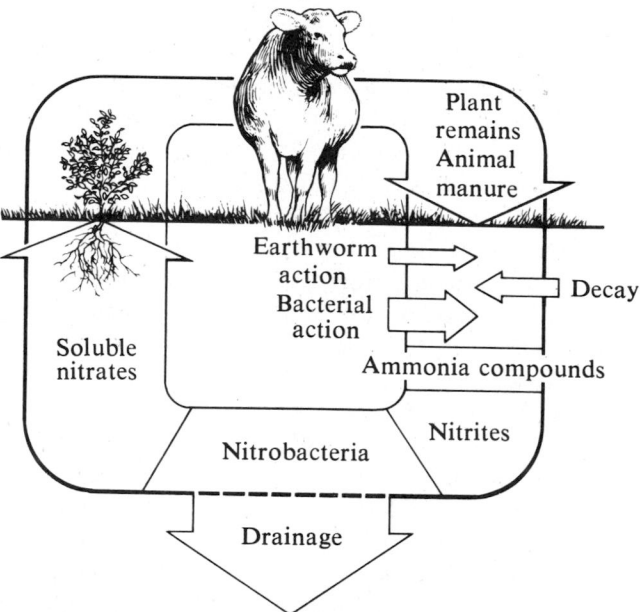

In its simplest form, the nitrogen cycle involves the conversion of atmospheric nitrogen to forms available to plants. As plant and animal materials decompose, earthworms and microorganisms convert these nitrites to nitrates, the form of nitrogen which plants utilize.

The intake and release of nitrogen in soils is achieved through a series of complicated biochemical transformations called the nitrogen cycle. Basically, nitrogen is added to the soil in the form of crop residues, green manures, ammonium and nitrate salts in rains, farm manures, or commercial fertilizers. This nitrogen undergoes many changes, especially when associated with organic matter. Proteins in organic matter are decomposed, and finally the nitrogen is changed into a nitrate form that higher plants or soil microorganisms can use. In this form, it can also be lost in volatilization or in drainage.

Nitrogen from organic matter is released slowly in a process called mineralization. In this way, a large amount of nitrogen is protected from loss but after being released through a natural decaying process, remains unavailable to higher plants. The entire process results in the release of ammonia, a form of nitrogen that is readily used by soil fungi and plants. In addition, certain bacteria, such as azotobacter, can use this form of nitrogen to produce nitrate nitrogen as an end product.

Chemical nitrogen fertilizers are a soluble form of nitrogen that is immediately taken up by plants. This results in luxury consumption and a much-too-rapid growth of plant stalks and foliage. Animals seem to sense when plants have too high a nitrogen content and will not eat them when something else is available. Forage containing high levels of nitrates can produce nitrate poisoning in cattle, and soil runoff in the form of nitrates can contaminate groundwater and pollute rivers.

Nitrate fertilizers also inhibit the production of ethylene in the soil, a gas important to soil and plant health. In addition, because there are large amounts of petroleum products used in producing chemical nitrogen fertilizers, they have become more scarce and expensive. As the supply of oil products decreases, nitrogen fertilizers will be harder to get and increasingly expensive.

Synthetic Forms: There are several main chemical fertilizers usually available for soil application. Urea is a synthetic containing 45 percent nitrogen. Composed of two parts of ammonia and one part of carbon dioxide, urea is a solid material manufactured from air and natural gas or coal. It can be dissolved and used as a leaf spray. Because it is similar to the natural urea in animal urine, it can burn plants if not handled carefully. In addition, synthetic urea contains biuret, a compound toxic to many plants when applied to soil or sprayed on foliage.

Urea-form, a derivative of urea, contains 37 to 39 percent nitrogen. It is a combination of urea and formaldehyde, the powerful preservative used in embalming fluids. Formaldehyde is dangerous to bacterial life in the soil.

Anhydrous ammonia, a by-product of the oil industry, is the most potent high-nitrogen fertilizer, containing about 82 percent nitrogen. Anhydrous ammonia comes bottled in cylinders for direct injection into the soil or for mixing with irrigation water. When anhydrous gas is dissolved in water, the resulting solution is sold as aqua ammonia, with a 20 to 24 percent nitrogen content.

Anhydrous ammonia is extremely caustic. Inhalation can cause death, and frostbite or extreme burns follow skin contact. Agronomists recommend that it be applied deeper and farther away from crop roots than any other chemical fertilizer. If it is put too close to the plant row, roots will be severely injured.

Organic Sources: Although none of the sources of organic nitrogen are as high in their nitrogen content as chemical fertilizers, they have many advantages. Many release their nitrogen slowly, over long periods of time, and do not have the tendency to burn plants as do chemical fertilizers. Manure is one of the best all-around fertilizers, although it does not have a particularly high nitrogen content. It is widely available and helps to build organic matter in the soil, a condition important to the action of soil microorganisms that release nitrogen. Rabbit droppings are one of the highest in nitrogen at 2 to 2½ percent. Hog and cow manures contain the least nitrogen. Manure should be kept indoors for best results; weather leaches out important nutrients.

NATURAL SOURCES OF NITROGEN

	Nitrogen (approx. %)
ANIMAL MATERIALS	
Bone meal (black)	2
Bone meal (raw)	2–4
Bone meal (steamed)	2–3
Bone tankage	3–10
Dried blood	10–14
Eggshells	1
Feathers	15
Fish (dried, ground)	8
Manure	
Cattle (excrement)	trace
Cattle (urine)	1
Horse (excrement)	trace
Horse (urine)	2
Poultry	2
Rabbit	2
Sheep (excrement)	1
Sheep (urine)	2
Swine (excrement)	1
Swine (urine)	trace
Meat meal	9–11
Oyster shells	trace
Sewage sludge (activated)	6
Sewage sludge (digested)	2
Wool waste	4–6
PLANT MATERIALS	
Beet waste	trace
Brewery waste	1
Castor pomace	4
Coffee waste	2
Corn fodder	trace
Corn silage	trace

	Nitrogen (approx. %)
Cornstalks	1
Cottonseed meal	7
Felt waste	14
Gluten meal	6
Grape pomace	1
Hay	
Alfalfa	2
Bluegrass	1
Clover	2
Cowpea	3
Millet	1
Pea	2–3
Red clover	2
Salt	1
Soybean	2–3
Timothy	1
Vetch	3
Leaves	
Apple	1
Cherry	1
Grape	trace
Oak	1
Peach	1
Pear	1
Raspberry	1
Nutshells	3
Oats, green fodder	1
Peanut shells	1
Pine needles	1
Seaweed dry)	1–2
Seaweed (fresh)	trace
Tea grounds	4
Tobacco stems	3
Wheat bran	3

Other sources of nitrogen are not as available as manure and are probably more expensive. Cottonseed meal, at 7 percent nitrogen, is somewhat acidic and is good for blueberries and other acid-loving plants. If applied to other vegetables, add lime. Feather meal, an excellent source of slowly released nitrogen, is a by-product of the poultry industry and contains about 15 percent nitrogen. Blood meal, although rich in nitrogen, is hard to get. Because of its expense, it is best used only on small plots or perhaps on ornamentals. Fish scraps are high in nitrogen.

Sewage sludge can be used as a nitrogen fertilizer on some crops. Activated sludge contains more nitrogen than digested sludge by as much as 4 percent and is usually sterilized before being made into fertilizer. It is generally not recommended for use on vegetables or plant parts eaten directly, but otherwise is considered safe.

Legumes: Legumes and a few non-legumes have the ability to fix nitrogen in the soil from vast quantities of atmospheric nitrogen available—about 75 million tons per acre. Nitrogen fixation actually occurs through the action of bacteria contained in root nodules ranging from a pinhead to a BB in size. These bacteria are known as *Rhizobium*. *R. meliloti* affects sweet clover and alfalfa, *R. trifolium* the clovers, and *R. japonicum* affects soybeans.

The *Rhizobium* can fix a surprising amount of nitrogen per acre, especially when associated with sweet clover or alfalfa. In a ten-year experiment at Ithaca, New York, researchers found that alfalfa fixed 251 pounds of nitrogen per acre, sweet clover 168, red clover 151, soybeans 105, and field peas 48. For optimum results, proper aeration, drainage, moisture, pH, and calcium are important. In soils high in nitrogen, nodulation and fixation are reduced. Legumes are virtually essential to crop rotations on an organic farm.

See also AZOTOBACTER, CARBON-NITROGEN RATIO, COMPOSTING, FERTILIZER, LEGUME, MANURE, SEWAGE SLUDGE, SOIL DEFICIENCIES.

NODE

A node is the point on a stem at which a leaf, bud or branch originates. The space between nodes is called the internode. The presence of nodes distinguishes an underground stem from a root. New plants arise from nodes in propagation by suckers, stolons, rhizomes, and runners.

NODULE

A nodule is a rounded mass of irregular shape, such as the tubercle found on the root

Through the action of bacteria contained in root nodules, legumes change atmospheric nitrogen into forms available to plants.

of a legume, which contains colonies of nitrogen-fixing bacteria.

See also LEGUME.

NORWAY SPRUCE
See CHRISTMAS TREE FARMING, SPRUCE

NPK

NPK is the abbreviation for nitrogen, phosphorus and potash, the major plant nutrients.

The NPK ratio is understood to mean the proportion of these three ingredients in a fertilizer. Thus, a fertilizer labeled 10–10–5 contains 10 percent nitrogen, 10 percent phosphorus and 5 percent potassium (potash). The manufacturers and blenders of chemical fertilizers are able to mix a fertilizer to almost any NPK ratio but this is more difficult with organic fertilizers.

See also FERTILIZER, CHEMICAL.

NUBIAN GOATS   *See* GOATS

NURSE CROP

A nurse crop is sown to give protection to another crop. For example, crimson clover is often sown with a nurse crop of buckwheat or cowpeas to protect it from the sun. Usually the nurse crop is thinly sown and is cut as soon as the main crop has become established and no longer needs the protection.

See also COMPANION PLANTING.

NUTGRASS   *(Cyperus esculentus)*

Also called nutsedge, nutgrass is very difficult to eradicate once it gets beyond the hand-picking stage. Trials have shown that it is severely discouraged by growing a heavy cover of cowpeas on the plot for one or more summers. As soon as possible, in early summer, sow cowpeas thickly, apply a large amount of compost and allow them to become heavily matted to shade the soil. The vines should be plowed or dug into the soil in October.

NUTRIENTS   *See* FERTILIZER

NUTSHELLS

Nutshells are often used as a mulch or for composting. The composition of nutshells varies according to the nuts. Almond shells and pecans decay readily; black walnut shells which contain greater amounts of lignin, take longer; filberts and English walnuts decompose without trouble. Analysis of coconut shells is given as 2.5 percent nitrogen, 1 percent phosphoric acid and 2.5 percent potash.

See also MULCH.

NUT TREES

In addition to producing a nutritious and valuable crop, nut trees are attractive, hardy, very productive, and easy to plant and care for. They range in size from small bushy plants, like the filbert, to spreading protective giants, like the black walnut. Land planted with nut trees can also be used to grow crops such as lettuce, radishes and potatoes that do not require full sun for best growth. Nut trees eventually provide high-quality lumber.

Pound for pound, very few crops can match nuts for food value. They are rich in protein, oils, calcium, phosphorus, iron, and vitamins. Often substituted for meat, they are our most concentrated food, having a higher proportional food and calorie value than meats, grains, fruits, or vegetables.

Nut trees grown in the United States include the almond, black walnut, butternut, Chinese chestnut, chinquapin, English walnut, filbert, heart nut, hickory, pecan, and pistachio.

Where to Plant: Nut trees can be used as ornamentals around the home and to provide shade for livestock in pasture. They can be planted along roadsides and streambeds, providing the land is well drained, and they often form part of a permanent fencerow. Planted on steep hillsides they are used to prevent erosion, and they can make productive a spot too stony or rough to be tilled.

For maximum production, the planting site should be well drained and fertile. Avoid frost pockets. Try to plant on hillsides and in places with good air drainage.

Spacing: Root systems of nut trees are extensive. Mature pecan trees have a root spread at least twice that of the branches, and the roots of four or five evenly spaced trees will occupy most of the soil on an acre. Only by providing and maintaining adequate space for the roots of each tree can the mineral nutrients and moisture required for best growth and largest crops be assured. Allow sufficient sunlight to reach lower limbs and encourage the productivity of these limbs. As a rule, allow about 50 feet between nut trees in all directions. Pecans may be planted 35 feet apart in rows spaced 70 feet apart. Chestnuts should be spaced about 30 feet apart. Filberts can be grown as close as six to eight feet, in which case they form a dense shrub.

Before the trees reach their full size, ground under them can be planted with vegetables, fruits or smaller trees which can be removed when they begin to compete for nutrients with the nut trees.

Choosing Trees: Consult local nurseries and the state experiment station for information on varieties suited to local conditions and climate. Newly developed varieties, like the Carpathian walnut, are hardy enough to produce good crops even in the North. When planning a nut orchard, keep in mind that certain species are self-sterile; that is, they *must* be cross-pollinated with pollen of another variety if satisfactory crops are to be produced. These include the almond, chestnut and filbert. Though all walnut, pecan and hickory species are self-fertile, cross-pollination is recommended to insure a better set of nuts with larger and better filled kernels.

If possible, choose a medium-size budded or grafted tree. Small trees are likely to be stunted, unless specifically tagged as one-year trees, and larger trees often suffer in transplanting.

Planting and Culture: Keep tree roots covered and moist until you are ready to plant. If not to be planted immediately, they should be heeled-in for protection. *See also* HEEL-IN.

The best time to plant depends on the climate. Where the earth does not freeze, trees may be planted in December or January. In

NUTRITIVE VALUE OF NUTS PER CUP

Nut	Calories	Protein (gm.)	Fat (gm.)	Calcium (mg.)	Iron (mg.)	Vit. A (IU)	Vit. B₁ (mg.)	Vit. B₂ (mg.)	Niacin (mg.)	Vit. C (mg.)
Almond (unblanched, shelled)	848	26.4	76.8	361	6.2	. . .	.25	.67	4.6	trace
Brazil nut (shelled)	905	20.2	92.3	260	4.8	trace	.86	. . .	. . .	. . .
Cashew (roasted, shelled)	1,312	41	109.6	104	11.2	. . .	1.4	.40	4.8	. . .
Coconut meat (shelled)	359	3.4	34.7	21	2	. . .	.10	.01	.2	2
Filbert (shelled)	1,520	28.8	138.4	656	8.8	224	.88	. . .	. . .	. . .
Hickory nut (shelled)	1,616	35.2	152.8	. . .	. . .	. . .	. . .	. . .	. . .	. . .
Peanut (roasted, shelled)	1,272	60.8	100.8	168	4	. . .	.72	.32	36.8	. . .
Pecan (halved)	696	9.4	73	74	2.4	50	.72	.11	.9	2
Walnut, black (shelled)	672	18.3	58.2	83	2.1	70	.33	.11	1.2	. . .
Walnut, English (halved)	645	15	64.4	83	2.1	30	.48	.13	1.2	3

the North they should be planted in late fall or early winter, after they have become completely dormant.

Holes for trees should be large enough so the root is covered and not bent in an unnatural position. Trim the ends off any broken roots. Set the tree one to two inches deeper than it grew in the nursery. Settle the roots gently as you fill the hole with moist, rich topsoil. Tamp firmly to avoid air pockets. Water well to settle the soil, leaving a slight basinlike depression to catch rain. Stake trees where winds prevail, and wrap the trunks loosely with burlap, cornstalks or similar materials during the first winter. This will prevent drying and sunscald. Protect the tree's tender bark from rodents and rabbits by pushing a ring of wire mesh about ten inches wide into the ground around the tree.

The tree must be thoroughly watered as soon as it is planted. Soak the ground so that the water remains on top for several minutes. After growth starts in the spring, water the trees thoroughly once a week, unless there has been a heavy rain, but be careful not to over-water. Nut trees do not flourish in a swamp.

Following planting, cut back the top of the young tree to match the pruning done to the roots. At one year, the top should be cut off six or seven buds above the graft union and the cut surface sealed. Stake one shoot to form the tree trunk and pinch back other growth above the union to strengthen the lower trunk.

Mulch around each tree with compost to conserve moisture and provide a continual supply of nutrients. The most economical way to maintain soil fertility is through the use of winter-hardy, leguminous green manures. Summer legumes may be used in addition to winter legumes in young nonbearing orchards if enough open ground is maintained around the trees to prevent too much competition for nutrients and moisture. *See also* COVER CROP, GREEN MANURE.

Harvesting and Storing: For the mildest, best flavor and lightest color, nuts should be hulled within a week of harvest, and then washed thoroughly. The nuts should be stored in a cool, dark, well-ventilated place. A period of curing, from two to six weeks, is recommended before use. Cracked nut meats are best stored in the refrigerator or freezer to keep oils from turning rancid.

See also entries for individual nuts, INSECT CONTROL, ORCHARD.

NYMPHAEA

Nymphaea is a genus of aquatic flowers consisting of about 40 species of showy flowers which float on top of the water, or stand near the surface. The flowers, which are white, pink, red, yellow, or blue, can open during the day or night, depending on the species. The large, usually round leaves are dark green on top and liver-colored underneath. Both leaves and flowers float at the ends of long rubbery stems arising from rootstocks that are buried in mud at the bottom of the pond. All species are perennial, but some are tender in cool climates. Numerous hybrids have been developed.

Culture: *Nymphaea* may be propagated by seed or root division. The seed is sometimes very hard, and will germinate more quickly if filed or sawed. It may then be started in a pot submerged in water indoors, or may be rolled in a ball of clay and dropped into the pond where it is to grow. Similarly, roots may be divided and started indoors in a submerged pot, or may be planted immediately in the pond, where they will need to be anchored with a weight. Tuberous plants are always started indoors until new tubers have developed. All need rich soil and full sun, and should be submerged under one to two feet of water.

It is a good idea to grow all water lilies in bushel-sized tubs, as this makes moving them easier. In northern areas, all tropical species must be taken out of the pond and stored damp in a cellar over the winter.

Fill the container with four parts rich soil and one part rotted or dried cow manure. Press the roots into this mixture and cover the surface with a layer of pebbles or sand to keep soil from washing out. Place the tub on some flat rocks on the pond bottom. Hardy water lilies can have nine to 12 inches of water over them, while tropicals should be submerged in only four to six inches of water.

Three species are commonly known as lotus. They are *N. caerulea,* Egyptian blue lotus; *N. Lotus,* the Egyptian white lotus; and *N. stellata,* blue lotus.

Grow Nymphaea Lotus *in a large tub at the floor of the pond.*
(Courtesy of Longwood Gardens)

European white water lily or platterdock (*N. alba*) is hardy, with flowers four or five inches across that are open all day. Variety Candidissima has early-spring blooms which continue until frost. Rubra is a red variety.

N. capensis, the Cape water lily, is a tender species with leaves that grow to 16 inches in diameter. Its large, light blue flowers, six to eight inches across, open four days in a row, instead of the usual three.

One of the largest is the Australian water lily (*N. gigantea*) with leaves 18 inches across, and flowers growing to 12 inches. Flowers are light blue, with petals tipped with dark blue, and they open seven days each.

The yellow water lily (*N. mexicana*) grows from a tuberous rootstock, which spreads by means of runners. Bright yellow, four-inch flowers open for the afternoon, standing several inches above the water.

The fragrant water lily (*N. odorata*) has small flowers, about three to five inches across, that appear in the morning. The type is white, but pink and yellow varieties are known to grow wild in the eastern United States.

A tender species which grows in Africa (*N. micrantha*) has elliptical leaves about six by ten inches, and deep blue flowers which will open only when the sun shines.

The India red water lily (*N. rubra*) is almost as large as gigantea. It is a night-blooming species, open until almost noon of the following day.

Pygmy water lily (*N. tetragona*) has flowers that are under two inches across, and leaves about three to four inches in diameter. It is a hardy species, growing as far north as Ontario. Flowers are white or yellow, and they all open in the afternoon.

Magnolia or tuberous water lily (*N. tuberosa*) is one of the handsomest, with white flowers four to nine inches across. The variety Richardson has so many petals they form a globe when open. Hybrids are pink, red and yellow.

See also LOTUS.

NYSSA

Nyssa is a genus of marsh trees grown in the southern United States for ornament. They are grown from seed, and sold burlapped and balled.

Cotton gum or large tupelo (*N. aquatica*) grows to 100 feet, has seven-inch, smooth edged leaves, and dark blue fruit less than an inch long.

Pepperidge, also called sour gum (*N. sylvatica*), grows to about the same size, but has leaves about half as large. It is difficult to transplant this species from the wild state, but the bright red fall foliage makes the pepperidge attractive as an ornamental. It is suited to rich, moist garden soils.

O

OAK (*Quercus*)

The oaks are beautiful landscaping trees and are a prized source of fine lumber. The wood is much used in flooring and furniture and makes excellent firewood. Oak leaves are lobed or toothed, except on the live and willow oaks. A few species are evergreen. Oaks flower early in the spring, and many have edible acorns, popular with squirrels, birds, pigs and, at one time, with people.

Oaks are very long-lived, but somewhat slow growing. Specimens over 800 years old have been found. With a few exceptions, they prefer a rich, fairly heavy and damp clay soil. Oaks are usually propagated by planting the acorns in the fall as soon as they drop from the tree. Acorns can also be stored over the winter in damp moss or sand. Sometimes cuttings are taken or layers are used to increase evergreen species, and the hybrid oaks are propagated by grafting in the winter under glass. All except the white oak transplant easily.

There are over 200 species of oaks. A few, such as the chinquapin oak, are shrubby, but most are handsome shade trees. A few of

Common Name	Botanical Name	Height in feet	Evergreen	Region
Black oak	Q. velutina	100		Widely distributed
California field oak	Q. agrifolia	70	Yes	Southern California
Cork oak	Q. Suber	60	Yes	South
Engelmann oak	Q. Engelmanni	40	Yes	Southwest
Holm oak	Q. Ilex	60	Yes	South
Laurel oak	Q. Laurifolia	60	Yes	Central states, South
Live oak	Q. virginiana	60	Yes	South
Maul oak	Q. chrysolepis	80	Yes	West
Pin oak	Q. palustris	80		Central states, North
Post oak	Q. stellata	100		Widely distributed
Red oak	Q. rubra	90		East
Scarlet oak	Q. coccinea	80		Widely distributed
Shingle oak	Q. imbricaria	60		Central states
Swamp white oak	Q. bicolor	60		Widely distributed
Valley white oak	Q. lobata	100		California, South
Water oak	Q. nigra	80		South, Coastal states
White oak	Q. alba	100		Widely distributed
Willow oak	Q. phellos	60		Widely distributed
Yellow chestnut oak	Q. Muehlenbergii	100		Widely distributed

The white oak is highly valued for its lumber and is one of the largest and hardiest shade trees.
(Courtesy of U.S. Forest Service)

the medium-sized oaks are evergreen, but the larger ones are deciduous and hardy.

See also ACORN.

OAT HULLS   *See* HULLS, MULCH

OATS   (*Avena sativa*)

Oats rank highest in protein and rival wheat as the most nutritious of the cereal grains. New varieties can yield as much as 22 percent protein on a dry basis. Oats out-rank other cereal grains in thiamine (.82 percent), calcium (1.6 percent), iron (4.1 percent), and fat (7 percent), but rank lowest in carbohydrates (70.2 percent).

Planting: Oats like more water than other cereal grains, and will in general per-form better on fertile clay loams, although they will grow on any fairly fertile soil. It is possible, too, that soil can be too rich in nitro-gen for oats. If a previous oat crop was dark green in color and much of it fell over (lodged) before harvest, use no nitrogen but add ten pounds of phosphorus or potassium per acre. If the oats are short and light green and ripen to a flat tan, the soil needs 60 pounds of nitro-gen, 15 pounds of phosphorus and 20 to 30 pounds of potassium. Such amounts of fertilizer can be added organically at a reasonable cost. A green manure crop with added stable manure turned in, lime, and two tons of phosphate rock per acre applied every three years should be sufficient for a good yield.

Plant spring oats early. Oats like cool, moist weather. Ground for planting should be plowed and disked in the fall so that it will warm up faster in the spring. The finer the seedbed, the better. As soon as you can get in the fields in the spring, broadcast or plant by drill at a depth of two inches. The usual rate for oats is 2½ bushels per acre, but if you are broadcasting you might want to plant three bushels per acre to get a good stand. If broadcasting, run over the field with a har-row when you are finished, to bury the seed. Planting is similar to wheat planting.

In the garden, broadcast your seed by hand, scattering it as evenly as possible over the plot. Run the tiller over the ground lightly.

Oats should be planted in soil that has been kept relatively weed-free, since you won't be able to cultivate once the crop is planted.

Pests and Diseases: Oats have fewer enemies than other grain crops. An occasional insect pest is greenbug, a type of aphid usually controlled by a natural predator. Destroy volunteer oats, wheat and barley which could serve as a host for the insect.

Crown rust is the most important disease of oats. Preventive maintenance is important. Buckthorn is an alternate host, so destroy buckthorn bushes in nearby fields or gardens. Resistant varieties also help to prevent the disease.

Septoria leaf blight, another fungal disease, attacks many cereal crops including oats. Crop rotation and the use of resistant varieties are the best defenses.

Harvesting: Oats can be harvested for grain, hay or silage, although the latter is impractical for a homestead. For grain, harvest (with a grain combine) when the oats are dead ripe, or cut and windrow the oats when they are not quite ripe. The stalks will ripen in the windrow and the grain can then be combined directly from the windrow with a special combine attachment.

Small patches of oats are best handled as hay. Cut the oats before they are dead ripe when they are in the early milk stage and allow them to dry on the ground for a day or two. Stack, cover with plastic to keep off the rain, and feed stalk, grain and all to livestock, or store the hay loose in the barn. Larger acreages can be harvested and baled with a secondhand baler bought from a used equipment dealer or at a farm auction. Bales are easy to stack in the barn. If you can find a neighbor who builds haystacks, see if he can tell you how to build an outdoor haystack that doesn't need to be covered; it is a dying art.

Oats can also be harvested when grain is just beginning to harden by bundling and shocking like you would wheat. This way, the bundles can be stored in the barn, stacked like wood with the grain heads inside to protect them from rats. Feed the whole oats as needed. Rodent control will be necessary if the grain is stored this way, so keep several cats in the barn near the oat stack.

Oats for your own use can be threshed and winnowed the same as wheat.

Using: You can feed oats, stalk and all, to most animals. Ground or rolled oats can be fed with corn to dairy cattle, and whole oats (hulls and all) are excellent poultry feed.

Unfortunately, removing the hull from oats is a process not yet practical for the homesteader. Commercial oat processors roast the grain at 180°F. (82.22°C.) for an hour and a half to make it easier to hull, then rub the grains lightly between emery stones or Carborundum disks set so precisely that they just rub off the hull and do not damage the groat. Modern mills use a centrifugal impact huller with a rotor that throws the grains against a hard rubber liner. The force of the impact knocks off the hull and blows it away. The grain or groat is then passed through steel rollers and dried for oatmeal.

You might be able to remove some of the hulls by putting some grain in the blender and running it lightly. Hulls are not good tasting, despite their value in the diet as fiber, so oats are usually grown primarily for livestock feed.

Varieties: Common white oats are the most widely grown. They are spring planted and harvested in midsummer. Red oats are planted in the southern and south central states in fall for harvest the next summer. They require a mild winter. Naked oats are a rarely grown third type.

Except for the difference in planting time, the distinction between white and red oats is often vague. Many varieties of each have both types in their parentage. There are many varieties of oats available, but the life of any one variety is apt to be short—about five to ten years, or the time it takes disease organisms to become adapted to the variety's inbred resistance. In addition, new varieties such as Dal and Otee are being developed for high protein content. Some older varieties have been proven reliable even today—Cherokee, Clinton and Bonda among them. These three enjoy a good milling reputation, providing a high amount of oatmeal per total weight. However, no one variety of oats seems better for oatmeal than another. Your best bet when choosing a variety of oats is to check with your extension agent or with neighboring farmers and find out what varieties of oats they grow.

OCOTILLO   *See* VINE CACTUS

ODONTOGLOSSUM

Only a few species of this epiphytic orchid are cultivated in this country. They are natives of mountainous regions in Central America and must be grown in a cool greenhouse. Their showy flowers are borne on long, slender stalks, usually in racemes, and one to three inches wide. Slightly curled leaves rise from each pseudobulb.

O. grande, the tiger or clown orchid, has large, waxy, long-lasting flowers, yellow and striped with brown, with the lip white. It blooms in late summer or early fall. *O. pendulum* bears drooping sprays of delicate violet and pink flowers in the spring.

O. crispum has many variations, ranging from a pure white to yellow and rose, including various highly spotted forms. As many as 20 blooms may spring from each spike. It is sometimes called a perpetual bloomer, because it may flower at different times of the year as the bulbs are completed; most often, however, it blooms in early spring.

There are over 100 species and many more hybrids of *Odontaglossum,* of all habits and colors, but most of them are difficult to obtain.

See also ORCHIDS.

OGDEN, SAMUEL ROBINSON

(1896–   ) In 1929, Sam Ogden and his family left their established city life for a life of self-sufficiency in the Vermont countryside. It was not easy, and in *This Country Life* (1973) Ogden explains his philosophy and offers some practical advice to those who think they might like the rural life. Another book, *Step-by-Step to Organic Vegetable Growing* (1976), is valuable reading for organic growers seeking to produce superior vegetables.

Over the years Ogden's bountiful organic harvests have become something of a legend in Vermont, and many area restaurant chefs have come to him for produce.

His other works include *America the Vanishing: Rural Life and the Price of Progress* (ed., 1969); *How to Grow Food for Your Family* (1942); *New England Vegetable Garden* (1973); *Pan and Griddle Cakes* (1973).

OIL SPRAY   *See* DORMANT-OIL SPRAY

OKRA   (*Abelmoschus esculentus*)

Okra is primarily a hot-weather tropical vegetable that can be grown in both northern and southern gardens. A tall-growing annual often called gumbo, it grows best in the southern states, where two crops of it can be grown in a single year.

Culture: The spring okra crop can be planted as soon as all danger of frost has passed. In most mild regions, plant the fall crop from June 1 to July 1. The fruits can be harvested from 55 to 65 days after seeding, depending on the variety. Always plant seed when the earth has warmed, since okra is a warm-weather plant and will not stand cool weather and soil.

Planting: Okra thrives in any well-drained, good garden soil in full sunlight. If the soil is wet, the seed tend to rot, so good drainage is necessary. Okra is hard to transplant, but in very northern places the seed can be started in cold frames or hotbeds and transplanted into the garden with caution.

Although okra will do well in any kind of ground, thorough preparation of the soil is very important. These woody plants can take on all the food given them. Because okra grows rapidly, nitrogen is particularly needed. Poultry manure is splendid material for okra beds. Since it is very strong, only about one-tenth as much chicken manure as other animal manures can be used. Compost, leaf mold, peat moss, and wood ashes can be used to advantage to improve poor soil in the garden. Peat moss and leaf mold are usually acid and a slight amount of lime should be used along with either of these two materials. These soil builders should be plowed under in the winter well before the planting time, or in a small home garden they can be spaded under in the early spring.

The rows should be at least three to five feet apart. The stalks are bushy and can become quite large when well fertilized and during rainy seasons. Scatter the seed in drills or plant loosely in hills and cover to a depth of one to two inches, according to the compactness of the soil. The seed should be separated three or four inches to allow space for the development of the stems. If weather is warm, germination should take place within a few days. But if there is a heavy rainfall in the meanwhile, the soil should be lightly cultivated between the rows and the crust broken up over the seed by means of a garden rake. This is suggested where the soil contains clay or is heavy. Sandy loam will probably not need any such treatment, as the seed will come through when the soil has been drained or the water has been evaporated by the action of the sun. After plants become established, thin them to stand 15 inches apart and mulch lightly.

Insects: The okra plant is not subject to attack from many insects, but the bollworm may be a problem. It bores into the pods and thus injures them. The stinkbug also attacks the pods, piercing them and extracting the juices. Since damage from the latter occurs late in the season, the loss is very little. Blister beetles and leaf beetles often feed upon the foliage of okra but these pests do little harm to the pod and scarcely influence the production of pods at all. Handpicking usually keeps these insects well under control. *See also* INSECT CONTROL.

Harvesting: For continuous production, pods should be gathered every day when they are one to four inches long, depending on the

Okra pods should be harvested daily when they are one to four inches long and still soft.

variety. They should still be soft and the seed should be only half grown if pods are to be eaten. If it is necessary to keep the pods over 24 hours, they should be spread out in a cool place and slightly moistened. They should be given ventilation because they become heated when kept in closed crates or boxes.

Varieties: The Dwarf Green Long Pod matures in 50 days, as does the Perkins Mammoth, sometimes called Green Long Pod. White Velvet takes 60 days to mature but this is the standard okra for many markets in the South. The Clemson Spineless okra mature in about 60 days and has uniform dark green spineless, long pods. Emerald is another variety often planted.

OLD-MAN-AND-WOMAN
See HOUSELEEK

OLD-MAN'S-BEARD
(*Chionanthus virginicus*)

Sometimes called the fringe tree, this exceptionally beautiful shrub of the Olive family bears loose panicles of pure white, scented flowers in June, and egg-shaped dark blue berries in the fall. In autumn, the foliage turns a glorious yellow. It grows about 20 feet or so high in reasonably good, moist loam soils and full sun, and in the wild is hardy north to New Jersey in sheltered positions. A later-blooming variety, the Chinese fringe tree, *C. retusus,* is somewhat less hardy and grows ten to 12 feet high. Both are propagated by seed, layers or cuttings, or by budding or grafting onto the ash.

OLEANDER (*Nerium Oleander*)

This spectacularly beautiful evergreen shrub or small tree is hardy in Florida and southern California, and sometimes is grown in slightly cooler regions where winter protection is provided. It grows from eight to 20 feet high, with white, pink, red, or purple flowers that are often double. The most popular variety is called the rosebay because of its rose-colored, long-lasting double blooms. There are deep cream and velvety crimson varieties, and some with single peach-blossom-pink blooms. Scented varieties may be listed as *N. odorum.*

Culture: Oleanders are used outdoors for specimens, hedges and sidewalk plantings. The rosebay is a favorite street or avenue ornamental. It is able to stand hot, dry, dusty conditions and prefers a sunny location. It likes a sandy soil and will give an incredible profusion of blooms if fed with compost, rotted manure or other organic fertilizers. A mulch and heavy watering in drought periods are also advised. A rapid grower, the oleander can easily be pruned to be a medium-sized or large, wide shrub or a handsome symmetrical tree. It blooms from May to October. Propagation is by layers, or by cuttings of mature wood started in winter in porous soil.

Where it is not hardy, the oleander is often grown as a highly decorative tub plant or as a potted plant for the house. In tubs, it needs a soil made up of equal parts of sand, loam, peat moss, and leaf mold or humus. With careful pruning, it can be shaped into a pleasing form in late winter. Keep it outdoors during the summer months then, just before frost, bring it indoors to a cool spot such as the cellar. Water only occasionally during this rest period and don't fertilize the plant. Before putting it outdoors in the spring, water and feed regularly through the blooming period.

In the house, oleanders in pots will flower from the middle of spring to early summer, if they have been kept fairly dry and at a temperature of close to 50°F. (10°C.) during the winter. Put them in a sunny window and increase the watering about the first week in March. The plants should be sunk in the sunny garden bed for the summer.

The sap of oleander is extremely poisonous, and small children should be cautioned against it.

OLEARIA *See* TREE ASTER

OLEASTER (*Elaeagnus angustifolia*)

Also called the Russian olive, the oleaster is a shrub or small tree growing ten to 20 feet high. It is hardy in the far North and is planted throughout the United States for its handsome silvery foliage and fragrant yellow, bell-shaped flowers. The sweet, mealy berries are edible. The shrub is useful for wildlife plantings and provides homes and food for bees. The dry, fallen leaves are sometimes eaten by cattle, goats and sheep. The shrub is highly resistant to drought and wind, and tolerant of alkali and city smoke. As a windbreak or shelterbelt, oleasters can be planted five to six feet apart. They are also good for seaside gardens.

Oleaster does well on many sites, and on soils from sandy and dry to alkaline and it will succeed in partial shade. But for best growth in the garden, it prefers a moist, rich soil and open sunlight. It makes a good street tree if the lower branches are pruned while the tree is young. Stratified seed sown the second year will give new plants. The shrub can also be propagated by cuttings, grafting or layering.

OLIVE   (*Olea europaea*)

The olive is a hardy evergreen tree of the subtropics whose fruit is pickled or made into olive oil. It is a very beautiful tree and exceptionally long-lived. Some specimens in the Mediterranean area have been bearing over 1,500 years. Of the hundreds of varieties cultivated most come from France, Italy, Spain, and Tunisia. In the United States, olives are grown commercially mainly in lower California and parts of Arizona. There the trees are generally about 25 feet high, with silvery foliage and fragrant panicles of white blooms, followed by plumlike fruits in late autumn.

Planting and Culture: The olive tree likes heat and needs a long, comparatively dry season. Most species endure temperatures as low as 15°F. (−9.44°C.), but the fruit itself is injured by the slightest frost. Although it grows well in the lower South, it sets fruit only occasionally there because of the relatively high humidity.

Olive trees are propagated by seed or cuttings. A common practice is to change the variety of older trees by top-grafting. Olive trees are not exacting as to soil requirements, providing they have good drainage. Open, sandy loams or clay loams are ideal. In poor soils, nitrogen is usually the crop-limiting element. Olives are moderately tolerant of salt and alkaline soil. Irrigation is practiced in most commercial groves, and the fruit is commonly

thinned to overcome the trees' tendency to alternate bearing. Correct pruning and spacing of the trees are vital, as shade can considerably lower yields. The few pests and diseases are easily controlled by sanitation.

Harvesting: When planted from 25 to 40 feet apart, the trees start to bear in four to eight years, but 12 to 15 years are required for a full crop. Two tons to the acre is the average yield. The oil content of ripe California olives varies from 18 to 25 percent. Between 50 and 60 gallons of oil of all grades are usually obtained from each ton of olives pressed.

Olives for pickling are usually gathered in autumn while they are still green, though sometimes not until they are ripe and black. They must be harvested by hand and handled carefully to avoid bruising. Some pickling is done in brine, but most methods involve the use of lye. When the olives are used for oil, cold and hot pressing methods are employed, the latter extracting the inedible oils which are used in soapmaking and other cosmetic and pharmaceutical preparations.

OMPHALODES   *See* NAVELWORT

ONCIDIUM

The hallmark of these orchids is their numerous spectacular flowers on stems several feet long. The long, branched clusters of *O. varicosum,* the most commonly grown type, are very beautiful, the blooms often being nicknamed "dancing dolls." Although the leaves may be only eight inches long, the flower spray is frequently five feet in length with 250 bright yellow flowers the size of a 50-cent piece. It is fall blooming.

Other varieties with somewhat shorter stems and larger flowers are *O. papilio,* the butterfly-orchid, which blooms most of the year in the greenhouse; *O. ampliatum,* a compact variety sometimes grown on a chunk of osmunda fiber wired to a slab of wood; *O. flexuosum, O. ornithorhynchum, O. splendidum,* and *O. sphacelatum,* all rich yellow, marked with brown or green. These are only the most popular of the oncidiums—over 300 species and many more varieties are known and occasionally offered by growers.

See also ORCHIDS.

ONION   (*Allium Cepa*)

Gardeners have grown onions since ancient days. In the days of the Pharaohs, Egypt was famed for the mildness of its onions. The choice of varieties extends from the satiny, globular-rooted Bermuda type to the cylindrical leek.

Onions are relatively easy to grow provided the garden soil is rich, fertile and reasonably well drained. The topsoil should be deep and should contain an ample supply of humus. If the soil is exceptionally sandy or very heavy, incorporate well-rotted horse manure, leaves or other organic material the season before planting. Dry soil will cause onions to "split," forming two small bulbs instead of normal growth.

The use of lime may be necessary to offset excess soil acidity. If finely crushed limestone is used, this may be incorporated in the soil at any time previous to planting.

Planting and Culture: Onions can be propagated by small bulbs known as sets, by seed or by transplants. The easiest and often the fastest method for the home gardener is sets, but seed are less expensive and better for large-scale plantings.

Sets: These dwarf onion bulbs have been grown from seed planted very thickly within the rows. They are usually of the Ebenezer type, although other white-, brown- and red-skinned varieties are available. Contrary to the beliefs of many gardeners, the best sets are not necessarily the largest. The preferred size is about ½ inch in diameter, with smaller ones lacking in vigor and larger sets often going to seed.

You will find that it pays to plant sets carefully, stem end up. Place them four to six inches apart in the row and cover them with ¼ inch sifted compost. Water well and firm the soil. One pound of sets is enough for 50 feet of row.

Planted as early in the spring as possible, the sets will grow rapidly. They demand only shallow cultivation or weeding. By five weeks the young plants should have made good growth. If pulled at this stage they are scallions or green bunching onions.

Seed: Onions grown from seed mature in about 130 days but offer a much wider range of varieties than those grown from sets. Seed longevity, however, is only one year. One ounce of seed is sufficient for 100 feet of row. Seed should be in the ground just as early as possible, even before the last frost. It should be planted thickly and evenly in a shallow drill, covered with ½ inch of sifted compost and firmed. Careful weeding of the rows and the same general care should be given as for onions grown from sets.

Plants: Because of the necessity for an early start so that the plants may be benefited by the long daylight hours and mature before the arrival of summer drought, many gardeners purchase young plants. But to obtain fine young plants, true to type and free from disease, you may decide to grow your own seedlings with the aid of a cold frame. You will then be in a position to transplant the seedlings to the garden the minute the ground is in a condition to receive them.

Bulb formation: The length of time needed to form edible bulbs is determined by the amount of daylight the plant receives and not by the maturity of the plant.

This explains why some types of onions form bulbs in certain localities and not in others. There are onions which form bulbs when receiving only 12 hours of daylight daily (Yellow Bermuda and White Creole, for example). Ebenezer and Yellow Globe Danvers require 13 hours of daylight each day to bulb. Such types as Red Wethersfield require as much as 14 hours.

Insects: The average garden-grown onion is relatively free from plant disease and insect pests, although the onion root maggot can be troublesome in some localities until the garden soil has been properly conditioned by the liberal use of properly composted organic humus. As a deterrent, some gardeners have found that radishes interplanted between rows of onions act as a very satisfactory trap crop. The onion root maggot prefers the radish root and infests it instead of the onion. When they become infested, pull up the radishes and destroy them.

The full-grown onion maggot is legless, pearly white and about ⅓ inch long. The body tapers to a point at the head. This insect is very similar to the cabbage maggot.

The onion maggot seldom attacks any crop except onions, but it will attack them throughout the growing season. Onions planted for sets are more susceptible than large onions; white varieties are more likely to be damaged than yellow ones and red varieties are least likely to be damaged.

Damage is most severe when the onions are small. One maggot is capable of destroying many seedlings by destroying their underground parts, whereas a single large onion may harbor several maggots without being destroyed. The maggot damage to onion seedlings not only reduces the stand but causes the remaining plants to be less uniform in size. This lack of uniformity is of considerable importance when onion sets are grown.

The maggots usually gain entrance to larger onions near the base where they attack the roots and sometimes burrow upward as much as two inches. When damaged onions are put into storage, they decay and cause sound bulbs to rot. A layer of sand added to the top layer of soil will deter onion maggots. Cull onions, if planted in intervals, will attract the maggot and prevent damage to the main crop.

The onion thrips is slender, light yellow to brown, very active, and almost too small to be seen with the naked eye. Onion thrips feed on onions, beans, cabbage, and on a large number of other crops and weeds.

This insect, unlike most others, scrapes the surface of a leaf with its mouthparts and laps up the sap that flows from the wounded tissue. Small whitish blotches appear where thrips have fed. Heavily infested plants become stunted, the leaves become bleached and die back from the tips, abnormally thick necks are produced, and the bulbs fail to develop normally.

It is not uncommon for large fields of onions to be destroyed by onion thrips during July and August. Injury is most severe during hot, dry seasons.

Harvesting: Onion sets mature in about 100 days and, as the plants approach maturity, the tops gradually fall to the ground. When most of the tops are down, the remainder are generally broken down by running the back of a rake over them. A day or two later the onions should be pulled and left on the surface of the ground to cure. They are then gathered and the tops clipped off about an inch from the bulb. To complete their curing, spread them loosely in a shed or airy lean-to where they may dry until cold weather arrives. To store for the winter, place onions in orange crates, net bags or other ventilated containers and move to a cool, dry cellar. If you lack a storage cellar, onions in open containers may be stored in some airy place, such as an attic. Provided they are dry, slight freezing does not injure them, although they should not be handled while frozen.

Varieties: Ebenezer is usually grown from sets and matures in 105 days. Sweet Spanish Hybrid is a high yielder with a mild flavor. Yellow Bermuda has a growing period of 95 days and produces mild, medium-sized bulbs. Another early variety is Crystal White Wax which matures in 95 days. It is a favorite in the South. Evergreen Long White Bunching has a long growing period of 120 days. It is produced in clusters and used for scallions.

See also ALLIUM, LEEK, SCALLION, SHALLOT.

ONOBRYCHIS

In Europe and parts of Asia, *O. viciifolia* is grown for forage for livestock, but here its lovely racemes of white, pink or rose blooms make it an attractive perennial for the border or massed planting. It is sometimes called sainfoin or holy clover and grows two feet tall, with prickly pods. It does well in sandy, poor soil. Sow the seed in spring or summer for bloom the next year. They should be planted ½ inch deep where they are to flower.

ONONIS   *See* RESTHARROW

ONOPORDUM   *See* SCOTCH THISTLE

OPHIOGLOSSUM

The adder's-tongue fern, *O. vulgatum,* grows about a foot tall, with narrow fronds. It is not an especially handsome fern. Damp meadows are its usual habitat, and it is grown occasionally in the wild garden or in fern plantings.

See also FERN.

OPHIOPOGON

This lilyturf is hardier than its relative, *Liriope,* surviving up to the latitude of New York. It is especially popular in California. An evergreen ground cover, it prefers sandy, moist banks and thrives under trees. There are two varieties, *O. japonicus,* ten inches high with underground stolons and small violet flowers in loose racemes, and *O. Jaburan* (often sold as *Mondo Jaburan*) with white blooms, leaves over a foot long and a thick mass of roots. A variety of the latter has white-striped leaves. Both bear pea-sized blue berries, and are easily propagated by division.

See also GROUND COVERS.

OPIUM POPPY
(Papaver somniferum)

This herb has been grown for over a thousand years as a source of opium gum, a sleep inducer found in the milky juice of the unripe pods. The seeds today are used for flavoring. Opium poppy is a vigorous annual about three to four feet high, with showy single or double, red, white, pink, or purple blooms four inches across. The strain with fringed petals is sometimes called the carnation poppy.

See also POPPY.

OPULASTER   *See* NINEBARK
OPUNTIA   *See* PRICKLY PEAR

ORACH   *(Atriplex hortensis)*

The orach is a plant of the Spinach family whose leaves are used in the same manner as spinach. Foliage should be used when quite young because of its short-lived tenderness and flavor. Orach succeeds best if sown where it is to grow, in rich, moist soil. Seed should be sown in rows eight inches apart. When plants are two inches high, they should be thinned to six inches apart in the rows.

ORANGE   *(Citrus)*

The common or sweet orange (*C. sinensis*) has many popular varieties of commercial importance. The sour or Seville orange (*C. Aurantium*) is used mainly as a rootstock. Although the orange can be grown commercially only in warmer parts of Florida, California, the Mississippi Delta and the lower Rio Grande Valley, many varieties are suitable for greenhouse growing in the North. Citrus fruits, including the orange, will grow readily in any well-drained soil, but prefer a medium loam.

Culture: Orange trees, like all other citrus trees, are evergreen and can be planted any time of the year except in the colder months of December, January and February. For the best results, plant in March, April or May when weather conditions are most favorable.

When you are ready to plant your orange tree, dig a hole about three feet deep and two feet wide. Place your tree upright in the center of the hole. Then fill in with soil, packing it tightly but gently around the ball, filling the hole to about one inch below the bud union, or the place the tree was grafted to the rootstock. Water well, putting in enough water to wet it right down to the roots.

Pruning: Pruning causes new growth which produces better fruit. All old growth that has died back should be cut off. Any branches that cross each other and cause damage by rubbing should be thinned out to eliminate that condition.

Types: Mandarins as well as tangerines are members of the species *C. reticulata*. The bergamot orange (*C. Aurantium* subsp. *Bergamia*) is more closely related to the lemon. There are early- and late-ripening varieties, as well as midseason ones. For example, along southern California coasts, Valencia, which is a late-maturing type requiring high heat, ripens during the second summer following bloom. Washington Navel ripens in fall or winter of the same year it blooms. It's grown in areas with hot summers.

See also CITRUS, FRUIT TREES, ORCHARD.

ORANGEBERRY
(*Triphasia trifolia*)

Grown for ornament in the Deep South and along the Pacific coast, this spiny shrub has very fragrant flowers resembling orange blossoms. The berry-type red fruit has a spicy pulp, but it is not often eaten. Orangeberry, also called limeberry, is frequently used for hedges.

ORANGE GUM
(*Angophora costata*)

This tall tree, also called the gum myrtle, is generally planted only in Florida and southern California. It is a relative of the eucalyptus, with showy white flowers in clusters. Propagate by seed sown in flats in summer and give it ordinary garden soil.

ORCHARD

Fruit growing success at home is not achieved easily. The selection of nursery stock, the procuring of varieties that are best adapted to your particular climate and soil, and the proper arrangement, spacing and planting of these varieties are of prime importance.

Location: Orchards are a long-term investment, whether grown on a large or small scale, and consideration should be given to all the factors involved in selecting the best site. An error in planting annuals can be corrected the following year, but site selection must be a rather permanent decision for the orchardist. Constantly lower yields may result from even a slight deviation from the optimum location and a mistake in this initial step can seldom be remedied during the entire life of the orchard. In other words, conscientious management cannot offset the consequences of late spring freezes and water-logged soils.

Soil and topography are the most important factors to consider in choosing a location for an orchard. Before selecting a site, the home orchardist should study winter and spring temperatures, moisture, soil and site conditions, and the suitability of a certain kind of fruit for a given region. In addition to these factors, the commercial grower must also consider transportation and marketing facilities.

Temperature: Temperature is the most important climatic factor affecting the geographic distribution of fruits. It is also the one over which man has the least control. Therefore, check carefully with local growers, extension horticultural specialists and the local office of the United States Weather Bureau regarding frequency of frosts and extremes in temperatures in past years in your area. Extremely cold winters (from -20 to $-40°F.$ [-28.89 to $-40°C.$]) or violent temperature fluctuations in the winter can prove fatal to any orcharding venture. For profitable fruit production it is necessary for the trees to experience an uninterrupted rest period during the winter when life processes are held at a minimum.

Spring frosts shortly before, during or after the blossoming period constitute one of the major hazards to fruit growing. These are far more destructive to the fruit industry than early autumn frosts.

The leeward side of a large body of water usually experiences slow changes in temperature due to the tempering effect of deep water. A body of water that is large enough not to completely freeze over during the winter maintains a more even temperature throughout the year than a nearby equal area of land. Consequently, air masses passing over large areas of water will not vary as much in temperature as those passing over land. In spring, the air temperatures remain at a lower level and retard plant growth until after the date of frost injury. In autumn, the period for ripening of fruit is extended due to warmer temperatures near the shoreline.

Wind: Heavy winds which blow more or less continuously over an area are also undesirable. Strong winds during the period of blossoming often reduce the fruit set, with consequent reductions in the crop. If prevailing winds are from one direction, young trees tend to grow one-sided. This more or less throws the tree off balance and may cause it to break under the weight of its first heavy crop.

Light: The amount of sunshine directly affects the leaves' rate of food manufacture. This, in turn, affects the size and color of the fruit and the regularity with which the trees bear. In regions of Washington State, for example, where sunshine is relatively abundant, fruit production per acre is greater, and alternate bearing of light and heavy crops of fruit is much less pronounced, than in eastern states where there is more cloudiness during the growing season. The amount of sunshine may also be affected by the proximity of orchards to heavy industrial centers where factory smoke constantly clouds the sky.

Elevation: The elevation of the site in relation to land immediately around it is especially important in the prevention of frost and freezing hazards. Upland rolling or sloping fields which are not too steep for efficient orchard operations are the most desirable sites. Broad ridges or upland plains bordering depressions are also desirable. River bottoms or flat valley floors are definitely undesirable. During still nights the cold air drains from high lands into lower-lying areas, often resulting in damage to crops in these areas; those on higher elevations may escape injury. This is especially critical during blossoming. Trees should not be planted lower than 50 feet above the base of a slope. A difference of ten feet in elevation may make a difference of from five to ten degrees (F.) in the minimum temperature encountered. In some seasons, such differences would determine whether a crop failed or was full.

The colder temperatures at lower elevations may at first seem contradictory to some people, since it is true that air temperatures decrease with increased elevations. However, during clear, still nights there is a temperature inversion. This phenomenon takes place because the layer of air which lies next to the earth is cooler, and, as cold air is heavier than warm, it flows downward while warm air rises. Air stratification may at times be so critical that blossoms on the lower part of a tree may be destroyed while those in the upper part remain uninjured.

Soil: Fruit trees thrive in a wide range of soil types and their limits are less exacting than those of some other crops. However, experience indicates that soil alone may often cause a difference of 50 to 100 percent in yield.

The color of the soil gives an excellent index of its depth of drainage. Poor subsurface drainage results in inadequate aeration which causes mottling in the subsoil. These mottled colors are most usually brown and gray, yellow and gray, or yellow and brown. The depth of mottling corresponds to the depth of good subsurface drainage. If mottling occurs near the surface, soils are usually too poorly drained for a good orchard site. A simple method of studying subsoil colors is through the use of a soil auger of the type that removes a continuous core of soil. A more difficult, but better method is to dig a trench about two feet wide, several feet long and about six feet deep. This may seem like a lot of trouble, but when one remembers the years of work that may be wasted, every means should be used to insure success.

Often a very productive soil for farm crops may not be suitable for orchards and conversely, a less productive one in good physical condition may support an excellent orchard when properly managed.

The first requirement of a good orchard soil is proper drainage that permits aeration and extensive root development. Orchard trees are deep rooted when compared to most other crops. Consequently, the subsoil is more important than the upper layer of soil in selecting a proper site. When the subsoil is hard and impervious, trees often grow satisfactorily for a few years, but become weak when they mature. If a severe winter occurs, they may die.

Fruit trees will not tolerate wet soils during the growing season. After a rain the water table rises, but it should recede within a few days. If it does not, and groundwater persists within a foot or so of the surface during the critical blossoming and fruit setting period, many roots will die and the tree suffers. Sub-mergence of the root system for even a few days during the summer growing season when temperatures are high usually results in eventual death of the roots. A soil on which water stands for more than a week after a heavy rain is unfit for fruit growing. In most orchards, it is not unusual to find small depressions where water collects. These can be avoided, or drained by tile, if this procedure does not prove too expensive.

The rooting area for a fruit tree should be at least four to five feet in depth, but this depends somewhat on the region and soil type. Heavy compact soils are unfavorable since soil aeration is an important factor for deep-rooted, well-established trees. Under optimum conditions for plant growth, about half of the pore space, which in the average soil comprises about 50 percent of the soil volume, should be occupied by water and the rest by air. In compact soil the pores are very small and are filled with water so that the air is excluded.

Pollination: In many cases where the space is small and the would-be orchardist desires to have as many kinds of fruit as possible, single trees of individual fruits are planted with no thought as to whether they will be properly pollinated and thus bear fruit. It is a sad experience when an individual buys the best trees from the nursery, prepares the soil with organic materials, carefully plants the trees and tenderly cares for them year after year, only to find out that although he has beautiful trees which blossom each spring, few, if any fruits develop.

There are several factors which cause unfruitfulness among fruit trees. Several of them arise from an imbalance of nutritional elements needed by the tree for fruit formation. However, the most common factor in small backyard orchards is improper pollination.

When fruit trees reach a certain age, depending on the variety and the nutritional status of the tree, flowers are formed. These flowers consist of two principal parts: the male pollen producers (stamen and anther) and the female pollen receivers (pistil and stigma).

Pollination refers to the transfer of pollen from the anthers to the stigma of a flower. Self-pollination refers to the transfer of pollen from the anthers of a flower to the stigma of the same flower or a flower of the same variety.

Cross-pollination refers to the transfer of pollen from a flower on one fruit type to the stigma of a flower of a different variety. Pollination does not mean that fruit will be produced, since the pollen of many fruit trees will not fertilize the flowers of the same variety or those of some other varieties.

Self-unfruitfulness, in the strict sense, means the inability of a tree to produce fruit with viable seeds following self-pollination, while self-fruitfulness involves the production of fruits with viable seeds. Cross-unfruitfulness takes place if one fruit type, when used as the pollenizer of another, is unable to produce sufficient fruits for the production of a commercial crop. If fruits are produced readily through cross-pollination, the varieties are said to be cross-fruitful. Most of the fruit types display rather definite patterns of self- and cross-unfruitfulness among the different varieties.

Some fruit trees are sufficiently self-fruitful to be dependably productive if planted alone. However, there are many other fruit varieties that will not produce fruits if planted alone, or bear if planted with some other varieties. It is therefore extremely important that the varieties which are planted be either self- or cross-fruitful. When cross-fruitful types are planted, it is important that they be planted close enough to insure adequate transfer of pollen by bees and other insects.

The value of the pollenizer depends on several factors. Certain trees are not cross-fruitful because their blooming seasons do not overlap sufficiently. Certain two-variety combinations may be unfruitful because of the difference in age at which they form their first flowers. Also, combinations that consist of trees that bear annually and those that bear every other year will not produce full crops each season. The use of a third variety in such cases to supplement pollination of the annual-bearing tree will remedy the situation. The most frequent reason for failure of cross-pollination between varieties is their close relationship. The unfruitful combinations in most instances are comprised of a fruit tree and its bud mutation or "bud sport."

Where cross-pollination is necessary and there is not room for more than one tree, trees may be topworked to more than one variety. This is a grafting or budding procedure that involves the placement of two or more varieties on one tree. Many nurseries sell two-in-one, or three-in-one trees which contain selected varieties which are cross-fruitful in respect to each other. Information on how to topwork your trees may be obtained from your State Agricultural Experiment Station or the United States Department of Agriculture.

If more than one tree of a particular fruit is necessary and there is not room for the standard trees, it is possible to buy dwarf trees which may be planted much closer together.

Apple: Pollination tests have shown that cross-pollination is essential for a full commercial crop. To insure high yields, it is now generally conceded that all apple varieties should be interplanted with other varieties that blossom at the same time.

A few fruits such as Jonathan, Baldwin, Rome Beauty, Gallia Beauty, and Yellow Newtown will sometimes produce a partial crop when self-pollinated, but Baldwin is the only variety of any commercial importance which has been reported to produce a commercial crop under these circumstances.

Varieties which have proved to be ineffective as pollenizers in cross-pollination are Arkansas Black, Baldwin, Blenheim, Canada Reinette, Crimson Bramley, Fall Pippin, Idared Gravenstein, Red Gravenstein, Mutsu, Rhode Island Greening, Ribston Pippin, Roxbury Russet, Stark, Stayman Winesap, Staymared, Summer Rambo, Tompkins King, Turley, and Winesap.

There are many apples which are cross-unfruitful with related varieties, mutations or "bud sports." A few examples are Cortland and Early McIntosh; Rome Beauty and Gallia Beauty; Delicious, Golden Delicious and some of the red sports; and Jonathan, Northern Spy and Red Spy. Although Grimes is unrelated to Arkansas, it will not fertilize that variety.

Apricot and nectarine: Of the important varieties grown in America, all are self-fruitful.

Peach: Most of the varieties are self-fruitful and may be planted singly or in blocks of one variety. The only self-unfruitful type widely cultivated is J. H. Hale. If you select this one, grow another cultivar nearby.

Pear: Most pears are completely or partially self-unfruitful. For this reason, one tree of another variety is planted for every 15 to 20 trees of the main variety or, in the home garden, at least two, different types are grown. Almost any two varieties are compatible for pollination, with the exception of Magness and Waite and Bartlett and Seckel.

Plum: The group is represented by three distinctly separate types: European, Japanese and American. Of the European varieties, Iroquois and Stanley are self-fruitful. Others such as Bradshaw, Imperial Gage and Italian Prune are self-unfruitful in most environments.

In general, the members of the Japanese group are self-unfruitful and sometimes several different varieties must cross-pollinate in order for fruit to set. Formosa, Inca, Eldorado, and Gaviota are examples of virtually self-unfruitful Japanese varieties.

Of the American types, De Sota, Hawkeye, Miner, Wild Goose, and Wolf are self-unfruitful. Surprise is the best pollenizer of these types.

Quince: All quince varieties grown in United States are self-fruitful. These include Orange, Smyrna, Champion, and Meech.

Sour cherry: The common varieties of sour cherries are self-fruitful provided a large population of pollinizing insects is available.

Sweet cherry: Most varieties of sweet cherry are self-unfruitful and many are compatible only with certain specific other varieties. Bing, Emperor Francis, Lambert, and Napoleon will not pollinate each other. Ask your nurseryman or extension fruit specialist before you select varieties.

Planning: Before planting the orchard, a plan must be decided on for the arrangement of the trees. Orchard trees are generally planted according to some definite system. The three most common arrangements of trees in an orchard are the square, the quincunx or diagonal, and the hexagon or triangle. Where the land is rugged and steep a fourth system, the contour arrangement, is best.

The square is the usual arrangement in most sections and makes orchard operations, such as mowing, easier. In this system a tree is set in each corner of a square of determined size. If filler, or temporary, trees are used one

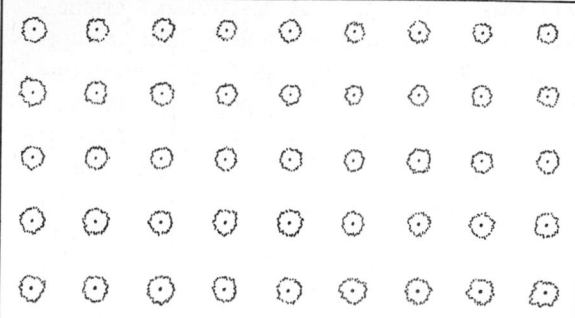

Square

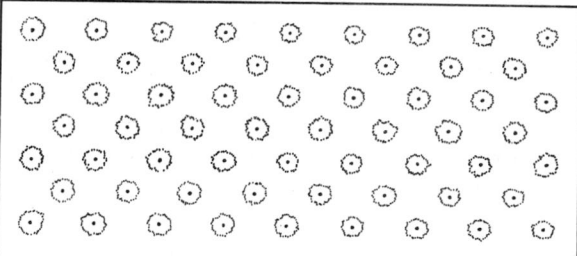

Quincunx

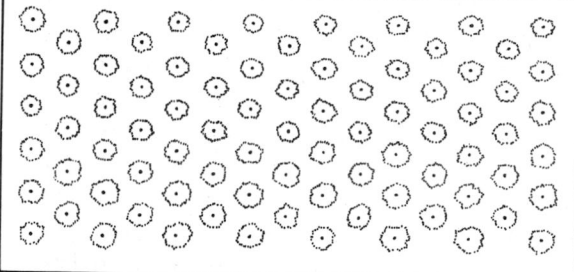

Hexagonal

On flat land, orchard trees can be arranged in many ways. The traditional square pattern allows for easy cultivation. With diagonal and hexagonal systems, more fruit is produced per acre, but cultivation is rather difficult.

may be set between every two trees in the row and another row of fillers set between each two permanent rows. Filler trees are removed after the trees begin to crowd each other too much.

The quincunx is very similar to the square, except that there is a tree in the center of each square. The center tree is semipermanent and is usually removed after the trees become very large. This method is particularly desirable when alternate rows are planted to different varieties. Generally, more fruit can be produced over a longer period of time since a larger number of trees can be planted to the acre. A disadvantage of this system is that cultural practices must be carried out on the diagonal.

When the hexagonal system is used all trees are equidistant from one another. With this system, 15 percent more trees can be planted to the acre than with the square system.

The contour system is the most feasible arrangement for planting an orchard on a hillside. In contour planting on sloping land, all trees in any row are planted at the same elevation. Obviously, the tree rows will not be equally spaced in all parts of the orchard.

The first step in laying out a contour planting is to decide upon a minimum allowable interval between rows. This distance will depend on the kind and varieties of fruit trees planted. The first contour line should be laid out at the highest elevation. The line is projected on the contour in both directions to the limits of the area to be planted, by using an engineer's level and rod and sighting from a fixed point. Then proceed to the steepest slope in the orchard below the first line and establish a point at the minimum distance between rows below the first line. A line is then projected in both directions from this point in a manner similar to that used in establishing the first line. If at any place in the orchard the distance between two adjacent lines becomes twice the minimum interval, a new line is laid out on the contour between them.

The planting distance must be determined principally by the size the trees are likely to attain at maturity. This is largely dependent upon the type of fruit, the type of tree (dwarf, semidwarf, standard), the variety, the fertility and depth of the soil, and the amount of rainfall or available moisture. The trees must be sufficiently far apart to allow the sun to hit the lower branches if fruit of satisfactory quality is to be grown on the lower parts of the trees. For information on specific planting distances, *see* Fruit Trees.

Planting: Fruit trees may be planted in the spring or fall. In the milder parts of the United States where minimum temperatures are not likely to go below 0°F. (−17.78°C.), they may be planted in the late fall before the ground is frozen. Peaches, apricots and other tender fruits often suffer considerable winter injury in more severe climates and should therefore be planted in spring. Spring-planted trees should be set as early as the ground will permit.

When trees are obtained from the nursery, they should be heeled in to keep them from drying out. Select a place that is protected from excessive exposure and where the soil is well drained. Dig a trench deep enough to accommodate all the roots, throwing the soil in a mound along the south side of the trench. Open the containers in which the trees were shipped. If you don't, heating may occur within the package, injuring the trees. Cut the bundles and separate the trees from each other,

making sure that you can distinguish the varieties from each other. Place the trees close together in the trench row and slant them toward the south to prevent sun injury. Fill the trench with soil, being sure all the roots are covered. Trees heeled in in this fashion may be held for a considerable length of time before they are permanently planted in the orchard.

Mulching: Mulching in the orchard is an attempt to imitate nature and allow litter to accumulate beneath the trees. This conserves moisture and adds nutrients to the soil. When one observes the trees that grow in forests where natural mulch materials are constantly being built up on the soil, it is not difficult to understand that this type of ground cover is extremely important.

It is extremely important to maintain the organic quality of soils. Cultural systems that do not include annual replenishment of organic matter gradually devitalize the soil and result in poor tree growth and fruit production.

Clean cultivation was practiced by orchardists when it was found that sod orchards did not do well because of the competition between trees and ground cover. The conversion to clean cultivation was rapid and during the early part of this century it became the accepted practice. The immediate effect of clean cultivation was an invigoration of trees and stimulation of growth. The more frequent and thorough the cultivation, the better the results appeared to be. However, no one realized that the reason the trees grew so well was because continual cultivation had placed organic materials near the surface of the soil where oxidation and decomposition could take place rapidly.

During the time that the organic matter persisted and continued to break down, good results were obtained. However, this method not only accelerated the utilization of organic matter, but left the soil unprotected from erosion. The organic matter became exhausted and resulted in a breakdown of the soil structure. Soils that had originally been friable and moisture retentive were found to run together into a sticky mass when rain fell and they became severely eroded.

Orchardists who argue for clean cultivation claim that mulching is not unlike sod culture. However, the two are quite different. A mulch eliminates the competition between trees and ground cover for water and nutrient materials, increases the penetrability of water and retards runoff, and prevents heavy evaporation of soil moisture. Organic mulch materials gradually break down and form humus. In short, mulches in the orchard offer much the same advantages as do garden mulches. There is another important advantage to the mulched orchard. Mulch reduces to some extent the amount of bruising of the windfalls and fruit which falls during the picking operation. This fruit is also cleaner than where clean cultivation is practiced.

One of the problems in a large mulch orchard is to secure sufficient litter. There are three common sources of such material. It may be grown within the orchard, produced elsewhere and hauled into the orchard, or purchased from an outside source.

Mulching materials that may be utilized include a wide variety of substances. The cut plant material of a large group of field and cover crops is available. Summer cover crops that may be planted in the orchard and cut for mulching material include soybeans, cowpeas, millet, Sudangrass, buckwheat, lespedeza, crotalaria, and sesbania. Orchard winter cover crops that may be cut for mulching purposes include rye, wheat, vetch, crimson clover, sweet clover, alfalfa, and kudzu. Besides these materials, many other substances are often available. Stone mulches are effective. For some other suggestions, *see* MULCH. When mulching with low-nitrogen materials such as straw or ground corncobs, add a nitrogen supplement to the soil.

Winter Care: To protect trees during fall and winter from rabbit and rodent damage, use a screening about 18 inches high and nine inches in diameter that is firmed into the ground. Aluminum foil is also effective around trees, and prevents sunscald as well. Remove piles of brush and stones where rabbits often nest.

See also entries for individual fruits, FRUIT TREES, INSECT CONTROL, MULCH, PRUNING.

ORCHARDGRASS
(Dactylis glomerata)

Orchardgrass is used in many pasture mixtures. A hardy perennial grass growing up to three feet tall in dense clusters, it is widely adapted in the North and upper South. Although more heat tolerant than timothy or Kentucky bluegrass, orchardgrass grows best at cool temperatures. Only moderately cold-hardy, it will often winter-kill in the North if a good snow cover is lacking. It thrives in moderately acid to neutral soils, and prefers shallow to deep gravelly loams, but will tolerate poorly drained clay and very moist conditions to some extent. Although orchardgrass is a fierce competitor for available nutrients, it does fairly well on infertile soils with low applications of fertilizers. It is particularly use-

Used in many pasture mixes, orchardgrass is highly productive and nutritional and will tolerate even the poorest of soils.
(Courtesy of U.S. Department of Agriculture)

ful when grown in shaded areas, such as orchards.

Orchardgrass reproduces by seed and asexually by runners. Orchardgrass is usually easily established in its area of adaptation.

Although orchardgrass is generally cut after blooming, for the highest nutritive value it should be cut earlier. When harvested at the vegetative growth stage, orchardgrass approaches the feeding value of alfalfa. Aftermath forage, the second growth after cutting, is leafy, palatable and of good quality.

Only recently has orchardgrass received emphasis as a cultivated crop. Leafy, nutri-

tional and productive, it can be used for pasture, hay and silage. For pasture, it is best suited to early spring grazing and to rotational, not continuous, grazing. Good results are achieved when it is seeded with ladino or white clover. Sow seed in the fall and allow grazing animals to trample it in the soil for spring growth. When grown for hay, orchardgrass can be grown by itself or with tall-growing legumes such as alfalfa. Once established, the stand should be managed to favor the alfalfa. Late-maturing alfalfa cultivars are especially useful.

ORCHID CACTUS
See EPIPHYLLUM

ORCHIDS

The orchid is one of the most admired, and least understood flowers in the world today. There are over 15,000 kinds of wild orchids. They are scattered over the entire earth, from high on tropical mountains to the tundras of Alaska.

Orchids are divided into three groups, epiphytic, semiterrestrial and terrestrial. Epiphytic orchids are those that live on trees, rocks or logs, but not upon the ground. Their roots are anchors only and do not supply food. Instead, they derive sustenance from the air and from decayed matter which builds up in the roots. Semiterrestrial orchids need a porous growing mixture for their fleshy roots. Terrestrial orchids grow in the soil; a common soil mixture is fine for these. Many of the terrestrial orchids are native to this country

Showy orchid

Yellow
lady's slipper

Purple-fringed
orchid

There are many native orchids just as beautiful as the exotic hybrids. Showy orchids and yellow and pink lady's slippers grow in moist woodlands throughout eastern North America. Purple-fringed orchids can be found in meadows and bogs.

and are valuable plants for special places in the outdoor garden.

Most of the exotic orchids suitable for indoor culture are epiphytes of tropical climates. They are very exacting in their tempera-

ture, humidity, light, and rest-period requirements but, if closely observed, they are not all that difficult to grow. There are thousands of orchids from which greenhouse gardeners can choose, the most popular and spectacular being the various species of *Cattleya, Cymbidium, Dendrobium, Epidendrum, Stanhopea, Laelia,* and *Vanda*. In a sunny window or under artificial lights in the home, moth orchids (*Phalaenopsis*), *Dendrobium nobile* and *Cattleya labiata* can be grown.

The rock, wild or bog garden is ideal for the hardy native terrestrial orchids, many of which can be purchased from wild flower nurseries. The best time to transplant is in the fall, for spring moving is apt to injure the tubers.

In general, these orchids need a peaty, fibrous soil which is moist and acid. Their native conditions should be duplicated as carefully as possible. They all need partial shade, and benefit immeasurably from a winter mulch of several inches of leaves, or a couple of inches of peat moss.

The best of the native orchids are the familiar lady's slippers (*Cypripedium*), found in bogs and woods; the fringe orchids (*Habenaria*), which grow in bogs and damp meadows; the purple-hooded orchid (*Orchis spectabilis*), a native of moist woods; the twayblades or scutcheons (*Liparis*), growing to eight inches tall; and the ladies' tresses (*Spiranthes cernua*), a fall-blooming, white-flowered orchid about a foot tall.

Others a little more difficult to transplant but worth trying are the rose pogonia or adder's-mouth (*Pogonia ophioglossoides*), a bog plant with rose purple blooms in summer; puttyroot (*Aplectrum hyemale*), which grows in forests and has yellow brown flowers; the dragon's mouth (*Arethusa bulbosa*), with yellow-fringed purple blooms, and which grows eight inches tall in acid bog soil; the swamp pink (*Calopogon tuberosus*), very similar to the dragon's mouth but taller; and the rattlesnake plantain (*Goodyera pubescens*) and its related varieties, suited to dry, open sites in the wild garden.

Growing Medium: All orchids need good drainage and an abundance of air about their roots. Epiphytic species are usually grown in shredded bark, peat, or perlite or in a special fiber obtained from the rhizomes of certain ferns. This material is called osmunda fiber and can be purchased from nurseries and plant supply houses. Unlike bark or perlite, osmunda provides the correct aeration and drainage and also feeds the orchids as it decays, making fertilization almost unnecessary.

Unfortunately, little is known about the exact nutrient requirements of many orchids and a hit-or-miss feeding program can easily ruin the chances of bloom. Diluted manure water and organic fish fertilizer, however, seem to work out well.

Terrestrial orchids are best potted in mixtures of osmunda, loam or leaf mold, sand, and well-rotted manure. Compost can be substituted for the manure, and peat moss or sphagnum for the leaf mold. In any case, the medium must be very rich and porous, like that offered by the forest floor where most of these orchids grow in their natural state.

When potting all indoor orchids, the bottom third of the pot should be filled with gravel or broken crock to insure good drainage. Most orchids need repotting every two years.

Light, Watering and Humidity: Practically all indoor-grown orchids will benefit from as much light as you can give them. However, direct, hot sunlight can burn the plants, so some shading may be necessary during the summer from perhaps 11:00 A.M. to 3:00 P.M. A semishaded porch or a lathhouse is a good summer home for them. The plants can also be suspended from the limbs of trees. In the winter, give them every bit of sun you can, preferably that from a southern window. Light requirements can be judged by studying the foliage. If the growth looks dark green, weak and soft, your orchids need more light. If it is hard, yellowish and leathery, they are getting too much sun.

Proper watering is very important. Most orchids should be watered abundantly during vigorous growth, but the growing medium should be allowed to become almost completely dry between waterings. Once a week may be fine. Be especially careful not to overwater during the winter. Wait until the osmunda looks light brown and bone dry, then dip the plant in a tub or sink for a thorough soaking. The best rule is when in doubt, don't water!

Humidity is not as critical a factor in orchid growing as many people believe. Placing the pots on a tray of pebbles and water, and spraying the foliage with a mist-type sprayer on bright days, will generally provide ample humidity. To make sure the roots never stand in water, the pots can be put on slats or mesh over the tray, or stood on inverted pots. If you grow your orchids in a glass or plastic-enclosed case, ventilate carefully so that the humidity does not remain constantly at a very high level. On cold, dark days of winter, fairly dry air is best. Try to give them some fresh air every day, but avoid drafts. As a general rule, the higher the light intensity and/or the temperature, the greater the humidity required.

Temperature: This, more than any other factor, will determine the kinds of orchids you can grow. There are three temperature classifications:

Warm—65 to 70°F. (18.33 to 21.11°C.) by day, 60 to 65°F. (15.56 to 18.33°C.) at night: *Bulbophyllum,* the mottle-leaved *Cypripediums,* some *Oncidiums, Phalaenopsis, Pleurothallis, Vanda.*

Intermediate—60 to 70°F. (15.56 to 21.11°C.) by day, 55 to 60°F. (12.78 to 15.56°C.) at night: *Cattleya, Coelogyne, Cycnoches,* some *Cypripediums, Epidendrum, Laelia, Odontoglossum, Oncidium, Stanhopea.*

Cool—55 to 60°F. (12.78 to 15.56°C.) by day, 45 to 50°F. (7.22 to 10°C.) at night: *Cymbidium,* the plain-leaved *Cypripediums, Dendrobium, Miltonia,* some *Odontoglossums.*

These are *winter* temperatures. In the greenhouse you may be able to grow species in all the classifications by careful regulation of ventilation, placing the cool-loving plants farther from the source of heat than the warm-loving ones, and so on.

But in the home, the cool ones are generally out of the question because modern heating systems make it difficult to find spots cool enough for them. *Temperatures are critical with most species.* Even a variation of five degrees (F.) for more than very short periods can make the difference between good growth and poor growth, between flowers and no flowers.

However, the warm and intermediate types include such vast numbers of species that only the most avid fancier will be disappointed if he cannot grow the relatively few cool ones in his home. Often varieties of a cool species can be found that will thrive under warm conditions. Some genera, incidentally, like the *Cattleyas,* are so diverse that it is possible to have different species in bloom every month of the year.

Starting with Orchids: The beginner is advised to purchase as his first orchid a blooming-size plant of a popular genus such as the *Cattleya.* Many orchids take three to seven years from seed to bloom, and starting with seedlings can mean a long wait that could dampen your enthusiasm. Blooming-size plants can be obtained for only a few dollars.

Study any books on orchid culture that you can find. Visit orchid greenhouses in your area. The American Orchid Society, Botanical Museum, Harvard University, Cambridge, MA 02138, publishes a most helpful magazine.

And most important of all, study your conditions. Note the temperature and light intensity in various spots. You may want to experiment with artificial light, or build a home-made orchid case for better control of conditions. You can use simple plastic enclosures for humidity control, thin curtains for shade, and an inexpensive heating cable to take the chill off cold nights.

See also entries for individual orchids, HOUSE PLANTS.

OREGANO   *(Origanum)*

Oregano is the mystery plant of the herb world. There is no agreement as to which species of the genus *Origanum* is referred to by the common name oregano.

O. heracleoticum, which some herbalists call winter marjoram, is a perennial native to Greece and the island of Cyprus. It isn't fully acclimated to harsh winters, so in the northern area of the United States, it should be treated as a tender perennial. A dense system of fine roots produces a low-growing, almost creeping plant with very hairy leaves. The flower stalks grow erect, about 12 inches tall, and develop at their ends small clusters of white flowers. The seeds are light brown and particularly tiny.

O. vulgare, the species most often sold as oregano, is also a perennial and a native of the Mediterranean. It, however, is quite hardy. The plant is erect, rising to two feet in height. It has dull, gray green, oval leaves, far less hairy than those of *O. heracleoticum.* The flowers can be pink, white, purple, or lilac.

Whichever species is selected, the flavor is the heart of oregano's usefulness. It is valued for its use in pizza, spaghetti sauce and other Italian dishes. Add the leaves, fresh or dried, to any of these dishes. Oregano is also a flavorful garnish for beef or lamb stews, gravies, soups, salads, or tomato juice. *O. heracleoticum* is limited to such uses, but *O. vulgare* has many other uses as well.

O. vulgare has an ancient medicinal reputation, the Greeks having used it both internally and externally, as an antidote to narcotic poisoning, convulsions and dropsy.

More recent herbalists have listed it as mildly tonic, diaphoretic, carminative, stimulant, and useful as an emmenagogue. They have noted that its warming qualities have made it useful as a liniment. A frequently mentioned toothache remedy is oregano oil. Moisten a bit of cotton with a few drops of the oil and place it on the aching tooth. A warm infusion of oregano is said to spur the fever and eruption of measles and to be helpful in cases of nervous headache.

Because of the strong balsamlike odor of the whole plant, it has had some use in potpourris, sachets and aromatic waters, although it takes a secondary role to sweet marjoram in such applications. The flower tops of the plant yield a dye which, though of limited durability, dyes wool purple and linen red brown.

Plants can be started from seed, cuttings or, in the case of *O. vulgare,* from divisions of the mature roots. Soil need only be moderately fertile, though good drainage and tilth are essential. Planting outside with a distance of 12 inches between plants should be delayed until danger of frost has passed. Hoeing and weed control are important; mulching with

Oregano leaves can be picked fresh throughout the summer and harvested for drying when the white flowers appear.

cocoa hulls or hay helps to keep the plants clean. Water requirements are minimal and generally supplied by average rainfall.

As soon as the white flowers appear, oregano is ready for harvest, unless of course, continued picking for fresh use during its growth prevents it from flowering. Even then oregano should be trimmed about six weeks after planting by cutting off all shoots to within one inch from the growing center. This practice stimulates dense, bushy growth.

Oregano can be hung inside or spread outside in the sun to dry. It dries very fast and retains most of its aroma and flavor. Rubbing the dried material through a fine screen prepares the oregano for culinary use.

See also HERB.

OREGON GRAPE   *See* MAHONIA

ORGANIC MATERIALS
See COMPOSTING

ORGANIC MATTER

Soil organic matter is a mixture of naturally occurring materials, including plant and animal remains. It is the product of decay processes that are continuously occurring.

Produced in living organisms, it is composed of a great many compounds of carbon. In soils, it occurs in admixture with inorganic soil constituents, which are derived from rocks and minerals. The type of vegetation, the nature of the soil population, drainage, rainfall, temperature, and management, all affect the kind and amount of the organic matter. A soil developed under deciduous forest in a cool, humid climate obtains most of its organic matter from the leaf fall on its surface, and the organic material is concentrated in the upper few inches of the soil. A grass/prairie soil receives residues from a large mass of fibrous roots and has a fairly uniform distribution of organic matter to a considerable depth. Little organic matter is found in arid soils where vegetation is sparse, because the raw materials are lacking.

Organic matter has been correctly called "the storehouse of the soil's nutrients." It is vital to soil because it improves the tilth, structure and water-holding capacity of the soil, aids in nitrogen fixation, makes nutrients available to plants, and helps to control soilborne plant diseases. Moreover, recent research has shown that soil organic matter acts as a buffer between soil microorganisms and the toxic chemicals that most farmers still insist on pouring into the soil.

Because of its vital role in the soil and in plant nutrition, organic matter is central to the organic method. The principal point of composting, mulching and applying animal and green manures is the building and maintenance of soil organic matter.

In most instances, if the gardener takes care of his garden soil's organic matter, the remainder of his gardening problems will take care of themselves. The garden soil will have the nutrients—in available forms—necessary to produce healthy plants. It will hold water, mitigating the effects of droughts and of high winds and heavy rains.

Most of these benefits of soil organic matter are due to the never-ending decomposition of plant and animal residues, which are ultimately converted into simple inorganic compounds, such as carbon dioxide, water and nitrates.

It is not very helpful to try to distinguish between relatively undecomposed residues on the one hand, and material in a more advanced state of decay on the other, although the term "humus" often is applied to the latter.

Soil Microorganisms: Wherever plants grow, their roots, leaves, stems, and twigs are the raw material for the organic-matter process, and all the intermediate substances between them and their simple end products, the inorganic compounds, make up the organic fraction of soils. A part of it is living—the cells of such microorganisms as bacteria, molds and actinomycetes.

The changes brought about by the chemical activities of these living cells are far more important than it might seem from their proportion by weight. Their most important function is to break down complex organic materials. If organic matter were an end product rather than an intermediate product in the biochemical factory of the soil, sooner or later it would contain all the carbon dioxide from the atmosphere.

The organic fraction is not a mixture of inert substances accumulating by reason of their immunity to microbial attack. Whenever fresh residues are applied, the decomposition of "humified" materials already present is speeded up, so that complete turnover of the organic matter eventually occurs.

This microbiological activity is vital to soil health. Manure, compost, green manure, and other organic matter are literally food for soil microorganisms, greatly increasing the numbers and disease preventing powers of beneficial organisms. Proper soil nutrition, which stimulates microorganisms, creates a kind of dynamic, flexible equilibrium.

Because of this, disease organisms are quickly chewed up and destroyed, or kept dormant and in check, by the already-established beneficial microflora. Many studies have shown that a soil occupied by healthy flora prevents disease organisms from establishing themselves in numbers that can cause symptoms in plants. Thus, plants grown in such soils tend to suffer less from diseases than those grown in soils with low organic matter contents.

Unfortunately, commercial agriculture makes little use of these facts. Chemicals which are applied to control plant diseases indiscriminately kill the microorganisms present in the soil. Rather than practice this chemical overkill, farmers must learn to use legume cover crops and organic amendments in their soil management systems. In these ways, they encourage a wide variety of soil flora and fauna to interact and establish a complex biological community. The greater the complexity (the more varied the constituents), the greater the stability of such a community.

Nutrient Content: Organic matter is a source of plant nutrients, particularly nitrogen, phosphorus and sulfur.

Nitrogen: Soil organic matter usually contains 5 or 6 percent nitrogen. The significance of the processes that convert the large organic reserves to usable forms can be seen easily, and the importance of continual turnover of organic matter as a factor in soil fertility also becomes apparent.

Crops in an organic garden get nitrogen from the decomposition of organic matter caused by bacteria and earthworms. In the process, the microbes liberate nitrogen gas into the air. Long ago, when the first life appeared on the earth, there was very little nitrogen in the atmosphere. The fact that the bulk of our atmosphere today is nitrogen is a legacy from eons of bacterial work. By growing legumes and by adding compost, the farmer provides food for the bacteria and thereby increases the nitrate content of his soil.

Phosphorus: Soil organic matter contains much less phosphorus than nitrogen, but it is enough in many soils to account for more than half of all the phosphorus present. In addition, organic matter influences the availability of soil phosphates.

Organic acids and humus created when plant and animal matter decay engage the iron and aluminum in the soil. These elements are the very ones that form insoluble compounds with phosphorus. What happens in a humusy soil is that iron and aluminum stay busy with the humus and up to 25 percent of the phosphorus is released to be used by plants.

Potassium: Organic matter is also vital in making potassium available to plants. Over 99 percent of soil potassium is bound up in mineral form, unavailable to plants. The remainder, in the soluble form that plants can use, is quickly leached out of soil unless there is an abundance of tiny, negatively charged surfaces in the soil. Organic matter particles have negatively charged surfaces. The positively charged potassium atoms are attracted to these surfaces and are held there electrically.

Organic matter acts like a magnet in the soil, drawing and holding most of the potassium until plants call for it. The rest of the potassium is still floating in the soil's moisture. These three forms (mineral, bound and solution) are in equilibrium. As plants draw the dissolved potassium from the soil moisture, an equal amount of electrically bound potassium detaches itself from the particle surfaces and becomes readily available. An equal amount will eventually leave the minerals in the soil and attach itself to the organic matter particles. Thus the system stays in balance.

Other nutrients: Sulfur is a constituent of proteins and is present in plant and animal residues and in soil microbes. Like nitrogen and phosphorus, it must be converted to a soluble inorganic form before it can be assimilated by growing crops. The conversion of organic sulfur compounds to sulfate is therefore an important part of the organic matter process. Because protein breakdown is involved, this phase of the sulfur cycle is linked to the carbon cycle.

Another way organic matter functions as a source of plant nutrients is through release of absorbed cations—calcium, magnesium and potassium.

Like soil clays, colloidal particles of the organic fraction are negatively charged and attract positively charged ions to their surface. On a basis of unit weight, the retentive capacity of organic matter is greater than that of the most reactive clays, so the importance of this material in plant nutrition is far beyond its weight percentage.

Nutrient elements, such as iron, which form highly insoluble inorganic compounds under conditions frequently encountered in soils, may not be present in soil solution in sufficient concentration to permit the best plant growth. The formation of iron-organic complexes, however, makes the iron more available. It has been known for many years that so-called iron-humate is a good source of iron for plants growing in solution culture.

The formation of metal-organic complexes sometimes stabilizes a soil nutrient that otherwise might not be retained in sufficient quantities for good plant growth. Adequate amounts of available boron usually exist in soils with high organic matter content—an indication that organic matter can protect the boron against leaching without making it unavailable.

The presence of organic matter tends to lower the ability of the soil pH to change when acid or alkaline materials are added. Soils high in organic matter require more lime to bring them to neutrality than soils low in organic matter, if other factors are comparable. On the other hand, organic matter lessens the effect of acid-producing fertilizers.

Physical Properties: Perhaps the best-known functions of organic matter are those relating to physical properties.

An adequate level of organic matter improves soils that are too heavy and those that are too light. A heavy clay soil may be hard to work and slow to absorb water and may tend to puddle, so that rainfall or irrigation water has a tendency to run off rather than soak in. Such a soil is also likely to be poorly aerated.

Organic matter makes heavy soils more friable—easier to work—and promotes a crumbly structure. It stabilizes the soil crumbs so that they are held together under the slaking action of water. As a result, the soil absorbs water more rapidly. Runoff and erosion decline. A more porous structure permits better aeration in the root zone. Less crusting permits better emergence of seedlings.

On the other hand, the faults of light, sandy soils are that they will not hold much water since water penetration of sand is too rapid. Aeration is good, but there is likely to be a deficiency of nutrient elements. Organic matter improves the water-holding ability of such soils and enhances the supply of nutrient elements. These elements are less susceptible to leaching when organic matter is present, because of its ability to absorb them. Other nutrients are slowly made available as needed during decomposition of organic matter.

These desirable physical properties are not entirely dependent on a high organic matter level. It is important to remember that soil organic matter is in equilibrium with its environment and that the level that can be maintained depends on soil texture, management techniques and climate.

Long before the modern soil scientist appeared on the scene, farmers were well aware of the importance of soil organic matter. Perhaps they also realized that the manure they turned under did not last very long in the soil. Although it is true that there are few soil properties that are not affected directly or indirectly by organic matter, it is also true that much of the value of soil organic matter results from its breakdown. The key to management of this valuable soil constitutent is in control of the organic matter process so that the desired by-products are obtained.

ORGANIC METHOD

The organic movement had its inception in the ideas and experiments of Sir Albert Howard. These experiments took place in India, over a period of 30 years. Howard was a British agronomist who noticed that plant and animal diseases were more prevalent on government farms than on neighboring farms. He noticed that the Indian farmers did not make use of artificial fertilizers. In order to develop a system of farming that would keep disease to a minimum, Sir Albert decided to use the methods of the natives, but with scientific management.

Howard's development of natural gardening and farming methods was partly a response to necessity. Since the area of India where he worked was so poor that local farmers couldn't afford to buy imported fertilizer, Sir Albert had to devise ways to recycle the natural nutrients available locally—the manure of animals and the waste plant materials that would otherwise be burned or overlooked. He saw that many potential sources of plant nutrients weren't being used because the native farmers didn't understand their value.

Sir Albert's practical solution to the Indian farm problem was the Indore method of composting. He taught farmers to combine rough weeds and crop wastes in layers with high-nitrogen manure and a little soil, making a pile that soon heated up to over 150°F. (65.56°C.) as a result of the multiplication of bacteria and fungi. Lacking machinery and power, the native farmers had no mechanical means to deal with those wastes. By composting, however, they were able to break down stalks and leaves and to create a valuable soil conditioner and fertilizer that would replace the nutrients and humus removed from the soil by crops.

Howard's theories of agronomy went beyond immediate practical problems, however. He was disturbed by the trend of the scientific community toward advocating synthetic substitutes for many natural commodities, a trend largely based upon the discoveries of the nineteenth-century German chemist, Justus von Liebig. Hailed as a pioneer of a new age of science, von Liebig had demonstrated the chemical composition of plant matter simply by burning it and then analyzing the ash for nitrogen, phosphorus and potash, ignoring the organic portion of the plant. The chemical fertilizer industry was created out of the ash of von Liebig's experiment. Salesmen told farmers that N, P, and K were all that mattered in the soil, and that by replacing those chemicals in the form of a powder, they could assure fertility indefinitely.

Sir Albert perceived in von Liebig's doctrine something extremely dangerous—the rupture of the cycle of life. Under the "scientific" system of farming, soil became primarily something to hold up the plants so that they could be fed with artificial solutions. The age-old rhythms of nature that had built the soil were violated. Sir Albert began preaching that it was possible for thinking farmers to preserve the cycle of life by returning plant and animal wastes to the soil, by countering insects by non-poisonous means, and by avoiding the synthetic, soluble fertilizers with their burden of toxic residues. If the cycle of life wasn't preserved, Howard maintained, future generations would be faced with declining fertility, hunger, and increases in disease and pollution.

In his work, Sir Albert broke away from

the accepted research procedures. He shunned the fragmented approach of the agricultural stations. Instead of growing plants in pocket-sized plots, he farmed a large acreage for more than 25 years. He proved conclusively that the use of chemical fertilizers was degenerating plants, animals and, due to the poor nutritional quality of the food produced, even people.

In 1940 Oxford University Press published Howard's important book, *An Agricultural Testament*. Its general theme is that present-day agricultural research is obsolete and that the use of chemical fertilizers is far from the answer to the maintenance and perpetuation of soil fertility. The book brought neglected organic matter back into the limelight in the equation of soil functioning, but created hardly a ripple in agricultural scientific circles.

More recently, however, scientists have been forced to confirm the warnings issued in *An Agricultural Testment* and interest in the methods of Sir Albert Howard has been renewed. In the United States, the organic movement was spearheaded by the late J. I. Rodale, an early reader and follower of Howard. Today, these ideas and discoveries are being tested not only on the Rodale experimental farms, but also in various universities and research stations throughout the world.

ORGANIC PHOSPHATES

The organic phosphate insecticides include demeton, diazinon, dimethoate, EPN, malathion, mevinphos, parathion, schradan, and TEPP. They work by inhibiting nerve and muscle response, and were originally developed for use in chemical warfare.

These highly toxic chemicals have no place in the garden. Application of many of them requires the wearing of respirators and protective clothing. Diazinon is extremely toxic to honeybees; TEPP and parathion are lethal to all warm-blooded animals, and can be absorbed right through the skin.

Organic phosphates are nonpersistent, broad-spectrum insecticides, meaning that they affect organisms other than target pests, but have the advantage of breaking down into nontoxic materials sooner than chemicals such as the chlorinated hydrocarbons.

See also INSECTICIDES.

ORGANIZATIONS, ENVIRONMENTAL

Environmental Action: This organization began as an offshoot of Environmental Teach-In, Inc., and of Earth Day, held April 22, 1970. EA succeeded Environmental Teach-In in 1970, actively lobbying for conservation issues and publishing a 16-page, twice-monthly ecology newsletter called *Environmental Action*.

One of EA's first campaigns was to "bust" the Highway Trust Fund and to create an EA affiliate, the Highway Action Coalition. EA also led a lobby for the Clean Air Act of 1970, mobilized citizens to support occupational health and safety legislation, and brought suits to disclose the phosphate content of detergents. EA helped stop the sale of herbicide 2,4,5–T. In addition, the organization leads a national coalition to lobby for transportation, energy conservation, solid wastes resource recovery, nuclear power, and recycling.

Partially funded by non-tax-deductible contributions, EA is also sponsored by the Environment Action Foundation, which conducts research and educational programs in support of local conservation groups. EA publishes many citizen action books, including *Earth Day: The Beginning, Earth Tool Kit* and *Ecotage!*

Environmental Defense Fund: In 1967 a group of scientists and lawyers established the Environmental Defense Fund (EDF) as a national legal action force for protection of the environment. EDF directs its tax-deductible contributions to the support of a staff, 700 volunteer scientists and several lawyers who engage in courtroom battles for conservation.

EDF has been involved in hundreds of court cases to protect environmental health, water quality, energy conservation, urban planning, recycling, and wildlife and resource conservation. Many of these cases are national. One major crusade of the fund is directed against man's contact with carcinogens, cancer-causing substances.

Grants from the Ford Foundation and other philanthropies help support the staff, which includes a small, full-time group of scientists, and lawyers with substantial litigation experience. EDF also has 50 staff members who man a national headquarters and five regional offices.

Friends of the Earth: FOE lobbies actively for proenvironment legislation. It was founded in 1969 by former executive director of the Sierra Club, David Brower, as a united force "committed to the preservation, restoration and rational use of the ecosphere." FOE is international, with affiliates in Yugoslavia, the United Kingdom, France, Germany, Holland, and Sweden.

FOE was the first ecology organization officially to denounce the war in Southeast Asia as "an ecological disaster." It also initiated an international coalition which sought a moratorium on nuclear reactors. The central theme of FOE is energy conservation. Founder Brower urges the public to use 10 percent less energy every decade, rather than the 125 percent more he claims it uses.

Four full-time Washington lobbyists are members of the FOE staff. They work with congressmen, staff and committees to promote proecology legislation, to draft bills and to enlist sponsors. One example of this was their work on wilderness areas in national forests. FOE publicly supported legislation to require sustained-yield forestry by timber companies on the land they own.

National Audubon Society: NAS began in 1898 as a society which lobbied through state and federal legislatures to protect non-game bird species from market gunners who sought their plumage or flesh. The society is responsible for the well-being of roseate spoonbills, woodpeckers, whooping cranes, and other species.

Today, the society has members in over 300 chapters which campaign for the protection of wildlife, birds and much more. NAS has led crusades to save the alligator, spotted cats, sea turtles, the whale, and the timber wolf. NAS was also the first conservation organization to protest the use of DDT and other lethal pesticides. During the 1973–74 energy crisis, NAS had its largest membership growth ever.

NAS owns 40 sanctuaries of up to 26,000 acres, maintained by Audubon wardens. Members participate in camps and nature centers and sponsor and attend ecology lectures. NAS consults and advises communities planning nature centers, in addition to sponsoring world tours and international symposia on environmental affairs.

The Nature Conservancy: The Nature Conservancy is the only nonprofit membership organization in the United States which directs its efforts entirely to the preservation of land. It was established in 1916 and incorporated in 1951.

The Nature Conservancy has protected about 700,000 acres of forests, swamps, marshes, prairies, mountains, and beaches through 1,200 projects in the United States. TNC protects wildlife areas in three ways: purchasing land through public subscription, accepting land donations, and obtaining acres for local, state and federal agencies, with the understanding that these agencies will later reimburse TNC.

The preservation of the Great Swamp at the Virginia and North Carolina border is credited largely to TNC efforts. The organization has also saved two Vermont mountains; Lignumvitae Key and Shell Key in Florida; Tubbs Island (a 330-acre wildlife sanctuary in San Francisco Bay); and a 60-acre marsh in Arizona with rare orchids, Canelo Hills Cienaga.

Sierra Club: The Sierra Club has joined with other groups to help ban DDT, to persuade Congress to drop the SST, to stop predator poisoning, to extend the Everglades National Park, and to protect other national parks. In 1972, it began a study of national energy policy. One of its major projects involved saving the Grand Canyon from a proposed dam project.

This last campaign resulted in advertisements in the *New York Times* and *Washington Post,* which led to the Internal Revenue Service's 1966 decision to drop the club's tax-deductible status as a nonlobbying group. The decision led to serious financial strain on the club, which was faced with having to launch publicity efforts and campaign aggressively for members without being able to offer tax deductibility. These campaigns succeeded.

Sierra Club has numerous supporting subdivisions. The Sierra Club Foundation funds the club's legal, scientific and literary projects and programs. In 1970, the Sierra Club Legal Defense Club was established. It later challenged the Trans-Alaska Pipeline, the California Water Project and the Four Corners coal-burning programs.

The Wilderness Society: This society began in 1935 as a group of eight men who sought protection of wilderness in public parks and forests in the United States. The society today protects 250 units of land totaling 65 million acres owned by the U.S. Forest Service, the Bureau of Sport Fisheries and the National Park Service. The society was primarily responsible for passage of the Wilderness Act of 1964, which provided protection for ten million wildlife acres.

The Wilderness Society also supports individual and citizen group efforts to protect the wilderness. It leads workshops, seminars and expeditions on horseback, canoe and foot. *The Living Wilderness* is the society's official publication.

ORIENTAL FRUIT MOTH

This pest was introduced from the Orient in the early part of the century and has since become a major plague of peach crops in this country. The moth is gray with brown markings. Eggs are flat and white and are laid on leaves and twigs just after the trees flower. The first brood of pinkish larvae emerges soon after and feeds on terminal shoots, causing them to wilt, turn brown and eventually die. Later in the summer, more serious damage is done as larvae enter fruits and feed on the central flesh.

Sometimes a slightly gummy substance appears on the fruit surface, but usually larvae enter at the stem ends and leave no telltale evidence behind them.

Proper pruning is a most important basic control measure, as is the elimination of cullage and garden trash. Annual spring cultivation destroys some of the cocoons and overwintering larvae.

Several parasites and predators of Oriental fruit moths which appear naturally in unsprayed orchards have been discovered. Field mice eat cocoons from tree trunks, lacewings feed on eggs, and the eggs of the *Trichogramma* wasp parasitize those of the moth. Of all the beneficials, *Macocentrus ancylivorus* has been found to be most effective. These tiny wasps parasitize the strawberry leaf roller as well, and strawberries planted in or near the orchard will attract them.

Oriental fruit moth larvae cannot survive where there are no late-ripening peaches. Thus, if the larvae are consistent pests in your orchard, it may be advisable to grow only early-fruiting varieties.

See also INSECT CONTROL.

ORIENTAL POPPY
(Papaver orientale)

A vigorous, long-lived perennial that springs from strong, deep-growing rootstocks, the Oriental poppy is a good choice for the perennial border. The enormous flowers, from six to 12 inches across, are brilliant scarlet with purplish bases, though the flowers of hybrid varieties can be white, salmon, crimson, orange, shell pink, lavender, or mahogany. Its blooming period is May and June. The poppy reaches a height of four feet though shorter varieties, good for the rock garden, do exist.

Poppies have two disadvantages, however. The foliage dies down by midsummer, leaving gaps in the border, and the hybrid varieties are likely to self-sow, resulting in undesirable colors. The second problem can be prevented by picking off the faded flowers. Plant poppies in a rich loam in full sun or very light shade with the crown of the plant three inches below the soil surface. This is very important as most failures are due to shallow planting. Planting time is from late July to September. Avoid moving them once established.

Brilliant Red is classic scarlet with a black blotch; Pinnacle is a bicolor with a white center shading through pink to scarlet on the ruffled petal edges; Helen Elizabeth is a pure pink without blotches; and Barr's White is white with purple block blotches at the base of the petals. Poppies make good cut flowers if the open ends of the cut stems are burned to prevent bleeding.

ORNAMENTAL

Any plant that is used primarily for decoration, rather than for food, fodder, lumber, or other purposes, is called an ornamental. Usually ornamentals have showy flowers, fruits or foliage. The category includes many shrubs, trees and annual and perennial flowers.

See also ANNUALS, PERENNIALS, SHRUBS.

ORNAMENTAL GRASSES
See GRASS, ORNAMENTAL

ORNAMENTAL TOBACCO
See Nicotiana

ORNITHOGALUM

The tender species of these bulbs, often called chincherinchee or star-of-Bethlehem, are grown indoors, while the hardy ones are usually relegated to the wild garden because of their habit of spreading and becoming serious pests. The most common hardy variety, *O. umbellatum,* grows to a foot tall, with green-edged white flowers in racemes. Two others, *O. pyramidale* and *O. nutans,* reach two feet in height.

Culture: The tender species are grown in the border in the South, and elsewhere in sunny windows or the cool greenhouse. They do best in a mixture of two parts of loam and one part each of sand and leaf mold or peat moss, with some bone meal and dried manure added. In a large pot, plant six bulbs one inch deep, any time from September to February. Water well after planting, then sparingly until growth begins. Thereafter, give weekly feedings of liquid manure and plenty of water until the foliage begins to die off. A temperature not exceeding 60°F. (15.56°C.) is best. The bulbs increase rapidly and can be propagated by means of the small bulbs growing around them. These will flower two seasons after planting.

The best indoor varieties are *O. arabicum,* with two-foot-tall clusters of big creamy white, black-centered flowers that smell like ripe apples; *O. caudatum,* three feet tall with green-centered blooms; *O. thyrsoides,* with pale yellow flowers; and *O. miniatum,* popular for its bright golden yellow flowers.

See also Bulb.

ORRIS   (*Iris*)

Orrisroot is obtained from two species of iris (*Iris* x *germanica* var. *florentina* and *I. pallida*), perennials native to southern Europe and cultivated chiefly in Italy for their fragrant rootstocks. Powdered orrisroot is used principally as a scenting agent in perfume and cosmetics. The plants grow well in a variety of soils and flourish in rich, moist loam, but roots grown in rather dry, gravelly soil appear to be the most fragrant.

Orris grows best in full sun and is readily propagated by division of the old plants, which may be set either in spring or fall, about a foot apart in rows spaced conveniently for cultivation. It requires three years to produce a marketable crop of roots. After the roots are dug at the end of the third season, they are peeled and dried in the open air. The delicate fragrance develops as the roots dry. The yield is from five to six tons of dry root per acre every third year under good conditions.

OSAGE ORANGE
(*Maclura pomifera*)

The osage orange has spiny branches and can be trained as a thick, impenetrable hedge. As such, it is an excellent wildlife plant. Left alone, it grows into a beautiful tree, 40 to 50 feet high, with very glossy foliage and dense heads of greenish flowers. The striking green fruits, up to five inches in diameter, look like lobed grapefruits, but are not edible. The trees are often used for shelterbelts.

Osage orange does well in ordinary or poor soil, and is hardy in all but the extreme northern regions. The wood is very elastic, and the Indians of the Southwest, where it grows wild, used it for bows. A strong fiber is obtained from the bark, and the bark of the roots yields a yellow dye. The osage orange is propagated either by seed soaked in water at least a day before planting, or by cuttings.

OSMANTHUS   *See* TEA OLIVE

OSMOSIS

Basically, the term osmosis refers to the diffusion which takes place through a semipermeable membrane separating two solutions of unequal concentrations. The membrane usually divides a solvent (such as water) or another dilute solution from a more concentrated solution. Osmosis tends to equalize the concentrations of the solution by allowing the solvent or more dilute of the two solutions to move through the membrane.

Osmosis is extremely important to living cells which characteristically are surrounded by semipermeable membranes and depend on osmosis for the transport of nutrients and water throughout the plant tissue. The soil's nutrient solutions are absorbed through the microscopic membranes on the root hairs of plants, and osmotic pressure is created in the roots. This pressure is responsible in large measure for the rise of sap up the stem. A similar process occurs in the cells of the plant when nutrient solutions in the sap permeate the walls of the cell.

OSMUNDA

These hardy ferns are very easy to grow. Both the cinnamon fern (*O. cinnamomea*) and the interrupted fern (*O. Claytoniana*) are good for massing in damp or wet, partly shady spots. The royal fern (*O. regalis*) likes sunlight and will thrive in very wet places like bogs, meadows or the edges of a brook or lake, if its crowns are above the high-water line. The soil should be rich and fertilized with manure or compost. The fruiting fronds of the cinnamon and royal ferns resemble flower heads. All three species are propagated by spores, and grow two to three feet tall, occasionally much taller.

Both the cinnamon and the interrupted ferns form large, fibrous root masses, often several feet square, above the ground. Called osmunda fiber or osmundine, this material is a growing medium for orchids. It is rich enough to feed an orchid for up to five years and is also extremely tough.

See also FERN.

OSTRICH FERN
(*Matteuccia pensylvanica*)

A tall-growing, very handsome subject for the fern garden, ostrich fern has running rootstocks that send up new plants to give a dense, massed effect. The foliage fronds are borne on short stalks and may be as long as ten feet, but more often are about five or six feet. The fern grows wild in the East, and is easily propagated by division of the rootstocks.

Another species belonging to this genus,

M. Struthiopteris, is more frequently cultivated. Plant it in partial shade in a deep mixture of good loam and swamp muck or leaf mold, with part of the crown left exposed above the ground. Mulch it lightly with leaves until it is established, and soon there will be a luxuriant thicket.

See also FERN.

OSWEGO TEA   *See* BEE BALM

OTAHEITE APPLE
(*Spondias cytherea*)

A tropical fruit tree growing to 50 or 60 feet high, the Otaheite apple bears clusters of white flowers and fruits that look like big yellow plums. The fruit is used in preserves. A tender tree whose cultivation in this country is limited to the southernmost part of Florida, the Otaheite apple is not particular in its soil requirements. It is best propagated by shield- or T-budding.

Two other varieties, the purple mombin (*S. purpurea*) and the yellow mombin or hog plum (*S. Mombin*), have smaller fruit that is a popular treat in the tropics. Both of these have greenish flowers.

OTAHEITE GOOSEBERRY
(*Phyllanthus acidus*)

The berries produced by this 20-foot Florida tree are used for preserves. It has clusters of small red flowers, and is propagated by seed or green cuttings. Give it a somewhat sandy, medium fertile soil and full sun.

OTAHEITE ORANGE
(*Citrus* x *limonia*)

This miniature orange tree is a popular, attractive plant for a sunny window or for a cool greenhouse. It grows two to three feet tall with glossy leaves and waxy white, pink-tinted flowers. The fruits are very numerous, shaped like lemons but a bright orange in color. One plant in a five-inch pot may carry over a dozen of the fruits, which are smaller than common oranges and less acid. Otaheite orange likes a humusy soil made up of equal parts of sand, loam and leaf mold or compost, with dried manure and bone meal added.

See also FRUITS, GROWING INDOORS.

OXALIS

Often called wood sorrel, these perennial bulbous plants grow six to 12 inches in height. They have clover-shaped leaves that fold up at night and abundant bright yellow, white, pink, or red flowers. Native to South Africa and South America, most species are best grown in greenhouses in North America. Some, however, thrive outdoors in the South and a few can be grown in northern gardens.

The common white wood sorrel (*O. Acetosella*) is one of the first wild flowers to bloom each spring. It needs a rich woods soil and shade. Unlike most species, it is very hardy and can withstand severe winters.

Violet or purple wood sorrel (*O. violacea*) likes the same conditions and can be grown as far north as Maine if planted deeply enough to escape freezing.

Bermuda buttercup (*O. Pes-caprae*) can be grown in very warm frostfree areas and has even become a weed in parts of southern Europe. It has bright yellow flowers and, since it is low growing, is a fine choice for the sunny border or rock garden.

O. rosea also does well in the sunny rock garden provided the soil is fairly moist. Flowers of this species are pink.

Plant bulbs in autumn, two inches deep and three inches apart. They like a sunny location and soil liberally enriched with compost.

For indoor culture, pot them in a soil mixture of two parts of loam to one each of sand and leaf mold or compost, with a sprinkling of bone meal added. Six bulbs can be fitted into a six-inch pot. Put them in a cool, dark place, giving little water until growth starts. Then move them to a sunny window, water well and feed with liquid manure. When bloom is finished, reduce the watering until the foliage matures. Store bulbs in the pots until early fall, then divide and replant.

The best varieties for indoor culture are *O. adenophylla*, pink; *O. Bowiei,* rose purple and summer blooming (this one can be planted outdoors and treated like gladiolus); *O. Pes-caprae,* the Bermuda buttercup, yellow; *O. enneaphylla,* white; *O. Ortgiesii,* yellow; and *O. rubra,* pink, lilac or white.

Oxalis is propagated by seed, offsets or root divisions.

OXISOL   *See* LATOSOLS

OXLIP   (*Primula elatior*)

A member of the Primrose family, the oxlip thrives in any good garden soil. This low-growing perennial reaches eight inches and has yellow flowers about one inch in diameter in spring. It should receive ample shade and moisture during summer.

See also PRIMROSE.

OXYGEN

The most widely distributed element in nature, oxygen makes up nearly half of all terrestrial matter. It forms approximately 21 percent by volume of the atmosphere; 87 percent by weight of all the water on the earth; and over 40 percent of the human body.

Plants and soil organisms cannot live without oxygen. Plants obtain this vital element through photosynthesis and respiration. The roots of most land plants (except rice, which can be grown underwater) need oxygen for their life processes and for best growth. Soil microorganisms break down organic matter in the soil, using up oxygen and releasing carbon dioxide to be used by the aboveground parts of the plant. The larger the organic matter content of the soil, the better the process proceeds.

In a well-aerated soil, the composition of soil air is similar to that of the atmosphere above the soil. When oxygen supply is cut off from the roots of most plants by flood, by compaction or through overuse of chemical fertilizers, roots suffocate and die. In soil severely lacking in oxygen, absorption of nutrients by the roots is poor, and root growth is poor. Anaerobic bacteria, those bacteria that thrive in airless soil, are stimulated to destroy valuable compounds and produce toxic amounts of hydrogen sulfide gas. Denitrification also proceeds faster, showing up in the lowered content of crude protein in plant tissues.

Plants that normally grow on well-drained and aerated soils usually are most sensitive to lack of oxygen. Even plants such as cranberries, which can remain under water during a long dormant period, will suffer from poor aeration in summer when the plant uses more water and nutrients.

See also AERATION, SOIL COMPACTION.

OYSTER PLANT   *See* SALSIFY

OYSTER SHELLS

An excellent source of calcium (ranging from 35 to 55 percent), oyster shells are ground and marketed commercially. Ground oyster shells can be added to the compost heap to insure an adequate calcium supply, or they may be mixed in sparing amounts with other organic materials for direct application to soil. The shells also contain over 40 percent carbon dioxide and lesser amounts of aluminum, copper, iron, magnesium, manganese, phosphate, silica, zinc, organic matter, chlorine, fluorine, and nitrogen. Ground oyster shells are used as a source of calcium for poultry.

P

PACHYSANDRA
See GROUND COVERS

PAEONIA   *See* PEONY

PAINTED DAISY   *See* PYRETHRUM

PAINTED LADY   *See* PYRETHRUM

PAINTED-TONGUE
(*Salpiglossis sinuata*)

The striking, highly colored, gold-banded and veined flowers of the painted-tongue resemble ornate petunias. The funnel-shaped blossoms come in a wide variety of bright colors and make excellent cut flowers. These tender annuals grow to three feet high but often need support as the stems are weak.

Sow the seed in peat pots in early March, moisten, and keep in a warm place (about 75°F. [23.89°C.]) until seedlings emerge. Thin them to one per pot before planting them outdoors, pot and all, when all danger of frost is past. Encourage bushiness by pinching out the tips.

PAK-CHOI   *See* CHINESE CABBAGE

PALM

Palms are evergreen shrubs and trees found in tropical areas. They vary in height from a few feet to 200 feet. Basically, they are divided into two groups, those with feathery foliage and those with fan-shaped leaves. Some are hardy enough for landscape work in lower California and warmer southern states. Smaller ones are good choices for tolerant house plants.

Planting and Culture: An all-purpose soil will suffice for most species. Some prefer a soil kept evenly moist, while some prefer a soil kept somewhat wetter. Species vary in preference for light from those that thrive in a sunless north window to those that thrive in an east or west window. Since palms do not branch, damage to their terminal leader results in the eventual death of the stem. A few types of palms can be propagated by division, but most are seeded. However, young plants are often unattractive, so most people purchase established plants.

Types: Some of the palms which make good house plants are described below:

Caryota: These are clumping palms with scalloped foliage on tall stems. *C. mitis* is known as the tufted fishtail palm and *C. urens* as the toddy fishtail palm.

Chamaedorea: Most of these form clumps and have feathery foliage. The popular parlor palm comes from this group, and is called Collinia or good-luck (*C. elegans*); it also comes in a miniature variety incorrectly called *Neanthe bella.*

Chrysalidocarpus: These are graceful, feathery, clump-forming palms. The best is the butterfly palm, *C. lutescens.*

Daemonorops: These tropical, spiny shrublike palms are sometimes grown in the very warm house. They are known as ground rattans or rattan vines.

Howea: These feathery palms, also called Kentia, are attractive. The sentry palm (*H. Forsterana*) and curly palm (*H. Belmoreana*) are prominent species.

Rhapis: These have a very oriental look. From this genus, the lady palm (*R. excelsa*) makes a good choice.

For outdoor use, some of the more hardy fan palms are Australian cabbage palm (*Livistona australis*), Chinese fan palm (*L. chinensis*), desert fan palm (*Washingtonia filifera*), Guadalupe palm (*Brahea edulis*), lady palms (*Rhapis* spp.), Mediterranean fan palm (*Chamaerops humilis*), Mexican blue palm (*Brahea armata*), needle palm (*Rhapidophyllum hystrix*), palmettos (*Sabal* spp.), and San Jose palm (*Brahea Brandegeei*).

See also HOUSE PLANTS.

PAMPASGRASS
See GRASS, ORNAMENTAL

PANAMA-HAT PLANT
(*Carludovica palmata*)

A tropical tree whose leaves are made into panama hats, this palmlike plant grows six to eight feet tall in the greenhouse. It has no trunk, the fan-type leaves being borne on stalks. The pinkish or green white flowers are borne in clusters, and the fruit is a berry which is ornamental for a short time after bursting open.

Sow the seed in moist sphagnum moss, or propagate by division in early spring. The panama-hat plant likes a humusy soil with excellent drainage, and it requires plenty of moisture while growing. Feed liquid manure once a month. It prefers nearly pot-bound conditions, and a night temperature of 55 to 60°F. (12.7 to 15.5°C.). Some shading over the glass is recommended to prevent burning of the foliage by strong sun. A dwarf species, *C. humilis,* is also grown occasionally.

PANAMA ORANGE
(*Citrus mitis*)

This small tree is occasionally grown in the Deep South. It bears small, orange yellow flowers and fruit about an inch in diameter, with acid pulp. The fruit is used like the common orange, and the tree is worth planting in those southern states where the orange is not hardy.

PANDANUS

This genus, commonly called screw pine, is native to tropical places such as Madagascar, the Solomon Islands, Timor, and Polynesia. It is known for its tolerance to home or apartment conditions. Leaves with sawtooth edges are arranged like arching lances in a spiral. Screw pines are best for house plants when young, since they become large, send out aerial roots and drop lower leaves when mature.

An all-purpose soil is required. The soil should dry between waterings. Light from an east or west window is sufficient. Propagation is achieved by rooting suckers with bottom heat.

For larger house or tub patio plants, *Pandanus Veitchii* with its white and green variegated leaves is the most popular. *P. Veitchii* var. *compactus* and *P. pygmaeus* last longer and take less room.

See also HOUSE PLANTS.

PANICGRASS   *(Panicum)*

There are many annual and perennial species of panicgrass, adapted to a wide range of soil and climatic conditions. Most of them are grown for forage or grain, but gardeners plant them occasionally for their flowers which are borne in feathery clusters and make good dried flowers.

The seed is sown in early spring, ⅛ inch deep in patches, and the plants are thinned to three inches apart. The perennials can also be divided in the fall.

Blue panicgrass (*P. antidotale*) is drought resistant, but not winter-hardy and is grown in the southern parts of the Great Plains and the Southwest. It prefers sandy loams and well-drained, fertile clays, moderately acid to slightly alkaline and of good depth. It is not as important a range grass as some of the other species.

Guineagrass (*P. maximum*), a forage grass in the South, tolerates a high degree of acidity. A perennial, it has leaves up to two feet long but very narrow, and flower clusters 18 to 24 inches in length. It is a bunch-type grass.

Paragrass (*P. purpurascens*) is another southern grass, a perennial that grows in neutral to highly acid soils. It requires very moist conditions and tolerates some flooding. A forage grass, it has erect stems up to ten feet high, and creeping stems that spread as much as 20 feet, rooting at each joint.

Proso millet or broomcorn millet (*P. miliaceum*) is an annual, grown for centuries for grain and fodder. It will tolerate moderate acidity and prefers deep, sandy loams and dry to moist conditions. It is most often cultivated in the Great Plains for its shiny white seed, and grows three to four feet high, with drooping flower clusters.

Switchgrass (*P. virgatum*), a vigorous perennial, prefers sandy loams that are reasonably well supplied with moisture. It grows up to six feet tall, and is hardy from Maine southward. It is often grown as an ornamental grass, having flower clusters up to 18 inches long.

Vine mesquitegrass (*P. obtusum*) likes sandy loams and well-drained clay, neutral to moderately alkaline. It tolerates slight salinity, and prefers dry conditions. A drought-resistant perennial, it is grown mostly in the southwestern states.

PANICLE

A panicle is an elongated, pyramidal flower cluster. It has a single main stalk that bears no blooms, but that has numerous branched flowering stalks arising from it. Technically, it is a compound raceme. Panicles are characteristic of plants like yucca, oats and catalpas.

PANSY (*Viola tricolor*)

The pansy is a wonderful flower for massing or edgings in borders and beds. If you live in an area where only slight frosts occur, it will produce cut flowers all winter long. Otherwise it will bloom through the early spring, summer and fall.

There are varieties that grow over four feet tall, "jumbos" that have blooms four inches across and special varieties for the cool greenhouse. They come in blue, apricot, white, purple, red, or orange, all with fascinating markings and lovely, velvety faces.

Pansies are quite hardy, withstanding temperatures down to 15°F. (−9.44°C.) if given a light covering of salt hay, dry leaves or straw through the winter. They feed heavily and prefer a cool, moist soil and a rich mulch. Use manure, compost, woods soil, leaf mold, or sawdust and shavings mixed with sheep or poultry manure. The mulch feeds them richly—they are surface feeders—and keeps the roots cool in summer, warm in winter.

The pansy is essentially a cold-weather plant, so if you want to keep them over the summer, plant them where they will have a few hours' shade each day. They are best raised from seed every year, as old plants put forth fewer flowers. Seed can be sown in spring for fall bloom, or started indoors in January or February for late spring and summer bloom.

Most often, pansies are sown in August in the cold frame or seedbed for early spring

Pansies favor cool temperatures and must be planted in a moist, shady spot if they are to bloom throughout the summer months.

bloom (they are particularly beautiful interplanted with tulips). Always purchase the best seed obtainable. Sow seed not more than ⅛ inch deep in rows, and keep them shaded and moist. Transplant seedlings to a nursery bed or permanent position as soon as they are large enough to handle and mulch them lightly. If you sow seed in the cold frame in late August, the plants must stay there over the winter.

New plants are easily rooted from cuttings made from the side shoots in August. Set the cuttings out and treat them the same as seed. Feedings of manure water will make them grow fast and healthy.

For biggest blooms, trim your plants to from four to six shoots after they start flowering, and if you wish to exhibit them, remove all blossoms up to three weeks before the show.

After hot weather sets in, the pansies bloom so fast you won't have the time to pick them from a large bed or walk. So another trick is to shear them, leaves, blooms and all. In other words, cut them in two. This will set them back for awhile. The plants, now rid of the burden of producing so many flowers, will green up and start blooming all over again. Never allowing seed to form prolongs bloom.

PAPAW   (*Asimina triloba*)

Native to the northern and eastern sections of the United States, the papaw is often grown as an ornamental shrub or fruit tree. The deciduous foliage is large and handsome, but gives off an unpleasant odor if crushed. The white to lavender flowers bloom in early spring and the delicious, custardy fruit ripens in September or October.

When growing papaws from seed, it is best to plant or stratify the seed after they have been removed from the fruit. The seed frequently wait until the second spring to germinate and it can take six to eight years from seed to the first fruit. Papaws can also be propagated by layering in autumn or by root cuttings. The plant requires moist, fertile soil with good drainage and dislikes transplanting.

The fruit should be allowed to ripen and drop from the tree naturally. When the skin is yellow brown to brown, it is ready to be eaten.

Hardy Michigan Banana is the most popular type of papaw, having a flavor suggestive of bananas.

PAPAYA   (*Carica*)

Papayas are called the "melons that grow on trees." The fragrant yellow or orange fruit varies in size from two to 20 pounds, and has

The fruit of the papaya contains riboflavin and thiamine and more vitamin C than oranges, but is too perishable for shipping and will grow in just a few areas of the United States.

a soft, melting texture when ripe. It is highly perishable. The flavor has been compared to that of peaches, cantaloupes and strawberries. Papayas have a milky juice and black seed, both rich in papain, an enzyme used to tenderize meats. They are rich in vitamins A and C, as well as riboflavin and thiamine. The vitamin C content is higher than that of oranges and strawberries.

The plant itself has various medicinal uses: to cure chronic diarrhea in children, to slough ulcers, to retard tumor growth, and as a blood coagulant. Fresh, mashed papaya is used as a moisturizer when applied to the face.

Papaya trees are planted eight feet apart. They like a rich, moist soil and thrive on well-decomposed compost, aged chicken manure, blood meal, cottonseed meal, and other organic plant foods rich in nitrogen. Papayas are propagated by seed. The trees begin to bear about nine months after planting. A tree lives about four years, but it is a common practice to replant every year or two, as the fruit get smaller after this.

The papaya tree usually grows up to 15 feet in height, and the fruits ripen from midwinter to early spring. It is hardy only in the lower tip of Florida, sometimes in mid-Florida and Southern California if protected. The trunk resembles that of a palm tree and is topped with a cluster of huge, deeply lobed leaves.

Papaya plants may be male, female or perfect (producing male and female flowers). Long, hanging flower clusters distinguish the male papaya. These ordinarily do not produce fruit. Female and perfect plants have flower clusters at the base of the leaf next to the stem. One male plant per 20 to 25 female plants is best for fruit production. The papaya may suffer a change in sex due to severe pruning or injury.

PAPRIKA   (*Capsicum annuum*)

Paprika is one of the less pungent varieties of red pepper and is widely used as a condiment. It has long been grown for export in eastern and southern Europe and successfully cultivated in the United States. The substance giving red peppers their pungent properties is produced almost entirely in the thin papery tissues to which the seeds are attached. Even in the mild paprika pepper this is somewhat pungent. The degree of pungency of ground paprika may therefore depend on the thoroughness with which these tissues are removed. Removal of the seeds and papery tissue results in a mild product, while grinding the whole fruit results in a product of more pungency. The seeds add a nutty, oily flavor. The so-called Spanish paprika is the milder type.

The paprika pepper, like the more pungent varieties, is well adapted to southern warm areas from the eastern coastal plain to California. When the weather is warm and sunny, fruit is produced throughout the season and ripens uniformly. However, if there is much rainy and cloudy weather at the blooming stage, the plants sometimes fail to set fruit, and if such weather prevails late in summer the fruit will not color properly and may be damaged by disease.

The paprika pepper grows on a large variety of fertile soils but thrives best on a warm, mellow, well-drained, sandy loam or clay loam type. The plant is propagated exclusively from seed, which may be planted in seedbeds or directly in the field. In beds the seed is sown as early in spring as possible, and the seedlings are then ready to be planted in the field as soon as the danger of frost has passed. They are spaced 12 to 18 inches apart, in rows 30 to

48 inches apart. If there is favorable weather early in spring the seed may be planted directly in the field by drilling in rows three to four feet apart and covering with one inch of soil. When the plants are two to three inches high they should be thinned to stand 12 to 18 inches apart in the rows and missing places filled in as necessary. Frequent shallow cultivation is necessary, and this must be continued throughout the long growing period of the crop.

Fruits of various degrees of maturity are found on the plant in summer and fall because the flowers are produced over a long period. Only fully mature fruits should be picked. Therefore, the harvesting must extend over several months, and the field must be checked at weekly intervals when good ripening weather prevails.

See also PEPPER.

PARASITE

A parasite is a plant or animal that takes its sustenance from another living organism, or host. The host may be weakened, injured or killed by this relationship.

Some parasites, such as tapeworms, some nematodes and viruses, operate from within the organism. External parasites include mistletoe, ticks, dodder, and some fungi.

Fungi, viruses, bacteria, and nematode infestation are called pathogens, as they are the agents of disease. This is in contrast to the nonparasitic diseases, which are due to environmental or nutritional factors unfavorable to the plant or animal, or to some abnormality in its constitution. Often the nonparasitic diseases, such as those caused by a deficiency

or unbalanced supply of nutrients or factors such as unfavorable weather, can weaken a plant so that it is more susceptible to damage by parasites.

Eradication or prevention of the parasitic diseases is achieved by proper nutrition, sanitation, rotations, breeding for resistance, biological control, and various measures affecting the soil and air environments of the host.

See also DISEASE, INSECT CONTROL.

PARASOL FIR
See UMBRELLA PINE

PARATHION
See ORGANIC PHOSPHATES

PARLOR MAPLE
See FLOWERING MAPLE

PARNASSIA

This low-growing hardy perennial, called grass-of-Parnassus, grows wild in damp or wet, shady places throughout the Northern Hemisphere. Good for the wild garden, most species are best suited to the edges of bogs and ponds. Sow the seed in peaty, very moist soil in spring or fall. They can also be propagated by division. *P. glauca* is common in the East and sometimes grows to 24 inches tall. Two less common varieties are *P. palustris* var. *californica,* about 15 inches tall, and *P. fimbriata,* one foot or less, found in the West. All are long-lived, showy plants, with white or yellow, green-veined flowers nearly two inches across, appearing from June to September.

PARROT'S-BILL
(*Clianthus puniceus*)

A very beautiful spring-blooming vine, parrot's-bill is grown outdoors in Florida and Southern California and in the cool greenhouse elsewhere. The flowers are red or white, three inches long and borne in clusters, and the plant will grow five feet tall or taller trained on a trellis. It is propagated by seed or cuttings, and potted in a mixture of two parts of loam to one each of sand and leaf mold or compost, enriched with manure. Outdoors it does well in ordinary garden soil and full sun. Another species, *C. formosus,* the glory pea, grows up to four feet tall and bears scarlet, purple-blotched flowers. It is propagated by grafting on the bladder-senna (*Colutea arborescens*), which is also a member of the Pea family.

PARSLEY   (*Petroselinum*)

Grown extensively in many vegetable gardens, parsley is a biennial herb most often treated as an annual.

The culinary uses of parsley are many. Its crisp green leaves are flavorful and nutritious additions to salads. Parsley can be sprinkled over potatoes—whether mashed, whole or salad style—and its use in flavoring sauces, soups and stuffings is extensive.

Planting and Culture: Parsley is usually planted in March or April. It is a biennial which does well either in open sun or partial shade. Any ordinary garden soil which does not dry out too rapidly, is rich in nitrogen and is not excessively alkaline, is suitable.

Since parsley seeds germinate slowly, it is best to soak them in lukewarm water for 24 hours before planting. The seeds usually require four weeks to germinate. One packet of seed should sow a 100-foot row. Place seed in a shallow trench that has been fertilized with compost and well-rotted manure and cover with about ¼ inch of fine soil. Plant rows about 12 to 16 inches apart. For a thick growth, unwanted seedlings should be thinned so that the mature plants stand at least six inches apart. The leaves also may be clipped. To avoid damaging the shallow roots while weeding, plant radishes among the parsley. The radishes will force out weeds and help to mark the parsley rows.

Parsley will overwinter if given the protection of a light mulch during severely cold weather. One of the earliest green plants to show in the spring, parsley blossoms in the second year. To prevent the herb from going to seed, the blossoms, which look like Queen-Anne's-lace, should be cut off as soon as they appear.

In the fall the herb may be dug up, potted and brought indoors where it will continue to provide fresh leaves throughout the winter months. Care should be taken to dig up as much of the root as possible, and some of the outside foliage should be cut from the plant. Potted plants may also be started from seed indoors.

Harvesting: The first tender sprigs may be cut as soon as the leaves are well formed. From then on, the leaves, with a portion of the stem, may be cut as needed. Customarily, the outer leaves only are cut. This practice permits the heart of the plant to continue to grow and produce more leaves.

For use as flavoring, the leaves may be cut

and dried. The tender parts of the stems are cut from the plants and placed on a screen in a shady, dry, well-ventilated location. When thoroughly dried, they may be crushed and stored in small, tightly covered containers.

Parsley may also be frozen for winter use. Pinch off the foliage and spread it on a cookie sheet. Quick-freeze and store, airtight, in a plastic bag to use a little at a time.

Varieties: Champion Moss Curled is mild in flavor and crisp. Giant Italian is a strong producer. Hamburg is favored for its prolific growth and hardiness and its thick, edible root.

PARSLEYWORM
See INSECT CONTROL

PARSNIP   (*Pastinaca sativa*)

In the East and North, this root vegetable can be left in the ground all winter and dug up as needed for cooking. Freezing seems to improve the texture and gives parsnips a sweeter, more delicate taste. In southern and western states where winters are mild, parsnips should be planted in fall and grown for a winter crop, because spring planting extends the warm growing season too long, making the parsnips woody and tasteless.

Planting and Culture: Since parsnip is a long-season crop, seed should be sown as early in spring as possible. Fresh seed should be secured each year. Slow to germinate, the seed should be soaked overnight before being planted out in a rich, deeply spaded, light soil. A generous amount of compost or some other humus should be added to enrich the soil and to provide good aeration and uniform moisture distribution.

Plant the seed thickly in rows about 18 inches apart. Radish seed should be planted alongside to mark the rows and keep the soil's crust from hardening before the parsnip seedlings appear. It is wise to mulch the rows after planting as the soil must remain cool and moist during the long germination period when the seed are in danger of drying out.

As the radishes become of edible size, pick

Parsnips can be harvested in the fall or left in the ground all winter and lifted in the spring after the tops start to grow.

them, and weed and thin the parsnip seedlings to stand six inches apart. Cultivate cleanly all season until the foliage touches between the rows.

Harvesting: Parsnips may be harvested at times when the ground has little else to offer. They may remain in the ground over winter and be dug up during a thaw, or they may be harvested just before the ground freezes hard and then stored in a root cellar for winter use. If left in the ground until spring, dig as needed until the new tops start to grow; then dig all that remain and store them in a cold place to prevent sprouting. After the growth of new tops begins, the roots lose flavor and soon become lean and limp as well as tough and stringy.

Hollow Crown is the all-time favorite variety. White Model and All American are also good. Premium is a variety suitable for shallow soils.

A good way to prepare parsnips is to parboil them, slice them, turn them gently in butter until golden brown, and serve.

PARTRIDGEBERRY
(*Mitchella repens*)

Thriving under evergreens where it forms dense mats, the native partridgeberry is one of the finest ground covers for deep or half shade. Its leaves are small, shiny, roundish, evergreen, and sometimes marked with white lines. In spring appear small, very fragrant blossoms that are usually white with pink throats. Edible but tasteless, bright scarlet berries develop later in the season. These are especially attractive to birds.

See also GROUND COVERS.

PASQUE FLOWER   *See* ANEMONE

PASSIONFLOWER   (*Passiflora*)

Passionflowers are tender or half-hardy climbing vines with attractive white, pinkish or blue flowers. Native to tropical America and to various temperate regions of Europe, the plant was named for the religious symbolism that early missionaries discovered in the structure of its flowers.

Most of the nearly 400 species are grown as greenhouse ornamentals or, in temperate regions, used to decorate patios and garden walls. However, a few passifloras, such as *P. edulis,* are grown commercially for their sweet, edible fruit. The fruit of this species has a thick, leathery, deep purple hull, and is about the size of a plum. Its flavor is described as a combination of the flavors of peach, apricot, pineapple, guava, banana, lemon, and lime.

Fragrant golden pulp sacs containing edible black seed fill the inside of the fruit. This pulp may either be scraped from the hull and served separately or spooned directly from the halved fruit. In Australia, New Zealand and Hawaii, quantities of passion fruit are grown yearly, and are extremely popular as flavorings and as pie or fruit salad ingredients. The fruit is also a great favorite in England, where it is imported mainly from Australia and New Zealand.

The passion fruit is never picked from the vine, but ripened fruits fall to the ground where they are gathered. Partially ripe fruits allowed to ripen off the vine have a woody off-flavor.

Planting and Culture: The plants respond well to barnyard or poultry manure, but are not particular about soil type, provided there is good drainage, as they use only a moderate amount of water. Full sun is necessary for flower and fruit production.

Mature vines will stand cold down to 28°F. (−2.22°C.), while young vines are even more tender. Besides being prey to heavy frosts or extreme heat, the vines are short-lived and must be replaced every eight years. Getting little plants started is a tedious task, requiring propagation by seed or cuttings.

Harvesting: Passion fruit vines produce two crops a year. The winter crop, the smaller of the two, blossoms in October and ripens in March and April, while the summer crop blossoms in April and matures from July to September. Between the fourth and fifth year, a vine is in full production and, under favorable conditions, can produce up to 40 pounds of fruit yearly.

Numerous flowers will develop along a vine, but the last produced may not set fruit. When a number of fruits have set along a branch, there is a short cessation of fruit setting. Later, after the first-set fruits begin maturing, flower setting may resume for the remainder of the flowering period. This alternation of setting and cessation of fruit setting results in several sections of a vine bearing fruit, with fruitless spots in between.

Other species of *Passiflora* include the maypop or wild passionflower (*P. incarnata*), which produces edible fruit. It is one of the hardiest of the passifloras and can be grown from Virginia to Texas. The small flowers are white or lavender and the fruit are bright yellow. Another hardy species is the blue passionflower (*P. caerulea*). Its flowers are much larger and more striking. Although it is capable of enduring some frosts, it does best when grown in very mild regions or in a frost-free greenhouse.

PASTURE

A pasture is a field of vegetation (generally consisting of grasses and legumes) which is harvested directly by grazing animals.

See also FORAGE, HAY, LEGUME.

PATHOGEN

A living organism which causes a disease is called a pathogen.

See also DISEASE, PARASITE.

PAULOWNIA

This is a small genus of trees in the Figwort family that is native to China. The foliage resembles that of the catalpa, with large heart-shaped leaves, sometimes lobed, and clusters of showy lavender to white flowers. The fruit is a large capsule with winged seed, and remains on the tree into the winter.

Used mostly from Washington south as specimen trees, they are generally hardy as far north as Montreal, sending up vigorous shoots as much as 15 feet tall in a single season. They prefer rich loam and a protected situation. Propagation is by seed, cuttings or by rooting leaves cut when they are one inch long.

P. Fortunei grows to 20 feet, with ten-inch leaves and showy clusters of flowers blooming before the leaves are open. Flowers are four inches across, and colored white with purple spots in the throats.

The empress tree (*P. tomentosa*) has large erect clusters of violet gloxinialike flowers with panicles sometimes growing a foot long. Leaves measure up to 12 inches. The tree is hardy throughout the southern and central United States.

PEA   (*Pisum sativum*)

There are various kinds of peas, including those with a high sugar content (wrinkled seeded) and those with less sugar (smooth seeded), field peas grown for forage and silage, and edible-podded types. The cultural methods are virtually the same for all.

Planting and Culture: Cool weather is essential for growing peas. When temperatures are high, blossoms do not set and pods dry up or fail to fill unless the roots are kept cool by a heavy mulch of organic matter. In the South and in the warm parts of California, gardeners should grow their peas during fall, winter and early-spring months.

Soil: The pea grower must regulate his planting according to his particular soil conditions. Heavy soil calls for a shallow seeding, and light soil for deep planting. If the peas are planted too deeply in a heavy clay soil, heavy rains before the plants are up can form a hard crust that will make it difficult for the peas to break through. To avoid this problem, work the soil deeply until it is quite flaky.

Should the ground be hard and dry, deep planting is essential to provide the moisture necessary to germinate the seed. Plenty of organic matter worked into the soil will help improve the soil. A good, well-rotted manure should be applied and turned under before planting.

The pea, being a legume, absorbs its supply of nitrogen from the air after germination. Bone meal is a fine source of nitrogen until then. It has a slow action in the soil and cannot harm any crop. A suggested organic fertilizer for peas consists of one part dried blood (usually obtained from slaughterhouses),

If successive sowings are made every ten days throughout the spring, fresh sugar peas can be harvested from April or May to late June.

one part bone meal and one part greensand, potash material or granite dust. This fertilizer should be applied at the rate of from ¼ to ½ pound per square foot of soil surface.

Planting: It is best to start early with this crop and, to insure a continuous early summer harvest, to buy varieties that mature at different times. Check with your local weather bureau or extension service for information on the best planting date for your area. The tall varieties should be planted about ten days later than the low bush varieties.

To encourage rapid germination, soak the seed overnight. This will soften the seed coat and cause tiny sprouts to appear. Immediately before planting, inoculate the sprouted seed with an appropriate nitrogen-fixing bacteria. *See* LEGUME INOCULATION.

Low bush peas are planted in drills about two inches deep in light sandy soil, and about one inch deep in heavy or claylike soil. Later plantings should be twice as deep. Late plantings are subject to greater heat when they come up and deeper planting and mulching will insure more moisture and greater coolness. The seed can be scattered freely in the drill, not less than one inch apart. As the plants come up they can be thinned to stand two to three inches apart. One pound of seed is enough for a 100-foot row.

High varieties are planted somewhat differently. The seed are planted in double rows 30 to 36 inches apart. The rows can consist of two parallel drills six inches apart, or one trench six inches wide and four inches deep. Plant seed about 2½ inches apart and cover them with enough soil to half-fill the drills or trench. After the plants have emerged, finish filling-in the rows. Planted in this way, about one pound of seed will plant a double, 100-foot row.

No variety of peas will amount to much without the proper support for the plants. The best ones are made of brush that has plenty of twigs and has its bark intact. Placed firmly in the ground between the rows, this "brush fence" should stand about four or five feet high.

Many gardeners prefer to use a fine-mesh chicken-wire fence instead of the brush since it may be used season after season. Wire should be securely fastened to stakes placed at six-foot intervals down the rows. Small-meshed wire is best because it sags less than the larger-meshed kind.

Insects and Diseases: There are a few common diseases of peas. Their severity is usually determined by climatic conditions. Fungi which cause root rot may destroy the entire pea crop. A good control is to rotate the crop with unrelated crops each season. Do not plant peas on low-lying spots where drainage is poor. The same measures are valuable in controlling wilt, bacterial blight and anthracnose. If you are having trouble with damping-off, you may be planting your peas too deeply. For some suggested crop rotations using peas, *see* CORN, WHEAT.

Many kinds of insects may attack peas, but only two are serious pests. The pea aphid attacks young vines and sucks the juices from the developing tips. The pea weevil infests the pods. For help in controlling them, *see* INSECT CONTROL.

Harvesting: Green peas should be harvested when they are young and tender. If left to hang on the vines too long, they become starchy and hard. They should be shelled and cooked within an hour or so after picking because in two hours after picking the sugar begins to turn to starch. Although still edible, they are not as sweet. Tearing or jerking pods

Adequate support is absolutely necessary for peas. A brush trellis made from dried tree branches or sticks does very well. A fine-meshed chicken wire fence has the advantage of being permanent.

from the vines injures the plants so much that they may stop bearing pods. Since peas mature rapidly, plan to preserve the surplus by canning, or preferably, freezing. Peas can also be dried. Shell and blanch for 15 minutes over steam. Dry in the sun or use another method of drying. *See* DRYING FOOD.

Edible-pod varieties should be harvested when the peas are just beginning to form. At this stage, the pea and the pod are stringless and can be eaten together. Peas alone can be eaten at a later stage, but they must be picked while still young.

Varieties: A number of pea varieties are available. The familiar green peas come in extra-early, dwarf and large varieties. Extra Early Alaska is the earliest dwarf available; it is hardy, wilt resistant and matures uniformly. Improved Laxton's Progress is an early dwarf that grows to about 16 to 18 inches high and produces large pods of uniform size. Little Marvel holds the peas in picking condition longer than other varieties. Burpee's Blue Bantam produces well over a long period if the pods are kept picked. Lincoln, which reaches 30 inches in height, is a good freezer that produces through July. Wando, a good main-crop pea, stands hot, dry weather well, and is a good canner and freezer.

Edible-pod peas are also called snow peas and sugar peas. They are eaten pod and all and can be used raw in salads, steamed or stir-fried with Chinese foods. Melting Sugar is a tall-standing variety, producing four- to five-foot vines that must be staked. Dwarf Gray Sugar is an early, hardy and disease-resistant dwarf.

Other types of edible peas are brown crowder peas, available in several varieties, and black-eyed peas. The latter can be eaten fresh or dried for later use.

PEACH   (*Prunus persica*)

The popularity of peaches in this country goes back to colonial days, when they were first introduced here. Peach trees can be grown almost anywhere, although chief commercial centers are in the Northeast, Southeast, Midwest, and Pacific Coast regions.

Peaches (and other stone, or drupe, fruits) have distinct winter and growing season temperature requirements. Where peaches are grown commercially, winter temperatures are sufficiently low and last long enough to bring the trees out of the rest period without damaging the root or top system severely. Generally, an exposure of about 700 hours of temperatures below 45°F. (7.22°C.) is needed to break the rest period, depending upon the fruit and variety. For example, American plums need more cold than peaches, and Elberta, an important peach variety, requires more cold than the Babcock variety. When selecting a peach variety for your home grounds, be sure to use varieties recommended for your area.

When it comes to minimum temperatures, peaches (and apricots) are the least hardy of the stone fruits. Although well-hardened trees are often able to withstand temperatures as low as −10°F. (−23.33°C.), peaches produce best where the mean summer temperature is 75°F. (23.89°C.) or above. This explains why many northern commercial peach belts are on the leeward side of large bodies of water, such as the southern shore of Lake Erie and Lake Ontario and the eastern shores of Lake Michigan. Peaches are also grown successfully on steep slopes throughout the Appalachian Piedmont area where the hilly terrain creates good air circulation. Air movement raises temperatures that might otherwise freeze buds or blossoms on frosty nights.

Planting and Culture: Except in the areas where winters are very mild, peaches should be planted in spring rather than in fall. Plant the trees as early as the ground can be prepared, and on a day when the soil is not too wet.

Any soil is satisfactory for growing peaches, but the best ones are sandy loams, light clay loams or sands. A light, well-aerated soil is especially important in northern regions where heavier ground would only prolong the growing season.

To plant, dig a hole large enough to hold the roots without crowding or bending them. Prune off broken roots and cut back any that are very long. Set the tree so that the bud union is at or near the surface of the soil. Fill-in the soil, tamp it down, water the tree, and wrap the trunk loosely with burlap or building paper. This will protect it from rabbits, mice and sunscald. Tie the wrapping loosely so that it does not bind the bark.

During the summer, the tree should be watered every eight to ten days according to the weather. Keep the area weed free and use plenty of mulch to save water. In general, the root system of peaches is less extensive and shallower than those of apple and pear, so peach trees suffer more quickly from drought and weed competition.

By the third year after planting, the tree should be ready to bear lots of fruit. Fertilize well before the autumnal rains begin. Prune it well in late winter or early spring. You may wonder where the fruit will come from. However, you will be very much surprised when spring comes and the tree begins to bloom.

Pruning: Any sucker growth that comes up from the trunk should be cut off smoothly using a sharp knife. If not cut out, it will grow faster than the main trunk and the tree will soon turn wild. Limbs that are crossed or out of line should be cut out. The tree will grow only as well as it is trained. Incidentally, by cutting it back when you prune, the tree will grow wide instead of tall and you won't need a ladder to pick the fruit.

Thinning: Overbearing weakens peach trees so that they are much more subject to winter injury. Also, fruit size suffers when too much fruit is allowed to mature, and flavor may also suffer. Almost all varieties need some thinning, some much more than others.

Thinning should be done as soon as the June drop has slowed down. Usually the rule for thinning is to leave one peach to each four to six inches of fruiting wood. Or, calculating it by leaf growth, one peach may be matured to every 50 to 75 leaves.

Most accurate thinning can be done if the peaches are removed by hand, working along each branch in turn. But an approximate job may be done by tapping the branches two feet from the tip with a piece of rubber hose attached to the end of a broomstick. A little practice with the truncheon method is needed, but it is much faster than hand thinning.

Insects and Diseases: Diseases affecting peach trees are varied. Of the virus diseases, peach yellows and little peach are the most common. Symptoms of peach yellows include premature ripening, drooping, pale green to yellow color, and clusters of yellow-leaved shoots along the trunk and main branches. Cultivated plums are common carriers of the virus. Peaches should not be planted within ½ mile of plums in regions where peach yellows is rampant. Little peach has similar symptoms and should be controlled in a similar manner.

A common pest is the peach tree borer whose eggs are laid in the bark or below the soil line of the tree. To kill off the borers, scrape away the soil from the top three inches of the main underground root and expose it to winter cold. By spring, the orchard or garden should be free of borers.

Borers already at work inside the trunk bark can be spotted by little piles of sawdust-like frass outside their holes. They can be dug out with a knife, or crushed with a wire run into their holes. Brown rot, caused by a growth of fungus on the growing peach, can be controlled in harvested fruit by submerging affected fruit in water at 130°F. (54.44°C.) for 1½ minutes. As this fungus infects fruit largely through insect injuries, the control program should involve keeping down populations of such insects as the plum curculio and oriental fruit moth.

Harvesting: Peaches are ripe when the green color in the skin changes to deep yellow. Fully tree-ripened fruit has more sugar and less acid than fruit picked half-ripe. When the flesh gives way to a light pressure of the thumb, the peaches are ready to pick.

Remove the fruit from the tree by tipping and twisting it sideways. If ripe, the fruit will come loose easily. A direct pull makes a bruise and, once bruised, the fruit spoils rapidly. If it is picked carefully, ripe fruit may be stored from several days to two weeks in a cool cellar. When it is stored, it should be sorted every other day to remove fruit which is beginning to soften.

To freeze peaches, peel and slice them and put them immediately in bags. In this way, their flavor is preserved for up to six months.

Varieties: There are many hardy varieties of peaches suitable for growth in the United States. Glo Haven produces a firm, juicy flesh which retains its high flavor when canned or frozen. Elberta is an early variety, ripening in early August. Golden Jubilee is suited to the cooler climates of the New England and Great Lakes regions, as is Reliance.

PEACH TREE BORER
See INSECT CONTROL

PEACOCK FLOWER
See POINCIANA

PEACOCK IRIS
(Moraea neopavonia)

A species of tender iris native to South Africa, it is grown in this country only in California and Florida. It grows one to two feet tall, with bright red, one-inch flowers spotted at the base with blue black or green black. Varieties have unspotted yellow flowers, bright purple with blue black spots, and white flowers with blue spots. Cultivation is the same as that for common iris.

See also IRIS.

PEANUT   *(Arachis hypogaea)*

Usually grown in the warmer regions, peanuts can mature as far north as New England in a soil that is rich in humus. Although they are semitropical, the light frosts of early spring or late fall do them little harm. They do require a long growing season, and have become one of the chief crops in the South. Through special growing methods they can be grown with reasonable success in the North as well, even in the severe New England climate.

Planting and Culture: Work the soil deeply, and thoroughly turn in compost, aged manure or leaf mold if necessary. Peanuts can be planted, shell and all, or may be hulled first. Although hulling reportedly hastens growth, if the red skin of the nut is torn, the seed will not germinate. Choose large seeds for rapid growth and high yield.

In the South, the kernels are planted at least four inches deep, but, in the North, plant no deeper than 1½ inches. Shallow planting will encourage quicker growth, and prevent damp rot in case of a cold, wet spring. Plant four kernels to a mound, with mounds 18 inches apart in rows two feet apart. In the central part of Massachusetts, peanuts may be planted during the third week of April. Subtract a week if you live 100 miles further south, or add a week if you live 100 miles further north.

If the days are cool and cloudy, the peanuts will take some time to germinate and send up tender shoots. Do not be discouraged if plants fail to appear in seven days.

When the plants are six inches tall, begin cultivating the rows. This will aerate the soil and keep down weeds. After plants have attained 12 inches, hill the rows as you would potatoes, hilling the soil high around each plant. This is very important, for, as the branches grow, their lower leaves drop off. In place of the discarded leaf, a long, pointed peduncle appears. As it grows it will force its way into the mounded soil, and there form a peanut pod at its very tip.

After the plants have been properly hilled, mulch between the plants with at least eight inches of straw or grass clippings. The decaying material will not only keep down weeds, but, each time it rains, juices will be carried down to the hungry roots. Thin the plants to about ten inches apart. Your peanut plants, thus treated, will require no more attention until harvesttime.

Harvesting: Peanuts are ready to be harvested when the leaves begin to turn yellow, the kernels develop and the veins in the pods

Peanuts are harvested when the leaves have yellowed, the pod veins darkened and the kernels fully developed.
(Courtesy of U.S. Department of Agriculture)

darken. This may coincide with the arrival of the first frost in your area.

Lift the peanut bush gently out of the ground and shake it free of dirt. Check the planting site for any peanuts that may have broken off from the bush. Pick the peanuts from the bush and store them in shallow trays in a warm, dry place. It will take at least two months of drying before the nuts are ready to be roasted.

Save the largest and best formed of your crop for next year's planting.

Varieties: Jumbo Virginia and Early

Spanish are hardy in the North as well as in the corn belt. Jumbo Runner yields large, sweet nuts. Spanish peanuts are heavy-bearing, dwarf bushes.

PEANUT HULLS

Rich in nitrogen, peanut hulls and shells can be advantageously used in mulching and composting. Peanut shells contain 3.6 percent nitrogen, .7 percent phosphoric acid and .45 percent potash, while peanut shell ashes contain .8 percent nitrogen, .15 percent phosphoric acid and .5 percent potash.

PEAR (*Pyrus*)

Pear trees fit well into an organic homestead. Pear trees are quite hardy and grow well on deep, well-drained loam soil with ample moisture. A heavy mulch or permanent leguminous cover crop produces the best growth. Avoid excessive nitrogen fertilization—it encourages disease—but mulch or barnyard manure is perfectly safe.

Planting and Culture: Dwarf pears are generally planted 12 feet apart in each direction; full-sized trees, 16 to 20 feet apart. Nearly all varieties require cross-pollination; any two varieties that blossom at the same time will cross-pollinate each other. Pear trees are well adapted to espalier training, and thus are a good fruit for small gardens.

Pears are generally planted as one-year-old whips, which are headed back to 30 inches. At the end of the first summer, all except three evenly spaced branches are removed. Each year, these are headed back moderately and three or four shoots are left to make secondary branches. Once the tree comes into bearing, only a little pruning is necessary. Remove enough wood to induce new shoot growth and thin to prevent overbearing.

Insects and Diseases: Fire-blight fungus is one of the most serious pests of pears. Very few trees are completely resistant and those that are usually produce poorer fruit.

Fire blight attacks leaves, flowers, fruit, branches, and trunks, making the infected portions blackish as if they had been scorched. There is no known cure for the blight except surgery. Trees should be inspected for blight every two or three days from blooming time to midsummer. When it is found, the infected portions should be cut out, using sterilized instruments. The cut should be made at least six, and preferably 12 inches back toward the roots. All material removed should be burned.

Pears are not bothered by many other diseases or insects, but occasionally scabs, psyllids, curculios, or codling moths may attack them.

Pear scab appears as a velvety olive-green spot on the fruit, becoming black and scabby at maturity. On the leaves the scab makes black spots. The disease is favored by warm, damp weather which also fosters blight. Remove any leaves or fruit infected with scab, and keep the area under the tree free of fallen leaves and fruit.

Psyllids are jumping insects which produce a honeydew that invites infections of fungal molds harmful to the tree. The insects attack the blossoms and prevent fruit set. The best preventive measure is a thorough dormant-oil spray in the spring.

Varieties: Among the favorites of the disease-resistant varieties are the Bartlett, Seckel, Clapp Favorite, Gorham, and Kieffer. Other blight-resistant varieties include Orient, Moonglow and Magness. These bear hardy, sweet fruit. Colette is a dwarf variety which ripens in mid-August to early September. Winter Nelis is a tasty, yellow green pear that bears very large fruit. Beurre Bosc and Beurre D'Anjou produce hardy fruit.

PEARLBUSH   *See* EXOCHORDA

PEAT

Peat is the naturally occurring, partially decomposed remains of plants, accumulated over centuries under moist, cool conditions. Peat is used as a soil amendment, as fuel (particularly in Ireland and the British Isles), as mulch, and as potting soil. Peat differs from muck in that muck soils are composed of highly decayed materials; in contrast, the components of peats can be easily identified, especially in the upper soil horizons.

There are three types of parent materials for peat deposits, each producing a distinctive type of peat. Sedimentary peat consists of mixtures of water lilies, plankton, decomposed pond weeds, and algae that have decomposed on the floors of ponds. It makes a very unsatisfactory growing medium and has no value as a soil conditioner.

Fibrous peat consists of decayed reeds, grasses or sedges, or hypnum or sphagnum moss. Fibrous peats are generally good soil conditioners. Reed or sedge peat is brown to red brown and is finer textured and less acidic than sphagnum peat or peat moss. Both have a good moisture-holding ability (although peat moss is superior) and both make good mulches, topdressings for lawns, components of potting soil, and material for rooting cuttings.

Woody peat results from the breakdown of accumulated material from trees, shrubs and undergrowth from the forest floor of the swamp. Brown or black when wet, it is not highly valued as an addition to compost or as a soil conditioner but, when fully decomposed, yields a superior soil for growing vegetables and other crops. Deposits of woody peat in the United States are mostly confined to Michigan, New York and Wisconsin.

For most gardeners, peat is an excellent soil amendment. It loosens heavy soils, binds light soils, holds vast amounts of water, increases aeration, aids root development, and stops nutrients from leaching away. It can be added to the soil or used as a mulch. When dry, it will absorb up to 15 times its weight in water. Its effect on soils is to make a "crumb" structure that holds much more water due to the increased surface area of the soil particles. Soil-held moisture is not only vital in preventing drought damage, but it is also necessary to carry in solution the nutrients the plant must have to grow. Proper amounts of moisture also aid the soil organisms to break up the organic compounds into usable forms.

Like other organic materials, peat acts as a buffer against toxic substances. Peat moss contains no weed seeds, no plant disease organisms, no insect eggs or larvae. It is biologically sterile. It will clear up unbalanced soil conditions, such as an overload of alkalis or residues of certain chemical fertilizers. Large applications of peat have restored many such soils to production.

For all its good points, peat moss is not a miracle soil amendment. While some sedge peats do contain as much as 3 percent nitrogen, this is released slowly, over many years. Compost or materials like leaf mold are preferable to peat moss because they have more nutrients which are in a readily available form.

The amount of peat moss to use depends on the physical condition of your soil. If it is already open and friable, it naturally will need less than a sandy or clayey soil. In general, if you are not incorporating any other organic materials, one part of peat to two of the soil is a good rule. For every three inches deep you dig, work in a one-inch layer of peat moss. Aim for a mixture that, when squeezed in the hand while damp, holds its form when released but crumbles apart when lightly touched.

The acidity of peat is not troublesome unless you are growing alkaline-loving plants or incorporating huge amounts of peat. If you need to neutralize the acid, add about a cupful of lime to each bushel of peat. *See also* ACIDITY–ALKALINITY.

The gardener who has no manure and who starts out the season without any compost can use peat humus, the black, completely decayed end product of peat decomposition. It is sold under several trade names. It is an excellent soil builder and fertilizer when mixed with animal matter such as dried blood or bone meal.

Some recommendations for using peat: acid-loving plants thrive in a soil made up of 50 percent loam, 50 percent peat. In the wild garden, use two parts of peat to one of loam. Established lawns can be top-dressed with ½ inch of peat moss twice a year, and poor spots renovated by mixing in a like amount, plus organic fertilizer, before reseeding.

Shredded sphagnum is an ideal medium for starting seeds, but once the seedlings are up they should be fed with a weak solution of compost or manure. To root cuttings, use equal parts of sand and finely sifted peat moss. In the greenhouse, sedge peat makes a good substitute for leaf mold.

Peat moss is a fine mulching material. However, a summer mulch of peat moss alone should not be made more than an inch deep. A deeper mulch will soak up and hold rainwater rather than passing it down to the soil. A winter mulch three to four inches deep will stabilize underground temperatures and prevent heaving. The coarser grades of peat moss make good livestock bedding and poultry litter.

For many years, farmers avoided peat soils, just as they avoided the mucks. The soils invariably had drainage problems, their structure was difficult to manage and they lost fertility quickly. All of these difficulties can be overcome, however, and the organic soils are intensively cultivated today.

See also MUCK SOILS.

PEA WASTES

There are several kinds of pea wastes and all can be obtained in large quantities from canneries. The shells and vines make an excellent livestock feed that is returned to the soil in the form of manure. If the pea wastes show signs of disease, burn them and use the ashes as fertilizer. Pea pod ash contains almost 3 percent phosphoric acid and 27 percent potash. Composted, the pea wastes break down rapidly.

PECAN   *(Carya illinoinensis)*

A genus of the Walnut family, pecans are native to the lower Mississippi Valley and are cultivated throughout the mild regions of the United States. They require a slow, hot growing season at least 180 days long. The trees are hardy, blooming late in spring and summer. They are grown for ornament, shade and for the savored nuts they produce. Pecans are rich in vegetable proteins, phosphorus, thiamine (vitamin B_1), calcium, and iron.

Planting and Culture: Grow in soils which are well drained and deep, since the roots grow deep in the ground. Allow 70 feet of space for branches and roots to spread when the trees mature. Fertilizing with manure insures a healthy yield. Mulching is also recommended.

Fall planting is easiest. Plant nuts two to three inches deep to protect against freezing temperatures. For spring planting, stratify the seed in moist sand or moss. Plant in layers, two inches apart.

Pecans can be stored in covered containers and placed in a refrigerator for up to six months.

Varieties: Recommended southern varieties include Stuart, Mahan-Stuart, Wichita, Schley Paper Shell, and Cape Fear. Northern varieties include Major, Surecrop, Missouri Hardy, and Giles.

Giant Mahan Paper Shell pecans produce more meat per pound than most other nuts. These trees are early-producing and hardy growers, with large kernels, and thin-shelled nuts. Colby pecans, first introduced by the University of Illinois, are early to mature and are more easily grown in the North. The variety is recommended for areas where pecan trees are usually difficult to grow. The thin-shelled Colby is good tasting and meaty. The Peruque pecan is the pecan with the thinnest-shelled nut; it is perfect for eating, baking and salads. It cracks easily, and its meat comes out neatly in complete halves.

See also HICKORY.

PEDICULARIS

Commonly called lousewort or wood betony, *Pedicularis* is a large genus of the Figwort family. These annual or perennial herbs are native to North America, with some species growing as far north as the Arctic Circle. They are often planted in the border or rock garden even though they are partially parasitic on the roots of other plants. Finely divided, fernlike leaves surround showy spikes of yellow, white, purplish, rose, or red tubular flowers. *Pedicularis* thrives in a woodsy loam and can be propagated by seed or division.

Wood betony, *P. canadensis,* is a common woodland flower growing to 1½ feet. It has soft, fernlike leaves and dull reddish or yellowish flowers that bloom from April to June. *P. lanceolata* grows to three feet and has yellow flowers. A native of California, *P. densiflora* has crimson flowers about an inch long.

PELARGONIUM *See* GERANIUM

PELICAN FLOWER
(*Aristolochia grandiflora*)

A species of the Wild ginger family that is closely related to Dutchman's-pipe, this native of the West Indies is best suited to greenhouse culture. It is a woody, purple-blotched, climbing vine that produces one tubular, yellow green, malodorous flower. The flower, which can be up to eight inches in diameter, ends in a long, thin, taillike appendage. The flower of the variety Sturtevant is 18 inches wide with a tail three feet long. The plants require rich soil and a warm, humid atmosphere. Propagation is by cuttings, layering or seed.

PENICILLIN *See* ANTIBIOTIC
PENNISETUM
See GRASS, ORNAMENTAL

PENNYROYAL

There are two different types of pennyroyal, English (*Mentha pulegium*) and American (*Hedeoma pulegioides*). English pennyroyal is a member of the Mint family; the American species is not. English pennyroyal is a creeping perennial with a peppermint odor and a lavender-blossomed flower stalk. Native to the Near East, it is cultivated as a medicinal, culinary and aromatic herb. Both varieties make good insect repellents.

American pennyroyal is an annual found in dry soils from Nova Scotia and Quebec to the Dakotas and southward. Both the dry herb and the oil distilled from it by steam distillation are marketable products.

The specific name for English pennyroyal comes from its long-recognized value as an insect repellent; *pulices* means "fleas." Its old botanical name, *Pulegium regium,* is another reference to the repellent properties of this herb, and an indication that even royalty had to deal with body lice and fleas. The ancient Greeks and Romans valued this herb for its medicinal value in treating gout, ulcers and even whooping cough.

The history of American pennyroyal begins with its use by the Indians and white settlers. The Onondagas tribe named it "smelling herb" because of its mintlike aroma. The

Mohegans made a tea out of it that soothed the stomach. White settlers used it as a diaphoretic, antispasmodic and cure for arthritis. These medicinal uses by Indian and white settlers led to the inclusion of American pennyroyal in the list of official drug plants from 1831 to 1916. Its oil was considered an intestinal irritant and abortion-causing agent from 1916 to 1931.

Both species are found in the herb garden, and American pennyroyal is also a common wild plant in many parts of this country.

American pennyroyal grows well on average soils and is frequently abundant on sandy or gravelly slopes. In field planting, the seed is sown in fall. Cover it no more than ¼ inch, since it rarely germinates if planted at a greater depth. It must be sown thickly to assure a full stand in early spring because much of it is lost in winter. For best results, clean cultivation and freedom from weeds are essential. In the garden, pennyroyal prefers light shade.

The crop is harvested early in summer, when the plants are in full flower. It is dried, preferably in the shade, and the large stems are then removed to improve the quality of the product. The herb is stored in tightly sealed, nonmetallic containers.

English pennyroyal can be started from seed, but germinates slowly. As a perennial, it it best started from cuttings or root divisions. It roots easily if kept moist.

Herbals list both American and English pennyroyal's properties as stimulant, carminative, diaphoretic, and antispasmodic. The herb is commonly infused as a tea and taken in doses. The aroma of pennyroyal is also useful in sachets and fragrant bags, since it repels moths and gives clothing a fresh scent. Pennyroyal shoots are also used in cooking.

PEONY   (*Paeonia*)

A beautiful and outstanding perennial, the peony produces a showy array of blooms during the months of May and June. Although the flowering season lasts only a short while, the peony retains its pretty green foliage until frost. Once started, this hardy perennial will produce blooms year after year with a minimum of attention.

Planting and Culture: Since the peony is seldom transplanted, it is wise to prepare a deep bed and enrich the soil generously with compost and well-rotted manure. Bone meal is also frequently used.

Roots may be planted from late August until hard frost. The ground should be prepared one to two weeks ahead of planting time so soil may settle. This prevents sinking and insures that the crown is not buried. Select root divisions with at least three eyes. Hollow out a sufficiently large hole for each clump and place the growing points or eyes just below the soil surface so that the buds will be about one inch deep. Planting too deeply is the most common reason for failure to bloom. Tamp the soil firmly around the root and water deeply. Place new clumps about three to five feet apart, allowing room for full development of each plant. Peonies may be planted either in full sun or in partial shade, but not close to trees or shrubs. Mulching is usually desirable the first winter but is not necessary after that.

Beginning in early spring, peonies may need support. Barrel hoops and stakes will do, but welded iron rod supports will last for years. If the size of the flower is important for cutting or for show, disbud by removing the two side buds as each group of three forms. If you don't

disbud, the flowering period will last longer. In
the fall cut off the foliage as soon as it is wilted
by frost. This will prevent possible spread of
disease. It is wise to side-dress older plants
from time to time with compost, well-rotted
manure and bone meal.

Propagation: Peonies are propagated by
root division. The clump need not be disturbed
for as long as ten or even 20 years, but if the
flowers grow small and the stems are crowded
it is best to divide the clump. Early fall is the
best time to divide roots. Loosen the soil at
least 18 to 20 inches around the plant and
about 12 inches deep. Lift the clump and let
roots dry in the sun for two or three hours.
Gently wash off surplus earth and cut the
stems to two inches. Bend the large clump
carefully to find the weakest parts and divide
there. Cut with a sharp knife. Then subdivide
each section into strong roots leaving at least
three eyes on each section for planting.

Varieties: The herbaceous peony that dies
down in autumn is the type most commonly
grown. There are several distinct forms of this,
of which the doubles are the best known. This
form produces flowers so completely covered
with petals that the center is never visible.
Good varieties are Festiva Maxima—white
flecked with red; Felix Crousse—rose red; Karl
Rosenfield—dark red; Myrtle Gentry—very
fragrant light pink; Edulis Superba—pink. The
single, Japanese and anemone-form peonies all
produce flowers with one or more rows of
outer petals surrounding a dense central cluster
of exaggerated staminodes. The flowers are
large and spectacular, but not nearly so well
known as the doubles, which tend to stay in
bloom longer. A newer form of herbaceous
peony is the estate peony which has extra-large
double blooms, and grows to three feet in
height. Among varieties of estate peony are
Angel Cheeks, Best Man, Moon River, and
Pink Parfait.

Far more unusual than any herbaceous
peony is the tree peony, a shrub producing
woody tapgrowth which does not die down in
autumn and should never be cut off except to
remove dead or diseased wood. To plant, dig
a hole two feet deep and three feet wide, filling it with a rich mixture of topsoil, leaf mold
or old compost (avoid manure) and a pound of
bone meal. Soil should be neutral to slightly
alkaline, not acid, so add limestone if needed.
Allow the soil to settle for a week or more.
Tree peonies are grafted on herbaceous peony
roots, and it is important to have this graft
union planted exactly four inches beneath the
surface. These plants thrive on organic matter,
so top-dress with rich compost each year. Do
not allow grass to grow under the dripline of the
branches. The bushes grow four to five feet tall
and up to six feet wide. Under good culture the
flowers can be eight to 12 inches across. Plant
tree peonies in a slightly shady location out of
strong winter winds, and protect the woody top
growth the first winter. Popular varieties include Jitsugetsu Nishiki and Banks.

See also PERENNIALS.

PEPPER　(*Capsicum*)

The garden pepper belongs to a different
botanical family from that of the black pepper.
Peppers are bushy plants generally treated as
annuals in cold climates, though in warm places
they are true perennials. Five or six plants will
supply the average family with plenty of peppers for table use. The fruit is attractive when

used with other vegetables for table arrangements and in salads, it provides a touch of color as well as nutritive value. Peppers are a fine source of vitamins A and C.

Planting and Culture: Since the pepper is a very tender vegetable and one which requires a long growing season, the plants must be started inside about eight to ten weeks before the garden planting date. One packet of any variety will provide more than enough plants for the average family. Seed can be started in flats or flowerpots in a sunny window, hotbed, or a cold frame.

Put a layer of pebbles or coarse material for drainage in the bottom of flats or flowerpots, and fill to ½ inch of the top with a finely screened mixture of one part sand, one part loam and one part compost.

Keep the containers evenly moist until germination has occurred and the seedlings are growing well. When the plants have at least their first pair of true leaves, move to flats, allowing each plant at least two inches in all directions. To prevent wilting and sudden death of young plants from fungus infections, be very careful not to overwater, especially during damp cloudy weather.

When the weather has become warm, and absolutely all danger of frost is over, set the pepper plants in a sunny location in the garden in rows two to three feet apart, with 18 to 24 inches of space between the individual plants. They will grow in any well-prepared garden soil and do not require a great deal of fertility. During very dry weather give the plants an occasional, thorough watering. Mulching the plants with grass clippings or hay will save work by smothering the weeds, and by holding moisture in the soil.

Because the pepper plant's requirements are so similar to those of the tomato, many gardeners when setting out a planting of tomatoes, substitute pepper plants for tomato plants here and there throughout the planting. Peppers are also often grown amid flowers and shrubs.

Insects and Diseases: Peppers are not especially susceptible to insect pests. Sometimes when the plants are first set out, cutworms cause damage, but they can be quite easily controlled by placing cardboard collars in the ground around the stems.

The most serious disease is mosaic, a virus infection. Leaves become malformed, mottled in color, and the plants are stunted and eventually die. Remove and destroy affected plants at once. Wash hands and tools before touching healthy plants.

Pulverized dry peppers, when mixed with water and a little soap, make a good insect repellent. Caterpillars, ants, spiders, and tomato worms will be discouraged by an application of this mixture. *See also* DISEASE.

Varieties: Peppers are classified as either sweet or hot. The sweet-fleshed varieties are perfect for slicing, salads and stuffing. California Wonder, Pimento, King of the North, and Canape Hybrid are good sweet varieties. Bell Boy Hybrid and Yolo Wonder, both sweet varieties, have the advantage of being resistant to tobacco mosaic. Red Chili, Long Red Cayenne, Hungarian Wax, and Tabasco are good hot varieties. Hot peppers are good for sauces, flavoring and pickling, either fresh or dried.

| PEPPERBUSH | *See* CLETHRA |
| PEPPERGRASS | *See* CRESS |

PEPPERMINT   (*Mentha piperita*)

Peppermint is a perennial herb frequently found growing wild in moist, open woodlands throughout the eastern half of the United States. The volatile oil, widely used for flavoring chewing gum, confections, and dentifrices and in medicines, is the principal marketable product. The leaves are often used for teas, and the plant is commonly recommended as an herbal remedy for a variety of complaints.

The plant is shallow rooted, with pointed, oval leaves attached to square, purple green stems. Flowers are small and violet colored, forming at the ends of the shoots. Seeds are small, round and dark, and, as with most mints, do not always reproduce true to the parent plant.

Peppermint is a good companion plant for cabbage which it protects from the white cabbage butterfly. It can be planted or strewn between cabbage plants, but must be watched closely because of its tendency to spread.

Planting and Culture: Peppermint requires a fertile, moist soil that is weed-free. The best way to establish peppermint is to plant several plants in a separate bed. Space plants two feet apart; they will propagate themselves rapidly and fill up the intervening space. As soon as runners begin to spread, begin hand-weeding the bed. Mulching, if done at all, should be thin, its purpose to keep plants clean.

Harvesting: Plants can be harvested when lower leaves begin to yellow, or when plants begin to flower. As soon as these indications appear, cut off the entire plant an inch above the ground. The second harvest will be smaller, and may be done as soon as the plants are large enough to handle.

Strip the leaves from the stems and dry them in warm shade. Do not allow dead stems or leaves to lie on the bed over winter. Instead, mulch with a two-inch deep layer of compost and rotted manure to protect runners and hasten decomposition of crop residues.

See also HERB, MINT.

Best started from plants, peppermint will quickly send out runners to establish a permanent bed.

PEPPERTREE   *See* SCHINUS

PEPPERWORT   (*Marsilea*)

These aquatic herbs do not have flowers, but are interesting for their floating, clover-shaped leaves. They are very easy to grow in pools or aquaria. *M. quadrifolia* is a hardy plant that may become a pest by completely choking a pool. *M. Drummondii*, sometimes called nardoo, is grown outdoors in the Deep South, but elsewhere is suited to greenhouse pools and aquaria. Reproduction is by spores.

PERENNIALS

Any plant which lives for more than two years is considered a perennial. This includes woody plants like trees, shrubs and many vines, but usually when the gardener speaks of perennials, he is referring to herbaceous perennials.

Perennials are adapted to a wide variety of conditions. Some are found growing wild in wet spots; others thrive on rocky hillsides or dusty, gravelly soils; some live in rich bottomlands. A few of them are practically "live-forevers." Others start to fail after the second year or die out after three or four years.

Beautiful perennials for any setting are numerous, but even the most confirmed enthusiast will admit that you can't make a whole garden or even a whole border of perennials and get constant bloom through the season. Most perennials have comparatively short blooming periods. In England, where pure perennial gardens are quite common, the damper climate makes for longer bloom, but in most of the United States the climate usually just won't allow it and it is necessary to fill in with annuals and bulbs.

Soil: A rich soil, not too heavy, is best for practically all perennials. It should be light and crumbly, well drained but moisture retaining, amply supplied with humus.

The best way to provide this is to dig at least 18 inches deep and work in a three-inch layer of leaf mold or peat moss, plus a one-inch layer of rotted manure or compost. Increase these amounts if your soil is poor.

Propagating: The perennials that are true to species are most easily propagated by seed. They may be sown in spring or midsummer, in a well-prepared seedbed or in pots or flats in a cold frame or greenhouse. Seed will give strong plants by fall, that will bloom the following year. Aquilegias and other seeds that germinate readily may be sown where the plants are to grow. Seeds of a few perennials, such as phlox, must be sown immediately after ripening or they will not germinate. It's a good idea to have a special propagating bed somewhere in your garden for starting new plants and storing surplus ones.

Many durable perennials may be propagated by division of their mature root clumps. Others can be started from late-summer cuttings of main shoots.

Most perennials should be divided and reset every three or four years.

Transplanting: Thin your seedlings as soon as they have their first true leaves, and give them plenty of room at all times. Transplanting seedlings or plants started from root division or cuttings is best done in the fall, at least four to six weeks before freezing weather is expected. Eight or ten weeks before is even better in order to let the plants get well established. Always water thoroughly when transplanting.

Mulching: Mulching in late fall is recommended, even if plants are winter-hardy in your region. After frost has penetrated the ground an inch or so, apply a mulch three to six inches thick, depending on the severity of your winters. It should be a light mulch, such as straw, pine needles, fresh or partly decayed leaves, peat moss, or salt hay. Be careful not to smother any plants that have evergreen leaves. Mulch under these, and use evergreen boughs to protect their upper portions. Many growers believe in leaving a two- to three-inch mulch under their perennials all year round.

See also BORDER, PROPAGATION.

PERESKIA

Native to the West Indies and Central and South America, these leaf cacti have wheel-shaped flowers that vary in color from cream to red and leaves which are very much like those of nonsucculents. Plants may be leafy trees, shrubs or vines. Spines are present at leaf axils.

Any well-drained cacti soil is fine. Pereskias tolerate more water and less sun than most cacti. An east window is fine for them, but the soil should still dry between watering periods. Cold temperatures will cause the plant to drop leaves. Propagation is by cuttings.

Recommended species include *Pereskia aculeata,* lemon vine or Barbados gooseberry, or better still, colorful sports *P. a.* var. *Godseffiana, P. Bleo* and *P. grandifolia,* rose cactus. Fruit will be unlikely under home or greenhouse conditions.

See also CACTI, SUCCULENTS.

PERIWINKLE   (*Vinca minor*)

The name periwinkle is believed to be taken from *pervinka,* the Russian name of the

flower, which itself is derived from *pervi* (first), since it is one of the first flowers of spring. *V. minor* and other subspecies are native to Europe and found in the British Isles. They have become naturalized in the United States. Periwinkle was originally recognized as an astringent and nervine.

Also known as creeping or running myrtle, periwinkle is a trailing, hardy evergreen often used as a ground cover for shady areas. It is also a fine plant for edging a window box or for growing in hanging baskets or vases.

V. minor is a hardy trailing plant with wiry stems, shiny leaves and small blue or white

Because of its shade tolerance and very long flowering period, periwinkle is a fine choice for underplanting large, hardwood shade trees.

flowers. *V. major* has larger flowers and in some varieties, leaves variegated creamy yellow. Not hardy in the North, it is generally used for window boxes, and will stand more sun than *V. minor*. Both species are usually propagated by division or by shoot cuttings rooted in a sand/soil mixture in the cold frame in summer. Pinch the tips of young plants to make them fuller.

PERSIMMON   (*Diospyros*)

Persimmons do well in a wide range of soils including poor ones. General procedures regarding planting, mulching and fertilizing persimmons are similar to those for other fruit trees.

Planting and Culture: Persimmons must be purchased as very young trees because they have a long taproot which cannot be transplanted when it is older. The trees should be allowed a space 18 to 20 feet in diameter in soil that is well drained. The young trees should be set about an inch deeper than they grew in the nursery, and should be mulched well to conserve the soil moisture. Fertilizer may be supplied by a mulch of strawy manure applied in the early spring.

The trees throw up a quantity of suckers which must be removed each year in order to prevent formation of a thicket. These young trees cannot usually be transplanted successfully to increase the garden stock. If transplanting is attempted, almost all of the top must be cut back, and a large section of root must be dug with each sucker. It is easier to increase a planting by starting seedlings. These may be grafted in mid-May of the following year. Grafting cannot be done as early on persimmons as

Persimmons should be picked while still firm, then allowed to finish ripening in a warm room.

on many fruit trees, because they start their growth late in the season.

Persimmon trees require very little pruning. The only trimming that should be done is to remove broken branches—the wood is fairly brittle and breaks easily—and to open up the top occasionally.

Harvesting: Since thoroughly ripe American persimmons are soft and not easily handled, they should be harvested while still a little firm and allowed to finish ripening in a warm room, or should be left hanging on the tree into the winter months. Frozen persimmons will retain their flavor when picked and thawed.

Completely ripe fruit is very sweet and may be blanched, peeled, individually wrapped, and frozen for winter use. Japanese varieties are so sweet that they may be dried and eaten like figs.

Varieties: In the northern areas up to Rhode Island and across to the Great Lakes and Iowa, the American persimmon is hardy. Japanese varieties are able to withstand winter temperatures down to 10°F. (−12.22°C.), which confines them to an area south of the Ohio River and to the Pacific coast. Most frequently grown in this country among Japanese varieties are Tanenashi, which is self-fertile; and Hachiya, and Fuyu, which must be cross-pollinated.

See also FRUIT TREES, ORCHARD.

PESTICIDE

A pesticide is a substance used to kill unwanted animal life. Pesticides are the most drastic measure a gardener can resort to, and should only be considered after preventative measures and lesser deterrents (traps, repellents and scares) have been tried.

Organic gardening practice rules out synthetic, chemical pesticides. The power of such commercial products upsets the ecology of the garden to such an extent that pest resurgences are common. Also, the chemicals are most often toxic to humans, and are ingested on sprayed and dusted crops and in drinking water.

Organic gardeners have found several natural pesticides that offer all the power they need. While these plant-derived products may also be used to excess (even a garlic spray

can seriously harm beneficial insects), they are safe to humans.

See also GARLIC, PYRETHRUM, QUASSIA, ROTENONE, RYANIA, SABADILLA.

PESTS   *See* INSECT CONTROL

PETASITES

Early in spring these members of the Daisy family send up spikes of fragrant lilac to white flower heads from fleshy perennial roots. Mats of low-lying woolly leaves soon follow. Because they spread quickly and easily by root runners, petasites are useful for covering barren spots where little else will grow. They are increased by division or by seed.

Winter heliotrope or sweet coltsfoot (*P. fragrans*) grows to one foot and has evergreen leaves and small purple flower heads.

Fuki (*P. japonicus*) is used for food on its native island off the coast of Siberia. The stems are eaten as a vegetable and the flower buds serve as a seasoning herb. It grows to six feet and has round leaves four feet wide.

PETUNIA

The bedding plant industry produces more petunias each year than any other annual; it alone probably accounts for close to 50 percent of all annuals grown. This great popularity is easily accounted for. Petunias are highly adaptable, doing well in rich or poor soils, under moist or dry conditions, in full sun or part shade. They can be used for edging, container work, mass bedding, or spotting wherever a bright accent is needed. They come in single or double forms in almost any color, including many bicolors. The F$_1$ hybrids produce so many flowers at the peak of the season that the foliage is hidden from view.

Planting and Culture: Petunias take a long time to reach flowering size, so they must be started indoors about ten weeks before the last frost, or around March 1 in the North. Seed is very fine and needs warmth to germinate. Use a soilless mix (you can make your own by combining equal parts of perlite, vermiculite and milled sphagnum), or combine two parts good loam, one part sand and one part milled sphagnum. If the soil is unsterilized, cover it with a thin layer of fine perlite or vermiculite. Sow seed on top of the medium—do not cover it—firm lightly, and water thoroughly with a fine mist spray. Cover the seed flat with glass or plastic and a single sheet of newspaper, put it in a sunny place or under fluorescent lights, and try to maintain an even temperature of 70 to 75°F. (21.11 to 23.89°C.). Higher temperatures will not harm seed. After germination occurs five to seven days later, remove the glass, shade seedlings for one day with the newspaper, and then give strong light and cooler temperatures. Transplant into flats or peat pots when the second set of true leaves appears, usually about one month after sowing. Rather than go to all this trouble, most gardeners prefer to buy plants in spring. Select young, compact plants with good foliage color and few flowers rather than larger plants in full bloom. The latter are usually heavily rootbound and take a longer time to recover from transplanting shock when set out in the garden.

Types: There is little difference between Grandiflora and Multiflora petunias. Multifloras are generally less ruffled and the flowers are slightly smaller than Grandifloras, but this is a matter of degree only. To prevent petunias from looking straggly and overgrown in late summer, keep the seedpods picked off and pinch back the side shoots frequently. Surprisingly few gardeners use petunias as cut flowers. Those who do usually have the most compact, tidy plants. In areas with hot, humid summers, petunias are prone to botrytis, a disease which disfigures the leaves and flowers. Some of the newer varieties are resistant. Petunias which have consistently done well in wet and dry summers at the Rodale Research Center near Emmaus, Pennsylvania, include the following: Coral Satin, coral pink; Happiness, strong rose pink; Cherry Blossom, cherry pink with a prominent white throat; Red Joy Improved, red; Champaigne, an aptly named off-white; and Sugar Plum, a heavily veined orchid pink.

PFEIFFER, DR. EHRENFRIED E.

(1899–1961) A student of Rudolf Steiner, Dr. Pfeiffer was for many years the foremost proponent of bio-dynamic gardening methods in the United States. He spent most of his life in the scientific study of the relationship of plants to the humus-forming processes in the soil.

See also BIO-DYNAMIC METHOD.

pH

The term pH is the method of expressing the amount of soil acidity or alkalinity.

The letters refer to potential hydrogen, and indicate the breakdown or ionization of water into the hydrogen ion (a positively charged atom), and an oxygen/hydrogen ion (a negatively charged molecule unit consisting of one hydrogen and one oxygen atom). Since water is a very stable compound, only a very little of this ionization actually takes place.

Nevertheless, soil alkalinity or acidity is determined by this breakdown. It is caused by the reaction of various mineral and organic compounds with moisture in the soil.

The acidity–alkalinity scale ranges from 0 to 14. The low end of the scale indicates acid, and the high side is alkaline. Neutral soils have a pH of 7. Soils usually run from 4.5 to 8.5. Soils testing 4 to 5 are very acid or sour, and relatively few plants will tolerate them. Similarly, soils of over 7.8 are too alkaline or sweet for most plants to thrive.

In general, most common vegetables, field crops, fruits, and flowers do best on soils that have a pH of 6.5 to 7; in other words, on a soil that is slightly acid to neutral. Especially if plenty of organic matter is present in the soil, most plants will generally do fairly well on soils that have a lower or higher pH. A few plants, such as azaleas, camellias and gardenias do best on a very acid soil.

See also ACIDITY–ALKALINITY, LIME.

PHACELIA

A genus of annual or perennial herbs of the Waterleaf family, these North American natives are easy to cultivate if given a sunny location and good garden soil. The blue, purple or white bell-shaped flowers grow in loose, one-sided clusters, often with decorative, sterile white anthers protruding from the bells. The velvety leaves are reddish when young. Phacelias are attractive to bees.

Easily propagated by seed, phacelias do not transplant well and should be sown directly into the garden. Perennial species may be prop-

agated by division. They thrive in any good garden soil.

California bluebell (*P. campanularia*) is an eight-inch annual with blue flowers and white anthers, used in masses as a low border. Its blossoming period lasts about one month.

Also called California bluebell, *P. minor* var. *whitlavia* grows to 1½ feet and has purple or blue flowers. Variety Gloxinoides has white flowers with blue centers.

Fiddleneck (*P. tanacetifolia*) grows to three feet, with slender hairy leaves, and blue or lilac blossoms, both stamens and style protruding.

PHALARIS   *See* REED CANARYGRASS

PHASE

A phase, more specifically a soil phase, is a subdivision of a soil type based on some important deviation such as erosion, slope, stoniness, or soluble salt content. It marks a departure from the normal soil type already established. Thus, a Cecil sandy loam, eroded phase, or a Hagerstown silt loam, stony phase, are examples of soils where distinctions are made in respect to the phase.

See also SOIL.

PHASEOLUS

Phaseolus is a genus of the Pea family, that includes a number of important garden beans as well as the scarlet runner bean, an ornamental. Beans grown for food in this country belong chiefly to the species *P. vulgaris,* and include kidney beans, string beans, and several varieties dried and sold as navy beans and marrow beans. Variety Humilis is the bush bean. Another important bean in this genus is the lima bean, *P. limensis.* Not included in the genus are broad beans, genus *Vicia,* and soybeans, genus *Glycine.*

Phaseolus generally have twining vines, three-part leaves and pea-type, clustered flowers of red, yellow, purple, or white. Flat pods appear during or soon after flowering.

Most members of this genus are now classified as members of the genus *Vigna,* except the scarlet runner bean (*P. coccineus*). It is a tender perennial often grown as an annual. A quick-growing climber with showy red flowers, it is a good choice for screening or covering unsightly fences and buildings.

See also BEANS, KIDNEY BEAN, LIMA BEAN.

PHELLODENDRON

Phellodendron is a genus of ornamental trees of the Rue family. Though phellodendron is called the cork tree, cork actually comes from the cork oak, *Quercus suber.* Growing to 50 feet in some species, the hardy cork tree has attractive dark green foliage and a rounded head. Inconspicuous dioecious flowers are followed by clusters of black berrylike fruit which persist long after the leaves have yellowed and fallen. Both fruit and leaves are aromatic.

Cork tree thrives in almost any soil, and is easily grown. Propagation is by seed, root cuttings or greenwood cuttings. The most commonly cultivated species are Amur cork tree (*P. amurense*), which grows to 50 feet and has deeply furrowed gray bark, and *P. chinense,* which grows to 30 feet and has a smooth brown bark.

PHILODENDRON

Members of the Arum family, philodendrons are native to the West Indies and tropical America. Their distinctive foliage and tolerance of average household conditions make them excellent and attractive house plants. The heart- or arrow-shaped leaves, which vary considerably in size, can be entire or split, glossy or dull, variegated or plain. Some species form vines, others rosettes. Aerial roots are frequently produced.

Planting and Culture: Philodendrons like a well-drained, all-purpose soil that is kept evenly moist, but not soggy. Light requirements vary and even north windows will provide enough light for some species. Growth is best when the roots are somewhat cramped. Propagation is by tip cuttings or stems with at least two joints. Many can be rooted in water.

Types: Vining types include *P. scadens* subsp. *oxycardium,* a very hardy and tolerant plant that responds well to bark slab or trellis training; *P. hastatum,* a vigorous climber with arrow-shaped leaves; and Burgundy, a hybrid with reddish stems, reddish juvenile leaves and reddish backs on mature leaves. Good self-heading choices are *P. bipinnatifidum,* a slow grower with split leaves; *P. Selloum,* with large, deeply lobed leaves; and *P. Wendlandii,* also called the bird's-nest philodendron, with paddle-shaped leaves. One popular split-leaf type once called *P. pertusum* is actually the juvenile stage of *Monstera deliciosa,* the Swiss-cheese plant or cut-leaf philodendron.

See also HOUSE PLANTS.

PHLOX

This large genus of annuals and perennials contains some of the most important garden flowers. By choosing carefully among the species and hybrids, the gardener can have phlox in bloom from April well into September.

The American native blue phlox (*P. divaricata*) is a spreading plant of delicate appearance growing a foot high and covered with pale lavender blue flowers in April and May. It does best planted in the lightly shaded wild garden or naturalized in open woods in well-drained soil. If space permits, allow it to spread into large airy drifts—this intensifies the effect of the pleasing color. It is one of the most easily grown wild flowers and is a fine companion for all spring bulbs. Leaves which fall on it in autumn should be left in place so long as there is no danger of smothering. They will provide winter protection and summer mulch which will slowly decay and fertilize the phlox. Rabbits are the only pest.

Mountain or moss pink (*P. subulata*) quickly forms mats of evergreen, needlelike leaves about four inches high which are invisible under the blanket of red, pink, blue, or white flowers in early spring. It needs sharp drainage and soil in full sun that is neutral or slightly alkaline and not too rich. This plant is very popular, but is too frequently seen planted in situations inappropriate for it. Though widely promoted as a ground cover, it is usually unsuitable for this purpose unless the gardener is willing to spend tedious hours pulling out the many weeds which sprout in the mats. Once grass has invaded the clumps, it is all but impossible to extract. Do not use moss pink to edge a flower bed because it spreads too rapidly. It is widely available in dozens of named varieties, but many of the reds and pinks come in artificial, fluorescent shades that clash with other flowers, and the blue shades are often dull and muddy. Pay careful attention to color when buying plants, or choose the white form, which is often the most effective in combination with other spring flowers. Moss pink is best used among rocks where it can be given plenty of room, or cascading over low retaining walls. A setting against rocks brings out the delicacy of the flowers and foliage. Cuttings root easily in damp sand.

A taller phlox which blooms in June and July is the 30-inch *P. carolina,* sometimes called *P. suffruticosa.* The best variety is Miss Lingard, which produces large panicles of white, fragrant flowers in early summer and again in fall if the first flowers are cut off. This one is more tolerant of light shade than garden phlox, and requires the same culture.

Planting and Culture: Garden phlox is often called the backbone of the summer garden because no other summer-flowering plant has such a long bloom period or so wide a range of bright colors. The plants grow mostly two to four feet tall with large domed panicles consisting of many individual flowers or pips atop the stems. Colors include white, all shades of pink and red, and lavender blue to deep purple. The flowers often have an eye of a deeper shade or a contrasting color. Many are fragrant. If the main flower head is cut off when faded, side shoots with smaller clusters will develop and extend the blooming season. If the stems at the front of the clump are cut back in June, they will flower at a lower height than the ones in back. Seed should never be allowed to form because the vigorous seedlings produce flowers of poor color and will crowd out the parents.

Garden phlox does best in full sun, in a location where air circulation is good. The soil should be rich in compost and moist but well drained. The plants require a great deal of water in summer, so mulching is desirable. The clumps will need to be divided every three or four years or they will decline in vigor and flower only in spring or fall. Replant only the largest divisions from the outside of the clump. Set the crowns one inch below the soil surface and space plants two feet apart.

The main enemy of phlox is mildew, a whitish mold growth which forms on the leaves. This does not seem to damage the plants greatly, but it does render them unsightly and spoils enjoyment of the flowers. Mildew spreads quickly in humid, stagnant air and there is no way of preventing it, but there are measures the gardener should take to control it. Never wet the foliage when watering phlox—put the hose on the ground and let the water soak in slowly around the roots. In spring thin the clumps by cutting out at the ground all but four of the stems. This may seem drastic, but it will improve air circulation and cause the remaining stems to develop larger flowers and more side shoots than they would otherwise. Even young plants should be thinned, but the procedure is especially beneficial to old clumps which have begun to lose their vigor. Plant phlox where air can circulate freely around them, avoiding locations near walls or heavy shrubbery.

Varieties: The many named varieties of garden phlox are mostly hybrids of the American species *P. paniculata*. Those of the B. Symons-Jeune strain were developed by a British Army captain and include many of the finest varieties. Consult nursery catalogs and choose colors that appeal to you most, paying careful attention to descriptions.

Seeds of the Drummond phlox should be sown in beds and borders in early autumn for germination the following spring and a profusion of deep pink and purple flowers throughout the summer.

The annual phlox used for mass bedding is *P. Drummondii* and its varieties. They bloom quickly from seed, which is best sown after frost where the plants are to flower. Make successive sowings to extend the bloom period. All are easily grown in good garden soil. The whole range of phlox colors is available in seed mixtures. One form, Twinkle, has frilly, star-shaped flowers.

PHOENIX TREE
(*Firmiana simplex*)

Popular through the lower South to California, this tree grows about 30 feet tall and has heart-shaped leaves a foot wide. The small, yellow green flowers are borne in clusters up to 18 inches long. The odd fruits are pods which split open to expose the seeds clinging to their leaflike segments. Both pods and flowers make this an interesting ornamental for the home grounds. It is often planted along streets. The phoenix tree is also known as the bottle tree, the Japanese varnish tree and the Chinese parasol tree.

PHOSPHATE ROCK

An excellent natural source of phosphorus for fertilizer use, phosphate rock or rock phosphate varies somewhat in its composition depending upon its source. Generally, it contains 65 percent calcium phosphate or bone phosphate of lime as well as other compounds and trace minerals, including calcium carbonate, calcium fluoride, iron oxide, iron sulfide, alumina, silica, manganese dioxide, titanium oxide, sodium, copper, chromium, magnesium, strontium, barium, lead, zinc, vanadium, boron, silver, and iodine.

The phosphate rock sold on the market today is different from that of a few decades ago. Phosphate rock today has been ground finer than talcum powder, so that a significant part of it is gradually available to the plant. The particles are small enough that organic acids and carbon dioxide produced by the plant roots and bacteria in the soil can break them down quickly.

Phosphate rock is scarcely soluble in water, does not leach out, and is lost in the soil only through cropping. Finely ground phosphate rock is available to the plant as it needs it. Plant roots give off carbon dioxide and certain organic acids which make available the phosphate rock in the soil for plant use. Unutilized phosphate rock remains unchanged in the soil until roots develop in its vicinity.

Research has shown that use of phosphate rock may result in added profits, since it is initially cheaper than superphosphate, and, in the presence of organic matter, becomes available to plants over a long period of time.

In most grain-growing areas, the limiting factors in production are poor physical structure and inadequate amounts of phosphorus, nitrogen and water. Limestone and phosphate rock have been used to eliminate these confining factors. This is done by applying them not to the grain crop but to the legume and grass in the rotation in quantities large enough (1,000 to 2,000 lbs. per acre, depending on soil test) to insure immediate response and maximum growth. The legumes supply the soil with nitrogen and, together with the grasses, add active organic matter which improves the physical structure of the soil and increases its water-holding capacity.

Apply about ten pounds of phosphate rock per 100 square feet of garden space along with 25 pounds of manure. Spread manure first, work it in, then add the phosphate rock a month or two later. Sprinkle the ground phosphate evenly over the soil surface and allow it to leach into the soil. On lawns, use one pound per ten square feet.

Colloidal (Soft) Phosphate Rock: Soft phosphate rock is surface mined from the abandoned settling basins of former hard phosphate rock mining operations in Florida. Although not as high in total phosphoric acid content as hard phosphate rock, it does contain about 20 percent P_2O_5 as well as over 25 percent lime and other trace minerals. It is a very fine material (70 percent passes through a 200-mesh screen when wet), but granular enough in consistency out of the bag to be run easily through all common types of fertilizer spreaders without packing or clogging.

Like hard phosphate rock, the soft kind stays where it's put when applied and does not move or dissolve into the soil solution. It is of little value, therefore, to apply it to the surface of the soil or sod, such as in a hay meadow or pasture, unless it is to be plowed under.

Phosphorus from either soft or hard phosphate rock is most available to crop plants when it has first been acted upon by soil microorganisms. For example, when the phosphate is incorporated with compost, manure or a green manure crop, the population of microorganisms is multiplied manyfold, and the humic acids they secrete will work to decompose the phosphate rock much more rapidly.

The only plants that use phosphate rock well in its raw, insoluble form are the legumes and other aggressive calcium feeders. The reason for this lies in the mechanism of absorption: the phosphorus in soft types is almost invariably in combination with some form of calcium. Root hairs coming into contact with particles of soft phosphate rock absorb the calcium first. This frees the bound phosphorous ions which are then absorbed in turn.

For this reason it is important not to apply lime at the same time you apply phosphate rock. The plants will take up the more readily available calcium from the lime instead or from the phosphate rock. Moreover, there is sufficient calcium already present in the phosphate rock to furnish most of the plants' requirements. Alfalfa and sweet clover are especially active in their use of this mechanism and should be used whenever possible as catch crops to be tilled under. Following the breakdown of these catch legumes and the decomposing action of the microorganisms associated with them, the crop plants that follow will absorb phosphorus much more readily.

There has been considerable controversy about the role of pH as it relates to the use of raw, slow-release phosphate materials, but it seems to be the case that in situations where soil organic matter is adequate, a pH of near neutral (7) is best. There is, however, no hard rule for all conditions, and care should be taken not to interfere with the calcium uptake mechanism described above by applying large amounts of lime.

Soft phosphate rock should be applied at a rate approximately double that of hard phosphate rock; two tons per acre is recommended for areas where soil tests show available and reserve phosphorous levels to be low. One such application is usually adequate for five to eight years. Because available phosphorus will always be much less than total phosphorus in phosphate rock, it is better to apply as much as you can afford at full strength than to spread it out over a large area at reduced rates. Where application is banded or put in hills, much less will be required, but it will not last beyond one season.

Superphosphate: The principal difference between superphosphate and phosphate rock is that the former is treated with sulfuric acid to make it more soluble. The result is mono-calcium-phosphate, a slowly water-soluble phosphate, and calcium sulfate, a highly soluble neutral salt. One of the deleterious side effects of sulfur is that it promotes the proliferation of sulfur-reducing bacteria which work to break down the sulfur. These sulfur-reducing bacteria feed on a fungus whose function is to break down cellulose in the soil. The end result of the use of superphosphate, therefore, is an imbalance in the microbial population in the soil and the buildup of harmful salts. It is also highly energy-intensive to manufacture.

Moreover, many of the important trace elements present in phosphate rock are inactivated in superphosphate processing. Such elements as boron, zinc, nickel, iodine, and others are available in phosphate rock but not in superphosphate.

See also BONE MEAL, FERTILIZER, PHOSPHORUS.

PHOSPHORUS

A major element in plant nutrition, phosphorus is essential for healthy growth, strong roots, fruit development, and greater resistance to diseases. The decomposition of organic matter in the soil is very important to the amount of phosphorus available to plants. The carbonic and nitric acids present when organic matter decomposes are necessary to release phosphorus for plant use.

Without phosphorus, plant growth stops. Plants won't mature as they should. Scientists think that lack of phosphorous content in the plant cells greatly hampers the rate of cell division.

Deficiency: The quickest indicator of phosphorous deficiency is a red purple discoloration of stems, leaf veins and leaves of vegetable plants. The short supply of phosphorus triggers production of sugar which in turn forms anthocyanin, a purple pigment.

Corn leaves may first appear a darker green when young if phosphorus is lacking, then leaves and stalks exhibit the purplish color. Defective ears are abundant, and rows of kernels are crooked and incomplete. Tomatoes become red purple on the underside of their leaves if phosphorus is absent from the soil.

NATURAL SOURCES OF PHOSPHORUS

Material	Phosphoric Acid (approx. %)
Activated sludge	3-4
Apple pomace (ashed skin)	3
Banana waste (ash)	2-3
Castor pomace	1-3
Citrus waste (ashed skin)	3
Cocoa waste	1-2
Cottonseed meal	2-3
Dried blood	1-5
Hoof and horn meal	2
Manure	
Cow (fresh)	trace
Cow (dried)	1
Goat and sheep (fresh)	1
Goat and sheep (dried)	1-2
Horse (fresh)	trace
Horse (dried)	1
Poultry (fresh)	1-2
Poultry (dried)	2-3
Swine (fresh)	trace
Marine products	
Fish (dried, ground)	7
Lobster waste	4
Shrimp waste (dried)	10
Pea waste (ash)	3
Rapeseed meal	1-2
Raw sugar waste	8
Silk mill waste	1
Tankage	2
Wood ashes	1-2
Wool waste	2-4

Leaves are small and stalks too slender. *See also* SOIL DEFICIENCIES.

Sources: Where high organic matter content is maintained, phosphorous deficiency hardly ever appears because the natural phosphorus in the soil is more readily available. Every soil should have some phosphorus added occasionally, especially if the land is heavily cropped.

The most useful form of phosphorous fertilizer for the organic grower is phosphate rock. Finely ground phosphate rock is soluble in water and remains useful to plants for a number of years. Phosphate rock is normally applied at the rate of ten pounds per 100 square feet of garden space along with 25 pounds of manure. Work in the manure first, then broadcast the phosphate rock and allow it to leach into the soil.

Bone meal—steamed, raw or charred as bone black—is another good source of phosphorus, but is expensive to use. It has the drawback of taking a long time to decompose and release phosphorus to the soil. Raw bone meal has a relatively high nitrogen content and will reduce soil acidity because of its calcium and lime content.

See also BONE MEAL, FERTILIZER, PHOSPHATE ROCK.

PHYLLANTHUS

Occasionally called *Xylophylla,* these tropical shrubs are sometimes grown as curiosities in the greenhouse. They have odd branches that flatten out to resemble leaves, but no true leaves. Foliage flower, *P. angustifolius,* grows eight feet tall with clusters of small red flowers borne on the edges of four-inch-long, leaflike branches. *P. arbuscula,* sometimes called the seaside laurel, is 15 feet tall with white flowers. Both need a well-drained, humúsy soil in the warm greenhouse. Propagate by cuttings of the leaflike branches. Another popular species is *P. acidus,* the Otaheite gooseberry which grows wild in parts of Florida.

See also OTAHEITE GOOSEBERRY.

PHYSALIS

Known as ground cherry, these herbaceous annuals and perennials of the Nightshade family are grown for ornament as well as for their edible fruit. The large, papery fruit cases keep for several weeks and are used in dried flower arrangements.

The plants are usually trailing or creeping and bear small yellow, blue or white axillary flowers. Most species prefer a warm, sunny bed and need a long growing season to develop color in the calices. Annuals are best propagated by seed sown early indoors and transplanted to the garden bed as soon as the soil is warm. Perennials may be propagated by root division.

P. Alkekengi, the winter cherry or Chinese lantern plant, is sometimes grown for its orange

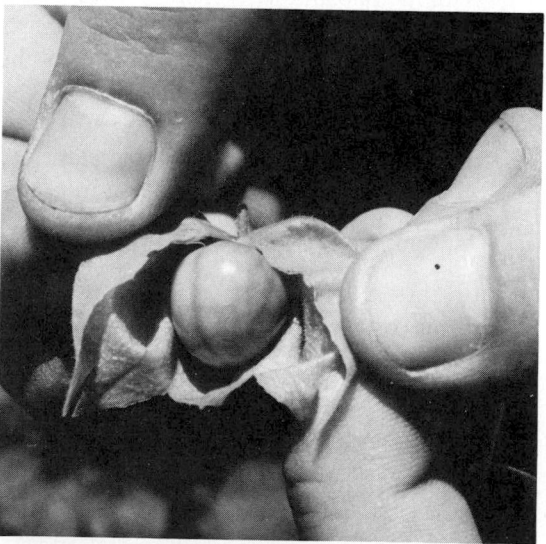

Tomatillo or Mexican ground cherry (Physalis ixocarpa) *is grown for ornament as well as for its edible yellow fruit.*

to yellow, papery, two-inch lanterns. It grows from long, fleshy underground stems which spread rapidly and become a nuisance in the garden if not planted in a confined area.

Tomatillo (*P. ixocarpa*) is a Mexican native which has been grown in northern gardens. An annual growing to three or four feet, the tomatillo has ¾-inch yellow flowers spotted with black and a fruit calyx veined with purple. It is also called the Mexican ground cherry.

Cape gooseberry (*P. peruviana*) is a tender tropical perennial with an edible yellow berry enclosed in a long pointed calyx.

The fruit of the strawberry tomato, husk tomato or dwarf cape gooseberry (*P. pruinosa*) is quite similar to that of *P. peruviana,* but is distinguished by its hairy stems and fruit calyx. It is also edible.

PHYSOCARPUS   *See* NINEBARK

PHYSOSTEGIA

Physostegia is a genus of hardy, native American perennials and a good choice for the border or wild garden. Commonly called obedient plant or false dragonhead, the plants have slender spikes of rose purple, pink or white flowers which resemble miniature snapdragons. They grow two to four feet tall, have neat, lance-shaped toothed leaves, and make compact clumps in a short time. Physostegias bloom in July and August and make long-lasting cut flowers.

The plants prefer a rich, moist soil in either full sun or partial shade. In the spring, they may be propagated by seed or division of clumps.

P. virginiana is the most cultivated species, having flower spikes up to eight inches long. Summer Snow is a white-flowered variety and Vivid, an autumn bloomer, has dark pink blossoms.

PICEA   *See* SPRUCE

PICKLEWORM
See INSECT CONTROL

PIG

Hickory-smoked bacon and ham, fresh, tasty pork, lard and sausages for the whole family—that's what keeping a couple of pigs on your homestead can mean. A home-raised porker, 200 to 225 pounds when killed at optimum slaughter weight, will dress out at about 30 percent waste, which means that you will lose only 60 pounds as offal, hide and bone. Pigs are among the easiest animals to keep and feed.

It's best to buy weaned, eight-week-old pigs, choosing the largest and strongest-looking animals in the litter. Buy pigs only from a reliable breeder who has wormed them and clipped their teeth. Select barrows—castrated males—weighing between 25 and 40 pounds, with short legs, compact shoulders and plump hams. Watch the ads in your local farm newspaper in fall and spring for feeder pigs.

Housing: There are two methods of raising pigs—the pasture system and confinement. For one or two feeder pigs, the latter is probably better because it takes less of a capital outlay initially. A sanitary pigpen is easy to

Perhaps the most sanitary way to house pigs is in a pen with a raised, slatted floor. Because the animals are easily sunburned, some kind of shelter must be provided.

build, and most experiment stations have plans for these. Pigs are clean animals, and given a clean yard they will leave their droppings in one corner.

One good type of housing is a raised pen with a slatted floor for droppings and urine to fall through. The pen should be about eight feet by eight feet, with a floor constructed of 2x6's separated by ⅞-inch spaces. Spacing is crucial—wider spaces will cause the pig to get his feet caught and smaller spaces will block up with droppings.

Surround this floor with strong fencing attached to stakes driven deep into the ground along the sides. The slatted floor can be rinsed with a hose daily, and the area under the pen can be turned into a compost heap. If you can build on a slight incline, so much the better—it will make cleaning easier. Be sure to provide some sort of shade inside the pen for the hog. Pigs stand cold weather well, but they sunburn easily and must have a refuge from direct sun. Provide a trough for food and a constant supply of fresh water.

Pasture: Hogs can also be raised on pasture, but they require a heavy, hogproof fence, and an electric or barbed wire added to the inside of the fence about three inches off the ground to keep the animals from rooting underneath. Pastures should be rotated yearly because of the parasites which overwinter and infest swine the following summer.

Good pasture can supply from 20 to 30 percent of the hog's total feed requirements. Alfalfa, clover and rape or a mixture of rape and oats are good hog pasture. Sudangrass, sorghum and soybeans make good summer pastures, with rye, ryegrass or winter barley later in the season. An acre of good forage along with a supplementary grain ration will handle up to 20 pigs weighing 100 pounds apiece.

A movable, easily constructed shade is used in the pasture if no natural shade is available. Self-feeders and -waterers can be home-built to plans provided by experiment station bulletins.

Feeding: Young pigs weighing 22 pounds or less need a diet of 22 percent protein. Pigs weighing up to 77 pounds need 16 percent protein. A 40-pound animal eats about 2¾ pounds of cereal grains and drinks about one gallon of water daily.

If a hog is confined, you can supply a large part of the feed for it from garden wastes—pea vines, cabbage leaves and the like—plus table scraps and leftover meat scraps. They will also eat leftover eggs, extra milk or whey from cheesemaking, alfalfa, comfrey, and Jerusalem artichokes. If pastured, hogs can even dig the artichokes by themselves.

Hogs can also be fed grains. Corn is generally preferred, and hogs eat it directly off the cob. Wheat is a good substitute, but should not be ground too finely because it forms dough balls in the mouth of the animal. In fact, corn and wheat can be fed with protein supplements as a complete diet. Grains such as sunflower seeds or millet should only make up 50 percent of the diet. Oats and potatoes are acceptable feeds, but should make up no more than one-third of the diet. Soybeans should not be fed to a hog, as they produce "soft" pork. So do peanuts, a popular feed in the South. Hogs on pasture can be allowed to forage, or you can cut forage and bring it to a confined animal.

A mineral supplement of two pounds of oystershell or ground lime to two of bone meal and one of salt, fed one pound to every five pounds of feed, will take care of mineral needs. The supplement can be mixed with coarsely ground feed.

Care: Pigs kept over winter need good shelter and adequate straw bedding. If you don't have a small pen for the hogs, you can easily remodel a corner of an existing structure to do the job. During the winter, pigs must have green feed or vitamin and protein concentrates.

In addition, clean, fresh earth should always be available to pigs in confinement. Pigs will root in a trough of earth and get trace minerals unavailable to them when confined.

PIGEON

Pigeons and squabs can be profitably raised on the small homestead. Although they require good housing, they can be raised anywhere in the United States.

Breeds: You should begin breeding with not less than four pairs of mated breeders. (Pigeons mate for life and are sold in pairs.) Buy good stock from a registered breeder. You might be able to find a breeder in your area by checking at a local feed and grain store.

The following breeds are recommended for beginners. They are good producers and raise large, broad-breasted squabs: White King, White Carneaux, Giant Homers, and Giant Runt.

Housing: Twenty-five pairs of breeding pigeons may be kept in a pen and loft. The loft must be dry and draft-free. Pigeons need sunshine, and a flying pen is usually constructed in the front of the loft, extending up to the roof, so the pigeons can fly and sun themselves. A pen 6 by 10 by 7 feet high is sufficient. The loft and pen must be mouse- and ratproof. Use fine wire mesh.

The loft floor should be smooth so it can be easily scraped. Put two inches of fine gravel on the floor. Open-front lofts can be built in warmer climates, but lofts with opening windows for summer ventilation should be provided in cooler climates.

Never give the pigeons nesting material. It is useless and messes up the floor. Cheap nesting bowls, made of pulp and available at a feed store, will keep eggs and squabs together. After a few months' use they may be discarded and replaced with new ones.

Each breeding pair will need two nests—one for the current squabs and another for the start of a second nest when the first squabs are about two weeks old. Orange crates stacked on top of each other with plywood between them serve well as nest boxes and are cheap to replace.

Pigeons are very clean and love to bathe. A large pan filled with three inches of water should be placed in their flying pen on warm mornings. After several hours, remove the pan, empty, and wash. Pigeons kept in a dry loft and allowed to bathe regularly don't have insect pests. Keep the floor clean and clean nesting boxes of manure at least every six months.

Feeding: If you can't raise your own grains for feeding, buy whole, unmixed grains. These are cheaper than commercial pigeon feed. Use whole yellow corn, wheat, red millet, sorghum, peas, or vetch. Never feed bread or table scraps, and feed lettuce or greens only occasionally. Pigeons need grit in their crops to help them crack grains and to aid in producing food for their squabs. Keep small boxes of red pigeon grit available in the pen. The birds need a constant source of fresh, clean water. Make sure they cannot get their feet into their water supply, or they will bathe in it.

Care: Pigeons mate at six months. The female lays two eggs which hatch in 18 days. The male helps with the nesting, sitting on the nest from early morning to late afternoon. The female sits during the rest of the day. Knowing this pattern may help in sexing pairs. Males also tend to be more aggressive, larger and have a coarser appearance.

During incubation, a substance called "pigeon milk" forms in the crops of both adults. This is fed to the young for the first five or six days after they emerge. After about their sixth day, they are able to digest grain which is fed from the crops of the parents. Since the parents feed their young shortly after eating, squabs are quick to be affected by moldy or sour grain.

Slaughtering: Squabs are ready to be killed at 28 to 30 days when the feathers under the wings are just past pinfeather stage; they should not be kept longer. They will not have left the nest at this stage.

Squabs should be dry-picked, never scalded. After picking, wash and place the carcasses in a pail of cold water for half an hour. If selling to someone outside your household, do not remove the feathers from the heads since these identify the birds as squabs, not mature pigeons. Dry and pack. For home use, dry, remove head and feet, and eviscerate. Leave the carcass whole or split it. Freeze in pairs.

PIGWEED   *See* WILD PLANTS, EDIBLE

PIMBINA   *See* CRANBERRY TREE

PINCHING

Pinching is a method of pruning in which the tender growing tips of plants are nipped off with the nails of the first finger and thumb. The objective of pinching off the top bud is to develop the side buds in the axils of the leaves into side shoots, giving the plant a stocky, well-branched appearance. Pinching is often recommended over shearing. Because the cutting force of pinching is limited to thumb and fingernail strength, only tender, new growth can be cut.

House plants which are pruned by pinching include English ivy, fuchsia, geranium and flowering maple. Annuals include cosmos, marigold, verbena, ageratum, and snapdragon; perennials include delphinium and phlox. Pinching is often done also to encourage sturdier growth in vegetable plants, such as tomatoes.

See also PRUNING.

PINCUSHION CACTUS

This name is commonly applied to two groups of cacti, the *Mammillaria* and the *Coryphantha,* both of which are favorite subjects for potted culture or the outdoor desert garden. Nearly all flower regularly, and many bear bright red fruit. Spines are produced in bunches at the end of each knoblike protuberance.

Golden-stars (*M. elongata*) forms dense, erect clumps, each prominence tipped with long golden spines. The flowers are white or yellowish. A cultivar, lace cactus (*M. e.* cv. 'Minima'), is a diminutive form with large, white, bell-shaped blooms. Old-lady (*M. Hahniana*) is globular in shape, covered with snowy hair that gets thicker with age, and bears rose carmine flowers. Snowball (*M. candida*) is neatly clustered, with dense white spines and rose flowers. Powderpuff (*M. bocasana*) has white silky hairs, white blooms, and single spines on each cushion or areole. Bird's-nest (*M. camptotricha*) carries as many as eight curving, yellow, papery spines on each areole. The clusters of feather cactus (*M. plumosa*) are completely hidden in the woolly hair and mass of short spines. Its small, bell-shaped, white flowers bloom in spring. Other varieties have delicate pink flowers, and some have as many as 60 spines per cluster. The *Coryphantha* are similar to *Mammillaria* in both habit and bloom.

Both lend themselves well to miniature desert gardens in simple or ornate containers.

See also CACTI, HOUSE PLANTS.

PINCUSHION FLOWER
See SCABIOSA

PINE   (*Pinus*)

Pine trees are widely cultivated as ornamentals and for timber and pulpwood. More than 50 species are grown in this country. They vary from about 25 to over 150 feet in height.

Planting and Culture: Pines do best when planted on a northern slope in a light soil that is not too rich. A southern exposure with no protection from late-winter sun will brown the needles, as will dry scorching winds. The long taproot offers some protection against dry soil and extended rainless periods, but makes transplanting difficult.

Although certain horticultural varieties of pine must be propagated by cuttings, most species are increased by seed planted in late spring. Plant fully ripe seed in a well-prepared bed and, as soon as it has germinated, mulch the rows lightly with straw or pine needles. In one or two years, the seedlings can be transplanted to the nursery or set in their permanent position.

In fall, winter or spring, examine the longest branches for a cluster of buds and carefully remove the central bud. The remaining ones will develop into strong lateral branches. Avoid cutting.

Types: The white pine (*P. Strobus*) is the most beautiful of the northeastern evergreens. Some of its forms are dwarf, others have variegated foliage and one is columnar. The Swiss stone pine (*P. Cembra*) is suitable for large specimen trees on estates; it is slow growing and bears edible seed. The Austrian pine (*P. nigra*), like the Japanese black pine (*P. Thunbergiana*), is planted throughout the country and is especially adapted to city growing. The latter is a very rapid grower. The rugged but not very handsome jack pine (*P. Banksiana*) is often grown on northern dunes. It has scraggly branches and twisted needles, but in the spring it bears oddly shaped flowers of great beauty that take 15 years to develop into hard cones.

The Swiss mountain pine (*P. Mugo*) is a widely cultivated species that assumes different forms under various conditions of soil and climate. Though occurring frequently as a prostrate shrub, in its native home it is a 60-foot tree with a girth of nine to ten feet. It is perfectly hardy, fine for low, massed plantings and the foliage does not turn brown, as does that of many evergreens when they drop their old leaves.

The foliage of Norfolk Island pine (*Araucaria heterophylla*) is a bright grass green and the branches are produced in regular whorls of five at short but regular intervals, making it a very pretty and symmetrical plant. It is one of the most popular house plants. The Norfolk Island pine will stand a great deal of neglect so long as it is in a cool place and the soil about its roots is kept moist.

Insects and Diseases: Blister rust, a deadly disease of white pines, is spread by currant and gooseberry bushes. Don't plant pines near these plants. Blister-rust cankers on pines should be cut out immediately and burned.

See also CHRISTMAS TREE FARMING, FIR.

PINEAPPLE   (*Ananas*)

The pineapple, a native of northern South America, was widely distributed throughout tropical regions of the world long before the discovery of America. This plant found its true home in Hawaii, but exactly when it was first planted on this island is not known.

Planting and Culture: The plant is grown from slips taken from the base of the fruit, from the crown that issues from the top of the fruit, or from suckers that grow from the lower part of the stem. It is not grown from seed. Seed-producing varieties are avoided because the development of seeds in the flesh of the pineapple spoils it for canning. When fully grown, this plant is from three to four feet high and bears over 100 long, somewhat spiny leaves arranged spirally on the central stem. The root system is comparatively shallow and must have its nutrient materials in the top few inches of the soil.

For a good crop of pineapples, soil must be loose and light. Preparation begins six to eight months before planting. All vegetation is carefully worked in. To increase the rate of the composting of the vegetable matter in the soil, plowing and harrowing are repeated several times. Occasionally, subsoiling may be practiced to increase drainage, an important factor in the growth of pineapples. Contour planting minimizes erosion and, in fields having a considerable slope, terracing is used.

Pineapples are planted in spring or fall, depending upon soil and weather conditions. The rows in the field are formed by strips of mulch paper which tend to prevent the growth of weeds, conserve moisture and increase the temperature of the soil. The mulching paper is put down with a machine which covers both edges of the paper with soil to hold it down. The paper is marked to show the spots through which the slips are to be planted.

After the slips, which have been collected from old plants, have been distributed along the lines of paper, the planters begin their operations. A narrow steel trowel is plunged through the mulch paper at the spots marked. A hole is made with a deft twist of the wrist and a slip is thrust into the hole at the same time the trowel is being withdrawn in such manner as to let the soil pack around the base of the slip. An average of about 10,000 plants are planted to the acre. Sometimes shade is provided for certain varieties by means of lath strips.

The first evidence of fruiting in a plant is the appearance of a red bud or flower cluster in the center where the new leaves have been forming. In this cluster are approximately 150 spirally arranged flowers which open when the cluster has reached a length of two or three inches. The petals are pale blue, and the flowers generally open progressively upward. Each flower blooms for a single day. The petals wither and drop off while the remainder of the flower develops into one unit of the multiple fruit. The fruits are mature and ready for harvesting about 20 months after the plants are set out.

After the fruits are harvested, the old plants are pruned by removing superfluous suckers in preparation for the second or "ratoon" crop. Each of the one to two suckers which are allowed to remain on the old plant will produce a pineapple which will mature in about one year.

Pineapples are popular house plants. To grow a potted pineapple, cut the stem from a plant with a bit of the flesh attached and scrape off the pulp. In a small bowl, grow the stem cutting in water until roots form. Then place it in a pot filled with a mixture of half sand, half soil and plenty of compost. Your plant should grow and develop a large, flavorful fruit.

Varieties: The varieties most commonly grown are Red Spanish, Porto Rico and the smaller Abbaka. Smooth Cayenne is used for canning.

PINEAPPLE GUAVA   *See* GUAVA

PINE BEETLE

The pine beetle is a short-legged, stout, ⅛-inch-long insect that tunnels through pines to deposit its eggs. Beetle damage, which is especially acute following drought, can be kept to a minimum by properly thinning pine stands and removing damaged, old or unhealthy trees. Infested treetops will turn yellow or red in winter.

See also INSECT CONTROL.

PINE NEEDLES

Like other leaves, pine needles are valuable fertilizers and mulches. They break down slowly since their resins and turpentines counteract the actions of bacteria and water. Small quantities can be mixed in with fertilizers of other kinds, especially as part of the plant matter of the compost heap. Larger quantities may be used for mulching trees; but considerable quantities should be piled separately and exposed to the influence of the weather so that

Two to four inches of pine needles can be used to mulch areas where a slight acidity is tolerable. (Courtesy of Longwood Gardens)

they may gradually break up. The nitrogen content of pine needles is estimated at about .5 percent but they have a high acid content. Mix them with extra lime or use on acid-loving plants such as the rhododendron or azalea.

See also MULCH.

PINKROOT   (*Spigelia marilandica*)

This hardy, native perennial herb occurs in rich open woods from North Carolina to Ohio and south to Florida and Texas. It grows one to two feet high and, in June and July, produces tubular red flowers with yellow throats.

Although the plant is generally found under partial shade, it may be grown in the open in rich, moist, loamy soil. It is propagated either by seed or by division of old roots.

Seed may be sown either in midsummer in a well-prepared seedbed or in fall, after having been gathered, mixed with moist sand and kept in a cool place until ready for sowing. In spring, when the young plants are a few inches high, they are set in their permanent location, spaced 18 inches apart in rows at least three feet apart. The old roots are divided when dormant, so that each division consists of a portion of the root with one or more buds and a number of the small rootlets. They are set in the same manner as the seedlings. Thorough cultivation to control weeds is necessary.

PINKS   *See* DIANTHUS

PIP   *See* LILY

PIPER

All of the members of this large genus require a moist, tropical atmosphere and in this country are generally confined to greenhouse culture. Pipers are herbaceous or woody shrubs, vines or trees that bear tiny, dioecious flowers and globular berries.

Of great commercial importance is *P. nigrum,* from which we get black and white pepper. The yellow red berries are harvested before ripening and allowed to dry until black and wrinkled. Removing the berry's outer skin produces white pepper.

P. Cubeba is a climbing or treelike vine whose berries are used for medicinal purposes in the East Indies.

P. ornatum is a tropical vine grown for its variegated leaves, which are spotted pink when young and white when mature.

PIPE VINE   (*Aristolochia durior*)

Dutchman's-pipe is the common name for this woody vine, whose small flowers look like miniature pipes. The yellow green flowers, tipped purple brown at the lobed opening, are suspended at the ends of slender tubes three inches long. They bloom in early summer. The heart-shaped leaves grow from six to 14 inches wide and form a dense cover, making the Dutchman's-pipe an excellent screen if trained on a trellis.

Usually grown from seed, this native of eastern North America will prosper if given a moist, rich soil and sun or partial shade. It often grows to 30 feet.

PISTACHIO   (*Pistacia vera*)

The pistachio is a spreading deciduous tree bearing the yellow green nut considered a delicacy here and on the Mediterranean, where it is native. Leaves of the pistachio are compound and alternate. The trees are dioecious with the inconspicuous flowers being all male on some trees and female on others.

The Chinese pistachio (*P. chinensis*) grows to 60 feet, and is grown principally for ornament, or for rootstocks on which is grafted *P. vera*. Propagated mostly by budding or grafting, pistachios are grown only in California in this country, where they find the dry climate they need.

Varieties which are considered best for nut production are Trabonella, Kerman and Aleppo, with Peters for the pollinator.

Space the trees 20 to 25 feet apart. If your garden space is minimal, graft a branch from a male tree onto the female tree, making only one tree necessary.

PISTILLATE

Pistillate is an adjective used to describe a female flower, that is, one bearing pistils but no stamens.

PITCHER PLANT

There are several different plants known as pitcher plants, including members of the genus *Sarracenia* and the genus *Nepenthes*.

Nepenthes are insectivorous, semiwoody, climbing plants native to tropical Asia as far south as northern Australia. They are called pitcher plants because an extension of the leaf midrib broadens into a pitcher-shaped vessel, often brightly colored, and with a large or small lid. The pitchers fill with a viscous liquid, and often contain enough water after a rain to drown small animals or birds. Insects become trapped in the pitchers where they are then digested.

Inconspicuous flowers, borne in clusters, are male on some plants and female on others. Seed is contained in a leathery capsule and is produced when both male or female plants are present.

Propagation is by cuttings or seed, at a temperature of 80 to 85°F. (26.67 to 29.44° C.), using sphagnum and peat moss in a glass jar or case. After being thoroughly rooted, they may be removed to hanging baskets under the roof of the greenhouse, where they should be shaded, with temperatures of 68 to 77°F. (20 to 25°C.) and 90 to 100 percent humidity. Some of the smaller varieties can be grown in a large, covered terrarium with a thermostatic tropical fish heater. A growing medium of two parts sphagnum moss to one part osmunda fiber is best and must be kept wet constantly.

Various species of the *Sarracenia* genus (closely related to *Darlingtonia*) are also known as pitcher plants. These are perennials found in wet, peaty woods and are somewhat easier to cultivate at home. They are distinguished by their large basal leaves which are shaped like pitchers and which trap insects by attracting them to a honeylike substance secreted by glands in an upper area of the pitcher. Beneath these glands is a smooth wall that makes clinging very difficult, so that insects slip into the bottom of the pitcher. They are prevented from ascending the walls of the pitcher by hairs that slope downward. The insect is dissolved by juices in the pitcher. The genus occurs almost exclusively east of the Mississippi, and is protected in North Carolina.

They may be grown in a bog or wild garden or in a terrarium as long as their native growing conditions are approximated as closely as possible. Full sun is best. Plant in a mixture of fine loam and sphagnum moss, and keep moist. Propagate by seed or root division in early spring.

See also DARLINGTONIA.

PITTOSPORUM

This is a genus of evergreen trees and shrubs native to Asia, a few South Pacific islands and Australia. Some are used in California, Florida and the Gulf states as hedges and windbreaks. One variety is grown in greenhouses for its thick, leathery foliage. Small purple, red or yellow flowers are fragrant in some species. The trees are propagated by seed, greenwood cuttings and grafting.

Karo (*P. crassifolium*) is used as a windbreak in California. It is a shrub or small tree, growing to 30 feet in New Zealand. Leathery leaves measure three inches long, and the red or purple flowers hang in terminal clusters.

Tawhiwhi (*P. tenuifolium*) is a dense tree good for screening because it will stand close clipping. It is also called kohuhu and black mapau.

Japanese pittosporum (*P. Tobira*) is the species used for greenhouse culture. It has yellow white fragrant flowers in terminal clusters. It is also used in warm climates as a hedge shrub.

Victorian box (*P. undulatum*) is used as an avenue tree in Southern California, and is also planted for its fragrant flowers. The tree grows to 40 feet, and the leaves measure six inches in length.

Queensland pittosporum (*P. rhombifolium*) is also grown as an avenue tree, and has yellow orange fruits which remain decorative for a long period. It grows to 80 feet, has leaves about four inches long, and white flowers.

Tarata (*P. eugenioides*) is used in clipped hedges and for ornamental plantings in California. It is a tall slender tree.

PITYROGRAMMA

Once classified as *Gymnogramma*, these tropical ferns are grown mostly in greenhouses or homes with relative humidity levels of 40 percent or better. They are good plants for a terrarium when small and immature. Pityrogrammas prefer an all-purpose soil kept evenly moist; an eastern, western or lightly shaded southern exposure; and temperatures of 50 to 55°F. (10 to 12.78°C.) nights and 70°F. (21.11°C.) days.

Some good species include silver fern (*P. calomelanos*) whose fronds are three feet long, ten inches wide and silver white on the backsides; gold-fern (*P. chrysophylla*), with fronds that are sulfur yellow on the reverse; and golden-back or California gold fern (*P. triangularis*), with seven-inch fronds that are yellow orange on the backsides. It grows to about a foot high.

See also HOUSE PLANTS.

PLANE TREE (*Platanus*)

This genus of the Platanus family contains six species of handsome deciduous trees that are characterized by large patches of flaking bark and dense maplelike foliage. The trees thrive in rich, moist soil, and will stand severe pruning. The flowers are ball-like with male and female separate but on the same tree. The fruit is a ball-like mass.

The spreading London plane (*P. x acerifolia* or *P. x hybrida*) grows to 140 feet and is hardy except in the coldest parts of the United States. Its leaves are blunt tipped and three- to five-lobed.

Buttonwood or eastern sycamore (*P. occidentalis*) is a very large tree with a thick trunk and grows to 150 feet high. It is not as good for city planting as London plane but is hardy in the woodlands.

PLANTAIN LILY   *See* HOSTA, LILY

PLANT BREEDING

Since Neolithic times man has attempted to control and improve his crops through the breeding of improved plant varieties. The earliest technique, pure-line selection, is still practiced by home gardeners. Beginning with a mixed population of plants, the breeder selects and saves the seed of those that appear to have the characteristics desired—early fruiting or high yield or resistance to a particular virus, for example. The plants resulting from the saved seed are judged again for desirable traits, and the best seed is once again saved. Though such methods can result in greatly improved varieties, pure-line selection is limited in that only those genetic combinations found in nature can be utilized. Varieties in which a desirable trait is discovered may also have undesirable traits, and in pure-line selection there is no way to transfer the desirable trait to another variety.

The basis of modern plant breeding is crossing or hybridization. By fertilizing one plant with the pollen of another, the plant breeder can produce new varieties rapidly. The home gardener can produce hybrids by choosing a blossom whose pollen is ready, carrying it to the other blossom as soon as it opens, and dusting the pollen over it, covering the pistil. The plants resulting from the seed of plants fertilized in this way will be a combination of the two parent varieties.

More recent developments in plant breeding concentrate on the internal workings of plants. Breeders can transfer genes responsible for desirable traits to other varieties. Such research has produced the high-protein opaque-2 corn with its favorable balance of amino acids, as well as crops resistant to disease, insect attack, flood, drought, and other adverse environmental conditions. Further work is being done on the fusion of cells from diverse species. An example of this work is the synthesized grain, triticale, a cross between wheat and rye.

Plant scientists have focused on solving the hunger crisis by producing high-yielding varieties of the staple grains. With these varieties yields sometimes increase fivefold. Unfortunately this research has often produced varieties dependent on irrigation, chemical fertilizers, pesticides, or other costly cultural techniques. In addition, farmers are likely to plant only the variety which promises the highest yield. Such monoculture allows the possibility of total crop failure if, for example, a virus to which the variety is not resistant unexpectedly attacks. For these reasons some research now emphasizes the development of a population of many improved varieties, a land race composed of several individual plant types which, as a whole, can be depended upon to produce a good crop.

See also CROSSING, HYBRID, RESISTANT VARIETIES, TRITICALE.

PLANT DISEASE   *See* DISEASE

PLANT FAMILY
See BOTANICAL NOMENCLATURE

PLANTING BY THE MOON
See MOON PLANTING

PLANTING DATES

The best time to plant seed or transplant seedlings depends upon the crop you are planting and the climate in your region. Hardy crops such as onion and certain greens prefer cooler temperatures and can be planted as soon as the ground can be worked, regardless of the last frost date. Cold-sensitive plants such as tomato and pepper cannot be set out until the soil has warmed thoroughly and all danger of frost has passed. Obviously, planting times are

EARLY PLANTING DATES FOR VEGETABLES MARCH 20–APRIL 10

| Crop | Planting dates for localities with average last freeze on— | | |
	Mar. 20	Mar. 30	Apr. 10
Asparagus, plants	Feb. 1–Mar. 10	Feb. 15–Mar. 20	Mar. 10–Apr. 10
Bean, lima	Apr. 1–June 15	Apr. 15–June 20	Apr. 15–June 30
Bean, snap	Mar. 15–May 25	Apr. 1–June 1	Apr. 10–June 30
Beet	Feb. 15–May 15	Mar. 1–June 1	Mar. 10–June 1
Broccoli, plants	Feb. 15–May 15	Mar. 1–20	Mar. 15–Apr. 15
Brussels sprouts, plants	Feb. 15–May 15	Mar. 1–20	Mar. 15–Apr. 15
Cabbage, plants	Feb. 15–Mar. 20	Feb. 15–Mar. 10	Mar. 1–Apr. 1
Carrot	Feb. 15–Mar. 20	Mar. 1–Apr. 10	Mar. 10–Apr. 20
Cauliflower, plants	Feb. 10–Mar. 10	Feb. 20–Mar. 20	Mar. 1–Mar. 20
Celery and celeriac	Mar. 1–Apr. 1	Mar. 15–Apr. 15	Apr. 1–Apr. 20
Chard	Feb. 20–May 15	Mar. 1–May 25	Mar. 15–June 15
Chervil and chive	Feb. 10–Mar. 10	Feb. 15–Mar. 15	Mar. 1–Apr. 1
Chicory, witloof	June 1–July 1	June 1–July 1	June 10–July 1
Collard, plants	Feb. 15–May 1	Mar. 1–June 1	Mar. 1–June 1
Cornsalad	Jan. 1–Mar. 15	Jan. 15–Mar. 15	Feb. 1–Apr. 1
Corn, sweet	Mar. 15–May 1	Mar. 25–May 15	Apr. 10–June 1
Cress, upland	Feb. 20–Mar. 15	Mar. 1–Apr. 1	Mar. 10–Apr. 15
Cucumber	Apr. 1–May 1	Apr. 10–May 15	Apr. 20–June 1
Dandelion	Feb. 10–Mar. 10	Feb. 20–Mar. 20	Mar. 1–Apr. 1
Eggplant, plants	Apr. 1–May 1	Apr. 15–May 15	May 1–June 1
Endive	Mar. 1–Apr. 1	Mar. 10–Apr. 10	Mar. 15–Apr. 15
Fennel, Florence	Mar. 1–Apr. 1	Mar. 10–Apr. 10	Mar. 15–Apr. 15
Garlic	Feb. 1–Mar. 1	Feb. 10–Mar. 10	Feb. 20–Mar. 20
Horseradish, plants		Mar. 1–Apr. 1	Mar. 10–Apr. 10
Kale	Feb. 20–Mar. 10	Mar. 1–20	Mar. 10–Apr. 1
Kohlrabi	Feb. 20–Mar. 10	Mar. 1–Apr. 1	Mar. 10–Apr. 10
Leek	Feb. 1–Mar. 1	Feb. 15–Mar. 15	Mar. 1–Apr. 1
Lettuce, head, plants	Feb. 15–Mar. 10	Mar. 1–20	Mar. 10–Apr. 1
Lettuce, leaf	Feb. 1–Apr. 1	Feb. 15–Apr. 15	Mar. 15–May 15
Mustard	Feb. 20–Apr. 1	Mar. 1–Apr. 15	Mar. 10–Apr. 20
Okra	Apr. 1–June 15	Apr. 10–June 15	Apr. 20–June 15
Onion, plants	Feb. 10–Mar. 10	Feb. 15–Mar. 15	Mar. 1–Apr. 1
Onion, seed	Feb. 10–Mar. 10	Feb. 20–Mar. 15	Mar. 1–Apr. 1
Onion, sets	Feb. 1–Mar. 20	Feb. 15–Mar. 20	Mar. 1–Apr. 1
Parsley	Feb. 15–Mar. 15	Mar. 1–Apr. 1	Mar. 10–Apr. 10
Parsnip	Feb. 15–Mar. 15	Mar. 1–Apr. 1	Mar. 10–Apr. 10
Pea, black-eyed	Apr. 1–July 1	Apr. 15–July 1	May 1–July 1
Pea, garden	Feb. 1–Mar. 15	Feb. 10–Mar. 20	Feb. 20–Mar. 20
Pepper, plants	Apr. 10–June 1	Apr. 15–June 1	May 1–June 1
Potato	Feb. 10–Mar. 15	Feb. 20–Mar. 20	Mar. 10–Apr. 1
Radish	Jan. 20–May 1	Feb. 15–May 1	Mar. 1–May 1
Rhubarb, plants			Mar. 1–Apr. 1
Rutabaga	Jan. 15–Mar. 1	Feb. 1–Mar. 1	Mar. 1–Apr. 1
Salsify	Feb. 15–Mar. 1	Mar. 1–15	Mar. 10–Apr. 15
Shallot	Feb. 1–Mar. 10	Feb. 15–Mar. 15	Mar. 1–Apr. 1
Sorrel	Feb. 10–Mar. 20	Feb. 20–Apr. 1	Mar. 1–Apr. 15
Soybean	Apr. 10–June 30	Apr. 20–June 30	May 1–June 30
Spinach	Jan. 15–Mar. 15	Feb. 1–Mar. 20	Feb. 15–Apr. 1
Spinach, New Zealand	Apr. 1–May 15	Apr. 10–June 1	Apr. 20–June 1
Squash, summer	Apr. 1–May 15	Apr. 10–June 1	Apr. 20–June 1
Sweet potato, plants	Apr. 10–June 1	Apr. 20–June 1	May 1–June 1
Tomato, plants	Apr. 1–May 20	Apr. 10–June 1	Apr. 20–June 1
Turnip	Feb. 10–Mar. 10	Feb. 20–Mar. 20	Mar. 1–Apr. 1

EARLY PLANTING DATES FOR VEGETABLES APRIL 20–MAY 10

| Crop | Planting dates for localities with average last freeze on— | | |
	Apr. 20	Apr. 30	May 10
Asparagus, plants	Mar. 15–Apr. 15	Mar. 20–Apr. 15	Apr. 10–Apr. 30
Bean, lima	May 1–June 20	May 15–June 15	May 25–June 15
Bean, snap	Apr. 25–June 30	May 10–June 30	May 10–June 30
Beet	Mar. 20–June 1	Apr. 1–June 15	Apr. 15–June 15
Broccoli, plants	Mar. 25–Apr. 20	Apr. 1–May 1	Apr. 15–June 1
Brussels sprouts, plants	Mar. 25–Apr. 20	Apr. 1–May 1	Apr. 15–June 1
Cabbage, plants	Mar. 10–Apr. 1	Mar. 15–Apr. 10	Apr. 1–May 15
Carrot	Apr. 1–May 15	Apr. 10–June 1	Apr. 20–June 15
Cauliflower, plants	Mar. 15–Apr. 20	Apr. 10–May 10	Apr. 15–May 15
Celery and celeriac	Apr. 10–May 1	Apr. 15–May 1	Apr. 20–June 15
Chard	Apr. 1–June 15	Apr. 15–June 15	Apr. 20–June 15
Chervil and chive	Mar. 10–Apr. 10	Mar. 20–Apr. 20	Apr. 1–May 1
Chicory, witloof	June 15–July 1	June 15–July 1	June 1–20
Collard, plants	Mar. 10–June 1	Apr. 1 June 1	Apr. 15–June 1
Cornsalad	Feb. 15–Apr. 15	Mar. 1–May 1	Apr. 1–June 1
Corn, sweet	Apr. 25–June 15	May 10–June 15	May 10–June 1
Cress, upland	Mar. 20–May 1	Apr. 10–May 10	Apr. 20–May 20
Cucumber	May 1–June 15	May 15–June 15	May 20–June 15
Dandelion	Mar. 10–Apr. 10	Mar. 20–Apr. 20	Apr. 1–May 1
Eggplant, plants	May 10–June 1	May 15 June 10	May 20–June 15
Endive	Mar. 25–Apr. 15	Apr. 1–May 1	Apr. 15–May 15
Fennel, Florence	Mar. 25–Apr. 15	Apr. 1–May 1	Apr. 15–May 15
Garlic	Mar. 10–Apr. 1	Mar. 15–Apr. 15	Apr. 1–May 1
Horseradish, plants	Mar. 20–Apr. 20	Apr. 1–30	Apr. 15–May 15
Kale	Mar. 20–Apr. 10	Apr. 1–20	Apr. 10–May 1
Kohlrabi	Mar. 20–May 1	Apr. 1–May 10	Apr. 10–May 15
Leek	Mar. 15–Apr. 15	Apr. 1–May 1	Apr. 15–May 15
Lettuce, head, plants	Mar. 20–Apr. 15	Apr. 1–May 1	Apr. 15–May 15
Lettuce, leaf	Mar. 20–May 15	Apr. 1–June 1	Apr. 15–June 15
Mustard	Mar. 20–May 1	Apr. 1–May 10	Apr. 15–June 1
Okra	May 1–June 1	May 10–June 1	May 20–June 10
Onion, plants	Mar. 15–Apr. 10	Apr. 1–May 1	Apr. 10–May 1
Onion, seed	Mar. 15–Apr. 1	Mar. 15–Apr. 15	Apr. 1–May 1
Onion, sets	Mar. 10–Apr. 1	Mar. 10–Apr. 10	Apr. 10–May 1
Parsley	Mar. 20–Apr. 20	Apr. 1–May 1	Apr. 15–May 15
Parsnip	Mar. 20–Apr. 20	Apr. 1–May 1	Apr. 15–May 15
Pea, black-eyed	May 10–June 15	May 15–June 1	
Pea, garden	Mar. 10–Apr. 10	Mar. 20–May 1	Apr. 1–May 15
Pepper, plants	May 10–June 1	May 15–June 10	May 20–June 10
Potato	Mar. 15–Apr. 10	Mar. 20–May 10	Apr. 1–June 1
Radish	Mar. 10–May 10	Mar. 20–May 10	Apr. 1–June 1
Rhubarb, plants	Mar. 10–Apr 10	Mar. 20–Apr. 15	Apr. 1–May 1
Rutabaga	Apr. 1–May 1	May 1–June 1	May 1–June 1
Salsify	Mar. 20–May 1	Apr. 1–May 15	Apr. 15–June 1
Shallot	Mar. 15–Apr. 15	Apr. 1–May 1	Apr. 10–May 1
Sorrel	Mar. 15–May 1	Apr. 1–May 15	Apr. 15–June 1
Soybean	May 10–June 20	May 25–June 15	May 25–June 10
Spinach	Mar. 1–Apr. 15	Mar. 20–Apr. 20	Apr. 1–June 15
Spinach, New Zealand	May 1–June 15	May 1–June 15	May 10–June 15
Squash, summer	May 1–June 15	May 1–30	May 10–June 10
Sweet potato, plants	May 10–June 10	May 20–June 10	
Tomato, plants	May 5–June 10	May 10–June 15	May 15–June 10
Turnip	Mar. 10–Apr. 1	Mar. 20–May 1	Apr. 1–June 1

different in different areas. Gardeners in high-altitude or northern regions may not be able to plant until several months after those living in milder areas.

The charts presented on pages 879 and 880 are useful planting guides only in a very general sense. The specific date of the last killing frost will vary from year to year in your region and may even occur several weeks after the "average last frost date" calculated by the state extension service in your area. However, if you follow these suggested planting dates *and* keep track of local weather reports, you will be able to have an early and productive garden. When frosts are predicted, cover plants with hotcaps or a light mulch. Turn the sprinkler on extremely sensitive plants and let it run all night. This will lessen the danger of frost damage.

See also Cloche Gardening, Frost.

PLATANUS   *See* Plane Tree

PLATTERDOCK   *See* Nymphaea

PLATYCERIUM
   See Staghorn Fern

PLATYCODON
   See Balloon Flower

PLOWING   *See* Cultivation

PLUG PLANTING   *See* Lawn

PLUM   (*Prunus*)

No matter where you live, you can have red, purple or golden yellow plums. Many new hardy varieties have been developed, as well as early, midseason and late-bearing strains, and the beauty of their masses of white flowers in the spring is an added inducement to growing them around the home.

There are four types of plums: American, Damson, European, and Japanese. Some varieties in each type will suit your area and general conditions.

Planting and Culture: Well-drained soil is especially important to plums. The European and Damson do best in heavy loam soils, while the Japanese prefer light, sandy loams. The American types thrive on a wide range of soils, but in general prefer ground suited to peaches. With the use of compost and natural fertilizers, vigorous growth occurs. Fertilizing too heavily, which is almost impossible with natural materials, will stimulate too much growth and delay bearing. On the home grounds, a mulch, renewed yearly, is the best practice. In orchards, late-summer-sown cover crops like clover, buckwheat, oats, or barley are recommended.

Planting: Most plums are self-fertile; two varieties are not necessary for pollination. *See also* Orchard.

Where winters are comparatively mild, plums may be planted in fall. The trees are stronger where fall planting is possible, and will go into their first growing season in the garden better prepared for whatever setbacks may come if their roots have had a chance to become established before leaves, demanding moisture, open in spring. Where winter temperatures fall below 0°F. (−17.78°C.), spring planting is advisable. Trees should be completely dormant when planted.

Where plums are to be planted in a home lawn, a circle at least six feet in diameter should be cleared of all grass and other roots, and the soil should be stirred to a depth of ten to 12 inches. A good supply of phosphorus and potash may be dug in at the same time. If these take the form of phosphate rock and granite dust, they will slowly become available to the young tree over the course of several years.

Plum trees need a space 18 to 24 feet in diameter after the trees are fully mature. When planting Japanese plums, try to give them a situation where the spring growth will not start too early, so that their blossoms will be delayed until the last of the spring frosts are past. Damsons and native species take less room than the large and spreading European and Japanese types.

Make the hole large enough to contain the roots without cramping. Cut off any roots that are damaged or that are too long. Set the tree at the depth at which it grew in the nursery. Firm the soil well as it is filled in around the roots and water it well before adding the last two or three inches. As soon as the young tree is planted, paint the trunk with white paint or wrap it loosely in several thicknesses of roofing paper. On milder winter days, heat from the sun may become quite intense on a tree's dark bark, causing the sap to rise. If nighttime temperatures drop below freezing, the sap can even freeze, causing the bark to split. White paint, or white wrappings, prevent the bark from absorbing so much heat.

Pruning: After the trees come into bearing, pruning should be limited to removal of dense top wood, damaged wood and crossing branches. If there is little of this to remove, some of the more rampant new growth should be cut out each year to encourage production of new fruiting spurs and to stimulate some new growth during the coming year. A tree should never be allowed to come to a standstill in its growth—it should make a little new growth each year, but not too much. This is especially important in the Japanese varieties whose fruit is grown on new wood. With plum trees, it is better to prune too little than too much. The trees are very easily thrown out of balance, and too much pruning may force them to develop overly dense tops.

Many varieties of plums tend to overbear when the season is favorable. Not only does the size and quality of the fruit suffer when too much fruit is allowed to mature, but the weight of so much fruit may break branches, or even split the trunk of the tree. Moreover, where the fruits touch one another, brown-rot fungus sets in and spreads from fruit to fruit. To avoid this, wait until after the normal June drop, then thin the fruit so that it hangs freely. Fruit should be permitted to remain no closer than one to three inches apart when thinned.

Pests and Diseases: Plum trees are all susceptible to heart rot which is the result of careless pruning practice. When pruning a plum, cut all limbs as short as possible. Stubs which are too long to heal invite the entry of bacteria to the heartwood, and heart rot results.

Most of the insect enemies of plum have already been covered under entries for other fruits or, under INSECT CONTROL. The only other serious pest is the bird population, which flocks around the plum trees almost as enthusiastically as around the cherries. If you have the room, plant enough mulberries close by to distract the birds, because one thing that they love more than plums and cherries, is a tree of ripe mulberries.

If you keep poultry, plant plum trees in your poultry yard and you'll never be troubled with the plum curculio, which causes wormy fruits. The chickens and ducks will eat the bugs wholesale. Dormant sprays and regular sanitation take care of other pests.

Harvesting: For canning or jelly making, plums may be picked as soon as they have developed their bloom. At this point they are slightly soft, but still retain some of their tartness and firmness. For dessert, they should be allowed to become fully ripe on the tree. When ripe, many of them will be very soft and should not be handled excessively. At this point, however, they are most delicious and naturally sweet.

Plums suitable for drying are usually distinguished by the fact that they will hang on the tree long after they are fully ripe, and develop more sugar as they hang. Home plum drying is usually practical only where the climate is very dry at harvesttime. Where early fall rains or heavy dews may be expected, the crop may be damaged or completely ruined before it is dry.

In commercial orchards, prune trays are placed beneath the trees when the fruit is ready to fall. The trees are shaken until the prunes drop into the trays. Then the trays are moved to the sunny drying yard and kept off the ground to allow full circulation of air. Fruit is stirred regularly to expose all sides to the sun. On a small scale, fruit may be protected from dew or rain by moving it indoors, or covering it with tarpaulins.

In northern climates and those with wet fall weather, plums may be dried in a specially constructed dryer, or they may even be dried in an ordinary oven if it can be closely regulated. After removing the fruit from the tree it should be spread in drying trays which will fit the oven. Fruit should be no more than one layer deep in each tray, and a little space must be left between the fruit to permit the air to circulate. It is then placed in the oven, which has been set for 110 to 150°F. (43.33 to 65.56°C.). The fruit must be stirred frequently. Total oven dry-ing time is usually between four and six hours. If the plums are soaked in hot water for 20 minutes before oven drying, their skins are made more permeable and they dry more quickly. However, some loss of nutrients takes place during the soaking. Drying is complete when the fruit feels tough and leathery, but is still soft inside. If it is stored for two or three weeks in an airtight container, a more even distribution of the moisture takes place, and the outside becomes less tough. At the end of the drying period, the prunes may be frozen, if desired, or stored in a cool, dry cupboard.

Varieties: American—Surprise and Wolf are large, highly productive trees bearing medium-sized red fruits. De Sota, Hawkeye and Wild Goose are high-yielding when planted with Surprise as a pollinator.

Damson—The best Damson is Shropshire, which produces terrific yields of dark purple fruits. A similar variety, with larger, better-quality fruits in somewhat less abundance, is the French.

European—All the Europeans are medium or large trees, hardy eastward from the Great Lakes region. Stanley and Italian Prune give dark blue or purple fruits. Imperial Epineuse has perhaps the sweetest fruits of all, borne on a big, vigorous tree. Iroquois is another self-fruitful, fairly hardy variety.

Japanese—All the best Japanese have red or red purple fruits, and most of the trees are quite large. Formosa, Burbank, Satsuma, Inca, and Santa Rosa are probably the all-around favorites. Abundance is also good, but its very juicy fruits do not store well.

The native beach plum (*P. maritima*), which grows wild along the Atlantic coast as far south as Virginia, does well in the home garden. Other species of wild plums thrive in fencerows and brushy woodland from Ohio to the Rockies. Fruit from these wild varieties is rather astringent but makes delicious jams and jellies.

See also FRUIT TREES, ORCHARD.

PLUMBAGO

Also known as leadwort, this genus of about a dozen species of small tender shrubs is grown outdoors in the South and in cool greenhouses in the North, for the phloxlike flowers which are borne all summer. For northern gardens, they may be grown in pots which can be used on the terrace or patio, and returned to the greenhouse to dry and rest in the fall. About February the foliage is cut back severely, and brought into the light at about 65°F. (18.33°C.) to start their growth for the coming year. When grown outside in warm climates, the growth is cut back in spring to one inch above the ground. Old flower stalks must be removed to insure continued bloom. Propagation is by seed, cuttings or division. Young shoots are pinched back several times to promote bushy growth.

P. auriculata, growing to five feet, has blue flowers with individual florets ¾ inch across. Variety Alba has white flowers.

P. indica has red purple flowers, and, with support, is a partial climber.

P. scandens is white flowered, a native of tropical America. It is either climbing or trailing.

P. larpentae (now called *Ceratostigma plumbaginoides*), also commonly called leadwort, is a dwarf, spreading perennial used for edging and in rock gardens. It grows to one foot or less, and is covered with brilliant peacock blue flowers in August and September when few other blue flowers are in bloom. The leaves turn reddish in fall. Propagation is by division. It is hardy in the South, but must be given a winter covering of evergreen boughs or straw in northern areas. It will do well in sun or partial shade.

PLUM CURCULIO

The plum curculio is a stout brown beetle, mottled with gray and marked with four humps on the back. It appears in the orchard about the time the trees blossom. The curculio feeds on small fruit, leaving crescent-shaped cuts in the skin. An egg is laid under each crescent, and the hatching grubs feed within the fruit, which usually drops and decays. The grubs then abandon the drops to pupate below ground.

Gather up the drops daily, before the grubs can escape to the earth, and bury them away from the orchard in a deep hole or let them rot in the heart of the compost pile. If you knock branches with a padded pole, the curculios will drop to a tarp spread below.

See also INSECT CONTROL.

PLUMEGRASS
See GRASS, ORNAMENTAL

PODOCARPUS

This genus of evergreen trees and shrubs, mostly native to the Southern Hemisphere, was formerly included in the Yew family, but now for technical botanical reasons has been given a family of its own, Podocarpaceae. With one exception (*P. alpina*), they are grown outdoors in this country only in the warm parts of California and Florida. Elsewhere they are grown in tubs in the greenhouse.

Male and female flowers occur on separate trees, the male flowers catkinlike, the female flowers inconspicuous and followed by a plum-shaped red, purple or yellow fruit on a fleshy stalk. The attractive leaves are flat and narrow.

P. alpina is a dense small-leaved tree growing to about 15 feet. The fruit is a small red berry. The tree will stand some frost.

P. andinus, the plum fir, grows about 30 feet tall, with small leaves striped white below and yellow white plum-shaped fruit, about one inch in diameter.

P. elongatus is grown in California as a shrub, and elsewhere as a greenhouse plant.

P. macrophylla is a slightly smaller tree, but bears leaves three to four inches long. The half-inch fruit is green purple, on a fleshy purple stalk.

Podocarpus thrive in sandy peat or loam. Propagation is by seed or cuttings.

PODZOL SOILS

A widespread and important group of soils under the pre-1965 soil classification system, podzol soils formed in cool-temperate, humid climates from the remains of forests or heaths. Podzols were characterized by an acidic, gray white A_2 horizon, and a B horizon with high aluminum, iron oxide and organic matter contents leached from the higher horizons. Most of these soils are now classified as spodosols.

See also SOIL CLASSIFICATION.

POGONIA

Rose pogonia or snakemouth, *P. ophioglossoides,* is the only cultivated species of the *Pogonia,* a genus of orchids growing in North American bogs, and hardy to Newfoundland. It can be grown only in the shady bog garden, in strongly acidic soil or in sphagnum moss. Reaching a height of 21 inches, the pogonia has a single four-inch leaf and, in June or July, a nodding, pink or rose pink flower whose lip is fringed or crested with yellow brown hairs. It is about one inch in diameter, with petals and sepals about equal. A pogonia will occasionally bear two flowers.

See also ORCHIDS.

POINCIANA   (*Caesalpinia, Delonix*)

Popular throughout the tropics, this beautiful flowering tree or shrub is easily and quickly grown, and with its broad, spreading crown and filmy foliage is well fitted for shade and ornament in yards and parks. The blooms come in a variety of colors and often flower at different times.

Planting and Culture: Grown mostly in Florida, California and the Gulf states, poincianas are started from seed which have been soaked in warm water before being sown in sandy soil. Young plants in windy environments should be staked to help keep them erect, and all poincianas should be watered throughout the summer until established. Poincianas grow from 12 to 18 inches a year, and can grow as high as ten feet after several years. They are usually insect and disease free.

Types: Attractive choices for landscaping include *D. regia, C. Gilliesii,* and *C. pul-*

cherrima. D. regia is the royal poinciana native to Madagascar and East Africa. It is often called flame tree, peacock flower and flamboyant, because of its yellow-striped, bright scarlet flowers. It rapidly attains a height of 20 to 40 feet. Barbados pride or dwarf poinciana (*C. pulcherrima*) grows to ten feet and produces yellow orange flowers. Bird-of-paradise bush (*C. Gilliesi*) has showy yellow blooms.

At one time poinciana leaves were infused as a tea for treating liver infections and the flowers were an ingredient of eyewash solutions and gargles.

POINSETTIA   (*Euphorbia pulcherrima*)

Poinsettia is one of the most favored Christmas flowers. As a tropical American species of euphorbia, it is most popular as a potted plant. It is suitable for garden culture in frost-free regions and is considered a shrub, growing to ten feet or sometimes twice that height under proper conditions.

Care during Blooming: Protect the poinsettia from draft, keeping it in a temperature of less than 70°F. (21.11°C.) in the daytime and not lower than 60°F. (15.56°C.) at night. A sunny window, preferably protected by a storm sash to prevent cold drafts, is a good place to keep potted poinsettias, as they require a lot of sun. Water every day from above with tepid or slightly warm water. Never let the soil dry out, yet do not keep it soggy. Excess moisture is sure to shorten the period of the plant's attractive display of red, white or pink flowerlike bracts.

Even if kept under perfect conditions, the plants will drop their leaves later in the winter until only the red bracts remain at the top. This is the natural behavior of the poinsettia, for it requires a resting period after it has bloomed. When the lowest leaves begin to drop, gradually withhold water, and finally let the soil dry out completely. When only the naked stems remain, store the pot in a warm, dry place until early May without applying any water.

Spring and Summer Care: In May, shake the old soil out of the pots and repot in fresh, rich soil. The soil should consist of garden

Poinsettias require plenty of sunlight, daily waterings and a temperature of 65 to 70°F. (18.33 to 21.11°C.).

loam, sand and leaf mold, to which a small quantity of dried manure may be added. Cut down the stems to within two or three eyes or buds from the base. Water and sink the pot outdoors in a sunny spot level with the soil surface. Soon after the plants are set outdoors, new shoots grow from the eyes. During the summer the plants grow into large, well-branched specimens. Plants must receive full light and sunshine throughout the day and lots of moisture.

Fall Care: In the fall, when the temperature drops to 45 to 50°F. (7.22 to 10°C.) at night, take the pots up and give them a sunny place indoors where the temperature does not fall below 65°F. (18.33°C.). Plenty of sunshine is imperative, and with judicious watering the plants will again be a blaze of color at Christmas.

Propagation: Poinsettias are propagated by cuttings taken in March. The tops which are removed before the plants are repotted are suitable for cuttings. Divide them into four- to six-inch lengths and place in warm water for about 15 minutes. This stops the sap from flowing too freely. Dip the lower end into powdered charcoal and insert the lower third into sharp sand for rooting. A temperature of 65°F. (18.33°C.) must be maintained during the rooting process. Keep them in a sunny location. When roots have formed, set them in small pots, water and keep shaded for a week or two. As top growth increases, repot into larger containers. From now on they are handled in the same manner as the mother plant.

See also HOUSE PLANTS.

POISON ASH *See* POISON SUMAC

POISON DOGWOOD
See POISON SUMAC

POISON ELDER
See POISON SUMAC

POISON IVY (*Rhus radicans*)

The poisonous properties of this plant are attributed to a yellow, slightly volatile oil which occurs in the resin ducts of leaves, flowers, fruits, and the bark of the plant. Only the wood, pollen and leaf hairs are not poisonous.

Contact with poison ivy causes inflammation and swelling of the skin, followed by intense irritation and blisters. Often the skin breaks, the liquid escapes, and scabs or crusts form. Symptoms may appear from a few hours to several days after contact. Some persons are apparently more susceptible at certain times than at others. Also, contact with the plant at different times during the season may result in varying degrees of infection and skin irritation.

It is generally advisable to consult a physician for treatment. If contact with poison ivy is known or suspected, immediate lathering with a strong alkaline (laundry) soap with frequent rinsing can prevent inflammation and blistering. The alkaline soap emulsifies the oil and by thorough rinsing, this may be removed from the skin.

Identification: Poison ivy varies in growth habit from dwarf and erect forms to straggling or climbing types that produce aerial rootlets which anchor the vines to fences, walls or trees. Slender, creeping rootstocks grow from the base of the stems and run underground for several

Poison ivy is most often found in rich woodlands, but it also thrives in open fields, hedgerows and waste spaces.
(Courtesy of U.S. Department of Agriculture)

yards. Short, leafy stems emerge from the soil from these rootstocks.

The leaves of poison ivy are alternate on the stem and are divided into three leaflets; each is oval shaped, pointed at the tip and tapered to the base. The terminal leaflet is longer stalked than the two lateral ones. The leaf surface, contrary to popular notion, may be *either* glossy or dull green, and smooth or somewhat hairy. Leaf margins may vary from entirely straight to toothed or somewhat lobed. In deep shade or in dry weather, leaves may be light green, yellow green, or even red. In autumn, they turn yellow and bright red before falling.

The light green flowers, borne in clusters, often pass unnoticed. The gray white, berrylike fruit measures up to about ¼ inch in diameter and contains a one-seeded pit. Stripes make it

look like the segments of a peeled orange. These fruits persist on the shrub through the winter and are eaten by some 55 different species of birds in the United States which help to disperse the seed over a wide area. Because some plants produce only male flowers, fruits are not always found on a green plant.

Poison ivy, though often found in rich woods, also thrives in dry, rocky fields, pastures, fencerows, banks and waste places. In being cautious for its presence, one should not mistake Virginia creeper or moonseed for poison ivy. Virginia creeper has five leaflets and moonseed is only three-lobed. Hog peanut, another plant sometimes confused with the pesty ivy, does have three leaflets, but has pink or white flowers, produces a pod, and is a twining-type vine.

Control: Large infestations of poison ivy can be controlled by mowing close to the ground in midsummer, then plowing and harrowing, or grazing sheep or goats. For smaller patches, the roots may be grubbed out.

Poison ivy will eventually die out if you keep it clipped to within an inch or two of the ground with a power mower. Grasses will tend to crowd it out, and it can't get enough height to put out leaves.

Under trees or along a fence where it may be difficult to mow regularly by machine and where plowing is not feasible, try smothering the ivy with tar paper or cardboard. A deep mulch of straw or other material will also be effective, as well as more attractive.

Vines growing up fences or trees can be handled by cutting each one near the ground and, several days later, pulling out the wilted plants. Wear gloves and protective clothing. When finished, wash well with any yellow soap, such as Fels Naphtha. If plants are burned, do not stand in the smoke because the infection-causing oils may stick to particles of soot and be carried to the skin.

Helpful control information is found in the Department of Agriculture Bulletin A1.9: 1972/*Poison Ivy, Poison Oak and Poison Sumac: Identification, Precautions and Eradications,* which may be obtained from the Superintendent of Documents, United States Government Printing Office, Washington, DC 20402. The main control methods described are cultivating, mowing or cutting, grubbing out roots, spraying, and smothering. A most effective way of eradicating young plants is to put on a long-sleeved jacket and leather gloves and pull them out by hand, as fast as they appear, destroying the roots.

Remedies: Among the popular remedies for poison ivy are the topical application of the juice of the aloe vera plant, Fels Naphtha soap, vitamin E, linseed oil, plantain tea or juice, and hardwood ashes and green bean leaves. Vitamin C taken internally may also help relieve the itching.

Jewelweed (*Impatiens capensis* or *I. pallida*), also referred to as touch-me-not because its seedpods explode when touched, is a member of the Impatiens family. It grows wherever poison ivy is found and can be recognized by its smooth leaves that gleam like mercury when held under the water. Jewelweed juice squeezed onto the blisters has a soothing effect and helps the blisters dry up rather quickly.

Poison oak (*R. diversiloba*) can be controlled by the same methods used to eradicate poison ivy.

POISON OAK   *See* POISON IVY

POISON SEGO   *See* ZIGADENUS

POISON SUMAC   (*Rhus vernix*)

This bog bush, also known as swamp sumac, poison dogwood, poison elder, poison ash, or thunderwood, can be more poisonous than its near relative, poison ivy. The conditions of poisoning and the toxic principles are the same as for poison ivy.

Its green white berries distinguish poison sumac from the harmless staghorn sumac and smooth sumac, both of which have red berries. Some confuse green ash with poison sumac; however, green ash has only one stem per plant and the leaf margin is toothed, while poison sumac produces a clump of stems and has leaves with unbroken margins.

This is a coarse shrub that grows from six to 20 feet tall, with smooth, gray bark and smooth branches. There are from seven to 13 leaflets per leaf, and autumn foliage is orange to scarlet in color. The yellow green flowers may be male or female and are arranged in a spreading or pendulous branch arising from the point of leaf attachment to the stem. Flowers appear from May through July; the globular fruit ripen from August to November and are conspicuous all winter.

Poison sumacs are most common in wet places, such as in bogs and swamps or along streams and ditches. In contract, the harmless sumacs grow only in well-drained soil or even fairly dry soils. Control recommendations made for poison ivy are applicable to poison sumac, with the added caution that this plant is even more toxic.

See also POISON IVY.

POKEBERRY   *See* POKEWEED

POKEWEED   (*Phytolacca americana*)

Pokeweed is a native perennial plant which occurs frequently in moist rich soil along fences and in uncultivated land throughout the eastern half of the United States. The root and the berries are used in medicine.

Also known as pokeberry and inkberry, pokeweed is a poisonous wild shrub growing to ten feet high. Its highly toxic root resembles horseradish. The plant produces white flowers and dark red berries. Umbra (*P. dioica*), another member of this plant family, is often grown as an ornamental evergreen tree in California, where it sometimes grows as high as 50 feet.

The herb's generic name, *Phytolacca,* comes from the Greek *phyton* (plant) and *laca* (crimson lake) referring to its use as a dye plant. Pokeweed was surreptitiously employed in dyeing wines in Portugal and France. The herb also went into the making of tinctures, ointments and poultices to reduce glandular swellings and rheumatism.

Pokeweed is usually found growing wild, and is rarely cultivated. It thrives in deep, rich soil well supplied with moisture and may be readily grown from seed sown early in spring in rows four feet apart and barely covered. The seedlings should be thinned to stand about three feet apart in the row. The plant develops long, thick, fleshy roots. At the end of the first year these may be turned out without great difficulty. When the plants are older they are much more difficult to "harvest."

In some regions, pokeweed continues to be used to treat rheumatism and swellings, but this is not recommended since overdoses may cause convulsions and death. The shoots of young plants are often eaten like asparagus, but when the plant matures it is quite unpalatable and could be toxic.

See also HERB.

POLEMONIUM CAERULEUM
See JACOB'S-LADDER

POLLEN

The tiny, invisible grains of pollen produced by the male part of a flower, the anthers at the top of the stamens, are the agents—when carried by wind, bees and other insects—that fertilize the female part of the flower and give rise to the embryo in the seed. Though only $\frac{1}{100}$ inch in size, under the microscope, pollen can be seen to be of many shapes: spiked, knobby, eight sided, or like burrs, dumbbells or Christmas tree ornaments, and in many colors: gold, brown, blue, red, and green. In some species, such as squash, there are separate female and male flowers; and in others, such as holly and the maidenhair tree, there are separate whole female plants and male plants.

Pollen is produced in a four-chambered area in the anthers. Even when very young the chambers contain large cells called microspore mother cells, which all eventually divide into four new cells, the microspores. These develop into pollen grains. Then their nuclei divide forming two halves or two new cells within the grain, one called the tube cell and the other the generative cell, and it is by means of these that the pollen is able to reach the female part of the flower and fertilize the egg. Meanwhile, the wall of the microspore has become thick and covered with spikes, spines, ridges, or whatever markings are characteristic of its species. At this time the walls of the anthers disintegrate so that the pollen can escape, or be rubbed out on the body of a bee, or other pollinator. As soon as the pollen grain gets to the stigma, it sends down a pollen tube from one cell. The generative cell divides to form two male gametes or sperms, one of which travels down to fuse with the female gamete or egg cell, and the other becomes the primary endosperm nucleus by fusing with the two polar nuclei in the embryo sac. Thus a food-storage part of the seed is created in the endosperm. It provides food when, after germination, the embryo begins to grow.

The ability of pollen grains to survive, travel and fertilize is amazing when it is realized that their life span may be only two or three hours, that hot sun can kill them and excess moisture can cause them to swell and burst. Sometimes they travel miles before alighting on the stigma of a flower no larger than the head of a pin.

Pollen is a very rich food. Fed to baby bees by the nurse bees in the hive, its high content of protein, vitamins and minerals makes them grow amazingly fast. Certain Indian tribes collected pollen for soups and gruel, and believed it gave them great vigor. And some modern doctors credit the health-giving properties of unfiltered, uncooked honey to the numerous pollen grains it contains.

See also BEES, ORCHARD, POLLINATION, SEED.

POLLINATION

Pollination is the process by which pollen from the anther or male part of a plant is transferred to the stigma at the top of the female part. On the stigma, a pollen tube is generated. Through this tube, the two sperm cells travel downward toward the ovary. Fertilization takes place when one sperm cell joins with the egg nucleus and the other with the endosperm part of the egg cell which eventually supplies nourishment to the growing embryo.

Types of Pollination: Cross-pollination is the transfer of pollen from the anthers of flowers of one variety to the stigma of a flower of a different variety. This may occur between squash and gourds when they are visited and cross-pollinated by bees on the same day. It is necessary with apple and pear flowers if the trees are to bear fruit. Cross-pollination results in plants that are usually very healthy and vigorous.

In horticultural terms plants are called fertile if, after pollination, they have the ability to set and mature fruit with viable seed. They are called sterile if unable to do so either because of nonfunction of the pollen, the ovules or both—sometimes simply because they do not mature at the same time. The term "fruitful" is used if the plants set a commercial crop, and "self-fruitful" if the varieties set good crops with their own pollen. Some plants produce edible fruit without fertilization; they are seedless and are called parthenocarpic.

Compatible pollen is that which can continue to develop on the female part of the flower pollinated and can reach the ovule in time for successful fertilization. This is especially important for certain fruits where two varieties are needed for fertilization to take place. Where the trees or bushes are near enough together and pollination is effective enough to produce fruit of commercial value, the plants are called "cross-fruitful." These plants have blooming periods which overlap at the same or compatible ages, either annually or in alternate years; they are also not too closely related. Many varieties of apples are ineffective as pollinizers in cross-pollination and all European pears are self-unfruitful. So are all American quinces, but most peaches, apricots and nectarines, on the other hand, are self-fruitful.

Several other terms are used by orchardists to describe ways in which the pollen of one plant is unsuitable for another; but if all relations are productive, the plants are called "interfruitful" and "interfertile." Trees having those relations are the goal of the orchardist. *See also* ORCHARD.

Bees often affect crossbreeding, even of ordinarily self-pollinated plants. And because pollen is so delicate, nearly 90 percent of the world's plants have to depend on bees, both tame and wild, moths, wasps, fleas, beetles, and other insects. Pollen sometimes travels to other plants by the help of wind, birds, snails, bats, and even on animals' fur and men's clothing.

Plants pollinated by insects and animals do not need to produce as much pollen as those which rely on the wind. It has been estimated that one sorrel plant can produce almost 400 million pollen grains per year. The grains that escape into the environment may be so rugged that they persist for millenia where they have been deposited on the earth. Scientists have found enough pollen grains in the Sahara desert to prove that that area was once a forest, and students of pollen layers in bogs can trace the vegetation of surrounding areas over the years so exactly that they can date when the climate was right for spruce, when right for pine, when right for birches, willows and certain grasses.

Flowers are constructed so that pollinators such as bees and beetles are attracted to them by color or fragrance, or when some flies are

As the bee moves from flower to flower collecting nectar, he picks up pollen grains from the anthers and deposits them on the stigmas where the pollen tubes grow down and fertilize the female cells.

the pollinators, by an odor of decay. The insect searching for nectar picks up some pollen on its body, and at the same time deposits another plant's pollen on the stigma.

Many plants can be pollinated only by certain insects. The yucca moth, for instance, collects pollen from the yucca plant's anthers and places it on the stigma so that the larvae, when they grow from the eggs she simultaneously deposits, will have yucca seeds to eat when they emerge. One African orchid with a

12-inch-long, pollen-lined tube and with its nectar at the bottom of this tube can only be pollinated by a hawk moth which has a foot-long tongue. The fig wasp is the one insect able to get pollen from the wild Capri figs necessary to pollinate cultivated Smyrna figs, which must be cross-fertilized this way in order to bear fruit.

Plant Breeding: Artificial pollination is practiced by many hybridizers and orchardists. They effect cross-pollination by carrying the pollen from one plant when the pollen is ripe and rubbing it gently on the other blossom when it opens or when the stigma is developed and sticky. Removal of stamens will make it easier. It is necessary to keep the blossom wrapped, however, to keep the bees from pollinating it before and after the artificial pollination. If the two flowers are not ripe at the same time, the pollen can be saved and put on the stigma of the other flower at a later time.

The ancients' knowledge of plant breeding was lost for many centuries until, in 1717, Thomas Fairchild made the first plant hybrid by placing pollen from a carnation on the female flower of a sweet William. Since then, thousands of hybrids have been developed, including 15,000 crossbreedings of roses, 8,000 of tulips and over 4,000 of China asters. Some commercial crops are characteristically cross-pollinated, such as sugar beets and the cucurbits as well as many popular ornamental shrubs, perennials and trees. In recent years frozen pollen has been used for difficult species such as the McIntosh apple, with the pollen flown in to the orchard and applied by hand.

All modern plant breeding depends in one way or another on the discoveries of the Austrian monk, Gregor Mendel, whose lifework, published in 1866, was devoted to the study of the heredity of peas. The Mendelian Law states that self-pollinated plants have offspring like themselves (homozygous), while cross-pollinated plants, because of different heredities, produce a dissimilar second generation (heterozygous). *See also* MENDEL, GREGOR.

See also BEES, FRUIT TREES, ORCHARD, PLANT BREEDING, POLLEN.

POLYGONATUM
See SOLOMON'S SEAL

POLYGONUM

Also known as knotweed or fleeceflower, this genus of the Buckwheat family contains a number of ornamentals as well as common weed pests such as smartweed and knotweed. Most are trailing or climbing annual or perennial vines. The small pink or white flowers grow in terminal clusters or spikes, and are attractive to bees. Annuals are started from seed. Perennials may be started from seed or may be propagated by woody cuttings or by division.

Japanese knotweed or Mexican bamboo (*P. cuspidatum*) is a perennial shrub which dies back to the root each year. It is a rampant grower that may easily become a pest.

The perennial mountain fleece (*P. amplexicaule*) grows to three feet and in late summer bears rose red or white flower spikes up to six inches long. It is recommended for the border.

Prince's feather (*P. orientale*) is an annual which may also be grown under lights indoors. It grows to six feet, with large hairy leaves and pink or rose flower spikes 3½ inches long.

Silver-lace vine (*P. Aubertii*) sometimes also called China fleece vine, grows to 20 feet, with masses of fragrant white flowers in late summer. It is hardy to New York.

See also SMARTWEED.

POLYPODY   (*Polypodium*)

This large genus of ferns includes both hardy and tender species that grow in all parts of the world. Polypodies are generally easy to raise and some species make good house plants. Nearly all develop from a rhizome, or fleshy rootstock, and have shallow roots. Propagation is by spores or division.

The common or European polypody (*P. vulgare*) grows on rocks, trees, walls, and banks throughout western North America, Europe and Asia. The evergreen fronds are six to ten inches long and have deeply cut, rounded pinnae. Other names for this fern include adder's foot, golden maidenhair and wall fern.

Hare's-foot fern or golden polypody (*P. aureum*) is a coarse tropical fern with fronds a foot wide and up to four feet long. A good house plant, it will thrive in moist humus in an east, west or lightly shaded southern window. It appreciates a nighttime temperature of 50 to 55°F. (10 to 12.78°C.) and a daytime temperature not above 70°F. (21.11°C.). Propagation is by division of the creeping rhizomes, which resemble rabbit's feet.

Resurrection fern (*P. polypodioides*) grows in trees in the southern states and in tropical America. During dry seasons the foliage curls up into a dry mass, and opens again to continue its growth when the weather is moist.

Rock polypody (*P. virginianum*) is similar in appearance to *P. vulgare* and is widely distributed throughout eastern North America.

Strap fern (*P. phyllitidis*) is native to southern Florida and southward. Its shiny, leathery fronds, up to three feet long, often have wavy margins.

See also FERN.

POME

A pome is a fleshy fruit with an inner core and seeds that are enclosed in parchmentlike casings. Apples, pears and quinces are pomes.

POMEGRANATE   (*Punica*)

The pomegranate is a thick-skinned fruit, about the size of a large orange, that contains a great number of agreeably acidic red seeds. The word pomegranate also refers to the attractive tree or shrub that bears the fruit, but which is sometimes grown solely for ornament.

One of the most famous pomegranate hedges in the Southwest is the one which lines either side of the roadway leading to the Santa Ana Botanic Garden. In early summer the brilliant hibiscuslike flowers present a dazzling blaze of color, and the big, fall-ripening crimson fruits weigh down the pliant branches with their heavy load. There are many varieties on the market, but Wonderful and Spanish Ruby are the most highly recommended.

Pomegranates are easily propagated from hardwood cuttings taken in midwinter during the dormant period. Planted in deep, heavy loam, they grow quickly into large, eight-foot bushes. They thrive anywhere in the Southwest's warm, arid regions and tend to produce the most luscious and juicy fruit when temperatures are very high. Under optimum conditions, pomegranates begin producing fruit several years after the shrubs are set out.

The common variety of pomegranate (*P. granatum*), growing from ten to 20 feet high, is hardy as far north as Maryland on the eastern coast, but California and Florida are best suited to its culture. For fruit growing, plant the trees about 15 to 20 feet apart. Cut out shoots coming out of the base to keep the tree more compact, and remove dead wood and interfering branches to keep the tree vigorous and healthy.

As an ornamental, the pomegranate makes a fine hedge. It blooms in spring and the attractive fruit ripens in summer.

PONDS

A homestead or farm fish pond can cost you from a few dollars up to several thousand, but it can return you thousands of dollars in fish crops, fun, fire and drought insurance, and a stable water table. In fire protection alone, an adequate available source of water can save your home or barn. Using the pond for supplementary irrigation can mean higher yields or an entire crop saved from drought.

The average pond is from ½ to three acres in size. It's far from being just a hole scooped out of the ground in any old place. Don't try to build a pond without expert help, as nine out of ten ponds built by farmers alone fail. Only an expert can allow for all the conditions of rainfall, silting, seepage, and so on that a pond has to cope with. Your county agent, the Soil Conservation Service, the Agricultural Extension Service and private pond contractors can help you.

Watershed: The proper-size watershed is very important. Five acres of cropland or ten acres of pasture or woodland are generally needed to "feed" an eight-foot, one-acre pond. A much smaller watershed, of course, will do if you can find a brook or spring to supply some of the water.

Don't dam a stream unless it has a very small watershed. Otherwise it may wash out the dam. You can divert part of a stream with pipe, tile or ditches to feed the pond on a bypass basis, or use diversion ditches to channel runoff into it. Some naturally wet spots make ideal ponds, but dig them out sufficiently; a shallow pond breeds mosquitoes and is rapidly overgrown with weeds.

Water must never flow over your dam. You'll need a broad, well-sodded spillway about two to three feet below its top, to carry away heavy overflow. You can also have a "trickle tube," a vertical drainage pipe with its open end six inches below the level of the spillway, and connected to a pipe running through the dam into the outside overflow. This will keep the spillway from being constantly wet, which would kill off the grass.

Fence the pond to protect it from cattle. A multiflora rose hedge makes an attractive barrier, and is also a fine bird refuge. You can turn in sheep during the day—they rarely break down the banks—and cows at night, since they almost never go near the water after dark.

Stocking and Feeding: The Soil Conservation Service or state or commercial hatcheries will supply the proper kind of fish for your pond. One hundred to 300 fingerling bass to 1,000 bluegill fingerlings per acre is the usual ratio in many areas. The bass feed on the young bluegills, keeping their populations down. Crappies, sunfish and trout are used in other regions.

How you feed the algae and plankton in your pond will determine the quantity and quality of your fish harvest. One thousand pounds of compost, or 500 pounds of finely ground phosphate rock satisfies a one-acre pond. These fertilizers may be spread in equal amounts once a month from May to September. During the summer, these materials feed the minute organisms which the fish eat. This microscopic plant life is the green scum which forms on a pond in summer. If the water in your pond is clear for more than a foot down, there are not enough algae—fertilize quickly.

But don't overfertilize. Too much could drastically reduce the oxygen content of the water and injure the fish. If excessive feeding results in very dark, scummy water, add some lime. Never use copper sulfate to clear the water since, in quantities greater than two parts per million, it will kill every living thing in the pond.

Silt, too, is an enemy of algae, so if there are cultivated fields or other erodible land in the watershed, manage them according to approved soil conservation methods to keep soil out of the pond.

Care: Constant fishing is necessary to keep the pond from becoming overstocked. *Fish are a farm crop.* You can't overfish. In fact, most ponds would produce twice as heavily if more fish were harvested. You can harvest more than 300 pounds of fish per acre per year from a good pond (more than the amount of beef you could raise on the same area!). You should remove at least five pounds of fish per acre each week. That's a lot of vital protein for your whole family.

Around your pond try to create the best possible conditions for wildlife. Fertilize the dam area and plant it to grasses and a legume like the tall sericea lespedeza, which will provide cover and food for birds and small animals. Plant a willow or two, and other shrubs and trees nearby. Your pond will soon play host to all kinds of birds, plus insect-eating frogs and snakes, and perhaps even muskrats or raccoons.

See also AQUACULTURE, LILY POND, WATER GARDEN.

POPLAR   *(Populus)*

In this genus are a number of well-known, quick-growing trees, including the aspens and cottonwood. Most are hardy and rather short-lived. They are considered ornamentals and many hybrids have been developed for reforestation and farm woodlots. The flowers appear in early spring in hanging catkins.

The white poplar or abele (*P. alba*) is the only species that does well on dry soils. It grows from 30 to 60 feet tall, and one variety, the bolleana poplar, is of a columnar habit. The Lombardy poplar (*P. nigra* cv. 'Italica') is also columnar. Both are popular for screen plantings, but the Lombardy poplar rarely lives more than 20 years. The black poplar (*P. nigra*) is a wide-spreading tree from 40 to 80 feet tall, with twisted leaves that quake in the slightest breeze.

Others with shimmering leaves are the quaking aspen (*P. tremuloides*), the European aspen (*P. tremula*), the large-toothed aspen (*P. grandidentata*), the cottonwood or balsam poplar (*P. balsamifera*) and the Carolina poplar (*P. canadensis*). The Berlin poplar (*P. x berolinensis*) is a very hardy columnar tree often used for windbreaks in the prairie states. Balm-of-Gilead (*P. x gileadensis*) is not as hardy as the other poplars; its buds are made into cough medicine. All of these grow to 50 feet or taller. *P. simoni,* the shortest poplar, grows 20 to 30 feet high. There are many other poplars, not as widespread as these, and several varieties with weeping forms.

Since their seed does not often come true, poplars are usually propagated by hardwood cuttings that are buried in sand over the winter.

See also TULIP TREE.

POPLAR   (*Papaver*)

The true poppies are annuals or perennials growing from six inches to four feet high. Some of them are among the showiest plants in the garden, having huge, brightly colored flowers. Many poppies make long-lasting cut flowers if the bottom inch or two of the sappy stems is burnt before putting them in water.

Poppies like light soils, sandy or even gritty in texture, with good drainage and lots of humus. Dig the bed at least 18 inches deep, and mix in manure, leaf mold and sand. Full sun and plenty of room to grow are also vital.

Annual Species: The annuals include the free-flowering tulip poppy (*P. glaucum*), which especially likes loose soil and is a biennial in warm climates. The corn poppy (*P. Rhoeas*) is the famous one that grows in Flanders fields and inspired the artificial poppies distributed on Memorial Day. The Shirley poppy was developed from the corn poppy, and if given ample room, both of these will make handsome

plants up to three feet across, with spectacularly lovely flowers. The opium poppy (*P. somniferum*) is a very tall, wide poppy that also needs plenty of space and a sandy loam soil. *P. pavoninum* is a one-foot-tall, hairy annual.

All the annual poppies suffer from transplanting, so sow the seed where they are to grow whenever possible. Unless the winters are very severe, sow in early fall for germination the following spring. Otherwise, plant seed in early spring.

Perennial Species: The short Iceland poppy (*P. nudicaule*) and the tall oriental poppy (*P. orientale*) are favorite hardy perennials of great beauty. Like all the perennial poppies, they need a rich soil for superlative bloom. The Iceland poppy in particular requires perfect drainage, or it will rot off. It will bloom the first year from seed, and self-sows freely, but is not truly perennial in this country.

Oriental poppies want a mulch of rotted manure in the fall, removed in spring, and they need staking. They are long-lived and get more beautiful each year. Any transplanting should be done in August, just after the foliage dies down. Propagating can be done then, too, by cutting the taproots of mature plants into small pieces and planting them in sandy loam soil.

Another perennial is the alpine poppy (*P. Burseri*), a very low grower which is excellent for the rock garden. It self-sows freely, prefers a gritty soil, and may be treated as an annual.

Sow the seed of perennial poppies under glass or in the cold frame. Transplant to a mixture of equal parts of loam, sand and leaf mold, and plant them in their permanent spots as early in the spring as possible. Or sow in summer where you want them to grow, covering the seed very lightly and sprinkling gently every other day. Always thin to provide ample room.

POTASH

One of the three major plant nutrients, potash or potassium oxide is essential for the development of strong plants. It is composed of two parts potassium and one part oxygen, K_2O. Potash is concerned chiefly with plant sugar manufacture. It helps plants to resist diseases, protects them from cold and protects during dry weather by preventing excessive losses of water.

Potash can do more than any other mineral to counteract excesses of nitrogen. While excess nitrogen may cause plants to lose their resistance to disease, a good supply of potash will increase resistance.

Deficiency Symptoms: Plants with potassium deficiencies produce poor yields of crops. The leaves sometimes get yellow streaks or spots on them, and leaf edges and tips become dry and scorched. In corn, the ears that do develop are small and poorly developed and the space between leaf nodes is abnormally short. Stalks are generally weak and dwarfed in appearance, and have a tendency to lodge.

Potassium-deficient plants have poorly developed root systems. Fruits ripen unevenly and are soft. Carrots showing potash deficiency exhibit curled leaves, beets grow tapered roots instead of fat bulbs and the leaves of radishes are deep green in the centers with scorching on the edges. *See also* SOIL DEFICIENCIES.

Chemical Sources: America's main source of chemical fertilizer potash is the vast deposit of potassium chloride salts in our south-western desert. Some people think this fertilizer is "natural" because it was deposited there by natural means, but muriate of potash, as it is commonly called, is a deposit of an ancient ocean and has more in common with the salty environment of the seas than with productive natural soils. Moreover, it leaves residues of chlorine in the soil. Natural mineral and organic sources of potash do not carry this chlorine residue.

Potash supply has long been a problem for eastern and midwestern farmers, because many soils in temperate regions are inherently deficient in this element. On the other hand, many soils in arid regions have good natural potash reserves.

Natural Sources: There are three sources of potassium used by organic gardeners and farmers: plant residues, manures and compost, and natural mineral sources like granite dust or greensand.

Plant residues, manures and compost bring to the soil potash that is free and available. But even in highly fertile soils the supply of this free potassium is rarely enough to meet the needs of a growing crop. So during the growing season the roots of plants come in contact with potash "locked up" in the soil's minerals and make it available.

If your soil does not have sufficient reserves of potash in its mineral structure, you are likely to have a potash deficiency. Natural mineral fertilizers—granite dust and greensand—are the ideal solution because they supply the mineral potash reserves that plants can draw on throughout the growing season. Natural minerals for potash are useful even if you use compost or manure, as the potash from these organic sources can be washed out of the soil or used up by plants. The best plan is to use both organic and mineral potash sources—organic for short-term potash release and mineral for the long term. An added advantage of that plan is that the organic material you add will stimulate soil bacterial activity which makes it easier for the mineral potash to be released.

Granite dust is now the most widely used natural potash mineral. Granites from different areas have varying potash contents, but the average is from 3 to 5½ percent. Fineness of grind of the material should be considered when buying a potash mineral, because the more finely ground material will release its nutrients quicker.

Greensand is another common source of potash and contains more potash than granite

NATURAL SOURCES OF POTASH

Material	Potash (approx. %)	Material	Potash (approx. %)
Manure		Kentucky bluegrass	2
Cattle (fresh excrement)	trace	Pea forage	1
Cattle (dried excrement)	2	Red clover	2
Cattle (fresh urine)	1	Salt	1
Duck	1	Soybean	1-2
Goat and sheep (fresh excrement)	trace	Timothy	1
Goat and sheep (dried excrement)	3	Vetch	2
Goat and sheep (fresh urine)	2	Winter rye	1
Goose (fresh)	1	Leaves	
Horse (fresh excrement)	trace	Apple	trace
Horse (dried excrement)	2	Cherry	1
Horse (fresh urine)	2	Grape	trace
Pigeon (fresh)	1	Oak	trace
Swine (fresh excrement)	1	Peach	1
Swine (fresh urine)	1	Pear	trace
		Raspberry	1
Natural Minerals		Straw	
Granite dust	3-6	Barley	1
Greensand marl	7	Buckwheat	2
Basalt rock	2	Cornstalks	1
		Millet	3
Plant Materials		Oat	2
Beet waste	1-4	Rye	1
Castor pomace	1-2	Sorghum	1
Cottonseed meal	2	Wheat	1
Fly ash	12	Tobacco stems	5-7
Garbage	2-4	Vegetable waste	1
Hay		Wood ashes (broad leaf)	10
Alfalfa	2	Wood ashes (coniferous)	6
Cowpea	2	Wool waste	1-4

dust. It comes from deposits left by ancient oceans, and contains trace minerals, including silica, iron and magnesium. It has the ability to absorb large amounts of water and provides an abundant source of plant-available potash.

Hardwood ashes are rich in potash, but should only be used on acid soils. The minerals will leach into the soil when the material is wetted.

See also FERTILIZER, GRANITE DUST, GREENSAND.

POTASH ROCK

A naturally occurring rock containing a high percentage of potassium, potash rock is one of the most effective potassium fertilizers, and when finely ground makes its nutrients readily available to growing plants.

Potash rock may be used in any quantity, usually ½ ton per acre, or about 2⅓ pounds per 100 square feet of garden area. It contributes a wide variety of minerals which are readily available when organic matter is added to the soils. Potash rock may be applied directly to the soil or may be added to the compost pile.

See also FERTILIZER, GRANITE DUST, GREENSAND, POTASH.

POTASSIUM

One of the three essential elements (along with phosphorus and nitrogen) needed by growing plants, potassium is usually referred to as potash when fertilizer is discussed.

See also FERTILIZER, GRANITE DUST, GREENSAND, POTASH.

POTATO   (*Solanum tuberosum*)

In almost any part of the country, the home gardener with sufficient garden space and a cool, dark storage cellar may grow and store potatoes by the organic method. Until recently potatoes could be grown only in cool areas, but now with improved varieties and better cultural techniques, they can be grown where summers are fairly hot if they are sufficiently mulched.

Soil: Potatoes need a moist, acidic soil with a pH of less than 6. Soils with a higher pH tend to harbor potato scab, a fungal disease that lives in the soil for many years. On the other hand, potatoes grown in extremely acidic soils are often small and of poor quality though free of scab. Before deciding where to plant potatoes, test the soil in several places on your property. If it is all too alkaline, try growing a green manure crop and plowing it under the autumn before seeding. Or, add pine needles or other acidic plant material to the soil.

Fresh manure must never be used on potato land. If well-rotted manure is used, it should be plowed or raked under the topsoil the autumn before planting. For a 100-foot row, use ten wheelbarrow-loads of rotted manure and mix it in well so that it does not burn the tubers.

Planting and Culture: Seed potatoes certified free of disease may be purchased from seed dealers. Unless the gardener has been able to save some of his own which he knows are healthy, certified seed potatoes are safest to plant. The best ones are small and do not need cutting. Each potato, or piece, contains one or more eyes and weighs one to two ounces. If cutting is necessary, make certain that plenty of flesh remains around the eyes

Each seed potato or piece should contain at least one eye and should weigh one or two ounces.

since plants must live on this stored food while sprouting. Cut seed should be allowed to dry 24 hours before planting.

Depending on the size and the number of eyes, five to eight pounds of potatoes are needed to plant a 100-foot row. The trenches or drills are five inches deep and the pieces of tuber are placed every 12 or 14 inches. Early varieties are planted about two weeks before the last killing frost. Late varieties may be planted to mature as late as the first fall frost. Early crops, growing while the weather is still cool, are less likely to be bothered by disease than late varieties. Seed for late crops should always be chosen from the disease-resistant strains.

As soon as planting is finished, a mulch of straw or hay ten to 12 inches deep should be applied. This will keep the soil moist and cool, and foster healthy potatoes.

A popular method of growing potatoes

above the soil is to plant them on leaves with a cover of mulch. Leaves are piled over the potato patch the previous fall to a depth of three feet and left there for the winter. By spring they have packed down and earthworms are working through them. Potatoes are planted by laying the pieces directly on the leaves, in rows where they are to grow. The seed is then covered with 12 to 14 inches of hay or straw. More mulch is added later, if tubers appear through the mulch. When harvesttime comes, the mulch is pulled back and potatoes are picked up and put into their sacks, with no digging necessary. Pests are deterred by the mulch system.

Insufficient potash in soil can result in potatoes which become soggy when cooked. A potash deficiency can be corrected by adding about ¼ pound per square foot of a natural potash mineral such as greensand, granite dust or pulverized feldspar to the soil. These natural minerals also contain the trace elements which are essential to normal healthy growth.

A good fertilizer for potatoes may be made by mixing one part cottonseed meal, one part dried fish meal, one part bone meal, two parts greensand, and two parts ground phosphate rock.

Insects and Diseases: In the garden, the insects and diseases injurious to potato plants can be controlled by removing insects as soon as they appear, giving them no chance to breed. The Colorado potato beetle and red slugs appear frequently. Sometimes blister beetles enter the garden and raise havoc among the potato plants. In the small garden, it is wise to place handpicked pests in containers of kerosene.

There are about 60 diseases of potato plants, but many of them are local and unimportant. Where the air is particularly moist and cool, early blight may kill the vines. Late blight may also occur and cause tuber rot. Unusually warm, dry weather may result in tip-burn or hopper-burn which destroys the foliage. Common scab is disfiguring to the potato and can be avoided by keeping the soil acid. Applications of lime or wood ashes should not be used if this is to be accomplished.

Harvesting: Potatoes are ready for harvest when the majority of the tops have withered. Early potatoes may be dug for table use at any time. But for storage, the potatoes should be fully mature. They may be left in the ground as much as four to six weeks if the weather is not too warm or too wet. After they are dug they should be allowed to dry as quickly as possible, and then should immediately be stored in a cool dark place. Stored in the light, they may turn green, and greened potatoes should not be eaten.

Varieties: Kennebec and Katahdin are recommended as late potatoes resistant to late blight and certain virus diseases, but not to scab. New Norland and Norgold Russet are resistant to scab and are very heavy producers as are Superior and Chieftain. Irish Cobbler and White Cobbler are old favorites grown in all states and considered excellent choices for home gardeners. Russet Burbank is widely grown in the Northwest, but, because it tends to produce misshapen tubers, it is not recommended for the amateur grower.

See also INSECT CONTROL, SWEET POTATO.

POTATO BEETLE
See INSECT CONTROL

POTENTILLA

Also known as cinquefoil and five-finger, this genus of the Rose family is composed mostly of perennial and woody plants native to the northern temperate regions. Showy and easy to care for once established, potentillas make good choices for beds, borders and rock gardens. The strawberrylike flowers are usually red, yellow or white, though varieties and hybrids come in pink and orange as well. Heights range from six inches to two or three feet.

Potentillas thrive in a cool, well-drained loamy soil. Although they prefer full sun, some species will spread and bloom in partial shade. All species are hardy, though some hybrids require a light covering of leaves in winter.

Herbaceous types can be propagated by division of the roots in autumn or early spring

The roselike flowers of potentilla appear in late summer and continue through early fall.

or, in some cases, by seed sown in the cold frame in spring. Woody species are best increased by cuttings of wood taken in midsummer and stored in sand in a cool place for several months. Best garden varieties are *P. argyrophylla,* with silvery foliage and clusters of one-inch amber-colored flowers; *P. fragiformis,* with velvety strawberrylike leaves and ¾-inch golden flowers; *P. fruticosa,* a three-foot shrub bearing yellow, white or red orange flowers from June to frost; *P. fulgens,* with yellow flowers, or scarlet in some varieties; *P. nepalensis,* two feet tall with clusters of pink flowers; *P. nitida,* a low-growing silky mat with one-inch rose-colored flowers; and *P. recta* cv. 'Warrenii', 2½ feet tall with showy yellow flowers.

POT LAYERING   *See* LAYERING

POTTING   *See* HOUSE PLANTS

POULTRY

Raising poultry offers a number of benefits to the small farmer. Most breeds of poultry will provide high-quality meat, fresh eggs, fertilizing manure, and feathers.

Before buying any kind of poultry, however, certain considerations must be taken into account. Are the birds to be for egg laying or meat production? How many can be kept and what is the cost compared to store-bought eggs and meat? Are they to be raised for personal consumption or profit? Choice of breeds should be determined on the basis of purpose. Though there are breeds that are both fair layers and meat producers, such as Rhode Island Reds or the various breeds of Rocks, even the best of these birds will not out-produce a breed specifically bred for one purpose. Therefore, if egg production is more important than meat production, White Leghorn hens or Khaki Campbell ducks should be chosen. Conversely, if meat production is more important, a meatier, blockier breed such as the Cornish hens or Embden geese would be a better choice.

Poultry raising does not have to be limited to food production. There are exotic breeds of chicken that can be raised for show, and fancy ducks are fun just to have around. Poultry catalogs, available from advertisements in farmers' magazines, list a wide variety of ducks, geese, chickens, exotic breeds of pigeons, as well as several breeds of turkeys and guinea hens.

Before you decide on any breed of poultry, consult breeders' magazines, catalogs, books, magazine articles, and talk to people in your area who are raising the kind of poultry in which you are interested. If you can find a professional breeder, as opposed to a commercial poultry farmer, so much the better. Investigate breeding methods, housing and general management techniques, production, and marketing.

Many breeds available today are the result of years of scientific breeding, and the prospective buyer should be aware of those that have been developed for very specific purposes. For instance, some layers won't set since broodiness was bred out to prevent interruption in egg laying, an important consideration for commercial egg production.

It is also helpful to know how long it takes to produce birds for market or table use: layers,

12 weeks; turkeys, 26 weeks; and hens, 24 weeks. Weights and ages may vary depending on the breed, so know your stock and its growth and maturation rates.

Housing: Housing for most kinds of poultry does not have to be elaborate. In many cases, you can build adequate structures yourself, or even remodel existing buildings on your farm to meet the needs of various types of poultry. Geese and ducks can be raised entirely on range, and many farmers allow their poultry to wander about the farm, picking up insects and foraging for greens. Feed companies have plans for homemade poultry feeders and equipment, and many books on raising poultry give plans and ideas for housing. Plans for small houses for poultry can also be obtained from your county agent or from the USDA.

Floor space required for various types of birds varies, as do their housing requirements. Layers need three to four square feet or more per bird, depending on breed, while broilers need only ¾ to one square foot. Turkey hens should be given four square feet apiece, mixed flocks, five, and toms, six. Provide breeder flocks of ducks with four to six square feet per bird. If you can give birds more than the minimum amount of room, so much the better. The crowding of birds in commercial poultry establishments is one reason that disease is such a serious problem.

If you plan to brood chicks, poults, ducks, or geese, the simplest way—barring natural motherhood—is to use an infrared light. This type of brooder can be installed in just a few seconds. Follow safety precautions for the equipment you will be using.

Feeding: Any meat or egg is only as good as the feed the bird gets. Your best bet for economical production of both meat and eggs

If allowed to wander around fields and yards, chickens will be able to find nourishing seeds, insects and fresh greens to supplement their diet.

is to grow your own grains, compound your own feeds and grind them yourself. If you do it yourself, you can be sure of what's being fed to your birds. On the other hand, if you don't have the room, the time or the inclination to grow your own grains, it will probably be cheaper for you to buy the grains and mix your own feed from them. As a last resort, feed commercially compounded feeds, but be sure they don't have medications already added. Your problems with disease, providing you buy clean stock and allow them plenty of room, adequate diet, and range, will probably be minimal. In any case, if trouble erupts you can provide specific medications if you have a large investment in your flock. Medication added to the food is costly for you and totally inappropriate on an organic homestead.

Another advantage in making your own feed is that you can store the feed unground. Ground feed allowed to stand for more than two weeks loses a considerable proportion of its vitamin and mineral content. By grinding your own, you can be sure your stock is getting the freshest feed possible.

Feed formulas are suggestions only. You can make substitutions in them to form a satisfactory ration for your birds. Formulas will also vary with the region, and you can use the crops grown in your region to compound a balanced poultry formula. Contact your state experimental station and ask for their poultry ration formulas.

Some birds need more grain than others. Broilers and layers require more grain than geese, who can live on range after the first few weeks and only need to be fed grain for fattening. During the spring and summer, birds can forage for green crops and eat insects.

In late summer and fall, feed lettuce, lawn clippings, kale, cabbage, Swiss chard, or beet tops. Green food is a problem in wintertime, but some pasture can be obtained from rye or winter wheat. Clean legume hay is also good. Many farmers find that sprouted grain makes an excellent chicken feed. The grain does not have to be threshed, but can be soaked and fed right in the stalk. *See* BARLEY.

Problems and Diseases: Many diseases are common to all poultry. The best treatment for most poultry disease is prevention. When buying stock, buy birds whose parents have been vaccinated against Newcastle, pullorum and laryngotracheitis. Some commercial hatcheries are certified as being pullorum-clean and offer a vaccination program for day-old chicks at extra cost. Proper diet and clean, dry, ventilated but draft-free housing are important factors in disease prevention along with clean, fresh feed and greens.

Viral coccidiosis is a persistent disease affecting mostly young birds. It is highly contagious and birds that become affected should be isolated from the rest of the flock. Different forms of the disease affect chickens, turkeys, and, rarely, ducks. Affected stock become listless, feathers become ruffled, and in advanced cases backs become hunched and droppings bloody. In advanced cases it is useless to try to cure the disease and stock should be drowned or otherwise disposed of. Cleanliness is of extreme importance both inside and outside the house when dealing with infected stock. Contact your vet for treatments.

Respiratory diseases such as infectious bronchitis, infectious coryza, chronic respiratory disease, infectious sinusitis, and infectious synovitis sometimes affect poultry flocks. Such diseases are difficult to cure without the use of antibiotics. In any case, you should contact your vet if your flock is having problems and follow his recommendations. Keeping the stock healthy and in good condition will prevent stress and lessen susceptibility to most ailments. Remember not to use the meat or eggs of sick birds.

Other poultry diseases are of less importance to the homesteader. Many of them are endemic to large flocks and confinement and do not occur on a small farm with a small flock.

Parasites are a problem, however, and are difficult to eliminate entirely. Commercial growers resort to pediculicides and insecticides to clean up feather lice and scaly leg mites, but you can counter these problems by allowing your birds access to outside runs where they can dust themselves. If the birds are confined,

PERCENTAGE COMPOSITION OF POULTRY MANURE

Source	Nitrogen	Phosphoric Acid	Potash
Chicks, baby (fresh manure)	1.7	1.3	.7
Chicks, baby (dried manure)	4.5	3.5	1.9
Chicks, growing (fresh manure)	1.6	.9	.6
Chicks, growing (dried manure)	5.4	3.6	2.4
Duck (fresh manure)	1.1	1.4	.5
Hen, laying (fresh manure)	1.1	.8	.5
Hen, laying (dried manure)	4.1	3.7	2.3
Turkey (fresh manure)	2.	1.4	.6

Source: U.S. Department of Agriculture.

place a box with dolomitic limestone or ordinary soil in the henhouse.

In addition to the various diseases and parasites, cannibalism may become a problem in your poultry flock. This can result from overcrowding, excessive lighting or heat, boredom, or poor diet. It begins with one bird picking at another's toes or the base of his tail. Injured or trapped chickens are especially vulnerable to attack and may be mercilessly picked until they are killed and eaten by the other birds.

Whenever a bird has been injured, place it in isolation until the wounds have healed completely. Prevent overcrowding by gradually increasing the size of the birds' available space as they grow. Feed them a high-protein diet and a wide variety of feeds. Of course, if there is an aggressive leader who initiates the picking, he should be removed from the flock.

Litter: A practice that makes healthier and more productive chickens is deep litter, sometimes called built-up litter. Simply let the litter accumulate to a depth of at least six to eight inches instead of cleaning out the poultry house every couple of weeks. Biological activity in the litter, just as in a compost heap, produces huge amounts of rich food.

Litter-reared chickens need no animal proteins or mineral supplements added to their feed, and if pastured or given ample green feed in addition, will need no vitamin A and D supplements. Antibiotics are also produced in the litter—litter-raised poultry is remarkably free from disease. In addition, chickens will eat the larvae of insects laid in the litter. Good litter materials include peat moss, straw, ground corncobs, wood chips, sawdust, and peanut hulls.

Poultry manure is a valuable source of humus and nutrients for the soil. It exceeds all other farm manures in fertilizing value. Under average conditions, it is safe to estimate that in most flocks about 150 pounds of manure are produced per layer per year. Poultry manure is high in nitrogen but low in phosphoric acid and potash, so supplement it with natural ground phosphate and potash rock. Phosphate rock will also help fix the nitrogen in the manure, and deep litter will cut down on the nitrogen loss by absorbing the liquid portion of the droppings.

See also individual entries for other fowl.

POWDERPUFF
See PINCUSHION CACTUS

POWDERY MILDEW
See DISEASE

PRAIRIE SMOKE   *See* GEUM

PRAYER PLANT   *See* MARANTA

PRAYING MANTIS
See MANTIS, PRAYING

PRICKLY ASH   (*Zanthoxylum*)

Members of the Citrus family that are considered pest plants, these shrubs or small trees grow to heights of between 12 and 25 feet. Branches, stems and twigs all have sharp ½-inch thorns in pair at the base of the leaves. Northern prickly ash (*Z. americanum*) is slightly taller than the southern species (*Z. clava-Herculis*) and can be grown in most parts of North America.

While the leaves and somewhat fleshy fruit (red brown when ripe) are pleasantly aromatic, their taste is disagreeably pungent. Seeds are shiny black, about ⅛ inch long. Flowers are yellow green and open before the leaves appear.

Prickly ash inhabits rich, moist woods, thickets and riverbanks, and also thrives at edges of woodlands. Eradication of these thorny shrubs can be accomplished by grubbing out the roots.

PRICKLY GREENBRIER
(*Smilax hispida*)

This shrubby tendril climber has firm black thorns ¼ to ½ inch long that can tear clothing or scratch unprotected skin. The deciduous leaves are oval or heart-shaped, and in their axils are clustered small, dioecious, carrion-scented flowers. The green black berries are globular and usually one seeded.

A slow grower with an eventual height of over 20 feet, the prickly greenbrier throws up stems from a common rootstock and may be controlled by digging this out. It is usually found in a rich, moist woodland soil.

The stems remain green all year and are much used in winter bouquets. All native species of the greenbrier are protected in Florida.

PRICKLY PEAR   (*Opuntia*)

The prickly pear is one of the most important members of the Cactus family. Some are called cholla. They may be flat or cylindrical in shape, a few inches high or over ten feet tall.

The hardiest opuntias are *O. humifusa* var. *austrina,* the common wild prickly pear of the northeast and central states, and *O. polyacantha,* the low, round-stemmed cholla, which thrives outdoors up to North Dakota. Both of these grow on sandy soil, often along shores, and have three-inch yellow flowers. They are easily transplanted from the wild or propagated from stem cuttings.

The outdoor culture of the rest is confined to the Southwest, but they are favorite greenhouse and house plants all over the country. Nearly all have extremely sharp spines arising from masses of short, barbed hairs, and white, yellow or red flowers. The handsome fruits of many species are edible and choice.

Some of the smaller ones for window gardens include the thimble tuna (*O. sphaerica*), a dwarf, red-flowered type that grows in clusters; cinnamon cactus (*O. microdasys* var. *rufida*), with green pads spotted with short spines, and yellow or orange flowers; fairy needles (*O. Soehrensii*), growing in clusters with long spines and yellow flowers; rose tuna (*O. basilaris*), with pretty rose red pads and large pink blooms; and rabbit's ears (*O. microdasys*), similar to cinnamon cactus but with plushy golden spines, and *O. tuna* is a low, prostrate cactus with yellow, red-tinged flowers and pear-shaped fruit called tuna.

There are also many large prickly pears, suited to greenhouse culture. They can be grown in tubs and put outdoors as garden accents in the summer. *O. cylindrica* grows up to ten feet tall and is sometimes without spines. *O. imbricata* is about the same height, but shrubby and with large purple blooms. *O. fulgida,* eight feet tall, has a woody trunk and pink flowers. Nopal (*O. Lindheimeri*) grows about 12 feet tall and has three-inch yellow blooms and two-inch purple fruit. The Indian fig (*O. Ficus-indica*) is cultivated throughout the tropics for its big, juicy, edible red fruit. It is treelike, often 15 feet high and usually spineless.

See also CACTI.

PRIMROSE   (*Primula*)

There are hundreds of primroses suitable for greenhouse culture, flower borders, rock gardens, or for naturalizing woody landscapes. Most are low growing with a leafless flower stalk rising from a rosette of leaves. Flowers come in many colors, growing solitary, in flat-topped clusters, in whorls around the stem, or in dense, round heads.

Planting and Culture: Most species will grow well only under climatic and soil conditions similar to those found in their native habitat. A few adaptable species have less exacting requirements and are reasonably easy to grow in American gardens if certain basic demands are met.

In most areas of the United States, primroses must be shaded from direct sun. Where temperatures are high at midday, a northern or eastern exposure with afternoon and midday shade is best. Some species prefer to grow under deciduous trees such as birches which provide light shade all summer. The north side of a deciduous shrubbery border is also suitable for the earliest-flowering types.

While soil and moisture demands vary, a good general rule is to provide a rich loam high in humus which drains readily. Soggy soil in winter will rot the roots and crowns of primroses. Dig in plenty of leaf mold, peat, compost, or well-rotted manure, and add enough sand and gravel to insure good drainage. Bone meal and wood ashes are good fertilizers. Top-dress annually with compost since primroses are heavy feeders.

Water frequently during the heat of summer to prevent the soil from drying out and to prevent infestation of red spiders. Wet the foliage on both sides at each watering.

A winter covering of some loose material like pine needles, evergreen boughs or oak leaves will help to prevent heaving during alternate periods of freezing and thawing. Avoid using leaves that mat heavily.

Propagation: Seed of most hardy primroses requires a period of freezing to induce germination. This can be accomplished in several ways. Sow seed in late fall or early winter in a cold frame or raised protected bed on a light soil containing peat, sand and loam. Seed will germinate in spring. Transplant seedlings first to nursery beds, then to their permanent positions in late summer or early fall. Water frequently until established. Alternatively, seed may be sown in flats which are kept in a shaded place outdoors or in an unheated building through the winter and placed in the cold frame for germination in spring. See that the flats do not dry out during the chilling period. A third way is to sow in flats which are put in plastic bags and kept in the freezer for two to four weeks, then brought into a cool (45 to 55°F. [7.22 to 12.78°C.], preferably), light place for germination. Seed of some primroses germinates very slowly, so don't be in a hurry to discard ungerminated flats. Transplant seedlings into peat pots or other flats, and set them in their permanent location as soon as they are strong enough.

Plants are more frequently propagated by division. When clumps have become large, they should be lifted and divided, usually about every two or three years. If they are left too long, they may stop blooming. The division should be done as soon after flowering as possible, except in the South, where it is done in early fall.

Each clump consists of one large and several smaller crowns. Separate these and plant them individually, taking care that soil does not fall into the center of the crown. This seems to cause it to rot.

Types: The best-known primroses belong to the vernal group. *P. vulgaris,* the common wild primrose of England, bears pale yellow flowers on individual stalks just above the foliage in spring. *P. veris,* the cowslip, and *P. elatiar,* the oxlip, are similar to each other. Their clusters of nodding yellow flowers are held on stems well above the foliage. These two species and *P. vulgaris* have been crossed to produce *P.* x *polyantha,* which is the most widely grown of all primroses. A great many colors and forms are available, such as the Pacific Giants and Colossea hybrids. All primroses in this group grow well in humus-rich soil and partial shade, but they need to be lifted and

Polyanthus is a hybrid primrose which blossoms very early in spring and often continues flowering until early summer.

divided every few years and replanted in enriched soil. Their evergreen leaves should be lightly covered in winter.

Many primroses do best in rock gardens, but they can be grown in the flower bed if adequate drainage is provided. Dig gravel and sand into the soil, and mulch the plants with stone chips to protect the crowns from excess water. *P. Auricula* is a European alpine species which has produced hybrid forms amenable to these conditions. Fragrant, "eyed" flowers in several colors are produced in umbels on six- to eight-inch stems above evergreen rosettes. *P. denticulata* has round heads of numerous lavender pink flowers in early spring. There is also a white form. The toothed leaves disappear in winter, leaving a dormant bud at the soil surface. Protect it with stone chips.

P. Sieboldii from Japan is easy to grow under the same conditions that suit the vernal primroses. It has crinkly, scalloped leaves that appear late in spring from a mat of rhizomes at the soil surface. The flowers, usually pink and sometimes having lacy petals, are borne in umbels well above the leaves. There are rose and white forms available as well as pastel bicolors. Divide the clumps just after flowering if the plants stop blooming well. This species tends to go dormant in summer, especially if the soil becomes dry. Mark its position so it is not dug up by mistake, because it will revive the following spring.

P. japonica is one of the candelabra primulas, so called because the flowers are produced in successive tiers on stalks that grow one to three feet high. It prefers bog or waterside conditions, but will do almost as well in a shady garden bed if watered heavily during summer months. The plants should be covered with an airy mulch after the large leaves disappear in late fall. *P. japonica* self-sows abundantly,

gradually forming colonies in this way. Flower color is magenta to crimson and white forms are to be had.

PRIVET   (*Ligustrum*)

This is a genus of shrubs or, occasionally, trees of the Olive family, native to Asia, Australia and the Mediterranean region. Several species are used in this country for hedges and windbreaks. Many are very hardy, dense and glossy-leaved, and some are almost evergreen. Leaves grow in white terminal clusters, and may be either fragrant or malodorous. They are easily grown in almost any soil, and are propagated by seed, cuttings or, in the choice species, by grafting.

Common privet (*L. vulgare*) will grow to 15 feet, with slender spreading branches and dense flower clusters followed by black berries.

California privet (*L. ovalifolium*) is upright and rather stiff, half-evergreen, with leaves to 2½ inches long. It is tender in the colder climates.

L. Ibota and *L. obtusifolium* is a hardy Japanese form with wide-spreading branches. It grows to six feet. Small nodding flower clusters bloom in June, followed by black berries that remain on the shrub most of the winter. Variety Regelianum is a denser and lower-growing form which looks good in front of higher shrubs.

Amur privet (*L. amurense*) is the hardiest, growing well in regions where other privet may be winter-killed. It will grow to 15 feet, and bears light green foliage and dark berries.

L. indicum is an evergreen species, but can be grown only in Southern California and Florida and the Gulf states. Wax-leaf privet

(*L. japonicum*) is also evergreen, and grows farther north; its oval leaves are about three inches long and leathery. *L. lucidum,* also evergreen, grows to a 30-foot tree in the Deep South. It is used frequently for street planting.

L. Quihoui, a six-foot Chinese shrub, is hardy in protected positions in the North. Flowers grow in clusters six to eight inches long and appear in August and September.

See also HEDGE, SHRUBS.

PROPAGATION

Most succulents can be easily propagated by means of a single leaf cutting or "slip."

Almost all flowering and cone-bearing plants can be propagated sexually by seeds and also asexually (or vegetatively) by cuttings, division, grafting, or layering as well as from bulbs, corms, rhizomes, offsets, and runners. Seeds are the common method for reproducing most vegetables, annuals, biennials, perennials, and many trees and shrubs. But fruit trees, many house plants and hybrid ornamentals are grown from cuttings or are grafted or bud grafted in order to maintain a pure strain and quickly procure plants identical with their parents.

The parent characteristics are preserved by asexual means because after the plant has been cut and wounded, the cells begin to proliferate tissues which will eventually grow into new plants, if the moisture and temperature are suitable for promoting new growth. An atmosphere of high humidity and a rooting medium such as moist sand provide the best conditions. Then the cuttings are transplanted when the new roots have been established.

Cuttings: Rooting mediums used for cuttings include combinations of moist sand and peat moss, peat moss and vermiculite, or sphagnum moss or perlite, or some other combination of those ingredients, as well as plain moist sand. When rooted, the cutting is moved to a richer medium with loam, leaf mold or compost in it. Both the softwood cuttings made from the current year's growth and the hardwood cuttings from older wood can be grown in these combinations.

House plants of certain species, including succulents, begonias and African violets, can be propagated from leaf cuttings, taken with or without the leafstalk or petiole. Root cuttings can be taken from house plants at repotting time, and from various perennials in spring, summer or fall, depending upon the plant. (Root cuttings also propagate weeds, as most gardeners know from their experience with quackgrass, which will grow up into a new plant from every piece of root left in the ground.)

Division: Propagation by division of the mature plant is a practice both common and advisable for perennials like iris and aster, which run out if their clumps are not split up every few years. Peonies, phlox, daylilies, and rhubarb should also be divided when they become too big and overcrowded. Among house plants, snake plants, ferns and African violets are divided when they outgrow their pots, or when they push up new small crowns around the base of the mother plant. To divide dahlias, it is necessary to separate the tubers, which are short, thick, underground food-storing structures, leaving one or two eyes and a piece of stem connected to each tuber.

Grafting: The two plant parts used in grafting are said to "take" when the wounds of the stock (or underpart of the graft) and the scion (or upper inserted part) finally heal, and the living tissues of the two parts grow together and work as one plant. The first agent of healing is a callus tissue which forms on each part, and eventually from this callus—or from alongside it—the new roots and new shoots are formed.

Layering: Layering, either by bending a section of a living shoot or branch into the ground, or by wrapping it in moist sphagnum moss, is another common method of propagation. Layering in the soil is done in one of several ways to induce roots to grow from the stem of the mother plant. This is a simple and easy method to use with such shrubs as forsythia, mock orange and the bramble fruits. With air layering, the wrapped stem on the plant is tied tightly in polyethylene to exclude drying winds, and left for a period of six months or longer until roots are formed.

Runners: Propagation from runners is possible with many spreading or vining plants such as strawberries and wandering Jew, which really layer themselves. New plants can be gotten from suckers of shrubs such as lilac, snowberry and Japanese quince.

All these methods of making new plants from old will save you money and may even improve quality, when you divide only your best plants, graft your own best fruit trees, take cuttings of your most vigorous and healthy plants, and save your own seeds.

See also BULB, CUTTINGS, DIVISION, GRAFTING, HOUSE PLANTS, LAYERING, SEEDS AND SEEDLINGS.

PRUNING

The natural form of the plant is usually beautiful and should be preserved, but sometimes it is necessary to control the plant's growth. Pruning involves trimming out unwanted or unhealthy plant growth to benefit the remaining portions of the plant. It is done for one of many reasons:

1. To remove dead or injured members; this should be done anytime you see dead or injured parts of a plant.

2. To check the growth of plants where space is limited. If you want to grow plants that, when mature, are too large for your grounds, you keep them within limits by pruning.

3. To thin plants that have become too dense to admit light and air to the area in which they are planted, or on which interior branches, leaves and fruit do not receive enough sunlight.

4. To encourage root growth and to prevent dieback of the branches.

5. To alter intelligently the form and size of plants for design purposes. Pruned hedges

and sculptured plants are examples of this form of selective pruning, as are the various espaliered plants.

6. To rehabilitate shrubs that suffer from neglect, poor growing conditions or diseased parts.

7. To encourage fruit, flower or foliage production, or to stimulate the growth of larger flowers and fruit.

The season for pruning varies with the type of plant that you want to prune and with the results you wish to achieve through pruning. Some pruning can be done at any time suitable to the gardener's convenience, while other must be done during a specific season. Pruning is not a mysterious process but a standard garden technique. Above all, it requires an understanding of the growth habits of plants, and an appreciation of the way each individual plant develops and what shapes it assumes as it matures. If you have any questions, consult your county agent.

Although plants have different shapes when mature, they have similar structures. Before discussing pruning, one must know the names of certain structural members. The trunk is the main support of a tree or shrub, and is considered to be that part of the plant from the ground to the lowest main branch. If a plant has several trunks, they are called stems.

There are four kinds of branches. The leader is the main branch; it points skyward and is generally a continuation of the stem or trunk. Side branches that grow from the trunk are called primary scaffold branches and branches that grow from these are secondary scaffold branches. Small branches called laterals grow from the leader or scaffold branches. Branches grow longer from the terminal buds at their tips; this is called primary growth.

When branches grow thicker, it is called secondary growth. Branches growing from the end of a branch are called terminal growth. The angle formed between two branches, or a branch and the trunk, is called a crotch.

There are three other branches you will be concerned with in pruning: suckers, spurs and hangers. Suckers grow from roots, trunk or large branches. If they grow from branches,

Use hand pruning shears to snip off only the smallest twigs and branches.

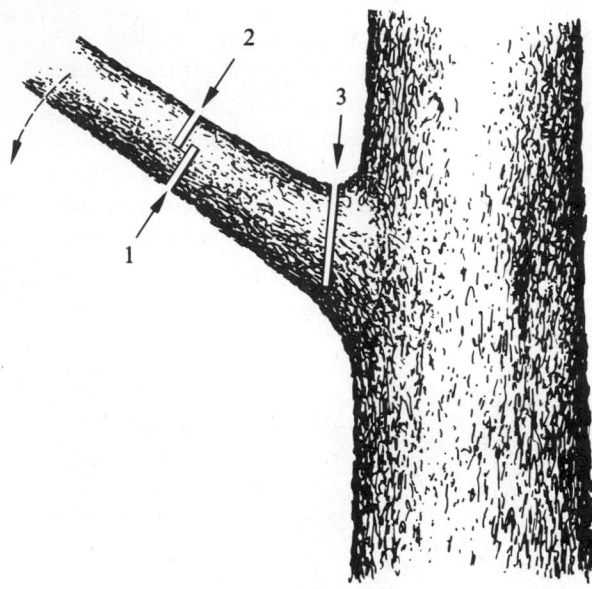

To remove a large limb without tearing the tree's bark, begin by sawing upward into the branch, about one foot from the trunk. Make the next cut an inch further from the trunk, sawing downward until the branch falls. Then saw off the stub as close to the trunk as possible, and coat the exposed surface with tree-wound paint.

they are also called watersprouts. They are usually removed by pruning. Spurs are short laterals, often fruit-bearing, which are thick and have visible growth rings. Hangers are branches that droop; they are thin, weak, slow growing, and are usually removed.

Basic Pruning Methods: To prune shrubs and trees around your home, you'll need a number of tools. A pair of hand pruning shears is a necessity; you will also need a pair of long-handled lopping shears for hard-to-work places. Saws are necessary for cutting heavy branches. There are two types of pruning saws: one has a large, curved handle and a straight blade with coarse teeth and comes in a variety of sizes,

and the other is a small saw with a blade that folds into the handle. For pruning hedges, you'll need a pair of hedge shears.

Always use the proper tool for the job. For branches thinner than ½ inch in diameter, use the hand pruning shears. Very hard wood or branches larger than 1½ inches in diameter should be cut with a saw. For branches intermediate in size, use the lopping shears. The hedge shears should be used only for pruning hedges. They will have to be trimmed whenever the new growth reaches two to three inches or they will look ragged.

Make all cuts clean, as close to the trunk or branch as possible, and just above a bud. Dress wounds larger than a penny with special tree wound dressing, *not* household paint. If you are pruning a diseased plant, dip your pruning tool in denatured alcohol after cutting.

Pruning large branches: Pruning heavy members of big trees is not an easy job for the amateur. Cut the branch in stages. The first cut is an undercut about a foot from the trunk. Saw about a third of the way through the branch. Next, make a cut about an inch further from the trunk, from the top of the branch. Continue cutting until the branch falls off, leaving a one-foot stub. Remove the stub by cutting back cleanly to the larger member; paint the wound with wound dressing.

This type of pruning cut should always be used for lateral branches about ¾ inch in diameter. If you don't use this type of cut, the branch may tear bark from the larger piece, providing a way in which insects or disease can enter the plant.

Pinching: Pinching is a simple method of pruning, and the most convenient tools are your thumb and forefinger. You can prune many small plants by carefully pinching back soft growth, and can dwarf conifers somewhat by pinching out terminal buds. As you walk through your garden, nip off random growth, break out small twigs and branches that interfere with the form or size of the plant. This can be done whenever the need arises.

Pinching is necessary is some plants to produce more foliage or to encourage better blooms. For example, commercial florists pinch mums to make them more bushy and create more blooms. All mum plants should be pinched at least once. Pinch off the terminal stem when the young plant has grown to eight to ten inches high, and pinch soft growth periodically until the plant has several side stems and is bushy.

To make house plants bushier, pinch off the growing tip of each stem. This will actually slow the growth of the plant, but by activating the dormant axil buds below the pinched point, will produce more stems and foliage.

Disbudding is similar to pinching and is usually done either with the thumb and forefinger or with a small, sharp knife. To disbud, pinch off the side buds early in the season before they are fully developed. The object is to produce fewer and handsomer blossoms on such plants as roses and mums. With side buds removed, the strength goes to the terminal bud, resulting in a larger flower.

Flowering Ornamentals: If you prune your ornamentals during the year, you won't have to do any major pruning. When you cut flowering sprays for summer decoration, cut them from misshapen parts of the plant. The underground sprouts that come up around the bases of older plants should be dug out with a spade, and long, whiplike shoots that develop from the base or lower branches should be cut back to two leaves. In the winter, prune out a quarter of the oldest branches in bushes older than five years.

To prolong blooming, snip off flowers that are past their prime. Although impractical in a large garden, this can be done with your favorite—or most valuable—plants.

Fruit Trees: When fruit trees are young, pruning can be done in midsummer, but as they mature, it becomes a winter or early-spring operation, done when the tree is dormant and leafless. At this time of year, the framework and branches are easily distinguished. The *best* time to prune a fruit tree is during March and April, but pruning can be done as late as blossoming without serious damage. Summer pruning should be limited on mature trees to removing watersprouts and broken limbs.

Pruning should also be done at planting time regardless of season. At planting and during the first few years, pruning is primarily a training operation directed toward establishing a strong tree framework. Too much pruning can stunt tree growth. Pruning during the bearing years consists of removing weak wood, thinning the branches, controlling height and width, and repairing damaged limbs.

The framework of a tree consists of several branches growing laterally from the main leader. There are a variety of methods of developing a framework for fruit trees. For example, apples are often trained to a modified leader system, which consists of a strong leader framed by several strong laterals. The advantage is a strong, rather open framework. Another system used for apple trees and common for peaches, apricots and nectarines is the open-center system. There is no leader on trees trained by this method but several strong branches form a bowl-shaped scaffold, allowing light to reach fruit in the center of the tree, producing nutritious and better-colored fruit.

For best results with fruit trees, start with an unbranched whip of good size. Do not prune when planting, but after the tree has become established, select the main laterals, spaced six to eight inches apart. Be careful to examine the crotch angles when selecting laterals. From the structural standpoint, the weakest part of any tree is where the upper side of a limb joins with the trunk at the crotch. The smaller the angle between the branch and the central leader, the weaker the crotch. Thus, by selecting only branches with wide angles (30 to 70 degrees), this crotch weakness is reduced.

On some trees, one branch may develop into a leader similar to the central leader of the tree. If allowed to continue, this condition will result in a forked tree, which is structurally weak, and under the weight of a heavy crop of fruit the tree may split into two parts. The vigorous branch should be suppressed by cutting off the branch just above the first good lateral branch growing toward the outside of the tree. This is known as heading back and may be applied to almost any branch. By cutting to an outside lateral, the limb is encouraged to spread out rather than to continue growing straight up. If by heading back a branch is reduced to less than 30 inches, it should be completely removed.

A condition may be found on a tree where several branches originate at the same point on a limb. This may appear as a fork or whorl. It is recommended that all the branches be removed but the one with the largest diameter.

As the tree ages, the rate of growth diminishes until the tree bears fruit. Growth after this serves to fill out the tree. To a young tree, pruning is an invigorating process that tends to delay the time of fruiting. Consequently, prior to bearing, as little wood as possible should be removed from the tree. Small branches and short stubby spur growth should be left since fruit develops from this wood. Once the main

lateral branches have been selected, pruning should be limited as much as possible to removing broken limbs or correcting bad situations. The general tendency is always to overprune a young tree.

After the fruit tree has begun to bear fruit, it should be pruned every year to encourage the development of good-sized, high-colored fruit. The way to prune a bearing tree is to start on the top and sides of the tree and work in toward the trunk. Detailed pruning, cutting branches ¼ inch and less in diameter with a pair of handshears, is very time consuming. Generally a saw, loppers or pole pruners are used to make cuts on larger branches, those greater than ½ inch in diameter. Limbs arising from the center of the tree that are smaller in diameter than the main laterals or that interfere with the branches on the main laterals should be removed or suppressed. It may be necessary to head back some branches or to eliminate whorls and forks as previously described.

The severity of pruning depends upon the kind of fruit. Very little wood if any should be pruned from pear trees. Train to a modified leader, prune sufficiently to prevent them from growing too much in a season, and trim side branches frequently. Peaches should be trained to open-center systems. Establish plums and cherries early because they are likely to bleed where branches older than a year are removed.

More detailed information can be obtained from your county agent.

Grapes: Grapes must be pruned each year to keep the vines within reasonable limits, maintain vigor and assure fruit of good quality. American grapes bear only on new wood—the shoots that start in the spring from buds formed the previous summer on canes which themselves had developed during that year.

European wine grapes bear on the current year's wood. These are pruned to a stump, from which several fruiting canes emerge in the spring. American grapes generally are trained to a trellis with a main trunk and two or four laterals which are allowed to produce a few, carefully spaced branches.

Shrubs: There are two types of shrubs. On one, blooming occurs on buds formed the previous season. These should be pruned in late spring immediately after flowering. If pruning is done during the dormant season, much of the flowering wood will be removed. Among these are azalea, bridal wreath, dogwood, forsythia, French hydrangea, lilac, mock orange, climbing roses, snowball viburnum, wisteria, and white fringe.

Other shrubs bloom on buds of the current season's growth. These should be pruned during the dormant period in winter or early spring. They include butterfly bush, clematis, highbush cranberry, honeysuckle, matrimony vine, bush roses, and rose-of-Sharon.

When shrubs have been neglected, are full of suckers, are ill-shapen, or primarily include a tangle of weak growth, you may need to do the most drastic type of pruning—cutting the entire plant down to the ground. Leave just a few inches of growth. This type of pruning is done in the early spring, and results in a new top for the shrub. As the young shoots grow they can be thinned or pruned to produce a shapely shrub. This method is advised for deciduous plants such as forsythia, snowberry, weigela, and others that are vigorous growers.

Hedges: If you keep your hedges clipped, shear them with a sharp hedge shears every time new growth reaches two to three inches. Use a string or cord stretched between two stakes of equal height to keep the top of the hedge even, and hold shears flat against the hedge when you're trimming it. Although you can trim the sides to grow vertically, it is better to bevel the sides and make the hedge 1½ times wider at the bottom than at the top, tapering them from a broad base to a narrower top. If your hedge is vigorous, it should be trimmed when required, even two to three times a season as necessary. For informal hedges, trim to keep in shape, and trim out dead wood and diseased growth.

Evergreens: Some broadleaf evergreens can be pruned freely, but you must be cautious with citrus and magnolias as well as other species. Older wood heals poorly, and should be pruned in summer only. However, cherry laurel, euonymus, hollies, mahonias, and others may be trimmed freely, preferably in spring as new growth hardens.

Azaleas may be pruned in late spring for best bloom in the future.

Dwarf and prostrate junipers are never pruned. Larger trees should be trained to a central leader with side shoots retained. They can be pruned anytime if you are careful to retain the natural form of the plant. Slant all cuts inward and downward so the cut ends will be hidden from sight.

In pruning pines and similar trees that grow similarly with branches radiating from the trunk in whorls like the spokes of a wheel, pinch back the young "candle" growth when small to encourage the development of many small branches. Shorten small branches in spring by cutting at a fork. Remove only the previous season's growth. If you feel you must work on your pines, you must trim the entire tree. Each "candle" which forms at the end of the branches must be cut back, preserving the size relationship between the central candle and the surrounding, smaller ones. Prune before the candles are fully developed in the spring just when they are beginning to break through their papery sheaths. Use a sharp knife. Specimen plantings of firs, spruces, and hemlocks should not be pruned. If a small tree is desired, many dwarf forms are available.

Roses: Except for fall removal of unusually long tips of tall canes, pruning of bush roses should be done in the late spring as soon as the leaf buds have begun to swell and all danger of severe freezing weather has passed. Autumn pruning should only be resorted to if the roses are in danger of being broken by wind, sleet or snow. This time would vary from February in Georgia to mid-April in our most northern states. Climbing roses should be pruned just after blooming. The same rule applies to such shrub roses as hugonis and the rugosas. Ground-covering types of roses such as wichuraiana or Max Graf, require little or no pruning other than the removal of dead or offending branches and may be done at almost any time.

Use a sharp pair of shears that will make a good clean cut. Ragged, crushed or mutilated cuts encourage stem fungus and borers rather than clean healing or callusing. Cut about ¼ inch above a bud or "eye" that points to the outside rather than the inside of the plant. Make a slanting cut in a direction parallel to the angle of the bud above which you cut. A touch of antiseptic tree paint on the wound will discourage stem fungus or stem borers from entering the wound before a callus forms.

In pruning hybrid tea roses, the grower is limited by the space allotted to each plant. The food of the rose is produced in the plant's foliage and the amount of foliage is largely dependent on the amount of wood remaining after pruning. If too much is taken off the top, the plant's ability to produce food is affected, and fewer blooms are produced.

Roses spaced 15 to 20 inches apart should be pruned to eight to 12 inches. For spacings of 20 to 30 inches, prune to 12 to 18 inches. For 30 inches apart or wider, prune to 18 to 24 inches. The pruning heights help to determine the size and number of blooms produced by the plant during the growing year. Therefore, the larger roses grow, the stronger and more productive they will be.

First prune all injured or diseased wood, then remove crossed or interfering branches. Weak branches less than ¼ inch in diameter can also be removed. Finally, cut back the bush to the desired height and shape. For the most blooms, varieties that produce a few tall, heavy canes from the bud should be permitted to retain more height than the varieties that break readily from the bud.

Floribunda roses bloom profusely if allowed to grow freely. Select varieties according to mature height and prune them only as necessary. Heights of three to 4½ feet with hundreds of blooms are not uncommon among the tall-growing floribundas, while low-growing ones will flower quite heavily at heights of two to 2½ feet or less.

The ramblers, or small-flowered climbing roses, are very vigorous growers and each year they send up many shoots from the bud. Each cane should be cut back close to the ground as soon as it has finished blooming. If they are grafted plants, cut only above the union. The young shoots which grow up in the spring and summer should be tied to a support as they will produce blooms the following spring.

Large-flowered climbers are handled in a slightly different manner. Because they do not produce as many annual canes as the rambler roses, a proportionately smaller number of canes should be removed. A good rule is to remove as many old canes each year as there are new ones produced. Always remove the oldest canes, the ones with the darkest and roughest bark, as closely to the ground as possible without injuring the plant. The new canes should be tied to a support.

Everblooming and climbing hybrid tea roses arc the most restricted growers of all climbing roses and need little or no pruning other than the removal of injured or diseased wood and withered blooms immediately after blooming. The blooms should be cut off just above the first leaf below the withered bloom.

Bramble Fruits: Pruning most of the bramble fruits is relatively simple. Canes grow to full height one year, and thc next year send out fruiting laterals. At the end of the season, they die back to the ground level. With spring-bearing plants, remove the spent canes as the crop finishes. Everbearing varieties should be cut in fall when the fruit-bearing canes are spent.

In fall, cut the canes to a height convenient for picking, and in spring, after buds have swollen, cut plants back to this height. Spray the cuts with wound dressing.

In pruning raspberry canes, remove dead canes and those growing outside the row. Then prune those in the row that are too small and weak to produce a good crop. If the plants are vigorous and overly crowded, remove some of the large canes. The amount of thinning varies with conditions, but it is generally desirable to keep the hedgerow not more than 15 to 18 inches wide, with not more than four or five canes per row foot. Head-back all remaining canes to a height of about 24 to 30 inches. If a trellis is used, the canes can be higher.

The new shoots of black and purple raspberries are ordinarily pinched off during the growing season when they are 18 to 24 inches high. This is done to induce lateral branches to grow from the main stem. At the dormant season, any canes not pinched should be cut back to 24 to 36 inches and all lateral shoots pruned back to about six inches. Remove all dead, weak, injured, or diseased canes. Burn these to prevent spread of disease.

Bush blackberries usually have stronger, sturdier canes than raspberries and should be pinched back in the summer when they are 30 to 36 inches long. Winter pruning will consist of cutting out weak, dead or diseased canes, cutting back those which were not pinched, and shortening the laterals to eight to 12 inches.

Blueberries: The blueberry produces fruit on wood of the previous season's growth. The largest berries are borne on the most vigorous wood. Most varieties tend to over-bear and unless part of the buds are pruned, the berries are small and there is little new growth for the next year's crop. Pruning is usually started at the end of the third season the plants have grown. The erect-growing varieties, such as Bluecrop, Dixi, Jersey, Rancocas, and Stanley, need to be thinned at the center, whereas Blueray and Homebell are especially spreading. Their lower, drooping branches may require pruning. The amount of pruning necessary depends on plant vigor; the more vigorous the plant the less pruning needed. Leave equal amounts of well-spaced one-, two- and three-year growth.

Remove only the low-spreading branches next to the ground, and leave the erect branches or shoots. If the center of the bush is dense, the weak and the older branches should be removed.

Red Currants: Late winter is the best time to prune red currant bushes. Remove canes four years old or older, low-growing canes that drop to the ground when heavy with fruit, broken or diseased canes, and the weaker one-year shoots. After pruning, an ideal bush might consist of about five one-year shoots, four two-year canes, three three-year canes, and possibly two or more four-year canes.

Gooseberries: Gooseberries may be pruned in late winter. Remove dead or broken canes, then those branches that are borne around the lower part of the bush—those low enough to touch ground when loaded with fruit. Canes more than four years old usually are too weak to be productive, so they should be eliminated. Save equal amounts of first- second- and third-year growth. This is usually the only pruning needed, although it may be desirable to remove a few twigs here and there.

See also entries for individual plants, BRAMBLE FRUITS, FRUIT TREES, GRAPE.

PRUNUS

This genus of the Rose family includes about 200 small trees or shrubs that bear stone fruits. Cherries, plums, almonds, apricots, and peaches are members of the genus. Leaves are alternate and mostly simple, flowers are white or pink and fragrant, and the fruit is characterized by its single pit or stone.

Most of the species are hardy in the North, though after a severe winter flower buds may be killed. They like neutral to slightly alkaline, loamy soil, but are easily grown in almost any ground. Propagation is by seed, by wood cuttings under glass, or by budding.

See also entries for individual fruit.

PTERIS   *See* FERN

PULMONARIA

Also called lungwort, this genus of perennial European herbs is a member of the Borage family and is closely related to the forget-me-not. The blue to lavender flowers are funnel shaped and appear in terminal clusters. The leaves, which are sometimes mottled, are larger at the base of the plant and become fewer and smaller as they progress up the stem.

Pulmonarias prefer a light, moist soil and partial shade. They are easily propagated by seed or division of the creeping rootstock. Clumps should be divided every three or four years to maintain vigor.

Bethlehem sage (*P. saccharata*), which grows from six to 18 inches tall, has white-spotted leaves and red violet flowers that bloom in April or May.

P. angustifolia grows from eight to 12 inches tall and produces lavender blue flowers in May. The leaves are not spotted.

P. montana has bright green, unspotted leaves and violet flowers that bloom in April. Its height ranges from six to 20 inches.

P. officinalis has white-spotted leaves and reddish flowers which later turn violet. It grows from six to 12 inches tall.

PULSATILLA   (*Anemone*)

Known as pasque flower, this member of the Buttercup family is grouped in the genus *Anemone,* and is similar to anemone except in fruit. It is a hardy perennial growing to about one foot from long-stalked clusters of finely divided basal leaves. The flowers are cup shaped and can be purple, lilac or white, two or three inches across. The clusters of its seed-fruits are silky. Pulsatillas may be raised from seed planted immediately after ripening, or by division. The plants prefer shade.

American pasque flower (*A. patens*) blooms in April or May before the leaves develop. The violet flower is raised above the low leaf clump.

A. vernalis, the European pasque flower, has flowers purple outside and white inside. *A. Pulsatilla,* the common pasque flower, has blue to lilac flowers, and other varieties have red flowers or variegated foliage.

PUMPKIN   *See* SQUASH

PURPLE BONESET
See JOE-PYE WEED

PURPLE COCKLE
See CORN COCKLE

PURPLE CONEFLOWER
See ECHINACEA

PURPLE ROCKCRESS
See AUBRIETA

PURSLANE   (*Portulaca oleracea*)

This low-growing perennial which is commonly considered a weed in the United States, is cultivated in some circles as a potherb. It has nondescript yellow flowers and grows close to the soil and sends out thick reddish stems with succulent green leaves. Allowed to grow freely, it will ultimately rise from the ground and develop single or double multicolored flowers. Both stems and foliage are meaty and oily.

Purslane was first introduced into Europe as a salad herb in the fifteenth century. The herb has also been recognized in the past for its medicinal value. Culpeper and other ancient herbalists believed it was an effective treatment for fevers and inflammations. When mixed

The weed purslane or moss rose can be cultivated as a salad herb or ornamental in rock gardens and low plantings.

with honey, the plant's juice was used to help treat coughs and shortness of breath. The culinary uses of purslane accounted for much of its popularity. Europeans and travelers to the New World spread the use of this nutritious herb.

Today, purslane is grown, when it *is* grown, for its use in preparing vegetables or as a salad ingredient.

As an ornamental, purslane is useful in rock gardens and for low borders and edgings. It is also a valuable plant to place between stones in paved areas, and makes a good grass substitute in hot, dry locations.

The most popular species is *P. grandiflora,* commonly known as rose moss, which has low, slender stems, short leaves and one-inch bright-colored blooms.

The plants will grow in almost any garden soil, but do best in well-drained loam. Seeds are usually sown in April. They require moisture to germinate, but once started, will survive almost desert dryness.

PUSSY WILLOW   (*Salix discolor*)

The pussy willow, known also as the glaucous willow, is a shrub or small tree which is native to the eastern United States. It seems to prefer wet places, but may easily be transplanted to dry areas. The lance-shaped leaves are dark green above but white with hairs beneath. The most distinguishing feature of this willow is the soft, silky catkin. These catkins (or flower clusters) appear in March before the leaves unfold. The male plants can be recognized by the yellow anthers of the stamens which give the male catkins a golden tone. The female catkins consist of a cluster of beaked pistils which produce seed bearing long silky down.

Twigs of pussy willow may be forced into bloom in late winter by placing their bases in water indoors. Such twigs often form roots and if set out in soil later, will grow into new plants.

PYCNANTHEMUM
See MOUNTAIN MINT

PYRACANTHA

This genus of evergreen thorny shrubs and climbers of the Rose family has orange red berries that remain on the plants all winter. They are tender to frost, except *P. coccinea,* which is fairly hardy to Massachusetts. White flowers appear in clusters during the summer, and the leaves are simple and alternate. Pyracantha may be propagated by seed, layering, cuttings, and grafting. They prefer sunny, well-drained habitats, and are used for specimen shrubs, hedges and espaliers.

Firethorns should be pruned carefully and lightly after bloom, as the berries are produced from the remaining flowers.

P. angustifolia grows to 12 feet, with branches sometimes prostrate, and is distinguished by its matted, dense flower cluster.

P. coccinea, scarlet firethorn, is the hardiest species, growing to 20 feet. It has long, toothed leaves and bright red berries.

P. crenulata is erect, growing into a small tree of 12 to 20 feet.

P. gibbsi or *P. atlantoides,* Gibbs firethorn, has glossy leaves and late-ripening red berries. It is hardy from Washington, D.C., southward.

PYRETHRUM

This name is given both to *Chrysanthemum coccineum* and to an insecticide derived from the flower heads of this very popular summer-blooming perennial herb.

The plant, which is sometimes called painted daisy or painted lady, grows one to two feet tall and has fernlike leaves and big, showy daisylike flowers in white, pink, red, or lilac. A favorite border and potted plant with many named varieties, pyrethrum likes a rich soil and a compost or rotted manure mulch, and is best propagated by root division in the spring. Set the plants about 12 inches apart. Flowers bloom in June and July, and are long lasting when cut.

The flower heads, dried and powdered, are used in insecticidal sprays and dusts. Pyrethrum insecticide is rather expensive, but it is not harmful to plants, and is regarded as the least toxic to man and animals of all insecticides. It is effective against a large number of soft-bodied insects that attack plants, man and animals.

Sometimes pyrethrum is mixed with a sesame oil by-product, with a substance called asarinin that occurs in the bark of the southern prickly ash tree, or with other plant extracts that enhance its effectiveness. But it is also mixed commercially with many other compounds, some of which may be quite toxic. Pyrethrum can be obtained pure only from veterinarians or pet shops. It kills pests by rapidly paralyzing them, but it has little residual effect and must be applied directly to the insects.

The striking, continuously blooming pyrethrum is not only a fine border plant, but also a potent insect repellent.

PYRUS   *See* PEAR

QUACKGRASS   (*Agropyron repens*)

Like many other weeds, quackgrass has a "Jekyll-and-Hyde" personality. In certain situations, it can be extremely useful. It binds loose soil and prevents erosion on steep, sandy slopes. Also, it provides good forage where better grasses will not thrive, particularly in some areas of the West.

But, for the most part, quackgrass is a troublesome pest. Although it prefers acid, moist soil, it will do well under all sorts of conditions and it increases by both seed and underground stems called rhizomes.

Quackgrass grows 18 to 30 inches tall and produces great quantities of seed on straw-colored spikes above the hairy leaves. These seeds can retain their ability to germinate for four years or longer. They are difficult to distinguish from the seeds of other common grasses.

Seed or pieces of rhizome may be introduced into new areas in topsoil brought in to make new lawns, in manure, in mud on the wheels of implements, on shoes or the feet of animals, or in hay or other forage.

The rhizomes, often several feet long, spread laterally in the upper three to six inches of soil. New plants can be produced at each node (joint), so that the weed quickly honeycombs the soil with a dense, extremely tough sod.

Quackgrass infesting a vegetable garden often makes such prolific growth in the spring that seedlings are greatly handicapped. A badly infested plot should therefore be planted only to crops with vigorous seedlings, or to transplanted crops. Cabbage, corn, squash, and tomatoes are good choices. Their roots can easily penetrate the mass of rhizomes, and since these plants are widely spaced, it is easy to hoe around them.

Control Measures: Constantly removing new top growth will reduce the food reserves in the rhizomes, thus weakening them. Therefore, hoe or cultivate frequently during the growing season. Always use a hoe or cultivator with a sharp blade. Tined tools will not completely sever the top growth from the underground parts.

Sometimes in extreme cases, the rhizomes can be raked up and hauled away, but this means a loss of considerable valuable organic matter. Spading late in the fall will kill many of the rhizomes by exposing them to drying and freezing. Thereafter, pull stray shoots by hand.

A mulch of plastic, boards or similar materials is also effective. Even better is a deep mulch of organic materials, which, at the same time it is smothering the quackgrass, will add organic matter and have other beneficial effects. A mulch should give a complete kill if left on the ground for one season.

Some crops make a dense shade that will smother quackgrass. Squash and pumpkins are excellent, particularly when planted closer together than usual. Until they make a heavy growth, hold down the quackgrass by frequent hoeing.

In making a new lawn or planting ornamentals or small fruits, heavy mulching or tilling for a season is necessary to eliminate serious infestations. If you choose the tillage method, use a tined cultivator that will lift the rhizomes to the surface and expose them to drying.

Always use organic matter to prepare the soil for a new lawn so that the grass will quickly make a tight sod that will crowd out the weed. Keep the lawn watered well and clip it weekly to a height of 1½ inches.

Sometimes ryegrass, included in lawn seed mixtures to provide quick cover, is mistaken for quackgrass. However, you can recognize ryegrass by its fibrous roots instead of rhizomes, and smooth leaves rather than hairy.

On a farm-scale, frequent tillage throughout the season is the best way to control quackgrass. The weed must never be allowed to make abundant top growth, for this means abundant rhizome growth. By plowing it under, you force the plants to send up long shoots from deep below the surface. Late fall tillage can expose many rhizomes to freezing, and close grazing will reduce the weed's vigor in pastures. In row crops, a cultivator fitted with sharp duckfoot shovels will cut the shoots and leaf growth without injuring crop roots. Good smother crops are buckwheat, millet, Sudangrass, and closely drilled soybeans. Always sow only certified seed, guaranteed to be free of quackgrass.

QUAIL

Recent experiments prove that it is possible to raise quail profitably on the small homestead. Quail are very efficient in converting grain into eggs that are almost identical nutritionally to chicken eggs. About 20 quail will provide enough eggs for the average family year-round. As far as meat production is concerned, chickens are slightly more efficient.

The Coturnix quail, a Japanese breed, is a very efficient converter of feed to eggs. Other breeds, such as the native bobwhite, are not as efficient for egg production although they may be hardier.

Buy quail from a reputable breeder. It is usually cheaper to buy fertile eggs and hatch them yourself than to buy chicks. Figuring on a 60 percent hatch rate and allowing for half the batch to be cocks, it takes about 70 eggs to produce 20 mature hens. Incubation requirements for quail eggs are the same as for chicken eggs, except that quail eggs require more humidity. Both types of eggs require careful checks on incubation temperature, humidity, ventilation, and position and turning of eggs to get good hatch rates. Incubators can be purchased new or used.

Housing: As a rule, try to allow one square foot of floor space per quail. Egg production drops significantly outdoors due to fluctuations in temperature and lack of light, and will be low indoors if less than .2 square foot of space is allowed per bird.

A variety of housing facilities can be adopted. A cage 3 by 7 by 3 feet can be built on a frame in an entryway or in another larger room. Cover all sides, top and bottom with wire mesh; droppings will drop through the mesh on the floor below and can be cleaned away. Such a cage can be moved outdoors during the summer if you wish.

A larger cage can be built in an existing structure. A cage constructed on the second floor of a chicken house should be about 20 feet long, 5 feet wide, and 8 feet high, and covered with nylon mesh on sides and top. The advantage of such a cage is that the birds are able to fly and exercise themselves. The floor is covered with about two inches of gravel which is changed frequently.

Quail can also be raised outside, either in some sort of outdoor cage or in the wild. If you are building a cage, be sure to cover it with wire or nylon mesh or they will fly away.

The sexual development of quail depends to a large extent on light. The longer their exposure to light, the faster they mature. Hens should be exposed to light 24 hours a day until they begin to lay, and then 16 to 18 hours a day to maintain egg production. Birds raised for meat gain fastest when they get only eight hours of light per day.

Feeding: Coturnix can be fed on a starter mash of 28 percent protein and a layer mash of about 21 percent protein. Quail are switched from the starter diet to the layer diet after five weeks. Formulas for the two feeds are similar. One hundred pounds of the layer formula would consist of 35 pounds of protein concentrate (vs. 58 pounds in the starter mash) mixed with 15.25 pounds each of cracked corn, oats, wheat, barley, and four pounds of bone meal. The poultry concentrate contains vitamins and minerals not found in sufficient amounts in the grains, but necessary for development of the birds.

To help beat the high cost of grains, you can give your quail wild plants and garden wastes as part of their diet. Turnip greens are especially nutritious. Insects, attracted to a 15-watt light bulb strung above the cage, make an excellent source of protein.

Quail must have a constant source of pure, clean water. Use small poultry watering jars.

Diseases: Quail are generally quite hardy. If you get started with healthy birds, feed them properly, and keep equipment and cages clean, you are not likely to encounter problems. Quail are, however, prone to the same disorders as other poultry. For information on common poultry diseases, *see* POULTRY.

Meat and Eggs: Quail should be slaughtered for meat at six weeks. Dry-pick the birds, eviscerate them, and remove heads and feet. Due to the small size of the bird, it is more practical to cook quail whole than to debone it. Whole quail can be stewed with vegetables or stuffed and roasted. The meat tastes rather like chicken, although it is slightly gamier.

About 20 Coturnix quail will produce enough eggs to satisfy the needs of an average family.

Quail eggs can be used like regular chicken eggs, and fried, scrambled or hard-boiled (five minutes). Figure 50 quail eggs to a dozen of chicken eggs. Pickled quail eggs are a delicacy and may be a profitable homestead sideline, as may the meat, which may be sold to gourmet shops or urban specialty food stores.

QUAIL BRUSH
(*Atriplex lentiformis*)

This gray-foliaged shrub, grown mainly in southern California, reaches a height of about eight feet and is often used for hedges. It is salt tolerant, does well in almost pure sand and will stand a high degree of heat and drought. Propagation is by cuttings. The *Atriplex* genus also includes several troublesome weeds, notably the greasewood or saltbush of the West, and a garden vegetable, the orach.

QUAKER BONNET   *See* LUPINE

QUAKER-LADIES
(*Hedyotis caerulea*)

Sometimes called bluets and innocence, this spring-blooming perennial suits the wild garden. It prefers a very moist spot with its roots in cool water, and can be found growing wild in mountain meadows and on flat, wet rocks along stream banks. The plant is delicate and tufted, about seven inches high, with little blue or white flowers. The clumps can be dug from the wild and increased by division. *H. purpurea* has bright purple or lavender flowers and is widely cultivated in the rock garden. Creeping bluets (*H. Michauxii*) are similar but with creeping stems. All are found in the eastern United States.

QUAKING ASPEN   *See* POPLAR

QUAMASH   *See* CAMASSIA

QUAMOCLIT   *See* STAR-GLORY

QUARANTINES

The Plant Quarantine Act of 1912 is designed to prevent the spread of injurious insects and plant diseases. According to this law, the secretary of agriculture has the power to prohibit or regulate the importation and interstate movement of all plant materials that may harbor pests.

Ball and burlap nursery stock from foreign countries, for instance, cannot be brought into the United States, because the soil around the roots might carry pests. Many other plant materials, including propagative parts, fruits, vegetables, cut flowers and plant products, are also regulated. An example of this is the prohibition against the importing of elm seeds from Europe, which might spread the Dutch elm disease. Certain other plant materials may be imported or moved across state lines only under permit and upon inspection by the USDA.

The law is revised whenever a pest becomes controlled or a new disease or insect appears. Information on current regulations can be obtained from your extension agency or from the Animal and Plant Health Inspection Service, 14th St. and Independence Ave., SW, Washington, DC 20250.

Most states have their own quarantine laws controlling the movement of suspect plant materials across their borders.

See also INSECT CONTROL.

QUARTZ

A combination of silicon and oxygen, quartz is one of the most common of all solid minerals. It may be colorless and transparent, or colored. Many semiprecious gems are forms of quartz. The crystals usually vary from a fraction of an inch to several inches in length, but one three feet long weighing 500 pounds was found in Maine.

Although it is everywhere—in beach sand, granite, gravel, and practically all soils—quartz is of no importance to the soil. It greatly resists weathering, remaining intact after all other rock components have disintegrated into soil materials. Tiny quartz crystals may dissolve over many years, but no plant nutrients are released and no clay is formed as they do.

See also MINERAL ROCKS.

QUASSIA

Chips from the quassia tree are sold for brewing an insecticidal spray. Simply place the chips and some larkspur seed in water and bring to a boil for about an hour. Cool the tea and syringe it on the infested plants. Without harming beneficial insects such as ladybugs and bees, quassia infusion works to eliminate aphids, sawflies and various caterpillars.

QUEEN-ANNE'S-LACE
(*Daucus carota*)

Also known as wild carrot, this plant is sometimes a nuisance weed, cropping up in gardens and crowding out useful grasses from fields and pastures. For this reason, it is often called devil's plague. The other common names such as bird's-nest and crow's-nest weed refer to the plant's flat-topped clusters or umbels of tiny white or yellow green flowers. Queen-Anne's-lace is found throughout the United States. It grows one to three feet tall, with umbels up to five inches across. It is hardy and spreads rapidly. Serious infestations on farms are best controlled by plowing the weed under just before it blooms.

Sometimes, a garden annual, *Trachymene coerulea,* is incorrectly called Queen-Anne's-lace. It grows two feet tall, with pure blue flowers.

QUEEN OF THE NIGHT
See SELENICEREUS

QUEEN PALM
(*Arecastrum Romanzoffianum*)

This feather palm reaches a height of 50 feet or more when grown outdoors. It is used widely as a street tree in Florida and California. Elsewhere it is a popular subject for the warm greenhouse. In pots, its leaves do not reach the ten-foot length they often do when it is grown outdoors, but they are very thin and feathery and the fruits hang in large attractive clusters. In the greenhouse, queen palm does best with a soil high in humus and plenty of moisture in the air as well as in the soil.

QUEEN'S CRAPE MYRTLE
See LAGERSTROEMIA

QUENOUILLE

Used in France for centuries, this system of training ornamental trees and shrubs is rarely seen here. The idea is to produce a perfect cone shape by tying down the lower branches and pruning the upper ones. It involves considerable patience and work.

QUERCUS   *See* OAK

QUICK FREEZING
See FREEZING FOOD

QUICKLIME   *See* LIME

QUILLAJA   *See* SOAPBARK TREE

QUINCE   (*Cydonia*)

The quince is a beautiful tree bearing valuable fruit, but commercial quince orchards are rarely seen today, though the tree is easy to grow and a real addition to the home grounds.

The fruit of the quince cannot be eaten raw, having a sour, astringent taste, but when it is cooked this changes to a piquant flavor that is quite pleasant. Quince preserves and jellies are delicious, and the fruit can also be used to give a guavalike flavor to apple and pear preserves and other cooked fruit dishes. Served alone, quince is excellent stewed, or cored and baked with their centers filled with honey. The fruit is high in calcium, phosphorus and vitamins A and C, and contains appreciable amounts of potassium and iron. When cooked, vitamins A and C are lost.

Culture: The quince is a shrublike tree that grows up to 25 feet high. It's best to plant two-year-old nursery trees, about 15

The fruit of the quince is too sour to be eaten raw, but is delicious when stewed, baked or made into preserves and jellies.

feet apart each way. They will yield best and live longest in a moist but well-drained, deep clay loam. Use fertilizer sparingly. A mixture of wood ashes, phosphate rock and potash is sufficient for growth. Apply and maintain a ring mulch of well-rotted compost, hay or other suitable material after planting, and no further feeding should be necessary. The trees will begin to bear five to six years after they are set out, and should continue producing well for up to 40 years.

A little heading-back to correct straggly growth is usually the only pruning a young quince requires. Useless and interfering branches and twigs should also be cut out. Do all pruning in late winter or early spring. Some thinning may be needed if the tree over-bears in any year.

The fruit must be picked and handled carefully to avoid bruising the delicate skin. When ripe, the quince will fall into the hand after a slight tugging. Quince can be stored two months or longer after harvesting, but do not keep them near apples or pears, which will absorb their strong odor.

Varieties: Orange and Champion quince produce large, round fruit and ripen early in October. Van Deman Smyrna, Fuller, and Cydonia are popular in the Midwest and California.

Flowering Quince: Closely related to the garden quince is the shrub known as the flowering quince (*Chaenomeles*). Its fruits are small and only used occasionally for preserves. However, its showy spring bloom makes it a prized specimen plant and a favorite for hedges. The best-known species is the Japanese flowering quince (*C. speciosa*) which has scarlet, pink or white blooms and spiny branches, and grows four to six feet tall. The lesser flowering quince (*C. japonica*) has red flowers, stays under three feet and is valued for its ability to stand city conditions. All of these like full sun and a medium-fertile soil.

See also FRUIT TREES, SHRUBS.

QUININE BUSH   (*Garrya*)

This hardy ornamental is not considered especially pretty, but is grown occasionally in the West from California to Oregon. Often called the silk-tassel tree, the quinine bush bears silver gray flowering tassels in hanging clusters through the winter. The dark evergreen foliage is similar to that of laurel but is even more resistant to pollution and smoke. The fruit is a round, velvety, inedible berry. Most species grow only six to 12 feet high, but at least one (*G. elliptica*) may achieve a height of about 25 feet. It will grow freely in any fairly fertile soil, but it needs some shelter from cold winds.

QUININE TREE   (*Cinchona*)

The bark of this tropical tree is the source of quinine, a drug important in the treatment of malaria. One variety is grown in the United States; it is of little ornamental value and suited only to the southern part of Florida.

R

RABBIT

Rabbit raising is becoming increasingly popular as organic farmers strive to attain self-sufficiency in meat production. An excellent source of protein-rich meat, rabbits can be raised with few complications.

The beginning rabbit raiser will do quite nicely with three does and one buck. The best varieties for meat production are the New Zealand White, the New Zealand and the Californian. They are good breeders and produce a high percentage of edible meat. Although the Flemish Giant is one of the largest in size, it is not as productive as the other breeds and yields a dress-out percentage far less than New Zealands or Californians. When buying stock, look for rabbits that are of good size, raise good-size litters to slaughter age, and produce good-quality fryers. One of the best ways to learn about rabbits is to attend a rabbit show, where the connoisseurs of rabbit raising and production can inform you of the do's and don'ts of raising a good herd.

Housing: No matter how good the stock, all your effort will be wasted if the rabbits are subjected to poor management and poor living conditions. A serious rabbit raiser must understand that producing fine meat from good stock requires more than just keeping ol' Peter Cottontail in a cardboard box. Rabbits need good ventilation, plenty of feed and fresh water, and ample room in which to roam and raise a litter.

Each rabbit in the herd should be given its own cage. Bucks and does should be kept in separate quarters when they are not ready to breed, and young does should also be separated. If kept together in the same cage, two young does may ride each other. This can cause false pregnancy in the doe that is ridden. She will act as though she is pregnant, refusing to breed and even gaining weight and making a nest. This false pregnancy lasts 15 to 20 days. Afterwards she can be bred.

Ample ventilation and sunlight are necessary. Ideally, a hutch specifically constructed for rabbits makes the best home, but henhouses and garages can be converted to satisfactory rabbit houses. Within the building, cages of one-inch, 12-gauge galvanized mesh should be hung from the rafters. This protects the rabbits from snakes and rats and makes care and feeding much simpler.

The normal cage size is one square foot for each pound of rabbit. Wire floors make cleaning and general maintenance easy. Some breeders complain that wire floors cause sore, bloody feet in rabbits. This condition is generally a function of genetically inherited thin pads and is not caused by the wire floors. Urine-soaked wood floors are unsanitary and hard to clean. Rabbits will chew on the wood and can become ill.

Care and Feeding: Fresh water should be available to the rabbit at all times. This can be provided through a plastic bottle fitted with a special dewdrop nozzle or by an ordinary watering trough. Whatever type of system is used, it is necessary to change the water daily.

Rabbit feed should be placed in an all-metal container and fastened to the side of the cage. Special hoppers can be purchased from supply houses or, the homesteader may prefer to make his own from an old coffee can. Cut down one side of the can to within two inches of the bottom, then continue cutting halfway around the body of the can. Fold this cut part flat across the opening and fasten it in place with rivets or a piece of fine wire. Crimp all sharp edges. This leaves a two-inch-deep, semi-circular dish attached to a closed, half-cylinder. It can be attached to the cage with heavy wire and, if desired, painted with nontoxic paint.

Rabbits, like all other livestock, require grains in their diet. The belief that rabbits love leafy, green vegetables and thrive on them is only a half-truth. An overabundance of the water-rich, leafy vegetables will cause bloat and scours in the herd.

Pelletized or commercial feeds may seem easier to manage, but they are much less nutritious than homegrown natural foodstuffs. For best results, mix your own rabbit feed from readily available materials. In this way, you can guarantee a feed that is specifically tailored to the needs of the rabbits during specific periods in their life cycles.

The tendency to overfeed is a big problem in rabbit care. Each rabbit's needs are different and are best recognized by closely watching the animal's feeding habits for a period of several days. Remember that when root crops or green feed are fed to the herd, the ration of dry feed should be reduced. Dry does in breeding conditions consume 3.8 percent of their live weight

FEED MIXES FOR BUCKS, DRY DOES AND DEVELOPING YOUNG

	Pounds
Whole oats or wheat	15
Barley, milo or other grain sorghum	15
Alfalfa, clover, lespedeza, or pea hay	69.5
Salt	0.5
Whole barley or oats	35
Alfalfa or clover hay	64.5
Salt	0.5
Whole oats	45
Soybean, peanut meal or linseed pellets	15
Timothy, prairie or Sudan hay	39.5
Salt	0.5

HIGH-PROTEIN MIXES FOR PREGNANT AND NURSING DOES

	Pounds
Whole oats or wheat	15
Whole barley, milo or other grain sorghum	15
Soybean or peanut meal pellets	20
Alfalfa, clover or pea hay	49.5
Salt	0.5
Whole barley or oats	35
Soybean or peanut meal pellets	15
Alfalfa or clover hay	49.5
Salt	0.5
Whole oats	45
Linseed pellets	25
Timothy, prairie or Sudan hay	29.5
Salt	0.5

daily. Bucks and young does consume about 6.7 percent of their live weight daily.

Breeding: When starting your herd, be sure you have male and female in your stock. Many rabbit breeders complain that their stock is not producing and then realize they have two rabbits of the same sex. You can determine the sex of a rabbit by holding a rabbit on its back and clearing the tail from the hind end. The male testicles usually protrude quite prominently. The female reproductive organ forms a slit on the rear ventral side. The sex of older does is easy to ascertain because the slit becomes more prominent as does age.

One buck can service as many as ten does. Breeding takes place at nearly any time. Always bring the female to the male to avoid fights. Mating is completed after a few minutes or when the buck drops over on its side.

The gestation period is approximately 31 days. Five days before delivery, the doe should be given a metal nest box and a supply of old hay and straw for nesting. The box should have an opening about six inches from the floor. The young bunnies, born hairless and with eyes closed, will open their eyes at ten days and soon begin to hop about the cage. At eight weeks, the young rabbits will be ready for slaughter and the doe can be rebred. The doe should not be left barren for too long, or she will become permanently sterile. Breeding every eight weeks will produce about four litters a year. Three does in a herd, producing around seven young in a litter, will provide enough rabbit meat for one meal a week for a year.

Breeding records are important to the rabbit raiser, for they indicate the time that new offspring can be expected, as well as the size of the litter, and the birth weight and lineage of the new arrivals. This information is essential in managing a healthy, productive herd and useful in controlling breeding stock.

Disease Control: Rabbits are prone to illness which is usually caused by poor management or unsanitary living conditions. Sore hocks, for example, result from rough or wet floors. In this condition, the pads of the rabbit's hind feet become inflamed, producing an unhappy rabbit who loses vitality and weight if the condition is not cared for immediately. Change the bed frequently or run the rabbit on dry soil to correct the problem. Severe cases can be treated by cleaning the pads with soap and warm water and then, after drying, dabbing the area with iodine.

Small mites which invade the external ear of the rabbit produce ear mange. Fluid released from infected areas hardens into irritating scabs. An animal infected with ear mange will continually scratch the infected ear with its hind leg, thereby scratching open the scabs and causing further infection. A solution of one part camphorated oil and five parts heavy mineral oil should be applied to the area daily until the infection heals.

Vent disease, or inflammation of the sex organs, can be controlled by applying a lotion of one part calomel to three parts lanolin. The disease will not afflict healthy animals if they are bred with care.

Colds and pneumonia may be caused by raising animals in drafty environments. It is wise to consult a vet about these and other serious ailments.

Slaughtering: The first slaughtering experience for a new rabbit raiser is often harrowing. The rabbit must be gently restrained and hit forcefully on the head. A good, clean clout will be less painful to the rabbit than a half-hearted one that doesn't do the job. After the rabbit has been killed, the head should be removed immediately for good bleeding. Suspend the carcass from wires thrust through both hind hocks. Cut off the front feet. Pruning shears will suffice. Cut through the skin around each hock, and then make a slit through the skin from each hock to the crotch. Peel the skin from the carcass, starting with the hind legs.

Eviscerate the animal by making an incision along the belly and removing all the innards. Then cut up the carcass—one cut behind the front shoulders, one ahead of the hindquarters and just behind the rib cage.

Preventing Rabbit Damage: Wild rabbits are often one of the gardener's worst headaches. They love to eat vegetables and the young shoots of many plants.

One of the best rabbit repellents, and one which is perfectly safe for plants, is powdered phosphate rock. Sprinkle it gently on seedling leaves as soon as they emerge. Dried blood sprinkled around the roots is another tried-and-true repellent. Others include powdered aloes dusted on the plants, and a solution of cow manure and water applied as a spray. Onions also seem to repel rabbits, and an occasional row of them interplanted with your other crops can be quite helpful.

A light sprinkling of red cayenne pepper on garden plants will discourage rabbits from invading the garden. A dusting of fish tankage and bone meal will turn the sensitive noses of the rabbits in another direction. A crop of soybeans planted adjacent to the garden will divert rabbits. This method saves the time and expense of reapplying a spray or dust after each rain.

A poultry fence is initially more expensive but it is a permanent solution. It must be at least 30 inches high and stoutly anchored on stakes or piping.

Fruit trees require a cloth or heavy paper wrapping, or a wire mesh cylinder around their trunks to keep rabbits from gnawing on the tree bark in late winter and early spring. Strips of aluminum foil wrapped around the trunks protect fruit trees not only from rabbits but also from sunscald during the warm days of winter. Lower branches can be wrapped in the same manner, leaving enough overlap so the foil can expand as the tree grows.

Rabbits shy away from anything with the odor of meat or blood on it. Rub a piece of liver or meat on the trees or spray a mixture of one tablespoon blood to two gallons water onto the tree trunks. Some gardeners report that animal lard smeared on the trunk is also an effective repellent.

RABBIT MANURE

Rabbit manures differ in analysis according to the kinds of feed the animals were given, but an average sample of rabbit manure is rich enough in nitrogen to produce good heating in a compost heap. On the average, the manure assays out at 2.4 percent nitrogen, 1.4 percent phosphorus and 0.6 percent potassium.

The manure can be applied to the soil as it is taken from the hutches or dug in. It can be used on lawns, between vegetable rows or around trees and shrubs all through the year. A large doe and her four litters which total 28 to 32 young a year will produce approximately six to seven cubic feet of manure annually.

The manure can also be mixed with a small amount of soil, kept moist and used as needed. It may be composted with plant wastes to cut down the odor and to improve the nutrient balance. Sawdust, straw, dry leaves, grass, and similar dry materials are often used for litter in the hutch, producing an excellent compost when the droppings and urine are caught and absorbed by these materials.

Rabbit manure compost has been called one of the finest soil builders for the garden.

Large applications of the fresh manure, however, should not be used on crops like potatoes, sugar beets and cereals, or on young deciduous trees and shrubs, because burning may result.
See also MANURE.

RABBIT-TAIL GRASS
See GRASS, ORNAMENTAL

RACEME

A raceme is a long flower cluster arising from a central axis. All the flowers are on short stalks springing from a single main stalk. Flowers are usually borne on small stalks of equal length and the central axis continues to grow during flowering as flowers open in succession from below. When the flower stalks are all on separate branches arising from the main stalk, the cluster is called a compound raceme or panicle. If each flower arises directly from the main stalk with no stalk of its own, the form is known as a spike.

RACHIS

The elongated axis of a flower stalk, or the main leafstalk from which two or more leaflets arise, is called a rachis.

RADISH   (*Raphanus sativus*)

The radish is one of the first recorded cultivated vegetables and dates back to earliest historical times. The name "radish" comes from the Latin, *radix,* meaning a root. Although radishes do not supply many nutrients, they are a good source of vitamin C, and make a tasty appetizer or salad ingredient.

A hardy, quick-growing crop used in succession planting, radishes are very easy to cultivate and can be grown in any part of the country if planted at the proper time. They are frequently used to mark rows in the garden because of their quick germination and rapid growth. Radish seed is often mixed with slow-germinating beet seed so that the radishes will mark the beet row and make hoeing easier.

Planting and Culture: There are three types of radishes: the early, the midseason and the late.

Early: The early, or spring, radish requires the cool spring or fall months to develop well. While spring radishes may be sown during the warm months, they seldom produce good, edible roots then. Instead, roots are very small and pungent, and the plants soon shoot to seed. Radishes prefer a cool, moist, loose, and fertile soil. If planted in heavy soils, the roots are apt to be misshapen and have a number of fibrous lateral roots. Compost or well-rotted manure may be used in large amounts in growing early radishes. The spring types will mature in 20 to 30 days. Succession plantings can be made a week apart during April and May, beginning as soon as the ground can be worked. For fall crops succession plantings can be made during August and September.

Sow the seed in rows 12 to 18 inches apart, and cover it ½ inch deep. Thin the plants to about one to two inches apart in the row. Radishes grow so quickly they do not need much care, and cultivation is almost unnecessary. Since the roots are small and essentially surface feeders, deep hoeing and raking does more harm than good. Radishes may be a nuisance because they have to be planted so often for a continual supply, but they make up for this by not requiring much attention after planting.

Midseason: In general, the soil and fertilizer requirements of midseason or summer radishes are the same as those of the early types, but summer varieties are much more heat resistant. Summer radishes should be sown about ¾ inch deep, in rows about ten to 15 inches apart, and thinned to three to five inches apart in the row. Since these roots require a longer period to develop (30 to 40 days) and will withstand heat, seed may be sown in successive plantings every week from May to the middle of August.

Late: Late or winter radishes do well in the North only during the fall months, but they can be grown throughout the winter months in the South. Because of their large size, they must have more generous spacing than the other two types. Winter radishes are generally sown ¾ inch deep, in rows 18 to 20 inches long with six inches between plants in the row. Sixty to 70 days are required to mature a crop from seed.

Most of the winter radish crop is harvested after the first fall frost and placed in storage. Place them in a well-drained, straw-lined trench and cover them with two or three alternating layers of straw or leaves, and earth. Radishes are extremely cold resistant and can be kept in storage for up to three or four months.

Insects and Diseases: If radishes grow rapidly enough, they are little bothered by disease. Insects, however, may be a problem. Leafhoppers will attack leaves only if they have been allowed to dry out. Root maggots can be discouraged by growing radishes in soil that has not grown another member of the Cabbage family in three years. If maggots, wireworms or borers are excessively active, however, large quantities of unleached wood ashes should be raked in along the rows.

Radishes are sometimes planted as a trap crop to attract root maggots away from onions. Maggot-infested radishes are then removed and discarded.

Liberal amounts of mature compost will also discourage pests. *See also* INSECT CONTROL.

Harvesting: Harvesting consists of merely pulling the radishes from the ground. The early ones can be harvested when they are big enough to eat, usually about 20 to 30 days after planting. The summer radishes can be harvested in five to six weeks, and the winter radishes can be either pulled in about nine weeks for immediate use, or left in the ground until frost comes.

Varieties: Spring varieties include French Breakfast, Champion, Red Boy, and Burpee White. The best summer types are White Icicle, Scarlet King, All Season, and Silver Dollar. Hardy winter types are White Chinese and Black Luxury.

RAGWEED   (*Ambrosia*)

There are several causes of hay fever—and one major cause is plant pollen. In spring, pollens come primarily from trees; in summer, from grasses and plantains; and in autumn, from ragweeds, principally from the common ragweed (*A. artemisiifolia*) and the giant ragweed, or kinghead (*A. trifida*). Both species are native annuals which grow in moist, waste places.

Common ragweed grows from one to three feet tall. It usually has alternate leaves on the

Common ragweed is one to three feet tall with coarse leaves and numerous petalless flowers that produce a tremendous amount of summer pollen.

upper branches and opposite leaves with two or three leaf divisions on lower stems. The nut-like fruits are ⅜ inch long with four to seven short, stout spines and, at one end, a beak.

Because there are no ray flowers, it may appear that the plant is not in flower and so does not produce pollen. However, abundant pollen is produced on the petalless flowers.

Giant ragweed is a robust grower, commonly six feet tall, and sometimes as much as 15 feet. Leaves are all opposite and three parted, except for those near the top.

A good all-round soil improvement and weed control program can help keep ragweed in check. Regular mowing in midsummer prevents production of pollen and seed.

See also WEEDS.

RAGWORT   (*Senecio*)

Ragwort or groundsel is the name of several relatives of the cineraria and candleplant. Often grown outdoors in the border, ragworts can also be grown indoors or in the greenhouse as potted plants, with seed sown in April producing bloom in December. Most ragworts prefer a well-drained garden soil and full sun, and if brought indoors they must have a cool location, good light and plenty of water. Propagation is by seed, cuttings or division.

Dusty-miller ragwort (*S. Cineraria*) is a hardy perennial growing to 2½ feet. Its silver foliage is somewhat woolly and its yellow or cream-colored flowers are small, daisylike and clustered. Seed may be started indoors in March and planted out in early May after all danger of frost has passed. Plants should be set one foot apart each way.

German ivy (*S. mikanioides*) is a climbing tender perennial with shiny, evergreen leaves and clusters of small yellow flowers. It is a hardy house plant and does well in the sunny window box. Propagation is by cuttings taken during the growing season and rooted in sand or water.

Golden ragwort (*S. aureus*) grows from one to two feet tall and has golden yellow flowers that bloom in late spring or early summer. It prefers a moist location with full sun, but will tolerate partial shade. Propagation is by division.

Leopard's-bane (*S. Doronicum*) grows to two feet and has showy yellow flowers with golden centers. They flower in late April. This hardy perennial is propagated by seed sown early in spring or by division in spring or fall.

Purple ragwort (*S. elegans*) is a hardy annual whose yellow-centered purple flowers bloom all summer long. Seed can be sown outdoors in April, or indoors in March. Plants are set out after frost danger is past.

Tansy ragwort (*S. Jacobaea*) grows to three feet and has yellow, daisylike flowers. This plant is a pernicious weed that is taking over pastures and fields in California and areas of the northwestern United States. It also contains a toxic alkaloid that is dangerous to grazing animals.

RAIN

In many areas rainfall is one of the most important factors in determining what may be grown. East of the Alleghenies there is an annual rainfall of from 35 to 50 inches which is sufficient for most garden plants. Any summer droughts that occur will have little effect on crops grown in organically managed soils.

Moving westward the forests are gradually replaced by grassland and the average rainfall lessens until desert where very few things will grow without irrigation. Along the upper Pacific coast and through the Northwest, however, the heaviest rainfall in the United States occurs.

Deficiency of rainfall, the organic gardener knows, does not have to mean poor crops. What matters most is how the rainfall is conserved. Organic methods hold runoff to a minimum, and water infiltration and storage are increased as the organic matter content of a soil is built up.

See also DRY WEATHER GARDENING, MULCH.

RAINTREE   *See* SAMAN

RAISIN

Raisins are the dried fruits of the sweet Vinifera grapes. Most of the United States raisin crop is grown in the San Joaquin Valley of California, where the Thompson Seedless, Black Monukka and Muscat grapes thrive. Grapes to be used for raisins should be harvested between August and November, or before the fall rains ruin the crop. When picked, the grapes are left in trays or other suitable receptacles where they dry in the sun for two to four weeks. Four pounds of fresh grapes will yield one pound of raisins. Raisins are high in calcium and iron.

See also DRYING FOOD, GRAPE.

RAKING

In making a seedbed the gardener uses a rake to pulverize his soil. It is necessary to have the soil finely textured so that small seeds, such as those of lawn grasses or flowers, will make maximum contact with the soil particles and thus be helped to germinate. Raking breaks up the clods and smooths the seedbed. It also conserves soil moisture by making a blanket of particles that prevents its escape. It aids the decomposition of organic materials that supply plant food and kills weed seedlings. Finally, raking encourages roots to develop rapidly, strongly and deeply. Soil in good tilth, amply supplied with organic matter, is the easiest to crumble and pulverize.

Always keep your steel-tooth rake sharpened, and work backwards so that you do not walk over and compact the raked area. Never attempt to rake when the soil is wet, or its structure will be damaged. A harrow is merely a large rake used for bigger areas than the garden.

RANUNCULUS

This genus of the Buttercup family includes the familiar buttercup or crowfoot among its more than 300 species. Some weedy, woodland species contain an acidic caustic juice or sap that can blister the skin of some people. The sap of most is poisonous if taken internally.

Native buttercups are perennial and annual herbs with finely dissected leaves and flowers that are yellow, white or red, with five separate petals and sepals and many stamens. When the flower matures, the head consists of many hard fruits called achenes. Most native species are propagated either by seed or root division.

A common European species, occasionally used here in rock gardens, is *R. acris*. This species has glossy, yellow flowers and its double variety is known as Flora Pleno.

The buttercup most popular in Europe and with florists in America is an intensely cultivated Asian species known as *R. asiaticus*. It surpasses other European and American species in beauty of form and color. Its cultivated forms are generally divided into two groups, the Persian buttercup, which has numerous varieties with many different forms and colors, and the turban buttercup, which has large spherical flowers shaped somewhat like small peonies. The flowers of both forms are usually double, about two inches across, and are found in almost every shade except blue. Some are variegated and striped in different colors, and suggest pompon dahlias in texture and beauty.

Unfortunately, the group is not as popular in the United States as it is in Europe due to the culture that it requires. These buttercups bloom in this country in late May to early June. They should be planted in a moist, rich soil where some shade is present during the warmer parts of the day. The roots resemble miniature dahlia tubers. They are not hardy north of Washington, D.C., and should be lifted after the foliage shows signs of withering or "ripening off," usually in late August. The tubers are then dug up, cleaned, and stored in a cool root cellar until the following spring, when they can be divided and planted as soon as the danger of frost is past. Plant about two inches deep and four inches apart. Propagate them by division to retain the choicest colors.

See also TROLLIUS.

RASPBERRY   *(Rubus)*

These prickly stemmed bramble fruits of the Rose family are native to the temperate regions of the Northern Hemisphere. Most species are intermediate between an herb and a shrub since the root is perennial but the stems die back during the second season after fruiting. The everbearing species, on the other hand, bears terminally and continuously, all summer.

Canes of the American red raspberry (*R. idaeus* var. *strigosus*) and European red raspberry (*R. idaeus*) grow upright throughout the season; those of the blackcap raspberry (*R. occidentalis*) grow more or less upright the first season but later droop near the tip and may strike root.

A few raspberry bushes planted in spring will begin bearing fruit the following year.

adapted. Others that are popular throughout most of New England, New York, the Great Lakes region, and the Middle Atlantic states are Newburgh, Taylor and Early Red. In the Pacific Northwest, Canby, Buckeye, September Red, Durham, and Willamette are widely grown. Two varieties, John Robertson and Reveille, are recommended for the Middle Atlantic states and other areas where winter temperatures frequently fluctuate above and below freezing. Good midseason varieties for the Northeast are Ott's Pennridge and Hilton, considered to be the largest of all red raspberries.

Blackcap or black raspberries are generally less hardy than red and yellow varieties and cannot be grown in the extreme north. Preferred varieties include Allen, Bristol, Cumberland, Dundee, and Huron for the East and, for the Midwest, Alleghany, Black Hawk, Black Knight, Cumberland, and Logan.

Purple-fruited raspberries are very vigorous and productive but their fruit is somewhat less desirable than that of the red and yellow types. Amethyst, Clyde, Marion, Purple Autumn, and Sodus are recommended for the Northeast and Midwest.

See also BRAMBLE FRUITS.

The red raspberry is the most important species among the bramble fruits, since it is good for desserts, jams and freezing. It is one of the hardiest fruits and can be grown throughout much of Canada and Alaska as well as the continental United States. However, since it is not heat resistant, it is rarely grown in southern states.

Red and yellow varieties withstand cold weather better than black and purple types. Of the red varieties, Latham is the most widely

---

RAT   *See* RODENT

RATIBIDA

This genus of annuals and perennials of the Daisy family is one of the several genera known as coneflowers. The flowers closely resemble black-eyed Susans, having yellow ray-flowers and brownish or purplish disks, but the disks are higher than those of *Rudbeckia,* and the foliage is more finely cut.

Two species, both natives of the American prairie states, are popular garden plants. Both are easily raised from seed in any good garden soil. The seed of the annual *R. columnifera* (sometimes erroneously called *R. columnaris*) is sown where the plants are to stand early in spring. *Columnaris* grows to 2½ feet and has hairy, somewhat coarse foliage and yellow flowers two to three inches in diameter. One variety, Forma, has brown purple rays, and another variety has double flowers.

R. pinnata, the perennial species, grows to four feet, with larger, coarser foliage. The flower, which is like a sunflower except for its raised cone, grows to five inches in diameter, with yellow rays and a brownish disk. Seed started early indoors will bloom the same year.

See also RUDBECKIA.

RAVENNAGRASS
See GRASS, ORNAMENTAL

RECEPTACLE

The widened, flower-bearing end of a stem which contains the floral organs is called a receptacle. Rose hips and strawberries are receptacles, botanically speaking, and so are the fruits of many other plants, either wholly, or in the early stages before they mature. In some plants, like the oleaster, the receptacle resembles a berry and is often mistaken for a true fruit.

See also FLOWER.

RED BLACKBERRY
See LOGANBERRY

REDBUD   (*Cercis*)

These handsome shrubs or small trees are especially valued for their very early bloom and easy cultivation. Rarely requiring pruning, they bear small, showy rose pink or rose purple blooms in generous profusion before most other flowering shrubs come into flower. Redbuds do not like heavy or wet soils and do best in light shade in an open-textured, sandy loam. Plant container-grown or balled trees in the spring.

The American redbud (*C. canadensis*), which is hardy over most of the country, rarely grows over 20 feet tall in cultivation. It has three-inch pods, heart-shaped leaves that turn yellow in fall, and pealike, rose purple flowers that blossom in spring before the leaves appear. Some of its varieties have double flowers or white flowers. Love tree or Judas tree (*C. Siliquastrum*) is similar to American redbud, but is hardy only to southern Oklahoma and lower Maryland. It prefers a sunny situation but can withstand light shade.

See also SHRUBS.

RED PEPPER   *See* CAYENNE

RED SPIDER MITES
See HOUSE PLANTS, INSECT CONTROL

RED VALERIAN
See CENTRANTHUS, VALERIAN

| REDWOOD | *See* SEQUOIA |
| REED | *See* CATTAIL |

REED CANARYGRASS
(*Phalaris arundinacea*)

Because of its ability to flourish on water-logged land, this vigorous, tall-growing grass is very effective in preventing gully formation and in binding soil. On upland soil, it continues its growth and remains green during midsummer drought. It is suited to a wide range of climate. In the United States, it is well adapted to the area north of Kentucky, Arkansas and Kansas and also to the higher areas further south and in the Pacific Coast states.

In general, the best time to plant reed canarygrass is when the gully is wet and will stay in that condition for at least three weeks. Early spring and late summer are favorable times. Late spring seedings too often suffer from summer heat, while late fall ones may be hit by winterkill.

A truckload of green hay will cover 500 feet of gully bottom, five feet wide. Tamp or poke the hay into the mud to get it in close contact with the moisture, thereby preventing its washing out while new sod is starting. Green shoots start in a week, while roots form in about two weeks.

Reed canarygrass can be propagated from sod or stems, but seed is preferred. Since germination rate is often low, test the seed before you decide how much to plant. A minimum seeding rate is about eight pounds of viable seed per acre. Cover with not more than ¼ to ½ inch of fine soil.

As a vigorous, tall-growing grass that thrives on poor, soggy lands, reed canarygrass makes an excellent ground cover for riversides and gullies susceptible to erosion.

Canarygrass in a waterway can be cut twice a year and used for hay or grass silage. It produces good pasture, although livestock generally do not like it as well as bromegrass or bluegrass.

REGAL LILY   *See* LILY

REGOSOL   *See* AZONAL SOIL

REPOTTING   *See* HOUSE PLANTS

RESISTANT VARIETIES

Resistant varieties of plants are those which, for a number of reasons, are especially able to withstand insect or disease damage. Using resistant varieties makes it easier to avoid reliance on chemicals. It does not interfere with the work of beneficial insects and fits in well with other organic methods of plant protection.

Many plants are naturally resistant to certain insects, viruses, bacteria, or fungi. Their color or flavor may be unappealing to the pest or they may possess certain biochemical or structural features that discourage intrusion. They may have resistance to a whole race of pathogens or only to a particular species.

As new types of pests evolve, plant breeders try to develop new plant varieties able to resist them. Usually, they try to breed plants that are partially resistant to, or at least tolerant of, a large number of diseases and insects. Varieties developed for this broad resistance are able to sustain some degree of infection or injury with few serious effects. Tolerant plants survive and produce a crop despite pest problems by regenerating tissue fast enough to remain healthy. Some plants are able to lose up to 30 percent of their leaf mass without lessening their yield much.

It's important to remember that healthy plants of any sort are more vigorous and better able to stand up to insects and diseases. Some research points to the conclusion that insects prefer plants grown in a soil with an improper balance of nutrients. Thus, the gardener who takes good care of the soil and uses plant varieties resistant to local pests is working with a double advantage.

Both insect and plant varieties are subject to change and react to local conditions. Therefore, a resistant variety may not work well in all areas. An insect variety may overcome a plant's defense mechanisms by mutating, and new disease strains evolve continually. These factors necessitate the development of new resistant varieties. Consult the state experiment station for advice on varieties resistant to pests in your area.

See also INSECT CONTROL.

RESTHARROW   (*Ononis*)

These hardy, perennial members of the Pea family have butterfly-shaped flowers that bloom throughout the summer. Flower colors range from pink to purple. *O. rotundifolia*, *O. hircina* and *O. spinosa* are the most commonly grown species. They are somewhat shrubby and grow from one to two feet high. Good plants for the border or the wild or rock garden, restharrows are easy to grow if given a moderately rich soil and a sunny location.

The seed is sown indoors in a cool place or in the cold frame in March, or outdoors in April. They should be barely covered. Transplant plants to their permanent spots, and after they flower, lightly prune the larger species into pleasing shapes. In late fall, cut down the flower stems and give the plants a manure mulch for the winter. Restharrows should be taken up and divided every fourth year.

RESURRECTION PLANTS

These interesting plants have the ability to curl up in dry periods and appear dead. However, when they get water, they quickly spring into growth again. They can repeat this "death-and-resurrection" cycle over and over again.

The one most commonly known as resurrection plant is *Anastatica hierochuntica,* a desert plant that folds up into a tight little ball until it receives moisture, and then becomes a foot-wide, fernlike plant. If given a sunny, warm place and sandy soil, seed sown in spring will produce plants with small, green white flowers by summer. The plant can be stored on a shelf for many years in its resting state.

The resurrection fern (*Polypodium polypodioides*) is an epiphytic fern which grows outdoors in the Southeast. Its gray green fronds are about six inches long and up to two inches wide.

A small, tufted plant of the southwestern desert, *Selaginella lepidophylla* is also called resurrection plant. Its bright green leaves turn dull brown when dry.

RETARDING

Retarding is the opposite of forcing, and is a method commonly used to slow the growth of plants like hydrangeas, Easter lilies and azaleas so that they flower at a later date. Cold storage may be used to retard Easter lily bulbs, while deep, unheated but covered pits, or special houses where light and temperature can be controlled, are commonly used for retarding other bulbs and many plants. In most cases, darkness and a temperature of around 40°F. (4.44°C.) are essential.

REX BEGONIA   *See* BEGONIAS

RHAMNUS

This genus of the Buckthorn family includes several plants, all of which do best in medium-rich, moist soil. The common buckthorn (*R. cathartica*) is a hardy, thorny shrub about 18 feet high, with black berries and inconspicuous spring flowers. Though not very ornamental, it is occasionally used in hedges. The evergreen coffeeberry (*R. californica*) is planted in the South and in Pacific Coast states as a bee plant. It grows over six feet tall and has small clusters of long-lasting greenish flowers and berrylike purple black fruits. Bearberry (*R. Purshiana*), which grows only in the Northwest, is a tall shrub whose dried bark is the source of the laxative, cascara sagrada. Its dark green leaves turn yellow in the fall and its red berries turn black. Alder buckthorn (*R. Frangula*) grows about 15 feet tall, is very hardy, and is esteemed for its brilliant yellow autumn foliage. The Indian cherry (*R. caroliniana*) grows somewhat taller, but is hardy only as far north as Nebraska. Both have red berries that change to black.

RHAPIS

Two species of rhapis or lady palm are grown in this country. They have reedy stems and grow in dense, bushy clumps. Popular potted plants for the house or terrace they can also be grown outdoors in southern Florida and southern California. They prefer a soil made up of three parts loam, one part sand, and one part leaf mold, humus or compost. A nighttime temperature of 55 to 60°F. (12.78 to 15.56° C.) and a relative humidity of 40 to 50 percent are ideal. Give them very little water in the winter and, in the summer, feed them once a month with liquid manure. Propagation is by seed or suckers.

R. excelsa grows to over five feet and its leaves have five to seven segments. *R. humilis* is not quite as tall, but it has leaves that are more finely divided.

RHIZOME

A rhizome, also called a rootstalk, is an underground stem or branch found on many perennial plants. It is thick and fleshy, and serves as a storage place for food gathered by the roots it sends out. Unlike true roots, most rhizomes tend to spread laterally, acting as an active means of vegetative reproduction and giving rise to new shoots. They may also exhibit buds or scalelike leaves. Rhizomes can be easily divided in spring or fall to make new plants.

RHODODENDRON

Rhododendrons are among the most beautiful spring-blooming garden perennials. Several hundred varieties of these broad-leaved evergreen or deciduous shrubs, from six inches to 40 feet high, are grown in temperate North America.

Planting and Culture: Rhododendrons thrive in a location that is sunny in the morning and offers protection from the hot afternoon sun. Planted along the north side of a house or beside evergreens such as hemlock or spruce, they will receive all the shade they need. Rhododendrons are especially magnificent against a backdrop of pine trees where they receive a constant mulch of needles as well as filtered sunlight. However, they should not be planted near deciduous trees such as elm, oak or maple, which monopolize the water supply.

Wind protection is almost as important as shade since exposure to strong gusts may injure leaf tips and result in dead leaf margins. If it is not possible to plant the shrubs where they will be adequately sheltered, a lath screen should be raised over them and allowed to stand for the first two or three years of growth.

Soil: One of the requirements for these plants is a distinctly acid soil (pH 4.5 to 5.5). It should be well drained but supplied with ample moisture at all times, much as a forest floor is. Rhododendrons definitely do not like heavy clay soil or lime.

Do not attempt to acidify the soil with chemicals such as aluminum sulfate which will injure the roots, or ammonium sulfate, which is changed quickly into a nitrate that yellows the leaves and causes poor growth.

A good planting mixture is one part decayed oak or other hardwood sawdust, or leaf mold or acid peat, to two parts loam. Hardwood sawdust or leaf mold contains tannin, which is beneficial to rhododendrons. All these materials also retain moisture in the soil, helping to make the cool, moist environment the roots like.

Planting: Transplanting should be done in favorable weather during the spring or early fall months. Rhododendrons, like their relatives the azaleas, are surface feeders and should not be planted too deeply. Dig the hole two to three times the size of the root ball—at least two feet deep and two or three feet wide for average nursery stock. Put some of the soil mixture on the bottom, and set the plants no deeper than they grew in the nursery. Fill in slowly, tamping the soil. Then soak thoroughly with water.

Rhododendrons are such prolific bloomers that they tend to exhaust themselves. By removing faded blossoms, the plant is spared the energy normally expended in developing seeds.
(*Courtesy of Longwood Gardens*)

If you are moving wild rhododendron shrubs from the woods to your garden or if you are transplanting nursery-grown stock from one place to another, special care should be taken to keep the roots moist and unexposed to the elements. Dig a trench at least 15 inches deep around the plant, or thrust a sharp spade to its full depth and cut a circle around the plant. Lift it carefully with a large ball of dirt and place it immediately in the prepared site. Water thoroughly once the shrub has been planted.

The final step in planting rhododendrons is to provide a permanent, deep, well-rotted acid humus mulch. Use three or four inches of decaying sawdust, pine needles or acid peat moss, or six to eight inches of oak or other acid leaves. Do not mound up the material but make a basin around the base of the plant. The feeder roots will spread into this mulch and find optimum living and feeding conditions there. Pruning at the time of planting is not necessary.

Care: With proper soil preparation and a good mulch, watering will rarely be necessary, but if your rhododendrons should require watering in hot, droughty periods, soak the soil thoroughly, rather than sprinkling it. Plenty of moisture is especially vital in the growing season after flowering. In extremely dry periods, soaking may be necessary once or even twice a week, but no more frequently. Waterlogging the soil will injure the plants.

Fertilizing is usually unnecessary, but if your plants do not seem to be growing at their best, five pounds of tankage or cottonseed meal per 100 square feet can be spread on the mulch and allowed to wash in. Fish meal, fish oil emulsion or blood meal are also good.

After the plants have finished blooming,

it is wise to remove the flower heads before the seeds form. This will result in more blooms the following year. There is a knack to removing them; just the bloom cluster should be snapped off. Removing too much will mean no flowers the next season.

Pruning is done after the blooms fade, and should be limited to taking out weak and dead branches, and cutting old ones back lightly to make a well-shaped shrub.

In the winter in areas that have weather at least as severe as that of lower New England, a covering of evergreen boughs or dried cornstalks is advisable.

Propagation: Growing rhododendrons from seed is fairly simple, but few seedlings are likely to be as good as the parent plant. The seed can be sown under glass in a finely sifted, peaty mixture that is acid in reaction. The seedlings usually take several years to reach flowering size after they are transplanted to pots.

Cuttings are difficult to root and require careful control of temperature and humidity. Commercial growers use a slightly acid sand/peat mixture and an electric hotbed where the bottom temperature can be kept at 70 to 75°F. (21.11 to 23.89°C.). Ordinary layering or air layering is probably easier for the gardener. Both air layering and the taking of cuttings should be done with soft wood during the early part of the growing season. Grafting, by side, saddle or veneer grafts on popular species in a propagating frame or greenhouse in spring, is a method of propagation commonly used by commercial growers.

Types: The named varieties of rhododendron available from nurseries are legion. Practically all of them are hybrids of the native *R. catawbiense* or similar species which have been crossed with Oriental or European species. The flowers come in every color and shade from white, cream and pink to yellow, orange, crimson, mauve, lavender, bright blue, and deep purple. Most are bell shaped, and some are spotted handsomely.

There are rhododendrons suitable for ground covers, many fine dwarfs for the rock garden, and larger ones for background use or for use in bigger places. Rhododendron specialists may list 250 or more varieties in their catalogs, with new ones being added every year. Size and color are the main distinguishing factors to consider, since most rhododendrons are hardy to near or below 0°F. (−17.78°C.).

See also EVERGREEN, GRAFTING, LAYERING.

RHUBARB   (*Rheum Rhabarbarum*)

Rhubarb is not a finicky plant. It can be grown anywhere, although cool seasons and freezing winters are most to its liking. The cold produces a delicate pink shade on the stalks and makes them look quite appetizing.

Planting and Culture: Rhubarb is usually propagated by division of the fleshy roots known as corms. These may be obtained from a seed supplier, nurseryman or from a friend with an established rhubarb patch. Each piece must have a good, strong eye.

In most temperate regions, the corms are planted in early spring, but in milder regions, they can be planted in late autumn after the foliage of the mother plants has died down. Select a rich, well-drained, loamy soil well supplied with organic matter. Plant the corms about three or four inches deep or so that the buds are two inches below the surface. Distance between rows is four to five feet and between plants within the row, two to three feet, depending on the richness of the soil and the vigor of the varieties selected.

Do not pull rhubarb from first-year or crown-piece settings. First-year roots should have their initial growing season to develop firm roots, and removal of the stalks will only cause the roots to put forth more leaf and top growth. Feed plants regularly from year to year, heaping compost or manure around the plants in fall and incorporating it in early spring. Remove the flower stalks as soon as they appear for, though they are striking and ornamental, they exhaust the plant and tend to lessen the quality and quantity of the edible stalks. Rhubarb patches will continue to produce for many years, though some growers prefer to divide clumps after five or six years and replant the divisions in an enriched soil.

For winter harvests or early spring crops, rhubarb can be forced. Select two- or three-year-old roots in the fall and place them in a shallow box. Cover them with about one inch of light soil, peat or sand, and let them remain out-of-doors until several light frosts have occurred. Then, bring these roots indoors and plant them in pots or flats and place them in a warm, dark cellar or a hotbed.

A much simpler, though perhaps less reliable, method of forcing involves simply placing a keg or bucket over the crowns where they grow in the garden. Pile fresh manure around the bucket and mulch with straw. This provides the necessary warmth and forces the plant to seek the light by growing taller than if left in the open. If the bucket is set over the crowns in late February, fresh rhubarb can be harvested by mid-March.

Insects and Diseases: For the most part, rhubarb is not troubled by insects and disease. Occasional leaf eaters can be easily checked by handpicking. Cut out flowering growths which take nourishment away from the plants and reduce their vigor.

Root damage can be recognized by the appearance of limp, discolored stalks early in the season. The root may be so extensively damaged that it will die during its winter dormancy. Foot rot, or phytophthora crown rot, is the most serious of rhubarb diseases. As the infection spreads, first one stalk and then another will wither and die. The only preventive measure is to remove the plants and give the soil in which they were grown plenty of sunlight.

Harvesting: Never use a knife to harvest rhubarb stalks. Instead, grasp them near the ground, twisting sideways. If breaking the stalk leaves a short piece attached to the crown, carefully remove it. Parts of stalks allowed to remain on the crown will deteriorate and may encourage the formation of rot. Never eat rhubarb leaves; they are poisonous.

Varieties: Canada Red is an extra tender and sweet variety, perfect for canning or freezing. Valentine is very sweet and requires little sugar. MacDonald and Ruby are bright red in color and have a tender texture. Victoria is an old-fashioned variety, less desirable since its stalks are thick and green with a tart flavor.

RIBBONGRASS
(*Phalaris arundinacea* var. *picta*)

This perennial relative of reed canary-grass has narrow, foot-long, white-striped green leaves and a dense flower panicle. It grows to six feet and is a popular ornamental in a border or in a waterside setting.

Ribbongrass does best in rich, loamy, fairly moist garden soil and can be increased by division.

See also GRASS, ORNAMENTAL; REED CANARYGRASS.

RIBES   *See* CURRANT

RICE, CULTIVATED
(*Oryza sativa*)

Rice is one of the oldest cereal crops. It has been cultivated in the Orient for more than 5,000 years. Although Oriental farmers often raise small crops of rice, so far most of the rice farming in the United States has been done on large, commercial farms in Texas, Louisiana, South Carolina, and California. Seed is spread from airplanes on huge paddies, and herbicides and insecticides are used to keep insects and weeds to a minimum. Since rice is considered only a commercial crop, little technology has been developed for small-scale production. The farmer who wants to grow rice for his family must rely on hand labor, but the work is interesting and rewarding.

Planting and Culture: If you want to grow rice successfully, you must provide it with the cultural and climatic conditions to which it is accustomed. This means you will need full sun and a minimum of 40 days with temperatures above 70°F. (21.11°C.). Fluctuating or low temperatures decrease the disease resistance of rice plants and night temperatures below 60°F. (15.56°C.) stunt growth. An abundant supply of fresh, preferably running water is a necessity. Ideally, the water should be warm enough to promote maximum plant growth and vigor. If water is being taken from a well or cold lake, dig a small warming basin where it can collect before it reaches the paddy.

Seed: Rice seed should be tested for its viability before it is planted. To do this, place seed in a bucket or other container full of water, adding a few tablespoons of salt. With your hands swirl the seed around in the water. Viable seed will sink. Skim off floating seed and repeat the process until no more seed float. Rinse salt off the viable seed by placing them in a strainer and running cold water over them.

The viable seed must then be soaked. Fill a small cotton bag or burlap sack with the seed and tie it closed. Place the bag of seed in a bucket or, if it is a large amount, in a plastic wading pool. Run a hose into the container and fill it with enough warm water so that the water trickles over the edge. Allow the rice to soak for 25 to 30 days in a warm place. This soaking begins germination and kills weak seed. After the soaking, allow the seed to dry in the open bag for a day.

Preparing the paddy: While the rice is soaking, prepare your rice paddy. The bottom of the paddy must be flat so that the water depth will be equal all over the paddy. Select fertile loam and till to a depth of one foot. Dig a trench round the perimeter of the paddy 1½ feet deep and six inches wide, placing the extracted soil on the outer edge of the trench to form a dike. Line the trench and cover the dike with sheets of plastic to help keep water from soaking out into adjoining fields.

Planting the seedbed: In most parts of North America, rice must be grown from transplants so seed should be planted in a small bed before it is moved to the paddy. Select a sunny, warm spot in the garden and water it well. Broadcast the sprouted seed and cover them very lightly with sand. Then lay a small amount of fine rice straw or a light net over the area. Water frequently and, in about one week, tiny shoots will appear. When plants are about four or five inches high and have been in the seedbed about one month, they are ready to transplant to the paddy.

Transplanting: Since you will be relying on manual weeding rather than herbicides, seedlings must be set far enough apart to allow for hand weeding during the growing season. Make rows in your paddy at least six to eight inches apart. Wet the soil in the seedbed until it is muddy. Pull the seedlings out of the bed, being careful not to damage the roots. Plant two or three plants in bunches six to eight inches apart.

After transplanting, keep water in the paddy to a depth of one inch for 20 days, regulating the flow of water so the depth is constant all day long. Water need not be kept at a constant depth at night. If seedlings fall over, push them back into the ground. They should establish roots in three days to a week.

Care: After this initial period, water only in the morning so afternoon sun will warm the soil around the plants and stimulate development of new shoots. Weed if necessary, and check for insect pests. After about a month and a half, the rice will begin to head. At this stage, it is crucial to keep the paddy covered all day with one inch of water. Too much wind and rain can retard pollination.

As rice ripens it will yellow, and the heavy, maturing heads will bend over. When the majority of plants have bent over, stop flooding the paddy and allow the rice to dry out for two weeks or longer.

Harvesting: Harvest by hand with a scythe or sickle, and bundle. Stack bundles in the barn or, if covered, outside, to dry for two weeks. Thresh and winnow like wheat. *See* WHEAT.

Removing the hull from the grain is a problem. In Japan, farmers can buy a small hand mill that dehusks the grains well. You might try using one of the methods suggested for dehulling oats. *See* OATS.

RICE FLOWER   *(Pimelea)*

The rice flowers are low evergreen shrubs, generally grown as greenhouse plants. They grow two to three feet tall, with small, pretty, white or rose pink flowers in heads or clusters surrounded by red bracts. If given a cool, humid spot in the greenhouse with shade in the summer, they make an attractive display. The seed is sown in late winter or spring, ⅛ inch deep, in equal parts loam, sand and leaf mold or compost. Rice flowers may also be propagated by rooting two- or three-inch cuttings of the young shoots one inch apart in a well-drained sand/peat mixture in March. Cover with glass and place in a shaded area where the temperature is about 55 to 60°F. (12.78 to 15.56°C.). During vigorous growth, rice flowers should be syringed on bright days and given a weekly application of liquid manure. Pinching back will make them bushy. After flowering, they are usually cut back and repotted.

RICE HULLS

Although often considered a waste product, rice hulls are very rich in potash and make an excellent soil conditioner. They decompose readily when worked into the soil and increase the humus content.

See also HULLS, MULCH.

RICE, WILD   (*Zizania aquatica*)

Wild rice is far more nutritious than ordinary rice, containing more protein and slightly more fat. It is not polished and its delicious flavor makes it a gourmet favorite, particularly as a stuffing for wildfowl. It can also be boiled for dessert, ground for porridge, or milled as flour. Many species of wild ducks are major consumers of wild rice, and it is the main feed for waterfowl on the Mississippi flyway.

Wild rice grows on single stems which are usually five to ten feet tall, with branching seed heads about 24 inches long. The husks are about an inch long and, when ripe, contain slender grains of a dark slate color. The plant is a self-seeding annual.

Planting and Culture: Wild rice will grow practically anywhere in the United States. Small farm ponds, if fairly shallow around the edges and fed by streams, can supply a fairly large crop. It grows best in quiet, pure water that is from one to six feet deep. Stream banks, ponds, lakes, and the floodplains of rivers with rich muddy bottoms are native habitats. It prefers a slow current of about a mile an hour and never grows in stagnant lakes or pools. The water level must be fairly constant during the growing season since an excessive rise will drown the plants and prevent reseeding.

To plant, scatter seed over the surface of the pond at the rate of a bushel per acre. Good seed will sink quickly. The best planting times are just before ice forms in the fall and as soon as the ice breaks up in the spring. Fall-planted rice often runs the risk of being eaten by migrating ducks.

Seed lying in the soft, rich mud sprout early in the spring, the first shoots appearing above the water in June. The first leaf is a "floater" which soon dies and is followed by the main stem. One seed can produce several flowering stems. A panicle then forms, its blossoms pollinated by the wind. In Minnesota, the seeds ripen on the heads early in September and harvest begins then. Seeds ripen over a ten-day period, so a bed must be harvested three times to get most of the crop. Nonshattering varieties need only be harvested once.

Soon after harvest, the plants are frozen in for the winter and when the spring rains raise the water level, the old plants are torn up by the lifting ice. The straw is either cast up on shore or sinks, adding fertility to the bed.

Harvesting: The Indians of Minnesota traditionally harvest wild rice in pairs. As the husband poles a canoe through the rice, his wife bends the stalks over and strips the rice from the heads with two rounded sticks. The rice is dried in the sun on a blanket, then parched or roasted in an oven at a low temperature. Indians remove the hulls by dancing on the grain in a shallow tub, but you can try putting the rice kernels in a burlap bag and stepping on it or hitting it with a baseball bat. Gentle rubbing also loosens the hulls eventually. Kernels may be shaken in a basket in front of a fan to remove chaff. Rice for commercial use is handpicked for hulls and poor kernels. Place the grain in plastic bags and store in the freezer.

Varieties: Two major varieties of wild rice are available. The most widely sold one is Angustifolia, a tall type that reaches heights of five to six feet. Brevis grows only three feet. In addition, a few cultivars with nonshattering seeds have been developed. These are excellent choices since the seed will not fall into the water before harvest.

Wild rice seed can be purchased from Wild Life Nurseries, PO Box 399, Oshkosh, WI 54901 and H. G. Hastings, Box 4088, Atlanta, GA 30302. Don't try to plant the store product; only unhulled seed will sprout.

RICINUS   *See* CASTOR BEAN

ROCKET

Two members of the Mustard family are commonly called rocket. One is grown in the vegetable garden as an annual salad plant (*Eruca vesicaria* subsp. *sativa*), and the other is an old-fashioned, ornamental perennial (*Hesperis matronalis*).

The edible rocket or rocket-salad is a dense, low-growing plant with long, smooth bright green leaves and white or yellow flowers. It grows best during cool seasons and is most often grown as an early spring green. Sow seed ½ inch deep in a moist soil. When the plants are two to three inches tall, thin them to stand about six inches apart. Leaves can be harvested six weeks after planting and plants will continue to put forth succulent growth until midsummer when the flowers develop.

Ornamental rocket is sometimes listed as dame's rocket or dame's violet. It is a coarse, tall plant with spikes of purple flowers that bloom from June to August. It thrives in practically any soil and will readily establish itself in a shady spot. Garden volunteers are common, so avoid planting dame's rocket in the flower bed.

ROCK FERTILIZERS

Rock dusts are some of the most abundant, naturally occurring sources of plant nutrient materials. Solid rocks, in various parts of the earth, contain all of the natural elements except nitrogen. Through the action of organic matter, they break down and produce a continuing supply of minerals. These, together with the organic contribution of living and once-living plants and animals, are the main components of soil.

When rock fertilizers such as granite dust, phosphate rock, or greensand are added to the soil with organic matter, they slowly break down and supply their nutrients over a long period of time. They improve the soil's physical structure and water-holding capacity and do not slow the activities of soil bacteria.

Since rock dusts cannot supply nitrogen, they should always be applied with fresh organic matter such as raw manure or newly incorporated green manure. These materials not only supply nitrogen, but also help to release the nutrients in the rock powders. If your soil is alkaline, this is especially important, since rock fertilizers tend to break down more slowly under alkaline conditions. Never apply the dusts with lime.

In applying rock dusts, avoid simply broadcasting them on the surface of the soil. Instead, disk them under and quickly incorporate them into the ground. As a general rule, flower gardens require about five to ten pounds rock dust per 100 square feet. Vegetable gardens should be fed about ten pounds per 100 square feet, and lawns about five pounds per 1,000 square feet. Feed trees 15 to 100 pounds per tree and roses and shrubs about one pound per bush.

It is important to remember that natural rock fertilizers are not immediately soluble, and one application will last for as long as five or ten years. Instead of feeding the plant by a hand-to-mouth method, when you use natural rocks you are putting plant nutrients in a controlled-release soil bank.

Most recommendations for phosphorus are given in terms of pounds of superphosphate per acre. A good rule of thumb when using natural rock is to merely double the application: for every 100 pounds of superphosphate prescribed, apply 200 pounds of phosphate rock. Since phosphate rock is usually about half as expensive as superphosphate, your investment will be about the same.

Phosphate rock is normally applied at the rate of 1,000 pounds to the acre. Two thousand pounds per acre will probably suffice for five years. Application costs are cut if you apply a five-year dose at one time.

Determining the proper application rate for potash rock fertilizers is slightly more complicated, as their quality and degree of fineness vary. If a soil test shows that your soil is low in potash it is not unreasonable to apply as much as three tons of granite dust or 500 pounds of greensand per acre.

For soils that need only a moderate amount of potash, an application of two tons of granite dust or 200 pounds of greensand to the acre is adequate.

With mild sources of potash like basalt and diabase dusts it is necessary to make fairly heavy applications. This is also true of rock dusts used mainly for their trace element value and not for basic nutrients like phosphorus and potash. In some cases these may be obtained for a small fee from quarries that have the waste dusts on hand.

See also Basalt, Fertilizer, Glauconite, Granite Dust, Greensand, Mineral Rocks, Phosphate Rock.

ROCK GARDEN

By combining the rough texture of stone with the delicacy of alpine flowers, a rock garden can become one of the most interesting and beautiful garden forms.

The art of rock gardening is based upon the forms and character of mountain landscapes. On the upper slopes of great mountains, above the line of trees, the soil is thin and mixed with rock chips and bits of moss. Rocks are everywhere. Even though at first glance the landscape looks desolate, it has certain aspects of a garden. The rigors of the climate have weeded out shrubs, vines and grasses, leaving only rock plants anchored in the veins of soil between the boulders. Some plants, like the lichens, are growing on the bare faces of the rocks themselves.

Iceland poppies, saxifrages, campanulas, and sempervivums are at home on high mountain slopes. The short growing season and long months of dormancy are just what they like. Take these beautiful plants down to a lower altitude where there is plenty of warm soil and long months of sun and they will soon be crowded out by the more numerous and faster-growing plants native to that environment.

Long ago, skilled gardeners realized that if the beauty of the high mountain slopes were to be captured in a sea-level garden, it was not enough to bring just the plants—the sheltering rocks must be brought too. Rocks must be set into the ground in such a way as to re-create the soil-filled fissures, rock chips and humus that the alpine plants found so inviting in their original homes. A few rocks scattered on the surface of a bare bank would not do. Finally, if the most difficult mountain plants were to be grown, their roots should be enabled to reach down into moving water—not into a stagnant pool.

Site: Although a slope is a natural place to build a rock garden, many successful ones have been made on once flat ground that has been scooped out to make a flowing contour. A slope simplifies drainage and, if facing north, will shade the garden. Shade and a short growing season are important to many rock garden plants. In their mountain home, alpine plants get only a month or so of warm weather and they are dormant the rest of the year. Although you can't give them the cold, damp weather they are used to, shade helps simulate dormant conditions. Many successful rock gardeners cover plants with a mulch during all but the summer months to stretch their dormant period.

Where a rock garden is to be made in full sun, it is best to plant with a northeastern exposure, especially avoiding a southwestern exposure if the summers tend to be hot and dry. Where more rainfall occurs, southern and western exposures can be used.

Most rock plants are more resistant to drought than they are to excessive moisture. For this reason it is safer to lean toward the dry side when selecting a site for your rock garden. Don't locate it where the plants will be subject to the drip from trees. Good drainage is also important, particularly for the larger, deep-rooted plants.

Soil: A loam, sandy loam or peat soil is most suitable for a rock garden. Avoid a heavy clay soil at all costs, or be prepared to enrich it with large amounts of organic matter.

Usually it is a good idea to make your own soil mixture: Dig out the site to a depth of 18 inches, and replace the existing soil with a mixture of equal parts of loam, sand, and leaf mold or similar humus material.

Where alkaline-loving plants are to be grown, make 5 to 10 percent of the mixture limestone chips, pulverized clean clam-, oyster- or egg-shells, or ground limestone. To create acid conditions, use oak leaf or pine needle mold or acid peat.

Some rock gardeners cover the soil after planting with a stone mulch made of crushed rock the size of peas. This helps to keep the moisture in and the heat out, and also prevents winter heaving. Evergreen boughs, salt hay or leaves also provide good winter protection for most rock garden plants.

Setting the Rocks: Remember, it is the part of the rocks that lies *below the soil* that is important. Actually, you should be more concerned about the *spaces between the rocks,* than about the rocks themselves. Here are some general rules to follow in doing rock work:

1. Use quarried stone. Rounded rocks are too difficult to fit together tightly, and eventually they work loose.

2. Don't use stones of many different types. You are making a garden, not a collection of geological specimens.

3. Every rock should be set firmly in the ground. It shouldn't move when walked on. At least one-third of the stone should be

buried beneath the surface.

4. Slope the top surface of the rock back into the bank behind it, so that water will flow back into where the roots of your plants are.

5. Don't let overhanging rocks block rain from plants below.

Recommended Plants: Here are some of the better-known and more easily grown rock garden plants.

Aubrietas are spreading plants with red, pink, lilac, or purple flowers. The color of aubrieta flowers varies greatly, because the plants seldom come true from seed. Seed, however, is often easier to find than plants. Once an exceptional color appears, the plant that has borne it may be propagated by division in August and September.

Basket-of-gold (*Aurinia saxatile*) is a spreading ten-inch-high clump with clusters of bright gold flowers. Flora Pleno has double flowers.

Bellflowers (*Campanula*) should be in every rock garden. The tussock bellflower is the one most frequently available and from June to October bears violet blue or white cups on ten-inch stems. *C. Elatines* var. *garganica* is smaller and fussier. For it a gritty lime soil with leaf mold, and shade are recommended. In June and July it has open violet flower stars above an attractive foliage of sharply notched leaves.

Bloodroot (*Sanguinaria canadensis*) can be depended upon to produce its large white flowers in April before any of its leaves appear. It grows wild in rich acid soil and in shady spots but does not seem too exacting for a rock garden. There is also a double-flowered form which is rare.

Columbine (*Aquilegia*) is a hardy perennial with nodding white, red, yellow, or blue flowers that bloom in May and June. The native plant *A. canadensis,* with its red and yellow flowers on twelve-inch stems, and *A. caerulea,* with large blue and white flowers, are popular species. *A. flabellata* var. *pumila,* a Japanese dwarf, has large blue flowers with inner petals of pale yellow. There are many species of columbine to choose from and varieties offer a wide selection of colors.

Dwarf geranium (*Geranium sanguineum* var. *prostratum*) has rosy-veined pink flowers from May to August.

Helianthemums are evergreen or half-evergreen shrubs that produce showy flowers in June and July. Flower colors range from white to shades of yellow and red, and there are many bicolored varieties. A spread of 18 inches or more should be allowed for each plant.

Moss pink (*Phlox subulata*) is a spreading mat with clusters of light blue, purple, pink, red, or white flowers standing two to six inches above the ground.

Pasque flower (*Anemone Pulsatilla*) has a clump of ferny foliage supporting large cup-shaped purple, blue or reddish flowers on eight-inch stems. White and brown varieties are available.

Pinks (*Dianthus*) are fine contributions to the rock garden. *D. gratianopolitanus* produces a mat of gray green foliage and showy, rose-colored flowers. Its height is less than 12 inches. *D. deltoides* is the readily available and super-invading maiden pink from which self-sown seedlings spring up everywhere. Its grass-like leaves form a dense mat.

Rock cress (*Arabis alpina*) is a hardy perennial with woolly gray leaves and sprays of white flowers. There are also single pink and double white forms.

Sedums are easy to grow and prefer poor soil. Those most readily available are fast-invading creepers but others of a clump type, with flowers of various colors, will behave well in the rock garden.

Sempervivums are available in large variety, with some blooming in June and others as late as October.

Speedwell (*Veronica*) includes several invading plants such as *V. pectinata,* which forms a gray carpet with blue flowers, and *V. repens,* which forms a mossy mat with blue or pink flowers. *V. incana* grows from 12 to 18 inches high and has clumps of silvery leaves and spikes of blue flowers in June and July.

Thrift (*Armeria*) is a hardy, low-growing perennial with rosettes of evergreen leaves and small white, pink or lilac flowers.

Thyme (*Thymus*) forms a spreading carpet with purple or white flowers. A few species are not invasive. The foliage is very aromatic, so many thymes are used for flavoring.

Virginia bluebell (*Mertensia virginica*) has lavender blue flowers in April on one- to two-foot stems. It likes a rich acid soil with at least half shade. After flowering, the leaves disappear until the following spring. It is on the protection list of several states.

See also entries for individual plants, WALL GARDEN.

ROCK PHOSPHATE
See PHOSPHATE ROCK

ROCKROSE   (*Cistus*)

Members of the Rockrose family, these low, summer-blooming, evergreen shrubs are generally hardy only in the South and along the Pacific coast. They need a sunny position and friable, well-drained soil slightly on the alkaline side. As rockroses do not transplant easily,

they are best moved when young or raised in pots until they can be planted in their permanent locations. Propagation is by seed, layering or cuttings of side shoots taken in fall and grown in sand under glass.

A charming shrub for the rock garden, *C. crispus* grows less than two feet high and has red purple blooms. *C. ladanifer* grows to five feet and has large white flowers that bloom in June. Both *C. villosus* and *C. albidus* have rose purple, yellow-centered blooms and grow to heights of three and six feet respectively. The tallest rockrose is *C. laurifolius,* which grows to six feet and has white, yellow-centered flowers borne in showy clusters. There are many varieties and hybrids.

See also HELIANTHEMUM.

RODALE, JEROME IRVING

(1898–1971) The founder of Rodale Press, Inc., J. I. Rodale became known as the world's foremost advocate of organically grown foods and natural food products while serving as publisher and editor of *Organic Gardening and Farming* and *Prevention* magazines. In addition, he was a playwright, writer, patron of the arts, manufacturer, and a general critic of the conventional medical and agricultural establishments.

Born on New York City's Lower East Side, he was one of eight children of a grocer. By his own admission he was a sickly child, subject to attacks of dizziness, colds and headaches, as well as being nearsighted and a poor athlete. Through a series of self-improvement and body-building courses, he overcame many of these handicaps. As his health improved, so did his determination to succeed at anything he

J. I. Rodale

lowed up with publication of a number of other magazines. Rodale's publishing efforts in the late thirties, which centered around his literary interests and his attempts to learn how to write more effectively, were more successful. His *Word Finder,* sold under his own imprint through direct mail, became the first of many such best-sellers.

In 1940, Rodale and his wife, Anna, purchased a farm in Emmaus and began to implement the theories of Sir Albert Howard, a British agronomist who believed that crops raised with fertilizer derived from natural animal and vegetable wastes were healthier than those raised with chemical fertilizers. JI integrated Howard's basic tenets with his own intrinsic belief in the interrelatedness of nature, and formulated the *organic* method of building soil health. In 1940, JI published the first edition of *Organic Farming and Gardening,* laying the foundation for broad-based acceptance of the organic movement.

Rodale criticized conventional ideas of gardening and large-scale agriculture, and warned against the use of chemical fertilizers and pesticides. He praised composting, the value of earthworms, stone mulching, companion planting, and the benefits of certain insects. He also became one of the first advocates of the back-to-the-land and self-sufficiency movements in the early 1940's.

Receiving only ridicule from the government and the agricultural industry, JI, in 1947, formed the Soil and Health Foundation, a nonprofit research foundation which awards grants to individuals and groups performing research in areas of organic interest.

Rodale was more interested in the health and nutritional aspects of gardening and farming than in actually tilling the soil. He was concerned with how foods were grown and their

tried, a quality which became ingrained in his character and helped him through many crusades against skeptics.

After graduation from high school, he studied accounting at night at New York and Columbia Universities, becoming an accountant for the Internal Revenue Service and then for a number of private corporations. While working as an accountant, JI had gone into the electrical manufacturing business with his brother, Joseph, and in 1930 they moved their firm from New York City to Emmaus, Pennsylvania. In 1930, JI entered publishing, with a small tabloid entitled the *Humorous Scrapbook.* The venture soon failed but was fol-

effect on nutrition. His lifelong concern with health came to fruition when he published the first issue of *Prevention* in June of 1950. JI thought there was a real need for a magazine like *Prevention* to translate studies from medical and academic journals into easy-to-read stories about health accessible to the layperson. He advocated good diet and the use of natural vitamin and mineral supplements. He won many converts as he battled the FDA, AMA and countless governmental bureaucracies on issues related to food processing, artificial additives, pollution of the environment, the evils of sugar, and the low minimum daily requirements set by the federal government for vitamins.

In 1960, JI left the publishing activities of his company to his son, Robert, and pursued myriad personal ventures. His primary passion became playwriting. His plays, which are performed today by high school, college and community groups, are morality plays about nutrition and health. He approached these unlikely themes with the same tenacity and defiance of convention that characterized his earlier battles with the agricultural and medical establishments.

His diversity of interests was clearly shown in the variety and number of publications which he founded, and in their treatment of topics ranging from the environment to foreign languages to theater news and crafts: *Compost Science* (1960); *Health Bulletin* (1963); *Quinto Lingo* (1964); *Rodale's New York* (1966); *Theatre Crafts* (1967); *Fitness for Living* (1967); *Environment Action Bulletin, Executive Fitness* and *Organic Food Marketing* (1970).

Among his many books are: *Pay Dirt* (1945); *The Healthy Hunzas* (1948); *The Organic Front* (1948); *The Health Seeker* (1962); *Our Poisoned Earth and Sky* (1964);

Walk Do Not Run to the Doctor (1967); *Natural Health, Sugar and the Criminal Mind* (1968); *The Prostate* (1968); *Natural Health and Pregnancy* (1968); *Happy People Rarely Get Cancer* (1970); and *Your Blood and Its Pressure* (1970).

RODENT

Rats and mice can cause serious problems on the farm or homestead. Each year in the United States, rats ruin food worth millions (some say billions) of dollars. For every two-dollars' worth of food one rat eats, he damages another four-dollars' worth and contaminates an additional six-dollars' worth, according to researchers at North Carolina State University. When one adds to this mouse damage in the home and orchard, one begins to realize how destructive rodents are and how draining their damage is to small farm or homestead budgets. Steps should be taken to eliminate not only the rodents themselves, but their sources of food and their shelters as well.

The major source of rodent damage is the Norway or brown rat (*Rattus norvegicus*). He is ably assisted by his cousins the black rat (*Rattus rattus*) and the house mouse (*Mus musculus*). Other relatives, the field mouse and the pine mouse, cause damage to orchards and in gardens.

Rats are among the most ingenious creatures known. They police their population so the number of rats does not exceed the food supply by killing or driving out weak rats. A healthy rat can fall 50 feet without serious injury, and can swim half-a-mile in open water or up sewer lines against swift currents. It can dive through a plumbing trap, gnaw through adobe brick, cinder block, oak planks, and, occasionally, through metal conduits.

Rat and mouse control are linked on the homestead or farm. Although mice are more of a problem in the house, rats can infest both the house and barn and are a more significant problem in sheds and other outdoor buildings. Even though you may succeed with ease in temporarily reducing the number of rats on your property, you will have to keep after your work to keep the population down permanently. Sanitation around the house and barn is vital.

Sanitation: Sanitation means general cleaning, eliminating sources of food for rats and mice, and destroying rodent nests. Begin by sealing all stored food from rats and mice. That does not necessarily mean rat proofing an entire building, since many buildings are impossible to completely rat-proof. Cement foundations, metal nailed over rat holes, metal flashings on doors and window frames, and self-closing devices on doors all help, but are not fail-safe. For best results you must rat-proof specific containers, rooms or bins in your buildings.

Dried and bagged food of all kinds should be stored in tight cupboards or preferably in glass jars or tin boxes with tight-fitting lids. Table scraps not fed to animals must be scrupulously composted; rat-proof compost bins are desirable, but proper composting *will not* draw rats.

Food that needs to be cured or hung for long periods of time can be hung in attics, garages, or storerooms in ways that protect it from rodent infestation. One way is to hang the foodstuffs from a wire strung from one wall to another. Simply punch a hole in the center of large metal disks and slip them over the wire about a foot from each wall. Rodents can't get around the disks. If you have a beam flush against the ceiling of a building, cover both ends of the beam with tin to about two feet from the wall on either end. Rats won't be able to maintain a footing on the metal surfaces of the beam ends. Drive nails into the beam for hangers.

Don't let surplus garden crops stand for extended periods or overwinter in the garden. Shred, plow under, or otherwise dispose of anything rats would enjoy, particularly mature sweet corn. Baled straw often contains wheat that was not threshed out properly at harvesttime and rats or mice will burrow into the bales for the grain. Do not store baled straw in a barn, or, if you do, use the bales as soon as you can.

Keep all livestock and pet feed in metal containers. Steel 55-gallon drums are ideal for the purpose, since they can still be purchased cheaply or be had for free. Be careful not to use drums in which toxic chemicals have been shipped or stored and wash all drums out thoroughly. Pieces of roofing tin weighted down with a rock or piece of cement block will cover the barrels. Set the barrels on pallets or a platform to keep them off the ground so they don't rust out. In four drums you can store all the feed six chickens and a pig need in a year.

Larger farms and homesteads need larger grain-storage facilities. There are many metal bins and cribs on the market. Old wooden cribs can be partially rat-proofed with hardware cloth or pieces of roofing tin, but rats will always find a new place to gnaw through.

If constructing new buildings, don't put wooden or composition floors in them unless you really need them. Of course, rats can get into dirt-floored buildings easily enough but they don't often stay because there is no place to hide. If you build a building with a floor, build it up off the ground so that a dog or cat can get underneath the building to chase a rat. Feed your barn cats underneath the floor of the building to encourage them to hunt there.

Keep all piles of wood and lumber up off the ground with planks and posts. Get rid of piles of rocks, old boards and junk.

Feed your chickens and other animals carefully so that they finish their grain and don't spill it. Don't leave mash or other food out overnight when rats are active. Rats will attack baby chicks, unless the hen fights them off, so any building in which you are raising chicks should be rat-proof.

Poisons: Poison is a less than completely satisfactory means of eliminating rats and mice. Poisons like arsenic and strychnine are effective killing agents, but rats who watch other rats die a violent death by strychnine seem to put two and two together and avoid the bait. Besides, such poisons are extremely dangerous to children, pets and farm animals, even if placed in bait stations along rat runs.

Rats sometimes learn to avoid the safer, newer anticoagulant poisons that have been so effective over the past ten years. These poisons often require repeated feedings before they will kill and a rat that gets sick may avoid eating the poison again—it seems to associate the odor of the bait with its sickness. Rats have also shown some tendency to become immune to anticoagulants.

Bait must be placed properly to have greatest effect. Place baits in runways or places where rats seek shelter, but cover them well so that domestic animals or children will not find them. A board may be leaned against the wall over the bait, or the bait may be covered with a box with two-by-three-inch holes in both ends. Rats deprived of earlier hiding places by the cleanup of their shelters may be enticed to the bait when it is enclosed in a new hiding place.

The most satisfactory results from poisons are obtained when prebaiting is done. Prebaiting is simply offering a variety of unpoisoned baits for the rats to sample, and then using the most popular—with poison added—in bait stations. Many different substances can be used as bait since rats are omnivorous: liver, bacon, cheese, chicken entrails, canned fish, cornmeal or oatmeal, green corn, bananas, raw eggs, or dried milk.

Traps: Trapping rats works but is not extremely effective. It is best used in combination with other controls. By far the safest trap to use on the ground is something like a Hava-hart live trap because you can free other animals that might get stuck in it. Bait the cage with grain, bread or bacon and set it in a runway. The rats may avoid it the first few nights because they are suspicious of anything new in their environment. As they get used to the trap, however, you should get results. Drown the rats you catch in this type of trap.

A spring-type rat trap can also be used. Nail it to a beam or fasten it to a pipe that has become a runway for rats. Bait should be firmly tied to the trap, and, once mounted, it can be left in place.

Mice in the Orchard: The field mouse and the pine mouse often live in orchards and damage fruit trees. The field or meadow mouse is rather stocky, short legged, short eared, and usually black and gray. The pine mouse is generally much smaller in size and has a very short tail. Its fur is dull chestnut and of very soft texture.

Field mice are not difficult to control in the orchard. They rarely burrow below the ground, and they feed on the trunk, not the roots of trees. If the orchard is mulched, be sure to pull the mulch a few feet away from the trunk in the fall. Field mice build nests in mulch but are hesitant to run around in the open once cold weather sets in. Placing a wire cylinder around the trunk of each tree is also effective against field mice.

Pine mice are often very difficult to control. Persistence is necessary. Dig some of the soil away from the base of the tree in the fall and fill it in with cinders. Spread cinders in a circle to at least three feet from the trunk. The sharp cinders will help prevent the rodents from tunneling in the soil. Regular snap-back mouse traps can be effective if carefully set in the runs.

RODGERSIA

These hardy summer-blooming perennials have bronze leaves and showy, feathery flower clusters up to a foot long. They like a soil high in organic matter, lots of moisture and partial shade. Give them plenty of room, for they have spreading rootstocks. A light covering in the winter is desirable in the northern states. *R. tabularis* grows three feet tall, with white flowers and *R. podophylla* up to five feet with green or yellow white flowers. Both are propagated in early spring, by division of the rootstocks.

ROMAINE LETTUCE
See LETTUCE

ROMNEYA

These tender perennials have beautiful, enormous white flowers, up to six inches across. They grow six to eight feet high with spreading rootstocks. The best-known species is *R. Coulteri,* the California tree poppy. Because they are difficult to grow, romneyas are best started in pots. As soon as the seed are ripe, they should be sown and barely covered in a sand/peat mixture. Putting seedlings under a bell jar will aid their growth. Temperature should be kept at 60°F. (15.56°C.) or slightly less. When transplanting, disturb the roots as little as possible. Give plants a soil high in sand and peat and a position in a sunny border with excellent drainage. Romneyas are occasionally grown in northern greenhouses.

ROOT

A root is the portion of a seed plant that originates at the lower portion of the axis of a plant embryo or seedling. It gathers and absorbs food and moisture from the soil, stores these materials, and transports them to the upper parts of the plant. Actually, the first function is carried on by the tiny root hairs or tips, and the second and third by the larger, more easily seen roots. The big roots also serve as anchors that hold the plant in the soil.

ROOT CROPS

Any crop whose edible portion is taken from under the ground is called a root crop.

Popular garden ones are beets, carrots, onions, parsnips, potatoes, salsify, sweet potatoes, and turnips. Actually, the onion is a bulb, and the potato, a tuber, but both are considered root crops.

See also VEGETABLE GARDENING.

ROOT CUTTING
See BRAMBLE FRUITS, CUTTINGS

ROOT DIVISION   *See* DIVISION

ROOT-KNOT   *See* NEMATODE

ROOT PRUNING

Root pruning is practiced to encourage the development of fibrous roots which are the plants' suppliers of food and water. Plants that are being readied for transplanting or that need invigorating, and trees whose roots are overtaking gardens, lawns and paths are often root pruned.

When fruit trees consistently fail to set fruit, though all other conditions are favorable, the grower may resort to root pruning. In the fall a trench about two feet deep and six feet from the trunk is dug around the tree. The trench exposes the big anchor roots for cutting. If no big roots are found, there is very likely a wild taproot that must be located and cut. Any ornamental tree that has spread its roots out into areas where they are not wanted can be treated in the same way. A metal or cement barrier set in the trench will prevent subsequent spread.

When planning to move a deciduous shrub, it's a good idea to prune its roots by forcing a sharp spade into the soil close to the stems during the summer. In response to the pruning, the plant will develop more fibrous roots and so become easier to take up in the fall. Sometimes judicious root pruning will force a recalcitrant flowering shrub into bloom. A system of root pruning and top pruning is sometimes used to keep tub plants small.

In the nursery, trees and shrubs are either lifted several times or planted wide apart and root pruned regularly until they are sold. Both these methods force trees and shrubs to develop a mass of fibrous roots rather than a few heavy, wide-spreading ones that would make them difficult to move and establish successfully. In nurseries, special machines are used to cut the roots under as well as around the plant.

See also PRUNING.

ROSE   (*Rosa*)

Roses have been known throughout the Northern Hemisphere as far back as literature records. Early poets of Greece, China and Persia all sang praises of the rose. Dried roses have been found in Egyptian tombs. An indication of the rose's antiquity is the fact that the name for it is almost the same in every European language.

Planting and Culture: Roses require sun, free circulation of air, and porous, well-drained, acid soil with a pH of 5 to 6. Full sun for eight hours a day is best, but six hours' sun, provided they are morning hours, is sometimes sufficient.

Roses planted too close to buildings or fences, where air does not circulate freely through their canes, are subject to mildew. It is best to provide trellis support for climbers that are intended to decorate buildings or walls.

A three-foot space between vine and house will not only provide air space, but will facilitate painting the building.

The best rose plants to buy are two-year-old field-grown budded stock. Roses may be planted in fall or spring. Most nurseries dig their roses in the fall, store them through the winter, and ship in spring. If you purchase them in fall and hold them for spring planting they should be heeled in at the bottom of an 18-inch trench, covered with loose soil, and mulched after the ground is frozen.

Preparing the bed: Soil should be trenched and prepared to a depth of 24 inches for best results. Experiments have proven that roses planted in more shallowly prepared soil will give results equal to those of roses in deep beds during the first year, but after the second year the roses in 24-inch beds are superior.

In preparing a rose bed, a few inches of topsoil are removed and saved. Then another few inches are removed and discarded. A mixture of half-rotted manure and humus is combined with the reserved soil which is then returned to the bed. Allow it to settle for two weeks before planting.

If drainage is a problem, a special drainage system may be installed in the rose bed. When the soil has been removed to a depth of 24 inches, the hardpan below is broken up with a pick or mattock. A four-inch layer of gravel, cinders or rubble is placed in the bottom of the trench before the enriched topsoil is returned to it. Where the ground is very poorly drained, drainage tiles are laid from the rose bed to carry off seepage from the gravel layer at the bottom of the bed.

Planting: A hole slightly larger in diameter than the spread roots of the plant should be dug when planting, barely deep enough to bury the bud graft. Soil is mounded in a cone shape in the center of the hole, and the plant seated upon it. If any of the roots are damaged, they should be pruned to behind the damage. Long straggly roots also are cut back, and the tips of most others removed. The hole is half-filled with soil, and a pail of water poured into it, to wash soil among the small rootlets. When the water has seeped away, the hole is filled to ground level and tamped around the plant. Canes are then pruned to six to eight inches above soil level.

Care: Roses need plenty of water when the season is dry, but it should be supplied at weekly intervals in quantities large enough to reach the deepest roots rather than in small daily doses. Watering done in the morning of a sunny day will be less likely to cause mildew than if it is done in the evening, when foliage may remain wet overnight. Allow the water to dribble slowly from the hose under the bush, rather than to flow from a spray which will wet the leaves.

To conserve moisture when the weather becomes hot and dry, a mulch may be spread around the plants. Compost, buckwheat hulls, ground corncobs, straw, decayed or shredded leaves, or lawn clippings may be used. If peat moss is used, it should be moistened before application. It is advisable to mix a nitrogenous fertilizer with the mulch, particularly if corncobs are used.

A formula developed especially for spring and summer rose feeding contains the following: two parts fish meal, two parts dried blood, one part cottonseed meal, one part wood ashes (if soil is very acid), one part phosphate rock, and one part greensand. The first three ingredients supply nitrogen, wood ashes supply potash, and phosphate rock and greensand provide phosphorus. Application of this fertilizer may be repeated in monthly doses, ending August 1 in the North, September 1 in midsections, and October 1 in the South.

Winter protection: Most bush roses need winter protection in areas where temperatures fall below 10°F. (−12.22°C.). It is standard practice to mound the soil around the plants to a depth of at least eight inches. Canes are drawn upright, and the longer ones trimmed to 30 inches. After the soil is thoroughly frozen and field mice have found their winter quarters elsewhere, a mulch of straw, leaves or garden refuse mixed with manure may be filled in between mounds. Further protection is seldom necessary, unless the plants are exposed to drying winter winds. Burlap held by stakes may be used to shield the bed from strong winds.

Winter cover should be removed before growth starts in the spring. Mulch should be raked away, and the winter's manure cultivated into the top layer of soil. The bed is then left to bake under the warm spring sun until the time arrives for covering with the summer mulch.

In sections where winters are extremely severe it may be necessary to protect climbing roses and ramblers. The only way to give them adequate cover is to take them down from their supports, gather the canes in a horizontal bundle on the ground, and cover them with soil. After the ground is thoroughly frozen a straw mulch may be spread over the soil.

Tree roses are difficult to protect in an upright position, because even when they are in burlap cases the drying winter winds, which do more damage than low temperatures, still reach them. The best protection can be given only when the tree top is bent down to the ground and the canes are covered with soil. If the plant must be encased in an upright position, pack straw and leaf mulch around it, but watch out for field mice inside the cover.

Pruning: Bedding roses are pruned in the spring when new shoots are about ¼ inch long. Dead wood—all wood with brown, dried or shriveled bark—is trimmed off first. The plant is then inspected for injury, and any canes injured by the winter winds or ice are trimmed back. Rough, gnarled branches with weak twigs, and thin weak shoots are removed next. Then the remaining branches are shortened by one-third their length if many flowers are desired, or two-thirds the length for larger but fewer blossoms. For exhibition bloom the canes are cut back to six or eight inches.

Large-flowered climbing roses are pruned in early spring in much the same way as bedding roses. Tree roses are also pruned in spring. These are cut back more severely than bush types to control their shape. Species roses are pruned very little, except to remove dead wood in early spring and overgrown canes after blooming. These varieties are left to develop their own graceful shapes.

Ramblers are pruned in spring, only to remove the dead wood. Their heaviest pruning is done immediately after blooming, when all canes that have flowered are cut back to the ground. Canes will grow as much as 20 feet before the end of the summer, and the following year's bloom will all be borne on wood developed after pruning.

Cut flowers: Unlike other flowers which last longer when cut early in the morning, roses should be cut late in the day. Experiments have shown that a rose cut after 4:30 P.M. will last ten hours longer than one cut at 8:00 A.M. The reason for this is thought to be the extra supply of sugar that the leaves store during the day. Sugar is manufactured in daylight. During the night it travels to the roots and other parts of the plant. After long daylight hours the leaves are saturated with sugar, so this can be used to nourish the flowers after they are cut.

Everblooming roses should not be cut below the second leaf axil on the cane if the bush is expected to continue to bloom. Later blooms will arise from the lower leaf axils. The fewer leaves removed from the plant, the more flowers will follow. If the flowers are allowed to remain on the plant until the petals fall, the old bloom should be pinched off just above the top leaf.

Propagation: Rose cultivars are seldom grown from seed because seed-grown plants will not carry the hybrid characteristics. It is possible to propagate species from seed, but, for the results achieved, it requires more work than most gardeners are willing to do.

Seed: Several methods of handling rose seed are suggested. The seed is contained in a fruit called a hip, which forms in the receptacle at the base of the flower. Hips are collected when fully ripe—usually just before the first frost.

One method of growing roses from seed is the "ripening" method. Hips are mashed to make a pulpy mash, and this is permitted to ferment at about 40°F. (4.44°C.) for 60 to 120 days. "Ripening," a process thought to aid in germination, takes place during this period. After fermentation, seed are washed and layered in humus in a flat or flowerpot, and placed outdoors on the north side of a building to refrigerate.

A second method of handling seed is to remove it from the hips and, without fermenting, to place it in leaf mold or peat moss in a flat or pot outside. Weathering during the cold months seems to help the seed to germinate.

The simplest method is to plant the seed directly in the garden in the fall. If this method is adopted, seed should be sown about an inch deep, and six inches apart. After germination, plants may be moved to stand a foot apart and permitted to grow for two years before taking their place in the shrubbery border.

Cuttings: A practical method for propagating roses true to the parent is by using cuttings or slips. Take cuttings from the healthiest plants, at a point where the cane breaks with a snap. If the cane bends, the wood is too tough. If it crushes, it is too green. A point below the sixth set of leaves on a shoot that has just finished blooming usually has the right texture.

Remove the two bottom sets of leaves, leaving the two nodes. (Nodes are the joints on the stem from which the leaves grow.) Cut off just below the two top sets of leaves, and discard the stem tip.

Slips may be set directly into an existing rose bed, or they may be started in a protected place where they will receive morning sun only. Insert them in the ground up to the remaining leaves, and firm the soil around them. Peat moss may be sprinkled around them lightly, and they are covered with glass jars, which are pushed securely into the soil. They are then watered well with a light spray from the hose. It is rarely necessary to water them because the moisture which condenses inside the glass jar will keep them sufficiently wet.

New shoots will appear within three or four weeks. Jars are not removed until the cuttings have roots enough to supply plenty of moisture to the leaves. This may not be until the following spring. Cuttings may be made any time from June until the first frosts. If they are made during July or August, it is well to shade them from the afternoon sun.

Runners: Some climbers and shrub roses spread by means of root runners, which send up shoots at a distance from the parent plant. When these shoots have made a root system of their own, they may be severed from the parent and moved to a new location. Many ramblers will root where the tip of a branch touches the ground. Thoroughly rooted tips may be cut from the parent canes, and the new plant moved.

Diseases and Insects: Weakened roses are subject to many fungus and insect infestations. Whether rose plants are weak or strong they are always subject to some diseases and pests, but many organic gardeners find that their well-fed and properly mulched roses are no more subject to these disorders than are more rugged garden specimens.

A few simple sanitary measures are recommended for gardeners who prefer not to use chemical sprays. Garden trash and mulches should be removed from rose beds early in spring so that the bare soil is exposed to sun for at least a month. This drying process kills many spores and fungi which may have wintered in the mulch or soil.

Rose leaves that fall from the plants during the growing season may be assumed to be harboring an insect or disease, and should be removed to the compost pile as soon as possible. Leaves on the plants which show signs of disease or insects are best removed, also.

The most common fungus diseases which attack roses are:

Black spot: Irregular circular spots with radiating margins (mycelium) appear on the leaves and sometimes also on canes. The leaves turn yellow and fall. Gather and dispose of infested leaves. Mulch the ground thoroughly and cultivate every spring.

Canker: Infection from fungus may occur in open wounds in the canes and prevent the wound's healing. Canker occurs most often in wounds made during the winter, and when plants are covered. Canes should all be inspected in spring, and damaged tissue cut back.

Prompt pruning of cankered canes is the best control. Be sure to disinfect shears after using them.

Chlorosis or mosaic: This is a virus disease that turns leaves yellow along the veins. It is more prevalent in greenhouses than outdoors. Plants attacked must be destroyed to prevent spreading. Make sure plants are well supplied with iron, nitrogen and potassium.

Mildew: This appears as a white powdering over leaves and canes, and causes buds and leaves to become dwarfed and gnarled. Ramblers are likely to show mildew in spring and bedding roses in late summer, especially after a prolonged period of wet weather. Full sun and adequate ventilation are the best preventives. Care should be taken never to wet foliage with the hose, especially late in the day when the sun will not have time to dry it before evening.

Rust: Orange brown powdery spore masses appear on under-leaf surfaces. Infested leaves should be destroyed.

Where one disease or another is difficult to control, special varieties resistant to that disease may be planted. Many of the newer roses are being bred especially for their hardiness and disease resistance. Lists of them may be found in any nursery catalog.

Sucking insects which attack roses are aphids and rose leafhoppers. Chewers that like rose flavor are rose sawfly, whose slug-like larvae skeletonize the leaves; rose chafer or rose beetles which attack buds and flowers; Japanese beetles, which eat the flowers; rose curculio and climbing cutworm, both of which bore holes in buds; leaf cutters that nip circular holes out of leaves; leaf rollers which tie up leaves; stem girdlers that tunnel in twigs to cause swellings; and rose midge, a small fly that lays eggs near flower buds, in order to supply its offspring with tender rose petals.

Many of these insects may be handpicked. According to organic gardeners, not many of them attack plants grown with proper sanitary control of soil, mulched, and given plenty of food and a reasonable amount of year-round care.

Species and Varieties: Linnaeus, in 1762, described 14 rose species, a number which he soon increased to 21. After Linnaeus had pointed the way, other botanists followed with more and more complete classifications. By the mid-twentieth century Arnold Arboretum had classified 296 species, and there are even more today.

Species described by botanists are pure strains. They do not include crosses, hybrids, doubles, bud mutations, and sports which, though not recognized by academic botanists as separate species, account for 95 percent of the roses listed in current catalogs. True species roses include dog rose (*R. canina*), China rose (*R. chinensis*), damask rose (*R. damascena*), musk rose (*R. moschata*), and swamp rose (*R. palustris*). It has been estimated that through the latter half of the nineteenth and the first half of the twentieth centuries at least 16,000 varieties of roses were developed from these and other species. Each year sees a new crop of hybrids presented to the gardener.

One of the oldest hybrids developed in the United States is Champneys' Pink Cluster, a cross between a China rose and a musk rose developed in Charleston, South Carolina, in 1810, and later sent to a Parisian florist. It later became known as the Noisette.

In 1817 a rose named the Bourbon rose appeared in a planting of China and damask roses in a garden on the Isle of Bourbon, possibly a cross between *R. indica* and *R. gallica* or *R. centifolia*.

These two, the Noisette and Bourbon, were the chief varieties used by the hybridizers of the early nineteenth century. It is believed that in combination they produced the first of the modern hybrid perpetuals.

The Empress Josephine, in her celebrated gardens at Malmaison, collected all the varieties of roses obtainable in her day. It has been estimated that at the time of her death in 1814, Malmaison gardens contained approximately 250 varieties.

The first hybrid tea rose, La France, was developed in 1867, a cross between the hardy perpetual Mme. Victor Verdier and the tea rose, Mme. Bravy. But it was not until after 1911, when a hardy understock of the multiflora was used in its graft, that the hybrid tea rose became popular. Thousands of hybrid teas are now listed in rose growers' catalogs.

With so many roses to choose from, the gardener may want help in planning his or her rose garden. Each year the American Rose Society in Harrisburg, Pennsylvania, issues *A Guide for Buying Rose Plants*. This leaflet is free upon request. It summarizes the society's national reports on the most successfully grown varieties of the previous year, and lists newly developed hybrids as well as old favorites.

Classes: Roses may be divided into three main groups, according to use. These are bedding roses, climbing and creeping roses, and shrub roses. Within each group are several classes of cultivars.

Bedding: Bedding roses include teas, hybrid perpetuals, hybrid teas, and polyanthas. They are used in freestanding beds and in low borders. Their average height is about 30 inches to three feet.

Tea roses were derived mainly from *R. odorata*. They are everblooming, but are not hardy enough to endure extreme winters in the northern states. Colors range from white through pink to rose, with some yellows, but no deep shades.

Hybrid perpetuals, the hardiest of the hybrids, were most popular in the latter part of the nineteenth century. They range in color from white through pink to deep red, but offer no yellow shades. They bloom mainly in the spring, with a light secondary bloom in the fall if conditions are right. The principal ancestors of the hybrid perpetuals are *R. chinensis* and *R. damascena.*

Hybrid tea roses are very complex in origin, developed mainly from hardy perpetuals crossed with *R. odorata.* They have long pointed buds and large handsome flowers in all shades and combinations of colors. They are everblooming and hardy.

Polyantha hybrids, also called floribundas, are derived from the baby rose (*R. multiflora*), from which they take their clusters of flowers, and from hybrid perpetuals, which give them great hardiness. Floribundas are becoming increasingly popular for their resistance to disease, their wide color range, and their abundance of blossoms throughout the season.

Climbing: Climbing roses are of two types —those with flowers in clusters, called ramblers, and those with single large flowers, designated as large-flowered climbers. Creeping roses are climbers adapted to trailing along banks or walls. Their flowers are generally small, but they are hardy and provide an attractive ground cover.

Ramblers are varieties of *R. polyantha,* derived principally from *R. multiflora* and *R. wichuraiana.* They are generally hardy in latitudes where peaches can be grown commercially. They are rapid growers, producing canes as long as 20 feet in one season. Many varieties are susceptible to mildew. Colors range from white through pink to deep red. Ramblers bloom only once each year.

Most large-flowered climbers were developed from hardy teas or hardy perpetuals, and are called climbing hardy teas or climbing hardy perpetuals, "C.H.T." or "C.H.P." Their color range includes yellows, deep shades and bicolors. They may or may not be hardy and everblooming, depending upon their parent stock.

Because of their vigorous growth, ramblers are best suited for positions where a high vine is desired. They may be trained to overhead trellises and supports, or to high pillars for vertical accents. Climbing hybrid teas and climbing hybrid perpetuals do not make as much growth in one season and are better suited to lower supports, such as fences. Trained horizontally along a fence, they will bloom more freely than on an upright support. Bloom buds will arise from almost every leaf joint of a horizontal cane.

Shrub: Shrub roses are species roses which may be planted in borders of deciduous shrubbery like forsythia and weigela. All are hardy, and in fall many bear attractive hips which are a valuable source of vitamin C. Chief among these are the rugosas (*R. rugosa*). *See* RUGOSA ROSE.

Hybrid sweetbriers were developed from common sweetbrier (*R. eglanteria*). They are tall and graceful and have scented foliage. Colors are pink, white, yellow, and copper.

Scotch roses, the burnet of northern Europe, are descended from *R. spinosissima.* They are very hardy and are useful in hedges.

R. palustris may be naturalized in low, swampy locations where other roses will not grow. *R. rubrifolia* is useful chiefly for its interesting reddish foliage.

Tree roses, or standard roses, are special adaptations of shrub roses, and may be grafted from any bedding variety. They are used as accents or specimen plants in the garden, and require special winter care in cold areas.

See also MULTIFLORA ROSE, PRUNING, SHRUBS.

ROSE ACACIA   *See* LOCUST

ROSEBAY   *See* OLEANDER

ROSE, CHRISTMAS
See CHRISTMAS ROSE

ROSE HIPS

Rose hips are the vitamin C-laden fruit of the rose. After the blossoms fade and the petals drop, rose hips appear as pulpy seed-pods of different sizes and colors. Most varieties of roses have a few hips the size of peas or marbles. Rugosa roses often have hips the size of crab apples, and in great profusion. In addition, the rugosa rose hips contain an exceptionally high quantity of vitamin C. *See also* RUGOSA ROSE.

A handful of rose hips can provide the vitamin C value of 60 oranges; a half-cup may contain as much as 1,200 to 1,800 milligrams of natural ascorbic acid, depending on variety and growing conditions. Wild hips are also rich in vitamins A, B_1 and B_2 and many minerals. In Norway and Sweden, the wild hips are collected in the fields and woods and made into soups, stews, preserves, sauces, and juices to fortify the vitamin-poor winter menu. During World War II they were the sole source of vitamin C in some areas, and their consumption is given partial credit for the general good health of many people during those lean war years.

The rugosa rose produces hips that are larger and richer in vitamin C than those of other varieties.

Rose hips should be gathered when they are fully ripe, but not overripe. They should be bright scarlet. If orange, they are under-ripe; if dark red, overripe. Some varieties won't ripen until after the first frost, and some people believe that frost improves their flavor. It has been shown that roses grown further north produce hips with higher quantities of vitamin C, one of nature's apparent compensations for a more severe winter. The easiest method of preservation is to pack the hips in mason jars and seal, freeze and store them for up to six months.

Rose hips have a flavor both fruity and spicy. Some people enjoy eating them fresh, right off the bush in early fall. Most often, though, they are collected, trimmed and cooked slightly before being used. They can be preserved, with some nutritional loss, by drying, and rose hip purée can be frozen or canned for easy addition to fruit juices, soups and sauces.

Guidelines to follow for processing the hips before serving are:

1. Wash the hips, then chill to inactivate the enzymes which might cause loss of vitamins.
2. Trim the hips with a pair of scissors, removing both blossom and stem ends.
3. Use stainless steel knives, wooden spoons, earthenware or china bowls, and glass or enamel saucepans. Copper or aluminum utensils will decrease the vitamin C content.
4. Cook quickly in a covered pan to prevent further vitamin loss.

A liquid extract can be made by adding one cup trimmed hips to 1½ cups boiling water. Cover and simmer 15 minutes. Let the mixture stand in a pottery or china bowl for 24 hours. Strain off the extract, bring it to a rolling boil, add two tablespoons lemon juice for each pint of extract, pour into jars, and seal. The extract can be added to many recipes by using from ¼ cup to one cup of the liquid in vegetables, stews, meat loaves, soups, and salad dressings or as a moistening agent in spreads. In Sweden, a soup made from rose hips is a popular dish served either as an appetizer or a dessert. The hips are ground and then boiled for ten minutes, then strained and again brought to a boil and thickened and extended with a mixture of four teaspoons flour and two cups cold water. This soup may be sweetened with honey and served hot or cold, often with a dollop of whipped cream added.

See also ROSE, RUGOSA ROSE.

ROSE MALLOW   *See* HIBISCUS

ROSEMARY   (*Rosmarinus officinalis*)

The spicy, aromatic leaves of this perennial evergreen shrub are used fresh or dried in a number of dishes as well as some medicines and cosmetics. The mature bush develops a woody stem, boughs of evergreen needles, and blue flowers that bloom in the spring. A member of the Mint family, the herb grows one to three feet high.

Rosemary is a well-known symbol of fidelity and remembrance in Christian weddings and funerals. According to legend, the Virgin Mary draped her cloak over a white rosemary bush during the flight from Egypt. The plant turned the same color as her garment, and hence was given her name.

The name rosemary is actually derived from the Latin *ros* (dew) and *marinus* (of the sea) because the plant's native habitat is close to the Mediterranean coast. Many people believe Roman conquerors brought it to northern Europe and England, where it was used as a balm, a curative tonic, a nerve-calming tea, and even in wine.

Planting and Culture: In the North, rosemary does well in a sheltered position, but in the South it is a common, perennial hedge plant. To propagate, take cuttings about six inches long. Root them in a sand/loam/leaf mold mixture in the cold frame or cool greenhouse. In the spring, set them outdoors in the same type of soil. Once or twice each season, the growth can be pruned back several inches.

Rosemary flourishes with occasional watering, but demands well-drained alkaline soil. All varieties grow best in sunny or slightly shady areas, but most cannot be exposed to temperatures below 27°F.

(−2.78°C.). In cold climates, the plants should be brought indoors or covered with bushel baskets or burlap bags.

Harvesting: To harvest rosemary, cut individual branches and strip the leaves from the stems. Stripped leaves can be dried in the shade on screens or paper.

In the kitchen, rosemary flavors beef, veal, pork, lamb, stuffings, soups, sauces, and salad dressings. Rosemary tips can be added to white wine or brandy to make a sauce for any dish.

Medicinal uses of rosemary are many. Young rosemary tips added to one pint of boiling water make a tea that is said to cure headaches and promote sleepiness among the restless. This tea is also believed helpful in insect control when used as a spray.

As a cosmetic, rosemary can be used in mouthwashes. It is also used in hair tonics for dandruff.

This herb is often grown merely for its decorative value and pleasant scent in the garden. Stale indoor air can be freshened by rosemary.

See also HERB.

ROSE MOSS   *(Portulaca grandiflora)*

Rose moss, an annual flower that thrives under the most trying conditions of heat, drought and poor soil, has narrow, succulent leaves that are completely hidden in a blanket of gaily colored blooms. For a summer edging, window box or rock garden, probably nothing surpasses the rose moss which is sometimes called garden portulaca. The single or double flowers, which are borne on trailing stems up to four inches long, are white, pink, yellow, red, or purple, and up to 1½ inches across.

Rose moss likes a dry, sunny situation. The seed is best sown when the weather warms up, in late May or June, but the blooming season is short, so it's a good idea to sow at monthly intervals through the summer. The young plants are easy to transplant. The plant self-sows freely, but volunteer seedlings should not be used because of the possibility of mixing in plants of the wild type which have inferior flowers.

See also PURSLANE.

ROSE-OF-HEAVEN   *See* LYCHNIS

ROSE-OF-SHARON
(Hibiscus syriacus)

Sometimes called shrubby althaea, rose-of-Sharon is a handsome, late-flowering (midsummer through October) deciduous shrub. It grows from six to 12 feet high or higher, and its lower branches can be pruned out to give the shrub a treelike shape. A longtime favorite in gardens, it is hardy in most of the United States if given plenty of sun and moderately fertile soil that is neither too wet nor too dry.

Plant in spring and cut back all shoots to within about two inches of their base to get the plant started growing vigorously. Prune each year in spring before growth starts, aiming at developing a shapely bush form. Cuttings of growing wood taken in July will root under glass in a few weeks. You can also take cuttings of mature wood in early winter, store them in a cold place covered with sand, and plant them in the open as soon as the soil is dry enough to work freely.

There are many varieties and forms. Some of the best are Jeanne d'Arc, a spectacular double white; Paeoniflorus, white with pink shading; Ardens, lavender; Bluebird, lavender blue; Anemone, bright pink; and Lucy, semi-double rose pink.

The name rose-of-Sharon is also applied to *Hypericum calycinum,* a Saint-John's-wort. This is an evergreen shrubby plant growing a foot or less high, which is useful as a ground cover in shade and sandy soil. Its large yellow flowers are in bloom from July to September.

ROSE PINK   *(Sabatia angularis)*

Native to North America, this member of the Gentian family grows best in freshwater bogs or salty, moist sand. It has spikes of white, pink or lilac flowers that bloom throughout the summer. Height varies from several inches to 1½ feet.

Sea pink (*S. stellaris*) is a closely related species that grows along the eastern coast. Its late summer flowers are pink or white with yellow eyes. It does well in partial shade or full sun and tolerates slightly acid soil.

Since both plants are protected in several states, they should not be transplanted from the wild. They can be propagated in fall or early spring from ripened seed sown in light soil.

ROSE POGONIA   *See* POGONIA

ROSETTE

A rosette is a cluster of stalkless leaves that radiates from a single point on a stem apex in some palms, but more often grows from the base of a plant. The name comes from its resemblance to the form of a rose bloom. The houseleeks are notable examples of plants with rosette form, and many biennials have rosette forms their first year.

ROTARY TILLAGE

Rotary tillage methods have been developed because of the need to simplify and speed up the process of preparing soil for planting. Ordinary tillage methods require the use of a plow, disk and harrow before seed can be planted. Sometimes a field is also dragged to break up clods and firm the seedbed. Rotary tillage equipment can do all three jobs in one operation. In addition, it incorporates crop wastes and other organic matter into the soil much more efficiently than the plow-disk-harrow combination. Plowing tends to bury organic matter too far below the surface to permit optimum decay and breakdown by microorganisms. Rotary tillage mixes organic matter into the soil evenly throughout and to the full tillage depth.

Farm-scale rotary tillage is steadily growing in popularity, but it has so far failed to be adopted by the great majority of farmers. There are a number of reasons why farmers have tended to stay with their old practices. Larger tractors able to pull four- and five-bottom plows have become common and have made plowing more rapid. Tillers are more difficult than plows to operate in rocky ground. Perhaps most important, some farmers feel that tillers require a larger initial investment and greater maintenance expense. By contrast, the plow is one of the simplest tools used by man and has been tested and proven in field use for thousands of years. Any new implement coming along to challenge the supremacy of the plow competes with centuries of tradition.

In the garden, however, tillers have actually replaced the plow as the most common

In rotary tillage, the seedbed is plowed, disked, harrowed, and dragged in a single operation.

power tillage tool. The reason for the garden popularity of rotary tillers is easily explained. A plow requires the horsepower and traction of at least one real horse to work efficiently. It is expensive to build comparable pulling power into a small garden tractor, but a very efficient tiller can be built using a small engine.

Selecting a Tiller: For best results in your garden, don't buy an underpowered tiller—six horsepower is the absolute minimum, and seven or eight horsepower is better. The extra money spent for the extra horsepower is worth it.

Tillers have either front- or rear-mounted blades or tines. You can push down on the handles of a front-mounted tiller to make it bite deeper. When you hit the brake of a front-mounted tiller, it can't go forward so the blade continues to turn in place, going deeper into the soil. If the soil is hard, the vibrations of a front-mounted machine will rapidly tire you.

A rear-mounted tiller won't vibrate when soil is tough, but it will lunge ahead, dragging you along with it. Some people say the rear-mounted type is easier to maneuver. In good soil, you can set a rear-mounted tiller for depth and speed, and all you have to do is follow it through your garden.

Both kinds have their limitations, and work best if you are gentle with them in heavy soil or when cultivating sod. Make several passes over the ground for best results.

Tillers come with several kinds of tines. Three-bladed chisel tines are cheap and work well for cultivating, except that they tangle easily if you are trying to incorporate plant residues into the soil. Slicer tines will dig deeply, but will also clog. Either bolo or slasher tines are recommended; both dig deeply into the soil and neither clogs readily when used on plant residues. Bolo tines can be used on bigger tillers, can move more soil, and can be operated at a higher speed than other types of tines.

Using: A rotary tiller can be used to work the ground for planting. Set your depth gauge, and, in heavy sod, make a light pass over the ground. If you have the time, let the ground dry out before going over it for a second time, working at right angles to the first pass. Then go over the ground a third time, working it into a fine, crumbly texture. Don't fight your machine—let the brake bar and the tines do the work. A rear-mounted tiller works better at this job since there is no brake bar to fight.

When using a tiller (especially on soil that is low in organic matter) take care not to pulverize the soil too thoroughly. If soil is overtilled, the tilth of the soil can be harmed and packing will result. If soil is poor, use the slowest efficient tine speed. Make sure the soil is not too wet or too dry when tilling is done.

After planting, your tiller can become a weed cultivator if you have allowed enough space for the tiller to run between rows. As soon as your plants are above ground, you can start cultivating between rows with the tiller, and if you do not dig too deeply, you won't have to worry about burying the new plants. You can sometimes buy special plant shields that fit your tiller and can be used during cultivation to prevent dirt falling on your plants.

Front-end tillers can be modified to cultivate between narrow rows by removing outer tines and turning the remaining tines inward.

Tillers can be used for renovating berry patches and ripping out runners, for cultivating or incorporating mulch into the soil in an orchard, or, when set at a three-inch depth, for cultivating asparagus beds in the spring. Tillers will also mix compost and turn the litter in a chicken house.

Care: Keep the oil bath around the worm gear at the specified level. If the tiller is chain-driven, the chain and bearings should be lubricated when and if the manufacturer has suggested it.

The engine requires more care. Oil should be kept at the proper level in the crankcase. It should be changed as frequently as recommended (usually every 25 operating hours, and sooner if the tiller is operated in extremely dirty conditions), and should be replaced with the proper fluid. In summer, SAE 30 weight oil is used and SAE 5w–20 or 5w–30 in winter. Clean the air cleaner frequently, and always change it when you change the oil. Keep the motor clean generally, and clean out the carbon in the exhaust ports from time to time.

See also GREEN MANURE.

ROTATION

Crop rotation is a regular scheme of planting in which different crops or covers make different demands on the soil each year. A four-year rotation might involve the use of corn, oats, clover, and wheat in four fields of similar size. Each year the farmer would grow all four crops but each in a different field. The fifth year corn goes in where it was at first and the repetition starts. Depending on his needs, the farmer may have a three-year, a five-year or an even longer rotation schedule, sometimes leaving a perennial like alfalfa in each field for two or more years. This requires careful planning of both time and place, and the right division of the farm into smaller units. It may take several years of trial and error to get just the right rotation for all the factors involved, since each farm has its own individual characteristics. Once rightly established, however, the rotation can continue indefinitely.

Disease Control: Crop rotation plays a vital role in controlling root diseases. In the absence of their host plants, root-dwelling fungi tend to die out in the soil. Failure to practice crop rotation can lead to heavy losses from parasitic fungi as well as from nematodes and insects whose populations build up in soils repeatedly planted with susceptible crops.

Crop rotation has been the most commonly used management practice for achieving soil sanitation in fields and gardens. Rotations are especially useful in controlling those fungi that cannot survive long in the soil in the absence of their host plants. Such organisms as those responsible for bean blight, anthracnose and blackleg in cabbage are controlled by three- or four-year rotations with other crops that these organisms do not attack. Rotations are also effective in minimizing the nematode and soil-borne root diseases of many vegetables, including blackrot of carrot, phoma rot of celery, blackleg of crucifers, fusarium wilt of watermelons, fusarium basal rot of onions, fusarium root rot of peas and beans, and verticillium wilt of strawberries.

Insect Control: Rotation also helps reduce damage by those insects that attack only a few kinds of plants. Growing plants of any kind on the same land year after year produces a condition favorable to the insects that attack that crop.

Chinch bugs are controlled by planting legumes or other immune crops in place of corn, wheat, barley, oats, or rye. A rotation to avoid two successive crops of corn on the same land will do much to prevent injury by the corn root aphid, the seed-corn maggot, the northern corn rootworm, the southern corn-stalk borer, and the sugarcane beetle. A four-year rotation of corn, soybeans, small grain, and clover is recommended in the North Central states to control the European corn borer.

Planting pastureland the first year of its cultivation to crops other than corn, lettuce, onions, potatoes or other root crops tends to prevent damage by sod webworms, white grubs, wireworms, and cutworms.

A cropping system of wheat following wheat favors an increase in infestation by the Hessian fly, the false wireworm, the winter grain mite, the wheat jointworm, the wheat stem sawfly, and the wheat strawworm. Wheat plantings may be broken by planting oats, buckwheat, corn, or sorghum in fields infested by the Hessian fly. Legumes or sorghum are recommended to break the cycle for the false wireworm; corn, sorghum, cotton, or clover for the winter grain mite; rye, barley, oats, or buckwheat for the wheat jointworm; and barley, oats, flax, corn, or mustard for the wheat stem sawfly. Since wheat is apparently the only host of the wheat strawworm, any other crop will break its cycle.

Peanuts, soybeans, velvet beans, and crotalaria provide good food and cover for the adult white-fringed beetle and its grubs, but grasses, including corn and the small grains, are poor foods for the adult beetles. When the succession of crops is a legume followed by oats, corn and cotton, the population of grubs in the soil does not increase enough to do much damage to susceptible crops.

The native white beetle grubs and those of the Japanese beetle, the European chafer, the

Asiatic garden beetle, and the oriental beetle feed on a wide range of garden and field crops, grasses and nursery plants, but they do not thrive in plantings of white clover, red clover, alsike clover, sweet clover, alfalfa, soybeans, buckwheat, or orchardgrass. The proper use of legumes in the rotation cycle in cultivated fields, or in combination with grasses in pastures, reduces the possibilities of infestation.

The best rotation for keeping wireworms at a low level is three or five years of alfalfa followed by one year of potatoes, and one or two years of other truck crops, such as sugar beets, corn, beans, or peas. In regions east of the Rocky Mountains, wireworms thrive in land devoted to hay crops or small grains. They are best controlled by rotations that include legumes (alfalfa, sweet clover, red clover, or soybeans), by not planting susceptible crops two successive years and by clean cultivation.

Garden Rotations: Vegetable and flower rotation systems that follow the same principles as those of field rotations have also been developed. Among vegetables, plants are classified according to their needs. The first group is comprised of heavy feeders such as corn, tomatoes and members of the Cabbage family. In the next group are the legumes. They are often planted directly after, or the season after, vegetables of the first group in order to help the soil recover from the heavy demands of those crops. The third group includes light feeders such as root vegetables, bulbs and herbs. In a rich, humusy soil, the second and third groups may be switched and the legumes not planted until last.

Rotation in the flower garden is more complicated since many of the plants may be perennials. However, the principles should be kept in mind when you move some of the perennials or when you seed annuals.

In the first group of the flowers are members of the Cabbage and Buttercup families which are heavy feeders. The common species include adonis, alyssum, anemone, aubrieta, candytuft, clematis, columbine, delphinium, helleborus, larkspur, meadow rue, monkshood, nigella, peony, rocket, and wallflower. Wild poppies, carnations and mignonette are also heavy feeders which demand large amounts of organic matter and which leave the soil depleted.

The leguminous flowering plants of the second group form one of the largest and most important groups. The most common ones are: acacia, baptisia, bush clovers, cassia or senna, coral tree, false acacia, false indigo, golden chain tree, honey locust, kudzu vine, laburnum, licorice, lotus, lupine, mimosa, redbud, sainfoin, scarlet runner bean, Scotch broom, sweet pea, wisteria, and yellowwood. Although not in this group, all the flaxes are soil benefactors and for cultivation purposes may be classed in the second group. Their fine root structure has an excellent soil-loosening effect.

The third group consists of light feeders. Lilies and all bulbous plants including those with fleshy roots such as iris, and those plants with delicate growth and high aromatic quality are classed here. Some of these may grow naturally under rather poor conditions, but remember that, under cultivation, unusual demands are made on them. They are forced to give up their naturally chosen habitat and companions. Fertilizing for this group of plants, though it can be lighter, is no less essential. Use well-decayed compost. One family belonging here has special interest in that its members are helpful companions to delicate, warmth-loving plants. The Spurge family has between 700 to 1,000 species, most having a milky juice, and many being fleshy, desert or warm-climate plants. Best known are castor bean, crown-of-thorns, poinsettia, and snow-on-the-mountain. They seem to radiate a certain warmth into the soil around them that helps plants which need a little coddling, perhaps because they, too, are far away from their native habitat.

See also FALLOW, PERENNIALS, VEGETABLE GARDENING.

ROTENONE

Rotenone or derris is a plant-derived insecticide that has been found to be harmless to warm-blooded animals. Do not buy rotenone that has been adulterated with synthetic toxins—check the label. Rotenone has little residual effect, and the period of protection it offers is short.

The roots of a native weed, devil's shoestring (*Tephrosia virginiana*), contain up to 5 percent rotenone.

Rotenone, like other organic insecticides, should be used only if both preventative measures and less powerful deterrents (traps, repellents and scares) have failed.

ROUGHAGE

Roughage is a coarse bulky feed high in crude fiber and relatively low in the percentage of its digestible portion. Hay, straw, stover, and other animal feeds are called roughage.

ROYAL FERN   *See* OSMUNDA

ROYAL LILY   *See* LILY

ROYAL PALM   (*Roystonea*)

This genus of feather palms contains several outstanding species widely planted as specimen or street trees in the tropics and in central and southern Florida. In Florida, the most popular species is the Cuban royal palm (*R. regia*), which grows to 50 feet or taller, with leaves up to 15 feet long. The Caribbee royal palm (*R. oleracea*) grows over 100 feet high and is frequently used to line broad avenues. The Puerto Rican royal palm (*R. borinquena*) is best suited to lawn planting, since it grows to only about 35 feet.

Royal palms bear flowers and small fruits though these are often concealed by the large fronds. All are tender and rarely successful in the greenhouse.

RUBBER PLANT   (*Ficus elastica*)

This common house plant of the Fig family has four- to 12-inch, glossy dark green leaves and grows to 100 feet in its native habitat, though it is less tall when under cultivation. It is a native of tropical Asia, and in this country will grow outdoors only in the southernmost parts of Florida, Texas and California. Though it will tolerate average household conditions, drafts or sudden temperature changes usually cause it to drop leaves. It is wise to mist rubber plant foliage occasionally.

The plant grows best in all-purpose soil kept evenly moist and in a spot with an eastern, western or shaded southern exposure. It produces one main stalk, which becomes unsightly after about three years. At that stage the top portion is usually air-layered to produce a smaller plant for removing the growth tip has little effect on shape. The root system tends to accept being pot-bound, so an eight-foot specimen can thrive in a ten-inch pot.

See also HOUSE PLANTS.

RUBIA

This genus of hardy herbs of the Madder family contains one economically important species, *R. tinctorum,* a three-foot perennial with roots used in making dye. It has hairy leaves and clusters of yellow green flowers. Although not often cultivated as an ornamental, it will do well in practically any soil if given a sunny position.

RUBUS

The *Rubus* or bramble genus of the Rose family has hundreds of species and countless numbers of hybrids and varieties. Of those cultivated in the United States, the most important are the blackberry, boysenberry, dewberry, loganberry, and raspberry.

Though most species are cultivated for their edible fruits, some which do not produce good fruit are grown solely for ornament. Among these are the flowering raspberry (*R. odoratus*), which has clusters of fragrant purple flowers, the swamp dewberry (*R. hispidus*), a semievergreen trailing plant that makes a good ground cover in shady places, and the Rocky Mountain flowering raspberry (*R. deliciosus*), which grows to six feet and has showy white flowers.

Species grown both for ornament and for edible fruit include the cutleaf blackberry (*R. laciniatus*), the sand blackberry (*R. cuneifolius*), and the wineberry (*R. phoenicolasius*).

Propagation is by seed, root cuttings or suckers.

See also entries for individual plants, BRAMBLE FRUITS.

RUDBECKIA

This genus of the Daisy family produces flowers with raised, dark conical centers. They are also called coneflowers and do well on average or even dry soil as long as full sun is provided. The perennial kinds must have soils that are well drained in winter.

The showiest rudbeckias are varieties of the black-eyed Susan (*R. hirta*) called gloriosa daisies. They produce large single or double flowers in shades of yellow, orange, mahogany, or yellow zoned with mahogany. These grow on two-foot stems above hairy foliage. Gloriosa daisies are biennials that should be treated as annuals since they bloom heavily the first season and rarely the second. They self-sow heavily and are easily grown from seed started indoors.

One of the best perennial rudbeckias is the variety Goldstrum derived from the species *R. fulgida.* Its flowers resemble black-eyed Susans and bloom from July to the end of September on strong 2½-foot plants, which can be left undisturbed for four or five years before dividing. To prolong bloom water Goldstrum well in dry periods.

Golden Glow (*R. laciniata* cv. 'Hortensia'), a perennial often seen in old gardens, has smooth, deeply cut leaves and produces double yellow flowers atop seven-foot stems for a long period in late summer. It spreads vigorously, and clumps of it live for many years in the most neglected situations. A newer, more desirable form is *R. l.* cv. 'Goldquelle', which grows to only 2½ feet and spreads more slowly. It produces double flowers from July to September and requires little maintenance.

See also RATIBIDA.

RUGOSA ROSE   (*Rosa rugosa*)

The rugosa rose is a vigorous, attractive shrub which produces large, fragrant blossoms almost continually during the growing season. In the fall, these blossoms are succeeded by brightly colored hips, the vitamin-laden fruit of the rose. Though the hips of a few other species have a higher concentration of vitamin C, they are neither so large nor so numerous as those of the rugosa. *See also* ROSE HIPS.

The rugosa is a multipurpose plant. It is attractive to birds, makes an excellent windbreak, is resistant to insect attack and plant diseases, and requires no pampering or pruning. It grows up to six feet tall and can endure cold, heat, dryness, poor soil and even salt sea air. Many consider the wrinkled foliage of the rugosa even more attractive than that of the more tender garden-variety roses.

The plant is a native of China, Korea and Japan and is one of about 200 different species of roses grown in the temperate and subtropical regions of North America. Because it is a distinct species, it can reproduce itself from seed. Over the years, horticulturalists have selected and hybridized rugosa roses, seeking to produce plants with larger blooms and exotic colors. Some of these propagated varieties are sold by nurseries for use as hedging. Among them are some with increased yields of exceptionally large rose hips. These include Hansa, with violet red blossoms and a clove fragrance, and Rubra, a spreading plant with deep crimson blossoms.

See also ROSE.

RUMEX   *See* SORREL

RUMINANT

Any animal which chews its cud, brings up its food, and rechews it prior to swallowing a second time is called a ruminant. Cows, sheep and goats are ruminants.

Thanks to their sectioned stomachs, ruminants can use an extremely large amount of roughage and bulky feeds in their diets. The rumen, a sort of fermentation vat, takes up about 80 percent of the total stomach size. Innumerable bacteria which live in the rumen supply the enzymes that break down the fiber and other parts of the feed. In this way, they build protein from simple nitrogen compounds and make available various essential vitamins.

RUNNER

Prostrate shoots which root are known as "runners." Runners, such as those on strawberry plants, are often used for propagation purposes, since all that is needed in order to start plants from them is to separate the rooted joints from the shoots of the parent plant.

RUNNING MYRTLE
See PERIWINKLE

RUSH	*See* CATTAIL
RUSSIAN OLIVE	*See* OLEASTER
RUST	*See* DISEASE

RUTABAGA   (*Brassica Napus*)

The rutabaga is an excellent nutritious late-season root crop that can easily be stored in pits or in moist sand in the cellar for three to four months. Rutabagas are sometimes called winter, yellow or Swedish turnips, but they are bigger and hardier than the common turnip, and they take longer to mature. They are best planted July 15 or later, in a moist, rich soil. Though they can be harvested after a frost, they must not freeze or their keeping quality will be impaired.

Sow the seed in drills. One ounce is sufficient for 400 feet of drill. Space the plants 12 inches apart. Rutabagas are good winter stock feed, and seed is often sown a month earlier in order to make big roots for this use. Use two pounds of seed per acre drilled or five pounds broadcast.

To grow rutabagas for seed, apply a heavy mulch to the patch. Uncover the plant early in spring and tie the seed stalk to a stick. Break off the mature seed stalk and store it in a dry place. Seed, which are viable for four years, can be removed when dry.

The best yellow varieties are Laurentian, Western Perfection, Superba, Improved Long Island, and American Purple Top Yellow. There are also several fine new white Macombers with especially sweet flesh. Macombers

can be planted several weeks earlier than yellow rutabagas without developing tough flesh.

See also TURNIP.

RYANIA

The roots of the ryania shrub yield a mildly alkaline insecticide that poses no danger to humans and other warm-blooded animals. It is sold as a dust, and can be mixed with water to make a spray. Ryania is effective against the codling moth, oriental fruit moth, corn borer, cranberry fruitworm, cotton bollworm, and other insects.

While ryania is classified as an organic insecticide, it should only be resorted to if both preventative measures and less powerful deterrents such as traps, repellents and scares have failed to give good results.

RYE   (*Secale cereale*)

For 2,000 years rye has been widely planted, largely because it is a cool-weather crop that will produce on land too poor to grow wheat. In the United States, rye is valued for pasture and green manure, especially since new breeding methods have increased growth and yields. Dairymen grow rye for late fall and early spring pastures and plow under the residue.

Ryegrass (*Lolium* spp.) is not a true rye. It grows only a foot tall and has no grain value, but can be used as a cover crop in the home garden. Sow it after vegetables are harvested, allow it to grow through the fall, and till it

Rye is a cool-season crop that produces well on fairly poor soils, but the grain is not especially valuable as animal feed.

under the following spring before planting. This is an inexpensive way to add nitrogen to the soil. Rye can also be planted between corn rows before harvesting to provide erosion control during the winter, and green manure when plowed under in the spring.

Planting and Culture: Rye grain can be sown any time from late summer to late fall, but should be planted early enough so that it can get a good start before the cold weather hits. If you are planting for grain, use about 1½ bushels of seed per acre; for grazing, use two to 2½ bushels per acre. Halve these quantities in a semiarid climate. Plant by drill, or broadcast as you would winter wheat.

Insects and Diseases: Few insects damage rye extensively, but it is susceptible to ergot disease. Ergot is a fungus that replaces rye kernels with black growths called sclerotia or sclerotium rot, which is poisonous to both animals and humans. Destroy the grain or soak infested rye in a 20 percent solution of table salt in water until the ergot bodies rise to the surface. Wash the seed before planting.

Rye is also afflicted with stem rots and smuts, but crop rotation and the use of resistant varieties solve that problem. Anthracnose seldom is severe on a well-balanced, fertile soil.

Harvesting: Rye will ripen just ahead of winter wheat, but it yields less. Average harvests are about 30 bushels to the acre so that it is not an especially valuable crop for the homesteader. The grain is not as palatable to animals as other grains. Rye doesn't make good hay, either, although horse farmers like rye straw bedding for fancy race horses. For home use, harvest as you would wheat and grind in a blender or mill.

Varieties: The best varieties for grain in the South are Florida Black, Abruzzi, Explorer, and Gator. Dakold is a northern variety of long standing, and Balbo has been a favorite for centuries. Adams, Caribou and Pierre are other varieties grown in the North. Other varieties are available, and new varieties hit the market from time to time.

See also WHEAT.

S

SABADILLA

Sabadilla is an insecticidal dust made from the seed of a South American and Mexican plant of the Lily family. Suppliers of the dust and the seed caution users that the product can irritate mucous membranes.

Sabadilla is effective against many pest larvae, grasshoppers, aphids, the squash bug, lygus bug, harlequin bug, chinch bug, and blister beetle.

SAFFLOWER   (*Carthamus tinctorius*)

This hardy annual, which is ornamental when grown in clusters, grows from one to three feet tall and has dark green leaves and orange flowers. The seeds yield an oil which is used in salad and cooking oils as well as in paints and varnishes. The flowers are used as a dye for silk, an ingredient in rouge, and a colorant and flavoring for gravies and soups. Because of its use as a saffron adulterant, the plant is often called false saffron.

Safflower is a native of the mountainous regions of southwest Asia and Ethiopia, and is extensively grown in India. It is a valuable commercial crop of the western Great Plains and north central California.

Safflower seed should be sown directly into the bed in April since seedlings do not transplant well. In some areas, safflower is seeded by airplane and later the seed is disked

into the soil. The plants will be ready for harvest in August, approximately 120 days after planting.

In California, safflower is grown in rotation with rice on high water-table land, but it also grows well in poor, dry soil, in full sun. Yield is from 350 to 1,500 pounds per acre on dry land, up to 3,400 pounds per acre on irrigated land.

SAFFRON CROCUS   *See* CROCUS

SAGE   (*Salvia*)

Sage represents a large genus comprising more than 500 species of annuals and perennials of the Mint family. They are distributed all over the world and are cultivated as herbs for their medicinal, culinary and ornamental value.

Sage leaves grow in pairs on square stems. They are usually oval or lance shaped and toothed, and are sometimes hairy or woolly. Flowers grow in spikes and are red, blue, white, purple, or pale yellow. Usually members of the genus grown for their flowers are known as salvias or flowering sage, and those for seasoning or medicine, as sage.

Sage was once considered a panacea for illnesses, particularly those linked with aging. Sage was believed to be a cure for tuberculosis and a treatment for snakebites. Its generic name, *salvia,* means "health" or "salvation." Native to the Mediterranean, the herb was introduced to Europe by Roman legionnaires. Later, it became a valuable export item in East-West trading.

Many fine varieties are half-hardy, and can be carried over winter if roots are lifted and stored away from frosts. Some are hardy in most parts of the United States, while others must be treated as annuals throughout the country.

The sage used for seasoning (*S. officinalis*) is a hardy perennial or partly woody shrub with woolly white leaves and shorter spikes of purple, blue or white flowers.

Planting and Culture: *S. officinalis* makes its best growth in a rich clay loam with a good supply of nitrogen, but it will grow in a wide range of soils if they have a reasonably high nitrogen content and are well drained. In the northern states sage will not survive winter if soils are wet when they freeze. Sage will withstand temperatures lower than 0°F. (−17.78°C.) if protected by snow or a mulch of leaves or straw.

Sage may be propagated by stem cuttings, which can be rooted easily in sand and then planted 12 to 18 inches apart in rows three feet apart. For larger plantings, seed may be drilled directly in the field about ¾ inch deep in rows three feet apart. Sow seed early in spring, as soon as the ground is warm. A few plants set in a corner of the garden will furnish enough leaves for ordinary family use.

Harvesting: The leaves should be harvested before the plant blooms. The tops should be spread on screens and dried in a well-ventilated room away from direct sunlight. When they are thoroughly dry, remove the stems and pack the leaves in closed containers.

Use the leaves sparingly to season stuffing

Sage leaves reach their peak in flavor and aroma just before the plant blooms.

for pork, ducks or geese. The powdered leaves rubbed on the outside of fresh pork give it a flavor resembling that of stuffed turkey. Crush the fresh leaves and blend them with cottage or cream cheese. Steep the dried leaves for tea.

Although most uses of this herb are culinary, sage is still listed as an official medicine in the United States. It is used as a wash for treating mouth sores and as a gargle for sore throats. Sage tea is also a home remedy for fever and even nervous headaches.

See also HERB, SALVIA.

SAGITTARIA

A genus of perennial water or bog plants of the Water-plantain family, sagittaria has arrow-shaped leaves and clusters of white, buttercuplike flowers in summer. Flowers are male or female, both growing on the same plant. Plants can be grown from seed in boxes and sunk in ponds or aquariums, or grown from dividing the rootstock in late fall or early spring.

S. Engelmanniana is native to the central and northern Atlantic coast. It grows to 1½ feet, with eight-inch arrow-shaped leaves.

S. latifolia grows to four feet, with dark green leaves and 1½-inch flowers. The large starchy roots were used as potatoes by the Indians and called wapatoo.

Giant arrowhead (*S. montevidensis*) is a six-foot-tall tropical native. Flowers are two inches or more across, with brown purple spots at the base of the petals.

Old-world arrowhead (*S. sagittifolia*) grows to four feet, with arrow-shaped leaves and flowers spotted purple at the base. The roots are eaten in the Orient. Flore Pleno is a double-flowered variety.

SAGO PALM   (*Cycas revoluta*)

Native to Japan, the sago palm grows to a height of ten feet and is crowned with a whorl of five-foot leaves. Only one whorl is produced a year, but with care the old leaves may be made to last for two or three years. The foliage is dark green. The individual leaves are long and flat, and composed of a long central stem to which the pinnae are attached in two rows. When the new leaves come out,

they are upright and unroll just like the fiddle-head fern fronds but as they grow older they gradually drop until they are horizontal or slightly drooping.

The sago is easy to grow, and succeeds well in the varying temperature of a living room and in almost any well-drained soil. It does best in a rather warm greenhouse and should be given plenty of water. It is much used for funeral wreaths.

SAINFOIN   See ONOBRYCHIS

SAINT AUGUSTINE GRASS
See LAWN

SAINT-JOHN'S-BREAD
See CAROB

SAINT-JOHN'S-WORT
(*Hypericum*)

Several members of the genus *Hypericum* are called Saint-John's-wort. Most are weedy, roadside perennials often grown in rock gardens and naturalized borders. Common Saint-John's-wort (*H. perforatum*) has yellow flowers and black-spotted leaves. It blooms throughout the summer in all parts of North America. Less familiar species include great Saint-John's-wort (*H. pyramiditum*) which grows to about four feet and pale Saint-John's-wort (*H. ellipticum*) which is found in marshes and waterways throughout the North.

The Saint-John's-worts are surrounded with legends that go back to the days of witchcraft. At that time, it was believed that hypericum collected on Saint John's Eve (June 24) offered protection against witches and evil spirits. The plant was also valued in medicine. An infusion of one ounce of the herb to a pint of boiling water was given to help treat lung and urinary disorders. The plant was also used in treating battle wounds.

Common Saint-John's-wort is easily grown in dry, light soil and part shade. Propagation is by seed or division.

SAINTPAULIA
See AFRICAN VIOLETS

SALAL (*Gaultheria Shallon*)

The salal is an evergreen shrub which grows from one to five feet tall with long racemes of white or pink flowers and small purple black fruits. It is hardy from Washington south to central California. Salal does best in an acid sandy soil and in a partly shaded location. Propagation is by seed, layers, suckers, root division, or cuttings of half-ripened wood under glass.

Another member of this genus is wintergreen (*G. procumbens*), a low-growing evergreen that produces red fruit.

See also WINTERGREEN.

SALINE SOIL

Saline soil is another name for white alkaline soil. Under hot, arid conditions, soluble salts may accumulate on the surface of soils whenever the groundwater comes within a few feet of the surface. During dry periods the surface of these soils is covered with a salt crust, which is dissolved in the soil water each time the soil is wetted.

Saline soils have an uneven surface covered with small puffed-up salty spots a few inches high. Salts congregate in the areas that remain moist longest after the onset of drought.

Saline soils normally show no difference in structure among the several horizons. This would indicate a resistance to change and weathering in these soils. Usually they are low in humus, because the natural vegetation cannot make much annual growth on them. The salts usually present in the soil are the sulfates and chlorides of sodium and calcium, though nitrates occur in a few places, and magnesium sometimes constitutes an appreciable proportion of the cations. Under these conditions, the pH of the soil is below 8.5.

The excess salts are soluble and can be leached out of the soil with no rise in pH, but the leaching water must be low in sodium.

See also ALKALI SOILS.

SALIX *See* WILLOW

SALPIGLOSSIS *See* PAINTED-TONGUE

SALSIFY (*Tragopogon porrifolius*)

Salsify is a hardy biennial, native to the Mediterranean and southern England, and naturalized as a wayside weed in the United States and Canada. The nutritious root is cooked like carrots or beets. The plant grows three to four feet high, with a white-skinned, deep taproot.

The Spanish oyster plant (*Scolymus hispanicus*) is often called golden thistle and is similar to salsify. Even better in flavor, some people say, is black salsify (*Scorzonera his-*

panica) which has a black-skinned root. Its leaves are often used in salads.

Salsify earned the names "oyster plant" and "vegetable oyster" from the oysterlike flavor of its root.

Since salsify is a long-season crop, its seed should be sown as early in the spring as possible. Sow it in deep, rich soil, such as sandy loam and provide generous applications of well-rotted manure. Plant the seed ½ inch deep in rows 18 inches apart, and thin young plants to four inches apart. One ounce of seed will plant a 50-foot row, and produce sufficient salsify roots for the average family.

Frosts improve the root's flavor and texture. Dig part of the crop in the fall, and store it like turnips in the cellar for winter use. The remainder of the crop can be dug in the spring. If the winters are not too harsh, a mulch will let you dig the roots as you need them during the cold months.

SALT HAY

Hay obtained from lowlands near bodies of saltwater, and commonly used as a mulch, is called salt hay.

See also MULCH.

SALTY SOIL   *See* SALINE SOIL

SALVIA

Salvia is the name generally given to sage when it is cultivated for ornamental rather than for medicinal or culinary purposes. Many species are hardy, but the best-known salvia is the scarlet sage (*S. splendens*), a tropical perennial used as an annual in beds and borders. Its brilliant red blossoms appear in early summer and continue until frost.

Planting and Culture: Seed of all species is usually started indoors in February or March, and plants set outside after the last frost. Because the seed requires both warmth and light to germinate, it should be sown shallowly in flats. Keep the flats in a warm (75°F. [23.89°C.]), light place until germination occurs. Transplant the seedlings before they become overcrowded. When the young plants are six to eight inches high, pinch them back to encourage lush growth.

Hardy perennial species can be direct-seeded in late spring or autumn. Planted before mid-April, the plants will flower their first year. Once established, they will thrive for many years. Some species may require spacing.

Not all of the hardy salvias are reliably perennial in the North. Some must be replaced every two or three years. Salvias are most likely to die out in heavy soils that stay wet in winter, so plant them in well-drained soil in full sun. Most are quite drought resistant. In areas where there is no continuous snow cover, mulch the plants in winter.

Types and Varieties: Besides the popular red varieties of *S. splendens,* there are white and pastel shades of rose, purple and salmon available. The paler colors tend to burn out in full sun, so grow them in shade.

The mealy-cup sage (*S. farinacea*) is another warm-climate perennial grown as an annual in the North. It can grow to four feet in rich soil, and has thin spikes of small blue or white flowers. It is at its best in late summer and early fall. This salvia is more subtle than showy and looks best planted in large masses to give a cool, restful effect. It flowers better in sun than in shade.

S. pratensis is very showy, producing three-foot sprays of lavender blue flowers in June from a basal rosette of leaves. It tends to be biennial, so keep some seed-grown replacements in reserve.

S. Jurisicii is a very hardy dwarf from the Balkans which forms mats of foliage and grows eight inches high. The violet blue flowers are produced from June through summer if dead flower heads are removed regularly.

Many gardeners consider *S.* x *superba* to be the best of all perennial salvias. It is quite hardy, growing 2½ to three feet high and as wide. The glowing red purple flower spikes are produced all summer if the plants are not allowed to go to seed.

See also SAGE.

SAMAN   (*Samanea Saman*)

In the United States, the saman, also called zamang or raintree, can be grown only in southernmost Florida, although it is a very popular shade tree everywhere in the tropics. It grows 50 to 80 feet tall and very wide, often spreading to 100 feet. Its vast number of leaflets fold up at night or just before rain. The showy yellow flowers are borne in heavy round clusters, with the pink stamens extending beyond these. The pulpy fruit pods may be eight inches long, and in some regions give the tree the name of monkeypod. Propagation is by seed.

SAMBAC   (*Jasminum Sambac*)

Sambac or Arabian jasmine has shiny leaves and hairy branches and is an extremely tender climbing shrub. Although it cannot withstand frost, it makes an excellent conservatory plant. It bears clusters of very fragrant white flowers that turn lavender with age. Like the other jasmines, it prefers full sun, and a fertile, friable soil.

SANDBUR   (*Cenchrus pauciflorus*)

Because this grass plant produces a bur with spines stout enough to penetrate the flesh of man and animals, causing punctures which lead to inflammation and infection, it is very obnoxious. At beaches, the burs mix with sand along the shore and puncture the skin of swimmers or sunbathers. They also adhere to clothing and get entangled in the fur of domestic animals.

The grass flower is enclosed by a hairy, spiny bur which is composed of many bristles. Each bristle holds backward-curving barbs that enable the spines to work into flesh. Seeds in the bur can live in soil for at least four years and probably longer.

Since the sandbur is an annual plant, reproduction occurs only from seeds contained in the burs. Seeds are spread by burs carried on man or animals or floated along the shore from one place to another.

Sandbur plants can be eradicated by burning the burs with a flame burner. Because burs are produced so close to the ground, mowing is ineffective.

SANDY SOIL

Sandy soil is composed of large, irregular particles that permit water to enter between them and pass through the soil so rapidly that it dries out quickly. Sandy soils are quite susceptible to leaching. The addition of organic matter is especially important in improving the structure of sandy soils.

See also ORGANIC MATTER.

SANSEVIERIA

Commonly called bowstring hemp, mother-in-law's-tongue and snake plant, this genus of perennial herbs belonging to the Lily family is easy to grow and tolerant of average household conditions. Some kinds can be grown outside in the South.

Sansevieria prefers an all-purpose soil and moderate light, though even dim light is sufficient for growth. The plant should be thoroughly watered and allowed to dry out before being rewatered, and the leaves should be sponged frequently. Native species produce clusters of pale flowers on slender stalks, but cultivated species seldom flower. Propagation is by division of the fleshy root or by leaf cuttings set in sand.

S. zeylanica, a native of Ceylon, is the most often cultivated species. The 2½-foot leaves, which are concave in the middle, are transversely striped with light green or gray, and the green white flowers are 1½ inches long.

S. hyacinthoides, an African native, grows to 1½ feet. Its flat leaves are 3½ inches across, margined with yellow and banded crosswise with lighter green. The flowers are green white, 1½ inches long and fragrant.

S. cylindrica, also from Africa, is a five-foot species with thick cylindrical leaves that are striped and banded with dark green. The flowers are white or pink tinged.

SAP

The juices of a plant, specifically the liquids which circulate through its vascular tissues, are known as sap. The term may be used to designate the liquids that enter through the roots and circulate upward to the leaves, or to describe the liquid that returns from the leaves, carrying sugars to the roots, flowers or seeds.

SAPINDUS   *See* SOAPBERRY

SAPODILLA   *See* SAPOTA

SAPONARIA

This genus of the Pink family is commonly called soapwort because its stems and leaves form a soaplike lather when crushed and mixed with water. Hardy annuals or perennials that are native to the North Temperate Zone, soapworts produce clusters of showy white, pink or rose-colored flowers that are long lasting when cut. They are good choices for the border or rock garden and are easily propagated by seed or division. Full sun and a well-drained garden soil are best for soapworts.

Bouncing Bet or soapwort (*S. officinalis*) is a perennial that grows to about three feet. It produces dense clusters of one-inch pink or white flowers that bloom from May to September.

S. Ocymoides, a trailing nine-inch perennial, is a rock garden favorite whose purple flowers bloom all summer. Varieties produce flowers ranging in color from white to crimson.

SAPOTA (*Manilkara Zapota*)

This tropical American tree is variously classified as *Pouteria Sapota, Sapota achras* and *Achras Zapota*. Common names include nispero, nazeberry and sapodilla. It yields a plumlike brown fruit called the sapodilla. An evergreen growing to 100 feet, the sapota has stiff, glossy leaves and small white flowers. It is best grown in frost-free regions in rich sandy loam. Propagation is by seed, budding or grafting, but seeds produce inferior trees.

The bark of the sapota yields a milky sap used in the production of chewing gum. Its hard, durable wood was once used in woodworking.

SAPROPHYTE

A saprophyte is a plant which lives upon dead and decaying plants. It has no chlorophyll so cannot manufacture its own sugar and starch, and must obtain them from its host. It does this with the help of the bacteria and fungi which are involved in the decomposition of decaying plant matter.

SASSAFRAS

The sassafras is a handsome ornamental tree of the Laurel family. It has an aromatic bark and clusters of pale yellow flowers that appear in April and May before or at the same time as the light green leaves. Dark blue plumlike fruits follow soon after. Common sassafras (*S. albidum*), which grows to a height of 60

The sassafras tree can be immediately recognized by its smooth, lobed leaves, its aromatic bark and bright green twigs.

feet or more, is generally cultivated from Maine to Michigan and south to Florida and Texas.

Sassafras trees prefer a warm, sunny spot and ordinary garden loam. Propagation is by seed or suckers, and transplanting is usually done while the tree is still young since with age it develops long taproots.

The root bark is often infused in water and taken as a tea or spring tonic. Scientists have found that safrole, an aromatic oil and the major chemical constituent of sassafras root bark, is carcinogenic, so the tea should be avoided.

SATINFLOWER   *See* SISYRINCHIUM

SATINPOD   *See* HONESTY

SAVORY   (*Satureja*)

Both summer and winter savory are herbs especially prized by particular cooks and companion planters. Like that of many other herbs, savory's primary use has shifted over the years from medicinal to culinary.

Savory is also as important in the garden as it is in the kitchen. Summer savory is considered an excellent companion plant for onions and green beans, because it aids their growth

Leaves and stems of savory can be used fresh throughout the season, but for drying they should be cut when the flowers begin to appear.

while providing an attractive border.

Savory is useful for flavoring many foods. Winter savory is an ingredient of several liqueurs and can be added to various poultry and vegetable dishes. Summer savory, however, has many more culinary uses. Its minty flavor is welcomed whenever stuffings, canned vegetables or salads are being prepared. It also makes a pleasant tea when one ounce of the herb is infused in one pint of boiled water.

Summer Savory: Summer savory (*S. hortensis*) is an ancient herb, native to the Mediterranean region. Virgil, the ancient beekeeper and poet, grew savory for his bees because it enhanced the flavor of their honey. The herb was used to treat asthma, digestive disorders, and even deafness. The Romans enjoyed its hot, peppery flavor in sauces and vinegar. Summer savory is a member of the Mint family and is generally cultivated as an annual in gardens in this country. It grows well under a wide range of soil and climatic conditions and generally reaches a height of about 18 inches.

It is grown easily from seeds sown early in spring in rows three feet apart. Plant the seeds ½ inch deep at the rate of ten to 12 to the foot. The plants will form a solid row if spaced three to four inches apart. Only a few feet of row are needed to furnish enough of the herb for family use.

The tender leaves and stems may be used anytime during the season, but for drying, six to eight inches of the top growth should be cut when blooming begins. Sometimes two or more crops can be harvested in one season.

The top growth cut from the plants may be tied in small bunches or spread on screens or paper to dry. When thoroughly dry, the leaves should be stripped from the stems and stored in closed containers. Care should be taken to remove all small pieces of woody stems.

Winter Savory: A hardy perennial native to southern Europe, winter savory (*S. montana*) has small white or purple flowers and grows to one foot tall. It is often used in the perennial bed or border as a low hedge or accent plant.

Savory prefers a light, sandy soil and full sun. Seeds can be sown directly in the garden early in spring or in a cold frame or window box, and the plants transplanted to the garden when two or three inches high. Several plants set 16 to 18 inches apart should provide ample leaves for flavoring.

The tender tops and branches can be cut for use during the season in the same manner as summer savory or thyme. The leaves and flowering tops to be dried for winter use should be cut at the beginning of the flowering period. The herb can be hung in small bunches or spread on screens to dry. Remove them from the stems and store for use as needed.

See also HERB.

SAWDUST

Sawdust, the wood particles left over when wood is sawed, is useful to gardeners as a fine natural mulch and soil conditioner. Sawdust aerates the soil and increases its moisture-holding capacity. One of its major drawbacks, however, is its low-nitrogen content (about .1 percent). Overuse of fresh sawdust without also adding high-nitrogen materials may cause a nitrogen deficiency. Well-rotted sawdust can be used anywhere.

Sawdust is a valuable mulch if used intelligently. Raw sawdust is not manure or compost and cannot substitute for them. It should not be worked into the soil deeply.

Plant vegetable seeds in the usual way after the soil has been fertilized according to its needs. Then spread a band of sawdust about four inches wide and ¼ inch thick on top of the planted row. The mulch will help reduce crusting of the soil and allow the young seedlings to push through easily.

When the plants are about two inches high, apply a one-inch layer of sawdust over the entire area between the rows. Weeds more than one inch tall should be killed by cultivating or hoeing before applying the mulch. Weeds less than an inch tall will be smothered. Weeds that grow through the mulch can easily be pulled out by hand when the ground is moist after a rain. Do not cultivate; this will mix the sawdust with the soil and destroy its value as a mulch.

Some people are afraid that the continued application of sawdust will sour their soil, that is, make it too acidic. A very comprehensive study of sawdust and wood chips made from 1949 to 1954 by the Connecticut Experiment Station reported no instance in which sawdust made the soil more acid. It is possible, though, that sawdust used on the highly alkaline soils of the western United States would help to make the soil neutral, a welcome effect.

In soils of low fertility sawdust mulches may cause nitrogen deficiency. Watch your plants carefully during the growing season. If they become light green or yellowish in color, side-dress with a high-nitrogen fertilizer such as cottonseed meal, blood meal, compost, manure, or tankage.

Sawdusts are receiving attention as high-carbon material for use in composting sewage sludge. Sludge/sawdust compost is a particularly balanced soil conditioner.

See also FERTILIZER, MULCH.

SAWFLY

See BRAMBLE FRUITS, INSECT CONTROL

SAXIFRAGE   *(Saxifraga)*

This genus includes a large and varied number of perennial plants which can be grown in the rock or wall garden or on rocky slopes or ledges. Most form a rosette of basal leaves, either fleshy or tufted, sending up slender sprays of pink, white, purple, or yellow flowers whose sepals, petals and stamens are in multiples of five. In the wild, the rosettes spread by offsets into broad mats or mounds, much in the manner of the familiar hen-and-chickens.

Planting and Culture: Seed may be sown in late summer in protected beds or cold frames. Sow it on a layer of fine gravel covering a perfectly drained soil composed of half leaf mold and half gravel and sharp sand. Clumps may be increased from their offsets, which root easily in the same mixture used in the seedbed. After becoming established, they need little winter protection in most climates. Most prefer a gritty, gravel soil derived from limestone. A mulch of limestone chips helps protect the rosettes from excess moisture. Saxifrage means "rock breaker," and the plants prefer to grow in rock crevices. Few can endure the full force of the summer sun, so they should be planted in a lightly shaded location or on a north or east slope. They must be watered in the heat of summer, but, in winter, water should never stand on the roots or crown.

Types: The encrusted saxifrages form tight rosettes of silvery leaves with white encrustations along the edges. *S. paniculata* is typical of this group. It has small white flowers, speckled purple or crimson, on 20-inch stems above five-inch rosettes of silvery leaves. Many hybrids with leaves and flowers of various colors have been developed.

The mossy saxifrages form mats of finely divided, soft evergreen leaves which send up eight-inch stems bearing many small white or pink flowers in spring. These will do well in the lightly shaded wild garden if the soil is very well drained and enriched with leaf mold. To keep the clumps from dying out in the center after flowering, work in leaf mold mixed with sharp sand. *S. caespitosa* is one of the best mossy saxifrages. It has leaves divided three or more times and produces eight-inch sprays of white flowers.

Typical of a group of tufted saxifrages is *S. Burserana,* which forms cushions of pointed, stiff gray leaves. The solitary white flowers measure about one inch in diameter and bloom very early. There are many named hybrids, many of which are suited to the dish garden as well as the open rock garden.

One of the more easily grown saxifrages is london pride (*S. umbrosa*), which does well in woods soil in part shade. The rosettes of dark green scalloped leaves form clumps which produce one-foot sprays of light pink flowers in summer.

Early saxifrage (*S. virginiensis*), a native of rocky eastern woodlands and meadows, is reliably perennial in the wild garden. It is adapted to a temperate climate and needs no lime. The rounded green leaves are reddish beneath, and the numerous white, fragrant flowers are carried on substantial, rather hairy stalks in early spring.

Strawberry geranium (*S. stolonifera*) is almost the only saxifrage grown as a house plant. It is also called mother-of-thousands and Aaron's-beard. The kidney-shaped leaves are marked white on top and red underneath, and grow from a low rosette that sends up white flower sprays in the summer. Propagation is by the strawberrylike runners.

SCABIOSA

Also known as mourning bride and pincushion flowers, these members of the Teasel family are easy to grow in a well-drained garden soil and full sun. The flowers, which have long, stiff stems and are long lasting when cut, come in colors ranging from white through yellow, blue, rose, red, maroon, and dark purple. Good in the border or cutting garden, scabiosas generally grow from 1½ to three feet tall.

Annual species are propagated by seed, which is sown outdoors in mid-spring in a sunny spot where the plants are to stand. Sometimes seed is started indoors in March and the plants set out in May. Perennial species can be propagated by root division in early spring after two or three years' growth. Young plants should be pinched back to encourage bushiness and flower heads should be kept picked to extend the bloom period.

S. atropurpurea, an annual growing to 2½ feet, has white, pink, red, or purple flowers that bloom from July to September.

S. caucasica is a hardy perennial growing to 1½ feet. It has grayish foliage and delicately tinted white, blue or lavender blue flowers that bloom from July to frost.

SCABWORT   *See* ELECAMPANE

SCALE INSECTS

Scales are small, prolific insects that suck the juices of plants. The young are either born live or hatched from eggs under the mother's shell. Clustered on the leaves, bark or fruit of plants, they appear as tiny, immovable dots. Some species resemble overlapped mollusk shells and others have a soft, cottony appearance. Plants infested with scale become stunted, pale and, where fruits are affected, deformed.

The most injurious scale insect is the San Jose scale, a small black or brown insect that attacks orchard trees. The oystershell scale, which is gray brown, attacks roses, lilacs and peonies as well as other shrubs and trees. Black scale produces a destructive sooty mold on olive and citrus fruit trees. The gray white scurfy scale attacks elms, willows and dogwoods.

Scraping the bark of affected trees will reduce an infestation, and dormant-oil sprays are often used to smother scales which have spread over a large area.

See also HOUSE PLANTS, INSECT CONTROL.

SCALLION

A scallion is actually a young onion pulled before the bulb has formed. It is also a name popularly used for young "bunch" or green onions which are sown thickly and harvested when of edible size.

Planting and Culture: Scallions can be grown from sets or from seed. A simple way to grow green onions from sets, and the method employed by many home gardeners, is to plant bulb sets early in the spring and to pull the green onions when they attain desired size. Sets should be placed three to four inches apart in rows 12 to 18 inches apart. Sets may also be planted in the fall early enough to become established before the ground freezes. Scallions are perennial and can be overwintered with some protection such as a loose mulch of leaves or straw.

Scallion seed may be planted in early spring or, if given winter protection, in late fall. Fresh seed should be planted thickly, in rows 12 to 18 inches apart, and covered with ½ inch of sifted compost. One packet of seed will sow a 25-foot row.

Scallions prefer a moderately acid soil (pH 6 to 6.5) that is rich in available plant food. They will tolerate a slight amount of shade, but prefer open, moist, sunny conditions. During dry weather, sufficient water should be provided to supply the natural requirements of the plants. This is best done by a thorough, slow flooding of the area during the cool of the evening.

Harvesting: Green bunch onions are harvested as soon as they are eight to ten inches tall and ½ inch thick. Sixty days is the usual maturation period for scallions. Several pullings are usually made. Remove the largest plants each time, leaving the others to develop. Before eating or cooking, the roots are trimmed and the outer skin is peeled off, leaving the stem clean and white.

Varieties: Southport White Globe is widely used for the production of green bunch onions from seed. It requires less peeling than most varieties. Hardy White Bunching, Yellow Globe Danvers, Long White Bunching, and Evergreen White Bunching are also popular varieties.

See also ONION.

SCARBOROUGH LILY
See VALLOTA

SCARIFICATION

Seeds of plants such as apple, beet, canna, carrot, celery, Kentucky coffee tree, honey locust, impatiens, moonflower, morning-glory, pansy, parsley, parsnip, sweet pea, and the stone fruits have very hard coats which must be bruised before germination can take place. The process by which the coat is altered and made permeable to gases and water is called scarification. In nature, scarification is the natural result of the seed's exposure to prolonged periods of freezing and thawing or to wind and rain. When the gardener or seedsman gathers seeds at the end of a season and places them in storage, he eliminates this period of natural weathering and must find other ways to break down the seed coat. Large seeds such as certain nuts and stone fruits can be tapped with a hammer. Others, such as beet and Kentucky coffee tree, benefit from a quick hot water treatment in which boiling water is poured over them. Pea seed can be placed between damp towels and kept in a warm spot for a few days before planting. There are also a number of mechanical aids which may be used to file or scratch the surface of the seed coat.

SCARLET LIGHTNING
See LYCHNIS

SCHINUS

The members of this small genus of resinous trees are also known as peppertrees. They are grown mostly for their decorative fruit. Leaves are compound and alternate, flowers appear in small white clusters, and the fruit is a small purple, pink, red, or white berrylike drupe. Male and female blossoms appear on different trees. Two species grown in California south of San Francisco are the California peppertree (*S. molle*) growing to 20 feet, with rose red fruit; and the Brazilian peppertree (*S. terebinthifolius*) also called Christmasberry tree for its bright red fruit.

SCHISANDRA

Members of a genus of ornamental woody climbers belonging to the Magnolia family, schisandras have bright green leaves and axillary clusters of white, pink or red flowers. Most species are dioecious, and a vine of each sex must be planted to produce the orange or scarlet berrylike fruit which ripens in late summer. Schisandras will grow from ten to 20 feet tall if given a moist sandy loam and partial shade. Propagation is by seed, greenwood cuttings under glass, layering, and suckers.

S. chinensis, the only species hardy in the North, grows to 25 feet and has dark green leaves, pink white dioecious flowers and deep red berries. *S. coccinea* grows from South Carolina to East Texas. Its monoecious flowers are crimson and its berries scarlet.

SCHIZANTHUS
See BUTTERFLY FLOWER

SCHLUMBERGERA
See THANKSGIVING CACTUS

SCILLA

Sometimes called squill, this small bulbous perennial of the Lily family is easily and quickly cultivated and self-sows freely. It is especially adapted for borders and rockeries, and is among the very first to bloom in early spring. The broad leaves are grasslike, and the blue, rose or white flowers are borne in clusters at the top of naked stems.

The Spanish bluebells and wood hyacinths are actually members of the endymion genus, but are often confused with scillas. They bloom at the same time as Darwin tulips, in May.

Plant bulbs in early autumn about three inches deep in humusy, well-drained soil. Fertilize with bone meal or dried sludge. Bulb offsets are taken after the foliage has withered.

The early-blooming squills include *S. bifolia,* which produces deep blue flowers very early in spring; *S. siberica,* whose Prussian blue flowers bloom with chionodoxa in April; and *S. tubergeniana,* with silvery white to blue flowers. All these grow four to six inches tall, and do well in full sun or light shade.

SCION

A scion or cion is a detached plant shoot prepared for use in grafting. It has one or more buds. Inserted in a rootstock, it reproduces the tree or shrub from which it was taken, rather than the tree or shrub whose root was used.

See also GRAFTING.

TREES AND SHRUBS FOR SCREENING

Plant	Botanical Name	Height (ft.)	Width (ft.)
DECIDUOUS			
Aralia, five-leaved	*Acanthopanax sieboldianus*	9	6
Barberry, Japanese	*Berberis Thunbergii*	5	4
Barberry, mentor	*Berberis mentorensis*	6	6
Birch, European white	*Betula pendula*	30	5
Buckthorn, common	*Rhamnus cathartica*	12	6
Chokeberry	*Aronia* spp.	12	8
Crab, Siberian	*Malus baccata* cv. 'Columnaris'	15	10
Euonymus, compact winged	*Euonymus alata* cv. 'Compacta'	6	4
Euonymus, European	*Euonymus europaea*	12	8
Hawthorn, cockspur	*Crataegus cuneata*	5	4
Hawthorn, Washington	*Crataegus Phaenopyrum*	25	10
Honeysuckle, Tatarian	*Lonicera tatarica*	8	8
Hornbeam, American	*Carpinus caroliniana*	18	5
Hornbeam, European	*Carpinus Betulus*	20	6
Lilac, Chinese	*Syringa* x *chinensis*	12	15
Lilac, common	*Syringa vulgaris*	20	15
Locust, erect black	*Robinia Pseudoacacia*	25	10
Magnolia, ash	*Magnolia Ashei*	25	15
Maple, amur	*Acer Ginnala*	20	20
Maple, Norway	*Acer platanoides* cv. 'Erectum'	30	8
Ninebark, mountain	*Physocarpus malvaceus*	5	5
Oak, English	*Quercus robus* cv. 'Pyramidalis'	50	10
Poplar, Lombardy	*Populus nigra* cv. 'Italica'	90	4
Privet, common	*Ligustrum vulgare*	8	3
Viburnum, arrowwood	*Viburnum acerifolium*	6	5
EVERGREEN			
Arborvitae, American	*Thuja occidentalis*	30	5
Bay, common	*Laurus nobilis*	40	15
Fir, white	*Abies concolor*	100	30
Hemlock, Canada	*Tsuga canadensis*	80	30
Hemlock, compact Carolina	*Tsuga caroliniana* cv. 'Compacta'	50	15
Holly, Japanese	*Ilex crenata*	10	6
Juniper, columnar Chinese	*Juniperus chinensis* cv. 'Columnaris'	60	15
Laurel, mountain	*Kalmia latifolia*	6	6
Pine, white	*Pinus strobus*	30	10
Spruce, Japanese	*Picea Maximowiczii*	75	20
Yew, Hatfield	*Taxus* x *media* cv. 'Hatfieldii'	10	8
Yew, Hicks	*Taxus cuspidata* cv. 'Hicksii'	10	8

SCOTCH THISTLE
(*Onopordum Acanthium*)

The prickly Scotch thistle is occasionally planted in sunny borders where the soil is well drained but not very rich. It grows five to eight feet high and needs plenty of room. The leaves which may be as long as a foot are silvery and tipped with spines. The purple flower heads are big and round shaped. Two other varieties, *O. bracteatum* and *O. tauricum,* grow about six feet tall, with white or pale purple flowers and yellowish spines. All are biennials and should be propagated by sowing the seed ⅛ inch deep in spring.

SCREEN PLANTS

Screen plantings provide privacy by screening out objectionable features of the landscape. They also may serve as a windbreak.

Where space is limited, screening should be provided by a single variety of tree or shrub. On the other hand, if more room is available, a screen planting of a variety of subjects will make a more interesting landscape picture.

Listed on the opposite page are plants recommended for screen planting. Narrow trees will require less trimming to keep them within bounds. Wider trees and shrubs should be used only where space is not limited.

See also EVERGREEN, LANDSCAPING, SHRUBS.

SCREW PINE   *See* PANDANUS

SCROPHULARIACEAE

This large family, also called the Figwort family, contains about 200 genera and 2,600 species, including herbs, shrubs and a few trees, the majority of which grow in temperate regions. The flowers are generally distinguished by their five petals joined to form two lips around a tubular calyx and a united corolla. There are usually four stamens, two long and two short.

Prominent members of the Scrophulariaceae are foxglove, snapdragon, linaria, calceolaria, veronica, pentstemon, monkey flower, and mullein.

SCRUB PINE   *See* PINE

SCUTELLARIA   *See* SKULLCAP

SEA BUCKTHORN
(*Hippophae rhamnoides*)

Brought into this country during colonial days, this shrub or small tree is noted for its gray foliage and numerous orange yellow berries, which ripen in September and persist throughout the winter. Its inconspicuous yellow flowers appear in April.

Most plants reach a height of about 15 to 30 feet, and are erect and spiny branched, with a rounded top. Sea buckthorn is often recommended for seashore planting because of its tolerance to wind and salt spray and its ability to stabilize dunes. When grown in a well-drained sandy soil, the sea buckthorn will produce numerous suckers and remain shrubby. In better soil it will grow into a small tree.

Propagation is by seed, root cuttings and layering. The home gardener, however, will do best to purchase sea buckthorn plants from a nursery. In order to have an annual crop of berries, it is necessary to grow both male and female plants. Pruning is rarely necessary.

SEA DAHLIA   (*Coreopsis maritima*)

A member of the Daisy family and a native California plant, the sea dahlia bears large, bright yellow flowers in early spring and is very showy when planted in masses. In California, the bloom period extends from February to May. A bushy, two-foot perennial that annually dies back almost to the ground, the sea dahlia is frequently treated as an annual. The top is trimmed back after flowering or, in some cases, the plant is replaced with a later-blooming annual. It grows readily from seed, which can be sown either directly in the garden or in flats for later transplanting. Sea dahlias grow well in sandy, well-drained soil, and are not usually troubled by insects.

See also COREOPSIS.

SEA GRAPE   (*Coccoloba Uvifera*)

These tropical trees are grown along the coasts of Florida and California and in greenhouses farther north. They should be given a moist, rich sandy soil and high temperature. The sea grape, which grows to 20 feet, produces clusters of small, fragrant white flowers and edible purple fruits that are used in pre-

serves. The glossy, leathery leaves are about seven inches long and five inches wide. Propagation is by seed, layering or cuttings of ripe wood.

SEA HOLLY   *See* ERYNGIUM

SEA KALE   (*Crambe maritima*)

Sea kale, or scurvygrass, is a large, coarse plant with blue green leaves and clusters of white flowers. Unlike the closely related colewort (*C. cordifolia*), which is grown for ornament, this plant is raised for its tender young shoots which are blanched early in spring and used as a vegetable similar to asparagus.

Sea kale thrives in rich, well-manured soil. It can be propagated by seeds or root cuttings. If seeds are used, plant them one inch deep in a well-prepared bed. Thin them to stand five to six inches apart in the row and, the following spring, move them to the permanent bed. If cuttings are used, plant them directly in their permanent location, spaced three feet apart. Root pieces should be four to five inches long.

Culture of sea kale is similar to that of rhubarb. Fertilize the beds each year and, at the close of the season, remove all dead leaves. Mulch the plant crowns with compost or manure.

The tender shoots can be harvested for a short period during the second season after plants are set in the permanent bed, but a full crop should not be cut until the plants are three or even four years old. When leaf shoots appear in the spring, hill-up the soil around the sprouts or invert a large flowerpot over them.

Shoots are cut when they are five to eight inches long.

SEA SQUILL   (*Urginea maritima*)

This half-hardy member of the Lily family is not commonly grown in the United States, although it is widely cultivated in the Mediterranean region for its medicinal value. A big, scaly bulb that prefers fairly mild temperatures, the sea squill bears small white flowers on foot-long racemes in the fall. Straplike leaves up to 18 inches long appear after the bloom period. In their native habitat, sea squills grow in sandy soil either inland or near the shore. They are sometimes called sea onions.

SEAWEED

The use of seaweed or kelp as a fertilizer dates back many centuries. In 1681 a royal decree regulated the conditions under which seaweed could be collected on the coast of France. The kinds that might be collected and the manner in which they should be used were specified. Recently, however, seaweed has been recognized as much more than a mere ingredient of compost heaps. Research indicates that seaweed has a chelating ability, and that it improves cation exchange in garden soil and releases locked-up minerals.

Seaweed has also been recognized for its ability to pass its high potash content on to potatoes, beets, cabbage, and other plants that thrive on large amounts of potash. The potash content of seaweed is twice that of barnyard manure.

Growth-producing hormones have also been discovered in ordinary seaweed. The growth stimulants gibberellin and auxin derived from seaweed are absorbed into the stomata of leaves, resulting in better plant growth and development.

Recent findings show that high concentrations of seaweed keep seedlings from becoming leggy. Mixed in with garden soil, it will keep plants from growing too large and make them easier to transplant.

Plants given seaweed show increased ability to withstand light frosts. Crop yields of tomatoes, sweet peppers and corn are increased as are the insect and disease resistances of these crops. The auxins in seaweed are even said to inhibit development of fusarium on tomatoes. Seaweed applications are also believed to control red spider mite infestation of orchard trees.

Seaweed is also valued by gardeners because it is free from weed seeds, insect eggs and plant diseases.

Types: Seaweeds used as fertilizers belong to two main groups found throughout the Northern Hemisphere. The first group consists of relatively small plants whose growth is usually dense. They are called rockweeds and grow on the rock bottoms between high and low water. They are easily collected by pulling or cutting from the rocks. There are innumerable rockweed species, but knobbed wrack and bladder wrack are the most common. Both plants are distinguished by air-filled vesicles which enable them to reach the surface when the tide comes in, and thus receive more light for photosynthesis.

The other group, sublittoral brown weeds known as laminaria, oarweeds or tangles, contains much larger plants which appear to have a root, a stem and a single large leaf. This similarity with land plants is very superficial for, in fact, these various parts do not function like their counterparts in land plants. Weed beds are often dense and growth is usually about 20 to 30 tons per acre. In May, the old growth is detached and cast onto the beaches and the plants develop a new frond. The detached fronds decay rapidly and should be collected as soon as possible for composting.

A third type, the giant kelp, grows off the coast of California. They are brown weeds and both annual and perennial types abound. Some of them exceed 200 feet in length. They shed their fronds between April and June and decay rapidly if the water temperature exceeds 76°F. (24.44°C.). Like other brown weeds, they are cast ashore during storms.

Composition: The chemical constitution of seaweeds is markedly different from that of the land plants. In general, land plants owe their rigidity to cellulose, whereas seaweeds contain only about 5 percent cellulose and owe their mechanical strength to alginic acid. The food reserve of land plants is starch; that of marine plants is laminarin. Mannitol takes the place of the sugars found in land plants. Alginic acid, laminarin and fucoidin are found only in seaweeds.

The most interesting feature of seaweeds is their substantial amounts of many different trace elements. Barium, chromium, lead, lithium, nickel, rubidium, silver, strontium, tin, and zinc have all been found in seaweed, along with traces of arsenic, boron, cobalt, molybdenum, and vanadium. The amount of these trace elements as well as the quantities of nitrogen, phosphorus and potassium varies widely from season to season. The chlorophyll content of seaweed is almost as high as that of alfalfa.

Uses: Alginic acid, the primary component of the fronds, is very susceptible to bacterial attack. This property is undoubtedly the basis of seaweed's activating energy in a compost heap. When only limited quantities are available, seaweed is best used as a compost accelerator. In two days, 200 pounds will heat to 100°F. (37.78°C.). When this is used as the core of a compost heap, the heap will be ready for use in six weeks. When only small quantities are available, the weed should be chopped and soaked overnight in hot water (one gallon to two pounds of weed). Pour this mixture over the compost heap. With dry, milled weed a temperature of 140°F. (60°C.) is sufficient, but fresh, chopped weed should be scalded and soaked initially at 160 to 180°F. (71.11 to 82.22°C.).

A number of commercial seaweed extract concentrates are available.

SECHIUM

S. edule is the only member of this genus of the Gourd family. It is a perennial tropical American vine of which almost every part is useful for food or forage. Its dark green or white fruit, commonly called chayote, choyote, christophine, or mirliton, is pear shaped, three or four inches long, and fleshy. Sechium can be creamed, baked or boiled and used in sauces, puddings and salads. It can be served as a cooked vegetable. It tastes somewhat like delicately flavored summer squash. The tubers, branches and young shoots are also used as vegetables, while all parts of the plant, including the leaves, make good fodder for livestock.

Planting and Culture: Since the vine thrives only in areas where frost does not penetrate the ground deeper than one inch, its culture is generally confined to the southernmost

The large, greenish fruit of the sechium plant can be eaten like squash or used in salads, puddings and sauces.

parts of the country. Sechiums are planted in the spring with harvest beginning at the end of the rainy season and lasting until frost. Each vine can be expected to produce between 50 and 100 fruits. The entire fruit is planted in a rich, well-drained soil with the stem slightly protruding above ground. Since the vines can grow up to 50 feet long, the plants should be spaced eight to ten feet apart and given a trellis or arbor for support. Large tuberous roots are formed during the second season.

Because the flowers are male or female and both kinds of flowers are not always found on the same vine, it may be necessary to plant more than one vine.

SECOND PLANTING
See SUCCESSION PLANTING,
VEGETABLE GARDENING

SEDGE PEAT   *See* PEAT

SEDIMENTARY ROCK

Sedimentary rocks are formed either by the precipitation of mineral matter from solution at or near the surface of the earth (rock salt and gypsum are common examples) or by the secretions of organisms. Limestone, coal and peat are examples of sedimentary rocks.

See also MINERAL ROCKS.

SEDUM

This genus of succulent perennials and annuals belongs to the Jade-plant family. It includes many common house and garden plants, including the stonecrops, gold moss and donkey's tail. Sedums are popular choices for low borders and rock and wall gardens because of their spreading habit, easy cultivation and resistance to drought. The star-shaped flowers are yellow, white, pink, red, or occasionally blue. The leaves are succulent.

Planting and Culture: Primary requirements for successfully growing sedums are good drainage and sun. They quickly rot when kept too wet or when they are in contact with rotting moist organic matter. If the soil is heavy or rich with humus, a layer of sand or fine gravel on top will help preserve the pulpy foliage. Propagation is by seed or cuttings. The stems with roots at their joints easily make new plants when moved. Cuttings may be made at any time in the year, though spring or summer, during the period of greatest growth, is best.

Types: *S. acre* is called gold moss, golden carpet or wall pepper. It has very small evergreen leaves and yellow flowers that bloom from late spring to midsummer. It grows to five

Because of their capacity for spreading and their excellent drought resistance, the sedums do especially well in rock and wall gardens.

inches and is best propagated by cuttings or by division of the plants. This is the common stonecrop which is used as a cover plant in rocky places. It thrives in poor, dry soils.

S. album is a dark green creeper that forms evergreen mats. Its white flowers bloom in midsummer.

S. brevifolium has rows of tiny leaves on four sides of the stem. Its white flowers bloom in July.

S. dasyphyllum is one of the best sedums. It makes small evergreen tufts with tiny flesh

pink and yellow flowers rising on slender stems above the foliage in July.

S. Ewersii is a somewhat tender evergreen which may die back but comes up again from the roots. It is 12 inches tall, with pink to lavender flowers in late summer. A dwarf form, Homophyllum, is available which grows only two inches high. Either may be grown as a house plant.

S. hispanicum is an annual or biennial species used in the rock garden. It has gray green foliage and pinkish flowers in midsummer.

S. kamtschaticum forms a dark green mat and has orange yellow flowers that appear in midsummer and continue through early fall. It is best propagated by seed or self-layering. The most common variety is Variegatum which has white or light green leaf margins. The subspecies Ellacombianum is another popular type which has much denser clusters of deep yellow flowers and grows a bit taller than other members of this species.

S. Morganianum is a common house and greenhouse plant which can also be grown in the sunny wall or rock garden. Known as donkey's tail, or burro tail, it is a drooping, leafy sedum with stems that reach lengths of three feet. Flowers are red or deep pink and appear on the ends of these trailing stems in early spring. Propagate this species by cuttings. Any ordinary garden soil will support donkey's tail.

S. pulchellum, called widow's-cross or flowering moss, grows to one foot, with slender trailing branches crowded with narrow leaves and rose purple flowers. It blooms in spring and early summer.

S. rupestre is a gray green creeper with yellow flowers in summer. In dry weather and in fall its leaves turn red.

S. spectabile is a common erect perennial growing one foot high, with three-inch fleshy light green leaves and numerous ½-inch pink flowers in September. Many cultivars are available, including several with brightly colored flowers and a few with variegated foliage.

S. Telephium is called live-forever or orpine. It is erect, to two feet, with three-inch leaves and red purple flowers in late summer.

SEED

A seed is very efficient reproductive structure produced by flowering plants and conifers. It has a protective seed coat, and contains an embryo of a new plant and very often a food supply that nourishes the embryo after germination. The endosperm or food storage area of corn seeds also nourishes the seedlings.

The embryo is formed after pollination of the female gamete, or egg, in the ovule by the male gamete from the pollen grain. When the fertilized ovule develops, it is usually encased in a fruit or pod, though seeds of conifers are naked. After fertilization, the seed itself remains more or less dormant until conditions of moisture and warmth promote germination.

Seeds are dispersed in many ways. The pods of some plants, such as violets, phlox, balsam, and witchhazel, explode and shoot out their seeds. Other plants such as dandelions, milkweed and thistles, have seeds that float on the wind. Blue thistle seeds are said to be blown sometimes for 1,000 miles. Quite a few seeds have wings to help them travel by air for short distances. These include maple, elm, box elder, basswood, and ash seeds. Others blow along the ground, like bluebell and yucca seeds. Heavier seeds such as those of pecan, walnut, coconut, horsechestnut, and buckeye trees, though they usually fall to the moist earth, can also travel by water. Seeds in cones and in sycamore balls travel by water at times, too. Fruit seeds and stones are deposited by man and animals in many places far from their point of origin. Birds carry seeds of digested berries, including those of honeysuckle, dogwood, poke, hackberry, mulberry, buckthorn, and mistletoe. Animals' fur and people's clothing catch cockleburs, burdock, devil's horns, Spanish needles, and other prickly seeds and carry them to other places. Small rodents take and hide the seeds of acorns, corn, sunflowers, and all kinds of nuts. Some pods, such as those of the poppies and the American lotus, merely drop their seeds like salt from shakers when the wind hits them. Even coasting on the snow or ice can be a method of dispersal. It is characteristic of the seedpods of the locust trees that cling on the trees until winter.

When a dry seed is given water, its colloids take up the moisture and soften the seed coat, often in a matter of hours, though sometimes of days. The enzymes in the protein system become active, and increase the metabolism rate in the cells; new energy becomes available for further development. Then water uptake and respiration continue while new materials for growth are being synthesized as the enzymes reduce the fats, proteins and carbohydrates stored in the seed to simpler compounds. These compounds then are transported to the root- and shoot-growing tips that emerge from the seed when cell division begins.

Seed Certification: Most states in the United States have a seed-certifying agency which sets up production standards and inspection methods to assure good genetic qualities of the seed produced for sale. Since pure seed comes only from self-pollinated plants or

The various sizes and shapes of seeds reflect the many ways in which they are dispersed.

of registered seed (or of one of the other classes) and is the kind produced in largest volume for sale to growers.

Stock seed is the term used by companies that provide foundation seed to contracted growers who in turn produce more seed for the companies. The seed companies maintain strict standards and supervise the fields of the individual contractors during the season.

Many high-grade seeds are hybrid cultivars, produced by the repeated crossing of two or more lines of parentage. This is accomplished by using inbred lines of seeds or by asexual propagation. The so-called F_1 generations are of very mixed ancestry and do not breed true from seed. However, they do produce plants of hybrid vigor. In F_2 and succeeding generations, the seed quality deteriorates and usually the seed is not worth using. Thus, yearly production of F_1 seed is required for healthy, vigorous crops.

See also GERMINATION, POLLINATION, SEEDS AND SEEDLINGS.

certain species in nature (the kind of seed said to come true), all other commercial seed developed by hybridizers and cross-pollination needs to be classified when certified.

The first class, breeder's seed, is seed that originates with the sponsoring plant breeder, and is the essential source of all certified classes. Foundation seed is a progeny, handled so as to maintain the highest possible standard of genetic purity and identity. This class is called select seed in Canada. Registered seed is the progeny of foundation seed (or breeder's seed) and is required to meet very high standards. Certified seed, the fourth class, is the progeny

SEEDS AND SEEDLINGS

The qualities, characteristics and forms of the seeds produced by plants vary greatly according to species or variety and environment. Some seeds are ready to germinate right after they are produced and others need a period of dormancy or a period of cold before they will grow. Some grow quickly, and some take a long time to reach maturity.

The way you harvest, ripen and store seeds depends upon germination requirements and the factors that influence the dormancy of each type of seed. For example, some seeds, including many tree seeds, must never be allowed to dry out before planting. For shipping these seeds should be collected as soon as they are ripe and carefully packed so they cannot dry out. Most other seeds must be stored in a dry, dark place but may require scarring or a special cold treatment before they will break dormancy and germinate.

Dormancy: There are several reasons that a seed remains dormant. Some, such as those of walnut, olive, peach, plum, lettuce, and many flowers and shrubs, have very hard coats which must be injured before they begin to absorb water and germinate. In nature, winter heaving and weathering scarify the seeds, but the gardener or grower must do it himself by tapping them with a hammer, filing them or rubbing them with sandpaper. *See* SCARIFICATION.

Certain tropical and desert seeds have an inhibitor in the seed coat and must rest until weather conditions develop which can break down the inhibitor. Seeds of some palms and orchids have embryos so tiny that they must grow during a quiescent period before they are able to germinate. Other seeds have a rather short period of so-called internal dormancy while they are drying out after being freshly harvested. The dry storage breaks this dormancy, which is a shallow one compared to the deep dormancy of winter-dormant seeds. Deep dormancy requires long periods of moisture and chilling. Seeds that are doubly dormant need both seed coat and embryo treatments before dormancy is broken. Various shrubs and trees, because of having double dormancy, need two years before they germinate.

Cold Treatment (Stratification): The amount of time needed for cold treatment

varies. Seed of cedar of Lebanon, which will stay viable for six months, only need two months for stratification. Plants like alder and chestnut need three months; shadblow, horsechestnut and shellbark hickory need four months. A few plants need both a warm and a cold period of stratification: cotoneaster, bearberry, dogwood, yews, and some of the barberries and junipers. Some lilies, viburnums and the tree peony all need a spell of moderate temperature followed by cold. Unless kept in the refrigerator, such seeds are planted during the summer, kept moist, and allowed their cold dormancy during the following winter.

To stratify seeds in the refrigerator, mix the seeds with slightly moistened sand, peat moss or sphagnum moss, or a mixture of sand and moss or sand and vermiculite. Store them in polyethylene bags. After a spell in the refrigerator at 40°F. (4.44°C.), watch for the beginnings of germination and when you see the seeds are starting to grow, bring them out and sprinkle them on flats, adding a little water daily so they will stay moist. Three months is the usual storage time needed for maples, barberry, birch, bittersweet, flowering dogwood, and fruits like cherries, currants and gooseberries. Two months will suffice for pines, most spruces, false cypress, and arborvitae.

Germination: Too much or too little water at the time of germination affects seeds. Celery, for example, needs a great deal of water, but spinach does not. Other seeds that do not need very much water (though a lot does not harm them) include cabbage, turnip, sweet corn, cucumber, onion, carrot, and tomato and many herbs. Those needing quite a bit more are beans, peas, beets, and lettuce.

Of course other conditions and the natural longevity of seeds also contribute to the success of germination. Onions are only considered to be viable for a year, along with leeks, parsnips, salsify, and corn; whereas pea, bean, cabbage, and cauliflower seeds will last for three years and melon up to seven years.

Be sure to inspect seeds received or saved to make sure that they are clean, all of one kind, uniform in size, and plump and fresh looking. If in doubt, put the seeds through a germination test by scattering a specific number of seeds between two damp towels. Place them in a warm, dark place and, after the required germination period, count how many have sprouted. If it is less than 50 percent, consider using other seed.

Too rich a soil in the seedbed is not advisable, and any break in the water supply can be fatal. Also fatal is an inadequate supply of oxygen, which is sometimes brought about when seeds are planted too deep to get good air circulation, or when a very wet season swamps them and cuts off air.

Saving Your Own Seed: In saving your own tree seeds, give them one to three weeks to dry on a screen or canvas. If you save cones for seed, dry them out for two to 12 weeks (or in an oven for a few hours at 115 to 140°F. (46.11 to 60°C.)—unless they are red pine seeds which need five or six hours at 170°F. [76.67°C.]).

To save seeds from berries or grapes, roll the berries with a rolling pin, whirl them in a blender, or trample them in a tub to crush the pulp. Then wash the seed quickly and clean it by hand. Another method is to put the berries in water and let them ferment for two or three days and then separate the seed from the pulp. Do not leave them in water too long or they may sprout. This method is used for saving the seeds of serviceberry, privet, honey-suckle, rose, mountain ash, holly, Russian olive, and huckleberry as well as those of the bramble berries.

The gardener who has a special variety of vegetable or flower which cannot be found in seed catalogs, may find seed saving worthwhile. If you wish to maintain the quality of the strain, you must take the same precautions that professional seed growers take. You must allow only your best plants to set seed. The plant which produces the largest seedpod is not necessarily the one with the best seed. Plants which grow as you want next year's crop to grow should be chosen for seed. Lettuce which is early to head and slow to bolt should be marked. Spinach which produces the most leaves should be used. If an early crop is wanted, for plants like corn or tomatoes, then the first fruits should be saved.

Some vegetables, such as the root vegetables, parsley, cabbage, and Brussels sprouts, are biennials and will not produce seed the first year. If you wish to save seed from these, the roots must be saved in cool storage and planted out the second year to produce seed.

Also keep in mind that it's not a good idea to save seed from a hybrid plant. Hybrids are produced by crossing, so they may not breed true or have the outstanding characteristics that you would like.

The safest way to propagate seedlings true to the parent plant is to be sure that there are no other varieties of the same species or, sometimes even of the same genus, growing in the neighborhood. If this is not possible, blossoms of the seed-producing plant must be protected from pollination by stray insects. If paper bags are used to cover seed heads, hand-pollinating is necessary. This is done with a small, soft brush which is brushed over the stamens and pistils of each flower. The paper bag is kept on the flower until fruit has begun to form. Sometimes it is necessary to cover the plant again when the seed is almost ripe, to prevent birds from harvesting the crop.

Drying: Whenever possible, seed should be allowed to dry on the plant. This is important with beans and peas, corn, root vegetables, and spinach. Seed embedded in soft fruit should be left on the plant and not harvested until the fruit is somewhat overripe. Tomatoes, squash, cucumbers, and eggplant are done this way. When fruits are taken indoors, the seeds should be scraped out and soaked a day or more in water. Like berries, they will start to ferment. Careful watching is necessary at this stage. When it has fermented a little, the pulp may be loosened by rubbing it between the hands. Then lift the seeds and dry them on sheets of paper.

All seed should be thoroughly dry before it is stored. Drying should be done in a warm room which has good ventilation. As it dries, stir the seed occasionally to prevent mold.

Storage: Handmade paper folders make good storage containers because they permit some air circulation, but they are easily entered by rats, mice and insects. Most seeds are best stored in metal cans or glass jars. Storage in the dark is preferable to storage in the light. Most seed retains its highest viability when stored at humidities below 65 percent. Optimum temperatures for long-term storage are between 0 to 32°F. (-17.78 to $0°C.$). Moisture and temperature are interrelated so that if one is high, the other must be sufficiently low to insure seed viability. For most seeds, a relative humidity of 50 to 60 percent and a temperature between 32 and 50°F. (0 and $10°C.$) are preferred.

Planting: Sterile containers, planting material and soil are advisable to protect germinating seeds and young seedlings from disease such as the fungus disease, damping-off. However, it should be remembered that some growers have found that the bacteria and actinomycetes in unsterile compost attack damping-off fungi. These organisms also encourage seedling growth. Sphagnum moss may also have antibiotic capacities. A good mixture for planting consists of equal parts of milled sphagnum moss, perlite and vermiculite—all natural materials with the capacity to hold water.

Pasteurizing or sterilizing the soil: Soil will be free of certain pathogens if it is heated in a 130°F. ($54.44°C.$) oven for 30 minutes. At 120°F. ($48.89°C.$) nematodes are killed; at 130°F. ($54.44°C.$) botrytis is controlled; at 140°F. ($60°C.$) most plant pathogenic bacteria as well as worms, slugs and centipedes are killed. It takes 150°F. ($65.56°C.$) to kill soil insects; 155°F. ($68.33°C.$) to kill viruses and up to 160 to 180°F. (71.11 to $82.22°C.$) to be surely rid of weed seeds and disease microorganisms. Since many microorganisms are beneficial to plant growth, completely sterile soil should be used only at the earliest stages of growth, before the first transplanting.

You can sterilize tools and containers by boiling them for ten or 12 minutes, cleaning them with rubbing alcohol or soaking them in a 10 percent solution of laundry bleach. Plastic flowerpots or flats can be dipped into water heated to 158°F. ($70°C.$) for three minutes. The small, compacted peat pots available at most garden centers are generally already sterile, but if they have been sitting around in open bins at the store, it may be wise to use hot water when adding water to make them swell up into little pots. They should be watered and squeezed out at least half an hour before using, but preferably six or eight hours before.

It is possible to buy very small electric sterilizers that will treat a bushel of soil, but heating soil to high temperatures has toxic effects. It concentrates salts and destroys organic matter. Therefore, the safest method of treating soil is pasteurization.

Sowing: Hardy and quick-growing annual flowers and vegetables are usually started in beds in the garden. More tender plants, slow-growing plants, those which take a long time to germinate, and those with seed so fine that weeks are required to develop the seedlings into manageable plants, are usually planted indoors. Perennial flowers may be started indoors in midwinter and may be expected to bloom the first year from seed. They may also be sown in spring, in a special outdoor nursery bed and then transplanted in fall to their permanent garden positions. Biennials may be planted in midsummer, at about the time seed normally ripens on the plants. Planted outdoors in spring, they grow much larger and produce more seed the following year. In unreliable climates it is best to overwinter biennial plants in a cold frame.

For early vegetables, seed may be sown indoors and the plants hardened in a cold frame or in a sheltered place outside before they are set in the garden. Such vegetables as cucumbers and squash, normally planted directly in the garden, may also be sown inside in pots or paper containers. At the normal time for planting in the garden, if all danger of frost has passed, these early plants may be set out without disturbing their roots.

Seeds planted outside are usually planted in the soil in which they will grow during the entire season. The soil must be properly pre-

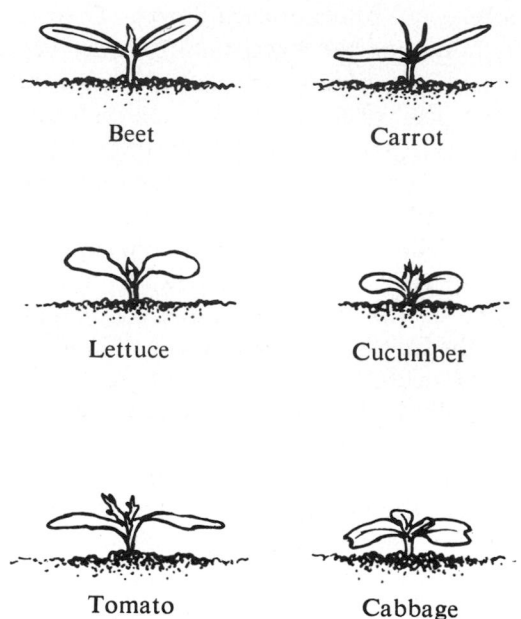

To avoid confusion when weeding and thinning, learn to recognize the common vegetable plants in their seedling stage.

pared in advance, by adding manure, compost, bone meal, or whatever that particular vegetable or flower needs to grow though not so much of it that the seedlings will grow too fast and be leggy. If the seed is to be planted in rows, a drill or trench may be made by using the edge of a board to keep the row straight.

Depth of planting depends upon the size of the seed, the consistency of the soil and the season of the year. The usual rule is to plant a seed at a depth that is three or four times the size of its diameter. This rule is modified by soil. Heavy clay soil is damper so seeds need not be planted as deeply. Sandy soil will dry out faster at the top, so the seed may need to be planted deeper in it. Seed should never be overwatered during germination, nor should it be kept too cold. If the soil is heavy and wet, it will be cold beneath the surface early in spring. Seed will germinate more rapidly if it is sown on the surface. When the soil is warmer, seed can be planted further down. Since seeds need air as well as water during germination, keep the tilth of the soil granular so that air may penetrate to the depth of the seeds and they can breathe.

Fine seed should be sprinkled on top of the soil and firmed with a board, the back of a hoe or with the hand. A very slight sifting of sand or fine compost over it will help keep it moist. Sand will also help to control damping-off, and will rebuff slugs and snails, which molest young seedlings. Summer-planted seed almost always needs to be firmed. Spring-planted seed may or may not need it, depending upon soil and weather. Summer-planted seed should also be covered with a sheet of paper, straw, or a shading device to protect it from drying until germination.

Seed sown indoors should be planted in soil that is not too rich. Soil should be of a texture which will hold moisture, but which will also drain well. The usual rule is half garden loam to half sand.

If the seeds are planted in a pot, the bottom quarter of the pot should be filled with broken pieces of pottery or with gravel to provide drainage. In a flat, the bottom quarter to half of the flat should be sphagnum moss. Soil which is added to cover these layers should be moist. Seed should be thinly sown. If more than one kind of seed is planted in a container, the seeds should be chosen to germinate at about the same time so that all will be ready for transplanting together.

After the seeds have been placed in rows, sand or fine compost is sifted over them to the correct depth, which is never more than three or four times the diameter of the seed. Firm the soil and water it, either from above with a very fine spray or from below, by plunging the container into water almost as deep as the soil. When wet patches begin to appear on top of the soil, remove the container from the water and drain.

Care: Seed flats may be covered to preserve surface moisture until germination starts, but the cover should be removed occasionally for ventilation or if fungus appears. The temperature for seed germination may usually be somewhat higher than what the plants will stand after growth has started. It can be 70 or 75°F. (21.11 or 23.89°C.) when seeds are germinating, but should be reduced to 65°F. (18.33°C.) when the leaves appear. Soil should be kept moist, but not wet, during this period.

As soon as the first green begins to appear, the covering should be removed and the seed pot or flat placed in a southern window. Gradually, as the seedlings sprout and the roots stretch down into the pot, watering may be lighter and less frequent, but the container should never be permitted to become dry. If seedlings are too thick they must be thinned immediately. Occasionally when fine seed is planted, it will come up unevenly, with thick patches in places in the pot. These patches should be thinned with tweezers, or excess seedlings cut off with nail scissors so as not to injure the roots. Crowding at this stage will almost inevitably result in damping-off.

Transplanting: When seedlings are ½ inch to one inch tall, they should be transplanted to stand two inches apart in a flat. The usual rule is to transplant when the first pair of true leaves has formed. By this time seedlings will have developed roots that are long in proportion to top growth. Soil in the new flat may have a small amount of compost mixed with the loam and sand, but the mixture should not be too rich. If the roots must seek further for food, they will build a strong, healthy root system, which is more important to the plants at this point in their growth than height of stem. Some plants benefit from a second transplanting which develops even stronger root systems. If the plants are grown in a tightly closed greenhouse, they should, at this stage, be given carbon dioxide during the days, either in gaseous or liquid form. This encourages photosynthesis.

About two weeks before the seedlings are to be planted in the garden, they should begin their hardening-off. At first they should be set outside in the middle of the day. Gradually the period when they are left outside may be lengthened into the cooler parts of the day. If a cold frame is available they may be placed in the frame with the sash lifted at midday. Watch them carefully to see that they do not wilt and keep them sheltered from the wind.

Most plants benefit from being sunk lower than they were in their flats. Transplanting should be done on a cloudy day, early in the morning or in the evening when the sun will not shine directly on exposed roots. If possible, for several days after transplanting, plants should be protected from the direct rays of the sun by newspapers folded to a hot-cap shape. They should be watered as soon as they are placed in the ground, and the soil around them should be kept moist until they are established. A cutworm collar is necessary in most gardens to protect the young seedlings. This may be a piece of cardboard or stiff paper about three by five inches, which is wrapped loosely around the stem and sunk about an inch in the soil.

See also COLD FRAME, GERMINATION, HOUSE PLANTS, VEGETABLE GARDENING.

SELAGINELLA

This genus contains a large number of species, most of which are tropical or subtropical natives. The feathery, mosslike foliage comes in various shades of green and tints of bronze or blue, making selaginellas popular terrarium and greenhouse plants. Often used to cover unsightly spots such as those under greenhouse benches, or the surface soil of large tub plants, selaginellas quickly form a dense growth when given a shady location and moist humusy soil. Selaginellas, which are flowerless annuals and perennials, will also grow outdoors in frost-free areas.

Propagation is by spores, layering or ½-inch cuttings from old plants. To plant the spores, scatter them over the surface of the soil, cover with a little finely screened soil and water them. Place a glass over the flat and put it in a shaded area where the temperature is about 70°F. (21.11°C.). Small plantlets should appear within several weeks.

S. Kraussiana, or trailing spike moss, is a bright green, mossy African perennial used for cover. The varieties Brown, a dwarf club moss, and Aurea, variegated club moss, are excellent in terrariums. *S. pallescens,* or sweat plant, has bright green leaves to one foot in length and is grown as a fern. It requires high humidity. *S. Martensii* has vivid glossy green foliage and is used as an ornamental. Resurrection plant (*S. lepidophylla*), a desert native of Texas and Central America, is often sold as a dry brown ball which, when moistened, becomes a mossy plant about four inches tall. This cycle can be repeated over and over again without harm to the plant.

See also FERN, HOUSE PLANTS.

SELENICEREUS

Often called night-blooming cereus or queen of the night, these epiphytic cacti of tropical American origin bear large, fragrant, white to yellow flowers that bloom at night. Selenicereus are not very spiny and can either trail or climb by means of aerial roots. Since their height can reach 15 feet, selenicereus is perhaps best grown in the greenhouse or in frost-free areas, outdoors.

Give it a moist humusy soil and sun from an eastern or lightly shaded southern window. Propagation is by stem tip cuttings. Good species include *S. Macdonaldiae, S. pteranthus* and *S. Urbanianus.*

See also CACTI, HOUSE PLANTS.

SELENIUM

Selenium is a trace element which must be present in soil in a minute quantity of no more than .1 to .3 part per million. In amounts over three parts per million in cattle feed, it can be toxic. Soils are seldom deficient in selenium and, because of its toxic nature, it should not be added to soil.

SELF-POLLINATION
See ORCHARD, POLLINATION

SELF-STERILITY
See ORCHARD, POLLINATION

SEMPERVIVUM   *See* HOUSELEEK

SENECIO   *See* RAGWORT

SENNA   (*Cassia*)

This tropical genus of the Pea family, which includes several hundred herbs, shrubs and trees, is grown both for its ornamental and for its medicinal value. Most species can be grown outdoors where winters are mild. Senna leaves and pods have been used as cathartics since the ninth century. The sennas, which prefer sandy loam and full sun, have finely cut, compound leaves and showy flowers with five equal petals. Propagation is by seed or, more often, by division.

Golden-shower (*C. fistula*) is a small tree from India which is grown commercially for its black pods that are used as purgatives. The leaves and yellow flowers are often steeped in boiling water to make a purgative beverage.

Pink shower (*C. grandis*) is a 50-foot tropical American tree which has drooping clusters of rose pink flowers and dark brown pods.

Wild senna (*C. marilandica*) is a hardy, shrubby perennial that may be planted in the border and grows from New England south. It has feathery, light green leaves, bright yellow flowers and flat pods, and may grow four feet tall. Wild senna is an effective cathartic. Propagation is by division.

Wormwood senna (*C. artemisioides*) is a six-foot shrub with narrow silver leaves, light yellow flowers and brown pods. It grows in dry places in California.

See also HERB.

SENSITIVE PLANT   *See* MIMOSA

SEPARATION   *See* DIVISION

SEQUOIA

Only two species of these enormous trees of prehistoric origin, the redwood and the giant sequoia, still exist. The redwood or coast redwood is classified *S. sempervirens,* while the giant sequoia or giant redwood is variously called *S. Wellingtonia* or, more properly, *Sequoiadendron giganteum.* Some nursery catalogs call it *S. gigantea.* Both are found mainly in California and Oregon and are the biggest and probably the oldest evergreens in the world, some being well over 300 feet tall and more than 2,500 years old. Much smaller specimens are occasionally found in the East, but the climate there is generally unsuitable, because the sequoia is a mountain tree and the redwood likes rain and fog. In England, many country estates boast wellingtonias reportedly produced from sequoia seed brought to England by the Duke of Wellington.

Redwood is an important timber tree. Its burls, sold by florists for centerpieces, sprout quickly and freely when put in water.

SERICEA   (*Lespedeza sericea*)

A perennial lespedeza, sericea is an excellent soil-building legume. It is frequently grown in the South for hay or pasture or to improve soil. Sericea prefers a firm seedbed and shallow planting, but it is prolific even in poor soils.

To produce a good crop, ordinary sericea must be cut early in spring. If you use it as hay feed for livestock, be sure to cut it before it reaches 15 inches in height. Leave two to three inches of stubble to develop new growth.

No more than two cuttings of hay, or one cutting followed by a seed crop, should be harvested annually. Avoid grazing sericea in late summer when its roots are preparing for next year's growth.

See also LESPEDEZA.

SERVICEBERRY
See AMELANCHIER

SESAME   (*Sesamum indicum*)

Native to Africa and the warmer parts of Asia, sesame was one of the first oilseed crops ever cultivated by man, and its seed has been a staple food and oil source throughout history in the Near, Middle and Far East. Ancient Egyptians and Persians ground the plant into a flour used for making bread, and the Romans flavored their butter with sesame oil. Both seeds and oil are widely used today throughout the world.

The oil yielded from sesame seed has long provided the basic fat in the diets of citizens of the Near East, especially those of Turkey and Syria. The oil is rich in calcium and vitamin C and the seed itself contains a certain amount of lecithin and vitamins E and F. The seed's nutlike flavor enhances salad dressings, candies, butters, and baked goods. Hulled seeds can also be eaten raw or toasted, much like sunflower seeds.

Planting and Culture: Sesame is a drought-tolerant plant well adapted to the climatic and soil conditions of the cotton-growing areas of the South and Southwest. Its combination-type root system, consisting of a taproot and numerous secondary roots, allows it to use subsoil and surface moisture very effectively. Though it will grow under a wide range of soil conditions, sesame does best in well-drained fertile soils. Besides having a dependable yield and a relatively low production cost, sesame is a short-season crop which can be used effectively when combined with other cash crops, grasses and legumes in a diversified system of farming. Sesame is a crop that tends to deplete the soil of essential minerals and to destroy its physical structure, while legumes and grasses tend to have the opposite effect.

Sesame should not be planted until all danger of cool weather is past. Planting dates may be as early as March 15 in the South and as late as June 15 in the North. Generally, sesame can be planted shortly after cotton in cotton-growing areas and after sorghum in sorghum-growing areas.

Most varieties mature in 90 to 120 days, depending upon the strain and the growing conditions. The pod, about the size and shape of a peanut pod, is borne on each leaf axil and contains seeds the size and shape of tomato seeds. Commercial types have semishattering pods and can be machine harvested.

In the United States, sesame is often cultivated as an ornamental. It is a hardy plant with white blossoms, green pods and wrinkled leaves.

See also HERB.

SET

The term "set" is used to describe the successful pollination of the blossoms of a plant. It is used especially in reference to fruit trees, which are said to "set fruit" when the ovary begins to swell and show the beginnings of a fruit form.

Small bulbs, corms and tubers are also sets. Onion seeds sown thickly in the fall produce dwarfed bulbs which are planted the following spring as scallion sets.

SEVENBARK   *See* HYDRANGEA

SEWAGE SLUDGE

Sewage is the total organic waste and wastewater generated by residential and commercial establishments. Sewage sludge is settled solids combined with varying amounts of water, and containing dissolved or solid materials that have been removed from sewage by screening, sedimentation, chemical precipitation, or bacterial digestion.

Although until recently, most sewage sludge was dumped into the ocean, burned or buried, there is increasing interest in the use of sludge as a soil amendment. The use of human wastes as fertilizer is, of course, ancient and still widely practiced in the Orient. Only since the 1960's, have various United States cities been marketing composted sludge as a fertilizer. Other cities are making sludge available to gardeners and farmers for application to agricultural land.

There are several forms of sludge available. Some have been activated with beneficial bacteria and others have had little or no treatment.

Unactivated: Raw sludge has simply been treated by way of gravity settling. Its major drawbacks are a foul odor and the fact that pathogens may be present.

Not all unactivated sludge has a foul odor. Some has been subjected to anaerobic fermentation in a digester and is virtually odorless. It is called digested sludge. The sludge is first allowed to settle and drain by gravity. The conventional anaerobic digestion system takes about ten to 14 days from the time the sewage reaches the sedimentation tank. The digested solids are pumped onto sand or gravel filter beds for drying. The dry material is removed and used for soil improvement. Some cities still incinerate their digested sludge, but the rising costs of fuel make incineration an expensive option. Ocean dumping of sludge is gradually being discontinued for environmental reasons.

Digested sludge may also be air-dried, centrifuged or heat-dried. Pathogens may persist to some extent, but die off further after soil application.

Digested sludge has about the same fertilizer value as barnyard manure. Its nitrogen content varies from 1 to 3 percent, and it averages less than 1 percent phosphorus. Sludge benefits plant growth by adding trace elements, and it improves the moisture-holding capacity, porosity and aggregation of soil. It has a detectable odor, which may be eliminated by curing in a pile for several months during warm weather. Avoid application during cool weather or on frozen ground.

Activated: Activated sludge is produced when sewage is agitated by air bubbled rapidly through it. Certain types of active bacteria coagulate the organic matter; this settles out, leaving a clear liquid that can be discharged into streams and rivers with minimal pollution.

Activated sludge is generally heat-treated and dried before being made available to gardeners and farmers. Its nitrogen content is between 5 to 6 percent; phosphorus from 3 to 6 percent.

The best use that can be made of sludge is in composting. The composting of sludge is a relatively inexpensive disposal method that provides a source of fertilizer for nearby farmers and gardeners.

The greatest obstacle to an increased use of sludge as an agricultural fertilizer is the problem of heavy metal contamination from industrialized city wastes. Heavy metals in sludge do present a potential danger to land and livestock, and for this reason all sludge should be tested for heavy metal concentrations before it is applied to the land. Research by the USDA, EPA and many state universities into heavy metal contamination has shown that the only way to clean up sludge is to separate industrial pollutants from the rest of the sludge. The heavy metal to be most concerned about is cadmium. Although other heavy metals can pose health problems for humans, most would have to be present at such high levels that plants could not grow on them. Cadmium, however, will endanger animals before it affects plants. The maximum permissible amount of cadmium in sludge to be spread on agricultural land is 50 parts per million. The ideal goal for continuous use of sludge is less than 15 ppm, but at 50 ppm the sludge is considered safe for a one-time use. Currently, researchers are studying the effects of continuous application of heavy metals. The evidence to date indicates that plants take up as much heavy metals in their first year of sludge treatment as they do after five years of continuous application, despite the fact that heavy metals do build up in the soil.

Composting of sludge before application has been proven to inhibit the uptake of heavy metals by plants, and organic matter in the soil has been shown to do the same. Liming of soil also decreases heavy metal uptake by plants.

Farmers and gardeners who wish to use sludge should first contact their sewage district and request an analysis of the heavy metal content. They should also ascertain whether there are any dangerous chemicals being dumped into the sludge by local industries. If unsure of the analysis of the sludge, contact your state agricultural school for guidance on using the material. Further information on using sludge which contains heavy metals may be obtained from the regional offices of the U.S. Environmental Protection Agency and the Biological Waste Management Laboratory of the U.S. Department of Agriculture, Beltsville, Maryland.

Pathogens and parasites present in human excrement represent another potential danger if raw or digested sludge is used on land. Human excrement should never be used as fertilizer without proper treatment. Composting sludge aerobically eliminates the pathogen danger since the high temperatures reached during composting kill off pathogenic organisms in the sludge.

Various processes have been worked out for composting large quantities of sludge. A process perfected by USDA scientists handles 50 tons of filtered sludge—a rate capable of serving a city of 200,000 to 500,000. The entire composting process takes seven weeks. Wood chips or bark are mixed with the sludge at a 3:1 ratio. The mixture is then piled eight feet high over a 12-inch base of wood chips covering 70 feet of perforated pipe hooked up to an air pump. The entire pile is covered with a 12-inch layer of screened compost, which acts as a filter to prevent obnoxious gases from escaping into the atmosphere.

The pump forces air down through the pile of sludge and through the perforated pipe. The oxygen in turn stimulates bacteria to act upon the sludge/chips mixture, and for the three weeks the material is composted in this manner, temperatures reach as high as 175°F. (79.44°C.)—high enough to kill off pathogens present in the sludge. After the three weeks of composting, the compost is moved to a stockpile where it is cured for four weeks. After a final screening to remove large pieces of bark, the odorless product is ready to apply to agricultural land.

Applying Sludge to Cropland: Experiments in Wisconsin have produced the following general recommendations for applying sludge to cropland:

1. Maintain a record of heavy metal additions and keep the total loading within acceptable limits. Keep the soil pH at 6.5 or higher to prevent potential toxicities.

2. Avoid applying sludge on soils where the risk of surface or groundwater contamination is high. This includes soils with a high water table, soils subject to ponding and flooding, soils underlain with bedrock at two feet or less, steeply sloping soils, and very sandy soils.

3. Minimize potential health problems for man and animals. Do not eat uncooked root crops or other vegetables, especially leafy vegetables, grown on sludge-treated land for one year following sludge application. Do not feed green forages to milk cows for two months or to other animals for two weeks following the sludge application.

4. Maintain good soil management on areas to be treated with sludge. This includes annual soil testing and use of soil conservation practices to reduce runoff and erosion.

Rate of application: Apply sludge at rates consistent with the nitrogen requirement of the crop to be grown. Generally six to ten tons of sludge (dry weight basis) per acre are required annually if the sludge is surface applied, or three to five tons per acre if the sludge is injected into the soil and immediately incorporated. Only dried sludge should be allowed to lie on the surface for any amount of time. Liquid sludge should be incorporated the day it is applied to avoid odor problems.

Dewatered sludge may be dumped on a field and spread in a four-inch layer with a crawler. This layer is then plowed under at the end of the day. With this method, an acre is given 20 to 25 tons of sludge and should not need to be refertilized with sludge for ten to 15 years. By using this method, you assure that only safe levels of trace minerals will be present. Sludge can be applied the next year if heavy-feeding crops are being grown on the land.

Crop recommendations: Although it is possible to spray irrigated row crops with liquid sewage sludge, flood irrigation will do more to prevent any possibility of surface contamination. Sludge can also be applied to row crops in its composted and heat-dried forms much the same as manure.

Whenever sludge in any form is applied to the surface of pasture and forage crops, sufficient time must be allowed for precipitation to wash off the sludge before harvest or grazing. Using the forage too soon after sludge application may create problems with metal or pathogen ingestion by animals. It is best to apply sludge immediately following clipping. Sludge injection through chisel subsoilers is possible at almost any time so long as animal and equipment traffic are delayed until sludge is absorbed by the soil. Composted sludge can be incorporated into the soil prior to fall or spring plowing. Apply dry sludge at the rate of ten to 15 tons per acre.

Either composted or heat-dried sludge can be easily applied to growing lawns. There may, however, be a temporary odor problem when turf is wet. The best times to apply sludge to lawns are late in March and early in September. When using sludge for new lawns or in reconditioning old stands of grass, prepare the seedbed by mixing the sludge with the soil. Use one part sludge to two parts soil if the soil is of a heavy clay texture. Spade the ground to a depth of at least six inches, making sure the sludge and soil are thoroughly mixed. Avoid having layers of sludge and layers of soil in the seedbed.

As a fertilizer for well-established lawns, the sludge should be applied in the winter and early spring months when the ground is frozen. Cover the lawn with a half-inch layer of sludge. This cover will insulate grass roots from the harmful effects of alternate freezing and thawing.

You can use dried sludge, liquid sludge or dewatered sludge on a garden. Dried sludge can either be worked into the soil like compost, or used as a specific fertilizer and incorporated into the soil around specific plants. Dried sludge may also be applied as a mulch, since its nitrogen content is not high enough to burn plants and its nutrients are released slowly. Liquid and dewatered sludge should be applied to the garden on a one-shot basis, and worked into the top six to ten inches of soil immediately.

See also FERTILIZER.

SHADBLOW   *See* AMELANCHIER

SHADE-TOLERANT ORNAMENTALS

A gardener looking for ornamental plants to grow in a shady location should first deter-

SHADE-TOLERANT ORNAMENTALS 1017

mine how much shade he has. The quality of the soil and the degree of dryness or moisture vary greatly from one shaded garden to another and also determine what can be grown in your garden. Experiment to find what will do best.

Light Shade: Locations in light shade will support a great variety of ornamentals. Light or broken shade can be found under deep-rooted, high-branched trees with naturally open crowns. Among these are apple (if kept pruned), ash, birch, hickory, locust, and some oaks. Many of these trees leaf out late in spring so before that they can serve as ideal companions for native woodland ferns and wild flowers, all spring bulbs except late tulips, and many of the early-flowering perennials. Locations in half-shade get several hours of morning or afternoon sun, but are shaded the rest of the day.

Certain cultural practices contribute to successful gardening under trees. Prune the trees so they branch high and the crowns are reasonably open. This helps to admit light and insure good air circulation. Where soil is hard and compacted, as it often is under old trees, loosen it to spade's depth and dig in plenty of humus in the form of leaf mold, compost or rotted manure, adding sand or gravel if drainage is a problem. An abundance of organic matter in the soil will insure that small plants with limited root systems can compete successfully with the trees for nutrients. Even the most deeply rooted trees take most of their nutrients and much of their water from the topsoil and thus compete with smaller plants.

A good way to establish a ground cover under such trees is to plant it in rich soil in low, bottomless boxes set on top of the ground and banked with compost or leaf mold. As the plants spill out and root, water them frequently and add humus. This method saves the ground cover from having to compete directly with tree roots. Top-dress the beds annually with compost if possible, and give flowering ornamentals a fertilizer rich in phosphorus.

Annuals which prefer to be partly shaded from direct sun include begonia, coleus, impatiens, monkey flower, and torenia. Some which do well in sun to light shade are ageratum, alyssum, calendula, clarkia, geranium, lobelia, nicotiana, pansy, petunia, rudbeckia, salvia, and snapdragon.

All of the following biennials and perennials will thrive in light shade: aconitum, ajuga, anemone, arabis, astilbe, azalea, bee balm, bergenia, bleeding-heart, bugbane, candytuft, cardinal flower, columbine, coralbells, Christmas rose, daylily, epimedium, evening primrose, forget-me-not, foxglove, globeflower, hosta, many irises (except tall-bearded), lamium, leopard's bane, lily-of-the-valley, loosestrife, primrose, pulmonaria, spiderwort, sweet woodruff, violet, and Virginia bluebell.

Perennials which prefer full sun but tolerate light or half-shade include: anchusa, a few asters, baptisia, boneset, many species of campanula, some daylilies, Chinese delphinium, edelweiss, false lupine, fraxinella, geranium, many lilies, liriope, lupine, meadow rue, meadowsweet, oriental poppy, peony, physostegia, and rudbeckia.

Heavy Shade: Relatively few plants will grow in the perpetual shade of a stand of evergreens, though some of the acid-loving native wild flowers may survive there. Dense-foliaged, surface-rooting deciduous trees such as Norway maple or beech also create heavy shade but certain plants can be grown beneath them. In heavily shaded areas, try tuberous begonia, European cyclamen, impatiens, Peruvian lily, periwinkle, rhododendrons, Saint-John's-wort, valerian, and sweet violet.

SHALLOT   (*Allium Cepa*)

A small onion of the multiplier type, the shallot seldom forms seed and is propagated by

Like all of the alliums, shallots are most easily propagated by means of small cloves or sets.

means of the small cloves. Cloves are the divisions into which the plant splits during growth. The top of the cloves should be planted even with the soil and not covered by it, because shallots grow above ground. They need shallow cultivation and should be kept free of weeds. For specific soil requirements, *see* ONION.

Shallots are ready to be harvested when their tops wither and fall over. If you choose to use the leaves for seasoning, cut the tops before they wither, taking care not to cut any new leaf growth coming up from the central stem.

SHASTA DAISY
(*Chrysanthemum maximum*)

Shasta daisies are bushy, upright plants with single or double, daisylike white flowers. They are often used in the border. The yellow-centered flowers, which can reach a width of six inches and bloom from June until frost, make excellent cut flowers.

These hardy herbaceous perennials grow two to four feet high. They require full sun and a moderately rich soil that is moist but well drained. Overly wet soil favors the growth of verticillium rot, which attacks the roots and causes the plants to suddenly wilt and die. Infected plants should be removed from the bed.

To maintain vigorous growth, Shasta clumps should be divided every second year. These clumps should be set about one foot apart in groups of three or more.

A few of the many named varieties include Polaris with branching stems and seven-inch blooms; Alaska, a popular and very hardy single; Marconi, a long-blooming double white; and Little Miss Muffet, a semidouble, 14-inch dwarf with a moundlike growth habit. Double varieties often do better if planted in light shade rather than full sun.

SHEEP

Sheep are a warm and friendly addition to any homestead. Easy to care for and fun to manage, they repay their owners with bountiful meat and wool harvests. They produce marketable meat in less than half the time cattle require, and are much easier to butcher.

Breeds of sheep can be broken down into

four main types: fine-wools, medium-wools, long-wools, and meat-types.

The fine-wools are adaptable to many different environments and are frequently found in the Southwest. Rambouillet is a fine-wool type yielding eight to 12 pounds of fleece per head. It is an open-faced breed, which means that wool does not grow on or near the eyes. Rambouillets will breed any time of the year. The Debouillet is another variety of medium size which also produces an excellent wool crop.

Of the medium-wools, the Columbia, the first breed of American origin, is the most popular. Sheep of this breed are large in size and prolific. Corriedales, a New Zealand breed, produce heavy fleeces and mature early. The Romney and Lincoln are the favored breeds of the long-wool variety. They are known for their adaptability to cold, wet climates.

The large, popular Hampshire is recognizable by its black face and narrow muzzle. The Suffolk and Shropshire are other large varieties bred for meat production.

Housing: Only simple accommodations are needed for a flock of sheep. A three-sided structure is sufficient in regions where winters are not too severe. You should provide approximately 15 square feet per sheep in a closed-off shelter. Indoor and outdoor feeders and provision for free-choice fresh water and salt must be made to maintain a healthy flock. A good bedding of straw on the floor of the shelter will insulate the building during the winter and if freshened periodically it will prevent the sheep's wool from becoming soiled and matted.

The biggest chore of the spring season is clearing the shelter of the manure and straw bedding which has accumulated over the winter. The manure can be used as fertilizer, composted, or sold to someone who can make use of it. A thorough cleaning of the shed floor and application of fresh bedding will start the new season.

On the homestead, sheep should not be run with cattle or hogs, although they can be kept near goats. Good meadow fencing is necessary to keep predators out and contain the flock.

Feeding: Sheep will be quite content to act as meadow lawn mowers by feeding on forage grasses. The best pastureland can support as many as 15 ewes and their lambs per acre. If land is too poor to provide enough food by itself, use a supplement of grain feed. One-third to one-half pound per day per ewe of corn, oats, milo, or barley should be fed. Feedlot sheep (those without access to pasture) should be fed at least two to four pounds of hay and about a pound of grain per head per day. A mixture of 60 percent oats, 25 percent corn or sorghum grains and 15 percent wheat bran is recommended.

Be sure to rotate forage pastures to prevent the ewes from contracting worms. Commercial wormers should be administered to sheep once every six months to insure against internal parasites. An alternative to a commercial product for worming is a diatom flour fed free-choice with salt.

Diseases and Parasites: When purchasing sheep, reject all animals with disease symptoms. Foot rot is a bacterial disease which causes the hoof to separate from the underlying tissues. A foot infected with the disease will carry an odor of decay. Mastitis is another condition to check for when buying sheep. Lumps or hardness in the udder indicate its presence and ewes infected with it will be unable to nurse offspring. Also beware of spreading or missing teeth, an indication of age.

Good nutrition and management will prevent practically all sheep diseases. Liver fluke can be avoided by keeping sheep away from stagnant water. Anthrax, the worst killer, can be prevented by not letting your sheep graze closely on sparse late-summer pastures. Anthrax germs live in the soil and on short grass and can be picked up by the animal.

Traditionally, sheep were dipped in a disinfectant to control parasites. Today, however, many sheepmen have stopped dipping their sheep. Most dips contain arsenic or DDT, neither of which is safe for the animals. Stay away from phenothiazine, too—this powerful worm-killer affects the sheep's body growth and metabolism, and may well be responsible for today's big lamb losses and the increase in "mystery" diseases. Pasture rotation is a better preventive of worms and parasites.

Breeding: Breeding activity varies among breeds and even between individuals within a breed. Many types have a restricted season based on daylength, temperature, and the age of the ewe. In most cases, the breeding season occurs between late July and early December. Within this season, ewes over nine months old enter heat every 16 to 17 days with each estrus lasting about 72 hours. The duration of pregnancy is approximately 145 days so that a late fall breeding will result in lambs arriving in late March or April.

One ram introduced into a flock will service 30 ewes. The rams should be marked at the time of breeding by painting the brisquet (lower chest) of the ram with artists' oil paint diluted with motor oil. Change the color on the brisquet every 16 days for easy detection of ewes which come into estrus after the initial breeding. The marking of the ewes by the rams during mating allows the shepherd to approximate when lambing will occur and to detect infertile rams.

Before breeding, sheepmen flush their ewes. Flushing is simply feeding on lush pasture or increased grain rations to encourage weight gain. As weight gain increases, the ewes drop more eggs and increase the possibility of multiple births.

Lambing: As the time for delivery draws near, the demands on the mother's body will necessitate a slight increase in feed rations. Some shepherds include about a pint (¼ to ½ pound) of molasses in the ration to protect against lambing paralysis. Lambing paralysis is characterized by stiff limbs in the mother ewe, listless walking, twitching muscles, grinding of teeth, and even death. Overly fat ewes are especially susceptible to this condition. For this reason, be careful not to overfeed during the early gestation period.

Wheat in the ewe's ration prevents stiff-limb disease in unborn lambs. Deficiencies of vitamin E and selenium are the causes of this disease.

Lambing time is the most demanding of all periods in the shepherd's schedule. It is wise to prepare for it by stocking up on essential supplies such as clean towels, iodine (to be used when cutting the cord), a sharp knife, alcohol, and cotton swabs. These items should be placed in a can or other sealable container and kept in the shed where they will be used when lambing starts.

Simple lambing pens to separate the ewes and their offspring from other members of the flock should be ready and waiting. A 3-by-5-foot, hinged, two-sided wooden fence to be placed in a corner is sufficient to segregate the pair. Be sure the rungs of the pen are low enough and close enough together to prevent mothers and lambs from trying to escape.

Keep a constant watch on the flock to detect any change in the behavior of pregnant ewes. Labored breathing, listlessness and loss of appetite are sure signs of an impending birth. When the ewe decides to lie down and wait, try to encourage her to make herself comfortable *inside,* not outside, the shelter.

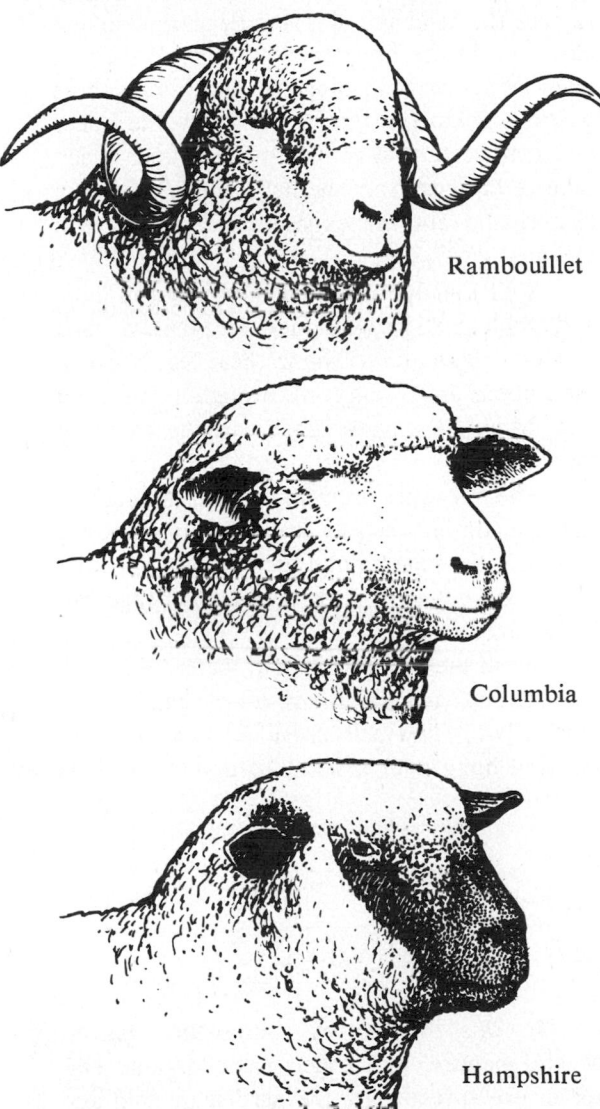

Rambouillet

Columbia

Hampshire

Sheep are classified as wool or meat producers. Of the wool types, Rambouillet and Columbia are very popular in this country, while the black-faced Hampshire remains the most popular meat-producing breed.

Cold drafts and wind can hinder a successful birth and result in the loss of a lamb.

The usual labor lasts an hour. Allow the ewe to conduct the delivery unassisted for the first 45 minutes, or slightly longer if things are progressing normally. To assist the ewe, pull on the emerging lamb's front two legs only when the ewe is contracting. There are frequent complications in birth; many lambs do not emerge hoof first. After disinfecting and lubricating your hands with alcohol and petroleum jelly, try to dislodge any limbs bent within the womb. This insures a comfortable delivery and prevents internal injuries to the mother.

The first few hours of life are critical for the newborn lamb. As soon as the lamb is completely dropped, begin to rub it briskly with clean towels or other cloths to get its circulation going. Lambs can also be immersed in warm water to get their bodies functioning. The anal passage should be wiped and the nose cleaned with cotton swabs to aid breathing. Cut the cord about six inches from the lamb's body and douse the area with iodine. The cord itself will dry up and fall in a week's time.

It is very important that the lamb nurse as soon as possible after birth. Try to encourage it to suckle by placing your finger in its mouth and, when it begins to suck, transferring it to the mother's udder. Give the ewe's nipple a few determined pulls to start the flow of colostrum. If there is no milk or if the lamb will not cooperate, have a bottle of substitute handy. Three cups milk, one tablespoon sugar, one beaten egg, and one tablespoon cod-liver oil will do the trick.

After one week to ten days it is time to dock the lamb. At birth, it has a long tail resembling a dog's tail. To prevent feces build-up, the tail is clipped with a special docking instrument. Cut it about two inches from the rump. Apply iodine and, to stop the bleeding, wrap a string tightly around the wound. A walk in cool air will encourage the blood to clot. After 15 minutes, the string can be removed. Lambs will frequently be traumatized by the pain, but they will resume normal activity in a few hours.

Lambs will begin feeding about two weeks after birth. Offer them a creep feeder, fashioned to allow only small-headed animals access to the feed. The ewe and lamb should be fed separately for the first few days after birth, or until the lamb is strong enough to ward off the jealous advances of other mothers.

Shearing: Sheep are shorn in the spring but, in special cases, they may be shorn in early summer, or in autumn, as preparation for breeding.

Shearing the ewes before lambing frees the birth passage and keeps the wool from being soiled. Shearing can best be learned from someone who is an old hand at the art. Sheep will yield approximately ten pounds of wool per animal.

Slaughtering: To slaughter your sheep, you need a .22 rifle, a special table or butchering "cradle," a meat saw, sharp butchering knives, containers for catching the blood, and a large sink in which to wash the carcass.

For about a day prior to slaughtering, withhold feed but not water from the animal. This will prevent the stomach from being too full and will make removal of the gut much simpler. Clean and assemble your equipment, then lead the sheep from its pen to the butchering table. Handle the animal gently, placing one hand under its throat and the other hand under the opposite flank.

Shoot the sheep in the center of the forehead. Lift the body onto the table and, with a sharp, pointed knife, slit the throat. Let the blood drain out into a container beneath the table. After bleeding, turn the sheep onto its back and cut down the center of the belly. Make sure you cut only through the skin.

Before continuing with the butchering, remove the head and, if it is to be used, skin and clean it. At the breastbone, pull back the pelt from the breast, skinning the neck as much as possible. Skin the forelegs down to the knees and remove the lower part of each one. Then remove the pelt from the belly, slit it down the center, and cut the exposed breastbone with the meat saw.

Split the throat and remove the windpipe and esophagus. Skin hind legs and remove back hooves. Make an incision in these legs between the tendons and string cord through it. You can now hang the carcass and continue skinning the sides.

The intestines are removed through an incision made in the belly wall. The viscera are removed, the paunch and liver cut out, and the diaphragm cut so that the heart and lungs can be removed.

Wash the carcass in tepid water. Cover it with netting, and hang it in a cool place for a day or two. The pelt should be covered with salt and hung over a fence to dry before it is tanned.

SHEET COMPOSTING

In this method of composting, leaves, weeds, manure, and other waste organic materials are spread over the garden or field and worked into the soil to decompose. To incorporate the compost, pass over the covered area with a rotary tiller. This chops the material so that it breaks down faster. Add lime, nitrogen fertilizers, bone meal, tankage, or dried blood, phosphate or potash rock before cultivating again.

See also COMPOSTING.

SHEPHERDIA

This genus of the Oleaster family includes three species, two of which are cultivated. Both of these are extremely hardy, grow far into the North, withstand winds, and thrive on poor soils where few other plants could survive. They have opposite leaves, inconspicuous yellow flowers and a fruit which is a small drupe. *S. argentea,* commonly called buffalo berry, silver buffalo berry and silverleaf, is a prickly shrub or tree growing to 18 feet, with silvery foliage and edible yellow or red fruit which is used for jelly. *S. canadensis,* also called buffalo berry, grows to about eight feet. Its leaves are green above and silvery beneath, and its fruit is flat tasting but edible.

SHODDY   *See* WOOL WASTES

SHORT-HORN GRASSHOPPER
See LOCUST

SHORTIA

This genus of the Diapensia family contains several species of stemless evergreen herbs or shrubs that spread by creeping rootstocks. In early spring, shortias produce a solitary, bell-shaped white flower atop a stalk arising from a cluster of roundish, leathery leaves. These perennial plants are useful in rock gardens and for planting under acid-loving shrubs. Shortias need an acid soil rich in humus and require regular mulching with oak leaf mold. Propagation is by runner or division.

Oconee bell (*S. galacifolia*) is native to the mountains of North Carolina. It grows to eight inches and has roundish, wavy-margined leaves and nodding white flowers, or, in variety Rosea, rose ones.

Fringed galax or fringe-bell (*S. soldanelloides*), a Japanese species, grows from two to four inches tall and has rose flowers paling to white or light pink at the edges. It thrives in alpine or rock gardens.

Nippon-bell (*S. uniflora*) is similar to oconee bell, but has leaves that are more heart shaped.

SHREDDER

Machines that shred and chop plant matter make composting much simpler and faster. Compost shredders help the home gardener to make compost in as little as 14 days. Cut-up leaves, weeds and other organic materials also make better mulch than whole materials do, because they hold moisture and form a thicker blanket which discourages weeds. Breakdown of shredded materials in the compost pile is faster, since a finer-textured heap heats up more quickly. Shredders are also used to grind and pulverize finished compost, which is ideal for lawns and for use in flower beds and in greenhouse benches and pots.

See also COMPOSTING.

SHRIMP PLANT
See HOUSE PLANTS

SHRUBBY ALTHAEA
See ROSE-OF-SHARON

SHRUBS

Shrubs are woody plants growing from a cluster of main stems, as distinguished from trees which usually grow from a single stem or trunk. Some small trees branch so close to the ground that for practical garden purposes they may be grouped with shrubs. Some of these will be found among the lists which follow.

Both evergreen and deciduous varieties of shrubs are useful in the home grounds. For the best year-round landscape, they should be mixed. Other characteristics which should be taken into account in planning shrubbery plantings are: *flowering*—blooming period, color and fragrance of blooms; *foliage*—color and texture; *fruiting*—ornamental value and quality; *location*—suitability of shrubs chosen for problem spots that are wet, dry or shady.

Planting and Culture: Soil requirements differ for various shrubs. In general, evergreens need an acid soil rich in humus, but with not too high a nitrogen content, while deciduous shrubs need richer soil, and may be given topdressings of compost or rotted manure. A leaf mulch under most shrubs will replenish organic matter in the soil. Unless fungus disease is a problem, leaves should be left where they fall, and may be supplemented by liberal mulching with grass clippings, peat, corncobs, straw, composted sawdust, or leaf mold. Bone meal may be added, and wood ashes are also beneficial if extreme acidity is not necessary to the species.

Most shrubs can be planted in either spring or fall. One useful rule is that leaf-dropping species should be set out while dormant—at least a week before the leaves appear in spring or at least a week after they have fallen in autumn.

If you are not ready to set the shrubs in their permanent place when they arrive, you will have to heel them in. Dig a trench and place the shrubs, roots down, in it. Then throw soil over them and water them well. They can be kept in this manner for a long time. If you are going to plant them in a few days, you can coat the roots with thick, souplike mud and stand them in the shade, covered with wet burlap. This is called "puddling," or "mudding." It can also be used to protect the roots from drying out if they are planted on hot windy days.

Dig holes large enough so that the roots will not be cramped. Fill the bottom of the hole to the desired height with topsoil and firm it down well. Then place the plant in the hole, with the roots puddled if necessary. After making certain that the roots are well spread and that any broken ones are cut off, fill in the hole with soil and tamp it down well. Leave a shallow depression around the newly planted shrub so that water will collect there and provide plenty of moisture.

Unless you have done so previously, shape the shrub, cutting back at least a third of its height. This applies to all woody plants except evergreens. Few shrubs require staking.

The following shrubs are difficult to move, and should always be purchased balled and burlapped: abelia, common bayberry, buckthorn, cotoneaster, inkberry, magnolia, rose-of-Sharon, snowball, and yew.

Pruning: Unless shrubs are intended to be used as hedges, their pruning should be light after they are established, consisting mainly of cutting back dead wood, removing faded flowers before fruit, which might tax the strength of the plant too greatly, forms, or cutting back overgrown specimens that have become leggy.

Any shrub which blooms early in spring on

wood grown the previous year should not be pruned until after the blooming period. Azalea, deutzia, forsythia, lilac, magnolia, mock orange, pearlbush, redbud, rose, spirea, Korean spice viburnum, and white fringe tree all bloom on last year's wood. If an attractive fruit is expected to follow the flowers, pruning should be limited to cutting out leggy growth, removing old wood, and shaping. If the shrub is a slow-grower like lilac, pruning should be very light. If it grows as rapidly as forsythia, it may be cut back drastically each year to produce more graceful growth for the following year.

Shrubs that bloom on new growth should be pruned very early in spring or in late winter. These include abelia, beautyberry, bladdernut, crab, goldflower, honeysuckle, hydrangea, hypericum, privet, pussy willow, rose-of-Sharon, summersweet, and New Jersey tea.

Shrubs that bloom in summer and fall and spring-blossoming varieties that bear desirable fruit are pruned just before growth starts in spring.

Pruning should be done primarily to keep shrubs in good health, rather than to restrain their growth. If small plants are required, specimens which naturally remain small should be planted. Large-growing species should not be barbered to small sizes and shapes. A shrub will be more graceful and will blend itself into the landscape much better if it is allowed to grow naturally. The one exception to this rule is for sculptured forms which are required in formal gardens.

Most shrubs will be improved by the removal of old wood from their centers. Many shrubs send up suckers which should be removed. Study the individual growth habit of each shrub and determine how to encourage it rather than to place it under restraint.

If shrubbery has become too thick and too high, which may happen in foundation groupings where unfortunate plantings of large-growing varieties have been made, it is best to remove some of the old shrubs and to replace them with lower-growing species. Dwarf varieties of almost all deciduous and evergreen shrubs have been developed. In addition, there are several naturally low-growing woody plants, including Chinese azalea, Japanese barberry, lowbush blueberry, alpine currant, and creeping juniper.

Drought-tolerant, Tender Shrubs: Some corners of southern gardens are sunny and dry out quickly, and for these locations shrubs that will grow with a moderate amount of water are required. These include Australian bluebells, plumbago and most of the roses.

Hardy Shrubs: In severe climates, such as that of northern Minnesota, native shrubs are more hardy than many of the standard cultivated kinds. Fewer varieties of native shrubs are found than farther south, but proper selection will provide for blooms from earliest spring to midsummer, and colorful fruit and foliage from then to late fall and early winter. Suitable native shrubs include arrowwood, low birch, buckthorn, northern sand cherry, black chokeberry, cranberry bush, gray dogwood, red-berried elder, hawthorn, hazel, fly honeysuckle, leatherwood, mountain maple, red osier, sumac, and smooth winterberry.

The most hardy rose for northern gardens is the meadow or smooth rose, so called because it is often without prickles. It will grow to seven feet in a sunny location, and bears pink blossoms in spring.

Moisture-tolerant Shrubs: In low, swampy areas where the soil may be quite acid, only a few selected shrubs can be grown. Among the most attractive of these are many varieties of arrowwood, swamp azalea, blueberry, buttonbush, black and red chokeberry, inkberry, nannyberry, pussy willow, swamp rose, Saint-John's-wort, spicebush, viburnum, and smooth winterberry.

Shade-tolerant Shrubs: Many shrubs tolerate shade for more than half the day. They are arrowwood, azalea, buttonbush, chokeberry, gray dogwood, hills-of-snow hydrangea, nannyberry, California privet, rhododendron, snowberry, spicebush, sumac, and weigela.

Others which will stand partial shade are: prickly ash, box, alpine currant, goldflower, Tatarian honeysuckle, Japanese hypericum, jet-bead, flowering raspberry, rose-of-Sharon, summersweet, sweet shrub, white fringe tree, and witchhazel.

Flowering Shrubs: Some of the most spectacular of the flowering shrubs are also tender, and cannot be grown in the North. The following are successful only in southern states: tender azaleas, camellias, lantana, oleaster, and royal poinciana.

Hundreds of varieties of rhododendron and azaleas make a dazzling spring showing further north, and a few are hardy as far north as New England. Other hardy shrubs which bloom where winters are extreme are flowering cherries and crabs, European cranberry bush, deutzia, dogwoods, forsythia, hawthorn, honeysuckles, hydrangea, certain magnolias, mock orange, Japanese quince, redbud, rose-of-Sharon, snowball, snowberry, spirea, sweet shrub, and long-blooming weigelas.

Edible-fruited types: Shrubs which serve as ornamentals and can also supply food for the family make themselves doubly valuable. Many bush-fruits supply large quantities of vitamin C, particularly some of the lesser-known and lesser-used berries and haws.

The European or Asiatic blackthorn or sloe is a tall twiggy bush whose white flowers open earlier than its leaves. Its edible berries are a bright blue in fall.

If your soil is acid, consider planting blueberry bushes. Their sizable, frosty blue fruit is both attractive and flavorful, and the small bell-shaped white flowers are pretty. Blueberries save their finest appearance for later in the season, when the autumn foliage takes on a brilliant scarlet color.

Several species of cherry serve as ornamentals. Nanking cherry is an early-flowering species which opens its white blossoms early in April. The cherries, which develop in June, are sweet and may be juiced to make a delicious drink.

Purpleleaf sand cherry is a medium-sized plant with red purple foliage that remains unchanged throughout the growing season. It produces edible purple black fruit in fall.

Sand cherry, western sand cherry and beach plum are often used to hold sandy soil in place. All have whitish flowers and berries which are wonderful for jam and jelly.

The cranberry bush has fruit rich in pectin, ideal for jams and jellies. Various varieties are excellent ornamentals, offering attractive flowers and foliage. Another viburnum whose fruit is rated valuable for jelly and jam is the native blackhaw, a tall bush, with oval blue black berries.

The alpine currant opens its spicy yellow blossoms in May. Its large black fruit which ripens in late summer is somewhat like a gooseberry in shape and flavor.

The elderberry or American elder has long been a favorite roadside shrub. The juicy, purple black berries ripen in August. Since they are coarse growers, elders are not recommended where space is limited.

(*continued on page 1030*)

RECOMMENDED SHRUBS FOR THE HOME GROUNDS

Common Name	Botanical Name	Height (ft.)	Flowering Period	Flower Color
Abelia, glossy	*Abelia* x *grandiflora*	6	June-October	pink
Aralia, five-leaved	*Acanthopanax sieboldianus*	9	May-June	green
Arborvitae, dwarf red	*Thuja plicata* cv. 'Cuprea'	4		
Arrowwood	*Viburnum dentatum*	15	June	white
Ash, prickly	*Aralia spinosa*	30		
Azalea, Chinese	*Rhododendron molle*	3	May	yellow
Azalea, snow	*Rhododendron mucronatum*	6	May	white
Azalea, swamp	*Rhododendron viscosa*	6	June-July	white
Azalea, yodogawa	*Rhododendron yedoense*	6	May-June	purple
Barberry, Japanese	*Berberis Thunbergii*	5	May	yellow
Bayberry, common	*Myrica pensylvanica*	9		
Beautyberry, purple	*Callicarpa americana*	6	May	blue
Beautybush	*Kolkwitzia amabilis*	8	May	white, pink
Birch, low	*Betula pumila*	15		
Blackhaw	*Viburnum prunifolium*	15	May	white
Blackthorn	*Prunus spinosa*	12	May	white
Bladdernut	*Staphylea colchica*	15	May-June	white
Bluebells, Australian	*Sollya heterophylla*	6	June	white
Blueberry, highbush	*Vaccinium corymbosum*	15	May-June	white
Blueberry, lowbush	*Vaccinium angustifolium*	1	May-June	white
Box, common	*Buxus sempervirens*	12		
Buckthorn, common	*Rhamnus cathartica*	12		
Buttonbush	*Cephalanthus occidentalis*	10	July-August	white
Camellia, Japanese	*Camellia japonica*	20	October-May	pink, red
Cherry, cornelian	*Cornus mas*	20	April-May	yellow
Cherry, Nanking	*Prunus tomentosa*	5	March-April	white
Cherry, sand	*Prunus pumila*	8	May-June	white
Chokeberry, black	*Aronia melanocarpa*	6	May	white
Chokeberry, red	*Aronia arbutifolia*	8	May	white
Cinquefoil, shrubby	*Potentilla fruticosa*	3	June-October	white, yellow
Cotoneaster	*Cotoneaster multiflorus*	8	May-June	white
Crab, cut-leaf	*Malus toringoides*	20	May	pink, white
Crab, Parkman	*Malus Halliana*	15	April-May	pink
Crab, Siberian	*Malus baccata* cv. 'Columnaris'	15	April-May	white
Crab, Soulard	*Malus* x *Soulardii*	14	May-June	pink
Cranberry bush	*Viburnum trilobum*	12	June	white
Cranberry bush, European	*Viburnum Opulus*	12	June	white
Currant, alpine	*Ribes alpinum*	4	May	yellow

Common Name	Botanical Name	Height (ft.)	Flowering Period	Flower Color
Deutzia, lemoine	*Deutzia lemoinei*	5	May	white
Dogwood, dwarf flowering	*Cornus florida* cv. 'Pygmy'	4	May	white
Dogwood, gray	*Cornus racemosa*	15	May	white
Dogwood, Kousa	*Cornus Kousa*	20	June	white
Elder, American	*Sambucus canadensis*	8	June-July	white
Elder, red-berried	*Sambucus pubens*	15	May-June	white, yellow
Fetterbush, mountain	*Pieris floribunda*	5	April-May	white
Firethorn, Laland	*Pyracantha coccinea*	20	May-June	white
Forsythia	*Forsythia* x *intermedia*	10	April-May	yellow
Fuchsia, hardy	*Fuchsia magellanica*	12	June-July	red, purple
Goldflower	*Hypericum Moseranum*	2	June	yellow
Hawthorn, English	*Crataegus laevigata*	15	May	white
Hazel, European	*Corylus Avellana*	25		
Holly, Japanese	*Ilex crenata*	10		
Honeysuckle, Amur	*Lonicera Maacki*	10	May	white
Honeysuckle, fly	*Lonicera Xylosteum*	10	May-June	white, yellow
Honeysuckle, Tatarian	*Lonicera tatarica*	8	May-June	white
Huckleberry, black	*Gaylussacia baccata*	3	May	white
Hydrangea, French	*Hydrangea macrophylla*	5	June-July	white, pink
Hydrangea, hills-of-snow	*Hydrangea arborescens*	4	June-July	white
Hydrangea, oakleaf	*Hydrangea quercifolia*	4	August	white
Hypericum, Japanese	*Hypericum japonicum*	2	June-August	yellow
Inkberry	*Ilex glabra*	8		
Jetbead	*Rhodotypos scandens*	6	May-October	white
Juniper, Andorra creeping	*Juniperus horizontalis*	3		
Juniper, Chinese	*Juniperus chinensis*	6		
Juniper, Rocky mountain	*Juniperus scopulorum*	30		
Lace shrub	*Stephanandra incisa*	8		
Lantana	*Lantana montevidensis*	3	June-July	pink, purple
Laurel	*Laurus nobilis*	30		
Laurel, great	*Rhododendron maximum*	12	May	pink, white
Laurel, mountain	*Kalmia latifolia*	6	June	pink, white
Leadwort, cape	*Plumbago auriculata*	5	June-September	blue, white
Leatherwood	*Dirca palustris*	6	May	yellow
Lilac	*Syringa vulgaris*	20	June	lilac, white
Magnolia, lily-flowered	*Magnolia quinquepeta*	8	April-May	white, purple
Magnolia, star	*Magnolia stellata*	10	April-May	white
Mahonia, holly	*Mahonia Aquifolium*	4		
Mahonia, leather-leaf	*Mahonia Bealei*	6		
Maple, dwarf amur	*Acer Ginnala*	3		
Maple, Japanese	*Acer palmatum*	20		

Common Name	Botanical Name	Height (ft.)	Flowering Period	Flower Color
Maple, mountain	*Acer Glabrum*	20		
Mock orange	*Philadelphus coronarius*	8	May	white
Nannyberry	*Viburnum Lentago*	30	May	white
Ninebark	*Physocarpus opulifolius*	8	May	white
Oleaster	*Elaeagnus angustifolia*	20	June-July	yellow
Orange eye	*Buddleia Davidii*	15	June-July	white, purple
Osier, red	*Cornus sericea*	10	June-July	white, yellow
Osmanthus	*Osmanthus* x *Fortunei*	8	June-July	white
Pearlbush	*Exochorda racemosa*	8	April-May	white
Pine, mountain	*Pinus Mugo*	30		
Plum, beach	*Prunus maritima*	10	June	white
Plumbago, Chinese	*Ceratostigma Willmottianum*	4	May-July	blue, purple
Poinciana, royal	*Delonix regia*	30	July-August	red
Privet, California	*Ligustrum ovalifolium*	15		
Pussy willow	*Salix caprea*	20		
Quince, Japanese	*Chaenomeles speciosa*	6	June-July	red, pink
Raspberry, flowering	*Rubus odoratus*	6	July-August	white
Redbud	*Cercis canadensis*	25	April	pink, red
Redbud, western	*Cercis occidentalis*	15	April	red
Rhododendron, Catawba	*Rhododendron catawbiense*	8	May	red, purple
Rhododendron, Fortune's	*Rhododendron Fortunei*	8	May	lilac, pink
Rose, alpine	*Rhododendron ferrugineum*	5	June-July	white, pink
Rose, baby	*Rosa multiflora*	10	June-August	white, pink
Rose, hugonis	*Rosa hugonis*	8	April-May	yellow
Rose, meadow	*Rosa blanda*	7	May-July	white, pink
Rose, rugosa	*Rosa rugosa*	6	May-June	white, pink
Rose, Scotch	*Rosa spinosissima*	4	June	yellow, white
Rose, swamp	*Rosa palustris*	7	May-July	white, pink
Rose-of-Sharon	*Hibiscus syriacus*	10	August	white, purple
Saint-John's-wort, shrubby	*Hypericum prolificum*	4	July	yellow
Serviceberry	*Amelanchier alnifolia*	15	April	white
Snowball	*Viburnum Opulus* cv. 'Roseum'	10	May-June	white
Snowberry	*Symphoricarpos albus*	3	July-September	pink
Spicebush	*Lindera Benzoin*	12	April-May	yellow
Spirea, Bumalda	*Spiraea* x *Bumalda*	3	July-August	white, pink
Spirea, Japanese	*Spiraea japonica*	6	May-June	pink
Spirea, Vanhoutte	*Spiraea* x *Vanhouttei*	6	April-May	white
Sumac, fragrant	*Rhus aromatica*	6	May	yellow
Summersweet	*Clethra alnifolia*	10	July-August	white, pink
Sweet shrub	*Calycanthus floridus*	6	May-June	purple
Tea, New Jersey	*Ceanothus americanus*	3	June	white

Common Name	Botanical Name	Height (ft.)	Flowering Period	Flower Color
Viburnum, Korean spice	*Viburnum Carlesii*	4	May	white
Wahoo	*Euonymus atropurpureus*	15	May	purple, red
Weigela	*Weigela floribunda*	10	May-June	red, pink
Weigela	*Weigela florida*	8	May-June	pink, purple
White fringe tree	*Chionanthus virginica*	20	May	white
Winterberry, smooth	*Ilex laevigata*	12		
Witchhazel	*Hamamelis virginiana*	15	October	yellow
Wolfberry	*Symphoricarpos occidentalis*	5	June	white, pink
Yew, Japanese	*Taxus cuspidata*	20		

Japanese quince is an early-flowering border shrub useful in any sunny location. It blooms and bears fruit well even when clipped. For a taller variety, you might choose the common garden quince. While it lacks the glossy foliage of the Japanese forms, it offers larger pink white flowers and larger fruit.

High on the vitamin C list is the fruit of the rugosa rose, a hardy species of rose that may be grown in hot dry places, in severe winter latitudes, in rich or poor soil, and even near the sea. A full-grown plant will attain 15 feet, with glassy, somewhat crumpled foliage and white, pink or purple flowers in spring. Rugosa hips are useful for their extract, which may be added to fruit juices, jellies, or other foods for additional vitamin C. *See also* RUGOSA ROSE.

Forcing Shrub Blossoms: Many early spring-flowering shrubs will provide flowers during the late winter months if branches are cut and brought into the house. Varieties which open their blossoms before their leaves are especially suited for forcing. At any time after its leaves have dropped in fall, forsythia will open its flowers indoors. Branches cut in December may take four or five weeks to bloom, while those cut nearer to the natural outdoor blossoming period will open more quickly. Bloom may be hastened if the branches are sprayed daily with warm water.

Other shrubs which may be forced indoors include cornelian cherry, crab, magnolia, pussy willow, quince, redbud, serviceberry, and spirea. Color is completely lacking in some of the more delicately tinted blossoms when they are forced. In others, the color grows stronger as the forcing time approaches normal flowering time.

See also entries for individual shrubs, EVERGREEN, FORCING, LAYERING, PRUNING.

SIDALCEA

Also known as false mallow, this genus includes annual and perennial flowers that resemble small hollyhocks. Sidalceas grow to three feet and have alternate, palmate leaves and spires of white, pink, red, and purple flowers that bloom in June and July. Plants planted in rich sandy soil can be propagated from root divisions or from seed.

Wild hollyhock (*S. malviflora*) has rose,

pink or white flowers, while *S. candida,* a Rocky Mountain native, has pure white ones.

SILAGE

Silage is a succulent forage such as corn, alfalfa, grass, or sorghum which is cut into short lengths and preserved by compaction and fermentation in the absence of oxygen.

A silo is any building or other storage receptacle for preserving cut green feed in the absence of air. It may have wood, stone, metal, glass, or earth as its air-excluding walls, or the silage itself may serve as a barrier.

See also HAY.

SILENE   *See* LYCHNIS

SILK-TASSEL TREE
See QUININE BUSH

SILK TREE   (*Albizzia Julibrissin*)

The silk tree belongs to the Legume family. Although *Albizzia* is a genus of tropical shrubs and trees, the silk tree is hardy as far north as Boston. It is a small tree with a broad-spreading crown and compounded leaves which have the feathery appearance of acacia or mimosa leaves. It produces exotic-looking, light pink feathery flowers in slender-stalked, compact heads. The fruits are flat pods measuring about five inches long and one inch wide.

The silk tree is highly ornamental, and tends to create a distinctly tropical atmosphere in a northern garden. New plants can be easily propagated from seed under glass.

SILT

A primary source of plant nutrients, silt is a loose, unconsolidated mineral material with particles much smaller than sand yet larger than clay particles.

SILVER-DOLLAR
See HONESTY

SIMPLE LAYERING
See LAYERING

SISYRINCHIUM

Known also as blue-eyed grass or satinflower, this genus of small half-hardy-to-hardy perennials of the Iris family has plants with grasslike leaves and clusters of yellow, blue or red purple flowers. They grow wild in rich meadows and swamps, but may be easily grown in the border if given a moist, rich garden soil. They may also be naturalized in the wild garden. Propagation is by seed or division of the clumps.

S. angustifolium grows to one foot and has violet blue flowers that bloom in June. Native to Oregon and California, *S. californicum* is called golden-eyed grass for its bright yellow flowers. It grows to 1½ feet.

SKIMMIA

These slow-growing evergreen shrubs belong to the Rue family and are hardy south of Washington, D.C., and on the West Coast.

They make good city plantings because they tolerate smoke and other environmental pollutants. They can also be grown in the greenhouse in pots containing a sandy mixture of peat and loam.

Skimmias prefer a sandy peat soil and partial or full shade. In cool regions, they may be grown in pots and set out on a porch or shaded walkway during the summer months.

S. japonica is the most common skimmia. It has male and female flowers that usually occur on separate plants. The small white flowers bloom in April and May. Male plants flower more profusely than female specimens, but the females put forth red berries that remain on the bushes from late fall through early spring. To encourage berry formation, plant one bush of each sex or plant one male for every three females.

S. Reevesiana is a smaller, more tender plant whose flowers contain both stamens and pistils. It is, however, less hardy than *S. japonica* and considered inferior.

SKULLCAP   (*Scutellaria*)

Members of a genus of annual and perennial herbs of the Mint family, skullcaps are small plants, growing no more than a foot tall. They have silvery foliage and spikes of scarlet, yellow, blue, or violet flowers that are followed by cup-shaped seedpods. Propagation is by seed or division.

S. indica var. *parvivolia,* sometimes listed as *S. japonica,* has gray green foliage and intense blue flowers in dense four-inch clusters. It grows to six inches. *S. orientalis* has gray green

foliage and yellowish flowers. *S. alpina,* with clusters of purple and white flowers, grows to ten inches and is a rapid spreader. All species flower in mid to late summer.

SKUNK

Studies of skunks show that their principal food is insects that are injurious to plant life. In fact, skunks deserve much credit for digging out the june bug and May beetle in both larval and adult stages. Ripe fruit constitutes an important part of skunk diet, but it is usually gathered from the surface of the ground where it would otherwise be wasted. In addition, skunks eat mice and injured or dead birds. Sometimes skunks invade beehives in their search for food. Damage can be prevented if hives are placed on benches or stands.

SLAG   *See* BASIC SLAG

SLIP

A slip is a cutting taken from a plant for propagation purposes.

See also CUTTINGS.

SLIPPERWORT   *See* CALCEOLARIA

SLUDGE   *See* SEWAGE SLUDGE

SLUGS AND SNAILS

Slugs and snails are members of closely related families in the Mollusk phylum. Both have soft bodies and secrete a silvery mucus that appears in trails across the garden and over plants. Snails carry a shell about with them.

Slugs and snails would be little more than curiosities if it weren't for their appetites. They are apt to nibble at the low-lying parts of many crops. These mollusks usually travel and eat by night.

Dry, cold periods and daylight hours are spent hiding beneath boards and plant debris, so control of them depends on ridding the garden of such shelter. Slugs and snails are repelled by a mulch of oak leaves or tobacco stem meal. A drenching of wormwood tea will deter them. Hellebore has long been used to keep slugs from grapevines. A dash of salt will cause them to shrivel up. The pests are attracted to stale beer, and will drown in a bit of the liquid set out in jar lids.

Among their natural enemies are ladybug larvae, snakes and turtles.

Slugs and snails are not insects but rather mollusks with soft, unsegmented bodies. They are covered by a thick mucous membrane which leaves a silvery trail wherever they travel.
(Courtesy of U.S. Department of Agriculture)

SMARTWEED (*Polygonum*)

A number of these pest plants contain juices that are bitterly pungent or peppery and cause smarting or irritation when in contact with the eyes and nostrils. Occasionally they cause a skin rash in people who are particularly sensitive.

The weak, reddish stems, willow-shaped leaves and greenish flowers of the mild water pepper cause irritation when brought in contact with the eyes.

The mild water pepper (*P. hydropiper-oides*) is probably the most irritating. Found primarily in damp or wet places, it has weak, reddish stems, willow-shaped alternate leaves and greenish flowers. Another widely found species is the lady's thumb smartweed (*P. persicaria*). This differs from the water pepper in having a somewhat triangular, purple thumbprint on each leaf.

Frequent mowing will prevent seed set and improved drainage will discourage these plants.

See also POLYGONUM.

SMILACINA

Also known as false Solomon's seal, this genus of the Lily family contains a number of perennial herbs useful for naturalizing with ferns and semiwild garden plants, in partly shady corners of the garden. They grow well in any moderately rich garden soil with plenty of moisture, and are propagated by division of the rhizomes. Pale green white flower clusters at the top of the plant are followed by very showy red berries. The leaves are simple and alternate, with parallel veins.

The most frequently cultivated species is *S. racemosa,* commonly called false spikenard or treacleberry. It grows to three feet, with individual leaves six inches long and red berries. The plants are very showy when grown in colonies under trees, both during the blooming season and in fall when the red berries ripen. Birds are fond of the fruit, and probably help to establish the plant in new areas. Try growing them from seed extracted from the berry pulp and sown in an outdoor bed, or buy plants. Avoid digging them from the wild.

SMILAX

These thorny vines of the Lily family which climb by tendrils are mostly native to North America. The most common species are called greenbriers and catbriers. They grow in any moist garden soil where partial shade is provided. Although they are sometimes considered ornamentals, their use in gardens is limited since they tend to form impenetrable thickets.

Other species are strictly tropical plants that can only be grown in the greenhouse. The familiar baby smilax or smilax asparagus is sometimes classified as a member of this genus but is more properly called *Asparagus asparagoides*. It is a tuberous-rooted vine with deep green leaves and white or yellow flowers. Trained on strings in the greenhouse, it requires the same cultural conditions as the true smilax.

Of the hardy species, sawbrier or wild sasparilla (*S. glauca*) is the most widespread shrubby type. It has dark blue berries and thick roots which were used by various northern Indians to make bread and soup. Carrion flower (*S. herbacea*) is a hardy herbaceous vine that grows in open fields throughout Canada and the eastern United States. Its leaves can be gathered and used as a potherb.

SMITHIANTHA

Smithianthas, sometimes listed as members of the genus *Naegelia,* are perennial tropical herbs of the Gesneria family. Raised in warm greenhouses, they usually grow to two or three feet. They have soft heart-shaped leaves and clusters of tubular flowers that are about 1½ inches long and colored red, yellow, purple, or white.

Propagation may be by seed, by division of tubers, or by offsets. Soil must be rich in humus and well drained. In the greenhouse the plants should be slightly screened from full sun, especially when flowering. After flowering, the pots with tubers are placed below the bench and allowed a period of rest during which they are kept almost dry. Seed is sown in well-drained peaty soil in late winter to early spring. Cuttings may be rooted at the same time. The blossoming period will be from September to November.

The difference between species is mainly a matter of size and color. *S. cinnabarina* is two feet high and has cinnabar red flowers that are spotted with white and swollen toward the base. The leaves are covered with reddish hairs. *S. multiflora* grows to about 1½ feet, and has white flowers with a slightly swollen tube. *S. zebrina* is taller, growing to three feet. Its hairy leaves are red or brown along the veins, and its flowers are red with yellow spots and contracted at the base. *S. hybrida,* a hybrid of *zebrina* and *multiflora,* is a short plant with hairy leaves and creamy blossoms.

SMOTHER CROP

A smother crop is a crop, such as buckwheat, that is thickly sown in a field overrun with weeds. As the term implies, the purpose of the seeded crop is to smother the weeds. Later all the vegetation, weeds and crop, can be worked like a green manure crop into the soil.

SNAILS   *See* SLUGS AND SNAILS

SNAKEMOUTH   *See* POGONIA

SNAKE PLANT   *See* SANSEVIERIA

SNAKES

There are about 220 distinct kinds of snakes on the North American continent. All are beneficial to mankind since they consume enormous numbers of harmful rodents and insects. The United States has only four major types of snakes with defense mechanisms which sometimes prove hazardous to man: the rattlesnake, the copperhead, the cottonmouth moccasin, and the coral snake.

SNAP BEANS   *See* BEANS

SNAPDRAGON   *(Antirrhinum)*

These hardy perennial or annual flowers can be divided into three groups: tall—to four feet; intermediate—to 1½ feet; and dwarf—to one foot. Popular for the color they add to the flower garden, snapdragons are also fine for cut flowers. The tall sorts add a spire effect to the border.

Planting and Culture: Seed may be planted directly outside when the soil has warmed up, but an early start indoors lengthens the flowering season. Start seed indoors at least eight weeks before the last severe spring frost in your locality. Plant the seed in flats, or in pots if you prefer, in regular light garden soil. Either scatter the seed or plant it in rows on the surface, covering it lightly with approximately ⅛ inch or less of soil. Tamp the soil lightly to make good soil-seed contact, but be careful not to pack it. Keep the soil moist and place the container in a warm location, as the seed requires warmth for good germination. Be sure to provide good air circulation to minimize the chance of seedlings damping-off. The seed may be rather slow in germinating, but after the true leaves have formed, the growth is usually rapid. Thin or transplant seedlings to other flats or 2¼-inch peat pots. When sunny spring days come along, set the flat of young seedlings outdoors, bringing them in at night. The plants will develop and grow faster in the open ground if they are permitted to harden off for at least a week outdoors before transplanting to the permanent garden location.

Snapdragons prefer a sunny location and a well-drained soil that is moderately rich. Before planting the seedlings or seed, add some compost or leaf mold to the soil, mixing it well. Set the seedlings about eight to ten inches apart in rows or in groups as you prefer. Water the seedlings for several days until their roots are well established. Water throughout the season during dry spells. To encourage the growth of flower-bearing side branches, pinch out the central bud. By keeping faded flowers cut, you will also encourage more blooming.

When the taller varieties begin to look tired and faded, about midsummer, cut them back to about four inches from the ground, top-dress with rich compost and water regularly with compost tea or dilute fish emulsion. This will usually cause them to produce another crop of flower spikes in late summer and fall.

Varieties: Plant breeders have done much work on the snapdragon, perfecting bigger blooms, longer spikes, double flowers, and rust-resistant strains. It is important to select rust-resistant varieties because this disease can be a serious handicap. The three-foot Rocket series is an excellent heat- and rust-resistant tall variety available in individual colors or as a mixture. Little Darling is a 12-inch semidwarf which branches heavily, has open-faced flowers and is excellent for bedding. Floral Carpet grows to only eight inches and can be spaced six inches apart. It does form a solid carpet of color when in bloom, but is less heat tolerant than Little Darling.

SNEEZE-WEED   *See* HELENIUM

SNOUT BEETLE
See CURCULIO, INSECT CONTROL

SNOW

Although snow does not contain any appreciable quantity of plant nutrients, it often acts as a natural buffer or mulch, helping to protect the soil and plants it covers from severe freezing and heaving. In some cases, the gradual thawing of snow improves the soil's texture.

SNOWBALL   *See* VIBURNUM

SNOWBERRY

Snowberry is the common name applied to two different plants, *Symphoricarpos albus,* the snowberry bush, and *Gaultheria hispidula,* a snowberry vine.

Snowberry bush is a member of the Honeysuckle family. It is a hardy, three-foot shrub, easily grown anywhere in North America. It has oval leaves, pinkish flowers and fat white berries. The bush is propagated by seed, cuttings, suckers, or division of roots. It does well in full sunlight or shade and has no particular soil requirements.

Snowberry vine is a creeping evergreen of the Heath family that grows in cold, wet, wild places in the northern part of the United States. It can be grown in wild gardens or rock gardens only under evergreens and only where the summers are not too hot. The flowers are white small bells, and they are followed by white berries of the same size. This vine is propagated by cuttings and division.

Snowdrops will bloom very early in the spring if the bulbs are planted in late summer just three inches deep.

SNOWDRIFT
See SWEET ALYSSUM

SNOWDROP   (*Galanthus*)

Members of the Amaryllis family, these attractive plants bloom for weeks in early spring, often before the snow completely disappears. Common snowdrop (*G. nivalis*) grows to about one foot high. Its solitary, nodding, bell-shaped flowers are green inside and white outside. *G. n.* cv. 'Flore Pleno' is a double form. It does best in light, moist, humus-rich soil and partial shade. Giant snowdrop (*G. Elwesii*) grows to about 1½ feet and should have a bit more sun and sandy soil. Mulch it with compost in fall.

For best effect, mass plantings of snowdrops should be made. Plant bulbs around Labor Day, placing them three inches deep and three inches apart.

See also BULB.

SNOWDROP TREE   (*Halesia*)

Growing on the banks of streams from Virginia and Illinois south to Florida, the beautiful snowdrop or silverbell tree bears clusters of pendent, white, bell-shaped flowers which appear with the leaves in early summer. Winged, light brown fruits, which are oblong, and rather fleshless, dry drupes, appear soon after. One of the loveliest of small hardy trees, the snowdrop tree can be kept small by proper pruning. Care should be exercised in pruning, since the flowers bloom on twigs produced the previous season. The snowdrop tree prefers a rich, well-drained soil and a protected site. It grows best in a sunny position, but will tolerate light shade. Propagation is by seeding or root cuttings.

SNOWFLAKE   (*Leucojum*)

A genus of bulbous plants of the Amaryllis family, leucojums produce drooping white flowers. Spring-flowering species put forth narrow basal leaves along with the flowers, and summer and fall species flower before leaves appear. Bulbs are planted four to five inches deep in sandy soil, and left undisturbed.

Spring snowflake (*L. vernum*) has solitary flowers that appear about a month after snowdrops bloom. These are white, tipped with green, and are borne on stalks nine to 12 inches high.

Summer snowflake (*L. aestivum*) grows a little taller, with its blossoms in clusters of two to eight per stalk.

Autumn snowflake (*L. autumnale*) has very slender stalks on which one to three blossoms open. This species is more tender than the others, so it needs winter protection in the North.

SOAPBARK TREE
(*Quillaja Saponaria*)

Although occasionally grown in Florida and Southern California, this evergreen tree comes from South America. It is fairly ornamental and grows to a height of 60 feet, but it is of interest chiefly for its bark, from which a lather can be worked up.

SOAPBERRY   (*Sapindus*)

The soapberry is a tropical American tree or shrub, whose berries are rich in saponin, a substance used for cleansing. The tree does best in dry, sandy or rocky soil, and can be propagated by seed or cuttings made in spring.

Soapberry is grown in southern Florida for ornament. *S. Drummondii* is a deciduous tree growing to 50 feet, with ten-inch clusters of yellow white flowers followed by yellow berries which turn black.

S. Saponaria is an evergreen that grows to 30 feet, bears flowers in ten-inch white clusters and produces shiny yellow brown fruit.

SOAP PLANT   See Zigadenus

SOAPWORT   See Saponaria

SOD

The upper stratum of the soil which is filled with plant roots and supports a thick stand of grass or other vegetation is called sod.

SODIUM

Sodium is a micronutrient not absolutely necessary for plant growth though it is present in all plants. Soil scientists do not seem to know a great deal about the action of sodium in small quantities. Excessive amounts of sodium can create serious problems. Soils with a high sodium content in the surface horizon are detrimental to plant growth and are classified as saline or sodic soils.

See also ALKALI SOILS, SALINE SOIL.

SOIL

Soil is the loose top layer of the earth's surface, which supplies plants with nutrients and minerals and which serves as a medium in which root systems develop. More specifically, soil is any part of the earth's surface which displays a soil profile and has recognizable horizons. The soil profile is a vertical cross section of earth, as you might see on a roadbank. It consists of a series of horizontal layers, called horizons, beginning at bedrock and progressing through various layers of subsoil to the uppermost layer of topsoil. The horizons are used by scientists as a means of classifying soils. *See also* SOIL HORIZON.

Soils are composed of several different components. Organic matter, minerals and other solid materials form a basis for the soil. Liquids (water) and gases (air) fill the gaps between soil solids. The amount and state of these elements vary greatly and depend on a variety of conditions, such as the amount of rainfall or the degree of compaction.

The organic fraction of soil varies greatly depending largely upon the soil's parent materials. The topsoil of an active garden or farm might consist of about 49 percent minerals and only 1 percent organic matter. In a virgin prairie soil, the organic matter content may be more than 10 percent and some soils might contain as much as 20 percent organic matter.

The deeper one penetrates the soil, the less organic matter one finds; at a depth of about 30 feet there may be only one-eighth of 1 percent.

The mineral portion of the soil also varies considerably in composition. The size of the mineral particles is very important to the soil. The ability of the soil to absorb water, its porosity and its tilth all depend on the size of the soil particles. Numerous other factors, including nutrient availability, are directly affected by soil particle size.

The majority of soil minerals are made up of only eight elements. These are (in order of decreasing abundance): oxygen, silicon, aluminum, iron, calcium, magnesium, potassium, and sodium. All the other elements occur in smaller quantities, although this does not mean that they play an unimportant role in plant growth, or, indeed, in animal nutrition and human health. Mineral elements occur in the soil as part of simple compounds or as complex silicates, which appear in a great number of colors and compositions. Due to various chemical reactions, weathering and leaching, these are broken down into secondary silicates which form the basis for clay minerals, the principal component of the clay portion of the soil.

How Soil Is Formed: Originally the entire earth was one mass of rock and the only living things were microbes—single-celled organisms. Through their activities, these bacteria and fungi liberated carbon dioxide and certain organic and inorganic acids. These had a solvent action upon rocks, beginning a process that broke them down into soil. The dead bodies of these early organisms were the beginnings of the organic matter that, when mixed with the tiny fragments of rocks, would form the first soil. The action of heat, cold, wind, rain, glacier movement, and other physical, chemical and biological factors soon contributed to the process. The difference in temperature between day and night caused expansion and contraction, producing open seams in the rock that permitted water to enter deeper into the rock. Freezing and thawing and other weathering detached rock fragments which were in turn acted upon and further broken down. The process of decomposition by water is called hydrolysis. Soluble materials may be lost in hydrolysis unless trapped by chemical reactions that change them to less soluble forms.

Eventually the decaying remains of primitive plants such as lichens and mosses began to cover the exposed rocks. Living moss grew on other exposed surfaces, its minute tentacles penetrating the rock and aiding in the decomposition of the rock surfaces. Slowly, a film of soil began to form over the rocks, providing the foothold for the plants in the next phase of soil evolution—the ferns. Gradually as the soil thickened, other higher plants and trees began to grow. Finally, jungles and rain forests came into being, further adding to the layer of decomposing organic matter on the earth. The whole process took millions of years to accomplish.

Soil was formed not only from the original bedrock, but also from rock that had been moved by glacial and other natural forces. Soil continues to be formed and is constantly being created by the same forces which formed it originally. Bedrock is still gradually turning to subsoil. It takes these processes perhaps 500 years to make one inch of soil.

Texture: Soil texture is related to the size of the mineral particles in the soil and, in fact, to the relative proportion of various particle-size groups in a specific soil. You can ascertain to some extent the texture of your soil by performing a simple test. Pick up a pinch of soil between your fingers and rub your fingers together. Sand feels gritty. Silt is powdery, like talcum powder. Clay is hard when dry, slippery when wet, and rubbery when moist.

These three substances, sand, silt and clay, in varying proportions, determine the texture of soil. Sand particles are the largest of the three measuring from $\frac{1}{50}$ to $\frac{1}{500}$ inch. When predominant, sand particles form a coarsely textured soil. Silt particles range from $\frac{1}{500}$ to $\frac{1}{2,500}$ inch, and clay particles are less than $\frac{1}{12,500}$ inch—so small they cannot be seen with an ordinary microscope. Sand and silt particles are chemically stable in the sense that they retain the same chemical composition as the mother rock from which they came, but clay particles are very reactive, constantly taking on and giving up ions of other elements in the soil.

Clay particles along with humus serve as a storehouse of soil nutrients. Sand and silt (and to some extent humus) serve as the determinants of soil texture. A clay soil contains about 60 percent clay, 30 percent silt and 10 percent sand. Clay loam consists of 35 percent clay, 35 percent silt and 30 percent sand. Loam, the most desirable soil in texture, contains 10 percent clay, 50 percent silt and 40 percent sand.

Structure: Soil structure depends on the grouping of individual particles into larger clusters. The most important are sphenoidal particles called granules if they are loose and do not swell much when wetted. If especially porous, they are called crumbs. Although no one knows for sure how crumbs form, scientists do know that organic matter contributes significantly to the formation of a good soil structure. In addition, the presence of earthworms aids in maintaining soil structure.

Good granulation or crumb structure of the heavier soils is essential for healthy crops.

Sandy soils show little if any granulation, due to the coarseness of their component particles. The structure of such soils is best improved by the addition of large amounts of organic matter and by planting sod crops. Organic matter will help to bind soil particles and hold water in the soil.

Heavy clay soils are also helped by the addition of organic matter—but this must be done carefully. If clay soils are tilled when too wet, they become dense and practically impervious to water and air. When dry, they are hard and dense. Plowing a wet clay soil can result in a cloddy, unsatisfactory seedbed. Clay soil will benefit from applications of organic matter and from sod crops grown in a good rotation. *See also* Soil Compaction.

Porosity: Pore space, or porosity, is associated with both texture and structure of soils. Pore spaces are large in coarse, sandy soils or in those with well-developed granulation. In heavy soils containing mostly fine clay particles, the pore spaces may be too small for plant roots or soil water to penetrate readily. Good soils have 40 to 60 percent of their bulk occupied with pore space, which may be filled with either water or air, both of which are important.

As in all other soil relationships, a satisfactory balance between water and air is important for productivity. Too much water slows the release of soil nitrogen, depletes mineral nutrients, and otherwise hinders proper plant growth. Too much air speeds nitrogen release beyond the capacity of plants to utilize it, so that much of it is lost. The stored water in an overly aerated soil evaporates into the atmosphere and is lost to plants.

Water: Soil water occurs in three forms, designated as hygroscopic, gravitational and capillary. The hygroscopic soil water is chemically bound in the soil constituents and is unavailable to plants. Gravitational water is that which normally drains out of the pore spaces of the soil after a rain. If drainage is poor, it is this water that causes the soil to be soggy and unproductive. Excessive drainage hastens the time when capillary water runs short and plants suffer from drought.

It is the capillary water upon which plants depend very largely for their supply of moisture. Hence the capacity of a soil to hold water against the pull of gravity is of great importance in ordinary agriculture. Organic matter and good structure add to the supply of water in soils.

Plants cannot extract the last drop of capillary water from a soil, since soil moisture tends to resist the pull exerted by the plant roots. The point at which the attraction of soil materials and the pull of plant roots are just equal is called the "wilting coefficient" of a soil. This term is used to express the level of soil moisture at which water becomes unavailable to plants. In other words, it represents the percentage of water in a soil at the time the loss from transpiration exceeds the renewal of the water by capillary means. Medium-textured loams and silt loams, because of the faster rate of movement of moisture from lower depths to the root zone within them and because they can bring up moisture from greater depths than either sands or clays, provide the best conditions of available but not excessive soil moisture and promote the best plant growth.

See also Aeration, Carbon, Carbon-Nitrogen Ratio, Humus, Mineral Rocks, Nitrogen, Organic Matter, Soil Conservation.

SOIL ASSOCIATION
See Haughley Experiment

SOIL CLASSIFICATION

The soil classification system presently used in the United States is called the Comprehensive Soil Survey System and supersedes earlier attempts at developing a comprehensive system for classifying soil structure. It was adopted in 1965 after seven preliminary approximations (drafts) were circulated for comment from the scientific community.

The new system offers several advantages over previous classification systems. It is based on the properties of soils as they are found in the field. These properties can be verified empirically and quantitatively. The names chosen for soils, especially in the broader classifications, give a definite idea of the soils' properties. Based on Latin and Greek roots, they can be understood by scientists throughout the world. For example, under the present system, soils found in dry climates are grouped in the order Aridisols (a combination of the Latin *aridus,* dry, and *solum,* soil).

A specific soil is classified according to a system of categorical nomenclature very similar to botanical nomenclature (*see* BOTANICAL NOMENCLATURE). The order, the broadest grouping, is based primarily on soil morphology with soil genesis a consideration, since soils of similar genesis tend to be similar. Suborders are subdivisions which emphasize genetic similarities such as wetness, climate or vegetation. The great group includes soils with similar diagnostic horizons; subgroups are a subdivision of this group, and include soils with closely related horizons. The properties of the family are similar soil pH, texture, temperature, and mineral content. The series, or more specific grouping, is essentially unchanged from previous usage and refers to soils developed from the same parent material by the same genetic processes with horizons of similar arrangement and content. The only variation between soils in the same series is in the depth and content of the surface horizons, and even these should not vary greatly.

The accompanying chart describes the recently adopted soil orders in terms of the old classification systems. Characteristics of each order follow.

Alfisols: Generally lying in humid areas and productive when cultivated, alfisols have gray to brown surface horizons and subsurface accumulations of clay. They are usually moist but may dry out somewhat during the dry season.

Aridisols: Generally low in organic matter, Aridisols are mineral soils located in dry regions. They have not been subjected to leaching in the upper horizons, and can be fairly productive if irrigated.

Entisols: These soils lack natural genetic horizons or show only the beginnings of such horizons. They vary in productivity and fertility and are found in a variety of climatic conditions.

Histosols: Developed in a water-saturated environment, Histosols have a high content of organic matter, with much of the organic tissue undecomposed. If drained, they can be quite productive, and when they are cultivated the original tissue tends to disappear.

Inceptisols: These are young soils with varying productivity formed from the alteration of parent materials rather than from accumulation.

Mollisols: Soils with surface horizons high in organic matter and a black color are called Mollisols. They do not solidify when dry. Mollisols have formed in areas of extensive grassland or in forested areas, and they are present in some of the richest agricultural land in the world.

Oxisols: Highly weathered soils, they are characterized by the presence of a deep subsurface horizon high in clays and iron and aluminum oxides. They are seldom used for crop production at present, and not very much is known about them.

Spodosols: These soils contain a light-colored, subsurface horizon of organic matter and aluminum oxides. Spodosols are coarse textured and generally low in fertility. They are most common in cold, humid regions.

Ultisols: Moist soils that were formed on old land surfaces and still retain some minerals are called ultisols. They have large amounts of iron oxides in the surface horizons and are characterized by a yellow color, are weathered and slightly acidic. Ultisols usually are located in areas with good moisture and long growing seasons and are productive when well managed.

Vertisols: Vertisols have a high content of swelling clays that develop wide, deep cracks when dry. Some surface matter leaches or moves into the cracks, thus "inverting" the soil structure. Although cultivated in some parts of the world, they are generally infertile.

NEW SOIL ORDERS AND THEIR OLDER EQUIVALENTS

New Order	Approximate Equivalents
Alfisol	Many planosols and gray-brown podzolic, gray-wooded, noncalcic brown, degraded chernozem, and some half-bog soils
Aridisol	Desert, red desert, sierozem, solonchak, some brown and red-brown and associated solonetz soils
Entisol	Regosols and azonal and some low-humic gley soils
Histosol	Bog and half-bog soils
Inceptisol	Ando, tundra, some brown forest, low-humic gley, and humic gley soils
Mollisol	Chestnut, chernozem, brunizem (prairie), rendzina, some brown forest, and associated solonetz and humic gley soils
Oxisol	Latosols and most groundwater laterites
Spodosol	Podzols, groundwater podzols, and brown podzolic soils
Ultisol	Red-yellow podzolic, red-brown lateritic, and associated planosol soils
Vertisol	Grumusols

Source: Soil Survey Staff, Soil Conservation Service, USDA. *Soil Classification: A Comprehensive System* (Washington, D.C.: United States Government Printing Office, 1960).

SOIL COMPACTION

Soil compaction, the hardening of soil into an impenetrable mass, results from poor cultural practices and the frequent passage of heavy machinery. Plants growing on compacted soil cannot develop healthy roots. By loosening lower soil levels with a subsoiler and by using green manure crops, the gardener can encourage deeper root penetration. To prevent compaction the gardener should try not to use heavy tractors and implements on plowed land unless they are necessary and should use lightweight machinery whenever possible.

See also AERATION, COMPOSTING, COVER CROP, GREEN MANURE, MULCH, ROTARY TILLAGE.

SOIL CONSERVATION

The conservation of our agricultural resource base is one of the most important tasks facing Americans today. There are about 438 million acres of harvestable cropland in the United States and although this seems like an unlimited amount of land, it is very small in the face of the growing worldwide need for increased amounts of food. Unfortunately, Americans have a poor record when it comes to soil conservation. The agricultural history of this country in the last 300 years is, with few exceptions, one of wholesale soil exploitation.

Many American farmers traditionally worked a piece of ground until it was worn out and unproductive and then moved on to other fertile land. The effects of this blatant disregard for soil were dramatically experienced when thousands of acres of once-rich prairie land in the Great Plains turned into the dust bowl, necessitating continuing government soil conservation programs for helping farmers in planning conservation methods for their farms.

Severe erosion problems are best managed in consultation with a professional. The Soil Conservation Service of the U.S. Department of Agriculture maintains expert personnel in almost every county in the United States and upon request, these individuals will study specific farms and make recommendations about how each piece of land can best be handled.

To make matters easier, experts have established eight classes of land. Land in Classes I, II and III is suitable for cultivation. Class I land requires no special conservation techniques other than continued maintenance of soil fertility. Classes II and III require more erosion-preventing measures. Class II needs only simple conservation measures but Class III land care involves measures such as terracing, drainage improvement, cover cropping, and crop rotations, either alone or in combination. Class IV land should only be cultivated occasionally and, whether cultivated or not, requires special conservation practices to control erosion. Class V, VI and VII lands are suitable for permanent vegetation, but not for cultivation. Class VII land requires special conservation practices while Class VI land is less severely restricted in use. Finally, Class VIII land is not suitable for forests, cultivation or grazing, and is extremely rough, sandy, wet, or dry.

To be truly effective, soil conservation must begin at home—each farmer must practice methods to prevent erosion and to reclaim eroded land. This can sometimes be done by following good but often neglected farming practices such as strip-cropping, cover cropping, stubble mulching, contour planting and plowing, and building up the amount of organic matter in the soil. In a long-term Texas study, it was discovered that the presence of a soil cover was quite significant in preventing erosion. Most erosion occurred in April and May because soil was bare at that time, awaiting planting.

Types of Erosion: Erosion can be caused by either wind or water. Wind erosion is a problem primarily of poorly managed, sandy, cultivated soil, but some wind erosion occurs in every state. The Soil Conservation Service estimates that there are 14 million acres of currently cultivated land that should be seeded to grass to prevent wind from eroding the soil. Stubble mulches are always recommended to prevent soil blowing. *See* STUBBLE MULCH.

Water erosion occurs everywhere. It is one of the primary means by which soil is created in

For the home gardener, bench terracing is one of the best methods of controlling hillside erosion and increasing garden space. The levels can be held in place by railroad ties, sod or stone walls.

the first place. However, when water erosion occurs on cultivated soil, it can destroy the utility of the land, creating unreclaimable gullies and washing away tons of topsoil. Scientists recognize several types.

Splash erosion: This occurs when raindrops beat bare soil into a muddy stream, splashing globules of soil and water two to three feet high and as much as five feet in distance. Although the force of the raindrops may seem negligible, they pack quite a wallop, moving as much as 20 miles per hour, and occasionally more. If the soil has a good cover of vegetation or is high in organic matter (such as in a forest), the soil will absorb both the water *and* the impact of the drop. On bare land the raindrops not only splash the soil around but also destroy soil structure; this is particularly a problem with fine-textured soils.

Gully erosion: This process occurs mostly on cultivated soils. Small channels or rills are formed by runoff water flowing downhill. These channels deepen and widen during subsequent water flows, and if the erosion process is not checked, they can become extremely large. Although small gullies can be reclaimed rather easily, the reclamation process for a large gully is lengthy and complicated.

Sheet erosion: The force of the drops packs the soil by moving the soil particles closer together. A surface forms that is virtually sealed when wet and, when dry, allows air and water to pass through it only slowly. As a result, water that at one time might have drained through the soil is forced to run off on top of the soil, carrying particles of soil with it. A less dramatic process than gully erosion, it is even more destructive because people do not realize how much soil is being lost until it is too late. Light-colored hilltops in the midst of a field with dark soil are the result of sheet erosion.

The easiest—and least expensive—method of erosion control is the maintenance of a continuing, close-growing cover of vegetation on the soil surface. This can be a combination of native grasses with small shrubs or trees, a good pasture on marginal land, or, in a farming operation, a green manure crop. Unfortunately, annual crops are not particularly effective in preventing soil erosion. There is a certain amount of time during which the soil is unprotected during any crop year, although this can be minimized by allowing crop residues to remain on the soil after harvest rather than plowing them under. Hay crops, harvested biennially or perennially, offer better soil protection, even after the hay has been cut. Grass crops can be used to improve pasture or grazing land, to prevent soil erosion and to allow the soil to absorb quantities of moisture. For best results, pastureland must not be overgrazed. The use of vegetative cover must function as part of an integrated effort tailored to the topography of the particular land in question, the region of the country in which it is located and the type of farming operation pursued. *See also* COVER CROP.

Besides growing a vegetative cover, other soil conservation measures may be necessary, and may range from the relatively simple and inexpensive to the complex and expensive, depending on the type of land and the results desired. Contouring, strip-cropping and terracing all have an important place in soil conservation since they prevent water from running downhill. The faster the water flows over a slope, the greater the erosion hazard, and the more damage it can do. As the speed of the water flow is doubled, its ability to damage soil is increased fourfold. Therefore, most soil conservation measures are aimed at either slowing the water as it runs downhill, or else shortening the length of the slope.

Contouring and Strip-Cropping: Contouring is a system of growing farm crops across the slope of the field. In most instances, the organic farmer combines this practice with strip-cropping by planting a variety of crops in rows perpendicular to the slope. Usually every other strip is hay or grass. The others may be planted to row crops, which are generally much less effective in preventing soil runoff. The hay or grass strips slow down and spread the water flowing from the strips planted to row crops, allowing the water to deposit whatever silt it has picked up.

The width of the strips, although sometimes determined by the type of crops grown and by local topographic conditions, is generally kept fairly wide, 40 to 50 feet being standard, so that strips can be worked easily with regular farm equipment. In some cases, strips can be much wider.

There are basically four kinds of strip-cropping. Field strip-cropping refers to strips of crops planted exactly parallel across a field. Such crops are generally not planted on the exact contour of the land. The method is best on smooth, long slopes. Wind strip-cropping is used on level land to prevent wind erosion. The strips are parallel across a field, perpendicular to the direction of the prevailing winds. Contour strip-cropping is the most widely practiced form of strip-cropping. Strips are laid out perpendicular to the slope of the land. On land of a 5 to 12 percent slope, this type of strip-cropping may be combined with terracing. Buffer strips are a more permanent form of strip-cropping. They may be wide or narrow, used in only part of a field, run downhill or located in irregular areas of a field—wherever continued plowing is not desired.

Terracing: Terracing is a centuries-old practice that, in the United States, originated from the practices of contour farming. Terracing today is done for several reasons—to preserve the integrity of a leveled piece of land and to prevent the soil from washing away, to make the rainfall run off sloping land slowly, or to hold it in the field until it can be absorbed by the soil. Terraces do this by reducing the slope of a piece of sloping land, by diverting the stream of water and carrying it across the piece of land, and by providing a channel that holds water until it can be used by the soil.

One advantage that terraces have over other types of conservation (for example, strip-cropping) is that *one* crop can be grown on a particular terrace. Terraces do not have to be strip-cropped for best results. Present-day terraces are built so that all types of farm machinery can be used on them, and channels or ditches are constructed so that it is not difficult for machinery to drive over them.

There are many different kinds of terrace construction but some are more common than others. Bench terraces are built on sharp slopes in order to reduce the slope to a series of narrow, level strips. Each terrace is held in place by a retaining wall of stones, grass-covered soil or other material. This kind of terrace is generally used in hilly areas of rather dense population. It is more costly than other types of terraces, and because it is used on steep slopes, these terraces are narrower and closer together than other types. Level ridge terraces have a ridge of earth on the lower side of a channel and are constructed where it is important to conserve water. The terrace construction makes it easier

In this terraced garden, the lower row of railroad ties is 40 inches high (five ties) while the succeeding rows are 48 inches high (six ties). Each terrace is five feet wide.

Whenever there is runoff from a field through terraces, the water must be discharged through some kind of outlet. The outlet may either be open and planted to grass, or drained by tile. An open water outlet must be planted to a fine-leaved grass and should be large enough to carry runoff from heavy rains.

Crop Rotations: Crop rotations are important in soil conservation and are simply good, commonsense farming practice. Crop rotation is defined simply as a sequence of crops grown in succession on the same fields. When well planned, crop rotations aid in building up the soil and enable plants to utilize nutrients efficiently. In addition, they serve as a form of erosion control. In a strip-cropping situation, for example, a good crop rotation will ensure that the same strips are not planted to row crops year in and year out. Instead, they will be used periodically for grasses or legumes that will not only enrich the soil but will also hold soil cover. Green manure crops will also build the amount of organic matter in the soil, adding to the ability of the soil to absorb water and lessening the damage that impact from rain will cause to bare soil.

for the water to be spread out and absorbed over a wide area.

A diversion terrace is built on a steep slope with serious erosion problems. It is cut deeply into the soil and it functions primarily to carry large quantities of water away from the slope. The terrace should never be plowed, and it is often difficult to cross with farm machinery. Land between diversion terraces should be contour farmed.

SOIL DEFICIENCIES

Plants are known to need at least 16 chemical elements. Of these elements, most are derived from soil solids: nitrogen, phosphorus, potassium, boron, calcium, chlorine, copper, iron, magnesium, manganese, molybdenum, sulfur, and zinc. The others, carbon, hydrogen and oxygen, are largely derived from the air and water.

A soil that lacks one or more of these essential nutrients is said to be deficient. Soils are seldom deficient in chlorine, molybdenum or sulfur. In fact, toxicity is a more common problem associated with these elements and the gardener should not try to add these minerals to his soil. However, deficiencies of the other elements frequently occur. Leaching and plant uptake are responsible for most soil deficiencies, but pH, cation-exchange, and organic matter content may also influence the amount of a soil nutrient actually available to plants.

It is possible to detect soil deficiencies by examining plants growing on the soil, and in fact, poor plant growth is a fundamental sign of a deficient soil. The trained eye can detect plant symptoms characteristic of specific nutritional deficiencies in the soil. Micronutrient deficiencies, for example, are best noted by observing "hunger signs" in plants. Experienced agronomists can often pinpoint a deficiency at first glance by noting such symptoms as the discoloration of a leaf or the peculiar shape of a fruit.

Detecting hunger signs in plants is one thing; diagnosing the cause of the hunger is another entirely. For example, a nitrogen deficiency may be signaled by the yellowing of leaves, but this can also be caused by improperly drained soil. Even an expert might not be able to tell which condition, it either, caused the yellowed leaves.

All things being equal, the gardener is well-advised to leave the diagnostic speculations to the experts and stick with a sound program of fertilizing and conditioning the garden soil with animal and green manures, compost, and rock powders. It is an established fact that soils with high levels of organic matter are seldom deficient in the essential plant nutrients. The beginning gardener may note hunger signs, but after a year or two of following the organic method, his plants should grow in full health. Many gardeners test their garden soils annually and fertilize them in ac-

cordance with test results. But just as many good gardeners heap on the mulch and compost, without testing and never find soil deficiency symptoms in their plants.

If a hunger sign does develop, or does persist, by all means have the soil tested and seek the advice of an expert, like your local county agent.

Nitrogen Deficiency: Nitrogen is especially important for vegetables since it is essential for the synthesis of natural proteins. Plenty of nitrogen gives a good normal deep green color to foliage and stems. In general, a nitrogen deficiency is characterized by slow growth, slender fibrous stems, and foliage and stems that fade to yellow in color.

Treatment: Animal manures are the best all-round organic fertilizers. Although rather low in nitrogen in comparison with some other sources, they add organic matter to the soil. Rabbit droppings and poultry manure are best, with pig and cow manure having the lowest nitrogen content of all barnyard manures. Compost the manure and use the compost as a fertilizer worked into the ground in fall or spring. You can also sheet compost with raw manure or use it as a mulch. Use ten tons per acre, or 25 pounds of dried, bagged manure per 100 square feet in the garden.

There are other, commercially available, sources of nitrogen. One of the best is cottonseed meal, which contains 7 percent nitrogen. If used regularly, it should be applied with lime since it is slightly acid. Feather meal is an excellent slow-release nitrogen fertilizer. Blood meal is expensive to use in quantity and sometimes difficult to buy, but it has a very high nitrogen content, and someone with a small garden which needs nitrogen quickly can best find it in this source. Fish scraps and sewage sludge are other sources of nitrogen. *See also* NITROGEN.

Phosphorous Deficiency: In general, plants which are deficient in phosphorus are slowed in growth. The underside of leaves assumes a red purple color, and the plants are slow to set fruit and mature. Fruit may drop prematurely.

Treatment: A high content of organic matter in the soil makes phosphorus more readily available. Add finely ground phosphate rock at ten pounds per 100 square feet of garden space, along with 25 pounds of manure. Work manure well into soil, then spread phosphate rock evenly on soil and allow it to leach into the soil. You can also use bone meal on small areas, but it is expensive to use and takes a long time to release its phosphorus for use by plants. *See also* BONE MEAL, PHOSPHATE ROCK, PHOSPHORUS.

Potassium Deficiency: Potassium deficiency is shown in reduced vigor and poor growth of plants. Frequently, leaves turn ashen and curl, later becoming bronzed. Older leaves exhibit these symptoms before young leaves and tips. Severe deficiencies almost always result in poorly developed root systems.

Treatment: By placing six inches of green matter to every two inches of stable manure in your compost heap, you supply adequate amounts of potassium for gardening purposes. Once the moisture of green plants is eliminated and the material is broken down, a great percentage of the solids consists of potassium. If your soil is particularly low in potassium, add potash rock, granite dust, wood ash, or some other potassium-rich organic material to the compost—or apply these materials directly to the soil. Heavy mulching also seems to help maintain the potassium supply. *See also* GRANITE DUST, GREENSAND, POTASH.

Boron Deficiency: A deficiency of boron causes plants to grow more slowly. Terminal buds die and the plants tend to become bushy. Later, lateral buds die, leaves thicken, and fruits, tubers and roots become cracked and discolored. Severe deficiency results in crop failure.

Treatment: Once organic-matter content of a soil is above 3 percent, soil seldom exhibits boron deficiency. Granite dust will supply boron, but few soils lack boron and there is greater danger from overabundance than from lack.

Calcium Deficiency: In general, plants exhibiting calcium deficiency are retarded in growth and develop thick woody stems. Terminal leaves and young branches are often deformed. The roots of many plants turn black and die.

Treatment: Use any good grade of ground natural limestone. About 60 mesh is a good grind. Where available, gypsum, oystershells and basic slag can be used. *See also* LIME.

Copper Deficiency: Copper deficiency is usually confined to peat or muck soils. Plants deficient in copper exhibit slow growth or complete cessation of growth. Shoot tips are affected first and eventually die back.

Treatment: Organic materials, natural rock fertilizers, and the soil itself supply enough copper for most plants. As with other micronutrients and trace elements, copper toxicity is a more common problem than copper deficiency.

Iron Deficiency: Insufficient iron in plants is characterized by spotted, colorless areas on young leaves. Yellow leaves appear on the upper parts of the plants. The growth of new shoots is affected and plant tissues may die if the deficiency is severe. Too much lime causes iron deficiency to develop.

Treatment: Plenty of manure, crop residues, dried blood, and tankage are the best materials to use in correcting iron deficiency.

Magnesium Deficiency: Magnesium deficiency is widespread in sandy soils. Plants deficient in magnesium are, in general, late to mature, and do not mature uniformly. They have poor market quality and exhibit a characteristic yellowing between the veins of older leaves. Leaves may develop bright colors.

Treatment: Add a quart of seawater to each 100 pounds of compost, or, use dolomitic limestone since this contains quite a bit of magnesium. *See also* LIME.

Manganese Deficiency: Plants deficient in manganese are slow to grow, and mature late and unevenly. The areas between the veins of leaves become yellow, then brown, while the veins remain green.

Treatment: Manganese shortage is likely to occur in a high organic soil that is too alkaline. Check soil pH, omit lime and work acidic materials such as oak leaves into the soil.

Zinc Deficiency: Zinc deficiency often occurs in peat soils. It is particularly characterized in plants by leaves which are abnormally long and narrow. The leaves may also turn yellow and be mottled with many dead areas. Since zinc deficiency tends to result in iron deficiency, the symptoms of both problems are similar.

Treatment: Use plenty of manure. Phosphate rock also contains traces of zinc.

See also entries for individual crops and elements, DISEASE, FERTILIZER, TRACE ELEMENTS.

SOIL HORIZON

All soils have a profile consisting of successive layers of soil and soil material running vertically from the surface to bedrock. These layers are called horizons. The horizons are described by field scientists according to their color, texture, consistency, structure, pH, boundary characteristics, and continuity. These diagnostic characteristics will vary according to geographic location and soil-forming factors, and soil scientists recognize 17 subdivisions of the principal horizons. Not every soil contains all horizons, but every soil has some of them.

The O horizons are organic horizons which form above the mineral soil from organic litter derived from plants and animals. They are dominated by fresh or partly decomposed organic material. They usually occur in forested areas and are generally absent in grasslands.

The most important soil horizons are the A horizons. These are mineral horizons lying at or near the surface of mineral soils. A_1, the topmost A horizon, features an accumulation of humified organic matter that gives it a dark color. A_2 is a lighter color and contains less organic matter. It is an area of high loss of clay, iron and aluminum oxides, and therefore has a corresponding concentration of materials resistant to leaching. A_3, a transitional layer between the A and B horizons, shares properties of both but is more like A_1 or A_2 than the B horizons. It is not always present.

The B horizons lie directly under the A horizons in a soil profile. They can be easily recognized by a distinct change in color, texture and structure. Usually the texture is heavier and the material is compacted. This is the region of maximum accumulation of materials such as iron and aluminum oxides and silicate clays. In arid regions, calcium carbonate, calcium sulfate and other salts may accumulate in the lower B horizon.

Below the B horizon begins a layer of unconsolidated material known as the C horizon and commonly called the subsoil. It may or

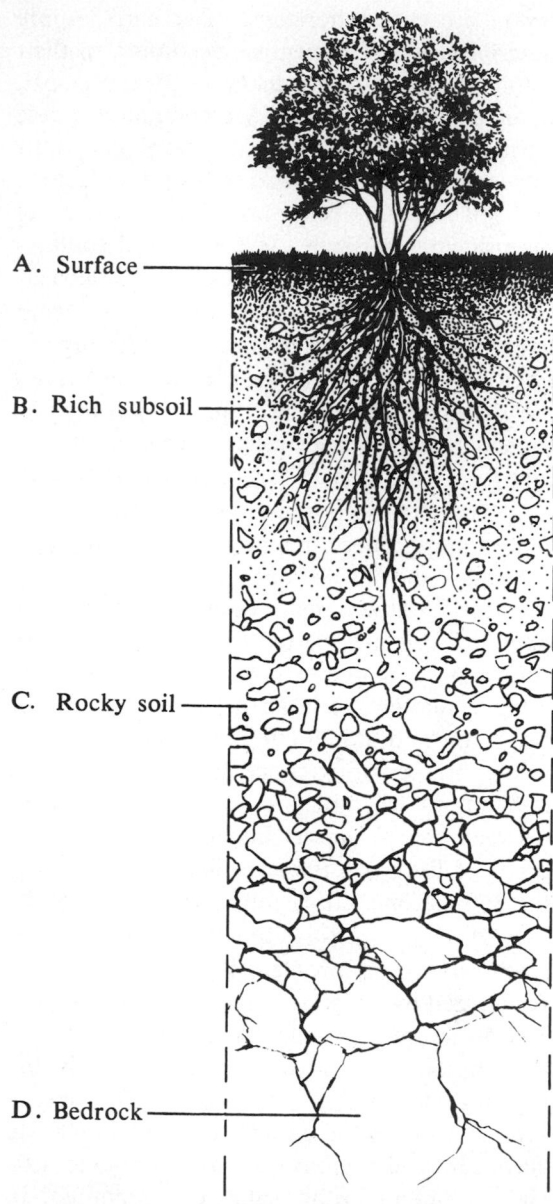

A. Surface

B. Rich subsoil

C. Rocky soil

D. Bedrock

The typical soil profile consists of a dark A hori-
zon rich in organic matter and humus, a heavier
B layer rich in minerals and a C or subsoil horizon
consisting of very heavy, often rocky soil. A layer
of bedrock usually lies beneath the C level.

may not be the same as the parent material from which the A and B horizons formed. It is not one of the zones of major biological activities and is little affected by soil-forming processes. Its upper layers may in time become a part of the other horizons as weathering and erosion continue.

The C horizon varies in depth, according to the geologic history of the deposits. If, for instance, the C horizon is of sedimentary origin, it may be either fairly shallow, as in the soils formed on outcropping red shale, or very deep, as in the soils of the coastal plain. If the C horizon is composed of residual rock deposits, its depth depends on the depth of the weathered material. Beneath this level is a level of consolidated bedrock, such as granite, sandstone or limestone.

SOIL PASTEURIZATION

Indoor gardeners and greenhouse users may find it necessary to pasteurize their soil before potting plants. This can be done without any expensive or cumbersome equipment.

Place soil three or four inches deep in a roasting pan and moisten it thoroughly. Make sure it is uniformly wet for best heat conduction. Stick a meat thermometer in the middle and bake at low heat until the oven temperature reaches 180°F. (82.22°C.). This is high enough to kill soil insects and microorganisms that may cause disease. Higher temperatures will destroy organic matter, damage soil structure and kill beneficial soil organisms. Whatever beneficial microorganisms are killed by pasteurization will be replaced by debris on the plant roots and by organic fertilizers.

To treat a seed flat for pasteurization, fill

the flat with soil and level with a stick (do not compact the soil). Cover with aluminum foil, stick a thermometer through the aluminum foil into the soil and pour boiling water over the flat.

See also SEEDS AND SEEDLINGS.

SOIL TEMPERATURE

Soil temperatures fluctuate just as much as air temperatures—at least to a depth of 20 inches. Below that, soil temperature seldom varies.

Soil temperature influences your gardening results in a number of ways. For example, germination of seeds depends upon warmth of soil below ground as well as upon air above ground. Cold soils also tend to make it difficult for plants to absorb phosphorus from the soil. Freezing and thawing of soils may improve the texture of cloddy soils, but it may heave crops (especially alfalfa) on bare, fine-textured soils.

A mulch or cover crop can help to regulate soil temperature to your advantage. Many soil scientists have found that an organic mulch acts both directly and indirectly to decrease the fluctuations in soil temperature. A mulch makes the soil warmer in winter and cooler in summer. A mulch also has an indirect benefit because it retains snow, which further protects the soil against temperature extremes.

The transfer of heat within the soil depends on the ease with which the heat can be conducted from particle to particle across the gaps in the soil which contain air when the soil is dry, and water when it is wet. The temperatures of the top three inches of very dark soils warm up much faster than those of light-colored soils. Sandy soils heat up the fastest, clay soils the slowest. Clay soils are cold in summer, partly due to their high specific heat and partly due to the constant evaporation from the surface which seldom dries.

See also FROST, MULCH.

SOIL TESTING

A good gardener wants to know as much about his soil as possible. The only sure way to find out what your soil needs is to test it— either by buying a soil test kit (they are available in varying degrees of sophistication) and testing the soil yourself, or by sending soil samples to a laboratory or to your State Agricultural Experiment Station. Actually, it doesn't hurt to use *both* methods; they can act as a check on each other, and your own soil tests, made periodically throughout the year, will supplement laboratory tests.

Taking a soil sample is the first step in making a soil test. A dry day in the early fall is the best time to sample your soil. That is the best time to test soil fertility and it is also the time when commercial laboratories are not as busy as in the spring.

A sampling probe is the best tool to use for obtaining soil samples. This device is a length of pipe with a sharp point for piercing the soil. If you don't have one, however, you can use a clean trowel or spade.

Dig a small hole, removing the earth to plow depth (about six to eight inches). Take a thin slice—about an inch thick—from the straight side of the hole. Trim the slice into thirds along its length; discard the two outer thirds, mixing the inner slice with other samples from the area tested.

With a sampling rod, one can take uncontaminated soil samples in a single step.

Take about six different samples from different places spaced more or less equally across the garden or field. Mix them together thoroughly, preferably in a plastic bucket, since rust flakes may alter the test results. Then take a sample from the mixture.

If your property contains decidedly different types of soil in different areas, you will need more than one test made. Take two or three samplings from each distinct area and mix these together, but keep the different area samples separate. For instance, if you have a big hill in back of your property where you have lawn or a small pasture and you also have a garden on low ground at the other end of your property, you will need to run two different tests. When you send in the two samples, specify that you want recommendations for growing lawn or pasture on the one, and recommendations for growing vegetables on the other.

On larger acreages, sampling is almost always done by field, because any treatment a farmer uses will generally be applied to the whole field. On a ten-acre field you might take six samplings from various spots and mix them together in one sample.

Your soil test kit will contain instructions about how to use its contents and how to test your soil. From your results, you will be able to determine generally what your soil needs. For example, if a pH test shows your soil to be too acidic, you can add lime to your plot, except where you want to plant acid-loving crops.

The advantage in using the soil-testing services of an extension agency or experiment station, however, is that soil scientists there can make recommendations based not only on your own sample, but on those of others in your region. The small cost of a test by the experiment station is often worth it.

You might want to engage the services of a commercial soil-testing laboratory. Although more expensive, these labs can run more sophisticated tests, including analyses for organic matter content, pesticide content or specific trace elements. In addition, many of them send field representatives to examine your site. Common sense should indicate, however, that a lab closely aligned with a fertilizer company might suggest that that particular brand of fertilizer be applied to your soil. It is best to avoid these connections.

A thorough analysis of your garden soil will include figures on the presence of the major nutrients—nitrogen, phosphorus, potassium—as well as trace elements. You'll get a reading on soil acidity, and perhaps an indication of the amount of organic matter in your soil.

You'll also get instructions for fertilizing your crops. Few laboratories will make recommendations specifically for organic gardeners. You will probably get test results and fertilizer recommendations resembling the following: "Use 200 pounds of limestone per 1,000 square feet. Use ten pounds of 10–10–10 per 1,000 square feet at planting. Side-dress with three pounds of ammonium nitrate per 1,000 square feet during the growing season." These chemical recommendations, of course, must be converted into their natural equivalents.

Here's how the editors of *Organic Gardening and Farming* suggest interpreting such test recommendations: Suppose your garden is 40 by 60 feet. That's 2,400 square feet, or about a sixteenth of an acre. First, follow the limestone application recommendation of 200 pounds per 1,000 square feet by putting down about 500 pounds of crushed limestone. For nitrogen, use manure. The optimum rate for manuring cropland is about 15 tons per acre. Thus, a 2,400-square-foot garden will require about a ton of manure. The phosphorus and potassium the recommendations called for—along with some trace minerals—will also be supplied largely by the manure. If you need more, apply 100 pounds each of phosphate rock and greensand or granite powder annually for three years. This will provide up to seven or eight years of fertilizing action.

SOLANUM

This very large genus of the Nightshade family includes the potato, tomato, eggplant, nightshade, and bittersweet as well as many other shrubs, vines and some trees.

See entries for individual plants.

SOLOMON'S SEAL   (*Polygonatum*)

Hardy perennials of the Lily family, Solomon's seals are often found growing in bogs and marshy places. In the garden they may be grown in moist, humus-rich soil among shrubs and ferns, or on the shady side of the house. The common name alludes to the scars

The hardy, perennial Solomon's seal is easily propagated by means of its blue or black berries or by division of the creeping rootstocks.

left on the creeping rootstocks by annual growth.

Graceful leafy stems arise from the rootstocks, with small white or greenish bell-shaped flowers growing from the leaf axils. Blue or black berries follow later. Native North American Solomon's seals are *P. biflorum,* which grows to three feet with four-inch leaves, and *P. commutatum,* an eight-foot species whose leaves are six inches long. *P. multiflorum* grows to three feet, and *P. latifolium,* to four feet. They are natives of Europe and Asia. All species bloom in spring and are easily propagated by seed or division.

SOPHORA

These ornamental shrubs or trees are grown mainly for their showy flowers and handsome foliage. Flowers may be white, pink, violet, or yellow. The trees' seedpods grow to ten inches long.

Most species can be grown in all but the coldest regions. They require fairly dry, deep, well-drained soil and full sun. Propagation is by cuttings taken in early summer or, in the case of the treelike species, from seed sown in spring or fall.

The Japanese pagoda tree (*S. japonica*) grows to 60 feet and is hardy north to Massachusetts. It is especially valuable for its late-summer flowers, which are yellow white and yield a yellow dye. Its leaves are a glossy dark green, and the tree is equally striking in winter because of its dark green branches. The trees tolerate heat, drought and city conditions. There is a variety with pendulous branches and another with variegated leaves.

The Kowhai (*S. tetraptera*) is a tender evergreen with fernlike foliage and delicate branches that grow in a zigzag habit. Clusters of deep yellow flowers appear in early summer. This tree can be grown in the Deep South and the mildest parts of California.

Mescal bean (*S. secundiflora*) grows to 50 feet. It has yellow green leaves and violet blue flowers that are very fragrant. It is hardy only in the Deep South and along the Pacific coast. The seedpods grow six to eight inches long and contain sophorine, a poisonous alkaloid.

SORBARIA

This genus of the Rose family contains both tender and hardy deciduous shrubs. Leaves are compound and pinnate, and the flowers are white and in small clusters, similar to those of spirea. The shrubs thrive in moist, rich soil and full sun. They may be easily propagated by runners, cuttings or seed.

S. Aitchisonii is hardy south of New York, grows to ten feet and blooms in July and August. *S. arborea,* equally hardy, grows to 18 feet. A shorter species, *S. sorbifolia,* which grows to six feet, is hardy throughout the United States and much of Canada.

SORBUS   *See* MOUNTAIN ASH

SORGHUM   (*Holcus sorghum*)

Sorghum grown in the United States falls into three classes: grain sorghums, sweet sorghums and broomcorn. Grain sorghum is most commonly grown in this country and is the principal feed grain in dry areas where corn does not yield well. Sweet sorghum can also be used as a feed grain, but is more often grown for the sweet sap that can be expressed from its stalks and reduced to sorghum molasses, a common sweetener in the South. Broomcorn is mostly grown for its straw that is used in brooms.

Planting and Culture: Grain sorghum is planted the same way as corn. Plant seed ten days after planting corn, or when the soil two inches deep registers 70°F. (21.11°C.) at noon on a soil thermometer. Plant two inches deep and four inches apart in rows 30 inches apart, closer in drier climates. The number of pounds of seed per acre varies with climatic conditions. If planted too thickly, sorghum has a tendency to lodge or bend over in heavy winds or rains. Southern farmers can plant sorghum in June after combining their wheat, and get two crops from the same field.

Sweet sorghum resembles grain sorghum at maturity except that it is three times as tall. It can be planted two inches deep in rows 40 inches apart with six inches between plants, or in hills with three or four plants to a hill. Plant broomcorn in the same manner.

Cultivation requirements for all sorghums are similar to those for corn, but no variety of sorghum requires as much fertilizer as does corn. About five tons manure per acre should be sufficient for sweet sorghum. Follow sorghum with green manure and apply finely ground phosphate rock every three or four years. Soil pH should be nearly neutral—6.5 or 7. Cottonseed meal and tankage are both good fertilizers for sorghum.

Insects and Diseases: In the South, seed is often infested in the field with rice weevil and Angoumois grain moth. These pests cause problems in stored grain. *See* WHEAT for suggestions for minimizing insect damage to stored grain.

Some of the same insects that attack corn also attack grain and sweet sorghums and broomcorn. Damage will rarely be serious. The sorghum midge attacks sorghum crops in the blooming stage in the Gulf Coast to the South Atlantic states, and the best defense is to cover the heads with a paper bag when the plants are about to bloom. Bags should be removed shortly after blooming since they create perfect conditions for the corn earworm and the corn leaf aphid.

Grain sorghum diseases include a variety of bacterial leaf diseases that are especially common in humid areas. The most important ones are bacterial leaf spot, bacterial streak, gray leaf spot, rough spot, sooty stripe, target spot, and zonate leaf spot. Crop rotations, sanitation and the use of disease-resistant varieties help prevent or combat these diseases.

Downy mildew is a serious and spreading disease of grain sorghums. Diseased parts show a white down on the underside of the leaf. This releases spores, which cause lesions on the plants, and leaves eventually shed. Though mildew-resistant hybrids are available, you should avoid growing sorghums near Sudangrass in areas where this disease is a problem. The Sudangrass becomes heavily infected and can contaminate the soil for years.

Maize dwarf mosaic (MDM) is a serious pest of grain sorghums. Johnsongrass serves as an overwinter host for this virus. Aphids feed on the Johnsongrass and then carry the virus to grain crops. Typical symptoms are stunted growth, discoloration of the head, and light and dark green mottling of the leaves. Select resistant varieties and plant the crop a little late in the spring.

A number of stalk and root rots damage grain sorghum. Use varieties resistant to these diseases.

Harvesting: Seed heads of grain sorghum will shatter if left in the field too long after ripening. When seeds are ripe, cut off the seed heads with about a foot of stalk attached. Tie the heads together into bundles and hang them in the barn or spread no more than three bundles deep to dry. In the North, grain sorghum must often be harvested when green and left to mature in the barn, especially when the weather is wet. If allowed to dry in the field, the seed heads will often mold. Plots over one-quarter acre should be harvested with a grain combine.

Sweet sorghum should be harvested when seeds are no longer milky but still in the tough, doughy stage. When your thumbnail can no longer cut the seed, the ideal harvesting time has passed. Harvest the stalks by first stripping off the leaves (feed these to your livestock), then cutting them off close to the ground with a machete or corn knife. The seed heads can be cut off the stalks all at once, and the bundles can then be pressed for juice.

Broomcorn must be hand-harvested in the late-bloom stage before the seeds have fully matured. The top brush is cut off with six inches of stalk attached. Dry the brushes for three weeks before using.

Using: Clusters of grain or sweet sorghum can be fed to chickens at the rate of one cluster to six chickens with an equal amount of other grain. Animals do not do well on sorghum alone.

For home use, seed must be threshed. Hold a cluster of seed heads over a bucket and rub it back and forth between gloved hands. Hulls and stem bits can be winnowed out of the grain by pouring back and forth between

As soon as seeds are ripe, grain sorghum heads can be cut, tied together and hung or spread to dry in a cool, shady place.

two buckets in front of a fan. Grind the seed in a blender or mill—use two-thirds sorghum to one-third wheat or make your own mixture. The resulting flour can be used in bread, cookies or pancakes.

Stalks can be fed to animals as fodder or used for bedding.

To make syrup from sweet sorghum, run the stalks through a press to crack the tough outer stalks and press the juice from the inner pulp. The juice collects in a barrel and then flows into a long evaporator pan with three or four baffles where the green liquid is cooked slowly over a steady fire. As the liquid runs along the length of the pan, nonsugar substances rise to the surface and are skimmed off. By the time the syrup reaches the lower end of the pan, it is a clear liquid that forms strings when the ladle is lifted out of it. The finished syrup is run off, bottled and allowed to cool rapidly. Some places in the South still maintain sorghum cooking operations where you can take your cane and have syrup made for a fee.

You might be able to make enough syrup for home use by crushing the stalks in a leaf shredder and pressing the juice from them with a cider press. The trouble with this method is that there is not enough pressure provided by the cider press to completely extract the juice from the stalks. Heat the juice in a pot on the stove. Syrup reaches its proper density at 226 to 230°F. (107.78 to 110°C.). A syrup hydrometer should read 35 to 36° Báume when the syrup is ready. The syrup should be allowed to cool to 180°F. (82.22°C.) before it is poured into containers. Old-timers say the best syrup is made on clear, cold days.

Broom making can be a profitable sideline for a homestead since over 1,000 brooms can be made from an acre of broomcorn, but it is a complex craft. Brooms are made traditionally in many styles. Your best bet, if you'd like to learn how to make brooms, is to visit a local broom maker and learn the art from him.

Varieties: Grain sorghum seed is brown white with tinges of yellow and red. The plant reaches 4½ feet in height, and yields about 100 to 180 bushels per acre on unirrigated land. Browner seeds have a higher tannin content, making them less palatable to cattle. However, the lighter-colored varieties which are more attractive to cattle are also more prone to bird damage. Some varieties are bred to contain more tannin in the milk stage, when seeds are most likely to be damaged by birds, and to become lighter in color as they mature. Hybrids with a high degree of resistance to common diseases of grain sorghum are available and so are hybrids that tolerate a shorter growing season.

Many say that the best syrup comes from the long-season varieties of sweet sorghum. Wiley, Brandes, Honey, and Sart are recommended for the South. Dale and Tracy are shorter-season varieties for central to northern regions. Sugar Drip can be grown even farther north.

There are several varieties of broomcorn grown commercially and classified according to their use in the broom. More information about broomcorn can be obtained from the National Broom Council, 333 North Michigan Avenue, Chicago, IL 60601.

SORREL (*Rumex*)

The Latin name of the genus for sorrel, *Rumex,* describes the spear-shaped leaves of these plants. Sorrel is traced back to the reign of Henry VIII, when it was used as a spice and meat tenderizer. The leaves were boiled as a substitute for spinach. Sorrel earned its common nickname "green sauce" when the English used its mashed leaves, vinegar and sugar to make a sauce dressing for meat and fish.

Sorrels are strong-rooted perennial weeds, some of which are cultivated for their edible leaves. They have long panicles of tiny green or white flowers, and are easily grown from seed sown in early spring. Garden sorrel

(*R. Acetosa*) grows up to three feet tall. Its basal leaves are eaten as greens. Herb patience or spinach dock (*R. Patientia*) is twice as tall and also bears leaves that are fine for salads and add tang to soups and drinks. French sorrel (*R. scutatus*) is a very low-growing species with fiddle-shaped leaves. The spinach-rhubarb (*R. abyssinicus*) grows eight feet tall. Its leaves are used like spinach and the stalks like rhubarb in pies. Curly or sour dock (*R. crispus*) and sheep sorrel (*R. Acetosella*) are both very weedy and may spread if planted in gardens.

The tuberous roots of canaigre (*R. hymenosepalus*) are an excellent source of tannin. This three-foot-tall, spring-blooming perennial, which is propagated by seed, roots or root crowns planted in the fall, has been introduced as a crop for sandy soils in the Southwest. The roots are harvested in the summer and dried. Indians have used them for centuries for tanning leather. Yields of fresh roots as high as ten tons per acre are common.

Planting and Culture: The best sorrels for garden culture are French sorrel, garden sorrel and spinach-rhubarb. All of these grow well in any rich soil, but French sorrel prefers a dry, sunny location and garden sorrel thrives in moist areas.

All species can be started from root divisions or from seed planted outdoors in March or April. When the shoots are one or two inches high, they are thinned. Mulching is then desirable, especially for moisture-loving garden sorrel. The seeds should be harvested soon after they appear in the spring. Removing the pods will help rejuvenate the plant and keep it producing green leaves through the fall. The citrus-flavored leaves can be harvested at any time, and used immediately. Drying does not preserve their flavor.

Using: Contemporary uses of sorrel are mainly culinary. The plant's leaves are boiled and served as a vegetable with butter. The famous French provincial *soupe aux herbes* includes sorrel leaves. Sour dock is one of the best and most widely found wild greens. It is cooked like spinach, and its roots are highly prized as a blood medicine. The leaves of sheep sorrel are somewhat bitter, but may be used in salads or cooked until tender and made into vegetable pies. French gardeners would not consider their vegetable gardens complete without some sorrels grown for the table.

See also HERB.

SOTOL   (*Dasylirion*)

These desert plants grow from central Texas to Arizona and south into Mexico. Also known as beargrass, they produce flowers resembling those of the lily, on stalks usually growing about 20 feet high. Sotol does best in full sun, and can stand intense summer heat and a small amount of frost. Soil should be a well-drained, sandy loam. *D. texanum* has a short or underground trunk. Spoon flower (*D. Wheeleri*) is a much taller species.

SOUR GUM   *See* NYSSA

SOUTHERN MAIDENHAIR
See VENUS'S-HAIR

SOUTHERNWOOD
(*Artemesia Abrotanum*)

Southernwood is a cousin of the herbs tarragon, wormwood and mugwort, although its herbal properties are somewhat less valued. It is said to have astringent, anthelmintic and deobstruent qualities, but its chief function is decorative.

A hardy perennial growing to five feet, southernwood roots well in almost any soil, and its toughness makes it desirable for city plantings. Its gray green foliage is finely divided and some varieties have lemon or tangerinelike aromas. It thrives in full sunlight. Propagation is best accomplished by cuttings or root division.

SOW

To sow is to scatter, broadcast or drill seeds. Sowing generally results in a rather dense population of plants.

SOW BUG   *See* INSECT CONTROL

SOYBEAN   (*Glycine Max*)

The soybean is a legume that has been grown for millennia, but is only now becoming important in the United States. Soybeans have a high protein content of over 40 percent. Not only are they an important component of animal feed rations, but, supplemented by grains and nuts, they can form the major source of protein in vegetarian diets for humans as well. The soybean supplies half the total vegetable fats and oils consumed in this country, acts as a meat extender when ground, and can be textured, flavored and cooked to resemble meat. Soybeans can also supply soybean milk for lacto-vegetarians or for those allergic to other kinds of milk. Flour made from the beans is a nutritious addition to many foods.

Planting and Culture: Soybeans do not respond well to direct fertilization, although fertilizer applied to a previous crop might affect the soybeans. Trace-element deficiencies sometimes appear, but in a rotation using both animal and green manures such deficiencies will probably be prevented.

Soybeans do best in well-drained soil with a pH between 6.5 and 7, but respond well in heavy clay soils, too. They can also be planted in a variety of ways and will respond well provided moisture and soil conditions are good.

Plant soybeans only after the soil has warmed in late spring, about a week after the optimum time to plant corn. Soybeans can be planted through June and even in July in areas below 40 degrees latitude and still have time to mature before frost.

Plant the beans 1½ inches deep early in the season. Later in the season, when soil is drier, seed should be planted three to four inches deep. Plant eight beans per foot of row. A variety of low-cost inoculants are available from seed catalogs and in hardware stores to improve yield and increase the ability of the plant to fix nitrogen in the soil.

The advantage of planting soybeans in rows is that you can cultivate them. Begin cultivation as soon as possible after planting. Cultivate between the rows with a tractor or tiller, and if you have the time or a small enough stand, hoe between the plants, since clean cultivation increases yield. You can run a rotary hoe over beans in a field even before sprouts emerge. With a tractor and cultivator, you have to wait until the plants are a few inches high before cultivating, even if you are using shields. As the beans grow, adjust the shields and increase tractor speed so that dirt rolls around the base of the plants—but be sure that a ridge does not form as it will create problems in machine harvesting. Stop cultivating when the beans are about knee-high to avoid serious damage to the plants or roots.

Soybeans can also be broadcast and then worked into the ground with a tiller, or, on a larger acreage, with a rotary hoe. Plots planted in this way are difficult to cultivate and will be weedier. However, if you follow a well-cultivated crop with soybeans, you will have fewer weeds.

Insects: Fortunately, soybeans have few serious problems from either insects or diseases. Problems with insect pests may be developing in different regions of the country, however. The Mexican bean beetle in the Middle Atlantic states, the velvet bean caterpillar in the South and the Japanese beetle in the Northeast may become pests in the future, but they can be controlled by natural predators and viral diseases. Other insects that occasionally bother soybeans, but less seriously, are bean leaf beetles, cutworms, wireworms, white grubs, grasshoppers, leafhoppers, and army worms.

Harvesting: Harvesttime depends on how you intend to use your beans. For table use, soybeans can be harvested in the green-pod stage when the beans are still green and tender. At this stage, you can harvest, cook and freeze them like peas. The best way to hull them is to steam the pods for about ten minutes, then pour off the water. Mature soybeans are easier to hull but hulling is still a slow process.

Harvesting the beans in the green stage can stretch over several weeks as the beans nearer to the base of a plant mature more quickly than the ones at the top of the plant. The green plants, once the beans are picked, can be cut and dried for hay.

Large patches can also be harvested as

Although soybeans can be picked in the green pod stage for home use, most are harvested for animal feed when fully ripe and dry.

hay. Bean hay takes longer than clover hay to cure, so plan to cut and dry it during August when the chances of rain are less.

Soybeans can be plowed under as green manure when the pods are just beginning to form, or at least before they are far enough along to reseed.

For feeding to rabbits and chickens, cut the soybeans when the pods are fully formed but the plants are still leafy. Bundle them and place them in a corner to dry. Feed plants and all. For other animals, mill the beans and add them to ground grain feed. About 200 pounds of soybean meal per ton of corn and oats makes an adequate ration.

Most soybeans, however, are harvested with a grain combine when fully ripe. The plants are left to dry in the field, leaves turn yellow and drop off, and the brown-colored stems and pods are left standing until thoroughly dry. When moisture content falls below 13 percent, the beans can be safely harvested.

Small quantities of beans can be cut and threshed by hand. Cut off the plants, stuff them in burlap bags, and tramp and beat the bags or drive over them with a vehicle. Most of the beans fall to the bottom of the bag and can be winnowed by pouring from one bucket to another. *See* WHEAT.

Store soybeans as you would wheat—in large, clean bins or, if in smaller amounts, in clean, tightly covered barrels. Rodents do not seem to like soybeans as much as grains, so rodent damage is not as much of a problem.

Varieties: There are two types of soybeans grown in this country. Although all varieties of soybeans are edible, soybeans grown for human food are called "edible soybeans" because they taste less oily than other kinds when eaten raw. Kanrich, Frostbeater, Pickett, Prize, Kim, and Disoy are popular varieties.

Most other varieties are grown for animal feeding and are adapted to different areas of the country. Check to see what varieties your neighbors are planting and find out which varieties fit your own cropping needs.

SPADING
See CULTIVATION, TRENCHING, VEGETABLE GARDENING

SPANISH BROOM
See WEAVER'S BROOM

SPANISH MOSS
(*Tillandsia usneoides*)

This epiphyte, which requires support from a bark panel or tree, has long, slender, mosslike, gray stems covered with tiny leaves and very small inconspicuous flowers. In its native southern states, long strands of Spanish moss hang gracefully from the branches of trees. It is seldom cultivated and in some regions is a serious pest.

When used as a mulch, Spanish moss will form a good covering without packing excessively. Plants will not penetrate a mulch of Spanish moss and, since it decomposes slowly, it must be removed before cultivation.

SPANISH NEEDLE
See BEGGAR'S TICKS

SPATHE

A spathe is a hoodlike leaf which covers a flower or inflorescence. The spathe may be fleshy and colored like a petal, bladelike or papery. The calla lily has large white or yellow cornucopia-shaped spathes. The spathes of most of the members of the Iris family are the papery coverings over the flower buds, which dry and curl up on the stem below the flower after it has opened.

SPEARMINT   *(Mentha spicata)*

Spearmint is a well-known mint frequently found growing wild throughout the eastern half of the United States. The leaves and flowering tops are widely used for seasoning meats and beverages and the volatile oil distilled from the whole herb is used for flavoring chewing gum, dentifrices and medicine. A pleasant herb tea is also made from the plant.

Spearmint is easily grown in any fertile, fairly moist soil. In general, it should be treated like peppermint in the garden. *See* PEPPERMINT.

Fresh leaves and leafy stem tips may be picked at any time. For drying, it is best cut just as flowering begins. Dry the leaves carefully in the shade.

See also HERB, MINT.

SPECIES

The two-word Latin name for a plant consists of the genus name, followed by the species. A species is a subdivision of a genus, whose member plants resemble each other to such an extent that they might all have had a common parent.

See also BOTANICAL NOMENCLATURE.

SPHAGNUM MOSS

Sphagnum moss collected from bogs has an important place in the nursery. Its excellent moisture-holding property makes it useful as a packing material for plants which are to be shipped through the mail. It is also a fine medium for seed germination. Since it is rela-tively sterile, there is no need to apply chemical protectants to the seeds or the seeding medium to prevent damping-off. With its ability to retain moisture, it also reduces harm from overwatering.

SPICEBUSH   *(Lindera Benzoin)*

Also called spicewood and Benjamin bush, this native plant is one of 60 species of a genus

The true alpine strawberry is not a variety or strain but represents a species completely separate from the common garden strawberry.

The crimson berries of the spicebush appear in fall just as the leaves are turning bright yellow.

The leaves were once brewed for tea, and the bright red berries were used as a spice by the colonists.

SPICEWOOD   *See* SPICEBUSH

SPIDER FERN   *See* FERN

SPIDER FLOWER
(*Cleome Hasslerana*)

This tropical American native is a good choice for the back of the border. It grows three to five feet tall with a thorny stem, spidery purple stamens and white, pink, yellow, or lavender flowers that bloom throughout the summer until frost. Giant Rose Queen and Helen Campbell are two popular varieties.

Though the spider flower self-sows readily, the seedlings do not produce showy flowers. Fresh seed should be sown annually in the spring. The spider flower prefers a sandy soil and full sun.

See also CLEOME.

of aromatic trees and shrubs of the Laurel family.

Spicebush is hardy throughout most of the United States. It grows from eight to 15 feet high, and starts and ends its season in a blaze of yellow. Early in spring the blossoms, and in fall the foliage, turn bright yellow. Originally a swamp shrub, it prefers a moist, partially shaded site but will grow in almost any soil or location. It may be propagated by seeds sown as soon as they ripen, or by cuttings rooted in sand.

SPIDER LILY   *See* HYMENOCALLIS

SPIDER MITES

Mites are not insects, but rather belong to the class Arachnidae, along with ticks, scorpions and spiders. Adults lack antennae and have simple, not compound, eyes. Some, such as the grasshopper mite, are beneficial predators of plant pests. Many more are harmful

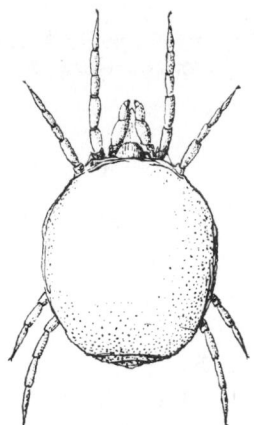

Less than ⅟₅₀-inch long, spider mites appear as tiny red dots on the underside of foliage. Wash infested plants with a strong spray of water.
(Courtesy of U.S. Department of Agriculture)

to plants, animals and man. Several species of red mite damage fruit and shade trees. Cyclamen mites, broad mites and other soft-bodied species feed on greenhouse plants and ornamentals. Acarid mites live in all sorts of organic substances, including stored food, bulbs and plant debris.

Of the plant-feeding mites, spider mites are the most injurious to agricultural crops. They pierce the upper epidermis of plant leaves, extract the juices, and cause foliage to yellow, wilt and eventually drop. Many of these mites spin protective webs which may not damage plants, but which often ruin the appearance of flowers. Adults hibernate during winter, then lay eggs on leaves and stems in spring and summer. Eggs hatch in three to five days and, a week later, young mites reach maturity. Spider mites are generally warm-weather breeders, the number of generations increasing as the temperature rises.

During cool, damp periods spider mites are usually kept under control by their natural enemies. The ladybug is the best-known predator, but lacewings and predaceous mites are also capable of destroying the pests in unsprayed orchards and gardens. Predatory mites can be purchased commercially and provide efficient, practical controls for infested house plants and garden crops. They perform best at temperatures below 75°F. (23.89°C.) and may be irritated by bright light. Monitor the pest population closely, introducing more predators as necessary.

Serious infestations can also be controlled by frequent sprayings of cold water. Orchards suffering from spider mites might benefit from a high-pressure spray of flour, buttermilk and water. Proportions suggested by a Purdue University specialist are 5 pounds of flour, 1 pint of buttermilk and 25 gallons of water. The mixture is very sticky and suffocates the mites without hindering plant transpiration or respiration. Spray thoroughly after leaves have matured and mite populations have reached about three per leaf.

See also HOUSE PLANTS, INSECT CONTROL.

SPIDER PLANT
(*Chlorophytum comosum*)

This common house plant is characterized by its arching, grasslike leaves and its plantlets that form at the ends of long, thin stems. Clusters of small white flowers are borne in the centers of the plantlets. The roots are white and fleshy.

Spider plants are vigorous growers capable of thriving under a variety of locations. However, they do best in the bright but indirect light of a southeastern window where average temperatures are between 55 and 70°F. (12.78 and 21.11°C.). Water thoroughly and evenly and, where humidity is low, mist the leaves every day. Plants can be propagated any time by division of the roots or by layering the plantlets. *See* LAYERING. Any standard potting soil will suffice.

SPIDERWORT   *See* TRADESCANTIA

SPIKEGRASS
See GRASS, ORNAMENTAL

SPINACH   (*Spinacia oleracea*)

One of the most important potherbs cultivated, spinach is rich in vitamins and minerals. It is an especially good source of vitamins A and C.

Planting and Culture: Any good, well-drained garden soil will suit spinach provided it is not acid. The preferred pH is between 6 and 7. Soils that are more acidic should be limed at whatever rate is indicated by a soil test. Spinach requires an abundance of plant food, especially nitrogen. The soil should be well spaded to a depth of six inches with well-rotted manure or compost incorporated. Lime only after the manure has been added.

Spinach is a cool-season crop which should be planted in the open ground as early in the spring as possible. It can also be planted in the fall, or just before the ground freezes in early winter. Protect it with a mulch of hay, straw or leaves. This crop will be ready to use very early the following spring. You may also be able to plant during an early February or March thaw. For spring planting, weekly

sowings can be made, the last one 50 to 60 days before hot summer weather is expected.

One packet of seeds plants 25 feet or one ounce of seed plants 100 feet. Cover the seeds with ½ inch sifted compost and firm well. Rows should be 12 to 15 inches apart, and plants three to four inches apart in the row.

If the season is dry, the garden should be thoroughly soaked late in the day. During the growing period the soil should be kept well loosened and weeds kept down.

Diseases: Spinach blight begins as a yellowing and mottling of the leaves and eventually halts the plant's growth. It is a virus disease transmitted from one plant to another by insects. Where it is known to be in the neighborhood, the resistant varieties should be planted.

Harvesting: Spinach is usually harvested by cutting the whole plant, but it may also be harvested gradually by cutting the outside leaves and allowing the small center leaves to continue growing. The drawback to this method is that the crinkled leaves are difficult to remove without damaging the plant. Plants are considered mature when about six or more leaves have grown to a length of seven inches.

In order to preserve the largest possible amount of the vitamins and minerals in spinach, the leaves should be washed as quickly as possible, without soaking, and dried by whirling in a salad basket. Water left on the leaves dissolves vitamin C, sugars and minerals, and spoils the flavor of the cooked product. To cook, heat as quickly as possible in a small amount of water, then reduce the heat and cover, allowing it to steam. The spinach is ready to serve after about five minutes or as soon as the leaves have wilted.

Varieties: There are two types: one with crumpled leaves, of which Long Standing

Bloomsdale and Virginia Savoy are the most popular; the other with thicker, smoother leaves, as typified by King of Denmark and Nobel. Neither of these go to seed as readily as the others.

Varieties recommended for freezing are: Giant Nobel, Viking, Long Standing Bloomsdale, Northland, and Hybrid No. 7.

Disease-resistant varieties include Winter Bloomsdale, Hybrid No. 7 and Melody Hybrid.

New Zealand spinach (*Tetragonia tetragonioides*) is not true spinach and does not resemble spinach in growth pattern, but when cooked and served there is little difference between them. It has the great merit of flourishing in summer heat, and as its leaves are picked, others grow to replace them. Because of the outer shells, seed should be soaked in water or scored before planting.

Malabar spinach (*Basella alba*) is another excellent substitute for spinach, either cooked or raw. It can be grown on a fence and will thrive in warm weather. It is susceptible to frost injury.

See also VEGETABLE GARDENING.

Cold and heat resistant, New Zealand spinach is unrelated to garden spinach, but when cooked and served there is little difference between them.

SPINDLE TREE   *See* EUONYMUS

SPIREA   (*Spiraea*)

This is a genus of mostly hardy deciduous flowering shrubs of the Rose family, and includes many of our most widely grown garden species. Many hybrids have been developed that grow well in almost any site, but do best where there is a reasonable amount of moisture and full sun. Most types can be grown anywhere south of central Ohio.

Leaves are alternate, usually toothed, and stalked. Flowers are small but arranged in large showy clusters, sometimes flat topped and sometimes in dense spikes. Early-flowering varieties are usually white, but the summer-flowering ones tend toward pink and red.

Propagation is by seed, cuttings, branched tips, or layering. Early-flowering species are pruned after blooming only to remove dead wood. Later-flowering kinds are pruned more severely early in spring.

S. alba, meadowsweet, is a summer-blooming, four- to six-foot shrub with leafy clusters of white flowers.

S. x *Bumalda* is one of the best known of all shrubs. Many hybrid varieties are available including Anthony Waterer which is a late-bloomer with crimson flowers.

S. cantoniensis is not quite hardy in northern areas. It is a bushy shrub to five feet tall, with early-blooming masses of white umbels.

S. japonica grows four to six feet tall and forms a vaselike shape. It bears loose clusters of pink flowers in the summer.

S. x *Margaritae* is a small hybrid which bears bright pink flowers from July through September.

Bridal-wreath is the common name for both *S. prunifolia* and *S.* x *Vanhouttei,* two early-flowering white species. The former has double blossoms, while the latter produces heavy masses of single ones. *Vanhouttei* is very hardy and makes a good shrub for city culture.

Another hardy species is *S. Thunbergii,* a handsome shrub growing to five feet. Small clusters of white flowers appear early in spring and the foliage turns red in fall.

S. tomentosa, called hardhack or steeple-bush for the steeple shape of its flower clusters, is low, grows in moist places, and bears rose purple flowers in late summer.

S. trilobata resembles *Vanhouttei* but is smaller in all its dimensions. It grows to four feet, and its leaves are usually three lobed.

SPORE

Spores are reproductive cells that develop into plants without union with other cells. This is a kind of asexual reproduction that occurs in some of the lower orders of plant life, notably ferns, common mosses, lichens, fungi, algae, and some unicellular forms of plant and animal life. Unlike seeds, spores contain no embryo, but they take the place of seeds among the plants in which they occur.

SPORT

A sport is a sudden variation, or mutation, in a plant gene which causes an offspring to differ from its parents in some marked characteristic. The result of such a change is also called a sport.

Such mutations are most common in seedlings but they may also occur on the branch of an older plant where flowers or fruit may differ from those borne on other branches of the same plant. The fruit now known as the nectarine first appeared on a branch of a peach tree.

Until recently, horticulturists waited for mutations to occur accidentally among their plants. Desirable changes were passed on to succeeding generations by developing seed strains from the mutant, or by propagating asexually. Scientists are now interested in radiation-induced mutations and have been experimenting for many years with plants changed by radiation.

SPRAYS   *See* INSECTICIDES

SPROUTING SEEDS

Sprouted seeds contain significant amounts of vitamin C, as well as vitamin A. In addition, they contain calcium, iron, phosphorus, potassium, and other minerals. Their carbohydrate content is quite low, however, so sprouts are fine for dieters. In the sprouting process starches are converted to simple, easy-to-digest sugars.

The most commonly sprouted seeds are wheat, mung beans, alfalfa, and soybeans. The list of seeds that can be sprouted is practically endless, however, and includes lentils, sweet corn, unhulled or unpearled barley, rye, lima beans, sunflowers, oats, navy beans, clover, pea, parsley, millet, flax, fenugreek, unhulled almonds, brown rice, radish, carrot, broccoli, and many more grain and vegetable seeds.

One important point to remember is to use only untreated seeds. Purchase certified organically grown or untreated seeds from mail-order seed companies, buy seeds packaged especially for sprouting at natural food stores, or use seeds you have grown yourself. Most commercial seeds are treated with chemicals to kill diseases and they should not be sprouted for table use. Seeds should always be of the current crop to insure full germinating power. Keep them stored in a cool, dry place.

Preparing: Although special sprouting equipment, like covered sprouting dishes and mesh caps that fit over standard canning jars, is available, you can use ordinary kitchen containers for sprouting. Any widemouthed jar, shallow bowl, strainer, colander, pie pan, or similar container that can be covered is fine.

Soak about a cup of seeds overnight in plenty of water. Drain and wash several times with warm (not hot) water, discarding broken or imperfect seeds.

Pour off the soaking water (save for watering plants or use in soups or casseroles), and put the seeds in your sprouting container.

If you use a strainer, put a saucer underneath to catch the rinse water. If you use a bowl or jar, cover the top with cheesecloth pulled taut and attached by a string or rubber band around the container mouth. Turn the bowl or jar upside down on two blocks or jar lids so that the rinse water can run freely into a dish underneath.

Keep the container in a warm spot and flush and rinse the seeds three or four times daily. A spray is handy for this.

In three to five days sprouts are ready to be removed and stored in the refrigerator. You can discard the loose skins if you wish, but they are fine roughage and can be eaten with the sprouts.

In the Japanese method, a series of shallow trays with small holes drilled in their bases are mounted one on top of the other. This setup, now available commercially, makes it easy to sprout several different kinds of seeds at one time. Wash the different seeds separately and put them in the individual trays. Then pour water over the top tray and let it seep down to moisten and rinse the whole unit.

Using Sprouts: Wheat and sunflower seed sprouts are most delicious when the sprout is the length of the seed. Mung bean sprouts are best when 1½ to three inches long and alfalfa sprouts when one to two inches long. Pea and soybean sprouts are good short or long. Lentil sprouts mold quickly so they must be used when about one inch long. In general, the longer the sprout, the more nourishment it contains, but most sprouts taste better when short. If the sprouts get long enough and are exposed to sunlight for a day, they will often send out tiny leaves which develop vitamin A and chlorophyll.

Sprouts are very versatile. They can be used whole in Chinese dishes, salads and casseroles. Some, such as alfalfa sprouts, make a nutritious and unusual breakfast food.

Some people who find it hard to develop a taste for soybean and certain other sprouts steam them over very low heat for ten to 15 minutes, or sauté them in a little butter and water in a covered pan about ten minutes. They can be roasted or included in various egg dishes.

SPRUCE   (*Picea*)

The spruces are members of the Pine family, with a single trunk, whorled branches, four-sided needles, pendent or berrylike cones, and catkinlike flowers. The genus includes many fine ornamental, timber and pulp trees. Their habit of growth is pyramidal and they may be grown in almost any well-drained soil with sufficient moisture. They are shallow rooted and easily transplanted. Dense foliage makes them useful as hedges and windbreaks.

The black spruce (*P. mariana*) is one of the few spruces that will grow in moist, low places. It is very hardy, but is of little interest as a landscape tree because it becomes scraggly with age. This spruce, which grows to a height of 30 feet or more, is the source of spruce beer, spruce gum and valuable timber.

The blue spruce (*P. pungens*), or Colorado blue spruce, grows to 140 feet in the wild and has 1¼-inch blue green needles and cones to four inches. In the variety Koster, branches are drooping and needles are bluer.

Engelmann's spruce (*P. Engelmannii*) is a tree of the Rockies, thriving at high altitudes. Growing to 150 feet, it has close-set branches and blue green needles. Varieties offer silver

Engelmann's spruce is a native of the high-altitude regions of Colorado but can be grown successfully as an ornamental in the East.
(Courtesy of U.S. Forest Service)

needles, bluish needles or drooping branches.

Norway spruce (*P. Abies*) grows to 150 feet, with horizontal branches and drooping branchlets. It is grown as a forestry crop as well as an ornamental. The needles are shiny and dark green. Of the many varieties, one has variegated needles, several are dwarfs, and one is prostrate.

The red spruce (*P. rubens*) is used chiefly for paper pulp, and is rarely cultivated.

The Sitka spruce (*P. sitchensis*) is a beautiful tree which grows to 180 feet, with needles colored silver above and glossy green below. The wood is used to make the sounding boards of musical instruments.

The white or skunk spruce (*P. glauca*) grows to 70 feet, and is the principal spruce of the Arctic. Many varieties are available.

SPURGE   *See* EUPHORBIA

SQUAB   *See* PIGEON

SQUASH   (*Cucurbita*)

The squashes are members of the large genus of annual, trailing or climbing vines which also includes the pumpkins and gourds. A truly native American plant, the squash flourishes in practically every part of the country where enough moisture is available.

Classification of the various pumpkins and squashes is confusing since each species contains cultivars called winter and summer squashes and pumpkins. In the United States, winter squashes are those that are eaten when mature and that can be stored for several months. Unlike summer squash, they have hard rinds and are baked, rather than boiled for table use. Pumpkins are orange, spherical winter squash. All species succeed in reasonably rich soil, although they favor a sandy loam. You will find them easy to cultivate.

Planting and Culture: Squash prefers a slightly acid soil with a pH of 6 to 6.5. A well-drained bed containing a supply of humus and rotted manure will produce healthy plants. Regardless of the condition of the garden, greater success will be assured if you add compost to each hill.

Butternut and acorn are winter squashes, hard rinded and good keepers.
(Courtesy of U.S. Department of Agriculture)

Squash seed should not be planted until all danger of frost has passed. Bush or summer squash should be spaced four to five feet between hills; running vines need ten to 12 feet. Six seeds to a hill covered with an inch of soil will be sufficient. Thin each hill to the two best plants. Squash seeds remain viable for up to four years and one packet of seed will plant ten to 12 hills.

Where the growing season is short, squash plants should be started indoors about a month before they can be planted outdoors. Squash roots resent being disturbed, so seed should be sown one to a pot indoors. Outdoors, set two seedlings in each hill. The first flowers of indoor plants which have been set out should be removed to encourage more fruit production.

Insects: The squash vine borer bores down the stem of the plant, causing the leaves to die off. To remove the borer, slit the stem lengthwise at the injured point. If the damaged stems are buried under a little soil, roots will set and new growth will begin.

The squash beetle leaves its eggs on the top and underside of the squash leaves. Eggs should be handpicked and crushed.

A box is an effective protection against squash enemies. A wooden or fiberboard box, about 18 inches square and 12 inches deep, with no top or bottom, should be placed over each hill. Stretch a piece of cheesecloth over the top of the box and secure. Similar protection can be built with barrel staves or stakes.

Dusting with wood ashes may also discourage insect pests which plague your plants. Be sure to cover the stems and the base of each plant, two areas most affected by squash enemies.

Harvesting: Summer squash should be picked when the skin is soft enough to be penetrated by a fingernail. Remove all fruit at this stage, in order to keep the vines bearing. Winter squash may be left on the vines until the danger of frost is at hand. Cut the fruit from the vines two weeks before frost and allow it to cure in the sun. If squash is damaged by frost, store it indoors for several days in a room where the temperature is at least 70°F. (21.11°C.).

Summer squash does not store well and should be eaten when picked. Winter squash should be stored in a dry cellar. The best temperature for stored squash is around 50°F. (10°C.). Check the winter squash frequently for the development of mold. If mold forms, wipe it off with an oily cloth. If carefully stored, squash should last until the following spring.

Varieties: Recommended summer squash (*C. Pepo*) varieties include the vegetable marrows such as Small Sugar; the summer crooknecks and cocozelles; pattypans such as White Bush Scallop; and black and gray zucchini cultivars. Of these, crookneck and zucchini are preferred. Most varieties mature within 60 days and produce an abundance of fruit.

Among winter types (*C. maxima, C. moschata* and *C. Pepo*), the most popular are Blue Hubbard and Hubbard, Buttercup, Butternut, Mammoth, Quaker Pie, Turban, and the acorn types such as Table Queen. Most of these are good keepers if stored at about 45 to 60°F. (7.22 to 15.56°C.) in a well-ventilated place. Both winter and summer strains come in bush as well as vine varieties and there are several miniature-fruited cultivars.

SQUASH BUG
See INSECT CONTROL

SQUILL   *See* SCILLIA

STACHYS

Also known as betony and woundwort, this genus of coarse herbs and shrubs of the Mint family contains a large number of annual and perennial species found mostly in temperate regions. They prefer moist, sandy loam and full sun.

S. affinis, the Chinese or Japanese artichoke, has edible white tubers that are planted in April and harvested in October. A perennial growing to 1½ feet, this species has white or pink flowers and lance-shaped leaves. *S. byzantina,* lamb's ears or woolly woundwort, is a hardy perennial with purple flowers and a coat of silvery "wool." Another hardy perennial, *S. grandiflora* grows to a height of one to two feet and produces showy violet flowers. Varieties offer white, rose or deep purple blooms.

STAGGERBUSH   *See* LYONIA

STAGHORN FERN   (*Platycerium*)

A genus of ferns with fronds shaped like a stag's antlers, these natives of the tropics are found on tree trunks, branches, old plants, or rocks. Some are grown principally in greenhouses, but others will thrive as house plants if given good care. Staghorns have two kinds of fronds—the fertile fronds, which are antler-shaped segments growing 1½ to five feet in length, and the sterile fronds, which are circular or shield-shaped leaves enclosing the roots and embracing the trunk or branch on which the plant lives. Roots are embedded in a mass of decayed sterile fronds, and sometimes pierce the bark of the tree, but are not parasitic. Rather, they are epiphytes and draw their moisture from the air.

The staghorn fern commonly grown as a house plant is *P. bifurcatum,* which has gray green drooping fronds from one to three feet in length. It is grown in a basket or attached to pieces of charred wood, cork or cedar. Its base should be enclosed with osmunda fiber and the plant should receive plenty of indirect light and frequent syringing. Water it directly only if it droops. Division of plants is accomplished by wiring a piece of the plant to a new branch or to a piece of wood and keeping it shaded and damp until roots form. This can be done only in a humid, warm greenhouse.

A large form with five-foot fronds is the *P. coronarium,* native to Java. *P. grande,* which comes from Australia, has six-foot fronds almost free of the hairs which are common to others. A deep green species is *P. Hillii,* with short, erect fronds which grow to about three feet. Triangle staghorn (*P. Stemaria*) has graceful, drooping, three-foot fronds which are twice forked. Another attractive form is the Java staghorn (*P. Willinckii*), whose fertile fronds are clustered in three and whose segments are long and narrow.

STAKING PLANTS

Vegetables are staked or supported to keep the fruit off the bare ground or to save space. Ornamental plants are staked to protect naturally upright, often top-heavy growth from breaking under heavy winds or to curb a natural tendency to sprawl.

Vegetables: In the vegetable garden, stakes are placed before the plants or seeds are in the ground. Supports for tomatoes may be stout 2x2 stakes or square supports similar to those used for peonies. The plants may be tied to successive wires of a fence as they grow

When staking tomato plants, tie thick twine securely but loosely to avoid cutting the stem.

together at the top, tripod style, and the seeds planted in the center between them. Poles for beans should be sunk two to three feet in the ground before seeds are planted.

Flowers: Many annual flowers profit from staking. Tall snapdragons, calendulas, annual campanulas—all have a tendency to sprawl unless they are given some support. If their main stalks are tied to an upright support when they are about six to eight inches tall, the later growth will be much more erect.

Supports used for bulbs, such as gladiolus, or for tubers, such as begonias, should be placed before the corm or tuber has been planted. If the stake is not placed until the shoot emerges from the ground, the gardener runs a risk of piercing the bulb with it, and perhaps killing a valuable plant.

Some perennials, such as peonies, which put forth many stalks, must be supported as a mass. Four stakes may be set into the ground around them in the form of a square and wire or heavy twine strung between the tops of the stakes. For peonies, the support should be placed when the leaves are less than a foot high. Train the growth up through the support. When the leaves and flowers have fully matured, they will lie over the top wire or twine and hide it from view. A similar support is useful for tall-growing oriental poppies.

Some slender-stemmed shrubs which have been bred for large flowers, such as some roses, require stakes. Tall perennials such as delphiniums, foxglove, hollyhocks, lilies, and others, may be more compact when they are given support that forces each stem to grow perfectly upright. A denser mass of bloom will result from such treatment. With both shrubs and perennials, stakes may be placed near the center of the plant and left from year to year. If the

taller. Peas are usually supported on chicken-wire fencing, but a framework of twigs pruned from shrubbery may also be used. If the twigs are freshly pruned from spring-flowering shrubs and immediately thrust into the ground, some of them may root, affording a supply of new, young shrubs.

Poles for pole beans are usually young sapling trunks, cut during the winter and trimmed for the purpose. They may be set erect at each hill, or three poles may be tied

stakes are unsightly after the plants have been pruned or have died back, remove them and drive shorter stakes in the same holes to mark their positions. This will prevent root damage which might occur if the regular stake is not thrust back into the same hole.

Chicken-wire fencing in one- to three-foot widths may be used to support other plants that will grow through the wire and hide it. It is particularly good around chrysanthemums, dahlias and other bushy plants or, in the vegetable garden, for staking beans and peas. The fencing may be formed into a circle or irregular shape to contain a clump, or it may be used as a double-row fence, with the row of plants between two lengths of chicken wire.

Materials: Materials used for staking may be purchased or culled from garden prunings of various sizes, thicknesses and strengths. A gray-barked twig will disappear from view more readily in the border than a new dowel. Stakes for smaller annuals need not be more than ½ to ¾ inch thick. Dahlias and hollyhocks need inch-thick stakes. Corner stakes for peonies should be at least as thick as a broomstick because they may have a sizable load when rain-filled blossoms lean on them. Some of the shorter annuals and perennials do best when permitted to grow up through an untrimmed twiggy stake or a framework of such stakes.

String or twine for tying will be less visible if colored green, tan or gray, rather than white. If wire is used, it should be well covered with plastic, paper or string coating. This will protect the stem from burning and chafing under a midsummer sun. Wires used to support small trees and shrubs are inserted in lengths of rubber hose.

First tie twine or wire to the stake at the desired height. Then tie it around the stem of the plant, leaving a loop large enough to permit later growth, but not large enough to allow the plant to blow around inside its support. Avoid slipknots; they may tighten and constrict the plant.

STALK BORER

Stalk borers are larvae that eat their way through the stems of weeds and many flowers and vegetables, including corn, potatoes, tomatoes, and eggplant. Infested stems wilt and snap off.

To help prevent an infestation, keep down weeds in the garden. Affected plants can sometimes be saved by slitting the infested stem and plucking out the borer.

See also INSECT CONTROL.

STAND

A dense planting of a crop in a given area is called a stand.

STANDING CYPRESS   *See* GILIA

STAR APPLE
(*Chrysophyllum Cainito*)

A tropical evergreen tree of the Sapodilla family, which is grown both as an ornamental and for its fruit, the star apple can be grown only in frost-free sections of Florida or in the greenhouse. The oval leaves are leathery, with golden hairs underneath, and the clusters of small flowers are purple and white. The edible fruit is smooth, white or light purple, and about the size of an apple. The fruit has pumpkinlike seeds arranged in a star-shaped pattern.

Propagation is by seed or cuttings of ripe wood placed in moist heat. Star apples often grow to 50 feet if given a rich, sandy soil.

STAR-GLORY
(*Ipomoea Quamoclit*)

This vigorous, handsome climbing vine is good for screening porches and trellises, or for growing in window boxes or tubs. Also known as cypress vine and cardinal climber, it is popular in the South and California. Although a few related species are perennial, star-glory is a tender annual. It grows 20 feet tall and has striking bright red flowers and feathery foliage. It blooms very freely in full sun if given a fairly rich soil.

Seed should be sown early, indoors or in a cold frame or cool greenhouse. Transplant seedlings outdoors after all danger of frost has passed. They like a fertile soil, well supplied with humus, but too much nitrogen will produce lush foliage and few flowers. Space plants about 12 inches apart.

STAR-OF-BETHLEHEM
See ORNITHOGALUM

STATICE   (*Limonium sinuatum*)

Statice or sea lavender is a half-hardy biennial usually grown as an annual in the ornamental rock garden or flower bed. It reaches a height of about two feet and has angled stems with clusters of papery white, yellow, red, blue, or purple flowers. The flowers appear in mid to late summer and are excellent for cutting and drying.

To propagate, sow seed indoors or under glass in late spring and transplant to the sunny garden after danger of frost has passed. Plants thrive in any rich, fairly moist garden soil.

STEEPLEBUSH   *See* SPIREA

STEINER, RUDOLF

(1861–1925) A noted author, lecturer, playwright, and producer, Steiner believed that through meditation man could truly know himself and, by extrapolation, understand the meaning of education, agriculture and the arts. His lifelong search for the harmony and balance he believed existed between the physical and spiritual worlds led him to develop a philosophy of life which gave a common thread to his diverse interests. Simply stated, Steiner believed that everything on the planet performed a unique and vital function essential to the well-being of the whole, with no one element, including man, deserving a destructive superiority over another.

Today his ideas are most widely applied to agriculture. His "bio-dynamic" concept, which holds that the earth is a living substance that needs to be replenished and revitalized through organic means, is a basic tenet of organic farmers and gardeners the world over.

Steiner also invented his own type of healing by applying nature's balanced cycle of integration and disintegration to human beings.

He considered illness an interruption of this balance, and believed that it could be prevented by following nature's rhythm and cured with various vegetable and mineral preparations.

Perhaps Steiner's greatest achievement lies in education. It was his belief that maturation occurs in three specific stages during a child's life, and that it is the responsibility of the teacher to recognize and encourage signs of personal growth and development. Schools that adhere to his philosophies are in existence all over the world.

Steiner is also known for his work with the mentally handicapped for whom he established communes where each one according to his ability contributed something to the preservation and growth of the entire community. Living in small families with two "parents," they learned self-reliance, responsibility and a measure of independence by growing their own food, making bread and caring for farm animals, as well as practicing various crafts and skills.

STEM

A stem is the main aerial axis of a plant. It bears buds and shoots instead of roots and is usually above ground, though perennials may have underground stems called rhizomes or rootstocks. Being a continuation of the root, the stem has an internal structure similar to that found in the root, but it also has layers of cells whose function is to stiffen the plant and raise it above ground. In woody plants, this tissue has the ability to persist through the winter and bear buds which will develop the following year. In herbs, the stem dies to the ground each year. A trunk is the stem of a tree. A stalk is the stem of a leaf or flower. A bulb, tuber, corm, or rootstock is a specialized stem.

STEPHANANDRA

Stephanandras are graceful Asiatic shrubs valuable for planting in borders and on rocky slopes. They have small, alternate leaves and clusters of white flowers at the tips of the stems. Stephanandras are propagated by seed, cuttings or division and are easily grown in any garden soil.

S. incisa, growing to eight feet, has dense masses of slender branches with sometimes drooping and deeply lobed leaves which turn purple in autumn. It is hardy south of New York. *S. i.* var. *crispa* is a dwarf form growing only two feet high and three feet across, and therefore useful along foundations or at the base of larger shrubs. Its dense, zigzag branches add winter interest. It flowers in June and is hardier than the tall form. *S. Tanakae* is slightly hardier, with larger leaves that turn yellow, orange and scarlet in autumn.

STERILITY
See ORCHARD, POLLINATION

STERNBERGIA

Also known as winter daffodils and lilies-of-the-field, members of this genus of bulbous herbs of the Amaryllis family have yellow, crocuslike flowers that bloom in spring or fall.

From each bulb spring one or two flowers on separate stems six to eight inches long. Grass-like basal leaves are ¾ inch wide and eight to 12 inches long.

Bulbs are planted in August, four to six inches deep in an exposed site in full sun. A well-drained bed on the south side of a wall or building is a perfect location for sternbergias. After planting, sternbergias should be left undisturbed for years, and will develop from bulblets into clumps. Foliage persists through the winter, dying back in the spring. If the bulbs must be lifted for any reason, they may be moved when the leaves have completely died.

The "lilies of the field" mentioned in the Bible are thought to have been *S. lutea* which still grows in Palestine. Each bulb of that species produces six to eight leaves and one to four flowers that bloom in spring. *S. Fischerana,* a spring bloomer, is a good rock garden subject.

See also BULB.

STEWARTIA

Also known as stuartia, this genus of deciduous trees and shrubs of the Tea family is native to Asia and the southern Atlantic coast of the United States. Stewartias have a smooth, flaking bark, white, camellialike flowers and toothed, bright green leaves that turn orange or scarlet in fall. A rich, moist mixture of peat and loam, and partial shade produce the best growth. Propagation is from seed, layers or cuttings of half-ripe wood under glass.

Japanese stewartia (*S. Pseudocamellia*), which may be grown as far north as Massachusetts, has a reddish, flaking bark and showy white flowers with orange or blue anthers. It grows to 50 feet tall. Silky camellia (*S. Malachodendron*) is a 12-foot shrub that is not hardy north of Virginia. Its showy white flowers have bluish anthers. Mountain camellia (*S. ovata*), a ten- to 15-foot shrub hardy south of New York, has white flowers with orange anthers.

STIPA   *See* GRASS, ORNAMENTAL

ST.-JOHN'S-WORT
See SAINT-JOHN'S-WORT

STOCK   (*Mathiola incana*)

Also called gillyflowers, these biennial or perennial plants, which are usually treated as half-hardy annuals, grow from one to three feet high and bear racemes of fragrant, single or double flowers in many shades of yellow, white, red, blue, and purple. The soft, gray foliage and beautiful flowers, which last well in the garden or cut, make an attractive display in beds and borders.

Stocks are cool-weather plants and will not set flower buds if night temperatures stay above 60°F. (15.56°C.). Plant them early so that they make their main vegetative growth before hot weather sets in. In northern areas, sow outdoors when peas are planted (about April 1) in very well drained soil that is not too rich. Use only the seven- or ten-week varieties. The tall Imperial and Column stocks are suitable as outdoor plants only in mild winter areas, where they are sown in fall, grow through the winter, and flower in early spring before the weather becomes hot.

Seed may also be started in February or early March in well-drained soil in a cool spot indoors or in the cold frame. Cover the seed very lightly and water sparingly. When the seedlings are large enough to handle, prick them out into peat pots or into flats about three inches apart each way. Grow the plants in a cool (45 to 50°F. [7.22 to 10°C.]) location and plant them in their permanent positions as soon as danger of heavy frost is past. The blooming season of stock will not last much beyond early July in most areas, but it can be prolonged if plants are given afternoon shade. Imperial and Column stocks can be grown in the cool greenhouse (50°F. nights, 60°F. days [10 to 15.56°C.]) for late-winter cut flowers. They bloom in about six months from sowing, so sow them in late September for March cut flowers. Greenhouse stock sown before late July or after early February will produce only "blind" growth, and no flowers due to high temperatures and light intensity at the time when they mature.

Evening-scented stock (*M. longipetala* var. *bicornus*) has small lilac-colored flowers that open at night, filling the garden with fragrance. Its foliage is inconspicuous, so the plants should be surrounded by more showy flowers. Sow the seeds outdoors in April and thin plants to stand six inches apart.

STOLON

A stolon is an aboveground, spreading stem that strikes root at its tip and sends up new shoots from each node.

STONECROP   *See* SEDUM

STONE MULCHING   *See* MULCH

STORAGE

The principal methods of storing perishable foods are canning and freezing. Present-day economic pressures, however, have caused more people than ever to rely upon home food resources and to take a new interest in other forms of preservation to complement these methods. Drying, the oldest process known, has gained popularity, despite some criticisms about the time it takes and the unfamiliar appearances and flavors of dried foods. To save time and money, many gardeners are using other methods to store fresh produce for long periods of time.

Underground Storage: This is an inexpensive means of preservation, which costs practically nothing in maintenance and construction after initial building expense. If certain basic guidelines are followed, root crops, cabbage, onions, pumpkins, late squashes, and many tree fruits can be kept fresh throughout the winter in cellars, pits, cold frames, and other underground storage structures.

Harvest should take place before the fruits and vegetables have a chance to become overripe and only the very best produce should be stored. Squashes, in particular, must be handled with extreme care to prevent decay caused by even the slightest of scratches and scrapes.

Never store fruit near potatoes, turnips or cabbage. The gases released by apples and certain other fruits will cause vegetables to overripen or sprout. If you must store fruit with vegetables, wrap it in paper or maple leaves before placing it in barrels. This will also prevent the absorption of odors.

Before storing, root crops need to be cleaned. Rubbing a soft cloth lightly over the vegetable or gently rinsing it under running water usually suffices, but if you rinse, allow excess water to evaporate before storing.

Small containers are necessary in most storage areas. Wooden boxes used to ship fruits are ideal units for cellars or other large storage rooms. Pack the produce in these boxes or in other containers with dry, crisp leaves, hay, straw, sphagnum moss, or crumpled burlap as insulation. Boxes should be stacked on 2x4's and separated from the floor and other boxes by more 2x4's. This allows air to circulate.

Pails, baskets and watertight barrels are other good storage containers. Bins (four inches above the floor) can be constructed for permanent use to accommodate potatoes and other root crops. Metal containers, galvanized or patch-painted to prevent rust, also serve well in storage areas. Layers of hay, straw or burlap insulation must alternate between layers of produce with insulation on top. Orange crates and mesh bags are excellent receptacles for onions and other foods requiring good air circulation.

Pits, cold frames and tiles: Storage pits can keep root crops close to a desirable temperature of 32°F. (0°C.). The pit should be dug in well-drained ground, and lined with straw and leaves. After the produce is placed inside, the pit should be topped with several inches of soil and a heavy mulch. Several pits can be dug to store fruits and vegetables separately.

A cold frame also serves as a fine storage area. If insulated with straw or leaves, and lined with an impervious material such as hardware cloth, it will protect the contents from rodent and other animal infestation.

A storage device suggested by Purdue University is the underground tile. Buried upright, in a well-drained, shaded area, a tile 30 inches by 18 inches can accommodate three bushel baskets of fruit or vegetables. Field tile is best because it is porous, but hard burned vitrified or concrete tile may also be used. After the tile is filled with food it should be covered with a deep mulch of straw, hay or leaves. A wire screen placed on top, held in place by a rock or another tile, will protect the stores from weather and animal vandals.

Barrel root cellar: An effective, small-sized root cellar for the home garden can be made from a wooden barrel set in a trench. Nowadays, barrels are hard to find, but you can check for them at hardware stores, lumberyards and country food stores.

The trench should be slightly larger than the barrel, so that stones or bricks can be placed on the bottom to facilitate drainage. Set the barrel at about a 45-degree angle in the trench. Cover it with six inches of dirt, six inches of straw or leaves and finally with two more inches of dirt to hold the other material in place. After the barrel is laden with food packed in sand, the cover is put in place, and then a foot of straw is placed upon the cover, with a board and rock on top as an anchor.

Aboveground Storage: Mound storage is one form of top-of-the-ground storage. A mound is started with a layer of mulch, followed by the fruits or vegetables, and then more hay, leaves or straw. This, in turn, is covered with soil and boards. A ventilation pipe can be added through the center of the mound and supported by stakes, but this pipe should be capped during freezing weather. A drainage trench around the mound completes the structure. All produce should be removed from this aboveground storage area at one time after it is opened. Several of these storage areas

STORAGE REQUIREMENTS FOR FRESH PRODUCE

Commodity	Preparation	Temperature/Humidity	Optimum Storage Time
Apple	Wrap in oiled or shredded paper. Handle carefully to prevent bruising.	AH	4 to 8 months
Asparagus		BH	3 to 4 weeks
Bean/Pea	Shell. Dry 30 to 60 minutes in a warm oven.	V	Indefinite
Beet/Carrot/Turnip	Remove tops. Do not wash. Pack in straw.	BH	5 to 7 months
Cabbage	Remove outer leaves.	BH	1 to 4 months
Celery	Do not wash. Place in peat or sand.	CH	4 to 6 weeks
Endive/Escarole	Place in moist sand or peat.	BH	2 to 3 months
Garlic	Dry bulbs in the sun. Bunch and hang them in a well-ventilated place.	CL	6 to 7 months
Hot pepper	Dry on the vine.	V	Indefinite
Kohlrabi	Remove leaves and roots.	CH	1 to 3 months
Onion	Dry bulbs in sun. Remove tops and place bulbs in bins or braid tops and hang bulbs.	CL	5 to 7 months
Orange		AH	6 to 10 weeks
Parsnip/Salsify	Leave one inch stem.	BH	5 to 9 months
Peach	Do not use fully ripe fruit. Do not wash.	BM	3 days to 2 weeks
Pear	Wrap in newspaper.	BH	2 to 3 months
Pepper		DM	2 to 3 weeks
Plum	Do not use fully ripe fruit.	BM	4 to 6 weeks
Quince	Do not use fully ripe fruit.	AH	2 to 3 months
Squash/Pumpkin	Cure in the field or indoors. Leave one inch stems.	EL	4 to 6 months
Sweet potato	Cure in sun for about 3 weeks.	EM	1 to 3 months
Tomato	Store only green ones.	EM	4 to 6 weeks

A   30 to 32°F. (−1.11 to 0°C.)   B   32°F.(0°C.)   C   32 to 42°F. (0 to 5.56°C.)

D   42 to 50°F. (5.56 to 10°C.)   E   50 to 60°F. (10 to 15.56°C.)

H   85 to 95% humidity   M   75 to 85% humidity   L   65 to 75% humidity   V   below 65% humidity

may be required to store enough food for an entire season.

Another aboveground method is to use bales of hay as the insulating material instead of earth. After the winter is over the hay can be used as mulch.

Cellar Storage: Cellars make excellent, spacious storage areas, especially if they have earthen floors which aid in keeping food cool and moist. If an earth-floored cellar is not available, part of a regular basement can serve just as well.

The key to constructing a storage cellar is in providing insulation and ventilation. Temperature and humidity must be controlled in order to maintain the correct conditions for keeping produce. Generally, this means lowering the usual basement temperature to between 30 and 40°F. (−1.11 to 4.44°C.). Fruits and vegetables store best at 32°F. (0°C.), but since there is a possibility of the food freezing at temperatures lower than this, the ideal temperature of a storage room is 35 to 40°F. (1.67 to 4.44°C.). Humidity for storage of most fruits and vegetables should be around 80 percent. Root crops such as beet, turnip, and carrot require slightly more humidity and squash and melon need a drier atmosphere.

When building a storage cellar in a basement, locate it away from pipes and chimneys, preferably in the northeast or northwest corner. An eight-by-ten-foot room will hold 60 bushels of goods, or enough to serve an average family for a year. The area should be constructed near a window for ventilation purposes, but the window should be shaded to keep out sunlight. With this arrangement the air will remove gases which cause sprouting, while the sunlight will be unable to affect the vegetables.

If the inside temperature is above 40°F. (4.44°C.) and it is cooler outside, the window should be opened. When the temperature in the cellar is down to 35°F. (1.67°C.), the window should be closed. Wooden louvers will block sunlight while the window is open, and, if they are covered with copper screening, rodents will be unable to enter.

Proper insulation helps to regulate the temperature and humidity within the room. This calls for moisture-vapor barriers, such as damp-proof paper, tar or asphalt, on both the inside and outside walls. The walls can be insulated with boards or by loose fill, in amounts determined by the temperature of the surrounding basement. A 2x4 frame, sheathed on both sides, with three-inch insulation batts between the studding, usually suffices. The door should also be protected with four inches or more of insulation. Some homemade storage cellars utilize cellar steps and window wells.

Home cellar storage areas must be kept clean. Walls and ceilings should be whitewashed, the floor swept frequently, and dead materials removed. Spring cleaning is imperative.

Regardless of the method, stored produce should be carefully checked to avoid loss from decay, growth or shriveling. Remove decaying vegetables immediately, and reduce temperature if vegetables begin to grow. Finally, wrap or lightly moisten any vegetables that begin to shrivel.

STORAX   (*Styrax*)

These deciduous or evergreen shrubs are prized for their fragrant, showy white flowers, which grow in loose drooping clusters and bloom in late spring or early summer. Flowers are followed by egg-shaped, dry drupes. The alternate leaves are oval or elliptical and toothed. The storax, or snowbell, prefers a warm sandy loam and full or partial sun.

Fragrant snowbell (*S. Obassia*) is a very showy shrub that grows to 30 feet but can be kept trimmed to about ten feet. It does best in slight shade with protection from strong winds. It blooms in early summer. Japanese snowbell (*S. japonica*) is a striking shrub that is hardy as far north as Massachusetts and also blooms in early summer. Snowdrop bush (*S. officinalis*) is a very tender species that is widely grown in California. Mock orange storax (*S. americanus*), not to be confused with the common mock orange (*Philadelphus*), is grown throughout the South.

STOUT, RUTH

(1891–   ) Ruth Stout is known to gardeners everywhere as the person who originated the year-round mulched, no-work garden. When she began gardening in the late 1920's and early 1930's, Ruth was a conventional gardener, but, by thinking for herself and carefully observing the results of her trials, she began to develop methods of her own that often defied gardening "experts."

Many gardeners mulch their gardens during the summer with whatever materials are at hand—grass clippings, leaves, weeds, hay, or straw—and in the fall or the following spring, they spread compost on their gardens and turn everything under. Ruth Stout developed a method that offers the advantages of this practice without the work. Since about 1943 she has used a permanent eight-inch straw mulch. She throws other vegetable matter on the straw—grass clippings, vegetable wastes, stalks

from old plants, weeds. Whenever the mulch begins to thin or weeds grow through the mulch, she adds more straw. As the mulch decays it enriches the soil underneath enough that no compost or fertilizer is required. Soil can be made more acid by adding cottonseed meal or peat moss, or more alkaline by adding ground lime. When planting, Ruth pulls back mulch from the rows, plants her seeds, and when they sprout, pulls the mulch around the tiny plants.

With this method, composting, tilling and weeding are unnecessary. Ruth eventually found that her soil was so fertilized by the decaying mulch that she didn't have to thin any crops besides corn and parsnips. Her method and its results were reported in a series of articles in *Organic Gardening and Farming* (beginning in 1953) and elsewhere, and in a series of books. Some of her gardening books in print include *The Ruth Stout No-Work Garden Book* (with Richard Clemence, 1971), *How to Have a Green Thumb Without an Aching Back* (1955), *Gardening Without Work* (1961), and *I've Always Done It My Way* (1975).

STOVER

Dried stalks of corn or sorghum from which the seed or grain has been removed is called stover. It is frequently used as fodder.

STRAIN

A strain is a group of plants within a variety that has similar morphology but has some physiological distinction, such as improved strength, color or texture, which persists through all generations of the plants. Strain is a horticultural term rather than a botanical term. It is used most often by seedsmen who develop slight improvements in plants through selection, and name the improved seed a strain of that variety.

STRATIFY
See SEEDS AND SEEDLINGS

STRAW

Straw, which is made up of the stalks or stems of farm crops, is commonly used as a mulch and compost material. If you compost large quantities of straw, incorporate considerable amounts of nitrogen in the form of green or animal manures. In this way, the bacteria

that break down the straw into humus will not deplete the soil of the nitrogen that is needed by growing plants.

It is also recommended that the straw be chopped. If mixed with other materials that hold water, or if composted with large amounts of barnyard manure, long straw offers no trouble, though heaps of it cannot be turned easily and take longer to break down. Weighing down the material with a thicker layer of earth might speed decomposition. This also preserves the moisture inside the heap. *See also* COMPOSTING.

If a large straw pile is allowed to stay outside in the field where deposited by the thresher, the bottom of it will weather and decay into a slimy mass rich in fungi, while the inside will be decomposed by fungi. This predigested material is excellent for compost making and mulching. Some of the fungi associated with straw are the types that form mycorrhizal relations with the roots of fruit trees, evergreens, grapes, and roses, so straw mulch will benefit these plants not only as a

MINERAL VALUE OF STRAWS

	Calcium %	Potash %	Magnesium %	Phosphorus %	Sulfur %
Barley	.4	1.0	.1	.1–.5	.1
Buckwheat	2.0	2.0	.3	.4	?
Corn stover	.3	.8	.2	.2	.2
Millet	1.0	3.2	.4	.2	.2
Oats	.2	1.5	.2	.1	.2
Rye	.3	1.0	.07	.1	.1
Sorghum	.2	1.0	.1	.1	.2
Wheat	.2	.8	.1	.08	.1

Source: U.S. Department of Agriculture.

moisture preserver but as an inoculant for mycorrhizae.

Straw makes an excellent mulch for most plants. As lower layers of the mulch break down, they enrich the soil. If mulching with straw alone, however, add supplementary nitrogen to the soil.

STRAWBERRY   (*Fragaria*)

Strawberries are hardy, perennial herbs grown throughout the United States and in most parts of Canada and in Alaska. They grow best in cool, moist states, and, with special treatment, strawberries can be grown in the hot Gulf states. Although cultivated in Europe since about the sixteenth century, the strawberry was not truly popular as a fruit until the advent of the Hovey seedlings, grown in the vicinity of Boston about 1840. These are thought to have been developed from the species *F. vesca,* which is responsible for the late-bearing qualities of many of today's everbearings. *F. chiloensis* and *F. virginiana* were also used in developing modern varieties.

Planting and Culture: Strawberries may be grown in any soil which is not too alkaline, too dry or in need of drainage. Best soil is a light, rich loam with plenty of humus and a pH factor between 5 and 6.

If strawberries are to be planted in the spring, prepare their bed the previous fall on a plot which has been cultivated for two years. This will be free of the beetle grubs and wireworms which may infest soil in which sod has recently been turned.

A site which slopes slightly is best for perfect drainage. Water must never be allowed to stand on a strawberry patch during the

If the soil is rich and the plants are given plenty of light and water, 100 feet of row will produce 50 to 75 quarts of spring strawberries.

winter. A southern slope will encourage earlier blossoming and earlier fruit but this may not be desirable in areas where late frosts often nip the flower buds, unless protection can be given during such emergencies. Frostbitten blossoms may be distinguished by their darkened centers.

Barnyard manure may be turned under in fall at the rate of 500 pounds to each 1,000 square feet of proposed strawberry patch. At the same time compost or leaf mold may be stirred into the top layer of soil. If no manure is available, leaves and lawn clippings may be worked into the soil at the rate of five or six bushels to each 100 square feet, accompanied by liberal dressings of cottonseed or dried blood meal, ground phosphate rock and bone meal. Limestone should be avoided unless the soil is very acid—below pH 5.

Planting: As soon as the soil is workable in spring, the plants may be set. The number of plants needed, provided space is not limited, may be calculated by the family capacity for strawberries, figured at the rate of 50 to 75 quarts of spring berries or 75 to 100 quarts of everbearing from 100 feet of row.

Young plants with vigorous roots should be used. First cut out damaged or diseased leaves or roots. The hole dug for each plant should be large enough to hold the roots without crowding. A mound of soil is heaped in the center of the hole, and the plant seated on the mound with roots pressed firmly into the soil all around the base of the mound. Each plant should be set so that the soil level will naturally cover all the roots, but will not cover any of the small leaves which are beginning to develop in the crown. The hole should be half-filled with soil. Pour water in to wash the soil around the roots. Then fill the rest of the hole and firm the soil around the plants. A berry box or basket may be inverted over the newly set plant to prevent drying during the first few days. From beginning to end of the planting operation, the roots should never be exposed to sun or drying winds. If the day is sunny, the plants should at all times be shaded. A damp layer of sphagnum moss or a piece of wet burlap may be placed over the receptacle containing the plants to prevent drying. Remove one plant at a time. Soil should be kept moist for several days after the plants are set.

Strawberries may be grown by the matted-row system, the spaced-row system, the hill system, by the stone-mulch system, or by a combination of some of the above systems with the permanently mulched garden system.

Matted rows: With this system many commercial growers plant entire fields each spring for the following spring's production. After bearing, the plants are plowed under and new plantings are made again the following year. Plants are set 18 to 42 inches apart in rows three to 4½ feet apart, depending upon how many runners the particular variety can be expected to make, and what type of cultivation will be used. Most of the runners are permitted to grow during the first season, with only the fruit buds being removed to strengthen the plants. A mat is formed which may be straightened and maintained at the desired width by cultivation. For ease in harvesting, the best width is three feet or less. Twin matted rows are sometimes made six to 24 inches apart, with wider paths between one pair of twins and the next.

Spaced rows: This system is most often used for varieties which are slow to send out runners and produce daughter plants, or for any variety when especially fancy fruit is desired. Because of the extra work involved, the system is not widely practiced. The daughter plants are spaced at definite distances by covering selected runners with soil until the desired number of daughter plants is obtained for each mother plant. Either later formed runners are removed as they appear or all surplus runners are removed at one time.

In the Cape Cod, Massachusetts, region, spacing is used rather extensively. Mother plants are set about 12 inches apart, and two runner series are allowed to form, one with three and the other with four daughter plants.

Hills: In the hill system, plants are close together and runners are pruned off or prevented from rooting new plants. Plantings are usually made in double or triple rows in which plants are placed 12 to 18 inches apart, with a 20- to 24-inch alley between each double or triple set.

No daughter plants are allowed to develop in the hill system. Fruit production is entirely dependent upon the yield of the mother plants. Individual plants become quite large and bear more than those in the matted-row system.

The matted-row and hill systems are both temporary, the plants being plowed under after their year's, or at most two or three years', production is finished. The spaced-row system may be carried on indefinitely. A variation of the spaced-row system is used in a stone-mulched bed.

Stone-mulched bed: To prepare the stone-mulched bed, the ground should first be well plowed or spaded, for this will be the last treatment the soil is given. Apply a generous dressing of compost. Rows of stone about two feet wide should then be laid with a soil space of about ten inches width in between. The stones should be dug into the ground a little to provide as flat a surface as possible. The level of the soil should be even with that of the stones. The labor involved in handling and laying the stones is significant, but this method will minimize maintenance, once established.

The strawberry plants are planted in the soil rows about two or three feet apart. The blossoms should be removed the first year to enable the plants to become established and produce runner plants.

The stone-mulched plot should be a "permanent" plot. To relocate it every couple of years would entail a great deal of work. By keeping the plants well nourished and properly spaced, and seeing that every plant that has produced a crop is replaced by a runner plant,

a vigorous, heavy-bearing strawberry patch can be maintained for many years.

Permanently mulched bed: A self-perpetuating bed under permanent mulch may be freshly planted or may be started from an already established strawberry patch. Soil should be prepared as described earlier. Plants are set 12 inches apart in rows 2½ feet apart. As soon as they are set, the soil in the rows and in the paths between is covered with a six-inch layer of mulch of grass clippings, straw, ground corncobs, pine needles, or chopped leaves. Plants are well watered, and are left to develop runners throughout their growing season. If new plants have been set, all fruit buds should be removed, to permit all the strength to go into runner development. Though runners seem to sit on top of the mulch, they will send roots down through it to the soil below. As the mulch decomposes during the summer, the layer will shrink from six to about two inches, and newly rooted plants will be only slightly above the soil level.

If an old strawberry patch is being used to prepare a permanently mulched bed, the procedure is the same as that followed during the second year of a new bed. Preparation of the bed for the following year begins with harvest of this year's strawberries. As the picker harvests, he marks with pegs or plant markers the best-bearing plants in each row, trying to space markers about ten to 12 inches apart down the row. When all berries have been harvested, all the unmarked plants are pulled out and mulch is removed. The strawberry patch now contains single rows of plants spaced ten to 12 inches apart. Well-rotted manure, compost, decomposed sawdust plus cottonseed meal, or enriched leaf mold are now worked into the top layer of soil. If the soil is too alkaline, a generous amount of peat moss is incorporated around each plant. The soil is smoothed out, and a six-inch mulch is again placed around plants which are ready now to form runners which will supply young plants for next year's bearing.

By careful selection of the best bearers, a strawberry patch can be made to bear a larger crop with each succeeding year. The heavy mulch during the summer will preserve soil moisture for the young rooted runners, and the decomposed layer of mulch on top of the bed will enrich the soil, which gradually becomes blacker and more mellow.

Strawberry barrel: Strawberries may be grown in holes in the sides of a barrel, if garden space is limited, although the yield will naturally be small.

Everbearing berries are usually used for a strawberry barrel. Two-inch holes are drilled in the sides of the barrel, spaced about six inches apart each way. The barrel is then placed where it will stand, giving it as much sun as possible. Rich garden loam is placed inside, to the level of the first row of holes. Plants are inserted through the holes, and their roots spread. Another layer of soil is filled in on top of the roots, to the level of the next row of holes, and plants are inserted through the second row. This is continued until the barrel is filled.

Various improvements may be made to the strawberry barrel. To make watering easier, insert a perforated pipe in the center of the barrel through which water or liquid manure may be poured. If you wish, the pipe can be filled with manure so that, when water is applied, nutrients leach into the soil. The barrel may be mounted on a small wheeled platform so it can be turned to face the sun.

A variation on the strawberry barrel is the tiered-hoop strawberry bed. This is built above the garden level with successively smaller metal hoops, each about six inches deep. Soil is filled in the hoops, and a water pipe is incorporated in the center. Plants are set in the setbacks between the hoops. The advantage of this arrangement over the barrel is that all the plants may receive their share of sun.

Irrigation: Strawberries need plenty of water, especially during their bearing period. Everbearing varieties such as Ogallala, Ozark Beauty and Gem should be kept moist during the entire summer in order to produce. A heavy mulch will help preserve soil moisture, but during periods of extreme drought it may be necessary to irrigate plants. A test for soil moisture may be made by digging down six to 12 inches, taking a handful of soil, and forming a ball with it. If the soil forms a moist ball, no water is needed. If it breaks up and crumbles, the strawberries need additional water.

Winter mulch: Strawberries grown in the North must be mulched over the winter in order to prevent heaving or drying. The mulch should not be applied until the garden is frozen. If plants are covered too early, while the soil is still warm, they may be stimulated into new growth and will be more vulnerable to the cold when it comes. In the latitude of New York State the mulch should be placed over the bed during the latter part of November.

Straw or pine needles makes the best winter mulch. A layer about four inches deep should be placed over the entire bed. If the area is not usually covered with snow, it may be necessary to anchor the mulch with cornstalks or twigs.

When the weather begins to turn warm, and the ground thaws in March, the winter mulch should be first loosened, and then removed entirely. It may be stacked beside the garden to use later as summer mulch after the bed has been renovated, if the permanently mulched system is being used.

Diseases and Insects: Strawberry diseases are best controlled by the following sanitary practices:

1. Select varieties that grow vigorously and are resistant to diseases in your area.

2. Buy disease-free stock from reputable nurseries that sell plants monitored by state plant inspection services.

3. Rotate your berry patch regularly or, in the case of the permanent bed, replace old plants with runner plants each year.

Red stele, the most serious fungus disease of strawberries in the United States, causes plants to wilt and sometimes die just before fruit starts to ripen. Like other fungi, it is most active in wet weather, and may sometimes disappear in warm, sunny weather. Fruit from affected plants is small, sour and few in number. Control is best achieved by removing any plants with coarse roots with no branching rootlets, by correcting any faulty drainage that may exist in the bed and, most important, by planting resistant varieties.

Verticillium wilt, another fungus disease active in cool, humid weather, causes the margins of the outer leaves to dry up and turn dark brown so that plants appear dry and flattened. If you suspect verticillium wilt in your area, do not plant strawberries in soil in which tomatoes, peppers, potatoes, or other strawberries have grown in the last two years. Varieties that display best resistance to verticillium are Blakemore, Catskill, Guardian, Redchief, Sunrise, and Surecrop.

Insects that may threaten strawberries include two kinds of aphids—the leaf aphid and the strawberry-root aphid—and two kinds of mites—the cyclamen and the spider mites.

Root weevils and crown borers also appear occasionally. Best control of all strawberry pests is to shred plants and plow the patch each fall, then locate your new patch at least 300 feet away, if possible. *See also* INSECT CONTROL.

Varieties: Strawberry varieties are constantly being improved and new ones are added to the seed and nursery catalogs each year. In selecting the variety for your garden, consider insect and disease resistance, ripening season, fruit size, productivity, and most important, hardiness. Listed below, according to their suitability to various major geographical zones, are the most reliable varieties.

Canada and the North: Hardy varieties, to be planted in sections where the winters are extremely cold or where temperatures go below 10°F. (−12.22°C.) without accompanying snow, include Catskill, Chief Bemidji, Dunlap, Royalty, Sunburst, Totem, Trumpeter, Veestar, and Vibrant.

Northeast and North Atlantic states: Varieties recommended for this region are Catskill, Cyclone, Dunlap, Empire, Fletcher, Midland, Midway, Ogallala, Premier, Sparkle, Surecrop, and Trumpeter.

Middle Atlantic states: Atlas, Guardian, Jerseybelle, and Raritan are preferred.

Midwest and Central states: Atlas, Guardian, Midway, and Surecrop are recommended.

Pacific Coast: In Washington and Oregon, Northwest, Olympus, and Tioga are grown; in California, Aliso, Salinas, Tioga, and Tufts are recommended.

Florida, Gulf states and Southern California: Apollo, Atlas, Blakemore, Dabreak, Earlibelle, Florida Ninety, Pocohontas, Streamliner, Sunrise, and Tennessee Beauty are the varieties recommended for these regions.

STRAWBERRY TOMATO
See PHYSALIS

STRAWBERRY TREE
(*Arbutus Unedo*)

An ornamental, large evergreen shrub, the strawberry tree has handsome dark green leaves and clusters of small white flowers which resemble lily-of-the-valley. The red, strawberry-like fruit gives the shrub its common name. The flowers and fruit appear simultaneously during the winter months, and the fruit is edible. The ultimate height of this shrub is about ten feet. It does best in well-drained soil and in a wind-protected location.

See also SHRUBS, UNEDO.

STRAWFLOWER
(*Helichrysum bracteatum*)

Strawflowers are tall robust annuals that may attain a height of three feet. They supply attractive material for dried bouquets. Cut the stems when flowers are about half open, strip off the leaves and hang stems in bundles, blossom end down, in a shady, well-ventilated place until dry.

Seed may be sown outdoors with marigolds and zinnias, but for earliest bloom it should be started indoors in April. The plants will stand some cold but are best set out after the danger of frost has passed. Avoid grouping strawflowers in a border with bedding annuals because the plants are coarse and rank. Grow them in a row in the vegetable garden. Very rich soil will cause heavy foliage growth and few flowers. Monstrosa is a tall form growing to 30 inches. Tom Thumb is an 18-inch dwarf. Colors include red, pink, yellow, purple, and white.

STRELITZIA REGINAE
See BIRD-OF-PARADISE

STRING BEAN   *See* BEANS

STRIP-CROPPING

Strip-cropping is a general term for the practice of growing crops in alternating bands which serve as barriers to both wind and water erosion. The strips are usually planted across the slope of a field, with every other strip planted to grass or hay. These grassy strips prevent erosion by slowing down and dispersing the water running downslope. At the same time the silt suspended in the water is deposited in the grassy strip.

See also SOIL CONSERVATION.

STUARTIA   *See* STEWARTIA

STUBBLE MULCH

Under this system, a continuous cover of crop residues or other organic materials is maintained on the land during the period between harvest and the establishment of new crops, as well as during the cultivation of row crops. The basic idea is to till the soil without inverting or burying the residue.

In the arid parts of the country, mulch tillage or stubble mulching has been proven successful. Erosion and water runoff have decreased, and yields are at least as high as those under clean cultivation. Soil scientists are still debating the advantages of mulch tillage in the eastern half of the nation, where the chief problem is in maintaining high yields while preserving the soil and water conservation benefits of the mulch.

Stubble mulching creates an environment in which moisture, temperature, aeration, and location of food for microorganisms are similar to those of a grassland or forest, where a protective cover of living and dead residues is maintained on the soil surface.

STUMP REMOVAL

There are several ways to remove tree stumps:

1. Pull out the stump with mechanical equipment.

2. Blast with explosives (not practical near buildings or landscaped areas).

3. Use chemicals made for killing and disintegrating stumps.

4. Cut the stump at the ground level, cover it with soil and keep the soil moist. To hasten decay, bore several vertical holes in the stump before covering it with soil.

5. Burn the stump with charcoal, coke or coal in a metal container such as a five-gallon paint can. Remove the top and bottom of the can and punch draft holes in the sides near the bottom. Put the stove on top of the stump, or down over it, and build the fire, starting it with kindling wood. Add charcoal, coke or coal. In burning a large stump, move the stove as each section is burned.

6. Dig out the stump. Using a grub hoe, mattock, axe, shovel, and some muscle power, dig a trench about two feet deep around the stump where the roots enter the ground. Cut the roots as close as possible to the stump, and roll or slide the stump out of the hole. This is least difficult when the stump is tall and a tow chain or something similar can be used. Instead of taking the stump out, you can dig a very deep hole beside and under it and let it drop down. Be sure the hole is deep enough to bury the stump several inches deep. Pack the soil well.

See also LAND CLEARING.

STYRAX   *See* STORAX

SUBSOIL   *See* SOIL

SUBSOILING

Subsoiling involves tilling, but not inverting, subsurface soil to break up dense layers that restrict water movement and root penetration. It is necessary only where a hardpan exists and hampers garden or farm productivity. The basic idea of subsoil tillage or chisel plowing is to get water and organic matter deep into the soil while disturbing the land's surface as little as possible. In most instances, subsoiling involves cutting up the land with a subsoil chisel to a depth of from 16 to 30 inches or, with heavy single-chisel implements, to over five feet.

Subsoiling can be carried out at any time when the land is not frozen or covered with a growing crop, but it is advisable to subsoil at the driest time of the year. The subsoil shatters most easily at this time and, by subsoiling in the dry months, the cuts will be open to receive the water of the fall rains and winter snows.

Since subsoiling leaves residues on top of the soil, it reduces runoff. Tests at the University of Nebraska Experiment Station have shown that the runoff from plowed land is from two to three times as great as that from subsoiled land. Research at the Idaho Experiment Station has revealed that 4 percent more of the moisture received was retained under subtillage methods than under one-way disking and moldboard plowing ones.

Besides controlling erosion, subsoiling tends to boost yields. In southern Idaho, where the annual rainfall is about 15 inches, experiments have clearly shown yield advantages of three to four bushels of wheat per acre gained from subtillage. In areas of greater rainfall, subsoiling has not made appreciable differences in the yield figures, but it is well to remember that the practice saves the soil and helps insure continued high yields.

Poor subsoils can also be improved by growing deep-rooted legumes after the land has been chiseled. As the roots of these plants decompose, they put organic matter down deep into the subsoil and leave channels to facilitate water intake. Alfalfa and sweet clover have long been the standard plants for soil conditioning. Other legumes are presently being tested.

See also AERATION, HARDPAN.

SUCCESSION PLANTING

Gardeners seeking maximum production from limited space commonly plant a second crop on the same land either before or soon after the first crop is harvested. String beans, for example, are commonly planted as a succession crop to beets, and carrots often go in when early lettuce or spinach is harvested.

Plan your garden to have a constant supply of a variety of vegetables throughout the season. There are vegetables for early planting and vegetables for late planting. There are vegetables for summer harvesting and for fall harvest. There are plants which get a vigorous start in early spring when temperatures are low and moisture high, and there are those that do better later on.

Although a little more care may be needed to realize a good uniform stand from summer-sown seeds than from spring-sown seeds, weed control and pest control are far easier in summer-sown garden rows.

Seeds should be sown just a trifle deeper and a little more thickly in summer-fitted gardens.

Where water is readily available, moisten the seedbed frequently. This prevents crusting of soil until the seedlings have emerged. If water is not available by garden hose, it is very helpful to soak the furrow bottom before seed is sown. A few gallons are sufficient for a 30- to 50-foot row. Seed sown directly on the moistened furrow bottom and covered as usual germinate more uniformly and more promptly than seed sown in dry soil.

Summer seeding time for any variety of vegetable depends mostly upon three factors. These are 1) the natural frost-hardiness or lack of hardiness of the vegetable; 2) the usual date of occurrence of the first killing frost in the area; and 3) the usual onset of growth-stopping freezes that affect freeze-hardy vegetables like cabbage.

In order to plan your successions, you'll have to know how many days will pass between planting and maturity. This information is listed in seed catalogs, on seed packets and in many different garden books and pamphlets. Time of maturity often varies with the variety. For example, Sparkler radishes take about 25 days to mature, whereas White Chinese, another variety, takes about 60 days.

Also keep in mind those plants which may be planted before the last killing frost in spring. Some vegetables in this category are cabbage, chives, garlic, lettuce, onion, pea, radish, and turnip. By planting them early, you will be able to harvest the first crop earlier, and, of course, plant the second one earlier as well.

Try not to plant members of the same family in succession. Root crops, for example, take a great amount of potash from the soil. To follow radishes with turnips, both root crops, may undermine the soil's supply of potash and result in poor crops later on. The same is true of leaf crops which require a great amount of nitrogen. *See also* VEGETABLE GARDENING.

Succession Cropping: Succession cropping is also practiced by farmers in many parts of the country. Dozens of double-crop possibilities exist. Both crops may be harvested as grain, or as silage or as a combination of the two. You can also plant a grain or silage nurse crop, such as oats, in combination with a hay or seed crop. In many cases, the best combination is to chop small grain (barley, wheat, oats, rye) for silage, then plant corn for silage. If there are early spring rains, small grain

silage usually yields well. By harvesting small grains in early spring, you can plant double-crop corn close to the traditional corn planting date.

In some north central states, you can double-crop corn for silage after harvesting barley for grain, because barley matures earlier than wheat or oats. In the lower Midwest, corn can be double-cropped after almost any small grain but the corn-growing season will be shortened and yields reduced accordingly.

In the Middle Atlantic states, the most common combinations are corn (harvested for either grain or silage) after taking off first-cutting hay, and barley followed by either soybeans or corn silage.

The main restraints on double-cropping are loss of fertility and soil moisture and overextension of the growing season. Sustained double-cropping requires much heavier applications of phosphorus, potash and nitrogen to maintain natural fertility levels. Soils low in organic matter will not sustain double-cropping for long, and yields will diminish dramatically. This same point of diminishing returns is reached rapidly when anything less than optimum moisture conditions prevail at planting and germination times.

SUCCULENT FEEDS

Succulent feeds are those high in water content, such as pasturage and silage.

SUCCULENTS

In the horticultural sense of the word, succulents are xerophytic plants which have fleshy leaves or stems or both. Through evolution these plants have adapted to dry habitats by reducing their body surfaces to lower loss of water through transpiration. Their fleshiness gives them a natural capacity for water storage which enables them to survive periods of drought. Many have unusual or bizarre shapes. Their root systems are often shallow to take advantage of any short-lived surface moisture. These characteristics make them excellent plants for garden, house and greenhouse.

Planting and Culture: Most succulents require a well-drained soil which can be made from one part coarse, washed builder's sand and one part roughly screened compost or leaf mold. One cup steamed bone meal and one cup hoof and horn meal per bushel or one tablespoon each for every two quarts of the soil mix is also beneficial. Outdoors, any well-drained garden soil is satisfactory. Gravel or sand can be used to improve drainage.

For best results with succulents, use clay pots that have drainage holes. Set pots in a sunny southern or eastern exposure either indoors or outside, and make sure the soil dries between applications of water. Water should flow from the drainage hole and the excess water should be discarded. A period of slow growth or dormancy usually occurs in winter. When it begins, fertilization should be stopped and water applied only about once a month. Because of the great number of species covered by the term succulents, cultural hints are generalized. Entries on specific species should be consulted for more details.

Many succulents can be treated as garden plants and some, such as many sedums, are even winter hardy at temperatures below 0°F. (−17.78°C.). They are ideal for rock gardens. As house plants they can be placed outdoors in the summer in a semishaded area. If periods of prolonged rain occur, potted succulents may require removal or protection to prevent root rot. Many can be moved to full sun after their adjustment from indoors to semishade is complete.

Blossoms on succulents vary from masses of tiny flowers to large blossoms. These flowers are beautiful and have attractive hues. Most succulents require a resting period and somewhat cooler temperatures in the winter in order to produce blossoms in the spring. In

Apart from their use in rock gardens, sempervivums are effective along dry walls, stone steps and terraces.

general, temperatures of 50 to 60°F. (10 to 15.56°C.) and water applied once a month from November through February produce spring flowers on succulents.

Some succulents can be propagated from seed. Many are propagated from suckers, leaf cuttings and stem cuttings. These should be removed during active growth and allowed to form a wound callus in a dry place. Otherwise, the cuttings will rot.

Types: There is an unending array of succulent plants. The most popular succulents are undoubtedly cacti, which are treated separately in this book under their own heading. The South African equivalents of American cacti, *Euphorbia,* vary in shape from that of a baseball, *E. obesa,* to a Medusa's head, *E. caput-Medusae.* Some, such as members of the Spurge family, are even garden plants. The Stonecrop family to which the sedums belong also contains many other excellent genera such as *Crassula, Echeveria, Graptopetalum, Kalanchoe, Rochea,* and *Sempervivum.* The Fig-marigold family contains interesting genera such as *Conophytum, Fenestraria* and *Lithops.* The Milkweed family contains *Caralluma, Ceropegia, Hoodia, Hoya, Huernia,* and *Stapelia,* and the Lily family contains *Gasteria* and *Haworthia.*

See also CACTI, HOUSE PLANTS.

SUCKER

A sucker is a shoot from the root or lower stem of the plant. The word refers especially to shoots arising on trunks of trees below the main branches. In some cases, as in lilacs, the suckers arising from the roots may be used to propagate the plant. In other plants, where an improved variety has been grafted on an unimproved rootstock, a sucker arising from the root or stem below the graft will produce an unimproved variety plant, and should be immediately removed. Suckers on fruit or ornamental trees are thought to rob the top of the tree of food.

The term sucker is also applied to water sprouts, the vertical shoots which sometimes arise on the branches of trees, especially when the root-branch balance has been upset by too severe pruning or by injury to a branch.

SUCKERING	See BRAMBLE FRUITS
SUDANGRASS	See GREEN MANURE

SUGAR WASTES

Sugar manufacturing produces several waste products. Most of these are filter material, often made of bone transformed into charcoal, when filled with residues from the sugar. This material is sold as bone black. Its phosphorous content is above 30 percent, its nitrogen value around 2 percent, its potassium content variable.

Raw sugar wastes show a content of over 1 percent nitrogen and over 8 percent phosphoric acid.

SULFUR

Sulfur is a nonmetallic element that occurs naturally in several forms. It is generally classified as a trace element, but it is of major importance to plant growth. Some plants, such as cabbages, contain more sulfur than phosphorus. When oxidized in well-aerated, warm soil, sulfur combines with other elements to form sulfates, such as calcium sulfate (or gypsum), potassium sulfate, ammonium sulfate, and zinc sulfate. In waterlogged soils sulfur can be changed into unavailable sulfides which encourage sulfur-working microorganisms.

Sulfur is not retained by soil particles in the way other trace elements are. It can be leached below the root zone, especially in sandy soils. Therefore, the availability of sulfur will vary considerably during a season, depending on the kind of soil.

All soils contain sulfur, but it is not always in available form. Wherever sulfur-containing fuels are consumed (in practically any industrialized area), sulfur is washed into the soil by rain. This should provide an adequate amount of sulfur for crops.

Sulfur deficiency does occasionally occur, and causes yellowing of plant leaves. It can be distinguished from nitrogen deficiency because the leaves do not completely dry out. Legumes, particularly alfalfa, have high sulfur requirements, so deficiencies usually show up first in these crops. Corn, small grains and grasses rarely show sulfur deficiencies. Since some water contains a high amount of sulfur, watering can often take care of sulfur deficiencies.

As a Fungicide: Sulfur has been used as a fungicide for thousands of years, but organic growers believe that it can disturb soil microorganisms and have a bad effect on beneficial insects. Sulfur applications may also damage cucurbits and roses.

Many people cannot grow grapes without resorting to sulfur fungicides to kill mildew. Usually this is because they have planted their vines in areas with high humidity and slow air movement. Grapevines should not be troubled by mildew if grown in sunny locations on slopes with good air drainage, if properly pruned during the season for maximum air circulation and light penetration, and if cultured organically.

Sulfur is used by growers of other fruits, to rid their trees of both fungal diseases and mites. Research in biological insect controls has shown that sulfur is lethal to many beneficial insects that, left to themselves, can take care of a number of important pests. Sulfur should be used only as a last resort in the orchard. Sulfur and oil sprays should not be used within a month of each other.

SUMAC (*Rhus*)

The sumacs are especially valued for their magnificent brilliant red autumn foliage and hairy red fruits. They are shrubs or small trees that do best in dry soils of near-neutral pH. They can be grown easily from seed, and are hardy over most of the United States.

Fragrant sumac (*R. aromatica*) is a dense shrub growing to eight feet. Its yellow flowers appear in spikes in early spring, and the foliage is quite fragrant. The scarlet or smooth sumac (*R. glabra*) bears red fruit clusters that can be soaked in water to make a pleasantly tart, pink drink. It grows to 20 feet tall and has dense clusters of greenish flowers that bloom in early summer. The staghorn sumac (*R. typhina*) is a large ornamental growing to 30 feet or taller. It has dense clusters of greenish flowers. Dwarf sumac (*R. copallina*) grows as a shrub or small tree up to about 12 feet tall, and stands city smoke very well. *R. trilobata,* also called skunkbush or squawbush, resembles fragrant sumac, but it is neither as beautiful nor as aromatic as that species. The sourberry (*R. integrifolia*) is an evergreen shrub or small tree growing to 25 feet and hardy only in the southernmost parts of the country. Its pale pink flowers bloom in March.

The leaves and flowers of the sumacs are high in tannin, and their shallow, spreading roots are valuable for preventing erosion.

See also POISON SUMAC.

SUNFLOWER   (*Helianthus*)

The sunflower is a tall, coarse annual herb that resembles a colossal daisy. Commercially it is one of the most important herbs in the world today. The plant is grown as an ornamental or for its seeds, which are a valuable source of vitamins and minerals.

The sunflower is native to the Americas. The Indians used its seeds as a source of meal, and the sun-worshipping Incas of Peru attached a religious significance to it and used the plant as an accessory in their religious rites.

The Spanish conquistadores and other visitors to the New World carried the seeds of the "floure of the Sunne" back to their homelands where the exceptional nutritional worth of the plant was at first ignored.

From the point of view of the gardener, growing sunflowers is an enjoyable occupation. When the plants are young, their heads will turn to face the sun each morning. There are many varieties, including some that do not produce seed. These are used chiefly as ornamentals. Some flowers resemble giant black-eyed Susans, while others are huge, beautiful pompons resembling chrysanthemums.

The head of the giant sunflower is packed with protein-rich seeds suitable for both livestock and human consumption.

Planting and Culture: Sunflowers grow very well with mild, organic fertilizers, and they have few insect pests, so seldom need to be sprayed. For giant-sized heads, space the plants at least three or four feet apart, but for production of seed, space them more closely. Overcrowding causes plants to fall in heavy winds.

Grown on a large-scale, sunflowers can be a valuable cash crop. They will grow successfully on any land that will produce a field of corn. A light loam is preferable to a heavy, wet soil. The field should be prepared by plowing, disking and smooth harrowing, similar to the preparation made for planting corn.

When grown commercially, a green manure crop should be planted in the field the previous fall. The soil should be tested for acidity and ground limestone applied if necessary to bring the pH to between 6 and 8. The plants require plenty of nutrients and manure may be applied at the rate of ten tons per acre.

Plant three pounds of seed per acre, using a two-row corn planter. Space the seeds at two-foot intervals in rows 36 to 42 inches apart. The plants should be cultivated twice.

As the plant matures, the head will grow heavy and the stalks may need some kind of support. A gentle looping of two or three stalks together will help the plants withstand damaging winds. In a small garden, sunflowers should be planted in the back or along the perimeter of the property.

Harvesting: Sunflowers can be harvested as soon as the backs of the seed heads are brown and dry. At this time, the inner rows are ripe, but need drying. To harvest, cut off the heads with about a foot of the stalk attached. The stalks are tied together, and the heads hung in an airy barn or loft to dry. When thoroughly dry, remove the seeds by rubbing the heads lightly. If stored in airtight containers, their food content and vitamins will remain in good condition for a long time.

The sunflower is a remarkably versatile commercial plant. Each part of the plant has an economic use: the entire plant can be used as fodder for livestock and poultry, the flowers yield a yellow dye, the pith of the stalks can be used to make paper or as a mounting medium for microscope slides. Since it has a specific gravity lower than cork, pith also can be used for making life preservers and belts.

Although used primarily as a protein-rich feed for livestock, sunflower seed and oil are also eaten by people. The seeds can be used like nuts or ground into a meal and used in baking or as a supplement to a variety of dishes. Sunflower seeds are increasingly sold as a snack which is particularly popular in Russia. Industrially the oil is used in the manufacture of soaps, candles, burning oils, Russian varnishes, and Dutch enamel paint.

Varieties: The most interesting sunflowers are those that produce seed. While these come in dwarf, semidwarf and tall varieties, the best kinds for the average gardener or homesteader are the common garden sunflower (*H. annuus*) and the giant sunflower (*H. giganteus*), also called the Indian potato. The common garden sunflower sometimes reaches heights of ten to 12 feet, with blossoms one foot or more in diameter. The plants are widely cultivated in the United States, the Soviet Union, India, South America, Canada, and Egypt. It is the state flower of Kansas.

The giant sunflower is a strong-growing perennial that climbs to 12 feet or more and bears a huge flower packed with big seeds suited for harvesting and eating. Most popular and widely grown of the giant varieties is the Mammoth Russian, which matures in about 80 days. Besides being the largest and tallest of all sunflowers, it bears big, striped seeds that are thin-shelled, meaty, and rich in both flavor and food value. The plants' towering, husky stalks make excellent screens or field backgrounds. When grown close together, their broad leaves block the sun from weeds.

Sunflowers suitable for growing in the flower garden are the small-seed types such as thin-leaved sunflower (*H. decapetalus*) and ashy sunflower (*II. mollis*). These grow from three to five feet high and branch freely from the leaf axils, producing many small flower heads rather than a single large one. The seed is about one-third the size of a corn kernel.

Petals can be shades of yellow, mahogany and purple, and some flowers have a broad band of a contrasting color around the center. All make very good cut flowers for large arrangements. These sunflowers are especially attractive to the smaller seed-eating birds such as goldfinches and chickadees, which will harvest the seeds themselves. Hummingbirds will visit them for nectar and small insects. Color Fashion, Autumn Beauty and Italian White are single-flowered mixtures. Teddy Bear grows to three feet, produces fully double yellow flowers, and is one of the best for cutting.

SUNROSE   *See* HELIANTHEMUM

SUNSCALD

Sunscald, which causes a burning or browning of plant tissue, is a result of intense heat or cold and exposure to sun. It is followed by a cankerous infection. This may occur in summer, but it is more serious when it occurs on tree bark during the winter. Treat winter sunscald by cleaning out the bark and coating it with tree wound paint to prevent infection.

SUPERPHOSPHATE
See PHOSPHATE ROCK

SWAINSONA

Also known as winter sweet pea, pepperbush and darling pea, this genus of Australian herbs or subshrubs of the Pea family can be grown outdoors in the warmest sections of the country and in the house or greenhouse elsewhere. The pealike flowers, which form racemes, are blue violet, red, pink, and occasionally white.

Winter sweet pea (*S. galegifolia*) is a sprawling or partly climbing shrub with clusters of red flowers. Its varieties have white, pink, rose, or violet flowers. *S. Greyana* has whitish woolly young foliage, with erect stalks of pink flower clusters.

Swainsona prefers a moist, humus-rich soil and full sun. Propagation is by seed or cuttings.

SWAMP SUMAC
See POISON SUMAC

SWATH

A swath is the path cut in one course by a scythe or mower or a windrow of grass or grain cut by such an implement. The term sometimes refers to a crop or row ready for harvest.

SWEET ALISON
See SWEET ALYSSUM

SWEET ALYSSUM   (*Lobularia*)

Sweet alyssum's greatest assets are its easy culture, its profuse bloom over a long period and its general pest resistance. Often grown in straight rows along the edge of beds, it is equally effective in masses in informal beds.

Seed may be planted in the tulip bed or other spring bulb beds, and after the bulbs have finished blooming the sweet alyssum will act as a camouflage to hide the wilted leaves of the bulbs. Other common names for sweet alyssum are snowdrift and sweet alison.

Planting and Culture: For early bloom, seed should be sown in the open ground as soon as it is workable. Sweet alyssum, like many other hardy annuals, may also be sown late in the fall for very early spring bloom. Sweet alyssum will self-sow. Sometimes germination takes place the following spring, but if growth starts in the fall, mulch the plants loosely.

A well-prepared soil, rich in compost, will insure a strong growth and fine blooms, but sweet alyssum seems to thrive in soil and under conditions that hamper other plants. Prepare the soil for planting and cover the seed with about 18 inches of soil. Sow thinly because the germination rate is high. Seedlings can be thinned out or transplanted. During the summer, shearing the plant tops every few weeks will remove some fading flowers and stimulate the plants to produce more blooms.

Sweet alyssum may also be grown in pots for winter blooming. It will bloom within a month after sowing in pots. Plants from the garden may be brought indoors in the fall before severe weather sets in. Carefully lift them and reset with as much earth as possible adhering to the roots. Select pots large enough to accommodate the roots conveniently. Keep the plants pinched back to force them into a bushy and well-branched form.

Varieties: Carpet of Snow with its dainty, pure white flowers gives the impression of a white carpet. The plants grow about four inches high and spread considerably so they are fine for wide edgings. Little Gem, which is also white, is a favorite for narrow edgings. Royal Carpet has rich royal purple flowers and grows low and spreading. Violet Queen is a deep shade of violet and keeps its color throughout the season.

See also ALYSSUM.

SWEET BASIL	*See* BASIL, SWEET
SWEET BELLS	*See* LEUCOTHOE

SWEET CICELY (*Myrrhis odorata*)

Growing two to three feet tall, this decorative perennial belonging to the Carrot family has delicate, fernlike leaves and umbels of attractive white flowers. Its pungent scent, light airy appearance and attractiveness to butterflies make it a popular choice for the herb garden or border.

A relative of the carrot, sweet cicely is native to England but is widely grown throughout Europe and North America as an attractive, aromatic border plant.

This herb is native to England, but is found throughout Europe and to a lesser extent in the United States. Although the plant has no recorded history as an aromatic, its botanical name comes from the Greek words for perfume. Sweet cicely was once used to treat coughs, and was a stimulant and tonic for adolescents and women and is still a folk remedy for coughs and bladder disorders. Wine made from its roots was used to treat dog bites, and a cicely ointment was said to help skin eruptions and gout.

Cicely prefers a rich crumbly soil and full sun. Its seeds, which are slow to germinate, should be planted in the fall. Germination is sometimes sparked by alternating freezing and thawing. Perhaps the best way to grow sweet cicely is to purchase several plants from a grower and let them reseed themselves. Cicely can also be divided, preferably in the early spring as soon as the shoots appear.

Harvesting can be done anytime. Collect the leaves when green and fresh for use in vegetables, salads or pastry fillings. They usually are not dried. The roots are eaten like fennel. Some enjoy sweet cicely purely for its lovagelike fragrance.

See also HERB.

SWEET CLOVER   *See* CLOVER

SWEET COLTSFOOT
See PETASITES

SWEET FLAG   (*Acorus Calamus*)

A hardy perennial belonging to the Arum family, sweet flag has spikes of light green flowers that appear in June, and slender, lily-like leaves that can grow as much as six feet long. It prefers wet soil and full sun and is most effective when grown in clumps. Propagation is by division.

Sweet flag is a lemon-scented plant whose rootstalks are used to make sachets and perfume. It is a good choice for the bog or herb garden.

SWEET GUM
(*Liquidambar Styraciflua*)

The native sweet gum tree grows as high as 125 feet and is most noted for its lovely scarlet foliage in fall. It may be grown from Massachusetts southward along the Atlantic coast, and in many midwestern states south to Mexico. The sweet gum prefers moist, rich soil. It produces small flowers and shiny brown fruit. The star-shaped leaves are aromatic when crushed.

Sweet gum trees are extremely resistant to pests and diseases. They are particularly fast growing and healthy when placed along a riverbank or in a sheltered seaside position. Purchase balled and burlapped trees and plant them in early spring. Pruning is best carried out during the winter months.

SWEET MARJORAM
See MARJORAM, SWEET

SWEET PEA   (*Lathyrus odoratus*)

This vining annual produces masses of fragrant, pea-shaped flowers in every color but yellow during spring and early summer. Sweet peas need cool, moist weather to grow and flower well. They do best in the cool summers of the far northern states, but they also bloom well during the winter in those southern and western areas which are nearly frost-free. While some are more heat resistant than others, none will last long once hot weather sets in. If started early, sweet peas can be grown successfully in most areas where edible peas are grown.

Planting and Culture: Sow the seed as early in spring as the ground can be worked, about the same time as edible peas are sown. Soil should be heavily enriched with compost or manure. Vining types can be sown in single or double rows along a fence or trellis. Many gardeners place the seed three inches apart and one inch deep at the bottom of a three-inch trench, which acts as a catch basin for water. Bushy types can be sown about one inch deep in beds, and later thinned to stand ten inches apart. In many northern areas, sweet peas can be planted in late fall just before a hard freeze and they will germinate in early spring. Water standing on the seed through the winter, however, will cause it to rot, so make sure the soil is well drained. In mild-winter areas, sow seed in fall for winter bloom.

Once the plants are up, mulch them to conserve water; sweet peas will not tolerate dry soil. At the same time, apply a side-dressing of fertilizer rich in phosphorus and potassium and low in nitrogen to induce heavier flower production. Sweet peas make exceptional cut flowers, so take many bouquets from the plants. This will prolong the blooming season by preventing them from setting seed.

Varieties: There are several types available, all producing flowers on stems long enough for cutting. The vining types like Cuthbertson and Spencer sweet peas grow up to ten feet or more and need a fence to climb on. These can be grown as cut flowers in the vegetable garden simply by reserving several feet at the end of a pea row for them. The newer dwarf varieties are considered to be more heat resistant than the vining types. Knee-Hi and Little Elf sweet peas grow to three feet, and the compact vines tend to be self-supporting. The bushy 12-inch Bijou type is good for bedding and for growing in containers.

SWEET POTATO
(*Ipomoea Batatas*)

The sweet potato is very nutritious and is an important food in many tropical regions of the world. It is rich in vitamin C and contains more vitamin A than most other vegetables.

An acre of sweet potatoes requires 10,000 to 12,000 plants but 100 to 200 plants will produce an ample supply for the average family. Plants can be purchased from a nursery, or grown at home by sprouting four or five sweet potatoes in a shallow pan of water.

Planting and Culture: Sweet potatoes can be grown as a garden plant over a wide area of the United States. They prefer a sandy soil, but can be grown in a heavier soil if it is worked five or six inches deep. Ridging is also necessary if optimum size and quality are to be produced.

Start preparing ground for sweet potatoes during April. Make a furrow long enough to accommodate the plants you need with 12- to 18-inch spacing. Place an inch or two of well-rotted compost or manure in the furrow. Then ridge up the soil on top of this band of humus. Ridges should be at least ten inches high to prevent roots from growing too deep for easy harvesting.

Don't set out the plants until about a month after the average date of the last frost in your area. Sweet potatoes are members of the Morning-glory family and are very sensitive to frost. Use a rounded stick, like a broom handle, to push the roots of the plants four or five inches deep. Water plants after planting to settle the roots.

The area around the plants should be kept free of weed growth until the vines themselves shade out weeds. Don't worry too much about drought, because sweet potatoes like hot, dry weather.

Harvesting: Dig the potatoes with a pitchfork before frost hits the vines, for frost on the vines can damage the tubers below. To prevent spoilage, be careful not to damage the potatoes during digging. Let them cure on the surface of the ground for several hours after digging. This helps them keep better in storage.

Storage: If properly cured, sweet potatoes can be stored and enjoyed for several months. This can be done easily by placing the harvested roots in a well-ventilated place where temperatures are fairly high. For best results the temperature should be around 85 to 90°F. (29.44 to 32.22°C.) and should be held in that range for ten to 15 days. High temperatures are a deterrent to rhizopus rot, a disease which affects potato roots.

Following the curing period, the sweet potatoes should be stored at a temperature of about 50°F. (10°C.) with humidity between 75 and 80 percent. During the storage period the sweet potatoes should not be handled or moved until time for use. Storage temperature below 50°F. usually will favor decay.

Varieties: Centennial Sweet Potato is a bright copper-skinned variety and a high yielder. Porto Rico, Allgold and Georgia Reds are gaining popularity with sweet potato growers. Recommended dry-flesh types are Orlis and Yellow Jersey.

SWEET-SULTAN   *See* CENTAUREA

SWEET VIOLET   (*Viola odorata*)

A hardy perennial growing to eight inches tall, the sweet violet has heart-shaped leaves and white, violet or rose flowers. Of the more than 600 kinds of violets known, this species is considered the most fragrant. It makes beautiful edging or border plantings and will thrive in the shady rock garden. Sweet violet prefers a slightly heavy, moist garden soil and responds well to added compost. Propagation is by seed or by division after plants have flowered. The flowers and leaves are occasionally candied for use as confectionery decorations or eaten in salads and omelets.

Varieties that are not quite as tall include the Czar and Queen Charlotte, both with blue flowers. White Czar grows to four inches and has white blooms.

SWEET WILLIAM (*Dianthus barbatus*)

Sweet William grows one to two feet high and is topped with rounded clusters of fringed, single or double flowers. It is often used for borders and in flower arrangements because of its lasting quality and beauty. Flowers range in color from white to pink, and from red to scarlet with some striped varieties.

Sweet William is a fairly hardy perennial but, since it tends to deteriorate after several seasons, it is usually grown as a biennial. Once established in a well-drained, fairly rich bed in a sunny position, it will reseed itself from year to year.

To start plants, sow seed in early summer in flats or open beds. Transplant seedlings to their permanent position in September or October, spacing them 12 to 15 inches apart. The plants will blossom the following spring.

See also DIANTHUS.

SWEET WOODRUFF
(*Galium odoratum*)

Sweet woodruff is a low, spreading plant forming clumps about eight inches high. It has slender leaves borne in starry whorls and loose clusters of small, white flowers. The herb is used for aromatic, medicinal and culinary purposes.

The name woodruff is derived from the French *rovelle* (wheel), referring to the plant's spokelike leaf patterns. Woodruff was popular in the fourteenth and fifteenth centuries for its perfume and was often placed in musty rooms as a freshener. Its leaves were used to treat cuts and wounds. It was also used to cure liver disorders. Through the Middle Ages, it was a strewing herb on Saint Peter's and Saint Barnabas' Days.

Woodruff makes a charming ground cover under taller plants or in partial shade and can be grown as a perennial if winters are not too severe. In cold climates plants may be kept indoors or in a cold frame over winter.

Woodruff grows best in moist soil with a heavy mulch of humus and compost. Propa-gation is by seed, cuttings or division, but seeds take up to one year to germinate, while cuttings root quickly. Woodruff can also be grown as a potted plant indoors.

As a rule, the herb is not deliberately cultivated, but gathered wild. It may be harvested any time during the growing season. Until dried, its vanillalike fragrance is not apparent. Harvested woodruff should be chopped and dried in warm shade. It can be used to flavor wine, punches and fresh fruits. It makes a tasty jelly and a glaze for cooking chicken and venison.

See also HERB.

SWISS CHARD   (*Beta vulgaris*)

A member of the same group as the common beet, chard has a smaller, nonbulbous root. It is grown for its finely textured leaves which are used as a cooked green, like spinach. The leaf-vein is sometimes cooked alone like asparagus. Like beets and clover, chard is a very deep-rooted plant so it is useful in a garden where the subsoil requires aeration. Roots are known to penetrate as deep as six feet in a single season.

Chard will grow in any good garden soil in which lettuce thrives. It will do well in soil amply supplied with humus, in an open, sunny, well-drained location. Since it is slow to bolt, chard is often grown as a substitute for spinach during hot weather.

Plants should be spaced 12 inches apart in the row. A row 15 to 25 feet long is usually sufficient for a family of four, and may be expected to supply greens for cooking from July until frost. In very hot regions, plants may show a tendency to become exhausted, that is,

Harvest the outer Swiss chard leaves before they are one foot tall and have become tough.

to produce smaller leaves after a period of growth. When this happens, new seed may be planted for harvesting in a month to six weeks.

To harvest, gently pull the outer leaves from each plant. Within a week, the inner leaves will have reached harvest size and a new set will be developing. As long as the roots are not severed and the plants are kept thinned, chard will produce greens throughout the sum-

mer. To extend the season into winter, cover the plants with a deep layer of straw or similar mulch.

Varieties: The most common varieties are Fordhook Giant, Rhubarb Chard and Lucullus. All three are flavorful and heavy bearers.

SWORD FERN   *See* NEPHROLEPIS

SYCAMORE   *See* PLANE TREE

SYMPHORICARPOS

Members of this genus of hardy, deciduous shrubs of the Honeysuckle family are mostly natives of North America. They are usually planted for their clusters of berries and small flowers, and may be easily grown in almost any soil. The shrubs thrive in partial shade, and grow well even in urban areas. The most widely grown species is the snowberry (*S. albus*), a three-foot shrub with pink flowers and white berries.

Indian currant or coralberry (*S. orbiculatus*) is also a popular species, grown for its red purple fruit, yellow white flowers and attractive crimson autumn foliage. It grows five to seven feet tall, as far north as New Jersey or South Dakota. More winter-hardy is the wolfberry (*S. occidentalis*), a stiff five-foot bush with white or pinkish flowers and white berries. The handsomest fruit is produced by *S.* x *Chenaultii,* a five-foot hybrid with white-dotted red berries.

See also SNOWBERRY.

TABERNAEMONTANA

The crape jasmine or pinwheel flower (*T. divaricata*) is a lovely shrub hardy only in California and parts of Florida. Very fragrant, it grows six to eight feet high with shiny leaves and clusters of single or double white flowers. It needs full sun and a fertile, sandy soil rich in humus. Propagation is by cuttings grown in pots and set out in fall when the rooted plants are at least a foot tall. In areas where there is light frost, they must be protected with a bank of soil around them.

T. grandiflora is a slightly smaller shrub with yellow flowers that have no fragrance and is not very popular except in southern Florida.

TAGETES   *See* MARIGOLD

TAILFLOWER   *See* ANTHURIUM

TAMARACK   *See* LARCH

TAMARISK   (*Tamarix*)

Deciduous trees and shrubs highly tolerant of salt and sand, tamarisks or salt cedars are good plants for seaside gardens. The long, slender branches, minute scalelike leaves and graceful panicles of small pink flowers give this ornamental a delicate, feathery appearance.

T. ramossima grows widely through most of the country, especially in the West. About 15 feet tall, it has bluish foliage and white or pinkish blooms. Also with bluish foliage and pink flowers, the salt tree (*T. aphylla*), to 30 feet, is very tolerant of desert and alkaline conditions. It is hardy only in the South and Far West, where it is often planted as a windbreak. *T. chinensis* grows ten to 15 feet tall, has big clusters of pink blooms and is as hardy as the salt tree. *T. dioca,* a small shrub up to five feet high, is similarly hardy. In the West, many of the tamarisks are important bee plants. Propagation is by cuttings.

TANGERINE   (*Citrus reticulata*)

Also known as mandarin orange, this citrus fruit reaches the peak of its popularity around the Christmas season since it ripens somewhat earlier than most oranges and also because it is attractive to use for decorative purposes. The fruit has a rich, red peel that separates easily from the flesh. Dark green, glossy foliage makes the tangerine tree one of the most beautiful of citrus trees.

See also CITRUS, ORANGE.

TANNIA   *See* XANTHOSOMA

1107

TANKAGE

Refuse from slaughterhouses and butcher shops is called tankage. Depending on the amount of bone present, the phosphorous content varies greatly. The nitrogen content varies usually between 5 and 12.5 percent, the phosphoric acid content is usually around 2 percent, but may be much higher.

TANSY   (*Tanacetum vulgare*)

A hardy perennial growing to two or three feet, tansy has dark green, fernlike foliage and flat clusters of bright yellow, buttonlike flowers. It often appears as a weed along roadsides in the United States and Europe, though it is an attractive background plant in the ornamental garden. It is used as a flavoring agent in many contemporary recipes.

The name tansy is probably derived from the Greek *anthanasia,* meaning "immortal." From ancient days through to the American Revolution, tansy was used to preserve stored meats. In the sixteenth and seventeenth centuries, tansy was used in Christian springtime rites. It is one of the bitter herbs of Passover.

In colonial America, clumps of the plant were used as an insect repellent. Oil of tansy is still believed to repel pests when rubbed on the body.

Though tansies can be started from seed, it is best to propagate them by root division, setting the new plants about a foot apart. Plant them in a deep container and bury it in the garden bed. This prevents the root structure from crowding out neighboring plants. Tansies prefer fertile soil rich in nitrogen. They should

Tansy is an especially powerful seasoning, useful as a substitute for pepper.

be harvested at the peak of growth, before the leaves turn yellow. Leaves are dried in 90°F. (32.22°C.) shade for two days.

Although tansy has had a history of medicinal (tonic, nervine, skin treatment) roles, its contemporary uses are largely culinary. It is used in salad dressings, omelets and even in the manufacture of the liqueur chartreuse. Tansy was at one time used as a substitute for pepper. This sharply flavored herb should be used sparingly in the kitchen.

TAPIOCA PLANT   *See* MANIHOT

TAPROOT

A taproot is a large, straight root growing downward from the stem and having smaller, lateral roots branching from it. Because the root often penetrates deeply into the soil, moving plants with taproots is difficult.

TARNISHED PLANT BUG

This garden pest is an active, ¼-inch-long, brassy brown insect that sucks plant juices from young shoots, buds and fruits of many plants. The nymphs are shaped like the adults, but smaller and colored yellow green. It is best to handpick early in the morning, when the bugs are cold. A sabadilla dust will take care of serious infestations.

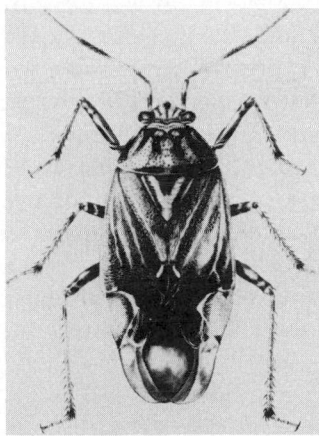

In the spring, the adult tarnished plant bug emerges from hibernation to feed on the leaves, flower buds and fruits of many economic crops.
(Courtesy of U.S. Department of Agriculture)

TARRAGON
(*Artemisia Dracunculus*)

Tarragon is an herbaceous perennial that grows to two or three feet if well kept. One of the curious aspects of tarragon is that it seems not to have any aromatic properties at all while it is growing. Not until the tops or leaves are harvested and dried do the oils concentrate and give off the characteristic tarragon sweetness, somewhat like the sweet aroma of freshly mowed hay.

Planting and Culture: The root ball is the key to propagating tarragon. Plants do not produce seed easily, nor can it be easily purchased. To propagate, divide a root clump in the spring, after the new shoots are at least two inches tall. Be sure to plant the divisions at least 18 inches apart, for tarragon's root structure spreads laterally rather than vertically. The sprawling, shallow root network dictates two other things: 1) that the gardener must take special care when cultivating not to damage the roots; and 2) that tarragon must get special winter protection, especially in the northern states. Extra-special care must be given during the first winter after transplanting, for the root umbrella will not have matured yet.

Tarragon likes moderate sun; try to offer it a little shade during the hottest part of the day. Plant it in fertile loamy soil that will retain moisture, but won't keep its "feet" wet. Heavy mulching is advisable.

Harvesting: Cuttings may be taken for kitchen use early in the spring and summer. When the leaves begin to yellow, harvest the whole top by cutting it back to about three inches above ground. Yellowing indicates either maturity or lack of nutrients. If the discoloration comes in early July, odds are that the plant

Highly valued as one of the finer culinary herbs, tarragon leaves are delicious additions to various fish, cheese, egg, and green vegetable dishes.

is mature. In any case, the discoloration can't be reversed and so harvest immediately.

Dry the leaves quickly, either in a dry, warm, shaded, and ventilated area, or in the oven at low heat. The leaves brown easily, and reabsorb moisture quickly, so pop them into an airtight jar after drying.

Tarragon imparts a delicate, faintly sweet hint to light vegetable dishes and soups, mild cheeses, all kinds of egg dishes, and even the lighter white-meat recipes. Fish and white sauces are naturals for tarragon.

See also HERB.

TARWEED   *(Madia elegans)*

Tarweed is not a popular annual, although its flowers are very fragrant. It grows 18 to 24 inches tall, with small daisylike yellow flowers and long, narrow leaves. Chilean tarweed (*M. sativa*) is about twice as tall, with much smaller leaves and tiny yellow flower heads. Seeds are sown where they are wanted, in shade and ordinary garden soil. The tarweeds grow wild in the West.

TAXODIUM

The three trees of this genus are usually known as cypresses, although they are not related to the true cypress. The magnificent southern or bald cypress (*T. distichum* var. *distichum*) grows well over 100 feet tall and is an important ornamental and timber tree. It has graceful, feathery foliage that turns orange in autumn. In wild swamps it produces buttresses or "knees," thick woody root projections rising several feet above the water. It is hardy up to lower New England but is much smaller in the North. It will grow well on any fairly moist soil.

Pond cypress (*T. distichum* var. *nutans*) is similar but smaller and Montezuma cypress (*T. mucronatum*) is an enormous, very long-lived Mexican evergreen. Some 120-foot specimens have a trunk diameter of over 50 feet and an age equalling or perhaps exceeding that of our giant sequoias. It is occasionally grown in Southern California and Florida but is not hardy elsewhere in this country.

TAXUS   *See* YEW

T-BUDDING   *See* BUDDING

TEA   (*Camellia sinensis*)

The tea shrub is grown mainly as a curiosity in the United States rather than for ornament or the commercial production of tea. It grows as a shrub or small tree with leathery leaves and fragrant white flowers. Give it a moist, friable soil that is rich in humus. Fertilize the plant with manure.

See also CAMELLIA.

TEABERRY   *See* WINTERGREEN

TEA GROUNDS

Tea grounds or leaves are useful as a mulch or an addition to the compost heap. One analysis of the leaves showed the relatively high content of 4.15 percent nitrogen, which seems to be exceptional. Both phosphorus and potash were present in amounts below 1 percent.

TEA OLIVE   (*Osmanthus*)

These evergreen shrubs or small trees have fragrant flowers borne in clusters, and are favorite landscaping plants throughout the South and Pacific Coast states. They thrive in almost any soil that is not too wet or acid. Some of the ten species do well in a cool greenhouse, given a soil mixture of equal parts of loam, sand, and leaf mold or compost, plus some dried cow manure and a little bone meal.

O. fragrans, the most popular species,

grows ten to 20 feet high, with white flowers appearing in April. *O. heterophyllus* is a little taller and blooms in early summer. It is somewhat hardier than *O. fragrans,* useful as a hedge plant, and has forms with gold, purple and variegated leaves. Devilwood (*O. americanus*) is a small tree with fragrant greenish flowers, blooming in late spring.

The tea olives are propagated by seed (very slow germinating) or by cuttings of half-ripe wood taken in late summer and rooted under glass.

TEASEL   (*Dipsacus*)

Biennial or perennial herbs growing up to six feet tall, teasels have prickly stems and

At one time, the dried heads of common teasel were used to raise the nap on woolen fabric.

prickly, blue purple heads. At one time, common teasel (*D. sylvestris*) was grown commercially and the dried heads used to raise a nap on woolen cloth. Today it is naturalized throughout North America and is a pesky weed in some regions. Fuller's teasel (*D. sativus*) is sometimes grown in the garden for use in dried arrangements.

TEA TREE   *See* LEPTOSPERMUM

TELEGRAPH PLANT
(*Desmodium motorium*)

Growing about three feet high, with small lavender flowers and inch-long pods, the telegraph plant is not very showy. Its appeal lies in the small lateral leaves, which move in various directions according to fluctuations in temperature and light.

Though a perennial, the plant is best grown as an annual in the warm greenhouse. Seed should be sown in February in light, sandy soil. Placed in a humid spot, the seed will soon germinate, and the seedlings should be transplanted to a mixture of loam and leaf mold.

TEMPORARY MEADOW

A temporary meadow is a hayfield used for a short time, usually not more than one crop season.

TENDER

Tender plants are those susceptible to killing by freezing temperatures. Some plants that are hardy in areas of dry winters must be considered tender in regions where the winters are wet and slushy. Tender annuals are those which cannot be sown early enough to bloom outdoors north of a line from upper Virginia to Nevada.

See also FROST, HARDINESS.

TENDRIL

Tendrils are thin, wiry extensions of a leaf or stem, used usually to help a vine cling to a support. Some plants have very prickly tendrils to help them grip smooth surfaces, while others have threadlike coiling ones which adhere to a blank wall or rock face with amazing tenacity.

TENT CATERPILLAR

The larvae of several moths and butterflies are collectively referred to as tent caterpillars. The name is especially applied to *Malacosoma americana,* known as the eastern tent caterpillar and sometimes as the apple tent caterpillar. Tent caterpillars multiply rapidly and can defoliate many deciduous trees and shrubs over a wide area in a short time. Wild cherry and apple are most often attacked; peach, pear, plum, rose, hawthorn, and various shade and forest trees are occasionally infested. In spring, the pests' unsightly nests, or tents, are conspicuous on susceptible trees by the roadside or in neglected orchards. These caterpillars are abundant and troublesome for several years in a row; they often eat all the leaves on a tree, weakening but seldom killing it. Once the caterpillars mature, in early summer, they cause no further feeding damage.

Life Cycle: One generation of the eastern tent caterpillar develops in a year. Larvae are present in late spring, cocoons and moths in early summer and eggs for the remainder of the time.

The larvae, or caterpillars, hatch in spring from egg masses about the time the first leaves are opening. The young caterpillars keep together and spin threads of silken web. After feeding for about two days, they begin to weave their tent in a nearby tree crotch, sometimes joining with caterpillars from other egg masses. As the caterpillars grow, they enlarge the tent until it consists of several layers. In good weather, they leave the tent several times a day in search of food, stringing silk after them, while bad weather sends them between the layers of the tent. When they finish feeding on a tree, the caterpillars leave the nest and search for food. Upon reaching maturity they spin cocoons on tree bark, fences, brush, weeds, or buildings, or among dead leaves and debris on the ground. When full grown, about six weeks after hatching, the caterpillar is almost two inches long and sparsely hairy. It is black and has white and blue markings with a white stripe along the middle of its back.

The pupal cocoon is about one inch long and white or yellow white. In early summer, red brown moths emerge, and the females deposit masses of eggs in bands around twigs. The eggs are covered with a foamy secretion that dries to a firm brown covering that looks

The nests of the tent caterpillar should be torn out by hand and the surviving caterpillars burned.

like an enlargement of the twig. An egg mass usually contains about 200 eggs.

Control: You can control the eastern tent caterpillar by hand if you have only a few infested trees. Since many insects are concentrated in a few groups, they can be easily destroyed. Take action when you first see the nests, before the larvae start to feed. Tear the nests out by hand or with a brush or pole, and either crush any surviving caterpillars on the ground or burn them with a torch made from oily rags tied to a pole. If you elect the latter method, do not let the fire get out of hand. In winter, you can destroy the egg masses by cutting off the infested twigs and burning them. Remove wild cherry trees growing in the vicinity of orchards, if possible.

There are several natural predators of the tent caterpillar. Soon after the female moth lays her eggs, they are apt to be attacked by a minute wasplike insect known as *Tetrastichus*. This parasite measures only $1/16$ inch in length and is shiny dark green with red eyes and iridescent wings. It lays one egg in each tent caterpillar egg and the tiny white grub that soon hatches devours the egg of the pest. When the grub is full grown, it entirely fills the hard caterpillar eggshell and spends the winter in this snug retreat.

An important predator of a western species, the Rocky Mountain tent caterpillar, is a digger wasp labeled *Podalonia occidentalis.* This insect is somewhat less than an inch long and is entirely black with the exception of the abdomen, which is gleaming red orange with a black tip. Although the adult female parasite feeds entirely upon the nectar of wild flowers, her young are carnivorous and must have living flesh for food. To provide this, the wasp paralyzes the caterpillars with an anesthetic that she injects into the central nervous system. She drags the caterpillar to an underground burrow, lays an egg on the skin of the pest, covers up the entrance to the chamber, and hurries off to seek a new victim. The parasite grub soon hatches and drills into the body of the slumbering caterpillar and proceeds to feed. First it devours the nonvital tissues so that it may continue to have fresh food to eat. It keeps from fouling its food supply by delaying the evacuation of waste products until it reaches full size and emerges from the host carcass. The grub then constructs a tough, parchmentlike cocoon about itself and remains underground until the following spring when it transforms into an adult wasp.

Mature caterpillars that have escaped the digger wasps are often attacked by another parasite that you might mistake for a large housefly. Known as *Sarcophaga aldrichi,* its light gray thorax has three longitudinal black stripes and the abdomen is divided into alternating light and dark squares. These extremely beneficial flies insert their living maggots beneath the skin of caterpillars. The pests usually live long enough to spin their cocoons and transform to pupae before succumbing. When the maggots reach full growth, they emerge from the caterpillar cocoon and drop to the ground. After they have dug beneath the surface to escape natural enemies, their outer skin hardens into a dark brown, seedlike shell inside of which they transform to pupae. With the advent of spring, the pupae change to flies and emerge from the soil.

A commercially available pathogen, *Bacillus thuringiensis,* is a very effective control. Baltimore orioles have been known to clean up entire infestations, and the birds' hanging sacklike nests are a sign that your trees are insured against tent caterpillar trouble.

Similar Pests: The forest tent caterpillar (*Malacosoma disstria*) and the fall webworm (*Hyphantria cunea*) are sometimes mistaken for the eastern tent caterpillar. The forest tent caterpillar may be distinguished from the eastern tent caterpillar by a row of orange spots along its back. The caterpillars are found more often on forest trees than on fruit trees. They differ from other species in that they do not form webs.

The fall webworm makes a nest resembling that of the eastern tent caterpillar, but it is located at the tip of a branch instead of at the crotch. In addition, the fall webworm is smaller and more hairy, and is present from midsummer to autumn. It feeds on many kinds of trees, including most of those attacked by the eastern tent caterpillar.

These insects may be organically controlled in the same way as the eastern tent caterpillar. For more information, consult your county agricultural agent, state agricultural experiment station or state agricultural college.

See also INSECT CONTROL.

TERMINAL

A flower, leaf or other structure growing at the end of a branch or stem is said to be terminal. The term is generally used to distinguish such forms from those located elsewhere, such as on the sides of stems or branches (lateral), or flower clusters which rise from the leaf axils.

TERMINALIA

The Indian almond or myrobalan (*T. Catappa*) is the only ornamental species of this genus. It is a very popular street tree in southern Florida and the tropics. The foot-long leaves cast a heavy shade and turn a beautiful red before falling. It grows about 70 feet high and bears small greenish flowers and two-inch-long pods with edible seeds much like almonds. Other species of *Terminalia* are commercially valuable plants yielding various resins, tannin extracts and other products.

TERRACING

An effective way to control hillside erosion, terracing involves the building of embankments across the slope of a field. Usually the terraces or steps are separated by ditches which divert the runoff water and prevent it from flowing downslope.
See also SOIL CONSERVATION.

TERRARIUM   *See* HOUSE PLANTS

TERRESTRIAL

Terrestrial refers to plants growing in soil, in contrast to epiphytic plants which grow in the air or aquatic plants which grow in water.

TETTERBUSH   *See* LYONIA

TETTERWORT
(*Sanguinaria canadensis*)

This beautiful spring-blooming wild perennial is often called bloodroot because of its red root and sap. It has one large leaf six inches wide, a waxy, pink, many-petaled flower and a small fruit pod. Tetterwort prefers part shade and well-drained, rich woods soil that is near neutral. It is easily propagated by seed or root division.

TEUCRIUM

The most familiar teucrium is the hardy wall germander (*T. Chamaedrys*) used for medicinal purposes since ancient times. It grows about one foot tall and makes an excellent low perennial border plant or decoration for a rock garden. It has shiny green leaves and spikes of white-spotted red or purple flowers that appear in late spring and continue until early fall. Although it prefers frost-free regions, it will survive in most locations if adequate winter protection is given. In the spring, plant seeds or root divisions in a moderately sunny place where the soil is sandy. The plants should be spaced about one foot apart.

Of the other species, wood sage (*T. canadense*) is about the same size, purple flowered and grows throughout the East. *T. Marum* is a small shrub with very fragrant foliage and flowers, and *T. orientale* is a perennial herb that grows less than a foot tall, with feathery foliage and lavender or blue flowers.

TEXAS BUCKTHORN
See LOTI-BUSH

THALICTRUM

The pretty meadow rues are good perennials for sunny spots in the border, rock and wild gardens. About 20 species are grown in the United States, all blooming in early summer with big, showy panicles of flowers in a wide range of colors. They like a moist, loamy soil, and are propagated by division in spring, each plant often yielding a half-dozen new ones.

A Japanese rue (*T. kiusianum*) is especially pretty, growing prostrate or nearly so and producing a mass of mauve lavender blooms for up to two months. Its interesting leaves resemble the delicate foliage of a maidenhair fern. This species prefers shade and good drainage.

T. dipterocarpum grows a foot or so tall with pale red or lilac flowers. *T. minus* and *T. dioicum* are about the same size but have yellow green blooms. The handsome *T. aquilegifolium* grows two to three feet tall, with flowers ranging from white and pink to orange and purple in varieties, and blooms in June and July. The yellow-flowered *T. speciosissimum* is three feet high and July blooming, while *T. polygamum* has white flowers and grows up to six or seven feet.

THANKSGIVING CACTUS
(*Schlumbergera truncata*)

The popular crab or Thanksgiving cactus is a hanging plant with fleshy stems that serve as leaves, very handsome three-inch white and crimson flowers, and red berrylike fruits. An excellent house plant, it can be made to bloom several times during the winter by putting it in a room where the temperature is 60°F. (15.56°C.) or less and giving it about ten hours of light a day for four to six weeks. Flowers will appear ten to 12 weeks later. Forcing requirements for some hybrids may vary slightly.

See also EPIPHYLLUM.

THAWS

Early spring thaws followed by refreezing of the soil results in heaving, which can damage the root systems of many plants. Those most affected are lawn grasses and shallow-rooted perennials growing in moist soils with considerable clay or silt. The roots of the plants, thrown up out of the soil, could die from exposure to cold and dryness.

To protect plants, apply a thick winter mulch, but be sure to remove it early in the spring before the soil gets very wet from spring rains. Otherwise the plants may rot. Perennials should also be planted firmly in heavy soils, in the spring when possible, to get strongly established. Lawns should be rolled to correct heaving, but not immediately after a heavy rain if the soil is very moisture retentive, as this would cause serious packing.

Heaving is not the only problem associated with early spring thaws. Often, the warm period causes plants to put forth new growth which is killed when the temperatures drop again. Sometimes the plant itself is killed. Evergreens with high rates of transpiration require large amounts of water during warm weather. If the roots are unable to supply that moisture, the plant turns brown and may eventually die. In these situations, a winter mulch helps to keep the ground cool and moist.

See also FROST, MULCH.

THERMOPSIS

These showy perennial legumes are hardy in all but the coldest regions of North America. Given a light, well-drained soil and full sun, they bloom from early to midsummer. The flowers are yellow, pea shaped and clustered on long spikes. They are excellent as cut flowers.

The most common thermopsis is the Carolina lupine (*T. caroliniana*) which grows three to four feet tall and has flower spikes up to one foot long. Sow fresh seed in early summer for blossoming plants two years later. Or, plant root divisions of dormant plants. Set three to four feet apart, the plants can remain undisturbed for many years.

THINNING

Thinning is a term used for several garden operations. Sometimes it refers to the removal of certain seedlings in a row in order to give room to others. If the pulled seedlings are replanted, the procedure is called pricking out. Disbudding, the removal of some flower buds to make the remaining ones grow larger flowers, is also a form of thinning. Similarly, fruit growers often "thin out" some of the developing apples, peaches or plums in order to encourage fewer, larger fruits. When the term is used in relation to pruning trees and shrubs, it refers to the removal of extra branches.

See also PRUNING, SEEDS AND SEEDLINGS, VEGETABLE GARDENING.

THISTLE

Thistles are found in many plant genera. All of them are characterized by prickly leaves and spiny flower heads. Some species are cultivated as ornamentals, vegetables and as garden borders. More often, however, the thistles are considered weeds.

Gardeners dislike many species of thistle because they tend to overrun the garden and are difficult to eradicate. Russian thistle (*Salsola kali tenuifolia*), for example, is a dense plant that must be cultivated out of gardens and mowed out of roadsides and fencerows to prevent its profuse seeding. Canada thistle (*Cirsium arvense*) is one of the most widespread weeds in America. It has showy blue purple flowers and a deep root that cannot be destroyed by cultivation. It must be dug out. Any little pieces left in the ground will produce new plants.

Most of the ornamental thistles are less tenacious and do not spread as readily as the weedy species. The blue-flowered globe thistles of the genus *Echinops* are handsome plants with species growing from one to over six feet tall, popular for the hardy border. This genus grows best in sun and soil that is not too rich or moist. The blessed thistle (*Cnicus benedictus*) grows up to two feet tall with yellow blooms. An edible thistle is the milk thistle (*Silybum Marianum*), sometimes grown as a vegetable. The roots, leaves and flower heads can be eaten. It grows three feet tall or taller, with glossy leaves over two feet long and big red purple flower heads. Sow the seed ⅛ inch deep in spring in any fertile soil.

THOUSAND-FLOWERED ASTER
See BOLTONIA

THRIPS
See HOUSE PLANTS, INSECT CONTROL

THUJA   See ARBORVITAE

Although many gardeners dislike the coarse appearance of the globe thistle, others grow it for the lovely purple flower heads.

THUNBERGIA

These tender shrubs and vines have spectacular flowers and are very popular ornamentals in the South and California. Their lush growth makes them excellent for covering porches, trellises or small buildings. A number of them will thrive in the warm greenhouse in the North, in a loamy soil high in humus. They are propagated by layering or cuttings.

The black-eyed Susan vine (*T. alata*) is sometimes grown as a garden annual but more often it is potted and used as a house plant. It is a rapid climber, achieving heights of eight to ten feet in one growing season. From early summer to mid autumn, it puts forth many dark-throated yellow to white flowers. To propagate this plant, sow seed indoors, eight to ten weeks before the last frost date. Transplant them to hanging baskets or tubs when they are about three inches high. Allow about two plants to each six-inch pot.

Other species include king's mantle (*T. erecta*) which has white or bluish flowers and the widely cultivated blue trumpet vine (*T. grandiflora*) which is frequently grown under arbors and porches.

THUNDERWOOD
See POISON SUMAC

THYME   (*Thymus*)

Thyme is a small, shrubby, perennial herb that grows six to 12 inches high and up to two feet wide. It has oval, gray green leaves about ¼ inch long and loose spikes of pink or lavender flowers. Native to southeastern Europe, it is often planted as an ornamental along garden borders or in rock gardens. The leaves are widely used for flavoring foods and the oil distilled from the plant has many medicinal properties. Historically, the herb has been associated with happiness, health and bravery. It is mentioned in the writings of Theophrastus, Horace, Virgil, and Pliny and is said to have been one of the herbs upon which Mary and Jesus slept

Golden lemon thyme is commonly found in old country gardens of temperate regions where it has been planted as an evergreen border.

in Bethlehem. For this reason, it is found in many Christmas crèches and is frequently planted in church and monastery gardens.

In early Greece, thyme signified graceful elegance and was associated with romance. The Greeks used the herb as incense and strewed the floors of their churches and banquet halls with it. Later, during the age of chivalry, thyme, as a symbol of strength and bravery, was a common logo on knightly pennants.

In Renaissance England, when wits were keen and words well chosen, it was said that thyme could hardly enter a conversation between two people of quick mind without a welter of puns developing. The first allusion to the herb became jokingly known as "punning thyme." French Republicans embraced thyme as a symbol of their courage, and a sprig delivered to the door of a loyal Republican was a silent summons to a clandestine meeting.

Planting and Culture: Seed of common thyme (*T. vulgaris*) can be purchased from most suppliers but is sometimes sold under the name English, German winter, or French summer thyme. For best results, plant seed indoors in early spring. A temperature of around 70°F. (21.11°C.) is best for speedy germination, but once seed leaves develop, the temperature can be dropped to 55 to 60°F. (12.78 to 15.56°C.). Outdoor seeding is also possible in a well-prepared seedbed with rows spaced about three feet apart. For plant-breeding purposes, propagate from crown divisions or cuttings taken from mature plants.

Thyme is a hardy plant and will grow under almost any conditions, but a sunny spot with light, sandy or loamy soil is best. Fertilizing is usually unnecessary unless the soil is very poor. Since the plant grows very slowly in its early stages, and usually remains low and small, year-round weed control is essential. Cultivate the soil lightly and apply a mulch of cocoa hulls or straw. Care should be used when cultivating the smaller prostrate, lemon-scented mother-of-thyme (*T. Serpyllum*), which is an excellent ground cover.

Harvesting: Thyme should be harvested in midsummer, just before the flowers begin to open. A second growth will develop during late summer or early fall. Do not cut this at all, or if necessary, remove no more than the top third. Otherwise its winter hardiness will be sacrificed. The plants should be covered with a blanket of mulch and special care should be taken if winters are bare and temperatures fluctuate between severe frosts and warm spells.

To harvest, cut the entire plants 1½ to two inches from the ground. Spread them on papers and dry them in warm shade until the tiny leaves separate from the branches with slight pressure. Thyme poses no problem in drying and stores well at a low humidity. Stems should be discarded or composted.

Thyme is mentioned in all pharmacopoeias and its action is said to be antiseptic, antispasmodic, carminative, and antipyretic. Thyme, especially in teas, is said by herbalists to be an aromatic, diuretic, diaphoretic, and emmenagogic stimulant. In herbal medicine, thyme is generally used in combination with other remedies.

To make thyme tea, add one ounce dried leaves to one pint boiled water. Strain and cool. Honey can be added to the mixture. If refrigerated, this syrup is good for sore throats, coughing spells and colds. Thyme-based honey has been used for medicinal and culinary purposes since the days of ancient Romans and can still be purchased in some Greek import shops.

In the kitchen, thyme serves as a universal seasoning. One expert on herbal cookery suggests using thyme "as freely as salt—in other words, on everything." The herb is an especially good seasoning for red meat, poultry, fish, and vegetables. It is also used in flavoring stuffings, sauces, pickles, stews and soups.

Dried thyme flowers, like those of lavender, can be used to protect linen from insects. Essence of thyme is used in cosmetics and perfume.

Thymol is a valuable crystalline phenol which is an extract of essence of sweet thyme. It is a powerful antiseptic for both external and internal use. It is also employed as a preservative of meat, a deodorant and a local anesthetic.

See also HERB.

TIGERFLOWER   (*Tigridia Pavonia*)

The very pretty, summer-blooming Mexican tigerflower has sword-shaped leaves up to 18 inches high and flowers ranging in color from deep red to yellow, buff and lavender, with magnificently spotted centers. Though the flowers are not very long lasting, they make fine cut flowers and bloom in succession from July to frost.

Tigridias like sandy, well-drained soil and are fine accent plants for a sunny border. Well-rotted manure worked into the soil, plus an occasional feeding of liquid manure, will insure large, spectacular blooms. Plant the bulbs three to four inches deep in groups. Usually bulbs are dug up after the first frost and stored over winter in a cool, dry place. However, some gardeners have found that the plants can overwinter outdoors if protected by a heavy mulch. Seed can be saved and sown in late winter under glass or outdoors when the soil has warmed up. The bulbs are often eaten by Mexican Indians.

TIGER LILY   *See* LILY

TILIA   *See* LINDEN

TILLAGE
See CULTIVATION, ROTARY TILLAGE

TILLANDSIA

Only a few of the many epiphytic plants in this genus are found in the United States. One of them is the well-known Spanish moss (*T. usneoides*) that drapes cypress and oak trees so picturesquely in the southeastern states. Its threadlike stems and numerous tiny leaves get their sustenance from the air and rain, and the gardener need only drape some strands of the moss over a suitable tree to get dense garlands of it.

Most of the tillandsias are tropical plants and can be grown in the warm greenhouse. Their roots are generally wired to a board on which some osmunda fiber has been placed. The plants should be watered frequently in the spring and summer and less often during winter months. One of the prettiest species is *T. Lindenii* which has a basal rosette of foot-long leaves and big spikes of purple blooms with brilliant scarlet bracts. *T. fasciculata* has leaves up to 18 inches long and a six-inch spike of blue flowers.

See also SPANISH MOSS.

TILTH

Tilth refers to the physical condition of the soil as it relates to ease of tillage. It also refers to its fitness as a seedbed and its resistance to seedling emergence and root penetration. Thus, a soil with good tilth is one that is sufficiently loose in structure. It is well aerated and can be easily penetrated by roots. A friable soil, one that is easy to break, crumble or crush has good tilth.

See also SOIL.

TIMOTHY   (*Phleum pratense*)

Timothy is a perennial grass extensively cultivated for hay. It grows as high as five feet, depending on soil and climatic conditions. It thrives in almost any neutral or slightly acid soil, from sandy loam to poorly drained clay.

See also HAY.

TIP LAYERING
See BRAMBLE FRUITS, LAYERING

TISSWOOD
(*Halesia* spp., *Persea Borbonia*)

Tisswood trees generally belong to the genus *Halesia* or *Persea*. The halesias are also known as silverbell or snowdrop trees and are characterized by their hanging clusters of bell-shaped, white flowers that appear in spring. In autumn, dry winged seedpods develop and the leaves turn pale yellow. The trees are considered choice ornamentals for southern lawns. Two species, *H. carolina* and *H. monticola,* are hardy along the coastal regions of lower New England. Plant the trees in a sheltered location where the soil is fertile and well drained.

Sometimes, nursery catalogs list the tropical evergreen tree *P. Borbonia* under the name tisswood. Also known as red bay or Florida mahogany, this tree is grown for its heavy, rich green foliage that somewhat resembles that of the laurel. It can be grown in moist, even swampy, soils from Delaware, south to Florida.

TITHONIA

Members of this genus are native to desert and tropical areas, but some species can be grown as annuals in the North. Known as Mexican sunflowers, the plants have deep orange yellow, daisylike flowers that are available for cutting in late summer. The most widely cultivated species is *T. rotundifolia,* a hardy, six-foot plant with spectacular bright orange flowers. Start seed indoors in early spring for August flowers. Seed sown outdoors after frost will not produce flowering plants until September. Plants should be grown in a fertile, sunny location and spaced three to four feet apart. Torch and Grandiflora are popular varieties.

TOAD

The toad is a tailless, leaping amphibian, and a good friend to the gardener. Nearly 90 percent of a toad's food consists of insects and other small creatures, most of which are harmful to the garden. In three months a toad will eat up to 10,000 insects, 16 percent of which are cutworms. Dead or motionless food is of little interest. Only moving objects, apparently, make any impression on its sensory apparatus. A toad's tongue is attached at the front end of the mouth, and is an organ especially adapted for capturing insects.

The spring appearance of the toad varies with locality and temperature. In the northern states, toads begin to emerge from hibernation in the middle of March, but most do not appear until after April 1. The males usually enter the water before the females, but do not commence to sing until the end of April or early May, according to latitude.

It is not unusual to find hundreds of toads congregated in a small pond during the spawning season. Under normal conditions, the female begins laying at once, and may lay from 4,000 to 15,000 eggs, the process usually being completed within one day unless there is a sudden drop in temperature. The eggs are laid in the water, in long spiral strings of jelly. The hatching period depends upon the temperature. Below 65°F. (18.33°C.), it requires eight to 12 days, and above that temperature, three to eight days. Toads are thus born in the water and in it spend their early life in a larval, fish-like state, breathing by means of gills. The transformation of a tadpole to a young toad takes place sometime between 50 and 65 days after birth though under abnormal conditions it may require 200 days.

If the weather is moderate, toads may remain active from March to the middle of November. During the winter months they hibernate in the ground. The toad makes its burrow with its hind legs, digging backwards. As the animal descends, the dirt fills in over its head.

To encourage toads to stay near the

garden, provide a modest shelter so they can rest out of the sun. Cut a small entrance in a box or chip out an opening in the side of a flowerpot, and bury it a few inches into the ground, preferably in the shade. You might even provide a shallow pond for toads to sit in. On very hot, dry days, wet the shrubbery to keep these allies happy.

See also FROG.

TOADFLAX
See LINARIA, MOROCCAN TOADFLAX

TOBACCO (*Nicotiana*)

Indigenous to the Western Hemisphere, the tall, attractive tobacco plant is a member of the Nightshade family. Growing from two to eight feet tall, the tobacco plant has broad leaves a foot or more in length, and a stem covered by sticky hairs. Its two-inch flowers are white, rose or rose purple.

The species *N. Tabacum* has become one of the world's most valuable luxury crops. Several flowering species, however, are grown for ornament in the garden and for their fragrant blooms. Tobacco's rich, colorful history, its importance as an agricultural commodity in some southern states, and its many and varied uses require the plant be designated an herb.

In 1613, John Rolfe, the husband of the famous Indian princess Pocahontas, sent the first shipment of Virginia tobacco from Jamestown home to England. Although there is no substantial evidence that the plant was used seriously by the Indians who cultivated it, Old World settlers like Sir Walter Raleigh quickly tried to turn the American weed into a profitable cash crop.

Tobacco was not without enemies, however. Among them was King James I who disliked the odor of the "sot-weed," and even attempted to forbid its use in England. The planting of tobacco also generated opposition in the colonies despite the lucrative trade it created, because it tempted settlers to ignore food crops. In New England, smoking was outlawed as a nonproductive pastime. Despite evidence that smoking can increase the incidence of certain kinds of cancer, the use of tobacco has continued throughout the world and its production is still subsidized by some governments.

Planting and Culture: All varieties of the plant require the same culture. The seed should be sown in a rich, loamy, friable soil under glass in late winter. The temperature of the hotbed must not fall below 70°F. (21.11°C.). Some varieties require shade.

The plants should be set in rows three feet apart, 12 inches from each other and cultivated until they cover the soil. The tops are picked off just before flowering to prevent the plants from going to seed and suckers are removed periodically.

Harvesting: Tobacco is harvested when the central leaves have turned from dark to light green and the top leaves are still dark. Pull the leaves from the stalks and hang them in special curing barns. Different heat-curing processes take from three days to three weeks.

Tobacco is a difficult and highly labor-intensive crop. Nevertheless, it is a vital cash crop in many southern states and an important one in parts of Pennsylvania, Connecticut and Massachusetts, for the price of the commodity is kept high by government controls on production.

Tobacco requires a rich organic soil and frequent cultivation in its early stages of growth.

The dried leaves of the tobacco plant are sold in the form of cigars, cigarettes and pipe tobacco as well as snuff and chewing tobacco. Tobacco is also used in making nicotine sulfate, an early pesticide that is still available though it is not used as widely as it once was. (Some organic gardeners—a minority—regard nicotine sulfate as a permissible pesticide for limited use.) Gardeners have been known to make a pesticidal infusion from cigarette butts.

In folk medicine, tobacco found its way into many official pharmacopoeias. It was said to be sedative, diuretic, expectorant, and emetic. The smoke was blown into the ear to relieve earaches and applied as a poultice for beestings, swellings and sores.

There are other species grown for ornament. *N. Bigelovii* produces fragrant, tubular, nocturnal blooms of white, yellow, red, and purple. *N. alata,* known as flowering tobacco or jasmine, is also an ornamental plant known for its fragrant flowers, as is *N. sylvestris,* which produces a crimson bloom that remains open in the daytime.

An ornamental tobacco tree, *N. glauca,* grows to 20 feet with blue green leaves and yellowish flowers. This species is not suited to northern climes.

See also NICOTIANA.

TOBACCO WASTES

Tobacco stems, leaf waste and dust are good organic fertilizer, especially high in potash. The nutrients contained in 100 pounds of tobacco wastes are 2.5 to 3.7 pounds of nitrogen, almost a pound of phosphoric acid and from 4.5 to seven pounds of potassium.

These wastes can be used anywhere barnyard manure is recommended, except on tobacco, tomatoes and other members of the Nightshade family, because they may carry some of the virus diseases of these crops, especially tobacco mosaic virus.

Compost tobacco wastes, or use them in moderation in mulching or sheet composting mixed with other organic materials. They should not be applied alone in concentrated amounts as a mulch—the nicotine will eliminate both beneficial and harmful insects as well as earthworms and other soil organisms.

TOMATILLO   *See* PHYSALIS

TOMATO
(*Lycopersicon Lycopersicum*)

A fine source of the vitamins A and C, the common tomato is easily grown in almost any backyard. Because of its food value, many uses and ease of culture, the tomato is probably the plant most widely grown by the home gardener.

The origin of the tomato is obscure. Its name comes from the Mexican word *tomatl,* but until a comparatively recent date the tomato was grown as an ornamental known as the "cancer apple." Formerly it was believed to be poisonous and disease producing.

Planting and Culture: The tomato is a warm-season plant which requires a fairly long growing season. You may live in an area where seed can be planted directly in the garden, but in most regions they must be started in a hotbed or indoors.

Seeding: One ounce of seed can produce about 2,000 plants. If you buy a couple of generous packages of good-quality seed you should be able to produce about 300 plants. Leftover seed should be saved since tomato seeds remain viable for up to five years. You can also save seeds from healthy, vigorous plants (*but not from hybrids*). Pick tomatoes when they are dead ripe, mash them, add an equal amount of water, and keep the mixture at 70°F. (21.11°C.) for several days. Stir daily. Good seed will settle to the bottom, and the mixture will ferment. Pour off the water, pulp and floating seeds, wash the good seed and dry on paper in a shady place.

In February or March, or about ten weeks before tomato planting time in your area, arrange some sort of window box which can be placed in a sunny southern window. Almost any small wooden box with drainage holes will serve. Fill with a mixture of two parts pasteurized garden soil to one part pasteurized compost and one part vermiculite or perlite. *See* SOIL PASTEURIZATION. Tomato seed germinates best at about 70°F. (21.11°C.). The seed should be evenly spaced and planted two to three inches apart with three to four seeds to

the inch, ½ inch deep. Keep warm and dark until the seedlings appear.

Young plants should appear in from eight to ten days. As soon as the first leaves develop, set the plants in the sunlight or under a grow light. For the next two weeks they should be watered from the bottom so that the surface soil remains as dry as possible. This reduces the danger of damping-off. Place the seed flat in a pan containing shallow water and allow it to remain there until it absorbs the moisture it requires. Snip off spindly plants, and turn the flat daily so the plants will grow straight and not lean toward the sun. Feed weekly with manure tea or fish emulsion.

When they have one or two true leaves, the seedlings should be transplanted into individual containers that contain a richer soil. Increase the feeding of liquid fertilizer slightly. Give the plants three inches of space each way. The containers should be packed into a tray with soil to prevent drying.

When plants have formed two or more sets of true leaves they are ready to be hardened off. Withhold some water for about one week and then place the young plants in a cold frame, gradually exposing them to the outside air until they are able to stand outdoor temperatures. The process should take about two weeks. After plants have hardened off—and when all danger of frost is past—they can be transplanted into the garden but will require protection—baskets, hay bales, hot caps, or gallon jugs with the bottoms knocked out.

Tomatoes can also be started from seed in a hotbed which, when opened, can serve as a cold frame as well. In some places, tomato plants will grow from seed outdoors. You may also be tempted to buy plants. Purchase only those that are dark green, medium tall, heavy stemmed, and without open flowers or fruit. Plants may also come up in your garden. Such volunteers are generally hardy and well developed. Don't try to transplant them because the root system will suffer.

Soil: As warm-weather plants tomatoes require an open, sunny, well-drained location in the garden. Avoid poorly drained spots where rainwater tends to form a pool. Many diseases of tomatoes are associated with poor drainage.

The soil should be fairly light and porous, and should contain a fair amount of humus. If it is quite heavy and contains a large percentage of clay, you can improve its texture by adding peat moss or sand. For plant nutrients, turn under a green manure crop or fertilize well with compost. Tomatoes prefer a slightly acidic soil with a pH of 6 to 6.8.

Tomatoes should be mulched, if possible, once the soil has warmed. Mulches keep the soil moist and help keep fruit off the ground, preventing rotting. If your garden is under a permanent mulch, pull back the mulch around the areas where you plan to plant tomatoes to give the ground a chance to warm up.

Transplanting: If paper or peat containers have been used, the plants can be set in place without removing the containers. Squeeze them to loosen soil before placing them in the ground. Be sure to completely bury peat pots, however, since if any part of the pot is exposed it will draw water away from the roots.

The plants will overcome the shock of transplanting more quickly if supplied with a starter solution. Mix two parts water with one part sifted compost. Allow the mixture to settle. Apply this solution to the hole in which the plant is to be set and again after the plant has been firmed and settled in place.

Young plants are set out as early as possible to hurry their growth, and it is sometimes necessary to protect them against late frost damage. Invert peach baskets or paper bags over the plants during unusually cold nights.

An alternative to five-foot tomato stakes is this double ladder support which encourages free air circulation and, to some extent, conserves space.

Staking: Perhaps the most desirable method of growing tomatoes for the home gardener is to stake and prune them. More plants can occupy a given space this way, and the difficulties of cultivation are greatly decreased. Drive a five-foot stake into the ground alongside each planting spot. Plant seedlings deeply so that they send out side roots from the stem. This will help to anchor the plant as well as to feed it. Tie the plant to the stake with soft yarn or strips of old cotton cloth. Tie the yarn around the stake and loop it loosely just underneath a leaf node on the plant. This prevents injury to the rapidly growing stem.

Using this method, it is necessary to pinch out the side shoots so that the plant produces two main shoots which are tied to the stake. Remove all suckers except the first one. This is allowed to develop into a second stem, which is tied to the stake like the first one. Other suckers should be allowed to grow six inches long before they are cut off with a sharp knife. To limit the height of the plant, pinch back the top when it reaches the desired height.

Many gardeners grow tomatoes without staking or training. If you do this your total crop per plant may be larger, but your garden will support fewer plants. Staked tomatoes are more uniform in size, though not much larger than unstaked tomatoes.

If you decide not to stake plants, set the plants about four feet apart each way. Before the sprawling branches bend down to the ground, spread a layer of clean straw, dried grass or similar material around each plant to keep the fruits from coming into direct contact with the ground.

Pests and Diseases: Tomatoes have a built-in insect repellent called solanine that will repel many insect pests. The tomato hornworm is probably the most serious pest of tomatoes, although Japanese beetles, cutworms and other pests also bother the plants. Many of these can be controlled by interplanting with flowers or other crops. Nematodes can be discouraged by planting marigolds or even planting tomatoes in soil where marigolds grew the year before and virus-free nasturtiums will trap aphids. The hornworm, a green worm with white stripes, is also attracted to dill, and is easier to spot on those plants than on the tomato. It can be handpicked and dropped into a can of kerosene. Some easy-to-make sprays, such as red pepper or onion and garlic also serve as insect repellents. Cutworm damage can also be prevented by placing a paper collar around the stem, about an inch above and below ground level.

Many diseases plague tomatoes, but only a few are of major importance.

Blossom drop: Tomato plants often fail to set a normal crop of fruit because the blossoms drop off just when the flowers have matured. This may occur wherever tomatoes are grown, but the trouble seems to be especially prevalent where soil moisture is low and plants are subjected to hot, drying winds. Such conditions prevent blossoms from setting fruit, as do sudden periods of cool weather or beating rains. Loss of blossoms also results from infection by parasitic bacteria or fungi. Since large-fruited varieties of the Ponderosa type are very susceptible, do not grow these where summers are going to be hot and dry. Instead grow resistant varieties in hot climates, especially in the Southwest. Irrigate if possible, and avoid excessive applications of nitrogen, especially during early growth. Fruit set can sometimes be increased by shaking the plant in the middle of a warm, sunny day or hitting the top of the stake to which the plant is tied.

Blossom-end rot: This is a common nonparasitic disorder of tomato fruit. A water-soaked spot first appears near the blossom end of the tomato when the fruit is about one-third of the way to maturity. The spot enlarges and browns until it covers up to half the surface, and gets dark and leathery, flat or sometimes concave as it grows. No soft rot of the tomato occurs unless it also has been attacked by bacteria or fungi.

This disorder characteristically strikes during a long dry spell after the plants have grown fast and well during the earlier part of the season, and sometimes appears after rainy periods. A deficiency of calcium is the basic cause of the trouble, but that condition is aggravated by excessive water or nitrogen. An excessive amount of total salts also causes blossom-end rot because the effective amount of calcium salts available to the plant is cut. Control should begin with a soil test very early in the spring or fall to find out whether there is already a shortage of lime in your soil. To raise the pH value of your soil by one unit, use about ½ pound of finely ground limestone for each ten square feet. If soil pH needs to be raised more than one unit because it tests out to have a pH below 6, apply more lime. Add a little at a time, and expect effects to last about three years. In a dry climate, be especially careful not to make your soil too alkaline.

Curly top: Also called western yellow blight, curly top is destructive to both tomatoes and sugar beets and can trouble beans, spinach, squash, peppers, and table beets. It is carried by beet leafhoppers from weedy abandoned lands. It is prevalent in the West, western Nebraska and a few other states in the Midwest. Attacks may occur at any stage of the tomato's growth, causing leaflets to roll and turn over to expose their undersurfaces. Foliage becomes stiff and leathery. The petioles of the leaves curl downward. Branches and stems become very erect and the veins get purple in places. The plants are stunted and very few fruits ripen normally. Early tomatoes probably suffer more from curly top than late varieties, but both are susceptible. Luckily tomatoes are not a preferred host, and beet leafhoppers rarely breed on tomato plants unless they are planted right next to beets.

Control is difficult because the range of the leafhoppers is very wide. Set out transplants after the heaviest leafhopper infestation has passed. Consult your county agent for the right date in your area. Plant more closely than usual, even six inches apart. You can also plant in double-hill plantings with two plants set six inches apart in hills planted in 42-inch rows. Yield has increased and damage decreased on this type of planting. On small plantings shading of the entire area with slats or use of a muslin-covered frame will repel a good many of the insects and arrest the effect of the curly top disease if it is already transmitted to the tomatoes.

Damping-off: This wilt is caused by a fungus that attacks the stems at the ground level. The plants soon fall over and die. The disease can be combated by sterilizing planting soil and controlling excess moisture. Avoid overfeeding your seedlings and place them close to a lighted window or overhead fluorescent light.

Early blight: This disease is common and serious in the New England, Atlantic and central states but of minor importance on the Pacific coast. Symptoms may appear first on the stems as dark, slightly sunken areas with concentric markings. Small, irregular, brown dead spots appear early in the season on the older leaves and enlarge until they are ¼ to ½ inch in diameter. The spots are usually surrounded by yellow, and if there are many spots on the leaf, the entire leaf might be discolored. Most early blight injury occurs just as fruit begins to mature. High temperatures and humidity will cause much of the foliage to die and the fruit to be exposed to sunscald. The disease is easily spread. To avoid problems with early blight, sterilize soil for starting seedlings, use commercially grown seed or clean seed from your own plants, and do not crowd plants in a flat. If seedlings show signs of this disease, do not plant them in the garden.

Fusarium wilt: Although sometimes a major problem, this disease can be entirely avoided if you buy resistant varieties. It is characterized by an overall wilting of the plant, beginning with yellowing and death of the leaves from the base upward. Often the disease will not be evident until fruit begins to mature. Some controls include growing the plants on clean soil, rotating locations of tomato crops yearly (the wilt is a soil-borne disease), and planting seed in pasteurized soil.

Growth cracks: Cracks radiating from the stem or extending more or less concentrically around the shoulders of the fruit may seem normal, but in reality they invite infection and detract from the appearance of fruits. Cracking often appears during rainy spells that are hot and conducive to rapid growth. Another kind of cracking comes when there is a dry period followed by a rainy period during the ripening season. To control this condition refrain from applying water at crucial periods of the plants' growth. Sometimes the cracks heal before harm is done.

Late blight: A fairly common disease in certain parts of the East and on the Pacific coast, late blight occurs sporadically elsewhere. The older leaves of infected plants develop irregular, black, water-soaked patches. Eventually, leaves drop and the disease destroys the fruit. Sometimes there is a white, downy growth of the fungus on the lower surfaces of the leaves, and if the weather is warm and moist, the plant will look as if it had been enveloped by frost. Damage to the fruit is likely to occur on the upper half. The first sign is a green gray spot which becomes brown and hard. Infected plants must be dug up and destroyed or the blight will spread to other plants.

Leaf roll: During very wet seasons tomato plants frequently show an upward rolling of the leaflets of the older leaves. At first this rolling gives the leaflet a cupped appearance. Later, the margins of the leaflets touch or overlap. The rolled leaves are firm and leathery to the touch. One-half to three-fourths of the foliage may be affected. Plant growth is not noticeably checked, and a normal crop of fruit is produced. Frequently leaf roll occurs when tomato plants are pruned severely, and it is very common when unusually heavy rains cause the soil to remain moist for a long time. To prevent leaf roll keep tomato plants on well-drained, well-aerated soil, and protect them from prolonged periods of heavy rainfall if you can.

Root knot: Nearly invisible nematodes which attack the roots of various plants are found wherever tomatoes are grown, especially in areas where rotation is not practiced. The attack results in the formation of root knots or galls which range in diameter from a pinhead width to a full inch or more. Soon the whole outer area of the root is discolored, and may rot. The results are not apparent above ground except that plant growth and yield are retarded. Infected plants wilt very easily on a hot day, and they may be stunted in appearance and somewhat yellowish. Some are nearly killed.

The best control for nematodes is the planting of marigolds along with tomatoes or, even better, put tomatoes in parts of the garden where marigolds grew during the previous year. The root exudate from marigolds has a powerful inhibiting effect on nematodes, and remains effective in the soil for three years. Interplanting is effective the same year. Examine roots of plants and discard any with root knots or rotten roots. Never use soil known to have had a nematode infestation the previous season. Plant marigolds instead. Burn infected plants.

Septoria leaf spot: Not common in the South or on the Pacific coast, it occurs in the mid-Atlantic and central states and as far south as Arkansas and Tennessee, flourishing when temperatures are moderate and rainfall abundant. The disease destroys so much foliage that plants fail to make enough food to support an abundant crop of fruit. Absence of leaves exposes the fruit to sunscald. Fungus is most evident on plants that are just beginning to set fruit. The first symptom is the appearance of water-soaked spots on the older leaves. Spots are rough and circular, with gray centers and dark margins. Later, dark dots are evident in the centers where spores are produced. Eventually all the leaves are affected and drop off, leaving only a few at the stem top. Fruits are rarely attacked. To control, plow under all crop and weed refuse; the fungus will not overwinter on plant remains that are buried deep in the soil.

Soil rot: This disease can attack your plants no matter where you have your garden. It is caused by the same organism that causes damping-off. The first symptom is a brown, slightly sunken spot on the fruit, with sharply outlined (not smooth) concentric markings close together. It enlarges and often breaks open. Soil rot can invade either through wounds or through uninjured skin, and usually occurs during wet periods and on moist soils where the plants cover the ground or when the fruit has been splashed by rain. Avoid poorly drained soil, use a good mulch and use varieties proper for staking.

Sunscald: During hot, dry weather green tomatoes may develop sunscald. It is especially common on plants that have lost their foliage from other diseases. The difficulty is common in the Southwest. Symptoms, especially on young fruits, include a yellow or white patch on the side of the fruit toward the sun, which may remain yellow or turn blistery and later flatten to a large, gray white spot with a very thin paperlike surface. It is very likely that this spot will later become the site of a fungus infection. To control, protect plants from defoliation and from wilt diseases and leaf spot.

If excessive loss of protective foliage occurs, put a light covering of straw over the fruit clusters.

Tobacco mosaic virus: Also called tomato virus, it is found everywhere and infects many members of the Nightshade family. The green strain causes light and dark green mottling of the foliage, curling and slight malformation of the leaflets. If seedlings or young plants are infected, mature plants may be stunted, but later attacks do not reduce the size of the plant, especially if they do not occur until the fruiting stage. Yellow strains cause yellow mottling of the leaves and sometimes of stems and fruit, as well as curling, distortion and dwarfing of the foliage. Control is advisable, especially since an infected plant is susceptible to attack by a second virus.

The tobacco virus is usually transmitted by first handling an infected plant and then a healthy one, or even by brushing against first one then the other. Careful handling is important—wash your hands in soap and water or milk if you are handling more than one plant. Greenhouse plants are most susceptible to the virus since they are so frequently handled. A few insects, such as the potato aphid, also transmit the virus from plant to plant. The virus will live for several years in dried stems and leaves, in greenhouses and in soil, especially when one tomato crop is planted right after another in a warm climate. Garden soil does not seem to be the source of much infection, but seedlings intended for garden planting are often infected if grown in or near a greenhouse where the disease is present. The carryover may be due to aphids. Eliminate jimsonweed, nightshade, bittersweet, matrimony vine, ground cherry, and horse nettle growing near your tomato patch. Mosaic virus is present to some extent in practically all cigar, cigarette and pipe tobaccos, so smokers are very likely to carry the virus on their hands.

To control or at least reduce losses from tobacco mosaic, remove all infected plants among the seedlings and spray with milk any tomato seedlings suspected of contracting the disease. For full protection, repeat at least once. Burn infected plants or place in a good, hot compost heap. Sterilize soil in which seedlings are grown, especially when a new crop is put in where an old crop has recently been dug up.

Verticillium wilt: This is a problem in the West, some of the north central states and in the Northeast. Unless the soil is pasteurized regularly, it can also invade greenhouses. Infected plants show a slight wilting at the shoot tips during the day and yellowing of the older leaves. Eventually the crown of the plant loses all its leaves, the higher stem leaves look dull and the leaflets curl. Finally, only the leaves near the tips of the branches are alive, and if the plant fruits, the tomatoes are very small and unattractive. When the leaves have been infected, they show yellow areas at their margins in a V design. Eventually this tissue dies and the leaves drop off, but the fungus may have already invaded the vascular system and may be traveling to infect the whole plant. As with fusarium wilt, the best control is to locate seedbeds on soil that is free from the fungus. Use clean, pasteurized soil in flats, hotbeds, cold frames, and peat pots.

Harvesting: During the summer, tomato vines should provide a steady supply of fresh fruit for family use. Later, when the crop reaches its peak, you will probably want to preserve much of it for future use. Tomatoes and tomato juice can be preserved in a num-

ber of ways and frozen or canned. Whichever way you choose, you can plant varieties of tomatoes bred especially for your purpose.

After most of the tomatoes have been gathered, and before the first killing frost, you will find a large number of green tomatoes on the vines. This crop should be gathered and stored. Smaller tomatoes can be used for making relishes and a number of other dishes. Larger tomatoes may be wrapped individually in newspaper and placed about three layers deep in open boxes or crates to store in any warm place. The tomatoes will ripen without the aid of light.

You might want to continue your growing season indoors. For tips on raising tomatoes in the house, *see* FRUITS, GROWING INDOORS.

Varieties: There are dozens of varieties to choose from—and many more not available to the home gardener. Your choice of varieties will depend on what you want from your plants and what varieties grow best in your region. In a locality with a relatively early fall frost and short growing season, select a variety developed for early maturation. Such short-season varieties include Cold Set, Fordhook Hybrid, Highlander Spring Giant, and Sub-Arctic. There are tomato varieties available for slicing, special ones developed for canning and freezing, others that make good catsups and sauce. Special varieties such as cherry tomatoes or climbing tomatoes are also available. Varieties with an especially high content of vitamins C (Doublerich) and A (Caro-Red) have been developed.

Many choices are simply a matter of taste, and if you're just beginning to grow tomatoes, you may want to order seed from several varieties to decide which is your favorite. Then, too, if you have enough room you can plant a number of varieties for different uses, and also early-, middle- and late-maturing varieties so you can enjoy tomatoes throughout the summer. In general, avoid varieties developed for commercial use; these have thicker skins, are good shippers or all ripen at once—characteristics desirable for the commercial grower but out of place in the home garden.

Old varieties are available and new garden hybrids are being developed constantly. Many of the newer varieties are resistant to tomato diseases—an important factor if these diseases are a problem in your area. Consult your county agent for recommended varieties locally.

TOPDRESSING

Topdressing is the application of compost, lime, manure, and fertilizers to the surface of the soil. Usually the material is raked into the ground around growing plants and along rows. *See also* COMPOSTING, FERTILIZER.

TOPIARY

Topiary is the art of pruning and training vines, shrubs and trees into ornamental shapes, such as geometric designs or animal or human figures. The art was practiced by the Romans, but examples of topiary are not often seen today, except perhaps in formal estate gardens. In this country the best subjects for topiary work are arborvitae, privet and yew, though training vines (English ivy, hoya) on decorative wire supports is gaining much favor.

TOPSOIL   *See* SOIL

TORCH LILY   *See* KNIPHOFIA

TORREYA

Three of these handsome evergreen trees are grown in parts of the United States. They are relatives of the yew. The stinking cedar (*T. taxifolia*) is hardy only in the Deep South and lower California. It grows about 40 feet tall, and its shiny dark green, narrow leaves have a disagreeable odor when crushed. *T. nucifera* is somewhat taller and hardy throughout most of the country. The biggest one, *T. californica*,

The seldom-grown Florida torreya does best in shady, sheltered spots where the soil is loamy and very moist.

the California nutmeg, grows as high as 70 feet and has approximately the same hardiness range as the stinking cedar. All of them have single-seeded green or purple fruits, and do well in medium-fertile, reasonably moist soils if mulched.

TOUCH-ME-NOT *See* IMPATIENS

TOWEL GOURD *See* LUFFA

TOYON *(Heteromeles arbutifolia)*

This lovely shrub, sometimes called the Christmasberry or California holly, grows ten to 15 feet high with leathery, pointed leaves. The tiny white flowers are borne in heavy panicles in summer, followed by bright red or, occasionally, yellow berries. Branches are often used for holiday decorations. It is hardy from the Deep South to central California and may be increased by seed, layering or cuttings. Toyon prefers a sunny spot in a well-drained, loamy soil.

TRACE ELEMENTS

Chemical elements necessary to plants in small amounts are called trace elements. Soil scientists like to call these elements micronutrients.

In all, there are 16 elements known to be essential to plants if they are to grow and reproduce. They are carbon, hydrogen, oxygen, nitrogen, phosphorus, potassium, sulfur, calcium, magnesium, boron, manganese, iron, copper, molybdenum, zinc, and chlorine. Of these, all but carbon, hydrogen and oxygen must be provided through the medium of the soil. Of the soilborne plant nutrients, three—nitrogen, phosphorus and potassium—are necessary in substantial amounts, while the remaining ten are necessary in small amounts, leading to their respective classifications as major or macronutrients and as micronutrients.

Animals require all of the essential elements required by plants except boron. They also need sodium, cobalt, selenium, and iodine. Plants will take up these latter elements if they are present in the soil. If they are not available to the plants, they must be provided to grazing animals through feed supplements.

While it is important that the micronutrients be present and available in the soil, they must not be overabundant. An excessive quantity of any micronutrient brings a host of toxic conditions in plants and sicknesses in animals and people.

Scientists do not know much about how trace elements work. They do know that a soil rich in organic matter seems to supply plants with adequate amounts of most trace elements (exceptions are copper and manganese on some heavy peat and muck soils). They also know that if a trace element *is* deficient, a small amount is all that's necessary to correct the soil balance. On cropland well fertilized with manure and with a high organic matter content, one may never run into deficiencies of trace elements.

Unfortunately, years of poor farming practices have taken their toll. Although most soils contained a sufficient supply of these elements to sustain good plant growth, intensive cropping, erosion, fertilization with chemical fertilizers, and the replacement of manure-producing animals with machinery have caused widespread deficiencies to occur.

Natural Sources: Adding trace minerals in chemical forms such as borax, manganese sulfate, zinc sulfate, and the like can be highly dangerous. It is easy to use too much; more than an ounce of molybdenum to the acre, for instance, will make plants so toxic they will poison animals eating them. In some soils, only 20 pounds of boron per acre can ruin a potato crop. Each species of plant has its own requirements and tolerances.

Likewise, a tiny bit too much of one element can make it "displace" another. Some elements work best in a certain balance with others. Soil scientists do not yet understand completely how this balance works. For example, cobalt must have copper and iron pres-

PRINCIPAL TRACE ELEMENTS

Mineral	Region of Deficiency	Deficiency Symptoms	Accumulator Plants and Sources
Boron	Widespread	Dwarfing, heart rot, corking, stem cracking, and discoloration in plants	Melon Sweet clover Vetch Agricultural frit Granite dust
Calcium	Acidic soils in humid regions	Blackheart, internal tip burn, blossom-end rot, and cavities in plants	Bone meal Calcite Gypsum Limestone
Chlorine	Very rarely deficient	Wilting of top growth, stubby roots in plants	All green plants Rainwater
Copper	Atlantic coast states	Poor growth, dwarfing of tomatoes, dieback of citrus trees in plants; paralysis, anemia, falling in animals	Bromegrass Dandelion Kentucky bluegrass Redtop Spinach Tobacco Agricultural frit Sawdust
Iron	Southeast	Chlorosis in plants; anemia, salt sickness in animals	All green plants

Mineral	Region of Deficiency	Deficiency Symptoms	Accumulator Plants and Sources
Magnesium	Acidic, sandy soils	Mottling of flowers and leaves, blotching of fruit in plants	All green plants Dolomite Limestone Talc
Manganese	Many varied soils	Poor growth, chlorosis and poor leaf color in plants; poor milk production and deformity in animals	Alfalfa Bromegrass Carrot top Redtop Agricultural frit Leaf mold
Molybdenum	Many varied soils	Necrosis of leaf edges in plants	Alfalfa Vetch Agricultural frit Phosphate rock
Sulfur	Very rarely deficient	Necrosis of leaves, slowed growth rate in plants	Cabbage Legumes Gypsum Manure Plant matter
Zinc	West Coast and South	Poor fruiting, dieback in plants; hair loss, skin thickening in animals	Corn Ragweed Vetch Agricultural frit Manure

ent if it is to prevent certain cattle ailments. In another instance, boron and calcium must be in a proper balance for both to work best.

In addition, chemical trace-mineral ferti- lizers leach out rapidly and can "burn" plants because they are overconcentrated. They may react chemically with soil compounds to become fixed and unavailable to plants. These effects do not occur with organic matter, rock fertilizers or salts of trace elements that have been fused with glass and applied to soils. These last materials are available in many trace element forms and are sold as "agricultural frits" or "glasses."

The most reliable method for assuring an adequate supply of micronutrients is by thorough organic fertilization. Compost, mulch, leaf mold, natural ground rock fertilizers, and lime help provide a complete, balanced ration of both major and minor nutrients. The mineral rocks contain micronutrients that will be released in the soil as the rock particles decompose. Other good sources are seaweed and fish fertilizers, deep-rooted weeds that bring up minerals from deep in the subsoil, and sewage sludge. Be sure that the sludge you plan to use has been tested for heavy metals and that it has low concentrations of these dangerous elements; it is otherwise safe.

Besides supplying trace elements themselves, these materials upon decomposition release acids that make elements already present in the soil more available to plants.

Some plants—called accumulator plants—have the ability to accumulate trace minerals. See the accompanying chart for some examples.

See also entries for individual elements, FERTILIZER, SOIL DEFICIENCIES.

TRADESCANTIA

This is a common house and greenhouse plant, whose trailing habit and ability to grow under adverse conditions make it a good candidate for hanging baskets. Most species come from tropical America, although one is native to North America. Flowers are tiny and white, and the stemless leaves may be green, green and white, or blue green. Some species have leaves with purple undersides.

An all-purpose soil is used and allowed to dry between applications of water. An east, west or lightly shaded southern exposure can be utilized. Propagation is by stem tip cuttings.

Good species include giant white inch plant (*T. albiflora* cv. 'Albovittata'), wandering Jew (*T. fluminensis*) and common spiderwort (*T. virginiana*). The last is native and hardy over much of the United States.

TRAILING ARBUTUS
(*Epigaea repens*)

Sometimes called mayflower or ground laurel, trailing arbutus is one of the most fragrant of all wild flowers. It is a prostrate, hardy evergreen plant of the Heath family with tiny pink or white blooms appearing in spring. It must have an extremely acid soil containing lots of leaf mold. Perfect drainage and shade are also vital. It cannot be emphasized too strongly that this plant should never be dug from the wild, and that the flowers should never be picked from wild plants. It has all but disappeared from many areas, and is on the preservation lists of a number of states. It almost inevitably dies out when transplanted from its native habitat to the garden. Buy plants from wild flower nurseries, or if you are feeling ambitious, very carefully gather seeds from wild colonies. Sow them in sphagnum moss.

TRAINING PLANTS
See BONSAI, ESPALIER, PINCHING, PRUNING

TRANSPIRATION

Transpiration is not simple evaporation of water, but a complex process whereby moisture is "exhaled" from the leaves of plants. The water needs of the plant, its stage of growth and the weather all affect the rate of transpiration. It has a very direct effect on wilting and growth. Some plants have special mechanisms for controlling transpiration. The resurrection plant, for example, curls up into a tight ball to reduce moisture loss during dry periods.

See also LEAVES.

TRANSPLANTING

When seedlings are about a half-inch high or have their true leaves (those resembling the species, instead of the ones known as "seed leaves" which appear first), they have reached the proper stage for transplanting to other containers.

The containers for transplanting purposes are practically the same as those used for sowing. Select a somewhat richer potting mixture, so that the seedlings will have plenty of available plant food. Dampen the soil and fill the containers loosely. Smooth it off and press it down with a flat board. With a small round stick, make holes that are wide and deep enough to accommodate the seedling roots. Lift the seedlings carefully from their old flat, hold them in your fingers at the proper depth in the hole, and with the other hand press the soil firmly around the roots. The proper depth is one at which the roots are thoroughly covered and the plant supported. Air spaces around the roots are fatal. Those fine feeder roots which do not come in close contact with the soil will

dry out and the seedling will die for lack of food. Water thoroughly and shade from direct sun until the seedlings begin active growth.

Plants which are grown in the house are usually too tender to transplant directly into the garden. They must be "hardened off"; that is, gradually accustomed to outdoor conditions, so that there will not be any shock to check active growth. If they are very tender, they may be placed for a week or two in the hotbed or cold frame. Always transplant, if possible, on a damp, cloudy day.

The soil in your seedbed must be well fertilized and finely raked. Again, make small holes, deep enough to care for the seedling's roots without bending them up. Remove the plants from the cold frame with a ball of earth at the roots and trim off any broken roots. Insert the seedlings in the hole and firm the earth around the roots as well as around the stem. Both thumbs can be used to press the soil down properly. This eliminates air pockets around the roots.

In planting all kinds of plants, be sure to set the stock not more than an inch deeper than it grew in the nursery. This can be determined by the soil ring around the stems, and there is usually a difference in color above and below the old ground line.

Keep topsoil and subsoil in separate piles. Loosen the earth at the bottom of the hole and if the subsoil is very poor, dig deeper and add a layer of well-rotted manure or compost. Cover this over with some good loam so that the manure will not burn the roots, and then set in the tree or shrub. If the ground is very dry, fill the holes with water and allow it to drain away before planting. Fill in as much topsoil as possible around the roots and then finish off with the poorer soil, which can be enriched later with a topdressing of fertilizer. Tamp down the earth around the plant so that no air pockets are left, and water again. A shallow depression around each specimen will hold water until the roots take a firm hold. Later fill in with good soil, and keep it loose to hold the moisture in the ground.

After the tree or shrub is planted, it must be pruned at once, so that the shortened roots will be able to provide adequately for the top growth. Evergreens and other plants which are received with a large solid ball of earth in burlap bags need no pruning, but all deciduous stock (trees which lose their leaves in winter) must have the branches cut back at least 50 percent. Prune weak shoots first, then thin out those badly placed and shorten the others. Do not clip them all back to the same length, as this makes an ugly-looking tree or bush.

Tall trees and shrubs may need to be staked until they are well established. The best way is "guying," that is, placing three stakes in the form of a triangle around the tree, about eight feet from the trunk. Fasten three strands of heavy twine or wire, enclosed in a piece of rubber hose, around the trunk, about five feet from the ground. Run these to the stakes, leaving a little slack to allow for some play of the tree during a heavy wind. Wrap the thin-barked trees with burlap from the ground to the first limb to prevent sunscald.

If for any reason you are moving established trees or shrubs, the method will vary somewhat according to the plant and the season. If the specimens are large, have them moved by professionals. The main thing is never to let the roots be exposed to either sun or air. Tiny root hairs through which the specimens feed are very sensitive and cannot stand exposure. Plants moved with a ball of earth large enough to include most of the roots will suffer little shock on transplanting. Evergreens, especially, should have the additional protec-

tion of burlap wrapped around this earth ball. This keeps their roots safe from dry air and wind.

Water copiously before and after transplanting. A light mulch around newly planted stock will help to keep moisture in the soil so that the dormant (inactive) plants may be well nourished.

See also COLD FRAME, SEEDS AND SEEDLINGS, VEGETABLE GARDENING.

TRANSVAAL DAISIES
See GERBERA

TRAPS
See GOPHER, INSECT CONTROL, MOLE

TREASURE FLOWER
See GAZANIA

TREE

A vast number of ornamental varieties of trees have been developed for landscaping, but this should not blind one to the possibility of using fruit and nut trees in their stead. Most fruit trees put on a beautiful display of pastel flowers in spring, and many nut trees display brilliant foliage in fall. Both produce crops that can be put to good use.

Fruit Trees: In addition to the more popular fruit trees, there are a number of lesser known species (sometimes called "minor fruits") from which you can choose.

The persimmon (*Diospyros virginiana*) produces plump orange fruit, ripening in late fall *after* frost. This is an attractive medium-sized shade tree of pyramidal habit while young, becoming round-headed as it ages. The foliage looks something like that of the magnolia.

Many species of *Prunus* are valuable in the home landscape. Although susceptible to climatic extremes, the picturesque Asiatic Ansu apricot (*P. armeniaca* cv. 'Ansu') is worth consideration. Its plump deep pink flower buds are among the first to open and the small, red-cheeked apricots follow in summer. Several trees are necessary to insure proper pollination.

Not to be overlooked, either, is the wild plum (*P. americana*), a native species occurring in thickets along fencerows and woodland margins. It dominates the early-spring landscape with its foamy, honey-scented white blossoms, and provides a rich harvest of edible red plums in the fall.

Small red plums—cherrylike in size, shape and coloring—are the unusual fruits of the hortulan plum (*P. hortulana*), a single-trunked species of the central Midwest. Too tart in flavor to be eaten raw, the fruit is used to make jellies.

Mulberries (*Morus*) are often avoided because of the litter resulting from the fallen fruits and the mess left behind by berry-eating birds. Still, the mulberry is a valuable tree. Some forms such as the everbearing mulberry produce berries of excellent flavor, and most species are fast-growing, round-headed trees with dense, bright green leaves.

The downy hawthorn (*Crataegus mollis*) is the earliest flowering (early May) and one of the tallest of the hawthorns. Its fruits often reach an inch in diameter.

Another group of small trees contributing generously to the beauty and bounty of the landscape is the Juneberry or serviceberry genus (*Amelanchier*). They offer misty white flowers in early spring, large and often sur-prisingly sweet fruits in June and orange to terra-cotta and gold foliage in the fall. *A. laevis* is a small, multiple-trunked tree, and *A.* x *grandiflora* has a picturesque spreading growth habit and large white flowers in loose pendulous racemes.

Flowering Trees: Among the larger shade trees are a few with flowers so lovely that they are considered some of the handsomest ornamentals. The sweet or Spanish chestnut (*Castanea sativa*) has gorgeous white blossoms faintly tinged with red and is a favorite street tree in Paris. Locust (*Robinia*), tulip poplar (*Liriodendron Tulipifera*) and the Japanese pagoda tree (*Sophora japonica*) are all good shade trees with conspicuous flowers.

Many of the smaller trees, however, are more beautiful still and in many cases more suitable for the average yard. One of the best known is Japanese cherries (*Prunus yedoensis*), known as Yoshino. The flowers are delicate pink or white, fragrant, and appear in early spring. *Prunus subhirtella,* often the first to bloom, is a large treelike bush, 15 feet or more in height and as much across, literally covered with thousands of tiny soft rose pink flowers. A fine form of this so-called rosebud cherry is the weeping or pendulous type; another variety blooms in the autumn, in late October or early November. The double-flowered forms sometimes bloom a few days later than *P. yedoensis.*

Crab apple species vary in size, color of flower and fruit, and season of flower and fruit. Sargent's crab apple (*Malus Sargentii*) is very slow growing, and one of the best for a small yard. It seldom reaches a height of more than eight feet with a canopy approximately 12 feet in diameter when mature. The blooms are pure white, and the fruits dark crimson with a soft purplish bloom. The showy crab apple (*M. flo-*

ribunda) and its many forms are among the first to blossom. The flowers are rose fading to white, borne on a large treelike bush with wide-spreading branches. Fruits are red or yellow red. The carmine crab (*M.* x *atrosanguinea*) has rose purple flowers. Eley crab (*M. pur-purea* cv. 'Eleyi') has wine red flowers and foliage that is deep purple. The Bechtel crab (*M. ioensis* cv. 'Plena') has double white or rose-tinted blooms.

The double-flowering peaches flower early and stay in blossom longer than any other flowering fruit trees. The flowers occur in red, pink, white, and occasionally striped forms, with foliage ranging from pale green to purple. They bloom the third year and reach a height of eight to ten feet. Seedlings sprout from the fruits that drop on the ground, and may produce single flowers instead of double.

The apricot has such beautiful pink yellow flowers that it is widely cultivated in spite of tenderness. It blooms very early in the spring but often does not set fruit in the North.

Planting: Trees with delicate roots should be transplanted only in the spring. These include mountain ash, beech, birch, grafted cherry, dogwood, magnolia, and yellowwood.

Hardy varieties may be planted in the fall as well as in the spring. In the fall, the best months are September and October. March and April are the best months for spring planting. Among these are the elm, linden, pin oak, the Norway, silver, and red maples, most fruit trees, and most evergreens.

Large trees can be transplanted successfully with proper equipment, if you are willing to pay the added cost of handling the larger trees and have an experienced helper on hand, but it is better to use small specimens. Small trees can be transplanted more easily and will

Before planting a bare-rooted tree, prune away any broken or long roots and plunge the pruned root mass into a slurry of water, compost and seaweed concentrate.

adjust themselves more quickly to their new environment than large trees. A tree must build up its root system to balance the top before it will continue to grow. For example, a small tree, six to eight feet tall, will adjust itself more quickly than a tree 16 to 18 feet tall. At the end of four or five years the eight-foot tree probably will be as tall as the 16-foot tree and more vigorous. For this reason, nursery-grown trees are prepared for transplanting by pruning both the roots and tops.

Transplanting invariably involves injury and shock to the tree. It is your job to keep these effects to a minimum. Trim all injured roots and limbs, but keep the tree in balance while doing so, trimming the roots to keep their volume and extent in line with the branch system—and vice versa. Do not cut back the central leader of the tree.

Deciduous trees may be collected and moved with bare roots. Preserve as much of the root system in digging as possible. As soon as the tree is dug, wrap the roots with wet burlap to protect it until planting.

Evergreens should be moved with a ball of dirt, the ball wrapped in burlap and tied securely. The limbs should be pulled together in a bunch and tied to keep them from breaking as the tree is handled.

Trees should be set approximately the same depth or slightly deeper than they grew in the field or nursery. Spread out the roots of deciduous trees and work good soil in around them to eliminate air pockets. As soil is added it should be tamped with the feet. When the hole is about three-fourths full, add water until the soil is thoroughly soaked. After the water has been absorbed, the remainder of the soil should be added. Dish the soil slightly toward the center to bring water around the trunk.

Hardwood trees, such as the sugar maple, red oak and dogwood, are subject to sunscalding which results in the bark cracking. This is common at the base of the tree. Wrapping the trunk when the tree is planted will prevent this type of injury. Burlap, cut into six-inch strips, or specially prepared wrapping paper can be used. The trunk should be wrapped up into the branches. The wrapping may be left on until it falls off.

Stake the transplanted tree to prevent it from being whipped around by strong winds. One stake may be used and the tree trunk tied to it with some material that will not injure the tree. Wire, with an old bicycle tire between it and the trunk, is good. A triangle of three stakes also can be used with ties from each stake to hold the trunk of the tree. If the tree is likely to be damaged by animals, a wire enclosure should be provided around the stakes.

See also entries for individual trees, FRUIT TREES, NUT TREES.

TREE ASTER   (*Olearia*)

About 20 species of tree asters are grown in the Far West and Deep South. Some are bushy shrubs four to eight feet high, while other species grow as small trees up to 20 feet. *O. Haastii* is a little hardier than most and grows about six feet tall, with small clusters of white flowers that resemble asters. Other species have panicles of showy lavender blooms. They do well in any medium-fertile garden soil and are increased by seed or cuttings of half-ripe wood.

TREE MALLOW   *See* LAVATERA

TREE-OF-HEAVEN
See AILANTHUS

TREE PERCHERS   *See* EPIPHYTE

TREE STUMP
See STUMP REMOVAL

TRELLIS

A trellis is an open, wooden structure or latticework frame used as a screen or support for climbing plants and vines. A simple trellis is composed of light strips of wood or metal joined vertically and horizontally to a framework of heavier wood, with the space between the parallel laths about equal in size to the strips themselves.

More complex and ornate patterns such as diamond-, oval- and circular-shaped panels have been developed. These are decorative trellises and are intended to be kept free of heavy vines and other covering plants. This ornate form of trellising was once used in the stately, elegant gardens of the French aristocracy. However, almost nothing could be more out of place in the average American garden. The name trellis is now more commonly given to the wires on which espalier or other trained fruits are attached.

When used to support ivy, grapevines or flowering plants such as roses, the trellis is designed to be strictly utilitarian and inconspicuous so as not to detract from the beauty of the plant. The coloring of the trellis should also be subdued rather than striking in order to blend with the plant's coloring.

A trellis can also be used in the construction of an arbor.

TRENCHING

Trenching might be called a "soil exchange" process. Its aim is to exchange enriched surface soil with soil from lower depths. This puts fertile soil down deep, and brings about better structure, drainage and root development.

Usually a trench is dug 12 to 18 inches deep, and the soil removed from it is hauled to the other end of the area to be trenched. Then a layer half as deep is taken off from the next strip, enriched with rotted manure, compost, rock fertilizers, and other organic materials, and dumped into the first trench. This is then filled to its original level with the remaining soil from the lower part of the second trench.

This process is repeated until the last strip is reached, and this is filled with the soil from the first trench. Some gardeners bring up an inch or so of the subsoil in each trench and mix it thoroughly with the upper soil, thus making their soil fertile and friable to a greater depth each time they trench it.

Trenching is also the term applied to one way of planting asparagus. *See* ASPARAGUS.

TRICHOGRAMMA

The trichogramma is a tiny wasp parasite of many garden pests. Its eggs are commercially available for use by gardeners.

The female trichogramma lays her eggs inside the eggs of other insects by means of a pointed ovipositor. The young parasites hatch within the egg, eating up the contents and thereby preventing one more potential pest from entering the world. Among the garden and orchard enemies vulnerable to the trichogramma are the corn earworm, corn borer, cabbage looper, codling moth, pecan nut casebearer, greenhouse leaf tiers, cabbage worm, and tomato hornworm. The wasps have been especially valuable in helping organic apple growers to produce worm-free harvests.

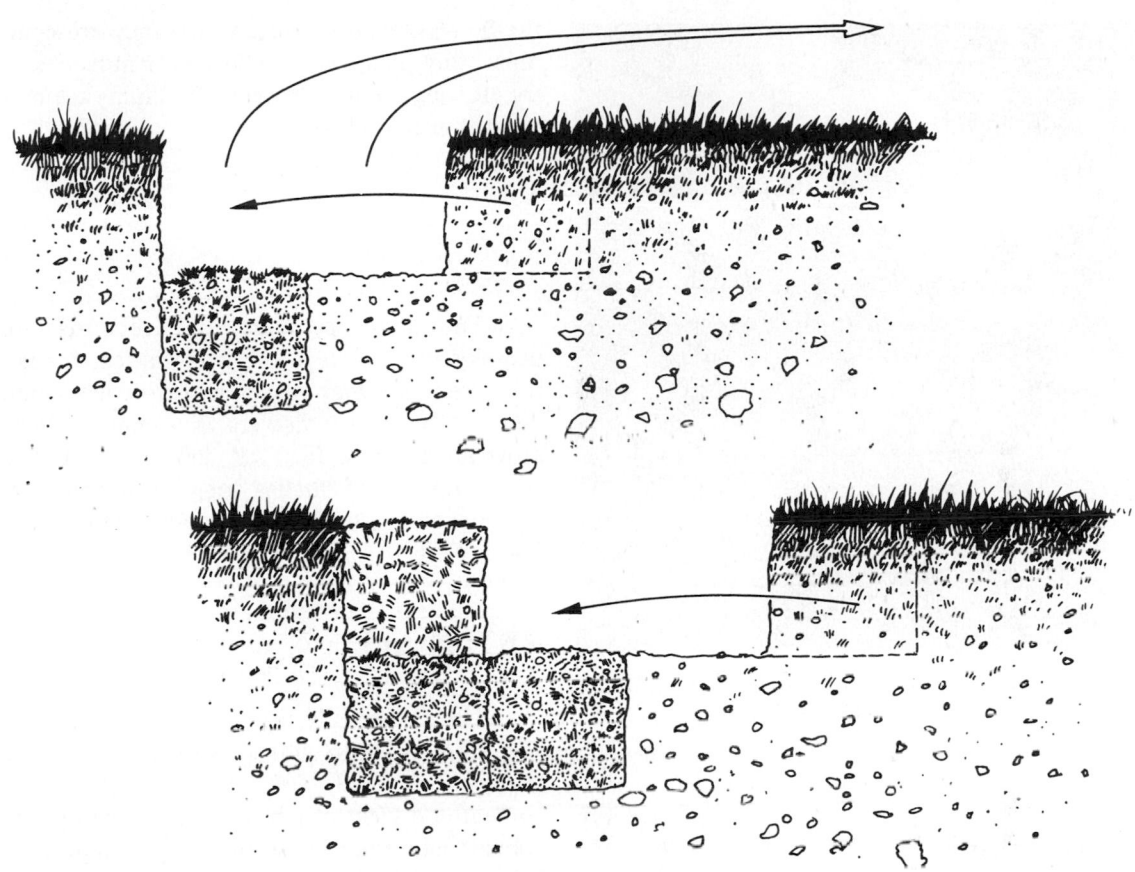

Trenching or "soil exchange" involves layering rich topsoil with poorer, heavier subsoil.

TRICHOSPORUM
See AESCHYNANTHUS

TRILLIUM

The trilliums or wake-robins are hardy perennials native to North America and are very well suited to the wild garden. They bloom in early spring, the flower stalks rising from heavy rootstocks characteristic of the Lily family to which they belong. Three-leaved stalks and three-petaled flowers distinguish the group. Sow the seed in a mixture of sand and acid peat in the cold frame and transplant to shady spots with a similar soil and ample moisture. Seeds require the cold of winter to break their dormancy. The roots can be divided in late fall or early spring.

The snow trillium (*T. nivale*) grows about six inches high with white flowers, while the purple trillium or squawroot (*T. erectum*)

Easily grown from seed, Trillium grandiflorum *has very large and stunning white flowers.*

is a foot tall with pink or purplish, disagreeably scented blooms. Toadshade (*T. sessile*) also grows a foot tall and has green or purple flowers. The hardy and very showy white trillium (*T. grandiflorum*) grows up to 18 inches tall and has large blooms that turn pale pink.

Though equally showy, the painted trillium (*T. undulatum*), which has beautiful crimson-striped white flowers, is far more exacting in its cultural requirements than the others. It demands a very acid soil in cool shade and perfect drainage. Try growing the others before attempting this species.

There are many other species and forms of trilliums, some hardy only in the South. As with many other wild flowers, gardeners should avoid digging trilliums from the wild or picking the flowers, even in areas where they are common. Buy plants from wild flower nurseries or try growing them from seed. Trilliums are best planted in colonies.

TRIOSTEUM

The horse gentians or feverworts are occasionally grown in the wild garden, though they are somewhat weedy and produce small, dull red or brown flowers in summer. They grow about three feet tall and have stalkless leaves up to ten inches long. Propagate by division and give them a woodsy, moist soil.

TRITICALE

The first totally man-made grain, triticale is a cross between wheat (*Triticum*) and rye (*Secale*). Triticale combines the high protein content and yield of wheat with the high lysine content and ruggedness of rye. Varieties are being developed that are adapted to climates unfavorable for wheat. Check with your state agricultural extension service to find out what varieties of triticale are recommended for your area.

Planting and Culture: Culture and seeding for triticale is very similar to that of wheat. Plant triticale as early in the spring as is practical for your area, and prepare your soil in the same way that you would for wheat. Do not plant triticale after the last week in May, and for silage plant before May 10. Seed at 60 to 100 pounds per acre, depending on your area and moisture situation, or just plant 100 percent of your normal wheat rate.

Fertilizer requirements are similar to those for wheat, except that triticale needs heavier fertilization for best results. It can stand heavier applications of manure and other nitrogen sources since it is not as susceptible to lodging as wheat. However, weeds are more of a problem, since triticale is slower growing than wheat. If possible, plant on clean ground that was in a heavily cultivated crop the previous year.

There are winter varieties of triticale available. To plant, seed at the same rate as winter wheat and observe Hessian fly planting dates. Fertilize heavier than winter wheat. If you graze your wheat, you can follow the same practice with triticale, and it is said to offer particularly heavy grazing in the spring. Triticale also makes good hay when seeded in old stands of alfalfa. Cut for the first time when the grain heads begin to turn down and for the second when the alfalfa is ready for cutting.

Harvesting: Winter wheat harvest will be about a week ahead of the harvesting date for a fall-planted crop of triticale. Likewise, the harvesting date for spring-planted triticale is also a week after the harvesting time for spring wheat. In any case, triticale should be at least four inches high if harvested for hay or silage to obtain best regrowth. Dry triticale harvests easily. If you are harvesting by hand, proceed as you would if harvesting wheat. If using a combine, slow the forward speed and cylinder down a bit, use less air and open the concaves up more than for wheat. Swathing is recommended.

There is little difference between triticale and wheat in cooking, and triticale can be substituted in recipes calling for that grain. Triticale, however, has a much higher protein content than does wheat.

See also WHEAT.

TRITICUM   *See* WHEAT

TRITONIA

These South African bulbs are often called montbretias or blazing stars. The beautiful yellow or orange flowers are borne on spikes two to three feet tall in summer. There are many named varieties that have blooms in varying shades from peach and bronze gold to purple. All have narrow, sword-shaped leaves.

The corms are planted about three inches deep and five inches apart when the weather has warmed up. South of Pennsylvania they are hardy without protection, and north of this they can sometimes be carried over the winter in the garden by mulching with strawy manure before the ground freezes hard. But usually it is safer to take them up and store them in a cool cellar. Tritonias like a fertile, friable soil with good drainage, and light shade. Work in a good feeding of well-rotted manure and bone meal before planting, and water well in dry weather.

T. crocata grows only a foot tall and is good for the front of a border. It can also be forced for winter bloom indoors.

TROLLIUS

Also called globeflower, these low perennial herbs of the Buttercup family have showy, frequently double, orange or yellow flowers that bloom in spring and early summer. The leaves are dark, bronzy green.

The species most planted in gardens is *T. europaeus* whose flowers have a ball-like appearance. The variety Golden Nugget grows to 1½ feet, and has large golden flowers. Orange Ball has large orange yellow flowers. All of these cultivars make fine cut flowers and bloom in May and June. Dwarf globeflower (*T. japonica*) is a fine rockery plant for a moist location and grows only about six inches high. Fortune is a favorite cultivar.

Trolliuses require a moist soil and thrive when planted in swampy parts of a rock garden, in wet beds or on margins of ponds and streams. In the border, give them a rich, humusy soil in partial shade. Seed requires cold temperatures to break dormancy and should be sown outdoors in a loamy soil in a shady location in September or April. In full sun they will need frequent watering.

Once these conditions are met, they will bloom for years with little additional maintenance. The plants are propagated either by seed or by division of the thickened, fibrous roots. Clumps need to be lifted, divided and replanted only every four to five years. This can be done in spring or early fall.

TRUMPET CREEPER
(*Campsis radicans*)

With its many aerial rootlets, this vigorous deciduous vine can climb as high as 30 feet, quickly covering unsightly wood or stone buildings. It has hairy leaves and showy red or orange, funnel-shaped flowers that bloom throughout the spring and early summer. A fairly hardy species that tolerates city conditions, the American trumpet creeper prefers a rich soil and full sun.

The Chinese trumpet creeper (*C. grandiflora*) does not grow as high, but its scarlet blooms are bigger and more showy. This species blooms in late summer and is hardy only in the South and along the Pacific coast. Both are easy to increase by seed, cuttings or layering.

TUBER

Tubers are short, thick, fleshy stems, usually underground, and bearing buds or "eyes." The potato and Jerusalem artichoke are common examples. Tubers should not be confused with tuberous roots, such as are found in dahlias and are merely swollen, food-storing roots. A few plants have tubers borne on their aboveground parts.

TUBEROSE   (*Polianthes tuberosa*)

The tuberose is one of the most fragrant of all summer garden flowers. A tender bulb of the Amaryllis family, it bears gorgeous spikes of waxy white blooms on three- to four-foot stems. There are double and single forms, all with bright green basal leaves up to 18 inches long. Single Mexican and the later-blooming Pearl are popular varieties.

As soon as all danger of frost is past, the bulbs can be planted three inches deep and six inches apart in fertile, friable soil and full sun. They can also be started in pots indoors and set out in early June. They grow well in large patio containers planted in multiples of three. Be sure they get ample moisture. In temperate areas the bulbs are taken up before the first frost, and stored at 65 to 70°F. (18.33 to 21.11°C.) for the winter. Propagation is by offsets, which will bloom late the second year.

TUFTED

A plant with many stems growing in close clusters or very tight clumps is said to be tufted. Many grasses as well as some sedums are tufted. Sometimes the plant is very densely tufted, in which case it is called a cushion plant. This tight-growing habit, commonly found in plants that grow in dry or high-altitude locations, helps them to survive by reducing transpiration.

TULIP   (*Tulipa*)

Tulips are bulbous plants which are natives of the Old World, where they occur in an area extending from the Mediterranean region to Japan. There are some 60 species and several thousand horticultural forms. They are doubtless the most popular bulbous garden plants.

Species Tulips: These tulips have been derived from wild species, and generally breed true from seed. Species tulips, also known as botanical tulips, are not generally grown in quantity as are the garden tulips. Most are early flowering and prefer a dry, sunny location. They are planted in groups in the border or rock garden. Among the best species are the dwarf *T. dasystemon* with violet and yellow flowers; lady tulip (*T. Clusiana*) with striped flowers; *T. biflora* with white and yellow flowers; and the many cultivars of *T. Fosteriana*, including Red Emperor or Madam Lefeber with bright red flowers, Gold Beater with golden flowers and Pinkeen with orange flowers.

Garden Tulips: The Turks appear to have been the first to develop the garden tulip,

Flowers of the breeder tulips appear in May and can be recognized by their rounded base and square-edged sepals and petals.

and they spread them over Europe. Since then the Dutch have been the great breeders of tulips. Most garden tulips were derived from innumerable crosses with the species *T. Gesneriana* and *T. suaveolens,* and the thousands of named forms which have since arisen. Garden tulips are divided into groups as follows:

Breeder tulips: These are tall-stemmed tulips which bloom in May. The flowers are distinctive in that they have a rounded base, while the sepals and petals have square ends. The Dutch varieties have oval or cup-shaped flowers mostly in shades of brown, purple, bronze, or red, but the base of the flower is white or yellow, and often stained blue, green or blue black. The English varieties have ball-like flowers, the base of which is yellow or white but not stained with any other color.

Cottage tulips: These are tall-stemmed, May-blooming tulips with self-colored, mostly pointed or rounded sepals and petals. The flowers in general have a square or somewhat rounded base and pointed or rounded tip.

Darwin tulips: These are the tallest of the self-colored May-flowering tulips. They may be recognized by the flower which has a somewhat rectangular base, while the sepals and petals are square-tipped or rounded.

Early tulips: These are the first of the tulips to bloom and follow close behind crocuses. They are chiefly dwarf in habit and may have single or double flowers in a variety of colors. Typical of the early tulips is the Duc van Thol.

Griegii tulips: These tulips have mottled or striped leaves and bloom later than most other types.

Lily-flowered tulips: These are tall-stemmed, May-flowering tulips with the sepals and petals distinctly long-tipped.

Mendel tulips: These are medium-early flowering tulips derived from crossing the Duc van Thol with the Darwin varieties.

Triumph tulips: These are tall, early-flowering tulips, blooming just after the early tulips.

Planting and Culture: In selecting tulips for the garden, the background must be considered. For instance, a yellow tulip would seem to be an intruder in front of a pink-flowered dogwood or a flowering crab apple tree, but would be fine near the violet blue racemes of Japanese wisteria (*Wisteria floribunda*). Matching the flowers of tulips with those of flowering shrubs and trees can be fun.

Tulips seem to be at their best in the garden growing with other plants, such as pansies, bluebells, forget-me-nots, rock cress, lungwort, Jacob's-ladder, English wallflower, bleeding-heart, doronicum, and the often harsh basket-of-gold. But they may also be planted together in groups in a bed or border to produce striking color schemes.

The bulbs grow best in well-drained light loam. The soil should be deep and enriched with plenty of well-rotted manure or compost to insure good plant growth and large flowers over a period of several years. Fertilizers such as bone meal, cow or sheep manure, or compost are excellent dressings. The best time to plant the bulbs is two to four weeks before the ground freezes, from October 1 to November 1; later planting may result in short stems and smaller flowers. Tulips will usually do better and bloom earlier in the sun than in half shade. Large bulbs may be planted deeper than small ones. The ideal depth is from four to six inches, and they should be about four to nine inches apart. If bulbs are planted too deep, they weaken as they push through the soil, but if planted too shallow, they may be heaved out of the soil, or possibly frozen. When setting the bulbs in the soil, give a half twist as though screwing the bulb into the soil; this assures that the base of the bulb is in direct contact with the soil.

Never cut the green leaves at any time; these leaves feed the bulb with new food to be stored for the next season. When the leaves begin to turn yellowish at the base and have a withered appearance, they can be pulled out easily from the soil. The bulbs are then more or less cured and may remain in the ground for at least two more seasons or even a third if the flowers have appeared well the last season.

Pests and Diseases: Tulips are subject to a few diseases. If the blossoms blister with brown or water-soaked spots on the petals, and if the leaves have greenish spots which gradually increase in size, the plants have fire blight. If this disease occurs in your tulips, cut off all the blooms and diseased leaves immediately to prevent its spread to the bulb. If the fungus has invaded the bulb, place it in the compost heap.

Insects such as the green peach or spinach aphid and the narcissus bulb fly may attack tulips grown in soils of low fertility. Another pest which attacks tulips grown in depleted soils is the millipede. The best remedy is to enrich the soil with compost and pulverized rock minerals.

Lifting and Storing Bulbs: Lack of flower development is a sign that the bulbs should be lifted and reset. Lifted bulbs may be reset in a new bed immediately, or they may be stored for the fall planting. Tulip bulbs do not usually last for years in the ground without special care. Left in the ground, they may rot during the summer from too much moisture or be eaten by rodents who love the juicy pulp.

Lifting: The first or second week in June is a good time to remove tulip bulbs from the soil. By this time the late Darwins have finished blooming. If you are too busy at the time, the bulbs may be removed as late as the end of the month. But, the sooner the better, as the stems will be firmer, and there will be less chance of their breaking. Stem and bulb must remain intact for proper curing.

Use a spade to lift the bulbs from the ground. A garden fork does not give the necessary protection during the lift. Insert the spade at least four inches from each tulip stem. Force the spade straight down to a depth of six inches.

Then, gently press down upon the handle, pushing outward, until the ground heaves and the plant moves. Bring the bulb to the surface and carefully shake it free of dirt, taking care not to snap off the stem. The new bulbs need the nourishment stored in the stem now that their soil food supply has been cut off.

Place your stemmed bulbs neatly in a pile until all have been taken up. If it is bright and sunny, protect the tender bulbs with a damp sack or heavy paper. Never expose tulip bulbs to the direct rays of the sun.

Hilling in: After your bulbs have been dug and each variety placed upon a separate pile, remove them to a protected part of your garden. In a vacant spot, dig a trench long and deep enough to accommodate all the bulbs. Carefully lay the bulbs in the trench and, before hilling in, stake or number each variety so you will know which is which when you lift them later.

Cover the bulbs with at least six inches of soil, but allow the green stems to remain exposed to the hot sun. As the sun dries the stalks, the food supply gradually trickles down to the bulbs. There, it is stored for next year's growth.

Removing: In about a week or two, as soon as the stems have turned yellow, remove the bulbs from the trench. Never allow them to remain hilled in more than three weeks, or they will rot. Run your fingers through the loose dirt after lifting, to get all the tiny bulblets that might have broken off. Spread the bulbs out on a flat surface in a heavy shade to dry for about an hour. Then continue removing the bulbs from the stems and casings.

As you begin your work you will notice that the bulbs are encased in a thick, brown pouch of clothlike fiber. Tear this apart, and remove all bulbs found among the different layers. No bulblet is too small to save. Even the tiniest grows to a reasonable size in one year. Besides the parent bulb, you will find as many as four or five bulblets with each stem. These smaller bulbs should be planted separately in the fall.

When the pouch is completely empty, throw it on a pile with the discarded stems. Later, this can be added to your compost heap or mulching material.

As the bulbs are removed from their casings, it is wise to place them immediately in trays specially built for tulip bulbs. These trays are nothing more than large squares with two-inch-high sides, and bottomed with heavy window screening to prevent the loss of tiny bulblets. If you have several different varieties, you might partition off the squares and save room. Some sort of legs, in the form of one-inch blocks should be nailed under each corner to allow a good circulation of air through the moist bulbs.

Don't forget to tag the trays if you have several varieties of tulips. This information will enable you to plant different arrangements in your beds next fall to create striking color effects in spring.

Storing: As soon as you have finished this phase of work, take the bulbs indoors immediately. Set the filled trays in a warm, dry place. The attic floor of your home or garage is excellent. Place the trays on the floor individually. That is, don't pile one on top of the other. And don't worry about the heat concentrating too heavily over the bulbs during the hot summer. It won't hurt them a bit. The hotter it is, the drier the air will remain. Tulip bulbs must be kept completely dry to prevent rotting.

Roll the bulbs back and forth in the trays several times during the first two weeks of curing to prevent moisture from gathering among the bulbs. One turning per week for the following month will finish the job. It is best to allow the bulbs to remain in their trays until planting time.

If your bulbs are bothered by mice, be sure to set traps or tack another sheet of window screening across the tops of the trays. Mice love the taste of tulip bulbs, and can put away quite a few by fall.

See also BULB.

TULIP POPLAR   *See* TULIP TREE
TULIP POPPY   *See* HUNNEMANNIA

TULIP TREE
(*Liriodendron Tulipifera*)

One of the finest lawn trees available, this stately tree of the Magnolia family grows up to 200 feet high, and has curiously shaped leaves and yellow green, orange-banded, tulip-like flowers that bloom in May or June. In several eastern states, it is valued as a honey plant, producing large quantities of dark red honey with a fine distinctive flavor. Also called the tulip poplar, the tree is hardy north to Massachusetts and Wisconsin. It thrives in a rich, moist soil and can be increased by stratified seed and grafting. The white, green-tinged wood is rated a poor choice for the fireplace but is a satisfactory furniture wood.

TUNA   *See* PRICKLY PEAR

TUNG-OIL TREE
(*Aleurites Fordii*)

In this country, the tung-oil tree is grown only in a narrow belt along the Gulf coast and upper Florida. The oil from its seed is used in making paint and varnish. The fruits fall to the ground in autumn and the oil is pressed out after they dry. The tree is of little ornamental value.

TUPELO   *See* NYSSA

TURF

Turf or sod can be cut from any good lawn planting and used to repair poor spots on lawns or laid on steep banks, the edges of paths and similar places. Usually sod is cut in strips about 12 to 15 inches for easy handling. If necessary, these can be kept for a couple of days stacked in shade, face to face. The soil on which the turf is to be laid should be prepared just as it would be for seeding a lawn, and the sod pieces carefully set down with their edges together. Thorough watering, plus rolling or heavy tamping, completes the job. Be sure to fill in any holes or ragged edges with soil. On steep banks, it may be necessary to peg them to prevent the sod from washing down in a heavy rain.

TURKEY

Turkeys can be a profitable sideline for the organic homesteader, particularly if he can grow the green feed on which the birds thrive, and if he can sell them at retail. If not, turkeys still make good eating, and a homesteader can raise a few to dress for table use for the family.

Stand warned, however, that these birds are difficult to raise. Turkeys are highly prone to disease and they are unintelligent. When young, they often starve to death without discovering their feed is right next to them. Mature hens are no smarter. They lay their eggs standing up, killing their unhatched young. The least scare sends turkeys piling into corners where they often suffocate.

Some of the most popular breeds are the White Holland, Bronze, Bourbon Red, and Narragansett. The new, smaller Beltsville turkeys, developed by the Department of Agriculture Research Center at Beltsville, Maryland, are gaining in popularity and find a good market throughout the year. Always buy quality stock from a reputable hatchery or breeder.

Housing: For retail production, start with newly hatched turkeys or "poults." A pen approximately 20 by 20 feet in a barn or poultry house will handle 100 to 150 poults until they are put on range at ten weeks of age. A raised wire porch the same size is necessary to keep the poults off the ground and reduce the danger of the highly infectious, fatal blackhead disease.

A good-sized electric brooder and hoppers for water and feed are other needs. Sand and shavings are usually used for litter in the poultry house. After they are two weeks old, the poults can go outside on the porch in good weather.

Care and Feeding: Grains are fed in addition to starter mash after the birds are two months old. Good commercial feeds for starting are available. Grain rations can be homemade if grains are raised on the homestead, or you can use a commercially made preparation. If the birds' entire lives are spent on wire, they should have fresh green feed, such as rape, oats or ladino clover, brought to them. Alfalfa, lettuce, cabbage, and other greens, less expensive than commercial pellets, can form as much as 25 percent of the ration. This can enable homesteaders to compete in price with commercial growers.

Turkeys on range will eat great quantities of forage, as well as pick up waste grain, weed seed and insects. An acre of good range gen-

An acre of good range can support about 100 turkeys, provided their diet is supplemented with whole corn, commercial feed, and milk or water.

erally supports 100 birds until they are six months old and ready to be slaughtered. Oats and rape make fine pasture for turkeys. For permanent pastures, a good mixture is red, ladino and alsike clover with timothy and Kentucky bluegrass. During the last five weeks before slaughter, the birds need plenty of whole corn to fatten them.

Excess milk from goats or cows can also be used in turkey feed. The liquid is used to moisten the mash. Feeders can be located inside the pen or outside in wooden troughs. Two inches of feeding space per bird is suggested.

Turkeys need water. This can be supplied by having fountains inside the pen or by attaching a water pan to the outside of the pen, allowing it to be more easily filled and cleaned.

Diseases: Turkeys are susceptible to many diseases. The most serious one is blackhead which is hosted by a worm common to chickens. Symptoms are droopiness and yellow droppings. Cage cleanliness and separation of turkeys from chickens help combat the disease. Turkeys housed on a raised sun porch are resistant to the disease. Turkey manure is an excellent fertilizer, so clean up and compost the droppings weekly.

Other diseases to which turkeys are prone include coccidiosis, pullorum, paratyphoid, and crop-bound. For control of these diseases, contact your county agent. In general, good stock, ample space, proper nutrition, and clean water and cages usually guarantee healthy birds.

For information on slaughtering turkeys, *see* CHICKEN.

TURKEY BEARD
See XEROPHYLLUM

TURNIP (*Brassica rapa*)

Turnips are treated in the home garden much the same as any other underground garden crop. One of the secrets of their good flavor is rapid growth, for which a good soil with a heavy supply of organic matter and phosphate rock is essential.

A loose, friable soil will prove most satisfactory for raising this short-season crop. Mulching the garden with grass clippings, hay and other organic mulches will further benefit turnips. If the soil is on the acid side, it is well to apply lime at the rate of ½ to one pound to each ten square feet.

Planting and Culture: Turnips can be planted as a spring crop, but must be put in as soon as the soil is workable so they can be harvested before hot weather. More often they are planted in fall.

Seed for late turnips should be sown during the latter part of July or early in August. Never cover turnip seed with more than ¼ inch of soil as they are very small and the tender young plants are easily killed when there is a thick layer of soil on top. The seed is sown in rows spaced 12 to 15 inches apart. These late plants, left in the garden all winter, will bloom and set seed the following spring.

Harvesting: Although rapid growth is needed for this crop, it bears watching. The turnips should not be allowed to grow too large or they will become woody and stringy and will be bitter tasting. If intended for storage, turnips should be dug before the first light frost. In the case of a mild winter, they can be left in the ground until after Thanksgiving Day.

After pulling up, turnips should then be topped and stored in the basement. The Swede or rutabaga turnip is generally conceded to be

Turnips should be harvested before they have grown too large and developed woody, bitter-tasting flesh.

the best variety for winter storage. If yellow turnips are preferred, plant American Purple Top.

Varieties: The types and varieties are many and take on various sizes and shapes. Some are flat, some are round, others are cylindrical. When grown under the same conditions, though, they all taste practically the same. Included among the more common varieties are the Extra Early Purple Top, Golden Ball, Large White and Large Yellow Globes, Snowball, White Egg, Red Top Globe, and Early Purple-Top Milan. Tokyo Cross is an early variety (35 days) which is valued for its resistance to virus and other diseases.

TWINFLOWER   (*Linnaea borealis*)

This Eurasian species and its American variety, *L. b.* var. *americana,* are trailing plants of the Honeysuckle family, with glossy evergreen leaves and pink, bell-shaped fragrant flowers. The American species is grown in the United States as far south as the latitude of Philadelphia, through the mountains of West Virginia, and across to the northern California coast.

Twinflower may be grown in the rock garden in an acid, moist, peaty soil, in a cool, partially shaded situation. Soil must be well drained for the plant to survive.

U

UDO (*Aralia cordata*)

This perennial herb, growing nine feet tall, is cultivated mainly for its edible young shoots. They have a bitter, turpentinelike odor which disappears when they are blanched, harvested and boiled in salty water. Udo needs a fertile, humusy soil, and is best planted in semishade in the wild garden. Propagate by division in the spring. Most people use it in salads or like asparagus.

ULE (*Castilla elastica*)

The ule or Panama rubber tree is a source of rubber in Central America. In the United States, it is grown only in the southernmost part of Florida, where it produces no rubber because the climate is not sufficiently warm.

ULMUS   *See* ELM

UMBEL

A cluster of flowers whose stalks arise from a single point on a stem is called an umbel. Sometimes several umbels are grouped together into one large one, which is called a compound umbel. Many herbs and flowers, as well as vegetables of the Carrot family (including parsnip and celery), have umbels, hence are called Umbelliferae.

UMBELLULARIA

The California olive (*U. californica*) is a handsome, aromatic evergreen. It is also called bay tree, pepperwood, balm-of-heaven, and California laurel. Growing 60 feet or taller, it bears dense clusters of yellow green flowers in late winter and early spring, followed by interesting berrylike fruits. It is hardy in the South and along the Pacific coast, and likes medium-fertile, moist soils. Propagation is by seed.

UMBRELLA LEAF
(*Diphylleia cymosa*)

A perennial for wild gardens in the southeastern states, umbrella leaf bears loose clusters of small white flowers and blue berries ½ inch in diameter. A huge leaf up to 18 inches wide arises from its base, complemented by two smaller, shorter-stalked leaves. Give it a cool spot, lots of shade and woods humus as a mulch.

UMBRELLA PALM
(*Hedyscepe Canterburyana*)

The umbrella palm can be grown outdoors in Florida and Southern California, and as a tub plant in the greenhouse. The beautiful feathery leaves appear in a dense cluster at the top of the trunk, along with the handsome flower panicles. Give it a humus-rich soil, water it generously during its growing season and shade it from hot sun.

UMBRELLA PINE
(*Sciadopitys verticillata*)

A tall evergreen, the umbrella pine or parasol fir is pyramidal in shape and grows over 100 feet high. Its dark, glossy, five-inch-long leaves—really stems assuming the functions of leaves—are arranged in umbrellalike whorls on the branches. A slow grower, hardy up to lower New England, it likes fairly moist, protected spots. Propagate by stratified seed, preferably in the cold frame, or by cuttings taken in the fall. It makes a very handsome ornamental.

UMBRELLA PLANT
(*Cyperus alternifolius*)

The many stems of this popular potted plant grow to about three feet tall and are topped with arching, umbrella-shaped leaves and small green flowers. It needs a wet soil and a temperature of 55 to 65°F. (12.78 to 18.33°C.). Propagation is by seed or cuttings

The home-potting variety of umbrella plant is easy to grow, requiring only plenty of water and a temperature of 55 to 65°F. (12.78 to 18.33°C.).

of leaf crown rooted in sand.

Another species, *C. Papyrus,* is an eight-foot-tall aquatic plant with stems clothed in sheaths which the ancient Egyptians used to make paper. It is a fine plant for a greenhouse pool.

Several other plants are also called umbrella plant, including *Peltiphyllum peltatum,* a perennial flower that grows wild in the swampy regions of Oregon and California. This umbrella plant has thick stems growing up to six feet tall and small pink to purple flowers. It will readily establish itself in any moist location. *See also* MOISTURE-LOVING PLANTS.

UMBRELLA TREE
(*Magnolia tripetala*)

The umbrella tree gets its name from the huge leaves, two feet long and half as wide, that radiate from the ends of the branches like umbrella spokes. It grows 30 to 40 feet tall, with big, creamy, cup-shaped flowers up to ten inches across. The flowers appear in late spring and have a disagreeable odor. It is planted for ornament from southern New England west to Nebraska, and likes a deep, fairly rich loam soil. Two other magnolias, *M. Fraseri* and *M. macrophylla,* have a similar habit and are sometimes called umbrella trees, but both have fragrant flowers. *Melia azedarach* is the Texas umbrella tree or chinaberry.

UMKOKOLO (*Dovyalis caffra*)

Also called kei apple, umkokolo is a shrub growing from ten to 20 feet high, with sharp thorns and tiny greenish flowers. It does well on sandy soils in Florida and California. The pulpy yellow fruits, about an inch in diameter, are edible when cooked, and taste much like cranberries. The Ceylon gooseberry or ketembilla (*D. hebecarpa*) is a similar plant hardy throughout the Deep South, with purplish fruits somewhat sweeter than those of umkokolo. Both species are unisexual so you must plant male and female specimens together in order to produce fruit. They are generally propagated by seed or budding.

UNEDO (*Arbutus Unedo*)

Also known as strawberry tree, this broad-leaved evergreen grows to 30 feet and is hardy in the South and along the Pacific coast. It bears orange red, edible but tasteless fruits that look like strawberries. The tiny pink or white flowers are borne in small drooping clusters. Another species, *A. Menziesi,* the madrone, has the same hardiness range but slightly bigger flowers, and is an important honey plant in California. It grows from 20 to 100 feet tall. Both species like well-drained soil enriched with peat, and shelter from wind. They are propagated by layering or by cuttings of ripe wood placed under glass in fall.

UNICORN PLANT
(*Proboscidea louisianica*)

The unicorn plant or devil's claw is a sprawling tender annual about three feet wide, with leaves up to ten inches across. It bears big, bell-shaped, yellow purple blooms in clusters and odd six-inch-long fruits that are pickled like cucumbers while still green. It can be started indoors and the seedlings hardened off and set out, about five feet apart each way, in any medium-fertile, near-neutral soil. A mulch is beneficial until the plants blanket the soil.

UNIOLA   *See* GRASS, ORNAMENTAL

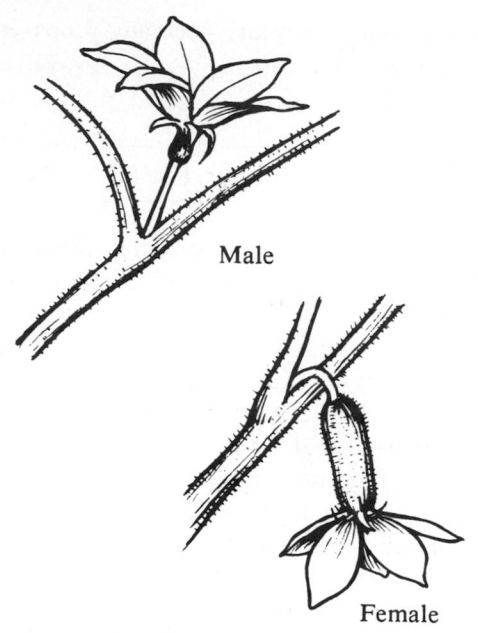

A monoecious plant, the cucumber produces both male and female flowers on a single plant.

UNISEXUAL

A flower containing only one organ of reproduction—either the male (stamen) or female (pistil) is unisexual. Plants that have separate male and female flowers on the same plant are called monoecious, while those having male and female flowers on separate plants are dioecious. Flowers that contain both male and female organs are called perfect.

See also FLOWER.

UNITED STATES DEPARTMENT OF AGRICULTURE
See GOVERNMENT SERVICES

UPLAND CRESS   *(Barbarea verna)*

Upland cress is the garden variety of yellow rocket or winter cress, which grows as a weed throughout the world. A tangy salad herb used alone or mixed with other greens, upland cress resembles watercress in appearance and flavor, but is much bigger, growing up to 18 inches tall. A hardy biennial, its seeds are sown in early spring in a medium-fertile soil. Plants should stand at least six inches apart. Cut the leaves often—the more you shear them, the faster the new, tender leaves spring up. If well mulched, upland cress will live over the winter and provide fresh leaves for spring salads. The plant flowers and goes to seed in midsummer.

See also CRESS, WATERCRESS.

URBAN GARDENING

In recent years, many people have discovered that gardening in the city is not simply fun, but is economical and produces better-quality food than is available in stores. Surprising yields of vegetables can be obtained from an intensively gardened, postage stamp-size backyard, and fruits and vegetables can be grown in containers on the roof, balcony or front porch. Some people manage to keep livestock in their backyards or on a roof; pigeons, chickens, bees, and rabbits can all be raised in the city if health codes allow and if the animals are not a nuisance to their human neighbors.

Although city gardening is similar in some ways to gardening in the country, it does require some special skills. Although city gardening has its disadvantages, one can learn to manipulate the microclimate of plants, in order to produce food over a longer period of time than would be possible in the country. By necessity, city gardeners learn to grow more produce in less space, increasing the theoretical productivity per acre.

There are many ways to maximize outdoor space for more efficient vegetable production. Use window boxes to grow small plants such as herbs, radishes, carrots, and onions. Plant vegetables such as lettuce, that, when cut, will continue to reproduce. Stick to compact varieties of plants that do not shade out other areas of the garden and avoid planting crops along a north wall. Build trellises or fences to utilize vertical space for plants such as tomatoes, peas, squashes, cucumbers, and beans.

Interplant slow- and fast-growing vegetables: the fast-growing vegetables will be harvested before they can crowd slower-growing plants. *See also* INTENSIVE GARDENING.

Some urbanites are fortunate enough to live in a city that has a community garden program. In many localities throughout the country, city governments, social agencies, industry, public institutions, churches, and private individuals have made land available to gardeners in their cities, often at no expense to the gardeners. Such programs are proving to be increasingly popular as the cost of food increases, and people seeking to raise their own food should investigate their own communities to see if there is already a community garden project there, or should try to initiate one on public land that is currently not being used.

URBINIA   (*Echeveria agavoides*)

This low succulent, grown in cool greenhouses and used often as a summer bedding plant, has pretty red flowers that rise on leafy stalks above its rosettes. Outdoors, it is grown mainly in the Southwest and other areas of dry winters. Urbinia needs a well-drained garden soil and full sun. Propagation is by offsets or cuttings of shoots.

URD   (*Vigna mungo*)

Also called black gram, urd is a bean grown for food in India and other hot countries, but rarely in North America. It is a spreading annual legume growing about two feet tall, with tiny yellow flowers and two-inch-long pods that hold the black beans.

UREA   *See* NITROGEN

URGINEA   *See* SEA SQUILL

URINE

The fertilizer value of livestock urine is not as well recognized by gardeners and farmers as it should be. Urine is high in nitrogen and potassium, containing two-thirds of the nitrogen and four-fifths of the potassium voided by an animal.

Use plenty of bedding to capture the urine, or, in barns, use a pipe arrangement to carry it from the gutters to a storage tank or pit. Soaked bedding or liquid can be applied at will to garden or field crops and pastures. Since urine is relatively concentrated, it should be applied sparingly and only in damp weather to prevent "burning" plants.

The Washington Experiment Station found that fertilization with urine alone produced extra-fine growth of grasses and clover much earlier in the spring than other types of feeding. (The elements in urine are more quickly available because they are in solution.) Urine is also an especially fine activator for converting crop residues to humus.

See also MANURE.

URSINIA

This genus of the Composite family contains several handsome annual and perennial species good for the border or greenhouse. Growing from several inches up to two feet tall, ursinias produce orange or yellow, daisy-like flowers with brown or purplish centers. *U. anethoides* is a two-foot perennial usually grown as an annual. Its flowers are bright yellow. *U. anthemoides,* a bushy annual growing less than a foot tall, has purple-based orange flowers. *U. sericea* has yellow flowers and grows to nearly three feet.

Ursinias need a light, well-drained soil and full sun. Propagation is by seed, which can be sown indoors in early spring with seedlings planted out later, or sown in January in the greenhouse to produce potted plants that bloom in early spring.

UTRICLE

A utricle is any small plant pouch such as the bladder of a bladderwort or the air cell of a seaweed. The term is also used to refer to any small, one-seeded fruit that ripens without bursting its outer sheath. Examples are the fruits of the buttercup and the beet.

UTRICULARIA

The bladderwort is found in swampy waters or the inlets of lakes, and can be grown in aquariums. It floats submerged near the surface, sending up clusters of pretty yellow flowers that rise above the water on stiff stems. On its delicate underwater branches are tiny sacs, less than 1/8 inch long, that catch insects.

Each sac or bladder is provided with a trapdoor, which springs open and sucks in minute water bugs or larvae that touch its bristly surface. Once inside, these organisms cannot escape and are digested by the plant. The bristle-trapdoor mechanism is so sensitive that even a microscopic paramecium can spring it. A single plant may have hundreds of these sacs, each of which can digest several insects at once.

Bladderwort is very hardy, and propagates itself by seed or by winter buds which rest on the mud during the cold season and develop into new plants in spring. There are approximately 200 species of bladderwort. Some tropical ones have blooms as lovely as orchids.

See also CARNIVOROUS PLANTS.

UVA-URSI
(*Arctostaphylos Uva-ursi*)

Commonly called bearberry or kinnikinnick, uva-ursi is a handsome, hardy evergreen ground cover. The sprawling stems are often six feet long, rooting at the joints to make a dense mat. It has white or pinkish flowers, red berrylike fruits and foliage that turns bronze in winter. Plant in early spring or late summer in the North, in a light, acid soil containing lots of sand and humus.

UVULARIA

Also called bellwort and merrybells, these spring-blooming, native wild flowers of the Lily family are good choices for the border or wild garden. The small, delicate, yellow green lily-like flowers nod from the stems and are usually hidden by foliage. *U. grandiflora* is a hardy 2½-foot-high perennial with large yellow flowers. Strawbells (*U. perfoliata*) is about four inches shorter and bears a single flower. Wild oats (*U. sessilifolia*) is over a foot tall, and makes a good ground cover.

Uvularias, which grow from thick, spreading rootstocks close to the surface of the soil, do best in light, humus-rich soil and some shade. Do not dig up wild colonies. Buy plants from a wild flower nursery.

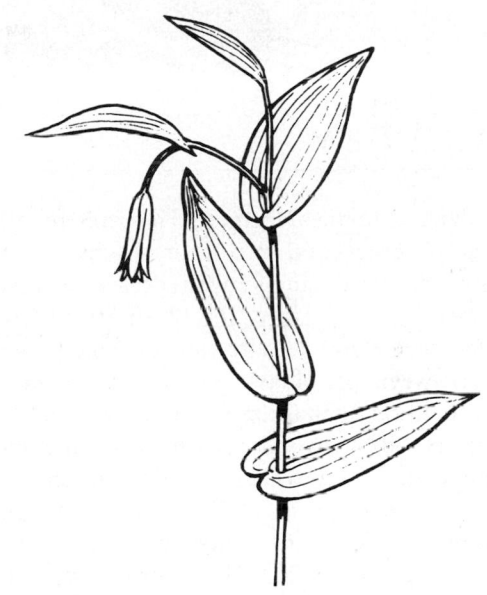

The wild uvularia or bellwort puts forth small, delicate yellow flowers in early spring.

VACCINIUM

Native to the Northern Hemisphere, this genus of erect and prostrate shrubs of the Heath family contains two species of great commercial importance, the blueberry and the cranberry. Both require an extremely acid soil, between pH 4 and 5 and the cranberry must have bog conditions. These two, and the cowberry (*V. Vitis-idaea*), which is sometimes planted in a cultivated "wild" garden, are among the few species of *Vaccinium* under cultivation. A few others are sometimes transplanted from the wild. The most suitable wild species are whortleberry (*V. Myrtillus*), dwarf bilberry (*V. caespitosum*), bog bilberry (*V. uliginosum*), and sparkleberry or farkleberry (*V. arboreum*).

Although they are spoken of as bog plants, blueberries will not tolerate a water table within one foot of the surface of the soil during the growing season. In most gardens, plants will have sufficient moisture if mulched with a thick layer of chopped oak leaves, pine needles or sawdust.

Cranberries cannot ordinarily be grown in the home garden or in most parts of the country. In order to grow them at all, a gardener must have a plentiful supply of acid water, a bog with a pH factor of 4.5 and a dam which will enable him to flood his bog during the season when temperatures drop below 26°F. (−3.33°C.). Because of these stringent requirements, cranberries are grown in only a few areas—in Massachusetts on Cape Cod, in New Jersey in the pine barren area and in Wisconsin.

Blueberry species include highbush blueberry (*V. corymbosum*) and lowbush or late sweet blueberry (*V. angustifolium*). Highbush is a shrub growing to 15 feet with fruit ⅓ inch in diameter. It is hardy north into Canada. Lowbush blueberry grows only one to two feet tall, but is also very hardy. Cultivars of both species are grown commercially.

See also BLUEBERRY, CRANBERRY.

VAGNERA   (*Smilacina*)

Vagnera is a genus of the Lily family which includes several perennial herbs called false Solomon's seal. A few are useful for naturalizing in partly shady corners of the garden where ferns and semiwild garden plants also grow. They grow well in any moderately rich garden soil with plenty of moisture and can be propagated by division. Pale green white flower clusters appear at the top of the plant, followed by berries similar to those of greenbrier. Leaves are simple and alternate, with parallel veins. The most frequently cultivated species are *S. racemosa,* commonly called false spikenard or treacleberry, and *S. stellata,* starflower or starry Solomon's seal. False spikenard grows to three feet, with individual leaves six inches long, and bears red berries. Starflower grows to about half that size.

VALERIAN   (*Valeriana officinalis*)

Often called garden heliotrope, this hardy perennial herb grows four to five feet tall, and has broad leaves and clusters of fragrant white, pink or pale violet flowers. Its heavy, strong-smelling, spreading rootstocks are dried and used for medicinal purposes. The herb is also used by gardeners to attract earthworms to the garden and as a companion plant. Like catnip, it attracts animals.

The Latin root word of this genus, *valere*, means to be in health, and refers to the herb's medicinal value. Traditionally, valerian has been used to treat bruises, relieve headaches, and, most important, as a sedative. One-half ounce of valerian root, skullcap and mistletoe added to 1½ pints of boiling water, covered and left standing for two hours is said to make a tranquilizing tea.

Valerian seed germinates so poorly that most gardeners prefer starting new plants from root divisions. The root can be split for transplanting in March or April, as soon as a crown appears on the rootstock. Plants should be spaced one foot apart in rows, which are also one foot apart. Valerian thrives in a rich rather heavy and moist loam.

Harvesting is best done in late fall. The roots are dug and the soil shaken out of them, before they are washed thoroughly. For drug use, roots are sliced lengthwise and dried at high temperatures.

A perennial sometimes called red valerian is *Centranthus ruber,* a two-foot-high plant with crimson flowers. The African valerian (*Fedia cornucopiae*) grows a foot tall, with dense clusters of red blooms. It is grown as a hardy annual and is sometimes used as a salad plant. The blue-flowered, perennial Jacob's-ladder (*Polemonium caeruleum*) is sometimes called Greek valerian. None of these are true valerians, however.

See also JACOB'S-LADDER.

VALERIANELLA

The leaves and stems of two species of valerianella are used for salad greens. The Italian cornsalad (*V. eriocarpa*) has rounded five-inch leaves and clusters of small blue or white flowers. Lamb's lettuce (*V. Locusta*) has rounded three-inch leaves and white flowers. Both grow to a height of one foot. The seeds are sown ½ inch deep in fertile, friable soil, from April to September, and the plants later thinned to stand three inches apart.

VALLARIS

These woody climbing vines are grown only in the Deep South. The most commonly cultivated species, *V. solanacea,* grows very tall and bears hairy leaves and clusters of fragrant white flowers. The one-celled fruits are four to six inches long. Vallaris does well in any medium-rich soil with good drainage.

VALLOTA   (*Vallota speciosa*)

The vallota or Scarborough lily is a member of the Amaryllis family and resembles amaryllis in every respect, except that the long straplike leaves appear at the same time as the flower stalk, instead of later. Flowering time is usually in spring or summer. The blooms are deep scarlet on stalks three feet high. Unlike amaryllis leaves, the leaves of the vallota should never be allowed to die off. Even during its winter semidormant period, water the plant enough to keep its foliage in good condition. Plant new bulbs in a rich, perfectly drained potting soil with the tip just protruding from the surface. The plants flower best when potbound, so do not disturb them unless they are grossly overcrowded. Plants suffer a setback if roots are broken. If repotting is necessary, do it in early spring before the plants flower. At this time small offset bulbs may be removed and potted individually. Old, potbound plants will require feeding every two weeks with a dilute tea leached from rich compost and/or dilute fish emulsion. They should be exposed to the full sun.

VALVE

Each segment or piece into which a pod splits is called a valve. Pea pods, for example, have two valves.

VANCOUVERIA

Vancouverias are evergreen shrubs which grow to two feet tall, with heavy creeping rootstocks. Their small white or yellow flowers are borne in drooping panicles. The most useful species is *V. hexandra,* a fine ground cover or border plant that is hardy in the South and along the Pacific coast. It needs a moist but well-drained, highly fertile soil and shade from hot sun. This species is easily increased by division of the rootstocks.

VANDA

Few orchids surpass vandas in the beauty of their foliage and flowers. Their straplike green leaves and the sprays of long-lasting blooms that come in a variety of colors make them popular house and greenhouse plants.

V. caerulea grows two or three feet tall, and has eight-inch leaves and light blue flowers tinged with darker blue. *V. tricolor,* also growing to three feet, has 18-inch leaves and fragrant yellow flowers that are spotted with brown and tinged with magenta at the mid-lobe. *V. teres* is often grown outdoors in tropical and semitropical areas. This orchid, a slender plant growing up to five feet tall, has pencillike leaves five inches long and pale rose blooms that are ringed by a red-spotted, yellow lip.

Vandas will bloom two or three times a year if given plenty of sun, high humidity, and frequent feeding and watering. They should be planted in sphagnum moss or in osmunda fiber mixed with pieces of charcoal.

Vandas have a monopodial growth habit, which means that their single stem grows higher each year, with new leaves springing from its tip. The flower stalk arises from the axils of the leaves, and aerial roots appear on the older portions of the plant. Should a plant become too tall, cut off the top part with some aerial roots attached and repot it. Vandas can also be propagated by taking off the young growths which spring from near the base of the stem.

See also ORCHIDS.

VANILLA

The vanilla orchid (*V. planifolia*) is a big-leaved epiphytic vine that produces numerous clusters of 2½-inch yellow and orange flowers in spring or summer. In its native habitat it will produce beanlike pods which, when processed, yield vanilla extract, a commercially important flavoring.

A pot containing several vines in osmunda fiber makes a handsome display for a window

Like the more widely grown planifolia *species,* V. pompona *or West Indian vanilla requires hand-pollination in order to produce the seedpods that yield vanilla extract.*
(*Courtesy of Longwood Gardens*)

garden or greenhouse, but vanilla orchids will not produce pods without artificial pollination. The plants need shade, frequent watering, high humidity, and a trellis on which to grow. Propagation is by seed or stem cuttings.

VANILLAGRASS
(*Hierochloe odorata*)

Vanillagrass is a perennial sweet-smelling grass that grows wild in the Northeast. It is not often cultivated in the garden, although its creeping rootstocks can be easily divided and transplanted from the wild. The leaves and brownish seed head grow about a foot high and are not especially ornamental.

VANILLA LEAF
(*Achlys triphylla*)

This spring-sown perennial grows to one foot high and has fan-shaped leaves that smell like vanilla when crushed. The flower heads are one inch long on spikes and have no petals or sepals. Vanilla leaf is a good border or wild garden plant. Sow the seed ⅛ inch deep in any fertile soil. The roots can be divided in early spring.

VARIATION

A variation is a dissimilarity in the character of an offspring from that of the parent. A variation may be temporary, with the third generation returning to the character of the original parent, or it may be permanent, with all future offspring retaining the variation which appeared in the second generation.

Temporary variations may be caused by growing conditions—unusual conditions of moisture, plant nutrients, sun or shade, soil acidity, or temperature. For example, plants that are tall woody shrubs or trees in the South often become two- or three-foot perennials when grown in the North, where they die back during cold winters. Cuttings taken from the northern plant and rooted in the South will develop into woody shrubs or trees.

Permanent or hereditary variation, in which the genes or chromosomes are changed, results in a sport or mutation. These permanent changes are now thought to be caused by gamma radiation.

See also SPORT.

VARIEGATED

Any leaf, flower or stem which has stripes, bars, blotches, or other markings of a different color from its ground-color is said to be variegated. Variegated markings are often irregular and are due either to the presence of two or more special pigments or, in the case of yellow or white coloring, to the absence of pigment from some areas of the plant surface.

VARIETY

A variety is a group of plants within a species that possesses the common characteristics of the species, but is distinct in some aspect, such as flower color, size or shape. When the character cannot be transmitted through the seeds, but must be propagated by cuttings from the plant, the offspring are called clonal varieties.

See also BOTANICAL NOMENCLATURE.

VARNISH TREE
(*Koelreuteria paniculata*)

The varnish or golden-rain tree grows to 40 feet tall with a spread of about 15 feet. It is a round-headed, feathery-leaved tree that bears papery pods and beautiful yellow flower clusters up to 18 inches long. It is hardy in all but the northernmost states. Give it an open position and fairly moist soil. Flamegold (*K. elegans*) is somewhat taller with bigger leaves, but is hardy only in central Florida and Southern California. Both are propagated by root cuttings and stratified seed. Prune trees only as necessary and only during winter months.

VEGETABLE BRAIN
(*Blighia sapida*)

This is a tropical African tree which is cultivated in southern Florida for its fruit, the akee, also called vegetable brain. Its leaves are oblong or oval and its flowers grow in fragrant clusters. The fruit is a three-celled capsule surrounded by a thick coating, or aril. The aril is the part used for food, though over- or underripe arils are said to be poisonous. The tree can be grown only in frost-free climates. Propagation is by seed or T-budding.

VEGETABLE GARDENING

Most people have turned to the organic

method primarily because of their vegetable gardens. Organically grown vegetables not only are free of the poison sprays, artificial colorings and preservatives found in most vegetables purchased in the market, but they often contain more vitamins. They are cheaper to grow and require no outlay for petrochemical fertilizers or insecticides which are usually unnecessary in the home garden anyway. Vegetables grown organically also taste better.

In order to eat foods from your own vegetable garden for as many months of the year as possible, you must plan your garden program before putting a single seed into the ground. A complete record of the space you used in a vegetable garden is an invaluable aid in planning your next garden. It is not enough to place the high vegetables on the north, the corn in blocks, and the asparagus where the tractor will not run it down. A map showing the pH of the soil in various garden areas should be made and kept up to date. Application dates for slowly available materials, such as phosphate rock, should be recorded. With such a record you can make a long-range plan of your garden that will be of inestimable help.

Location: On a small suburban lot, the vegetable garden can be placed at the back of the property where it will receive the least shade from buildings and trees. If you wish, it may be screened from the landscaped areas by plantings or fences.

Where limited space is not a factor in locating the garden, it is best planted near compost heaps, toolsheds and barns, but not too far removed from the kitchen. If the vegetable plot is distant from the house, a supplemental herb and salad plot, called a kitchen garden, and located near the kitchen door, is useful.

The ideal spot for a vegetable garden is an area that slopes gently toward the east, southeast or south. Good drainage is essential to the success of a garden, and a slope is likely to be well drained. A southern slope warms up early in spring and, with moderate protection, can be kept warm to prolong the growing season for several weeks in the fall. With judicious use of cold frames and hotbeds, the season may be stretched another four to eight weeks, making it possible for you to grow your own table greens two to three months longer than average without the use of a greenhouse.

In addition to having a favorable exposure, the vegetable garden should be placed away from shallow-rooted trees, such as elms, maples, poplars, and willows. Such trees not only rob the soil of food and moisture, but they seem to send all their roots into the plot.

Size: The size of the vegetable garden must ultimately be determined by what it is expected to yield—the quantity of food that your family can eat during the growing season, and the amount that can be stored fresh in the cold cellar, or can be frozen or canned.

Use the chart on the next page to help you estimate quantities to plant with reference to approximate yields. Your estimate should take into account the tastes of your family, your methods of preparing foods and the help available to you during peak harvest season.

It is easy to calculate the number of row-feet needed to grow vegetables like onions, beets, kohlrabi, or carrots where the whole plant is uprooted and used at once. Row-feet for vegetables that produce fruits or pods that are picked, leaving the plant to yield more, are not as easy to calculate. This is especially true in an organic garden, where increasingly rich soil and improved growing conditions after a few years of organic practice sometimes bring about phenomenal yields. Results, however, are limited by the length of the growing season, and by rainfall and temperature. Soil fertility and your cultural practices also influence results.

NUTRIENT REQUIREMENTS AND PLANTING DIRECTIONS FOR VEGETABLES

Crop	Nitrogen	Phosphorus	Potash	pH	Distance between plants (in.)	Distance between rows (in.)	Yield (per 100 row-ft.)
Asparagus	EH	H	EH	6–7	18	48–60	12–24 lb.
Bean, bush	L	M	M	6–7.5	4–6	18–24	50 lb.
lima	L	M	M	5.5–6.5	6–10	18–24	60–75 lb.
Beet, early	EH	EH	EH	5.8–7	3	12–18	100 lb.
late	H	EH	H	5.8–7	3	12–18	100 lb.
Broccoli	H	H	H	6–7	18–24	24–30	50 lb.
Cabbage, early	EH	EH	EH	6–7	15–18	24–30	100 lb.
late	H	H	H	6–7	24–30	24–30	175 lb.
Carrot, early	H	H	H	5.5–6.5	3	12–18	100 lb.
late	M	M	M	5.5–6.5	3	12–18	150 lb.
Cauliflower, early	EH	EH	EH	6–7	18–24	24–30	30 heads
late	H	H	EH	6–7	18–24	24–30	30 heads
Corn, early	H	H	H	6–7	12–18	24–36	100 ears
late	M	M	M	6–7	12–18	24–36	100 ears
Cucumber	H	H	H	6–8	36–60	36–60	150 lb.
Eggplant	H	H	H	6–7	24–30	24–30	125 fruits
Lettuce, head	EH	EH	EH	6–7	6–12	12–18	50 lb.
leaf	H	EH	EH	6–7	6–12	12–18	50 lb.
Muskmelon	H	H	H	6–7	48–72	48–72	50 fruits
Onion	H	H	H	6–7	2–3	12–18	75–100
Parsley	H	H	H	5–7	3–6	12–18	50 lb.
Parsnip	M	M	M	6–8	3–6	18–24	100 lb.
Pea	M	H	H	6–8	1–3	18–36	40 lb.
Potato	EH	EH	EH	4.8–6.5	12–15	24–30	75 lb.
Radish	H	EH	EH	6–8	1	12–18	1,200
Rutabaga	M	H	M	6–8	6–10	18–24	150 lb.
Soybean	L	M	M	6–7	6–10	24	50 lb.
Spinach	EH	EH	EH	6.5–7	2–6	15–24	50 lb.
Squash, summer	H	H	H	6–8	36–80	36–80	100 fruits
winter	M	M	M	6–8	48–120	60–120	100 fruits
Sweet potato	L	M	H	5–7	12–18	30–48	100 lb.
Tomato	M	H	H	6–7	24–48	24–48	200 lb.
Turnip	L	H	M	6–8	3	12–18	100 lb.

L Light   M Moderate   H Heavy   EH Extra Heavy

Only experience can accurately tell you how many vegetables can be grown in a given locality or a particular garden. However, there are some rules which will guide the beginner.

Snap beans and wax beans bear abundantly, but the peak of the crop lasts for a short period. A small number of seeds, or a few feet of row, must be planted in succession a few days apart to bear continuously through the summer. Lima beans will bear their main crop shortly after the first beans are large enough to pick, but given abundant water and a good mulch they will continue to bear until frost. Limas should be planted late—two to four weeks after the first snap beans—and the seed should be spaced two to three inches apart and plants thinned later. Peas, like snap beans, bear their main crop at one time and are then through bearing. But peas should be planted thickly. A hoe-width trench can be sprinkled with seed about two inches apart each way. To plant this thickly will require a pound of seed to 100 feet of row. One to two pounds of seed will grow enough peas for the average family.

Tomatoes may be grown in several different ways; each type of culture will produce a different yield per plant. If allowed to sprawl on the ground, the plants will need approximately nine to 16 square feet per plant—and will bear the largest amount of fruit each. Some of the lowest fruit on the plant may be lost to slugs, or never harvested because the lush foliage hides it until it becomes overripe. If plants are staked, they will bear less fruit because the cords used for tying tend to crowd the middle branches, but less will be lost. If the branches are kept pinched out at the leaf nodes, and only the main stalk is allowed to grow tall, the plants may be spaced 30 inches apart along a fence, and will yield the least per plant, but the most for the space. Depending on cultural methods, one to two dozen plants will grow all the tomatoes that most families will be able to use fresh in summer and canned in winter.

Swiss chard, an easily grown vegetable, is sometimes overplanted by the beginner. A row 15 to 20 feet long is sufficient for the average family. Cut the leaves from the outside of the plants, and they will be replaced quickly for more cuttings.

Other vegetables to be planted in small quantities include parsley, horseradish, peppers, rhubarb, and most herbs.

Spacing: By having calculated the number of plants needed to supply your family with vegetables, you have now arrived at the number of row-feet needed in the garden. To calculate the dimensions of the garden, you must also know how close together to plant your rows. Before arriving at this figure you must decide how the garden is to be cultivated, or if it is to be temporarily or permanently mulched.

A garden which is hoed by hand or cultivated by a rotary tiller or tractor will need more space between rows than a garden under an organic mulch. Each plant needs a certain amount of space and an open path must be left between rows if a machine is to pass without damaging the plants. The size of the path will, of course, depend on the size of your machine. The chart indicates a maximum area needed for power tool cultivation, and a minimum for crops under straw mulch. If mulched, your garden should need no cultivation except hand-weeding around young plants.

In a stone-mulched garden, rocks are set in paths two feet wide, leaving a foot between for planting. With this much space, almost any crop may be placed in any row, making rotation of crops a simple matter. Remember that stone mulching is permanent.

Planting Systems: By calculating the space between rows and the row-feet needed, you're now able to compute the area you need for your garden. In these calculations, you should remember that some crops can share the same space or use it in succession during the growing season, while others need the whole area throughout the season.

Perennial crops must be located where they will grow undisturbed for two to ten years and where they will not hinder tilling or machine cultivation. If necessary, give them a plot of their own, removed from the rest of the vegetable garden. These include all the perennials, such as asparagus, chives, horseradish, Egyptian onions, rhubarb, some herbs, and berries.

Annual vegetables that require sole possession of their garden space for the summer include lima beans, Swiss chard, cucumbers, eggplant, okra, onions, parsley, parsnips, peppers, sweet potatoes, late white potatoes, salsify, squash (both summer and winter), New Zealand spinach, tomatoes, and watermelon.

One other factor must also be considered, however. This is the grassy space needed at each end of the garden to allow a tractor to turn around if you plan to use a tractor to cultivate or plow your garden.

If the garden is on a slope, rows are usually planted to follow the contour, to avoid erosion. However, if the slope is very gentle and the garden will have a permanent straw or hay mulch, erosion will present no problem, and rows can be made up- and down-hill.

Permanent plantings, cold frames, stone-mulched beds, and hotbeds should be placed at one end of the garden. All of these need to be near the water supply.

In planning the row arrangement, the only invariable rule is that the tallest vegetables should be planted where they will not shade shorter ones. This is accomplished most easily by planting tall crops at one end of the garden. However, no crop should grow in the same place year after year, and even tall crops should be rotated yearly to cut down disease or to balance nutrient demands on the soil. Place them on the south side of a vegetable which will stand some shade. Shade-tolerant crops include lettuce, peas, cucumbers, kohlrabi, and scallions. Tall-growing corn may also be placed beside plants which will grow moderately tall by the end of the corn's growth. Among these are peppers, staked tomatoes and mustard.

Intercropping: Garden space may be saved by doubling rows of narrow-growing crops. Onions may be grown in double rows six inches apart. If they are mulched the double rows will not need weeding or much watering. Carrots, beets, parsnips, and turnips may be handled in the same way.

Radishes do not need a separate space in the garden plan. They mature so quickly that they may be sown in rows with slowly germinating seed, like carrots, and then pulled before they crowd the carrots. Melons and pumpkins may be started in the early corn, and will benefit from the shade corn provides for them in the hottest weather. By the time their fruits are ready for full sun to help them ripen, the cornstalks may be pulled out. *See also* COM-PANION PLANTING.

Succession planting: Some plants which may be grown and harvested early in the season and then supplanted by late crops are: bush beans, beets, cabbage, cauliflower, carrots, corn, kale, kohlrabi, lettuce, mustard, green onions, peas, early potatoes, radishes, spinach, turnips, and rutabaga. Early varieties of these vegetables are available. A short-season crop may be planted in spring, and replanted later in the year for a yield just before frost.

Almost all the plants on the list, except a few which thrive only in cool weather, may be used for later sowing. The exceptions are peas, which become too dry when the weather gets hot; kolhrabi which gets tough; and lettuce and spinach, which bolt.

Hot-weather varieties of most of these crops are offered by various seed companies. For example, Wando peas have been bred to be heat-tolerant. Early-planted heading lettuce may be followed in summer by heat-resistant leafing varieties, with curly endive and escarole planted in August to carry on even after the first light frosts. Seed catalogs indicate which varieties are best for spring sowing, for fall crops, for storage, or for freezing.

Disease and insect infestation will be kept to a minimum if plants subject to the same diseases and insects are not allowed to follow each other in the same bed. This particularly applies to members of the Cabbage family, beans, squash, cucumbers, and melons.

Starting Seed: Every gardener is eager to have early produce from his garden. One way to hasten early crops is to start many of them indoors before outdoor planting is possible. A few vegetables dislike transplanting, and must be sown directly in the garden for best results. Among these are peas, corn, carrots, and beans. Melons and squash may be started inside with special techniques, but they grow so rapidly outdoors that the early start seems to make little difference.

Tomatoes, peppers, eggplant, cabbage, cauliflower, and celery are usually started indoors or under glass. Seed for the large varieties of onions may also be started under glass, with the seedlings transplanted to the garden

before spring frosts are over. Cabbage, cauliflower and celery are normally started about six to eight weeks before time to transfer them to the garden. Tomatoes, peppers and eggplant cannot be planted in the garden until the soil is thoroughly warm, so their seed is started indoors about four weeks after the cabbage.

Seed is usually started in flats or in small pots, in a mixture of sand and garden loam. After the first true leaves have appeared, seedlings are transplanted to stand one to two inches apart in flats, or alone in small pots. The soil in the flat may be sterilized by pouring boiling water over it, or by baking it for an hour in the oven. It should not be rich; a poorer soil will encourage good root growth and discourage legginess. Flats should be kept in full sun during the day, and should have a temperature at night of no more than 60°F. (15.56°C.). If the plants grow too fast for the advancing spring, they may be held back and further prepared for planting out if they are transplanted once more.

Planting: At least a week before being planted in the garden, the seedlings should be hardened off. Hardening off may be done in a cold frame, ventilated by opening the sash during the day. Plants may be set outdoors in the daytime and brought in to a cool room at night.

When it is time to plant them, plants are set out in the garden in the evening or on a cloudy day. Every effort should be made to prevent the roots from becoming dry while the seedlings are in transit from flat to garden bed. The soil should be prepared in advance, a trench or series of holes dug for the plants, and a watering can or hose kept at hand to wet the soil as the small plants are placed. If they are being planted out very early in spring when frosts might still be in the offing, a protection of some sort should be provided.

If you are planting in rows between parted deep mulch, the mulch banks heaped up beside them will protect the seedlings. A pane of glass laid between banks of mulch and holes made for the plants will form a miniature cold frame for each plant. If this is not possible, a hot cap or a basket may be inverted over the plants and left there until danger of frost is past. It is best to shade the newly set seedlings for several days, even though the weather is warm. Plants set out in the middle of the summer may need protection from the sun for as long as two weeks until their roots have spread into the garden bed.

Seed sown directly in the garden is drilled or scattered in a trench. Planting depth depends on the size of the seed, but the usual rule is to cover the seed to four times its diameter. Finely sifted compost makes the best cover because it will not cake as clayey soil may do.

Late crops started in flats for later transfer to garden rows can be left outside in the shade to germinate. These flats may require a large percentage of humus to maintain sufficient moisture. More uniform moisture may be supplied to seedlings if a wick arrangement is set up when the flats are filled. To prepare a wick flat, a piece of muslin or burlap is cut to fit the bottom of the flat, with about a foot of the material overhanging at each end. The flat is then filled with soil, covering the wick. Seeds are planted in the flat in the usual way, and the flat is then placed over a large pan of water, with the wick hanging over each end into the water. If the pan is not allowed to go dry, the soil in the flat will remain uniformly moist until seeds germinate. *See also* TRANSPLANTING.

Mulch: Gardening experts agree that mulching during the hot summer months will produce good results in a home vegetable garden. Besides conserving moisture and cutting down labor required for weeding, an organic mulch breaks down gradually through the summer to add humus to the soil. Even if the mulch is raked away in fall or spring for plowing, a certain amount will have broken down and will be plowed into the soil. Earthworms thrive in the layer of soil just below the mulch, and carry on their work of aerating and enriching the soil.

What materials you use as mulch will depend upon what you can get in the neighborhood. Hay or straw are commonly used and spoiled hay may sometimes be purchased cheaply. Shredded leaves stored from the previous fall make excellent mulch. Sawdust or wood chips can be used around acid-loving berries and vegetables. Ground corncobs make a good mulch because their granular texture allows shoots to push through. Use these on an asparagus bed.

If the mulch is fine textured, as is shredded leaf mold or ground corncobs, it may be plowed under the spring after its use to increase the organic content of the soil. A coarse mulch which is high in carbon, such as straw or hay, breaks down slowly and if turned under without also adding nitrogenous material, it can rob the soil of existing nitrogen. A coarse mulch is either left on the soil year round, or it is raked away while the soil is being turned, disked or harrowed, and then immediately pulled back over the soil to protect it from drying out.

A permanent mulch has been used successfully in some gardens; Ruth Stout is the most famous advocate of this method. *See* STOUT, RUTH. In this method, the soil is permanently covered with a six-inch blanket of straw or other material, and it is never turned or harrowed. When planting is to be done, mulch is parted for rows or spots are cleared. Permanent mulching has been most successful where the original soil was porous, either sandy or gravelly, or where a large amount of humus had been incorporated with it for several years. Before beginning to grow a garden under permanent mulch, make sure soil texture is open. A heavy clay soil that has been plowed before the mulch's application will do well during the first year or two of permanent mulch, but eventually the clay will pack and a thin top layer of rich organic material will rest on a solid clay subsoil.

Stone mulching is similar to permanent straw mulching in that the bed is prepared deeply, fertilizers and supplements are added, and the stones are set in place to remain there for years. Stone mulch has one great advantage over straw mulch—a stone-mulched garden warms up earlier in spring than any other. The rocks absorb heat from the sun, and remain warmer than the air during the night hours.

If the whole vegetable garden is not stone mulched, a few stone-mulched rows at one end of the garden are useful for growing early vegetables, and for providing outdoor salad greens for six weeks longer in the fall. Seed of hardy herbs, such as parsley, dill and scallions, planted in fall, germinate early in the stone-mulched area. Early in spring, lettuce may be transplanted from indoor flats to grow under hot caps in a stone-mulched bed long before seed can be sown outdoors.

In autumn, hardy greens such as endive and escarole may be protected and kept growing in the stone-mulched beds until after Thanksgiving. In some regions, broccoli and Brussels sprouts in a stone-mulched bed will yield into the winter. Some root vegetables improve in flavor.

If, for any reason, a permanent mulch cannot be used in the vegetable garden a sea-sonal mulch may be spread between rows and around plants. In spite of the old belief that such plants as corn and tomatoes need to bake their roots, mulch has been shown to improve the yield even of these crops. Because the soil does not dry out as rapidly under mulch, plants are better fed, and the general health of the garden is improved. Less watering is needed during periods of drought, and weeding is cut to a minimum. *See also* MULCH.

Fertilization and Care: Not only do the nutrient needs of different vegetables vary, but sometimes the needs of the same vegetable vary from season to season. Early cauliflower, for instance, needs more nitrogen and phosphorus than fall crops need. Squash plants which will produce summer fruit are heavier feeders than squash which ripens its fruit in fall. Acid or lime requirements of various plants also differ.

The gardener must know what his soil lacks, and must make up for the lack for each of the plants he grows. Soil-testing kits, containing materials and information for simple quick tests, are available, and should be used often until experience will substitute for them. *See* SOIL TESTING.

Most vegetables will grow well in a soil with a pH between 6 and 8. Potatoes, parsley and a few other vegetables prefer a more acid soil, and will not grow well in the presence of lime. Take this into account when rotating crops. Limestone should be spread on portions of the garden where lime-loving vegetables are to be planted, and plants with a preference for acid soil should not be put in these areas until the lime has had time to leach away in two to three years.

Vegetables with high nitrogen needs benefit from being planted in the rows previously occupied by beans, peas, soybeans, or limas—legumes whose roots harbor nitrogen-fixing bacteria. Fast-growing vegetables which make a heavy growth in a season should be enriched with compost, rotted manure, or cottonseed or blood meal. These same heavy-feeding plants usually need more water than do those which make a smaller growth.

Manure water or side-dressings of cottonseed or blood meal may be given to any of the heavy-feeding vegetables during their fruiting period. Lima beans will bear longer and produce better-quality beans if given plenty of food and water while their pods are forming. It is best to feed tomatoes heavily only when the size of the fruit begins to diminish. Earlier feeding may delay ripening, while nitrogen fed at this time will help to make larger tomatoes.

Crookneck squash and zucchini are both heavy feeders, that need plenty of compost to start the season, and ample water in order to form their large fruits. Eggplant is another heavy-feeding vegetable that may be grown in a hill composed chiefly of manure and compost.

Moisture: Just as a plant's need for food varies at different periods, its need for water will also vary. Usually when it is producing its heaviest crop, the vegetable will need the most water, and lack of water will reduce the plant's resistance to insects and disease. Tomatoes, if given all the water they need while ripening, will bear a healthy, blight-free crop. As soon as they begin to feel a drought, brown blight spots will often begin to appear on the bottom of the fruits. Squash plants seem to be freer of squash beetles in a wet rather than in a dry year. Many organic gardeners report that as the moisture-holding humus content of their soil increases, Mexican bean beetle infestations wane.

Muskmelons and celery are two crops which need both abundant water and very well drained soil. Celery cannot be grown successfully in heavy clay soils. It must have light,

friable, but very rich loam, with plenty of moisture. Good melons may be grown on average soil if the hills are well composted and kept moist. Rich compost or rotted manure should be dug in where each hill will be planted. A six-inch flowerpot may be sunk in the center of the hill and kept filled with water. While small melons are forming on the vines, fill the flowerpot with manure water once a week.

Trenching: The European method of garbage trenching may be used to advantage where more garbage is available than can be used in compost heaps, or where compost heaps are prohibited.

A trench about a foot deep is dug across the garden in spring, and the soil left heaped up beside it. (The trench and heap of soil may both be temporarily covered with mulch to prevent drying.) Start at one end and work toward the other, filling the trench with garbage, pulling the soil over it and mulching. The entire row is left unplanted during the entire season, to permit bacterial action below ground to be completed.

Do not plant seeds or seedlings in a trench that contains a large amount of undecomposed garbage. The decomposition process temporarily depletes some soil nutrients.

Insect Pests: Many insect pests seem to disappear when healthy plants are grown organically. Plants given enough food, water and humus are comparatively free of such pests as squash bugs, Mexican bean beetles and aphids. A few of the larger pests, such as tomato worms and Japanese beetles, can be picked off by hand.

Cutworm damage can be minimized if plants are protected by paper collars. A 3 x 5 file card makes a collar of about the right size for most transplants. The collar is loosely wrapped around its stem, and thrust down into the soil, to make a fence against cutworms. *See also* INSECT CONTROL.

Slugs are pests that are attracted to mulch or loose debris in any garden. Actually, the slug helps to break down organic material and turn it into humus by digesting dead plant material under mulch, but it also feeds on growing leaves and vegetables. This is especially true during wet weather, when slugs surface to wet their skin. Slugs can be killed by sprinkling small quantities of ordinary table salt on their backs. Plants may be protected from them by pulling the mulch a few inches away from the stems and permitting the surface soil at the base of the plants to dry out. *See also* SLUGS AND SNAILS.

Birds help to rid the garden of many insects but at times, starlings and pheasants may do more harm than good to strawberries or peas. To keep birds away from these plants, or to keep rabbits and woodchucks out of newly sprouted succulent greens, use portable wire covers that may be moved from row to row. These may be made of three-foot wire fencing with 2-by-4-inch mesh, cut slightly longer than the rows. The fencing is folded down the middle to form a right angle, and the ends are folded over to make a triangular wall at each end. These tentlike protectors are then placed over the rows where they are most needed. They are also useful in early spring or late fall, when they may be covered at night with plastic, burlap or newspaper to protect the plants from frost.

Companion planting will deter many insects from damaging the garden. *See* COMPANION PLANTING.

Harvesting: Government studies have indicated that there is a wide variation in the nutrient content of vegetables, depending on their age when picked, the time of day of the harvesting, and whether the prevailing weather then was cloudy or sunny. Light has a remarkable effect upon the accumulation of vitamin C. Seedlings sprouted in light contain, after seven days, more than four times as much vitamin C as seedlings of the same age grown in darkness.

Fruit from the shaded side of a tree has been shown to have a lower vitamin C content than that from the sunny side, and even the sunny side of individual fruit has been found to have more than the shaded side. The changes in the amount of vitamin C in a plant under varying conditions of sunlight are noticed first in the leaves, though later differences may be observed in other parts, even in the roots.

Test results suggest that for the best vitamin C values, vegetables, especially leafy vegetables, should not be harvested before midmorning when weather is generally clear. If harvesting must be done after a cloudy day, collection should be made late in the afternoon.

See also entries for individual vegetables, PLANTING DATES.

VEGETABLE OYSTER
See SALSIFY

VEGETABLE SPONGE
See LUFFA

VEGETABLE TALLOW
(*Sapium sebiferum*)

The tallow is one of a genus of poisonous trees of the Spurge family which are native to China and Japan. Vegetable tallow grows to 40 feet in native surroundings, but may be somewhat smaller in the southeastern United States, where it is planted as an ornamental shade tree. Its inconspicuous flowers appear in terminal clusters, followed by half-inch seed capsules whose waxy coating is used in the Orient for candles and soap. The tree is easily grown in almost any soil. Propagation is by seed, cuttings or grafting.

VEGETATIVE REPRODUCTION
See GRAFTING, LAYERING, PROPAGATION

VELAMEN

The roots of tree-perching orchids and certain other epiphytes are covered with a whitish or greenish coating called a velamen. This corklike "skin" absorbs moisture and minerals from humus material and from the air. It also anchors the plant to the surface it is living on. The velamen serves the same food-gathering purpose as the root hairs of plants that live in soil.

VELVET BEAN   (*Mucuna*)

The velvet bean, a good forage or green manure crop, is an annual leguminous vine suited only to hot regions with long growing seasons. One popular species, the Florida velvet bean (*M. Deeringiana*), sends its vines sprawling 50 feet or more along the ground or climbing up supports and has lovely drooping clusters of purple flowers. All the velvet beans bear thick, sharp, hairy pods. Give them a sandy soil of medium fertility.

VELVET BENT   *See* LAWN

VELVETGRASS   (*Holcus lanatus*)

This perennial grass grows to two or three feet high and is covered with velvety hairs. It is a good ornamental grass, with leaves six inches long and clusters of green spikelets. Grow it in clumps, propagating it by division of the rootstocks in spring or fall. It likes a fairly moist, not-too-rich soil. There is also a variety with white-striped leaves.

VENIDIUM

This is a genus of annuals and perennials of the Daisy family. The leaves are hairy, gray green and deeply cut. The solitary flowers, which are often four inches across, are yellow, orange, or salmon with a band of purple at the base and a purple center. Members of the genus, which is native to South Africa, are usually grown as annuals outdoors, and sometimes as perennials in the greenhouse. They can be used for cut flowers, although the flowers close up at night.

For outdoor plants, seed is started early inside and plants set out in May. They thrive in any well-drained, sunny location, and are most useful in hot, dry areas. In regions with wet, humid summers they tend to stop flowering early.

V. decurrens is a perennial species growing to two feet, with dark-centered yellow flowers about 2½ inches in diameter. Flowers of cape daisy (*V. fastuosum*) grow to four inches across on three-foot stalks. They appear in mid to late summer and come in various shades of yellow and orange.

VENUS'S-FLYTRAP
(*Dionaea muscipula*)

Each leaf of this insectivorous perennial has two rounded lobes hinged like a bear trap.

The Venus's-flytrap is a native of the Carolina bogs, but can be raised at home in a miniature plastic greenhouse or terrarium.

Both halves have spines along the outer edges and three tiny spines on the inner surface. If an insect touches two of the three inner spines, the leaf folds and traps it; the insect is subsequently digested. In the spring the plant bears a cluster of small white flowers on top of a stalk.

Venus's-flytraps, which are native to the bogs of North and South Carolina, grow best in a humid, cool atmosphere in a constantly moist, acid medium with a pH of 4 to 4.5. A sphagnum moss or sand-acid peat moss growing medium is usually sufficient. Since the humidity levels in most homes are too low for Venus's-flytrap, it should be grown in a cool greenhouse or terrarium with southern or eastern exposure.

VENUS'S-HAIR
(*Adiantum Capillus-Veneris*)

Also called southern maidenhair, this fern has a slender black leaf stalk growing to 1½ feet. The leaves range from 16 to 20 inches long and the fan-shaped leaflets are ½ inch wide. Venus's-hair, which is usually grown as a greenhouse plant, grows outdoors in the temperate and tropical parts of this country and in the warmer parts of Europe. It should be given partial shade, a moist situation and protection over its roots in winter.

See also FERN.

VENUS'S LOOKING GLASS
(*Legousia Speculum-Veneris*)

An easily cultivated European annual of the Bellflower family, this hardy species grows to 15 inches tall and has purple, blue or white bell-shaped flowers that are ¾ inch wide. It grows in any good garden soil, and is a good choice for the sunny rock garden, though it is rarely seen in North America.

VERATRUM

Members of this genus of hardy perennial herbs of the Lily family grow four to nine feet tall, and have white, yellow or purple flower clusters at the tops of the stems. Veratrums, also known as false hellebore, are sometimes grown in the border or the wild garden, or naturalized along streams. Propagation is by seed or division of the fleshy rootstock.

Skunk cabbage (*V. californicum*) grows to six feet, with 16-inch leaves and 1½-foot panicles of green-spotted, white flowers. *V. nigrum* is a four-foot species with narrow clusters of black purple flowers. American false hellebore or Indian poke (*V. viride*) is the most hardy species, and grows in swamp woods from Georgia to Minnesota and New Brunswick. Often reaching seven feet tall, it has foot-long pale green leaves and yellow flowers in long clusters. The entire plant of Indian poke is poisonous and the roots of all veratrums are extremely poisonous.

VERBASCUM

This genus of biennial and perennial herbs of the Figwort family is native to the Mediterranean though most species have been naturalized throughout the Northern Hemisphere. Verbascums or mulleins, good ornamentals for the border, have soft, gray green foliage and dense spikes of yellow, orange, red, purple, or white flowers. Some species, however, are rapidly spreading weeds which may become a nuisance. Verbascums grow easily in any dry, warm soil with some sun, and are propagated by cuttings, division or seed.

Moth mullein (*V. Blattaria*) is a six-foot biennial with smooth, dark green leaves and yellow flowers forming a loose cluster. Purple mullein (*V. phoeniceum*), a perennial, has wrinkled, dark green leaves in a basal rosette, and woolly purplish flowers. The common mullein (*V. Thapsus*), also called velvet plant, candlewick and flannel-leaf, is a five-foot biennial that is covered with a yellowish felt and produces yellow flower spikes from June to September. Dried leaves of this plant have been used in various household remedies.

VERBENA   (*Verbena* x *hybrida*)

A tender perennial, garden verbena or vervain is usually treated as an annual. It is a trailing plant growing about a foot tall with white, yellow, pink, or red flowers in clusters. There are many named varieties, several of which are often grown indoors or in the greenhouse. Since their introduction to the United States, vervains have often been found in waste areas and on roadsides. Plants prefer wet areas, such as swamps and riversides.

The name vervain is derived from the Celtic *fer,* "drive away," and *werfan,* "to throw," apparently a reference to the diuretic properties of the herb. Verbena has also been used as a tonic and expectorant. In China, it is used to relieve rheumatism, and as an astringent and vermifuge. Centuries ago, verbena was linked to witchcraft and magic. In ancient days, it was bruised and worn around the neck

Several varieties of the low-growing garden verbena are raised for their white, pink, yellow, or red flower clusters.

as a charm against headaches and venomous bites. Some even believed the herb was used to treat the wounds of Christ on Calvary.

Sow the seeds in March in a sand-soil mixture in the cold frame or cool greenhouse, and transplant seedlings outdoors after all frost is over. Those with choice colors should be propagated by cuttings, which can be made by shearing off the plants in late summer and cutting the young shoots which then spring up. Root these under glass and plant them outdoors in the spring.

Among the other verbenas are blue vervain (*V. hastata*), four feet tall with blue flowers, and moss verbena (*V. laciniata*), a spreading, lilac-flowered species that thrives in the rock garden. Both require the same culture as the garden verbena.

VERBESINA

Members of a genus of annual and perennial American herbs of the Daisy family, verbesinas are often grown in the wild garden or, in warmer climates, as shrubs. They have clusters of yellow, orange or white flowers that bloom in late summer or early autumn.

A three-foot annual which is sometimes grown in Florida, butter daisy (*V. encelioides*) has golden yellow flower heads two inches across.

VERMICULITE

Vermiculite is a mineral containing mica that is processed and used as a medium for starting seedlings and rooting cuttings. When vermiculite ore is heated to about 2,000°F. (about 1,100°C.) in processing, moisture within it turns to steam and pops the granules to many times their original size. This rapid expansion leaves countless tiny air cells within the mineral, which provide room for water and air. When seeds are germinated or plants rooted in vermiculite, the medium supplies them with water and air with which to grow and develop dense root systems. Vermiculite can contain several times its own weight in water but even when the medium is thoroughly wet, ample air circulates about plant roots, helping to avoid damping-off.

Vermiculite is also used for mulching or as a soil conditioner to lighten and aerate heavy clay soils and help sandy soils to retain moisture. However, it does not do this job as well as organic matter, which, in addition to providing moisture and air, feeds plants.

Vermiculite can also be used for storing

Because of its high air- and water-holding capacity, vermiculite is an excellent rooting medium.

bulbs and winter vegetables, and as a base for floral arrangements.

VERNONIA

Members of this genus of shrubs, trees and perennial herbs of the Composite family have slender leaves and showy clusters of purple, pink or white flowers that bloom in late summer or early fall. Tall ironweed (*V. altissima*) grows from five to nine feet tall and has one-foot leaves and purple flowers. *V. novaboracensis* grows to about six feet and bears purple flower heads surrounded by bristles. Both are hardy to Massachusetts.

Vernonias, which are propagated by root division, like a moist, rich soil and sun.

VERONICA

Veronica is an ornamental, low-growing perennial with woody stems, gray green hairy leaves and spires of blue flowers that bloom from May through July. The veronicas are good ground covers and are also used for the border and rock garden. Most species grow readily in rich organic soil, and can be propagated by division after blooming. They require full sun and good drainage.

Of the many species of veronica, the most widely grown are the speedwells (*V. gentianoides*, *V. incana*, *V. longiflora*), cat's-tail (*V. spicata*), and germander (*V. Chamaedrys*). *V. gentianoides* has white to pale blue flowers and grows to about one foot. It is tolerant of some shade but must have a well-drained location. *V. incana* is somewhat taller, and *V. longiflora* grows up to three feet. All three species are excellent subjects for small beds or perennial borders.

Cat's-tail is particularly valuable in the garden bed since it blooms from July to September and has bright blue, pink or purple flowers. Several hybrid varieties are available including a white-flowered form and a dwarf type.

Germander grows wild throughout eastern North America. Its flowers are deep blue on two-foot stalks. This species is somewhat coarse and tends to spread.

VERVAIN   *See* VERBENA

VETCH   (*Vicia*)

The vetches are annual or biennial legumes widely used for green manures or forage, or as winter cover crops in the South. They produce high-quality hay, pasture and silage. There are about 150 species in the genus. Cultivated vetches are native to Europe and Asia. Viny, tendrilled plants with pinnate foliage, vetches bear large flowers and elongated, compressed pods with rounded seeds.

Any vetch can be planted in the fall in the southern United States and on the Pacific coast, but hairy vetch is the only winter-hardy variety in other areas. If it is sown in the fall, the land will be completely covered and protected from wind and water erosion by winter. The other vetches are usually spring planted, seeded with small grains for hay, pasture or silage, or plowed under as a green manure.

Vetch makes a palatable and luxuriant pasture, but should be used for pasture only when the ground is dry. This prevents soil compaction.

Winter or hairy vetch (*V. villosa*) is extremely hardy in the northern states, and is adapted to both heavy and light, sandy soils. Spring vetch (*V. sativa*) is half-hardy and best adapted to well-drained soils. New varieties of considerable merit have been developed in recent years.

V. Faba, the broad bean, is an erect annual which grows three to five feet tall and produces edible seed. It is grown extensively in the United States and Europe where summers are cool and damp. The cow vetch (*V. Cracca*) is an ornamental perennial that climbs up to five feet and has showy white or lavender flowers in small racemes. The seeds are sown in early spring.

Crown vetch (*Loronilla varia*) is a closely related legume cover crop which is an extremely effective erosion control plant. *See also* CROWN VETCH.

VETIVER   (*Vetiveria zizanioides*)

A perennial grass growing six to eight feet tall, vetiver is cultivated in the South for its thick, aromatic roots that are used in making mats and screens. Oil from the roots is used in perfumes.

Vetiver will grow in almost any soil, but does best in light, sandy soils, because they make harvesting the roots easier. Propagation is by divisions of the old clumps, which are planted in spring or fall, about five feet apart each way.

VIABLE

Seeds which are alive and capable of growing are said to be viable. Some seeds remain viable for only a matter of months, while others keep their germinating power for 20 years or longer. Many vegetable seeds are viable for an average of two to three years.

See also GERMINATION.

VIBURNUM

This large genus of popular ornamental shrubs and trees of the Honeysuckle family has numerous members which are native throughout the Northern Hemisphere. Many of the viburnums are brilliantly colored in autumn, and carry ornamental fruits which attract birds. The evergreen species are hardy only in warmer climates, but the deciduous ones are hardy as far north as Massachusetts. Leaves are opposite and simple, the spring flowers are colored pink or white. The fruit is a drupe or haw.

Viburnums will grow in almost any soil. They are propagated by stratified seed, hardwood cuttings, greenwood cuttings under glass, or by grafting. Some species are grown in the greenhouse for forcing.

V. acerifolium, dockmackie, grows to six feet. It has maplelike leaves, and three-inch clusters of white flowers followed by purple black fruit. Leaves are rose-colored in fall. It does well in dry places.

V. alnifolium, hobble-bush, grows to ten feet, with wrinkled leaves that turn purplish in fall, and persistent purple black berries. White flowers appear in five-inch clusters. This bush prefers a moist and half-shaded position.

V. Carlesii has fragrant white flower clusters that open early in spring along with the leaves. It is not usually a very vigorous shrub.

V. cassinoides, Appalachian tea, is a compact, round-headed shrub of 12 feet. It has clusters of creamy white flowers in June, succeeded by green to pink to blue black fruit in fall. Appalachian tea grows well in moist situations.

V. dentatum, arrowwood, grows to 15 feet, with coarsely toothed leaves and clusters of white flowers; blue black berries appear later. The plant is good for shady moist spots, and flourishes under trees.

V. Lantana, wayfaring tree, is the species commonly called viburnum. It thrives in drier locations than most viburnums, and grows vigorously to 15 feet. White flower clusters are followed by red berries that turn black in winter. The foliage is light green and wrinkled, turning deep red in fall.

V. Lentago, nannyberry, is a 30-foot tree with lustrous leaves, creamy white flowers and black berries. It may be distinguished in winter by its long pointed buds. It is hardy throughout the United States and in southern Canada.

V. lobophyllum grows to 15 feet, and has heavy clusters of scarlet berries in fall.

V. molle, poison haw, makes a dense 12-foot growth. In winter the bark appears flaky with light gray young stems. The berries are dark blue. It can only be grown in southern and central states.

V. Opulus, European cranberry bush, has three-lobed leaves that turn crimson and orange in fall. Its flowers are white and appear in early summer. The berries are scarlet. Variety Nanum is dwarf; variety Roseum, the common snowball bush, has round heads of sterile flowers; and variety Xanthocarpum has yellow berries.

V. plicatum var. *tomentosum,* Japanese snowball, is one of the handsomest viburnums. It has wide-spreading horizontal branches with clusters of conspicuous white flowers and fruit which is scarlet, turning black. While not hardy in the coldest parts of the United States, it may be grown in the North, along the Atlantic seaboard to Maine. It requires an open, sunny position.

V. prunifolium, blackhaw, is a wide-spreading shrub or small tree growing to 15 feet, with handsome foliage, white flowers and blue black fruit. It grows on rocky hillsides from Connecticut to Florida.

V. rhytidophyllum is a ten-foot evergreen species, with dark green wrinkled leaves and yellow white flowers. The fruit turns from red to black. This species must be planted in a protected position, but it is at home where temperatures do not go below 0°F. (−17.78°C.). It tolerates full sun or partial shade.

V. rufidulum, southern blackhaw, grows to a 30-foot tree in the South, but is a shrub in the North. It has shiny dark green leaves, with rusty brown hairs on the leaf and flower stalks. Flowers are white, and the fruit is blue.

V. Tinus, laurustinus, is evergreen, and hardy only in the South. It grows to ten feet tall, with flowers varying from pink to white. The berries are black. *V. Tinus* is sometimes grown in northern greenhouses. Many cultivars are available.

V. trilobum, cranberry bush, is very much like *V. Opulus.* Its large three-lobed leaves turn scarlet in fall, and the clusters of scarlet berries remain until spring.

V. Wrightii, leatherleaf, is a ten-foot shrub, which blooms a bit later than other species. In fall, it bears so many scarlet berries that branches are often weighed down to the ground.

See also ARROWWOOD, SHRUBS.

Whether grown indoors or out, victorias are annuals which form neither rootstocks nor tubers and must be raised from seeds each spring.
(Courtesy of Longwood Gardens)

VICTORIA

The enormous leaves of these water lilies grow up to six feet across with upturned margins that make them look like giant floating pans. *V. amazonica* is found only in the tropics, but *V. Cruziana* is a spectacular plant for water gardens in the North. Its fragrant white flowers turn deep pink the second day after blooming. The leaves have handsome radiating colored veins, which so reinforce the leaf that it can support weights of 100 pounds or more. Sharp red spines cover the undersides of the leaves and stems.

For best growth, victorias need a very rich soil and a large pool, for as many as ten huge leaves may be produced from one plant. The seeds are sown in pans containing a sand/soil mixture early in March, and the pans are submerged in a tank of water several inches deeper than the pan. In a few weeks, two floating leaves will appear. At this point, seedlings should be potted in three-inch pots in three parts rich soil to one part sand. After they make dense root growth, transplant to six- or eight-inch pots. Keep the water in the tank fresh.

When the water temperature of the pool is about 75°F. (23.89°C.), work into the soil about a two-inch depth of manure plus some bone meal, and plant the lily. It will reach giant size in about two months.

Except in the long growing season of the South, the seedpods will not ripen on the plant, so cut them off at the first light frost. Put them in a tub of water in the greenhouse, being careful of the sharp spines, and in a month or so the seeds will come free from the pods. They can then be buried in moist sand and kept at approximately 60°F. (15.56°C.) until they ripen, becoming very dark in color. To make it easier for the seeds to germinate, they are filed or cut to puncture the hard shells before planting. Longwood Gardens, Kennett Square, Pennsylvania, has a large collection of these and other water lilies.

VICTORIAN BOX
(*Pittosporum undulatum*)

This evergreen tree grows to 40 feet and is cultivated in California and the southern states as an ornamental. The shiny green leaves are oblong and four to six inches long. Fragrant white flowers appear in terminal clusters and seed capsules are about ½ inch long. This box, which is also called cheesewood, is propagated principally by grafting, but also by seed sown in a cool greenhouse or by half-ripened wood cuttings.

See also PITTOSPORUM.

VICTORIAN HAZEL
(*Pomaderris apetala*)

An ornamental tree of the Buckthorn family, the victorian hazel grows to 20 feet and has oval, woolly white leaves three to four inches long, and loose clusters of small green white flowers. *P. phylicifolia* is a four-foot shrub of the same genus. Both are propagated by cuttings of half-ripened wood in early summer.

VIGNA

These tropical vines are legumes used commonly for forage or green manuring in the central and southern states. *V. unguiculata* subsp. *sesquipedalis,* the yard-long or asparagus bean, is a long trailing vine with yellow or lavender flowers and fleshy pods as large as three feet long. The catjang (*V. u.* subsp. *cylindrica*) is similar but has much smaller pods. *V. unguiculata* is the edible cowpea. All of them are grown as annuals and should be inoculated.

See also COWPEA.

VINCA   *See* PERIWINKLE

VINCETOXICUM
(*Cynanchum ascyrifolium*)

The vincetoxicum, often called the mosquito-trap because its white flowers trap small insects, is a hardy perennial with hairy leaves and fruit like that of the milkweed. It is easily grown in a variety of soils.

VINE

A vine is a plant with a long, supple stem incapable of supporting the weight of the plant. Many species of climbing plants are beautiful and useful in the garden. Vines make the hard surfaces of garden walls and houses look softer while at the same time, decorating them. They may also be trained to grow on trellises to enclose outdoor living areas.

Many varieties of plants are called vines. Vines can be evergreen or deciduous, annual or perennial, herbaceous or woody. Some have dense foliage and others have lacy, delicate leaves. Some climb by adhesive disks, others attach themselves to supports by means of tendrils, and still others twine around their support.

Morning-glory, honeysuckle and wisteria belong to the twining group. Tendril bearers include grapes and gourds. Latticework used to support these should be thin enough so that the tendrils or stems can easily encircle it. The stems of self-clinging vines grow modified roots which secrete an adhesive substance that effectively glues the vine to its support. English ivy and other vines in this group do not need trellising when grown against walls.

In selecting vines for any location it is important to consider their means of support. Those planted against the walls of a house should not cling to the house itself, but should have the support of hinged trellises which can be unhooked and lowered without damaging the vines, when maintenance has to be performed on the house wall. Some climbing vines, like wisteria, make too heavy a growth to be suitable for planting against a house.

Planting and Culture: There are general rules regarding the care of vines. Many vines send out top growth comparable in mass to that produced by a small tree, so proper soil preparation is essential, especially for woody vines expected to occupy one space for many years. Since the soil around the foundation of buildings is often of poor quality, before planting make a hole three times deeper and wider than the size of the root ball, and open up the bottom of the hole to ensure good drainage. Incorporate well-decayed compost and topsoil. Mix more compost with soil to fill in around the ball of roots. Tamp down the soil mixture in the hole, and level the top of the ball of roots with the ground. As the soil and ball settle, fill in with soil around the roots. When the hole is nearly filled, run a slow stream of water in from the hose, letting it run until the water is down below the roots. This will further settle the soil and fill up any air pockets. Fill in with soil and finish planting by making a well around the vine to hold water.

During the summer months cover the ground over the roots with a good mulch, and renew the mulch as it breaks down.

Vines should not be planted close to the foundation wall of a house when there are wide, overhanging eaves, but should be placed 12 to 15 inches out from the wall. If eaves are narrow, plant the vine six inches from the support. Autumn is a good time to plant vines. Water deeply in dry spells, especially if the vine is planted near a wall. Soil near a house foundation is usually drier than the soil several feet away from the house.

Regular pruning and training are necessary to keep most vines from outgrowing their allotted space. Left unattended, vines growing on walls or arbors will quickly smother what they were supposed to beautify. Heavy, dense growth full of dead wood also invites pests and disease. Begin training the plant while it is young, guiding the stems in the direction you want them to grow. Some vines may have to be tied to their support at first. Try to develop a basic framework of stems, and maintain this by shaping and pruning when the vine has matured. Prevent stems from intertwining and choking each other. As a rule, cut back more heavily than you think you should. Hard pruning usually induces vigorous growth and good flower production.

Cold hardiness varies with species and climate. Marginally hardy vines can often be wintered successfully if they are planted against

The vine Aristolochia durior *or Dutchman's-pipe has huge, heart-shaped leaves and greenish flowers shaped like meerschaum pipes.*
(Courtesy of Longwood Gardens)

a south wall or other sheltered spot out of the prevailing winds. Be sure all vines are watered well in late fall before the ground freezes. A good precaution to take in very cold areas is to mound up soil or mulch around the base of the plant in fall. When mulch is used, even if the top growth winter-kills, the crown will stay alive to send up new growth in spring.

Types: Blood trumpet (*Distictis buccinatoria*) is a splendid climber that will cover a large space on fence or wall. The reddish trumpet flowers with yellow throats have a long flowering season, and the rich green leaves make an effective background for them.

Carolina jasmine (*Gelsemium sempervirens*) is a fine winter-flowering climber for a mild climate. It has bright green foliage and begins to flower at the end of December. Its golden yellow trumpet-shaped flowers continue until April. Plant it in a sunny position. It may be trained on a trellis to flank the front door of a house, or on an arch over a garden gate.

The various clematis species and varieties are among the choicest of hardy vines. All need trellis supports. The large-flowered hybrids are especially useful as accent plants and for covering small spaces because they are not rank growers.

Cross vine (*Bignonia capreolata*) is a useful screening plant in warm regions. It thrives in deep, rich soil and should be watered thoroughly once a week if the weather is hot and dry.

Cup-of-gold (*Solandra guttata*) is a good choice where a vine is needed to cover a large surface. Planted beside a garage, it will climb to the roof. It grows luxuriantly in a mild climate, but is sensitive to frost. Give it a warm position. The large, yellow, cup-shaped flowers measure six to eight inches across and the still larger, bright green leaves make a fine background for blooms.

Easter lily vine (*Beaumontia grandiflora*) has beautiful foliage as well as flowers. Leaves are up to ten inches long with prominent white veins. The white, lilylike flowers blossom from April to June and are very fragrant. Easter lily vine requires a deep, loamy soil and extremely warm, even tropical, weather. It does not succeed as a potted plant.

English ivy (*Hedera helix*) is a tough, adaptable old standby for covering walls, banks and old trees in sunny or shady locations. It is self-clinging. The Baltic variety is the hardiest evergreen in the North. Large masses of it can look somber and dull, so use it in combination with showier plants.

Gold guinea plant (*Hibbertia scandens*) is an attractive evergreen vine from western Australia. Its branches are densely covered with handsome dark green leaves. In summer it is covered with quantities of brilliant yellow flowers that resemble single roses.

Grapes should not be overlooked as ornamental vines. They are unexcelled as covers for arbors and porches where their fruit is easily accessible at harvesttime. They require less care and maintenance than ornamental vines.

Several flowering honeysuckles make striking ornamentals. Hall's Japanese honeysuckle (*Lonicera japonica* cv. 'Halliana') has sweetly fragrant flowers and vigorous evergreen leaves. Use it in the garden only where it can be severely restricted, bearing in mind that birds are fond of the fruit and may spread the plant into areas where it is not wanted. The vine is very difficult to eradicate in parts of the East, where it has become a pest. Trumpet honeysuckle (*L. sempervirens*) grows in frost-free regions. It produces clusters of inch-long trumpets throughout the summer. It is a good vine for small spaces, and can be allowed to climb up old shrubs like lilacs. The flowers attract hummingbirds. It prefers a cool, shady location.

Madagascar jasmine (*Stephanotis floribunda*) is a choice and lovely evergreen vine. The clusters of waxy, white, tubular flowers are delightfully fragrant. This climber needs light shade during the hottest hours of the day.

The Morning-glory family has many fine members. *Ipomoea Nil* cv. 'Scarlet O'Hara' has flowers of a brilliant and unusual shade of red. Moonflower vine (*I. alba* or *I. leptophylla*) has large, fragrant white flowers, which open in the evening and close before noon the next day. These plants grow quickly and produce flowers from seed in a short time. Plant in good ground in full sun.

Potato vine (*Solanum Wendlandi*) and love-charm (*Clytostoma callistegioides*) are two good vines to plant side by side. The former is deciduous and the latter evergreen. They both have lilac flowers and will decorate a wire fence or wall for a long time. Love-charm will start to flower in April and continue through May into June, while the solanum will flower during summer and early autumn.

Star jasmine (*Trachelospermum jasminoides*) comes from the Malay Peninsula. This jasmine may be grown as a shrub if carefully pruned and will form a strong framework of branches. It may also be used as a ground cover on a low, sloping bank, or on level ground. The star jasmine may be trained up either side of a group of windows or over a door. The fragrance of the white flowers is exquisite.

Tara vine (*Actinidia arguta*) is a twiner with red-stemmed, glossy dark green leaves that climbs to 25 feet. It produces edible fruit. Heavy feeding causes rank growth. It must have a strong support.

Trumpet creeper (*Campsis radicans*) is self-clinging and will grow rampantly to 30 feet but can be pruned to any height. Give it plenty of space because its underground runners send up stems among neighboring plants. The large orange red trumpet-shaped flowers are borne in July and August, and are highly favored by hummingbirds.

Winter creeper (*Euonymus Fortunei* var. *radicans*) is an evergreen, self-clinging vine that does well in sunny or shady locations. The variety Vegeta has showy orange fruit in fall similar to that of American bittersweet. It is good for growing along masonry walls and old trees.

Many wisteria species are hardy and long-lived ornamental vines. Chinese wisteria (*W. sinensis*) has purple and white flowers and is the most popular. Japanese wisteria (*W. floribunda*) flowers two or three weeks later in the summer. It grows to 30 feet and bears long, grapelike clusters of violet blue or white fragrant flowers in spring. It requires rich soil. It is best to buy container-grown or balled and burlapped grafted nursery plants, because seedlings generally take many years to flower. Wisteria must be pruned heavily each year to keep it in bounds and flowering well, unless a large space is allotted to it.

See also entries for individual vines.

VINE CACTUS
(*Fouquieria splendens*)

This huge cactus, which grows ten to 20 feet tall or taller, is sometimes called ocotillo, coach-whip or Jacob's-staff. It has many prickly, rigid stems and bears small crimson flowers in beautiful ten-inch clusters in spring. It is hardy only in the Southwest and is very popular as a hedge in desert gardens. It is also a favorite subject for arid greenhouses in the North.

VINEGARWEED
(*Trichostema lanceolatum*)

Native to California and Oregon where it is used in wild or rock gardens, this herb belongs to the Mint family. It is commonly called blue-curls for its arched, protruding flower stamens. The blue flowers are attractive to bees. Vinegarweeds like dry, sandy soils and full sun.

VIOLA

The violas, including violets and pansies, are popular bedding, edging and rock garden plants. They bloom profusely in spring and into summer, and have long-lasting flowers, good for cutting. The colors range from white through many shades of yellow, red and blue.

Violas like rich, humusy soil and full sun, but will tolerate some shade, especially during hot weather. Though violas are usually treated as biennials and their seed sown in summer, some can also be treated as annuals. Sow seed in September or early in the spring in the cold frame or greenhouse. The rootstocks may also be divided at these times, and cuttings of young shoots a few inches long can be taken in late summer and rooted in a shaded cold frame, to be transplanted outdoors in early spring. A mulch of compost and leaf mold is good with all types of violas.

Numerous varieties of sweet violet (*V. odorata*) are grown for winter bloom. Seed is sown outdoors in spring and the plants are moved to the cool greenhouse or cold frame in late summer. If the plants are brought into a warm place, they may be attacked by red spider mites unless the atmosphere is kept moist. While grown outdoors they need a deep, rich soil, plenty of moisture and semishade. Freezing when in the cold frame will damage them. The long-flowering hybrid strains are particularly good for window boxes.

There are many named varieties of violas. Most of them are crosses of *V. cornuta*, *V. gracilis*, *V. lutea*, *V. tricolor*, and *V.* x *Wittrockiana*. Blue Perfection has light blue to mauve flowers and Arkwright Ruby has red ones. Chantreyland is a beautiful apricot-colored type and Purple Bedder has big purple flowers with yellow eyes. The smaller violas are often more reliable and longer-lived than the larger pansies. Gardeners report they have picked bouquets of some violas from mid-March until after the plants were covered by winter snows.

The native violets, such as *V. blanda,* *V. canadensis, V. cucullata, V. sororia,* and others, are often planted in the wild garden. They are hardy and can be planted outdoors or in an open cold frame in autumn. They have runners which can be easily rooted to make new plants. *V. pedata* likes open, dry locations. Some of these violets can be transplanted from the wild, and a number of them make good ground covers in semishade. Give them a woodsy soil. They will do especially well where they can get their roots under rocks or stones to keep them moist and cool.

See also BORDER, PANSY.

VIOLET   *See* VIOLA

VIPER'S-BUGLOSS   (*Echium*)

Viper's-bugloss is a member of the Borage family. Native to Europe and Asia, the common viper's-bugloss has become naturalized throughout the eastern United States. The plants are bristly, with alternate simple leaves and blue, pink, purple, or white flowers which bloom in spikes. Some species are quite showy and are cultivated outdoors or under glass in any well-drained garden soil that is not too rich.

In warm climates viper's-buglosses become shrubs, and some species are grown in California as ornamentals. *E. fastuosum,* a five-foot shrub, and *E. Wildpretii,* which grows as a biennial, are found only in the eastern United

States. *E. vulgare,* also known as blueweed, blue thistle and blue devil, is a weedy biennial growing to about two feet tall with pink flowers which turn blue. It is commonly seen along roadsides in the eastern United States.

VIRGINIA SNAKEROOT
(*Aristolochia Serpentaria*)

This hardy herb of the Birthwort family is cultivated in some places for its root, which is thought to have medicinal value. It grows to about three feet and has a wiry stem, heart-shaped leaves and small, irregularly shaped flowers. Because it is a woodland plant, it must be grown in a sheltered, partly shaded spot, in rich soil which has plenty of humus. Propagation is by seed.

VIRGINIA STOCK
(*Malcolmia maritima*)

A small fast-growing annual of the Mustard family, Virginia stock has oval leaves and red, pink, lilac, or white flowers that are followed by erect seedpods. Virginia stock flourishes in ordinary soil and full sun and grows to less than a foot tall. Seed should be sown successively from early spring on if blooms are wanted all summer.

VIRGINIA WILLOW
(*Itea virginica*)

This shrub of the Saxifrage family is grown along the Atlantic coast, from New Jersey to Florida. It bears fragrant, showy white flower clusters which open in June and July. Although usually a moderate-sized, three- to five-foot plant, it sometimes reaches a height of ten feet. Oval leaves turn red in autumn. The Virginia willow prefers moist, rich soil, and is propagated by division.

VIRUS   *See* DISEASE

VITEX   (*Vitex Negundo*)

This 15-foot-tall deciduous shrub, which is hardy to lower New England and southern Illinois, bears lovely spikes of tiny lilac or lavender flowers in late summer and fall. It is often grown as a bee plant. The stems may die out over the winter, but new vigorous shoots will come up in the spring. The chaste tree (*V. Agnus-castus*) grows to ten feet and has scented leaves and showy spikes of lilac flowers. There are also varieties with white blooms. Propagation is by seed or by cuttings of young shoots under glass. Vitex grows well in ordinary garden soil, with some sun.

VITIS   *See* GRAPE

VITTADINIA

These are woody perennials of the Composite family which grow in both north and south temperate Pacific islands. The only cultivated species is *V. australis,* a somewhat hairy one-foot plant which grows from a thick rootstock. Alternate, obovate leaves are either entire or three-lobed. The solitary flowers have white rays and yellow disks. Flower heads are surrounded by rows of overlapping bracts. Vittadinia is grown only in warm climates, and propagated by seed or division.

VRIESIA

These tropical epiphytic plants of the Pineapple family are grown in greenhouses for their striking foliage rosettes and exotic flowers. Vriesias can be grown outdoors in southern Florida, where their dense clusters of stiff, spiny, sometimes variegated leaves often spring from the trunks of living trees. In the greenhouse they are rooted in rich, sandy soil, kept shaded during the warm months, and watered heavily during their summer growing season, though only lightly through the winter. Propagation is by seed, division or offshoots.

V. fenestralis has 1½-foot green leaves with dark veins and brown tips and pale yellow flower spikes growing from spotted green bracts.

The leaves of *V. hieroglyphica* are banded and irregularly marked with dark green above and brown purple below. The flowers are yellow.

V. Saundersi also has yellow flowers, but has stiff, fleshy, grayish leaves dotted with purple brown.

V. splendens, which grows to three feet, has yellow white flowers enclosed in bright red bracts and one-foot leaves banded with brown.

WAKE-ROBIN   *See* TRILLIUM

WALLFLOWER
(Cheiranthus Cheiri)

A perennial of the Mustard family, the wallflower is grown in England and throughout Europe along fences and walls. In this country, only the cool moist climate of the Pacific Northwest favors their growth and bloom. They grow up to 2½ feet, with slightly hairy, narrow simple leaves, and fragrant clusters of stocklike flowers. Colors range from yellow, to orange yellow and red brown. Since wallflowers are grown as biennials, wallflower seed must be planted early in spring or fall for bloom the following spring, before the onset of hot weather. Colors do not always come true from self-sown seed, so wallflowers are sometimes propagated by cuttings. These may be wintered in pots in the cold frame, and set out in spring as soon as the ground is open. Wallflowers prefer full sun and an enriched, moist garden soil.

WALL GARDEN

A wall garden is a planting against a wall of a building; a freestanding wall or a terrace retaining wall; a masonry wall built with niches or planters intended to hold potted plants; or a dry wall with soil pockets in place of mortar, the pockets planted with rock-garden material or vines.

For the first type of planting, the following shrubs, trees and vines are especially recommended. For espaliered specimens trained to decorate the wall, choose fruit trees, such as apple, peach and pear. Suitable shrubs include buddleia, cotoneaster, euonymus, forsythia, Laland pyracantha, snowball, and winter jasmine. Good vines for training against buildings include many roses, wisteria, ivy, clematis, matrimony vine, bittersweet, grape, trumpet vine, and innumerable annuals and perennials.

Niches or planters built into walls usually have an architectural purpose and should be used accordingly. If the niche is away from the ground, plants which may be used will be temporary, probably replaced every year, and chosen from greenhouse or window box material. Provision is made in some modern patio architecture for permanent plantings in set-back sections of masonry walls. Soil in such set-backs must be well drained, with a thick layer of rubble 18 to 24 inches below the surface, and tiles laid from the base of the planting to open ground.

Dry Wall: Dry wall planting is usually done on a wall which is used to retain a steep terrace. This wall is best planted while being constructed. Walls over four feet high should be made of masonry or concrete. A foundation trench 12 to 18 inches or so deep must be dug at the base of the dry wall. Fill in the area that

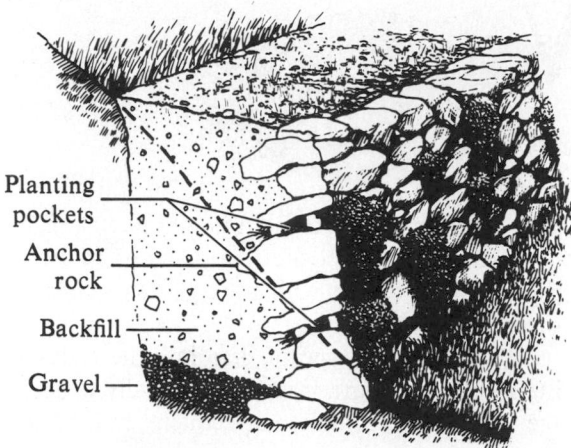

A stone wall is an ideal, attractive place to grow certain kinds of ferns, sedums, sempervivums, pinks, campanulas, and other mat-forming plants with fairly fine root systems.

Planting pockets

Anchor rock

Backfill

Gravel

will be behind the wall with six inches of good drainage material, like gravel, pebbles and broken brick. Then add finer gravel and sand and let it settle. Largest stones are set in the trench, flat side down. Soil is packed between the stones of each succeeding course as it is laid. Stones should be placed as they are in a rock garden, with the narrowest faces on the surface and the deepest dimension running back into the wall. Be sure that the joints of each layer of stones are lapped by stones on the next layer for increased strength. The flat surfaces of the rocks are slanted downward on the inside of the wall, to help carry moisture to the roots of wall plants. The face of the wall should slant back two inches to the vertical foot, to provide a shelf at the front edge of each stone for catching water. Thickness of the wall at the base should be approximately half the height.

As the stones are laid in the wall, rock plants may be placed upon them, roots spread

and covered with well-enriched sandy loam. Occasional pebbles should be placed between the courses of stone to take the weight of the wall off the roots of the plants. If planting is done after construction, the soil should be moist and crumbly, rather than too wet or dry.

Plants suitable for this type of garden will be the same as those which may be used in a rock garden. The following are especially recommended: adonis, alyssum, bellflower, bugleweed, candytuft, chain fern, Christmas fern, coralbells, creeping gypsophila, dwarf iris, glory-of-the-snow, grape hyacinth, hepatica, moss phlox, moss pink, polypody, poppymallow, prostrate veronica, rock cress, sea lavender, sedums, Siberian squill, snowdrops, snow-in-summer, soapwort, and thyme.

A freestanding dry rock wall may be built like the terrace-retaining wall, if made double, with the core between its two sides filled with soil. Great care must be taken when constructing such a wall to provide drainage at its base, so that water entering at the top will not find its way out through the rocks at the side. The soil exposed through the wall may be planted with trailing vines, with perennial or annual flowers, with rock plants, or with hedges or dwarf evergreens.

See also Rock Garden.

WALNUT   *(Juglans)*

The genus *Juglans* includes many ornamental, timber and edible-fruited trees. Persian walnut (*J. regia*) is an excellent nut tree that produces fine cabinet wood. American black walnut (*J. nigra*) is also valued for its nuts and wood. Butternut (*J. cinerea*) and heart nut (*J. ailanthifolia* var. *cordiformis*) are discussed in separate entries in this book.

Planting and Culture: All species of walnut grow best in a fertile, neutral or slightly acid silt loam that is at least five feet deep. Coarse, sandy soils or clay soils underlain with hardpan are not at all suited to walnut production.

Select a protected, sunny spot for your trees. Most species make fine lawn trees since their shade is not too dense. Black walnut trees, however, should not be placed near the vegetable garden since their roots contain substances that are harmful to tomatoes and other crops.

In late winter or early spring, purchase vigorous stock from a nursery. In most cases,

Drive over walnuts to split the hulls, then remove the nuts by hand.

the trees you purchase will be year-old, grafted specimens, about five to eight feet tall. Smaller seedlings that have not been grafted are less expensive but they are not as sturdy or disease resistant as the grafted types.

Plant nut trees 40 to 60 feet apart, allowing a depth of two to four feet for the taproot. Stake each tree as you would any fruit tree and water deeply. If it has not already been done for you, cut back the tree to within four or five buds above the graft union. The one shoot you tie to the stake will form the tree's trunk. As growth begins, rub off all buds that arise on the lower section of the tree. After this initial training, little pruning is needed other than spring thinning and removal of damaged limbs.

Soil cultivation is necessary whenever the weeds become out-of-hand. Most growers plant a cover crop of purple vetch or clover each fall and plow it under the following spring. This not only adds organic matter and nitrogen, but it also helps break up the soil so that water can penetrate more easily.

Since walnuts are deep rooted, they do not always receive sufficient moisture. Mature trees have roots up to nine or ten feet long and water must be regularly supplied to them. This is especially important during flowering and the first five to six weeks of fruit set.

Harvesting: Three to five years after grafted trees are set out, they will begin producing a crop. To harvest, place a sheet beneath the tree and shake the limbs vigorously. Since most species drop ripe walnuts over a one- to two-month period, you will probably have to shake the limbs about once a week for several weeks.

If fully ripe, Persian walnuts are fairly simple to hull by hand. Black walnuts and butternuts, however, are very hard shelled. Use a hammer to hull these or, for large quantities, drive over them.

Persian: Persian walnuts are mostly confined to regions where winter temperatures do not fall below −10° F. (−23.33°C.). The Carpathian types are the hardiest varieties and and will succeed in parts of Canada. Their greatest weakness is that they leaf-out early in the spring, and may be injured by a late-spring frost. Secondary buds will come on later and produce leaves and new growth, but no nuts.

The trees make beautiful ornamentals, growing somewhat the shape of but eventually much larger than apple trees. They grow quite rapidly under good conditions. Nuts mature in a comparatively short season, ripening from mid-September to early October in the northern United States.

Persian walnuts, especially the Carpathians, are quite free of serious diseases and insect enemies, though some varieties are troubled with leaf spot or walnut anthracnose. Carpathians are more resistant to the brooming disease than the other walnuts. Their most serious insect pest is the butternut curculio, whose larva infests both the terminals of the new growth and the nuts. Apple and plum curculio may also attack them. In some locations husk maggots darken the nuts, and the affected shucks do not open up normally, making the harvesting more difficult. Some of the best varieties are Concord, Eureka and Payne in California and Franquette and Eureka in the Pacific Northwest. Clinton, Colby, Greenhaven, Lake, and Somers are Carpathian varieties that can be grown in the Northeast.

Black: Black walnut trees sometimes grow as high as 100 feet tall. They thrive anywhere where temperatures do not drop below −20°F. (−28.89°C.). They make fine ornamental trees and produce rich, oily nuts which are packed with vitamins and good flavor. The nuts fall from the trees during frosts. They are enclosed in a thick, pulpy husk covering a black ridged surface, and are hard to crack.

Although seedlings are often used to start walnut trees, planting the nuts themselves is an easier and less expensive method of propagation. Soil should be fertile and deep for best growth. Woodlands, fence corners and stream banks make good tree sites. Plant seeds in the fall and spring. Sod or leaves should be scraped off a planting site which is at least 15 square inches in size. Dig two- to three-inch-deep holes, planting two to three nuts in each hole. Space the holes about 20 feet apart.

The trees take ten to 20 years to produce the black veneer which brings high prices in the lumber market. The wood is used in paneling, cabinetwork and furniture making. Pruning is recommended when the walnut is grown for lumber, in order to develop long, straight logs. Prune in the fall, as soon as the tree is four or five years old.

There are more than 100 varieties of black walnut. Some are better than others for planting. One of the oldest varieties, Thomas, is still one of the best. Other hardy varieties include Michigan, Snyder and Sparrow. Ohio and Stabler are better for warm regions.

See also BUTTERNUT, HEART NUT, NUT TREES.

WANDERING JEW
See TRADESCANTIA, ZEBRINA

WATERCRESS
(*Nasturtium officinale*)

A member of the Mustard family, watercress is a hardy perennial that grows best in gently flowing, cool water. It is native to the

A bed of watercress established along the banks of a flowing stream will provide cuttings each spring and fall.

sure their container is set in a cool, only partially sunlit spot.

As soon as the plants are large enough to handle, set them out in a convenient elbow along the banks of a stream. The best time to do this is during April and May. An established bed will provide cuttings each spring and fall. Care must be taken that the water is clean; otherwise the cress is not fit to use. The windowsill method of growing watercress in pots set in water is excellent for a winter crop. Seedlings mature in about 50 days.

Watercress has medicinal, culinary and ornamental uses. In addition to its wealth of vitamin C, watercress contains iron, iodine, sulfur, copper, and manganese. It makes an excellent food for those with near-anemic blood or skin disorders. As a garnish, it enhances many dishes and stimulates the appetite before meals.

northern United States, though it grows well in the South during the winter months. If you do not have a stream, you can grow watercress in containers filled with frequently changed water and sunk in the ground, or indoors in pots set in a tray of water.

Plants can be obtained from cuttings or seed. Sprigs will sprout in a glass of water, provided the water is changed daily. To start plants from seed, sow thinly in pots filled with a mixture of soil, ground limestone and sifted humus. Keep seedlings wet at all times and be

WATER GARDEN

A water garden is a decorative planting of aquatic herbs, trees and shrubs. It can be made in and around natural or artificial pools, ponds or brooks, or in a bog.

Pools and Streams: Natural bodies of water with native stones and plants make the best water gardens. Artificial brooks can also be constructed, using the same methods as for making lily ponds. Water lilies and other aquatic plants will grow well in brooks if they are at least 18 inches deep.

Large natural pools look best when surrounded with plants of varying sizes. Tall, vertical plants provide protection from wind and harsh weather, and give smaller plants shade. Perennials and dwarf pine and spruce trees are attractive at a pool's edge. Weeping willows

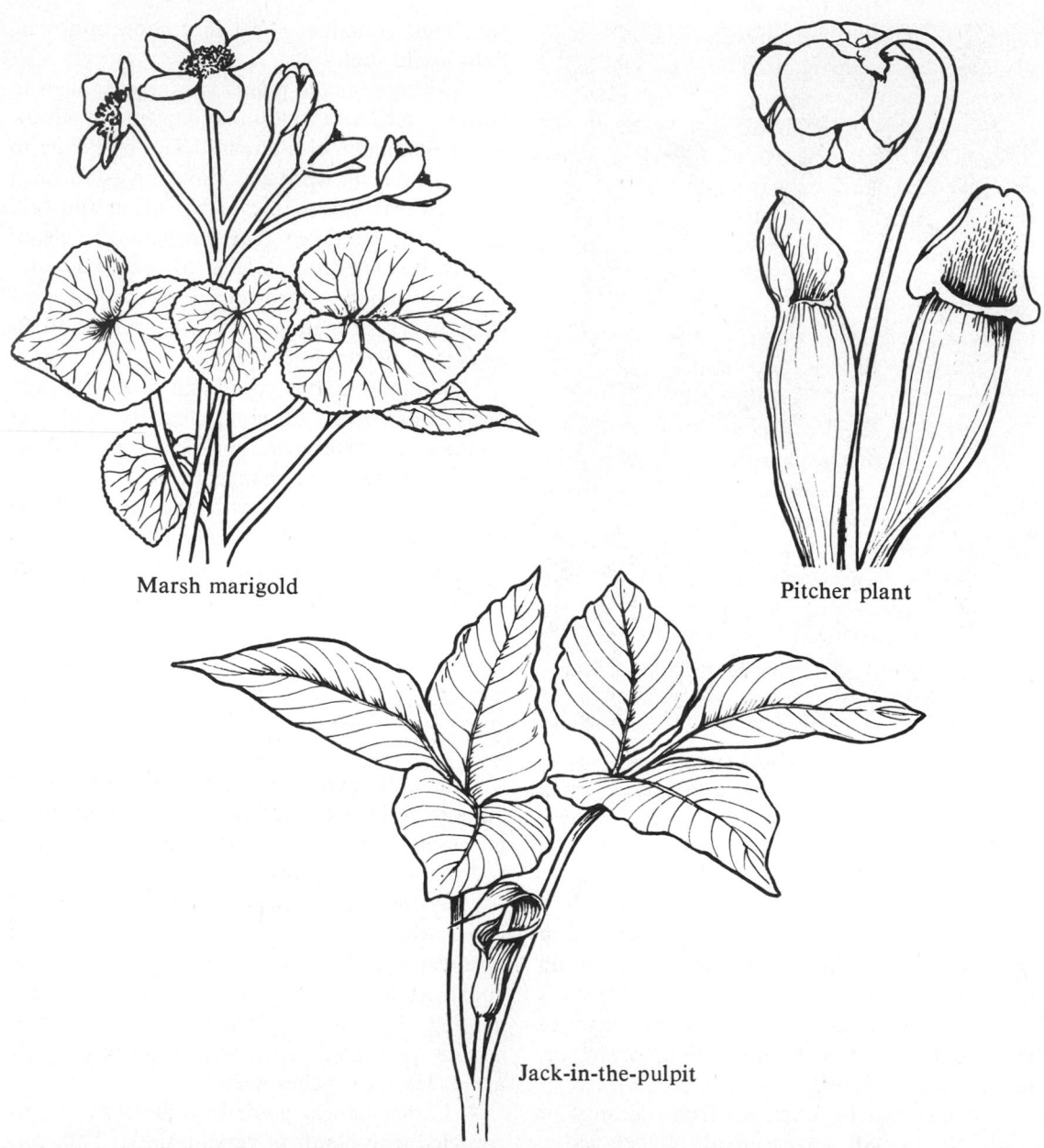

Marsh marigold

Pitcher plant

Jack-in-the-pulpit

The water gardener need not limit his plant selections to nursery-grown stock. The native bunchberry will form a lush, perennial ground cover in almost any wet location. Yellow-flowering marsh marigolds, Jack-in-the-pulpits and marsh ferns are abundant throughout the eastern United States and transplant easily. Pitcher plant is less common and should not be picked or transplanted.

(*Salix babylonica*), golden willow (*S. alba* var. *vitellina*), and weeping birch (*Betula pendula*), are low, dipping trees.

Arrowheads, azaleas and hydrangeas thrive at poolside. Plants and trees should be arranged so that sunlight is not blocked out of the pond and space is provided for growth.

Other suitable plants for a brook—and also for shallow parts of a sizable pond—include cattail, iris, lotus, papyrus, rush, sweet flag, water hyacinth, water poppy, and water snowflake. In general, any planting plan for a lily pond can be modified for a brook or pond.

Bogs: Where bog conditions prevail, a somewhat different approach is necessary. Boggy sites are usually found on the sides of lakes, streams and ponds, or in marshy hollows where the ground is of a distinctly peaty character. The soil is rich, acid, fibrous, and full of decayed humus material.

Usually such sites need only clearing to get rid of unwanted plants, and require no soil work other than digging. However, it is a good idea to prepare a compost for building mounds throughout the bog, and for mulching. Use pine needles, oak leaves, hardwood sawdust, manure, and similar acidic materials.

Bogs generally have low banks, not much more than a foot high. These can be planted to a large number of acid- and moisture-loving plants. Some of the best are eulalia (*Miscanthus sinensis*), horsetail (*Equisetum*), iris (*I. laevigata* and *I. sibirica*), marsh marigold (*Caltha palustris*), primrose (*Primula japonica*, *P. Bulleyana*, *P. chionantha*, and *P. helodoxa*), and willow herb (*Epilobium*). Suitable shrubs are bog laurel (*Kalmia polifolia*), bog myrtle (*Myrica Gale*), bog rosemary (*Andromeda Polifolia*), and winterberry (*Ilex verticillata*).

On the mounds, native orchids, the cypri-pediums or lady's slippers, are often planted. The leopard, meadow and turk's-cap lilies do well here, too, along with many of the trilliums and ferns that like boggy conditions.

Ferns also do well in wet depressions, along with arrowhead (*Sagittaria* spp.), bogbean (*Menyanthes trifoliata*), forget-me-not (*Myosotis sylvatica*), gentian (*Gentiana* spp.), pickerelweed (*Pontederia cordata*), flowering rush (*Butomus umbellatus*), and water arum (*Calla palustris*). *See also* MOISTURE-LOVING PLANTS.

Remember that a bog garden whether large or small should have a natural, informal look. Given the right conditions, you may even be able to create an artificial bog in a low spot in your garden. There, you can grow bog plants, shallow water aquatics and deep water plants all in one setting. A cascade or waterfall can be built if the water garden includes a brook. Imagination is often a more important ingredient in making water gardens than in designing any other kind of garden. A cool, serene, entirely naturalistic setting may be achieved by good planning.

See also LILY POND.

WATER HYACINTH
(*Eichhornia*)

A floating water plant that grows abundantly in freshwater streams and lakes in the Deep South, the water hyacinth has long been scorned as a weed pest in warm areas. It is very difficult to control or eradicate and can make waterways unnavigable. However, the common water hyacinth (*E. crassipes*) has fine feathery roots and makes an attractive plant for shallow pools.

Since the water hyacinth is so plentiful, it can be an important source of organic matter for southern gardeners. When dehydrated, it contains about 1 percent nitrogen and 4 percent potash. It is fine for adding to the compost heap or for use as mulch, and even makes an acceptable animal feed.

Although well known for their destructive influence in inland waters, water hyacinths are valuable in pollution control. Since hyacinths thrive on the pollutants nitrate and phosphate, and absorb cadmium and nickel from polluted water, they are expected to be of increasing importance in the filtering of industrial wastes and sewage plant discharges.

WATERLEAF   (*Hydrophyllum*)

A hardy perennial herb one to three feet tall, waterleaf has large compound leaves and clusters of bell-shaped, white or purple flowers that bloom in May or June. It grows from South Dakota and Quebec south to Kansas and South Carolina. Since the plant needs a shaded location and rich soil, it is most suitable for a wild garden.

WATER LILY
See LOTUS, NYMPHAEA

WATERMELON   (*Citrullus lanatus*)

A member of the Cucumber family, native to tropical Africa, the watermelon needs a long, dry growing season.

Planting and Culture: Soil, for good watermelons, should be light, fertile, deep, and well drained. A pH of 5.5 to 6.5 is preferred. Preparation of the soil should begin the fall before planting. At that time, turn under manure to a depth of six to eight inches. If there is a plentiful supply of manure on hand, dig in an inch layer of it all over the watermelon bed. If the supply is limited, a few forkfuls may be dug into the hills, and left to decompose during the winter, so that the nutrients have time to leach down into the soil to a depth where the vine's deepest roots will find them. A handful of phosphate rock and one of greensand or granite dust may be incorporated into the hills at the same time. Lime should not be used unless the pH is below 5.

In cool areas, or where the growing season is short, seed may be started indoors in peat or compressed manure pots and moved to the garden when all danger of frost is past. A greenhouse or hotbed makes it possible to start the seed eight weeks before field-planting time. If they must be started in the home, sow them just six weeks before field planting. Otherwise they will become leggy. Plant three or four seeds in each pot and thin to one vine. Later, when setting out plants, place three pots in each hill. After the vines have made a foot or two of growth, thin each hill to one or two vines.

If seeds are to be started directly in the garden, space hills six to 12 feet apart, depending upon the variety planted and the fertility of the soil. On rich soil with high summer temperatures, the plants will grow and fruit will set rapidly. In the South, practically all melons are started in the open. Seeds are planted ten to 14 days before the last expected frost, so that the seedlings will come up as soon as possible after the frost. If there is any danger that frost may overtake the seedlings, make two plantings in each hill a week apart, putting in half the seeds each time. A total of eight to ten seeds should be planted in each hill in a circle eight to 13 inches in diameter. Cover the seeds with an inch of soil. After the first true leaves appear on the young plants, reduce the number of plants to four or five per hill. Gradually thin them as they grow larger, until only one or two strong vines are left.

Mulching: Watermelon vines should be mulched to keep down the weeds and conserve moisture, but the mulch should not be applied until the soil is thoroughly warm. In the meantime, keep the area clean with shallow hoeing. Straw, hay or chopped leaves are the best mulching materials to use. Spread them in a six-inch mulch over the entire watermelon patch and draw the mulch up to the base of the vines. This should be done before fruits begin to form, because the small fruits may be damaged by handling. The best time to apply mulch is right after a rain, when the soil is thoroughly damp.

Thinning: Commercial growers often thin fruits on the vines in order to produce larger and more uniform melons and to speed ripening when no more than two melons are left on each plant. In the home garden, where melon size is not so important, the vines may be permitted to set more fruit, but late-set fruit should be removed. When too few hot days and warm nights are left for maturing fruit, all blossoms should be removed from the plants before they begin to develop. The sooner these are removed, the more plant energy will be diverted to the development of the early-set fruit.

Harvesting: Melons are most flavorful when permitted to ripen on the vine. Experience is the best judge of ripeness, and none of the many ways advanced to choose a ripe melon is infallible. According to Mark Twain, a green melon says "pink" or "pank" when thumped with the knuckles; a ripe one says "punk." A less subjective way to determine ripeness is to take a look at the melon and

New Hampshire Midget watermelon is well adapted to northern regions, has a growing period of about 80 days, and is resistant to most diseases.

vines. The fruit is apt to be ripe when the underside turns from white to yellow and at least three tendrils on each side of the melon are dead.

Varieties: Charleston Gray adapts to climates throughout the United States. It has an 85-day maturation period, and is fiber-free and disease resistant. Dixie Queen is wilt resistant and requires 90 warm days to reach maturity. Fordhook Hybrid bears small-seeded fruits and is hardy in the North. Also recommended for the North are Crimson Sweet, New Hampshire Midget, Golden Midget, and Sugar Baby. They are well adapted to cool climates and have growing periods of 65 to 90 days.

WATERSHED

All the land and water within a natural drainage area is called a watershed. For example, the Mississippi River–Missouri River valley is a watershed. Each river has a watershed, and streams feeding either of these drain watersheds.

By carefully studying the topography of an area, in their efforts for better water management, the Soil Conservation Service can establish a manageable section called a "small watershed."

WATSONIA

Watsonia is a genus of strong-growing summer-blooming bulbs of the Iris family. These South African natives are similar to gladiolus and have sword-shaped leaves and racemes of six-lobed, trumpet-shaped flowers that are good for cutting. Commonly called bugle lilies, watsonias are grown widely in California for hot-weather bloom.

The most commonly grown species is *W. Beatricis* that puts forth apricot-colored flowers from August to September. Many other species with white, red, pink, or purple flowers are available.

Watsonias prefer a sandy loam that has been well prepared and enriched with organic matter. An open, sunny location brings the best results. Plant bulbs in mid spring for blooms that summer. To grow especially strong specimens, plant bulbs three to six inches deep.

WATTLE   *See* ACACIA

WAX FLOWER
(Stephanotis floribunda)

Native to Madagascar, the wax flower or Madagascar jasmine is a twining woody vine of the Milkweed family that grows to 15 feet. It has opposite, four-inch leathery leaves and clusters of fragrant, waxy white, tubular flowers which bloom from April through October. In Hawaii, the flowers are used in making leis. Wax flower requires a warm, humid greenhouse (62 to 65°F. [16.67 to 18.33°C.] at night and 80 to 85°F. [26.67 to 29.44°C.] during the day), an all-purpose soil kept evenly moist and a northern exposure. Propagation is from cuttings of half-ripened wood.

WAX GOURD   *See* ZIT-KWA

WEAVER'S BROOM
(Spartium junceum)

The Spanish or weaver's broom is an almost leafless, ten-foot shrub grown along the Pacific coast for its profuse and fragrant, yellow pealike flowers. The clusters are often 15 inches long, and may be borne throughout most of the year in California. Native to southern Europe, weaver's broom will grow in any soil in a warm climate, and can be propagated by seed or cuttings.

WEEDS

Weeds are simply native plants that happen to be growing where you would rather have something else grow. Although the gardener must eliminate most weeds that compete with his crop, he should not be too quick to completely destroy all of the unwanted vegetation. Many weeds actually help the farmer. Deeprooted weeds make minerals available to plants and serve as trace-element accumulators. Those with strong roots break up hardpans, letting crop plants feed in the lower depths of the soil. Weeds conserve nutrients that otherwise would leach from bare earth. They add organic matter which improves soil aeration and water-holding capacity. In addition, they fiberize the soil so that the roots of plants spread out. Many serve as host plants for beneficial insect predators.

Weeds as Indicators: Weeds can tell you a lot about your soil—whether it is acid or alkaline, its soil type, how well it is drained, and so on. The following list of soil conditions and the weeds that they invite can be helpful to both the gardener and the farmer:

Acid soil: cinquefoil (*Potentilla*), hawkweed (*Hieracium*), knapweed (*Centaurea*), sheep sorrel (*Rumex acetosella*), spurrey (*Spergula*), stargrass (*Hypoxis*), and swamp horsetail (*Equisetum*).

Slightly acid soil: black-eyed Susan (*Rudbeckia hirta*), chickweed (*Stellaria*), daisy (*Chrysanthemum*), yarrow (*Achillea*).

Alkaline soil: goldenrod (*Solidago*), kochia, pickerelweed (*Pontederia cordata*), saltbush (*Atriplex*), saltwort (*Salsola*), samphire (*Crithmum maritimum*), yerba mansa (*Anemopsis californica*).

Sandy soil: goldenrod (*Solidago*), broom sedge (*Andropogon virginicus*), wild lettuce (*Lactuca canadensis*), onion (*Allium*) partridge pea (*Cassia fasciculata*), yellow toadflax (*Linaria vulgaris*).

Limestone soil: Canada bluegrass (*Poa compressa*), chamomile (*Matricaria*), madder (*Rubia*), pennycress (*Thlaspi arvense*), peppergrass (*Lepidium*), wormseed (*Chenopodium ambrosioides*).

Poorly drained soil: bindweed (*Convolvulus*), cutgrass (*Leersia*), foxtailgrass (*Alopecurus*), Joe-Pye weed (*Eupatorium*), hedge nettle (*Stachys*), horsetail (*Equisetum*), meadow pink (*Lychnis*), Saint-John's-wort (*Hypericum*), silverweed (*Potentilla anserina*), smartweed (*Polygonum hydropiper*), spiderwort (*Tradescantia virginiana*).

Hardpan soil: chamomile (*Matricaria*), horse nettle (*Solanum carolinense*), morning-glory (*Ipomoea purpurea*), field mustard (*Brassica rapa*), pennycress (*Thlaspi arvense*), quackgrass (*Agropyron repens*).

Weed Control: There are many effective methods of eliminating weeds in the field and garden without using harmful chemical herbicides. Declining soil fertility is one cause of weed growth. Many types of weeds appear to thrive only on soil that is low in some minerals and has an excess of others. As many farmers have learned, declining fertility lets such weeds as broomsedge and ticklegrass invade fields and pastures. Building up a soil organically, and providing well-balanced mineral fertilization is one of the best ways to lick the weed problem.

Cultivation: On large acreages and in some gardens, cultivation is necessary to keep weed growth at a minimum. Permanent mulching, as advocated by gardeners such as Ruth

Stout (*see* STOUT, RUTH) is not practical for farmers. They find chisel plows or rotary hoes more useful in eliminating weeds from their fields. A soil rich in organic matter is easily worked, and its cultivation and tillage can be timed advantageously. Enriched soil is in good shape after a rain and can be worked without causing clods to form. Spring tillage on a good organic soil makes a fine seedbed, and subsequent passes with a rotary hoe, chisel plow or cultivator can help to keep weed growth down. *See also* CULTIVATION.

Mulching: Mulching is one method of eliminating weeds in the garden. Straw, leaves and other organic matter can be piled thickly between rows and between plants in the row. A thick mulch will suppress weed growth, but even if weeds emerge they can be controlled by piling more mulch on them. Mulch also helps retain moisture in the soil, and enriches the soil as it decays. *See also* MULCH.

Natural control: The planned introduction of insects and fungus organisms that destroy weeds is a new and promising development. The prickly pear cactus, a pest on rangelands, has been controlled by a moth that tunnels through the weed. Klamath weed, a poisonous western pest, is falling to a tiny beetle who lives on nothing else. A moth has been found that controls ragwort, another poisonous range plant. Leaf beetles are being employed against the American lotus, an aquatic plant that crowds out duck-food plants in many waterfowl areas, and other insects are being used to control water hyacinth in southern waterways. Biological control of weeds is most useful when one weed is overrunning an area. Other weeds will come in to take the place of any weed taken out by biological controls, and so this technique is not useful for general weed control. Pastures, orchards and fields infested with specific weeds are the prime areas for biological control.

Biological weed controls are commercially available and can be found through a county agricultural extension agent.

Organic gardeners and farmers, by improving the soil and creating ecological diversity, are providing the conditions needed for naturally occurring biological control of weeds to operate. The artificial spreading of organisms that control weeds has certain indisputable advantages: it is cheap, it is natural and it restores nature's balance.

For more information on controlling or using weeds, *see also entries for individual weeds;* WILD PLANTS, EDIBLE.

WEEPING TREES

Trees, and even shrubs, with pendulous branches are referred to as "weeping." Weeping trees may be natural, as exemplified by the weeping willow, or may be artificially produced by grafting, as is often done with flowering crab apple or flowering almond. The latter are produced by grafting prostrate varieties on upright forms of the same species. Trees may be produced to weep from any height, and branches may be made to touch the ground, to hang loose above ground or to trail. Weeping trees are usually not planted among other trees or shrubs, but are either featured as accents in the garden, standing free and alone, or are used in a row to form an alley.

Naturally weeping trees may occur as sports in many families, though there are several species whose natural form is pendulous. Two species of naturally weeping willows are *Salix babylonica,* the common weeping willow which grows to 40 feet, and *S. blanda,* the Wisconsin weeping willow.

Another naturally pendulous tree familiar

east of the Rockies is the weeping American elm (*Ulmus americana* cv. 'Pendula'), a stately ornamental growing to 120 feet, and much used as a street tree. The Camperdown elm (*U. glabra* cv. 'Camperdownii'), which also has pendulous branches, is often grafted to make a small tree for the garden.

Weeping beech (*Fagus sylvatica* cv. 'Pendula') may grow to a height of 80 to 90 feet, with pendulous branches that completely hide the trunk.

Weeping birch (*Betula pendula*) has white bark and is especially handsome planted in groups near water.

There are several weeping trees that have ornamental fruits or flowers. Weeping cherry (*Prunus subhirtella* cv. 'Pendula') is a naturally pendulous flowering tree. Weeping white mulberry (*Morus alba* cv. 'Pendula') has heart-shaped leaves that turn yellow in fall and red fruits. Weeping hawthorn (*Crataegus monogyna* cv. 'Pendula') is an attractive tree with sweetly scented white flowers and scarlet berries.

WEEVIL
See CURCULIO, INSECT CONTROL

WEIGELA

Plants of this genus of handsome flowering shrubs of the Honeysuckle family bear white, pink or red tubular blossoms, about 1½ inches long, that open in spring and early summer. Among the cultivated species, there are many hybrids which are widely grown because they thrive throughout the country in any moderately moist garden soil. Where winters are severe, plant shrubs in a partially protected site. They require little attention and should never be pruned until after the blooming period, because flowers are produced on the growth made the previous year.

See also SHRUBS.

WHEAT   (*Triticum*)

Wheat belongs to the Grass family, and has been cultivated since 5,000 B.C.

Planting and Culture: Wheat is not difficult to grow. You can plant a small patch that will furnish part of your family's grain needs. The plant's straw can be fed to steers, used for bedding animals, employed as a mulch, or simply turned under in the field to provide organic matter in the soil.

To plant wheat, till a fine seedbed, then rake, disk or harrow the soil. Broadcast the seed and lightly rake the surface. That's all you have to do until harvesttime. On a small plot, you can broadcast the seed by hand, but larger plots can be planted more efficiently if some sort of mechanical device is used. Hand-cranked seed broadcasters are still being sold. These can be adjusted to the amount of seed you want to plant, but a great deal of the machine's efficiency depends on the speed at which you walk, and how fast you turn the crank. It is best to adjust the settings by following the directions provided with the unit.

A seed drill does a precise job of planting the seeds, in nice, evenly spaced rows at whatever depth you want. Secondhand drills can be bought at farm auctions or from farm equipment dealers. The drill, however, is not really necessary unless you are planting a large quantity of wheat.

Winter wheat must be planted after the Hessian fly ceases its activity in the fall. If planted before the "fly date," there is a high risk of crop infestation. Check with local farmers for the fly date in your area.

Early-planted winter wheat also runs the risk of "stool" or rapid fall stalk development. This condition increases chances that the wheat will be winter-killed. In some places, farmers graze fall stands of wheat to prevent stooling, but in muddy areas grazing by heavy animals such as cows or steers may cause soil compaction. Grazing should only be done when root systems are firmly established, about a month after planting. Chickens are best for grazing, since they do not compact the soil. They can also be turned into the field in the spring—six chickens to a patch 20 by 60 feet. They will cut yields somewhat, but they will also harvest their own food when they're in the field.

Wheat prefers a dry soil, and cannot stand acidity. Soil pH should be 6.4. Although wheat has low nitrogen requirements and lodges when overfed, some nitrogen should be provided through the addition of several tons of manure per acre.

In addition, wheat will benefit from two tons per acre of phosphate rock every four years. Sufficient potassium can be supplied by manure, green manure, greensand, or a commercial organic fertilizer. Fertilizing can be combined with a good five-year rotation for both garden and field. In the garden, a good rotation to use would be wheat, clover, sweet corn, peas, and beans followed by late-fall vegetables, tomatoes and then back to wheat. In the field, various rotations can be established if the basic rule of thumb of wheat followed by a legume followed by field corn is kept in mind.

If wheat follows a heavily cultivated crop and is planted in the fall when most weeds are already dead, the crop can get a good start in a weed-free soil. In the spring, wheat will begin growing ahead of the weeds.

Problems and Diseases: The biggest problem wheat growers face is "lodging"—the wheat grower's term for what happens when high winds or heavy rains knock ripening wheat down and make it devilishly hard to harvest. Recently, varieties with stiffer stalks have been developed, and they have solved the problem to some extent. Making sure your soil has enough potassium will also help.

Rusts, blights and smuts, once common wheat problems, have been largely overcome by breeding resistant varieties. "Take-all," a disease that can ruin an entire crop, is caused by a soil-borne organism. The disease seems tied to poor soil and rarely strikes crops in fertile ground. Using a good rotation can help solve the problem. If take-all hits your wheat crop, the entire crop, including straw, must be destroyed or the disease may spread.

Harvesting: As it ripens, wheat turns dull yellow, and the kernels become brittle. Winter wheat ripens about June 1 in the South, and much later in the North. Winter wheat is harvested in Canada about August 1. A half-bucketful of grain taken to the nearest mill or grain elevator can be moisture-tested to determine if the crop is ready to harvest. Moisture content should be 12 to 13 percent.

The best way to harvest more than a half-acre of wheat is by combine. The combine not only cuts the wheat, but it also threshes it. You might be able to get a neighbor to combine your crop for you if you don't have the equipment.

In the garden, you can harvest by hand with a scythe and if you can find a scythe with a grain cradle, so much the better. If you must thresh by hand, cut the wheat when it is still slightly green. The stalks should be yellow with green shot through them. Cut a two-foot swath, swinging the scythe with a natural, easy rhythm, and letting the blade swing against the stalks at a 45 degree angle. Take your time! You'll learn how to do it, especially if you have a large crop of wheat to harvest.

Wheat must be bunched for threshing. Use baler twine, and tie the wheat in bundles about eight inches in diameter. Shock these in the field or take them to the barn to dry. The grain will ripen in about two weeks, and can then be threshed.

To thresh your wheat, lay a large, clean cloth—an old sheet works well—on a hard surface. Lay a bundle of wheat on the cloth and beat it with a plastic baseball bat, a length of broom handle, a broken tool handle, or another appropriate device. The grain will shatter quite easily. What's left in the stalk can be fed to the chickens.

The grain must be cleaned further to get out bits of chaff and hulls. This can be done by pouring it from one bucket to another (allow a three- to four-foot drop) in front of a fan or in a stiff breeze. A seed cleaner, bought new or secondhand, can be used, but wheat can be ground into flour for table use without being perfectly cleaned of chaff. The extra chaff improves the fiber content of the flour.

Storage: Some insect larvae and eggs are often already present in the grain, so wheat storage is a problem. Weevils can be killed by heating the grain to 140°F. (60°C.) for half an hour. Insect activity can also be arrested by grain storage below 40°F. (4.44°C.), so if you don't have much wheat, it can be kept in the refrigerator or freezer.

For bin storage, begin by cleaning the bin well. Rat holes should be covered with tin nailed securely with roofing nails. Dust the bin with diatomaceous earth and treat the wheat by thoroughly mixing in diatomaceous earth at the rate of one cup to 25 pounds of wheat. Mix

thoroughly. Small amounts of wheat can be stored in steel drums covered with tin or wood covers.

Wheat that is to be used as chicken feed can be stored in the bunch, although it is more vulnerable to rodent and weevil attacks. One solution is to feed your entire crop from harvesttime until the corn is ready, thereby eliminating all wheat storage problems.

Using: Wheat is a versatile grain in the kitchen. You can grind grain into flour in the

Raw wheat can be ground in the blender for use as a breakfast cereal, toasted for a snack or milled to a finer flour for use in baked goods.

blender or use a mill. Grind the grain once a week, or when you need it. Wheat berries can be sprouted, coarsely ground or eaten raw as a hot or cold cereal. Any good natural foods cookbook will have many good recipes for using wheat.

Corn is more fattening than wheat, so you'll have to feed more wheat to animals to get a comparable weight gain, but animals prefer whole wheat to whole oats in their grain ration. Wheat may also be ground finely and used as a starter feed for chicks.

Types and Varieties: There are five commercially important wheats grown in the United States today.

Hard red winter wheat and *hard red spring wheat* are grown mostly west of the Mississippi and are used commercially for bread baking.

Soft red winter wheat is less tolerant of extremely low temperatures and requires more moisture than does hard red winter wheat. Both soft and hard red winter wheat are sown in the fall, make some growth and then lie dormant until spring. Soft red is grown in more humid regions of the country, from the Mississippi east, and in some places in the Pacific Northwest. It is used commercially primarily for making pastries.

Durum wheat is grown mostly in North Dakota and surrounding states. It is more drought resistant than any other type, and its primary commercial use is for spaghetti and macaroni products.

White wheat, grown in the Pacific Northwest and sometimes in the Northeast, is used commercially for bread.

You should plant the kind of wheat most suited to your area. Ask neighboring farmers what they plant, or check with your county agent. You'll find that soft wheat makes good bread when used at home.

Many varieties of wheat are available to choose from, but since cereal grains are harder to hybridize than corn you'll have a choice of only a few hybrids, and they will be expensive. New varieties of wheat offer high-yield, disease-resistant plants, with shorter, stiffer stalks to help combat lodging, the primary problem in wheat harvests.

You can buy certified, tested, cleaned seed, or you can go to a local mill or grain elevator and buy a few bushels of local grain. In either case, if you buy a nonhybrid variety you'll be able to save your own seed.

WHIP

A whip, also called a maiden, is a year-old shoot or stem of a woody plant, usually without branches.

WHISPERING-BELLS
(*Emmenanthe penduliflora*)

Also called yellow bells and golden-bells, this hardy annual of the Waterleaf family, which is native to California and Mexico, grows 12 to 18 inches high, and has segmented, slightly sticky leaves and branched clusters of drooping cream white or light pink bells. Seed may be planted indoors for early bloom.

WHITEFLY

Various species of whitefly are common pests of garden and house plants. The tiny adults, which have white, powdery wings, lay pale yellow or gray eggs on the underside of leaves.

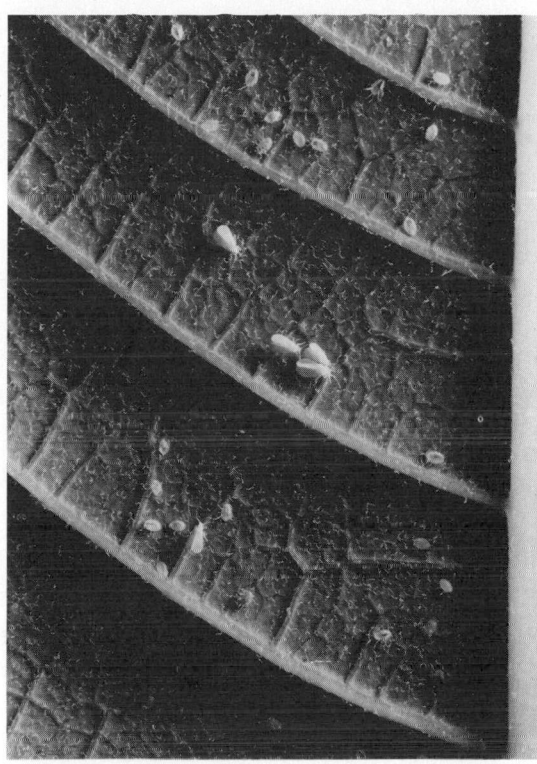

Whitefly infestations can be organically controlled with tobacco dust or a spray of tea or oil.

A parasitic wasp, *Encarsia formosa,* is now raised commercially as a biological control of whiteflies. The wasps lay their eggs in pest nymphs. Lacewings and ladybugs can also be purchased to keep down whitefly populations. Tobacco dust and tea, and ryania and oil sprays are also effective controls.

See also INSECT CONTROL.

WHITE GRUB

Grubs that live in the soil are often the larval stage of the Japanese beetle or june bug.

Plowing and hoeing throughout the spring will keep their numbers down. Grubs in lawns are best controlled by applying milky disease spores which are available commercially.

See also INSECT CONTROL, JAPANESE BEETLE.

WHITE WALNUT
See BUTTERNUT

WHORL

A whorl consists of three or more leaves or flowers rising in a circle around a stem.

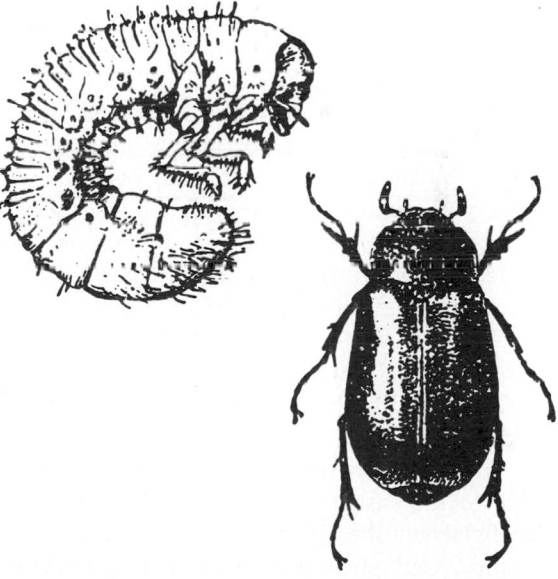

Like the closely related Japanese beetle, the june bug feeds on plant tissue at all stages of its development. Young white grubs are the most destructive, attacking the roots of potatoes, grasses and grain crops.
(Courtesy of U.S. Department of Agriculture)

WIGANDIA

Perennial, tropical American herbs of the Waterleaf family, wigandias are grown in California for their showy foliage. Their large leaves are covered with shining, stinging hairs, much like nettle leaves, and the white and purple tubular flowers grow in terminal clusters.

Wigandias, which grow from six to ten feet tall, are propagated by seed sown in winter under glass, or by root cuttings in spring.

WILDLIFE

A sizable and diverse wildlife population can often mean saving a whole crop from insects or disease. Some animals such as birds, foxes and weasels prey upon insects, mice, rats, and rabbits that may be destroying your crops. Others control weeds or cultivate the soil.

In order to create or simply maintain a healthy balance of animal life on your homestead, you must provide wildlife with adequate food and shelter. Avoid burning vegetation, extensive fall plowing, overgrazing, clear-cutting, and early clean mowing of pastures since these practices destroy the food and habitats of a vast number of helpful animals. Use of chemical pesticides and herbicides accounts for fantastic wildlife losses.

Building up the soil is one of the best ways to increase the numbers and variety of beneficial wildlife. Ecologists have found, for instance, that pheasants are usually abundant wherever corn and small grains are grown, and must have plenty of calcium. If the soil is lacking in this element, few pheasants will live in the area, no matter how plentiful the grain food. A study in Missouri showed that raccoons in areas with very fertile soil were often twice as big as those in regions where the soil was poor. Deer have been shown to avoid areas where the browse is low in cobalt.

Encouraging many different species of plants that create different types of habitats is another way to increase animal populations. Broad expanses of one crop or woodlots with but one tree species are inimical to a mix of animals. The bank, depths and margins of streams, marshes and ponds not suitable for crop production should be planted with vegetation that will attract birds and animals. The best plants to supply food and/or cover for waterfowl include muskgrasses, sago pondweed, wild rice, wild celery, duckpotatoes, wild millet, duckweeds, chufa, bulrushes, watercress, and wild water lilies.

Plant waste areas with a variety of plants that will offer cover and shelter to animals. Brushpiles are an excellent means of providing quick cover in barren spots where needed. A good brushpile is at least 15 feet wide and six feet high. It can be made in an unused fence corner, around a rock pile or at the head of a gully. The droppings of birds and animals will deposit seeds which should soon make a thicket of vines and berry bushes. You can also plant some sprouts of wild grape, Virginia creeper or bittersweet around the edges to speed up the process. It is also important to plant hedges, windbreaks, fencerows, and borders wherever crops are not being grown. After consulting the following list, check with your experiment station for other plants suited to your area.

Woodland Hedges and Borders

Bayberry	Honeysuckle,
Cedar, red	Tatarian
Coralberry	Oleaster
Dogwood, gray	Plum, wild
Hazel,	Rose, baby
American	Viburnum

Windbreaks and Shelterbelts

Ash, green	Mulberry
Box elder	Oleaster
Catalpa	Pine
Chokecherry	Plum, wild
Cottonwood	Privet
Elm, American	Rose, baby
Hackberry	Spruce, Norway
Honey locust	Spruce, white
Honeysuckle, bush	Sumac
Locust, black	Willow

Waste Areas

Bayberry	Hawthorn
Blackberry	Honeysuckle, bush
Chokeberry	Oleaster
Dogwood, gray	Plum, wild
Dogwood, silky	Rose, baby

See also BIRDS.

WILD PLANTS, EDIBLE

Edible wild plants are popular greens and vegetables in many lands. In early spring when cultivated greens are scarce, woods and fields will provide a bountiful harvest.

Wild plants are fine foods at other times of the year as well. Many of the best ones can be grown in the garden for a guaranteed supply. They will do well if their wild environment is duplicated.

Edible weeds are often among the best of natural foods. These plants have vigorous root systems that seek out more elements in greater variety than are taken up by garden crops. Consequently, they have higher vitamin, mineral and trace-element content than do a lot of their domesticated cousins.

For best flavor, always pick your wild plants when young and small. Remember to mix your weeds whenever possible; variety enhances flavor. Introduce them gradually, add-ing increasing amounts to dishes of more familiar garden greens. Don't hesitate to put them in the blender when making raw vegetable concoctions.

Never overcook wild plants, or use soda in cooking them. A tasty way to prepare many wild greens is to add them to lean, well-cooked salt pork. Cook no longer than ten minutes. Try flavoring them, too, with lemon juice, butter or vinegar.

The best edible weeds are listed on pages 1210 and 1211. Check with your county agent or state agricultural college about any other

Gather the young shoots of wild lamb's-quarters and prepare them like spinach or greens.

plants you find. Many cookbooks offer suggestions on how to prepare wild foods, and some are entirely devoted to wild food cookery.

Burdock (*Arctium Lappa*): The young stems are peeled and eaten raw or cooked; the pith of the roots is boiled like parsnips or used in soups.

Carrion flower (*Stapelia*): Gather the young asparaguslike shoots in late spring and cook them until tender.

Cattail (*Typha latifolia*): The rootstock can be used as a salad or cooked vegetable and the young flower heads for soup. Eat the early shoots raw or cooked.

Curly dock (*Rumex crispus*): Cut off the leaves close to the ground and cook them alone or with other greens.

Dandelion (*Taraxacum officinale*): This is one of the earliest greens, with leaves useful for salads or cooked like spinach, and roots that can be roasted as a coffee substitute. Pull up the plants while the bud is still tiny and furry. When white and fluffy, the plants are bitter.

Ferns (several species): Pick when the shoots, called fiddleheads, are still tightly curled and six to eight inches high. Cut them like string beans, boil, and serve on toast like asparagus. The rootstocks of some ferns can be eaten raw or boiled.

Ground cherry or husk tomato (*Physalis*): The berries, ripening in late summer and fall, can be eaten raw or used in preserves or pies.

Groundnut (*Apios americana*): The starchy underground tubers, available all year, can be parboiled and roasted or sliced and fried with butter. The seedpods may be cooked like string beans.

Jack-in-the-pulpit (*Arisaema triphyllum*): The starchy corms are baked or boiled in several waters to remove the extremely bitter juice. No other plant parts are edible.

Lady's thumb (*Polygonum persicaria*): The young leaves add an interesting flavor to salads.

Lamb's-quarters (*Chenopodium album*): The young shoots are cooked like spinach or boiled with meat.

Leadwort (*Plumbago scandens*): Very fiery, the crinkly brown tubers clinging to the roots fortify a salad better than the hottest radish.

Marsh marigold (*Caltha palustris*): The young spring growth is used as a potherb. Pick it just as the first flower buds begin to burst into bloom.

Milkweed (*Asclepias*): Young sprouts are cooked like asparagus or braised. A little later, the young stems and furry leaves are delicious, and finally, the roots and young pods are eaten raw or cooked.

Peppergrass (*Lepidium*): The young greens have a hot, biting flavor and are often used in salads with other wild plants, or as a flavoring for soups and blender drinks.

Pigweed (*Amaranthus*): The leaves and stems can be cooked like spinach.

Pokeweed (*Phytolacca americana*): The tender spring stalks are treated like asparagus, and the leaves cooked as greens. The roots are poisonous and the mature plant may also be dangerous.

Purslane (*Portulaca oleracea*): This herb is a decorative garnish for many dishes. It is fine in salads with other wild or cultivated greens. The stems and leaves can be cooked and used like okra.

Skunk cabbage (*Symplocarpus foetidus*): Boiled in several waters, the leaves lose their acridity and make tasty greens. The Indians also ate the underground parts.

Solomon's seal (*Polygonatum biflorum*): The rootstocks are boiled as a vegetable.

Young milkweed pods can be eaten raw or cooked; earlier in the summer, the shoots, young leaves and flower buds can be gathered for food.

Sorrels (*Oxalis*): Good sours that add an interesting tang to soups, salads and drinks; sometimes used like rhubarb in pies.

Sow thistle and Russian thistle (*Sonchus oleraceus* and *Salsola kali tenuifolia*): Young shoots are good raw or cooked.

Spatterdock (*Nuphar advena*): The seeds or starchy underwater roots are dried and ground into meal; the roots can also be eaten whole.

Spring beauty (*Claytonia virginica*): The small tubers when boiled for ten minutes, taste like potatoes.

Turk's-cap lily (*Lilium superbum*): The bulbs are used in soups.

Watercress (*Nasturtium officinale*): A favorite early-spring green eaten raw in sandwiches or salads, or cooked as greens.

Wild garlic (*Allium vineale*): Eaten raw, or used as a flavoring for poultry and meat.

Wild leek (*Allium tricoccum*): Fine in salads, or eaten with bread and butter like green onions.

Wild lettuce (*Lactuca*): Young leaves are good used sparingly in salads, or cooked like spinach.

Wild onion (*Allium canadense*): Can be eaten raw or used to flavor meats and poultry.

Wild primrose (*Primula*): When cooked like spinach, these are so flavorful they are called "butter weeds."

Wood lily (*Lilium philadelphicum*): The bulbs are used like potatoes.

In addition to these, there are hundreds of other, unrecognized edible wild plants. Many of them are regularly sold in the foreign markets of large cities. Some garden plants that are not usually eaten also yield edible parts.

The leaves of young violets, for instance, add a delicate taste to salads. In late summer, elderberry flowers are fine added to scrambled eggs or pancake batter. The leaves of white clover are delicious raw or cooked. Wild ginger, the leaves of horseradish and sweet potato, plantain, chickweed, pumpkin vines, and young blackberry plants—these are but a few of the many plants useful in the kitchen.

See also entries for individual wild plants.

WILD RICE   *See* RICE, WILD

WILLOW   (*Salix*)

Most willows are native to the Northern Hemisphere. Leaves are deciduous and lance shaped; flowers are male on one plant, female on another. Willows are distinguishable from their relatives, the poplars, by the property of erect, rather than droopy, catkins. Large species, which grow very fast, are sometimes planted beside more durable, slow-growing trees which need shade until well started. Weeping willows (*S. babylonica* and *S.* x *blanda*) should be grown near water in moist places. They may be easily propagated by cuttings or seed.

Black willow (*S. nigra*) has dark purple or black bark, and grows to 35 feet throughout North America. The bark is useful in making a quinine substitute.

Goat willow or sallow (*S. caprea*) is a shrub or small tree, up to 25 feet tall, bearing conspicuous bright yellow catkins, which appear before the leaves.

Golden osier (*S. alba* var. *vitellina*) has bright yellow twigs in winter. It is hardy everywhere.

Laurel or bay willow (*S. pentandra*) also has showy yellow catkins and reaches 25 feet.

Osier willow (*S. viminalis*) is grown in this country and abroad for its twigs which are used in basketmaking. When tops of a European specimen have been repeatedly cut back, it becomes the familiar "pollarded" willow of the continental countryside.

Pussy willow (*S. discolor*) is a shrub or small tree which grows to 18 feet. The catkins used for cuttings grow on female plants.

White willow (*S. alba*) grows to 75 feet, and bears finely toothed leaves lined with silky hairs.

WILT   *See* DISEASE

WILTING

Wilting is a loss of turgidity in plants caused by adverse environmental conditions, such as lack of moisture, or too much heat or wind.

When plant cells are filled with water, they are swollen like tiny balloons. Turgidity makes celery and lettuce crisp, and corn wide and lush, and flower heads erect. Loss of turgidity causes droopy plants, leaves that are curled up tight or folded, and twisted or wrinkled stalks.

Permanent Wilting: If plants don't get water after a prolonged period, permanent wilting may result. This is a very serious condition because it means that plant energy must go toward replacing root hairs that died from lack of water. If wilting has progressed to the stage where water is withdrawn from the green cells of the plant, the photosynthetic ability of the cells is injured for a long time, or even permanently. Permanent wilting retards or completely stops the growth of new organs.

Temporary Wilting: Unless the soil contains plenty of organic matter to take up excess water and then release it to thirsty plants, and unless tender plants are shielded from the direct rays of a hot summer sun and from hot, dry winds, plants are likely to wilt, through loss of cell water. As soon as the conditions are rectified, as they are with the coming of night, the plant cells immediately regain their turgidity and are bright and fresh and crisp-looking again.

Temporary wilting does not necessarily

mean a loss of vital activity. If water is restored to the plant soon enough, turgidity is reestablished and the plant resumes its vital activity. However, temporary wilting does slow down growth because it retards photosynthetic activity. It may also reduce yields.

Potted plants that are temporarily wilted can be revived by putting them into a moist atmosphere. This can be done by enclosing them in plastic or glass and standing them over water. Moist greenhouses will also revive wilted plants.

Flooding wilted vegetable or flowering plants with water will not work, because excess water hinders capillary action. When watering wilted plants, use water that is at about air temperature and introduce the water slowly. Many gardeners keep a barrel filled with water near the garden for this purpose. Shading the plants will also help.

To revive wilted cut flowers, try making a fresh cut at the stem tip without taking the stem out of the water.

WINDBREAK

A screen of living trees or shrubs planted at right angles to the prevailing winds will help hold down soil, keep snow from drifting over driveways and, when protecting a house, conserve fuel. Windbreaks affect air movement in such a manner that there is a slowing down in wind velocity as winds approach the break, even before the windbreak is reached. The effect of diminishing the wind starts a chain of favorable climatic influences, such as the reduction of evaporation, the lowering of temperature, the increasing of relative humidity in the air—all of which result in an increase of crops

Planted closely together, evergreens form a sturdy windbreak.

grown under the protective influence of shelterbelts.

Aside from their influences on crops, tree belts reduce soil blowing. The ability of wind to move and pick up soil particles is cut considerably, and even as little as a 10 percent reduction may mean the difference between considerable and very little soil blowing. A 50 percent reduction should practically keep the wind from moving soil particles.

It has been established that shelterbelts afford a protection on the leeward side to 20 times the height of the trees—that is, with a belt of trees 50 feet high, protection extends to a horizontal distance of 1,000 feet.

Make every effort to plant your windbreak where it will do the most good. Study the locations and relationships of the buildings and the grounds you want protected. Windbreaks are usually planted across the west and north sides of property, but many exceptions can be made, depending on local conditions and land configuration.

Try not to plant the screen too close to the garden it is designed to protect. Close planting will rob garden plants of moisture and nutrients. On the Great Plains, where the winds blow free in the wide-open spaces, windbreaks are planted at least 50 feet from field crops.

See also SCREEN PLANTS.

WINDOW GARDENING

Window gardening is one kind of gardening that can be enjoyed by urban apartment dwellers. It is also a means by which outdoor gardeners can lengthen their growing season.

In planning a window garden, first establish the day and nighttime temperatures of all the windows and sun porches you plan to use. Survey the light sources, both direct and indirect, natural and artificial, and check the source and kind of heat. All these factors will determine which plants you can grow and where you should put them.

Some plants do better in a south window and some in an east one; some need 12 hours of sunlight per day, while others are happy in a north window where they get no direct sunlight. In selecting plants for your window garden consider light, humidity and temperature requirements. Also consider the plants' sensitivity to any fumes that may be present in the house.

Keep your plants cool, as the florist does. You will be surprised to learn that most plants require a temperature far below that of the average home. Plants grow better when the night temperature is from 5 to 10 Fahrenheit

degrees (2.8 to 5.6 C.°) lower than day temperatures. Outdoors, this drop occurs after the sun sets. In extremely cold weather, window plants should be protected by drawing the curtains or shades or by placing paper between the plants and the windowpanes.

Light Requirements: See to it that your plants have plenty of light for growing and ample sun for flowering. Many plants may be grown in an unheated, fairly dark room but must later be brought to a sunny window for their blooming period. Remember that a green plant needs energy in the form of light. Some plants, such as the wax begonia, require little or no direct sunlight for blooming, while others, such as the geranium, require all the sunlight a south window can provide.

As a rule, flowering plants are more difficult to grow in the window garden than foliage plants because they need more light. Variegated foliage plants usually need more sun than their all-green counterparts that have more chlorophyll area.

Subdued light: Those plants that will tolerate the low light of a northern window are cast-iron plant (*Aspidistra*), Chinese evergreen (*Aglaonema*), dracaena, dumbcane (*Dieffenbachia*), fiddleleaf fig (*Ficus lyrata*), kangaroo vine (*Cissus antarctica*), nephthytis, parlor ivy (*Philodendron scandens*), pothos (*Epipremnum aureum*), rubber plant (*Ficus elastica*), screw pine (*Pandanus*), snake plant (*Sansevieria trifasciata*), and syngonium.

Moderate light: Some plants prefer the light found near an east or west window. These include African violet (*Saintpaulia ionantha*), air pine (*Aechmea*), aluminum plant (*Pilea Cadierei*), asparagus fern (*Asparagus setaceus*), begonia (*Begonia semperflorens*), bromeliads, caladium, citrus, dracaena, dumbcane (*Dieffenbachia*), fiddleleaf fig (*Ficus lyrata*), flame violet (*Episcia*), grape ivy (*Cissus*),

Moses-in-the-cradle (*Rhoeo spathacea*), nephthytis, peperomia, philodendrons, piggyback plant (*Tolmiea Menziesii*), pothos (*Epipremnum aureum*), prayer plant (*Maranta comosum*), umbrella tree (*Schefflera*), and wax plant (*Hoya*).

Direct light: Other plants require a very sunny situation, preferably near a southern window. Among these are coleus, crown-of-thorns (*Euphorbia Milii*), flowering maple (*Abutilon*), geranium (*Pelargonium*), ivy (*Hedera*), palms, shrimp plant (*Justica Brandegeana*), and velvet plant (*Gynura aurantiaca*).

These categories are not meant to be rigid; they are just suggestive. Your southern window might be shaded by a tree and be equivalent to an east window. You must experiment a bit until you find the best locations.

See also HOUSE PLANTS.

WINDROW

A row of a harvested crop, such as hay, raked up to dry is called a windrow. Any long loaf-shaped pile or stack of material, such as compost, can also be given the name.

WINE

Wine is usually made from the fermented juice of grapes or other fruits, but fine-tasting wines can also be made from flowers, beef marrow, herbs, or vegetables. Wine is sometimes fortified with distilled alcohol or flavorings to produce sherry, port, vermouth, and dessert wines, and it is distilled to make brandy.

Fruit Wine: Properly made, wine is quite stable when protected from air and light, and it is possible that juices were originally fermented to preserve the food value of fruit. However, preservation is a distant second aim of winemakers today. The modest percentage of alcohol in wine makes it a healthful and enjoyable beverage.

While good, sweet grapes, apples and other fruits often supply enough sugar for fermentation, many vintners find it necessary to add sugar or honey. Add too little, and the wine will be somewhat insipid and short-lived. Add more than the yeast can use (the little plants die when the alcohol reaches about 14 percent), and the resultant wine will be sweet. The hydrometer is a useful device that measures the percentage of sugar suspended in the unfermented juice to give an idea of just how much sugar or honey is needed. If you lack a hydrometer, it is usually safe to use two pounds sugar to each gallon juice. It's better to err on the dry side, for a wine can always be made sweeter. To produce a clear wine, siphon it off into a second container after its initial, violent fermentation. When the wine is quiet and most of its pulp and spent yeast lies at the bottom of the jug, decant it into bottles. Should the wine remain cloudy, stir in pieces of eggshell or isinglass.

Mead: A superb honey wine, or mead, can be made from apple or pear cider and honey. Add one pound of honey to each gallon of cider, and allow the mixture to ferment in a cool place. The hazy yeast that lives on the fruit will get the mead off to a violent start, and it is best to cover the fermenting vessel lightly to allow the carbon dioxide to escape. As the bubbling and frothing subsides, fit a ten-cent balloon or inexpensive air-lock on the vessel to keep air and fruit flies from turning the young wine to salad vinegar. After two or three months, when the mead is sending up only occasional bubbles, it can be bottled as a poor-man's champagne. Let the wine sit longer before bottling to produce a still wine.

Fruit mead is meant to be drunk young, but can be enjoyed at any stage of its development. Spice meads take longer to ferment and mature. A mead known well to Shakespeare, sack, is made by adding an infusion of rue leaves and fennel seeds to honey and water, mixing three pounds to the gallon.

Beer: By making beer at home, you can avoid the many chemicals that find their way into commercial brews. Brewing differs little from winemaking. However, beers are usually lower in alcoholic content (rarely higher than 6 percent) and have a somewhat bitter flavor (imparted by hops or tree roots). They are best activated with a purchased beer yeast. They are bottled when bubbling very slowly, and are drunk young. Good beers can be made from the young shoots and needles of the black spruce, from powdered ginger and from a number of other aromatic plants.

WINEBERRY
(*Rubus phoenicolasius*)

A bramble native to Japan and China but naturalized in the southeastern United States, the wineberry is grown both for ornament and for its edible berries. These are good for freezing and for jelly, but are rather flavorless when freshly picked.

The arching canes, which grow up to nine feet long and strike root where the tips touch ground, are covered with red sticky hairs and weak thorns. The leaves have three segments and purple veins, the small flowers are pink or white, and the bright red berries are surrounded by orange bracts until ripe. Berries grow on the canes of the previous year's growth.

Wineberries are easily grown in any good garden soil. They can tolerate some shade. Propagation is by root cuttings, suckers or seed.

See also BRAMBLE FRUITS.

WINTERBERRY   (*Ilex verticillata*)

An ornamental woody shrub of the Holly family, the common winterberry is native to North America and is often cultivated as a garden shrub. Also called black alder, it has bright red or yellow berries that remain on the branches long after the leaves have fallen.

Like other hollies, the winterberry does best in a northern or northeastern exposure. Sunlight encourages lusher growth, but shade makes the leaves a richer green. Winterberries thrive with a continuous mulch of oak leaves or peat moss, and with regular fertilizing with decomposed manure, preferably poultry droppings. The plants benefit from watering during dry periods in both summer and winter.

See also HOLLY.

WINTERBLOOM   See WITCHHAZEL
WINTER DAFFODIL
See STERNBERGIA

WINTER GARDEN CARE

Your garden not only requires care during the growing season, but also needs a certain amount of attention in the wintertime. This is especially true if you plan to store vegetables in your garden over winter. Mulch the garden well to prevent excessive freezing and thawing of the soil. With proper mulching, almost any fleshy-rooted vegetable can remain in the garden and be harvested when needed.

Some plants, such as dandelion, endive and lettuce, can be overwintered in such a manner that they will begin producing very early in the spring. But cabbage, carrot, horse-radish, kale, and spinach are all reasonably hardy vegetables that continue to produce during cold weather. All but horseradish should be mulched lightly.

Most of the plants in your garden are less hardy than these vegetables and may need special care in order to survive the winter. As a general rule, employ any cultural practice that will encourage plants to harden off before cold weather sets in. Unless the autumn is especially dry, discontinue watering several weeks before the first expected frost. In a dry autumn, wood ripens well, but if it is unseasonably dry just after the first heavy killing frost, good watering is advisable to make sure there is a normal amount of sap in the plants.

Mulching: By far the best kind of winter protection for plants is a mulch. If suitably mulched, the ground freezes little or not at all. Plant roots and soil organisms remain partly active and can start functioning in the early spring when sunny, windy days, followed by nighttime frosts, have a drying effect on vegetation. Under these early-spring conditions, unmulched evergreens often lose water through their leaves. Unable to replace it from the frozen soil, they often turn brown and die.

Snow is one of the best protective winter mulches, but over a large part of this country it cannot be depended on to give continuous protection during the really cold months. Frequently a midwinter thaw is followed by a cold spell and frost sinks deep into the ground.

Mulching biennial and perennial flowers, shrubs and trees is the last and the most important job of the year. It may make the difference between beautiful and healthy plants and sickly, insect-ravaged ones.

Do not apply mulch until the ground has been frozen slightly. This will insure complete dormancy of the plants under the mulch. If snow falls in the meantime, mulch over the snow. Do not be in a hurry in the spring to remove the mulch. Mulches should be removed gradually and only when plants have begun to renew growth in spring.

Mounding: Some shrubs and woody perennials can be protected most satisfactorily by mounding the soil around the plant's base. In most regions and for most plants, a six-inch to one-foot mound is adequate. Cut back tall plants and mulch the area well.

Covering: Biennials such as delphinium, foxglove, violas, and pansies which have a rosette of leaves near the surface of the ground must be protected during the winter, but cannot endure under a mulch which packs and excludes air. A suitable protection for such plants consists of an inverted box large enough to cover the plant with six or eight inches of plant mulch over and around the box. If leaves are used for mulching, wire screening over them, weighted down with stones or bricks, will keep the leaves in place.

Most plants are sufficiently protected if covered with a layer of autumn leaves, especially dry oak leaves which are the least apt to pack into a tight, compact layer. Of course, any leaves that are available may be used. Boughs of hemlock, spruce or other coniferous trees may be used as a protective winter cover for biennial and perennial herbaceous plants. Any material which will not pack, such as salt hay, straw, excelsior, wood shavings, rock or mineral wool, may be used for a winter mulch.

Wind Protection: Tender shrubs can be protected by wrapping them with rye straw. This protective covering should not be applied until the weather has become quite cold and the plants are completely dormant. For protecting such plants as boxwood and rhododendron against the biting winter winds, burlap screens or covers may be used. They break the force of the wind and still admit sufficient air to keep the plants in a healthy condition. Windbreaks may also be made of other materials such as bamboo or fiber matting, boards, poultry wire covered with heavy paper, a barrel with both ends removed, and hedges of such hardy plants as spruce or hemlock. Screens and cases are to be regarded as additional protection given after the ground has already been well mulched for the winter.

It produces small, solitary, white or pink flowers and tiny scarlet berries that are edible. A native western variety, *G. Shallon,* grows up to six feet tall. It has heart-shaped leaves, panicles of pink white flowers and dark purple fruits.

Wintergreen leaves and berries have long been valued as a flavoring for candy, medicine, chewing gum, perfume, tooth powder, and tea. It has also, traditionally, had uses in internal and external medicine.

Wintergreen requires a partly shady location and well-drained, sandy soil with a pH of 4.5 to 5.5. Wintergreen can be propagated by seed (although small seed makes it difficult), cuttings and layering. Divisions may be set out in spring or fall. Because of its many requirements, wintergreen makes a better wild garden subject than one for the herbiary.

It is quite difficult to establish plants taken from the woods. Nursery-grown stock is more satisfactory for transplanting, since it is ac-

WINTERGREEN
(*Gaultheria procumbens*)

A prostrate evergreen herb belonging to the Heath family, wintergreen is noted for its bright, stimulating taste and smell. These qualities have given it the nicknames spiceberry, teaberry and checkerberry. It is a hardy plant, found in scattered woods and clearings from eastern Canada south to the Gulf states, and especially at elevations of 2,000 feet or more.

Wintergreen is a low-growing, creeping plant. Its stems are half underground, and the plant rarely grows higher than four inches tall. Its oval leathery leaves are glossy green above, pale on the underside, and about an inch long.

Wintergreen is difficult to establish but success can be had if nursery-grown stock is planted in a partially shaded spot where the soil is very acid.

customed to artificial conditions. It should be planted on a shady slope and mulched with two to four inches of pine needles.

WINTERKILL

Winterkill of plants is caused by extreme cold, or cold greater than a given plant can withstand. Twigs and immature wood may be winter-killed, while the mature older wood remains untouched; or, the entire top of a plant may be winter-killed to the ground, though sprouts may appear later from the roots. A sudden drop in temperature early in winter is more likely to kill than the same drop late in the season, when new growth has become hardened.

See also FROST.

WINTER PLANTS

Evergreens are generally considered the backbone of winter garden design, but many deciduous trees and shrubs with valuable winter characteristics also offer beauty, color and interest during the colder months.

These include birches, the hardy crab apples, dogwoods, hawthorn, moosewood, and many willows. Many shrubs, including hollies, Japanese barberry, snowberry, and viburnums, also produce attractive berries. Colorful foliage during winter is offered by the cotoneaster, heather, some honeysuckles, and lavender cotton.

Some plants even produce blooms in cold weather. Among this group are rosebud cherry (*Prunus subhirtella* cv. 'Autumnalis'), Christ-mas rose, spring or winter heath, and some of the witchhazels.

See also entries for individual winter plants.

WINTER SAVORY   *See* SAVORY

WINTER SWEET PEA
See SWAINSONA

WIREGRASS   *See* BERMUDAGRASS

WIREWORM

These slender, jointed, usually hard-shelled worms are light to dark brown, and range in length up to 1½ inches. They are often confused with millipedes, which have many pairs of slender legs instead of the wireworm's three pairs, positioned well forward. They feed entirely underground, attacking the germinating seeds, roots, underground stems, and tubers of growing plants. Among the many vulnerable crops are potatoes, beets, beans, cabbage, carrots, corn, lettuce, onions, and turnips.

Wireworms are most likely to cause damage on poorly drained soil or on land that has recently been grass sodded. Newly broken sod should not be used for the garden if other soil is available. If sod must be used, it should be thoroughly plowed and stirred once a week for four to six weeks preceding planting. Stirring the soil exposes many of the insects and crushes many others. Enriching soil with humus will also improve aeration and reduce wireworm attacks. To control serious infestations, fallow the land in summer every two or three

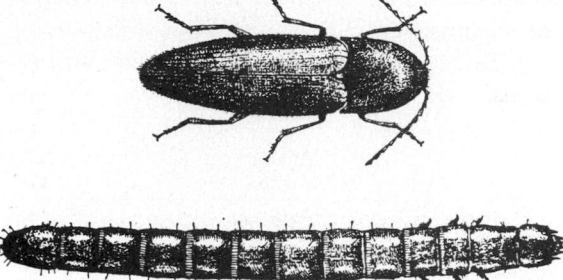

The larvae of click beetles, wireworms feed on underground stems, seeds and roots. Crop rotation is the best preventative measure known.
(Courtesy of U.S. Department of Agriculture)

years. It also helps to grow annual green manure crops, such as clover.

In the garden, wireworms can be lured to a half potato, with the eyes removed. Bury it an inch underground and pull it out after a day or two.

See also INSECT CONTROL.

WISTERIA

Deciduous woody vines of the Pea family that are hardy in the North, wisterias have velvety, compound leaves, large, flattened seed-pods, and drooping clusters of purple, lavender, blue, and white pealike flowers.

Wisterias can be grown in full sun or partial shade. Since they are vigorous and rapid growers, they require plenty of room and a very sturdy support. Plant the vines along the wall of a building or train them to freestanding trellises.

Prepare the soil to a depth of three feet, adding enough rotted manure to make up one-third of its bulk. Water the plants regularly until they are well established and then mulch them to keep the roots cool.

It is important to prune wisteria very severely annually, after the blooming season and before the growth of new wood. Vines that fail to blossom, should be pruned during the summer. If the vines are cut back to within six or seven buds, they should flower the next spring.

Japanese wisteria (*W. floribunda*) grows to 35 feet and has 18-inch clusters of blue flowers followed by velvety pods. Variety Macrobotrys has flower clusters to three feet long. There is also a white-flowered variety.

Chinese wisteria (*W. sinensis*) has 12-inch flower clusters that appear before those of Japanese wisteria. Both species are very showy and can be grown in many northern regions.

WITCHALDER   (*Fothergilla*)

A genus of the Witchhazel family, Hamamelidaseae, fothergilla includes plants which are grown for their attractive foliage and showy spikes of petalless white flowers. Dwarf alder (*F. Gardenii*) grows to three feet, and has spikes one to two inches long, while *F. monticola,* four to six feet, and *F. major,* to ten feet, have two-inch spikes. All are hardy south of Boston.

Fothergillas prefer a rich, moist soil, and are propagated by seed or layering.

WITCHHAZEL   (*Hamamelis*)

Native to low woods from Nova Scotia to Minnesota and south to Florida and Texas, this small genus of ornamental shrubs is sometimes called winterbloom because it blooms from October to April. Crumpled flower buds open into yellow blossoms which are followed by two-seeded, gaping capsules. The leaves, which turn yellow or orange in fall, yield a fluid which is used to make a tonic and astringent lotion. Easily cultivated in the garden or on the bank of a stream or other moist site, witchhazel is propagated by layering or by seed, which is slow to germinate.

H. virginiana, which is hardy from Canada southward, is a shrub or tree up to 15 feet tall. Its light yellow flowers bloom while the leaves

Witchhazel's ragged, bright yellow flowers are followed by seed which can be gathered and used for propagation.

are falling. *H. vernalis,* hardy from Philadelphia south, grows to six feet, and opens its yellow flowers during the winter. *H. japonica,* hardy throughout most of the United States, blooms between January and March. It grows to a small tree up to 25 feet tall. Flowers are bright yellow.

H. mollis is the showiest species, with leaves that are gray white beneath, and golden yellow flowers which bloom in February or March.

WOLFBERRY   *See* SYMPHORICARPOS

WOOD ASHES

A valuable source of potash in the garden, hardwood ashes generally contain from 1 to 10 percent potash and 1½ percent phosphorus. Wood ashes should never be allowed to stand in the rain, because their potash leaches away. They can be mixed with other fertilizing materials, side-dressed around growing plants or used as a mulch. Apply about 5 to 10 pounds per 100 square feet. Avoid contact between freshly spread ashes and germinating seeds or new plant roots by spreading ashes a few inches away from plants. Avoid using wood ashes around blueberries or other acid-loving plants, since they are alkaline. Only wood ashes, and not coal ashes, should be used in soil or compost.

See also FERTILIZER, POTASH.

WOOD BETONY   *See* PEDICULARIS

WOOD CHIPS

Like sawdust and other wood wastes, wood chips are useful in the garden. They can be used as a decorative garden mulch or as a component of compost. They have a higher nutritive content than sawdust, but, like sawdust, are low in nitrogen and may cause temporary nitrogen deficiency when added to soil. It is a good idea to compost chips before using them if your soil is coarse or loose. In any soil, nitrogen-rich material should be added with them. Pine chips have been found particularly effective in improving the soil because they require less nitrogen for decomposition. Other woods such as birch and oak work well also.

Another way to avoid nitrogen drain from soil when using fresh chips is to apply the chips ahead of a green manure crop, preferably a legume, or to allow about a year's interval between application of the chips and seeding or planting of the main crop.

Wood chips may also be used as bedding in the barn, stable or poultry house. Bedding soaked with urine and manure makes an excellent fertilizer which may be applied to the fields.

See also COMPOSTING, MULCH.

WOOD ROT

Wood decay in a living or dead tree is caused by fungus, which enters the tree through a wound in the bark. Heartwood rot in an old tree may be dangerous if it causes the tree to lose its mechanical support. The best remedy for tree rot is prompt attention to injuries, removing injured branches and filling cavities left by cleaning out dead tissue.

WOOD SORREL　　*See* OXALIS

WOODY PLANTS

Shrubs, trees or vines which do not die to the ground during the winter, and have buds above ground, are known as woody plants. These are distinct from herbaceous plants which die to the ground each year and have only underground buds.

WOOL WASTES

Also known as shoddy, wool wastes have been used by British farmers since the early nineteenth century. The wool fiber decomposes when in contact with moisture in the soil, and releases nitrogen for plant growth.

WORM
See EARTHWORM, INSECT CONTROL

WORMSEED
(*Chenopodium ambrosioides*)

A coarse, usually annual weed of the Goosefoot family, wormseed commonly occurs in waste places and is often cultivated throughout the eastern and southern parts of the United States. The seeds and the volatile oil distilled from the fruiting tops of the plant are used in the control of intestinal worms in livestock. American wormseed grows well under cultivation in almost any soil, but a good sandy loam and full sun are preferred.

WORMWOOD   (*Artemisia*)

Species of this large genus of aromatic and bitter perennials are cultivated as ornamentals, medicinal and culinary herbs and even as insect repellents. Wormwood is distinguished by its long stem with silky hairs, its gray green leaves and its tiny yellow or whitish flowers that bloom from July through October.

Easily cultivated and making small demands on soil fertility, wormwood is propagated by cuttings, root division in fall or seed sown in fall. Allow two feet between plants.

The entire plant is harvested in July and August and the stems and roots then discarded. The upper portions should be kept in a warm room until thoroughly dry. After removing coarse stems pack the remaining portions in airtight jars.

In the garden, wormwood is valued for its ability to repel flea beetles and cabbage butterflies. Absinthe (*A. absinthium*) is not a good companion plant, however. It secretes the toxic substance, absinthin, which inhibits the growth of neighboring vegetation.

This genus also includes tarragon (*A. Dracunculus*), a popular seasoning; southernwood (*A. Abrotanum*), a small, aromatic ornamental; Roman wormwood (*A. pontica*), an ingredient of vermouth; and sagebrush (*A. tridentata*), the silvery shrub of the western United States.

See also SOUTHERNWOOD, TARRAGON.

The entire wormwood plant can be harvested in middle to late summer and dried for use as an insect repellent.

WOUNDWORT   *See* STACHYS

WYETHIA

Members of a genus of western American perennial herbs of the Daisy family, wyethias grow one to three feet tall and have long, slender leaves and yellow flowers. They are sometimes transplanted to the wild garden, where they should be given a sunny spot. Propagation is by seed or division. *W. amplexicaulis* is a glossy-leaved, two-foot plant with yellow flowers that grow up to four inches across. *W. angustifolia* has similar flowers, but its foliage is hairy.

X

XANTHISMA

Members of this small genus of the Composite family thrive in full sun and poor soil, and will withstand drought and high winds. They are native to Texas. Star-of-Texas (*X. texana*) grows to three feet, and is a bushy annual which bears lemon-colored flowers.

XANTHOCERAS

The popular *X. sorbifolium* is a shrub which grows 15 feet tall and in spring bears beautiful long racemes of white flowers with yellow bases. It is hardy in most of the United States and grows well in any medium-fertile, well-drained soil. The leaves are feathery and stay green long into autumn. Propagate by means of stratified seed or root cuttings.

XANTHORHIZA

Yellowroot (*X. simplicissima*) is a low deciduous shrub that grows up to two feet high. It is hardy throughout most of the United States and thrives on moist, sandy banks. The tiny brown purple flowers are borne in drooping racemes in spring. The plant has interesting yellow roots and can be easily increased by division. It is a useful shrub for the wild or rock garden.

XANTHOSOMA

The rootstocks of these pretty foliage plants are much used for food in the tropics. Here they are popular ornamental and indoor plants. *X. Lindenii,* a fine plant for a warm window garden or greenhouse, has 19-inch leaves veined with white and a six-inch white spathe. The purple-veined leaves of *X. violaceum* are sometimes even longer and 1½ feet wide. The foot-long spathes are white. Both of these make good summer bedding plants. *X. sagittaefolium,* which is called yautia or tannia, has big leaves—up to three feet long and two feet wide. These species can be grown outdoors in extreme southern Florida. Xanthosomas need full sun, very rich, moist soil and heavy dressings of compost or rotted manure. Propagation is by division.

XERANTHEMUM

Long-lasting annuals of the Composite family, the xeranthemums or everlastings are often grown for dried flowers. Immortelle (*X. annuum*) grows to two feet tall, with white or lavender flower heads. Some of its varieties are double. Immortelle grows well in any soil and if grown as a tender annual will give very early bloom.

Everlastings should be dried slowly by hanging them upside down in the shade. Some gardeners dry them by completely burying the flowers in pots of dry sand, which are left in a warm room for several weeks. After this period the sand is poured off very slowly and the petals carefully cleaned off with a camel's-hair brush. Both these methods may also be used to dry other garden and wild flowers.

The name everlasting is given to many other plants whose flowers (or seedpods) can be dried and preserved. Some of these are the globe amaranth (*Gomphrena globosa*), thrift (*Armeria*), cockscomb (*Celosia cristata*), honesty (*Lunaria*), strawflower (*Helichrysum bracteatum*), winged everlasting (*Ammobium alatum*), and helipterum.

XEROPHYLLUM

The xerophyllums or turkeybeards have very narrow grasslike leaves and bear dense racemes of tiny white flowers in early summer. *X. asphodeloides* grows four or five feet tall in moist, acid, sandy soil and is usually found along the borders of pine-barren bogs on the Atlantic coast. *X. tenax,* sometimes called the fire-lily, grows on the Pacific coast in similar soils, and has leaves two feet long and an 18-inch flower cluster. Both can be transplanted to suitable spots in the wild garden.

XEROPHYTE

Plants which have special mechanisms to help them survive occasional or frequent long droughts are called xerophytes. Some plants like the cacti store water in their tissues, while others have foliage that rolls up tightly into a ball. Others have a varnishlike coating, or become very ashy-dry or actually fall—all means of reducing transpiration.

See also RESURRECTION PLANTS, SUCCULENTS.

Y

YAM (*Dioscorea*)

Yams are vines cultivated for ornament or for their edible tubers. They are native to the South Pacific islands, but their culture has spread to other tropical areas. Japan, China, Australia, India, Africa, the West Indies, South America, and the southern tip of Florida all grow yams. In many of these places, yams provide an important part of the diet. The sweet potato is sometimes called a yam, but it is of an entirely different genus (*Ipomoea*). *See also* SWEET POTATO.

Most yams do best in near-tropical climates. Their tubers may be planted any time of the year in warm, sandy soil. Place them two to three feet apart in rows about five feet apart. Some species produce their tubers above ground in leaf axils; others produce them so far underground that they are difficult to dig. For optimum yields, stake the vines.

The Chinese yam or cinnamon vine (*D. Batatas*) bears cinnamon-scented flowers and aerial tubers which are used for propagation, as well as large edible, deep-growing underground tubers. It is grown for ornament as well as for food and is hardy as far north as New York although it will not always produce edible tubers. The air potato (*D. bulbifera*) has no big underground tubers, but is grown in the South and in greenhouses for the odd tubers borne in the axils of the leaves which are sometimes eaten like potatoes. Yams contain more protein and less starch than potatoes.

The yampee (*D. trifida*) is another south-ern vine with small underground tubers, prized for their flavor, while the wild yam (*D. villosa*) grows along the Atlantic and Gulf coasts and has a woody rootstock. There are many other edible species, mostly tropical, some of which have tubers weighing up to 100 pounds.

YAM BEAN (*Pachyrhizus erosus*)

This tropical vine of the Pea family bears edible tubers and pods, but is rarely grown in this country. Its stems, which often reach a length of 15 feet and need support on a fence or trellis, bear six-inch leaves and clusters of lavender or deep pink flowers. The hairy red pods are up to six inches long, and each contains a half-dozen or more seeds. *P. tuberosus* is a species with white flowers and huge pods. Neither species will stand the slightest frost.

YANKEE BUG
See BLISTER BEETLE, INSECT CONTROL

YARROW (*Achillea Millefolium*)

Common along roadsides and in pastures in Europe and the United States, yarrow is a hardy perennial of the Composite family that usually grows in thick, bushy clumps. It has striking yellow, white or crimson blooms and finely divided gray green foliage. Some species such as *A. ageratifolia* are used for ground cover, and grow less than eight inches high, but most yarrows grow to heights of two to three feet.

Planting and Culture: Yarrow can be planted from seed or by dividing the root clumps of established plants. Seeds should be sown on fine, moist soil, preferably indoors during the early spring. Yarrow will grow in very poor soil where ordinary lawn grasses cannot grow and may be used as a grass substitute. Although fertilizing is largely unnecessary, annual applications of bone meal will promote growth. The herb's aroma will be more pleasing if it is grown in light, sandy soil rather than in heavy, clayey ground.

The plants need plenty of sun and should be spaced ten inches apart in an open bed. Yarrow has a tendency to become weedy and must be kept in bounds.

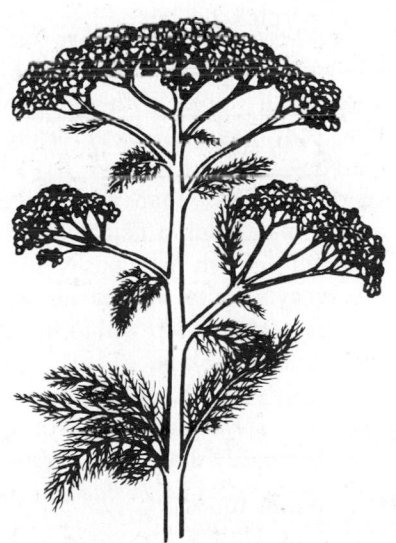

A hardy perennial with very soft, pale green leaves and white, yellow or pinkish flower heads, yarrow does well in the sandy soil of a rock garden.

Harvesting: The plant can be harvested beginning in June or July. Yarrow flowers, which can be dried and used in bouquets, bloom until October. The whole plant should be cut at the peak of flowering if you wish to use it as a medicinal herb. Chop the stem and leaves, and dry them rapidly at 90 to 100°F. (32.22 to 37.78°C.). If it is not dried rapidly and thoroughly, the plant will darken.

In the kitchen, yarrow has only a marginal use as an occasional stand-in for cinnamon or nutmeg.

See also HERB.

YAUTIA   *See* XANTHOSOMA

YAWWEED   (*Morinda Royoc*)

A small shrub about three feet high, the yawweed or royoc is hardy only as far north as central Florida and Southern California. It bears small white flowers in dense heads and fleshy yellow fruits an inch in diameter. The Indian mulberry (*M. citrifolia*) grows as a small tree in the same areas, and has big shiny leaves, small flowers and two-inch yellow fruits.

YEAST   *See* MICROORGANISM

YEDDO HAWTHORN
(*Raphiolepis umbellata*)

Popular in the Deep South and Southern California, the yeddo hawthorn is a rounded six-foot shrub, with clusters of shiny evergreen leaves, fragrant white flowers and purple black berrylike fruits. The Indian hawthorn (*R. indica*) is a similar shrub with pink blooms, and *R.* x *Delacourii* is a hybrid of the two, with a very compact growth habit. All three species do well in any medium-fertile soil that is not too wet or acid, and *R.* x *Delacourii* is a favorite for patio and terrace plantings. Yeddo hawthorns are also good shrubs for cool greenhouses in the North if they are given a humusy, well-drained soil. Propagate by seed or cuttings of ripe wood under glass.

YELLOWROOT   See XANTHORHIZA

YELLOWWOOD   (*Cladrastis lutea*)

The yellowwood or gopherwood tree grows 30 to 50 feet tall, and is hardy as far north as lower New England and Ontario. Its wood has a pronounced yellow color. In late June, the tree bears drooping 12-inch clusters of white flowers and flat pods. It is popular for its showy blooms and for its feathery foliage, which turns bright yellow in fall. It will thrive in practically any fairly moist soil and is propagated by seed in spring.

YERBA SANTA
(*Eriodictyon californicum*)

A shrubby perennial belonging to the Waterleaf family, yerba santa grows three to eight feet high and has aromatic, shiny leaves which are hairy underneath. The plant also has attractive clusters of lavender to white flowers that appear in late spring and early summer. It grows best in fairly moist soil of moderate fertility, primarily on the West Coast.

Yerba santa has been used as medicine in the southwestern United States. It is an expectorant and is added to drugs to mask their flavor.

YEW   (*Taxus*)

Yews are among the most beautiful and popular of the evergreens. They range from small shrubs to 60-foot trees, and bear scarlet berries that have small holes in them through which the tiny gray seeds can be seen. The wood is very strong and flexible and has been used for centuries to make bows. Both the leaves and the fruit contain a poison that is highly dangerous if eaten.

The Japanese yews will thrive on sandy slopes buffeted by driving storms. They keep their clean, fresh look, with thick velvety needles that stay beautiful even through the rigors of a New England winter. *T. cuspidata* is a more rapid grower than most evergreens and, though it may reach a height of 35 to 50 feet, it is usually grown as a bushy shrub. A variety, *T. c.* cv. 'Nana' makes an excellent hedge which is easy to keep within bounds. It is also a fine specimen plant.

The English yew (*T. baccata*) is a slow-growing tree, not often planted in North America. Though less hardy than the Japanese yews, there are a few varieties of *T. baccata* that are suited to northern gardens.

Ground hemlock (*T. canadensis*) generally grows less than three feet high and is hardy throughout most of the United States. It is often used as a ground cover under evergreen trees, but does not do well in exposed positions.

Yews are propagated by seed (very slow to germinate) or by cuttings taken in spring or fall.

See also EVERGREEN.

YLANG-YLANG   *See* ILANG-ILANG

YORK AND LANCASTER ROSE
(*Rosa damascena* cv. 'Versicolor')

This is a variety of the damask rose that bears both white and pink flowers on the same bush, as well as white-striped red flowers. The name refers to the Wars of the Roses, in which the house of York, represented by a white rose, fought the house of Lancaster, symbolized by a red rose. Like the damask, this rose is hardy to southern New England and grows as a shrub up to eight feet high.

See also ROSE.

YOUNGBERRY
(*Rubus ursinus* cv. 'Young')

This bramble fruit is a hybrid between a trailing blackberry and a southern dewberry. It bears abundant nearly seedless fruit that ripens a few weeks before that of boysenberry. Youngberries taste much like raspberries and are prized for juice, jams and dessert. Hardy varieties have been developed, but most need winter protection.

See also BRAMBLE FRUITS.

YUCCA

Yucca is usually thought of as a desert or semidesert plant, confined to dry areas of the South and the southwestern desert, but several yuccas are surprisingly hardy in the cool, moist regions of the North.

Yuccas are very handsome plants. Nearly all of the 40-odd species have stiff, swordlike silver green leaves, growing in a clump at ground level. From this clump arises a single leafless stalk bearing a magnificent spike of highly fragrant, waxy flowers.

Yuccas blend handsomely in borders, contrast beautifully with the shapes of both evergreen and deciduous shrubs, and can be planted to stand as majestic sentinels on either side of an entrance gate or door. They also serve well lining a driveway, fence or terrace wall, or as a dramatic living sculpture against low, craggy rocks. Finally, yuccas can be grown in tubs and moved around for special effects.

Planting and Culture: All yuccas require a sunny and fairly dry location with a light, sandy or gritty well-drained soil. Digging a deep hole and filling it with a sand-humus mixture will take care of this. Apply compost, bone meal and dried manure to the plants once each year. Watering should rarely, if ever, be necessary. Drought produces a lovely foliage and stem patina on desert-type plants. Yuccas generally flower only in alternate years, but the flowers last four to six weeks.

Yuccas are easy to propagate. They can be increased by seed, rhizome or stem cuttings, or by digging offsets from the side of an established plant.

In nature, the yucca is pollinated by a small white moth, the pronuba. This night-flying insect deposits her eggs in the seed vessel of a blooming yucca, then fertilizes the plant with pollen from another yucca. When the pronuba grubs hatch out, they find a goodly supply of seeds to eat, but leave plenty to produce more yuccas. Scientists call the yucca-pronuba relationship a perfect example of symbiosis, the mutual interdependence of two things in nature.

Types: Two species have trunks. The Joshua tree (*Y. brevifolia*) grows up to 40 feet high, its branches twisting into grotesque shapes. The Spanish bayonet (*Y. aloifolia*) is about 20 feet tall, and has very sharp-pointed, long leaves and spectacular white or purple-tinged flowers. Neither of these will stand wet winters, and they grow only in the South.

Our-Lord's-candle (*Y. Whipplei*) has short basal leaves but sends up great creamy spikes, bearing many blooms. It will not stand frost or wet soil.

Northern gardeners who have never grown the hardy yuccas are missing plants that add great beauty and accent to gardens. One of the best yuccas for northern gardens is the Adam's needle (*Y. filamentosa*), sometimes called needle palm. It is a deep-rooted, tough-fibered, handsome plant that has no trouble surviving rigorous New England winters. Its flower stalk may rise 12 feet or higher. *Y. flaccida* is a similar species.

Other yuccas for the North are *Y. glauca*, soapwell or soapweed, and *Y. elata*, soaptree, both good as far north as southern Minnesota if good drainage and shelter against harsh winds are provided. *Y. gloriosa* is reportedly even able to stand city smog. *Y. rupicola* is much the same as *Y. gloriosa*, except that its leaves droop over.

YULAN   *See* MAGNOLIA

Z

ZALUZIANSKYA

The fragrant night phloxes of this genus are tender annuals of the Figwort family. *Z. capensis* grows 15 inches high, and has tubular white flowers that are white on the inside and purple on the outside, while *Z. villosa* is about ten inches high, and has similar flowers that may be either white or lavender on the inside. The flower spikes open only at night and bloom all summer.

ZAMANG   *See* SAMAN

ZAMIA

Members of a genus of Zamiaceae, the zamias, also called coonties, can be cultivated indoors in a moist, warm greenhouse or outdoors in absolutely frost-free sections of Florida. They are curious palmlike plants, with stiff evergreen leaves at the top of a trunk. The trunk of *Z. floridana* is almost completely underground, but in *Z. integrifolia* it rises about a foot above ground. Both species bear six-inch-long woody cones. Zamias, which need a moist, sandy soil, are propagated by seed or offsets.

ZANTEDESCHIA   *See* CALLA LILY
ZANTHORHIZA   *See* XANTHORHIZA

ZAUSCHNERIA

This pretty perennial, often called the hummingbird's trumpet or California fuchsia, has small hairy leaves and brilliant crimson flowers that resemble fuchsias but bloom much later. The plant does well under dry conditions so it may not be hardy in eastern areas with wet winters. It grows about a foot tall. Propagate by seed or division and use soil that is not too rich.

ZEBRAGRASS
See GRASS, ORNAMENTAL

ZEBRA PLANT

There are two plants called zebra plant: *Aphelandra squarrosa* and *Calathea zebrina*. The former is the one commonly sold by florists as zebra plant.

Aphelandra, a tropical American native, has striking gray green or bright green leaves veined in white. The showy terminal spikes of red- or yellow-bracted flowers bloom in fall, but can easily be made to bloom in other seasons. Aphelandras prefer warm temperatures of 80 to 85°F. (26.67 to 29.44°C.) during the day and 62 to 65°F. (16.67 to 18.33°C.) at night. They need average humidity and moderate light. They are best potted in a humus-rich soil and kept slightly pot-bound. When blooming ends, prune lightly and decrease the amount of water so that the soil is dry, but do not allow the plants to wilt. At other times, keep soil moist. Propagate from cuttings of slightly ripened wood. Other popular species include *A. aurantiaca* cv. 'Roezlii' with orange red bloom, and *A. chamissoniana* with yellow flowers.

Aphelandra *zebra plants have strikingly deep green leaves year-round and showy red- or yellow-bracted flowers in the fall.*

Calathea zebrina is a popular indoor foliage plant, growing two to three feet tall, with leaves up to 18 inches long and a foot wide. The foliage is usually green striped with light yellow green and with red purple on the undersides.

C. zebrina can be grown outdoors in a moist rich soil in Florida and Southern California, and should be fed heavily with compost or rotted manure. In the house it needs a temperature between 75 and 85°F. (23.89 to 29.44°C.), with a moist atmosphere, shading from hot sun and biweekly feedings of liquid manure. Give it a sand-humus soil mixture and repot it only when it has become very pot-bound. There are many other varieties of *Calathea* growing from eight inches to over three feet tall, with variously colored and striped leaves.

ZEBRINA

These Mexican plants, with their graceful decumbent growing habit and colorful variegated foliage, make excellent hanging basket plants for the greenhouse or home. They are quite tolerant of adverse conditions. Variegated ovate leaves with a metallic sheen appear in red, purple, green, and white and usually have purple undersides. The plant has tiny purple flowers.

An all-purpose soil kept evenly moist is recommended and plants should be placed in an eastern, western or lightly shaded southern window. Propagation is by stem tip cuttings which root at the joints. Eventually the plants will require pruning, otherwise they develop a "leggy" appearance. Fading of color is usually an indication of insufficient light.

The most common zebrina is *Z. pendula,*

Not to be confused with Tradescantia, *the* Zebrina *form of wandering Jew is characterized by purplish, variegated leaves.*

often called wandering Jew. *Z. pendula* cv. 'Quadicolor' is a particularly colorful cultivar.

ZELKOVA

These ornamental, deciduous trees of the Elm family have serrated leaves, small flowers and one-seeded fruits. *Z. carpinifolia* is a round-headed 80-foot tree, which is hardy north to lower New England and south to Missouri. Its leaves turn red in fall. *Z. serrata* is a similar species though it is hardy throughout most of the country. Its leaves turn yellow or russet in fall. Zelkovas do well in a variety of soils, and are propagated by seed, layering or grafting.

ZENOBIA

A semievergreen shrub grown in the southeastern states, *Z. pulverulenta* reaches a height of six feet and bears blue green leaves. In late spring it has racemes of small white flowers. Give it a humusy, slightly acid soil, and mulch it heavily with leaves. It is occasionally forced in the greenhouse.

ZEPHYR LILY   *See* ZEPHYRANTHES

ZEPHYRANTHES

The zephyr or fairy lilies are summer- or fall-blooming bulbs which grow about eight inches high, with dainty, funnel-shaped white, yellow, pink, or red flowers. They are planted in spring in a sandy soil with ample humus, two inches apart and with the tips of the bulbs just under the soil surface.

Z. candida and *Z. Atamasco* are the hardiest species and can be left in the ground all winter as far north as Washington, D.C. All other species must be lifted before frost and stored in dry sand. They can be forced for indoor bloom by potting a half-dozen in a five-inch bulb pan in equal parts of loam, sand and peat moss. They benefit from a short cooling period before they are brought indoors but they should never be exposed to freezing temperatures. If they are allowed to dry off for a couple of months after blooming they will flower once again and perhaps even a third time in one year.

ZIGADENUS

A hardy perennial for the wild or bog garden, zigadenus has foot-long, grasslike leaves and a two- to three-foot stalk that bears a panicle of tiny white or yellow green flowers. It needs a moist, humusy, acid soil. Both the foliage and rootstock contain a dangerous alkaloid, which sometimes causes serious live-stock poisoning in the West. Some of the other names for species of zigadenus are soap plant, zygadene, death camas, and poison sego.

ZIGZAG CLOVER
(*Trifolium medium*)

Like all the clovers, zigzag clover is a legume that is useful for soil improvement. It is a one-foot-high perennial with zigzag stems and creeping rootstocks. The flowers are deep purple.

ZINC

Zinc is one of the most important trace minerals—and one of the most frequently deficient in soils. Scientists are just beginning to understand the vital role that zinc plays in plant, animal and human nutrition. Corn low in zinc displays a lack of tryptophan, one of the essential amino acids. Zinc has been found to be critical to growth in animals, and zinc deficiency can not only impair growth, but also delay healing and contribute to chronic disease.

A lack of zinc can be endemic in some soils, such as the particularly alkaline farmland soils of the West. Even on fertile, hilly land, zinc may be in short supply in badly eroded areas. Generally, however, soil with a high content of organic matter will have a sufficient amount of available zinc.

Zinc deficiency can and does occur on fertile soil that has had heavy applications of artificial fertilizer. Apparently the large amounts of nitrogen, phosphorus and potassium in the fertilizer tie up available zinc. In addition, low organic matter content and restricted plant root zones which have been caused by soil compaction or hardpans may contribute to lack of zinc.

Manure is by far the best organic fertilizer to use to maintain proper zinc levels in your garden soil. Soil experts of whatever persuasion agree that well-manured fields have not been found to be zinc deficient. Raw phosphate rock contains traces of zinc, too.

See also SOIL DEFICIENCIES, TRACE ELEMENTS.

ZINNIA

Zinnias have become one of the favorite and best all-purpose annuals. Their use in the garden is almost without limit. They may form a flowering hedge or serve in a mixed border. Smaller varieties are excellent for edgings or for the rock garden. Zinnias of all varieties make good cut flowers. When the plant was first introduced from Mexico, it was a small-flowered, coarse and unattractive plant. Today there are so many varieties of different heights, sizes of flowers and colors that it is best to consult seed catalogs for full descriptions.

Planting and Culture: Zinnias are easily

grown in almost any soil and survive in the hottest weather. They are warm-weather plants, so should never be sown until both the days and nights are warm and there is no danger of frost. The seeds are large and germinate quickly, often in four or five days. Sow seed in the open ground and cover the seed with about ¼ inch of soil. Because practically every seed will sprout, they may be planted ½ inch to one inch apart. If the ground is very dry, soak the soil to hasten germination. For earliest bloom, start seed indoors in late April.

After the seedlings have acquired their true leaves, they may be thinned to stand four or five inches apart. A final thinning should leave the plants ten to 12 inches apart for dwarf varieties, 16 to 18 inches apart for those of medium growth and up to 20 to 22 inches apart for the tall varieties. Zinnias transplant readily, so plants thinned out may be used else-

where. Although they stand transplanting at almost any stage, you will have stronger, well-branched plants if you transplant or thin zinnias when the plants are small.

Once the young plants have become established, you can forget about them for the rest of the summer. If you wish to cultivate, do it shallowly so as not to risk disturbing the roots. Do not overwater zinnias since wetness seems to help the foliage rather than the flowers.

Pinching is not important with zinnias. When the first center bloom has been cut the plants will branch freely. The dead flowers look unattractive, so keep them picked.

See also ANNUALS.

ZIT-KWA   (*Benincasa hispida*)

Also called the wax gourd, this tender annual vine bears a melon used in China for preserves. The zit-kwa grows as a long trailing vine with big leaves and handsome yellow flowers. The fruit is about a foot long and does not have a hard rind. Give it the same culture as melon or cucumber. It is a good ornamental for a sunny southern slope.

ZIZYPHUS   *See* JUJUBE

ZOYSIA

This creeping Asiatic grass has long been used for lawns and golf courses in the Deep South. Zoysia generally needs two seasons to become thoroughly established, and it browns soon after frost and becomes green slowly in the spring. However, it does well on most types

What zinnias lack in fragrance they make up in their limitless range of warm colors, their excellence as long-lasting cut flowers and their flowering season that lasts from June to October.

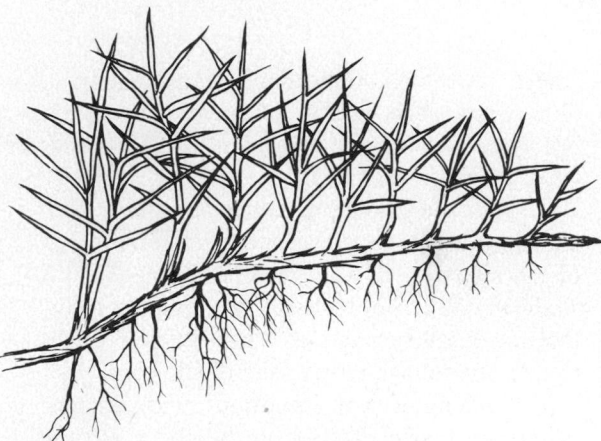

Once established, southern zoysia or Japanese lawngrass forms a very dense, lush ground cover which seldom requires mowing.

of soil, and maintains a dense, green turf even during long stretches of dry weather.

Zoysia is not seeded like most grasses, but planted in small round plugs, or in sprigs which are the strips of root and leaves pulled from these plugs. The plug method calls for the lawn-maker to dig holes two inches deep and about the same in diameter, spaced approximately one foot apart each way. The plugs are set firmly into these holes. Special plugging tools are available to speed up the job.

Good species include Koreangrass (*Z. japonica*) and Manilagrass (*Z. Matrella*). The latter is especially tolerant to salt spray.

See also LAWN.

ZUCCHINI   (*Cucurbita Pepo*)

Zucchini is a dark green and smooth-skinned summer squash whose complete botanical epithet is *C. Pepo* var. *Melpepo* cv. 'Zucchini'.

Zucchini seed is sown directly into the gar-den as soon as the weather has warmed. If started indoors, zucchini should be transplanted in a peat pot so as not to disturb its roots.

Like other members of the Gourd family, zucchini is susceptible to the striped cucumber beetle, and should therefore be planted in a different location each year. To control squash bugs, place a flat board on the ground under the plants. The bugs will cluster on its underside during the night and can be picked up and destroyed in the morning.

Popular varieties include Golden, Black and Hybrid zucchini. All are hardy and have maturation dates of 50 to 55 days.

See also SQUASH.

ZYGOCACTUS

See CACTI, EPIPHYLLUM, THANKSGIVING CACTUS

ZYGOPETALUM

These handsome epiphytic orchids have long leaves and racemes of large and showy, long-lasting flowers that bloom in winter and spring. *Z. Mackayi,* a popular and stunning variety, bears five or six three-inch blooms on each of its several 18-inch stems. The dingy yellow green flowers are spotted with purple, and the wide and ruffled white lip is striped with deep blue or purple.

Zygopetalums should be grown in osmunda fiber or sphagnum moss mixed with large pieces of charcoal, and kept moist at all times. They grow best in a cool (60 to 65°F. [15.56 to 18.33°C.]), shaded, well-ventilated greenhouse. Propagation is by division of the pseudobulbs.

See also ORCHIDS.

State	Average date of last frost	Average date of first frost	Length of growing season, in days
New Jersey			
Cape May	April 4	November 13	222
New Brunswick	April 21	October 19	181
New Mexico			
Roswell	April 9	November 2	208
Santa Fe	April 23	October 19	179
New York			
Binghamton	May 4	October 6	154
Buffalo	April 29	October 23	178
North Carolina			
Wilmington	March 15	November 19	274
Winston-Salem	April 14	October 24	193
North Dakota			
Fargo	May 24	September 27	134
Williston	May 14	September 23	132
Ohio			
Cincinnati	April 12	October 24	194
Cleveland	April 18	November 3	198
Oklahoma			
Miami	April 7	October 26	202
Oklahoma City	March 28	November 6	221
Oregon			
Medford	May 1	October 17	169
Portland	February 25	December 1	279
Pennsylvania			
Erie	May 1	October 11	163
Philadelphia	April 10	November 13	208
Rhode Island			
Kingston	May 1	October 14	166
Providence	April 14	October 23	190
South Carolina			
Charleston	February 19	December 10	294
Greenville	March 26	November 11	230
South Dakota			
Rapid City	May 7	October 4	150
Sioux Falls	May 5	October 3	152
Tennessee			
Chattanooga	March 26	November 10	229
Nashville	March 28	November 7	224
Texas			
Brownsville	February 15	December 10	298
Plainview	April 10	November 6	211
Utah			
Blanding	May 18	October 14	148
Logan	May 15	October 6	144
Vermont			
Bennington	May 15	October 4	142
Saint Johnsbury	May 22	September 25	126